SEMITIC LANGUAGES
OUTLINE OF A COMPARATIVE GRAMMAR

Page of David Qimḥi's philological treatise *Sefer Mikhlol* from the *Kennicott Bible*, Oxford, Bodleian Library, ms. Kennicott 1, fol. 443ʳ
(Courtesy Bodleian Library).

ORIENTALIA LOVANIENSIA
ANALECTA
——— 80 ———

SEMITIC LANGUAGES
OUTLINE OF A COMPARATIVE
GRAMMAR

BY

EDWARD LIPIŃSKI

UITGEVERIJ PEETERS en DEPARTEMENT OOSTERSE STUDIES
LEUVEN
1997

CIP Koninklijke Bibliotheek Albert I, Brussel
LIPIŃSKI Edward

Semitic Languages: Outline of a Comparative Grammar. — Leuven: Peeters, 1997. —
756 p.: ill., 24 cm. — (Orientalia Lovaniensia Analecta: 80).

D. 1997/0602/48
ISBN 90-6831-939-6 (Peeters, Leuven)

TO MAŁGORZATA

CONTENTS

PREFACE 17

ABBREVIATIONS AND SYMBOLS 21

I. SEMITIC LANGUAGES 23

  1. Definition 23

  2. Afro-Asiatic 24

    A. Egyptian 25
      a) Old Egyptian 25
      b) Middle Egyptian 26
      c) Late Egyptian 27
      d) Demotic 27
      e) Coptic 29
    B. Cushitic 29
      a) Bedja 31
      b) Agaw 32
      c) East Cushitic 32
      d) West and South Cushitic 33
    C. Libyco-Berber 34
    D. Chadic 39

  3. Proto-Semitic 41

  4. Classification of Semitic Languages 47

  5. North Semitic 50

    A. Palaeosyrian 50

    B. Amorite 52

    C. Ugaritic 53

  6. East Semitic 53

    A. Old Akkadian 53

    B. Assyro-Babylonian 54

    C. Late Babylonian 55

7. West Semitic. 56

   A. Canaanite. 56
      a) Old Canaanite 57
      b) Hebrew 57
      c) Phoenician 58
      d) Ammonite 60
      e) Moabite 60
      f) Edomite 61

   B. Aramaic 61
      a) Early Aramaic 61
      b) Official or Imperial Aramaic 63
      c) Standard Literary Aramaic 63
      d) Middle Aramaic 63
      e) Western Late Aramaic 65
      e) Eastern Late Aramaic 66
      f) Neo-Aramaic 69

   C. Arabic. 70
      a) Pre-Islamic North and East Arabian 71
      b) Pre-Classical Arabic 72
      c) Classical Arabic 75
      d) Neo-Arabic or Middle Arabic 75
      e) Modern Arabic 77

8. South Semitic 78

   A. South Arabian 78
      a) Sabaic. 79
      b) Minaic 80
      c) Qatabanic 80
      d) Ḥaḍramitic 80
      e) Modern South Arabian 80

   B. Ethiopic 81
      a) North Ethiopic 83
         Ge'ez 83
         Tigre 83
         Tigrinya 84
      b) South Ethiopic 84
         Amharic 84
         Argobba 84
         Harari 84

Gurage 85
Gafat 85

9. Language and Script 86
    A. Cuneiform Script 86
    B. Alphabetic Script 87
    C. Transcription and Transliteration 93

II. PHONOLOGY 95

1. Basic Assumptions 96
    A. Linguistic Analysis 96
    B. Consonantal Sounds 99
    C. Vowels 100
    D. Intonation 102
    E. Phonemes 103
    F. Voiced and Unvoiced Sounds 104
    G. Emphatic Sounds 105
    H. Proto-Semitic Phonemes 106

2. Labials 109

3. Dental Plosives 116

4. Interdentals 117

5. Dental Fricatives 122

6. Prepalatal and Palatal 126

7. Laterals 129

8. Liquids and Nasal 132

9. Velar Plosives 137

10. Laryngals, Pharyngal and Velar Fricatives 141

11. Synopsis of the Consonantal System 150

12. Vowels 152

13. Diphthongs 166

14. Geminated or Long Consonants 173

15. Syllable 178

16. Word Accent 181

17. Sentence Stress or Pitch 184

18. Conditioned Sound Changes 186

    A. Assimilation 186
       a) Assimilation between Consonants 187
       b) Assimilation between Vowels 190
       c) Assimilation between a Consonant and a Vowel . 190

    B. Dissimilation 191

    C. Metathesis 192

    D. Haplology 193

    E. Prosthesis 194

    F. Anaptyxis 195

    G. Sandhi 196

    H. Elision 196

    I. Hypercorrection 199

III. MORPHOLOGY 201

  1. The Root Morpheme 201

  2. The Noun 209

    A. Noun Stems or Patterns 209
       a) Simple Patterns 210
       b) Patterns with Diphthongs 212
       c) Patterns Extended by Gemination 213
       d) Patterns Extended by Reduplication 214
       e) Patterns with Preformatives and Infixes 215
          Preformatives '-/'- 215
          Preformative ya- 216
          Preformatives w-/m-/n- 216
          Preformative t- 219
          Infix -t- 220
          Preformative š- 221
       f) Patterns with Afformatives 221
          Afformative -ān 221

Afformatives *-iy/-ay/-āwī/-ya/-iyya* 223
Afformatives in *-t* 225
Other Afformatives 226
Afformative *-ayim/n* of Place Names 228
g) Nominal Compounds 228

B. Gender 229

C. Number 235
   a) Dual 236
   b) Plural 238
     External Plural 238
     Plural by Reduplication 244
     Internal Plural 245
   c) Paucative 251
   d) Collective Nouns 251
   e) Singulative 252

D. Case Inflection 253
   a) Diptotic "Ergative" Declension 254
   b) Use in Proper Names 258
   c) "Classical" Triptotic Declension 259
   d) "Adverbial" Cases 260
   e) Historical Survey of Case Inflection 262

E. The "States" of the Noun 265
   a) Construct State 265
   b) Predicate State 266
   c) Determinate State 267
   d) Indeterminate State 272
   e) Paradigms 274

F. Adjectives 278

G. Numerals 280
   a) Cardinals 280
   b) Ordinals 292
   c) Fractionals 294
   d) Multiplicatives 295
   e) Distributives 296
   f) Verbal Derivatives 296

3. Pronouns 297

A. Independent Personal Pronouns 298

B. Suffixed Personal Pronouns 306

C. Reflexive Pronoun 311

D. Independent Possessive Pronouns 312

E. Demonstrative Pronouns 315

F. Determinative-Relative Pronouns 324

G. Interrogative and Indefinite Pronouns 328

4. Verbs 331

A. Preliminaries 331

B. Tenses and Aspects 335
   a) Fully Developed System 335
   b) Simplified Systems 340
   c) Transitivity — Intransitivity 343
   d) Modern Languages 346

C. Moods 351

D. Actor Affixes 359
   a) Suffix-Conjugation 359
   b) Imperative 366
   c) Prefix-Conjugation 368
      Set I 369
      Set II 376

E. Stems and Voices 378
   a) Basic Stem 378
   b) Stem with Geminated Second Radical Consonant . 382
   c) Stem with Lengthened First Vowel 385
   d) "Causative" Stem 387
   e) Stem with *n*-Prefix 393
   f) Stems with *t*-Affix 395
   g) Frequentative Stems 402
   h) Reduplicated Biconsonantal Stems 405
   i) Stems with Geminated or Reduplicated Last Radical . 406
   j) Other Stems 407
   k) Verbs with Four Radical Consonants 407
   l) Passive Voice 408
   m) Recapitulation of Stems 409

F. Infinitive and Participle 415
   a) Infinitive 415
   b) Participle 419
   c) Neo-Aramaic Verbal System 421
   d) Participial Tense Forms in Other Languages . . 424

G. Particular Types of Verbs 425
   a) "Weak" Verbs 425
   b) Biconsonantal Verbs 436
   c) Verbs with Pharyngals, Laryngals, Velar Fricatives . 445
H. Verbs with Pronominal Suffixes 450

5. Adverbs 453
A. Adverbs of Nominal Origin 453
B. Adverbs of Place and Negatives 454
C. Adverbs of Time 458

6. Prepositions 459
A. Primary Prepositions 460
B. Prepositions of Nominal Origin 465
C. Compound Prepositions 469

7. Connective and Deictic Particles 470
A. Conjunctions 470
B. Presentatives 472
C. Subordinate Conjunctions 474
D. Copulae 475
E. Expression of Possession 480

IV. SYNTAX 481

1. Classes of Sentences 483
A. Minor Clauses 483
B. Major Clauses 484
C. Nominal Clauses 484
D. Verbal Clauses 487
E. Concord of Subject and Predicate 491

2. Nominal Phrases 494
A. Attribute 494
B. Apposition 496
C. Genitival or Subjoining Relation 497

3. Verbal Phrases 504

    A. Accusative 504

    B. Infinitive 508

4. Clauses 511

    A. Particular Types of Main Clauses 511

    B. Parallel Clauses. 515

    C. Subordinate Clauses 519

      a) Relative Clauses 521

      b) Temporal/Causal Clauses 527

      c) Final/Consecutive Clauses 533

      d) Substantival Clauses 535

      e) Conditional Clauses 536

V. LEXICON 543

1. Etymology 545

2. Derivatives 554

3. Languages in Contact 557

4. Internal Change 564

5. Proper Names 567

    A. Anthroponomy 568

    B. Toponymy 570

GLOSSARY OF SELECTED LINGUISTIC TERMS 575

BIBLIOGRAPHY 593

1. Semitic Languages in General 593

2. North Semitic 597

3. East Semitic 598

4. West Semitic 600

    A. "Canaanite" 601

    B. Aramaic 605

    C. Arabic 610

5. South Semitic 617

   A. South Arabian 617

   B. Ethiopic 619

6. Libyco-Berber 622

7. Cushitic 624

8. Chadic 627

9. Languages in Contact 629

10. Anthroponomy and Toponymy 633

GENERAL INDEX 639

INDEX OF WORDS AND FORMS 681

  Agaw 681
  Amharic 681
  Ammonite 684
  Amorite 684
  Arabic 685
  Aramaic, Mandaic, Neo-Aramaic, Syriac 696
  Argobba 702
  Assyro-Babylonian, Late Babyloninan, Old Akkadian . . . 702
  Bantu 713
  Bedja 713
  Chadic 714
  Coptic 714
  East and West Cushitic 714
  Egyptian 715
  Gafat 716
  Ge'ez 717
  Greek 720
  Gurage 721
  Harari 724
  Hausa 725
  Hebrew 725
  Hittite 731
  Latin 731
  Libyco-Berber, Numidic, Tuareg 731

Moabite 734
North Arabian 735
Oromo 735
Palaeosyrian 736
Persian 738
Phoenician and Punic 738
Rendille 740
Semitic, Common 740
Somali 742
South Arabian, Epigraphic 742
South Arabian, Modern 744
Sumerian 745
Tigre 746
Tigrinya 748
Ugaritic 749

TABLES, MAPS, AND TEXT FIGURES 753

PREFACE

Having taught the introduction to the Semitic languages and their comparative grammar for more than a quarter of a century, year by year, I decided finally to acquiesce to a long-standing suggestion and to undertake the task of publishing the results of my research and teaching in the form of a textbook. In fact, the usefulness of an outline of a comparative grammar of the Semitic languages is self-evident since the last original work of this kind was published twenty-five years ago by B.M. Grande, Введение в сравнительное изучение семитских языков, (Moscow 1972). This work was based mainly on the so-called classical Semitic languages, viz. Akkadian, Biblical Hebrew, Syriac, Classical Arabic, and Ge'ez, but paid little attention to other Semitic languages, both ancient and modern, and it abstained from a systematic treatment of the syntax and of semantic problems. However, it was felt in different quarters that it is important to draw the attention of the students to certain tendencies discernible in modern dialects and to clearly bring out the main common features of Semitic syntax. In addition, the material has increased considerably during the last decades and the need for a synthesis taking the new information into account was growing steadily. Finally, comparative Semitics without a broader Afro-Asiatic or Hamito-Semitic background is — in some areas at least — methodologically questionable, although C. Brockelmann's famous *Grundriss* and its epigones seem to neglect this type of comparisons. Yet, the right approach was already outlined in 1898 when H. Zimmern published his *Vergleichende Grammatik der semitischen Sprachen*, where he gives some paradigms showing the connections between Semitic and other Hamito-Semitic languages.

Designed to come out in the centenary of the completion of Zimmern's work, which resulted in the first comparative grammar of the Semitic languages ever published, the present book owes a similar approach to itself. Besides, as I.M. Diakonoff rightly stressed in 1988, the Afro-Asiatic language families "cannot be studied, from the point of view of comparative linguistics, in isolation from each other". The scope of the present *Outline* is thus larger, in a certain sense, that the one of earlier comparative grammars of the Semitic languages, but it is nevertheless intended primarily as an introductory work, directed towards an audience consisting, on the one hand, of students of one or several Semitic languages, and, on the other, of students of linguistics. Its aim is to underline the common characteristics and trends of the languages and dialects that compose the Semitic language "family" by applying the comparative method of historical linguistics. The object it has in view is not a mere juxtaposition of forms belonging to various languages, but a comparison and an explanation of the changes they incurred, seen in both a diachronic and a synchronic perspectives which must be used together, if some part of the evidence is not to be veiled. To avoid an excessive overloading of the text, references are given, as a rule, only when they cannot be found easily in current grammars of the particular languages.

No Semitist can be assumed today to be at home in all the Semitic idioms, and the present work relies to a great extent on publications of other scholars, especially of A.F.L. Beeston, J. Cantineau, I.M. Diakonoff, W. Fischer, I.J. Gelb, Z.S. Harris, T.M. Johnstone, E.Y. Kutscher, W. Leslau, E. Littmann, R. Macuch, S. Segert, W. von Soden. It is clear, of course, that the views exposed in this book differ some- times from the opinions expressed by the above-mentioned Semitists and by other scholars. Nevertheless, we deemed it unwise to explain here at full length why the preference was given to certain theories to the exclusion of others, and thus to corroborate our views by quoting litera- ture in extensive notes. The selection of linguistic facts and the degree of their condensation may also be subject to discussion and to criticism. For a more detailed presentation and analysis of linguistic data, how- ever, the advanced students should rather refer to specific grammars, a selective list of which is given in the bibliography, at the end of the vol- ume. In view of the great variety and intricacy of the material presented, especially from spoken languages and dialects, it is inevitable that incon- sistencies will appear in the transliteration and the spelling of Afro-Asi- atic words and phrases. For such occasional lack of uniformity and for certain redundancies, aimed at lessening the possibility of misinterpreta- tion, we must ask the user's indulgence.

It might also be useful to stress at the outset that the present work is intended as a compendious and up-to-date analysis of the nature and structure of the Semitic languages. It is a comparative analysis of a lan- guage family, not a comparative study of the views expressed by com- peting linguistic schools: Semitics is more wonderful than linguistics! Consequently, we do not attempt to apply the latter's arsenals of techni- cal vocabulary to the Semitic languages, but rather to present as clearly as possible the fundamental insights about the wide world represented by the history and the present reality of the concerned language family.

Part One is introductory. It situates the Semitic languages in the wider context of Afro-Asiatic or Hamito-Semitic language family, the five main branches of which are Semitic, Egyptian, Cushitic, Libyco-Berber, and Chadic. The Semitic group, the single languages of which are briefly described, includes such languages of antiquity as Palaeosyrian, Old Akkadian, Assyro-Babylonian, Hebrew, Phoenician, Aramaic, and Epigraphic South Arabian, as well as Arabic, Neo-Aramaic, and the contemporary languages of Ethiopia and Eritrea. The last section of Part One deals with the problems of language and script.

Part Two is devoted to phonology. The presentation of the basic assumptions is followed by a synchronic and diachronic description of the consonants, vowels, and diphthongs. Questions related to the syllable, the word accent, the sentence stress, and the conditioned sound changes are examined in this part as well.

Part Three concerns the morphology. After a preliminary section dealing with the problem of the Semitic root, the nouns, the pronouns, the verbs, the adverbs, the prepositions, the coordinative and deictic particles are examined from a diachronic and synchronic point of view.

Part Four treats of the main features of Semitic syntax, with questions such as classes of sentences, nominal and verbal phrases, particular types of main clauses, parallel, coordinate, and subordinate clauses. Diachronic factors come here distinctly to the fore in relation to word order, i.e. to the sequence in which words are arranged in a sentence. In fact, both fixed and free orders are found mingled in widely varying proportions in a great number of Semitic languages.

Part Five aims at presenting some fundamental insights about lexicographical analysis. Etymology, derivatives, languages in contact, internal change, proper names — these are the main questions examined in this part. It is followed by a glossary of linguistic terms used in Semitics, by a selective bibliography, by a general index, and by an index of words and forms.

It is a pleasure to acknowledge my gratitude to the many classes which have inspired the successive drafts of this grammar. I have profited in particular from a number of questions raised by my Kurdish students and from the constructive comments of those who have followed my seminars in the Department of Epigraphy at the Yarmouk University.

I also wish to express my sincere thanks to Mrs F. Malha for the great care and professional skill which she exercised in preparing the text for printing. Further, I cannot let go unexpressed my deep appreciation for the work realized by Peeters Publishers and the Orientaliste typography, whose skilful care is apparent over again in the way this book is printed and edited. Last but not least, I must thank my wife Małgorzata for helping me to bring this work to a happy end.

ABBREVIATIONS AND SYMBOLS

The Books of the Bible

Gen., Ex., Lev., Nb., Deut., Jos., Judg., I Sam., II Sam., I Kings, II Kings, Is., Jer., Ez., Hos., Joel, Am., Ob., Jon., Mich., Nah., Hab., Soph., Hag., Zech., Mal., Ps., Prov., Job, Cant., Ruth, Lam., Qoh., Esth., Dan., Esd., Neh., I Chr., II Chr., Sir., I En., Act.

Other Abbreviations

Acc., acc.	=	accusative
Amor.	=	Amorite
Arab.	=	Arabic
Aram.	=	Aramaic
ARM	=	*Archives royales de Mari*, Paris 1950 ff.
Ass.-Bab.	=	Assyro-Babylonian
ca.	=	*circa*, about
C	=	Consonant
cf.	=	*confer*, compare
Cl.Ar.	=	Classical Arabic
Coll.	=	Colloquial
cor.	=	corrected, corrects in
DN	=	divine name
E	=	Egyptian execration texts published by G. POSENER, *Princes et pays d'Asie et de Nubie*, Bruxelles 1940.
e.g.	=	*exempli gratia*, for example
EA	=	The El-Amarna tablets numbered according to J.A. KNUDTZON, *Die El-Amarna-Tafeln* (VAB 2), Leipzig 1915; A.F. RAINEY, *El Amarna Tablets 359-379* (AOAT 8), 2nd ed., Kevelaer-Neukirchen-Vluyn 1978.
E.S.A.	=	Epigraphic South Arabian
Fem., fem., f.	=	feminine
Gen., gen.	=	genitive
Hebr.	=	Hebrew
KTU	=	M. DIETRICH - O. LORETZ - J. SANMARTÍN, *The Cuneiform Alphabetic Texts from Ugarit, Ras Ibn Hani and Other Places* (*KTU: second, enlarged edition*), Münster 1995.
lit.	=	literally, etymologically
M.Ar.	=	Modern Arabic
Masc., masc., m.	=	masculine
M.S.A.	=	Modern South Arabian
msec.	=	millisecond(s)
Ms., mss.	=	manuscript(s)

Nom., nom.	=	nominative
n.s.	=	new series
O.Akk.	=	Old Akkadian
O.Bab.	=	Old Babylonian
Pers., pers.	=	person
Plur., plur.	=	plural
PN	=	personal name
Pr.-Sem.	=	Proto-Semitic
P.Syr.	=	Palaeosyrian
1Q, 2Q, 3Q, etc.	=	Texts from Qumrān grot 1, 2, 3, etc.
RÉS	=	*Répertoire d'Épigraphie Sémitique*, Paris 1905-68.
Sing., sing.	=	singular
TAD	=	B. PORTEN - A. YARDENI, *Textbook of Aramaic Documents from Ancient Egypt* I. *Letters*, Jerusalem 1986; II. *Contracts*, Jerusalem 1989; III. *Literature, Accounts, Lists*, Jerusalem 1993.
TSSI	=	J.C.L. GIBSON, *Textbook of Syrian Semitic Inscriptions* I. *Hebrew and Moabite Inscriptions*, 2nd ed., Oxford 1973; II. *Aramaic Inscriptions*, Oxford 1975; III. *Phoenician Inscriptions*, Oxford 1982.
Ugar.	=	Ugaritic
v	=	vowel
v̄	=	long vowel
vs.	=	versus, against

Symbols, Determinatives

/ /	enclose phonemic transcriptions;
[ ]	enclose phonetic approximations or reconstructed parts of a text;
( )	enclose words not found in the original, but needed in the translation;
*	indicates form or vocalization supposed, but not attested as such in texts;
<	signifies that the preceding form has developed from the following one;
>	signifies that the preceding form develops or has developed into the following one;
!	to be especially noticed, e.g. because of a new reading;
?	dubious reading or interpretation;
//	parallel with;
/	indicates alternative forms, appellations, symbols, when placed between two letters, syllables, words, etc.;
:	the colon indicates length in linguistics; it is generally replaced by the macron in the present *Outline*;
+	joins lexemes or morphemes forming one word.
-	hyphen used to connect the elements of certain compound words, as well as cuneiform and hieroglyphic "syllabic" graphemes pertaining to one word.
d	abbreviation of the determinative DINGIR, "god", in cuneiform texts;
ki	postpositional determinative KI, "country", in cuneiform texts;
LUGAL	small capital letters indicate logograms, sumerograms;
uru	determinative URU, "city", in cuneiform texts.

I

SEMITIC LANGUAGES

1. DEFINITION

1.1. The "Semitic" languages were so named in 1781 by A.L. Schlœzer in J.G. Eichhorn's *Repertorium fuer biblische und morgenlaendische Literatur* (vol. VIII, p. 161) because they were spoken by peoples included in Gen. 10,21-31 among the sons of Sem. They are spoken nowadays by more than two hundred million people and they constitute the only language family the history of which can be followed for four thousand five hundred years. However, they do not stand isolated among the languages of the world. They form part of a larger language group often called Hamito-Semitic, but lately better known as Afro-Asiatic. The existence of a relationship between Berber in North Africa and Semitic was perceived already in the second half of the 9th century A.D. by Judah ibn Quraysh, from Tiaret (Algeria), in his work known as *Risāla*. Ibn Quraysh is rightly regarded as one of the forerunners of comparative Semitic linguistics, based an Arabic, Hebrew, and Aramaic, but his intuition connecting the languages of this group with another branch of Afro-Asiatic, at least in some particular cases, did not yield fruit before the 19th century. A broader interrelationship was first recognized by Th. Benfey in his sole work on Semitic linguistics: *Ueber das Verhaeltniss der aegyptischen Sprache zum semitischen Sprachstamm* (Leipzig 1844), where he expresses the opinion that also Berber and "Ethiopic", i.e. Cushitic in his terminology, belong to the same large language family. As for Hausa, the best known of the Chadic languages, it was related to this group in the very same year by T.N. Newman who had appended a note on Hausa in the third edition of J.C. Prichard's *Researches as to the Physical History of Man* (vol. IV, London 1844, p. 617-626), and was then followed by J.F. Schön in the latter's *Grammar of the Hausa Language* (London 1862). The designation "Cushitic" was introduced by 1858, and the entire language family was named "Hamito-Semitic" in 1876 by Fr. Müller in his *Grundriss der Sprachwissenschaft* (Wien 1876-88), where Müller describes the concerned group of languages. J.H. Greenberg, instead, considering that this is the only language family represented in both Africa and Asia, proposed to call it Afro-Asiatic in his work *The Languages of Africa*, issued in 1963.

1.2. The languages in question are spoken nowadays in Western Asia, in North Africa, and in the Horn of northeastern Africa, but their oldest written attestations, dating back to the third millennium B.C., are limited to Mesopotamia, North Syria, and Egypt. Whereas the relation between the various Semitic languages can be compared with that of, say, the various Germanic or Romance or Slavic languages, Afro-Asiatic would more or less correspond to the group of Indo-European languages. The latter have a few points of contact with Afro-Asiatic, but these are scarcely sufficient to warrant assumption of any genetic connection; anyhow, this topic is outside the scope of the present study. On the other hand, there is a structural analogy between Afro-Asiatic and the Caucasian languages, as first shown by I.M. Diakonoff (*Semito-Hamitic Languages*, Moscow 1965) who reached the important conclusion that Afro-Asiatic belonged originally to an ergative language type, characterized by the opposition of a *casus agens* (nominative, instrumental, locative) to a *casus patiens* (accusative, predicative). The links of Afro-Asiatic with the great Bantu linguistic stock of Central Africa seem to be more precise, as indicated e.g. by the noun prefix *mu-* (e.g. Kwena *mu-rút-i*, "teacher", built on the stem *-rút-*), the reciprocal verb suffix *-án-* (e.g. Sotho *ho-óp-án-á*, "to be striking one another"; Swahili *patiliz-an-a*, "to vex one an other"), and the causative suffix *-ís-* / *-iš-* (e.g. Kwena *ḫu-rút-ís-á*, "to cause to teach"; Swahili *fung-iš-a*, "to cause to shut"). A reference to these languages will be made only occasionally, although there are many features of semantics and idiom which are common to African languages and to Semitic. For example, parts of the body are often used as prepositions and the extended metaphoric use of words, e.g. of the verb "eat", can lead to meanings like "win, gain, use", etc.

2. AFRO-ASIATIC

1.3. The languages that belong to the Afro-Asiatic group are classified in four main families, besides the Semitic family which will be described below. The pertinent observations are restricted here to the prerequisites necessary for an understanding and a reconstruction of Semitic linguistic history. A more detailed approach is unnecessary, since comparative Egypto-Semitic linguistics is still in its infancy, while

none of the other African members of the Afro-Asiatic group is known
from sources earlier than the 19th century, except ancient Ethiopic or
Ge'ez, which is a Semitic language, and Libyco-Berber, represented
by inscriptions only partly understandable in the present state of our
knowledge.

A. Egyptian

2.1. The Egyptian language was the speech of the Nile valley from the
earliest historical times until some time after A.D. 1000. Only Egyptian
and some Semitic languages have records from very ancient times. Even
in the third millennium B.C., however, these two branches were very
distinct. Among the similarities is the phonological system, although
next to nothing is known about the vowels of the older stages of Egyptian. The morphologies of Semitic and Egyptian were characterized by
consonantal roots which are combined with vowel patterns and affixes.
Both possess two genders (masculine and feminine) and three numbers
(singular, dual, and plural). Egyptian has a suffix verb form, namely the
old perfective or "pseudo-participle", which is related to the Semitic stative, and a prefixed form in $š/s$ which corresponds to the Semitic
causative stem. There are also some affinities in the vocabulary, independently from loanwords. Despite these analogies, the practical use of
Egyptian in morpho-syntactic analysis and in comparative Afro-Asiatic
studies in general is limited. This results partly from the current Egyptological research that too often postulates syntactic principles unheard in
language study and, therefore, cannot serve comparative purposes. There
is also the intrinsic default of the hieroglyphic writing system that lacks
any indication of vowels and geminations, while its limits are not compensated by any living tradition. Only Coptic dialects (§2.7) give some
insights into the latest phase of a number of grammatical categories in a
language that underwent important changes in the course of time.

a) Old Egyptian

2.2. The main sources for our knowledge of the language of the Old
Kingdom are the biographic texts, the royal decrees, and the Pyramid
texts discovered on the walls of chambers inside the pyramids of the
kings of the Fifth and Sixth Dynasties. These texts, which were incantations for the well-being of the dead king, show peculiarities of their own,

including very archaic linguistic features. Besides the old perfective, Old
Egyptian has a series of suffix-conjugations, which are peculiar to
Egyptian and are not paralleled in the other Afro-Asiatic languages.
Since Egyptian is linked by evident lexical and morphological isoglosses
with Semitic, Libyco-Berber, Chadic, and Cushitic, it is unlikely that it
could have diverged from common Afro-Asiatic before the latter had
developed its verbal system. Therefore, it stands to reason that Egyptian
has lost the prefix-conjugation in prehistoric times under the influence of
a Macro-Sudanic adstratum or substratum of the Nile valley, just as
Egyptian vocabulary comprises words alien to Afro-Asiatic but related
to Old Nubian, as *k3ỉ*, "to think out, to plan", vs. Old Nubian *ki-*, "to
think", *ỉrp*, "wine", vs. Old Nubian *orpa-gir*, "to make wine", negative
m vs. Old Nubian negative morpheme *m*. In another domain, Egyptian
religion presents the same basic characteristics as the Nilotic religion of
the Dhinka and Shilluk tribes of southern Sudan, the only ones of whose
religious ideas there is definite knowledge. However, because of the lack
of vocalization in Egyptian, it is extremely difficult to ascertain that the
Egyptian conjugation system had developed under a Nilotic influence.
For example, like Nilotic languages, Old and Middle Egyptian dispense,
as a rule, with any equivalent of a definite or indefinite article, but an
important feature of several Nilotic languages consists in showing definiteness by the use of verbal forms involving an internal vowel change,
viz. the "qualitative" (indefinite) and the "applicative" (definite); e.g.
Anyuk *a kïïo ki ğääy*, "I am paddling **a** canoe" ("qualitative"), *a kiia
ğääy*, "I paddle **the** canoe" ("applicative"). Now, such vocalic differences cannot be expressed in hieroglyphic script. We know at least that,
along with Nilotic languages, Egyptian has a special verb for "not-
knowing": *rḫ*, "to know", vs. *ḫm*, "not to know".

b) Middle Egyptian

2.3. Middle Egyptian is the classical stage of ancient Egyptian. It
developed from Old Egyptian and was based on the language spoken
towards the end of the third millennium B.C., being used for all purposes from that time until the mid-second millennium B.C. The suffix-
conjugations of Old Egyptian remained the major verb forms in use
through Middle Egyptian, but the influence of the spoken language is
reflected by the occasional use of forms which were to become standard
only in Late Egyptian. Middle Egyptian survived in later times for many
monumental inscriptions and for some literary compositions.

2.4. At least as early as the Middle Kingdom, a special system known as "group-writing" was devised for the transcription of foreign names and words, particularly Semitic. This system involves the use of certain hieroglyphic or hieratic signs indicating a consonant followed by a weak consonant or a semi-vowel (*ꜣ*, *i̯*, *w*, *y*). These "syllabic" signs are thought by some to represent Semitic syllables, but they are often combined with "alphabetic" signs marking just one consonant (Fig. 1). Besides, since the Egyptians did not distinguish between *r* and *l* in their script, they usually used the sign *ꜣ* to transcribe these two Semitic phonemes in Middle Egyptian texts (e.g. *i̯-ś-ḳ-ꜣ-n* = *'šqln*), but they represented them also by signs which Egyptologists transcribe with "*r*" and "*n*". There are also some hesitations in the transcription of Semitic voiced consonants, for instance in the name of Byblos, *Gbl* in Semitic but *K-p-n* or *K-b-n* in ancient Egyptian.

c) Late Egyptian

2.5. Late Egyptian shows striking differences when compared with Old and Middle Egyptian: the old verb forms were being replaced, definite and indefinite articles were used, many phonetic changes occurred, and numerous foreign words appeared. Fairly accurate deductions may be made about the phonetic value of the consonants and of the vowels thanks to cuneiform texts, particularly the Amarna letters from the 14th century B.C. It appears also, for instance, that the Egyptian phoneme interpreted as "*ṯ*" by Egyptologists corresponds then to Semitic *s* (e.g. Egyptian *ṯwf.y* vs. Hebrew *sūp*, "papyrus plant") and that the alleged "*ḏ*" is the phonetic equivalent of Semitic *ṣ* (e.g. Egyptian *ḏbꜥ* vs. Semitic *'ṣbꜥ*, "finger").

d) Demotic

2.6. Demotic was the ordinary language used for official acts and other documents, beginning in the 8th/7th century B.C. and continuing into Roman times, down to the 5th century A.D. Definite traces of dialect distinctions, which may be related to these of Coptic, are found in Demotic texts. Demotic is written from right to left, like contemporary Semitic alphabetic scripts. The signs comprise phonograms, word signs, and determinatives, and a single Demotic sign is often in origin a ligature of several hieroglyphs. In the Ptolemaic age it first distinguishes *l* from *r*.

SIGN	TRANS-LITERATION	OBJECT DEPICTED
𓄿	ꜣ	Egyptian vulture
𓇋	i͗	flowering reed
(1) 𓇌 (2) 𓏭	y	(1) two reed-flowers (2) oblique strokes
𓂝	ꜥ	forearm
𓅱	w	quail chick
𓃀	b	foot
𓊪	p	stool
𓆑	f	horned viper
𓅓	m	owl
𓈖	n	water
𓂋	r	mouth
𓉔	h	reed shelter in fields
𓎛	ḥ	wick of twisted flax
𓐍	ḫ	placenta (?)
𓄡	ẖ	animal's belly with teats
(1) 𓋴 (2) 𓊃	s	(1) bolt (2) folded cloth
𓈙	š	pool
𓈎	ḳ	hill-slope
𓎡	k	basket with handle
𓎼	g	stand for jar
𓏏	t	loaf
𓍿	ṯ	tethering rope
𓂧	d	hand
𓆓	ḏ	snake

Fig. 1. The uniconsonantal signs in the Egyptian hieroglyphic script according to A. Gardiner, *Egyptian Grammar*, 3rd ed., London 1957, p. 27.

e) Coptic

2.7. During the Roman and Byzantine periods Greek was the most common written language in Egypt, although Demotic was also widely used. As early as the 2nd century A.D. texts were written in Egyptian but in Greek letters, breaking with the hieroglyphic and Demotic traditions. These were not only horoscopes, magic spells, and the like, but also Christian translations of the Bible, followed by a Christian literature, written in Greek letters supplemented by seven characters taken from Demotic. The language was the one or the other of the Egyptian dialects as they were then spoken and are known as Coptic, from the Greek (*Ai*)*gyptos*, "Egypt". Aside from the rather slight difference of linguistic structure between Demotic and Coptic, there is a marked change in vocabulary and general tone due to the shift from paganism to Christianity, with its religious and ecclesiastical phraseology borrowed from Greek. In fact, Coptic literature is almost entirely religious and consists mainly of translations from Greek. Coptic dialects became progressively restricted after the Arab conquest of Egypt (A.D. 640). The Arabic writer Maqrizi, born in Cairo (1365-1442), still records that in his own day Copts in Upper Egypt spoke scarcely anything but Coptic. But it is generally assumed that Coptic died out as a spoken language during the 16th century, although a Coptic native speaker is attested at Asyût in 1672/3, while a few men in the village of Zainīya (northeast of Karnak) could understand usual Coptic liturgical texts as late as 1936. The Bohairic dialect is still the liturgical language of the Coptic Church, but the pronunciation is based on the values of the letters in Modern Greek.

B. Cushitic

2.8. The Cushitic family comprises about seventy mostly little-explored languages. There is, as yet, little agreement concerning the identification and classification of these languages that are spoken from the Red Sea littoral to the area south of the Horn of northeastern Africa (cf. Fig. 19). They are generally characterized in phonology by palatal consonants (*č*, *ǧ*, *ň*, *š*), by glottalized emphatics (*p* = *p'*, *ṭ* = *t'*, *č̣* = *č'*, *q* = *k'*), and by the absence or the limited use of pharyngals (*ḥ*, *'*) and of velar fricatives (*ḫ*, *ġ*), which have most likely disappeared like in several Semitic languages. Cushitic preserves some archaic Afro-Asiatic features in morpho-syntax, as verbal aspects, the "ergative" and the non-active cases of the noun inflection, the causative, passive, and reflexive

stems of the verb, but it frequently suffixes the characteristic morphemes, just as it uses postpositions rather than prepositions. The
pronominal elements and the basic vocabulary often show close relationship to Semitic. Instead, Cushitic is not-related to the Macro-Sudanic
languages which were used and written in northern Sudan: Meroitic, a
still imperfectly understood language which is attested from the 3rd century B.C. to the 5th century A.D., and Old Nubian which is known from
Christian writings dating from the end of the 8th century to the 14th century, and which is continued by the modern Nubian dialects of the Nile
valley and of the Kordofan hills. Cushitic consists of five main groups of
languages, that might be further subdivided.

The following diagram presents the main sub-groups:

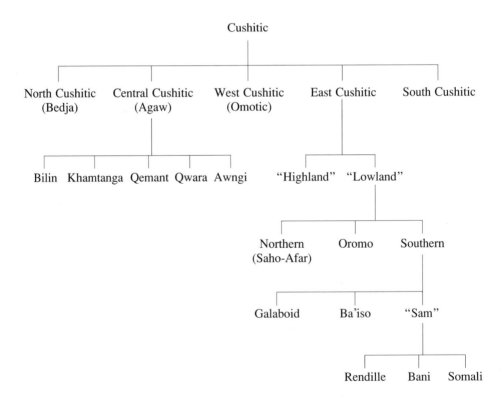

a) Bedja

2.9. Bedja or North Cushitic is spoken on the Red Sea littoral of the Sudan and in the hinterland, to the latitude of Kassala in the south. The Bedja tribes of eastern Sudan are essentially nomad pastoralists that belong to two main tribal confederacies: the Bisharin and Abdada, in the north, the Hadendowa, Amarar, and Beni 'Amar in the south. Their language, called also (To) Bedawi, presents striking morphological analogies with Semitic verbal stems, with the causative prefix *s-* (*gumad*, "to be long", *sugumād*, "to lengthen"), the reflexive/passive affix *-t-* (*kehan* "to love", *atkehan*, "to be loved"), and the intensive or "pluriactional" doubling of a radical (*dir*, "to kill", *mdedar*, "to kill each other"). Moreover, the conjugation of the finite verb parallels the Semitic imperfective, preterite, and probably jussive; e.g. present *'adanbīl* < **'adabbīl*, "I am collecting"; past *'adbíl*, "I collected"; conditional *'īdbil*, "I may collect", which has a present meaning in negative clauses (e.g. *k-ādbil*, "I don't collect") and seems to go back to a volitive form. As for phonology, Bedja has lost the Afro-Asiatic pharyngals and the emphatic consonants. The Bedja of the Sudan are probably the Medju of ancient Egypt and certainly the Blemmyes who used to raid Upper Egypt in the Roman period. They are called Βουγαειτοι in the Greek inscriptions of Ezana, king of Aksum in the mid-4th century A.D. (§8.11), and Βεγά in the "Christian Topography" written about A.D. 550 by Cosmos Indicopleutes who had travelled throughout the Red Sea trading area. In earlier times the Bedja speakers extended much further to the west across the Nile. They probably inhabited what is now called the Bayuda desert, about 200 km north of Omdurman. Remnants of these western Bedja are to be recognized in the Bedyat of Ennedi, whose royal clan, the Bisherla, is presumably of Bisharin descent. The Islamism of the Bedja, though fervid in some tribes such as the Hadendowa, is relatively recent, for Maqrizi (1365-1442) wrote of them as mostly heathen. Early Moslem monuments discovered in the area should be linked rather with the Arabs of the Beni Omayya tribe who had begun to cross the Red Sea as early as the 8th century. Thus, Moslem tombstones dating from the 8th to the 11th centuries (the earliest is dated from A.H. 153 = *ca.* A.D. 790) have been found in some places, while early Moslem stone-built towerlike tombs occur at Maman, about 100 km northeast of Kassala, and elsewhere. Circular stone graves with flat tops are presumably those of Bedja, either Moslems or no. In any case, many non-Islamic beliefs persist among the Bedja people until our days.

b) Agaw

2.10.   Agaw or Central Cushitic is constituted of a number of closely
related languages, that are not necessarily intelligible to speakers of
another Agaw idiom. These languages are spoken in Eritrea and in
northwestern Ethiopia, in a region where Semitic influence has been relatively strong. The Agaw people are believed to have once occupied
most of highland Ethiopia. Their present scattered distribution must be
the result of the Semitic expansion in this area (§8.9). The Agaw dialects
which are still living include Bilin, spoken in Eritrea around Keren,
Khamtanga, corresponding to the Khamta and Khamir varieties of Agaw
reported earlier in the northeastern part of the Amharic area (Wello
province), Qemant and the Qwara or Falasha dialects, north of Lake
Tana, and Southern Agaw or Awngi, spoken south and west of the lake.
At the request of James Bruce, the text of the Song of Songs has been
translated in 1769-72 from Amharic into three Agaw dialects, among
them into Falasha, and some Falasha prayer texts in Qwara, dating from
the 19th century, have been preserved. The Falashas, which claim to be
of Jewish descent, once spoke two Agaw dialects, and it is still customary among them to recite certain blessings in Agaw, including the Grace
after Meals. But they have almost entirely forgotten their former language with the exception of some outlying communities living in Qwara
before the Falasha emigration to Israel. The Falashas read the Bible in
Ge'ez and speak Amharic. The Agaw dialects are receding nowadays
before Amharic and Tigrinya, although Awngi seems to be in less danger of disappearing than the others. It is noticeable for having preserved
five basic verbs which belong to the prefix-conjugation, parallel to the
Semitic imperfective and perfective: *yinte*, "he comes" (vs. Semitic
y-'ty), *yage*, "he brings" (vs. Semitic *y-wgʿ*), *yigʷe*, "he remains" (vs.
Semitic *y-qūm*), *yaġe*, "he is, he becomes" (vs. Semitic *y-wqʿ*), *yaqe*,
"he knows" (vs. Semitic *y-wqy*). Otherwise, Awngi has a developed suffix-conjugation with a clear distinction between the main verb and the
verb of subordinate clauses. The Agaw dialects of the Qemant-Qwara
group possess the voiced velar fricative *ġ*, like Awngi, and also the velar
nasal *ng* (/ŋ/), as well as their labialized counterparts.

c) East Cushitic

2.11.   East Cushitic comprises a number of languages spoken in the
Horn of Africa and divided into "Highland" and "Lowland" East
Cushitic.

1° The main "Lowland" language is Oromo, formerly called Galla or Gallǝñña. It is spoken by some twenty million people living in Ethiopia and in northern Kenya, and it was once used also in northern Somalia. Oromo is thus, after Arabic, Hausa (§2.16), and Swahili (§1.2), the African language with the largest number of speakers, but it became a "written" language only in 1975, with the publication of the first Oromo periodical in Ethiopian script (§9.7).

2° Other linguistically important Lowland East Cushitic languages are the Konso in Ethiopia, the Saho-Afar in Eritrea and in the Djibouti Republic, the languages of the Galaboid sub-group, Ba'iso which is spoken on an island of Lake Abaya, and the so-called "Sam" languages, whose name is derived from a common root *sam ("nose"). The latter sub-group is important for comparative linguistics because of its prefix-conjugation with an aspectual distinction between perfective and imperfective. It comprises Rendille, spoken in Kenya, east of Lake Turkana (former Rudolf), Boni, attested mainly in Kenya, east of the lower Tana river, and the Somali dialects spoken by about five million people in Somalia, in eastern Ethiopia, and in northern Kenya. Instead, the total of Rendille and Boni speakers amounts only to a few thousand. Contrary to a Somali tradition, there is no reason to believe that their ancestors arrived from Arabia, although the Arabic peninsula was the origin of an increasing immigration, probably from the 8th century A.D. onwards, as well as the source of the Islamization of Somalia. There is a large body of Somali oral literature, including alliterative poetry. The name Somali first occurs in a praise song of Yeshaq I of Abyssinia (1412-1427).

3° Eastern Sidamo, now called Highland East Cushitic, was the main substratum language of South Ethiopic. This sub-family of East Cushitic is a compact group with seven or eight languages and several dialects spoken by some two million people. Hadiyya, spoken by about one million people, is its main representative nowadays; the other languages of this group are Kambata, Sidamo proper, Ṭembaro, Alaba, Qabenna, Darasa, and perhaps Burǧi.

d) West and South Cushitic

2.12. West Cushitic, also called Kafa group or Omotic — because it is spoken in the vicinity of the Omo river —, constitutes a family of some forty related languages spoken by about two million people in south-western Ethiopia. Among the Omotic dialects, which are considered by some scholars as a distinct branch of Afro-Asiatic, the best represented is the Walamo dialect cluster with more than one million speakers. Special attention was paid also to Moča, Djandjero, Madji, and Kafa. From the comparative point of view, Kafa, for instance, has only suffixed nominal and verbal formations, but it preserves the aspectual nature of the conjugation very well. Most verbal roots are monosyllabic and belong to the types C_1vC_2 or $C_1vC_2C_2$.

2.13. South Cushitic comprises languages spoken in Kenya and in Tanzania, like the Mbugu, the Iraqw, and the Dahalo. These languages — except Iraqw — are little known and some of them, as Mbugu and Dahalo, in Tanzania, are influenced by Bantu languages. There is no doubt, however, that the pronouns are Cushitic and that the conjugation belongs to the common Cushitic suffix inflection.

C. Libyco-Berber

2.14. Libyco-Berber dialects were formerly spoken in all of North Africa except Egypt, by the Tuareg of the Sahara, and by the Guanches of the Canary Islands (Fig. 2). Considerable interest in the spoken Berber languages and their origins had developed by the middle of the 19th century, but no written sources are available before some Shleuh manuscripts from the 16th or 17th century written in Arabic script, except a few short Berber sentences in an Arabic manuscript from the 12th century and a number of Berber words and proper names quoted in works of Arab mediaeval writers. The Libyco-Berber language is spoken by some twenty million people from the Siwa Oasis in Egypt to the Atlantic and from the Mediterranean southwards into the Sahara. It shows many correspondences of a phonological, morphological, syntactical, and lexical nature with Semitic, but these affinities can readily be explained within the general framework of Afro-Asiatic languages. Libyco-Berber preserves the features of an ergative language type to a greater extent than Semitic and its declension system is based on the opposition of an active subject case (*casus agens*) to a predicative or non-active case (*casus patiens*). In the singular, as a rule, the active subject case is characterized by the *u*-prefix, while the *a*-prefix is marking the predicative or non-active case (§32.1-7). Beside a stative conjugation (e.g. *ḥnin*, "he is gracious") and two non-aspectual tenses, viz. the imperative (e.g. *əlkəm*, "follow!") and the jussive (*-lkəm-*) (§38.2), which is used also in subordinate clauses, Libyco-Berber has two verbal prefixforms, viz. the imperfective and the perfective, that indicate the aspect, i.e.

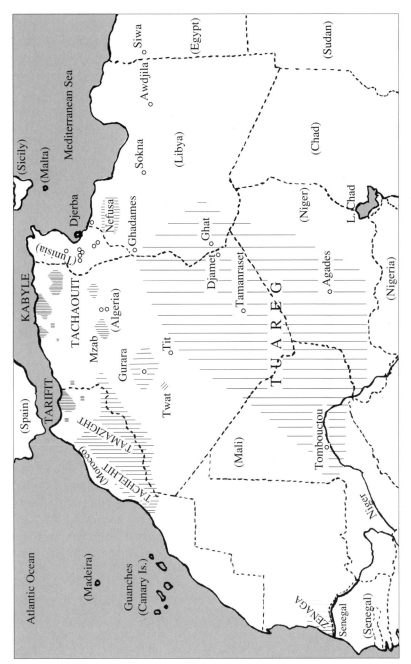

Fig. 2. Geographical distribution of Libyco-Berber

whether the action is considered as a lasting process or as a concluded action; e.g. the basic stem of *-lkəm-*, "to follow":

Aspect	Positive	Negative
perfective	*-lkăm-*	*-lkem-*
imperfective	*-lākkəm-*	*-ləkkəm-*

A vowel lengthening characterizes in Tuareg the intensive stem, like in some Semitic and Cushitic languages, and affixes may be added in all dialects to the verbal root in order to express the causative, reflexive or reciprocal, frequentative, or passive meaning of the verb. All these stems occur also in Semitic languages, except the last one which is paralleled by the Egyptian "pseudo-passive":

intensive stem, e.g. *-lkām-*; *-lākkəm-*;
causative *s*-stem, e.g. *-sərtək-*, "cause to fall";
reflexive / reciprocal *m/n*-stem, e.g. **mətrəg-**, "be freed";
frequentative *t*-stem, e.g. *-təffəġ-*, "go often out";
agentless passive *ttwa*-stem, e.g. **-ttwaddəz-**, "be crushed".

Despite numerous lexical variations (e.g. "fox", *uššən* in Kabyle but *ăbəggi* in Tuareg) and important phonetic changes (e.g. "heart", Tuareg *əwl*, Tachelhit *ul*, Tamazight *už*, Tarifit *ur*), Libyco-Berber is still essentially one language, the numerous dialects of which show but relatively slight differences, although Tuareg and some eastern idioms appear to be its most archaic forms of speech. Tuareg is important also because it has but few borrowings from Arabic, which are instead numerous in other Berber dialects, viz. Tarifit or Rifan in northern Morocco, Tachelhit or Shleuh in the south of the country and in Mauritania, Tamazight in the Middle Atlas region, Kabyle and Tachaouit or Chaouia in Kabylia and in the Aurès (Algeria), Zenaga in southwestern Mauritania, etc. However, the borrowings from Arabic are mainly lexical, exceptionally morphological or syntactical. In Tuareg, one must reckon also with possible loanwords from Songhai, an important isolated language spoken in Tombouctou (Mali), in the Niger valley farther south, and in the city of Agades in the Air oasis of the Sahara (Niger).

The term *ta-maziġ-t* is used nowadays in Moroccan and Saharan dialects to designate the Berber language in general, and someone speaking Berber is an *a-maziġ* (plur. *i-maziġ-ən*). The word *maziġ* has a long history, since it is attested as a North African personal name in Roman times, while some Libyco-Berber tribes are called *Mazices* or Μάζικες in classical sources. Ibn Khaldun (1332-1406) considers Mazigh as a forefather of the Berbers.

2.15. The Berber-speaking Tuaregs have a writing of their own, the *tifinaġ*, a plural apparently related to Greek φοῖνικ-, "Phoenician, Punic". Its origin may go back to the 7th-6th centuries B.C., as indicated by monuments and inscriptions ranging over the whole of North Africa. Most of the ancient inscriptions (about 1200) date however from the times of the Numidian kingdoms (3rd-1st cent. B.C.) and of the Roman Empire (Fig. 3). As a rule, they do not indicate vowels, not even the initial *u-*, *a-*, *i-* of the case prefixes which have thus to be supplied, e.g. *nbbn nšqr'* corresponding approximately to **i-nbabən n-u-šqura'*, "the cutters of wood (were)…" (Dougga, 2nd century B.C.). There is also a large corpus of Libyco-Berber proper names quoted in Punic, Greek, and Latin sources. However, it is not easy to connect the phonological, morphological, syntactical, and lexical elements of this antique documentation with the modern Berber forms of speech. The Numidic noun *gld*, "king", pronounced nowadays *žəǧid* in Tarifit because of the phonetic changes *g > ž* and *ll > ǧ*, gives a small idea of the problems facing the linguists. Nevertheless, the uninterrupted continuity of the Libyco-Berber idioms appears to be accepted nowadays by all reputable scholars in the field. The orthography of Tuareg in Latin characters, officially adopted in Niger and in Mali, does of course not reflect the dialectal richness of the language, although it undoubtedly presents some advantages.

The modern Berber dialects reflect the ancient loss of original gutturals, but they have more pharyngalized emphatics than Common Semitic, also more palatalized and fricativized consonants. The changes *d > ḍ, d > ṭ, d > ḏ, g > ġ, k > g, k > ġ, q > ġ, r > ṛ, s > ṣ, t > ṭ, s > ẓ* are quite frequent, as well as *g > ž, k > š, l > ž, ll > ǧ, ll > č, rr > ǧ, z > š (>h), z > ž, b > ḇ, d > ḏ, t > ṯ*; e.g. Tachaouit *ti-ġəṭṭ-ən*, "she-goats", to compare with Hebrew *gədī* and Arabic *ǧady*, "young goat". Besides, original pharyngalization can disappear (e.g. Tachaouit *ddəhhašt < *ta-ḍahḥākit*, "laughing"), a secondary pharyngal may be inserted before *t* (e.g. Tachaouit *əz-zəḫt < Arabic əz-zəyt*, "olive oil"; Kabyle *ta-ḇəġliḫt < ta-ḇəġlit*, "mule"), and various assimilations may occur (e.g. Tarifit *yəšša < *yikla*, "he ate").

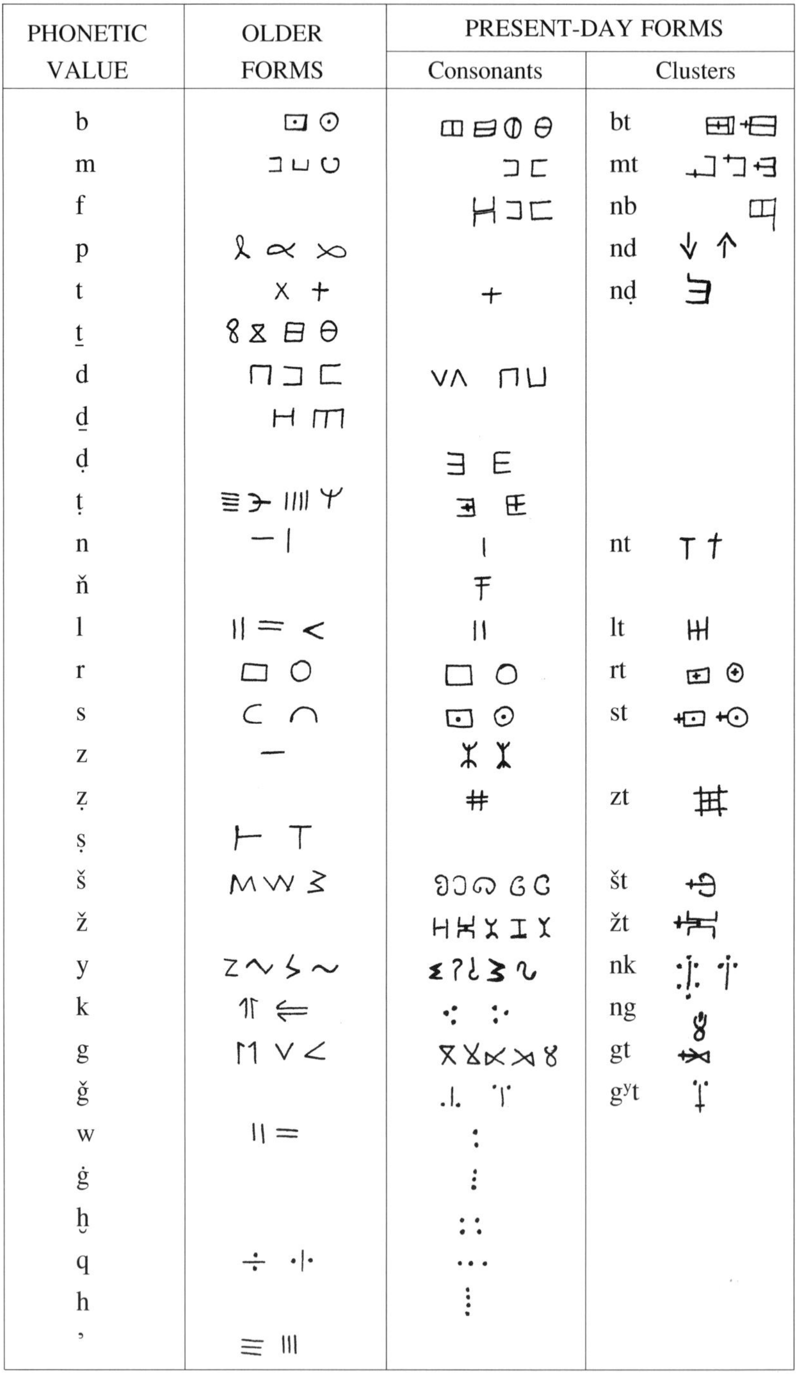

PHONETIC VALUE	OLDER FORMS	PRESENT-DAY FORMS	
		Consonants	Clusters
b			bt
m			mt
f			nb
p			nd
t			nḍ
ṯ			
d			
ḏ			
ḍ			
ṭ			
n			nt
ň			
l			lt
r			rt
s			st
z			
ẓ			zt
ṣ			
š			št
ž			žt
y			nk
k			ng
g			gt
ǧ			gʸt
w			
ġ			
ḥ			
q			
h			
ʾ			

Fig. 3. Libyco-Berber writing

D. Chadic

2.16.   The Chadic languages, so called from the name of Lake Chad, are spoken in Western and Central Africa, i.e. in northern Nigeria, northern Cameroon, western and central Chad, and, in the case of Hausa, Niger. They form the most variegated branch of Afro-Asiatic with some 125 different languages, a recent subdivision of which is presented in Fig. 4. The chief idiom of this family is Hausa, a large group that has only recently been described in a satisfactory way. The Hausa speakers constitute the single most numerous group in northern Nigeria and in southern Niger. The language has become the general *lingua franca* in northern Nigeria and the number of people speaking Hausa as a secondary language is considerable. Hausa is written traditionally in an orthography based on the Arabic alphabet, and an original Hausa literature does exist, composed mainly in the dialect of Kano which became the standard literary language. The dialect differences are not sufficiently serious to interfere with mutual intelligibility. As result of Islamic influence, numerous Arabic words have been borrowed, particularly in the spheres of religion, crafts, and technology. The importance of Hausa cannot be underestimated, but in general East Chadic languages, as Mubi, Kwang, Kera, Migāma, Bidiya, spoken in northern Cameroon and in the Chad Republic, seem to be more archaic and to provide more parallels to Afro-Asiatic. Distinctive Afro-Asiatic features that can be shown to exist also in Chadic are the affixed morpheme *t* with the triple function of feminine / diminutive / singulative (e.g. Hausa *yazo*, "he came", *tazo*, "she came"), the *-n/t/n* gender-number marking pattern in the deictic system (masculine, feminine, plural), the *m-* prefix forming nouns of place, of instrument, and of agent, the formation of noun plurals, among other ways, by adding a suffix *-n* and by inserting a vowel *-a-*, the formation of intensive or "pluriactional" verbs by internal consonant gemination, and an asymmetrical conjugational system involving suffixed feminine and plural markers in addition to pronominal prefixes. There are also some highly probable etymological connexions between Chadic and Afro-Asiatic. For instance, *mutu* means "to die" in Hausa, while the Old Akkadian corresponding verb is *muātu*. In both languages, *mutum* means "man". In East Chadic (Migama), *sín* means "brother" like in ancient Egyptian, while *náàsò*, "to breathe", corresponds to Egyptian *nšp*, to Semitic *našāpu*, and to Cushitic *néfso* (Boni), with metathesis. The Mubi aspectual opposition between *bēni*, "he built", and *binnǎa*, "he is building" (Mubi), is undoubtedly related to the conjugation of the Semitic verb *bny*.

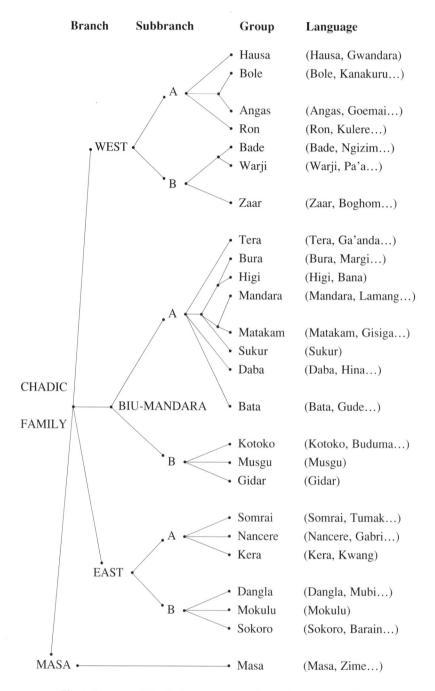

Branch	Subbranch	Group	Language

Fig. 4. Diagram of Chadic languages according to P. Newman (1977).

2.17.   The five branches of Afro-Asiatic are not really parallel to each other, because closer relations can be established between some of them. Thus Libyco-Berber is certainly closer to the Semitic branch than Egyptian or Cushitic, while Chadic languages, as far as known presently, are obviously the most distant from the other branches. Very characteristic of Libyco-Berber and of Semitic are the preserved features of the ergative language type, with identical morphemes indicating either the active subject or the predicate-object, both in the singular and in the plural. Also the system of conjugation in Libyco-Berber and in Semitic is built upon a "nominal" and a "verbal" bases, with the aspectual opposition of accomplished to unaccomplished. These two branches of Afro-Asiatic are thus closely related to each other, but this relationship can best be explained in the general frame of the whole language family. The interrelations between the five branches of Afro-Asiatic may therefore be represented schematically in the following way:

Proto-Afro-Asiatic

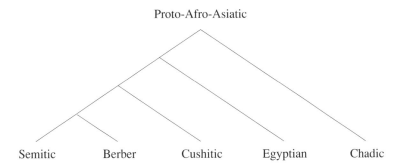

Semitic   Berber   Cushitic   Egyptian   Chadic

3. PROTO-SEMITIC

3.1.   The Semitic languages, although their number amounts to about seventy, have a much larger layer of common elements in their phonology, morphology, syntax, and vocabulary than the Afro-Asiatic group as a whole. They also share certain common features in their evolution, easily recognizable in ancient and in modern forms of speech. These common elements and parallel developments, maintained despite lapse of time and spreading over new areas, strongly support the family-tree theory which regards the dividing process that affects a homogeneous language — in this case the Proto-Semitic — as the main impelling power from which new idioms originated. This theory does not exclude,

however, concrete applications of the wave-theory that attributes common linguistic evolutions to the spreading of linguistic changes by contacts between dialects, that may lead to the emerging of a new local
koinè, of a new common language. In any case, neither the wave-theory
nor its variant, the peripheral hypothesis, correspond to the global evidence with distant Semitic areas, as Akkadian and Ethiopic, more alike
than are those which are not so widely separated. In other words, Proto-
Semitic is something more than a conventional name given to the whole
of elements shared by the family of languages under consideration. In
view of the relatively limited geographical dispersion of the ancient core
of Semitic languages and of the great measure of affinity between them,
the concept of Proto-Semitic would seem comparable to that of Latin
with regard to the Romance languages. The problems of the latter group
are, however, more manageable owing to the fact that the Latin language
is historically documented, while Proto-Semitic is a linguistic prerequi-
site the existence of which in prehistoric times is necessary for an understanding of the mutual relations and parallel developments of the historically documented Semitic languages.

3.2.   Since the Semitic languages go apparently back to a common origin, the question of the location of the speakers of this Proto-Semitic
language has been often considered of importance. Various regions have
been taken into account: Syria, Arabia, and Africa. No definitive
answer, however, can be given to this question without considering the
Afro-Asiatic linguistic interrelations. In fact, the sedentary or half-
sedentary protopopulation of North Syria and Mesopotamia was most
likely non-Semitic, as appears from the large number of non-Semitic
geographical names in Palaeosyrian and in Old Akkadian texts. Now,
geographical names, with the exception of newly founded settlements,
reflect an old and inherited linguistic tradition of the specific areas. As
for Arabia, this region could hardly have supported sufficient population
for such large waves of emigration before the domestication of the
dromedary in the second millennium B.C., while the Semitic languages
of Africa are grouped in an apparently peripheral area of Semitic and
their appearance in the Horn of Africa, midst Cushitic languages, is most
likely due to an ancient conquest and emigration.

3.3.   The problem of the original homeland of the Semites cannot be
examined historically without considering the linguistic relations
between the five branches of the Afro-Asiatic language family. The

main service that comparative linguistics can render to the investigation
of this prehistoric problem is not simply asserting the common origin of
the languages in question, but defining the degree of their divergence
and relating it to two variables: time and separation. Time is a variable
related to divergence in the sense that, under like circumstances, the
longer the time the greater the divergence. Separation is a variable in the
sense that parts of an original language community will tend to diverge
faster if they become completely separated as, say, Semitic and Libyco-
Berber around e.g. 1000 B.C. The similarities in language between peoples living so far away from each other are due, not to cultural contact
and borrowing, but to common linguistic tradition. Now, the most
numerous isoglosses and lexicostatistical convergences are precisely
those linking Semitic with Libyco-Berber, while the isoglosses and the
lexicostatistical factors connecting Semitic and Egyptian, on the one
hand, and Semitic and Chadic, on the other, seem to be the less important. Although the available data and the very incomplete lexicostatistical studies must be regarded as preliminary, the conclusion from purely
linguistic evidence seems inescapable that the Proto-Chadic languages,
followed by Egyptian, were the earliest to separate from the common
trunk, while Proto-Semitic maintained, for a certain time, closer language contacts with Libyco-Berber and with Cushitic. This implies that
the speakers of Proto-Semitic were still dwelling in Africa in the 5th
millennium B.C., in the Neolithic Sub-pluvial (*ca.* 5500-3500 B.C.),
when the Sahara's climate was much wetter, so that erosion took place
as in other moist temperate or subtropical regions, and there was a
proper system of rivers and vegetation consisting of grass with trees.
Settlement was undoubtedly widespread in the Sahara at that time, and
there is ample evidence of Neolithic culture with rock drawings showing
animals that no longer live there. A worsening of environmental conditions is indicated in North Africa *ca.* 3500 B.C. with disappearance of
vegetation, a major faunal break, desertification, and desertion. This
might have been the period when the speakers of Proto-Semitic passed
through the Nile delta from the West to the East, and reached Western
Asia, where written documents of the third millennium B.C. preserve
noticeable traces of Pre-Semitic and, in Mesopotamia, also of Pre-
Sumerian substratum. The collapse of the Ghassulian culture in Palestine
around 3300 B.C. and the Egyptian finds in southern Palestine from the
Early Bronze period I (*ca.* 3300-3050 B.C.) may testify to the arrival of
these new population groups. The Palestinian tumuli, belonging to the
culture of semi-nomadic groups during much of the fourth and third

millennia B.C., seem to confirm this hypothesis, since a very similar type of sepulture characterizes pre-historic North Africa, especially Algeria, and it is a typical feature of the old Libyco-Berber tradition. Thus, from North Africa, wave after wave of Semitic migrations would seem to have set forth. The earliest of these migrants, and those who went farthest to the East, were the Akkadians who, journeying along the Fertile Crescent through Palestine and Syria, and crossing over into Mesopotamia, reached Northern Babylonia *ca.* 3000 B.C. and founded the first Semitic Empire at Kish (§4.2; 5.2; 6.2). The Amorites (§4.1-2; 5.3) and their congeners would appear to have followed as far as Syria before 2500 B.C. The Southern Semites would seem to have reached the moister highlands of the Yemen and Ḥaḍramawt after 2000 B.C., following the collapse of the Early Bronze culture in Palestine, while the Ethiopians would have crossed over to the Horn of Africa when drier conditions prevailed in South Arabia *ca.* 1500-500 B.C. Since only the most primitive type of raft was needed to cross the Straits of Bab el-Mandeb or to make the short voyage across the Hanish Islands, a relatively early date for the beginning of the last mentioned migration would not be surprising. Semitic speakers settled among Cushitic pastoralists whose presence in the region probably goes back to 3500-3000 B.C. (Fig. 5). The Libyco-Berbers continued, instead, to occupy the original language area of the speakers of Afro-Asiatic. Their African origins may even be confirmed by a relationship of Afro-Asiatic with Bantu languages (§1.2) which form the central group of the large Niger-Congo family and whose homeland probably lies in the Nigeria-Cameroon area.

3.4. Although the discussion of these problems lies outside the scope of the present work, it is useful to add that any linguistic mapping a Afro-Asiatic speakers should be complemented by an anthropological approach. The data are not so abundant as might be wished, but enough evidence is available to establish the fact that the Afro-Asians belonged basically to the long-headed or dolichocephalic Mediterranean peoples widespread in distribution in Late Neolithic and Chalcolithic times. Further subdivisions of course exist, but they are generally too ephemeral to be helpful in this context. However, skeletal evidence seems to indicate that the same Neolithic peoples from North-Africa entered the Iberian peninsula and moved into the Egyptian upper valley of the Nile in pre-dynastic times. They are well represented by the ʾNaqāda cranial series, dated to the Amratian period (*ca.* 3500 B.C.), and their modern descendants — through frequently mixed with negroes — are found among the

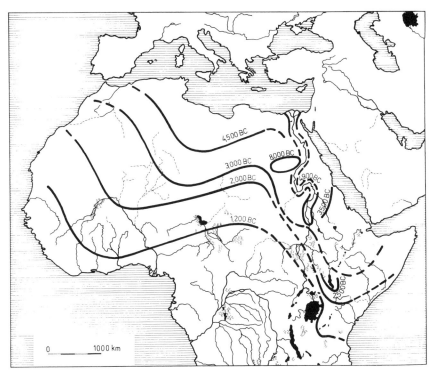

Fig. 5. The spread of the earliest pastoralists in Africa, *ca.* 8000-1200 B.C., according to
L. Krzyżaniak, *Schyłek pradziejów w środkowym Sudanie*, Poznań 1992, p. 158.

speakers of Cushitic languages in the Horn of Africa and the Bedja
people in the desert between the Nile and the Red Sea. Characteristic
artefacts of the Amratian period, suggesting connexions with prehistoric
Libyco-Berbers, are statuettes of bearded men wearing phallic sheaths,
like those of the Libyans in historical times. The Amratian culture seems
to have been absorbed by the Gerzean one, coming from Lower Egypt
where the latter's origins begin to be investigated. The predynastic population of Lower Egypt differed from that of Upper Egypt in having
broader heads, longer faces, and narrower noses. The subsequent racial
history of Egypt was to be that of a gradual replacement of the Upper
Egyptian or "Cushitic" type by that of prehistoric Lower Egypt. In
Palestine, instead, there was no drastic change in the main anthropological type during the transition from the Chalcolithic to the Early Bronze
age. Summing up, striking similarities link the physical characteristics of
the predynastic Egyptians, of the contemporary Bedja population and the
main Berber type, and of the Palestinian skeletons of the Early Bronze

age: dolichocephalic type, with a stature of a little less than 1.65 m. for
men and about 1.55 for women, with a projecting occiput and the chin
prominent. The dolicocephalic features are best preserved nowadays
among the Bedouin Arabs.

3.5. The spreading of Afro-Asiatic, thus delineated, implies a determinate type of linguistic expansion in Western Asia. Linguistic expansion
can take place by diffusion, infiltration, and migration. Whereas diffusion necessitates no permanent displacement of language carriers and
infiltration implies a movement of but a restricted number of individuals, migration signifies that whole tribes permanently displace themselves and spread over a new territory. These are the circumstances
obviously reflected in the settlement of Semites in Western Asia where
Semitic idioms replaced the substratum languages of the regions where
today Arabic, Neo-Aramaic, and Hebrew are spoken. The substratum
generally modifies the gaining language through interference, thus causing the spreading language to differentiate itself from the language of the
original linguistic homeland. Interference varies in degree and kind
chiefly in proportion to non-linguistic cultural receptivity or hostility.
Now, judging from the great similarity of the Semitic languages and
from their close relationship to Libyco-Berber, the influence of the linguistic substratum on Semitic must have been limited except in
Mesopotamia where the Sumerian adstratum played an important role.
Archaeological evidence from Palestine probably provides the correct
interpretation of this fact, viz. the location of the new Early Bronze I settlements shows a great shift from the preceding Chalcolithic pattern.
Areas densely settled in the Chalcolithic period were either totally or
partially deserted, and the new sites were usually situated in different
spots. Thus, the new migrants — Semites, in our hypothesis, — seem to
have brought an end to the Chalcolithic settlements in Palestine. This
indicates in turn that the Early Bronze age culture introduced by the
Semitic population groups lacked the receptivity required to be modified
in a very significant way through linguistic interference. However, the
Semitic tongues of the new territories followed together with other cultural features a path of historical development more or less divergent
from that of the Afro-Asiatic language of the original homeland. The latter, represented nowadays by the Libyco-Berber dialects, developed
independently from Semitic during a period of 5500 years or more, if we
except the borrowings from Punic and Arabic. This large span of time
seems to be sufficient for explaining the differences between Semitic

and Libyco-Berber, especially if we take into account the fact that the two groups were affected, respectively in Asia and in Africa, by neighbouring forms of speech which belonged to completely different language families.

4. CLASSIFICATION OF SEMITIC LANGUAGES

4.1. The distinct Semitic tongues are ranging from important languages with large literatures to language forms used over a limited territory and either entirely unwritten or possessing but a few preserved documents. Some are attested only in the third or the second millennium B.C., while other languages have been identified as late as the 20th century A.D. It was usual, until a short time ago, to group all languages into three great branches: the East Semitic represented by Akkadian, the Northwest Semitic with Canaanite, Ugaritic, Amorite, and Aramaic, and the South Semitic with Arabic and Ethiopic.

This classification was based on the view that the first division which Semitic underwent, before 3000 B.C., was between East Semitic or Akkadian and West Semitic. At a later date, but before 2000 B.C., West Semitic was believed to have split into a northern and a southern branch. Northwest Semitic further divided into Canaanite and Aramaic, while Southwest Semitic split into Arabic, on the one side, and South Arabian and Ethiopic, on the other. This conception can no more be sustained because of the discovery of languages that do not fit into any of those branches, and in view of doubts risen with regard to the classification of Ugaritic, Amorite, and Arabic.

4.2. The discovery of new types of Semitic speeches in Northern Syria, at Ebla, Tell Beydar, and Mari, as well as in the Kish area of Central Mesopotamia, reveals the existence of a group of dialects belonging to Semitic languages of the third millennium B.C. that were related to Old Akkadian and slightly less to Amorite. It is convenient to call "Palaeosyrian" those dialects that are attested by documents found in Syria, although the language shows a certain mixture (§41.28; 48.5), while some "literary" and lexical texts are duplicated at Fāra and at Tell Abū Ṣalābīkh (Iraq). The language may be linked to some extent with the writing system brought from Mesopotamia and thus partly represent the written Semitic of the place from which the script was taken *ca.* 2400 B.C., probably Kish (§5.2). Unfortunately, there is no way at present to check this hypothesis. It appears also that Palaeosyrian and Old Akkadian texts contain many proper names in which occurs an ending -*a* that qualifies the predicate state of the noun and that is attested also in some Amorite names, but does not belong to the living languages of the texts. One can assume therefore that this feature reflects an even older common stage of Semitic languages. Besides, Palaeosyrian dialects share certain linguistic features with Ugaritic, South Arabian, and Ethiopic, that obviously preserve some common archaic elements. The resulting picture shows therefore that there was no clear cut between East and West Semitic in the third millennium B.C. As for the greater affinity between Palaeosyrian and Old Akkadian, it is due to the use of the same type of script, borrowed from the Sumerians or Proto-Sumerians, and to the chronological and perhaps partly local vicinity of the written languages. The differences between the Semitic forms of speech obviously increased with the time.

4.3. There is also no clear cut between Northwest and Southwest Semitic in the first millennium B.C. For instance, some Early Aramaic dialects probably possessed the internal or "broken" plural, regularly found only in the South Semitic area, while some North Arabian languages used the prefixed article *han-*, attested normally in Canaanite languages of the first millennium B.C. Therefore, classifications based on important literary languages, as Arabic, Ethiopic, Hebrew, and Syriac, and the interpretation of other forms of speech as mere dialects of these literary languages cannot be sustained any more. For a time, varying in length in the various regions, all spoken dialects were of equal prestige, and the epigraphical documentation transmits fuller information on dialectal varieties than has since been available. But with the formation of literary languages in cultural and political centres, certain local dialects augmented their prestige and with their grammatical codification came some measure of petrifaction allowing for clearly cut linguistic features. A classification based on these standard languages does not reflect, of course, the variety of spoken dialects, the differences of which often increase with the time and in proportion as the geographical distances grow, thus blurring clearly cut linguistic divisions.

4.4. In conclusion, a subdivision of the Semitic language family should be based on the wide geographic distribution of the speeches, but take also into account, if feasible, the historically attested documentation. In ancient times, Semitic languages were spoken in Mesopotamia, Syria-

Palestine, Arabia, and Ethiopia. Beyond this area they have spread only as a result of later and historically known developments, i.e. migration, colonization, or conquest. It is convenient, therefore, to describe the Semitic languages and dialects roughly in the same geographic order, slightly corrected in view of some chronological considerations, since the linguistic material of the present survey extends in time over some 4500 years: from the mid-third millennium B.C., when we encounter the earliest written manifestations of a Semitic language (Palaeosyrian, Old Akkadian), until the present times, when some entirely unwritten forms of Semitic speech have been described and analyzed.

4.5.   Therefore, the present survey will distinguish a North Semitic grouping, to which belong written languages of the third and second millennia B.C. (Palaeosyrian, Amorite, Ugaritic), an East Semitic group with Old Akkadian, Assyro-Babylonian, and Late Babylonian, that cannot simply derive from the preceding stages of Babylonian, a West Semitic group with Canaanite (Hebrew, Phoenician, Moabite, Ammonite), Aramaic, and North Arabian languages (Thamūdic, Liḥyānite, Ṣafaitic, Standard Arabic, Neo-Arabic), and a South Semitic group with South Arabian and Ethiopian languages, both ancient and modern.

4.6.   This survey does not aim at giving a detailed description of all the Semitic languages. However, the lack of any up-to-date introductory work demands a summary presentation of the current knowledge in this field in order to clarify the concepts and the terminology adopted in the present comparative study. Although the latter has an introductory character, does not aim at exhaustiveness, and emphasizes the position of the great literary or standard languages, it also adduces evidence from other ancient and modern Semitic languages and dialects. Their position in the Semitic family has therefore to be briefly characterized. The terms "dialect" and "language" are taken here in their rough definition, the distinct forms of speech being called "dialects" when the differences are relatively small. In this approach, not only geographically different forms of speech may be called "dialects", but also historical stages of the languages considered, as Old Assyrian, Middle Assyrian, and Neo-Assyrian that together cover a span of 1500 years. In any case, no exact definition of "language" and "dialect" is feasible, and the "discovery" of a new Semitic language merely expresses the scholars' conviction that a type of speech appears sufficiently distinct from others so as deserve a name of its own.

5. NORTH SEMITIC

5.1. North Semitic is represented nowadays by Palaeosyrian (but cf. §4.2), Amorite, and Ugaritic. These are languages spoken and written in Upper Mesopotamia and Northern Syria in the third and second millennia B.C. They are known to us only through written records and cannot be subjected to strict phonetic analysis. However, their corpus expands steadily by the discovery of more written documents, that may reveal the existence of unknown dialects or even of new related languages, as was the case at Tell Mardikh/Ebla and at Tell Beydar, near Hassake (Syria).

A. Palaeosyrian

5.2. Palaeosyrian is represented by the "Eblaite" texts from Tell Mardikh/Ebla dating from the 24th century B.C. according to the "short" chronology (Fig. 6), by the tablets from Tell Beydar, going back to the mid-third millennium B.C. as well (Fig. 7), by the Pre-Sargonic and post-Ur-III texts from Mari, in Syria. Common scribal traditions and cultural elements are revealed by these documents and by texts from the area of Kish, in Mesopotamia, 15 km east of Babylon. It would be premature, however, to term that cultural entity "Kish civilization" and to contrast it too sharply with the Sumerian culture, especially with the written culture of Sumer. Palaeosyrian cuneiform script is of Sumerian or even of Pre-Sumerian origin and it uses Sumerian logograms or word signs, besides syllabic signs and auxiliary marks aimed at helping the understanding of the writing. It is impossible to consider the texts from different sites as written in one language spoken by a single people in the whole area extending from North Syria to Babylonia. However, the spoken languages may differ to various extents from a written *koinè* and, in any case, there are common features in the writing system, in phonology, morphology, syntax, and vocabulary. Further research and more discoveries are needed to establish how many written Semitic languages or dialects of the mid-third millennium should be distinguished in the area under consideration. Besides, the sources so far discovered — in particular the proper names — contain elements surviving from an older Semitic language that should also be studied and evaluated.

Fig. 6. Ebla Tablet TM.75.G.1377 Obverse
(Courtesy Missione Archeologica in Siria).

Fig. 7. Tell Beydar Tablet 2629-T-2
(Courtesy Euro-Syrian Excavations at Tell Beydar).

B. Amorite

5.3.   Amorite is the name given nowadays to a group of North Semitic
dialects spoken in North Syria and Upper Mesopotamia between the middle of the third millennium and the second half of the second millennium
B.C. These forms of Semitic speech are mainly known by the numerous
proper names — with specific grammatical forms — which appear in various cuneiform texts, by some loanwords borrowed by Old Babylonian
scribes, and by certain linguistic peculiarities occurring sporadically in Old
Babylonian texts, in particular those from Mari. Some Amorite names are
found also in Middle Egyptian execration texts from the 19th and 18th centuries B.C. Amorite was once called "East Canaanite" and is often considered as a Northwest Semitic language. The geographical area of the speakers of Amorite dialects and the relation of these speech forms to
Palaeosyrian suggest however to classify Amorite among the North Semitic
tongues and to consider "East Canaanite" as an inappropriate designation
of the language under consideration.

C. Ugaritic

5.4. Ugaritic is the name given to the Semitic language discovered in 1929 at Ras Shamra, the site of ancient Ugarit, on the coast of north-western Syria. Ugaritic was written in an alphabetic cuneiform script using 30 simple signs which, on the whole, present single consonantal sounds. The texts discovered at Ras Shamra and at Ras Ibn Hani, south-west of Ugarit, date from the 14th, 13th, and the beginning of the 12th centuries B.C. A few tablets in alphabetic cuneiform script were also found at other sites, notably in Palestine. Next to mythological and epic compositions, there are letters and administrative-economic documents that reflect a somewhat younger stage of the language.

6. EAST SEMITIC

6.1. East Semitic is represented by Old Akkadian, attested roughly from 2400 to 2000 B.C., by the various branches of Assyro-Babylonian (roughly 1900-600 B.C.), and by the Late Babylonian that cannot be derived from the preceding stages of Babylonian without admitting at least considerable interference from another Semitic language. "Akkadian" is the most diffused global appellation of these forms of speech; it comes from Akkad or Agade, the capital of the Semitic Empire of Sargon of Agade (*ca.* 2265-2210, according to a "short" chronology). Yet, to underline the distinction between Old Akkadian, on the one hand, and the Assyrian and Babylonian dialects of the second and first millennia B.C., on the other, the latter will generally be called "Assyro-Babylonian" in this *Outline*. Akkadian did use logograms or word signs, but was written mainly in syllabograms that also indicated vowels. However, this script was in several respects imperfect, owing to its Sumerian or Pre-Sumerian and thus non-Semitic origin.

A. Old Akkadian

6.2. If the Early Dynastic III or Pre-Sargonic texts from the Kish area (§5.2) are considered as written in an earlier dialect of the same language as the one used in the Semitic documents of the Empire created by Sargon of Akkad, Old Akkadian may be dated between 2350 and 2000 B.C. according to a "short" chronology. Like in the case of Palaeosyrian, its writing is of Sumerian or non-Semitic origin and has the same general characteristics, but cuneiform signs are generally used with their normal Sumerian value, contrary to the Ebla practice, and certain speech elements are not omitted in writing, as it happens frequently at Ebla and at Mari. On the other side, there seems to be no convincing way of deriving the earliest attested Assyrian or Babylonian texts from Old Akkadian, that obviously was a local dialect of northern Babylonia that owed its prestige and literary character to the fact of being spoken in the power centre of the Kish dynasties and of the Akkadian Empire.

B. Assyro-Babylonian

6.3. The huge number of private letters, contracts, public documents, and literary texts preserved makes Assyro-Babylonian one of the principal sources for ancient Semitic. Because of the cultural prestige of Babylonian, various local forms of Assyro-Babylonian were used in the neighbouring countries and served in the second millennium B.C. for purposes of State correspondence and for official documents in areas where East Semitic was not spoken. The outstanding case of this is the Amarna correspondence, chiefly from Syria-Palestine. By a gradual process, however, between the 8th and the 6th centuries B.C., Assyro-Babylonian died out as a spoken language and was replaced by Aramaic in its homeland. Its written use, however, continued until the 1st century A.D.

6.4. *Babylonian*, the dialect of the southern part of Mesopotamia, was also used as a literary language in Assyria. The Babylonians themselves were calling it "Akkadian". Within the Babylonian dialect one can distinguish the following periods: Old Babylonian (*ca.* 1900-1500 B.C.), Middle Babylonian (*ca.* 1500-1000 B.C.), and Neo-Babylonian (*ca.* 1000-600 B.C.). There are several sub-dialects in the Old Babylonian period. Thus, the existence of dialectal differences between North Babylonian and South Babylonian, and between the earlier Old Babylonian and the later Old Babylonian has to be pointed out. Besides, there are provincial dialects from Susa (Elam), from the Diyala region, and from Mari. In addition, literary compositions, which originated in the Old Babylonian or Middle Babylonian periods, continued to be copied in later times, generally conserving their original wording. The dialect of these literary texts has been termed Standard Babylonian (Fig. 8).

Fig. 8. Middle Babylonian fragment of the Gilgamesh Epic from Megiddo
(Courtesy Israel Department of Antiquities and Museums).

6.5. The various linguistic stages of *Assyrian*, the dialect of the northern part of Mesopotamia, can be divided into Old Assyrian (*ca.* 1900-1700 B.C.), with texts principally from commercial settlements in Anatolia, but written in the same dialect, Middle Assyrian (*ca.* 1500-1000 B.C.), with records strongly influenced by Babylonian, and Neo-Assyrian (*ca.* 1000-600 B.C.), which was Aramaicized in its final phase, especially in the northwestern regions of the Assyrian Empire and in the wording of contracts.

C. Late Babylonian

6.6. Late Babylonian is the written language of South Mesopotamia in the Persian, Seleucid, and Arsacid periods from *ca.* 600 B.C. onwards, while Aramaic and the practically unknown Chaldaean dialect were the spoken idioms which by a gradual process influenced the written language. Since people resorted in the Near East to professional scribes to have even their private letters written, read, and translated, the existence of Late Babylonian tablets belonging to this genre does not prove that Babylonian subsisted as a vernacular language at that time, although there were certainly educated people having a fairly good knowledge of the literary idiom. The latter does not seem to have borrowed an important part of its lexicon from Aramaic, but certain texts can hardly be considered as written in a truly Babylonian dialect, since their type of speech reveals a too far-reaching linguistic change in phonetics, morphology, and syntax, as the use of *iprus*-forms in the volitive functions of the Aramaic imperfect (§54.6) and the occasional transmutation of the stative into an Aramaic perfect (§38.10).

7. WEST SEMITIC

7.1.   West Semitic was traditionally divided into two groups, namely the Canaanite and the Aramaic, with Hebrew and Syriac as the main literary languages. In recent times, Amorite and Ugaritic have often been considered as older forms of speech of Canaanite despite the fact that they are morphologically and syntactically more distinct from Hebrew than the North Arabian languages. For this reason, Amorite and Ugaritic have been classified here as North Semitic tongues, while the North Arabian forms of speech will be viewed as the third main family of the West Semitic languages of Syria-Palestine and Northern Arabia.

A. Canaanite

7.2.   The name Canaanite, coined from the toponym Canaan, the ancient appellation of southern Syria and Palestine, will be used in the present work to designate, as a rule, the older stages of the Canaanite languages, known from sources of the second millennium B.C. The stages of the first millennium B.C. are classified, instead, as Hebrew, Phoenician, Ammonite, Moabite, and Edomite. The Hebrew language is the only one in this group that survived the Antiquity.

a) Old Canaanite

7.3.   Old Canaanite forms of speech of the second millennium B.C. are reflected to a certain extent in the Old Babylonian tablets from Hazor. They are attested directly by a number of short inscriptions found in Palestine (Proto-Canaanite) and in the Sinai peninsula (Proto-Sinaitic), some superimposed upon datable Egyptian objects. The whole series is variously dated by scholars from 1800 B.C. onwards. If the inscriptions on Phoenician arrowheads and the Gezer calendar are added to this group, the latter can be dated between the mid-second millennium B.C. and the 10th century B.C., and it represents the earliest purely alphabetic form of writing. Also the pseudo-hieroglyphic inscriptions of Byblos are most likely composed in a Canaanite dialect, but they cannot be considered as deciphered.

7.4.   The Amarna correspondence of the 14th century B.C. provides a large number of Canaanite glosses and linguistic peculiarities in its Babylonian cuneiform text. This material can be supplemented by the Canaanite words and forms occurring in eight texts found at Kāmid el-Lōz (Lebanon) and in a few scattered documents, by the Semitic loanwords in ancient Egyptian, and by the few words in Egyptian texts put into the mouth of Semites. Also this material is unmistakably Canaanite, but cannot be further defined with any certainty.

b) Hebrew

7.5.   Hebrew is the Canaanite form of speech used inland from *ca.* 1000 B.C. onwards. In the first millennium B.C., it comprised two main dialects — the Israelite in the north and the Judahite in the south — but the biblical text retained but a few traces of dialects that can instead be identified in the epigraphical material. Besides the Bible, the Dead Sea scrolls, the documents discovered in the Judaean Desert, the Mishnah, and the Tosefta belong to the period when Hebrew was still a spoken language, at least in some parts of Judaea. The last mentioned works are written in the so-called Mishnaic Hebrew, which existed previously for hundreds of years as a vernacular but became a new literary language only in the late first century A.D. Also some of the documents discovered in the Judaean Desert are written in this idiom and its influence can be detected already in the later books of the Bible, e.g. Qohelet, the Chronicles, and Esther. The Dead Sea scrolls have revealed some linguistic features that are parallel also to the particular Samaritan tradition of Hebrew, although Samaritan Hebrew, retained as the language of liturgy and revived as literary language from the 14th century on, exhibits innovative elements as well, developed under the influence of Aramaic and of the Arabic vernacular. Mishnaic Hebrew ceased to be spoken around 200 A.D., but it remained a written language that served for every written purpose and even flourished in poetry and literature. This later form of Mishnaic Hebrew was influenced by Biblical Hebrew and by Aramaic. As a result, this mixed idiom cannot be employed as a trustworthy basis for the study of spoken and literary Mishnaic Hebrew used in the earlier period. The same must be said about the "Masoretic" Hebrew of the 9th-10th centuries A.D. that serves as the main base for the grammatical investigation of Biblical Hebrew, though Elijah Levita (1468/9-1549) pointed already out that the Masoretic vowels and accents do not belong to the original text but had originated in post-talmudic times. In fact, although the consonantal text of the Hebrew Bible is generally speaking reliable from the linguistic point of view, its phonological and grammatical interpretation by the various Schools of "Masoretes" or traditionalists, especially that from Tiberias, is conditioned by their knowledge of the language spoken more than a thousand years before them and by the reliability of oral traditions underlying the reading of the Bible in Jewish communities whose vernaculars were mainly Aramaic or Arabic dialects. Since 1881 Hebrew again became a spoken idiom and it is nowadays the language of modern Israel, known as *ivrīt*. There was a certain impact of Yiddish on the early stage of modern Hebrew, since most of the Jewish immigrants who arrived in Palestine from eastern Europe prior to World War II were native speakers of Yiddish. Instead, the recent massive immigration of Jews from Russia brings about a Slavic impact on some aspects of spoken Hebrew.

Vocalized quotations of Hebrew words and sentences in the present *Outline* are generally based on the reading of the Tiberian Masoretes as preserved in the Ms. St. Petersburg B 19^A which was written in 1009 A.D. and whose vocalization was adjusted to the system of Aaron Ben-Asher. As a matter of fact, its vowel points and accents are almost identical with those of the Aleppo Codex pointed by Aaron Ben-Asher himself in the first half of the 10th century A.D. (Fig. 9).

c) Phoenician

7.6. Phoenician is the Canaanite form of speech used in the first millennium B.C. in the coastal cities of Byblos, Sidon, Tyre, in the

Fig. 9. Page from the Aleppo Codex with the text of I Chron. 2,26-3,4.

neighbouring towns, and in the various settlements and colonies established in Anatolia, along the Mediterranean shores, and on the Atlantic coast of Spain and of Morocco. The epigraphical material attests the existence of different dialects in the Phoenician homeland and overseas. In Carthage, a Tyrian foundation, the language developed a distinct form, called Punic (Fig. 10), that was also used in the Numidian kingdoms of North Africa. In its latest stage, documented down to the first centuries A.D., the Phoenician speech of West Mediterranean countries is called Neo-Punic and it is attested also in Latin script (Latino-Punic inscriptions). As far as our information goes, Neo-Punic continued to be spoken in North Africa until the 5th century A.D., perhaps down to the 11th century A.D. at Surt, in Libya, but Phoenician died out as a spoken language in the Levant at latest in the 3rd or 4th centuries A.D.

Fig. 10. Punic inscription from Carthage.

d) Ammonite

7.7. Ammonite, represented by a small corpus of inscriptions dated from the 9th to the end of the 6th century B.C., was a Canaanite form of speech, used east of the lower Jordan valley around Rabbath-Ammon, modern Ammān. It was probably more different from Hebrew than can be guessed from the unvocalized Aramaic script of the inscriptions.

e) Moabite

7.8. Moabite, represented by two inscriptions and a few seals dated from the 9th through the 6th century B.C., was a Canaanite idiom spoken east of the Dead Sea. Although the ninth-century B.C. Moabite inscriptions present the earliest "Hebrew" characters of the alphabetic script, their language cannot be regarded as an Hebrew dialect.

f) Edomite

7.9. Edomite, attested by a few inscriptions and seals dated from the 9th through the 4th century B.C., was the Canaanite idiom of southern Transjordan and eastern Negev. Despite our very poor knowledge of the language, palaeography and morphology reveal some specifically Edomite features.

B. Aramaic

7.10. Aramaic forms a widespread linguistic group that could be classified also as North or East Semitic. Its earliest written attestations go back to the 9th century B.C. and some of its dialects survive until the present day. Several historical stages and contemporaneous dialects have to be distinguished.

a) Early Aramaic

7.11. Early Aramaic is represented by an increasing number of inscriptions from Syria, Assyria, North Israel, and northern Transjordan dating from the 9th through the 7th century B.C. (Fig. 11). There are no important differences in the script and the spelling of the various documents, except for the Tell Fekherye statue and the Tell Ḥalaf pedestal inscription. The morphological variations point instead to the existence of several dialects that represent different levels of the evolution of the language. While the Tell Fekherye inscription (*ca.* 850 B.C.) seems to testify to the use of internal or "broken" plurals, the two Samalian inscriptions from Zincirli (8th century B.C.) apparently retain the case endings in the plural and have no emphatic state. The latter is also unattested in the Deir 'Allā plaster inscription (*ca.* 800 B.C.) and on the stele found at Tell el-Qāḍi (*ca.* 850 B.C.), and both do not use the determinative-relative *zy*. From the 8th century B.C. on, a standard form of the language prevails in the inscriptions, and even in the juridical and economic documents on clay tablets from Upper Mesopotamia and Assyria.

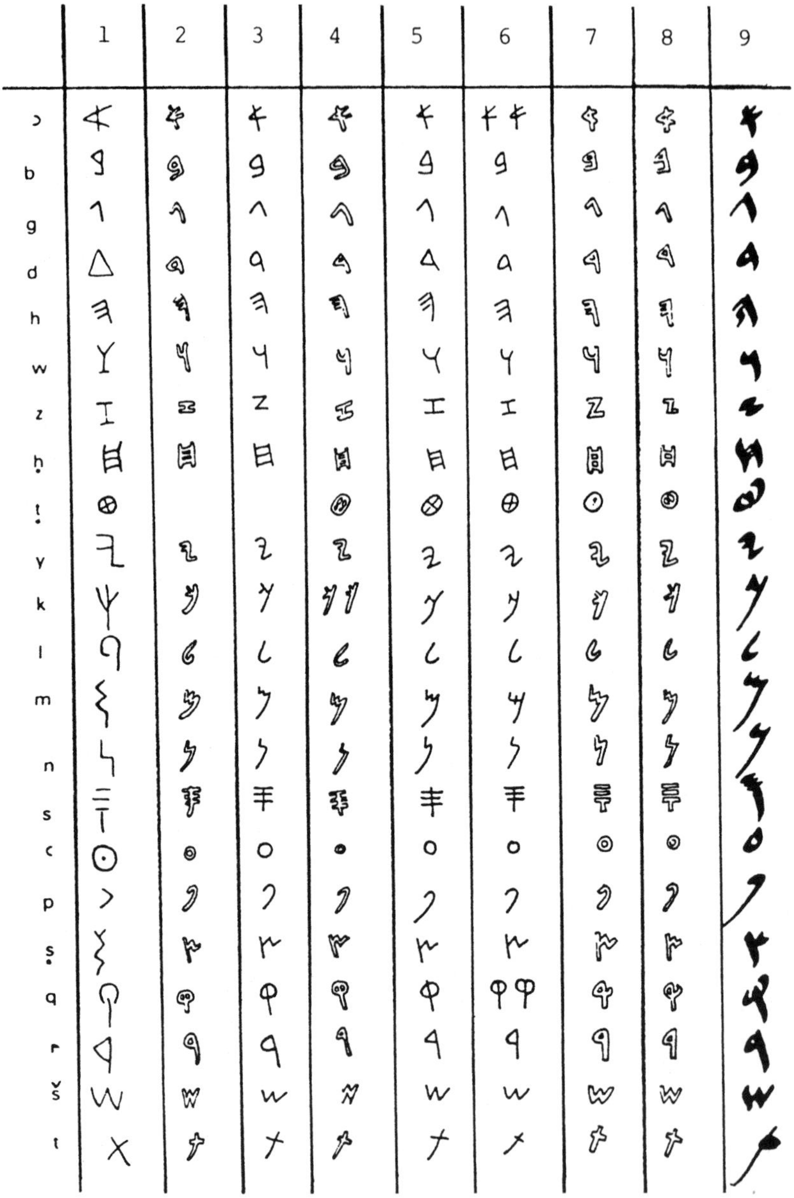

Fig. 11. Alphabetic scripts of Syria, Cilicia, and northern Transjordan in the 9th and
8th centuries B.C.:
1. Tell Fekherye, mid-9th century; 2. Kilamuwa (Zincirli), late 9th century; 3. Zakkūr
(Tell Afis), beginning of the 8th century; 4. Panamuwa I (Zincirli), early 8th century;
5. Sefire, mid-8th century; 6. Karatepe, mid-8th century; 7. Panamuwa II (Zincirli),
ca. 730; 8. Bar-Rakkāb (Zincirli), late 8th century; 9. Deir 'Allā, *ca.* 800.

b) Official or Imperial Aramaic

7.12. Official or Imperial Aramaic is the language of the Aramaic documents of the Persian Empire, but some authors apply this qualification also to earlier texts. Beginning with the 8th century B.C. Aramaic became the *lingua franca* of the Near East and it served later as the official language of the Achaemenian administration until the end of the 4th century B.C. It is the language of various inscriptions on stone, of the Aramaic documents found in Egypt, in the Wadi Dāliyeh (Samaria), and at Persepolis, as well as of the Aramaic letters and documents quoted in the Book of Ezra.

c) Standard Literary Aramaic

7.13. Standard Literary Aramaic is the literary dialect that emerged in the 7th century B.C. and subsisted alongside the Official Aramaic of the Achaemenian period. The Story of Ahiqar, perhaps the scattered phrases of the story from the tomb at Sheikh el-Faḍl, the Bar Punesh fragments, and the narrative in the Aramaic portions of Ezra are the earliest examples of this form of speech that is further used in the Book of Daniel, in the literary Aramaic compositions discovered at Qumrān, in the Targums to the Pentateuch and to the Prophets, known as Onqelos and Jonathan, in *Megillat Ta'anit*, and, at a much later date, in the "Scroll of Antiochus".

d) Middle Aramaic

7.14. Middle Aramaic is the name generally given to the Aramaic dialects attested from the 3rd century B.C. to the 3rd century A.D. Besides the texts in Standard Literary Aramaic and in a faulty Official Aramaic that survived in non-Aramaic speaking regions of the former Persian Empire, in Afghanistan, Pakistan, Turkmenistan, and in the Caucasus, there are a number of epigraphic dialects from this period.

7.15. The documents and the Bar Kokhba letters discovered in the Judaean Desert represent the *Palestinian Aramaic* of Judaea.

7.16. Documents written in *Nabataean* were also discovered among the scrolls of the Judaean Desert. Although they are basically written in Official Aramaic, they already contain elements of Middle Aramaic on the one hand, and of Arabic on the other, like the Nabataean inscriptions

and graffiti from Transjordan, North Arabia, Negev, Egypt, Greece, and
Italy. From the 2nd century B.C. to the 4th century A.D. Nabataean
Aramaic was the written language of the Arab population whose main
centre was Petra, historically attested from the beginning of the 4th century B.C. The Nabataean use of the Aramaic language and script continued a North Arabian tradition attested already in the 5th century B.C. by
the inscriptions of the oasis of Tayma' and somewhat later by the
inscription of Qaynû, king of Qedar, found at Tell el-Maskhūta (Egypt).
The last dated Nabataean Aramaic text dates from 356 A.D. There are
also a few inscriptions written in Nabataean Arabic (§7.38).

7.17. The *Palmyrene* inscriptions, dating from the 1st century B.C.
through the 3rd century A.D., are written in a West Aramaic idiom based
on Official Aramaic (Fig. 12). Traces of Arabic, which was the language
of a substantial part of the population of Palmyra, are detected in some
of these inscriptions, the language of which was also influenced by an
East Aramaic dialect.

Fig. 12. Palmyrene inscription from Malkū's tomb, dated A.D. 214
(Courtesy Ny Carlsberg Glyptotek, Copenhagen).

7.18. The *Uruk Incantation* text from the 3rd or 2nd century B.C., found in southern Iraq and written in cuneiform script on a clay tablet, is composed in East Aramaic, perhaps in the Chaldaean dialect.

7.19. Also the Aramaic texts of *Hatra*, *ca.* 100 km south-west of Mosul, show the influence of East Aramaic. They date from the 2nd and 3rd centuries A.D., and their language is closely related to Syriac. The inscriptions from Ashur and other sites in the area of Upper Tigris, all dating from the Late Parthian period, reflect a closely related form of speech and are written in the North Mesopotamian variant of the Aramaic script.

7.20. The earliest *Syriac* inscriptions from the region of Edessa, modern Urfa, go back to the 1st-3rd centuries A.D. and are all of pagan origin. Their script resembles that of the contemporary cursive Palmyrene inscriptions, but their language occupies an intermediate position between West and East Aramaic.

7.21. The *Aramaic logograms* in Parthian inscriptions, i.e. words written in Aramaic but read in Middle Iranian, are the precursors of the ideograms used later in the Pahlavi texts of the Sassanid dynasty (226-642 A.D.). The most important witnesses of this use of Aramaic logograms are the Avroman parchment from 52/3 A.D. and the inscription of the Herakles statue from 150/1 A.D. Despite the contrary opinion of some authors, also the *ca.* 2000 ostraca of Nisa (Turkmenistan), from the 1st century B.C., are written with Aramaic logograms, and this may also be the case of the inscriptions found at Toprak-kale, in Uzbekistan, and considered by their editors as Khwarezmian (Middle Iranian).

e) Western Late Aramaic

7.22. From the 3rd century A.D. on, positive distinctions between East and West Aramaic can be made on ground of vocabulary, phonology, morphology, and syntax. It is a period with abundant written material. West Aramaic consists primarily of material known from Palestine.

7.23. The *Jewish Palestinian Aramaic* of the Byzantine period is often called *Galilean Aramaic* since most of the material comes from Galilee, but this appellation may be too restrictive. The material consists of a variety of dedicatory and memorial inscriptions, but the dialect is best

known from literary works, such as the Palestinian Talmud, the Aramaic
parts of *Genesis Rabba*, of *Leviticus Rabba*, and of other Midrashim,
and from the Palestinian Targums, as best represented by the so-called
Neofiti I Targum from the Vatican Library and by fragments from the
Cairo Geniza.

7.24. *Samaritan Aramaic*, written in an offshoot of the Palaeo-Hebrew
script and spoken by Samaritans till about the 10th century A.D., is represented by the Targum to the Pentateuch, the Aramaic hymns preserved
in the liturgy, and such works as *Memar Marqah* and the *Asaṭir*.

7.25. *Christian Palestinian Aramaic*, sometimes called Palestinian
Syriac because of its script, was spoken by converted Jews living in
Judaea and in Transjordan at least from the 3rd-4th centuries A.D. until
the Arabization of Palestine. Besides some epigraphic finds, this dialect
is best represented by fragments of Bible translations from Greek, as
well as of translations of other Greek religious texts, such as the Melchite liturgy. The preserved sources date from the 5th-8th centuries
A.D., when the language was spoken, and from the 11th-13th centuries
A.D., when it was used only in the liturgy. The sources exhibit a dialect
closely related to Samaritan Aramaic (§7.24) and to Galilean Aramaic
(§7.23). Traces of Mishnaic Hebrew influence are found in this dialect.

f) Eastern Late Aramaic

7.26. Eastern Late Aramaic is represented by the literary languages
Syriac, Mandaic, and Jewish Babylonian Aramaic, as well as by the Aramaic logograms in Pahlavi and other Middle Iranian dialects.

7.27. *Syriac*, originally the dialect of Edessa, occupies an intermediate
position between East and West Aramaic. It is the best documented of
the Aramaic languages, with a large literature in both poetry and prose,
primarily of a religious Christian nature. Its oldest literary works go
back to the 2nd century A.D. and the language is used down to the present day, although Syriac was generally replaced by Neo-Arabic as a
spoken idiom from the 8th century A.D. on. One can distinguish Western and Eastern Syriac, but the differences are limited to some phonetic
features. Instead, there are two different vocalization systems and three
main Syriac styles of writing: the *Esṭrangelā*, a formal script which
resembles that of the Syriac inscriptions of the 1st-3rd centuries A.D.,

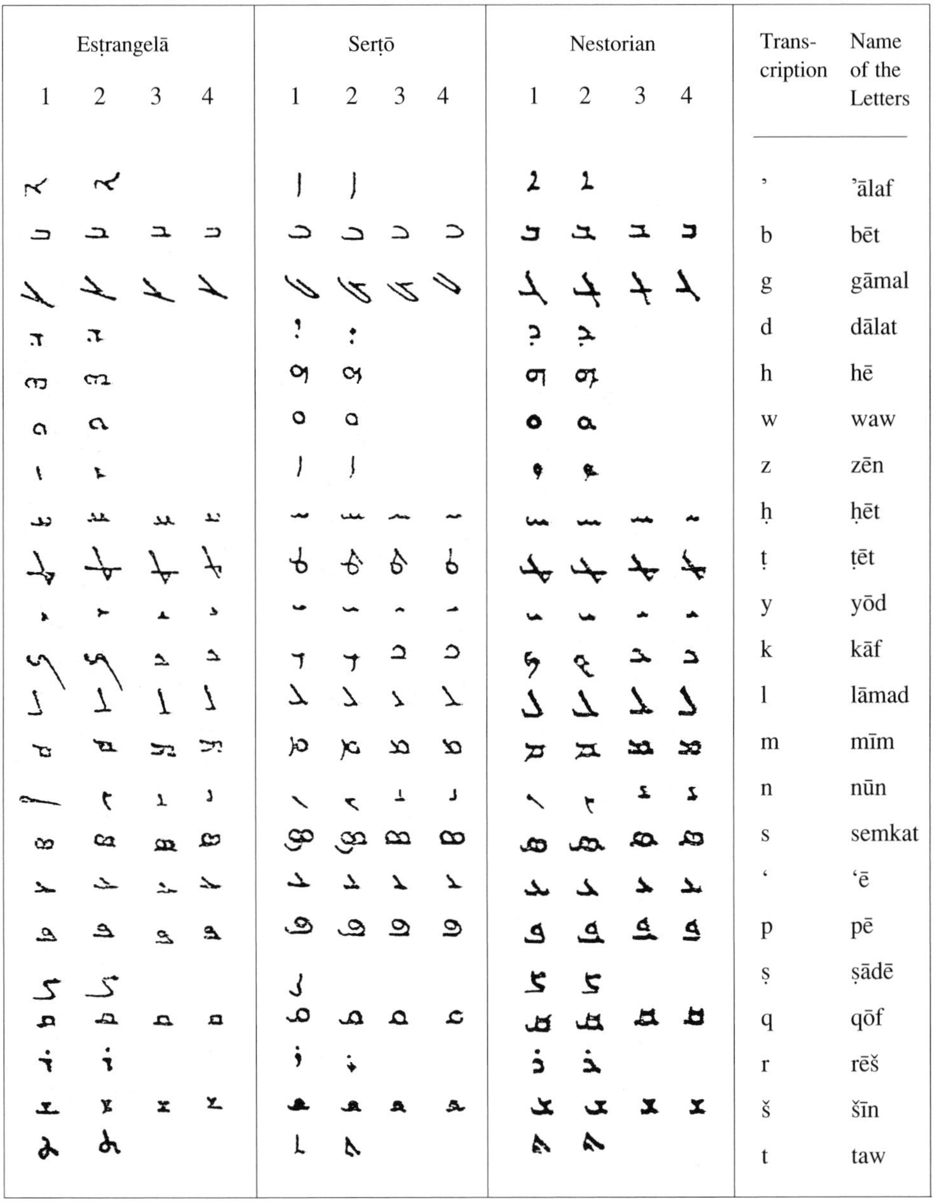

Estrangelā				Serṭō				Nestorian				Trans-cription	Name of the Letters
1	2	3	4	1	2	3	4	1	2	3	4		
												ʾ	ʾālaf
												b	bēt
												g	gāmal
												d	dālat
												h	hē
												w	waw
												z	zēn
												ḥ	ḥēt
												ṭ	ṭēt
												y	yōd
												k	kāf
												l	lāmad
												m	mīm
												n	nūn
												s	semkat
												ʿ	ʿē
												p	pē
												ṣ	ṣādē
												q	qōf
												r	rēš
												š	šīn
												t	taw

Fig. 13. Syriac Scripts.

the *Serṭō*, a developed cursive ordinarily used by the Jacobites in the West, and the Nestorian, another cursive variation used in the East. The majority of the Syriac letters have different forms depending upon their position in a word, whether at the beginning, middle or end, and whether they stand alone or are joined to others (Fig. 13). The works of Syriac grammarians, like Jacob of Edessa (7th century A.D.), have exerted an influence on both Arabic and Hebrew grammatical traditions.

7.28. *Mandaic* is the language of the Gnostic sect of the Mandaeans, whose origins are obscure. The sect flourished for a time in Upper Mesopotamia, around Harran, and then moved to southern Iraq and Iran where its adepts have still been identified in the 20th century, and a form of colloquial Mandaic has been recorded. The earliest Mandaic texts, known at present, date from the 4th-6th centuries A.D. and their major literary works may also have been written in that period. Besides, a large number of inscribed "magic" bowls, in Mandaic script and language, have been discovered in southern Iraq and Iran. They date from the 5th-7th centuries A.D. and their script represents a South Mesopotamian variant of the Aramaic script-type. Since Mandaic uses *matres lectionis* more than any other Aramaic dialect and does not follow any traditional orthography, it has been of great importance for establishing the phonology and the precise morphology of East Aramaic.

From the Canonical Prayerbook of the Mandaeans, ed. E.S. Drower (Leiden 1959).

7.29. *Jewish Babylonian Aramaic* is known primarily from the Babylonian Talmud, the Geonic texts, the *Book of Commandments* by 'Anan ben Dawid, the early Karaite leader, and the Jewish Babylonian incantations of the "magic" bowls from the Nippur region. These various sources, for which good manuscripts should be used, date from the 3rd through the 11th century A.D. Differences have been detected in the language of these texts spread over eight centuries.

7.30. The *Aramaic logograms* in Pahlavi and other Middle Iranian dialects are mostly derived from Official Aramaic, but some of them indicate changes due either to the influence of Late Eastern Aramaic or to errors made by the scribes who no longer knew the Aramaic language. Most useful is the *Frahang i Pahlavīk*, a kind of Aramaic - Middle Iranian glossary that might go back at least to the 7th century A.D.

g) Neo-Aramaic

7.31. Neo-Aramaic dialects are spoken nowadays by about half a million people living in various regions of the Near East or emigrated to other parts of the world. These dialects are the surving remains of the once widespread Aramaic languages, preserved by religious minorities in mountainous retreat areas. They are divided into three main groups.

7.32. *Western Neo-Aramaic* is still used by Christians and Moslems in the three villages of Ma'lūla, Ǧubb 'Adīn, and Baḥ'ā, about 60 km. north of Damascus. The language is reminiscent in many respects of the ancient Aramaic dialects of Palestine (§7.23-25). Characteristic of this Western form of spoken Aramaic are the changes $\bar{a} > \bar{o}$ and $p > f$, the use of the *y*-prefix in the 3rd person of the imperfect, etc. Western Aramaic is exposed to strong phonetic, grammatical, and lexical influences of vernacular Arabic.

7.33. *Ṭūrōyo* comprises the dialects spoken by Christians in the Ṭūr 'Abdīn area, near Mardin, in southeastern Turkey. These dialects occupy an intermediate position between Western and Eastern Neo-Aramaic. Like Eastern Neo-Aramaic (§7.34), they show a tendency to use the pharyngal *ḥ* and have developed a conjugation based on participles, but they exhibit the unconditioned change $\bar{a} > \bar{o}$ like Western Neo-Aramaic. A closely related idiom was spoken at Mlaḥsṓ, a village in the Diyarbakır province. The large emigration of the local population resulted in the creation of scattered Ṭurōyo-speaking communities in Western Europe.

7.34. *Eastern Neo-Aramaic*, called also "Modern Syriac" or "Assyrian", is the continuation of the eastern branch of Late Aramaic. There are archaic elements retained in Neo-Aramaic which are absent from Classical Syriac (§7.27), as well as innovations shared by Mandaic (§7.28) and by Jewish Babylonian Aramaic (§7.29), but lacking in Syriac. It is assumed therefore that Eastern Neo-Aramaic developed from a language similar to Mandaic and to Jewish Babylonian Aramaic, but there are no documents extant in this form of speech since it was not used as a literary vehicle. Neo-Aramaic dialects are used in Kurdistan, near the common borders of Iraq, Iran, and Turkey, in the neighbourhood of Lake Urmia, in Iran, and near Mosul, in Iraq. They are spoken both by Jews and by Christians of different denominations: Nestorians, Chaldaeans, and Jacobites. Benjamin of Tudela, who visited Kurdistan in the mid-12th century A.D., reports that the Jews living there were speaking Aramaic. Nowadays, however, most of the Jews have emigrated to Israel, while the emigration of Christians to the United States and to Armenia, Georgia, and Russia had already started as a result of World War I. The Christians write in the Nestorian type of Syriac script, used for printing periodicals, books, and pamphlets. The fairly uniform standard written language of these publications is based on the Urmi dialect. It gave rise to a spoken *koinè* that coexists nowadays with the dialects.

In this *Outline*, as at rule, references to Neo-Aramaic, made without further specification, point to the Eastern Neo-Aramaic.

C. Arabic

7.35. The earliest attestations of Arabic are a number of proper names borne by leaders of Arab tribes mentioned in Neo-Assyrian texts. While some of them bear Aramaic names, others have names that belong to a group of dialects now called Proto-Arabic or Ancient North Arabian. Various North Arabian populations have to be distinguished, differing by their language and their script, and above all by their way of life. While populations of merchants and farmers were settled in towns and oases, semi-nomadic breeders of sheep and goats were living in precarious shelters in the vicinity of sedentary settlements, and true nomads, dromedary breeders and caravaneers, were moving over great distances and living in tents. Different forms of speech have been distinguished, both urban and Bedouin.

a) Pre-Islamic North and East Arabian

7.36. Pre-Islamic North and East Arabian dialects use a variant of the South Arabian monumental script, that had developed from the common Semitic alphabet. Only the few Nabataean Arabic texts are written in Aramaic script.

7.37. *Liḥyānite* is the local dialect of the oasis of al-'Ulā, ancient Dedān, that had its own king in the 6th/5th century B.C. Liḥyānite should not be distinguished, as it seems, from the language of the so-called "Dedānite" inscriptions which antedate the period when Dedān was the residence of a Persian governor in the 5th century B.C. Then, from the 4th century B.C. through the 1st century B.C., the oasis was the capital of the kingdom of Liḥyān, which for nearly two centuries was home to a colony of Minaean tradesmen from South Arabia. Dedān and the neighbouring site of al-Ḥidjr (Ḥegrā') were occupied in *ca.* 25 B.C. by the Nabataean kingdom. Liḥyānite is represented by a series of graffiti and of mainly monumental inscriptions engraved in a variety of the South Arabian script.

7.38. *Nabataean Arabic* is represented by a few inscriptions in Aramaic script, that testify to the evolution of the language. While the case endings of the nouns are still used correctly in the bilingual Aramaic-Arabic of Oboda, dated *ca.* 100 A.D., there was no longer a fully functioning case system in the 3rd and 4th centuries A.D., as appears from the inscriptions of Ḥegrā' (267 A.D.) and an-Namāra (328 A.D.). Also in South Arabian, the case differentiation between *bnw* and *bny*, where it can be detected, has become merely vestigial by the 1st-3rd centuries A.D.

7.39. The so-called *Thamūdic* graffiti are named after Thamūd, one of several Arabian tribes mentioned in the Assyrian annals (*Tamudi*), in a Greek inscription of a Nabataean temple in northeastern Ḥedjaz, dated *ca.* 169 A.D., in a 5th-century Byzantine source, in North Arabian graffiti from the Tayma' region, in many passages of the Qur'ān, and in writings of Arab geographers. These sources make it clear that the

Thamūdaeans were living between Mecca and Tayma'. However, the name "Thamūdic" was incorrectly applied to various types of graffiti found throughout Arabia, dating from the 6th century B.C. through the 3rd or 4th century A.D. and belonging to different dialects. The oldest Thamūdic inscriptions, probably from the 6th century B.C., have been found in the northern Tayma' area.

7.40. The *Ṣafaitic* inscriptions date from the 1st century B.C. through the 4th century A.D. They are so called because they belong to a type of graffiti first discovered in 1857 in the basaltic desert of Ṣafā, southeast of Damascus. Many thousands of such texts, scattered over an area including southeastern Syria, Jordan, and North Arabia have so far been collected and in part published (Fig. 14-15). They are, to a large extent, memorial inscriptions that mention the name of the person and of his ancestors, often specify his job or the circumstances of his passage, and call on a deity to protect his memory and ensure peace to him. Since the Ṣafaitic graffiti have been found on the Nabataean territory and are contemporaneous with the Nabataean Aramaic inscriptions, some of them are likely to be written in Nabataean Arabic. In any case, Ṣafaitic texts do not belong to a single dialect, as shown e.g. by the use of two different articles, namely *h-*, which is very common in Ṣafaitic inscriptions, and *'al*, which is widely used in Nabataean Arabic proper names but appears exceptionally in names attested by the Ṣafaitic graffiti.

7.41. *Ḥasaean* is the name given to the language of the inscriptions written in a variety of the South Arabian script and found mainly in the great oasis of al-Ḥāsa', in the east of Saudi Arabia. South Arabian script was used also in southern Iraq ("Chaldaean" inscriptions) and on the East Arabian coast, from al-Ḥāsa' down to 'Omān, for the rendering of various local forms of East Arabian speech. These inscriptions can be dated from the 8th through the 1st century B.C.

b) Pre-Classical Arabic

7.42. Pre-Classical Arabic dialects, both urban and Bedouin, are described to a certain extent by early Arab philologists which have preserved some data on the forms of speech in the Arab peninsula around the 7th-8th centuries A.D. For the period from the beginning of the 2nd century B.C. through the 3rd century A.D. we actually possess the inscriptions from Qaryat al-Fāw, near modern Sulayyil, on the trade

Fig. 14. Three Ṣafaitic inscriptions on a boulder in Wadi Sirḥān (courtesy of Abdu-Aziz
al-Sudairi):
1° *lh lblm bn 'rm*, "(belonging) to him, to *Blm*, son of 'Amru";
2° *ldhbn nql bn mnhl*, "(belonging) to Ḏahbānu the carrier, son of Minhālu";
3° *ls²mt bn 'n'l*, "(belonging) to Śāmitu, son of 'Ān'il".

route linking Nadjrān with the eastern Arabian coast. They are written in
fine monumental South Arabian script, capable of expressing the phonetic features of Arabic unambiguously. They reveal the disappearance

Fig. 15. Ṣafaitic inscription on a boulder in Wadi Sirḥān (courtesy of Abdu-Aziz al-Sudairi): *l'bṣ 'ṭrw*, "(belonging) to Abūṣu, (man) of 'Aṭṭara".

of the nunation (e.g. *mn 'zzm* = Classical *min 'azīzin mā*, "from anyone strong") and of the case system (e.g. *lwldhw*, "for his child"), but attest the preservation of *š* (s^1) and *ś* (s^2), of *ḏ*, *ṯ*, *ḍ*, *ġ*, etc. However, dialects with and without case endings coexisted, and the -*t* of the feminine ending was preserved in some idioms, while it has dropped in others, except in the construct state. The consonantal text of the Qur'ān, written in a script developed from the Nabataean cursive, is most likely a literary expression of the urban dialect of Mecca and Medina in Mohammed's time. Thus the feminine ending -*t* is replaced by the *mater lectionis -h*, like in Aramaic, except in the construct state, where ancient Qur'ān manuscripts preserve the spelling -*t*. There was no longer a fully functioning case system in nouns and the case endings, when indicated in script, have probably lost their functional yield. The consonants not contained in the Aramaic alphabet are indicated by letters marking related sounds, according to a system already established at Tayma' in the Persian period. Thus $ḍ$, which was in Old Arabic an emphatic lateral $ś$, is signified by "ṣ" and $ẓ$, which was an emphatic interdental $ṭ$, is expressed by the corresponding dental "ṭ", just as $ṯ$ is indicated by "t" and $ḏ$ by "d" (Fig. 16).

c) Classical Arabic

7.43. Classical Arabic is the language of Pre-Islamic poetry, probably based on an archaic form of the dialects of Nadjd, in Central Arabia, shaped further to satisfy the needs of poetical diction and of metre, and standardized in the Abbasid empire, in the schools of al-Kūfa and Baṣrā'. Already before Islam, perhaps as early as *ca.* 500 A.D., this language was employed by poets whose vernacular may have differed strongly from the archaic Nadjdi dialects, thus testifying to the emergence of an Arabic *diglossia*, at the latest in the 6th century A.D. The early Arab philologists of the 8th-9th centuries A.D. have provided the consonantal text of the Qur'ān, that had become sacred very quickly, with a number of diacritical symbols in order to fix its pronunciation and to adapt it to the rules of Classical Arabic, without altering the holy text. However, despite the various vocalic signs and the symbols for *tanwīn* (nunation), *tā' marbūṭa* (feminine ending), *hamza*, the system of the "pausal" forms, etc., the language of the Qur'ān preserves certain features deviating from ordinary Classical Arabic and proving thus that the consonantal text has not been tampered with.

d) Neo-Arabic or Middle Arabic

7.44. Neo-Arabic or Middle Arabic is the urban language of the Arab Empire from the 8th century A.D. on, emerged from the Pre-Classical Arabic dialects. It did not arise as a result of the great Arab conquests, although Mesopotamia and Syria-Palestine provided the Aramaic linguistic substratum that stimulated the development initiated a few centuries earlier and apparent already in inscriptions and in the consonantal text of the Qur'ān. An important source for the investigation of early Neo-Arabic are South-Palestinian texts from the 8th-10th centuries A.D., as well as a bilingual Graeco-Arabic fragment from Damascus, dating back to the 8th century A.D., with the Arabic version of Ps. 78 written in Greek majuscules and thus exhibiting the vowel system.

Unbound	Bound to the right	Bound on both sides	Bound to the left	Transcription	Name of the letter
ا	ﺍ	—	—	', ā	'alif
ب	ﺏ	ـبـ	ﺑ	b	bā'
ت	ﺕ	ـتـ	ﺗ	t	tā'
ث	ﺙ	ـثـ	ﺛ	ṯ	ṯā'
ج	ﺝ	ـجـ	ﺟ	ǧ	ǧīm
ح	ﺡ	ـحـ	ﺣ	ḥ	ḥā'
خ	ﺥ	ـخـ	ﺧ	ḫ	ḫā'
د	ﺩ	—	—	d	dāl
ذ	ﺫ	—	—	ḏ	ḏāl
ر	ﺭ	—	—	r	rā'
ز	ﺯ	—	—	z	zāy
س	ﺱ	ـسـ	ﺳ	s	sīn
ش	ﺵ	ـشـ	ﺷ	š	šīn
ص	ﺹ	ـصـ	ﺻ	ṣ	ṣād
ض	ﺽ	ـضـ	ﺿ	ḍ, ṣ́	ḍād
ط	ﻁ	ـطـ	ﻃ	ṭ	ṭā'
ظ	ﻅ	ـظـ	ﻇ	ẓ, ṯ̣	ẓā'
ع	ﻉ	ـعـ	ﻋ	'	'ain
غ	ﻍ	ـغـ	ﻏ	ġ	ġain
ف	ﻑ	ـفـ	ﻓ	f	fā'
ق	ﻕ	ـقـ	ﻗ	q	qāf
ك	ﻙ	ـكـ	ﻛ	k	kāf
ل	ﻝ	ـلـ	ﻟ	l	lām
م	ﻡ	ـمـ	ﻣ	m	mīm
ن	ﻥ	ـنـ	ﻧ	n	nūn
ه	ﻩ	ـهـ	ﻫ	h	hā'
و	ﻭ	—	—	w, ū	wāw
ى	ﻯ	ـيـ	ﻳ	y, ī	yā'

Fig. 16. Arabic Script.

7.45. In almost all the Neo-Arabic dialects *ḍ* has merged with *ẓ*. In the dialects of the sedentary population, interdental spirants have shifted generally to the corresponding occlusives. The disappearance of the case and mood endings led to a more rigid word order in the clause, with a marked tendency to place the subject before the verb and to avoid the inserting of the object between verb and subject. The dual disappears completely in the verb, the adjective, and the pronoun, and its use with the substantive is limited. The relative pronoun becomes invariable, the asyndetic sentences become more frequent, the tenses are associated with the division of time, etc.

e) Modern Arabic

7.46. Modern Arabic dialects, spoken by some hundred and seventy million people, are no descendants of Classical Arabic but rather its contemporaries throughout history, and they are closely related to Neo-Arabic. From the sociological point of view the Modern dialects fall into Bedouin and sedentary colloquials. Among the Bedouin dialects, those of the North and Central Arabian 'Anoze, Shammar, Rwāla, and Dōsiri tribes are better known. According to geographical criteria, that imply different linguistic substrata, the following division emerges: 1° Ḥidjazi dialects in Saudi Arabia; 2° Southwest Arabian in Yemen and Zanzibar; 3° East Arabian dialects of Kuwait, Baḥrain, Qaṭar, and the United Arab Emirates, and the 'Omānī dialects in 'Omān; 4° North Arabian dialects in Iraq, in southeastern Turkey, in the Aleppo area and in oases of the Syrian desert, in Khuzistan (Iran), and in some villages of Uzbekistan; 5° dialects of Syria, Lebanon, Israel, Palestine, Jordan; 6° dialects of northern and central Egypt; 7° dialects of southern Egypt, Sudan, and Central Africa; 8° West Arabian dialects of the Maghrib with Malta and certain regions of western Egypt, to which the Arabic idioms of Muslim Spain (al-Andalus) and of Sicily were closely related. Except for Maltese, no spoken colloquial Arabic achieved official status as a written language, but there is some popular literature in various dialects. With the spread of literacy, *Modern Literary Arabic*, a direct offshoot of Classical Arabic, becomes more and more widely known and it is used today for almost all written purposes and for certain formal kinds of speaking. The Arabic which is used in ordinary conversation by all speakers of Arabic, no matter how well educated, is instead the colloquial Arabic in its different forms of speech.

8. South Semitic

8.1. The present summary exposition divides South Semitic into South Arabian, both epigraphic and modern, and in Ethiopic, with ancient Ethiopic or Ge'ez and various modern languages of Eritrea and Ethiopia, sometimes called "Ethio-Semitic" in order to distinguish them from the Cushitic languages of Ethiopia. This subgrouping of Semitic languages corresponds not only to geographical criteria, but also to shared linguistic features.

A. South Arabian

8.2. In Yemen, at the southern end of the Arabian peninsula, a sedentary agrarian civilization developed at least from the beginning of the second millennium B.C. At the end of the 8th century B.C. appear the oldest monumental rock and display inscriptions so far recorded. A total of at least 8000 such texts, whole or fragmentary, dating down to the 6th century A.D., have been so far discovered. Besides, hundreds of cursive texts incised with a stylus on sticks and palm-leaf stalks have been found in the Yemeni Djawf, but only some of them have been fully deciphered and published (Fig. 17).

Monumental	Ψ	٦	Ψ	ᴾ	♦	⊕	⋛	⟩	⊓	Χ
Cursive										
Transcription	h	l	ḥ	m	q	w	s^2	r	b	t

Monumental	ᴎ	ᴎ	ᴸ	Υ	Ӿ	♦	○	ᴎ	ᴴ	٦
Cursive										
Transcription	s^1	k	n	ḫ	s^3	f	'	'	ṣ(ḍ)	g

Monumental	ᴎ	⊓	⫿	Χ	H	ᴾ	𐤗	ᴎ	ᴾ
Cursive									
Transcription	d	ġ	ṭ	z	ḏ	y	ṯ	ṣ́	ṯ̣ (ẓ)

Fig. 17. South Arabian Alphabet.

Four principal languages, attested by epigraphical documents, have been discerned besides the modern spoken South Arabian idioms: Sabaic, Minaic, Qatabanic, and Ḥaḍramitic (Fig. 18). A number of ancient South Arabian linguistic features have been registered by early Arab grammarians and such occur also in the earliest materials of Andalusian Arabic in Spain, where many "Yemenite" tribesmen have settled in the 8th century A.D.

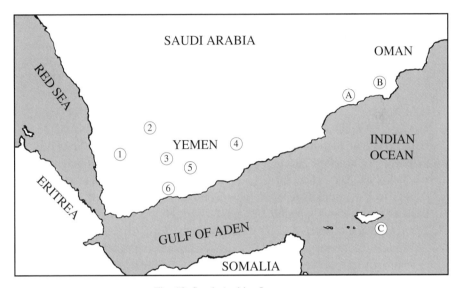

Fig. 18. South Arabian Languages

Epigraphic	Modern
1. Saba (Sabaic)	A. Mahra (Mehri)
2. Ma'in (Minaic)	B. Djibbāl (Śḥeri)
3. Qatabān (Qatabanic)	C. Soqoṭra (Soqoṭri)
4. Ḥaḍramawt (Ḥaḍramitic)	
5. Awsān (Awsānic)	
6. Ḥimyar (Ḥimyaritic)	

a) Sabaic

8.3. Sabaic is epigraphically attested from the 8th century B.C. through the 4th century A.D. in north Yemen, the realm of the ancient kingdom of Saba. In the 4th to 6th centuries A.D. its limits extended southward to include the region of Ẓafar, the centre of the kingdom of Ḥimyar, and eastward to cover the former Qatabanic and Ḥaḍramitic areas, since these languages had by then ceased to be used for epigraphic purposes. Besides, Sabaic inscriptions dating mainly from the 5th-4th centuries B.C. have been found also in Ethiopia. However, they may be written in an Ethiopian language not classifiable properly as Sabaic.

b) Minaic

8.4. Minaic inscriptions are attested at Khirbet Maʻin, ancient Qarnāwu, the capital of the kingdom of Maʻin, at Khirbet Barāqish, ancient Yaṯil, with a few texts from other sites in the east end of Yemeni Djawf. Besides, there are texts from the Minaean trading settlements at al-ʻUlā, ancient Dedān, and at Qaryat al-Fāw, and from scattered places outside Arabia, resulting from Minaean trading activities. Chronologically, these texts date from the 4th to the 2nd centuries B.C.

c) Qatabanic

8.5. Qatabanic monumental texts have been found in the Wadi Bayḥān, in the Wadi Ḥarīb, and on the plateau to the south of the two wadis. They date from the 5th century B.C. through the 2nd century A.D. The few inscriptions from the ephemeral kingdom of Awsān, at the southern marches of Qatabān, are in fact written in Qatabanic. To judge from the name ἡ Αὐσινίτη ἠϊών given to the East African coast in the "Periplus of the Erythraean Sea" (1st century A.D.), the people of Awsān had led the way in the South Arabian trade along the eastern coast of Africa for which the island of Soqoṭra was undoubtedly an important sailing centre (cf. §8.7).

d) Ḥaḍramitic

8.6. Ḥaḍramitic inscriptions have been discovered so far in the royal residence Shabwa, the capital of Ḥaḍramawt, and at several widely scattered sites, in particular at the trading settlement of Khor Rori, ancient Samhar, near modern Salālah, in ʻOmān. Their chronological spread is from roughly the 4th century B.C. to the end of the 3rd century A.D., when Ḥaḍramawt was conquered in its turn by Saba, after the Sabaean conquest of Maʻin and of Qatabān.

e) Modern South Arabian

8.7. The Modern South Arabian languages, which are now confined to a relatively small area in and around Ḏofār and to the island of Soqoṭra, are

the last vestiges of a group of closely related South Semitic languages
which were spoken in the whole of South Arabia. The modern languages
exhibit certain features, however, which are absent from Epigraphic South
Arabian, and it has been doubted whether they can be considered as
directly related to the old literary dialects. They share many distinctive features with Ethiopic. The main modern languages, spoken by some 30.000
people, are Mehri with the closely related Ḥarsūsi and Baṭḥari dialects,
Śḥeri, also called Djibbāli, and Soqoṭri. The special attention paid to the
Mahra tribe of this region by Arab historians and geographers was very
likely due to its peculiar culture and unfamiliar language, as it appears from
the typical description by Ibn al-Muḏǧāwir (13th century): "They are tall
and good-looking, and have their own language which none but they
understand". As for Soqoṭra, which preserved its Greek name of Island of
Dioscorides, it was inhabited in the time of the "Periplus of the Erythraean
Sea" by Arabs, Hindus, and by a Greek colony the going possibly back to
Hellenistic times. Its commercial importance was certainly great (§8.5).

B. Ethiopic

8.8.   Certain features in phonology, morphology, and syntax justify the
classification of the Semitic languages of Eritrea and Ethiopia into North
Ethiopic and South Ethiopic. Both are generally assumed to be derived
from a common Proto-Ethiopic, although the speakers of South Ethiopic
may descend from an earlier wave of Semitic immigrants (§8.9). The
phonological division between North and South Ethiopic is shown by
the Northern preservation of the pharyngals and laryngals. The main
morphological differences appear in the secondary South Ethiopic gemination of the second radical of the verbs in the perfect of the basic stem
(§41.53), in the widespread non-gemination of this radical in the imperfect (§38.7), and in the Southern sharp distinction in the conjugation of
main verbs and subordinate verbs (§39.12). The North Ethiopian languages include Ge'ez, Tigre, and Tigrinya, while South Ethiopic
includes Amharic, Argobba, Gafat, Harari, and Gurage (Fig. 19). The
close relationship between Tigre, Tigrinya, and Ge'ez has not yet been
sufficiently investigated. Therefore, the question whether Tigre and
Tigrinya are direct descendants of Ge'ez or not should remain open. An
answer cannot be provided easily since the majority of Ge'ez texts are
translations and there is no certainty, in particular, that their syntax has
not been influenced by the language of the original texts.

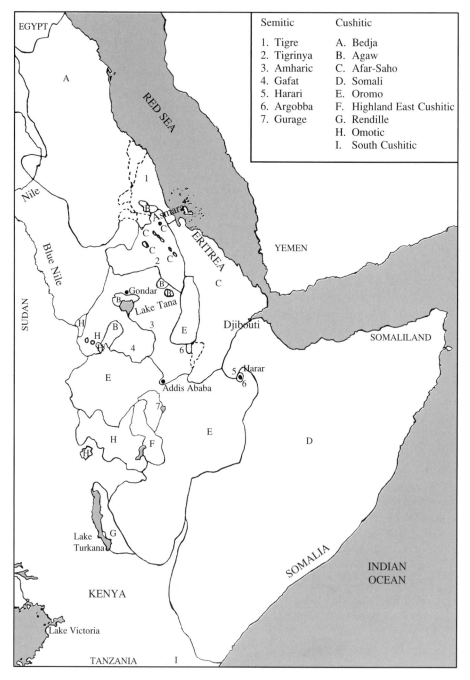

Fig. 19. Semitic and Cushitic languages of the Horn of Africa.

8.9. The Semitic languages of Eritrea and Ethiopia occupy a geo-graphical area in which Cushitic was and still is employed. When Semi-tes from ancient Yemen settled in Ethiopia, they imposed their South Arabian language on this Cushitic domain. A period of bilingualism fol-lowed, which still endures. The Cushitic group lost ground, but not with-out having an impact on the structure and vocabulary of the South Ara-bian idioms spoken by the conquering Semites. This influence of the Cushitic substratum on the Semitic languages of Eritrea and Ethiopia is a crucial problem of Ethiopic linguistics. In the north, the Cushitic lan-guages of Bedja, Agaw, and Saho-Afar appear as the linguistic substra-tum of Ge'ez, Tigre, and Tigrinya, and partially of Amharic and Gafat, while Eastern Sidamo or Highland East Cushitic covered the domain of Amharic, Argobba, Harari, and Gurage, which were influenced also by Oromo and by Somali (§2.9-11). The influence of the Cushitic is stronger in the south than in the north.

8.10. The South Arabian inscriptions found in Ethiopia, especially those of the 5th-4th centuries B.C., prove the existence of ancient rela-tions between southwest Arabia and Ethiopia and might indicate that Semitic was brought to Eritrea and to Ethiopia from Yemen in the first millennium B.C., if not earlier (§3.3).

a) North Ethiopic

8.11. *Ge'ez*, called also Ethiopic, is attested by epigraphic texts from the 2nd century A.D., especially at Aksum, in present-day Tigre province. It was the language of the Aksum Empire, which was con-verted to Christianity in the 4th century A.D. The Bible was translated from Greek into Ge'ez between the 5th and the 7th centuries A.D., although the oldest known manuscripts go back only to the 14th century. Ge'ez remained a spoken language until the end of the 9th century A.D. It survived as a literary language, as the language of worship and sacred literature, and it is still taught in the Church schools. However, no defi-nite conclusion concerning its ancient pronunciation can be drawn on this basis since present-day pronunciation of Ge'ez is influenced by the spoken language, and particularly by Amharic.

8.12. *Tigre* is spoken in Eritrea by seminomadic tribal communities numbering some 300.000 people. It is closely related to Ge'ez, although it is not certain that it is the direct descendant of the language of the

Aksum Empire. It was mainly influenced by two Cushitic languages: the
Bedja and the Agaw. The references to Tigre in the present *Outline* are
based in particular on the dialect of the Mansa' tribe.

8.13.   *Tigrinya* is spoken by some five to six million people, mostly
Christians, in the Tigre province of northern Ethiopia — hence Tigrinya
is called also Tigray — and in the central regions of Eritrea. Tigrinya is
thus, after Arabic and Amharic (§8.14), the living Semitic language with
the largest number of speakers. As in the case of Tigre, the language is
closely related to ancient Ge'ez; it was influenced mainly by Agaw.
Tigrinya literature, written in Ethiopic script (Fig. 21), is only in its
beginnings, but it is developing steadily with papers, magazines, and
books being produced. The earliest known document written in Tigrinya
is the code of customary law discovered at Sarda and dating from the
19th century A.D.

b) South Ethiopic

8.14.   *Amharic* is the official language of Ethiopia. It is spoken in the
central and southern highlands of the country by some fifteen million
people. The oldest Amharic documents actually known are songs from
the 14th century A.D. Amharic syntax and vocabulary are strongly influenced by Cushitic, and Amharic lacks the archaic features discernible in
other South Ethiopian languages. The absence of these features in
Amharic is due to the fact that it represents an innovated type of South
Ethiopic. There are dialect variations in Amharic which bear on phonology, especially regarding palatalization, also on a few grammatical
points, and on the vocabulary, with a marked difference between towns
and the countryside. The references to Amharic in the present *Outline*
are based on the literary language, unless stated otherwise.

8.15.   *Argobba* was still recently spoken in a few villages to the north
of Addis Ababa. It was spoken also to the south of Harar, but the language disappeared in favour of Cushitic Oromo. It is with Amharic that
Argobba has the greatest number of essential features in common.

8.16.   *Harari* is spoken in the city of Harar in eastern Ethiopia. Some
Harari texts, dating to the 16th century, are preserved in Arabic script
and more recent texts, from the 19th century, have been written in
Ethiopic script. Harari has several features in common with North

Ethiopic and the opinion was expressed that Harar was a military colony from northern Ethiopia. No extra-linguistic data help us yet in answering this question.

8.17. *Gurage* is a cluster of rather divergent dialects spoken to the southwest of Addis Ababa by a population numbering about 600.000 persons or more according to other estimations. The Gurage dialects are divided into three groups: a West Gurage group including Chaha, Eža, Ennemor, Endegeň, and Gyeto; an East Gurage group including Selṭi, Wolane, and the dialects spoken on the five islands of Lake Zway; and a North(east) Gurage group represented by Soddo or Aymallal, with a possible sub-group Muher, Gogot, and Masqan, which are alternatively considered as a sub-branch of West Gurage. From the three main groups of dialects, the Eastern ones come closely to Harari and have several features in common with North Ethiopic. There must have been a territorial continuity between the East Gurage and the Harari speakers, later disrupted by population movements.

8.18. *Gafat* was a Semitic language spoken in the region of the Blue Nile, in western Ethiopia. At present, the language disappeared completely in favour of Amharic. Its study is based mainly on a translation of the Song of Songs made from Amharic into Gafat in 1769-72 at the request of James Bruce and on the ample documentation collected in 1947 by W. Leslau from four native speakers. Gafat has some archaic characteristics and a number of features in common with the North Gurage dialect Aymallal, called also Soddo (§8.17). It is the only Semitic language preserving, e.g., the plural noun *kitač* (< *kitāti*), "children", related to ancient Egyptian *ktt*, "little one". It also preserved the noun *mossay*, "child", related to Egyptian *mś*, "child", from the root *mśі*, "to give birth". This word appears as *mossa* in Amharic and as *muča* in Oromo; the root is attested in Gurage with the meaning "calf", corresponding to Coptic *mase*, "calf": *mʷäsa* in Chaha, *mʷässa* in Muher, and *mossa* in Soddo. The Soddo and Gafat domains must have been once contiguous. Later, the movements of the Oromo tribes separated them.

9. Language and Script

9.1. Most languages have existed and still exist as purely oral forms of communication. Writing is no more than a secondary, graphic and largely inadequate representation of spoken language. There is even a greater difference between a living language and a "dead" language, deprived of sound and gesture. This was already perceived by Antoine Fabre d'Olivet (1768-1825) who refused to identify the letters and the vocalization of ancient Hebrew writing with actual phonetic elements, being aware that these elements are "signs" of the real words, as emphatically expressed but unskilfully worked out in his book *La langue hébraïque restituée et le véritable sens des mots hébreux rétabli et prouvé par leur analyse radicale* (Paris 1815-16). His "signs" were, in fact, the precursors of the phonemes as distinguished from their actual realization (§10.7). Yet, written records also present indubitable advantages and the debt of modern society to writing is enormous. Granted the importance of writing, in particular for the knowledge of ancient languages, a student of linguistics must remember that writing is still only a secondary representation of language, that it reflects a standard speech while true dialectal forms transpire but rarely, and that spoken language provides the final clue for understanding its written expression, formulated in common types of script the rigid conservatism of which helps concealing local pronunciations. A treatment of Semitic scripts lies outside the scope of the present work. However, since writing systems may condition and even influence linguistic data, the following aperçu deals with the essential facts of the Semitic writing systems.

A. Cuneiform Script

9.2. The written records of North and East Semitic, as well as the Amarna letters, make use of the cuneiform writing system, the graphs of which, when Semitic texts first began to be written in it, were arranged in vertical columns progressing from right to left. At a somewhat later stage, the texts were arranged in horizontal lines progressing from left to right. A graph in the cuneiform writing system is a wedge or a cluster of wedges imprinted in clay, or imitations of such imprints in other materials. Such a graph is called a "sign" and its referent in the language is called its "value". With the exception of Ugaritic, which uses alphabetic cuneiform signs, the elements of the cuneiform script consist of syllabic signs or syllabograms, of word signs or logograms, often followed by phonetic complements, and of determinatives that specify the class or category of the word which they determine, without being pronounced. Word dividers consisting in small vertical wedges occur irregularly in Old Assyrian texts and they are often used later in Ugaritic cuneiform alphabetic script.

9.3. The Sumerian or Pre-Sumerian origin of the cuneiform writing system, the local variations in the use of signs, and the changes occurring between earlier and later texts cause problems for the correct analysis of the Semitic phonology. The writing system was not designed for Semitic and palliatives, such as scribal conventions and later differentiations of signs, never reached a point where it could be said that every combination of phonemes found expression in the writing. In particular, the notation of pharyngals, laryngals, and semivowels, the distinction of interdentals and dentals, of voiced, unvoiced, and emphatic consonants belonging to the same "triad", the indication of the length of vowels and of the doubling of consonants never received a satisfactory and unambiguous solution. The indication of vowels by syllabograms is of considerable assistance to the linguistic analysis, but the distinction of *i* and *e* does generally not find expression in the writing. Thus, for instance, the cuneiform sign IB has the values *ib*, *ip*, *eb*, *ep*, but may also signify *yib* or *yip* at the beginning of a verbal form. The sign GIŠ has the values *iz*, *is*, *iṣ*, *ez*, *es*, *eṣ*, besides *giš*, the sign DI stands for *di*, *ṭi*, *de*, *ṭe*, and KI has the values *ki*, *qí*, *ke*, *qé*. In short, it is difficult, therefore, to reach phonetically satisfactory conclusions without using data drawn from comparative Semitic linguistics. Besides, the morpho-graphemic spellings like *qa-qa-ad-šu*, "his head", which are often described as reflecting the deep morphological structure of the language (*qaqqad* + *šu*), correspond to an actual pronunciation *qaqqassu*, in accordance with genuine East Semitic morpho-phonemic rules. In other words, also the consonantic elements require an appropriate evaluation and an interpretation. This applies in particular to the Ebla texts that cannot be understood by taking the cuneiform signs at face value, neither in Sumerian nor in Semitic words.

B. Alphabetic Script

9.4. The West and South Semitic languages, as well as Ugaritic, use consonantal alphabetic scripts developed from an alphabet created in

Canaan in the mid-second millennium B.C. and based on Egyptian hieroglyphic signs. While the Ugaritic script represents a cuneiform adaptation of this new writing system, the West and South Semitic languages used its original linear form which developed into two distinct types of letters: the so-called Phoenician alphabet with twenty-two letters and the South Arabian alphabet with twenty-nine letters. The main lines of the evolution of the Semitic alphabet are shown schematically in Fig. 20.

9.5. The Semitic alphabet was originally purely consonantal in character, probably because its creation was inspired by the Egyptian hieroglyphic "alphabet". However, the Ugaritic script of the 14th century B.C. already possesses two supplementary signs *'i* and *'u*, distinct from the original ' that received the value *'a*. These three signs could be used also to mark the vowels *a*, *i/e*, *u*, short or long, at least in Hurrian texts written in alphabetic cuneiform script. Besides, a fully developed use of *matres lectionis* or vowel letters appears in Aramaic and in Moabite as early as the mid-9th century B.C. Three or four consonantal signs of the Phoenician alphabet received a supplementary function in order to indicate long final vowels and, to a limited extent, even long medial vowels: *w* was used to mark *ū/ō*, *y* served to indicate *ī/ē*, *h* was used initially to mark final -*ē* and then also final -*ā*, for which also ' served in Aramaic, perhaps as early as the 8th century B.C., and later in Arabic. This vocalic use of the letters under consideration was borrowed by the Greeks together with the Semitic alphabet and was extended to short vowels, like in later Semitic texts. The ambivalent use of *w* and *y* allows sometimes for the possibility that either the diphthong *aw/ay* or a long vowel is represented in a word. Only Mishnaic Hebrew and some Late Aramaic dialects show the practice of indicating consonantal *w* and *y* by a double spelling *ww* and *yy*; e.g. Mishnaic Hebrew *ywwny* /*Yawnē*/ instead of Biblical Hebrew *ybnh* /*Yabnē*/; Christian Palestinian Aramaic *ḥyy'* /(*ḥ*)*ayya*/, "the life".

Greek o was not borrowed directly from Semitic but by application of the acrophonic principle to the Greek translation ὀφθαλμός of Semitic *'ayn*, "eye".

9.6. The use of the *matres lectionis* *w* and *y* is also attested in the South Arabian type of alphabetic script, with the same vocalic values *ū/ō* and *ī/ē*. Instead, there is no notation at all for *ā*, not even in the Pre-Classical Arabic inscriptions from Qaryat al-Fāw, written in monumental

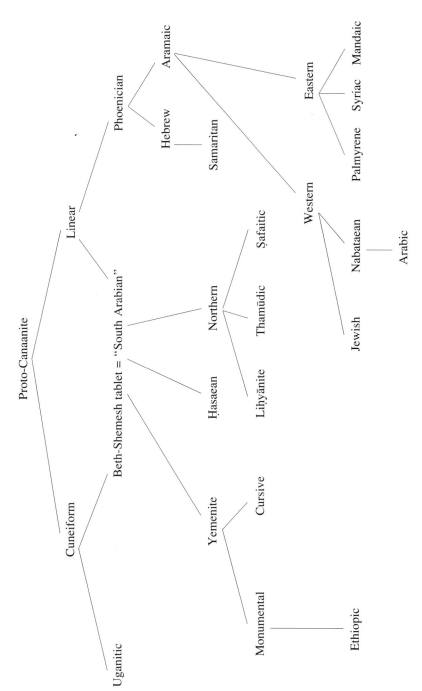

Fig. 20. Evolution of the Semitic alphabet.

South Arabian script (§7.42). However, the Liḥyānite inscriptions of the Hellenistic period follow the Aramaic scribal tradition and use *h* as a vowel letter for *ā*, e.g. *mh* /*mā*/, "what"; *'ḏh* /*'iḏā*/, "while". Occasionally, they indicate an internal long vowel as well, like in *'ḫwhm* /*'aḫūhum*/, "your brother".

9.7. The South Arabian script has been adapted in Ethiopic to denote seven vowels by a variety of changes in the shape of the consonantal symbols. Vowels have thus become an integral part of Ethiopic writing which assumed a syllabic character, comparable to some extent with the cuneiform writing system. The orthography, however, has two defects: it does not indicate the gemination or consonantal lengthening, and it uses the same set of symbols to mark the vowel *ə* and the absence of any vowel. Besides, the pronunciation of Geʿez preserved in the Ethiopic Church is influenced by Amharic. The latter uses the traditional Ethiopic syllabary with additional signs: it has thirty-three characters, each of which occurs in a basic form and in six other forms known as orders. In addition to these 231 forms, there are thirty-nine others which represent labialization and are usually listed as an appendix to the main list (see Fig. 21). Two additional symbols indicating gemination and non-gemination are often used in traditional grammars written in Amharic. The gemination is marked by a small *ṭə*, an abbreviation of *ṭəbq*, "tight", placed above the letter, while the non-gemination is marked by *la*, an abbreviation of *yälalla*, "that is loose", placed also above the letter.

9.8. Contrary to the other West Semitic languages, Phoenician did not use any vowel letters, except in a few forms brought about by linguistic change. In some Late Phoenician inscriptions from Cyprus and in Punic, however, *w* and *y* are exceptionally used as vowel letters in foreign names or words. Besides, the Late Punic and the Neo-Punic inscriptions did employ *w*, *y*, ', *h*, *ḥ*, and ʿ as vowel letters, according to two different systems (§21.14). The best represented system uses ʿ for *a*, and ' for *e* and *o*. In the second system, ' stands for *a*, *h* for *e*, and ʿ for *o*. Besides, *ḥ* can be used for *a*.

9.9. Vowel notation by means of *matres lectionis* does not fix the meaning and the reading of texts in an unambiguous way. Besides, there is a notable deficiency in the absence of any consistent marking of geminated or long consonants. These deficiencies have been partly obviated in the 7th-9th centuries A.D. by a complicated system of diacritical signs

Name of the letter	Transcription	Consonant + Vowel							Consonant + w + Vowel				
		1 ä/a	2 u	3 i	4 a/ā	5 e	6 ə/ø	7 o	1 ʷä	3 ʷi	4 ʷa	5 ʷe	6 ʷə
hoy	h	ሀ	ሁ	ሂ	ሃ	ሄ	ህ	ሆ					
lawe	l	ለ	ሉ	ሊ	ላ	ሌ	ል	ሎ			ሏ		
ḥawt	h < ḥ	ሐ	ሑ	ሒ	ሓ	ሔ	ሕ	ሖ					
may	m	መ	ሙ	ሚ	ማ	ሜ	ም	ሞ			ሟ		
šawt	s < š	ሠ	ሡ	ሢ	ሣ	ሤ	ሥ	ሦ					
rees	r	ረ	ሩ	ሪ	ራ	ሬ	ር	ሮ			ሯ		
sat	s	ሰ	ሱ	ሲ	ሳ	ሴ	ስ	ሶ			ሷ		
šat	š	ሸ	ሹ	ሺ	ሻ	ሼ	ሽ	ሾ			ሿ		
qāf	q	ቀ	ቁ	ቂ	ቃ	ቄ	ቅ	ቆ	ቈ	ቊ	ቋ	ቌ	ቍ
bet	b	በ	ቡ	ቢ	ባ	ቤ	ብ	ቦ			ቧ		
tawe	t	ተ	ቱ	ቲ	ታ	ቴ	ት	ቶ			ቷ		
čawe	č	ቸ	ቹ	ቺ	ቻ	ቼ	ች	ቾ			ቿ		
ḥarm	h < ḫ	ኀ	ኁ	ኂ	ኃ	ኄ	ኅ	ኆ	ኈ	ኊ	ኋ	ኌ	ኍ
nahas	n	ነ	ኑ	ኒ	ና	ኔ	ን	ኖ			ኗ		
ňahas	ň	ኘ	ኙ	ኚ	ኛ	ኜ	ኝ	ኞ			ኟ		
'alf	'	አ	ኡ	ኢ	ኣ	ኤ	እ	ኦ					
kaf	k	ከ	ኩ	ኪ	ካ	ኬ	ክ	ኮ	ኰ	ኲ	ኳ	ኴ	ኵ
ḵaf	h < k	ኸ	ኹ	ኺ	ኻ	ኼ	ኽ	ኾ			ዃ		
wawe	w	ወ	ዉ	ዊ	ዋ	ዌ	ው	ዎ					
'ain	' < '	ዐ	ዑ	ዒ	ዓ	ዔ	ዕ	ዖ					
zay	z	ዘ	ዙ	ዚ	ዛ	ዜ	ዝ	ዞ			ዟ		
žay	ž	ዠ	ዡ	ዢ	ዣ	ዤ	ዥ	ዦ			ዧ		
yaman	y	የ	ዩ	ዪ	ያ	ዬ	ይ	ዮ					
dent	d	ደ	ዱ	ዲ	ዳ	ዴ	ድ	ዶ			ዷ		
ğent	ğ	ጀ	ጁ	ጂ	ጃ	ጄ	ጅ	ጆ			ጇ		
gaml	g	ገ	ጉ	ጊ	ጋ	ጌ	ግ	ጎ	ጐ	ጒ	ጓ	ጔ	ጕ
ṭait	ṭ	ጠ	ጡ	ጢ	ጣ	ጤ	ጥ	ጦ			ጧ		
čait	č	ጨ	ጩ	ጪ	ጫ	ጬ	ጭ	ጮ			ጯ		
pait	p	ጰ	ጱ	ጲ	ጳ	ጴ	ጵ	ጶ					
ṣaday	ṣ	ጸ	ጹ	ጺ	ጻ	ጼ	ጽ	ጾ			ጿ		
ḍappa	ṣ < ṣ́	ፀ	ፁ	ፂ	ፃ	ፄ	ፅ	ፆ					
af	f	ፈ	ፉ	ፊ	ፋ	ፌ	ፍ	ፎ			ፏ		
pesa	p	ፐ	ፑ	ፒ	ፓ	ፔ	ፕ	ፖ					

Fig. 21. Amharic syllabary.

aiming at fixing the pronunciation of Syriac, Hebrew, Jewish Aramaic, and Classical Arabic, especially for the reading of the sacred texts. The pronunciation thus fixed was a traditional one, but no definite conclusion concerning the older vocalizations can be drawn on its basis.

9.10. The so-called Phoenician alphabet was used for Aramaic, Hebrew, the languages of Transjordan, and later for Classical Arabic, the script of which derives from the Nabataean Aramaic cursive. The twenty-two symbols of that alphabet could not express the Semitic phonemes which did not exist any more in Late Canaanite and Phoenician languages. In Early Aramaic, for example, the three sounds *ṯ*, *š*, and *ś* were all designated by the same symbol "š", except in the Tell Fekherye inscription of the mid-9th century B.C., where *ṯ* was indicated by the letter "s". The real phonemic status of the languages using the Phoenician alphabet can only be established by synchronic comparisons with cuneiform, hieroglyphic, and South Arabian spellings, or by diachronic references to later spellings, to much later diacritic signs, and eventually to the pronunciation of some consonants in modern conservative idioms such as Modern South Arabian. The use of diacritics is widespread and serves to distinguish various sounds expressed by the same consonantal symbol, e.g. in Arabic and in Neo-Aramaic. The oldest attestations of a diacritical dot distinguishing *d* and *r* are found in the Palmyrene inscriptions of the 3rd century A.D. and in Syriac. That "punctuation" system was further developed by Arab scribes who called it *naqṭ* and used diacritical dots to distinguish consonantal phonemes represented by the same characters. The use of these diacritics is attested in the earliest Islamic papyri and inscriptions from the 7th century A.D. A similar system was adopted in modern times to write spoken Aramaic that contains an expanded sound system comprising some thirty-one consonantal phonemes. Thus, by adding special diacritics to a number of the original twenty-two letters, new sounds are represented. With a simple dot placed under "g" one obtains *ġ*; with a small upside-down *v*-like diacritic under the same letter, one gets *ǧ*. Using the same principle one gets *ḫ* and *č* from "k", etc.

9.11. Different punctuation signs have been used in the alphabetic script to divide each two words of a text. They go back either to a vertical stroke used as word divider or to a pair of dots arranged like a colon (:), sometimes to three dots, placed one on top of the other, later reduced to one dot. The three systems are used in the Aramaic Tell Fekherye inscription of the 9th century B.C. The vertical stroke keeps with the tradition attested in Ugaritic by the small vertical wedge and anticipated in Old Assyrian texts (§9.2). This practice was continued in West Semitic inscriptions of the 11th and 10th centuries B.C., and in Epigraphic South Arabian, while the Moabite Mesha inscription uses small strokes to mark out sentences or contextual units. The three dots occur on the Lachish ewer from the 13th or 12th century B.C., in archaic Greek writing, and in two lines of the Tell Fekherye inscription. The pair of dots and the single dot are better attested. In particular, two square dots are employed as word dividers in the Ethiopian writing system, which uses four square dots arranged in a square pattern (::) as a sentence divider. In Masoretic Hebrew, instead, the pair of dots (:) is used as verse divider. From the mid-first millennium B.C., space was used to separate words in West Semitic instead of dots, and this practice began to be followed also by printers of modern Ethiopic texts. However, there are West Semitic inscriptions and even Ethiopian newspapers where the words are run together.

C. Transcription and Transliteration

9.12.   The transcription of Semitic words, which is employed in this work, follows the usual conventions and is based mainly on the standard form of the languages concerned. When the transcription differs from the simple transliteration of the signs, the latter is also given, for example in Nabataean Arabic: *fa-yaf'al lā fidā wa-lā 'aṯarā (pyp'l l' pd' wl' 'tr'*), "and he acted neither for reward nor for favour" (cf. § 38.11), or *ḏū 'asrā li-Ṯāǧ (dw 'sr' ltg)*,"who campaigned up to Thadj". Allophones are indicated only in special circumstances, in accordance with the requirements of an introduction.

9.13.   No attempt is made in the present *Outline* to deal in a systematic way with the problem of transliterating foreign names and words into a Semitic writing system, although occasional references to such transcriptions occur in the part dealing with phonology. A different but related problem concerns the use of one offshoot of the Semitic alphabetic script to write texts in another Semitic language. This is the case, in particular, of mediaeval Arabic texts written either in Syriac script and named *garšūnī*, or in Hebrew characters and called "Judaeo-Arabic". Besides, there are Hebrew texts, mainly biblical and liturgical, in

Arabic transcription, and there is a Berber translation of a Passover *Hag-gadah* in Hebrew characters. Such texts may have a great linguistic importance, but an *Outline* cannot enter into the discussion of questions they may raise and dialects they reveal. Instead, occasional reference will be made to the vocalized transcriptions of Punic words in the *Poenulus* of Plautus, and of Hebrew words in Origen's Hexapla and in a few other works.

II

PHONOLOGY

10.1. The sounds of speech can be analyzed from various points of view (§10.2). If the linguist and grammarian takes great interest in them, it is becáuse they are the phonetic manifestation of the morphemes which are the minimal units of any grammatical structure. However, he should bear in mind that the analysis of speech sounds of ancient languages is based mainly on their written notation which is imperfect and often conservative (§9.1). Thus, it does not reveal all the phonetic richness of the language and does not follow its evolution in an adequate way. The twenty-eight characters of the Arabic alphabet, for example, are generally believed to correspond quite well to the consonantal speech sounds of Classical Arabic. Yet, the famous Sibawayh's treatise on Arabic grammar, written in the 8th century, enumerates forty-two consonantal speech sounds registered in Arabic by this doyen of Semitic linguistics. Therefore, it is a matter of great methodological importance to distinguish between orthography and phonology in considering written documents. Although we are dependent on the orthography for discovering the phonology of ancient languages, we cannot base our phonological inferences on the statistical predominance of a conservative spelling in the available sources. Particularly interesting and more revealing are the lapses, as well as the transcription of one language in the alphabet of another when this script is inherently unfitted to be the vehicle for an automatic transcription. Such material, apart from a few scattered glosses, consists generally in proper names. Now, being part of speech, proper names change pronunciation along with the rest of the language and, therefore, their transcription in other languages may provide some help in following the evolution of speech sounds, often concealed by the conservatism of scribal practices. Although this phonetic material is in general limited and subject to mishearing, it cannot be neglected in the study of ancient languages and it will be used in the present work. As for the modern proununciation of Semitic languages, as the Ashkenazic, Sephardic, or Yemenite pronunciation of Hebrew, it is far from trustworthy in determining that of earlier periods, although relatively static and isolated communities, as those of the island Soqoṭra and of the montainous regions of ʻOmān, may preserve old South Arabian pronunciations and articulations.

1. Basic Assumptions

A. Linguistic Analysis

10.2. The linguistic analysis of the sound of language as a whole and of specific languages can be considered under three headings: 1° the study of the articulation of speech sounds; 2° the classification and description of speech sounds (phonetics); 3° the functioning of speech sounds in the language structure (phonemics). The study of the articulatory movements that produce speech sounds is prelinguistic, being concerned with physics and physiology. All the sounds of the spoken Semitic languages can be subjected, in one way or another, to experimental investigation: thus, spectrography observes speech displayed in the form of acoustic energy, airflow and intraoral pressure measurements aim at explaining the aerodynamic conditions of speech production, while glottography and laryngography help in stating the function of the glottis. These experimental procedures go over into the field of phonetics as soon as they describe the bases for the classification of speech sounds as such. Speech sounds can be classified first into consonants, vowels, and tones. It is customary to put phonetic symbols in brackets, e.g. [p], [a], but word stress is shown in the present *Outline* by an accent placed above the vowel of the stressed syllable, e.g. Arabic *kátaba*, "he wrote". In the international phonetic alphabet, the stress is indicated by an accent placed at the beginning of stressed syllables, e.g. *'kataba*.

10.3. The various sounds of Semitic languages, as far as known and described precisely, can be expressed in a fairly adequate way when one uses the symbols of the international phonetic alphabet (in brackets). However, for practical reasons, in accordance with the requirements of an introduction and with the widespread practice of teachers and students of Semitic, the system of transliteration has been kept as simple as possible, and traditionally employed symbols and diacritics have been used to a great extent. A synopsis of the two notation systems should make it clear.

Consonants

'	= [ʔ]	(glottal stop)
'	= [ʕ]	(voiced pharyngal)
b	= [b]	(voiced labial)

b̠ = [β] (do. spirantized)
ç = [ç] (fricative palatal)
č = [tʃ], [c] (voiceless palato-alveolar affricate)
d = [d] (voiced dental plosive)
d̠ = [δ] (do. spirantized or voiced interdental)
ḍ = [ḍ], [ɬ], [ɗ] (emphatic voiced dental, emphatic fricative lateral, velarized voiced dental)
d̰ = [d̠] (emphatic voiced interdental)
d̃ʸ = [d̠ʲ] (palatalized voiced dental plosive)
f = [f] (voiceless labiodental fricative)
g = [g] (voiced velar plosive)
g̠ = [γ] (do. spirantized)
ǧ = [ʤ] (voiced palato-alveolar affricate)
ġ = [γ] (voiced velar fricative)
gʸ = [gʲ] (palatalized voiced velar plosive)
h = [h] (voiceless laryngal)
ḥ = [ħ] (voiceless pharyngal)
h̠ = [x] (voiceless velar fricative)
h̠ʸ = [x] (palatalized voiceless velar fricative)
k = [k] (voiceless velar plosive)
k̠ = [x] (do. spirantized)
kʸ = [kʲ] (palatalized voiceless velar plosive)
l = [l] (liquid lateral)
ḷ = [ɫ] (velarized voiced lateral)
m = [m] (labial nasal)
n = [n] (dental nasal)
ň = [ɲ] (palatalized nasal)
ñ = [ŋ] (post-palatal or velar nasal)
p = [p] (voiceless labial)
p̠ = [φ] (do. spirantized)
q = [ḳ], [k'], [ḳ] (emphatic voiceless velar plosive, glottalized or velarized)
qʸ = [ḳ'] (palatalized and glottalized voiceless velar plosive)
r = [r], [R] (liquid trill, uvular trill)
ṟ = [ɾ] (velarized voiced trill)
s = [s] (voiceless fricative dental)
ṣ = [ṣ], [s'], [s], [ts] (emphatic voiceless fricative dental, glottalized or velarized, affricate)
ś = [ɬ] (voiceless lateral fricative)
ṣ́ = [ɬ] (emphatic lateral fricative)
š = [ʃ] (voiceless palato-alveolar fricative)
ṣ̌ = [ʃ'] (emphatic/glottalized voiceless palato-alveolar fricative)
s¹ = [ʃ] (voiceless palato-alveolar fricative)
s² = [ɬ] (voiceless lateral fricative)
s³ = [s] (voiceless fricative dental)
t = [t] (voiceless dental plosive)
ṭ = [ṭ], [t'], [ɬ] (emphatic voiceless dental plosive, glottalized or velarized)
t̠ = [θ] (voiceless interdental)
ṱ = [ṭ], [ɬ] (emphatic voiceless interdental, velarized)

ṭ = [ts]   (voiceless dental affricate)
tʸ = [t̠]   (palatalized voiceless dental plosive)
w = [w]   (voiced labial velar)
y = [j]   (palatal)
z = [z]   (voiced fricative dental)
ẓ = [ẓ], [ẕ]   (emphatic voiced fricative dental, velarized)
ž = [ʒ]   (voiced palato-alveolar fricative)
ź = [ɮ]   (voiced lateral fricative)

Labialized consonants are transcribed *bʷ*, *gʷ*, *ḫʷ*, *kʷ*, *pʷ*, *qʷ*. A dot under the letter indicates its emphatic pronunciation, e.g. *ḷ*, *p̣*, *ṛ*. The spirant form of *b g d k p t* in Hebrew and Aramaic is normally not marked (§11.10). Otherwise, if helpful for pointing out the etymology, underlined symbols *ḇ*, *g̱*, *ḏ*, *ḵ*, *p̱*, *ṯ* are used. Hebrew *dageš* forte and Arabic *šadda* are shown by geminating the consonant (e.g. *hammelek* [*ham:elek*], "the king"). Normally, Hebrew *mappiq* and Arabic *hamza* are simply indicated by transliterating *h* (e.g. *'arṣāh*, "her land") and ' (e.g. *ra'sun*, "head"). The medial and final vowel letters ', *h*, *w*, *y* of Hebrew, Aramaic, Syriac, Arabic, are not transliterated unless the orthography needs to be pointed out, but the long vowels *ā*, *ē*, *ī*, *ō*, *ū* thus indicated are shown in transcription (e.g. *yōm*, "day"; *samā*, "heaven").

Vowels

a = [ɑ]   (low, back)
ā = [ɑ:]   (long)
ä = [æ], [ɛ]   (higher-low, lower-mid))
ă = [ă], [ǎ]   (non-syllabic)
ã = [ɑ̃]   (nasalized)
ᵃ = [ă]   (non-phonemic)
e = [e]   (mean-mid, front)
ē = [e:]   (long)
ĕ = [ĕ]   (non-syllabic)
ə = [ə]   (lower-high, central)
i = [i]   (high, front)
ī = [i:]   (long)
ĭ = [ĭ]   (non-syllabic)
o = [o]   (mean-mid, back)
ō = [o:]   (long)
ɔ = [ɔ]   (lower-mid, back)
ŏ = [ŏ]   (non-syllabic)
ö = [ɵ]   (central)
u = [u]   (high, back)
ū = [u:]   (long)
ŭ = [ŭ]   (non-syllabic)

No graphemic distinction is made between long vowels resulting from a monophthongization or marked by a *mater lectionis*, and other long vowels: they are all indicated in this *Outline* by a macron, as in *ā*, *ē*, *ī*, *ū*. The same system is followed, as a rule, for Libyco-Berber, Cushitic, and Chadic, although specialists in the field and a recognized orthography of some languages, as Tuareg, Oromo, and Iraqw, duplicate the vowel symbol, as Oromo *beeka*, "he knows", instead of *bēka*. However, when there are two level tones, low and high, as in Rendille *géèl*, "to enter", the vowel symbol is doubled in this *Outline*. In the articulatory description of vowel height, some authors prefer the classificatory terms of "close", "half-close", "half-open", and "open" to "high", "mid", and "low" because of the belief that the former category provides clearer distinction.

Considering the various traditional pronunciations of Hebrew vowels and their intricate historical development, these distinctions will not be followed for Hebrew and Biblical Aramaic. Instead, a usual, mainly mechanical transliteration of Tiberian vowel signs (§21.19) will be adopted, as shown in the following figure with the letter ב (b) as example and with the names of the Tiberian vowel signs:

ב ba	ב bā/bǒ	ב be	ב bē
(*patah*)	(*qames*)	(*segol*)	(*sere*)
ב bi	ב bo	ב bu	ב bə
(*hireq*)	(*holem*)	(*qibbūs*)	(*šəwa mobile*)
ב bǎ/bᵃ	ב bǒ	ב bě	
(*hatef patah*)	(*hatef qames*)	(*hatef segol*)	

The "furtive" *patah*, which is an artificial ultra-short vowel *a* inserted in Hebrew before a final guttural (§27.10), is transcribed ᵃ like the *hatef patah* used in similar circumstances after a guttural. The *šəwa quiescens* of Hebrew, the *sukūn* and the *ğazma* of Arabic, which mark the absence of any following vowel, are not indicated.

B. Consonantal Sounds

10.4. Consonantal sounds are described in terms of points of articulation, i.e. of the various obstacles to the freely vibrating or moving air as it passes out from the throat passage. For instance, [p] is called a *labial* because both lips are brought together to produce the sound, as opposed to the [t], which is called a *dental* sound because the tip of the tongue is

at or near the upper front teeth. Both of these differ from *t* or [θ], which
is called an *interdental* because it is produced by placing the tip of the
tongue between the upper and lower front teeth, and from [k], which is
articulated with the back part of the tongue somewhere in the region of
the velum; hence it is called a *velar* sound. The sound of *palatal y* ([j])
is produced by placing the front (not the tip) of the tongue near or
against the hard palate. It differs from the *palato-alveolar š* ([ʃ]) formed
with the front of the tongue touching the hard palate near the alveolar
ridge. Both differ from the pharyngals and the laryngals which are articulated respectively in the *pharynx* and in the *larynx*. Consonants are also
described in terms of the activity of the air stream in the mouth and the
activity of the vocal cords. When the vocal cords are vibrating the sound
is said to be a *voiced* sound, as [b]; otherwise it is *voiceless*, as [p].
When the air stream must pass through a narrow opening, as in [f] or [s],
the sound is called a *fricative*. The air stream is continuous in the fricatives but interrupted in the plosives or stops, as [p], [t], [k]. This difference has important consequences for the phonology since stops cannot
be lengthened without changing quality, while other consonants, called
"continuants", may be articulated with greater length (§23.1). This may
vary from a slight lengthening in time of the pronunciation to much
more than double. In the case of the *nasal* consonants such as [m] and
[n], the velum is dropped and part of the air stream passes through the
nasal cavity. Another articulatory contrast opposes a lax articulation to a
tense one which is characterized by greater energy resulting either in consonantal lengthening, e.g. [m:], or in a sharper onset and/or wipe-off of the
consonant. The various points of articulation are represented in Fig. 22.

C. Vowels

10.5. Vowels may be described as sounds produced in a resonance
chamber such that there is a minimum of interference with the freely and
regularly vibrating air as it passes out from the throat passage. Vowels
are classified by two criteria: 1° tongue height and tongue advancement
or retraction; 2° lip spreading or rounding. According to the first criterion, the three basic Semitic vowels [ɑ], [i], and [u] can be described in
the following way: the vowel [ɑ] as in *kalb*, "dog", is the lowest of the
back vowels, since the tongue is bunched toward the back of the mouth,
but it is not high toward its roof. Instead, the vowel [i] as in *milk*, either
"king" (Phoenician) or "estate" (Arabic), is the highest of the front

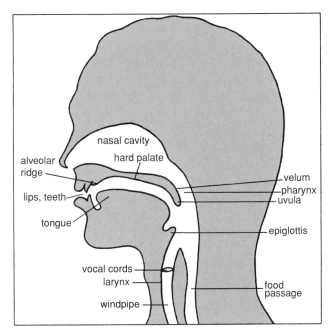

Fig. 22. Points of articulation.

vowels, since the tongue is bunched forward in the mouth and is high toward its roof. The vowel [u] as in *šulmu*, "well-being" (Akkadian), is the highest back vowel. The position of the tongue during the articulation of these three vowels is roughly indicated in Fig. 23. According to the second criterion, the vowel [ɑ] is open and has no significant rounding or unrounding, while [i] and [u] are close vowels, since the mouth opening is slight, but [i] is unrounded and [u] is described as a close rounded vowel.

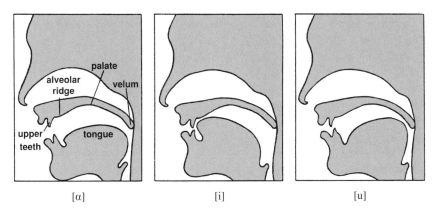

Fig. 23. Articulation of vowels.

D. Intonation

10.6.   The intonation is the rise and fall in the pitch of the voice. In the languages called tone languages, such as Chinese and most Bantu idioms, intonation distinguishes one word from another. This might have also been the case in the Sumerian or Pre-Sumerian language for which the Mesopotamian writing system was originally designed, since this would explain the number of homophonous signs in Akkadian, that may have been distinctive in Sumerian or Pre-Sumerian. The maximum number of tones systematically used in any one language to distinguish morphemes seems to be about five. Speakers may distinguish, for instance, among a high tone, a low tone, a falling tone, a rising tone, and a tone that falls and then rises. Semitic languages are not tone languages and, at present, the tone is not an integral part of any Semitic word. However, tone plays an important part in some Cushitic languages. High tone is indicated by an acute accent (*á*), while low tone is either left unmarked or indicated by a grave accent (*à*). In Oromo, for example, lexical distinctions may be based on tone, as in *gara*, "towards", and *gará* "stomach"; *bara*, "year", and *bará*, "learner". It is likely that the "Proto-Sam" sub-group of East Cushitic (§2.11) was a tone language distinguishing between high (*á*), low (*à*), and high-falling tone (*áà*), and that sex gender of nouns designating human beings or animals was specified in "Proto-Sam" by the high-low tone for the masculine and the low-high tone for the feminine (e.g. Rendille *ínàm*, "boy"; *inám*, "girl"). In Semitic, tone must have distinguished the preterite (**yíqtùl*) from the jussive (**yìqtúl*) (§38.2), and intonation can affect the meaning of whole sentences, that may consist of a single word (§50.3-4). In particular, intonation conveys shades of meaning which cannot conveniently be expressed by other means. Thus, in Old Babylonian, the two meanings of the interrogative *šarrānu... islimū* and of the declarative *islimū* are distinguished phonetically by intonation, with the pitch rising at the end of *šarrānu... islimū́*, "Did the kings make peace?", and fading at the end of the answer *íslimū*, "They made peace". The rising intonation may be indicated in cuneiform script by an additional vowel sign (*is-li-mu-ú*) but, in general, it is not practicable to mark this kind of intonation in Semitic orthography and there are no punctuation marks designed at signifying an interrogation or an exclamation.

E. Phonemes

10.7. Current linguistics distinguishes sharply between speech and language, between sounds and phonemes. In nearly every language the number of distinguishable sounds is often quite large and greater than the number of consonants and vowels indicated by a current writing system (§10.1). Instead, the number of *significant* differences is smaller and may correspond more or less to the number of consonants and vowels marked by a writing system. For instance, in Hebrew the word *pat*, "bit", begins with a voiceless labial plosive or stop; in *ṣippōr*, "bird", the internal consonant sound is a voiceless labial plosive geminated; in *ṣāpōn*, "north", the postvocalic *p* is spirantized and pronounced as a labial fricative [φ] or *p̲*. These various *p* sounds are said to be members of a class of sounds which, as a whole, is in contrast with other such classes, for instance with the class *b* represented in such Hebrew words as *bat*, "daughter", which begins with a voiced labial plosive, or *rabbīm*, "many", where the internal voiced labial plosive is geminated, or *'eḇed*, "servant", where the postvocalic spirantized *b* is pronounced as a labial fricative [β] or *ḇ*. Such a class of sounds is called a *phoneme*. It is customary to represent phonemes by symbols enclosed in slant lines, i.e. the phoneme /p/, the phoneme /b/, etc. The members of a phoneme are called its allophones. By grouping the sounds in such a way, one gets a limited number of phonemes in each language. Of course, phonemic distinctions differ from one language to another, hence each language has its own set of phonemes or distinctive sounds. Semitic languages have between 35 and 50 phonemes, that are consonants, short and long vowels, and intonations. When two words differ by only one phoneme, such as Hebrew *pat* and *bat*, the words are said to be a minimally distinct pair. In a minimally distinct pair of words, if there is a difference of only one distinction between the two phonemes in question, then the two phonemes are minimally distinct phonemes. Thus in Hebrew *pat* and *bat*, /p/ and /b/ are both plosives or stops, both are labial and the only difference is that /p/ is unvoiced and /b/ is voiced. The phonemes /d/ and ' or /ʕ/ in Arabic *damara*, "he perished", and *'amara*, "he lived long", are not minimally distinct, because one is plosive, the other fricative; one is dental, the other pharyngal; however, both are voiced sounds.

F. Voiced and Unvoiced Sounds

10.8.   The description of the minimal differences has a certain importance in comparative Semitic phonology, since the distinction between
voiced and unvoiced sounds, for instance, might not be an original feature of Proto-Semitic. In any case, the history of all languages that can
be followed over a long period of time shows that voiceless occlusives
become voiced. In this hypothesis, the original Proto-Semitic consonantal pattern could be compared with Sumerian and Chinese, where the
phonemic distinction between voiced and voiceless consonants is non-
existent. In Mycenaean Greek, this distinction is expressed graphically
only for the dentals, and it is missing in the Cypriot Greek syllabary.
Early evidence points to a similar situation in ancient Semitic. The historically attested spellings *'bd* and *'bt*, "to perish", *b'l* and *p'l*, "to
make", *kbd* and *kbt*, "to be heavy", *ndn* and *ntn*, "to give", *nbš* and *npš*,
"breath", "life", *nbk* and *npk*, "well", *šbt* and *špt*, "sabbat", "full
moon", *ḏū* and *ṯū* ("*šu*") > *še*, "this", "who", *ḏmr* > *zmr*/*dmr* and *ṯmr* >
šmr, "to guard", "to protect", *wṣt* and *wṣd*, "to be firm", etc., as well as
the Egyptian transcriptions *k-p-n* and *k-b-n* of *Gbl*, "Byblos", and the
frequent lack of differentiation between voiced and unvoiced sounds in
Semitic cuneiform writing may in fact suggest that /b/ and /p/, /d/ and /t/,
/ḏ/ and /ṯ/, /g/ and /k/, and perhaps some other similar pairs were originally allophones or free variations of the same labial, dental, interdental,
or velar phoneme. Still in prehistoric times, these allophones or phonetic
variants would have received a phonemic status in the languages concerned, but *b/p* is again treated as one phoneme in Neo-Assyrian. The
phonetic realization is another question, and spoken Semitic languages
show that voiced consonants may become voiceless in contact with other
consonants and in final position in the syllable, e.g. Neo-Aramaic *glabtā*
[*ġlapta*], "victory"; Tigre *'ādad* ['*ādat*], "number". Such a devoicing,
normal in speech, is well known in the spelling of foreign names and it
occurs in informal texts as well, e.g. the Syriac inscription *'Isḥāq bar
Dāwīt* or the Latin coin legend *Turris Davit*. A similar devoicing of
occlusives occurs also in some Indo-European languages, as in German
before other occlusives. Another development consists in spirantization
or palatalization of occlusives in order to ease the enunciation (§11.10;
18.5-6).

G. Emphatic Sounds

10.9. A different problem is raised by the Semitic emphatic sounds that are pronounced nowadays in the Ethiopian languages and in Modern South Arabian as ejectives, i.e. with vocal cords tightly closed and pushed upward, and followed by a glottal stop ': *p'*, *t'*, *s'*, *č'*, *k'*, also transcribed *p̣*, *ṭ*, *ṣ*, *č̣*, *ḳ/q*. Besides, there are pre-glottalized allophones pronounced with a closed and stationary glottis in the initial phase of the articulation, thus *'k*, *'s*, *'t*. In Arabic, instead, the characteristic articulatory feature of all the emphatic phonemes is the contraction of the upper pharynx, accompanied by a velarization; the latter can be seen by means of a radioscopy which shows how the emphatic phonemes are articulated with a raising of the back part of the tongue in the region of the velum. This velarization gives them, and the surrounding vowels, a sombre *u*-like quality that tends to spread over the whole word. It is uncertain which of these characteristics — glottalization in Ethiopic, velarization or pharyngalization in Arabic — should be considered as primary. However, ancient phonetic changes and transcriptions of the emphatics *ẓ* and *ḍ*, which probably originated from *ṯ* and *ṣ́*, support the primitive character of the pharyngalization which characterizes the Libyco-Berber emphatics as well. In standard Ugaritic, the following changes are ascertained: *ṯm'* > *ġm'*, "to be thirsty", *nṯr* > *nġr*, "to guard", *ṯr* > *ġr*, "mountain", *mṯy* > *mġy*, "to arrive", and perhaps *yqṯ* > *yqġ*, "to be alert". The appearance of the velar fricative *ġ* signifies that the pharyngalization of the interdental fricative *ṯ* had supplanted the basic character of this phoneme. A comparable phenomenon is attested in Aramaic by the spellings "q" and "'" used to mark *ḍ* < *ṣ́* and by the Neo-Assyrian transcriptions of this phoneme with *ḫi* or *qi*, like in *Ra-ḫi-a-nu* / *Ra-qi-a-nu* for *Raṣ́yān*. Since "q" marks a velar plosive and "'" was used to indicate also the voiced velar fricative *ġ*, while *ḫ* is a voiceless velar fricative, all the aforementioned changes and transcriptions point to a pharyngalization. Besides, the spreading of the velarization over the whole word, called *tafḫīm* in Arabic, may explain the variant forms of certain Semitic roots, such as *ḍḥk*, *ṣ́ḥq*, and *ṣ̌ḥq*, "to laugh", or *qtl*, *ktl*, and *qṭl*, "to kill", as well as the appearance of the vowel *u* in the neighbourhood of emphatics in East Semitic, for instance in *qurbum* instead of *qarbum*, "near", *inaṣṣur* instead of *inaṣṣar*, "he guards", etc. Because of this spread of the suprasegmental velarization, new emphatic consonants arose also in modern dialects. Their phonemic load, however, as far as it is to be considered, is very limited.

10.10.   The fact that the glottalization of emphatics is not found in Semitic outside Ethiopic, Modern South Arabian, and also Hebrew as pronounced by Georgian-speaking Jews, points to its being a secondary feature, but it cannot be ascribed to the sole influence of Cushitic. One should rather note that all these forms of speech are also characterized by an almost complete non-occurrence of the pharyngal ', that tends to be replaced by the glottal stop or by a glottalized velar plosive k' (among the Georgian-speaking Jews). Therefore the replacement of the pharyngalization or velarization of the emphatics by their glottalization may reflect the same phenomenon as the change ' > ', supported in Ethiopia by the influence of the Cushitic languages. As for the phenomenon q > ' in many Arabic urban dialects, in Tigre before a consonant, and in Hebrew as realized by some Jews of Algeria and Morocco, it must result from an articulation which is limited to the glottal contraction, without the retraction of the tongue and a raising of its back toward the soft extremity of the velum. Economy of effort seems thus to have brought about this development which does not indicate, therefore, that the dialects in question had a glottalized emphatic velar in an earlier period. The geographical setting shows, on the other hand, that this development did not happen under the influence of Cushitic (§18.8).

H. Proto-Semitic Phonemes

10.11.   The phonemes constitute the basic structure of the material of the language, and it is out of them that the words and the grammatical forms are formed. The phonemes of spoken Semitic languages can be described and analyzed on the basis of observation of what happens when speech is produced. The phonemes of ancient written Semitic languages are reconstructed on the basis of various indications, such as traditional pronunciation, description by mediaeval grammarians, transcriptions in other languages and scripts, orthographic peculiarities, and comparative Semitic linguistics. Although there remain doubts and uncertainties, while the laws of phonetic correspondences between the branches of Afro-Asiatic have not been sufficiently elucidated, the common Semitic or Proto-Semitic phonemic system can be reconstructed with a high degree of probability.

Consonants

	Plosive	Fricative	Lateral	Liquid	Nasal	Semivowel
Labial	*p b*				*m*	*w*
Dental	*t d ṭ*	*s z ṣ*	*ś ṣ́ (ḍ)*	*l r*	*n*	
Interdental		*ṯ ḏ ṱ (ẓ)*				
(Pre)palatal		*š*				*y*
Velar	*k g q*	*ḫ ġ*				
Pharyngal		*ḥ ʿ*				
Laryngal	*ʾ*	*h*				

Vowels

Low/open back velar *a* ([ɑ]).
High/close front palatal unrounded *i* ([i]).
High/close back velar rounded *u* ([u]).

Common Semitic or Proto-Semitic also possesses the three corresponding long vowels: *ā* ([ɑ:]), *ī* ([i:]), *ū* ([u:]). The vowels *e/ē* and *o/ō*
do not belong to the common Semitic phonemes, but they acquired the
phonemic status in several Semitic languages. They are intermediate in
height between the high vowels [i] and [u], and the low vowel [ɑ]. The
location of various vowels with regard to the front-back and high-low
dimensions is indicated in Fig. 24. Besides, vocalic functions of *l* and *r*
are identifiable in some forms of speech and numerous vocalic variations
are attested in Semitic since its most ancient historically attested phases.

	Front	*Central*	*Back*
high	[i]		[u]
mean-mid	[e]		[o]
lower-high		[ə] [ɵ]	
lower-mid	[ɛ]		[ɔ]
higher-low		[æ]	
low		[a]	[ɑ]

Fig. 24. Location of vowels.

Intonations

Besides the word-stress Semitic languages have various sentence
stresses or pitches, some of which have certainly a phonemic status
when used in concrete circumstances.

10.12. Proto-Semitic phonemes underwent a great variety of phonetic changes in the course of time. Prehistorical, i.e. reconstructed changes cannot be treated in the same manner as historically attested developments which are revealed by orthography and its deviations, by the modern pronunciation of native speakers, by comparative evidence, and by evidence from contact between languages. Only a careful consideration of historical changes enables us to draw any conclusions regarding prehistorical developments. The innumerable phonetic changes found in the history of Semitic languages represent three major types of phonemic development: 1° the phonemic shift consisting in the change of a phoneme of one sound-type into a phoneme of another sound-type (e.g. *ś* > *ḍ*); 2° the phonemic merger or total assimilation (cf. § 27.3-10), i.e. the coalescence of two phonemes resulting in the exclusive occurrence of either one of the two contrasting sound-units (e.g. *nt* > *tt*) or in the emergence of a new, possibly intermediate type (e.g. *ḏt* > *dd*); 3° the phonemic split consisting in a bifurcation of two phonemes out of the allophones of one initial phoneme, either short (e.g. *m* > *mb/p*) or double/long (e.g. *dd* > *nd*, *ss* > *rs*). The monophonemization consisting in the change from a cluster of two phonemes into a single phoneme is a phonemic merger, while the diphonemization consisting in an opposite development is a phonemic split. The phonemic loss (e.g. of the velar fricatives in Assyro-Babylonian) and the rise of a new phoneme by borrowing (e.g. of Turkish words in Neo-Aramaic) are two additional types of sound changes in a language. Prehistorical changes can be reconstructed by comparison also with Afro-Asiatic languages other than Semitic. The equations may become quite interesting when Egyptian, e.g., is compared with Semitic, since more radical divergencies are then revealed, independently from the conventional nature of Egyptological transcriptions. We may refer, for instance, to Egyptian *snb* = Semitic *šlm*, "to be healthy"; Egyptian *wdn* = Semitic *wzn* / *'zn*, "to be heavy"; Egyptian *ḥk3*, "rule" = Semitic *ḥqq*, "to be right".

10.13. All phonemic changes may occur either in all positions or only in specific ones. The former are usually called "unconditioned" and they are examined, as a rule, in the paragraphs dealing with the single phonemes (§11-22). The latter changes, termed "conditioned", correspond synchronically to conditioned allophonic variations and manifest themselves through assimilation, dissimilation, metathesis, prosthesis, anaptyxis, elision, etc. These changes are examined in the apposite paragraphs dealing with gemination and various conditioned sound changes

(§23; 27). Some general principles, which nevertheless require qualification, may usefully be posited at this point. These are four: 1° phonetic
change is usually regular in that it affects all the occurrences of a
phoneme in certain clearly definable positions in the utterance; 2° phonetic
shift affects, as a rule, all the speakers in a given speech community
together, since each man's pronunciation is governed by the general
conventions followed in his milieu; 3° the speakers of a given community are unaware of sound change, as this is not made consciously;
4° sound change affects only certain sounds in a given language at a specific period of its history.

2. LABIALS

11.1. Common Semitic or Proto-Semitic has two labial plosives,
voiceless *p* and voiced *b*; it has further a labial nasal *m* and a labial
semivowel *w*. Original /p/ is realized as the voiceless labiodental fricative /f/ in Arabic, in South-Arabian, and in Ethiopic; it probably originated through the spirantization of *p* into [φ]. Pliny's Latin *carfiathum*,
"autumnal", based on South Arabian *ẖrf*, "autumn", testifies to this
shift in South Semitic already in the 1st century A.D. and the Sabaic
transcription *blṭ* of Greek παλλάδ(ες) — designating the widespread
Athenian tetradrachms with the head of Pallas Athena — indicates that
the letter ◊ could not be used to express the Greek π. Ethiopic possesses, besides, a series of labialized consonants, in particular *bʷ*, *gʷ*, *kʷ*,
ẖʷ, *qʷ* (cf. §18.7).

11.2. The phoneme *p* occurs in Eastern Arabic dialects, but its use is
restricted to loanwords, e.g. *parda*, "curtain", from Persian *parde*; *pēp*,
"pipe", from English "pipe". In other dialects, however, and in the literary language, where a Persian, Greek, etc., word or name has *p*, the
Arabs pronounce it as [f] or [b]; e.g. Persian *pirind*, "sword", is pronounced in Arabic *firind* or *birind*. Also Ethiopic possesses a *p* in addition to the *f*. It is relatively rare in Ge'ez and its symbol does not occur
in the Aksum inscriptions. Its presence in some Semitic roots could
probably be explained as resulting from an original geminated *bb* as is
the case in West Gurage where the sound *p* is an allophone of *bb*; e.g.
Eža *däbbärä*, "he added"; Chaha, Ennemor, and Gyeto *däpärä*;
Endegeň *däppärä*.

11.3. Ethiopic possesses also a voiceless labial plosive *p* which is emphatic ([p']) and, like *p*, of rare occurrence. The shape of its symbol is imitated from *ṣ* and it is usually employed to transcribe Greek loanwords (e.g. *parāqlิṭōs* = παράκλητος; *ṭarappeza* = τράπεζα, "table"). However, this glottalized labial may well be of Cushitic origin. In East Gurage (Selṭi), the sound *p* alternates with *p*, and both *p* and *p* are variants of *b*. Nowadays, many Ethiopians substitute *b* for *p*, e.g. in *posta*, "post office", pronounced and even written sometimes as *bosta*. Pharyngalized labials are unknown in Classical Arabic and they play but a marginal role in modern Arabic dialects, e.g. in the minimal pair *bāba*, "its door", and *ḅāḅa*, "father".

11.4. Interchanges between *b* and *p* are frequent in Semitic languages and some of them go probably back to the time when *b/p* was one phoneme. When the allophones *b* and *p* reached a phonemic status, certain roots did not receive the same formalized expression in all the languages (§10.8), thus e.g. *p'l*, "to make", in West Semitic, but *b'l* in Ugaritic and Amorite (*i-ba-al-*). Nabataean *kpr'*, "the tomb", certainly corresponds to the usual *qbr'* with an additional change *q > k*. In Neo-Assyrian *b/p* is again one phoneme, with variant spellings, e.g. *Ar-pa-a-a* and *Ar-ba-a-a*, "Arab", where one should not assign the unusual value *bá* to the sign PA; *Nam-pi-gi* for present-day *Manbiğ*, in Aramaic "spring site"; *Ìl-pa-rak-ka*, Aramaic /'*Il-barak*/, "God has blessed". Caution is required in these matters because of the frequent lack of differentiation between voiced an unvoiced sounds in cuneiform writing, with the result, e.g., that the current Assyriological transcription *pelludû* or *pilludû* faces the Greek transcription βιλλοδω, "cult".

11.5. A non-geminated *b* in non-initial position can be spirantized into *ḇ* (§11.10), become *w*, and be reduced to the round vowel *ō/ū*. Different stages of this change are historically attested. E.g. Syriac *qwaz < *qbz*, "to leap", Ge'ez *ḍabsa* and *ḍawasa*, "to be weak", Amharic *säw* as against Ge'ez *sab'*, "man", Eastern Neo-Aramaic *qbāltā > qwaltā*, "complaint", illustrate the transition *b > ḇ > w*, which appears already in the Numidic transcription *'wdštr* of Punic *'bd(')štrt*, "Servant of Astarte". The further change is well represented in Neo-Aramaic (e.g. *gabrā' > gōra*, "man, husband"; *nabšā' > nōša*, "person, soul"), in Modern South Arabian (e.g. **lbn > lūn*, "white"), and in Modern Ethiopian languages (e.g. *'bn > Gurage ūn*, "stone"; *kbd > Harari kūd*, "liver"), but it is already attested by the Masoretic vocalization of

Hebrew *kōkāb* < *kawkab* < *kabkab*, "star", with a similar development of *p* in *ṭōṭāpot* < **ṭapṭapat*, "frontlet between the eyes". Sometimes the *b* disappears without leaving a trace in the labial vowel, especially in Amharic (e.g. *arat* for Ge'ez *'arba't*, "four").

11.6.   There are occurrences in which *b* alternates with *m*. This phenomenon is well attested in Palaeosyrian that exhibits spellings like *Ḥa-lam*[ki] for *Ḥalab*, "Aleppo"; *u₄-bu* for *u₄-mu*, "day"; *ba* for *mā*, "water". Such spellings must echo real allophones, instead of representing unheard values of cuneiform signs, since *m* reappears much later in the name of *Ḥalmān*, "Aleppo", explainable as *Ḥalam* + Aramaizing *-ān* (§29.54). The same phenomenon occurs also in Ethiopian languages, where *m* and *b* can occasionally alternate (e.g. Tigre *dabanā* and *damanā*, Soddo *dabäna* and *dämmäna*, "cloud"), *m* can change into *b* (e.g. Chaha and Eža *nəm* > Ennemor *nəm̱* > Gyeto *nəḇ*, "charm"), and intervocalic *m* > *b* passing through *ḇ* can become *w* (e.g. Gurage *amänägä* and *awänägä*, "to escape"; *dām* and *dāw*, "master"). Since there are archaic features in South Ethiopic, which shares many characteristics with South Arabian languages, it is not surprising that South Arabian *bn* corresponds to West Semitic *min*, "from". Besides, *ymmt* alternates in Ugaritic with *ybmt*, "daughter-in-law", Amorite *yamamu(m)* is the same word as *yabamu(m)*, "brother-in-law", ʼΙαμνια stands for Old Hebrew *Yabneh*, and various cases of substitution of *b* for *m* and vice versa are attributed to the Ṭayyiʼ and Bakr dialects in North and Northeast Arabia: e.g. *ḥabaltu* for *ḥamaltu*, "I carried", *maġaḥa* for *baġaḥa*, "he rejoiced", *bā smuk* for *mā smuk*, "what is your name?". The interchange of *b* and *m* is attested also in Andalusian Arabic; e.g. *qinnam* for *qinnab*, "hemp", *ġanība* for *ġanīma*, "booty". Sporadic examples occur in modern Maghrebine colloquials; e.g. *lbən* for *lmən*, "for whom?" Palaeosyrian *šar-mi-na*, dual of /*šarmīnu*/, and Assyro-Babylonian *šurmīnu*, "cypress", correspond to Aramaic *šurbīnā*, Syriac *šarwaynā*, and Arabic *sarw*, with a further change *b* > *w* or *m* > *w*. The change was certainly not carried through consistently in any dialect. Therefore Aramaic *bar*, "son", might be related to Babylonian *māru*, to Old Assyrian *merʼum*, to Middle and Neo-Assyrian *marʼu*, "son", as well as to the verb *brʼ*, "to shape, to create".

11.7.   The nominal prefix *m-* changes often into *n-* in Assyro-Babylonian words containing a labial, e.g. *napḥaru*, "total, sum". The same shift is sporadically attested in Aramaic, e.g. *nšpṭ* < *mšpṭ*, "judgement"; *nʻbṣ*,

"bowl-like leg"; *nqdš'* < *mqdš'*, "the sanctuary", at Hatra; *ndbkh* <
madbəḥā, "the altar", name given to the god of Akko in the Babylonian
Talmud (*'Abōdā zārā* 11b). This change occurs frequently in Libyco-
Berber (§ 29.26). Also the third radical *m* may change into *n*, as shown
by Palaeosyrian *kà-ma-tum* / *kà-na-tù-um*, related to Assyro-Babylonian
kalmatu(m), "parasite", "louse", and by Babylonian *pasāmu* / *pasānu*,
"to hide", or *baqāmu* / *baqānu*, "to pull away". The same phenomenon
is attested in Classical Hebrew with *śṭm* / *śṭn*, "to accuse". In Jewish
Palestinian Aramaic and in Mishnaic Hebrew the change *m* > *n* in final
position is very common, e.g. *drwn* < *drwm*, "south", *ḥkyn* < *ḥkym*,
"wise person", *'dn* < *'dm*, "man", but the opposite change *n* > *m* is
attested in *lšm* < *lšn*, "tongue, language". The occasional change *m* > *n*
in medial position is found in the Aramaic name *Ìl-šu-un-ki* = *'lsmk*,
"God is (my) support". The examples of the *m* / *n* alternation increase if
the broader Afro-Asiatic area is taken into account with, e.g., East
Semitic *wasāmu*, "to be fit, skilled", and Libyco-Berber *wsn*, "to be
skilled", attested already in Antiquity by the agent noun *mwsn* and per-
sisting nowadays in Tuareg *a-mūssen*, "skilled man".

11.8. The labial *m* can become *w*, passing through the spirantized *m̱*,
when *m* is in intervocalic or postvocalic position. This change is well
attested in Neo-Babylonian, as in *Šamaš* pronounced *Šawaš*, which is
written with *m* in cuneiform writing but transcribed *šwš* in Aramaic
(Σαος in Greek). The signs with *m* stand therefore for the phoneme *w*, as
in *A-mu-ka-nu*, *A-muk-a-nu* or *A-muk-ka-na*, transcribed *'wkn* in Aramaic. In identical conditions, *nwṭy* stands for "Nabataean" in Talmudic
Aramaic, but the *b* is preserved in *'rby* /*'Arbay*/, "Arab". The same
change *m* > *w* may explain the shift from Babylonian *I-lu-Me-er* to Aramaic *'lwr* and it certainly occurs in Gurage dialects (e.g. *awäd* for Ge'ez
ḥamad, "ashes"), where one also finds a probable hypercorrection of *w*
becoming *m* (Muher and Gogot *tamuyä* for **tawəyä*, "orphan"). In addition, the Middle Assyrian and Neo-Assyrian shift of intervocalic *m* to
glottal stop and long vowel (e.g. *dēq* < *de'iq* < *damiq*, "is good"), confirmed by Aramaic transcriptions (*ss* = *sās* < *sa'as* < *šamaš*), may imply
a previous spirantization of *m*.

11.9. There are some examples of inserted *b* or *p* after *m*, which cannot be interpreted as dissimilation of gemination, e.g. Palaeosyrian
zumūbaru, broken plural (§31.28) of **zambāru* < *zamāru*, "song";
Gogot *tambuyä* next to *tamuyä*, "orphan"; Amharic *qämbär* from Ge'ez

qamar, "yoke"; Spanish *Alhambra* from Andalusian Arabic *'al-Ḥamrā'*, "the Red (Castle)"; Αμβρι transcribing Hebrew *'mry*, "Omri"; Ιαμβλιχος used for *Yamlik*; Σαμψαι marking the proper name *Šamšay*; Mandaic *'mbr'* from *'mr'*, "sheep". A similar phenomenon is attested in Cushitic (e.g. Boni *šimir*, Somali *šimbir-ta*, Rendille *čimbir*, "bird") and in Indo-European languages, as in French *chambre* from Latin *camera* or in Greek ἄμβροτος, "immortal", from μορτός, "mortal". Therefore we cannot be sure that Greek λάμβδα reproduces a Semitic pronunciation of *lamed*. The original nasal may disappear in front of the inserted plosive, as in the secondary Greek form βροτός, "mortal". It is quite probable therefore that Eblaite *sí-piš* and Ugaritic *špš*, "sun", originated from **šampšu* or **šimpšu*, with an inserted *p* after *m*, like in Σαμψαι. However, also a secondary *m* may be inserted before *b*, as in East Gurage *əmbab*, "snake", and in the name of *Ḫumbaba*, both related to Harari and Arabic *ḥubāb*, "snake", and both attested also with the change *b > w* (Argobba *həwaw*, "snake"; Old Babylonian *Ḫuwawa*). But no evident case of such an insertion seems to occur before *p*.

11.10. The spirantization of labials, dentals, and velars in the various Semitic languages is well known. Although Aramaic *p* and *k* are never rendered in Demotic by *f* and *ḫ*, the spirantization is probably indicated by the Greek transcriptions of *k*, *p*, *t* in the Bible: the Septuagint transcribes these letters either by κ, π, τ, or by χ, φ, θ, but these two series of transcriptions do not imply regular positional variants as in the traditional Jewish reading of Biblical Hebrew and Aramaic, where the non-geminated consonants *b g d k p t* are spirantized in post-vocalic position. These positional variants are attested in the Middle Ages in all Jewish Arabic-speaking communities, including Spain, and in France. With the exception of a few communities, only some of the six consonants are realized nowadays in Hebrew as plosives and as spirantized or labiodental fricatives. Among the Samaritans, *b g d k p t* have survived only with one pronunciation except for *p*, which is pronounced *b* when geminated and mainly as *f* elsewhere. Instead, traces of the double pronunciation of *b g d k p t* can be detected in Neo-Aramaic, both Eastern and Western, but the plosive and the spirantized realizations have both attained phonemic status and are no more conditioned by their position. In Ṭūrōyo, however, there are hesitations in the pronunciation of *p* / *f*. In Eastern Syriac, *p* is never spirantized, except in the loanwords of some dialects. Arabic does not know spirantization of labials or velars, but the labials *b, m,* and the velars *k, q* can be spirantized in Ethiopic when they are not geminated. The spirant consonants are not phonemic in Ethiopian languages and they can appear as free variants. In Śḥeri (Modern South Arabian), neither *b* nor *m* may occur in intervocalic position, but there is either a compensatory lengthening of the vowel or a raising of a semivowel, facts that seem to imply a previous spirantization of the labials. In Assyro-Babylonian, spirantization of labials and of dentals cannot be detected, except in the case of *m* (§11.8), but there are some sporadic traces of spirantization of non-geminated velars *k, g,* indicated by signs with *ḫ*; they are not necessarily connected with post-vocalic position (e.g. the divine name *Nusku = Nušḫu*).

11.11.   The labial semivowel *w* has regular correspondences in all the Semitic languages. It may come from non-geminated *b* or *m* by spirantization, and from rounded phonemes *bʷ, gʷ, kʷ, ḫʷ, qʷ* in Ethiopian languages (e.g. Gurage *wäz < bʷäz,* "slave"; cf. §18.7); it may also result from a secondary diphthongization of a long vowel. The labial *w* can serve as a glide between vowels, especially after *u* (e.g. Assyro-Babylonian *pa-nu-ú-a = panūwa = panū'a;* Arabic *maqrū'a > maqrūwa,* "being read"), and also as an on-glide in initial position before *o, u* (e.g. Ethiopic *wof* and *of < 'ōp,* "bird"), and even before *a* (e.g. colloquial Arabic *wakkil < 'akkil,* "he fed"; cf. §19.24). In various diphthongs *w* may be reduced to a vowel, generally *ō* or *ū,* but also *ā (aw > ā)* (§ 22.1,3-4; 27.23-24). Similarly, Ethiopic labialized consonants followed by *ä* may alternate with consonants plus *-o (<-ō)*; e.g. Amharic *Gʷäǧǧam* or *Goǧǧam,* the name of one Ethiopian province.

11.12.   Phonetic *w* occurs as a speech-sound throughout the life of East Semitic, but its graphic notation in cuneiform syllabic scripts is imperfect and doubts have been cast on its phonemic status from the Old Babylonian period on. Since the phoneme *w* did not exist in Sumerian or Pre-Sumerian, cuneiform writing does not have any special signs to express it. The Semites were forced therefore to find ways of expressing *w* in their writing and they regularly used the sign PI in the function of *wi, wa, wu* (e.g. *sá-pu-wa-an,* "flexible [shoes]"). The initial *wa* was sometimes expressed also by *ù+a* or *ú+a,* as in *Ú-ar-ti-a /Wardiya/,* and by the sign É having the value *'à,* as in *'à-ba-al /wabāl/,* "transporting". Replacement signs with *b* and *m* were also used, as in Old Assyrian *Tan-bar-ta* and *Tan-mar-ta,* which are allographs of *Tan-wa*(PI)-*ar-ta.* These replacements show that the scribes were aware of the phonetic correlation of the labials *b*, *m*, *w* and that the apparent changes *w* > *m* and *w* > *b* in East Semitic are to be considered as graphic replacements or allographs and not as real phonetic developments. The sign PI having become restricted in later periods to the values *pi*, *pe*, except in archaizing script and in peripheral regions, its place in the system was taken by signs with *m* and *b*, probably following the occasional spirantization of these phonemes in the spoken language. In Middle Assyrian and in Neo-Assyrian, also the vowel-sign *u* could be used to indicate *wa*, as in *Ni-nu-u* for *Ni-nu-wa*, the other possibility consisting in not expressing *w* at all, as in *Ni-nu-a*, "Nineveh". The loss of *w* at the beginning of words can generally be assumed from the Old Babylonian period on.

11.13. A development *w* > *y* in initial position characterizes Amorite, Ugaritic, Aramaic, as well the "Canaanite" of the second and first millennia B.C. E.g. *yld*, "to bear", is in opposition to *wld* in the other Semitic languages. The use of the cuneiform sign PI to mark *yi*, *ya₈*, *yú* besides *wi*, *wa*, *wu* (§11.13) in texts influenced by Amorite, Ugaritic, and Canaanite (Amarna correspondence) witness to this development which had a repercussion on scribal habits. Initial *w* is preserved only in the conjunction *wa-*, "and", in the name of the letter *wāw*, meaning "hook", in a few loanwords and in foreign proper names. A South Arabian Sabaic inscription shows a dialectal tendency to replace *w* by *y* at the beginning of words and the same phenomenon is attested once in an Arabic Ḥidjazi poem where *yāzi'ahum*, "their commander", stands for *wāzi'ahum*. In Sabaic, fluctuation between the semivowels *w* and *y* is sometimes seen also in medial and final positions, e.g. in *kyn* against normal *kwn*, "to be", in *rḍw* and *rḍy*, "goodwill". The same fluctuation occurs also in Andalusian Arabic, e.g. *fawḥa* and *fayḥa*, "fragrant emanation", *hawba* instead of usual *hayba*, "gravity". It is encountered in medial position after a consonant in the Hebrew and Aramaic word *'aryē*, "lion", instead of common Semitic **'arwiy-*.

11.14. In Arabic there is a possible development *wu-* > *u-* and *wi-* > *i-* in initial position, especially in Hudhail, a Ḥidjazi dialect. These forms are written *'u-* and *'i-* in the Arabic sources, but the *hamza* is there a purely orthographic feature. Besides, some roots with first radical *w* have sporadically a variant with ', e.g. *'irṯun*, "inheritance", from *wariṯa*, "to inherit" (cf. §19.24). There is also the regular Arabic practice of substituting ' for *w/y* after *ā*, e.g. **ǧāwiz* > *ǧā'iz*, "lawful", **'iǧrāy* > *'iǧrā'*, "enforcement".

11.15. The labiodental *f* may result in certain conditions from the inter-dental *ṯ* and from a lisping articulation of *š* / *s* so that the sound produced is [θ] > [f] (cf. Greek θερμός, Latin *formus*, "hot"). This phenomenon is well-known to Arab grammarians and enters in their category of *'ibdāl luġawī* or "lexical substitution"; e.g. *ǧadaṯ* > *ǧadaf*, "grave, tomb"; *Maṣyaf* for Mediaeval Arabic *Maṣyaṯ*; Greek transcription Φέρεπ of the Syrian place name *Ṯārib*; Liḥyānite *Rubaf* for *Rubaṯ*. This phenomenon would explain the Egyptian pronominal suffix *-f* of the third person mas-culine singular and the Argobba prepositions *wəfč*, "inside", when com-pared with Harari *usṭu*, *tef*, "under", which possibly goes back to a **teš* alternating e.g. with Amharic *tačč*, and then by analogy *lef*, "on".

3. DENTAL PLOSIVES

12.1. Common Semitic or Proto-Semitic has two dental plosives, voiceless *t* and voiced *d*; it has further an emphatic plosive *ṭ* which was voiceless, as indicated by the traditional and colloquial pronunciation of Arabic, Ethiopic, and Hebrew. Like the other emphatic consonants, also in older Arabic, *ṭ* corresponded to a pair of non-emphatic ones, one of which was voiced and the other voiceless. It was therefore of no phone-mic significance whether the emphatic sound was pronounced with or without voice. Cuneiform spellings, as the sign DI used with the values *di/de* and *ṭi/ṭe*, and ancient Egyptian transcriptions of Semitic names, as *D-b-ḫ* for the toponym *Ṭú-bi-ḫi*, do not prove a voiced realization of *ṭ*, since the distinction between voiced and emphatic consonants of the same group is insufficient in both systems.

12.2. The tendency of voicing a voiceless *t* or *ṭ* is nevertheless attested in several Semitic forms of speech. The Jewish Sephardi communities of Italy pronounce Hebrew *t* as *d* and the voicing of final *t* into *d* also occurs in Ethiopia, namely in West Gurage and in Argobba. In Modern South Arabian languages, the post-glottalized *ṭ* (*t'*) has partially voiced and sometimes wholly voiced variants. In the Jewish Yemenite commu-nity, Hebrew *ṭ* is realized either as *ṭ* or as *ḍ*. The Arabic colloquials of North Africa also show a tendency of voicing *ṭ*; e.g. at Cherchel (Alge-ria), classical *naṭaqa* is pronounced *ndaq*, "he spoke".

12.3. When pronounced by Bantus and Uzbeks, who are unfamiliar with emphatic phonemes, Arabic pharyngalized dentals, either plosive or

fricative, often change into the corresponding labialized consonants, thus
$t > t^w$, $s > s^w$, etc. Instead of the back orifice, i.e. the upper pharynx, the
front orifice is contracted, i.e. the lips are rounded. Palatalization of dentals occurs in Western Neo-Aramaic (e.g. *berča* < *berta*, "daughter")
and especially in South Ethiopic: *di* > *ǧ* (§ 15.5), *ti* > *č*, *ṭ* > *č̣*. It is also
attested for Arabic *t* in a few Tunesian dialects, but the Maghrebine *t* is
mainly characterized by its affricative articulation *ț* [ts], widespread in
the urban dialects of Morocco and of several Algerian cities.

12.4. The precise phonological status of dental plosives in prehistoric
Afro-Asiatic raises some questions because of the traceable alternations
t / *k* and *d* / *r*. The first alternation occurs in Semitic pronominal elements (§36.6; 40.5,11) and it led in Cushitic to an opposition of masculine *k* vs. feminine *t* (§36.6). Instead of being original, this opposition
may result from a specialized function obtained by the allophones *t* and
k of the same phoneme. An example of a phoneme realized as [t] or [k]
is encountered nowadays in the Samoan language which is believed to
represent the oldest form of Malayo-Polynesian, also known as Austronesian. A change *t* > *k* took place in the Indo-European Lycian of
South Anatolia, at least in the consonantal cluster *tb* > *kb* (e.g. *kbatra* <
*tbatra / *twatra*, "daughter"), but an alternation *t* / *k* appears in other
circumstances as well (e.g. the PN *Krupssi-* transcribed Θρύπσις in
Greek). The alternation *d* / *r* has left traces in Cushitic and in South
Ethiopic (§17.7), and it occurs in languages of the Niger-Congo family
(e.g. Fulani *debbo*, "woman", plur. *rewḅe*). Further research is needed
in both cases.

4. INTERDENTALS

13.1. Common Semitic or Proto-Semitic has two interdental fricatives,
voiceless *ṯ* and voiced *ḏ*, i.e. [θ] and [δ]; it has further an emphatic fricative *ṯ̣*, which is often transliterated "ẓ". This consonant is represented by
a graphic symbol of its own in Ugaritic and in Epigraphic South Arabian, while a diacritical sign distinguishes it in Arabic from the emphatic
dental fricative *ṣ*. The following table gives but a very partial idea of the
development of the interdentals in the main Semitic languages and has
to be explained below.

Pr.-Sem.	Ass.-Bab.	Ugar.	Hebr.	Aram.	Cl.Ar.	E.S.A.	Ge'ez
ṯ	š	ṯ	š	ṯ > t	ṯ	ṯ	s
ḏ	z	d or ḏ	z	ḏ > d	ḏ	ḏ	z
ṱ	ṣ	ṱ	ṣ	ṱ > ṭ	ẓ	ṱ	ṣ

13.2. Palaeosyrian and Old Akkadian preserve traces of one interdental at least, namely the voiceless *ṯ*. In fact, the group of syllabograms consisting of the signs ŠA, ŠI, ŠU expresses the syllables *ṯa, ṯi, ṯu* (e.g. *u-ša-ab* /*uṯṯab*/, "he sits"), while the signs SA, SI, SU stand for syllables containing the Semitic phonemes *š* or *ś* (e.g. *u-sa-lim* /*ušallim*/, "he made good"). A third set of signs SÁ, SI₁₁, SU₄ interchanges frequently with the SA, SI, SU group and seems to indicate that the phonemes originally differentiated by the two rows of signs were tending to coalesce in the period under consideration. However, the regular occurrence of the SU₄ sign in the spelling of the independent and suffixed personal pronoun, as well as of the demonstrative of remoter deixis ("that", "those"), may signalize a phonetic distinction between the SU₄ sign, used initially to express the prepalatal *š*, and the SU sign employed originally for the lateral *ś*, e.g. in *su-ru-uš* (*śrš* = s^2rs^1), "foundation". In the case of the Old Akkadian demonstrative, this interpretation is supported by the parallelism between *su₄*, *su₄-a* and Qatabanian s^1w, between *su₄-a-tum* and Qatabanian oblique s^1wt, and between *su₄-nu-ti* and Qatabanian oblique plural s^1mt. As for the oppositions SÁ : SA and SI : SI₁₁ in Old Akkadian, one could mention *sá-lim* (*šlm* = s^1lm), "he is well", and *tá-sa-am-ma* (*tś'm* = $ts^2'm$), "you will buy", as well as *sa-am-si* (*śmšy* = s^2ms^1y), "my sun", and *ni-si₁₁* (*nś'* = ns^2'), "people". In Old Akkadian, Proto-Semitic *ḏ* and *ṱ* (*ẓ*) are expressed by the row of the signs ZA, ZI, ZU, that are used for the three dental fricatives *s, z, ṣ* (e.g. *zu'āzum*, "to divide", root *zḫṱ*). In Eblaite, instead, the voiced phoneme *ḏ* is indicated by the same signs as its voiceless counterpart *ṯ*, and both may be expressed also by the sign ŠÈ. No systematic distinction is made between *ś* and *š*, but traces of a distinctive sibilant seem to appear in the name of the Sun-deity **śpš*, written *sí-piš* (cf. *Taš-má-Sí-piš* // *Taš-má-*ᵈUTU), and in the expression *mu-da-bil sí-kà-ri* /*mudabbil sikāri*/, "storyteller", where **ḏikr* is spelt with ZI (*sí*) in agreement with Phoenician *skr* (§14.2).

Some irregularities occur in documents from Ebla where parallel texts quote e.g. the same city name as *Ma-ša-du*ᵏⁱ and *Ma-sa-ad*ᵏⁱ, thus obliterating the phonetic distinction between ŠA and SA. However, the overall picture corresponds to the Old Akkadian scribal practice.

13.3. The picture that emerges from the Old Babylonian period on in Assyro-Babylonian is that $t̠$, $š$ and $ś$ have coalesced into one phoneme $š$, expressed in the cuneiform writing by the signs of the set ŠA, ŠE, ŠI, ŠU, while the signs SA, SI, SU, SÁ, etc., were used to indicate the voiceless sibilant s. However, reservations have to be set forth in the case of the Mari and Qaṭara (Tell ar-Rimaḥ) texts, especially regarding the transcription of Amorite names (§13.4), and also in the case of Old Assyrian texts. These documents from Northern Mesopotamia still seem to reflect a distinction between $t̠$ on the one side and $š/ś$ on the other (e.g. *sa-am-si* < *śmt̠*), although the cuneiform signs of the different sets may occur in free interchange, e.g. *ú-sa-ás-ḫa-ar* next to *ú-ša-ás-ḫi-ir*, "he turned".

13.4. The cuneiform spelling of Amorite personal names clearly preserves the distinction between the interdental $t̠$ and the sibilants $š/ś$, that were coalesced into $š$ like later in Ugaritic; e.g. *Ia-šu-ub-^dDa-gan* /Yat̠ūb-Dagān/, but *Ia-sa-rum* /Yašarum/, *Sa-ap-si-A-du* /Šapši-Haddu/. However, the rare interchanges of ŠA, ŠI, ŠU with SA, SI, SU indicate that the development $t̠ > š$ must have begun in some Amorite dialects towards the end of the Old Babylonian period, e.g. *Sa-am-šu-^dIM* or *Ša-ap-ši* at Alalakh. The Proto-Semitic interdentals $d̠$ and $t̠$ ($ẓ$) were coalesced with the dental fricatives.

13.5. A chart of the principal signs involved in the discussion of early Semitic sibilants recapitulates the outline of §13.2-4 and offers a comparison with the situation in Ugaritic and Epigraphic South Arabian.

*Pr.-Sem.	P.Syr.	O.Akk.	Amorite	Ass.-Bab.	Ugar.	E.S.A.
$t̠a$	ŠA	ŠA	ŠA	ŠA	$t̠$	$t̠$
$t̠i$	(ŠI)	ŠI	ŠI	ŠI	$t̠$	$t̠$
$t̠u$	ŠU	ŠU	ŠU	ŠU	$t̠$	$t̠$
$d̠a$	ŠA	ZA	ZA	ZA	$d/d̠$	$d̠$
$d̠i$	(ŠI)	ZI	ZI	ZI	$d/d̠$	$d̠$
$d̠u$	ŠU	ZU	ZU	ZU	$d/d̠$	$d̠$
$ša$	SA/SÁ	SÁ	SA	ŠA	$š$	s^1
$ši$	SI/ZI	SI	SI	ŠI	$š$	s^1
$šu$	SU/SÙ	SU$_4$	SU/ZU	ŠU	$š$	s^1
$śa$	SA	SA	SA	ŠA	$š$	s^2
$śi$	SI/ZI/SI$_{11}$	SI$_{11}$	SI	ŠI	$š$	s^2
$śu$	SU	SU	SU	ŠU	$š$	s^2
$sa/i/u$	ZA/I/U	ZA/I/U	ZA/I/U	SA/I/U	s	s^3

13.6.   In Ugaritic, *ṯ* and *ṭ* generally retain their independence. However, there are traces of an initiating process *ṯ* > *š* appearing in the spelling *'aḥrṯp* of the name *'aḥršp* and in the use of a new sign **o** to mark both *š* and *ṯ* in three texts from Ugarit, which are written from right to left in a shorter alphabet of 22 letters (KTU 1.77; 4.31; 4.710). As for *ṭ*, besides the words in which an etymological *ṭ* is velarized into *ǵ* (§ 10.9), it can be replaced by a non-emphatic interdental in *ḥṯm*, "arrows", and in the theonym *ṯṭ*, occasionally written *ḥdm* and *ṯṭ*. In addition, the two words *ṯhrm*, "gems", and *lṭpn*, "kind", are spelt *ṯhrm* and *lṭpn* on one tablet (KTU 1.24), a phenomenon which seems to prelude to the Aramaic shift *ṯ* > *ṭ* and to the merging of the two phonemes. The interdental *ḏ* generally merges with *d* (e.g. *dbḥ*, "sacrifice"), like later in Aramaic, but some words preserve the etymological *ḏ* (e.g. *ḏr'*, "arm"), especially when the word contains a laryngal or *r*. In two texts (KTU 1.12; 1.24), all of the few occurrences of etymological *ḏ* are retained (e.g. *'aḥḏ*, "he seized").

13.7.   It is uncertain whether the Proto-Sinaitic inscriptions preserve the three interdentals, which merged in Canaanite with dental and palato-alveolar fricatives at the time of the Proto-Canaanite inscriptions using the short alphabet of 22 letters, that appears about the 13th century B.C. However, the biblical *shibbolet* story in Judg. 12,5-6 points to the existence of *ṯ* (*ṯblt*, "stream, flood") in Northern Transjordan, but the dialect referred to may be Aramaic instead of being Hebrew. Also Ammonite seems to have preserved *ṯ*, although the alphabet borrowed from the Phoenicians makes such assessments difficult. The Greek transcription Τύρος of the Phoenician place-name *Ṣr* might indicate that original *Ṯūr* was still dialectally realized with *ṯ* when it entered Greek under the form Τύρος, clearly differentiated from Σιδών (Phoenician *Ṣdn*) and from the later attested name Σο(υ)ρ, "Tyre". Ancient Egyptian *Ḏ-r* can simply transcribe *Ṣr*, since the "ḏ" of Egyptologists usually corresponds to Semitic *ṣ*.

13.8.   In Early Aramaic inscriptions the symbols "š", "z", "ṣ" stand also for *ṯ*, *ḏ*, *ṭ* respectively, except in the Tell Fekherye inscription where *ṯ* is transcribed "s". In the 8th century B.C. new spellings begin to appear, reflecting the shifts *ṯ* > *t* (e.g. *yhtb* < **yhṯb*, "may he bring back"), *ḏ* > *d* (e.g. *'ḥdwhy* < **'ḥḏwhy*, "they seized him"), *ṭ* > *ṭ* (e.g. *nṭr* < **nṭr*, "he guarded"). They should be distinguished from the assimilation *ṭṭ* > *ṭṭ*, as in *'ṭtr* > *'tr*, "'Attar". The phonetic process reflected in these changes lasted probably for several centuries and the dental realization of the interdentals did certainly not happen at the same time in all the Aramaic dialects. The opposite process of free spirantization of *d* > *ḏ* and *t* > *ṯ* cannot be assessed for Aramaic and Hebrew before the Hellenistic period.

13.9. In the North Arabian sphere, Pre-Classical and Classical Arabic maintain the three interdentals as independent phonemes and Classical Arabic uses the Aramaic symbols "d", "t", "ṭ" for *ḏ*, *ṯ*, *ṱ*. Hesitations occur in Palmyrene Aramaic, as *pḥd* and *pḥz* for *faḫḏ*, "clan, tribe". The usual Greek transcriptions are δ for *ḏ*, τ or θ for *ṯ*, and τ for *ṱ*. The Damascus fragment from the 8th century A.D. (§7.44) uses δ to transliterate Arabic *d*, *ḏ*, *ḍ* (*ṣ́*), as well as *ẓ* (*ṱ*). In fact, *ṱ* (conventionally transcribed "ẓ") appears to have become a voiced interdental [ḏ], which is attested in various Modern Arabic forms of speech, for instance in the Ḥawrān, in Syria (e.g. *ḏöfŏr*, "nail"), or in the Algerian cities that have preserved the Andalusian dialect of Arabic (e.g. *ḏuhr*, "mid-day"). In most dialects of the sedentary population, however, interdental fricatives have shifted to the corresponding dental plosives. Besides, readers of the Qur'ān who have no interdentals in their own language and try to pronounce them, often realize /ṯ/ as [s], /ḏ/ as [z], and /ḍ/ as [ẓ]. In cuneiform script, North Arabian *ṯ* is transcribed by *t*, e.g. in *Ia-at-ri-bu* /*Yaṯrib*/.

A particular feature of North Arabian inscriptions from the Tabūk (Saudi Arabia) and Ma'ān (Jordan) area consists in indicating the etymological *ṯ* by the sign for *ṣ́* (*ḍ*), e.g. *w-ḥdṣ́ ṣ́yt* = *w-ḥdṯ ṯyt*, "and he made a new sheepfold". This scribal practice is somehow related to the phonetic shifts *ḏ* > *d* or *ḏ* and *ḏ* > *ṯ* which are attested around the 9th century A.D. by the early South-Palestinian Arabic spellings *šaḥḥāṯ* for *šaḥḥāḏ*, "beggar", and *dm'rn'* for *ḏamā'irunā*, "our hearts". A voicing of *ṯ* is attested in the Ḥassānīya dialect of Mauritania, but its acoustic value is not identical with that of *ḏ*.

13.10. In Epigraphic South Arabian, the frequency with which *ṣ́* and *ṯ* appear as variant spellings in the same word (e.g. *ṣ́ll* for *ṯll*, "covering"; *ṣ́m'* for *ṯm'*, "thirst") suggests that the phonemic distinctiveness of these two letters was, to some extent at least, lost. An intermediate development phase seems to be attested by Sabaic cursive texts which indicate the etymological *ṯ* by the sign for *ṣ́* (*ḍ*), like in *mḍ'w* for *mṯ'w*, "they reached". In fact, this sign was borrowed by Ethiopic (*ḍappa*), but the phoneme in question merged with *ṣ* soon after the Aksum inscriptions (§ 16.4). A limited evolution may be assumed in ancient South Arabian also for the interdentals *ṯ* and *ḏ*, but different cases should be distinguished. Although *s³* and *ṯ* remained distinct phonemes in Minaic, it is *ṯ* that is used for the rendering of a non-Semitic /s/, as in *dlṯ*, "Delos", *tlmyṯ*, "Ptolemaios", and *'ṯrḥf*, "Osiri-Apis, Osarapis". Since the Phoenician dialect of Lapethos in Cyprus uses *š* in the same period to transcribe Greek /s/ in *ptlmyš*, "Ptolemaios", these transcriptions "ṯ" and "š" probably reflect a weakly enunciated Greek variety of the sound *s* which was likely to suggest a lisping effect, more appropriately noted by "ṯ" or "š" than by "s³" or "s". In Semitic, the hiss of *s* is very much stronger and more sibilant than the Greek *s* (§14.1). In Sabaic, however, Greek /s/ is represented by *s³*, except in the place-name "Ctesiphon", written *qṯwṣf* with *ṣ*, and there is one case in Sabaic from Haram where Semitic *ṯ* is spelt *s³*, i.e. [s]: *ys³wbn*, "he will reward". This would imply a local dialectal shift *ṯ* > *s* in the 1st-3rd centuries A.D. In addition, the sounds noted by *ṯ* and *s³* have fallen in Ḥaḍramitic together into a single phoneme noted indifferently by either letter, e.g. in the divine name *'ṯtr* or *'s³trm*. The same may have happened in the case of *ḏ* and *z*, though here seems to be a preference for noting the sound as *ḏ*, e.g. *'l'ḏ*, "Eleazos" (Ἐλεάζος), against Sabaic *'l'z*.

13.11.   In some Modern South Arabian dialects there is loss of distinction between *t* and *ṯ*, *d* and *ḏ*, *ṭ* and *ḏ̣* (e.g. North Mehri *ḏar*, South Mehri and Soqoṭri *ṭar*, "upon").

13.12.   In Ethiopia, Geʻez, Tigre, and Tigrinya lost the interdentals *ṯ*, *ḏ*, *ṭ*, that became *s*, *z*, *ṣ*. In Amharic, Argobba, Harari, and Gurage *ṯ*, *ḏ*, *ṭ* became *s*, *z*, *ṭ*, but [ṭ] can alternate in Gurage with the glottal stop and become *zero*. Most South Ethiopian languages testify thus to a different development of *ṯ* (*ẓ*) than North Ethiopic; e.g. Gurage *ṭäma-*, Amharic and Argobba *ṭämma-* vs. Arabic *ẓami'a*, Geʻez *ṣam'a*, "to be thirsty"; Gurage *aṭara*, Argobba *haṭṭära*, Harari *ḥēṭära*, vs. Arabic *ḥaẓara*, Geʻez *ḥaṣara*, "to fence in".

5. DENTAL FRICATIVES

14.1.   Common Semitic or Proto-Semitic has two dental fricatives, voiceless *s* and voiced *z*. It also possesses an emphatic dental fricative *ṣ*, which is voiceless. It is pharyngalized in Arabic, but post-glottalized ([s']) in Ethiopic and in Modern South Arabian. The Arabic *ẓ* is in reality the emphatic interdental *ḏ̣* < *ṭ* (§13.9).

It is noteworthy that the Arabic plain /s/ is of higher pitch than most allophones of English /s/, while the pharyngalized /ṣ/ displays a noticeably lower pitch than the English /s/, comparable with the low pitch of Russian plain /s/. Therefore, a Russian observer will be inclined to identify Arabic /ṣ/ with his own /s/. This might help, by analogy, to understand an ancient transcription of Semitic /ṣ/ by Hittite /s/ in *ku-ni-ir-ša* [konīrsa] rendering Semitic *qōnī* (*'a*)*rṣa*, "who owns the earth", while a cuneiform sign *za/ṣa* was also available. The three dental fricatives *s*, *z*, *ṣ* are often interchanged in Western Late Aramaic manuscripts dating from a period when Aramaic dialects were no longer spoken in Palestine and, as a consequence, the phonetic distinction of these consonants was blurred.

14.2. The cuneiform script does not distinguish the dental fricatives in an adequate way and a change in the writing practice occurred in the first centuries of the second millennium B.C., as explained in §13.2-4. Besides, Neo-Assyrian /s/ was palatalized into [š], as shown by Aramaic transcriptions, e.g. *mšn* /*masennu*/, "treasurer". A similar palatalization of /s/ is attested later in Arabia and in Ethiopia (§14.3). The devoicing of *z* < *ḏ* into *s* occurs in the Phoenician root *skr* < *zkr* < *ḏkr*, "to remember", and in the Late Punic spelling *s* / *st* of the demonstrative pronoun *z* / **zt* < *ḏ* / *ḏt*, transcribed in Latin as *syth*. In the 11th century B.C., both pronunciations *zkr* and *skr* are attested by the same name written *zkrbʻl* on three arrowheads and *ṯ-k-r-b-ʻ-r* in Egyptian transcription corresponding to *skrbʻl*. These variations most likely represent forms taken from different Phoenician dialects surviving later in Punic.

14.3. In the Arabic sphere, the North Arabian inscriptions, even the earliest Liḥyānic ones, use only the letters s^1 (*š*) and s^2 (*ś*), and the Sabaic tendency to merge s^3 with s^1 in the 5th-6th centuries A.D. (e.g. ms^1gd for the Aramaic loanword *masgad*, "house of prayer") is already attested in an earlier period by a text from the Haram area, where $'ks^1wt$, "garments", stands against standard Sabaic ks^3wy, "clothing". In Palmyrene inscriptions, etymological Arabic *š* is transcribed "š", as in $š'd$ ($s^1'd$), "lucky", and the original *s* appears also as "š", e.g. in $šh(y)mw$ (s^3hm), "arrow". Instead, the transcription of the etymological *ś* fluctuates between "s" and "š", as in *skr* / *škr* (s^2kr), "rewarding". When Nabataean Aramaic script was adopted for writing North Arabian, no use was made of the letter *samek* ("s") expressing the [s] sound, for this sound was obviously palatalized into [š] and could be indicated by the letter *shin* ("š") serving to indicate both /š/ and /ś/, which correspond to South Arabian s^1 and s^2. In the 8th century A.D., Sibawayh makes it clear that, in his time, /s/ had a point of closure between the tongue-tip and the hard palate, together with retroflexion of the tongue-tip, a description which identifies it with [š] (§14.4). The merging of /s/ and /š/ occurred also in Geʻez and in modern Ethiopian languages, but it is not complete. Although secondary palatalization of *s* into [š] is attested in Tigrinya, Amharic, Harari, and Gurage, it is unlikely that all the attested cases of etymological *š* may have been occasioned by palatalization. Some of them go back to earlier stages of Ethiopic and preserve the original phoneme.

14.4. The modern standard pronunciation [s] of Arabic *sin*, in which /š/ and /s/ had merged, must post-date Sibawayh's time. It introduces a clear distinction between *sin* and *shin* [š], which in Sibawayh's days had a point of closure "the same as for *g* and *y*, between the centre of the tongue and the soft palate", i.e. probably similar to the fricative palatal [ç]. The Damascus fragment from the 8th century A.D. (§7.44) transliterates the etymological *š* by χ (e.g. χεβιγοῦ for *šabiʻū*, "they were sated"), which serves for *ḥ* and *ḫ* as well (e.g. χουβζ for *ḫubz*, "bread"; λυχουμ for *luḥūm*, "meat" plur.), while etymological *s*, *š*, and *ṣ* are indicated by σ (e.g. σεμιγ for *samiʻ*,"he heard"; αφ.σελ for *'afsal*,"he abhorred"; σαγ[ιδ] for *ṣaʻid*,"it came up"). This transliteration shows at least that the modern standard *shin* was realized at that time as a complex sound, different from simple sibilants. Thus we may represent the development of the three sibilants indicated in Arabic as «š» in the following way:

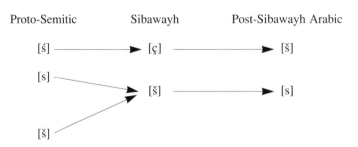

Proto-Semitic	Sibawayh	Post-Sibawayh Arabic
[ś]	[ç]	[š]
[s]	[š]	[s]
[š]		

The fricative palatal [ç] is still attested nowadays in Śḥeri, the speakers of which pronounce it with approximately the same tongue position as *š*, but there is no contact between the top of the tongue and the alveolar ridge. The air is pushed out over the tongue and the lips are simultaneously rounded and pouted. This sound derives from an original *ś*, as in *çeṭan*, "the Devil" (root *śṭn*), or in *çirif*, "noble" (= Arabic *šarīf*), but it can also be a palatalized variant of *k*, as in *çirś*, "belly" (root *krś*). This [ç] has phonemic status in Śḥeri.

14.5. Both changes *s* > *š* and *š* > *s* are attested in modern Arabic dialects but they are generally conditioned: under the influence of a following *ǧ*, *s* can change into *š*, but *š* can also change into *s*, e.g. *sǧī'* against classical *šaǧī'*, "courageous". There are also unconditioned variants, as *rafas* and *rafaš*, "to kick". In some Jewish Moroccan communities Hebrew /s/ and /š/ are both realized as a sound intermediary between [s] and [š], or as [s].

14.6. The substitution of *z* to *s* in the neighbourhood of an emphatic is attested in colloquials of central Syria, e.g. in *zaqf* < *saqf*, "roof". In contact with *q*, on the other hand, *z* becomes *s*, as in *sqōq* < *zuqāq*, "lane". In the colloquial of eṣ-Ṣalṭ, in northern Jordan, the difference between *s*, *z*, *ṣ* is suspended in the neighbourhood of emphatics, e.g. in *zirāṭ*, *sirāṭ* or *ṣirāṭ*, "way" (< Latin *strata*). The principle at work here is the phonological tendency which makes the whole word either emphatic or non-emphatic, and in the first case turns all or most consonants into emphatic ones (§10.9). This tendency is attested also in North Africa, e.g. in *ṣolṭān* < *sulṭān*, "master". The opposite shift *ṣ* > *s* is attested as well in mediaeval and in modern Arabic dialects. It may reflect dissimilation, as in the cluster *ṣṭ* > *sṭ*, or simple develarization.

14.7. The realization of Hebrew *ṣ* as a voiceless dental affricate [ts] by European Jews is probably to be considered as an innovation, although it seemingly corresponds to an old pronunciation of this dental fricative, at least in Late Antiquity, when *ṣpn*, "north", was transcribed by *tspn* in Demotic, and *ḥṣr*, "plant", by αστηρ in Greek. Also in Modern Ethiopian languages, viz. in Amharic and in Gafat, *ṣ* is often pronounced as an affricate [ts']. One should also mention the passage *ṣ* > *ṭ* in South-Amharic, Argobba, Gurage, and Harari under the influence of Cushitic.

14.8. In modern South Arabian languages, *ṣ* can be realized as *š*, e.g. in Mehri *šəba'*, "finger", as against *'əṣba'* in Śḥeri and in Soqoṭri.

14.9. In Ethiopian languages, as mentioned above (§14.3), the merging of /s/ and /š/ had already occurred in Ge'ez, that shows an arbitrary interchange of the two symbols "s" and "š". The palatalization of *s* into [š] led to the development of a new phoneme *š* for which an adaptation of the symbol for "s" is used (*šat*), found mainly in borrowed words. However, Tigrinya and Amharic have an etymological *š* in some genuine Semitic words and forms, like Tigrinya *šəm* beside *səm*, "name", *ḥammuštä*, "five", *šobʿattä*, "seven", the Amharic causative preformative *aš-* beside *as-* (§41.14). Therefore, one may wonder whether the articulated *š* of Ethiopic results always from a secondary palatalization of *s* or preserves an old pronunciation, at least in a number of cases.

14.10. The sibilant *s* is almost universal, but is was replaced by the rough breathing in Greek (e.g. ἑπτά / *septem*, "seven") and by *h* in Lycian (e.g. *mahana-* vs. Luwian *maššana-*, "god"), in Armenian, Persian, Modern South Arabian (§15.4), and eastern Polynesian (*Hawaii / Savaii*). The change of an original sibilant (*z*, *ž*, *š*) into *h* is attested also in the Tuareg dialects of Ahaggar and Air; e.g. *hik*, "make haste!", vs. Ghat dialect *zik*, Arabic *suq / siq*, "urge on!" (root *šūq*). If one takes this evidence into account, there is a strong case for regarding *š* > *s* (> *h*) as the primitive phoneme of the Semitic personal pronoun of the third person (§36.10,20), of the Afro-Asiatic prefix of the causative verbal stem (§41.11), and of the Semitic conditional particle (§61.2).

6. Prepalatal and Palatal

15.1. Common Semitic or Proto-Semitic has a voiceless fricative prepalatal or palato-alveolar *š*, i.e. [ʃ], and a palatal semivowel *y*, i.e. [j].

15.2. The changing practice of the cuneiform writing system with regard to the interdental *ṯ*, the dental fricative *s*, and the prepalatal *š* was described in § 13.2-4. In addition, the Middle Babylonian and Middle Assyrian orthographic change *š* > *l* before a dental is probably a scribal device that indicates a total reciprocal assimilation (§27.5) producing a geminated dental lateral of the *ś* type (§ 16.4), for which no adequate cuneiform signs were available; e.g. *kušda* > *kulda* [*kuśśa*], "come here!". This would explain the spelling *iu-se-bi-la* [*yuśśēbila*], "he has sent", in an Amarna letter from Byblos (EA 88,35) and the later Neo-Assyrian spellings like *issu* for *ištu*, "since", or for *išdu*, "foundation", very likely [*iśśu*]. Instead, Neo-Assyrian *š* was pronounced [s], as shown by Aramaic and Hebrew transcriptions, e.g. *nbwsmskn* for *Nabû-šum-iškun*. In consequence, since the Neo-Assyrian cuneiform spelling remained unchanged, West Semitic *s* was transcribed "š" in

Neo-Assyrian texts, e.g. *Mil-ki-a-ša-pa* = *mlkysp*, while West Semitic *š* was rendered by "s", e.g. *Sa-me-ri-na* = *šmryn*, "Samaria".

15.3. The prepalatal *š* merged with *s* in various Arabian and Ethiopian forms of speech, and finally developed into [s] in Arabic and in Ethiopic, despite some dialectal palatalizations of *s* into *š* (§ 14.3-4,7). It is unlikely, however, as stressed above (§ 14.3,9), that palatalization may have brought about the change of *s* into *š* in the various cases where modern Ethiopian languages have an etymological *š* which is not contiguous to a phoneme like *i* that may have occasioned the change *s* > *š*. In other languages, an unusual variation *š/s* occurs in some words, like *šabe / sebe*, "seven", in Assyrian and *šb'm / sb'm*, "seventy", in Neo-Punic that probably continues two different Punic dialects (§15.4). In Neo-Punic there is an occasional interchange between *š* and *s* in other cases as well, but mainly in foreign names from which one cannot infer that *š* and *s* were normally confused. On the contrary, the use of the Greek symbol Σ in Latino-Punic inscriptions to indicate *š* (e.g. ΣVMAR = *šmr*, "guardian") shows that the phonemic distinction between *š* and *s* was not lost.

15.4. A change *š* > *h* is attested in the Semitic personal pronoun of the third person (§36.10,20), in the causative prefix of the causative verbal stem (§41.11), and in the conditional particle (§61.2). A similar phenomenon occurs on a wider scale not only in Indo-European and other language families (§14.10), but also in Modern South Arabian, as shown by a comparison of some nominal and verbal roots in Mehri and in Śḥeri, while the situation in Soqoṭri is less clear and seems to reflect external influences. E.g.:

Root	Śḥeri	Mehri	Soqoṭri	
*šab'	šō'	hōba	yhobə'	"seven"
*šim	šum	ham	šem	"name"
*hamš	ḥīš	ḥayməh	ḥamoš	"five"
*šma'	šī'	hīma	hʸemaḥ	"he heard"
*šqiy	šeqe	həqu	ḥežə	"he watered"

15.5. In Modern South Arabian and Ethiopian languages, the palatalization of the velars (§18.6) increased the number of words containing the prepalatal *š*; e.g. Śḥeri *šurś* < *krś*, "belly"; Gafat *gäǧǧaš* < *gäǧǧaki*, "your (fem.) house". This is an old phonetic change, noticed already among the Mahra by Mas'ūdī in the 10th century A.D.: "they put *š* instead of k", he says. Besides, palatalization added $\check{c}$, $\check{z}$, as well as the corresponding glottalized emphatic $\acute{\check{s}}$ or $\acute{c}$, to the phonetic repertory; e.g. Śḥeri *širet* < *qryt*, "town"; East Gurage *bäče* < *bakaya*, "he wept". As for the palatal $\check{g}$, it may be derived not only from a velar (§ 18.6), but also from d; e.g. Gafat *təgälǧi* < *təgäldi*, "you gird yourself" (fem.); Harari *wŭläǧi*, "give birth!", from *wäläda*. Similar phenomena occur in Arabic and Neo-Aramaic vernaculars (§18.6). In Eastern Neo-Aramaic, for example, the voiced prepalatal $\check{z}$ is found in loanwords and in genuine Aramaic words in which $\check{s}$ is voiced by assimilation, e.g. in [*xežbōna*] < *ḥušbānā*, "bill".

15.6.   The palatal semivowel y has regular correspondences in the various Semitic languages. It is either original, or is derived from w (§11.13), or appears as a glide (§15.7), or results from a palatalization of l; e.g. Amharic *haya* < **kil'ā*, "twenty". In cuneiform script it is not marked in initial position, in which it disappears in Assyro-Babylonian leaving behind the vowel which accompanied it (e.g. *yi-* > *i-*, *yu-* > *u-*). The Old Akkadian spellings of the type *i-ik-mi*, "he captured", *i-ig-mu-ur*, "he conquered", probably indicate the preservation of initial y, also in cases of usual spellings without initial *i-* (cf. §22.13-14).

15.7.   The palatal y can serve as a glide between vowels, especially after i (e.g. Arabic *ḥaṭī'a* > *ḥaṭīya*, "sin"), and also as an on-glide in initial position, instead of a glottal stop; e.g. Arabic *yusr* < *'usr*, "captivity"; 'Omānī colloquial *yāl* < *'āl* < *'ahl*, "family"; Neo-Aramaic *yəmma* < *'emmā*, "mother".

15.8.   Palatalization plays an important role in Afro-Asiatic languages, not only in Semitic (§15.5). Therefore, any lexical study must take this widespread phenomenon into account. In Libyco-Berber, e.g., l is palatalized into $\check{z}$ in Tamazight (e.g. *už* < *ul*, "heart") and ll changes into $\check{g}$ in Tarifit (e.g. *a-fǧaḥ* < *fallāḥ*, "peasant"; *səǧəm* < *sallim*, "to greet"). Devoicing at the end of a word or of a clause may cause a further change $\check{g}$ > $\check{c}$, like in Tarifit *Mrič* < Melilla, also with the change l > r. The velar k is palatalized into $\check{c}$ in various circumstances, especially when it is contiguous to the vowel i / u; thus, the Old Egyptian pronominal suffix *-ki* of the second person feminine singular became *-č*, and it is conventionally transcribed "ṯ" by Egyptologists. The Egyptian name *nṯr*, "god", is believed to be related to Semitic *nkr*, "strange(r)", but it should perhaps be linked with Agaw *nkəra*, "soul, spirit". Also t may be palatalized as, for example, the Semitic noun *qāt-*, "hand", well-known in East Semitic, which corresponds to West Cushitic (Omotic) *kuč-*, *kis-*, "hand, arm". A systematic study of the Afro-Asiatic lexicon and of the palatalization rules in various languages is still a desideratum.

7. LATERALS

16.1. Common Semitic or Proto-Semitic had two dental laterals, voiceless *ś* and emphatic *ṣ́*, conventionally transcribed *ḍ*. They correspond to [ɬ] and [ɬ̣].

16.2. Non emphatic *ś* has a graphic sign of its own in Epigraphic South Arabian, namely *s²* (𐩦), and it is pronounced in Modern South Arabian by retracting the right corner of the mouth and forcing a stream of air between the teeth and the inside of the cheek at the right side of the mouth, with the tongue-tip in the *l*-position. This phoneme cannot be distinguished from *š* in the North and East Semitic languages, except in Old Akkadian where the sign su_4 seems to have originally expressed the prepalatal *š*, while the sign su indicated the lateral *ś* (§ 13.2). Otherwise, the merging of *š* and *ś* is apparently complete in all the languages attested in cuneiform script, and it seems therefore that *ś* has lost there its phonemic status. Neither do the Amarna glosses and the Egyptian transcriptions indicate that an autonomous phoneme *ś* existed in the Canaanite languages of the II millennium B.C. In the Amarna glosses, the sign *ša* can express *ṯa* (e.g. *ša-aḫ-ri* = *ṯ'r*, "gate"), *ša* (e.g. *ša-mu-ma*, *ša-me-ma* = *šmm*, "heaven") and *śa* (e.g. *ša-te-e* = *śdh*, "field"), while the Egyptian transcriptions *s* and *š* are interchangeable (e.g. *sk* and *šik* = *śk'*, "Soco"). In the Phoenician alphabet *ś* and *š* are expressed by one symbol with the obvious consequence that the alphabetic script of no West Semitic language is capable of distinguishing the two sounds without using diacritical signs.

16.3. Nevertheless, the word "ten", *'śr*, is written in Phoenician *'šr*, but its "feminine" form is spelt *'šrt*. The existence of both forms is best explained by an original *'śr*. Greek βάλσαμον and its derivatives are borrowed from Semitic *bśm*, "balsam-oil", and -λσ- transcribing *ś* clearly shows the lateral character of this phoneme. It might be a Phoenician loanword, but this is by no means certain: it can be directly borrowed from another Semitic language. The Neo-Assyrian transcription *Ka-[ma-]as-ḫal-ta-a* of the Moabite royal name **Kamōš-'aśā*, "Kamosh has made", indicates that *ś* was preserved in Moabite in the 7th century B.C. and that it was a lateral phoneme.

16.4. In Aramaic, the phonemic distinction of *š* and *ś* is demonstrated by Neo-Assyrian, Neo-Babylonian, Late Babylonian, and Elamite transcriptions. While *š* is regularly rendered by "s" in Neo-Assyrian and by "š" in Babylonian, the various attempts to indicate the strange sound *ś* reveal its different phonemic status: e.g. *śagīb*, "victorious", is transcribed *sa-gi-bi* or *ta₅-gi-bi*; *śhr*, "moon(-god)", appears as *śe-er*, *te-er*, *il-te-(eḫ-)ri*, etc., and *śmš*, "sun(-god)", is spelt *šam-si*, *ta₅-meš*, *il-ta₅-meš*, *il-ta-meš*, *il-te-meš*, *sa-mi-iš*, *ti-mi-iš*, etc., and in Egypto-Aramaic once also *smš*. The name "Chaldaean", *kśdy* in Aramaic and *ks²dy* in Sabaic, is written *Kal-da/dà-a-a* in Assyro-Babylonian, where the spelling clearly shows the lateral character of *ś*. The phonemic distinction between *ś* and *š* results likewise from the later shift *ś > s* in Aramaic, while *š* remains unchanged, as e.g. in *'əsar < 'śr*, "ten", and *ḥammeš < ḥmś*, "five", in standard Syriac. However, the Old Syriac inscriptions from the 1st-3rd centuries A.D. still preserve the spelling with "š"; e.g. *trt'šr'*, "twelve"; *śryn*, "twenty".

16.5. In Hebrew and in Arabic, the differentiation of *š* and *ś* is expressed by diacritical signs. The Masoretes indicate the graphic distinction by placing a point either above the right side of the symbol (for *š*) or its left (for *ś*). Arab philologists distinguished *šīn* (< *ś*) from *sīn* (< *š*) by placing three points above the right side of the letter (ﺵ) serving to express *šīn* (< *ś*), which in Sibawayh's time had a totally different articulation from the modern one, perhaps close to [ç] (§14.4). Spoken Arabic leaves no doubt about the original character of this differentiation. Instead, the graphic distinction introduced in Hebrew is absent from the Samaritan tradition and may be based on a comparison with Aramaic, since etymological *š* is written "š" in Jewish Aramaic texts, while etymological *ś* is rendered there by "s". In fact, the realization of *ś* is equal to that of *s* in all Jewish communities. However, the distinction made by the Masoretes is etymologically correct and it is confirmed by the incompatibility of contiguous *ś* and *l* in Hebrew roots. This also demonstrates the lateral character of original *ś*, since Semitic languages generally avoid homorganic radicals in contiguous position.

16.6. Ethiopic, which had the same development as Arabic in this case, borrowed the South Arabian letter *s²* (𐩦) to indicate *ś*, but this sound merged with the one expressed by s^1 (ᚺ) to become [s]. The existence of $\acute{s}$ at an early stage of Ge'ez is therefore attested in orthography, though the sound itself has disappeared. However, $\acute{s}$ and s are not confused in the early inscriptions.

16.7. The emphatic lateral $\acute{ṣ}$ ($ḍ$) has a graphic sign of its own in Epigraphic South and North Arabian, namely "ḍ", that was borrowed by Ethiopic to express the corresponding sound (ፀ). In Modern South Arabian languages, this phoneme is articulated like a voiced $\acute{s}$ (§ 16.2), i.e. like $\acute{z}$, without the glottalization which characterizes Modern South Arabian and Ethiopian emphatics. However, the original emphatic character of the sound is supported by its articulation as $ḷ$ in the Datīna dialect of South Yemen (e.g. *abyaḷ* for *'abyaḍ*, "white"; *ḷā'* for *ḍā'*, "he was lost") and by its merging with $ṣ$ in Ethiopic, soon after the early Aksum inscriptions, as well as in East and North Semitic languages, in Phoenician, and in Hebrew. The dialectal treatment of $\acute{ṣ}$ in a single text from Ugarit (KTU 1.12), where $\acute{ṣ}$ is expressed by $ṯ$ in *yṯḥq*, "he laughs", *ṯ'i*, "go out!", and *ymṯ'a*, "he finds", also supports its original emphatic character and indicates that $\acute{ṣ}$ had existed in North Semitic as an independent phoneme. Early Aramaic practice of indicating $\acute{ṣ}$ by "q" and the later spelling " ' ", e.g. in *'rq > 'r'*, "earth", confirm the independent phonemic status of $\acute{ṣ}$ and its emphatic character, expressed by the clear velarization of the sound symbolized by " ' " (§10.9). In Arabic $\acute{ṣ}$ is pronounced either as a voiced emphatic dental plosive [ḍ] or as a voiced emphatic interdental [ḏ̣], conventionally indicated by "ẓ". It loses sometimes its emphasis and is then reduced to [ḏ], as e.g. in *tōḏröbni*, "you smite me", in the Ḥawrān dialect.

16.8. The original lateral character of $\acute{ṣ}$ results not only from its pronunciation in Modern South Arabian and by its articulation as $ḷ$ in Datīna (§16.7), but also from ancient transcriptions. The name of the Arab god Ruḍā is transcribed in cuneiform script, in the 7th century B.C., by *Ru-ul-da-a-a-ú* and the description of *ḍād* given by the Arab grammarians leaves little doubt that $ḍ$ represented a lateral phoneme in early Islamic times. Andalusian Arabic *'al-qāḍi* was still borrowed in Spanish as *alcalde*, "mayor", *'al-bayāḍ*, "white", as *albayalde*, "ceruse", *'arrabḍa*, "suburb", as *arrabal(de)*. The loss of the lateral glide in Arabic is therefore a quite recent phenomenon, at least in some dialects.

16.9. The alternations between *ḍād* < $\acute{ṣ}$ and *shīn* < $\acute{s}$ in Arabic indicate that the two phonemes constitute a pair: *bašaka* and *baḍaka*, "to cut off", *ḥaša'a* and *ḥaḍa'a*, "to kindle the fire", *ḥaša'a* and *ḥaḍa'a*, "to be submissive", *ḥašama* and *ḥaḍama*, "to break", *šaḥaza* and *ḍaḥaza*, "to blind", *šafaza* and *ḍafaza*, "to kick", *'illawš* and *'illawḍ*, "jackal", *mašaġa* and *maḍaġa*, "to knot", *nāša* and *nāḍa*, "to carry", *waššaḥa* and *waḍḍaḥa*, "to explain". The corresponding alternation between *šīn* and *ṣāde* occurs in Hebrew *śāḥaq* and *ṣāḥaq*, "to laugh". These alternations reveal an emphatic and a non-emphatic pronunciation of the same roots, with the high probability that the latter reflects the loss of the emphasis, while the lateral glide of the phoneme was preserved (*ṣ́ > ś*).

16.10. The originally emphatic consonant *ṣ́* corresponds to a single non-emphatic one. It was therefore of no phonemic significance whether the emphatic sound was produced with or without voice.

16.11. The following table displays the development of the Proto-Semitic laterals in the Semitic languages taken into account.

*Pr.-Sem.	Ass.-Bab.	Ugar.	Hebr.	Aram.	Cl.Ar.	M.Ar.	E.S.A.	M.S.A.	Ge'ez
ś	š	š	ś	ś > s	ç	š	ś(s^2)	ś	ś > s
ṣ́	ṣ	s/ṭ	ṣ	q > '	ṣ́	ḍ/ḏ	ṣ́	ẓ	ṣ́ > ṣ

8. Liquids and Nasal

17.1. Common Semitic or Proto-Semitic has two dental liquids *l* and *r*, and one dental nasal *n*. The original phonemic distinction of these consonants in Afro-Asiatic is in doubt, considering the lack of a distinction *l* / *r* in ancient Egyptian and the frequent alternations (§17.3-6), exemplified by the noun "dog", *kar-* in some Chadic languages, *kan-* in West Cushitic (Omotic), and *kal-b-* in Semitic, with the gender determinant *-b-* of dangerous animals (§30.10). Although *l* / *n* / *r* still appear as allophones of the same basic phoneme in Palaeosyrian (Ebla) and in Gurage, their distinctive phonemic status is nevertheless established in common Semitic as known in historical times. The dental basis of articulation of these phonemes is supported by their traditional and modern realizations. However, *n* tends in some modern Arabic dialects toward a post-palatal *ñ* before most consonants, especially before velars and palatals, while *r* was realized as a uvular non-rolled [R] in one of the traditional European pronunciations of Hebrew and sporadically in Gafat. This uvular articulation would explain the occasional non-gemination of *r* in Gafat and its systematic non-gemination in the Masoretic vocalization of the Hebrew Bible. However, the Septuagint still shows gemination of Hebrew *r*, as Γόμορρα (Masoretic *'Ămorā*), Σάρρα (Masoretic *Śārā*), Χαρράν (Masoretic *Ḥārān*). The non-gemination of *r* might also result from the articulatory shift *r* > *ġ*, attested in some mediaeval Arabic dialects of Iraq and nowadays also in North Africa, e.g. *ġəǧəl* < *riǧl*, "foot"; *ḥəġmi* < *ḥarīm*, "wife". This phonetic phenomenon could be related to the appearance of the non-etymological cluster *r'* in the Aramaic *'r'm* of the Palestinian Targum for *'ărīm*, "he raised" (Gen. 29,11). Certain reservations have also been expressed concerning the dental nature of *r* and *n* because they are frequently contiguous to other dentals (e.g. *fard*, "single"; *ǧund*, "army"), while Semitic languages generally avoid homorganic radicals in contiguous position. However, the weakness of these phonemes may explain this apparent exception to the common trend. The variations in ancient and modern articulations of *r* have no phonemic value, but the emphatic pronounciation of *ḷ* and *ṛ* in certain Arabian words deserves a mention; e.g. (*'A*)*ḷḷāh*, "God"; *ṛāḥ*, "he went". As for the liquid *l*, it may be palatalized into *y* (§15.6).

17.2. The weakness of the liquids is amply exemplified at Ebla: e.g. *La-ru$_{12}$-ga-tù* / *A-ru$_{12}$-ga-tù*, a city name attested as *lrgt* at Ugarit; *'à-a-gú-um* < *hlk*, "to go"; *ša-mi-nu* / *šar-mi-na* (dual), "cypress". The common use of the cuneiform sign NI to indicate Semitic *ni*, *lí*, and *ì*, even in the same word *ì-lí*, "my god", reflects the weakness and the interchangeability of *l/n* (§17.3). The weakness of the liquids is confirmed by ancient Egyptian transcriptions of Semitic *l* and *r* with an *ꜣ* in the Middle Kingdom period, e.g. *i-ś-ḳ-ꜣ-n*, "Ashkelon", *i-ꜣ-ḥ-b-w-m*, "Rehob". Besides, several roots common to Semitic and Egyptian have *l/r* in Semitic but *ꜣ/i* in Egyptian; e.g. Semitic *karm-*, Egyptian *kꜣm*, "vineyard"; Semitic *qarb-*, Egyptian *ḳꜣb*, "intestines"; Semitic *libb-*, Egyptian *ib*, "heart"; Semitic *lb'-*, Egyptian *ꜣby*, "lioness". A similar situation results from a comparison of Semitic and Cushitic roots, e.g. Semitic *laḥām-* and Rendille *aḥam*, "to eat". In the first millennium B.C., the weakness of the liquids is reflected by the Aramaic verbs *hlk*, "to go", and *slq*, "to go up", with forms like *yəhāk*, "he shall go", and *hussaq*, "he was brought up" (§43.10). The loss of final *r* is frequent in Sabaic personal names, e.g. *whb'tt* < *whb'ttr*; final *l* and *r* are dropped occasionally in Jewish Babylonian Aramaic, e.g. *'m'* for *'mr*, "to say", while Gurage testifies to the occasional loss of medial *l* or *r*, e.g. in *weǧ* < *wld*, "boy", and *qema* / *qārma*, "gleanings". The same phenomenon is attested in Hebrew with *qīqālōn < *qalqalān*, "disgrace" (cf. Syriac *qulqālā*, "disgrace"), with *ḥăṣōṣərā < *ḥaṣarṣarat*, "clarion", in Nabataean with the proper name *'bd(')lg'* transcribed once Αβδαγης, and in Aramaic, e.g., *qīqiltā < qilqiltā*, "rubbish dump". The disappearance of the liquid is compensated by the lengthening of the preceding vowel. The frequent assimilation of *l* and *n* to the following consonant — and even to the preceding one (§27.3) — confirms the weakness of the liquids. One should also mention the change of intervocalic *n* into ' in Middle Assyrian and Neo-Assyrian, e.g. *da'ānu < danānu*, "might", *rēmē'ū < rēmēnū*, "merciful". However, the aforementioned losses of liquids and of *n* should be distinguished from morphological phenomena like the surrender of nunation and mimation in Arabic and in Assyro-Babylonian.

17.3. The interchange between *l* and *n* may be observed in various languages. In some Gurage dialects the change *l > n* occurs even in initial position, e.g. *laba > naba*, "waist". As a matter of fact, the original liquid *l* almost disappeared in West Gurage, but its substitution by *n* or *r* is accomplished under well-defined conditions. The change *l > n* occurs in initial position and in medial position when *l* was originally geminated; otherwise, *l* becomes *r*.

17.4. The shift *l > n* in initial position occurs sporadically in other Semitic languages as well. Thus, Hebrew *layiš,* Aramaic *laytā*, Arabic *layṯ*, and Greek λῖς are paralleled by Assyro-Babylonian *nēšu*, "lion". In the field of grammatical morphemes, the prefix *n-* instead of *l-* in the Eastern Aramaic prefix-conjugation (§40.23) and in the jussive of some South Ethiopian languages (§40.30) is to be considered as the result of an *l > n* shift, which should be distinguished from the morphological change consisting in the use of the jussive prefix *l- > n-* instead of the imperfective *y-*. The latter phenomenon can be dated in Eastern Aramaic to the 2nd-3rd century A.D., while the phonetic change *l > n* is already announced by the possible intermediary sound in *al-na-šuḫ*, "Nusku", in the 7th century B.C., and it is realized in *nhwy'*, "may he be", in the 4th century B.C., unless a different explanation is offered for this form. Sporadic occurrences of the interchange between initial *l* and *n* occur in Assyro-Babylonian (*lamṣatu / namṣatu*, "fly"), in a dialect of central Syria (*Nuḫašše / N-g-ś > Luḫuti / L'š*), and in Cypro-Phoenician (Λάρναξ *> Nrnk*, cf. Λευκωσία *> Nicosia*). They are attested also in the Daṯīna dialect of South Yemen (e.g. *laḥna mā laqbil* for *naḥna mā* *naqbil*, "we don't accept"), in Moroccan Arabic, and in Tigrinya (e.g. *nə* for *la*, "for"). The variation of *n* and *l* occurs in medial and final positions as well, e.g. *ban* for *bal*, "but", in North Arabian; *badengāl* for *badingān*, "aubergine", *fengāl* for *fingān*, "cup", *glem* or *qlam* for *ganam*, "sheep", *l-ḥāṣōn* for *'al-ḥāṣilu*, "briefly", etc., in Modern Arabic dialects; *'lk*, *bl*, *mtl* for *'nk*, "I", *bn*, "son", *mtn*, "gift", in Egypto-Phoenician; *ṣnm* for *ṣlm*, "statue", and *-mnkw* for *-mlkw*, "king", in Nabataean Aramaic; *kulkā* for *kunkā*, "seal!", in Old Assyrian. The existence of the articles *hn-* and *'l-* in North Arabian also suggests a change *hn-* > *'l-*, since the shift *h* > *'* is widely attested. The variation *l/n* is a surviving feature of Afro-Asiatic, as exemplified by a comparison of Semitic *lšn*, "tongue", with the etymologically and semantically corresponding Egyptian term *ns*, attested in Demotic as *ls* and in Coptic as ⲗⲁⲥ.

17.5. Interchanges between *l* and *r*, that certain languages like ancient Egyptian and Mycenaean Greek (Linear B) do not distinguish graphically, occur frequently in Libyco-Berber, where e.g. Tarifit *r* corresponds regularly to Tachelhit *l* (e.g. *awal* > *awar*, "word"), and such interchanges are also fairly common in Semitic. The *l/r* alternation is particularly frequent at Ebla, e.g. *Ìr-'à-aq-Da-mu / Íl-'à-aq-Da-mu*, i.e. /*Yilḥaq-Da'mu*/, "Damu caught up"; *'à-da-ru₁₂-um / 'à-da-lu-um*, i.e. *ḥdr*, "the interior"; the divine name *Iš-ḥa-ra / Iš-ḥa-la*. In Assyro-Babylonian the "stork" is called *laqlaqqu* or *raqraqqu*. Arabic *sāraḥa*, "to dispatch", corresponds to Hebrew and Aramaic *šlḥ*, "to send", and Sabaic *rzm*, "land-tax", is etymologically related to Arabic *lzm*. Liḥyānite *Ḥimrāg* is a phonetic variant of *Ḥimlāg*. Hebrew *gādal*, "to become big", corresponds to Gafat *gäddärä*, Harari *gädära* or *gōdära*, and East Gurage *gädärä*, *godärä*, or *gudärä*, "to be" or "to become big, great, tall". In West Gurage dialects, as mentioned above (§17.3), the change *l* > *r* occurs in non-initial position when *l* was originally not geminated, e.g. *gaméra* from *gəmäl*, "camel".

17.6. Interchanges between *n* and *r* are also attested, as Aramaic *br* against *bn*, "son". In West Gurage dialects, the non-geminated *n* becomes *r* in non-initial position, e.g. *ammärä* for Amharic *ammänä*, "to believe". The same phenomenon is sporadically attested in Neo-Assyrian, e.g. *qarṭuppi* < *qanṭuppi*, "stylus". Instead, in West Gurage *r* becomes *n* in initial position and in non-initial position when originally geminated, e.g. *qän(n)* for *qärr* < *qärn*, "horn". Similar changes occur in Chadic languages, e.g. Logone *ngun*, "belly", plural *ngwaren*.

17.7.   In the Central Mediterranean island of Gozo a peculiar shift *l* > *d* is attested in the Phoenician divine name *ṣdmb'l* < *ṣlmb'l*, "statue of Baal", and in the name of the island itself Γαυδος < *gwl*, nowadays Għawdex. Variant forms of this phenomenon, explainable by the close articulation points of *l* and *d*, occur in a number of languages. Thus the alternation *d* / *l* is encountered in Luwian and in Lycian (e.g. the Lycian PN *Dapara* transcribed Λαπαράς in Greek), probably in Proto-Berber (cf. Numidic *mnkd*, Tuareg *a-mnukal*, "king"). The change *l* > *d* is reported in the Bantu languages (e.g. Proto-Bantu *-tund-* < *-tunl-*, "teach") and a similar phenomenon, but not identical, can be observed in the Amharic variants *sədsa* (dissimilated from *səssa* < *səlsa*) and *səlsa* of the numeral "sixty", and in the change affecting the liquid *r* in the Amharic, Argobba, and Gafat word *qänd(ä)* < **qänr* < *qarn* (Ge'ez), "horn" (*nd* < *rn*), or in the Oromo word *sinra*, "wheat" (root *ś'r*), attested as *sənde* in Highland East Cushitic and in Amharic, and as *səndä* in Gafat.

17.8.   The insertion of a non-etymological *l*, *n* or *r* is generally the result of the dissimilation of a geminated consonant (§23.6-9), e.g. in Aramaic *hansāqā* < *hassāqā* < **haslāqā*, "to bring up". However, this explanation is hardly correct in cases like *han'ālā*, attested next to *he'ālā*, "to bring in", from the Aramaic root *'ll*. The insertion of *n* should be rather explained in this case as the marking of the nasalization of the following consonant, frequent in South Ethiopian languages, also with the original pharyngals *ḥ* and *'*, e.g. Amharic *ənqəfat* for Ge'ez *'əqfät*, "obstacle", with the loss of the original pharyngal. A nasal twang is quite audible with some Palestinian Arabs when they pronounce *'ain*, and Oriental Jews use a strongly nasalized *'ain* in Hebrew. An insertion of *r* before *'ain* occurs in Hebrew *śar'appīm* (Ps. 94,19; 139,23) for *śə'ippīm*, "anxieties", related to Arabic *šaġaf*, "passion, ardent zeal", and in *sar'appā* (Ez. 31,5) for **sə'appā*, related to Arabic *sa'af*, "palm leaves". An insertion of *r* before another consonant is encountered in Mishnaic Hebrew *ḥarṭom*, "nose", related to Arabic *ḥaṭm(un)* and attested next to the usual *ḥōṭām*.

17.9.   Plus-vocalic features of *l* and *r* are apparent also in Semitic. In classical Semitic languages, a sequence of abutting consonants generally may not belong to one syllable so as to form a "consonant cluster" (§24.8). Therefore, when a sequence of two consonants should appear in the beginning or at the end of a word, e.g. as the result of prefixing a morpheme or dropping the case endings, there is a wide tendency to use prosthetic or anaptyctic vowels. However, this rule does not apply to colloquial forms of Arabic, to Eastern Neo-Aramaic, to Amharic and other modern Ethiopian forms of speech, and even to some ancient Semitic languages, especially in the case of plus-vocalic sonorants or liquids (*l*, *r*) that may be followed by another consonant at the end of a word (e.g. *kalb*, "dog" in Arabic; *qart*, "city" in Phoenician), or be preceded by another consonant in the beginning of a word; e.g. *slābā*, "theft" in Eastern Neo-Aramaic; *ġlem*, "sheep" in colloquial Arabic; *brät*, "iron, rifle" in Chaha, a Gurage dialect. The only initial clusters which do occur in Amharic are those involving *l* and *r* as second member (*bl-*, *br-*, *gl-*, *gr-*, *kr-*, *qr-*, *tr-*); e.g. *graň*, "left-handed"; *krämt*, "rainy season". More possibilities occur in final position (*-fs*, *-nz*, *-st*, etc.); e.g. *näfs*, "soul"; *wänz*, "river"; *mängəst*, "government".

9. VELAR PLOSIVES

18.1.   Common Semitic or Proto-Semitic has two velar plosives, voiceless *k* and voiced *g*. It also possesses an emphatic velar plosive *q*, generally articulated as the emphatic consonant corresponding to *k* and therefore also transliterated *ḳ*.

18.2.   Sibawayh defines Arabic *q* as *maġhūra*, which does not mean "voiced" (*g*), as generally assumed, but "fortis". Nevertheless, certain modern Arabic dialects either support a voiced pronunciation or reflect the shift *q* > *g* (cf. §18.8). However, there was also a way of pronouncing *q* in Arabic that led to its occasional representation by "k" and *q* can alternate with *k* in modern Ethiopian languages. In reality, there was of no phonemic significance whether *q* was produced with or without voice, since the one emphatic velar plosive corresponded to a pair of non-emphatic ones: voiceless *k* and voiced *g*.

18.3.   The syllabic cuneiform writing system is, as usual, inadequate to indicate the distinction between *k*, *g*, *q*. Throughout the whole course of cuneiform writing no attempt was ever made to indicate the exact character of a final plosive: AG serves as *ag*, *ak* or *aq*, IG is used for *ig*, *ik* or *iq*, etc. For the initial plosives, a certain distinction is introduced from the Old Babylonian period on, e.g. between GA, KA, and even QA in certain regions like Mari and Eshnunna, but the emphatic velar plosive *q*

is generally indicated by signs with the "voiced" or "voiceless" consonant, e.g. KI serves for *ki* and *qí*, KU for *ku* and *qú*, but GAB is used for
gab and *qab*, and GIM for *gim*, *kim* and *qim*. The occasional orthographic
interchanges GA/QA, GI/KI, GU/KU may reflect a dialectal voiced articulation of *q* in some areas, but cannot prove the existence of two phonemes
/ḳ/ and /g̱/ in Assyro-Babylonian.

18.4.   In Neo-Assyrian [g] and [k] seem to be positional variants of the
same phoneme. The voiced pronunciation is attested in intervocalic position by Aramaic and Hebrew transcriptions, e.g. *mngsr* for *Mannu-ki-
šarri*, as against *tkltšr* for *Tuklat-Ištar* (> *Iśśar*; cf. §15.2).

18.5.   The spirantization or fricativization of non-geminated and non-
emphatic velar plosives is attested in various Semitic languages. The
occasional cuneiform spelling with signs of the series "ḫ" instead of
signs with *g/k* reflects this change, e.g. *ḫanāšu* instead of *kanāšu*, "to
bow". Such cases should carefully be distinguished, e.g., from the Late
Babylonian spelling *tamāku* of *tamāḫu*, "to seize", which simply signifies that the Aramaic verb *tmk* is used in this occurrence. Hebrew and
Aramaic spirantization of *k/g* follows the same rules as the spirantization
of labials (§11.10) and explains, e.g., why the Babylonian loanword
maḫāru, "to equalize in value", is borrowed in Syriac under the form
mkr, and why Babylonian *kimaḫḫu* [*kiwaḫ*], "grave", is attested in Aramaic as *kwk* (§63.9). In Neo-Aramaic, the spirantized velar plosives
attained phonemic status and their "hard" or "soft" pronunciation does
not depend on their position. In Modern South Arabian and Ethiopian
languages, the spirantization of velars is widely attested, but it is not
phonetically conditioned in the same manner in the various forms of
speech. The Ḥaḍramitic preposition *h-* resulting from the change *k > ḳ >
h* attained a phonemic status already in Antiquity, and a similar phonetic
situation may occur under certain circumstances in modern South
Semitic languages, especially in Amharic; e.g. *hulätt*, "two", vs. Tigre
kəl'ot. In Tigrinya, the non-geminated *k* is frequently spirantized into *ḳ*
or *ḫ* in post-vocalic position, and may be written then as *ḫ*; e.g. *käbiru*,
"he is rich", but *yəḫäbbir*, "he will be rich".

18.6.   The affricative pronunciation of *k > č* or *k > š*, of *q > č*, and of *g
> ǧ*, *g > č*, or *g > ž* is attested in Arabic, in Ethiopian languages, in Mod-
ern South Arabian, and in Neo-Aramaic (§15.5). In Classical Arabic, the
pronunciation *ǧ* is considered as the correct one (e.g. *daǧāǧa*, "hen"),

while the analogous tendency $k > č$ is viewed as a dialectal deviation (e.g. $dič < dīk$, "cock"). Palatalization of q into $č$ or $ǧ$ before or after front vowels (i, e) is common in Central Arabian bedouin colloquials (e.g. $sīǧān < sīqān$, "legs"), while North Arabian inscriptions from the Tabūk (Saudi Arabic) and Maʿān (Jordan) area seem to testify to an ancient conditioned $g > č$ change, indicated e.g. by the spelling *wtm* instead of *wgm*, "he was mourning", in a verb that was probably belonging to the *faʿil* class (*$wagim > $*$wačim$). A non-conditioned $q > č$ change occurred in the ʾAzd dialect of northern Yemen. In Cairene Arabic, both colloquial and literary, the original pronunciation [g] is either preserved or revived. The same is witnessed on the southern coast of Arabia and in early Andalusian Arabic, while [g] as well as [ž] are attested in Moroccan Arabic. This fricative variant [ž] is encountered also in Algeria and in southern Iraq. Instead, the devoicing $ǧ > č$ occurs in the dialect of Palmyra. Mainly in the neighbourhood of a palatal vowel, the direct change $k > š$ is attested in some Arabic colloquials (e.g. the feminine suffixed pronoun *-ki* becomes *-š*), in the Neo-Aramaic dialect of Maʿlūla (e.g. $k̲īfiš < k̲ēpiki$, "your stone"), in Modern South Arabian (e.g. *šubdet* < *kbdt*, "liver"), and in Ethiopian languages (e.g. *bäššä* < *bky*, "to cry", in Soddo, Northeast Gurage). In Modern South Arabian, the passage $g > ž$ is attested in Soqoṭri and Śḥeri (e.g. *žirit*, "slave-girl"), but not in Mehri ($gərēt$, "slave-girl"). The palatalization occurs extensively in both Soqoṭri and Śḥeri, but is rather unstable except for $ǧ$, where the influence of Arabic is a factor of importance. The sounds $ǧ$ and $ž$ interchange in South Ethiopic under Cushitic influence (e.g. Amharic *žəb* and *ǧəb*, "hyena").

18.7. A series of labiovelars g^w, k^w, q^w, and occasionally $ẖ^w$, occurs in all the Ethiopian languages, except in Tigre, Harari, and some Gurage dialects (§11.11). These sounds have a phonemic status and exist alongside the ordinary velars (e.g. $näk^w$, "I am"). The lack of traces of the Geʿez labiovelars in an unvocalized text is probably due to the fact that the new symbols for the labiovelars, developed from the signs for the velars, were invented at the same time as the vocalic signs. In Semitic the labiovelars phonetically conditioned occur in Arabic colloquials of Tripolitania and Morocco, and also in Mehri. Therefore, their development in Ethiopian languages cannot be ascribed solely to Cushitic influence, although their phonemic status is due to the impact of the Cushitic substratum.

18.8. Arabic *q* is almost invariably transliterated by Geʿez "g", but the lack of glottalization differentiated Arabic *q* from Ethiopic *q* and may explain this transliteration. However, the change *q* > *g* is actually attested in Ḥaḍramawt and in Ḍofār, thus in a region that had contacts with Ethiopia. It occurs also in the Mesopotamian *gǝlǝt*-dialects (*gǝlǝt* for *qultu*, "I said"), in some of the Arabic dialects spoken in the Chad-Sudan area, and in East Arabian where it may result from a partial assimilation by voicing, as in *bgara*, "cow", for *baqara*, after a change of the syllabic structure, or in *ibg*, "stay!", from *bqy*. Besides, there are many cases of written *g* for *q* in Mandaic (e.g. *g'yṭ'*, "summer", for Syriac *qayṭā*), and Hebrew *q* is realized in some Jewish Yemenite communities like /g/ or /ġ/. On the other hand, *q* becomes ' in some Arabic dialects, in the realization of Hebrew *q* among certain Jewish communities of Algeria and Morocco, and in Tigre at the end of a syllable (e.g. *lǝ'tal* for *lǝqtal*). In some Gurage dialects, the velars *k* and *q* can become *zero* in medial position (e.g. *ṭit* < *ṭǝqit*, "few"). The change *q* > ' happened probably as the result of an economy of effort (§ 10.10). This development seems to be different from an earlier change that occurred in Aramaic at least in two distinct phases, the first one consisting in the shift *q* > ʿ which is supported by the spectrographic analysis showing the *q* between *ḍ* and ʿ. The actual evidence is provided by the change *q* > ʿ in the Aramaic spelling of *ṣ̌* (*ḍ*) (§ 16.7). The second stage ʿ > ' is attested in Late Aramaic and in Neo-Aramaic (§ 19.14); it represents the widespread reduction of the voiced pharyngal ʿ to a glottal stop (§ 19.9-19).

18.9. The change *ǧ* > *y* is attested in some Arabic colloquials, especially in East Arabian; e.g. *ḥayar* < *ḥaǧar*, "stone". In some cases, the syllabic structure has been influenced by this change, as in *rīl* that in Kuwait means as well "man" (*rīl* < *ruyil* < *raǧul*) as "foot" (*rīl* < *riyl* < *riǧl*). In Baḥrain, e.g., *wēh* is monophthongized from *wayh* < *waǧh*, "face". It is noteworthy that a similar change is attested in Algerian Arabic by the word *msīd*, "mosque", and by the Maltese place name *Msida*, both from *mǝsyid* < *masǧid*, "mosque". Historical implications are obviously involved.

10. Laryngals, Pharyngal and Velar Fricatives

19.1. It is convenient to examine Semitic laryngals, pharyngal fricatives and velar fricatives in the same paragraph, because of their historic developments and of the way they are indicated in the various writing systems. These phonemes are often classified under the heading of "gutturals", a name which has been accepted in several circles even though it does not accurately describe all of them from the point of view of their articulation. Nevertheless, they share some common features and, among them, a tendency to be phonetically weakened and even reduced to *zero*, as in Amharic (§19.20). This phenomenon is paralleled in other Afro-Asiatic languages and in Indo-European, as shown by Hittite that has supplied the clinching evidence for the existence of laryngals and pharyngals in Proto-Indo-European (e.g. *paḫḫur*, "fire", Greek πῦρ).

19.2. Common Semitic or Proto-Semitic has two laryngals: one glottal plosive ' ([ʔ]) and one voiceless laryngal fricative *h*; they oppose each other as *spiritus lenis* and *spiritus asper* in Greek. There are two fricative pharyngals: voiceless *ḥ* ([ħ]) and voiced ' ([ʕ]), as well two velar fricatives, voiceless *ḫ* ([x]) and voiced *ġ* ([γ]). Of the two pharyngals, *ḥ* is essentially a pharyngalized laryngal, a fortis, while the air consumed by the voicing of ' leaves it as a lenis.

19.3. The syllabic cuneiform writing system disposes only of signs indicating ' and *ḫ*, while the twenty-two letters of the Phoenician alphabet are insufficient to express all the phonemes of the languages which have adopted it. Only the cuneiform alphabetic script of Ugarit and the South Arabian alphabet have adequate symbols for the laryngals, the pharyngals, and the velar fricatives, while Arabic uses diacritics in order to distinguish the various phonemes. The Assyriological practice of indicating etymological ' by '[1], *h* by '[2], *ḥ* by '[3], ' by '[4] and *ġ* by '[5] is followed in the present section. However, an articulated *ġ* is generally transliterated in syllabic cuneiform writing by *ḫ* and not by '.

19.4. Palaeosyrian and Old Akkadian writing allows distinguishing the laryngals, the pharyngals, and the velar fricatives.

19.5. The two laryngals ' ('[1]) and *h* ('[2]), as well as the two pharyngals *ḥ* ('[3]) and ' ('[4]), are indicated in two ways: 1° by *zero*, as in *a-bi* /'*abī*/, "my father", or *a-la-ga-am* /*halākam*/, "to go" (accusative), *il-ga*

/yilqaḥ/, "he took", a-li-dam /'alītam/, "upper" (feminine accusative), a-zum /'azzum/, "fierce"; 2° by special signs, such as MÁ, as in iš-má /yišma'/, "he heard", and É ('à), as in gu-la-'à-tum next to gu-la-a-tum and gu-la-tum (meaning unknown), or 'À-da /Hadda/ for the divine name, 'À-da-ša /Ḥadaṭa/, "Youthful" or the like, Ib-'à-lu /Yib'alu/ or /Yip'alu/, "(The god) made". The conventional transliteration of É as 'à does not indicate that the word or the name contains a true aleph, but expresses any of the '1 to '4 consonants. Besides, the pharyngals ḥ and ' influence, under certain conditions, the change of contiguous a to e, as in En-na-ì-lí /Ḥenna-'Ilī/, "My god is favourable", or Eb-du-ᵈRa-sa-ap /'Ebdu-Rašap/, "Servant of Resheph". This change does not affect the laryngals ' and h, which are therefore to be distinguished from the pharyngals ḥ and ' in Palaeosyrian as well as in Old Akkadian. Besides, ' is exceptionally indicated by 'à, while this spelling occurs frequently with h, thus differentiating the laryngal fricative h from the glottal plosive '. There is also a convincing way of distinguishing ' from ḥ in Palaeosyrian and Old Akkadian writing system. In fact, the phoneme ḥ ('3) when followed by the vowel a is expressed quite often by the sign É = 'à, e.g. da-la-'à-mu /talaḥḥamu/, "you will taste" (subjunctive). This spelling is at least a leftover from a period in which the phoneme ḥ was independent from '. Occasionally, however, also ' may be indicated by 'à, as in Old Akkadian 'à-zum /'azzum/, "fierce". In any case, there is little doubt that a phonemic distinction must have existed between, e.g., arābum, "to combat" (ḥrb), and arābum, "to enter" ('rb), but it may have disappeared in course of time (§19.11), giving rise to homophones.

   The change ʿa > ʿe occurs regularly at Ebla, but ʿ does not influence, as a rule, the vowel in the Palaeosyrian texts from Mari (but cf. §21.6).

19.6.   The two velar fricatives ḫ and ġ are both indicated in Palaeosyrian and in Old Akkadian by signs with ḫ, e.g. Ḫa-la-Il /Ḫāla-'Il/, "El is a maternal uncle", Ḫa-zi-ir /Ġazzīr/, "Hero". The fact that Old Akkadian maḫāru(m), "to equalize in value", or aḫāzu(m), "to seize", remained maḫāru(m), aḫāzu(m) in Old Babylonian, while Old Akkadian ṣaḫāru(m), "to be small", or ḫarā'u(m), "to empty", became ṣeḫēru(m), ḫerū(m), means that the voiced phoneme ġ in ṣġr and ġrw had definite characteristics which influenced the vowels and separated it from the voiceless ḫ of 'ḫd and mḫr. This a > e change proves conclusively that ḫ and ġ are to be distinguished.

19.7. In Amorite proper names written in syllabic cuneiform script, the laryngals are reduced graphically to *zero*, but ' and *h* are clearly distinguished in Amorite names found in Egyptian execration texts and in later alphabetic texts from Ugarit. The pharyngals are often indicated by signs with *ḫ*, e.g. *Ḫa-an-ni-*DINGIR */Ḥanni-'Il/*, "El is favourable", or *Ḫa-ab-du-ᵈḪa-na-at* */'Abdu-'Anat/*, "Servant of 'Anat", even at the end of a word, e.g. *Ya-ás-ma-aḫ-ᵈDa-gan* */Yašma'-Dagan/*, "Dagan has heard". However, *ḥ* and ' may be reduced graphically to *zero*, e.g. *Am-mu-ra-pí-i* */'Ammu-rāpi'ī/*, "The Ancestor is my healer", and *An-na-*DINGIR */Ḥanna-'Il/*, "El is favourable", contrary to *ḫ* and *ġ* which are always expressed by signs with *ḫ*, e.g. *Ab-di-a-ra-aḫ* */'Abd-Yaraḫ/*, "Servant of Yaraḫ", and *A-bi-ḫi-il* */'Abī-ġēl/*, "My father is snatched away (?)". An actual reduction of ' may occur when ' is contiguous to a labial, like in *i-ba-al* */yib'al/* or in *Da-mu* */Da'mu/* (cf. §45.7-8). This is easily explainable since the narrow orifice of the labial articulation scarcely affords a contrast to the narrowing of the pharynx. Whether this reduced ' was then lengthening the adjacent vowel or was simply absorbed by the labial depends on the interpretation of the second *i* in the name *ibȝfȋ* [*Yibāl-pī*] or [*Yibal-pī*] of a prince of *Mktry* */Magdalay/* in an Egyptian execration text (E 5), which provides a shortened form of the well-known Amorite name *I-ba-al-pi-El*, "The word of El has made". In any case, all the pharyngal and velar fricatives are clearly distinguished in parallel names attested in texts from Ugarit: e.g. *ḥn'il*, *'bd'nt*, *yšm'*, *'bdyrḫ*, *'abġl*. Therefore, there is no reason whatsoever to suppose that the articulation of these phonemes in Amorite was different from the one known from Ugaritic alphabetic texts.

19.8. In Ugaritic, all the laryngals, pharyngal and velar fricatives are indicated by a distinct symbol. Three cuneiform signs are used for the glottal stop ' according to its vocalization *'a*, *'i*, *'u*. These signs were employed also as vowels, not only in Hurrian texts, but even in Semitic when the etymological ' was not pronounced in postvocalic or intervocalic position; e.g. *qr'at*, "she called", corresponds to *qarāt* and not to **qara'at* (§45.8). However, personal names show occasional changes ' > ' (e.g. *'abdḥr* < *'bdḥr*), *ḥ* > *ḫ* (e.g. *'aḥrtp* < *'aḥršp*), *ḫ* > *ḥ* (e.g. *ḥnn* < *ḫnn*), *ḫ* > *ġ* (*'bdyrġ* < *'bdyrḫ*), as well as the reduction of ' and of *h* to *zero* (e.g. *'bdnt* < *'bd'nt*, *ḏmrd* < *ḏmrhd*). These changes already announce the later development of the phonemes under consideration.

19.9. In Assyro-Babylonian the laryngals and the pharyngal fricatives have been reduced to the glottal stop '. Yet the pharyngals *ḥ* and ' are often indicated in Old Assyrian by signs with *ḥ* showing that they were still preserving their phonemic status; e.g. *ḥapārum* /ḥapārum/, "to dig"; *raḥābum* /ra'ābum/, "to be terrified". In later periods, the glottal stop is omissible and could therefore be considered as an allophone of the *zero* phoneme, e.g. *ša-'-a-le* and *ša-a-le*, "ask!". In reality, however, the use of a particular form of the sign AḪ to indicate ' from the Middle Babylonian and Middle Assyrian periods onwards leaves little doubt about the phonemic status of the glottal stop. Besides, the older praxis of indicating /'a/ by "a" may as well lead to the conclusion that e.g. *ša-a-le* stands for /ša'al/ and that *a* is an allograph of ' or '-*a*. Dialectal variations could influence the standard practice of the scribes. In particular, it is generally assumed that gemination of *aleph*, retained in earlier periods, was lost in later dialects. On the synchronic level, Amorite influence can probably be detected in spellings like Old Babylonian *e-ḫi-il-tum* for *e-'-il-tum*, "debt", and Aramaic influence in the Neo-Assyrian form *ḫa-an-ni-e* for the demonstrative *anniu*, "this". The graphic notation of ', irregular and optional in medial position, is usually absent at the beginning of words. However, the conclusion that Assyro-Babylonian words could begin with a vowel, contrary to the classical Semitic rule, is unwarranted: the absence of a symbol does not necessarily coincide with phonetic reality, as shown e.g. by the glottal stop in English *an aim* contrasted with *a name* and by the very Neo-Assyrian variant *ḫanniu* of *anniu*. So does the presence of the symbol not always mean that a glottal stop has to be articulated, as shown e.g. by the Arabic *'alif 'al-waṣl* which is not pronounced in the classical language.

19.10. A partial identification of the etymological consonants which have coalesced in Assyro-Babylonian ' is at times possible, for *ḥ* and ' had influenced the change of contiguous *a* into *e*, e.g. *eṣēdu* / *eṣādu* (*ḥṣd*), "to reap"; *epru* ('*pr*), "dust". However ' and *h* did occasionally influence the same change *a* > *e*, e.g. *rēšu* (*r'š*), "head"; *ewûm* (*hwy*), "to be".

19.11. Assyro-Babylonian *ḥ* corresponds in general to *ḥ* or *ġ*, e.g. *ḥasīsu* (*ḥss*), "wisdom"; *ḥanāmu* (*ġnm*), "to grow rich"; *ṣeḥēru* (*ṣġr*), "to be small". However, it may indicate an etymological *h* in cases in which a change *h* > *ḥ* had occurred in a period in which Proto-Assyro-Babylonian still had an independent phoneme *ḥ*, e.g. *ḥakāmu*, "to understand" (< ḥkm). A general shift ḥ > ḫ occurred in Eastern Syriac and in Neo-Aramaic (§19.14). Instead, the exceptional Neo-Assyrian spelling ḫanāšu for kanāšu, "to bend", is the result of a spirantization of k (§18.5).

19.12. The Canaanite dialects of the second millennium B.C. possessed not only the two laryngals and the two pharyngal fricatives, expressed by distinct letters in the "Phoenician" alphabet, but also the two velar fricatives ḫ and ġ. While ḫ is indicated in Egyptian by ḫ, e.g. r-ḫ-b, "Rehob", ḫ is transliterated by ḫ, e.g. d-b-ḫ = Ṭú-bi-ḫi in an Amarna letter (EA 179). Semitic ʿ appears also in Egyptian as ʿ, e.g. ʿ-k-3, "Akko", while ġ is transliterated either by q (ḳ) or by g, e.g. q-ḏ-t or g-ḏ-t, "Gaza". These distinctions do not appear in the West Semitic alphabetic scripts of the first millennium B.C., when ḫ is represented by "ḥ" and ġ by "ʿ". However, e.g., the name of Gaza (ġzt), in Hebrew ʿazzā, is consistently spelt Γάζα in Greek and ġzt in Minaic inscriptions; the place-name ġufrā, "covert", in Hebrew ʿOprā, is called Γοφερα in Greek, while Akko (ʿky), in Hebrew ʿAkkō, appears in Greek as Ἄκη. Besides, e.g., Bethlehem (byt lḥm), in Hebrew Bēt-Leḥem, is transcribed Βηθλεέμ in Greek, but Jericho (yrḫw), in Hebrew Yərīḫō, appears in Greek as Ἐριχώ or Ἰεριχώ, and the proper name ʾbḫyl, in Hebrew ʾĂbīḫayil, is transcribed Ἀβιχαιλ. These examples indicate that a phonetic distinction between etymological ḥ and ḫ, as well as between ġ and ʿ, persisted in spoken Hebrew until the Hellenistic period. This phonetic distinction had a phonemic status allowing the Greek translators to discern, e.g., the ʿzry (< ġzr) hmlḥmh of I Chron. 12,1, who are "men valiant in battle", from the ʿzry (< ʿḏr) rhb, "the helpers of Rahab", in Job 9,13. In Phoenician, instead, nothing suggests the survival of a distinction between the velar and the pharyngal fricatives. Any real trace of this distinction vanished also in the pronunciation of Hebrew in Roman times, and St Jerome (348-420 A.D.) never represents ʿ by g, the same being true of the Punic passages transliterated in the *Poenulus* of Plautus.

19.13. In Aramaic, the situation is also quite clear despite the use of the "Phoenician" alphabet. The velar fricatives ḫ and ġ are always transcribed by ḫ in cuneiform script, e.g. Ba-ḫi-a-nu /Baġyān/, "the desired one". Instead, under different conditions, the pharyngal fricatives may either be transcribed by ḫ (e.g. Ḫa-ab-di-ia = ʿbdy) or by ʾ (e.g. Ba-ʾ-lu = bʿl), or correspond to an orthographic *zero* (e.g. Ab-di-ia = ʿbdy;

Ba-al = *b'l*). These different spelling conventions mean that the velar fricatives *ḫ* and *ġ* had definite characteristics which separated them from the pharyngal fricatives *ḥ* and ' despite the fact that the alphabetic script used the same letter "ḥ" for both *ḥ* and *ḫ*, and the same letter "'" for both ' and *ġ*. These phonemes probably remained independent until the Hellenistic period, while the increasing cuneiform use of signs with *ḫ* to transliterate the laryngal fricative *h* (e.g. *Na-ga-ḫa*-U.U /*Nagah-Hadad*/, "Hadad has shined") demonstrates the strength and the stability of this phoneme in the period under consideration. However, the *h* of the divine name *hdd* / *hd* is often reduced to ' or assimilated in personal names, perhaps under influence of Assyro-Babylonian *Adad* (e.g. '*dntn* < *hdntn*, "Hadda gave"; *mt'dd* < *mt'hdd*, "Protected by Hadad").

19.14. Middle Aramaic generally retains the independent articulation of the laryngals and of the pharyngal or velar fricatives, but original ' and *h* are liable to disappear in certain situations. The velar fricative ' may change into ', as in the Old Syriac proper names '*bdnḫy* < '*bdnḫy*, "Servant of Nuḥay", and '*bd't*' < '*bd't*', "Servant of 'Attā", while *ġ* changes into ', that is finally pronounced in Neo-Aramaic as an ' which is always retained. The *ḥ* tends to be articulated /h/ in the West, but it is pronounced as /ḫ/ in Eastern Syriac and in Eastern Neo-Aramaic. The consonants in question are frequently interchanged in Samaritan Aramaic, but the etymological spelling is generally retained in the other dialects. In Neo-Aramaic, the final syllable of a word was often written phonetically, but the actual tendency is to write it etymologically, e.g. *-leh* /le/ instead of earlier *-lē*. In loanwords the phonemes ', *ḥ*, ', *ġ* are also found, e.g. Arabic *ḥākim*, "ruler", is written *ḥākīm*, but is articulated [*ḥākim*], while Syriac *ḥakīmā*', "wise man", is pronounced [*ḥakkīma*]; Arabic *ġalaba*, "victory", is written *glabtā*, but articulated [*ġlapta*].

19.15. In Middle Hebrew, the process *ḫ* > *ḥ* and *ġ* > ' is complete, but the Jewish European tradition realizes *ḥ* as [ḫ], while it generally reduces ' to ' or to *zero*. Instead, no velar fricative articulation is attested among the Jewish Arabic-speaking communities, which all retain the pronunciation of the pharyngal fricatives. In the Samaritan pronunciation of Hebrew, the laryngals and the pharyngals are reduced to *zero*. It is possible that the Masoretes have aimed at preventing a similar development by means of their peculiar system of vocalizing the pharyngals in the biblical text (§27.10).

19.16. The laryngal ' was weak in Phoenician, as appears from the number of changes and elisions which it suffered. In Late Phoenician ' and ' seem to be losing their distinct consonantal values, as suggested by *bd'štrt* where ' occurs for '. In Punic, the gradual weakening and the final reduction of ', *h*, *ḥ*, ' to *zero* are seen from spellings like *ldn* for *l'dn*, "for the Lord", or *'d* for *'ḥd*, "one", from the frequent interchange of these letters in the orthography (e.g. *b'l'mn*, *bḥlḥmn*, *b'l'mn* for *b'lḥmn*) and from their use as vowel letters in Late Punic and Neo-Punic (§21.14). Latin transcriptions of proper names, like Hasdrubal (*'zrb'l*), Himilco (*ḥmlkt*), etc., cannot be considered as proofs of an actual articulation of Punic pharyngals, for the initial *h-* just reflects a fashionable Latin pronunciation.

19.17. In Arabic, the laryngals and the pharyngal and velar fricatives are generally retained. The laryngal *h* was pronounced distinctly in ancient North Arabian, since the divine name *Nhy* /Nuhay/ is transcribed ^d*Nu-ḫa-a-a* in Neo-Assyrian and *Nḫy* in Syriac (§19.14). However, there was a shift *h* > ' recognizable later in the prefix of the verbal form *'af'ala* < *haf'ala* or in the particle *'in* < *hin*, "if" .The Arabic sounds *ḫ* and *ġ* are usually represented in Greek by χ and γ. Also ' is transliterated by γ in the Damascus fragment (§7.44), e.g. λεγαλ for *la'all(a)*, "perhaps", but it is unlikely that something can be inferred from this fact. In vernaculars, dialectal changes *ġ* > ', *ḥ* > *h*, ' > *ḥ*, ' > ' are attested, and ' may disappear in certain situations, or be replaced by *w*, *y*, or be compensated by the lengthening of the contiguous vowel, e.g. in early South-Palestinian *tarawwas* far classical *tara''as*, "he became chief", *rayyis* far classical *ra'īs*, "head"; in Maghrebine *wekkǝl* for classical *'akkala*, "he made (him) eat", *mya* for classical *mi'a*, "hundred", *ūden* for classical *'udn*, "ear". These cases should be carefully distinguished from spellings like Safaitic *my*, "water", or *s¹my*, "heaven", where *y* is etymological, while it is replaced by *hamza* in Classical Arabic *mā'* and *samā'*. The etymological *y* is preserved also in the Neo-Arabic broken plural *'amyāh* instead of classical *'amwāh*.

19.18. In Sabaic, one of the three letters ', ', *h* is occasionally omitted in a place where it would normally have occurred. These omissions reflect a phonetic trend towards the reduction of these consonants to *zero* in certain circumstances, e.g. *yz* for normal *yz'*, "he shall do again"; imperfect *ts²r*, "she will be aware", against perfect *s²'rt* immediately before; the divine epithet *ṯwn* instead of the usual *ṯhwn*. This trend

appears also in cases where *'b*, "(my) father", and *'l*, "(my) god", are
reduced to *b* and *l* in compound personal names. In Ḥaḍramitic, the *'d* is
the equivalent of Sabaic *'d*, "to", which points to a change ' > ', widely
attested also in Modern South Arabian and Ethiopian languages.

19.19.   In Modern South Arabian, there is a shift *ġ* > ' and *ḫ* > *ḥ* in
Soqoṭri, as well as a tendency for both pharyngals to become glottals.
This trend is attested for ' also in Śheri and Mehri, although this consonant occurs explicitly as a radical. E.g. *'ḫ*, "brother", is articulated in
Soqoṭri as *əḥi* or *əhi*, while *b'l*, "possessor", is pronounced in Śheri *b'al*,
ba'l or *bāl*, with the vowel lengthened and realized with the pharyngal
constriction required for the pronunciation of '.

19.20.   Ge'ez had all the phonemes in question, except *ġ* that has
become ' in all the Semitic languages of Ethiopia. However, some
speakers of Tigrinya articulate the voiced velar fricative *ġ*, which exists
also in the Agaw dialects of the Qemant-Qwara group. In Tigre and
Tigrinya, etymological *ḥ* and *ḫ* have coalesced into *ḥ*, although the non-
geminated *k* is frequently fricativized into *k̠* or *ḫ* in Tigrinya (§ 18.5). All
the laryngal and pharyngal fricatives tend to become *zero* in South
Ethiopic. The *h* is still fairly common in Amharic, but it may be dropped
as well; e.g. the word for "fifty" may be pronounced *hamsa* or *amsa*.
However, in Harari, in Argobba, and in some Gurage dialects ', *h*, *ḥ* are
preserved in certain conditions, e.g. in Harari *ḥarāsa*, "to plough" (root
ḥrt̠); *hadāra*, "to pass the night" (root *ḫdr*); *sāma'a*, "to hear" (root
šm'). In modern North Ethiopic, on the contrary, ' may disappear altogether in word-final position (e.g. Tigre *mulu'*, "full", pronounced
[*mulu*]), while ' and ' may be in free variation with each other (e.g. Tigre
['*addəha*] or ['*addəḥa*], "noon"). The Amharic pronunciation, which
reduces the phonemes in question to *zero*, has affected the spelling of
Ge'ez texts, so that inconsistencies and interchanges blurred the orthography of many manuscripts.

19.21.   According to the Masoretic tradition, the laryngals and the
pharyngals, as well as *r* which shares several of their characteristics,
cannot be geminated in Hebrew and in Biblical Aramaic. In the
Ethiopian idioms in which gemination is a regular feature, all the consonants can be geminated except ' and *h*. In Neo-Aramaic, instead, the
doubling of the consonants has largely been eliminated and replaced
by the length of the preceding vowel. In Arabic, all consonants may be

subject to gemination (e.g. *fa''ala*, "he caused to make"), and this might have been the original situation also in the other Semitic languages. In any case, the Samaritan tradition geminates Hebrew *r* and this doubling of *r* is confirmed by the Greek transcriptions Χαρραν, "Harran", Σαρρα, "Sara", etc., while Late Babylonian transliterations of Jewish names, like *Mi-na-aḫ-ḫe-mu*, "Menahem", attest the gemination of pharyngals as well.

19.22. In conclusion, the correspondences of the laryngals, pharyngal and velar fricatives in the principal Semitic languages may be presented as follows:

Pr.-Sem.	P.Syr.	O.Akk.	Amor.	Ass.-Bab.	Ugar.	Hebr.	Aram.	Arab.	E.S.A.	Ge'ez
'	'	'	'	'	'	'	'	'	'	'
h	h('²)	h('²)	h	'	h	h	h	h	h	h
ḥ	ḥ('³)	ḥ('³)	ḥ	'	ḥ	ḥ	ḥ	ḥ	ḥ	ḥ
'	'('⁴)	'('⁴)	'	'	'	'	'	'	'	'
ḫ	ḫ	ḫ	ḫ	ḫ	ḫ	ḫ > ḥ	ḫ > ḥ	ḫ	ḫ	ḫ
ġ	ġ(ḫ)	ġ(ḫ)	ġ(ḫ)	ḫ	ġ	ġ > '	ġ > '	ġ	ġ	'

19.23. In the broader area of Afro-Asiatic, an alternation ' / *g*, independent from the Greek transcription of ' < *ġ* by γ (§19.12), can be observed when comparing Semitic and Cushitic roots; e.g., Hebrew *'ereb* / Somali *galab* / Rendille *geléb*, "evening"; Hebrew *'ēṣ* / Sabaic *'ṣ́* / Somali *geid*, "tree, wood"; Aramaic and Syriac *'all* / Oromo and Somali *gal* / Rendille *géèl*, "to enter". A similar *ḥ* / *k* alternation occurs e.g. between Semitic *ḥrṯ* and Libyco-Berber *krz*, "to plough"; Semitic *ḥšb*, "to assume", and Libyco-Berber *kašaf*, "to guess". Further research is needed in these comparative fields.

19.24. An initial ' may alternate with *w* (or *y*; cf. §15.7) without being the result of a change of *wa-* into *'a*, or in the contrary. This alternation rather implies the existence of variant on-glides, as in Arabic *'aḥad* and *wāḥid*, "one", from **ḥad* (§35.3); *'alifa* and *walifa*, "to be familiar"; *'asmā* and *wasmā'*, "the beatiful one", from **šmay/w*; classical *'anātun*, "languid woman", from Arabic *wanā* but Hebrew *'ānā*, "to languish"; in Liḥyānite *'āfaqū* for usual *wāfaqū*, "they agreed"; Old Babylonian *'aḫārum* and *waḫārum*, "to be behind". These analogical formations are particularly widespread in the Arabic verb, and the main methodological danger would consist either in considering colloquial *w*-forms as newly formed from classical verbs with initial glottal stop or in assuming a passage of verbs with first radical *w* from Stem I to Stem IV because they appear with initial ' in Andalusian Arabic or in modern dialects (§41.11). Besides, this ' may simply introduce a prosthetic vowel. Further research in this matter is needed throughout the whole Afro-Asiatic field, because the alternation ' / *w* appears also when comparing e.g. Semitic *waqru* and Egyptian *iḳr*, "excellent".

11. Synopsis of the Consonantal System

20. To summarize the evolution of the Semitic consonantal system in the principal languages of the group, the following table may be of some use:

Pr.-Sem.	P.Syr.	O.Akk.	Amor.	Ass.-Bab.	Ugar.	Hebr.	Aram.	Arab.	E.S.A.	Ge'ez
'	'	'	'	'	'	'	'	'	'	'
ʿ	ʿ('⁴)	ʿ('⁴)	ʿ	ʿ('⁴)	ʿ	ʿ	ʿ	ʿ	ʿ	ʿ
b	b	b	b	b	b	b	b	b	b	b
d	d	d	d	d	d	d	d	d	d	d
ḏ	ḏ	z	z	z	d/ḏ	z	ḏ > d	ḏ	ḏ	z
g	g	g	g	g	g	g	g	ǧ	g	g
ġ	ġ(ḫ)	ġ(ḫ)	ġ(ḫ)	ḫ	ġ	ġ > ʿ	ġ > ʿ	ġ	ġ	ʿ
h	h('²)	h('²)	h	'	h	h	h	h	h	h
ḥ	ḥ('³)	ḥ('³)	ḥ	'	ḥ	ḥ	ḥ	ḥ	ḥ	ḥ
ḫ	ḫ	ḫ	ḫ	ḫ	ḫ	ḫ > ḥ	ḫ > ḥ	ḫ	ḫ	ḫ
k	k	k	k	k	k	k	k	k	k	k
l	l	l	l	l	l	l	l	l	l	l
m	m	m	m	m	m	m	m	m	m	m
n	n	n	n	n	n	n	n	n	n	n
p	p	p	p	p	p	p	p	f	f	f
q	q	q	q	q	q	q	q	q	q	q
r	r	r	r	r	r	r	r	r	r	r
s	s	s	s	s	s	s	s	s	s(s³)	s
ṣ	ṣ	ṣ	ṣ	ṣ	ṣ	ṣ	ṣ	ṣ	ṣ	ṣ
ś	š	š	š	š	š	ś	ś > s	ç > š	ś(s²)	ś > s
ṣ́	ṣ	ṣ	ṣ	ṣ	ṣ/ṭ	ṣ	q > ʿ	ḍ / ḏ	ṣ́	ṣ́ / ṣ
š	š	š	š	š	š	š	š	s	š(sᐟ)	s
t	t	t	t	t	t	t	t	t	t	t
ṭ	ṭ	ṭ	ṭ	ṭ	ṭ	ṭ	ṭ	ṭ	ṭ	ṭ
ṯ	ṯ	ṯ	ṯ	š	ṯ	š	ṯ > t	ṯ	ṯ	s
ṱ	ṣ	ṣ	ṣ	ṣ	ṱ	ṣ	ṱ > ṭ	ẓ	ṯ	ṣ
w	w	w	w	w	w	w	w	w	w	w
y	y	y	y	y	y	y	y	y	y	y
z	z	z	z	z	z	z	z	z	z	z

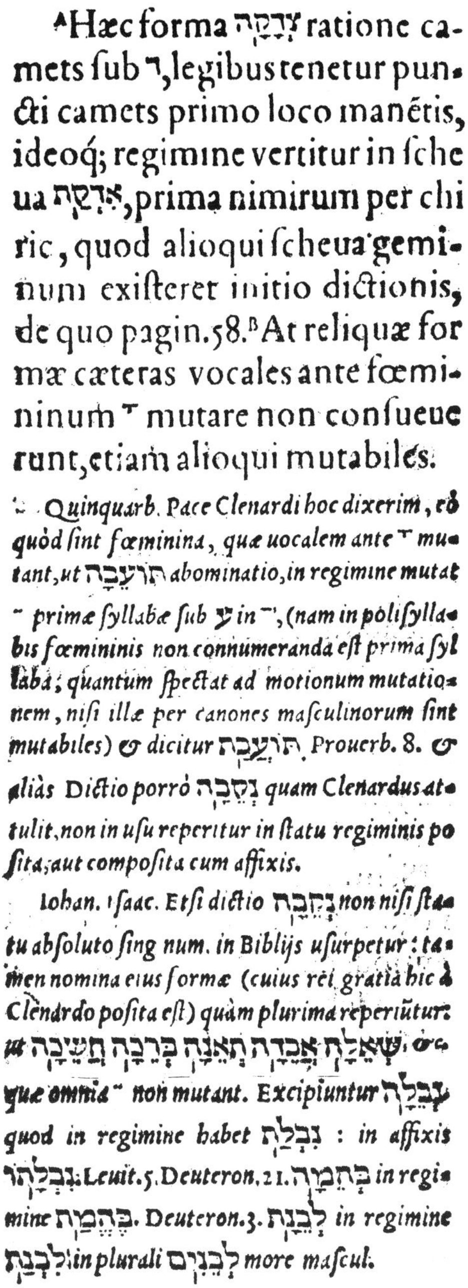

ᴬHæc forma צְדָקָה ratione camets fub ר, legibus tenetur pun-
cti camets primo loco manétis,
ideoq; regimine vertitur in fche
ua אִדְסַת, prima nimirum per chi
ric, quod alioqui fcheua gemi-
num exifteret initio dictionis,
de quo pagin.58.ᴰ At reliquæ for
mæ cæteras vocales ante fœmi-
ninum ᵀ mutare non confueue
runt, etiam alioqui mutabiles.

⸪ Quinquarb. Pace Clenardi hoc dixerim, eô
quòd fint fœminina, quæ uocalem ante ᵀ mutant, ut תּוֹעֵבָה abominatio, in regimine mutat
ᵀ primæ fyllabæ fub צ in ־, (nam in polifylla-
bis fœmininis non connumeranda eft prima fyl
laba; quantum fpectat ad motionum mutatio-
nem, nifi illæ per canones mafculinorum fint
mutabiles) & dicitur תּוֹעֲבַת, Prouerb. 8. &
aliàs Dictio porrò נְקֵבָה quam Clenardus at-
tulit, non in ufu reperitur in ftatu regiminis po
fita, aut compofita cum affixis.

Iohan. Ifaac. Etfi dictio נְקֵבָה non nifi ftatu abfoluto fing num. in Biblijs ufurpetur: ta-
men nomina eius formæ (cuius rei gratià hic à
Clenardo pofita eft) quàm plurima reperiutur:
שָׁאֲלָה אֲכָדַת תְּאֵנָה בְּרֵכָה חֲשֵׁיכָה &c.
quæ omnia ᵀ non mutant. Excipiuntur עֲבֵלָה
quod in regimine habet נִבְלַת : in affixis
נִבְלָתְהוּ Leuit.5. Deuteron.21. בְּחֶמְיָה in regimine בְּהֶמַת. Deuteron.3. לְבֵנַת in regimine
וְלְבְנַת in plurali לְבֵנִים more mafcul.

Fig. 25. Fol. 62/3 of the *Tabulae in grammaticam Hebraeam* by Nicolaus Clenardus (Cley-
naerts) (1493/4-1542), professor of Hebrew at Louvain in 1521-31, with comments by
Johan. Quinquarboreus (Cinqarbres) and Johan. Isaac Levita, in the Cologne 1561 edition.

12. VOWELS

21.1. Common Semitic or Proto-Semitic has three short vowels (§10.5): low/open back velar *a*, high/close front palatal *i*, and high/close back velar *u* with strongly rounded lips. It also possesses the three corresponding long vowels *ā*, *ī*, *ū*. Although additional vocalic phonemes have arisen in various Semitic languages, there are no sufficient grounds to suppose that other vowels belong to the original core of the Semitic phonemic system. The three vocalic -*a*-, -*i*-, -*u*- classes in the basic stem of the Semitic verb (§37.1; 38.3) and in the basic patterns of the Semitic noun (§28.5-12), the three Ugaritic *'a*, *'i*, *'u* signs for the glottal stop (§19.8), and the three vocalic phonemes of Classical Arabic show that these are the sole vowels constituting the vocalic core of the system. The situation is identical in Libyco-Berber. Besides, if one takes the evidence of primitive languages, such as those of America or as Australian Arunta, and considers the Bantu languages of Africa, there is a strong case for regarding *a*, *i*, *u* as primitive vowels, of which *e* and *o* are accidental variants, unless they result from diphthongs. However, the realization of the Semitic vowels *a*, *i*, *u* in actual speech can produce other vocalic sounds, mainly in the case of short vowels (cf. §10.11). There is a widespread tendency in Semitic to pronounce high and low vowels, especially when they are unstressed, as mid vowels [e], [ə], [o]. Thus short [i] and [u] tend to become [ə], as in Ethiopic (§21.30), and the same can happen with [ɑ] (§21.6-8,10,13). Besides, [i] can easily become [e] by lowering the tongue, [u] becomes then [o]. The lack of appropriate vocalic signs, especially for [ə] and [o], does often not allow determining the presence of these vowels in an accurate way, and "e" will then stand for [ə] and "u" for [o] (§21.3). On the other side, a stressed short vowel tends to become long, and its articulation may at the same time be lowered (e.g. *i* > *ī* > *ē*) or raised (e.g. *a* > *ā* > *ō*). Some of these new vowels may acquire a phonemic status in a determined language.

21.2. Despite their smaller number, the vowels are not second to the consonants with regard to their phonemic importance, as shown e.g. by Hebrew *'ab*, "father", *'ēb*, "bud", and *'ob*, "bag". These words differ by only one phoneme, which is a vowel. Statistical examination of the relationship between consonant and vowel shows that an average Arabic text contains *ca.* 52% of consonants versus 48% of vowels. Statistical samplings of an average Ethiopic text give similar results: *ca.* 55% of consonants versus 45% of vowels. Such statistical calculations offer a salutary corrective to the impressionistic approach to Semitic phonology, in which the vowel is considered just as a secondary modifier of a consonantal root.

21.3.   Besides *a, ā, i, ī, u, ū*, North and East Semitic languages possess the vocalic phonemes *e, ē*. The existence of the vowels *o, ō* cannot be proved directly, because the cuneiform writing system does not use special signs with *o*, while variants like *qurbu* and *qarbu*, next to *qirbu*, "near", do not point to [*qorbu*], but indicate the existence of dialectal variations. Even Ugaritic *'u < 'aw* cannot be considered as a conclusive proof of *'ō*, for the monophthongization *aw > ū* is as plausible as *aw > ō*. However, the vowels *o, ō* appear in Greek transcriptions of Late Babylonian words in the Seleucid period, e.g. οζον for *uznu*, "ear", ωει, for *ūmī* [*ūwī*], "days".

21.4.   The vocalic quantity in North and East Semitic can often be determined only by comparison with other Semitic languages and by application of phonetic principles. In fact, the rule that long vowels can be expressed in cuneiform writing by an additional vowel, as in the type *ka-a-nu* for *kānu*, "to be stable", or *ša-qu-u* for *šaqū*, "to drink", does not apply to the older phases of North and East Semitic, when this scribal convention was still unknown. Even in later periods, the writing itself rarely indicates length by inserting a vowel sign after the sign for open syllable (e.g. *ka-a, qu-u*).

21.5.   The alternating cuneiform notation of a long vowel in one case and of a "doubled" consonant in the other, e.g. *šarru-u-ti* and *šarru-ut-ti*, "kingship" (genitive), should presumably be considered as a spelling convention and not as a phonetic phenomenon which is usually described as doubling of the consonant to compensate for the shortening of the preceding vowel. This variation must represent two different scribal devices used to indicate a long vowel by writing an additional sign which expresses either the sole vowel (e.g. *šarru-u-ti*) or the vowel plus the consonant of the following syllable (e.g. *šarru-ut-ti*). The latter practice is just a particular case of the so-called "continuous" spelling in which the final consonant of one sign announces the initial consonant of the following sign without aiming at indicating its gemination, e.g. *li-il-lik-kà* instead of *li-il-li-ka* /*lillika*/, "may he come". Signs expressing consonant plus vowel plus consonant (C_1vC_2: *lik*) are not used to indicate geminated or long consonants, while pairs of syllabograms graphically doubling a consonant (vC_1-C_1v) may either indicate a gemination (e.g. *du-ub-ba* /*dubbā*/, "speak!", root *dbb*), or express the lengthening of the preceding vowel (e.g. *šarru-ut-ti* /*šarrūti*/), or be devoid of any phonetic significance (e.g. *Im-li-ik-ku-um*, variant *Im-li-kum* /*Imlikum*/). The alleged dialectal variation of Assyrian *-uttu* versus Babylonian *-ūtu* is hardly sustainable, for the spellings in *-ut-tu* /*-ūtu*/, etc., characterize the scribal practice at Ugarit, notably in the "General's Letter", at Boghazköy, in the Amarna letters from Amurru, etc., where they cannot be regarded as Assyrian dialect forms.

21.6.   The Palaeosyrian vowel *e* is secondarily derived from *a* under the influence of the consonantal phonemes *ḥ* and *ʿ*, as in *En-na-ì-lí* /*Ḥenna-'Ilī*/, "My god is favourable", *Eb-du-*^{d}*Ra-sa-ap* /*'Ebdu-Rašap*/, "Servant of Resheph", both at Ebla, or ^{d}*Eš₄-tár-ra-at* /*Eṭtarat*/, "Astarte", at Mari. The long vowel *ē* is derived at Ebla from a diphthong *-ay*, as in *Ti-iš-te-Da-mu* /*Tištē-Da'mu*/, "Damu has drunk", with a prefix *ti-* of the third person feminine because of the sex of the name bearer, regardless of the syntax of the name. A short *e* (rather than *i*) may result from the reduction of *a* in unstressed syllables; e.g. *ba-tá-qì i-dim* /*batắq yidim*/ next to *bí-tá-qì i-dim* [*betắq yidim*], "cutting by hand"; *ne-sa-qù(-um)* [*nešắqu(m)*], "to kiss"; *a-a-ù mi* /*(l)a'ắyu miy*/, "getting of water", with loss of initial *l* (§17.2), next to *lé-a-ù ma-a* [*le'ắyu maya*], "to get water", with initial sign NI. The long *ā* does not change into *ō*.

21.7.   In Old Akkadian, *e* is secondarily derived either from *a*, following the same conventions as in Palaeosyrian, or from *i*, as in *E-li-* /*'Elī*/ from *'ilī*, "my god". Long *ē* is derived from *i* followed by a "weak" consonant, as in *ip-te* /*iptē*/ from **yiptiḥ*, "he opened", from *a* plus a "weak" consonant, as in *be-lí* /*bēlī*/ from *ba'lī*, "my lord", from a diphthong *ay*, as in *Me-sar* /*Mēšar*/, from **Mayšar*, the deified "right", or from an original *ī*, as in ŠÁM-*me* /*ši'mē*/ from *ši'mī*, "prices" in the oblique case of plural. Vowel *i* changes into *u* before *š* (e.g. *ištu* > *uštu*, "from"; cf. §48.18) and before an emphatic consonant (e.g. *uṣārum* < **ḥiṣārum*, "court"), confirming the velarized nature of the emphatics (§10.9).

21.8.   In Amorite, the phonemic status of the short vowel *e* is uncertain, for *e* seems to be a positional variant or allophone of *i* in front of *ḥ*, *h*, *l*, *r*, e.g. *El* /'*El*/ or *Il* /'*Il*/. Instead, the long phoneme *ē* appears in Amorite *mēqtil* names (e.g. *Me-es₅-li-mu-um* /*Mēšlimum*/, "Well-doer") which formally are causative participles *muhaqtil > *muyaqtil > *miyeqtil > *mēqtil*, attested in Semitic as late as Neo-Punic (e.g. *myšql*, "honouring"; *myqm*, "raiser"). Some interchanges of *i* and *u* (e.g. *Bi-ni-* / *Bu-ni-*), of *a* and *u* (e.g. *Sa-mu-* / *Su-mu-*), and of *a* and *i* (e.g. *Ba-sa-ar* / *Bi-si-ir*), in words like *bn*, "son", *šm*, "name", or in the name of the mountain Bishir, may possibly suggest the existence of secondary vowels of the *ι*, *ü*, *o*, *ö* types, but Arabic parallel cases of dialectal *i* against *u* (e.g. *mishaf* / *mushaf*, "codex"), of *u* against *a* (e.g. *summ* / *samm*, "poison"), and of *a* against *i* (e.g. *lahya* / *lihya*, "beard") rather indicate that *binum* is used in one dialect, *bunum* in another, etc., and that these variations were originated under the influence of certain consonantal combinations.

21.9. From the three Ugaritic symbols *'a*, *'i*, *'u* we may probably infer that the Ugaritic vowel system corresponds substantially to that of Proto-Semitic (§21.1). The existence of the phonemes *ē* and *ō* cannot be deduced from the monophthongizations *'i* < *'ay* and *'u* < *'aw*, for *ay*, *aw* can also evolve into *ī* (e.g. *i-nu* < *yyn*, "wine" in Canaanite; Βιθια < *byt'n*, "House of the Spring" in Punic; Βυτυλλιον < **byt'l*, "House of El" in Phoenician) and *ū* (e.g. Μουθ < *mwt*, "Death" in Phoenician), like in Assyro-Babylonian (§21.10). In any case, syllabic transcriptions of Ugaritic names indicate a shift *ay* > *ī*, as in *Mi-ša-ra-nu* = *mšrn* /*Mīšarānu*/, from *mayšarānu (root *yšr*, "right"); *I-nu-ia* /'*Īnuya*/, from **'Aynuya* (root *'yn*,"eye"); *I-ia-um-mi* /'*Īya-'ummī*/, from **'Ayya-'ummī*,"Where is my mother?". Like in ancient Hidjazi poetry, also the diphthong *iya* can become *ī*, as in *Bi-di-'-lu* /*Bīdi-'Ilu*/, from **Biyadi-'Ili*,"By the hand of god". An occasional shift *ā* > *ō* occurs in personal names, e.g. *A-du-ni-*ᵈU /'*Adōnī-Ba'al*/,"Baal is my lord". It is attested also at Emar where the same persons are called *Da-a-du* or *Du-u-du*, *Ab-ba-nu* or *Ab-bu-nu*.

21.10. Assyro-Babylonian presents a vowel system identical with Proto-Semitic, but with the addition of the phonemes *e* and *ē*, which were secondarily developed at various periods from *a*, *ā*, *i*, *ī*. For *e* < *a* and *ē* < *ā* one can refer, e.g., to *šebēru* < *tabārum, "to break"; *qebēru* < *qabārum*, "to bury"; *qerēbu* < *qarābum*, "to approach", where *r* brings about the change *ā* > *ē*, like the velar fricatives (§ 19.11). Vowel *i* followed by any of the so-called "weak" consonants can change into *e*, e.g. *i-ru-ub* or *e-ru-ub*, "he entered", from *(*y*)*i'rub*. The change *i* > *e* can also occur before *r*, *ḫ*, *m*, e.g. *kal-be*, "dog" in genitive, from *kalbim*, while the shift *i* > *u* is attested mainly before emphatics and labials, like in *uṣṣu*, "arrow", from **ḫiṭṭu*, or *ummu*, "mother", from **'immu*. The vowel *a* characterizes many Old Assyrian words which have *i* in other dialects; e.g. *gamrum*, "expenditure", as against Middle Assyrian *gimru*. There is also a frequent *a/u* alternation; e.g. *azni* and *uzni*, "my ear". In Assyro-Babylonian, the original diphthong *ay* changes either to *ī* or to *ē*, e.g. *i-nu* or *e-nu*, "eye", from **'aynu*. In the writing system, the signs can often be read with *i* or with *e*, e.g. *gi/ge*, *ri/re*, *šìr/šèr*, *zik/zek*, *ib/eb*, *ir/er*, etc. In the late periods, the loss of final vowels occurs not only in the case of short vowels, as in *awīl*, "man", for the older *awīlu* (nominative), *awīli* (genitive), *awīla* (accusative), but also in the case of originally long vowels, as in *rab*, "chief", *nāš*, "holder", for the older *rabī*, *nāšī*, which were shortened in the intermediate period to *rabi*, *nāši*.

21.11. Late Babylonian reveals a certain tendency towards alphabetization of the syllabary with use of odd vowels. This tendency appears not only in the transliteration of Greek words like προστάτης, "chief", spelt *pu-ru-su-tat-te-su*, but already in the spelling of genuine Akkadian forms like *ú-zu-na-a-šu* for *uznāšu*, "his ears", *li-qí-bu-ni* for *liqbūni*, "may they speak", or *i-rak-ka-si* for *irakkas*, "he ties". These odd vowels are devoid of any phonetic value and should be explained on a purely graphic basis.

21.12. Old Canaanite, known by texts written in cuneiforms, displays the same vowel system as Assyro-Babylonian. However, the change *ā* > *ō*, expressed by cuneiform signs in *u*, is already attested at Hazor in the Old Babylonian period by the theophorous element *Ḫa-nu-ta* /'Anōt/ < 'Anāt, while North Semitic preserves the long *ā*: *Ḫa-na-at* (Mari), *A-na-tu/ti/te* (Ugarit). In the 14th century B.C., the shift *ā* > *ō* is shown at Pella, in northern Jordan, by the Amarna gloss *sú-ki-ni* /sōkini/ (EA 256,9), from *sākinu*, "prefect", against Ugaritic *sà-ki-ni* /sākini/, and it is confirmed in Jerusalem by the pronoun *a-nu-ki* /'anōki/ (EA 287,66.69), "I", against Ugaritic *a-na-ku* /'anāku/. The long vowel *ē* resulting from the monophthongization *ay* > *ē* is then found, e.g., at Byblos with the probable *qè-e-ṣí* /qēṣi/ (EA 131,15) from **qayṣu*, "summer", at Tyre with *mé-e-ma* /mēma/ (EA 148,31), plural of *may*, "water", and in Palestine with *ša-me-ma* /šamēma/ (EA 264,16), plural of **šamay*, "heaven", "sky".

21.13. The Phoenician vowel system can be partially reconstructed with the help of Assyro-Babylonian, Greek, and Latin transcriptions of Phoenician words and names. The many dialectal variations result from the geographic and chronological dispersion of the sources, that witness a number of varying pronunciations. The impact of the Old Canaanite change $\bar{a} > \bar{o}$ (e.g. *macom* /*maqōm*/ < *maqām, "place") becomes stronger in Phoenician after the accent shift to the last syllable and the lengthening of the stressed vowel, which created a new group of long $\bar{a}$ vowels. While the original vocalization of the verbal form is preserved e.g. in *Ia-ta-na-e-li* /*Yatan-'El*/, "El has given", in the 7th century B.C., the change *yátan* > *yatán* > *yatón* is attested in the same period by *Sa-mu-nu-ia-tu-ni* /*Šamun-yatōn*/, "Eshmun has given". The new long $\overset{\circ}{a}$ vowel, which resulted from the lengthening of *a* after the loss of a "weak" consonant, also changed into $\bar{o}$ and later into $\bar{u}$. Thus, the original vowels are still preserved in *Ba-'-li-ra-'-si* /*Ba'li-ra'ši*/, "Baal of the Cape" (9th century B.C.), but *a'* > $\bar{a}$ is finally reduced in Punic to $\bar{u}$, e.g. in *Rhysaddir* /*Rūš 'addīr*/, "Mighty Cape", and *a'* > $\bar{a}$ appears finally like $\bar{o}$ in *Anniboni* from *Ḥanni-Ba'l*, with the loss of final *l* or a change *l* > *n* (§17.4). In closed unaccented and in doubly closed syllables (e.g. Αννω for *Ḥannō*) the vowel *a* was short and remained unchanged, although it could be pronounced colloquially as *e* (e.g. *felu* < **pa'lū*, "they made"). Short *i* was rather lax and open, so that by the side of the usual Μιλκ-, *Gi(r)*-, there occur the variants Μελκ-, Γερ-, for *mlk*, "king", and *gr*, "devotee". The diphthongs *ay* and *aw* could develop to $\bar{e}/\bar{\iota}$ (e.g. σαμημ- /*šamēm*/, "heavens"; Βιθια /*Bīt-'ī(n)*/, from *byt'n*, "House of the Spring") and $\bar{o}/\bar{u}$ (e.g. Ιωμιλκου from *Yiḥaw-milk*, "May the king give life!"; Μουθ /*Mūt*/, "Death"). The use of the *matres lectionis* in Late Punic and Neo-Punic (§21.14) seems to reflect the lack of a phonemic distinction between *u* and *o*.

It is noteworthy that the letter *y* is used in the Latin transcription of the Punic passages in Plautus' *Poenulus* where we would expect *u* or *i*. One should keep in mind that the letter *y* was not yet used in Latin in Plautus' time, so that it must have been inserted into the Mss later. This happened probably in Accius' day, some fifty years after Plautus' death, when the latter's work seems to have been edited first. At that time, however, Punic was still a very alive language and the representation of a Punic vowel by *y* would normally signify that it was pronounced [ü] and corresponded to Ionic-Attic υ.

21.14. The more widely followed system of vowel letters in Late Punic and Neo-Punic can be schematized as follows:

"y" for *i* (e.g. *ṭyṭ'*, "Titus"), sometimes for *e* (e.g. *synṭr*, "senator");
"w" for *u* (e.g. *lwqy*, "Lucius"), sometimes for *o* (e.g. *rwm'n'*, "Romanus");
"'" for *e* (e.g. *p'lyks*, "Felix") and *o* (e.g. *'nṭ'ny'*, "Antonia");
"'" for *a* (e.g. *grm'nyqs*, "Germanicus").

A second, less successful but partly older system, uses "y" for *i* and "w" for *u*, like the first system. Besides, it uses "'" for *a* (e.g. *rm'*, "Roma"), "h" for *e* (e.g. *šhqnd'*, "Secunda"), and "'" for *o* (e.g. *'d'n* for *'adōn*, "lord"). In addition *h* and *ḥ* could be used for *a* (e.g. *hdn* for *'adōn*; *bḥrk'* for *barakō*, "he has blessed him") and *o/u* (e.g. *qlh* for *qolō*, "his stem"; *yhly'*, "Julia"; *šmḥ* for *šamō'*, "he heard").

21.15.   The vowel notation in Hebrew was limited before the 7th/8th century A.D. to the *matres lectionis* used at least from the 9th century B.C. (§9.9). Therefore, any investigation of ancient Hebrew vocalism is as difficult as that of Early Aramaic. The use of Masoretic punctuation indicating the vowels of the consonantal text began only five hundred years after Mishnaic Hebrew had ceased to be a vernacular. It was inspired by the Syrian practice of vocalizing the Bible by means of diacritic marks and it is nearly contemporaneous with the similar vocalization of the Qur'ān by early Arab philologists. The names and descriptions of vowel sounds in Arabic, Hebrew, and Syriac show that much of the phonological theory then current was common to the students of all three languages; e.g. *ptāḥā*, "the open one" in Syriac, is the vowel *a*, in Hebrew *pataḥ* and in Arabic *fatḥa*. From the fact that Syriac manuscripts with diacritical marks go back to the 5th century A.D. and that similar vowel signs, with similar values, were used for the sacred texts of the three languages we can safely deduce that the system of Eastern Syriac served as model for the Hebrew and Arabic vocalizations. Besides, Syriac influence is visible in writings on other facets of Hebrew and Arabic grammar, so that impact on the development of the vowel marks is not an isolated phenomenon.

21.16.   Within the Masoretic system itself three different traditions can be distinguished: the Babylonian one, the older stage of which is very close to the Eastern Syriac system, the Palestinian tradition, continued by the Samaritans, and the Tiberian one, which is not attested before the 9th century A.D. The first and the second of these vocalization systems indicate the vowels by means of supralinear signs, while the third one uses sublinear symbols (with one exception). There are a few notable differences in the qualitative distinction of vowels between these systems: the Babylonian and the Palestinian vocalizations do not distinguish *a* (*pataḥ*) and *e* (*segol*). The lack of this phonetic distinction in an ancient pronunciation of Hebrew is confirmed by the Greek transcriptions of the name of Esther as 'Αστήρ or 'Ασθήρ, which correspond to modern Jewish Yemenite pronunciation. Besides, the Palestinian system did originally not distinguish either *a* and *e* or *o* and *u*. The combination of vowel signs with the *matres lectionis* suggests a certain quantitative evaluation of the vowels. None of these systems allows for a distinction of earlier Hebrew dialects.

21.17. According to the older stage of the Babylonian system, consisting entirely of dots located above the letter and to the left of it, the vowels may be represented as follows:

ā	*a*	*e*	*i*	*o*	*u*

This system has probably led to some confusion because of the multiple use of the set of two dots, and it was replaced by a system in which *ā* is symbolized by a small *'ain*, *a* by the shape of *aleph* with one leg missing, and *u* by a small *waw*:

ā	*a*	*e*	*i*	*o*	*u*

The transcriptions *ā* and *a* are approximate and simply correspond to the system followed in the transliteration of Hebrew (§10.3). However, they may be correct since vowel quantity is phonemically relevant in modern Tigre precisely and exclusively in the case of *ā/a*. A similar situation cannot be excluded for Hebrew as pronounced in the Babylonian tradition.

21.18. The Palestinian system is not a crystallized one. A few mss. do not distinguish between *o* and *u*, while the use of two different symbols for *a* and *e* in some classes of mss. imply the existence of allophones. Besides, symbols for *a* interchange to some extent with *e* and *i* in many mss. Such variations appear to reflect different Palestinian pronunciations of Hebrew over a period ranging from the seventh to the tenth or eleventh centuries A.D. Like in the Babylonian system, the diacritics are located above the letter and a little to the left of it:

or	or			
a	*e*	*i*	*o*	*u*

This vocalization allows for a clear distinction of the basic vocalic phonemes of Common Semitic with the sole addition of the vowel *e*. This tradition was followed by the Samaritans with a few changes in the shape or the value of the signs:

$\underline{=}$	$\underline{\shortmid}$	$\underline{\vee}$	$\underline{\leq}$	$\underline{\wedge}$
a	*ö*	*e*	*i*	*u/o*

The transcription *ö* is approximate.

21.19. The Tiberian system was developed by the Karaite families of Ben Asher and Ben Naphtali. It prevailed in Hebrew manuscripts and later on in printed books. In this system, best represented by the St. Petersburg Codex B 19[A] and the Aleppo Codex, both vocalized by members of the Ben Asher family (§7.5), the Hebrew vocalic system consists of seven full vowels. Their values, as indicated below, simply correspond to the current transliteration of Hebrew:

$\overline{=}$	$\overline{\mathtt{.}}$	$\overline{\mathtt{..}}$	$\overline{\mathtt{.}}$	$\overline{\mathtt{.}}$	$\mathtt{.}$	$\mathtt{.}$
a	*ā*	*ē*	*e*	*i*	*o*	*u*
(*pataḥ*)	(*qameṣ*)	(*ṣere*)	(*segol*)	(*ḥireq*)	(*ḥolem*)	(*qibbūṣ*)

When a *waw* is adjacent to the letter followed by the vowel *u*, the three dots are replaced by a dot added to the *waw*. Besides these eight signs, an additional one $\overline{\mathtt{.}}$ (*šǝwā*) is used to indicated a *zero* vowel or a furtive vowel *ǝ*, often symbolized by *ᵉ*. This sign can be added to the vocalic symbols for *a*, *ā*, *e* to express furtive vowels of the same quality. In the original Tiberian pronunciation, the *qameṣ* was probably realized as a lower-mid, back [ɔ]. In the Jewish Sephardic tradition, instead, the *qameṣ* was considered as a representation either of a long *ā* or of a short *ŏ*. This tradition is phonologically justified for, e.g., the *qameṣ* stands for *ā* in *qām*, "he stood up", and it stands for *ŏ* in an original *kull*, "all". This pronunciation was officialized in the State of Israel and it is generally followed in the teaching of Hebrew. The corresponding transliteration is used also in the present work.

21.20. The vowel system of earlier stages of the Hebrew language can be learned to a certain extent from the transcription of Hebrew words and names in cuneiform, Greek, and Latin texts, as well as from epigraphy. Besides, the fragments of the second column of Origen's Hexapla (3rd century A.D.) contain a transliteration of the Hebrew Bible in Greek letters and the Dead Sea scrolls are characterized by an intensive use of

matres lectionis indicating medial and final vowels. These sources confirm the Canaanite shift *ā > ō*, but point to a dialectally differentiated situation of the diphthongs (§ 22.6).

21.21. Aramaic uses the *matres lectionis w, y, h*, and ' to indicate the
final and medial vowels *o/u, i/e*, and *a*, generally when they are long
(§9.5). However, in Mandaic each and every vowel, long or short, is
spelled *plene*, i.e. with the use of *matres lectionis* ', *h, w, y*, '. The
exceptions are rare, contrary to the practice in other Aramaic dialects,
where we have even long medial vowels without *matres lectionis*. The
use of *matres lectionis* increases with the time and the vowel *a*, initially
indicated only in final position by *h* or ', begins in the Hellenistic
period to be written *plene* with ' (in Mandaic also with ') even in
medial position (e.g. *b'tyn*, "houses"). In Late Aramaic, spelling tends
to be *plene*, even in the case of internal short vowels, except in Samaritan Aramaic. In Syriac, long final vowels *ē, ā, ō* that disappeared in
speech are in certain cases preserved in writing, e.g. *rby*, pronounced
rab, "my teacher".

21.22. Syriac is the only Late Aramaic dialect to have standardized
vocalization systems of its own, while Biblical Aramaic and the Targums or Aramaic translations of the Bible use the same systems as
Hebrew. There are two different methods of vowel notation in Syriac:
the Eastern system of dots, used by the Nestorians, goes back to the 5th
century A.D., while the Western one, used by the Monophysites or Jacobites, is based on Greek vowel symbols and probably does not antedate
the 7th/8th century A.D.

The Eastern Syriac vowel signs are located above or under the letter.
To indicate the vowels *o/ō, u/ū* and *ī*, they are combined with *matres
lectionis* which are widely employed in Syriac: the dot marking *o/ō* or
u/ū is used with the letter *w*, while the dot indicating a long *ī* is
employed with the letter *y*:

÷	∴	‾ or ⸚	⸗
a	*ā/ö*	*e/i*	*ē*
(*ptāḥā*)	(*zqāpā*)	(*rḇāṣā/zlāmā karyā*)	*rḇāṣā/zlāmā qašyā*

ȯ	ọ	⸌
o/ō	*u/ū*	*ī*
('*eṣāṣā rwīḥā*)	('*eṣāṣā 'allīṣā*)	(*ḥḇāṣā*)

The Western Syriac vowel signs use the Greek vowel letters mostly irrespective of their quantity:

ᵡ	ᵒ	ᵖ	ᴧ	ᴵ
a/ā	o/ō	e/ē	u/ū	i/ī
(ptōḥō)	(zqōfō)	(rbōṣō)	('eṣōṣō)	(ḥbōṣō)

21.23. In Aramaic as in Arabic, *ā* does in general not change into *ō*, except in Western Syriac and in Western Neo-Aramaic, at Maʿlūla, e.g. *pōrūqō*, "saviour", in Western Syriac, but *pārōqā* in Eastern Syriac. Besides, Western Syriac presents cases of a shift *ō > ū* and *ē > ī* (e.g. *rīšō*, "head"), while the old phonemes *ō* and *ū*, *ē* and *ī* merge in Samaritan Aramaic: their quality and quantity is conditioned by stress (on the penultimate) and syllable (open or closed), e.g. *rábbon*, "lord", but *rabbúni*, "my lord".

21.24. Pre-Islamic North Arabian inscriptions do not furnish sufficient indications for a full reconstruction of the vowel system. In some forms of speech, at least, that system differed appreciably from that of Classical Arabic, for the phonemes *ō* and *ē* certainly existed in Thamūdic and in Ṣafaitic. In fact, as a rule, neither the long vowels nor the diphthongs are indicated in Thamūdic and in Ṣafaitic inscriptions, e.g. *'n* for *'anā*, "I"; *tm* < *taym*, "servant"; *'s¹* < *'awš*, "gift"; *mt*, "death"; *bt*, "house". The diphthongs were certainly monophthongized *aw > ō* and *ay > ē* like in many modern Arabic colloquials. This is shown by Greek transliterations as Νοτεροs < *Ntyrw*, Ολεμοs < *'Ulaym*, Οσεδοs < *'ws¹d*, etc. Spellings like Μολαιχοs do not prove the contrary since Greek αι in those times was pronounced like ε (cf. Μολεχη). Instead, the diphthongs are partially preserved in Nabataean names, as results from Greek transliterations like Αυσαλλαs for *'wš'lh*. Greek transliterations show also occasional shifts *u > o*, *i > e*, *a > o*, and *a > e*. Thus in Nabataean Arabic names, *a* sometimes changes into *o*, probably due to the following emphatic consonant (e.g. Ροσαουαθοs = *Rḍwt* /*Raṣawat*/), and *a* followed by a laryngal changes into *e* (e.g. Κεειλοs < *Kahīl*). In Nabataean, long *ā* at the end of words was expressed by ' as in other Aramaic dialects, but in Thamūdic and in Ṣafaitic no long *ā* is indicated in writing; e.g. the demonstrative *ḏā* is written *ḏ*.

21.25. Pre-Classical Arabic, from which derives Middle or Neo-Arabic, as well as the modern colloquials, is best represented by the consonantal text of the Qur'ān. It does not indicate the short vowels, but contemporaneous Greek transliterations of Arabic names show that it possessed the vowels *a*, *ə*, *e*, *i*, *o*, *u*, e.g. Οβαιδαλλα βεν Αβιλαας τῶν βανι Ιεσχωρ [*'Obedallah bən 'Ab'ilaha' min banī Yəs¹ḥōr*], in the 7th century A.D. However, the phonemic structure of the short vowels was characterized by the opposition *a* : *i/u*, with allophones. The long vowels are indicated by *matres lectionis*: *w* and *y* express respectively *ū/ō* and *ī/ē*, while ' indicates *ā*, except at the end of feminine nouns in the "absolute" state where *h* is used as *mater lectionis* for *ā*, like in Aramaic, e.g. *klmh* /*kalimā*/, "speech". However, these letters may also be etymological, e.g. in *sw'l* /*sū'l*/, "demand" (root *š'l*), later shortened to *su'l* in a closed syllable, or *hdy* /*hadiy*/, "guidance" (root *hdy*).

21.26. Classical Arabic, formalized in the 8th-9th centuries A.D. by Arab grammarians, presents a vowel system which corresponds phonemically to the Proto-Semitic one with the three short or long vowels *a/ā*, *i/ī*, *u/ū*. The existing system of *matres lectionis* was complemented in the late 7th century A.D. by a system of diacritics inspired by the Eastern Syriac system: a dot above the letter for *a*, a dot under the letter for *i*, and a dot in the midst of the letter or to its left for *u*. Duplicated dots, placed in the same positions, indicated the nunation *-un*, *-in*, *-an* (*tanwīn*). This old system, attested in the 8th century A.D. by Kufic manuscripts of the Qur'ān, was expanded towards the end of the same century by additional diacritical signs, and the dots were replaced by other diacritics, used henceforth in Qur'ān and Ḥadīth manuscripts, i.e. from the 9th-10th centuries on:

∠	⟋	ᵖ
a	*i*	*u*
(*fatḥa*)	(*kasra*)	(*ḍamma*)

For the notation of long vowels, these diacritics are consistently combined with the matres lectionis ', *y*, *w* and added to the preceding consonant. A special symbol called *sukūn* (᷉) denotes the absence of a vowel; it is also called *ğazma* when placed on the final consonant of a word. In order to distinguish the glottal stop (*hamz*) from the *mater lectionis ā*, a sign called *hamza* (᷉) is placed above the letter '. To signify the reading *'ā* with the glottal stop followed by a long *ā*, another symbol is placed above the letter, namely *madda* (᷉). In the Qur'ān, however *madda* is used to indicate *ā'*, *ī'*, *ū'*. The prosthetic ' (§ 27.15), albeit traditionally written, is not supposed to be pronounced in the Classical language and it is therefore distinguished by a symbol called *waṣla* or *ṣila* (᷉), e.g. in *'sm*, "name"; *'bn*, "son".

21.27.   Early Arab grammarians and descriptive studies of modern colloquials reveal the extensive variations in the timbre of Arabic vowels.
The main tendencies are already described in the traditional Arabic
grammars which single out two principal phonetic phenomena: 1° *imāla*,
a non-conditioned palatalization *ā > ē*, e.g. *ṣēra* instead of *ṣāra*, "he
arrived"; 2° *tafḫīm*, a velarization *ā > ō*, sometimes conditioned by the
neighbourhood of emphatic consonants, but heard also, e.g., in *salōmun
'alaikum*. In modern colloquials, *ō* is often a free variant of *ū* (e.g.
bākōr, "fig", in Algeria), but it can also result from the contraction, e.g.,
of the pronominal suffix *-ahu > -ō*. In several dialects, the short *a* is
preserved, but *i* and *u* change into *ə*, unless they occur in a final closed
syllable where they are pronounced *e* and *o*, e.g. in Damascus. In some
colloquials of North Africa, all the short vowels are elided or reduced to
ə. Thus, the very short vowel *ə* can derive from original *a* (e.g. *ṣəhra*,
"rock"), *i* (e.g. *ḍəll*, "shade") or *u* (*bə'd*, "distance"). In general, the
variations can be very important as shown, e.g., by the different pronunciations of the word "name" in urban colloquials of Algeria: *īsəm* at
Algiers, *səm* at Djidjelli, *āsəm* at Cherchel. These developments are
partly depending on the Libyco-Berber substratum and adstratum.

21.28.   In Epigraphic South Arabian, no vowels are indicated, except
for the use of *w* and *y* ambivalently for either consonant or vowel notation. The spelling of the pronominal suffix *-hmw* indicates a pronunciation ending in *-u* and variant spellings like *ywm* and *ym*, "day", in the
same inscription obviously express the same pronunciation *yōm* or the
like. Similary, *y* might represent *ī / ē*. Instead, there is no notation at all
for long *ā*, except in two or three aberrant cases.

21.29.   In Modern South Arabian languages, vowel quality and quantity are closely related to stress. In Śheri and Soqoṭri, there is a large
range of vowels *a, e, ä, ə, i, o, ö, u*, which are generally long in stressed
syllables. In Mehri, there are five long vowels *ā, ē, ī, ō, ū*, and two short
vowels *ə* and *a*, which occurs only in stressed closed syllables. E.g.
kətōb, "to write", corresponds to *ktöb* in Śheri and Soqoṭri.

21.30.   Old Ethiopic or Ge'ez was at first written in a purely consonantal way, like Epigraphic South Arabian, but in the 4th century A.D. the
consonantal symbols were provided with regular vowel markings by
adding short strokes or circles and other alterations in the shape of letters. The vocalism which is manifested by this notation distinguishes

seven "orders" or syllabograms for each consonant, as can be seen in Fig. 21 (§9.7). These distinctions are essentially qualitative, with the probable exception of Ge'ez *ā* and *a*. Also in Tigre, vowel quantity is relevant phonemically only in the case of *a*/*ā*. Beside this case, the Proto-Ethiopic origin of the single modern Ethiopic vowels can be reconstructed as follows: *ä* < *a*; *u* < *ū*; *i* < *ī*; *a* < *ā*; *e* < *ay*; *ə* < *i*/*u*; *o* < *aw*. In classical Ge'ez, the vowel *a* is reduced to *ə* before laryngals and pharyngals. The Ethiopic change *i* > *ə* and *u* > *ə* is paralleled to some extent in Tuareg (e.g. ergative *ə-mnokal* < **u-mnokal*, "king"; *tə-barart* < **tu-barrart*, "girl"; plural *ə-nəsləm-ən* < **u-nəsləm-ən*, "Moslems"; non-active case *ə-lkas-ən* < **i-lkas-ən*, *tə-lkas-en* < **ti-lkas-en*, "gourds") and a similar tendency is widely attested in Arabic colloquials (§21.27).

21.31. The modern Ethiopian languages have several additional vowels, short and long. The two central vowels *ä* and *ə* are the most frequent ones, but they show variation in pronunciation depending on the surrounding sounds. All the vowels can be nasalized and the long vowels are generally phonemic. They may result from various phonetic developments, as disappearance of intervocalic, prevocalic or postvocalic consonants, or contraction of contiguous short vowels. Short vowels are liable to variation and allophones occur frequently. In particular, [ə] seems to function sometimes as an allophone of a *zero* phoneme. For further details, studies of the various languages and dialects concerned have to be consulted.

21.32. There is a widespread tendency in spoken Semitic languages to weaken short *-a-* to *-ə-* or *-e-*, and to *-i-*. The resulting vowel has an indistinct timbre, especially in an unaccented syllable preceding a stressed one. Very often such vowels disappear altogether. There is little doubt that this unconditioned weakening of *-a-* took place also in ancient Semitic languages, but it is concealed by the conventional and systematized spelling of the scribes. At Ebla, however, where there was obviously no longstanding tradition of writing the local idiom, the variant spelling of proper names reveal the same tendency. Thus, the same place name may be written *a-ga-lu*[ki] or *i-ga-lu*[ki], the same personal name may be spelt *a-da-ad-mu* or *i-da-ad-mu*, *'à-gi* or *i-gi*. At Ugarit, instead, the occasional change *a* > *i* results from a vowel assimilation and is thus phonetically conditioned; e.g. *'iḫqm* /*'Iḫīqam*/ < *'aḫqm*. There are also examples of a change *a* > *o* in close syllable, e.g. in the name *Šabbat(ay)* transcribed Σοββαθο(ς) in the 3rd century B.C. (§21.24).

13. DIPHTHONGS

22.1. Diphthongs are continuous monosyllabic speech sounds made by gliding from the articulatory position for one vowel towards that for a semivowel ("falling" diphthong), or the opposite ("rising" diphthong). They usually undergo a different development from that of their components. The combined sounds are subject to a number of conditioned changes which will be dealt with in the appropriate paragraphs. Some changes, however, are not conditioned: they affect, in particular, the falling diphthongs *aw*, *ay*, whose development presents several varieties. When the semivowel *w* or *y* is not long or geminated, as in *ayyābu*, "enemy", or *qawwām* "manager", the diphthong is often monophthongized. Thus *aw* is reduced either to *ā* or to *ō/ū*, and *ay* changes either to *ā* or to *ē/ī*.

22.2. Besides, diphthongs can arise when two vowels meet or they can originate from long vowels, the diphthongization of which leads to the creation of new nominal and verbal patterns. E.g. the colloquial Arabic verb *ǧawraba*, "he put on socks", derives formally from Stem III *ǧāraba* of the root *grb* (§22.17), with lengthened first vowel, while Stem II of the same verb means "to test, to try".

22.3. The phonetic shifts *aw* > *ā* and *ay* > *ā* are found in several Semitic languages. In Palaeosyrian, at Ebla, the variants *a-mu 'à-mu-tum* and *a-aw-mu 'à-mu-tum* /(y)a(w)mū hammūtum/, "hot days", both with the elision of initial *y*, suggest the dialectal coexistence of the diphthong and of the contracted form *ā* < *aw*, while the change *ay* > *ā* appears frequently, e.g. in *ba-tù* < *baytu*, "house", or in *Ba-na-a-ḫu* /Banā-'aḫu/, "The brother is nice". The name of Ebla itself, spelt *Ib/Eb-la*ki, later *E-eb-la-a-* or *I-ib-la-a* in Hurrian texts, testifies to this monophthongization, since it is still written *Yb3y* = *Yiblay* or *Yeblay* in an Egyptian execration text which mentions its Amorite king *Šmšwỉpỉrỉm* = *Šamšu-'app-'ilim*, "The sun is the face of God" (E 43). Also in Amorite names, we find the variants *Ia-aw-ṣí-*DINGIR and *Ia-ṣí-*DINGIR /Ya(w)ṣi-'El/, "El went out", with the change *aw* > *ā*, while the shift of final *ay* > *ā* appears e.g. in *Ra-ṣa-*ᵈ*Da-gan* /Raṣā-Dagān/, "Dagan is pleased". The shift *'ayn* > *'ān*, "eye", is implied at Ugarit by the spelling of ᵐ·ᵈIGI-*at* /'Anāt/, and the widespread change *ay* > *ā* is confirmed there by syllabic transcriptions like *Ma-ag-da-la-a* for *Mgdly*, *Šá-am-ra-a* for *Ṯmry*, etc., which indicate the monophthongization *ay* > *ā* at the end of a word. An earlier pronunciation is attested for the first place name by *Mktry* /*Mag-dalay*/ in an Egyptian execration text (E 5).

22.4. The change *ay* > *ā* is widely attested in Arabic. Thus, e.g. Ṣafaitic *my*, "water", and *s¹my*, "heaven", become in Classical Arabic *mā'* and *samā'*, while early Arab grammarians mention *'alāhā*, "upon her", for *'alayhā*; *salām 'alākum*, "peace upon you", for *'alaykum*; *ilāka*, "to you", for *ilayka*; *ladāka*, "with you", for *ladayka*, etc. In modern vernaculars, the change *ay* > *ā* occurs in closed syllables of the Syrian dialect of the Nusayris (e.g. *bāt*, "house", but *bayti*, "my house"), and before accented syllables in a few dialects of Southern Tunisia (e.g. *zātū́n*, "olives"; *baḍá*, "white"). In verbal roots with "weak" *w/y* as third radical, the singular of the base-stem shows the monophthongization *-aw* > *-ā* and *-ay* > *-ā* when the semivowel is not retained; e.g. *ǧafā* < **ǧafaw*, "he treated harshly"; *bakā* < **bakay*, "he wept". In fact, the termination *-a* of the perfect in Classical Arabic is not attested either in modern colloquials or in Ṣafaitic, judging from Greek transliterations like Μασαχηλος, Σαμαχηλος, etc. And a pronunciation *'atā*, *bakā*, etc., as in Classical Arabic, is unlikely in Ṣafaitic because of the spelling *'ty*, "he came", *bky*, "he wept", etc. The monophthongization of *-ay* > *-ā* seems to have taken place in Arabic quite late. E.g. the name of the Arab goddess al-'Uzzā is written *'zy* not only in the Nabataean name *'bd-'l-'zy*, "Servant of al-'Uzzā", but the Syrian writer Isaac of Antioch, in a poem describing events of *ca.* 457 A.D., still renders her name as *'wzy*. Also the frequent Arabic spelling of final long *ā* with a *-y* goes back to the Pre-Classical language in which the monophthongization had not yet taken place. But the final *-ay* becomes *-ā* in the interior of Ṣafaitic composite names, e.g. *wḥ'l* /*Waḥā-'Il*/,"God has revealed". This development is attested in most Semitic languages.

22.5. In Old Akkadian, the original diphthong *ay* changes to *ē* or *ī*, as in *Me-sar* < **Mayšar*, "right"; *e-ni-a* < **'aynīa*, "my eye"; *bí-tum* < **baytum*, "house". The original diphthong *aw* is reduced to *ū*, as in *u-mi-* < **yawmi-*, "day"; *u-su-zi* < **ušawṣi'*, "he led on". The reduction does not take place when the semivowel of *ay* is long or geminated, like in *a it-ti-in* /*ayyiddin*/, "may he not give". The same changes occur regularly in Assyro-Babylonian (§21.10), with the same exception of *ayy*, e.g. *ayyābu*, "enemy". In North Semitic, changes *ay* > *ā* (§ 22.2) and *ay* > *ē*/*ī* are attested at the same time, suggesting the existence of such unknown factors as the dialectal distribution, e.g. in texts from Ugarit (§ 21.9; 22.3).

22.6.   The shifts $ay > \bar{\iota}/\bar{e}$ and $aw > \bar{u}/\bar{o}$ occur in Old Canaanite (§ 21.12), in Phoenician and Punic (§ 21.9,13), and in ancient Hebrew, where spellings like *yn* in the Samaria ostraca instead of *yyn*, "wine", *'b* instead of *'wyb*, "enemy", and *'nm* instead of *'wnm*, "their sin", in a Qumrān fragment (4QPs 89), indicate the reductions $ay > \bar{\iota}/\bar{e}$ and $aw > \bar{u}/\bar{o}$. In Masoretic Hebrew, the diphthongs *aw* and *ay* remain generally unreduced when the semivowel was originally long or geminated (e.g. *ḥay < *ḥayy*, "living"), when the diphthong constitutes the final syllable of a word which is not in the construct state (e.g. *layl*, "night"), or when it precedes the enclitic particle *-h* expressing the direction (e.g. *šāmaymāh*, "towards heaven"). However, there is a tendency not only to preserve or to restore the diphthong, but even to split it into two syllables, e.g. *bayit < *bayt*, "house"; *māwet < *mawt*, "death".

22.7.   This tendency to expand and split the diphthongs radically differs from the general trend observed in Pre-Islamic North Arabian (§21.24) and in Arabic, except in the classical language which preserves the original diphthongs in medial position, but often reduces *-ay* to *-ā* at the end of words (§ 22.4). The reduction *-ay > -ē* is indirectly attested at al-Kūfa where Qur'ān codices frequently write *-'* instead of the final *-y* and where long *ā* was subject to *imāla* (§21.27). In the Syro-Palestinian dialects, the diphthongs *ay* and *aw*, followed by a consonant, are generally reduced to *ē* (e.g. *lēl < layl*, "night") and *ō* (e.g. *ṭōr < ṭawr*, "bull"). However, there are also cases of a monophthongization $ay > \bar{\iota}$ (e.g. *bīṭār < Syriac paytārā*, "farrier") and $aw > \bar{u}$ (e.g. *ġū'ān < ġaw'ān*, "hungry"). Instead, these are the best attested reductions of the diphthongs *ay* and *aw* in Arabic colloquials of North Africa; e.g. *bḥīra < buḥayra*, "pond"; *bīn < bayn*, "between", *mūǧa < mawǧa*, "wave"; *yūm < yawm*, "day". Cases of *aw* becoming *ū* are rare outside the Maghrib, but the change of initial $aw > \bar{u}$, as in *ūlad < awlād*, "children", is ascribed to the ancient Tamīm dialect of northeast Arabia.

22.8.   The contraction of diphthongs in Early Aramaic is attested in certain dialects and in certain circumstances. In the Tell Fekherye inscription from the mid-9th century B.C., the closed syllable of the non-suffixed construct state of *byt* in *bt hdd*, "temple of Hadad", shows the reduction, while the open syllable of the suffixed form *byth* is spelt with *yōd.* The monophthongization of *bayt* might have been *bāt*, as suggested by *Bat-ti-il-, Ba-ti-il-, Bathillo* in Latin transcription, i.e. */Bāt-'Il/*, an Aramaic divine name meaning "God's house", but the reductions *ay > ī* and *ay > ē* are also attested, e.g. by *E-ni-ìl* designating the same person as *A-i-ni-ìl*, "Eye of God", or by *Sa-mir-i-na* besides *Šá-ma-ra-'-in*, "Samaria". It is clear that forms preserving the diphthong *ay* and forms reducing it to *ā, ē,* or *ī* could coexist in the same area and in the same period. Also in later times, the diphthong *ay* could be either preserved or monophthongized. In Syriac, it is preserved unless occurring in a doubly closed syllable, e.g. *'aynā*, "eye", but *'ēn* in the construct state. In Eastern Neo-Aramaic the reduction *ay > ē* is general, e.g. *bēsa < baytā*, and *ē* shows a tendency to change into *ī*. A similar reduction occurs in Ṭūrōyo with the monophthongization *əy > i*; e.g. *mílef < máyləf*, "it is learned". Instead, the diphthong *ay* is generally preserved in Western Neo-Aramaic.

22.9. The parallel use of *'l yrwh* and *'l yrwy*, "let it not be sated", at Tell Fekherye, suggests a reduction to *-ē* indicated by *-h*, while *-y* probably represents either a historical spelling, inherited from an older stage of the language, or a secondary diphthongization *-ē > -ey*. Since the diphthong *-ay* at the end of perfect forms of the basic stem is invariably reduced to *-ā* (e.g. *banā < *banay*, "he built"), the reduction to *-ē* at the end of a word should be rather explained here by the contraction *-iy > -ī > -ē* (*yarwiy > yarwī > yirwē*), well attested in Aramaic by variants as *Zab-di-ia /Zabdiy/* and *Zab-de-e /Zabdē/, Ba-ni-iá /Bāniy/* and *Ba-né-e /Bānē/*, designating the same person.

22.10. The diphthong *aw* can be preserved in Aramaic or be reduced to *ō / ū*. The spelling with *w*, even in Early Aramaic inscriptions, does not allow deciding whether *w* indicates the semivowel, or is used as a *mater lectionis* for *ō / ū*, or is simply a historical spelling. E.g. the name *mwdd*, from the root *wdd*, "to love", appears in cuneiform transcription as *Mu-da-da, Mu-da-di*, and in Greek as Μωδαδ. In Syriac, the noun "death" is spelt *mawtā*, but its construct state appears as *mūt*, because the preservation of the diphthong would then result in a doubly closed syllable. In Eastern Neo-Aramaic, the diphthong is always reduced to *ō* (e.g. *mōtā*, "death"), unless the *a* is long or the *w* geminated, as in *qawwəma*, spelt *qāwemā*, "to get up, to go". The same reduction is applied to diphthongs originating from the change *b > ḇ > w*, as in *gabrā > gaḇrā > gawrā > gōrā*, "man". The *ō* shows a further tendency to change into *ū*. A similar monophthongization *əw > u* occurs in Ṭūrōyo (e.g. *ktúli* < **ktə́wli*, "I wrote"), while *aw* is generally preserved in Western Neo-Aramaic.

22.11. In Epigraphic South Arabian, variant spellings like *bt* and *byt*, "house", or *ym* and *ywm*, "day", even in one and the same text, indicate that both can be facultative variant orthographies for a single pronunciation, probably *bēt* and *yōm*, according to the modern Ḥaḍramawt colloquial which contracts *ay* into *ē* (e.g. *ēḍā* < *'ayḍan*, "also"; *'ēn* < *'ayn*, "eye"), and *aw* into *ō* (e.g. *yōm* < *yawm*, "day"); cases of *aw* becoming *ū* are rare outside the Maghrib. An alternative interpretation, which would introduce a distinction either between open and closed syllables, or between stressed and unstressed syllables, does not explain all the variant spellings *byt* / *bt* and *ywm* / *ym*, since they occur in the same forms, as *ywmtn* and *ymtn*, "the days".

22.12. In ancient Ethiopic or Geʿez the diphthongs appear in reduced form, e.g. *yom* < *yōm*, "today", *lelit* < *lēlīt*, "night", but there are many variations. In the modern Ethiopian languages, the number of divergent realizations of diphthongs is even greater. E.g., while the "threshing floor" is called *awd* in some Gurage dialects, it is *od* in others. Similarly, "sheep" is said *ṭay* (< *ṭāli*) in some Gurage idioms, why it is *ṭe* in other dialects. The reduction pattern appears to be *aw > o* and *ay > e*.

22.13. The diphthongs *iw, uw, uy* are reduced to *ū* in Assyro-Babylonian, e.g. *ūbil* < **iwbil*, "he brought"; *šūbil* < **šuwbil*, "send!", *šūšur* < **šuyšur*, "is kept in order". Original *iy* is instead monophthongized to *ī*, e.g. *īde* < **iydaʿ*, "he knows". In Arabic, instead, *iw* changes to *iy > ī* at the end of a syllable; e.g. *īqāʿ* < **'iwqāʿ*, "rhythm", from the root *wqʿ*. Also *uy* develops to *iy > ī*, sometimes to *uw > ū*; e.g. *bīḍ* < **buyḍ*, "layings (of eggs)", from the root *byḍ*; *mūqin* < **muyqin*, "certain", from the root *yqn*. When the Phoenician orthography was fixed, the suffix *-iy* of the first person singular was still pronounced *-iya* after nouns in the oblique cases, e.g. *'by*, "of my father". With the loss of final short vowels it was reduced to *-iy*, which in time was simplified to *-ī*, but the writing with *y* was preserved and even extended by analogy to nominative nouns (e.g. *'my*, "my mother"), despite the fact that Phoenician does generally not use any *matres lectionis*. The same development is attested in Palaeosyrian by synchronic variants; e.g. *i-a-la-nu* ['iyalānu] and *i-la-nu-um* or *i-la-núm* ['īlānum], "a large tree". In Hebrew, *uw* becomes *ū* and *iy* changes in *ī*; e.g. *hūšab* < **huwtab*, "he set"; *yīraš* < **yiyrat*, "he will inherit". Corresponding reductions are also common in Ethiopian languages.

22.14. The rising diphthongs *yi-* and *yu-* of the prefixed verbal forms of the third person are not indicated in Palaeosyrian, but they are probably signified in Old Akkadian by the spellings *i-ik-mi-* /yikmī-/, "he captured" (root *kmy*), *i-iš-e-* /yiš'ē-/, "he searched" (root *š'y*), *u-ub-lam* /yūblam/, "he brought" (root *wbl*), *u-ur-da-ni* /yūrdanni/, "it went down on me" (root *wrd*). Similar spellings occur in Old Assyrian; e.g. *ú-ub-lu* /yublū/, "they brought"; *i-iš-qú-ul* /yitqul/, "he weighed out". In Amorite, *yi-* is only expressed by *i-*, but *yu-* is attested by the name *Iu-um-ra-aṣ*-DINGIR /Yumraṣ-'El/, "El grieved". In Assyro-Babylonian, *yi-* is reduced to *i-* and *yu-* to *u-*. Also *ya-* is monophthongized to *i-*, e.g. *idu* < **yadu*, "hand", but the alternative spellings with *a-* and *i-* in Palaeosyrian indicate the change *ya-* > *yi-*, without monophthongization; e.g. *a-me-tum* /yamittum/ and *i-me-tum* /yimettum/, "right side". This change explains the form *yi-* > *i-* of the prefixed personal in most Semitic languages (§40.31) and, occasionally, of the first syllable *ya-* in the basic stem of verbs like *yāda'*, "he recognized"; e.g. in the Edomite proper name *Qwsyd'* transcribed Κοσιδη in a bilingual ostracon from the 3rd century B.C.

22.15. Secondary diphthongizations are to be found in Semitic languages when two vowels meet. In such a case, either the two vowels coalesce and there is crasis (e.g. Arabic *ī+ū* > *ū*; *ū+ī* > *ī*; Tigrinya *ə+a* > *ä*; Amharic *ə+a* > *a*), or a "hiatus-filling" semivowel *y* or *w* is produced. The so-called "weak" verbs, the root of which is monosyllabic and contains a long vowel *ā*, *ī*, *ū*, give frequently rise to such secondary diphthongs, e.g. *qūm*, "to get up", *śīm*, "to place", *kūn*, "to be". Thus, the active participle of *qūm* is in Aramaic either *qym* /qāyim/, or *q'ym* with a medial *mater lectionis*, or *q'm* with ' substituting the *y* after *ā*. While the form *qym* goes back to the 6th century B.C., the glottal stop replaces the glide *y* only in the 2nd century B.C. Also in modern South Ethiopic, the glottal stop may replace *w* or *y*, as in *e'ädä*, "to tell", and *we'a*, "to go down", in one of the Gurage dialects, against *ewädä* and *wəyä* in other dialects. The situation in Arabic is similar to that of Aramaic. In Pre-Classical Arabic, as apparent in the consonantal text of the Qur'ān, the active participle of the same verb is *q'ym* /qāyim/, "standing", which was reinterpreted in Classical Arabic as *qā'imun*. Such changes are well-known to Arab grammarians who call them *'ibdāl nahwī* or *ṣarfī,* "grammatical substitution", but consider usually that *hamza* is replaced by *wāw* or *yā'*, although the etymological form is, e.g., *miyar*, "provisions", while *mi'ar* is a secondary form historically. Ṣafaitic inscriptions use sometimes ' as in *k'n* /*kā'in*/, "being", but in some cases *y* is written even instead of an etymological ', chiefly in the neighbourhood of the vowel *i*, as in *hnyt* /*hāniyat*/, "maid" (root *hn'*). In Epigraphic South Arabian, there is no trace of the practice of substituting ' for *w/y* after *ā*, and the modern Arab colloquials are identical in this respect with the Pre-Classical language. E.g., in Syro-Palestinian dialects, the participle "seeing" of *šūf* is *šāyef* and, in Maghrebine dialects, the participle "lodging" of *bāt* is *bāyĭt*. Because cuneiform script lacks specific signs with semivowels, spellings like *ša-i-im, ša-i-mu*, "fixing" (root *šīm*), are ambiguous. Assyriologists explain them usually as *šā'imu*, but occasional Standard Babylonian forms as *da-a-a-ik* /*dāyik*/, "killing", seem to indicate that one should always read *šāyim*, etc. In Hebrew, the forms *qām*, "standing", *mēt*, "dead", imply the monophthongization of the secondary diphthongs: **qāyim > qām, *māyit > mēt*. In modern Ethiopian languages, *w* can be used in medial position as a transitional consonant between two vowels, e.g. *duwa* from Arabic *du'ā'*, "Muslim prayer".

22.16. There is a series of nominal patterns extended by a diphthong, like *fay'al, faw'al, fay'āl, fay'ūl, fu'ayl, fu''ayl, fī''awl*, known not only from Arabic but also from other Semitic languages. In particular, the patterns *faw'al* and *fu'ayl* — the latter used for diminutives — are attested also in Aramaic (e.g. *'lym*, "lad") (§29.10). The monosyllabic patterns *fayl* and *fawl* alternate sometimes with noun types *CīC* and *CūC* (§29.9), and a possible example of a *fayl* noun paralleled by a *CāC* type is provided by the word *bayt*, "house", apparently related to Cushitic *bati*, "roof" (Oromo), borrowed in Gafat with the same meaning.

22.17. Verbal Stem III with lengthened first vowel — attested in Arabic, Ethiopic, and Syriac (§41.5) — kan give rise to a secondary diphthong developed from the long vowel. This is perhaps non evident when comparing, e.g., Classical Arabic *ġawġa'a* or *ġawġā*, "to cluck" (of hens), with Syro-Palestinian colloquial *gāga*, because the verb derives from an onomatopoeia, but colloquial *ḥōrab*, "to strike up a war song", is best explained as **ḥawrab < ḥārab*, "to wage war", since *aw > ō* is the normal reduction in Syro-Palestinian colloquials. The existence of a *fā'ala* > *faw'ala* / *fay'ala* stem in Ethiopic is implied by forms of the types *qotala* and *qetala*. As for Syriac, e.g., the form *gawzel*, "he set fire on", is best interpreted as a Stem III *ā* > *aw* of the root *gzl*, "to plunder". These developments are important for a right understanding of the secondary stems of the monosyllabic verbs with a long vowel (§44.5-9).

22.18. Another type of secondary diphthongs can explain the formation of some secondary verbal roots with "weak" first radicals, e.g. *wld* / *yld*, "to bear" (§43.6-7). Thus in Ethiopian Gurage dialects, e.g., the prepalatal *y* can be an on-glide before the vowels *ä*, *e*, *ə*, *i*, e.g. *yärbat* and *ärbat*, "evening meal". In the same way, labial *w* can serve in South Ethiopic as an on-glide in initial position before *o*, *u*, e.g. *wof* and *of*, "bird". This phenomenon cannot be equated with the appearance of a diphthong at the beginning of a Berber noun to which the ergative *u*-prefix is added, e.g. *wagmar* < *u+agmar*, "horse"; *yiləf* < *u-iləf-*, "wild boar".

14. GEMINATED OR LONG CONSONANTS

23.1. Gemination or consonantal length can be justified etymologically or grammatically, but it occurs also when a long vowel plus a single consonant is replaced by a short vowel plus a doubled consonant, as in Hebrew *gəmallīm*, "camels", "dromedaries", plural of *gāmāl* (§24.7). Some Semitic languages and dialects are non-geminating in part or in general (§23.5). A compensatory lengthening of the contiguous vowel may then correspond to the gemination, as in Neo-Aramaic *dābāšā*, "bee", instead of *dabbāšā*. Gemination is phonemic in the Semitic languages in which gemination or lengthening of consonants is a regular feature, as it appears, e.g., from Arabic *kabara*, "to become great", and *kabbara*, "to make great", or North Ethiopic (Tigrinya) *qätänä*, "to be small", and *qättänä*, "to liquefy", *'abay*, "wild", and *'abbay*, "Blue Nile", and South Ethiopic (Gurage) *abar*, "dry season", and *abbar*, "young man", where gemination and non-gemination of *b* and *ṭ* constitute the sole phonemic difference between the two words.

It has been suggested that there may have been a phonetic difference in Semitic between long consonants and double or geminated consonants. In fact, there is a category of "continuant" consonants that can be held continuously, with variable tension but without changing quality, and a second category of so-called "kinetic" or "interrupted" sounds that cannot be so held. The first group comprises the nasal, lateral, fricative, and rolled phonemes, while the second one includes the plosives and the affricates (e.g. [t͡s]). The gemination of the phonemes of the second group does not imply length, properly speaking, but increased tension which is perceivable in the case of a voiceless plosive, while a voiced one is reckoned less tense since a considerable part of the air it uses is consumed by voicing alone. Therefore, really geminated voiced plosives have to be pronounced either by doubly stopping the chamber of the mouth and sucking in the breath, or by changing the quality, as /bb/ > [mb] or [b͟b], [dd] > [nd] or [d͟d], /gg/ > [ng] or [g͟g]. The first articulation is encountered, e.g., among native Ṭūrōyo speakers and among speakers of Western Neo-Aramaic who even insert an anaptyctic vowel between the geminated consonants; e.g. ameləl < amell, "he said to them" (Ǧubb ʿAdīn). Concrete examples of the second pronunciation in ancient Semitic languages are probably provided by such transcriptions as Σεπφώρα for Ṣippōrā, Ἀκχώ for ʿAkkō, Ματθαθίας for Mattityā, which aptly illustrate the changing quality of geminated plosives. In other circumstances or forms of speech, and especially in the articulation of "continuants", the so-called "doubling" of a consonant does not consist phonetically in its double articulation, but either in its lengthening or in its amplification. This may vary from a slight "tightening" or lengthening in time to much more than double. We keep nevertheless using the traditional terminology and the current notation of consonantal length or tension by transcribing the long or tense consonant twice, e.g. bb. This notation is interchangeable with the symbol /b:/ employed in the international phonetic system and with the capital letter B adopted by some authors.

23.2. Gemination is sometimes hardly audible, particularly at the end of a word (§24.5), where it is not recorded either in Amharic or in Hebrew, e.g. ʿam, "people", instead of ʿamm. However, it becomes evident when the final consonant is followed by a vowel, e.g. Hebrew ʿammī, "my people". Gemination is at times missing also in the middle of a word, as shown by the Masoretic notation məbaqəšīm (Ex. 4,19; 10,11), "seeking", instead of the expected *məbaqqəšīm. Besides, there is no regular marking of long consonants in cuneiform script and there is no such notation at all in Semitic alphabetic scripts, except in some rare cases (§23.3), until the introduction of special diacritics in Hebrew and in Arabic (§23.4).

23.3. Early essays aiming at indicating a geminated or long consonant are found, e.g., in the Hebrew Bible, where the variant spelling hrry of hry must express the plural construct state *harrē, "mountains". In Literary and Official Aramaic, spellings like ʿmm' for ʿammāʾ, "the people", or dššn and dššy' for the plural of the noun dašš(ā), "door", should be explained in the same way. Besides, it is very likely that at least the liquids and the nasal n, when geminated, were sometimes written in

Ṣafaitic with a double *l* and a double *n*, e.g. *kllhm* = *klhm*, "all of them", *ṭnn'l* = *ṭn'l*, Ταννηλος, "God has considered" or the like.

23.4. In the Hebrew vocalization systems, the symbol called *dageš* — generally a dot placed in the letter — is used to mark the gemination of a consonant, but it is in reality an ambiguous sign, since it can also indicate the lack of gemination and the plosive pronunciation of the consonants *b g d k p t*. This was probably the original function of the *dageš* used with the plosives, since these phonemes cannot be lengthened, properly speaking, but only amplified by other means, as a pronunciation with greater pressure. Only Arabic *šadda* (ˇ) indicates in an unambiguous way that the consonant is long or geminated, e.g. *'ammu*, "paternal uncle".

23.5. In principle, all the consonants can be geminated, but ' and *h* are not geminated in Ethiopian languages and the Masoretic punctuation of Hebrew and of Biblical Aramaic in principle excludes the gemination of the pharyngals (*ḥ*,'), of the laryngals (', *h*), and of *r*. In Neo-Aramaic, the doubling of consonants has largely been eliminated and replaced by the lengthening of the preceding vowel, e.g. *yāma* < *yammā*, "sea", but a secondary gemination can oppose a word to its counterpart characterized by a long vowel followed by the single consonant, e.g. */mīta/*, "dead" (masculine), and */mitta/*, "dead" (feminine). There are also non-geminating dialects in the modern Ethiopian languages, although gemination through assimilation occurs in these dialects as well, e.g. *wässe* < *wäsfe*, "awl", in a non-geminating Gurage dialect.

23.6. Assimilation and resulting gemination occur in all the Semitic languages and will be examined in the appropriate paragraphs dealing with conditioned sound changes (§27.3-7). Instead, dissimilation of gemination is a common Semitic phenomenon which is not conditioned by any particular phonetic environment. It amounts to a phonemic split or diphonemization, if the resulting sounds become significant (cf. §10.7,12), as in Neo-Arabic where the dissimilation may serve as means to distinguish verbal Stems I and II (e.g. *ġarmaš* < *ġammaš*, "to scratch", vs. *ġamaš*, in Lebanon). A geminated consonant can be dissimilated through *n* and *m*, through the liquids *l* and *r*, sometimes through ' and *y*. It should be stressed that the dissimilation of geminated plosives, especially when they are voiced, proceeds from the nature of these phonemes that cannot be lengthened, properly speaking, without changing quality. Thus there arise equations like /b:/ = [mb] or [lb]; /dd/ = [nd], [md], or [rd]; /ṭṭ/ = [nṭ], etc. The dissimilation through ' (§23.10) belongs to the same phenomenon, since the *p t k* series is "geminated" in some languages by spirantization or glottalization.

23.7. Dissimilation through *n* occurs in Palaeosyrian, e.g. *ṣí-na-ba-ti* (gen.) < **ṣibbātu*, "sunbeams", from a variant root *ṣbb* of Hebrew *ṣby*, "splendour", with a plural *ṣibǝ'ōt*. It is attested in Old Akkadian, e.g. by *Ḫa-an-za-ab-tum* as compared with *Ḫa-za-ab-tum* /*Ḫaṣṣabtum*/, a personal name derived from the root *ḫṣb*, "to break off". In Amorite, one can mention the names *An-du-ma-lik* = *Ad-du-ma-lik*, "Haddu is king", and ᵈ*Šamaš-ḫa-an-zi-ir* = ᵈ*Šamaš-ḫa-zi-ir* /*Šamaš-ġazzīr*/, "Shamash is a hero". Besides the frequent Babylonian form *inandin* < *inaddin*, "he gives", one can refer to *ta-na-an-zi-iq* = *ta-na-az-zi-iq* /*tanazziq*/, "you are angry". The geminated consonants of both verbs can be dissimilated also through *m*: *tanaddina* > *ta-nam-di-na*, "you give me", *anazziq* > *a-nam-ziq*, "I am angry". Dissimilation through *m* is attested also in Assyro-Babylonian *ṣumbu* < *ṣubbu*, "wagon" (cf. Hebrew *ṣabbīm*; Aramaic *ṣabbā*). The name of the Palestinian city Eqron /*'Aqqarōn*/ is dissimilated in Neo-Assyrian texts in *An-qar-u-na* and *Am-qar-u-na*, and the name of the Aramaic tribe *Gabbūl*, "kneader", appears as *Ga-am-bu-lu*, etc. The Aramaic personal name *ḥdy* /*Ḥaddiy*/, "rejoicing", is transcribed *Ḫa-an-di-i* in Neo-Assyrian and *Ḫa-an-di-ia* in Neo-Babylonian texts. The noun *kkr* < *krkr* (§27.3), "talent" (weight), may be dissimilated in Aramaic in *knkr*, with parrallel Coptic forms *ǧingōr*, *ǧingor*, and Greek κίνχαρες. The geminated *ṭ* of the Ammonite name *ḥṭš* /*Ḥaṭṭaš*/, also attested in Ṣafaitic and in Nabataean with a Greek transliteration Χαττεσος, is dissimilated in Neo-Assyrian texts in *Ḫa-an-ṭa-si* and in Neo-Babylonian texts in *Ḫa-an-ṭa-šú*. In Ethiopian Gurage dialects, e.g. *goǧǧo*, "hut", is dissimilated into *gonžo*.

23.8. Dissimilation through *l* is attested in Hebrew by *pltyš* in the Isaiah scroll 1QIsᵃ for *paṭṭīš*, "forge hammer". One can also quote *galmūd* < **gammūd*, "sterile", from the root *gmd*, "to be hard"; *zal'āpōt* < **za''āpōt*, "deadliness", from the root *z'p*, "to kill instantly"; *ḥlmš* = Assyro-Babylonian *elmešu* < **ḥammīš*, a precious stone, from the root *ḥmš*, "to be steadfast". The Assyro-Babylonian name of the reptile *ḥulmiṭṭu* corresponds to Hebrew *ḥomeṭ* and is obviously dissimilated from **ḥummiṭṭu*. In Arabic, there are several verbs without and with dissimilatory *l* in stem II, e.g. *faṭṭaḥa* and *falṭaḥa*, "to make broad"; *ḥabbaṣa* and *ḥalbaṣa*, "to mix"; *kaḥḥaba* and *kalḥaba*, "to strike"; *dammasa* and *dalmasa*, "to hide"; etc. The North Arabian name **Faddās*[1] is dissimilated in Nabataean in *pndšw*, but it appears in the Hebrew Bible as *pldš*. In Amharic and in Gurage dialects, one can mention *səlsa*, "sixty", dissimilated from *səssa* < *sədsa*.

23.9. Dissimilation through *r* is attested in Old Babylonian by *la-marsú-[u]m* < *lamassum*, "guardian she-angel" (ARM VI,31,19), in Aramaic by *kursi'* < *kussi'u*, "throne", by the name of Damascus: *Dammeśeq* > *Darmeśeq*, and by *šarbīṭ* < Babylonian *šabbiṭu*, "staff, sceptre", borrowed further by Hebrew (Esth. 4,11; 5,2; 8,4; Sir. 37,17). In Biblical Hebrew, the verbal form *yəkarsəmennāh* (Ps. 80,14) derives through dissimilation *ss* > *rs* from *yəkassəmennāh*, "it gnaws it", and the participle *məkurbāl* (I Chr. 15,27), "wrapped", is dissimilated through *bb* > *rb* from *məkubbāl*, attested in Mishnaic Hebrew. In Ethiopian Gurage dialects, the dissimilation through *r* is frequent, e.g.: *gərd* < *gədd*, "misery"; *korda* < *koddä*, "water bottle"; *irda* < *iddä*, "carding bow", etc. Rare examples of progressive dissimilation through *r* are attested in Hebrew with *dibrē* < *dibbē* (Assyro-Babylonian), "words", followed by the denominative verb *dibber*, *yədabber*, "to speak", and other derivatives, and in Arabic with *batta*, "to cut off", dissimilated in *batara* or in *bat(t)ala*, with *l* (§17.5).

23.10. The glottal stop serves for the disjunction of a geminated consonant in some West Gurage dialects, e.g. *gum'a* vs. *gumma*, "club"; *gun'är* vs. *gunnär/n*, "head". This feature can be interpreted as dissimilation of gemination. A similar phenomenon may perhaps be observed in Middle Assyrian and in Neo-Assyrian, in words like *bi-'-ti* < *bittu* < *bintu*, "daughter"; *pe-'-ta* < *pettu* < *pēntu*, "charcoal"; *sa-'-te* < **sattu* < *san/mtu*, "morning dawn", although the change *n* > ' is well attested in these dialects when *n* appears in intervocalic position (§17.2). However, this is not the case in the present examples, since the spellings *bittu* (*bi-it-ta-*, *bi-it-tá*) and *pettu* (*pé-et-tum*) are likewise attested in cuneiform texts.

23.11. The semivowel *y* serves, e.g., for the disjunction of a geminated liquid in the Arabic verbal form *ṭayla'* < *ṭalla'*, "he brought up", attested in Lebanon.

15. SYLLABLE

24.1. The syllable is a sound or combination of sounds uttered together or at a single impulse of the voice, and constituting a word or part of a word. Authors generally assume that every Semitic syllable originally began with one consonant and one only. However, at least in consequence of the phonetic and morpho-phonemic evolution of the languages, a word can also begin with a vowel or with a two-member cluster of consonants (§17.9). One might even invert the reasoning and conclude from spoken languages that the above-mentioned phonological principle of classical literary languages results from standardizing tendencies which aim at committing speech to writing.

24.2. Assuming that every syllable begins with a consonant, one can distinguish three types of syllables in Semitic: 1° an open syllable consisting of a consonant or a consonant cluster followed by a vowel, short (Cv, CCv) or long ($C\bar{v}$, $CC\bar{v}$); 2° a closed syllable consisting of a consonant or a consonant cluster followed by a vowel, short or long, which is followed in its turn by a consonant (CvC, $CCvC$, $C\bar{v}C$, $CC\bar{v}C$); 3° a doubly closed syllable consisting of a consonant followed by a vowel, which is followed either by a long or geminated consonant or by a two-consonant cluster, the first member of which is often a liquid ($CvCC$).

The orthographical ambiguity of syllabic cuneiform has a bearing on syllabic structure, especially in Palaeosyrian and in Old Akkadian. Thus, an orthographically open syllable may represent a syllable actually closed by a guttural, by a "weak" l (§17.2), or by a geminated consonant; e.g. Palaeosyrian *Da-mu* stands for the divine name **Da'-mu* and *kà-ma-tum* represents either *kal-ma-tum*, "parasite", "louse", or **kam-ma-tum*, with an assimilation *lm > mm*. On the other hand, one orthographically closed syllable may stand for two open syllables and represent a value of the type *CvCv*, unless one assumes that a short unstressed vowel was elided. Such elisions are not exceptional in the Old Babylonian of Mari (e.g. *ilkamma* for *illikamma*, "he came here"; §25.5) and they occur also at Ebla; e.g. Sumerian KU₄ ("to enter") = *ma-sa-gàr-tù-um* or *mas-gàr-tum* /*mašagārtum*/, probably "asylum", a nominal derivative in *ma-* (§29.21) from the causative **šagār* (cf. Arabic *'aǧāra*, "cause to enter" a sanctuary, "grant asylum") of the verb *ǧūr* (cf. Sabaic *gr*, "enter" a sanctuary). Instead, the often assumed hypothesis that two orthographically open syllables of the Ebla texts, as *ma-sa-*, may represent one closed syllable, thus *mas-*, is contrary to the old scribal practice, well-known from Old Akkadian, and it may lead to an incorrect interpretation of variant spellings. Such cases occur instead in Late Babylonian (§21.11).

24.3. Quantitatively, a syllable may be short, long or ultra-long: 1° a syllable is short when it ends in a short vowel (*Cv*: e.g. *bi-*, "in"); 2° a syllable is long when it ends either in a long vowel or in a consonant following a short vowel (*Cv̄*: e.g. *lā*, "not"; *CvC*: e.g. *min*, "from"); 3° a syllable is ultra-long, when it ends either in a consonant following a long vowel, or in a geminated or long consonant, or in a two-consonant cluster (*Cv̄C*: e.g. *qām*, "he stood up"; *CvCC*: e.g. *'amm*, "paternal uncle"; *kalb*, "dog").

24.4. The vowels are always short in a closed unstressed syllable and long vowels show a tendency to become short when their syllable closes. In Arabic, the shortening of long vowels in closed syllables became a general rule, e.g. *qam* < *qām*, "he stood up". However, there are exceptions in pausal forms of Classical Arabic, when the final vowel is dropped in pronunciation (e.g. *nāzilūn* < *nāzilūna*, "descendants"), and in the case of long consonants that can either be shortened (e.g. *ḍallūn* > *ḍā/lun*, "straying, erroneous") or be pronounced long in the beginning of the following syllable (e.g. *ḍā/llun*). This phenomenon leads to the elimination or restriction of syllables of the type *Cv̄C*, but opens the way to syllables of the type *CCvC*.

24.5. Also long or geminated consonants show a tendency to become short, especially at the end of a syllable (§23.2). This shortening is a general feature in Hebrew at the end of a word (e.g. *'am* < *'amm*, "people", with a plural *'ammīm*), while modern Ethiopian dialects can avoid it by splitting the long or geminated consonant by means of an anaptyctic vowel (e.g. *qurər* < *qurr*, "basket" in Gurage). In Arabic, this shortening appears, e.g., in *fa-qaṭ* < **fa-qaṭṭ*, "only", and in verbs with a second long or geminated radical (e.g. *ẓaltu* or *ẓiltu* < **ẓall-tu*, "I became"), unless the long consonant is split by an anaptyctic vowel (e.g. *ẓaliltu*).

24.6. Short vowels tend to become long in open and in stressed syllables. It is difficult to perceive this phenomenon in a correct way in languages written in cuneiform syllabograms (§21.5), but this is the case in certain forms of West Semitic verbs with last radical ' when the latter loses its consonantal value, e.g. Hebrew *qāra'* > *qārā*, "he called"; Arabic *nabbā* < *nabba'(a)*, "he announced". In Phoenician, the accent shift to the final syllable occasioned its lengthening with the eventual change *ā* > *ō*, e.g. *yátan* > *yatā́n* > *yatṓn*, "he gave".

24.7. There are also some cases of consonant doubling after a short open syllable (§23.1), e.g. in the Hebrew plural *gəmallīm* < **gəmalīm*, "camels", or in Aramaic *'attānā* < *'atānā*, "she-ass". This results in a change of the nature of the syllable in question which becomes closed and long.

24.8. There is a wide tendency in classical Semitic languages to eliminate two-consonant clusters at the beginning or at the end of a word by adding a supplementary vowel either between the two consonants or at the beginning, respectively at the end of the word. Beside the anaptyctic vowels of *qurər* and *ẓaliltu* (§24.5), one can refer to the Hebrew verbal form *nif'al*, "was made", differing from the corresponding Arabic form *'infa'ala* by the place of the supplementary vowel *i* which is added in Arabic at the beginning of the word, while it is inserted in Hebrew between the prefix *n-* and the first radical of the verb. In both cases, the addition of the vowel results in a new syllable *'in/fa'ala* or *nif/'al*. A vowel can also be added at the end of a word, e.g. to the imperative of the verbs with second long or geminated radical: *massi* or *massa*, "touch!", *firri* or *firra*, "run away!", both in Arabic. The same phonetic device is used in Tigrinya with nouns ending in a cluster of consonants; e.g. *kälbi*, "dog"; *'əzni*, "ear". Instead, Amharic often breaks final clusters by inserting an anaptyctic vowel *ə*; e.g. *əgər*, "foot"; *näbər*, "leopard". The Assyro-Babylonian imperative *dubub*, "speak!", has an anaptyctic vowel *u* splitting the geminated consonant. In all these cases, the addition of a vowel results in the appearance of a new syllable.

24.9. This tendency is absent from most modern colloquials and its partial absence may be traced back at least to the Late Antiquity and early Middle Ages. In fact, besides the two-consonant clusters formed with a liquid, like *naḥl*, "palm trees", or αρσ, "earth" (§17.9), one can point, e.g., to the transliteration κοδϭ of Hebrew *qdš*, "holiness", in Origen's Hexapla, to Masoretic Hebrew *štayim* and to Syriac *štā*, "two". Although the palato-alveolar *š* may conceal some phonetic affinities with liquids in these particular cases, the fluctuating pronunciations of Hebrew *šəwa* (§21.19) and of Syriac words, with or without an ultra-short vowel *ə*, at least announce the modern colloquials with, e.g., the imperative *ptuḥ*, "open!" in Eastern Neo-Aramaic, the perfect *ktəbt*, "I wrote" in urban Maghrebine Arabic, or the noun *krämt*, "rainy season" in Amharic. However, some modern Arabic dialects and Western Aramaic show a clear tendency to introduce prosthetic vowels in such cases; e.g. Neo-Aramaic *ebra*, "son"; *iftaḥ*, "he opened" (§27.17).

24.10. In Arabic colloquials, the loss of ancient short vowels in open syllables and the shift of the accent from the stressed syllable of Classical Arabic to the following one completely changed the syllabic structure of the language. The pattern observable in nouns and verbs can be schematized as $C_1 \acute{v} C_2 C_3 > C_1 C_2 \acute{v} C_3$. E.g. classical *qamḥ(un)*, "wheat", was pronounced *qamăḥ* in Pre-Classical and Middle Arabic; it later became *qamáḥ* and finally *qmáḥ*, after the loss of the short unstressed syllable. A similar evolution can be observed in verbal forms, e.g. *báraqa > bráq*, "it lightened", with the reduction of the perfect to one syllable. A parallel phenomenon is attested in the Neo-Punic of North-Africa thanks to the *matres lectionis* marking the stressed syllable in words like *ndʿr [ndár] < *nidr*, "vow"; *skʿr [skár] < *sikr*, "memory"; *qbʿr [qbár] < *qabr*, "tomb"; *ʿsʿr [ʿsár] < *ʿasr*, "ten". Like in Arabic, this phase was preceded by a dissyllabic realization of the nouns under consideration, as shown by Late Phoenician βααλ [*baʿal*] < **baʿl*, "lord"; Μααρ- [*Mahar-*] < *Mahr-*, "courier"; Αβεδμελεχε (vocative) [*ʿAbed-melek̠*] < **ʿAbd-milk*, "servant of the king". Also the Ethiopian languages make a fairly extensive use of prosthetic and anaptyctic vowels, but this does not lead to a radical elimination of original short vowels.

24.11. When vowels meet, a semivowel or the glottal stop is inserted in order to avoid the hiatus, unless there is elision or contraction (§22.15). The inserted *ʾ*, *y*, *w* introduce a new syllable.

16. WORD ACCENT

25.1. Orthography rarely indicates tone and stress. In Greek, tonal marks were added only in Alexandrian times and Hebrew accentuation was only introduced by the Masoretes in early Middle Ages. Yet, these elements are of the highest importance, above all if there is a stress accent with a phonemic status (§25.8). Now, in Semitic, an expiratory or stress accent exists in Hebrew, Aramaic, in certain Arabic colloquials such as the Syrian, and in certain Gurage dialects. The opposite, non-expiratory type of accent can be heard in Amharic and in Ethiopic in general, although the traditional pronunciation of Geʿez seems to show some principles for the stress of isolated forms and words. Early Arab grammarians did not deal with the subject and little can be said about "written" languages, although some variant spellings may reveal the impact of the stressed syllable or a shift in the position of the accent. Common Semitic or Proto-Semitic principles in this matter can only be highly hypothetical.

25.2. Considering modern colloquials from various regions, the word accent falls on the final syllable when the latter is ultra-long; e.g. *makātíb*, "letters", in the Arabic of the Ḥawrān, *něǧráḥt*, "I was wounded", in Maghrebine Arabic. The word accent may perhaps fall on the final syllable also when the latter is the result of contraction, e.g. Assyro-Babylonian *šanū́* < *šaniyu*, "second".

25.3. In other cases, the word accent does not fall on the ultima, even if it is long, contrary to the Jewish traditional pronunciation of Hebrew and of Aramaic. Generally, the stress falls then on the penult syllable which can be long or short, thus, e.g. in Maghrebine Arabic: *ríḥa*, "perfume", *ktěbna*, "we wrote"; in Arabic of the Ḥawrān: *katabúha*, "they wrote it", *katábū*, "they wrote"; in Syriac: *kétbat*, "she wrote"; *néhwē*, "he is". Concerning the 3rd person of the perfect in Geʿez, there is general agreement that the penult syllable is stressed, thus *nagára*, "he said"; the same situation is found in the South Ethiopian Harari, e.g. *säbára*, "he broke". The penult syllable is systematically stressed in the Samaritan pronunciation of Hebrew and Aramaic, e.g. *barášit bára ʾälúwem ʾit eššámem wit áreṣ*, "in the beginning God created heaven and earth" (Gen. 1,1). This accentuation seems to be confirmed by the *matres lectionis* of the Dead Sea scrolls, e.g. *swdm* /Sôdom/ in 1QIs[a] 1,10, against Masoretic *Sədóm* but in agreement with Greek Σόδομα.

25.4. However, in the Egyptian tradition of the Qur'ān reading, the position of the accent on the penult syllable is limited to the cases when the latter is long. Otherwise stress recedes until it meets a long syllable and, if there is no such, it comes to rest either on the first syllable of the word or on the antepenult, thus *qatálta*, "you killed", but *qátala*, "he killed"; *raqabatáni*, "you observed me", but *raqábatun* or *ráqabatun*, "slave". Besides, the final syllable of a noun in the construct state (§33.3) is considered as belonging to the following word, e.g. *ṭálaba/tu l-ʿílmi*, "quest of knowledge". The monosyllabic proclitic particles bear no stress.

25.5. It was assumed that the position of the word accent in East Semitic followed analogous principles, but such a reconstruction is based mainly on secondary deductions. However, *plene* writing occurs in accented syllables and does not necessarily mark phonemic length; e.g. Middle Babylonian *ma-a-ni* /*mánni*/, "who"; *še-e-mi-šu* /*šémišu*/, "his hearing"; *qá-a-ab-la-at ta-am-ti* /*qáblat tāmti*/, "the middle of the sea". But no systematic attempt was made until now to establish whether Assyro-Babylonian had an expiratory accent, which would have been a force in the word capable of bringing about, e.g., the reduction and complete elision of some vowels. Such elisions frequently occur in Mari letters (e.g. *il-ku* for *ílliku*, "they went", *te-še-em-ma* for *tešémmema*, "you will hear"), but they very likely reveal the stress accent of the Amorite linguistic substratum of the writers, and not that of Old Babylonian. However, Babylonian by-forms like *litmudu* / *litamdu*, "he understands", *damiqtu* / *damqatu*, "good" (feminine), are best explained by assuming stress on the first syllable.

25.6. The situation in some languages is the result of complicated developments, for which no clear phonological rules can be determinated to-day. Thus, the accentuation of the final syllable is dominant in the Jewish traditional pronunciation of Hebrew, but the accent falls on the penultimate in some particular cases, especially in "segolate" forms like *melek*, "king", as can be learned from Hebrew grammars. Also Phoenician, that appears to have had a strong stress accent, usually accentuates the final syllable of the word, which was tone-lengthened with the consequent change *ā* > *ō* (e.g. *yatṓn* < *yatán* < *yátan*, "he gave"). The place of the accent, and its strong stress character, may be judged from the apparent reduction of short unaccented vowels in the penult syllable (e.g. Ιεδουδ [*Yədū́d*] < *yadū́d*, "beloved").

25.7. Although it is difficult to generalize, the stress falls also in Modern South Arabian languages on the final syllable wherever there is no penult long syllable in the form under consideration. This tendency is even stronger in the Arabic dialects of the area, as in Ḏofār *ḥabál*, "pregnancy"; *gitlát*, "she killed". In Soqoṭri, however, stress is regularly on the penultimate and all the vowels are phonologically short. In some West Gurage dialects, the accent falls on the last syllable of the verbs, but on the penult syllable of the nouns, e.g. *tā'äbắ*, "he washed himself", but *wăka*, "beam". In Tigre, instead, stress is non-distinctive and shifts easily from one syllable to the other. It is also difficult to determine where stress falls in Tigrinya, though it falls usually on the final syllable of a word, but it is conditioned by the general sentence stress or pitch.

25.8.   An important question is whether word stress or tonic accent has or has not a phonemic status, in other words: whether there are tonemes in Semitic. In Masoretic Hebrew accentuation has a phonemic value in some grammatical constructs rather than in lexical items. Thus, the stress is a distinguishing feature between certain pairs of words, e.g. *bắnū*, "among us", and *bānū́*, "they built"; *bắʾā*, "she is coming", and *bāʾắ*, "she came"; *qū́mī*, "get up!" (feminine), and *qūmī́*, "my getting up" (infinitive); *šắbū*, "they returned", and *šābū́*, "they captured". A similar situation occurs in spoken Neo-Aramaic, e.g. *nášele*, "he is a man", and *našéle*, "he is their man". Instead, also lexical items can be contrastive in stress in West Gurage dialects: some verbs can be distinguished from certain nouns only through the place of the stress, which falls on the last syllable of the verb, but on the penultimate syllable of the noun, e.g. *eppắ*, "he made", and *éppä*, "toga"; *ēnzắ*, "he seized", and *énzä*, "thatch" (grass to cover the houses); *dekkắ*, "he is long", and *dékkä*, "long"; *wäkắ*, "he pierced", and *wắka*, "beam". Considering the existence of archaic features in South Ethiopic, one can assume that the word stress may have had a distinctive or phonemic status in Proto-Semitic, e.g. in the case of the preterite *yáqtul* / *yíqtul*, "he killed", and of the jussive *yaqtúl* / *yiqtúl*, "may he kill!" (§38.2), since the word accent seems to be the only distinguishing feature between this pair of verbal forms. But we are moving here on ground that has not been satisfactorily investigated, even if authors often assume that word stress is not phonemic in several Semitic languages, e.g. in Arabic and in Assyro-Babylonian.

17. SENTENCE STRESS OR PITCH

26.1.   Sentence stress or pitch affects the meaning of whole sentences, but it is not an integral part of any word. It gives expression to sentences and conveys shades of meaning which cannot conveniently be expressed by other means. In Semitic languages, declarative, exclamatory, and interrogative sentences generally differ merely in intonation, though sometimes — particularly in written language — a question may be introduced by a word indicating that the sentence is a question or the order of words in the sentence may differ from the ordinary one. Investigations into Semitic phonology and syntax must include intonation and pitch, but so far no serious work has been done on the subject, though much important material can be adduced from spoken and even "written" languages, especially from letters. We must therefore limit ourselves to some general observations on the falling and rising pitch patterns.

26.2. In a declarative sentence, the last syllable is generally lower in pitch than the penultimate. This common and spontaneous phenomenon has a repercussion on the traditional recitation of the Qur'ān and of the Hebrew Bible, and gives rise to the so-called "pausal" forms. Thus, in Arabic, final short vowels, case endings, and feminine noun endings are dropped (e.g. *kataba* > *katab*, "he wrote"; *malikun* > *malik*, "king"; *qāḍīn* > *qāḍī*, "magistrate"; *malikatun* > *malikah*, "queen"), with a consequent anaptyxis in monosyllabic roots (e.g. *'al-bakrun* > *'al-bakur*, "young [camel]"). In Masoretic Hebrew, stress retrocedes to the penult syllable (e.g. *'ānōkī́* > *'ānṓkī*) and a short accented vowel is lengthened or changes its quality (e.g. *máyim* > *mā́yim*, "water"; *'ereṣ* > *'ā́reṣ*, "earth"). Pausal phenomena occur also in modern Arabic dialects. In Yemen, e.g., either a nasalization may affect vowels standing in the pausal position (e.g. [*wallī́ⁿ*] for *walli*, "he went"), or pausal consonants may be pre-glottalized and devoiced (e.g. [*awlā't*] for *awlād*, "children"). In Syro-Palestinian and Egyptian dialects, vowel lengthenings (e.g. *byúktōb* for *byúktub*, "he will write"), diphthongizations (e.g. *yimšów* for *yimšū*, "they will go"), vocalic changes (e.g. *kalbi* for *kalba*, "bitch"), etc., may occur, but no accent shift has been registered.

26.3. In an interrogative sentence, on the other hand, the different speaker's commitment is discernible mainly from a higher pausal pitch. In other words, a question must be said with a rising tone, particularly toward the end when the latter corresponds to the point of greatest significance in speech; in any case, the last syllable must be heard as being on a higher pitch than the penultimate. This may be expressed in writing by the additional final sign *-ú* in *is-li-mu-ú*, "did they make peace?", in an Old Babylonian letter from Mari suggesting a pitch *islimú* instead of the normal *íslimū* (§ 10.6).

26.4. The exclamatory intonation implies a high pitch and a consequent shortening of the words, as shown by the "pausal" forms used in Classical Arabic for the vocative (e.g. *yā 'ammā*, "oh! uncle!") and even by the occasional dropping of the final radical of the word (e.g. *yā ṣāḥi < ṣāḥibu*, "oh! friend!"). This is confirmed by the apocopated forms of the jussive in various Semitic languages (§39.14-18).

26.5. The stress of conjoined clauses appears to be influenced in the main by the meaning of the sentence as a whole and, like the order of words in the sentence, is essentially governed by semantic considerations. In particular, logical hypotaxis seems to be indicated by the stress falling not on the verb of the main clause, but on the beginning of the logically dependent clause, especially when there is formal asyndetic parataxis (§55); e.g. Arabic *qul yáġfirū*, "tell that they should forgive". A sentence of any length has several accents, but only one of them is the main sentence stress. The place of the secondary accents is based principally on the word accent, which appears to be conditioned by proclitics, enclitics, subjoining words, though the interval between accents, whether primary or secondary, is scarcely more than two or three syllables; e.g. Arabic *kállimī rasúla lláhi yukállim...*, "speak to God's envoy he should speak..." In other words, sentence stress has a syntactical function.

18. CONDITIONED SOUND CHANGES

27.1. The natural tendency of the speaker is to limit effort in his speech and to avoid sharp shifts in the use of speech organs. This leads to a chain of assimilations of one sound to another. Only when this assimilation is particularly sharp is the change felt. At other times, a sequence of similar sounds demands a greater effort from the speaker and he tends to dissimilate them. Another type of change is metathesis, while elision, prosthesis, anaptyxis, haplology, etc., aim at facilitating or simplifying the emission of speech sounds in various ways. Hypercorrection is instead an intentional but erroneous correction of the spelling or of the pronunciation of a word.

A. Assimilation

27.2. Assimilation is the main type of conditioned sound changes. There is partial and total assimilation, contiguous and distant, progressive and more often regressive, and reciprocal assimilation. Assimilation may take place between consonants, between vowels, and between a consonant and a vowel. It amounts to a monophonemization, to a phonemic merger or shift, if the resulting sound becomes distinctive and significant (cf. §10.7, 12).

a) Assimilation between Consonants

27.3. Assimilation between consonants takes most often place between a liquid *l*, *r* or the nasal *n* and another consonant, the common type being here total regressive assimilation, perhaps better termed "anticipatory", since the vocal organs "anticipate" the position of the next sound.

The main types of Semitic consonantal assimilation are the following:

bk > kk	*nd > dd*	*rl > ll*
bt > pt	*nḏ > ḏḏ*	*rn > nn*
dn > nn	*nf > ff*	*rs > ss*
dš > ss	*ng > gg*	*rz > zz*
dt > tt	*nh > nn*	*sf > ss*
ḏt > dd	*nk > kk*	*ṣf > ṣṣ*
kr > kk	*nl > ll*	*ṣt > ṣṣ/ṣṭ*
ld > dd	*nm > mm*	*td > dd*
lk > kk	*np > pp*	*th > tt*
ln > nn	*nṣ > ṣṣ*	*tk > kk*
lq > qq	*nt > tt*	*tn > nn*
lr > ll	*nṭ > ṭṭ*	*tš > šš*
lš > šš	*nz > zz*	*ṭṭ > ṭṭ*
lt > ss	*qt > qṭ*	*tz > zz*
mb > bb	*rd > dd*	*ṯṯ > tt*
nb > bb/mb	*rk > kk*	*zt > st*

a) Thus, vowelless *n* assimilates regularly to a following consonant: e.g. in Old Akkadian and in Assyro-Babylonian **indin > iddin*, "he gave"; in Amorite *yanṣib > yaṣṣib*, "he raised"; in Phoenician and North-Israelite Hebrew **šnt > št /šatt/*, "year". In Thamūdic, in Liḥyānite, and in Ṣafaitic, the *n* is sometimes assimilated to a following consonant (e.g. *'t* /'atta/ < *'anta*, "you"; *mg't* < *manǧa'+t*, "feed-place"; *'ṯṯ* /'aṯṯat/ < *'anṯat*, "woman") contrary to Classical Arabic, but in agreement with certain colloquials where forms like *bitt < bint* occur occasionally, e.g., North Arabian *munḏū > muḏḏū*, "since"; Andalusian Arabic *'anta > att*, "you"; *kīn tarā > kittarā*, "you would see", with the auxiliary verb *kīn* (classical *kāna*) used to express an eventuality. In Sabaic, we find **s¹tnṣr > s¹tṣr*, "he summoned to his support"; in Ge'ez inscriptions *'ǝnza > 'ǝzza*, "while"; in Gurage *känfär > käfär*, "lip"; in Gafat *samat / samǝttä* vs. Amharic *samǝnt*, "week". The occasional or dialectal loss of a vowel may also lead to the regressive assimilation of *n*, as in ιβωρθ transcribing Late Babylonian *ina būrti*, "through the cistern".

b) Vowelless *l* assimilates to various consonants, most prominently in the case of the Arabic article *'al-* (e.g. *'al-šams > [aššams]*), but also in

Assyro-Babylonian (e.g. *nalšu* > *naššu*, "morning dew"), in Hebrew
(**yilqaḥ* > *yiqqaḥ*, "he takes"), in Aramaic (*'l dbr* > *'dbr*, "because
of"), in colloquial Arabic (e.g. *ma-qtel-nā-š* > *ma-qten-nā-š*, "he didn't
kill us"), in Tigre (e.g. *halla 'əl-ka* > [*hallakka*], "it is to you"; *mən
la-bet* > [*mənnā bet*], "from the house"). Instead, the assimilation of a
sibilant to *l* is exceptional, as in Palaeosyrian *su-lu-la-a*, "of the two
horns (of the moon)", from **sul-sul* (cf. Hebrew *salsillōt*, "shoots").

c) The assimilation of *r* to the following consonant is well attested in
various West Gurage dialects, e.g. *gurda* > *gudda*, "solemn oath";
bärzaz > *bäzāz*, "dream". It occurs in North and West Semitic, e.g.
kakkaru or *kikkār*, "round disk", "round loaf", "talent" (weight), to
compare with Sabaic *krkr*, Egyptian Demotic *krkr*, "talent", also with
Arabic *kirkira(tun)* used metaphorically to designate the callous protuberance on the breast of dromedaries which, when the animals lie down,
rests upon the ground "like a cake of bread" (E.W. Lane).

d) Also labials and dentals may be assimilated, as well as other consonants, e.g. in the Palaeosyrian noun *kak-kab* < *kabkab*, "star"; in the
Phoenician name of the god *mlqrt* < **milk-qart*, "the king of the city";
in Assyro-Babylonian **(w)ālidtu* > *(w)ālittu*, "the one who bore"; in
Hebrew and in Sabaic **'ḥdt* > *'ḥt*, "one" (feminine); in Hebrew **mit-
dabber* > *middabber*, "speaking to himself"; in Aramaic, the divine
name *'Aṯtar* > *'Attar*; in Ge'ez inscriptions *'əmbəḥəru* > *'əbbəḥəru*,
"from the sea".

e) Transcriptions of proper names in other scripts allow us to distinguish assimilations from elisions; e.g. Palmyrene *'bnrgl* < *'bd-Nrgl*,
"Servant of Nerigal", shows the assimilation *dn* > *nn*, as indicated by
the Latin form *Abinneric(h)us*; Old Syriac *'mšmš* < *'mt-Šmš*, "Handmaid of Šamaš", results from the assimilation *tš* > *šš*, as shown by
Greek Αμασσαμσης, etc.

27.4. Total progressive assimilation frequently occurs in verbal forms
with infix *t* (§41.25), e.g. in Assyro-Babylonian **uṣtabbit* > *uṣṣabbit*,
"he imprisoned"; **aṭtarad* > *aṭṭarad*, "I sent"; in Arabic **iṭtalaba* >
'iṭṭalaba, "he sought". It is attested in Hebrew with the pronominal suffix *-hū*, e.g. **yilkədenhū* > *yilkədennū*, "he shall capture"; *gəmālathū* >
gəmālattū, "she weaned him". There are also other cases, e.g. in Gurage
wäsfi > *wässe*, "awl"; in colloquial Arabic *niṣf* > *nəṣṣ*, "half".

27.5. Total reciprocal assimilation implies the change of both consonantal sounds in an intermediary one, e.g. in Classical Arabic **iḏtakara*

> *iddakara*, "he remembered", where the contact of the voiced inter-
dental *ḏ* with the voiceless dental *t* gives rise to the geminated voiced
dental *dd*. In Neo-Assyrian *ilteqe* > *isseqe*, "he took", pronounced
/*iśśeqe*/, the contact of the liquid *l* with the dental *t* gives rise to the
geminated dental lateral *ś* (§15.2).

27.6. Partial regressive or "anticipatory" assimilation occurs e.g. in
Geʽez *'agā'ɔzt* > *'agā'ɔst*, "lords", where the devoicing *z* > *s* partially
assimilates *z* to the voiceless *t*. In Maghrebine colloquial *šrapt* < *šrabt*,
"I drink", the devoicing *b* > *p* partially assimilates *b* to the voiceless *t*.
The change *nb* > *mb* occurs frequently, e.g. Arabic *'anbar* > *'ambar*,
"ambergris"; *minbar* > *mimbar*, "pulpit, rostrum"; Tigre *'ɔgɔl tɔnbar* >
tɔmbar, "in order that you live", *'ɔnbe* > *'ɔmbe*, "we said".

27.7. Partial progressive assimilation occurs frequently with verbal
infix *t* which changes into emphatic *ṭ* when it is contiguous to another
emphatic consonant, e.g. in Neo-Assyrian **aqtirib* > *aqṭirib*, "I
approached"; in Aramaic **yiṣtabbaʽ* > *yiṣṭabbaʽ*, "it is immersed"; in
Hebrew **niṣtaddāq* > *niṣṭaddāq*, "we shall prove our innocence"; in
Arabic, **iṣtabaġa* > *iṣṭabaġa*, "it was dyed". The assimilation is total
when the contiguous consonant is *ṭ* (§27.4). Another partial progressive
assimilation, frequent in Neo-Babylonian and in Late Babylonian, occasions the change *nk* > *ng*; e.g. *kangu* < *kanku*, "sealed"; *ramānga* <
ramānka, "you yourself".

27.8. There are also cases of non-contiguous assimilation between
consonants. Besides the possible occurrences which can be best interpreted in a different way (§10.8), one can mention the partial regressive
assimilation of voice in Gurage **timbäräkä* > *dimbäräkä*, "to kneel
down", and the partial progressive assimilation of voice in Gurage
ṭäpäbä > *'epäpä*, "to be narrow". Regressive nasalization explains the
West Semitic names *Minyamēn* < *Binyamēn* and Μιννναίος < *Bin-*
Nanay, while the latter's feminine counterpart Βαθναναία / Βιθναναία,
"Daughter of Nanay", remains unchanged. The trill consonant *r* occasions changes ' > ʽ and ʽ > *ġ* in Arabic where, e.g., *ġarb*, "West", and
its derivatives are etymologically related to Ugaritic and Epigraphic
South Arabian *ʽrb*. Inversely, Śḥeri *ġarb* and Mehri *ġōreb*, "base of
neck", correspond to Hebrew *ʽorep*, "base of neck", and Arabic *ʽurf*,
"mane (of a horse)". In Ḥaḍramawt colloquial, e.g., attention was paid
to *barraʽ* < *barra'* < *barran*, "outside", and to *raʽa* < *ra'a*, "behold!"

The influence of *r* also explains the prosthetic *'a-* in nouns like *'aqrab*, "scorpion", and *'akbar*, "mouse". In Arabic words borrowed by Libyco-Berber, *q* may change into *ġ* in the proximity of *r*; e.g. *-warġ-*, "yellow", from *wariq*; *-ġra-*, "to read, to study", from *qarā*, attested next to *ġr*, "to call". Besides, *r* may also cause the change of a non-emphatic consonant in an emphatic one in modern Arabic dialects, e.g. *ra's* > *rāṣ*, "head", at Aleppo; *darb* > *ḍarb*, "road, at Essaouira (Morocco). There are also examples of partial assimilation of non-emphatic to distant emphatic consonant, e.g. in Gurage *wädäqä* > *wäṭäqä*, "to fall".

b) Assimilation between Vowels

27.9. Assimilation between vowels is always at distance, since the structure of Semitic syllables does not admit contiguous vowels (cf. §22.15). Vowel harmony is widely attested in Semitic, especially in Assyrian. It can be partial, as in Assyro-Babylonian *ḫiblātu* > *ḫiblētu*, "damage" (progressive), or *uḫappi* > *uḫeppi*, "he struck" (regressive), or total, as in Palaeosyrian *'aḫírtum* > *i-ḫir-tum* [*'iḫírtum*], "issue", "rest", in Ugaritic **'allūpu* > *'ulp* /*'ullūpu*/, "prince", "chief" (regressive), or in Gurage *əbbut* > *əbbət*, "pile" (progressive). Typical cases of regressive total assimilation occur in Assyrian and in Classical Arabic when the vowel of the noun is assimilated to the vowel of the case ending, e.g. in Assyrian *qaqqudu*, "head" (nominative), *qaqqidi* (genitive), *qaqqada* (accusative); in Classical Arabic *'imru'un*, "man" (nominative), *'imri'in* (genitive), *'imra'an* (accusative). Vowel harmony occurs also after *-i/-ī* in the pronominal suffix *-hu/-hū* of Classical Arabic (e.g. **sāriqihū* > *sāriqihī*, "of his thief"; **sāriqīhu* > *sāriqīhi*, "of his thieves") and in Hebrew "segolate" nouns (e.g. *keleb* < *kāleb* < **kalb*, "dog"). The regressive total assimilation of vowels may take place in Tigrinya, e.g. *ṣälot* > *ṣolot*, "prayer"; *mädoša* > *modoša*, "hammer"; *nəgus* > *nugus*, "king"; *kəfu'* > *kufu'*, "wicked".

c) Assimilation between a Consonant and a Vowel

27.10. Assimilation between a consonant and a vowel can consist in the influence of the vowel either spirantizing the following labial, dental, or velar (§11.10; 18.5), or palatalizing the following velar (§18.6), e.g. in colloquial Arabic *dīk* > *dīč*, "cock". Also a preceding dental may be palatalized, especially in Ethiopian languages; e.g. Tigre *gəzaž(ž)e*, "my glass", as against *gəzāz*, "glass"; *masāničče*, "my friends", as against *masānit*, "friends". Assimilation can further consist either in the velarizing effect of an emphatic consonant which brings about a change of other vowels into *o* / *u* (§10.9; 21.27), or in the influence of pharyngals, laryngals, and velar fricatives which frequently occasion a vocalic shift *a* > *e* in North and East Semitic (§19.5; 21.6-7), but also in West Semitic, as it appears e.g. from the transcription Κοσιδη of the Edomite name *Qwsyd'* in a bilingual ostracon from the 3rd century B.C. Instead, the gutturals bring about a change of other vowels into *a* in Masoretic Hebrew (e.g. **yišloḥ* > *yišlaḥ*, "he sends"), in ancient Arabic dialects (e.g. *yafruġu* > *yafraġu*, "he is at rest"; *luḥd* > *laḥd*, "grave-niche"), and in modern Egyptian colloquials of Cairo and of the Delta (e.g. *yifassaḥ*, "he takes out for a walk", vs. *yikammil*, "he achieves"; *'allim*, "he taught", vs. *killim*, "he spoke"), where *a* appears also in contiguity with emphatics. However, this change presents some dialectal variations or is optional, as it appears from Arabic and from the Hebrew of the Dead Sea scrolls, where e.g. *šlwḥ* /*šəloḥ*/ (1QIs^a 58,9) stands for Masoretic *šəlaḥ*. The Masoretic vocalization is paralleled by the appearance of secondary *a*-timbre vowels next to the consonants ', *ḥ*, and sometimes *h*, which were normally vowelless, e.g. **rūḥ* > *rū^aḥ*, "breath", *Ya'qob* (Ιακωβ) > *Ya'^aqob*, "Jacob". This phonetic notation of the Masoretes aimed probably at insuring a distinct pronunciation of the gutturals and may not reflect any really spoken language. However, it is comparable to some extent with East Arabian dialects which are characterized by the change $C_1aC_2 > C_1C_2a$ when C_2 is *h*, *ḥ*, *ḫ*, ', *ġ*; e.g. *ḥamar* for *'aḥmar*, "red"; *mġarib* for *maġrib*, "evening" (but cf. §24.10). One should also mention the phenomenon attested in the Western Neo-Aramaic dialect of Ǧubb 'Adīn and in the Arabic dialect of surrounding villages where the long vowels *ō*, *ū*, *ē*, and *ī* are prounounced with an off-glide *a* before any consonant; e.g. Neo-Aramaic *kē^afa*, "stone". Besides the emphatics, also labial consonants may cause other vowels to change into *u*, e.g. **libb* > *lubb*, "heart" in Arabic (regressive assimilation).

B. Dissimilation

27.11.   Dissimilation is the reverse of assimilation, i.e. it is a diphonemization or a differentiation of two or more identical sounds in a word by substituting for one of them another sound of similar type or position. Dissimilation can be progressive or regressive, contiguous or non-contiguous. Abstracting from the differentiation of long consonants or the so-called disjunction of gemination (§23,7-10), dissimilation is most often non-contiguous. It results in the develarization or deglottalization of one of a pair of emphatic consonants, in the voicing or devoicing of one of the consonants, or in the dissimilation of two homorganic sounds. E.g. Aramaic *kṭl* and Arabic *qtl* may point to an original *qṭl*, "to kill", with the first or the second emphatic develarized (but see §10.9), and Gurage *ṭarraqqa* > *därraqqa*, "moon", shows a deglottalization of *ṭ* which changes into a voiced *d*, since *q* is voiceless. A dissimilation of voice is attested e.g. in Gurage *dəmʷd* > *dəmʷt*, "meeting place of two rivers", and a dissimilation of homorganic sounds appears e.g. in Arabic *layl*, "night", > *lūn*, "to spend the night", and in Amorite *kabkabbu*, "star", changing into *kwkb* in Hebrew and *kawkab* in Arabic, although a spirantization of the first *b* may have helped the process in this particular case. There is also dissimilation of homorganic sounds in Arabic **wawāqī* > *'awāqī*, "ounces"; *wuǧūh* > *'uǧūh*, "faces"; **Madīnīy* (< *Madīna*) > *Madānīy* > *Madanīy*, "Medinan", where the dissimilation of the long vowels *i* is qualitative (*ī* > *ā*) and quantitative (*ā* > *a*). A dissimilation of vowels occurs also in Syriac, e.g. *Šlēmōn* for Hebrew *Šəlōmō* and Greek Σαλωμων, and in Masoretic Hebrew, e.g. *heḥākām* for **hāḥākām*, "the wise man".

C. Metathesis

27.12. Metathesis or transposition of sounds in a word occurs in all the Semitic languages. It is related to the phenomenon aptly expressed by the phrase "his tongue tripped". Metathesis can be contiguous, that is, the consonants that undergo metathesis are in contact without any vowel between them, e.g. Hebrew *śimlā* and *śalmā*, "coat", or Sabaic *'wld* and *'lwd*, "children". It can also be non-contiguous, that is, the consonants are separated by a vowel, e.g. Phoenician *ḥls* /ḥalōṣ/, Early Aramaic *ḥsl* /ḥaṣal/, and Tigre *laḥaṣa*, "to save"; Hebrew *kebeś* and *keśeb*, "lamb"; Hebrew *təʿālā* and Arabic *talʿa(tun)*, "water-course"; Hebrew *'āṣam* and Arabic *ġamaḍa*, "to shut the eyes"; Geʿez *nakasa* and *nasaka*, "he bit"; Harari *sinān* < *lisān*, "language", with a concomitant change *l* > *n* (§17.13-14); Tigre *mawarri* and *marawi*, "sticks"; Neo-Aramaic [*sāḥɪd*] < [*ḥazɪd*] (root *ḥṣd*), "to harvest"; Gurage *käbäzä* < *käzäbä*, "to lie". Metathetic relations appear also in the larger Afro-Asiatic realm, as it appears e.g. from the East Cushitic verb *ḍal* / *d'el* ("Sam" languages,

Oromo, Saho), "to give birth", to be compared with Semitic (w/y)ld, or Oromo *dabra* or *darba*, "to pass", related to Arabic *dabara*, "to pass".

27.13. In general, there are not enough examples of metathesis in the same language to warrant a definite statement on the phonetic conditions in which metathesis occurs. However, there is little doubt that one of the consonants involved in many cases is either *l* or *r*, i.e. one of the two "liquids". Beside the examples quoted in §27.12, one may refer e.g. to the name of the Cassite goddess known in Babylonia as *Šumaliya* but called *Šnm* at Ugarit, with an additional change *l* > *n* (§17.3-4). Assyro-Babylonian *simmiltu*, "ladder", corresponds to Hebrew *sullām*, and Persian *ḫurma*, "date", is borrowed in ʿOmānī Arabic as *ḫumra*. Both *ʾarġal* and *ʾaġral* mean in Arabic "sluggish". To Geʿez *ʿaqrab*, "scorpion", corresponds Tigre *ʿarqab*, while Aramaic *tarʿā* < *ṯrġ* parallels "Canaanite" *ṯġr* > *šʿr*, "gate", "door", etc.

27.14. Another allegedly paradigmatic example is provided by the verbal infix and prefix *t* of the verbal stems (§41.20-32) which is generally believed to be subject to metathesis with the first radical of the verb in precise conditions, i.e. when the first radical is a sibilant *s*, *z*, *ṣ*, *š*. In Assyro-Babylonian, the infix can be prefixed to the verbal form, e.g. **ṣitbutu* > *tiṣbutu*, "to grasp"; **zitqāru* > *tizqāru*, "eminent". In Hebrew, the prefix is placed after the first radical (e.g. **yitšammer?* > *yištammer*, "he is on his guard"), instead of being totally assimilated to it, as in Pre-Classical Arabic (e.g. **yatṣaddaq?* > *yaṣṣadaq*, "he will prove his righteousness"). These explanations are not really convincing and another point of view will be presented below (§41.24-25). In Aramaic, at least, further research is needed to see whether there is metathesis of a *tfʿl* stem or simply an example of a *ftʿl* stem, as in *ʾestəmek*, "he leaned".

D. Haplology

27.15. Haplology is the omission of one of two contiguous and almost identical syllables which occurs occasionally in various languages and can also be expressed in writing. E.g. Syriac **ʾaryiyā*, "lion", becomes *ʾaryā*; Hebrew *bəbēt*, "in the house", can be reduced to *bēt*; *mäzässē*, "sieve", in one Gurage dialect, becomes *mässē* in another one. In Arabic, *tataqātalūna*, "you fight", may be reduced to *taqātalūna*.

E. Prosthesis

27.16.   In order to disjoin an initial two-consonant cluster by producing
a new syllable, a prosthetic vowel is generally prefixed to the first consonant. This prosthetic vowel can be *i, e, ə < i, ä, u*, and it is introduced
by ' or *h* in idioms which require the presence of an initial consonant,
either pronounced or simply written. There are also animal names with a
prosthetic *'a-* that form a special category (§27.8; 29.17). The use of
written *h* is limited to the Hebrew verbal stem *hitpa'el*, probably by
analogy with the stem *hif'il*, while the other languages, as Aramaic and
Arabic, use ', e.g. *'ifta'ala, 'etkəteb*. Instead of a prosthetic vowel, an
anaptyctic vowel can be used (§27.19). A third mean of disjoining a
two-consonant cluster is attested in Tigrinya and in Harari, where an
auxiliary vowel *-i* is added at the end of a monosyllabic root (§24.8);
e.g. Tigrinya *kälbi*, "dog"; *bägli*, "mule"; Harari *qäbri*, "cemetery";
säbri, "endurance". This *-i* is attested also with roots ending in a geminated consonant, as Tigrinya *ləbbi*, "heart". The final *-i* can be dropped
if these nouns are followed by another word.

The initial *h* of some North and West Semitic words borrowed from Sumerian, as *hbrk*, "steward", *h(y)kl*, "palace", *hyn*, the Hurrianized name of the god
Ea, is not a prosthetic letter, but a reflex of Old Sumerian *h*.

27.17.   Beside the cases of composite verbal forms with initial cluster,
already explained when dealing with syllabic structure (§24.8), one
ought to mention the use of a prosthetic vowel in nouns like Palaeosyrian *íṣ-ba-um /'iṣba'um/ < *ṣba'*, "finger"; Ugaritic *'uṣb'*, "finger";
'udm't, "tears"; Hebrew *'ašmoret < *šmrt*, "night-watch"; Arabic *'ibn*
< bn, "son"; Gurage *ərkus / ärkus*, "impure", from *räk(k)äsä*, "he was
impure"; Assyro-Babylonian *ikribu*, "prayer" (cf. §29.16); the Phoenician divine name *'šmn* = Εσμουνος *< šmn*, "oil", etc. The same development occurs in Western Neo-Aramaic (§24.9) and in some modern
Arabic dialects after elision of an original short vowel; e.g. *iblād* from
bilād, "broken" plural of *balad*, "country"; *inḥās* from *nuḥās*, "copper", both in Egyptian Arabic. The prosthetic vowel is employed also
with foreign names, as Late Babylonian *Ik-se-nu-nu* for Ξένων, Punic
'klyn for Κλέων, Hebrew *'ptlmys* and *'btlmys* for Πτολεμαῖος, Ge'ez
'əsṭifanos for Στέφανος, and Arabic *'Aflāṭūnu* for Plato, or with loanwords like Neo-Aramaic *'usṭol* for Russian стол, "table"; Amharic
əsport, "sport". The prosthetic vowel is not required when the initial
cluster contains a liquid or the palato-alveolar *š*, like in the sound *št*

(§17.9; 24.9); e.g. Neo-Aramaic *grībā*, "bushel", an Old Persian word already borrowed into Imperial Aramaic (*grb*); Hebrew *štē*, "two", although the Tiberian Masoretes were pronouncing it *'ištē*.

27.18. A so-called "prosthetic" vowel *ä* or *ə* occurs in modern Ethiopian languages, especially before *l*, *r*, *s*, *š*, without serving to disjoin an initial cluster, e.g. *äsok*, "thorn", in Gurage. The vowel *u* is found in Harari *urūs*, "head" (root *r'š*).

F. Anaptyxis

27.19. Anaptyxis is the insertion of a supplementary vowel in a word in order to disjoin a two-consonant cluster by producing a new syllable. It is also called "epenthesis". The anaptyctic vowel can be used at the beginning of a word (e.g. *nif'al* = N-stem) or at its end, especially when a two-consonant cluster was created by the loss of case endings (§24.8), e.g. in *kalbu* > *kalb* > *kāleb* or *kalib*, "dog". However, anaptyxis did not spread automatically to all doubly closed syllables, as shown by Phoenician *qart*, "city", or *milk*, "king", where the presence of a liquid can dispense from using the anaptyctic vowel (§17.9; 24.9). Modern Semitic languages permit similar consonant clusters in initial and final position; e.g. Amharic *krämt*, "rainy season" (pronounced also as *kərämt*); *mängəst*, "government" (§17.9). Even plosive clusters occur regularly in Maghrebine Arabic, as *ktub*, "books", *ktabt*, "you wrote". Also the connexion of a noun in the construct state with its complement can make the insertion of a vowel superfluous, e.g. in Assyro-Babylonian *ri-ig-ma-Adad* [*rigm-Adad*], "the voice of Adad"; *zi-ik-re-el-ka* [*zikr-elka*], "the mention of your god"; *ša-ak-ne-Ellil* [*šakn-Ellil*], "the trustee of Ellil". But the use of the anaptyctic vowel is attested in other cases for the same nouns: *ri-gim* < *rigmu*, *ša-ki-in* / *šá-kin* / *šá-kan* < *šaknu*, *zi-kir* < *zikru*. The systematic use of the anaptyctic vowel *e* in Masoretic Hebrew (e.g. *melek*, "king"; *māwet*, "death") is a unique feature which is not confirmed for a somewhat earlier period by Origen's Hexapla mentioning, e.g., κορβ for *qereb*, "middle"; αρσ for *'ereṣ*, "earth"; κοδὅ for *qodeš*, "holiness"; αρβ for *'ereb*, "evening", etc.

A widespread use of anaptyctic vowels gives a peculiar flavour to the Ebla texts where they cannot be reduced simply to a particular way of using the syllabograms; e.g. ^d*Sa-nu-ga-ru*$_{12}$, the Djebel Sindjar identified with the Moon-god and known later as *Šangar* or *Šaggar*, perhaps originally *Šañar*. A similar situation occurs with the Ethiopic syllabograms of the 6th order that are traditionally pronounced in Ge‘ez either vowelless or with the vowel *ə* < *i/u*. It stands to reason that these syllabograms were originally articulated with a very short vowel in all circumstances, thus e.g. *'adəbār*, "mountains", instead of the traditional *'adbār*.

G. Sandhi

27.20. Sandhi, meaning in Sanskrit "a placing together", designates the assimilative changes occurring in a word under the influence of neighbouring words uttered in consecutive speech. Thus, e.g., the spirantization of the consonants *b g d k p t* becomes operative also at the beginning of a word when the preceding one, uttered together in consecutive speech, ends in a vowel or in a consonant producing the spirantization. Sandhi is widely attested in Arabic, especially in the traditional recitation of the Qur'ān, e.g. in *Sūra* 24,44: *ḫalaqa kulla dābbatin*, "he created all the animals", is pronounced [*ḫalakkulla dābbatin*] with the dropping of the final -*a* of *ḫalaqa* and the assimilation *q-k* > *kk*. According to Sibawayh, to produce the phrase *hal* + *ra'ayta*, "did you see?", Tamīm speakers of Central and Eastern Arabia were saying [*harra'ayta*], with the assimilation *l-r* > *rr*; in Ḥedjaz, on the other hand, speakers pronounced it without assimilation. The sandhi-writing *'zlh* for *'zl lh*, "he went away" (cf. §65.4), is common in Galilean Aramaic and it became a rule in the Neo-Aramaic of Ma‘lūla. Similarly, the spelling *qwly*, etc., is used regularly in early South-Palestinian Arabic for *qul lī*, "tell me!". In Tigre, *halla 'əl-ka*, "it is to you", i.e. "you have", is pronounced [*hallakka*]. A sandhi-spelling, which involves the assimilation of *n* to the following consonant, is attested in some Old Phoenician inscriptions; e.g. *ḥṣ trb‘l byrm* for **ḥn yrm*, "arrow of Tūra-Baal, son of Yarīm". A similar development gave rise to the divine name *Mlqrt* < **milk qart*, "the king of the City", and to *mlkty* < **milk Kitti*, "king of Kition". In Hebrew epigraphy, the sandhi phenomenon leads to spellings like *ḥyhwh*, "Yahwe is alive", for *ḥy yhwh*.

H. Elision

27.21. Elision of vowels and "weak" consonants (*'*, *w*, *y*, *h*, *l*, *n*) is amply attested in Semitic languages, as already reported when dealing with these sounds.

27.22.   According to Sibawayh, in ancient Arabic dialects unstressed *i* and *u* were elided, thus reducing e.g. the dissyllabic nominal patterns *fi'il*, *fu'ul* to *fi'l*, *fu'l*, while *fa'il* and *fa'ul* were reduced to *fa'l* and the verbal forms *fa'ila* to *fa'la*. The elision of short vowels occurs also in modern Arabic dialects and in other languages under influence of a strong word accent (§25.5).

27.23.   When two vowels meet, either one is elided or a glide *w*, *y*, ' is produced (§ 22.15). When there is elision, following rules are generally applied: 1° the meeting of two like vowels results in the same long vowel, e.g. North Arabian *mnwt(w)* = Latin *Manavat* > *mnt* /*Manāt*/, one of the so-called "Allāh's daughters"; 2° the quality of the long or stressed vowel tends to prevail, e.g. Assyro-Babylonian *ibniū* > *ibnū*, "they have built"; 3° two phonetically distant vowels, like *a* and *i*, may produce a vowel with an intermediate point of articulation, e.g. Phoenician σαμημ- /*šamēm*/ < *šamayīm*, "heavens".

27.24.   Postvocalic and intervocalic ', *y*, *w* can be elided when they are not long or geminated. The remaining vowel is originally long and the process is practically identical with the contraction of the diphthongs *ay* / *iy* / *aw* > *ā* (§ 22.3-5); e.g. Punic *nasot* /*našṓt*/ < *našăti < *našá'ti*, "I carried"; Nabataean Aramaic *wldhm* for *wyldhm*, "and their children"; Pre-Classical Arabic *baqat* < *baqāt* < *baqiyat, "she remained"; colloquial Arabic *dale* < *dalā* < *dalaw*, "he drew". In West Semitic, at the time the orthography was fixed, the ' was still pronounced in some forms of the words where it was later elided. Thus, it is often kept as historical and etymological spelling without being articulated. This was probably the case also at Ugarit; e.g. the verb in *rḫt*[*h*] *yml'u* /**yumalli'ū*/, "they filled his hands" (KTU 1.16,V,28), was very likely pronounced [*yimallū*] or [*yumallū*] (cf. syllabic *ú-ma-lu-ú*; § 45.8).

27.25.   The *h* of the presentative *han (§49.6) may be elided in Ugaritic in intervocalic position: *wn* < *wa-hanna/*u* (KTU 1.3,V,38; 1.4,IV,50; V,6; 1.24,31), corresponding to the frequent Hebrew *wə-hinnē*. In Early Aramaic, at Tell Fekherye, there is elision of intervocalic *h* in pronominal suffixes: *klm* < *klhm*, *kln* < *klhn*, "all of them". Similarly, the *h* of the pronominal suffixes *-hu* / *-ha* is elided in Ethiopic (> *-u* / *-a*) and the masculine suffix *-hu* can be elided also in Hebrew (> *-ō*). It is omitted in the imperfect of the frequently used Ge'ez verbs *bəhla*, "to say", *kəhla*, "to be able", the imperfect being *yəbl*, *yəkl*.

Elision of *h* occurs further in North Gurage *hono*, "to be, to become" root *kūn*), when *h* is preceded by the *l* of the negative *al-*, thus *balonä*, "if he is not", for *balhonä*. In North Arabian, the elision of *h* is attested in the word *'ahl*, "family", "people", which is often written *'l* in Ṣafaitic; e.g. *ḏ-'l Ms¹k*, "from the people of Mašaku". A similar assimilation or elision must have occurred in the Libyco-Berber verb *llukk* < **hlukk*, "to tread on", and in the West Semitic forms *lk*, "go!", and *lkt*, "to go", of the very same verbal root.

27.26. The elision of an initial unstressed syllable *'a* occurs in Phoenician personal names (e.g. *Ḥīrṓm* < **'Aḥirṓm*), and also in some Aramaic names as *ḥlrm /Ḥīlarīm/* for *'Aḥīlarīm*, "May my brother be exalted!". Instead, Aramaic *ḥad*, "one", preserves the original monosyllabic character of the word (§35.3). The same phenomenon occurs in Mishnaic Hebrew, as shown e.g. by the name *L'zr* instead of biblical *'El'āzār*. This form is found in contemporary Palestinian inscriptions, in the New Testament (Λάζαρος), and in manuscripts not affected by hypercorrection (§27.29).

27.27. Also *l* and *n* are elided in certain conditions (§17.2). The nasal *n* is often assimilated (§27.3) or elided at the end of a word, like in Ge'ez *'ako*, "it is not", composed of the negative element *'a* and of the verb *kona*, "to be". An elision in the middle of a divine name is attested, e.g., by Neo-Punic *Abaddir* < **'abn 'addīr*, "Stone of the Mighty one". The liquid *l* can also be assimilated or elided, as the auxiliary *-al* in Harari before suffixes, e.g. *tisäbraš* < *tisäbralš*, "you (feminine singular) break", or the *l* of *B'l-šmyn* > *B'šm(y)n*, "Baal of the Skies", in various Middle Aramaic dialects.

27.28. The elision of the feminine ending *-t* at the end of a word is a widespread phenomenon attested in Semitic and in Late Egyptian (§30.4). If one hesitates to recognize this general trend in the Palaeosyrian personal name *Si-a-ḫa /Šī-'aḫat/*, "She is a sister" (rather "brother", *'aḫa*), from Tell Beydar (cf. §27.29), there is no doubt that the ending *-at* gave way to *-a* > *-ā* at some point in the history of several Semitic languages. The residual final *-a* was then indicated in Hebrew, in Aramaic, and in Arabic by the vowel letter *-h*, also by *-'*. It is uncertain whether *-h* functions already as *mater lectionis* in the Ugaritic equation *mḫrtt* = *mḫrth*, "plough-land", provided by parallel passages (KTU 1.6,IV, 3 = 14 cor. *mḫrtth*), but it is certainly used as a vowel letter from the 9th century B.C. on; e.g. Aramaic *ṭbh* in *tṣlwth ṭbh*, "praying to him is sweet"; Moabite *Mhdbh*, "Medeba"; Hebrew *m'h*, "hundred". In the first millennium B.C., final *-t* was dropped in Assyro-Babylonian pronunciation after *a / ā* and after *ē*; e.g. Neo-Assyrian *Ekallāte* transcribed *'glh* in Aramaic; *rēšāti*, "first fruits", transcribed *rsh*; *maqarrāt(e)*, "bales (of straw)", transcribed *mqrh*. The same process took place in Phoenician, first in the verb where this occurred before the fixing of the orthography (hence *p'l*, "she did"), later also in the noun where Neo-Punic spellings like *ṣdyq'*, "just", or *tm'*, "perfect", show the feminine ending *-ā* > *-ō*, confirmed by Latin transcriptions such as *Anna* for *Ḥnt*. The feminine ending *-t* was still preserved in Pre-Islamic North Arabian (e.g. Thamūdic *nqt* /*nāqat*/, "she-camel"; Liḥyānite *s¹nt*, "year"; Ṣafaitic *bkrt*, "young she-camel"; Palmyrene *'mt*, "folk"), but the spelling of feminine nouns in *-h* throughout the Qur'ān shows that final *-t* was elided in the Pre-Classical period and that the residual vowel *-a* was indicated by *-h*, that was already used as *mater lectionis* in Liḥyānite (e.g. *mh* /*mā*/, "what"; *'dh* /*'idā*/, "while"). A similar process occurred in Late Egyptian, as shown by number of Semitic and Greek transcriptions of Egyptian proper names; e.g. Aramaic *Pṭ'sy* for *P3-dì-3ś.t*, "Whom Isis has given".

27.29. In proper names, the elision of final consonants is attested in various places. At Ebla, e.g., the place name *Mug-rí-i*^{ki} occurs next to *Mug-rí-du*^{ki}, the personal name *A-mi-ì* occurs next to *A-mi-du* and probably designates the same person. In both examples, a hypocoristic suffix *-iy* is added to the name. At Emar, Hittite pseudo-hieroglyphic transcriptions, like *ma-li* for *malik*, *tà-ka* for *Dagān*, illustrate this phenomenon. In ancient South Arabian anthroponomy, the theophorous element *'Aṭṭar* occurs frequently without *r* at the end of a name.

I. Hypercorrection

27.30. Hypercorrection occurs when a speaker or a writer over-compensates for an error which he fears he might incur, as when an English speaker uses "whom" where "who" is required, since "whom" sounds more formal and hence seems, fallaciously, more correct. Such misplaced changes occur frequently in Mss., not only when a copyist endeavours correcting a normal scribal error, but especially when he tries to harmonize the idiom used by a writer with a "classical" form of the language. Thus, it can be shown, e.g., that Mediaeval copyists, and later the printers, tried to harmonize Mishnaic Hebrew with Biblical Hebrew because they considered departures from the latter one as mistakes. This "hypercorrecting" tendency let to a complete distortion of the linguistic structure of Mishnaic Hebrew in many manuscripts, printed texts, and finally grammars and dictionaries. E.g. the Mishnaic Hebrew word for "man" was *'ādān* instead of biblical *'ādām*, but the word was systematically "corrected" in more recent Mss., and it disappeared in printed texts. The pronominal suffix of the 2nd pers. masc. sing. was *-āk*, e.g. *dəbārāk*, "your word", but its vocalization was "corrected" into *-kā*, e.g. *dəbārəkā*. This phenomenon is not at all unusual where speakers and copyists try seriously to follow the rules of a "correct" language, but lack the necessary knowledge. Hypercorrection occurs also in Mandaic manuscripts, e.g. when scribes extend the archaizing spelling with *z* for *ḏ* to words in which *d* is etymological, thus writing *zeqlā* for *deqlā*, "palm-tree", *zəmā* for *dəmā*, "blood", etc. Fortunately, all these words with etymological *ḏ* and *d* are pronounced exclusively with *d* in colloquial Mandaic.

III

MORPHOLOGY

1. THE ROOT MORPHEME

28.1. The material of a language is generally taken to be its words. If Semitic languages can be considered as genetically related, it is because they exhibit a systematic correspondence of words in their morphology, especially in the inflectional patterns. Now, morphology is relatively resistent to radical linguistic mutation, but it may undergo a certain degree of change through internal diachronic development or by contact with other languages. This is the reason why a rather synchronic assessment of the characteristics of the Semitic root morpheme may differ somehow from a diachronic appreciation, as the one exposed in §28.4 ff. Most of the words of the historically attested Semitic languages are usually analyzed as being a combination of three consonants, and of one or more vowels. Such a conception was strongly advocated in the 10th century A.D. by Ḥayyudj of Fez whose ideas are generally followed up to now. According to this traditional grammatical analysis, the three consonants, called *radicals*, form the smallest lexical unit of the language and constitute the *root* morpheme (e.g. Arabic *ktb*, "to write"). This basic semantic element is assumed to be further qualified by a number of vowels or vowels plus consonants which either specify the meaning of the root and serve as lexical morphemes (e.g. *kitāb-*, "book"; *kātib-*, "writer"; *maktabat-*, "library"), or determine the grammatical category and act as grammatical morphemes (e.g. *kataba*, "he wrote"; *yaktubu*, "he writes").

28.2. The existence of biconsonantal roots in Semitic languages, besides the triconsonantal ones, cannot be denied, even apart from the roots that became biconsonantal in consequence of the dropping out of one of the radicals. Their number even increases significantly if one accepts that only two of the three radicals of the triconsonantal roots are the main bearers of the meaning and that the third one had at one stage the task of a determinant or modifier in very much the same way as occurs with vowels in the fully developed triconsonantal system. This is illustrated by the well-known example of the Hebrew verbs *prd*, *prm*, *prs*, *prṣ*, *prq*, *prr*, *prš*, etc., that have the radical *pr* in common and express the basic notion of "dividing".

28.3.   However, the Semitic triconsonantal or biconsonantal root, conceived as the smallest lexical unit, is only the abstract basis of a family of words used in the language and did never exist as a living reality in a spoken idiom. Such a situation does not occur in other language "families" where the roots also include vowels and can be pronounced by any speaker of the tongue under consideration. In English, for example, as in Indo-European languages in general, the roots include vowels and they constitute pronounceable realities, e.g. "to cut", "boy", "love". The same happens in languages as different as Chinese or Sumerian. In Sumerian, e.g., the root is a stable reality, as dingir, "god", gal, "great", d u, "to go", gub, "to stand". In fact, the morphological analysis of basic Semitic words and forms — especially the three -*a*-, -*i*-, and -*u*- classes of East Semitic and Arabic verbs (§37.1; 38.3, 15) — reveal a relative stability of radical vowels, which should therefore be regarded as forming part of the root. In other words, Semitic roots are *continuous* morphemes which are instrumental in derivation but subject to vocalic and consonantal change in this process which is based on continuous or discontinuous "pattern morphemes", both lexical and grammatical. However, for practical reasons and to keep in tune with the common usage of the Semitists, we shall often refer to the roots by indicating their sole consonants. This practice should be considered as a simple shorthand, without any morphologic bearing on the Semitic word structure.

28.4.   Contrary to the traditional opinion, the basic stock of the Semitic vocabulary appears to consist of monosyllabic root morphemes (e.g. *'ab*-, "father"; *ḫud*, "seize!") that can be extended by affixes, which are either lexical morphemes (e.g. *'ab-ūt*-, "fatherhood") or grammatical morphemes (e.g. *ya-ḫud-u*, "he seizes"). The derivational process can occasion phonetic modifications (e.g. *abbūtu*, "fatherhood" in Assyro-Babylonian), and further changes are due to the standardization of the monosyllabic root in accordance with a dissyllabic stem pattern, especially in the verbs (e.g. Arabic *ya'ḫud-u*), an evolution which took place already in the Proto-Semitic period. Despite these changes that Semitic has undergone, eight monosyllabic types of Semitic root morphemes can readily be distinguished in historical times, when complementary morphemes, like those specifying the grammatical gender (§30.10-11), were already agglutinated to the root. The root morphemes in question consist either of short syllables of the type Cv, or of long syllables as $C\bar{v}$, CvC and $C_1C_2vC_3$, or of ultra-long syllables, as $C\bar{v}C$, $C_1C_2\bar{v}C_3$, $C_1vC_2C_2$, and $C_1vC_2C_3$ (§24.3). Since the vowel length behaves like a consonant and since the initial or final two-consonant cluster is just a variant of a long or geminated consonant, one could also say that the monosyllabic roots are either short, or long, or ultra-long syllables. For clarity's sake, however, it is better to divide them into eight groups. Taking the three fundamental vowels a, i, u into account, one can then distinguish twenty-four sub-groups of monosyllabic roots. In this approach, the pronounceable two-consonant clusters are acceptable as well as in modern colloquials.

28.5.   There are three sub-groups of the Cv class, distinguishable on the basis of the vowels a, i, u. In general, these morphemes are proclitics or enclitics:

Ca: wa- > u-, -ma, "and"; ha- > a-, interrogative; ka-, "as, like"; la-, "truly";
       pa-/fa-, "and so, so that".
Ci: bi-, "in"; li-, "for".
Cu: lu-, "let it be, be it!"; du/tu, "that (one)" (cf. §28.6).

28.6.   The three sub-groups of the $C\bar{v}$ class are distinguishable on the basis of the long vowels $\bar{a}$, $\bar{i}$, $\bar{u}$:

$C\bar{a}$: $y\bar{a}$, "oh!"; $l\bar{a}$, "not"; $m\bar{a}$, "what?"; $q\bar{a}$, "gauge".
$C\bar{i}$: $k\bar{i}$, "because".
$C\bar{u}$: $g\bar{u}$, "voice"; $d\bar{u}$/$t\bar{u}$, "that (one)" (cf. §28.5); $l\bar{u}$, "truly"; $p\bar{u}$, "mouth".

The inflection of the nouns $q\bar{a}$, $g\bar{u}$, $p\bar{u}$ can bring about a change of the vowel, and their construct state may be used either with the -u of the nominative, or with -i attested also in the nominative and in the accusative, or with the vowel -a in the accusative; e.g. in Old Akkadian pu-i, pi-i, $pá$-i, "my mouth", pu-$šu$, pi-$šu$, $pá$-$šu$, "his mouth", all in the accusative. The Assyro-Babylonian nominative form qa-a confirms the $C\bar{a}$ pattern for the noun "gauge", while the Arabic construct state $f\bar{u}$ favours a $C\bar{u}$ root morpheme in the case of "mouth".

28.7.   The CvC class is well represented by monosyllabic nominal roots and verbal basic forms:

CaC: 'ab-, "father"; 'ah-, "brother"; had, "one"; ham-, "father-in-law"; yad-,
       "hand"; may-, "water"; ta'-, "ewe"; $gaš$, "come near!"; da', "know!";
       hab, "give!"; qah, "take!".

CiC: *'il-*, "god"; *bin-*, "son"; *ṯin-*, "two"; *šim-*, "name"; *din/tin-*, "give!";
   lid(ī), "bear!"; *lik*, "go!"; *rid*, "go down!"; *ṯib*, "sit down!".
CuC: *mut-*, "man"; *ruʿ-*, "companion"; *śu'-*, "sheep"; *ḫud*, "seize!".

Some specimens of this group may go back to a Proto-Afro-Asiatic pattern *CCvC* or *CvCC*, as a comparison with Libyco-Berber seems to suggest in a few specific cases. E.g. the Hebrew imperative *lēk* < **lik*, "go!", may originate from **hlik*, as Libyco-Berber *llukk*, "tread on!", would indicate, since the initial tense or long *ll* probably derives from **hl*. The Hebrew plural *mət-īm*, "men", is apparently related to the Libyco-Berber plural *midd-ən* or *mədd-ən*, "people", "men", where the tense *dd* suggests a link with Bantu *mu-ntu*, "man", and seems to imply a development *nt* > *tt* > *dd*, although Hausa *mutum* and East Semitic *mutu(m)* exhibit a non-geminated *t*.

28.8. The $C_1C_2vC_3$ class with a consonant cluster in initial position occurs frequently in modern Semitic languages, e.g. in Neo-Aramaic, but it was largely represented also in Pre-Classical languages, as shown e.g. by the imperative of triconsonantal verbs in the simple stem. However, there tend to be strict constraints on the formation of clusters in most languages; the best attested combinations involve one of the consonants *l, m, n, r* (§17.9), but labiovelar consonants (*kp, gb*) may play a role as well, since they are frequent in African languages (cf. §1.2).

$C_1C_2aC_3$: *rbaʿ*, "four"; *ṣbaʿ-*, "finger"; *ptaḥ*, "open!".
$C_1C_2iC_3$: *mri'*, "man"; *nzil*, "go down!".
$C_1C_2uC_3$: *d/ṯmur-*, "night-watch"; *sgul-*, "belonging"; *šmun-*, "olive-oil";
   ktub, "write!".

The clusters involved by these patterns are generally resolved in Classical languages by the addition of a prosthetic (§27.16-17) or an anaptyctic vowel (§27.19), which is often identical with that of the radical, particularly in the imperative of the simple stem: e.g. *'uktub*, "write!", *'inzil*, "go down!", but *'iftaḥ*, "open!", in Arabic; *kušud*, "seize!", *ṣabat*, "take!", but *limad*, "learn!", in Assyro-Babylonian; *'arbaʿ*, "four", in Hebrew and Arabic. Alternative forms with prosthetic or anaptyctic vowels can coexist, e.g. *Samun-* and Εσμουν-, the Phoenician divine name "Eshmun" derived from **šmun*.

28.9. The $C\bar{v}C$ class with an internal long vowel is well attested among nominal and verbal roots. This class comprehends, in particular, the so-called "weak" verbs of the type *śīm*, "to place", or *qūm*, "to get up", although there is a widespread opinion among scholars that Semitic and even Afro-Asiatic "weak" verbs have triconsonantal origins. They base themselves mainly on the Classical Arabic "weak" verbs. Now, Arabic morphology in general, and that of the verb in particular, reflects extensive late analogical formation, thus adapting monosyllabic roots to the triconsonantal system. This extensive analogical process makes Arabic less fitting for an analysis of the monosyllabic roots of the $C\bar{v}C$ class than most other Semitic languages. More insight might be found in Libyco-Berber verbs like *qqim*, "stay!", where the tense consonant *qq* could go back to a labiovelar q^w (§11.11; 18.7) and imply an original form *$q^w im$ in Proto-Afro-Asiatic. Such monosyllabic roots would simply require the transfer of some samples to the classes CvC or $C_1C_2vC_3$.

$C\bar{a}C$: *kāp-*, "rock"; *pān-*, "face"; *bāš*, "be ashamed!"; *šāl > sal*, "ask!".
$C\bar{\imath}C$: *zīm-*, "feature(s)"; *ṭīṭ-*, "clay"; *kīs-*, "bag"; *kīr-*, "oven"; *ṣīṣ-*, "flower"; *ṣīr > ṣir*, "begin!"; *śīm*, "place!".
$C\bar{u}C$: *būl-*, "livestock"; *kūb-*, "foetus"; *mūś-*, "night"; *nūn-*, "fish"; *sūq-*, "street"; *pūt-*, "forehead"; *kūn*, "be firm!"; *qūm*, "get up!".

One should note that the opposition $\bar{\imath}:\bar{u}$ is not absolute, as shown by words like *kīr-* in Assyro-Babylonian and *kūr*, "oven", in other Semitic languages, or *bīr* and *būr*, "well". The situation is here comparable with the opposition of voiced and unvoiced consonants (§10.8).

28.10. The $C_1C_2\bar{v}C_3$ class with a consonant cluster in initial position and a long radical vowel does not occur frequently, but its existence is firmly attested, in particular by some basic numerals.

$C_1C_2\bar{a}C_3$: *ḏrā'-*, "arm"; *ṯlāṯ-*, "three"; *ṯmān-*, "eight"; *tmāl-*, "yesterday".
$C_1C_2\bar{\imath}C_3$: *brīq-*, "pitcher" (Classical Arabic *'ibrīq*); **kdīś- > kdīš*, "cart horse, nag, jade" (Classical Arabic *'ikdīš* or *kadīš*).
$C_1C_2\bar{u}C_3$: *klūb*, "cage" (Greek κλωβός).

28.11. The $C_1vC_2C_2$ class is characterized by a long or geminated final consonant.

$C_1aC_2C_2$: *baqq-*, "gnat"; *ḥagg-*, "feast, pilgrimage"; *kapp-*, "palm of the hand"; *'amm-*, "ancestor, founder of a family"; *śarr-*, "chief, king"; *gal(l)*, "roll!"; *maš(š) > mass(i/a)*, "touch!".
$C_1iC_2C_2$: *'imm-*, "mother"; *zimm-*, "wound"; *libb-*, "heart"; *ṭill-*, "shade"; *šinn-*, "tooth"; *firr(i/a)*, "flee!"; *qirr(i/a)*, "be at rest!".
$C_1uC_2C_2$: *ḏubb-*, "fly"; *ḥurr-*, "cave"; *šušš-*, "sixty"; *gud(d)*, "kill!"; *dubb(u)*, "speak!".

28.12. The $C_1vC_2C_3$ class is a variant of the preceding one. Instead of the final long or geminated consonant, it has a two-consonant cluster at the end. This pattern characterizes many nominal roots and it constitutes the stem of the Assyro-Babylonian stative (*pars-*), with the exception of the 3rd pers. masc. sing. (*paris*, "is separated"). According to the common opinion, instead, the second vowel of the stem is to be considered as consistently suppressed. The following list includes only examples of nominal roots:

$C_1aC_2C_3$: *'amr-*, "order, word"; *ba'l-*, "lord"; *gadr-*, "wall"; *ḥamš-*, "five"; *kalb-*, "dog"; *malk-*, "king"; *'aśr-*, "ten"; *šab'-*, "seven".

$C_1iC_2C_3$: *biśr-*, "joy"; *nidr-*, "vow"; *sipr-*, "document, book"; *'igl-*, "calf"; *'iḏr-*, "help"; *śi'b-*, "gorge, ravine".

$C_1uC_2C_3$: *'uḏn-*, "ear"; *ḥušk-*, "darkness"; *'umq-*, "valley"; *ġunm-*, "booty"; *qudš-*, "holiness".

28.13. The enlargement of certain biconsonantal roots with *-ā* should be compared with the colloquial extension of Arabic pronouns to *anāya*, *əntāya*, "I", "you", with the Libyco-Berber use of an expressive particle *ay*, and with the widespread suffixing of an enclitic *-a* in various Agaw dialects, especially to the pronoun of the first person singular *an-a*, besides the normal form *an*. In fact, the Semitic enclitic *-ā* often occurs in cases where "my" is implied and it is probably related to a pronominal suffix of the first person singular (cf. §36.26). This enclitic produced derivatives that are sometimes considered as proofs of the original triconsonantal or dissyllabic character of the roots under consideration. Thus, some ancient Arabic dialects used *'abā* instead of *'ab*, "father", *'aḫā* for *'aḫ*, "brother", *yadā* for *yad*, "hand", *damā* for *dam*, "blood". These forms might be compared with Mishnaic Hebrew *'abbā*, "(my) father", and *'immā*, "(my) mother", that are unlikely to have been borrowed from the Aramaic emphatic state (§33.7). Now, Arabic *damawīy*, "bloody", instead of *damīy*, derives from such a secondary form *damā* with a *w*-glide separating the two vowels. A comparable phenomenon occurs in dialectal Aramaic with *dbhh*, "she-bear", and *šmh'*, "the memorial" (lit. "the name"), where a *h*-glide separates the two vowels *ā*, like in the name *'Abrāhām* < *'Abrām* and in the plural form of some nouns (§31.19). Similar enlargements of biconsonantal roots are found in Palaeosyrian and in Libyco-Berber. In Palaeosyrian, however, the *a*-vowel changed into *u* under the influence of the *w*-glide. Thus, we encounter at Ebla *ù-ḫu-wa-tum* /*'uḫuwātum*/, "fraternity"; *ṭù-bù-a-tum* /*ṭūbuwātum*/, "goodness"; *sa-zu-wa-tum* /*ša(w)ṣu(')wātum*/, "dismissal" (root *wṣ*, "to go out"). These forms go back to the following elements: *'aḫ-ā + atum*, *ṭūb-ā + atum*, *ša(w)ṣā(') + atum*. The original *a*-morpheme is preserved, instead, in Libyco-Berber, e.g. *ilsawən*, plural of *ils*, "tongue", and *ismawən*, plural of *ism*, "name". In reality, both are "sound" plurals of older internal plurals (§31.9) **ilsā* and **ismā*, corresponding to the Arabic internal plurals *'asmā'* of *'ism*, "name", and *'abnā'* of *'ibn*, "son". Such cases cannot advocate the alleged triconsonantal origin of the roots in question.

28.14.   The roots are sometimes called by linguists "full" and "free" morphemes. They are "full" morphemes because they have a more or less independent meaning, so that one or a series of full morphemes in isolation can be fairly meaningful. E.g. *kalb-* suggests a determined animal, a "dog", and *sipr- li-malk-* means "a book (belonging) to a king". They are "free" morphemes because they can stand alone as independent words. The "full" and "free" morphemes are not fully defined by their semantic and phonological properties. They also have syntactic properties which determine how they function with respect to the grammatical processes of the language. For example, *kalb-*, "dog", can function only as a noun, and never, say, as a verb, but the "full" and "free" verbal morpheme *ktub-*, "write!", is subject to a shift in grammatical class or part of speech when determinate lexical morphemes are added to it (§28.1). Conversely, some nominal morphemes may become verbal when an appropriate lexical morpheme is added to it; e.g. *ṯin-*, "two", gives rise to *ṯni(y)*, "double!", when the morpheme *-y* is suffixed to the root. In fact, this morpheme seems to have a causal function (§41.13; 43.11).

28.15.   The task of lexical individualization and grammatical categorization is assumed, indeed, by lexical and grammatical morphemes (§28.1) which are affixed to the root or infixed in it according to a series of well determined patterns. These morphemes are called "bound", because they cannot stand alone as independent words, and "empty", because they do not have an independent meaning, although they are not all empty of semantic content; e.g., the prefixed morpheme *ma-* forming nouns often implies a notion of place (§29.21), while the suffixed verbal morpheme *-ū* usually indicates the plural.

28.16.   Affixes and infixes have varying effects when they are added to roots. When *-īm* is added in Hebrew, e.g., to *kalb-* to form *kalb-īm*, "dogs", the effect is to further specify *kalb-* with respect to the number of animals being referred to. Both *kalb-* and *kalbīm* are nouns; adding the plural morphem *-īm* does not change the grammatical class of the word in question. Similarly, affixing the imperfect and indicative morphemes to the Arabic verbal root **ktub-* gives another verbal form *ya-ktub-u*, "he writes". On the other hand, *yaktubu* and *maktabat-*, "library", belong to different grammatical classes; *yaktubu* is a verb, the conjugation of which is examined in the corresponding chapter, but *maktabat-* is a deverbal noun, the pattern of which, etc., is dealt with in the chapter on nouns.

28.17. Accordingly, linguists often distinguish between "inflectional" and "derivational" affixes, or, to use older terms, "grammatical" and "lexical". However, derivational affixes do not always effect a change in grammatical class as in the example of *maktabat-*. The derivational suffix *-at-*, for instance, relates *malk-*, "king", and *malkat-*, "queen", yet both are nouns. Nor is a shift in grammatical class always signalled by an overt marker. E.g., *bēt-* and *ašar-* are basically nouns, meaning "house" and "place", but they can also be used as relative pronouns, with no affix (§57.5). As a rule, however, a shift in grammatical class is indicated by overt markers, as prefix, suffix, infix, and even vocalic change, as **ma-ktab-at-** vs. **ktub*.

28.18. The addition of affixes or infixes to roots is one way of constructing complex lexical items from simple ones and of indicating their grammatical function. There are various other ways of forming complex lexical units and expressing the relative function of various items in a sentence. Affixation and infixation involve adding an "empty" morpheme to a "full" morpheme or to a larger unit containing a "full" morpheme. Some words, by way of contrast, are formed by combining two or more roots. Thus, combining the preposition *ana*, "in", and the noun *šum*, "name", we obtain the East Semitic subordinate conjunction *aššu(m)*, "because" (§58.16). As for the grammatical function of different units in a clause, it can be expressed by their simple juxtaposition in a determined word order; e.g. *libb malkat*, "heart of the/a queen", where the *nomen regens* is followed immediately by the *nomen rectum*, with no affix in a Semitic language lacking a functioning case system in nouns.

28.19. On the basis of the categories for which certain classes of words inflect, three inflectional classes or parts of speech may be distinguished: nouns (§29-35), pronouns (§36), and verbs (§37-46). Uninflected morphemes are subdivided in adverbs (§47), prepositions (§48), connective and deictic particles (§49). These distinctions are based on the actual use of the parts of speech in Semitic languages. However, most adverbs and prepositions are derived from nouns, and the distinction between nouns and verbs is not clearly cut in Semitic and, in general, in Afro-Asiatic. There are many deverbal nouns and denominative verbs. The participle and the infinitive are verbal nouns, while the stative or suffix-conjugation stands on the threshold between nominal and verbal predication. Comparative Afro-Asiatic linguistics shows even that the distinction between verbal and nominal roots is not always clearly cut, because there are a number of Afro-Asiatic roots which are used both as nouns and verbs without distinctive affixes. In Somali, e.g., *qufaʿ* means either "to cough" or "cough", *gargar*, "to help" or "help", and *habār* "to curse" or "curse". In East Semitic, *qātu(m)* designates the "hand", but Somali *qād* < **qāt* is a verb meaning "to take".

2. THE NOUN

29.1. A noun is a member of a class of words which has a descriptive function and comprises substantives, adjectives, and participles, as well as numerals. These nominal subclasses are usually distinguishable through their various degree of subjection to the inflectional categories of gender, number, and case, and often also through their morphological type, called "stem", "noun-form", or "pattern", which is associated in several instances with a specific meaning or function. Semitic nouns are either primary or derived. They are primary if they correspond to a root morpheme, e.g. *'ab-*, "father". They are derived if their pattern represents an extended or modified verbal or nominal root morpheme, e.g. Arabic *'ubūwa*, "fatherhood".

29.2. In the following, the main noun patterns will be presented with their principal semantic fields, inasmuch as they can be established. For the identification of the patterns, either the symbols *CvC*, etc., or the usual paradigms will be used: *f'l* mainly for Arabic, *prs* for Assyro-Babylonian, *qtl* for most North and West Semitic languages. The same paradigms will be employed in the sections dealing with the inflection of the noun, viz. gender (§30), number (§31), case (§32), state (§33), as well as in the further chapters of this book.

A. Noun Stems or Patterns

29.3. Nominal patterns are said to be "simple" when they correspond to a root morpheme or appear as its allomorphs. They are "extended" either when preformatives, afformatives or infixes are added, when a diphthongization occurs, or when the whole root morpheme or one of its radicals are reduplicated. The "simple" patterns are distinguishable from each other by vocalization, by lengthening of vowels, and by lengthening or gemination of consonants. Hence it is evident that a purely consonantal script, e.g. Ugaritic or South Arabian, conceals a wide variety of morphological "simple" noun stems. The "extended" patterns are often discontinuous and may be superimposed on a root. E.g. Arabic *mağlis-*, "conference room", simply implies the prefixing of *ma-* to the verbal root **glis* (*i*-class), "sit down", but Aramaic *miškab*, "bed", is formed on the pattern ***miCCaC*** which is superimposed on the verbal root **škub* (*u*-class), "lay down". Considering the uncertainties resulting from lacking vocalizations, diachronic factors, and phonetic developments, we shall not enter in this *Outline* into a discussion of the vocalic components of discontinuous patterns.

a) Simple Patterns

29.4. The monoconsonantal ($C\bar{v}$) noun stems are fairly rare. The biconsonantal "simple" patterns can have either a short vowel (CvC), or a long vowel ($C\bar{v}C$), or a long second consonant ($C_1vC_2C_2$). They correspond all to the root morphemes of the same type (§28.6-7,9,11), but are subject to phonological developments according to the principles exposed in the section on phonology (§10-27). Their semantic field includes kinship (e.g. *'ab-*, "father"; *'aḫ-*, "brother"; *'imm-*, "mother"), parts of human body (e.g. *pū-*, "mouth"; *dam-*, "blood"; *yad-*, "hand"; *kapp-*, "palm of hand"), and basic numerals (*ḥad-*, "one"; *ṯin-*, "two").

29.5. The triconsonantal nouns with one short vowel of the type $C_1vC_2C_3$ (§28.12) are likewise subject to phonological developments, especially to anaptyxis (§27.19). E.g. *kalb-*, "dog", can become *kalab* in the construct state of Assyro-Babylonian; it develops to *kāleb > keleb* in Hebrew and to **kalab > kəlab* in Aramaic. In Arabic, the patterns *fa'al* and *fa'il* may occur as phonetic variants of *fa'l*; e.g. *nahr* and *nahar*, "river"; *ša'r* and *ša'ar*, "hair"; *ṭard* and *ṭarad*, "hunt". The same phenomenon seems to be attested in Palaeosyrian (e.g. *sa-ma-nu*, "oil"), unless such a spelling of stems belonging to the type $C_1vC_2C_3$ is to be attributed to the inadequate character of the writing system. These stems mostly denote concrete nouns, but they may convey abstract meanings as well; e.g. Assyro-Babylonian *šulmu*, "peace, well-being", Arabic *quds*, "holiness".

Hebrew nouns belonging to this category are called "segolates" since they are vocalized *e-e*, with two segols, in the Tiberian Masoretic tradition. It is worth noting that this segolization is still unknown to Origen (3rd century A.D.), barely attested in the Latin transcriptions of Jerome (348-420 A.D.), and apparently unknown to the author of the Latin transcriptions of Hebrew in the 10th-century Ripoll Ms. 74, where *kerem* appears as *charm* and *zemer* as *zambr*. In the Babylonian tradition, these nouns are vocalized *a-a*, while their Tiberian pausal vocalization is *ā-e*.

29.6.   Dissyllables with short vowels of the type *CvCvC* may be variants of the preceding group, occasioned mainly by anaptyxis, e.g. Palaeosyrian *ba-ša-nu-(-um)* and Arabic *baṯan(un)* vs. Babylonian *bašmu(m)*, "serpent"; *malik*, "king", from *malk-*; *kabid-* from *kabd-*, "liver". Others are adjectives, partially substantivized, as Arabic *ṯiqal*, "heaviness", to be compared with the broken plural *ṯiqāl* of the adjective *ṯaqīl*, "heavy"; or *kibar*, "greatness", to be related to the broken plural *kibār* of the adjective *kabīr*, "great". The second short vowel is lost in Syriac and in Neo-Aramaic, e.g. *ḥalba* < *ḥalab-ā*, "milk" (cf. §33.7). Numerous vocalic changes occur in modern Arabic dialects.

29.7.   Dissyllables with long vowel in the first syllable (*Cv̄CvC*) are either active participles of triconsonantal verbs (*CāCiC*), often substantivized as agent nouns, or patterns very rare outside Arabic. E.g. *kātib*, participle "writing" in Aramaic and substantive "scribe" in Arabic; *āliku(m)*, participle "going" and substantive "envoy" in Assyro-Babylonian. This pattern is attested also in Palaeosyrian; e.g. *kà-šè-bù(-um)* /*kāḏibum*/, "misleading", hence "liar"; *wa-zi-um* /*wāṣi'um*/, "going out", hence "quitter". It is subject to important vocalic changes in Hebrew and in Phoenician, e.g. **ṯāpiṭ-*, "judge", becoming *šōpēṭ* and later *šūfēṭ* in Punic.

29.8.   Dissyllables with long vowel in the second syllable (*CvCv̄C*) partially derive from monosyllabic morpheme roots of the type $C_1C_2\bar{v}C_3$ (§28.10), which reappears frequently in modern colloquials. E.g. *ṯalāt-*, "three", and *ṯamān-*, "eight", probably originate from **ṯlāt-* and **ṯmān-*, while the present colloquial forms of Damascus are *tlāt-* and *tmān-*. The patterns *CvCīC* and *CvCūC* are predominantly adjectival or participial, e.g. Arabic *kabīr*, "great"; Ge'ez *marir*, "bitter"; Hebrew *'āṣūm*, "strong". *CvCīC*, in particular, is used in Aramaic as a passive participle

(e.g. *kətīb*, "written"), while the same function is assumed in Hebrew by
the type *CvCūC*, e.g. *qātūl*, "killed". A similar use of both stems occurs
occasionally also in other languages, e.g. *karūbu*, "blessed" in Assyro-
Babylonian poetry; *qatīl*, "killed" in Arabic. In modern dialects, the
short vowels may disappear or be affected by a qualitative change; e.g.
kabīr, "great", becomes *kibīr* in Cairene Arabic and *gbīr* in a
"Mesopotamian" dialect. The patterns *CiCāC*, *CuCūC*, and *CaCīC* are
used in Arabic to form broken plurals, especially the first one (e.g. *riǧāl*,
"men"; *biḥār*, "seas"), which appears as an extension of the pattern
CiCaC (e.g. *ṣiġār*, "the small ones", cf. *ṣiġar*, "smallness"; *ʿiẓām*, "the
great ones", cf. *ʿiẓam*, "greatness"; see also §29.6). The same pattern
CiCāC is employed also for tools and instruments, e.g. Assyro-Babylonian *qināzu(m)*, "whip"; Aramaic *ḥimār*, "donkey"; Arabic *niṭāq*,
"belt". In some languages, the short vowel *i* is lost or changes into *ē / ə*,
and *ā* may become *ō*; e.g. Neo-Aramaic *ḥmāra*, "donkey"; Geʿez *qənāt*,
"belt"; Hebrew *ʾēzōr* < **ʾizār*, "belt".

b) Patterns with Diphthongs

29.9. Monosyllables with diphthong appear in Semitic (e.g. *bayt*,
"house"), particularly in Arabic: e.g. *yawm*, "day", *tawm*, "garlic",
ḥawr, "lake". They characterize the Andalusian dialect, as suggested by
rawz for *ruzz*, "rice", *ṣawf* for *ṣūf*, "wool". Since early Andalusian is
related somehow to ancient South Arabian (§8.2), the Sabaic patterns *fyl*
and *fwl* should probably be interpreted as *fayl* and *fawl*: e.g. *ʾys¹*, "man"
(cf. Hebrew *ʾīš*), *gyr*, "lime-plaster" (cf. Arabic *ǧīr*), *hyn*, "time" (cf.
Arabic *ḥīn*), *tyb*, "scent" (cf. Arabic *ṭīb*), *ṣwr*, "image" (cf. Arabic *ṣūra*).
Dissyllables with diphthong in the first syllable (*Caw/yCaC*) may have
different origins. E.g. West Semitic and South Arabian *hykl* or *ḥykl* goes
back to Old Sumerian (§27.16), while *kawkab*, "star", attested already
in Sabaic (*kwkb*), is based ultimately on the biconsonantal reduplicated
root *kabkab-*, known from Amorite onomastics. Ethiopic *ʾaydug*, "ass",
is used for *ʾāʾ(ə)dug*, while *ʾawnuq* or *ʾaynuq*, "she-camels", are internal plurals (§31.26-28) of *nāqa* in ancient Arabic dialects. Other Arabic
examples are *ḥaydar*, "small"; *šayham*, "hedgehog"; *fayṣal*, "arbiter".
Several nouns of this group are simply Arabic elatives introduced by
ʾa- (§34.5), e.g. *ʾawfar*, "more abounding", from *wafara*, "to abound".
The diphthong *aw* appears instead of *u* in Andalusian Arabic *lawbān* for
lubān, "olibanum", and in Sabaic *ḥwlm* vs. Arabic *ḥulm*, "dream", also
in *kawtar*, "generous", vs. **Kutar*, a divine name.

29.10. Dissyllables with the diphthong -*ay*- in the second syllable (*CvCayC*) and a dissimilated vowel *u* < *a* in the first one are largely used as diminutives, especially in Arabic; e.g. *kulayb*, "small dog" in Arabic; *'ulaym*, "young boy" in Aramaic; perhaps *ṣlym*, "statuette" in Sabaic. The pattern *f'wl* occurs in Epigraphic South Arabian mainly as a broken plural stem (e.g. *mdwr*, "territories"), but it is also encountered in proper names. It might be identical there with the Arabic *fiʿʿawl* pattern which occurs in some diminutives; e.g. *'iǧǧawl*, "small calf"; *ḥinnawṣ*, "piglet".

c) Patterns extended by Gemination

29.11. Twelve different noun stems with geminated second radical consonant are attested in Arabic, either with short or long second vowel, or with one of the diphthongs -*aw*-/-*ay*-. Most of these stems occur also in Assyro-Babylonian, while their number is somewhat reduced in other languages. The pattern $C_1aC_2C_2\bar{a}C_3$ is largely used in Semitic for names of professions, e.g. *gallābu(m)*, "barber" in Assyro-Babylonian; *mallāḫ*, "sailor" in Aramaic; *naǧǧār*, "carpenter" in Arabic; *rakkāb*, "horse-man" in Hebrew; *gabbār*, "workman" in Geʿez. The vowel *ā* should normally have changed into *ō* in Hebrew, but this did not happen for some unknown reason. Clear traces of this pattern subsist in Libyco-Berber; e.g. Tuareg *a-fərrad*, "sweeper"; *a-nəbbal*, "grave-digger". The same noun stem is employed for tools or instruments in colloquial Arabic (e.g. *kaddān*, "harness collar"; *zammām*, a kind of "bolt"), while Assyro-Babylonian uses patterns with vowels *ī* / *ū* for the same purpose (e.g. *ḥaṣṣīnu*, "axe"; *sikkūru*, "bolt"). The pattern $C_1aC_2C_2\bar{u}C_3$ is used instead of $C_1aC_2C_2\bar{a}C_3$ in Assyro-Babylonian *šakkūru*, "drunkard", and in a number of Syriac nouns, e.g., *gazzūzā*, "shearer"; *gazzūrā*, "butcher"; *dabbūḥā*, "sacrificer". Aramaic *ptwr*, "interpreter (of dreams)", should belong here too. The pattern appears also in Hebrew *'ammūd*, "column, pillar"; *ḥabbūrā*, "contusion", but belongs then to different semantic fields. Stems of the types $C_1vC_2C_2vC_3$ and $C_1vC_2C_2\bar{v}C_3$ are also employed throughout the Semitic languages to indicate adjectives with intensive meaning; e.g. *qattanu*, "very small" in Assyro-Babylonian; *šappīr*, "beautiful" in Aramaic; *'addīr*, "powerful" in Hebrew and in Phoenician; *qaddūs* or *quddūs*, "most holy" in Arabic; *da-nu-nu* /dannūnū̆/, "(are) very strong"; *ni-bù-ḫu* /nibbūǧū̆/, "(are) outstanding", and /ṭubbūḫu/ in Palaeosyrian, if *Ṭù-bù-ḫu*-ᵈ*À-da* means "Very slaughterous is Hadda". This pattern occurs in Libyco-

Berber adjectives as well; e.g. *a-məllal*, "white"; *a-wəssar*, "old". The pattern $C_1 \partial C_2 C_2 \bar{a} C_3$ is used in Tigre to form names of products or results of actions; e.g. *ḥərrād*, "what is slaughtered"; *səṭṭār*, "splinter". The same meaning characterizes the $C_1 i C_2 C_2 \bar{u} C_3$ pattern in Samaritan Aramaic; e.g. *ṣiyyūd*, "game"; *gizzūr*, "piece". The gemination is lost in Neo-Aramaic (e.g. *palāḥa* < *pallāḥā*, "worker") and in some modern Ethiopic dialects (e.g. *ḥaǧis* < *häǧǧis*, "new").

29.12. Dissyllables with geminated third consonant occur chiefly in Old Akkadian, in Assyro-Babylonian, and in Arabic, with different vowels. E.g. *baluḫḫu(m)*, "galbanum", and *ḫaluppu(m)*, "oak", are two Sumerian loanwords in Akkadian, while the etymology of Assyro-Babylonian *arammu*, "wharf, ramp", is unknown. In Old Akkadian, a suffix *-akku(m)* or *-ikku(m)* was added to several Sumerian loanwords, e.g. *išši'akku(m)*, "city ruler"; *gursidakku(m)*, "flour basket"; *nešakku(m)*, a priest. Other nouns are Semitic, as *kunukku(m)*, "seal", or *aḫuzzatu(m)*, "marriage". In Arabic there are a few nouns and adjectives of these patterns, e.g. *filizz*, "(non-precious) metal"; *ǧiṭamm,* "vast (ocean)". Aramaic nouns like *pərakkā*, "altar", and *kəlakkā*, "raft", are borrowed from Assyro-Babylonian.

d) Patterns extended by Reduplication

29.13. Patterns with reduplicated root morphemes are attested in most Semitic languages, e.g. *kabkab-*, "star" in Amorite, changed into *kakkabu(m)* or *kawkab* > *kōkab* in other languages; *qaqqadu(m)* < **qadqadu(m)*, "head" in Assyro-Babylonian; *galgal*, "wheel, globe", and *sirsur*, "broker", with vocalic dissimilation, in Phoenician, Hebrew, and Aramaic; *pirpira*, "butterfly" in Neo-Aramaic; *sansal* < **šalšal*, "chain" in Ge'ez. The vowel of the reduplicated base may change by dissimilation, like in *sirsur*; e.g. Hebrew *baqbūq*, "flask"; Mishnaic Hebrew *pilpēl*, "pepper". The pattern with complete reduplication of base is easily recognizable also in Libyco-Berber, especially in Tuareg, e.g. *tă-kəlkəbba*, "occiput", and *tă-kərkort*, "skull", both related to Assyro-Babylonian *gulgull(at)u(m)*, Hebrew *gulgolet*, Aramaic *gulgultā* (Greek Γολγοθά), and Arabic *ǧalǧala(tun)*, "skull".

29.14. Noun stems with reduplication either of the second or third consonant of the root morpheme ($C_1 v C_2 v C_2 v C_3$, $C_1 v C_2 C_3 v C_3$), or of both of them ($C_1 v C_2 v C_3 C_2 v C_3$), are attested in various Semitic languages. The first pattern occurs rarely in Assyro-Babylonian (e.g. *zuqaqīpu*, "scorpion") and in modern Ethiopian tongues, e.g. in Amharic *talallaq*, "great". The second one is encountered in Assyro-Babylonian (e.g. *kulbābu*, "ant"), in Aramaic (e.g. *marṭūṭ*, "lint"), in Hebrew (e.g. *ra'ănān*, "green"), in Arabic (e.g. *šumlūl*, "small amount"). Patterns with reduplicated second and third consonants of the root morpheme occur sporadically in Aramaic (e.g. *šəparpārā*, "brightness, morning light"), in Syriac (e.g. *šəlamləmā*, "complete"), in Hebrew (e.g. *'ăqalqallōt*, "crooked paths"), in Arabic (e.g. *'arakrak*, "thick"), in Ge'ez (e.g. *ḥamalmāl*, "green"), in Tigre (e.g. *hatamtam*, "babbling"), in Tigrinya (e.g. *səwunwun*, "movement"). Besides, this pattern is used in Hebrew for diminutives of colour names: *'ădamdām*, "reddish"; *yəraqraq*, "yellowish, greenish"; *šəḥarḥar*, "blackish".

e) Patterns with Preformatives and Infixes

29.15. Noun stems are extended by various prefixes, infixes, and suffixes. The main prefixes consist in a prosthetic vowel introduced by ' or sometimes ', in the morphemes *ya-*, *wa-*, *m-*, *n-*, *t-*, and *š-*. Both denominative and deverbal derivatives are represented in this large group of patterns.

Preformatives '-/-'

29.16. Patterns with a prosthetic vowel introduced by '- are well represented in Arabic. The most frequent of these is *'af'al* which forms elatives (§34.5), i.e. comparatives or superlatives (e.g. *'akram*, "nobler, very noble"; cf. *karīm*, "noble"), colour names (e.g. *'aḥmar*, "red"), and bodily qualifications (e.g. *'a'raǧ*, "lame"; cf. *'araǧ*, "lameness"). The pattern is attested also in Liḥyānite and in Nabataean Aramaic, especially with *'ṣdq*, "executor" (cf. Arabic *'aṣdaq*, "the most reliable"); e.g. *'n' ... 'ṣdq w-yrt ... 'by*, "I, ... the executor and the heir of my father ...". In Pre-Islamic North Arabian, this pattern may lead to the splitting of the long second radical; e.g. *'s²ll /'aslal/* against Arabic *'ašall*, "withered?". A few Hebrew adjectives are related to these categories (e.g. *'akzār*, "cruel"). The same pattern is used also for some animal names, e.g. *'arnab*, "hare" in several Semitic languages (but cf. *annabu*); *'anḫr*, "narwhal" (cf. *nāḫiru* in Assyro-Babylonian), and *'anhb*, "shellfish?" (cf. *nibu* in Assyro-Babylonian), both attested in Ugaritic. The noun stems *'af'ul*, *'af'ūl*, *'af'āl*, *'af'ilat*, *'af'ilā(')w* are employed in Arabic, in South Arabian, and in North Ethiopic to form "broken" or internal plurals (cf. §31.26-28). Patterns with prosthetic *i*- are attested in Assyro-Babylonian, e.g. *inṣabtu(m)* or *anṣabtu(m)*, "ear-ring, ring"; *ikribu(m)*, "prayer"; *išdiḫu(m)*, "profit"; *ipṭeru(m)*, "ransom".

29.17.   Some animal names containing the consonant *r* have a pros- thetic vowel introduced by ʿ instead of ʾ (§27.8); e.g. *ʿuṣfūr*, "sparrow, small bird" in Arabic (cf. *ṣippōr*, "birds", in Hebrew); *ʾrgl*, "locust" in Sabaic; *ʿaqrab*, "scorpion" in Hebrew, Aramaic, Arabic, Ethiopic; *ʿqšr*, a kind of snake in Ugaritic (cf. *qišr*, "slough" of a snake in Arabic). Per- haps the divine name *ʿAṯtar* is to be explained in the same way, since the antelope or gazelle is the holy animal of this deity.

Preformative *ya-*

29.18.   Patterns with preformative *ya-* are confined to names of animals and plants, and to proper names. E.g. *yaḥmūr*, "deer", and *yabrūḫ*, "mandrake", both in Aramaic, Hebrew, and Arabic; *Yaṯrib*, original name of Medina; *Yarmūk*, Yarmouk river; *Ygrš*, "Expeller", name given to a staff in Ugaritic.

Preformatives *w-/m-/n-*

29.19.   There are few nominal patterns having a particular meaning in South Ethiopic. In the Chaha dialect of Gurage, however, nouns of instrument are formed by the prefix *wä-* and the suffix *-ya*; e.g. *wädräg- ya*, "hammer", from *dänägäm*, "he hit"; *wänṭiya*, "filter", from *näṭäräm*, "it melted". This morpheme *wä-* derives from *mä-* that is used in the various Ethiopian languages to form verbal nouns. The shift could simply be explained by the tendency of Gurage to change *m* to *w* (§ 11.8). The nouns with prefix *wä-* belong therefore to the categories discussed in §29.20 ff.

29.20.   The patterns with preformatives *ma-/mi-/mu-* have the widest possible range of meanings, including nouns of place, instrument, agent, time, verbal nouns, and participles. Basically, the morpheme *m-* has an instrumental function and expresses the instrument or the means by which one performs an action. However, just like the instrumental and locative functions of the ergative case are closely related, so *m-* may also express the place where or the time when the action occurs. The unvocalized Ugaritic and South Arabian texts prevent us from further specifications, but other languages furnish valuable information concerning the use of different patterns, although no general rules can be established. The prefix *m-* is also attested in the other branches of Afro-Asiatic, thus in ancient Egyptian, particularly with nouns of instrument; e.g. *mnḫt*, "clothing", from *wnḫ*, "to clothe one's self"; *mrḫt*, "fat", from *wrḫ*, "to anoint"; *mḫnt*, "ferry-boat", from *ḫni*, "to row". In Hausa, e.g., several nouns in *má-* derive from the verbal root *kas-*, "to kill⁵, viz. *má-kás-áa*, "site of killing"; *má-kás-híi*, "weapon", i.e. "instrument of killing"; *má-kà-híi*, "killer". Various nouns of agent are formed with *m-* > *n-* in Libyco-Berber (§22.26), and nouns of place, etc., occur in Cushitic, e.g. *maḥdär*, "dwelling", in Qemant-Qwara; *mana*, "home, house" (cf. Egyptian *mnw*, Arabic *manāḫ*, Hebrew *mānōᵃḫ*, "halting place, resting place"), and *magālā*, "market place" (cf. Hebrew *ma'gāl* "encampment"; Punic **ma'gal* > Latin *magalia*, "enclosure"), both in Oromo.

29.21. The prefix *ma-* forms Semitic nouns of place, e.g. *ma-ša-ba-tum* /*mada'bātum*/, "dam structures", and *mar-a-tum* /*mar'aytum*/, "pasture-land" in Palaeosyrian; *maškanum*, "settlement" in Old Akkadian; *mūšabu(m)* < **mawšabu(m)*, "dwelling" in Assyro-Babylonian; *madbaḥ*, "place of sacrifices, altar" in Aramaic; *ma'ᵃrāb*, "west" in Hebrew; *maqōm*, "place" in Phoenician; *maǧlis*, "conference room, court" in Arabic; *maḥfad*, "tower" in Ge'ez; *mäqdäs*, "sanctuary", and *mängəst*, "kingdom" in Amharic; also in Ugaritic, as shown by the syllabic spellings *ma-aḥ-ḫa[-du]* (*m'aḥd*), "city"; *ma-a-al-tum* (cf. *ma'ᵃleh*), "height, step", and in ancient South Arabian, as apparent in place names like Μάριαβα (*Mryb*) or Μαίφα (*Myf't*). However, the prefix *mi-* is likewise used to form nouns of place in Hebrew (e.g. *midbār*, "desert"; *mizrāḥ*, "east"), in Aramaic (e.g. *miškab*, "bed, grave"), in Punic (e.g. *myqdš*, "temple"), often in Ge'ez (e.g. *məšrāq*, "east"), in Tigre (e.g. *məbyāt*, "dwelling place"; *məkwāl*, "hiding place"), and in Amharic (e.g. *məsraq*, "east"; *mərfaq*, "dining-room"), but rarely in Arabic where a noun like *miḥrāb*, "prayer niche", is borrowed from ancient South Arabian *mḥrb*, "audience room".

29.22. Instead, the prefix *mi-* is largely employed in Arabic for nouns of instrument, e.g. *miftāḥ*, "key"; *mizān*, "scale". It is heavily exploited in scientific and other modern coinages, e.g. *mizlaǧ*, "skate, ski". The same use is attested in Hebrew (e.g. *mismār*, "nail"; *mišqāl*, "weight"), which also employs the prefix *ma-* for the same purpose (e.g. *mazlēg*, "fork"; *maptē^aḥ*, "key"), as does Palaeosyrian (e.g. *ma-qar-tum* /*maqqartum*/, "chisel"; *ma-za-rí-gú* /*mazārīqu*/, "set of javelins"), Ge'ez (e.g. *malbas*, "dress"), and Amharic (e.g. *mälhəq*, "anchor"; *mänka*, "spoon"). In Tigre, the suffix *-i* is attached to the stem (e.g. *maktabi*, "writing implement"; *maṣaddaqi*, "altar"). This semantic use of the pattern occurs also in Libyco-Berber (e.g. *a-maddaz*, "mallet").

29.23.   The prefix *mu-* is used in Assyro-Babylonian for nouns of time (e.g. *muṣlālu*, "midday") and of extension (e.g. *mušpalu*, "depth"), whereas it appears in Arabic as a variant of *mi-* (e.g. *munḫul* / *munḫal*, "sieve").

29.24.   Some substantives are attested in Arabic with different vocalizations of the prefix *m-*, e.g. *maṣhaf*, *miṣhaf*, *muṣhaf*, "book, codex"; *maġzal*, *miġzal*, *muġzal*, "spindle". One should also notice that the local and instrumental acceptations are sometimes difficult to distinguish; in Hebrew e.g., *merkābā*, "chariot", can be regarded as a tool and as the place where the driver sits or stands; *maḥzīt*, "mirror", can be considered as an implement and as the surface on which something can be seen, and *migdōl*, "tower", is one of the defence means and a place (cf. Phoenician *magdōl).

29.25.   Patterns with prefix *m-* also serve to form various participles (§42.14-16) and derived verbal stems in Neo-Aramaic, also infinitives (§42.4, 7, 9), especially Aramaic infinitives of the basic stem, and verbal substantives or abstracts; e.g. *maqraba-*, "closeness" in Arabic; *mišpāṭ*, "judgement" in Hebrew; *maqlūm*, "burning" in Assyro-Babylonian; *məhrät*, "mercy", *məgbar*, "action", in Amharic.

29.26.   Patterns with prefix *n-* can either derive by dissimilation from stems with prefix *m-* when the root morpheme contains a labial, or be deverbal nouns formed from the verbal stem with preformative *n-* (§41.15-19). Both cases occur mainly in East Semitic, e.g. *naplaqtum* < *maplaqtum, "battle-axe" in Old Akkadian; *napḫaru(m)* < **mapḫaru(m)*, "sum" in Assyro-Babylonian, borrowed as *npḥr* into Aramaic; *nanduru*, "fearful", from the Assyro-Babylonian verb *nadāru*, "to be wild". The change *m-* > *n-* of the prefix appears exceptionally in other Semitic languages, with alternative forms as *ma-pá-ḫu(-um)* /*mappaḫum*/ and *na-pá-ḫu-um* /*nappaḫum*/, "bellows", in Palaeosyrian, and with the rare examples of *nbl'at*, "flames" in Ugaritic, and *nšpṭ*, "judgement" in Old Aramaic (cf. §11.7). However, the change *m* > *n* occurs frequently in Berber dialects when the root morpheme contains a labial or the labiodental *f*; e.g. *-nḇarš* < *-mbārǝk* < *-mubārak*, "blessed, lucky"; *-nǝḥšam* < *-*mǝḥkam*, "judge"; *-naġmar* < *-*mǝ'mal*, "hunter"; *-nǝzḏam* < *-*mǝṣdam*, "woodcutter"; *-nǝfsaḏ* < *-*mǝfsad*, "roper"; *-naẓum* < *-*maṣūm*, "fastener". This phonetic development is attested as early as the 2nd century B.C. by the nouns *nbb-n* < **i-mbabīn*[?], "cutters" (root *bbǝy*, "cut"), and *nbṭ-n* < **i-mbǝṭṭūn*[?], "splitters" (root *bḏu / bǝṭṭu*, "divide"), in a Punico-Numidic inscription from Dougga. Another dissimilation, viz. *ma-* > *wa-*, may occur in South Ethiopic; e.g. Amharic *wämbar* < **mänbär*, "chair"; *wänfit* < **mänfit*, "sieve"; *wättaddär* < **mäthaddär*, "soldier" (cf. §29.19).

29.27. In the Ethiopic dialects of the Gurage group, there are several nouns with a non-etymological prefix *ǝn-*, mostly before velars (e.g. *ǝnqolo*, "roasted grain", from *qollä*, "to roast"), but also before other consonants (e.g. *ǝnṭǝlfit*, kind of "hawk", from *ṭǝlfit*). This prefix occurs sometimes in other modern Ethiopian languages as well, e.g. in Amharic *ǝnqʷǝrarit*, "frog", as against Tigrinya *qʷǝr'a*. Besides, a preformative *nä-* can appear in the Chaha dialect of Gurage before a collective noun in order to express a plural or a great quantity, e.g. *nä-qǝb*, "a great quantity of butter". This element *nä-* corresponds to Amharic *ǝllä* with the *n* derived from an original **ll*.

Preformative *t-*

29.28. The patterns with preformatives *ta-/ti-/tu-* produce, for the most part, nouns derived from verbal stems. They characterize professional or social situations with reciprocal connotations, in conformity with one of the basic functions of the affix *t-*; they frequently form verbal nouns signifying an action, and sometimes occur with nouns of place, also with animal qualifications; e.g. *tù-la-dì* /tūladu/, "new-born crop" in Palaeosyrian; *takbaru*, "fattened sheep" in Assyro-Babylonian. Although less common than the patterns with prefix *m-*, those with *t-* are also widespread in Semitic.

29.29. A professional or social meaning appears already in Palaeosyrian and in Old Akkadian, e.g. *tá-aš-tá-me-lum*, "the man of the mourners" at Ebla, from **ṭml*; *tá-da-bí-lu* /tadābilu/, "interpreter", also at

Ebla (cf. Gafat and Gurage *däbbälä*, "to repeat"); *tamkārum*, "supplier, tradesman" from *makāru(m)*, "to give away". Assyro-Babylonian uses patterns with prefix *ta-* for *tamlāku(m)*, "counsellor"; *talmīdu(m)*, "disciple"; *targīgu(m)*, "evil-doer"; *tarbū(m)*, "pupil"; *tū'amu(m)*, "twin". Ugaritic does it for *tdgr*, "store-keeper", from *dgr*, "to heap"; Hebrew for *tōšāb*, "resident, metic", from *w̱tb*; *talmīd*, "disciple", from *lmd*; *tō'ām*, "twin", from *w'm*; etc.

29.30. Verbal nouns in *t-* signifying an action are well attested in Palaeosyrian (e.g. *tá-er-iš-tù-um* /*taḥeríttum*/, "ploughing"; cf. Libyco-Berber *takərza*), in Old Akkadian (e.g. *tamḥārum*, "battle"), in Assyro-Babylonian (e.g. *tarmiktum*, "layerage" or "soakage"; *tallaktu*, "going"), in Ugaritic (e.g. *trmmt*, "offering"), in Arabic (e.g. *tafrīq*, "partition"), in Hebrew (e.g. *təhillā*, "praise"), in Phoenician (e.g. *tklt*, "summing up"), in South Arabian (e.g. *tnḥyt*, "confession of sin"), in Ge'ez (e.g. *tafṣām*, "completing"), in Amharic (e.g. *tägbar*, "work"; *təmhərt*, "teaching"), in Aramaic (e.g. *takrīk*, "covering, garment"), in Syriac (e.g. *ta'dīrā*, "help"), in Neo-Aramaic (e.g. *tešmeštā*, "service"). However, semantic evolution into concrete nouns must be allowed for; e.g. *tamšīlum*, "image" in Assyro-Babylonian; *tip'eret*, "ornament" in Hebrew; *tärakäz*, "heel" in Amharic. Despite its late appearance in texts, the noun *targūm*, from *rgm*, "to utter, to speak", is implied already by Ugaritic *targumyānu* and Assyro-Babylonian *targumānu*, "interpreter", formed by the addition of the suffix *-yānu* or *-ānu* (§29.39).

29.31. Nouns of place with the prefix *t-* are found in Assyro-Babylonian (e.g. *tarbāṣu*, "fold"; *tapšaḥu*, "resting-place"), in Ugaritic (e.g. *trbṣ*, "courtyard"), in Hebrew and in Aramaic (e.g. *tēmān* < *taymān*, "south"). There are also ancient Semitic place names, like *Tadmer / Tadmor*, "Palmyra", that are formed with this prefix.

Infix -*t-*

29.32. Apart from the participles and substantivized infinitives of the verbal stems with *-t-* (cf. §41.20-32), nominal patterns with infixed *-t-* occur in East Semitic for adjectives with intensive meaning; e.g. *gitmālu(m)*, "perfect"; *pitluḥu(m)*, "awful". Their existence in North Semitic is ascertained by the Amorite names *Bataḥrum* (masc.) and *Bataḥra* (fem.), "chosen".

Preformative š-

29.33. Patterns with prefix *ša-* / *šu-* are employed in East Semitic for verbal nouns of the stems with preformatives *š-* and *št-* (§41.8-10,29), as well as for some elatives (cf. §34.5). E.g. *šūbultu(m)*, "present", and *šutābultu*, "interpretation" of omens, both from *wabālu*, "to bring"; *šagapūru(m)*, "very strong", from *gbr* / *gpr*. Apart from Assyro-Babylonian there are a few examples of these patterns in Palaeosyrian *sa-zu-wa-tum* /*ša(w)ṣu(')watum*/, "dismissal", in the Ugaritic proper name *Š'tqt*, "She-who-removes(-evil)", and in Aramaic nouns derived from verbal *šafʿel* stems (§41.10), e.g. *šuklālā*, "completion", from *šaklēl*, "to complete"; *šalhēbītā*, "flame", from *šalhēb*, "to kindle", borrowed into late Biblical Hebrew as *šalhebet*. This pattern, built like the verbal stem with causative preformative, is attested also in Libyco-Berber; e.g. Tachelhit *a-skərz*, "plough", "ploughshare", from *-kərz-*, "to plough".

f) Patterns with Afformatives

29.34. There are several noun patterns with afformatives or "nominalizers": *-ān* > *-ōn* > *-ūn*, *-iy* > *ī* and *-ay* > *ā*, *-āwī*, *-ya*, *-at*, *-ut*, *-it*, *-o*, *-när*, *-akku*, *-äňňä*, *-ā'u*, *-aym/n*.

Afformative -ān

29.35. The morpheme *-ān*, which is sometimes attached to other nominal patterns, occurs especially with adjectives and proper names formed as adjectives, with verbal substantives, diminutives, nouns of agent, and broken plurals. This pattern has similar functions in Libyco-Berber, e.g. *a-bərkan*, "black"; *a-šiban*, "bald". In Hebrew and Phoenician *-ān* usually changes into *-ōn*, and it develops later to *-ūn* (e.g. Ελιουν, "Most High"). However, there are some Hebrew nouns, like *šulḥān*, "table", and *qorbān*, "offering", where this change does not take place. Instead, Neo-Aramaic uses a variant morpheme *-ūn* to denote diminutives (§29.38).

29.36. Adjectives with the suffix *-ān* occur in Arabic (e.g. *kaslān*, "lazy"), Hebrew (e.g. *qadmōn*, "eastern"), Phoenician (e.g. *'lyn* = Ελιουν, "Most High"), Aramaic (e.g. *raḥmān*, "merciful"), Neo-Aramaic (e.g. *ḥaylānā*, "strong"). Numerous proper names belonging to this group are found in Assyro-Babylonian (e.g. *Šinnānu*, "toothed"), Ugaritic (e.g. *Nūrānu*, "luminous"), Aramaic (e.g. **Dahbān*, "golden"), Hebrew (e.g.

Šimšōn, "sunny" or "small sun"). The widely used hypocoristic suffix *-ān(um)* of personal names, which is attached also to verbal forms (e.g. *Yamlikān* in Amorite), goes back either to the adjectival or to the diminutive function of the afformative. The suffix *-ān* can be added to the afformative *-iy* (§29.41), especially in names from Ugarit (e.g. *Šapšiyānu*, "sunny" or "small sun"), but also in nouns of agent (e.g. *targumyānu*, "interpreter"; cf. §29.30,39). Conversely, the gentilitial endings *-iy* > *-ī* or *-ay* can also be added to the suffix *-ān* > *-ōn*, e.g. in Hebrew *qadmōnī*, "oriental"; in Phoenician *'štrny*, "(man) of Astarte"; in South Arabian *'lwny*, "(man) of Alw"; in Neo-Aramaic *ṭūranāyā*, "mountaineer". The number of adjectives in *-ānī* without any gentilitial connotation increases in Post-Classical Arabic; e.g. *ǧišmānī*, "corpulent"; *ruḥānī*, "spiritual".

29.37. Verbal nouns or abstracts in *-ān* > *-ōn* are attested in Assyro-Babylonian (e.g. *šulmānu*, "greeting, present, bribe"), Ugaritic (e.g. *zbln*, "sickness"), Arabic (e.g. *ḥafaqān*, "heartbeat, fluttering"), Hebrew (e.g. *qorbān*, "offering"; *zikkārōn*, "remembrance"), Aramaic (e.g. *šolṭān*, "power"; *puqdānā*, "order"), Geʿez (e.g. *rəšʾān*, "growing old"), Amharic (e.g. *səlṭan*, "authority"; *qʷənṭan*, "stomach-ache"). However, some nouns have a concrete meaning, like Palaeosyrian *i-a-la-nu* /ʾiyalānu/, "large tree", related to Hebrew *ʾyl*, Ugaritic *tlḥn* and Hebrew *šulḥān*, "table", Phoenician *ʾln* = *ʾalōn*, "god", or Arabic *qurʾān* from *qaraʾa*, "to recite".

29.38. Diminutives in *-ān* > *-ōn* occur in Assyro-Babylonian (e.g. *mērānu*, "whelp"), in Hebrew (e.g. *śahⁿrōn*, amulet called "little-moon"), in Arabic (e.g. *ʾaqrabān*, "small scorpion"), in Modern Hebrew where diminutives end in *-ón* with a feminine *-ónet* (e.g. *kalbón*, "small dog"; *siprón*, "booklet"). A great many Arabic names of the first Islamic centuries, and later still in the West, were formed with a suffix *-ūn* (e.g. *Ibn Ḥaldūn*, *Ibn Ḥalfūn*), which should be compared with the suffix *-ūn* appearing in Syriac names (e.g. *ʿAbdūn*) and in the Neo-Aramaic diminutives (e.g. *yalūnā*, "youngster"; *našūnā*, "little fellow"). Some Neo-Aramaic words have nowadays lost their original diminutive meaning (e.g. *ʾaḥūnā*, "brother"; *brūnā*, "son"), but they testify to the existence of a suffix *-ūn*, variant of *-ān*.

29.39. The nouns of agent formed mainly from active participles by addition of the suffix *-ān* are well represented in Assyro-Babylonian and in Neo-Aramaic. They do not imply any particular individualization of the person acting, contrary to the opinion of some authors. E.g. in Assyro-Babylonian, *nādinānu(m)*, "seller"; *šarrāqānu*, "thief"; *ummiānu(m)*, "master", from Sumerian u m m i a; in Neo-Aramaic, *katbānā*, "writer"; [*orāna*] < *'abrānā*, "passer-by"; also in Mishnaic Hebrew, *gozlān*, "robber"; *roṣḥān*, "murderer", etc.

29.40. Broken plurals in *-ān* are found in Arabic (e.g. *ġazāl*, "gazelle", plur. *ġizlān*; *qunwān*, "bunch of dates"; *ṣubyān*, "boys"), also in modern colloquials (e.g. *sīgān*, "legs"; *ḥörfān*, "lambs"), and probably in Epigraphic South Arabian. This use of the afformative *-ān* should be distinguished from the external plural *-ān* attested in several Semitic languages (§31.12).

Afformatives *-iy* / *-ay* / *-āwī* / *-ya* / *-iyya*

29.41. The gentilitial or adjectival suffixes *-iy-* > *-ī* and *-ay-* > *-ā*, the so-called *nisba*, are attested also in ancient Egyptian (e.g. *ḥmy*, "steersman", from *ḥm*, "to steer"; *rḥty*, "washerman", from *rḥt*, "to wash"; *Ḥr Nḥny*, "Horus of *Nḥn*"; *Nbty*, "the Ombite", from *Nbt*, "Ombos"). They most commonly signify an individual member of a social group and they are widely used as gentilitial and hypocoristic endings with Semitic and even non-Semitic proper names. The relation between these different functions of the suffix is not evident. The genitilitial ending, extended to professional qualifications, may have originated from a postposition, used also to form the genitive marker *-i* (§32.7). In this hypothesis, the hypocoristic ending should have a different origin and be related either to a form of diminutive (§29.42) or to the first singular pronominal suffix.

The difference between *-iy-* and *-ay-* seems to have been originally dialectal. In fact, the gentilitial formation *-ay-* does not exist in Old Akkadian and in standard Assyro-Babylonian before the Middle Assyrian period. Instead, in the Palaeosyrian texts from Ebla one finds the suffix *-ay-* (*kà-na-na-um/im* /Kana'nayum/, "Canaanaean"), which is also used later at Mari (e.g. *Ekallātayum*, *Elaḥutayum*). A parallel difference characterizes the hypocoristic ending which seems to be *-ay-* at Ebla (e.g. *En-na-ià*, *Ḥa-ra-ià*, *Iš-ra-ià*), whereas it is *-iy-* in Old Akkadian (e.g. *Ir-bí-ia*, *Ìr-su-ti-a*, *Ar-ša-ti-a*), and later in Old Assyrian and in Old Babylonian (e.g. *Sukkalliya*, *A-sí-ya*, *Ma-ti-ya*). The Amorite anthroponomy appears to distinguish the masculine hypocoristic suffix *-iya* (e.g. *Zi-im-ri-ia*, *Su-mi-ia*) from the feminine *-aya* (e.g. *ᶠMa-ar-ṣa-ia*, *ᶠIa-pu-ḥa-ia*). At Ugarit, this distinction lacks clarity, but *-aya* is generally used for feminine names. In subsequent times, there is a clearly cut division between

Aramaic, on the one side, and the bulk of West and South Semitic languages, on the other. While the Aramaic gentilitial and hypocoristic ending is -ay (e.g. Kaśday, "Chaldaean"; Ḥaggay, "[Born] on a holiday"), the suffix -iy > -ī is used in Arabic (e.g. Miṣrī, "Egyptian"), in Hebrew (e.g. Ṣīdōnī, "Sidonian"; Ḥaggī, "[Born] on a holiday"), in Geʿez (e.g. ḥarrasi, "ploughman"; rawwaṣi, "runner"). Under the influence of Aramaic, however, the hypocoristic ending -ay appears frequently in Hebrew names and in Assyro-Babylonian onomastics, where -ay is often written -a-a. The suffix -ī can be added to the afformative -ān > -ōn (§29.36).

29.42.   The hypocoristic function of -ay may have a bearing on its use in forming modern Ethiopic diminutives, e.g. Tigre ʼəgelāy, "little calf", from ʼəgāl, "calf"; dəggetāy, "small town", from dəgge, "town". However, an ancient use of this afformative to develop diminutives may be attested, e.g., by Arabic ǧady and Hebrew gədī, "young goat", when compared with Libyco-Berber -*ġəṭṭ-, "goat". The corresponding Tigre feminine endings -at and -it go probably back to -*ayt > -āt or -īt; e.g. ʼəgelat, "little calf" (fem.); ʼəlatit, "little well" (cf. §29.43).

29.43.   Afformatives employed in Tigre to produce diminutives (§29.42) are also used to form pejoratives and augmentatives. However, to form pejoratives, the masculine suffix -āy is added to feminine nouns, while the feminine suffix -at or -it is added to masculine nouns. E.g. betāy, "ruined house", against betatit, "little house"; ʼənesat, "worthless man", against ʼənesāy, "little man". Instead, augmentatives can be derived only from nouns ending in -at by substituting the suffix -āy for this morpheme; e.g. baʿāy, "large cave", from baʿat, "cave".

29.44.   A related suffix -āwī appears in Arabic with place names ending in -a/-ā (e.g. Makkāwī besides Makkī, "Meccan"; Ṣafāwī, "man from Ṣafā") and with some other nouns ending in -a/-ā, e.g. dunyāwī, "earthly, worldly", from dunyā, "earth, world". Examples occur already in Ṣafaitic, as l'bṣ ʿtrw /ʿAṭṭarāwī/, "(belonging) to Abūṣu, (man) from ʿAṭṭara" (Latin Otthara). This suffix -āwi is widely used in Geʿez, e.g. bāḥrāwi, "maritime"; sanbatāwi, "Sabbatical"; krəstiyanāwi, "Christian". It is also productive in Tigrinya (e.g. ʼənglizawi, "Englishman") and in Amharic, e.g. mängəstawi, "official", from mängəst, "state"; wättaddärawi, "military", from wättaddär, "soldier". This suffix may have existed also in ancient Egyptian as suggested, e.g., by ḥmww, "craftsman", from ḥmt, "craft"; ḥsw, "singer", from ḥśî, "to sing"; ḥk3w, "magician", from ḥk3, "magic".

29.45. The suffix *-ya* is used with the prefix *wä-* in some modern Gurage dialects of South Ethiopic to form nouns of instrument, e.g. *wädrägya*, "hammer" (cf. §29.19). Modern Arabic uses the suffix *-iyya* to coin the ever increasing number of abstract nouns corresponding to English "-ity", "-ism", "-ness"; e.g. *miṣdāqiyya*, "credibility"; *'uṣūliyya*, "fundamentalism".

Afformatives in *-t*

29.46. Noun stems with suffixes *-at* /*-ut* /*-it* have often an abstract or collective meaning and, when attached to masculine root morphemes, they produce feminine nouns (§30.1-3). By analogy, most nouns with a suffix in *-t* came to be regarded as feminine. Outside Semitic, nominal patterns with *-t* are attested in ancient Egyptian, not only in truly feminine nouns (e.g. *m3w.t*, "mother"), but also in abstracts (e.g. *i3w.t*, "old age") and in concrete nouns (e.g. *mḫ3.t*, "balance"). Cushitic nouns belonging to an old stock seem to confirm the originally collective meaning of the pattern; e.g. Oromo *abbōtī*, "elders" (cf. Amorite *abbūtu*); *ummata*, "people" (cf. Old Babylonian *ummatum*). In Libyco-Berber, the feminine singular is formed by prefixing and suffixing *t*, e.g. Tuareg *te-kahi-t*, "hen", from *e-kahi*, "cock". Some of the abstract nouns thus formed were subsequently used as masculine concrete nouns; e.g. Late Babylonian *pāḫātu*, "governor"; Phoenician *mmlkt*, "king"; Numidic *gldt*, "king"; Arabic *ḫalīfat-*, "deputy, successor".

29.47. The usual feminine ending is *-at-* in the singular (e.g. *šarratu*, "queen", from *šarru*, "king", in Assyro-Babylonian), but the tone-lengthening of *a* after the dropping of case endings (§32.15) gave rise in many Phoenician dialects to a new *-āt* that became *-ōt* and later *-ūt* (§21.13); e.g. *'amatu* > *'amāt* > *'amōt*, "maid". Some Palestinian place names, like *'Anātōt*, *'Aštārōt*, *Rāmōt*, and the Hebrew singular *ḥokmōt*, "Wisdom", may witness to the same phenomenon. The feminine plural ending was *-āt-*, but it became *-ōt* in Hebrew and in Phoenician, and even *-ūt* in Punic (e.g. *alonuth*, "goddesses"). In Geʿez, the ending *-āt*, with a probably original long vowel, produces abstracts like, e.g., *na'asāt*, "youth"; *qədsāt*, "holiness". Since this derivational suffix *-āt* is homophonous with the "feminine" plural mark (§31.15), it is quite possible that this ending is to be considered as an originally plural morpheme, indicating that some concrete plurals (e.g. "holy things") have shifted to the category of abstract or collective substantives (cf. §31.16).

The same remote origin might be ascribed to Amharic abstracts like *nafqot*, "longing"; *ämləkot*, "domination"; *sərqot*, "theft", that were perhaps borrowed from North Ethiopic. Modern written Arabic widely uses the *-āt* suffix to designate concrete or abstract entities, as *mu'assasāt*, "institutions", or *taqallubāt*, "fluctuations".

29.48. The original suffix *-ut* was probably added initially to root morphemes ending in *-ū* (e.g. Hebrew *kəsūt*, "covering"), but it served subsequently as *-ūt* to form abstracts derived from other roots and, in East Semitic, it produced the masculine plural forms of adjectives. Abstract substantives in *-ūt* occur in Palaeosyrian (e.g. *ù-mu-tum* /'ūmūtum/, "fattening"), in Old Akkadian and in Assyro-Babylonian (e.g. *šarrūtum*, "kingship"), in Hebrew and in Aramaic (e.g. *malkūt*, "kingship"), most likely in Phoenician (e.g. *mmlkt*, "royalty" > "king"), rarely in Ge'ez (e.g. *ḥirut*, "goodness") and in Arabic (e.g. *malakūt*, "kingship"). In Arabic, these nouns are rightly regarded as loanwords from Aramaic, and they are masculine. Also the exceptional Arabic adjectives in *-ūt* are borrowed from Aramaic substantives, as e.g. *tarabūt*, "trained, manageable", from *tarbūt*, "training", and they have no relation whatsoever to the East Semitic masculine plural of the adjectives, e.g. *dannūtu(m)* from *dannu(m)*, "strong, powerful" (cf. §31.16; 34.4).

29.49. The suffix *-it* was most likely added originally to root morphemes ending in *-ī* (e.g. Palaeosyrian *'à-rí-tum* /harītum/, "pregnant"; Hebrew *bəkīt*, "crying") and to gentilitials in *-iy > ī* (§29.41) in order to form their feminine (e.g. *Mō'ābīt*, "Moabite"), although a formation with addition of *-at > -ā(h)* is also attested (e.g. *Mō'ăbiyyā*). It served subsequently as *-ūt* to form abstracts in Palaeosyrian (e.g. *a-za-me-tù* /lazamītu/, "coercion", "spell-binding"), in Hebrew and in Phoenician (e.g. *rē'šīt*, "beginning"), in Aramaic (e.g. *'aḥărīt*, "future"), in Ge'ez (e.g. *qadāmit*, "beginning"), and in Amharic (e.g. *mädhanit*, "medicine"). In Neo-Aramaic, the suffix *-īt* forms singulatives (§31.40), e.g. *ḥiṭīṭā*, "a grain of wheat"; *'anḫīṭā*, "a grape". Modern Hebrew adds *-ít* to form diminutives, e.g. *kadít*, "little pitcher"; *kasít*, "little glass".

Other Afformatives

29.50. North Ethiopic has an *-o* suffix used with concrete and abstract nouns; e.g. Ge'ez *fətlo*, "spinning"; Tigre *məhro*, "teaching"; Tigrinya *'ətro*, "jar". It is attested also in Amharic, e.g. *zändo*, "python";

käbäro, "tambourine". Its origin is not clear. In Gurage dialects of South Ethiopic, there is an additional suffix *-när* serving to form abstract nouns, e.g. *näž-när*, "heaviness", from *nazä-m*, "to be heavy".

29.51. Nouns borrowed from another language are often extended by particular suffixes. Thus, Sumerian loanwords are characterized in Old Akkadian and in Assyro-Babylonian, among others, by the suffix *-akkum* (§29.12), derived from the Sumerian genitive morpheme -a k (e.g. *išši'akkum* from e n s í, "city ruler"), or by a geminated last radical, followed by *-ī'um* > *-ūm* (e.g. *kussī'um* from g u z i, "throne") or *-ā'um* > *-ūm* (e.g. *tappā'um* from t a b a, "partner"). This formation preserves the final vowel of the Sumerian word, but follows the Old Akkadian nominal pattern *purussā'* (e.g. *ḫuluqqā'um*, "destruction"), which is infrequent in later East Semitic, but is attested in Palaeosyrian (cf. ᵈ*Adammā'um*). Besides, it is paralleled by the Arabic *-ā'u* class (e.g. *ḫirbā'u*, "chameleon"), which is employed also for loanwords borrowed from Aramaic with the ending *-ā'* of the emphatic state (§ 33.7), e.g. *'aṯṯalāṯā'u*, "Tuesday". Several Arabic loanwords are used in South Ethiopic idioms of the Gurage group with the palatalized suffix *-äňňä* (and variants), e.g. *kətabäňňä*, "teacher", from Arabic *kataba*, "to write" (cf. §29.52).

29.52. In modern Amharic, nouns of agent are formed by adding the suffix *-(ä)ňňa* to loanwords denoting objects and occupations; e.g. *gazeṭäňňa*, "correspondent", from *gazeṭa*, "newspaper"; *muziqäňňa*, "musician", from *muziqa*, "music"; *əsportäňňa*, "sportsman", from *əsport*, "sport". However, the suffix is added also to Ethiopic words, e.g. *əgəräňňa*, "pedestrian". Abstract nouns are formed by adding the suffix *-(ə)nnät* to concrete nouns and to adjectives; e.g. *prezidentənnät*, "presidency", from *prezident*, "president". Parallel formations occur in Tigre, where a suffix *-ənna* or *-ənnat* is used to form abstract nouns; e.g. *qədəsənna*, "sanctity"; *wələdənnat*, "parentage". The two suffixes are interchangeable, e.g. *bəṣəḥənna* and *bəṣəḥənnat*, "maturity".

29.53. Suffixes of non-Semitic origin are added in Modern Hebrew and in Neo-Aramaic to Semitic nouns to form diminutives. Thus, the Yiddish suffix *-le* is used in nursery words and in proper names, e.g. *'ímale*, "little mama"; *'ábale*, "little father". The suffix *-čik* has a Polish origin, e.g. *baḥúrčik*, "little lad"; *ḥamórčik*, "little donkey". Instead, the suffix *-iko* is Judaeo-Spanish or Ladino, e.g. *ḫabériko*, "comrade".

Neo-Aramaic diminutives are characterized by the affix -ik- and by the
feminine gender indicated by the afformative -tā [-ṭa]; e.g. karm-ik-tā,
"small vineyard", from karmā, "vineyard".

Afformative -ayim/n of Place Names

29.54.   The place names ending in -ayim /-īm /-ām or -ayin /-īn /-ān are
no duals, but toponyms formed with an archaic locative morpheme
which probably consists of the gentilitial suffix -ay /-iy with the genitive
ending -i-, followed by the mimation or the nunation. The latter usage
was not general, as it appears, e.g., from the Egyptian execration texts of
the early second millenium B.C. with place names like Yb3y /Yiblay/,
"Ebla" (E 43), 'ky /'Akkay/, "Akko" (E 49), Mktry /Magdalay/ (E 5),
"Magdala", known also with an early change ay > ā (§22.3). The distinction of the cases is still preserved in the place name Ta-al-ḫa-yu-um
(nom.), Ta-al-ḫa-yi-im or Ta-al-ḫi-yi-im (gen.), Ta-al-ḫa-ya-am (acc.),
known especially from the Mari documents. The later reduction
-iyi- > -ī- allows at Ugarit for the orthographical distinction between the
petrified country name Mṣrm (/Muṣrīm/), "Egypt" as in 'il Mṣrm, "the
gods of Egypt", and the always productive gentilitial formation Mṣrym
(/Muṣriyyūma/), "Egyptians". The same reduction explains the forms
Na(ḫ)rīma/i in the Amarna correspondence, N-h-r-n in Egyptian texts of
the New Kingdom, and Nahrīn in Aramaic, while Hebrew has
Nah^arayim, "North Mesopotamia". A reduction ay > ā appears in
Dotayin = Dotān, 'Ēnayim = 'Ēnām, and Ḥoronayim (Hebrew) = Ḥwrnn
(Moabite). Arabic place names of Syria-Palestine ending in -īn may have
the same origin, e.g. 'Ib(il)līn from Hebrew 'Iblayim.

g) Nominal Compounds

29.55.   The process of word formation in Semitic includes coinage of
nominal compounds comparable to English words like "motel" from
"motor + hotel". Such blended nouns are no strictly modern innovations
in Semitic, since numerals as Assyro-Babylonian ištenšeret, "eleven",
from ištēn ("one") + ešeret ("ten", fem.), adverbs like Biblical Hebrew
šilšōm, "the day before yesterday", from šāloš ("three") + yōm ("day"),
and some Phoenician divine names as Mlqrt, "Melqart", from milk
("king") + qart ("city"), or 'štr'sy, from 'štrt ("Astarte") and 'sy
("Isis"), belong to this category. Similar formations occur in Gafat, e.g.
abälam^wä, "shepherd", from ab^wä ("father") + älam^wä ("cow"), i.e.
"father of cows"; g^wöräbetä, "neighbour", from *g^wörä ("neighbour")

+ *bet* ("house"); *əmmäǧätit*, "lady", from *əmʷä* ("mother") + *ǧätit* ("mistress"). Amharic has a considerable variety of compound nouns, but their components are written as separate words and may even be joined by *-ənna*, "and", but the plural marker (§31.17) is added to the second element, e.g. *mäkina näǧi-w-očč*, "car drivers", lit. "car-leaders"; *balä bet-očč*, "owners", lit. "master of a house" + plur. marker; *bal-ənna mist-očč*, "married couple", lit. "husband and wife" + plur. marker. Blending of words to form new nominal compounds plays an increasing role in Modern Hebrew; e.g. *migdalor*, "lighthouse", from *migdal* ("tower") + *'ōr* ("light"); *šmarṭaf*, "babysitter", from *šomer* ("guard") + *ṭap* ("little children"). Comparable compounds are widely used also in Neo-Aramaic; e.g. *qeštīmāran*, "rainbow", from *qešteh* ("his bow") + *māran* ("our Lord"), i.e. "the bow of our Lord"; *parḥalēle*, "bat", from *pāraḥtā* ("winged animal") + *lēle* ("night"), i.e. "the winged animal of the night"; *maršema*, "well-known", "famous", from *mārā* ("owner") + *šemā* ("name"), i.e. "the owner of a name". The most common formation consists of a noun in the construct state (§33.2-4) with a genitival qualifier (cf. §64.5), but other compositions occur as well.

B. Gender

30.1. Primarily gender has nothing to do with sex: human beings and animals with sexually distinct social or economic function have simply different names, as *'ab-* vs. *'imm-*, "father" vs. "mother"; *ḥimār-* vs. *'atān-*, "ass" vs. "she-ass". Only later was the attempt made to relate them according to their kinds and different patterns. People speaking Latin, Greek, Sanskrit, and the Slavic languages, for instance, are conditioned by three-gender language patterns, while Semites speak under the influence of a two-gender language system, although Semitic nouns have preserved some traces of a completely different grammatical gender institution (§30.10-11). Yet, in historical times, the Semitic noun has two genders, masculine and feminine, like the Romance languages, but Semitic pronouns and verbs carry gender characteristics in addition to the nouns. However, gender correlates with sex only in those nouns where sex in expressed semantically. The masculine possesses no special endings, except for the cardinal numerals (§35.4). Instead, the feminine is marked by the ending *-t-*, like in ancient Egyptian and in the other Afro-Asiatic languages. A particular feature of Libyco-Berber consists in both prefixing and suffixing the morpheme *t* in the singular, as in *ta-mġar-t*, "elderly woman", *t-uššən-t*, "she-jackal", *t-iləf-t*, "wild sow". However, the Libyco-Berber *t*-prefix belongs to the case markers *ta-*, *tu-*, *ti-* of the feminine or to their allophone *tə-* (§32.1), and the resulting forms cannot be assimilated, in consequence, to the Semitic abstract nouns with both prefixed and suffixed *t*; e.g. Old Assyrian and Old Babylonian *takšītum*, "large profit"; Hebrew *tarbīt*, "increase". In fact, the *t*-morpheme was used in Semitic to form collective and abstract nouns as well, e.g. *'ābōt*, "fathers" in Hebrew; *šarrūtu(m)*, "kingship" in Assyro-Babylonian; *ḫalīfat-*, "deputation" > "deputy" in Arabic. Originally it designated a female being only in nouns derived from a root morpheme signifying a male, e.g. Arabic *malikat-*, "queen", from *malik-*, "king"; Tigre *walat* (< **waldat*), "daughter", from *wad* (< **wald*), "son". Other feminine nouns were not characterized by this ending *-t-*, e.g. *'imm-* > *'umm-*, "mother"; *'atān-* > *'ātōn*, "she-ass". Hence the absence of the *-t-* morpheme does not necessarily indicate masculine gender (cf. §30.6), except for adjectives and participles that are not always recognizable by their form as such. Conversely, the appearance of so-called "feminine" endings with *-t-* in the plural of nouns of masculine singular does not demonstrate that the gender of the nouns in question is or became feminine. Such a proof can be provided instead by the gender of the adjectives, participles, pronouns, and verbal forms referring to the noun under consideration.

30.2. The widespread use of the morpheme *-t-* to indicate female beings led by analogy to the attribution of the feminine gender to most nouns ending in *-t-*, either collective or abstract, and even to the addition of *-t-* to some feminine nouns originally deprived of this mark, e.g. Assyro-Babylonian *erṣetu(m)*, *napištu(m)*, and *imittu(m)* as compared with common Semitic *'rṣ*, "earth", *npš*, "soul, person", and *ymn*, "right hand", or Palaeosyrian *i-ma-tum* /*'immatum*/, Gafat *əm*ʷ*it*, and Soddo (Gurage) *əmmit* vs. common Semitic *'imm-*, "mother".

30.3. The morpheme *-t-* was either attached directly to the root morpheme, — e.g. in Assyro-Babylonian *bēltu(m)*, "lady", and in Phoenician *qart*, "city", — or it was connected with the root by a vowel. The three formations in *-at-*, *-it-*, *-ut-* are attested, e.g. Assyro-Babylonian *šarratu(m)*, "queen"; Ge'ez *bə'əsit*, "woman"; Hebrew *malkut*, "kingship". A third pattern may occur with nominal bases ending in a consonant cluster, like *gabr-u*, "man", *warq-u*, "yellow-green", *ḫamš-u*, "five", *rapš-u*, "wide". Instead of adding the morpheme *-at-/-it-/-ut-*, the phonological solution may then be *-CC+t-* > *-CaCt-*, *-CiCt-*, or *-CuCt-*. The quality of the vowel occurring between the last two consonants of the base is not predictable but, as a rule, it is the same as that of the vowel which may occur in the same position in the stative (§38.3). The vowel is, in most cases, *i* like in *ḫamištu*; in a restricted number of cases *u*, like in *waruqtu*; rarest is *a*, like in *rapaštu*. This pattern is clearly attested in East Semitic and it subsists in Hebrew under the form of the feminine *segolata*, like *gəberet* < **gabirtu*, "lady", from the base *gabr-*; *ḥămēšet* < **ḫamištu*, "five", from the base *ḫamš-*; *'aḥeret* < **'aḫirtu*, "other", from the base *'aḫr-*.

30.4. The *t* of the most frequent ending *-at-* was eventually lost in many Semitic idioms from the first millennium B.C. on (§27.28), although it was consistently retained in the construct state (§33.19-20). Besides, it was preserved in the cuneiform writing. The ending of the absolute state was thus reduced to *-a*, which was indicated in some languages as Hebrew, Aramaic, and Arabic by the *mater lectionis hē*; e.g. Hebrew *'iššah*, "woman"; Aramaic *millah*, "word"; Arabic *ḫālah*, "mother's sister". The elision of *-t* in late Assyro-Babylonian is attested by Aramaic transcriptions as *rsh* for Neo-Assyrian *rēšāti*, "first fruits". The loss of the *t* in the endings *-it* and *-ut* is reflected, e.g., by Aramaic *mšqy*, "watering-place", and *malkū*, "kingship", as against *malkut* in the construct state. Transcriptions of the first millennium B.C. testify also to the elision of the feminine ending *-t* in ancient Egyptian.

30.5. A number of nouns may be either masculine or feminine, without any marking of the gender. E.g. Assyro-Babylonian *unqu*, "signet ring", *mušaḫḫinu*, "stove", Sabaic *nḫl*, "palmgrove", Hebrew *kerem*, "vineyard", Neo-Aramaic *šimšā*, "sun", Tigre *bet*, "house", are attested in both genders. The gender variation may also be dialectal; e.g. Assyro-Babylonian *nāru*, "river", is generally feminine, but it has masculine concord in Neo-Assyrian. Animal names can be feminine when they designate a female; e.g. *ṯa'lab*, "fox", can also mean "she-fox" in Arabic; *šōr*, "bull", can designate a "cow" in Hebrew, and *lb'* can be a "lion" or a "lioness" in Sabaic. On the opposite, *faras*, "mare", can also designate a "horse" in Arabic. Masculine concord may refer to species, abstracting from sex.

30.6. Besides the sex of human and animal beings, and the formal constitution of the noun with the ending *-t-*, some categories of nouns determine their feminine gender. Thus, names of cities and countries are generally feminine, but they tend to be masculine in Assyro-Babylonian because of the usually masculine gender of the word *ālu(m)*, "city", just as Hebrew place names beginning with *byt*, "house", are masculine, since *byt* is a masculine noun in Hebrew. In Ethiopic, gender usage is predictable only for nouns denoting human beings. Nearly all other nouns occur in either gender, but for some semantic fields there is a definite preference. Thus, names of months, stars, meteorological phenomena, rivers, metals, and weapons tend to be treated in Ethiopic as masculine. In Amharic, almost any noun can be treated as feminine if it refers to something female, relatively small, or toward which the speaker feels affection. E.g. *yəh mäṣhaf*, "this book", is masculine, but *yəčč mäṣhaf* is feminine because it might refer to a favourite booklet. Even the feminine pronoun *anči*, "you", may be applied in Addis Ababa to a male friend to show affection. Names of parts of the body, especially paired, are generally feminine in Semitic: *'udn-*, "ear"; *yad-*, "hand"; *'ayn-*, "eye"; *rigl-*, "foot"; *napš-*, "breath", then "throat" (§63.7); *šinn-*, "tooth"; *qarn-*, "horn"; *rūḥ-*, "breath"; etc. However, instances occur, even in literary texts, where such nouns are treated as masculine, although they are used in a proper sense; e.g. in Hebrew *yad* (Ex. 17,12) and *yāmīn*, "right hand" (Prov. 27,16); in Aramaic *'yn* (TAD III,1.1,157) and *rgl* (TAD III,1.1,170); in Christian Palestinian Aramaic *'dr'*, "arm", *lyb*, "heart", *'pyn*, "face"; in Neo-Arabic *kaff*, "palm of the hand", perhaps *yad*, "hand", and *riǧl*, "foot". In an Old Babylonian letter from Mari, e.g., the plural *qar-na-at na-li*, "horns of roebuck", is referred to by a masculine pronominal suffix (ARM XIII,55) (cf. §31.15). In these questions, dialectal differences and even personal preferences must obviously be taken into account. Besides, names of various tools are feminine (e.g. *ḥarb-*, "sword"; *kās-*, "bowl"), as well as names of different stuffs (e.g. *'abn-*, "stone"; *milḥ-*, "salt"). However, e.g. Tigre *madoša*, "hammer", and *gəndāy*, "log of wood", are masculine. In other words, no generalizations are possible.

30.7. Semitic languages show instances of nouns which can be either masculine or feminine (§30.5), as well as of nouns the gender of which changes when they are used in the plural. In Assyro-Babylonian e.g., *girru(m)*, "road, march", or *šamnu(m)*, "oil", can be either masculine or feminine in the singular. Instead, *ṭuppu(m)*, "tablet", is masculine in the singular, but can be masculine or feminine in the plural, and *libbu(m)*, "heart", is masculine in the singular, while its feminine plural *libbātu*(*m*) is used in the special acceptation of "heartstrings, anger". One can observe in Tigre, e.g., that inanimate feminine nouns may have a masculine singular concord when they are used in plural, e.g. *həta gərrum* (masc. sing.) *wanaččit* (plur. of fem. *wānča*) *ba*, "she has beautiful bracelets". In the Lowland East Cushitic languages of the "Sam" sub-group, there is a large noun class which is feminine in the singular and formally masculine in the plural, and there are traces of another class with the opposite gender-number relation.

30.8. In any case, the *formal* distinction between masculine and feminine is not an original feature of Semitic languages, as shown by the many basic feminine nouns without any special morpheme. This opinion is apparently confirmed by the South Ethiopic idioms of the Gurage group which have no feminine mark, although this situation may also reflect that of Highland East Cushitic. The distinction in gender is indicated by the verb or the pronoun referring to the noun. For the sex differentiation of animals, an additional word may be used: *täbat* or *wər* may serve to designate the male, *arəst*, *ast* or *äm* the female (*wər kutara*, "cock"; *arəst kutara*, "hen"). Other living beings have different root morphemes for the male and the female, e.g. *ärč*, "boy"; *gäräd*, "girl". However, the *-t* morpheme characterizes some feminine proper names and it occurs in a couple of substantives (e.g. *gregät*, "women of the same clan"), in the pronominal element *ebäryät*, "so-and-so" from the masculine *ebäryä*, and probably in *zak̲-it*, "this one". Other Ethiopian languages have gender specifiers for the male and female sex of animals and of human beings, although the *-t* morpheme is used to a certain extent as a feminine marker as well; e.g. Gafat *täbat bušä*, "boy", *ansətä bušä*, "girl"; Amharic *wänd ləǧ*, "boy", *set ləǧ*, "girl"; *täbat ṭəǧǧa*, "he-calf", *anəst ṭəǧǧa*, "she-calf".

30.9. It is interesting to recall here that no gender distinction based on sex existed in Sumerian that has a gender classification made on another basis entirely — that of animate and inanimate categories. The same gender classification exists, e.g., in the Algonquian family of North American Indians, while the Bantu languages of Africa and the Caucasian languages have many grammatical genders, including "human beings", "animals", "plants", "places", etc. The Bantu, e.g., divide things into eight to fourteen categories, which they designate by different prefixes. In the east Caucasian languages, as Chechen, Avaro-Andi, or Darghi, substantives are divided into two to six classes or genders.

30.10. Semitic languages preserve traces of a similar gender classification with a distinction, e.g., between wild animals and domestic animals. Thus, the postpositive determinant -*b* qualifies the grammatical gender of wild and dangerous animals; e.g. *əmb-ab* / *ḥub-āb*, "snake" (South Ethiopic; cf. §11.9); *'arn-ab-*, "hare"; *dub-b-*, "bear"; *ḏi'-b*, "wolf"; *ḏub-b* > *ḏub-āb*, "flies"; *ḍab-b*, "lizard"; *hab-b-*, "elephant"; *kal-b-*, "dog" (dangerous and originally a wild one), but still lacking the -*b-* in Cushitic and Chadic; *nuh-b*, "bee"; *'ank-ab-*, "spider"; *'aqr-ab-*, "scorpion"; *ġurā-b* / **ġāri-b*, "crow, raven", still lacking the -*b* in South Ethiopic (*qurä*, *kura*, etc.) and in Cushitic (*qura*, *ġura*); *ta'l-ab-*, "fox, jackal"; *qʷər'-ab-*, "frog" (Tigrinya), lacking the final *b* in *qʷər'a* (Tigrinya) and in other Semitic languages; *wärā-ba* or *urā-ba*, "hyena" (Harari, Gurage), related to Somali *warā-be* and perhaps to Egyptian *whr*, "dog", still lacking -*ba*. Instead, the postpositive determinant -*l* / -*r* qualifies the grammatical gender of domestic or tamed animals; e.g. *'imm-ar-*, "ram, lamb"; *baq-ar-*, "cattle"; *ḥilam-ār*, "donkey"; *ḥu/izz-īr-*, "swine, pig"; *kir-r-*, "lamb"; *laḥ-r-* / *raḥ-l-*, "ewe", attested as *laḥ*, without the final morphem -*l-*, in Somali and in Rendille (East Cushitic); *'ay-r-*, "ass-foal"; *taw-r-*, "ox" (cf. §65.5); *'ayy-al-*, "deer"; *fəyy-äl* / *fəǧǧ-älä*, "goat" (South Ethiopic); *gam-al-*, "camel, dromedary"; *nayy-al-*, "goat, roebuck"; *nam-l-*, "ant" (!); *'ag-al-* / *'ig-l-*, "calf"; *dawb-al*, "young ass" (Arabic); *ǧawz-al* "young pigeon" (Arabic); *kuta-ra*, "poultry" (Gurage). A significative example is provided by Gafat *anšə-lä*, "donkey" (Argobba *hansia*), which can hardly be separated from Sumerian a n š e, "donkey", and therefore seems to indicate that **hanše* was a West Asiatic culture word used around 3000 B.C. Some of these suffixed animal names and similar formations appear in other Afro-Asiatic languages as well; e.g. Egyptian *3-bw*, "elephant"; *iy-r*, "deer"; *s-rw*, "sheep"; Egyptian *d-b* and Highland East Cushitic *ló-ba*, "hippopotamus"; *zab-bä*, "lion", but *dáb-el*, "goat" (Saho); *bak-ál*, "kid" (Afar); Tuareg *a-gʸān-ba*, "crocodile"; Libyco-Berber *a-tbi-r*, "pigeon"; *a-ġy-ul*, "ass"; *izimm-ər*, "ram, lamb". This gender classification should thus go back to a common Afro-Asiatic background, just as the postpositive morpheme -*t* categorizing the collective or abstracts nouns, but it must be posterior to the domestication of animals, mainly in the seventh millennium B.C. Contrary to -*t*, however, the determinants -*b* and -*r* / -*l* became constituent elements of the concerned nominal roots in the historically known languages, although these formations were still operative in the late third or the early second millennium B.C., as shown by the Semitic name of the "dromedary", *gam-al-*, domesticated in that period in Arabia and still called *kām* (plur. *kám*) in Cushitic (Bedja), without the morpheme -(*a*)*l*. The same morpheme is prefixed in Libyco-Berber to **gam* / **kam*, intensified as usual to **ġam*; thus *a-l-ġ*ʷ*m* in Tachelhit, *a-ž-ġəm* in Tamazight, with the typical change *l > ž* of that dialect, and *a-r-ġəm* in Tarifit, with the regular Rifan allophone *r // l*. The East Cushitic name of the dromedary, *gāl* in Rendille and Boni, *gēl-a* (collective) in Somali, is best explained by the loss of intervocalic *m*, a development attested in Boni. Its Tuareg name *alam* has a different origin. It is the same word as Gafat *älam*ʷ*ä*, "cow", and it lacks the determinant *l*. There are also several exceptions in Semitic, but these are mostly either loanwords or derivatives.

30.11.   A number of languages distinguish a grammatical gender comprising names of parts of the body. Thus, in Proto-Semitic, the postpositive determinant -*n* qualifies this gender as shown by *'ud̲-n-*, "ear"; *āfu-na*, "nose" (Gurage, from Semitic *'anf* + *na*; Oromo *fuňňān*, with metathesis); *bat̲-n-*, "stomach"; *gaḥ-ān-* "belly"; *g*ʷ*ad-n*, "rib" (Ethiopic, Cushitic); *ḥiṣ-n*, "lap", "bosom", perhaps from the same root as *č̣ə-n*, "thigh" (Amharic, Gafat, Argobba, Gurage; cf. Oromo *činā*, "side"); *yam-an-*, "right hand"; *t̲ad-an/un*, "teat, udder"; *laš-/liš-ān-*, "tongue"; *'ay-n-*, "eye"; *pa-n-*, "face"; *pa'-n-*, "foot"; *qut̲-n-*, "small finger"; *qar-n-*, "horn"; *šin-n-*, "tooth"; *q*ʸ*ən-n*, "buttocks" (Gurage); also Oromo *af-ān*, "mouth", corresponding to Ge'ez *'af* and Harari *af*. The noun *t̲ad-an* (Arabic), *t̲d-n* (Ugaritic), *ša-du-un* (Amorite), "teat, udder", corresponds to a form without final -*n*, as Ugaritic *t̲d*, Hebrew *šad*, Syriac *t̲ədā*. The word "tongue" is attested without the gender morpheme in Egyptian (*ns*), in Libyco-Berber (*i-ls*), and in Chadic (**lš-*), while "ear" and "horn" lack it in Cushitic (**waž*; Omotic *qaro*). Interestingly *əzän* designates the "heart" in some Agaw dialects of the Qemant-Qwara group, *wazana* in Saho, *wadne* in Somali, etc., whereas "ear" is called *käzär(ä)* in the same Agaw dialects, with other names in various Cushitic languages.

C. Number

31.1.   Within the general domain of number expression, languages differ on the basis of whether they limit themselves to singular and plural, or include also dual and, sometimes, trial. Semitic languages possess three numbers: singular, dual, and plural. Besides, there are collective nouns (§31.38-39) and paucatives (§31.35-37). The latter category, attested at least in Arabic and in Ethiopic, needs further investigation. As for singulars, they denote either a single being or thing, as "man", or a group of beings or things regarded collectively, as "mankind". In all probability, the singular was originally the only number, while the plural was expressed by the collective singular, characterized in Semitic by a different pattern of the basic root, corresponding to the so-called "broken plural" (§31.23-34). The plural distinguished by additional morphemes from the singulars and from the collective singulars is then the result of a further development. Many language groups present plural formations radically different. In the Bantu languages, for example, the plural is distinguished from the singular by other sets of class-prefixes, e.g. in Class 1 (human beings) *mu-ntu*, "man", *ba-ntu*, "men"; in Class 7 (diminutives) *ka-ntu*, "little man", *tu-ntu*, "little men". Besides these general observations, the singulars do not require any particular presentation, except for the singulatives derived from collectives (§31.40-42).

a) Dual

31.2. The dual is formed by special endings attached to the singular. It serves to denote not only pairs of objects — mostly parts of the body occurring in pairs, e.g. the eyes —, but also to express simple duality. Its regular occurrence in Palaeosyrian, Old Akkadian, Ugaritic, Arabic, and in Modern South Arabian idioms indicates that its restricted use in other languages results from the widespread substitution of the plural for the dual.

31.3. Comparative analysis indicates that the dual is diptotic in all the Semitic languages, viz. it distinguishes only the nominative and a single oblique case (genitive-accusative). It is formed by adding -*ā* in the nominative and -*ay* > -*ē* / -*ī* / -*ā* in the oblique case. These dual morphemes are attached to the stem or to its "feminine" ending -*t*, and they are followed in the absolute state of the noun (§33.12) by nunation or mimation, which can be missing. E.g. Old Akkadian *bēlān*, *bēlīn*, "the two masters"; *bēltān*, *bēltīn*, "the two mistresses"; Thamūdic *h-bkrtn*, "the two young she-camels"; Ṣafaitic *n'mtn*, "two ostriches". The absence of nunation or mimation does not necessarily indicate its dropping in a later period. In Palaeosyrian, at Ebla, nunation is generally missing, e.g. *in ba-ta-a*, "in the two houses"; *al₆ su-lu-la-a* 1 ITI, "by virtue of the two horns of the moon".

31.4. In the Semitic languages which have lost the case endings (§32.12-18), the dual morpheme *-ay* of the oblique case is commonly used also in the nominative. It can be contracted to *-ē* (Arabic colloquials) or to *-ī > -i* (Modern South Arabian). In the absolute state, it is followed by the nunation in Aramaic, in Neo-Arabic, and in Modern Arabic colloquials, e.g. *qarnayin*, "horns" in Aramaic; *'ēnēn*, "eyes", and *'entēn*, "two eyes", in the Arabic dialects of Damascus and of Baghdad (§31.6). However, among modern colloquials, that of Ḥaḍramawt has *-an* for the dual in all cases, but the *ā* might result from a monophthongization of *ay* (cf. §22.4). In Hebrew and in Phoenician, we have mimation instead of nunation, e.g. Hebrew *raglayim*, "feet, paws"; Phoenician *'ḥym*, "two brothers".

31.5. The mimation is used also in Ugaritic, but the unvocalized texts and the contraction of the diphthongs reveal no formal distinction between the nominative and the oblique case. Authors generally believe that such a distinction has to be admitted since Ugaritic possesses the three basic cases (§32.13). However, this assumption is by no means certain, because the whole extension of the same single form for all cases of the dual in ancient Arabic dialects calls for caution. The attested Pre-Classical forms are *-āni* or *-āna*, in the construct state *-ā*. The *ā* of the oblique case might result from a contraction *ay > ā* (cf. §22.3-4).

31.6. A noun designating an object that comes naturally in pairs, in particular a part of the body, is generally used in the dual, but it may also appear in the plural when more than two are meant or when the word is used in a derived or different meaning. Thus, in Ugaritic e.g., besides the dual *qrnm*, "two horns", occurs also the feminine plural *qrnt* when more than two horns are meant, and besides the dual *ydm*, "hands", appears also the feminine plural in *'šr ydt*, "ten handles" or some similar tools. In classical and literary Arabic e.g., the dual "two hands" is *yadāni* in the nominative, but the plural of the same feminine noun is *yudīyun* or *'ayādin*, with various meanings. Instead, in most modern Arabic colloquials, the original dual ending is used as a "pseudo-dual", e.g. *'ēnēn*, "eyes", while "two eyes" is *'entēn* in Damascus and in Baghdad, with the dual ending added to the feminine morpheme *-t-*, thus *-tayn > -tēn*. A similar situation occurs in Modern South Arabian languages where original duals can function as plurals, and are so considered by native speakers (e.g. *naṣfi*, "halves", from sing. *naṣf*).

31.7. In Assyro-Babylonian, dual endings are replaced by plural endings from the Old Babylonian period on. However, they continue to occur with nouns that denote a pair of objects, but they are then used even if the number of these objects is more than two. When the same nouns occur with the regular plural ending, they have a different meaning. Therefore, the contrast between originally dual endings and plural endings is henceforth on the lexical level and it does not express any more the distinction between the numbers dual and plural. E.g., two or more "hands" are *qātā(n)*, while *qātāti* designates two or more "shares".

31.8. The same evolution is attested in Hebrew and in Punic. E.g., "six wings" are called in Hebrew *šēš kǝnāpayim*, with the dual ending, while the regular feminine plural *kǝnāpōt* means "extremities". In Punic, the dual ending occurs in *p'mm*, that refers to the paws of sacrificed animals, but the regular feminine plural *p'mt* is used when the word means "occurrences, times".

b) Plural

31.9. The plural may be formed in Semitic by the attachment of special endings to the singular or by the use of a noun pattern different from the one employed for the singular. The first type of plural is called "external" or "sound"; it may consist either in the lengthening of the characteristic vowel of the singular (§31.10-11), or in suffixing an ending *-ān(-)* or *-āt(-)* (§31.12-20). The second type of plural is referred to as "internal" or "broken" plural (§31.23-34). There is also a plural pattern in *-h* (§31.19), which could be related to the broken plurals, and a plural by reduplication of the root morpheme (§31.21-22). Besides, there are examples of double plurals, i.e. consisting in pluralizations of forms already plural. E.g. Arabic *qawl*, "saying", *'aqwāl*, "sayings", *'aqāwīl*, "ensembles of sayings"; Ge'ez *liq*, "elder", "chief", plur. *liqān* and *liqānāt*. Broken plurals, in particular, are sometimes further pluralized by an external plural (§31.25,28,33) and both forms may coexist (§31.33), e.g. in Ge'ez where the external plural ending *-āt* may be added to the broken plural, as in the case of *liq* and of *mǝsāle*, "proverb", plur. *'amsāl* and *'amsālāt*. Such a double pluralization is frequent in Berber dialects (§28.13).

External Plural

31.10. Comparative analysis indicates that the external plural of Proto-Semitic or Common Semitic is diptotic and that it is formed by the lengthening of the characteristic vowel of the singular. Thus, the plural of the nominative *kalbu(m)*, "dog", is *kalbū* and the plural of the oblique case *kalbi(m)* is *kalbī*. Similarly, the plural of the feminine nominative *kalbatu(m)*, "bitch", is *kalbātu(m)* and the plural of the corresponding oblique case *kalbati(m)* is *kalbāti(m)*. In the masculine plural of Old Akkadian and Assyro-Babylonian, the mimation of the singular is omitted, but it is preserved in the absolute state of plural North Semitic nouns, at least in Ugaritic, also in Hebrew and in Phoenician, while it changes to nunation in Aramaic (with the exception of Samalian), in Arabic, Moabite, Ammonite. It is as yet uncertain whether the Liḥyānite construct plural *bnw* /banū/, "sons", implies an absolute masculine plural *banūna*, like in Classical Arabic.

In Neo-Aramaic, the ending *-yāti* is the plural morpheme of the nouns ending in *-tā*; e.g. *šišiltā*, "chain", plur. *šišilyāti*. This formation is already attested in Late Aramaic; e.g. *bīrtā*, "stronghold", plur. *bīrānyāt* with a double plural termination *-ān + yāt* (§31.12; cf. Late Babylonian *bīranātu*).

31.11. The allophone *-ē* of the ending *-ī* in the oblique case of the plural is already attested in Old Akkadian. In the "plene" spellings *a-wi-li-e*, "men", *bi-ti-e*, "houses", which regularly occur in Old Assyrian and occasionally in Old Babylonian, the *-e* functions as the phonetic indicator of this long vowel. The later Assyro-Babylonian plurals *kalbē*, used also for the nominative, can best be explained by the common tendency of the oblique case to stand for all cases. This trend is well known from Hebrew (e.g. *sūsīm*, "horses"), Phoenician (ηλειμ = *'lm*, "deity", a plural in form), Aramaic (e.g. *millīn*, "words"), Neo-Aramaic (e.g. *tōrī/ē*, "bulls"), and modern Arabic colloquials (e.g. *ḥaddādīn*, "smiths"), but the distinction of the cases is preserved in the Samalian dialect of Aramaic (e.g. *mlkw*, "kings", but *mlky* in the oblique case), in the Canaanite dialect of the Gezer calendar (e.g. *yrḥw 'sp*, "months of ingathering"), in Classical Arabic (e.g. *sāriqūna*, "thieves", but *sāriqīna* in the oblique case), and most likely in Liḥyānite and in the earlier stages of South Arabian, as suggested by the construct state *bnw* and *bny*, "sons".

31.12. A masculine plural in *-ānu/ū* (nominative, e.g. *šarrānu*, "kings") and *-āni/ī* (oblique case, e.g. *ilāni*, "gods") appears in Assyro-Babylonian from the Old Babylonian period on, i.e. from the time when the distinction between the numbers dual and plural was abandoned. This apparent innovation might thus be explained as an expanded use of the originally dual ending -*ān* (§31.3), followed by the case markers -*u/ū* and -*i/ī*. However, one should bear in mind that the plural in -*n* is attested in Libyco-Berber as early as the 2nd century B.C., thus independently from any influence of Arabic, e.g. in the nouns *nbb-n*, "cutters", and *nbṭ-n* "splitters", of a bilingual Punico-Numidic inscription from Dougga. Besides, the same suffix forms the plural in Chadic (e.g. Logone *ngun*, "belly", plur. *ngwaren*), as well as the plural patterns *fiʿlān* and *fuʿlān* in Arabic (e.g. *ġizlān*, "broken" plural of *ġazāl*, "gazelle"). The apparently double indications of the plural in East Semitic -*ān-ū* or -*ān-ī* (e.g. *a-la-nu-ú*, "cities"; *a-la-ni-i-ka*, "your cities") could perhaps be compared with the addition of the plural ending -*āt* to the dual morpheme -*ēn-* in the colloquial Arabic of Baghdad (e.g. *sitt riġlēnāt*, "six pairs of paws"). The ending -*āni* < -*ānī/ē* is also used to form masculine plurals in Neo-Aramaic and it is rightly seen there as combining the element -*ān-* and the usual plural morpheme -*ī/ē*. The external masculine plural in Modern South Arabian languages is -*īn* or its allophone (e.g. *ġəfnīn*, "eyebrows"), while the most common feminine ending is -*ōtən*, -*tən* or an allophone (e.g. *ġəgōtən*, "girls"). In Geʿez, which kept only few traces of the dual, the external masculine plural ending can be also -*ān* (e.g. *masiḥān*, plural of *masiḥ*, "Messiah"), although the "feminine" suffix -*āt* is used for masculine substantives as well (e.g. *kahənāt*, "priests"; §31.15). Modern North Ethiopic still preserves the ending of the external plural -*an* in Tigrinya and -*ām* in Tigre, with the change *n* > *m*; e.g. Tigrinya *qəddusan*, "saints"; Tigre *qəddusām kətubām*, "Holy Scriptures". It is used mainly with participles and verbal adjectives. Significantly, the ending -*ān* appears in Aramaic as the feminine plural morpheme of the absolute state, as early as the ninth century B.C., and it is being substituted for the feminine ending -*t* of the singular (e.g. *malkān*, "queens").

31.13. Some nouns with the overt -*t*- mark of the feminine in the singular have a masculine and a feminine forms in the plural. E.g. Arabic *sanat(un)*, "year", has the plurals *sinūna* and *sanawāt(un)*, and *ri'at(un)*, "lung", corresponds to the plurals *ri'ūna* and *ri'āt(un)*. The plural *s*[1]*nn* /*šinūn(a)*/ is attested also in Ṣafaitic. In Hebrew, *šānā*, "year", has the plural *šānīm* in the absolute state, but *šənōt* in the construct state, while *'ăšērā*, "sanctuary", has both plurals *'ăšērīm* and *'ăšērōt*. The Aramaic noun *ginnā*, "garden", has the plurals *ginnīn* and *ginnayyā* or *ginnātā* in the emphatic state (§33.7). There seems to be no contrast between the two sets of forms that can be determined at present.

31.14. A similar phenomenon occurs in Assyro-Babylonian, in Ugaritic, and in Aramaic with nouns which do not have the feminine morpheme *-t-* in the singular. Thus, in Assyro-Babylonian, *bābu*, "gate", has the plurals *bābāni* and *bābāti*; *biblu*, "gift", is attested with the plurals *biblāni* and *biblāti*; *idu(m)*, "hand", with *idū* and *idātu(m)*. In Ugaritic, *r'iš*, "head", appears with the plurals *r'ašm*, *r'ašt* and *r'išt*; *grn*, "threshing floor", has the plurals *grnm* and *grnt*, while the word "wheat" (root *ḥnṭ*) is attested under the forms *ḥṭm* and *ḥṭṭ*. These nouns cannot be considered automatically as feminine, as shown by the plurals *nasīkāni* and *nasīkāti* of the name *nasīku*, "sheikh" or "prince" of the Aramaeans. In Imperial Aramaic, *yōm*, "day", has the attested plurals *yōmīn* and, in the construct state, *yōmāt*. Both forms of plural occur also in Hebrew (*yāmīm*, *yəmōt*) and in Phoenician (*ymm*, *ymt*), while the Ammonite phrase *ywmt rbm*, "many days", indicates that the morpheme *-t* does not change the gender of the noun, as shown by the masculine plural termination of the modifying adjective *rbm*. Some Neo-Aramaic masculine nouns have a "feminine" plural formation besides the regular masculine plural ending. This alternative plural regularly adds a special connotation and agrees with masculine forms of adjectives and of verbal pronominal affixes; e.g. *mārā*, "owner" (masc.); *mārī*, "owners" (masc.); *mārwātā*, "known owners" (masc.).

31.15. Some nouns, both masculine and feminine, without the *-t-* mark of the feminine in the singular, take the "feminine" ending in the plural. This phenomenon assumes larger proportions in Assyro-Babylonian and especially in North Ethiopic where the "feminine" plural ending *-āt* is widely used for masculine nouns. Also the external plural in *-očč* / *-ač*, used for both genders in modern South Ethiopic (§31.17) and in some Tigre nouns, originates from an ancient **-āti*, which was the ending of the plural oblique case: the vowel *i* caused palatalization of *t* and was absorbed in the palatal. In Assyro-Babylonian, some of the nouns in question are really feminine also in the singular, as e.g. *abullu(m)*, "city gate", plur. *abullātu(m)*, or *eleppu(m)*, "ship", plur. *eleppētu(m)*. Other nouns however, as e.g. *qaqqadu(m)*, "head", plur. *qaqqadātu(m)*, or *ikkaru*, "peasant", plur. *ikkarātu(m)*, are masculine in both numbers. A third group consists of nouns which are masculine in the singular, but are treated as feminine in the plural, e.g. *epinnu(m)*, "plough", plur. *epinnētu(m)*, or *eqlu(m)*, "field", plur. *eqlētu(m)*. The situation is similar in Ugaritic with nouns like *ks'u*, "chair", or *mṯb*, "dwelling", which have the plurals *ks'at* and *mṯbt*. We know at least that *ks'u* is also feminine in the singular. In North Ethiopic the ending *-āt* is used instead of the masculine plural morpheme *-ān* without influencing the gender of the nouns (e.g. Ge'ez *māy*, "water", plur. *māyāt*; Tigrinya *säb*, "person", plur. *säbat*), while the morpheme *-ān* (cf. §31.12) is employed for adjectives and participles (e.g. Ge'ez *ḥadis*, "new", plur. *ḥadisān*), and for a small number of substantives. In Tigrinya, the plural ending is *-tat* after vowels (e.g. *gäza*, "house", plur. *gäzatat*), even when the final vowel has only an auxiliary function (§27.16), as in *ləbbi*, "heart", plur. *ləbbətat* (cf. §31.20). Besides the plural ending *-očč* (§31.17), Amharic continues using the Old Ethiopic ending *-āt*, mainly with masculine nouns or with nouns unspecified as to gender, e.g. *ḥawaryat*, "apostles", *ləsanat*, "languages", *gädamat*, "convents". The wide use of the ending *-āt* can best be explained by the original function of the morpheme *-t-* forming collective nouns (§30.1). However, a side influence of the Cushitic adstratum on Ethiopic should not be excluded, since *-t-* is the most common Cushitic marker of the plural, also in Highland East Cushitic.

31.16.   For the adjective masculine plural, Assyro-Babylonian uses the morpheme *-ūtu*, in the oblique case *-ūti*, e.g. *rabiu(m)*, "great", plur. *rabiūtu(m)*, *rabiūti(m)*. This morpheme is homophonous with the derivational afformative *-ūtu* that forms abstract nouns (e.g. *šarrūtu*, "kingship") and, therefore, it is sometimes difficult to decide whether the noun ending in *-ūtu* is an adjective masculine plural, as *šībūtu(m)*, "elders, witnesses", or a substantive with collective meaning, e.g. *amēlūtu(m)*, "mankind". In the context, however, the question can be decided on the basis of grammatical concord.

31.17.   Contrary to Ge'ez and to the modern North Ethiopic, South Ethiopic has an external plural only. The Amharic broken plurals are borrowed from Ge'ez (§31.34) and the preserved patterns are no longer productive. South Ethiopic uses the ending *-očč* / *-ač* deriving from an ancient **-āti* as plural marker without making a distinction between the masculine and the feminine (§31.15). This plural morpheme is pronounced *-očč* in Amharic, whereas it is *-äč* in Harari and *-ač* in Argobba, Gafat, and the Soddo dialect of Gurage. East Gurage dialects add a vowel to the element *-č*: *-čä*, *-əččä*. E.g., the plural of *bet*, "house", is *betočč* in Amharic, whereas it is *bedač* in Argobba; the plural of *ənǧ*, "hand", is *ənǧəččä* in East Gurage. East Gurage dialects also repeat the last radical to express the plural (§31.22); e.g. *čulo*, "baby", plur.

čulalo; *gamela*, "camel", plur. *gamelalo*; *wagi*, "elder brother", plur. *wagigo*. Instead, West Gurage has no plural marker; thus, *färäz* means both "horse" and "horses"; *bet* is "house" and "houses". The number of the noun is indirectly reflected in the verb and in the pronouns. The same situation is found also in some Cushitic dialects of the region.

31.18. Aramaic uses the feminine plural morphemes to form the plural of some masculine nouns — mainly loanwords — ending in a vowel, thus *'āsē*, "doctor", plur. *'ās(^{a})wātā* in the emphatic state; *'aryē*, "lion", plur. *'aryāwān* and *'aryāwātā*; *kinā*, "companion", plur. *kənāwān* and *kənāwātā*; *korsē*, "seat", plur. *korsāwān*; *peḥā*, "governor", plur. *paḥ(^{a})wātā*. The same usage is attested in Arabic; e.g. *bāšā*, "pasha", plur. *bāšawāt(un)*; *'aġā*, "ag(h)a", plur. *'aġāwāt(un)*; *'ustāḏ*, "master", plur. *'ustāḏāt(un)* or *'asātiḏa(tun)*. Similar plurals occur in North Ethiopic, e.g. in Tigrinya where *gäza*, "house", has a plural *gäzawətti* besides the usual *gäzatat* (§31.15).

31.19. Sabaic plural patterns in -*h* are found with biconsonantal nominal roots in *'bh*, "fathers", *'mh*, "female clients, handmaids" (sing. *'mt*), and with the addition of an external feminine plural morpheme in *'mht*, "mothers". The plural in -*h* is attested also in Arabic (e.g. *šifāh*, "lips") and in Qatabanic (*'ḫh-*, "brothers", construct state), while the formation of the plural in -*ht* occurs in Palaeosyrian, with *gu-la-'à-tum* / *gullahātum* /, "cups", in Ugaritic, with *'amht*, "handmaids"; *'umht*, "mothers"; *'ilht*, "goddesses"; *qrht*, "towns", likewise in Minaic (e.g. *'ntht*, "women"; *'hlht*, "clans"), in Ḥaḍramitic (*'bhty*, "fathers", construct state), in Hebrew (*'ămāhōt*, "handmaids"), in Phoenician (*dlht*, "doors"), in Aramaic (e.g. *'imməhātā*, "the mothers"; *'ābāhātōk*, "your fathers"; *šəmāhāt*, "names" in the construct state), and in some modern Arabic colloquials, e.g. in the Ḥawrān (*'abbahāt*, "fathers"; *'ummahāt*, "mothers"). The Tigre plurals *'abayt*, "fathers", and *'afayt*, "mouths", have probably the same origin. In all these instances, the ending -*t* of the plural seems to be superimposed upon an earlier ending in -*h*.

31.20. The same ending -*āt* > -*ōt* of the plural is sometimes superimposed upon the singular ending -*t*. E.g. Assyro-Babylonian *išātu(m)*, "fire", plur. *išātātu*; *ṣuḥartu(m)*, "girl", plur. *ṣuḥartātu(m)* besides *ṣuḥarātu(m)*; Ugaritic *'aht*, "sister", plur. *'ahtt*, besides *'aht*; Hebrew *delet*, "door", plur. *dəlātōt*; *qešet*, "bow", plur. *qəšātōt*; Ge'ez *barakat*, "blessing", plur. *barakatāt*; Tigre *sadāyat*, "help", plur. *sadāyatāt*;

'āmat, "year", plur. 'āmotāt. This suffix -otāt < -atāt is common in Tigre with nouns whose singular ends in -at, but it is used also with other nouns; e.g. sərəq, "theft", plur. sərqotāt. The Tigrinya plural ending -tat appearing after vowels is probably related to these cases; e.g. gäza, "house", plur. gäzatat (§31.15); cf. mä'alti, "day", plur. mä'altat.

Plural by Reduplication

31.21. A plural formation by reduplicating the root morpheme is attested for some biconsonantal nouns, e.g. Palaeosyrian ḫa-ba-ḫa-bí (gen.), "hidden things" (cf. Arabic ḫab'), Hebrew mēmē, "waters" (construct state); Assyro-Babylonian birbirrū, "glare", with no singular but with the addition of the plural morpheme -ū; Aramaic rab, "great", plur. rabrəbīn (masc.) and rabrəbān (fem.); Syriac daqdəqē, "little ones"; ḥadhədānē, "certain ones", also with the addition of the usual plural ending; Sabaic 'l'lt, "gods", Hebrew pe, plur. pīpiyyōt, "cutting edges", with the addition of the -t morpheme. The repetition of the root morpheme is probably one of the oldest methods to express the plural. It is used in Chadic (e.g. Hausa dambe, "struggle", plur. dambedambe), to a lesser extent in Cushitic (e.g. Bedja san, "brother", plur. sanasanā), in Sumerian (e.g. kur - kur, "mountains"), and in the Malay language (e.g. rumah-rumah, "houses"), while ancient Egyptian initially reduplicated the hieroglyph to mark the dual and wrote it thrice to signify the plural. A similar practice is attested at Ebla where the triple writing AN.AN.AN may indicate the plural "gods", while the double writing AN.AN signifies "heaven". This type of plural marking is unlikely to have arisen from a distributive context (§35.22), for reduplication can have various functions. The addition of the usual plural morphemes (-ū, -īn / -ān, -t) should be considered as a secondary feature.

31.22. An analogous plural formation is attested in some South Ethiopian languages which express the plural by the repetition of the last radical, especially in Gurage (§31.17); e.g. čulo, "baby", plur. čulalo; wolla, "neighbour", plur. wollalu; ämar, "donkey", plur. ämararä; gʷäbbe, "brother", plur. gʷäbbabit, with addition of a -t. Also Amharic uses the repetition of a radical as a device to express the plural in a limited number of nouns, but this consonant is not necessarily the last one (e.g. wäyzäro, "lady", plur. wäyzazər), and the plural morpheme -očč can still be added to the extended root (e.g. wändəmm, "brother", plur. wändəmamočč). This partial reduplication occurs also in Chadic (e.g.

Hausa *magana*, "word", plur. *maganganu*; *kofa*, "door", plur. *kofofi*) and in Cushitic (e.g. Kafa *bāk-ō*, "cock", plur. *bākik-ō*; Somali *san*, "nose", plur. *sanan*).

Internal Plural

31.23.   Semitic internal or "broken" plurals are formed by the use of noun patterns different from those of the singular. The patterns so used are rightly regarded as original collectives and their function as plurals can only be established in the light of grammatical concord.

31.24.   The use of broken plurals is widely attested in Arabic and in Ethiopic, and it is more pervasive in ancient South Arabian than in any other Semitic language. Traces of broken plurals are also preserved in dialects belonging to Semitic languages in which these plurals are not regularly attested, and there are clear parallels in other branches of Afro-Asiatic, viz. in Libyco-Berber, in Cushitic, especially in Bedja and in Afar-Saho, and in Egypto-Coptic, where the Coptic internal plurals can hardly be considered in mass as a secondary development. Some of them may be quite archaic, as suggested by the old Egyptian plurals *ipw* and *ipn* of *pw* and *pn*, "this", or *ik3*, a rare plural of *k3*, "soul", attested besides the usual *k3w*. Therefore, the broken plurals may be regarded as Proto-Semitic, at least in the sense that the collective function of some of their patterns is common to several Semitic languages in different areas.

31.25.   Thus, Old Assyrian *ṣuḫrum*, the pattern of which corresponds to Classical Arabic *fu'lun*, has the collective meaning "the small ones", while the Assyrian individual singular is *ṣaḫru(m)*, "small". The same noun pattern is used in Old Akkadian and in Assyro-Babylonian for so-called abstracts like *dumqu(m)*, "goodness", which is in reality a collective noun "good things" derived from *damqu(m)*, "good". A restricted number of Assyro-Babylonian monosyllabic nouns preserve traces of a broken plural — sometimes called "infixed plural" — that parallels the Arabic pattern *fu''al* (e.g. *buhhal*, "free men"). These nouns form their plural on the pattern $C_1vC_2C_2a(C_3)$ to which the ending $-\bar{u}$ / $-\bar{\imath}$ or $-\bar{u}tu$ / $-\bar{a}tu$ of the external plural is added:

Sing.	Plur.
ab-u, "father"	*abba-ū > abbū*
aḫ-u, "brother"	**aḫḫa-ū > aḫḫū*
alk-at-, "way"	*alkak-ātu*
ark-u, "long"	*arrak-ūtu*
bakr-u, "young camel"	*bakkar-ī*
damq-u, "good"	*dammaq-ūtu*
daqq-u, "fine"	*daqqaq-ūtu*
ebr-u, "friend"	*ebbar-ūtu*
ḫanb-u, "voluptuous"	*ḫannab-ātu*
ṣaḫr-u / ṣeḫr-u, "small"	*ṣaḫḫar-ū / ṣeḫḫer-ūtu*
zikr-u, "man"	*zikkar-ū*

This pattern might be attested also in Palaeosyrian by e.g. *du-ba-lu* /*dubbaru*/, "pastures", a noun related to Aramaic *dabr-*, "pasture", and to Ethiopic *dabr*, "mountain". However, the Palaeosyrian orthography does not allow distinguishing patterns corresponding to *fuʿāl*, *fuʿʿal*, *fuʿʿāl* and *fuʿal*. Besides, both *fuʿal* and *fiʿal* are well represented in North Ethiopic by the pattern *CəCaC* (§31.31), to which *du-ba-lu* might be related as well. This kind of ambiguity does not occur in Hebrew where similar survivals of broken plurals — traditionally explained by a *dageš dirimens* — are preserved by the Masoretic vocalization of some Hebrew nouns. They generally have a superimposed external plural termination which causes the shortening $a > ə$ in the pattern $C_1vC_2C_2aC_3$:

Sing.	Plur.
səbak < *sbak-, "thicket"	*subbək-ō*
ʿēnāb < *ʿinb-, "grape"	*ʿinnəb-ē*
ʿăṣeret < *ʿaṣr-, "crowd"	*ʿaṣṣər-ōt*
ʿāqēb < *ʿaqb-, "heel"	*ʿiqqəb-ē / -ōt*
ʿēśeb < ʿiśb-, "herb"	*ʿiśśəb-ōt*
qešet < qašt-, "bow"	*qaššət-ōt*
miqdāš, "sanctuary"	*miqqədāš*

31.26. By far the most frequently used broken plural pattern in ancient Arabic, in Epigraphic South Arabian, in Geʿez, and in Tigrinya is *ʾfʿl* with the preformative *ʾa-*. The stem vowel is either *a* (*ʾafʿāl > ʾafʿal*) or *u* (*ʾafʿūl > ʾafʿul*). This stem is preserved in a few Amharic forms borrowed from Geʿez (e.g. *amsal*, "parables"; *adbar*, "mountains") and it was used in North and West Semitic, as well. The stem with vowel *ā* most likely occurs in *aḫlāmu*, the probable Old Babylonian designation of the Proto-Aramaeans and their congeners which must transcribe a native *'aġlām*, "boys, lads". It is probably found also in Palaeosyrian *ar-ša-lu* /'*arḍālu*/, "despicable (men)"; *a-sa-lu* /'*āšālu* < '*a'šālu*/, "rush"; *áš-kà-lum* /'*aṭkālum*/, corresponding to Hebrew *'eškōl* or *'aškōl* < **'aṭkāl*, "grapes". Vocalic variations as Ugaritic *'uṭkl* and Aramaic *'etkālā* might suggest that the pattern was broken. The stem with vowel *ū* ('*af'ūl*) is found in *'dqwr*, an Aramaic noun used in the Tell Fekherye inscription (9th century B.C.) and apparently employed as the broken plural *'adqūr* of *dqr*, "jug". This stem with the vowel *u* < *ū* is very common in Geʿez; e.g. *hagar*, "city", plur. *'ahgur*; *ḥaql*, "field", plur. *'aḥqul*. It is used also in modern North Ethiopic; e.g. Tigre *kaləb*, "dog", plur. *'aklub* next to *'aklāb*.

31.27.   Minaic plural stems with infix *-h-* are found in *bhn*, "sons", and *bhnt*, "daughters". They may occur also in Palaeosyrian, as suggested, e.g., by *gú-a-tum* /*quhatum*/, probably a plural of *qātum*, "hand", with the meaning "surety", "warranty", and by *sa-a-dum* /*šahadum*/, seemingly a plural of *šēdu(m)*, a barley species. The trace of such a plural, with the addition of the usual plural morpheme *-m*, probably occurs in Ugaritic *bhtm*, "houses", though it is often to be translated as a singular. The existence of such a plural may also be assumed for **mht*, "lands", in consideration of *mt kln*, "all the lands", in the Aramaic Tell Fekherye inscription, in which there are clear examples of syncope of internal *-h-* (§27.25), as well as some other possible instances of broken plurals (§31.26).

31.28.   Classical Arabic has thirty different patterns of broken plurals (Fig. 26), with short or long vowels, with diphthongs, some of them with geminated second radical (e.g. *kātib*, "scribe", plur. *kuttāb*), others extended either by the prefix *'a-* (e.g. *maraḍ*, "illness", plur. *'amrāḍ*) or by the suffix *-ān* (e.g. *ġazāl*, "gazelle", plur. *ġizlān*). Some of these patterns go probably back to the third millennium B.C., since they seem to appear in Palaeosyrian. There is also a pattern *fu'alā'*, used with nouns designating persons (e.g. *šā'ir*, "poet", plur. *šu'arā'*), but similar broken plurals have a wider range of application in Libyco-Berber (e.g. *-zlufa*, "rushes", from sing. *-zlaf*; *-ġbula*, "springs", from sing. *-ġbalu*), where they are attested already in the 2nd century B.C. as shown by *šqr'*, "wood", and *zl'*, "iron", in a Punico-Numidic inscription from Dougga. In modern colloquials, except in Yemen (§31.29), the patterns with the prefix *'a-* (§31.26) have almost disappeared and coalesced with other stems, deprived of their short vowel; e.g. both *'af'āl* and *fi'āl* became *f'āl*, which is a new, widely used pattern: *ḥarāf*, "lamb", plur. *ḥrāf* instead of *ḥirāf*; *ǧabal*, "mountain", plur. *ǧbāl* instead of *'aǧbāl* or *ǧibāl*. Four-consonant singular patterns have plurals formed on the stems *fa'ālil* and *fa'ālīl*, e.g. *kawkab*, "star", plur. *kawākib*; *šayṭān*, "devil", plur. *šayāṭīn*. For further details the grammars of classical and colloquial Arabic have to be consulted. It should be stressed here that some of the last-mentioned patterns are very old or are used also in other languages. Thus, the broken plural of the *fi'āl* pattern occurs in Palaeosyrian *mu-da-bil sí-kà-ri* /*mudabbil sikāri*/, "story-teller", lit. "teller of stories", while the Hebrew plural of "segolate" nouns derived from the type $C_1 v C_2 C_3$ (§29.5) is an external plural superimposed on a broken plural of the same pattern *fi'āl* > *f'āl*; e.g. sing. *malk-* > plur. **milāk+īm* > *m(ə)lākīm*. The same situation occurs in Samaritan Aramaic (e.g. sing. *rigl-* > *rēgāl+en*, "feet"). The pattern *fa'īl*, represented in Arabic by words like *'abīd(un)*, "slaves", and *ḥamīr(un)*, "donkeys", is likewise attested in Palaeosyrian, e.g. *sa-i-lum* or *sa-ì-lu-um* /*śa'īrum*/, "barley", as well as the pattern for four-consonant singular stems, but with a different set of vowels; e.g. *zu-mu-ba-ru$_{12}$* /*zumūbaru*/, "songs", from **zambāru* < *zamāru* (§11.9).

Patterns of "broken" plurals
in Classical Arabic

fa'al(un)	*fa'ala(tun)*		
f'ial(un)	*fi'ala(tun)*		
fu'al(un)	*fu'ala(tun)*	*fu''al(un)*	
fu'ul(un)			*'af'ul(un)*
fa'īl(un)			*'af'ila(tun)*
fi'āl(un)	*fi'āla(tun)*		*'af'āl(un)*
fu'āl(un)	*fu'āla(tun)*	*fu''āl(un)*	
fu'ūl(un)			
	fi'la(tun)		*fi'lān(un)*
			fu'lān(un)
fa'ālil(un)	*fa'ālila(tun)*	*fawā'il(u)*	*fa'ālā*
fa'ālīl(un)		*fawā'īl(u)*	*fa'ā'il(u)*
fu'alā'u			*'af'ilā'u*

Fig. 26.

31.29. As said above, the use of broken plurals is more extensive in ancient South Arabian than in any other Semitic language, inasmuch as it occurs even with *nisba* formations in -*īy*, e.g. *'ḥḍr*, "Ḥaḍramites".

The most used broken plural pattern is *'f'l* (§31.26), but its vocalization cannot be established directly. Since present-day Yemeni colloquials use the stem *'af'ūl* (e.g. *'amm*, "uncle", plur. *'a'mūm*), best attested in Ethiopic (§31.26,31), instead of usual Arabic *'af'āl*, one can assume that epigraphic *'f'l* (e.g. *nfs¹*, "soul, person", plur. *'nfs¹*) was vocalized similarly. Other attested broken plural stems of ancient South Arabian are *f'l*, *f'lt*, *f'wl*, *f'wlt*, *f'yl*, *f'ylt*, *f'lw*, *f'ln*, *'f'lt*, *'f'lw*.

31.30. The Modern South Arabian languages have broken plurals, the patterns of which show more similarity to those of Ethiopic than to those of Arabic; e.g. *aġā*, "brother", plur. *aġayw*; *gəwf*, "chest", plur. *gəwəft*. Another kind of broken plural has developed within these languages. It consists in the change of the last vowel *i/ə* of the singular into *o/u*; e.g. *fəlhi*, "foal", plur. *fəlho*; *nənhən*, "younger brother", plur. *nənyhon*.

31.31. In North Ethiopic the situation is similar to that of ancient South Arabian, with broken plurals showing the vocalic change of the singular basis, sometimes accompanied by the preformative *'a-* and/or the afformative *-t*. We give examples of the main patterns $CiCaC$ / $CuCaC$ > $CəCaC$ (e.g. Ge'ez *'əzn*, "ear", plur. *'əzan*; Tigre *karšat*, "belly", plur. *kəraš*; *'əgər*, "foot", plur. *'əgar*), $CaCāC$ (e.g. Ge'ez $q^wəy\ṣ$, "shin", plur. $q^wəyā\ṣ$; Tigre *ğəbbat*, "jacket", plur. *ğabāb*), $CaCaCt$ (e.g. Ge'ez *ṣaḥāfī*, "writer", plur. *ṣaḥaft*), $aCCāC$ (e.g. Ge'ez *zanab*, "tail", plur. *'aznāb*; *dabr*, "mountain", plur. *'adbār*; *ləbs*, "dress", plur. *'albās*; Tigre *kaləb*, "dog", plur. *'aklāb*; Tigrinya *färäs*, "horse", plur. *'afras*; *'əzni*, "ear", plur. *'a'zan*; *zämäd*, "relative", plur. *'azmad*), $aCCūC$ (e.g. Ge'ez *ḥaql*, "field", plur. *'aḥqul*; *hagar*, "town", plur. *'ahgur*; Tigre *daqal*, "mast", plur. *'adqul*), $aCCəC$ (e.g. Ge'ez *baql*, "mule", plur. *'abqəl*; *ṣāḥl*, "chalice", plur. *'aṣḥəl*; Tigre *dabər*, "mountain", plur. *'adbər*), $aCCəCt$ (e.g. Ge'ez *baḥr*, "sea", plur. *'abḥərt*; *nəsr*, "eagle", plur. *'ansərt*), and for four-consonant singular stems the patterns $CaCāCəC$ (e.g. Ge'ez *dəngəl*,"girl", plur. *danāgəl*; Tigre *manṣaf*, "carpet", plur. *manāṣəf*; Tigrinya *mändäq*, "wall", plur. *mänadəq*; *känfär*, "lip", plur. *känafər*) and $CaCāCəCt$ (e.g. Ge'ez *mal'ak*, "messenger", plur. *malā'əkt*). Additional or variant patterns occur in modern North Ethiopic: $aC_1aC_2C_2əC_3$ (e.g. Tigre *naggal*, "kid", plur. *'anaggəl*), $aCāCəC(t)$ (e.g. Tigre *walat*, "daughter", plur. *'awāləd*; Tigrinya *bätri*, "staff", plur. *'abatərti*; *bägli*, "mule", plur. *'abaġəlti*), $aC_1aC_2C_2it$ (e.g. Tigre *ğəna*, "child", plur. *'ağannit*), $C_1aC_2aC_3C_3əC_4$ (e.g. Tigre *šəngul*, "adult", plur. *šanaggəl*), $C_1aC_2aC_3C_3i(t)$ (e.g. Tigre *šəfta*, "rebel", plur. *šafattit*), $CaCāCi(t)$ (e.g. Tigre *masni*, "friend", plur. *masānit*).

31.32. A characteristic of broken plurals in modern North Ethiopic is the preservation of original diphthongs. E.g. the broken plural of Tigre *bet* < **bayt* is *'abyāt*, that of *ḥilat*, "strength, power", from the verb *ḥela* < **hayla*, "to be strong", is *ḥəyal*. The same occurs with a Tigre noun like *kokab* < **kawkab* < **kabkab*, "star", the broken plural of which is *kawākəb*. Other diphthongs reveal the use of a broken plural pattern which corresponds to ancient South Arabian *f'yl*. Thus, e.g., the broken plural of Tigre *zəlām*, "rain", is *zalāyəm*, and that of *ḥaṣur*, "enclosure", is *ḥaṣāyər*.

31.33. In modern North Ethiopic, there are many examples of external plural superimposed on broken plurals. Thus, several Tigre nouns of the pattern *CəCāC* have a plural *'aCəCCat*, where the *-at* ending probably goes back to the plural morpheme *-āt*; e.g. *kətāb*, "book", plur. *'akətbat*; *səgad*, "neck", plur. *'asəgdat*. This plural form occurs also with some other noun types like *kətəm*, "seal, stamp", plur. *'akətmat*, and with a metathesis when the second radical consonant is a guttural; e.g. Tigre *bə'ray*, "ox", plur. *'ab'arat* < **'abə'rat*; *wəhər*, "bull", plur. *'awhərat* < **'awəhrat*. Besides, the plural suffix *-āt* can be added optionally to the broken plural of the type *'aCCvC*; e.g. Tigre *mədər*, "land", plur. *'əmdār* or *'amdārāt*; *dəgəm*, "tale", plur. *'adgām* or *'adgāmāt*; *luḥ*, "board", plur. *'alwāḥ*, or *'alwaḥāt*, or *'alwəḥat* with vocalic changes next to the pharyngal *ḥ*. Some nouns of this group are used only with the additional external morpheme *-āt*; e.g. Tigre *bərə'*, "pen", plur. *'abra'āt* or *'abrə'at* with vocalic changes next to the pharyngal '. The external suffix *-at* > *-ət* is added also to broken plurals of the type *'aC₁aC₂C₂əC₃* when C_3 is a guttural; e.g. Tigre *kalə'*, "clay pot", plur. *'akallə'at* or *'akallə'ət*. Some nouns have alternative plurals, e.g. Tigrinya *täḥli*, "plant, tree", with a regular external plural *täḥlitat* (§31.15), a broken plural *'atəḥəlti*, and a combination of both in *'atəḥəltat* or *'atahəltat*.

31.34. Amharic has borrowed several broken plurals from Ge'ez. Besides the *aCCaC* type (§31.26), one should mention the *CäCaCəCt* pattern which is used for four-consonant singular stems and is the best represented; e.g. *mäṣaḥəft*, "books", from *mäṣhaf*, "book"; *mänabərt*, "seats", from *mänbär*, "seat". The plural *amaləkt*, "gods", is a form superimposed on the formally broken plural *amlak*, "God", coined from *malik*, "king", as a kind of *plurale maiestatis* (§50.24). The same pattern is used for *aga'əzt*, "sovereigns", plural of *əgzi'ə*, "sovereign", and for *anabəst*, "lions" plural of *anbäsa*, "lion". Instead, the plural of *nəgus*, "king", is *nägäst*, and the plural of *liq*, "learned man", is *liqawənt*.

c) Paucative

31.35. Paucative is a grammatical category expressing smallness of number or quantity. It is attested at least in Arabic and in Ethiopic, but may have existed in other Semitic languages as well. Further research is needed.

31.36. In Arabic, the paucative derivation is characterized by the prefix *'a-* with the following patterns: *'af'ul(un)* corresponding to the plural *fu'ul(un)*, *'af'āl(un)* corresponding to *fi'āl(un)*, *'af'ila(tun)* corresponding to *fa'ala(tun)* or *fi'ala(tun)*, and *'af'ilā'u* corresponding to *fu'alā'u*. E.g.:

Singular	Plural	Paucative
nahr, "river"	*nuhur*, "rivers"	*'anhur*, "some rivers"
bi'r, "well"	*bi'ār*, "wells"	*'ab'ār / 'ābār*, "some wells"
'ilāh, "God"		*'āliha*, "some gods"
qarīb, "relative"		*'aqribā'*, "some relatives".

31.37. Paucative is indicated in Tigre by the plural-type suffixes *-ām* for the masculine gender and *-āt* for the feminine. The suffixes are added to the basis of countable singulars, to the basis of diminutives, and to broken plurals. E.g.:

wa'at, "cow"	*wa'āt*, "a few cows"
habbeyāy, "small monkey"	*habbeyām*, "a few monkeys"
walatit, "little girl"	*waletāt*, "some girls"
'anhās, "houses"	*'anhesām*, "a few houses"
'akarrit, "hyenas"	*'akarritām*, "a few hyenas"

d) Collective Nouns

31.38. Collective nouns express a plurality of individual objects or persons, species of animals, plants, etc., under the singular form, e.g. Old Akkadian *ṣabūm*, "people, workmen"; Arabic *dam'(un)*, "tears"; Tigre *qaṭaf*, "leaves". As subjects of a sentence, the collective animate nouns may take their verbs in either the singular or the plural; they may be considered as masculine or feminine (§50.23). Collectives are often feminine in gender when they are considered as a plurality, e.g. *ummānum*, "army", and *nīšum*, "people", in Old Akkadian; *ṣo'n*, "small cattle", in Hebrew; *gabil*, "people", in Tigre. Besides being frequently equivalent to plurals, collectives are often difficult to distinguish from abstracts. On the other hand, no principle of classification differentiating individual from collective nouns is apparent from a mere inspection of the members of each class. There is no apparent reason why entities of such similar nature as Arabic *ḥimār*, "donkey", and *baqar*, "cattle", or *nasr*, "eagle", and *ṭayr*, "birds", should belong to different classes. Yet, there is a correspondence between determinate categories of beings and the linguistic classes: e.g. animals living in groups ("cattle", "birds") vs. animals living individually ("donkey", "eagle").

31.39. The presence of a collective noun does not imply the absence of either the countable singular or the plural. A singular may be derived from the collective noun by means of an afformative; such a countable singular is called singulative (§31.40-43). A plural form may exist beside the collective noun, derived either from the singulative, or directly from the collective in the absence of a countable singular belonging to the same root; e.g. Tigre *'addām*, "people, men", and *'addāmātāt*, "crowds".

e) Singulative

31.40. Nouns formed by the addition of the gentilitial suffixes *-iy > -ī*, *-ay > ā*, or *-āwī* (§29.41-42) can be considered as singulatives. The suffix *-ay* may also be used without any gentilitial connotation to form a singulative; e.g. post-classical Arabic *'askariyyun*, "soldier", from *'askarun*, "army"; Tigre *qadrāy*, "a gnat", from *qadar*, "gnats"; *təkenāy*, "a bug", from *təkān*, "bugs". This afformative may also express the notion "a piece of"; e.g. Tigre *'əčyāy*, "a piece of wood", from *'əčay*, "wood".

31.41. The more common afformative of the singulatives is *-at(un) > -ā/a* in Arabic, in Hebrew, and in Ethiopic. E.g. Arabic *ḥamām(un)*, "pigeons", *ḥamāma(tun)*, "single pigeon"; *ḥadīd(un)*, "iron"; *ḥadīda(tun)*, "a piece of iron"; *labin(un)*, "bricks", *labina(tun)*, "single brick"; Hebrew *'ŏnī*, "ships, fleet", *'ŏniyyā*, "ship"; *'ēber*, "pinions", *'ebrā*, "pinion"; *śē'ār*, "hair", *śa'ărā*, "single hair"; *šīr*, "songs", *šīrā*, "single song"; Tigre *rəšāš*, "lead", *rəšāšat*, "a piece of lead"; *bun*, "coffee", *bunat*, "a coffee grain".

31.42.   In Arabic, the active participle may function as a singulative of collective nouns of the pattern *faʿl* / *faʿal* which designate human beings; e.g. *šārib(un)*, "a drinker", as the singular of *šarb(un)*, "drinkers' company".

D. Case Inflection

32.1.   To what extent the Semitic languages originally possessed case distinctions is a debatable question. Ancient Egyptian, for instance, shows no trace of case inflection, and the syntactic relations of nouns were indicated either by the word order or by the use of prepositions and the like. Instead, Cushitic and Libyco-Berber have two basic cases, but they do not correspond exactly to classical usage. Thus, the familiar contrast of nominative and accusative, or subjective and objective, was originally replaced by one between "ergative" and "predicative", the former being used when the noun is acting (cf. Greek ἐργάτης) as instrument or subject, while the latter at once defines the predicate and the object, i.e. the non-active component of the sentence. This contrast is close to the distinction of the "agent case" (*casus agens*) and the "patient case" (*casus patiens*) in the so-called "ergative" languages, but the name *casus patiens* suits the Afro-Asiatic "predicative" only in part. The Cushitic case system appears quite clearly in Oromo which possesses an "ergative" in *-n(i)* (e.g. *namni*, "the man", subject case; *harkan*, "by hand", instrumental), with a plural in *-on(n)i* < *-ot-ni*, and a "predicative" in *-a* (*nama*, "the man", object case; *hama*, "bad", predicate), with a plural in *-ot-a*. There are other nominal suffixes in Cushitic, partly postpositions, and Southern Agaw (Awngi), e.g., has developed a rich operative case system. Instead, Bedja has a prefixed case marking with *ū-* (sing.) or *ā-* (plur.) for the subject case, and *ō-* (sing.) or *ē-* (plur.) for the object case. The feminine *t-* morpheme precedes the case marking (sing. *tū-* / *tō-*; plur. *tā-* / *tē-*). A similar situation is found in Libyco-Berber which shows close links with Semitic. It has two cases expressed by the vocalic alternation which affects the first syllable. The "ergative" is marked by *u*, generally reduced to *ə* after the feminine *t-*prefix and in Tuareg, while the "predicative" or non-active case is marked by *a* in the singular and by *i* in the plural. We can assume that the plural case marks were originally pronounced *ū* and *ī* so that, e.g., *wam-an* and *yam-an*, "water(s)" — a plural noun attested in all Berber dialects — can be interpreted respectively as **ū-am-an* and **ī-am-an*:

yəššur a-ġarraf s waman, "he filled the jar with water"; *aḏ yəksi yaman z gʷanu*, "may one draw water from the well" (both examples in Tarifit). The system may be presented schematically as follows, with the examples *a-funas*, "bull", and *ta-funast*, "cow", the vowels of the plural ending being those of Tuareg dialects:

| | masc. | | fem. | |
	non-active	ergative	non-active	ergative
sing.	*a-funas*	*u-funas*	*ta-funas-t*	*tu-funas-t*
plur.	*i-funas-ən*	*u-funas-ən*	*ti-funas-in*	*tu-funas-in*

Although authors generally believe that Semitic substantives and adjectives originally inflected for three basic cases, viz. nominative, genitive, and accusative, several facts suggest that Semitic nouns were initially diptotic and that two cases were distinguished like in Cushitic and in Libyco-Berber: the subject case or "ergative" in -*u* and the non-subject case or "predicative" in -*a*, which has a predicative function (§32.11; 33.5) and partly corresponds also to the two oblique cases of the "classical" languages, viz. the genitive and the accusative.

a) Diptotic "Ergative" Declension

32.2. The well-founded assumption that Semitic originally had two cases (§32.8-12), the "ergative" or "agent" case in -*u*, traditionally called "nominative", and the non-active or "predicative" case in -*a*, called "accusative", leaves us with the same morpho-syntactical opposition *u* : *a* as in Libyco-Berber. Several peculiarities of this diptotic system indicate that it is closely related to an ergative language structure: 1° the coincidence of the "nominative" case with the "instrumental" or "locative"; 2° the function of the non-active case in -*a* in intransitive verbal or nominal clauses; 3° its use to denote the construct state of the noun; 4° the existence of an absolute form of the noun which originally corresponded to the case in -*a*; 5° the use of pronominal affixes of the verb referring not only to the "agent" but also to the non-active component of the sentence (§36.16); 6° the lack of a common Semitic passive voice (§41.43). The questions related directly to the case system will be examined briefly in the following paragraphs.

32.3. In ergative languages, the active principle of a process is not viewed as the subject of the verb expressing the action, but as the instrument of its realization. This is the reason why the agent case, called "ergative", and the instrumental case coincide, as a rule, although historical developments often introduce a formal distinction between these two functions. For example, the Caucasian Chechen language distinguishes *küjgaca*, "with the hand" (instrumental), from *küjguo*, "the hand" (ergative), but the archaic form *küjga* still functions as ergative and as instrumental. This distinction was not introduced in Afro-Asiatic, which uses the same basic forms in both functions. In Libyco-Berber, e.g., the Tarifit clause *yəššur u-rgaz a-ġarraf s waman*, "the man filled the jar with water", contains two "ergative" cases and one non-active case, which indicates the object affected by the action. Thus, *u-rgaz*, "man", is an "ergative" singular and *waman < *ū-am-an*, "water", is an "ergative" plural which is introduced by the preposition *s*. As for *a-ġarraf*, "jar", it is the entity affected by the "filling", as indicated by the *a-* marker. Palaeosyrian ritual texts seem to preserve some archaic phrases with the "ergative" *u*-case used like in Libyco-Berber after a preposition, as a possessive, and as instrumental in a verbal clause, while the *a*-case may appear with the construct state; e.g. *ba ti-'à-ma-tù /mā tihāmatu/*, "the water of the sea"; *si-in I-li-lu*, "for Enlil"; É *ᵈI-li-lu*, "the house of Enlil"; *i-na-'à-áš na-'à-su I-li-lu /yinaḫḫaš naḫāšu Illilu/*, "he will certainly recover thanks to Enlil". Vestiges of the same system are preserved in Old Akkadian onomastics where the same "ergative" case in *-um* is still attested in names like *En-num-ì-lí*, "By the grace of my god", where */ḫennum/* is clearly an instrumental case, called "locative" in Assyriology, and *I-bi-ì-lum* or *Ì-lum-i-bí*, "God has named", with */'ilum/* indicating the agent (§32.18). Both names provide incomplete sentences, since the verb is missing in the first one and the subject in the second one, where the child is obviously understood. This particular example does not raise the question of the concord between verb and subject, because the god and the child are both masculine and both in the singular. However, the personals of the verb in the historically attested Afro-Asiatic languages agree with the agent in person, gender, and number, while the concord with the non-active component of the sentence is established in certain conditions by means of pronominal suffixes. A similar situation occurs in Caucasian languages, with the difference that the Semitic "ergative" finished by losing its instrumental function and became a nominative subject case, while the "predicative" became, by contrast, an accusative object case.

32.4. In intransitive utterances, the predicate is represented by the non-active case, like in Libyco-Berber where it is indicated by the *a-* prefix;

e.g. Tarifit *Muḥnd ḏ a-mqqran*, "Muḥend is great". The same morpheme *a* is suffixed to the nominal predicate in Palaeosyrian, Old Akkadian, and Amorite names, in Classical Arabic, in Geʿez, and in East Gurage (§32.11; 33.5; 54.2). The ending *-a* of the perfect in Classical Arabic and in Ethiopic (§40.3) has the same origin, since the perfect of the suffix-conjugation goes back to a stative which is basically a nominal predicate (§38.3). Instead, the "ergative" case characterizes the logical subject of these intransitive sentences, as shown e.g. by the Oromo clause *niti-n hamtu-ḍa*, "the woman bad-is", by the Amorite name *E-lu-ra-ma*, "El is high", or by the Tachelhit verbal clause *imdl u-fruḥ*, "the child is buried". In fact, however, the logical subject was originally conceived as the instrument by means of which the signified condition was actually realized, viz. being bad, high, buried, etc., while the non-active component of the sentence is expressed by the so-called "predicative accusative" (§52.8), e.g. Arabic *gāʾa rākiban*, "he arrived (as) a rider"; *tātūna 'afwāğan*, "you are coming (in) crowds". The personals of the verb agree always with the logical subject. The original system was later reinterpreted along the lines of the contrast of nominative and accusative.

32.5. The *-a* ending characterizes the construct state in Geʿez (e.g. *nəguša hagar*, "the king of the city") and in Amharic (e.g. *batä krəstiyan*, "house of Christian", i.e. "church"). This construction exactly parallels the syntax of the Libyco-Berber noun phrase with the *nomen regens* having the *a*-prefix, while the *nomen rectum* is marked by the *u*-prefix; e.g. *a-ham u-rgaz*, "the tent of the man"; *ta-ḍuṭ-ṭ w-ulli*, "the wool of the sheep". The noun determined by another noun can be regarded as a kind of recipient and be considered, therefore, as a non-active component of the phrase. The construct state in *-a* appears occasionally also in East Semitic, not only in the accusative (e.g. Old Akkadian *qīštašu*, "his gift"; Old Babylonian *mārašu*, "his son"), but also in the nominative, before pronominal suffixes; e.g. Old Akkadian *tērtakunu lillikam*, "may your instruction reach me"; Babylonian *alaktašu šaniat*, "his way is different"; *kī ṭuppaka pānam ul šuršu*, "why does your tablet not make it clear?"; *ummašu aḥāt* PN, "his mother is the sister of PN". This *-a* is usually explained as a paragogic vowel, but it should rather be considered as a vestige of an old syntactic feature, still operative in Ethiopic. Traces of a construct state in *-a*, used independently from the accusative, occur in Nabataean Arabic as reflected by the Greek transcription Αβδαδουσαρος, "Servant of Dusares", in Classical Arabic call phrases and exclamations (cf. §32.6), like *yā bna 'ammī*, "oh! son of my uncle!"; *rabbanā*, "our Lord!", and in Syro-Palestinian colloquials before pronominal suffixes; e.g. *'ummane*, "our mother", *darbane*, "our road", in the Ḥawrān dialect. Otherwise, no case endings are used in Modern Arabic and, in Classical Arabic, the construct state in *-a* occurs only when the *nomen regens* is an accusative. Cushitic Oromo distinguishes the subject case in *-n(i)* (e.g. *manni motti*, "the house of the chief") from the object case in *-a* (e.g. *mana motti*).

32.6. The existence of an "absolute" form or citation form of the noun is a characteristic of ergative languages. In Afro-Asiatic, this form coincides with the non-active *a*-case. This is the form of the Libyco-Berber or Cushitic noun given in answer to a question like: "what is the word for...?" The answer is, e.g., *a-funas*, "bull" in Tuareg, *i-rgaz-ən i-məqqr-an*, "big men" in Tarifit, *muk-a*, "tree" in Oromo. A similar situation can be assumed in the ancient Semitic languages before the development of a new case alignment. This would explain why a large number of words passed from Old Akkadian to Sumerian in a form ending in *-a*, such as d a m - ḫ a - r a, "battle", m a - d a, "country", and why several Semitic divine names also end in *-a*, like *Abba, Ela, Labba, Išḫara*, Palaeosyrian ᵈ*'À-da /Hadda/*, ᵈ*A-dam-ma*, etc. The same origin may be attributed to the ending *-ä* of the absolute state of the nouns in Gafat (e.g. *bäsärä*, "meat"; *afärä*, "earth, dust") and in some West Gurage dialects. Also the Classical Arabic vocative in *-ā / -an* may go back to this "absolute" form of the noun; e.g. *yā 'ammā*, "oh! uncle!"; *'a-rākiban kamīyan*, "oh! heroic rider!".

32.7. The genitive of the diptotic Semitic declension ends in *-a* (§32.12), the mark of the "predicative". To what extent this ending corresponds to an ancient usage is a debatable question, since it is the "ergative" that often denotes the genitive relation, like in Libyco-Berber; e.g. *a-ḫam u-rgaz*, "the tent of the man". One might posit an initial distinction between a genitive denoting an "agent" and a genitive denoting a "patient". Such a distinction inevitably touches upon the question of the ambiguous status of the so-called *genetivus obiectivus* (§51.12), i.e., the likelihood that, e.g., *ba'al hab-bayit*, "the owner of the house", may go back by nominalization to both *bā'al hab-bayit*, "he owns the house", and *nib'al hab-bayit*, "the house is owned (by him)". In Afro-Asiatic, the first clause would require the *a*-"predicative" **bayta* and the second one would use the *u*-"ergative" **baytu*, as indicated by Tachelhit *imdl a-fruẖ*, "he buried the child", and *imdl u-fruẖ*, "the child is buried". As for the "new" genitive marker *-i*, it is likely to have the same origin as the gentilitial suffix *-iy-* > *-ī* (§ 29.41), which may derive from a postposition. In Highland East Cushitic, e.g., there is a postposition *-i* which includes the idea "out from" or "away from"; e.g. Hadiyya *mene-i*, "from a man". The Semitic gentilitial suffix *-iy-* expresses a similar idea (e.g. *Makkī*, "from Mecca") and it is a postposition *-ti* that expresses the genitive relation in Oromo (Lowland East Cushitic) , e.g. *ilma nama-ti*, "the son of a man"; *manni kun* (subject) *kan* (object) *abbāko-ti*, "this house (is) the one of my father". Further research work is needed in this field; it should be made on a comparative Afro-Asiatic basis.

32.8.   There are only two cases in the plural and the dual of the Semitic languages (§31.3,10). Also in the singular, the diptotic declension characterizes Ge'ez, several nominal patterns of Classical Arabic (*'af'al*, *fu'al, fa'lān, fu'āl, maf'al*, the plural stems of the type *fa'ālilu*, etc., the stems ending in *-ā'u*), as well as many categories of proper names, and syllabic spellings indicate that the situation was similar in Amorite and in Ugaritic, at least in part with names ending in *-ān*, with some place names, and with theophorous elements.

b) Use in Proper Names

32.9.   Many nouns without any ending or with the ending *-a* appear in Palaeosyrian and Old Akkadian proper names, such as personal, divine, geographic, and month names, and among the Semitic loanwords in Sumerian. This situation can best be explained as still reflecting Semitic languages or dialects having no well-established declension, or using the non-active case with the ending *-a* as citation form (§32.6). Contrary to the case endings of the actually used Palaeosyrian, Old Akkadian or Amorite languages, this *-a* ending never appears as *-am(a)*, probably because it reflects idioms spoken before the introduction of the mimation (§33.13,15-17), the use of which is still inconsistent in Palaeosyrian and in the Old Akkadian onomastics in general.

32.10.   The divine names with no case endings (e.g. [d]*Ra-sa-ap*, [d]*Da-gan*, [d]*Ma-lik*) have been regarded by some scholars as vocatives in form. Plausible as it may appear for theonyms, this explanation cannot be accepted, because forms without case endings appear also among

Semitic toponyms (e.g. *U₉-ga-ra-at*ki, *A-ru₉-ga-at*ki, *Ba-sa-ar*ki, *A-šùr*ki), names of months (e.g. *Ba-ḫi-ir*, *Ḥa-ni-it*), and common words borrowed by Sumerian (e.g. d a m - g à r < *tamkār-*, "supplier, tradesman"; g a - r a - a n < *karān-*, "vineyard"; s a - t u < *śadw-*, "mountain"; š ú m < *ṭūm-*, "garlic") or used in anthroponomy (e.g. *Šu-ru-uš-ki-in*, "The root is firm"; *A-pìl-ki-in*, "The heir is firm"; *Li-da-at-*GI, "The progeny is firm"). Such words could not possibly be explained as vocatives. They rather reflect the stage of the language prior to the introduction of case marking, an explanation which is generally proposed for a few basic Libyco-Berber common nouns which are in the same situation, as *fad*, "thirst", *laẓ*, "hunger", *kra*, "(some)thing".

32.11. As for the ending *-a*, it is the morpheme of the predicative in Palaeosyrian, Old Akkadian, and Amorite proper names, always characterized by conservatism (e.g. *A-ba-Il*, "Il is father"; *Ìr-ra-na-da*, "Irra is exalted"; *Ba-aḫ-la-*DINGIR, "El is lord"; *Šú-ra-Ḥa-am-mu-ú*, "His ancestor is a rock"; cf. §33.13). The same *-a* morpheme still characterizes the predicate in Classical Arabic, in Geʿez, and in some Gurage dialects of South Ethiopic, in combination with the verb "to be, to become"; e.g. in Arabic: *kāna ʾaḫā lī*, "he was a brother to me"; in Geʿez: *konki bəʾəsita*, "you became a women"; *bərhānəka ṣəlmata kon-aka*, "your light has become for you darkness"; in East Gurage: *gid-dirän yəhanäl*, "he became big".

32.12. The morpheme *-a* can also be the morpheme of the genitive (§32.7) in Amorite and Ugaritic proper names (e.g. *Ḥa-ab-du-Ba-aḫ-la*, "Servant of Baal"; *Ha-ab-du-A-šu-ra*, "Servant of Ashur"; *ʾaṯr bʿl =* uruKI-dU-*la* /*Aṯru-Baʿla*/, "Settlement of Baal"), and it is used as such in a productive way with diptotic Ugaritic names (e.g. contrast subject cases *Nu-ri-ia-nu* and *Pu-lu-zi-nu* with genitives *Nu-ri-ia-na* and *Pu-lu-zi-na*). The ending *-a* is likewise the morpheme of the non-subject case of diptotic nouns in all the Semitic idioms which have preserved the case inflection.

c) "Classical" Triptotic Declension

32.13. The "classical" Semitic languages, Palaeosyrian and Old Akkadian included, present a somewhat different picture. With the exception of Geʿez, they possess three basic cases for the singular of most nouns, thus distinguishing one subject case or "nominative" ending in *-u*, and two non-subject cases, usually called "genitive" and "accusative".

32.14.   The genitive is a subjoined case (*nomen rectum*), determined by its antecedent which can be a preposition (§48.2), a determinative pronoun (§51.18-20), or another noun (*nomen regens*) in the bound form, called "construct state" (§33.2-4). Its ending is *-i* (cf. §32.7) with a possible allophone *-e*.

32.15.   The accusative is used for the object of a transitive verb and for the term of reference of an intransitive verb, such as an adjective, an adverb, etc. Its ending is *-a*, inherited from the *-a* of the unique non-subject case which has lost its predicative function with the exception of the formations still attested in Arabic and in Ethiopic (§32.11). It is uncertain whether this predicative function reappears in the Aramaic "emphatic" state (§33.7), but the *a*-case develops for sure from a nominal predicate through the participial predicate (e.g. *Qāma-Da'mu*, "Damu is standing") into the verbal perfect in *-a* (*fa'ala*; §33.5; 40.3).

32.16.   The singular endings *-u* and *-i* are quantitatively distinct from the corresponding morphemes *-ū* and *-ī* of the plural, to which they are related genetically. There is also quantitative opposition between the singular ending *-a* and the dual morpheme *-ā* of the subject case, but no functional relation connects these forms. The following picture of the case inflection emerges thus for the "classical" Semitic languages:

	Singular	Plural	Dual
Nominative	*-u*	*-ū*	*-ā*
Genitive	*-i*	*-ī/-ē*	*-ay*
Accusative	*-a*		

d) "Adverbial" Cases

32.17.   Old Akkadian, Old Assyrian, and Old Babylonian have also a dative-adverbial or terminative-adverbial case in *-iš* or *-eš* (e.g. *Idiglat-eš*, "into the Tigris") which expresses the idea "with, to, for". This morpheme occurs frequently with nouns forming elements of personal names (e.g. *Sar-ri-iš-da-gal*, "Rely upon the king!"), with infinitives (e.g. *na-da-ni-iš*, "to give"), with adjectives and participles, acquiring thus an adverbial meaning (e.g. *da-ni-iš*, "strongly"; §47.5). It is even used with words functioning as prepositions (e.g. *maḫ-rí-iš*, "in front of"), also at Ebla, as it seems (e.g. *a-li-iš*, "instead of"; *mu-lu-iš*, "in addition to"; *sa-da-bí-iš*, "on behalf of"). Beside the examples with *-iš*, there are several East Semitic forms with -*uš*, which might have developed secondarily from -*iš*. In reality, the morpheme *iš* is no case ending but a particle used mainly in ancient phases of Semitic as postposition, but employed also as preposition in Palaeosyrian, in texts from Mari (e.g. *iš maš-a-né-en*, "for a pair of shoes"; *iš na-ak-ri-im*, "to the enemy") and from Ebla (e.g. *éš* NÌ.KAŠ₄ *Ḫar-zú*ᵏⁱ, "for the journey to Harzu"; *éš* NÌ.KAŠ₄-*sù*, "for his journey"; §48.10). This double use of a particle as preposition and postposition is not exceptional in Afro-Asiatic and it may be compared with the parallel existence of the common Semitic conjunction *wa-*, "and", and of the East Semitic and South Ethiopic enclitic -*ma*, "and", which may have the same origin, since the alternation *w* : *m* is well attested (§49.1).

32.18. Besides the "classical" cases already considered, Proto-Semitic had a so-called "locative" in -*u(m)*, which should more conveniently be called "instrumental". Its traces survive in several Semitic languages, and there is little doubt that it coincides with the subject case, with which it formed the "ergative", as already mentioned (§32.3). The function of the instrumental / locative suffix -*um*/-*u* appears in Standard Literary Babylonian fixed phrases like *šēpū'a* (< **sēpū-ya*), "at my feet", and *rittū'a* (< **rittū-ya*), "in my fingers", and in a few Old Akkadian names, like *I-dum-be-lí*, "By the hand of my lord", and *En-num-i-lí*, "By the grace of my god". In Ugaritic, the instrumental suffix -(*u*)*m* used in one parallel member is balanced by a preposition in the other, e.g. *lqḥ 'imr dbḥ bydh // ll'a kl'atnm* (KTU 1.14,III,55-57), "he takes a lamb of sacrifice with his hand, a kid with both hands". The suffix -(*u*)*m* is preceded here by a morph (*ā*)*n* which appears in this position also in Assyro-Babylonian (e.g. *ṣuprānuššu* < *ṣupr-ān-**um**-šu*, "with his claws"). The pronominal suffix follows -*um* also in Palaeosyrian, at Ebla, as shown by *ma-za-lum-sù*, "for/with its/his messenger". Most of the nouns to which the ending -*um* is attached form adverbs or prepositions (§47.3); e.g. Old Akkadian and Assyro-Babylonian *balum*, "without"; Hebrew *pit'om*, "on a sudden", but not *šilšom*, "the day before yesterday" (§ 29.55). Forms without the final -*m* are attested already in Old Babylonian (e.g. *libbu*, "in the heart of, within") and could be compared with Arabic adverbs ending in -*u* (e.g. *fawqu*, "above"; *ba'du*, "later"; *taḥtu*, "below"), as well as with Syriac and Ge'ez adverbs with final long -*ū*, which may derive from an original -*um* > -*əm* (§47.3); e.g. Syriac *kaddū*, "sufficiently, enough"; Ge'ez *lā'lu* < *lā'lū*, "above".

32.19. The postposition -*iš* can be combined with the ending -*um* and alternate with a prepositional phrase, like in an Old Akkadian love incantation from Kish: *ki-rí-šum tu-ur₄-da tu-ur₄-da-ma a-na kirīm*, "to the orchard they went down (dual fem.), they went down to the orchard". The postpositive -*iš* can be used also with another adverbial ending -*am*; e.g. *ūmišam*, "day by day, daily" in Old Akkadian and Assyro-Babylonian. This ending -*am* is employed in Hebrew without the postposition -*iš* to form the adverbs *yōmām*, "by day"; *rēqām*, "empty-handed", etc. (§47.2). In view of the analogy with the suffix -*um*/-*u* (§32.18), we may surmise that the Aramaic adverbs such as *'ar'ā*, "on the ground, below", *bārā*, "outside", have the same ending -*am* without the final -*m* and with the consequent lengthening of the vowel (§47.2).

32.20. The Hebrew ending -*ā(h)* denoting a place relation (e.g. *Bābelāh*, "to Babylon") was regarded by some scholars as a survival of the accusative ending -*a*. However, Ugaritic has shown that the -*h* in question was originally a consonantal postposition expressing motion towards a place; e.g. *šmmh*, "heavenward"; *'arṣh*, "earthward". The weakening of this postvocalic -*h* (*-ah*) and the consequent reduction of the postposition to the vowel -*a* are already noticeable in Ugaritic, as shown e.g. by *š'a ydk šmm* (KTU 1.14,II,22-23) compared with *nš'a ydh šmmh* (KTU 1.14,IV,4-5), "he lifts his hands heavenward". This reduced directive postposition -*a* is preserved not only in Hebrew but also, as it seems, in Arabic, where it is regarded as an adverbial accusative (e.g. *šarqan wa-ġarban*, "eastward and westward"), and perhaps in Ge'ez (e.g. *bo'a hagara*, "he entered into the city") and in modern East Gurage dialects of South Ethiopic (e.g. *hadadəni gar garäni hid*, "each of them entered into his house"), but the concomitant use of verbs of movement, employed also with the accusative (§52.3), allows of the explanation of this -*a*/-*ä* morpheme as the ending of the non-subject case.

e) Historical Survey of Case Inflection

32.21. In East Semitic, case inflection is in full use down to the middle of the second millennium B.C. Subsequently, there was no longer a fully functioning case system in proper names and in nouns. From the Middle Babylonian period on, case endings on proper names were either dropped or drastically shortened. Many names are not declined at all, while others end either in a consonant or in a vowel, which is mostly *i*.

As for nouns, the ending *-u* often occurs instead of the *-a* of the accusative. At Emar, in the early 12th century B.C., the case system was not in full use any more and the irregularities are numerous. In the Neo-Babylonian and in the Neo-Assyrian dialects, all three endings *-u*, *-i/e*, and *-a* are encountered without reference to their syntactical function, while the plural is marked by *-ī/ē* or *-āni*, without any case distinction. This indicates that the vocalic endings of the singular, kept in writing because of the syllabic nature of the script, had been dropped in the spoken language or had become merely vestigial, and that there was no longer an operative case system. The syntactical function of the case inflection is taken over by word order, with the following scheme: object (accusative) precedes the verb, subject (nominative) precedes the object. The relation expressed by the former genitive is sufficiently indicated as such by its antecedent.

32.22. In North Semitic, case inflection is in full use down to the twelfth century B.C., as may be seen in Ugaritic nouns whose final consonant is ', vocalized *'a*, *'i*, *'u*, e.g. *ks'u* (nominative), *ks'i* (genitive), *ks'a* (accusative), "throne", *rp'um* (plural subject case), *rp'im* (plural non-subject case), "shades (of the dead)".

32.23. In West Semitic, case inflection is fully used in Old Canaanite, as may be seen in the Amarna glosses showing the *-u* of the nominative (e.g. *ṣú-ú-nu = ṣ'n*, "small cattle": EA 263,12), the *-i* of the genitive (e.g. *sú-ki-ni = skn*, "governor": EA 256,9), the *-a* of the accusative (e.g. *ma-aṭ-ni-a = mṭn'*, "supply": EA 337,9.21), the *-ūma* of the plural subject case (e.g. *ša-mu-ma = šmm*, "heaven": EA 211,17), the *-īma* of the plural non-subject case (e.g. *ša-me-ma*: EA 264,16), and the *-ā* of the dual (e.g. *ḫi-na-ia = 'ny*, "my eyes": EA 144,17).

32.24. In the "Canaanite" languages of the first millennium B.C. and in Aramaic, there is no longer a distinction between subject and non-subject plural forms, and the vocalic case endings of the singular disappear, and with them the entire case system. Therefore, the use of the Latin case names "nominative", "genitive", "accusative" in reference to these languages is more convenient than strictly scientific. It simply suggests the syntactical function of the nouns which is indicated by word order (§50.7,13,17-19) and by the optional use of a particle introducing the object of a transitive verb, the former accusative (§52.10-11), while the subjoined function of a noun, the former genitive, results from its place and from the bound form of its antecedent. The faint traces of case endings, the so-called "paragogic" vowels of the Hebrew grammar, have no longer a syntactical function. They may play an euphonic or rhythmic role, especially at the junction of a noun in the construct state with its complement, often in poetry and in proper names, e.g. *ʿAbdī-ʾĒl*, "Servant of God"; *bənō Bəʿor*, "son of Beʿor"; *Pənū-ʾĒl*, "Face of God".

32.25. Pre-Classical North Arabian had no longer a fully functioning case system in the 3rd and 4th centuries A.D., although the Nabataean and the South Arabian scripts continued to indicate final vowels indiscriminately (cf. §7.38, 42). The archaizing use of the case system in Classical Arabic derives from conservative dialects, standardized for diction in the schools of the Abassid empire (§7.43). In Neo-Arabic or Middle Arabic, and in the modern colloquials which developed from Pre-Classical Arabic, the case inflection does not exist. However, a few faint traces of case endings subsist in Bedouin vernaculars of the Arabian peninsula. In some dialects of Northern and Central Saudi Arabia, one encounters the nunation in the *-in* form (e.g. *darbin*, "a road"), apparently with the *-i-* of the former genitive, while *-u < -un* is preserved in some Yemenite colloquials when the noun is indeterminate (e.g. *baytu*, "a house", but *al-bayt*, "the house").

32.26. Because of the lack of vocalization in the script of ancient South Arabia, the construct external masculine plural is the one grammatical feature in which a case distinction would be apparent. In fact, we are limited to the contrast between the two forms *bnw* and *bny*, which testify to the existence of a subject case and of a non-subject case in the plural. However, this distinction is already blurred by the mid period of the epigraphical evidence, which means that the case differentiation had become merely vestigial by the 1st-3rd centuries A.D. The modern South Arabian languages do not possess any case distinction.

32.27. Geʿez distinguishes the subject case and the non-subject or oblique case, marked by *-a*. This morpheme is used in the expression of the direct object (e.g. *saba nasʾā kāhən maya*, "after the priest has taken water"), in the expression of place relation, where another explanation is however possible (§32.20), and in combination with the verb "to be, to become", where the morpheme *-a* expresses the syntactic predicative situation (§32.11). The same use of the suffix *-ä* is encountered in East

Gurage dialects of South Ethiopic, especially in the expression of the direct object. However, Ge'ez occasionally introduces the direct object by a prefixed *la-*, a feature paralleled in other Ethiopian languages. A few Greek transcriptions apparently show that Early Ge'ez had the *-u* (nominative) and the *-i* (genitive) case endings. If so, these were first reduced to *-ə*, and then disappeared. For proper names, Ge'ez has a particular case ending *-hā* for the accusative; e.g. *Dāwit walada Salomonhā*, "David begot Solomon".

32.28. Traces of a case distinction are preserved also in South Ethiopic where various developments can be observed. The South Ethiopic plural ending *-ač / -oč̆č̆* originates from the plural oblique morpheme *-āti* (§31.15, 17), testifying indirectly to the earlier existence of two distinct cases in plural nouns. There is a direct object marker in Harari which is *-u* after a consonant and *-w* after a vowel; e.g. *bidā'a-w musāfir-u yäthidādral*, "he administers the merchandise (and) the merchant(s)". This marker is identical with the postpositive definite article *-u* in Amharic (e.g. *betu*, "the house") and in Argobba (e.g. *bedu*, "the house"), and there is a corresponding *-i* morpheme in various Gurage dialects (e.g. *gari*, "the house"). It is a unlikely that these postpositive articles *-u / -i* have originated from the case vowel preceding the nunation, as in ancient South Arabian languages (§33.17). Their origin seems to be different (§33.14), although nunation appears in Amharic, in Argobba, and in Gafat when the definite noun is used as direct object (e.g. Amharic *bägun šättä*, "he has sold the sheep") and in some other phrase types. The definite article *-u* is occasionally paralleled in Amharic by *-itu* for the feminine (usually *-wa* < *-u+a*) (cf. §33.14).

E. The "States" of the Noun

33.1. The Semitic noun can appear in four different syntactic situations, which may imply four formally differentiated forms, called in the traditional terminology the "states" of the noun: the construct state, the predicate state, the determinate state, and the absolute or indeterminate state.

a) Construct State

33.2. A noun followed by a genitival qualifier, either noun (e.g. Classical Arabic *suyūfu l-'a'dā'i*, "the swords of the enemies"), or attached pronoun (e.g. Arabic *rabbuka*, "your lord"), or an asyndetic relative clause (e.g. Ṣafaitic *s¹nt b'yt ḥwlt m's*, "the year when Ḥawlat has overcome Ma'aṣ"; Arabic *ḥīna māta*, "the time he died"; cf. §57.5), is said to be in the "construct" state or in a "bound" form, as opposed to the "free" form.

33.3. As a general rule, a noun in the construct state has the stem form with no prepositive or postpositive article (§33.7-14), and with no additional mimation or nunation. This rule is followed already in Palaeosyrian; e.g. *a-za-me-tù du-ḫu-rí si-ne-mu* /*lazamītu duḫūli šinnīmu*/, "spell-binding of the rear of the teeth", in parallelism with "spell-binding of the tongue". However, the dual or plural morpheme and the case ending are usually added to the stem (e.g. Aramaic *'aynē 'ănāšā*, "the eyes of a man"; Classical Arabic *mālu tāǧirin*, "the wealth of the tradesman"), but they are capable of deletion, especially before pronominal suffixes (e.g. Assyro-Babylonian *māssu < māt-šu*, "his country"), and they may be not represented in the consonantal writing systems when they are reduced to a simple vowel (e.g. Phoenician *bt 'lnm*, "temples of gods"; Sabaic *rglhw*, "his two legs"). Besides, the article may be prefixed to the construct state in well defined circumstances, as in Modern South Arabian (§33.9) and in Tigre (§33.11).

33.4. At first sight, a different picture seems to emerge from Ge'ez and from Amharic that indicate the construct state by an additional ending *-a*, e.g. Ge'ez *nəguša hagar*, "the king of the city". This ending derives from the case-form of the non-active component of the sentence (§32.5) and it cannot be regarded as a simple paragogic vowel. The contraction of the vowels explains why Ethiopic nouns ending in the long vowels *-ā*, *-e*, *-o* remain unchanged in the construct, while those ending in *-i* have their construct in *-e*.

b) Predicate State

33.5. The standard form of the predicate state in a nominal clause (§50.6-10) corresponds in East and North Semitic to that of the absolute state (§33.15) or of the stative (§40.2ff.), e.g. in Old Akkadian: *Ea-ra-bí*, "Ea is great"; *Eštar-ra-bí-at*, "Ishtar is great"; *Ilū-da-nu*, "the gods are powerful". However, a form ending in *-a* is found in personal names regarded as Palaeosyrian, Old Akkadian, or Amorite (§32.11). It represents the case-form of the predicate in a nominal clause of an ergative language (§32.4), exactly as in Libyco-Berber; e.g. Tarifit *Muḥnd ḏ a-mqqran*, "Muḥend is great". In Classical Arabic, instead, the predicate of the nominal clause is in the nominative of the absolute or indeterminate state (§33.15); e.g. *'al-waladu ṣaġīrun*, "the boy is small". However, the *-a* of the predicate state subsists in Classical Arabic and in Ethiopic when the verb "to be, to become" is used (§32.4,11; 54.3), and it also explains the verbal perfect ending *-a* in both languages (§40.3), e.g. Arabic *malaka*, "he owns"; Ge'ez *qatala*, "he killed". This morpheme *-a* must go back to Afro-Asiatic since it occurs also with forms of the Egyptian old perfective or pseudo-participle, which presents a close resemblance with the Semitic stative; e.g. *ḥr-tì*, "you are content"; *šm-tì*, "she is gone"; *ḏd-kì*, "I am/was saying".

c) Determinate State

33.6. A noun which is neither a proper name nor in the syntactic situation of a construct or a predicate can be made "determinate" by an additional prefixed or suffixed morpheme which may mark individual determination, as when affixed to a substantive already mentioned or being in natural connection with a given situation, as in Arabic *man-i r-raġulu*, "who is the (i.e. "this") man?" (cf. § 33.10). It often marks class and species determination, as in Hebrew *habbāqār wə-haṣṣo'n*, "cattle and flock" (cf. § 33.8,10). It may also express the idea of "the particular one", as in Ṣafaitic *klmh h's¹d*, "a (particular) lion roared at him", and replace a pronominal suffix. The predicative in *-a* of the Palaeosyrian, Amorite, and Old Akkadian onomastics (§32.11; 33.5) appears to have such a secondary function when one compares names like *Su₄-be-lí*, "He is my lord", and *Su₄-be-la*, "He is **the** (particular) lord", or *A-bi₄-ì-lí*, "My god is my father", and *A-ba-Il*, "God is **the** (particular) father". The mimation, instead, seems to lack any connection with the determinate or indeterminate state of the noun, at least in the North and East Semitic languages (§33.16). As for the article proper, both definite and indefinite, it is a very late acquisition of the Semitic languages and, for that matter, of the Indo-European languages as well. This grammatical device, though not indispensable, contributed to the growth of identification, e.g. "the man" as distinguished from "man" in general. Enclitics are here much less frequent than proclitics, but they are attested in Aramaic (§33.7), in South Semitic (§33.14), and probably in North Semitic (§33.13).

33.7. The predicative morpheme -*a* might reappear in Aramaic with its determinative value as the postpositive article -*ā*, which character-izes the so-called "emphatic" state of the Aramaic noun, originally iden-tical with the determinate state (e.g. *malkā'*, "the king"). This mor-pheme -*ā* is indicated in writing by ' from the 9th century B.C. onwards and by *h* already in the 8th century B.C. at Hamath, in the word *mlkh*, "the king". In this particular case, therefore, either the original form of the postpositive article is preserved dialectally, or -*h* is already a simple vowel letter. In the first hypothesis, the Aramaic postpositive article is a suffixed pronominal element, like in South Semitic and probably in North Semitic (§33.13-14). This implies that the original morpheme *-ah* was weakened very early to -*a'* and finally reduced to a vowel -*ā* marked either by ' or by the *mater lectionis h*. In the "predicative" hypothesis, the original consonantal value of ' as a glottal stop is in doubt, and the usual transcription -*ā'* is more convenient than strictly scientific. Anyhow, this "emphatic" state became the common form of all the nouns in the Eastern dialects of Middle Aramaic and in Neo-Ara-maic. Its ending -*ā* is pronounced nowadays as a short vowel, since it is unaccented in speech, e.g. [*malka*] or [*malko*], "king". Other means ful-fil the former function of the "emphatic" state: the Neo-Aramaic of the Ṭūr 'Abdīn area (Ṭūrōyo) expresses definiteness by prefixing shortened allomorphs of the demonstrative (§36.36), thus ['*ū-malko*], "the king" (masc. sing.); ['*ī-barto*], "the daughter" (fem. sing.); ['*am-malkē*] < '*an-malkē*, "the kings" (plur.). In other Neo-Aramaic dialects, also in the Western ones, definiteness is expressed by proleptic pronominal suf-fixes added to the verb form; e.g. *pteḥlē-la* (fem.) *qōra*, "he has opened (**it**) the grave"; *yuspul-la ḥḍučča*, "they will take (**her**) the bride along" (Ma'lūla).

33.8. The determinate state of the noun is marked in the "Canaanite" languages of the first millennium B.C., in Pre-Islamic North Arabian, in Arabic, in Modern South Arabian languages, and in Tigre by a prefixed definite article. Its earliest attested form is *ha-*, used in Hebrew, Phoeni-cian, Ammonite, Moabite, Edomite, Liḥyānite, Ṣafaitic, Thamūdic, and in the Modern South Arabian languages where the definite article *a- / ä-* is prefixed to definite nouns the initial element of which is a voiced or glottalized consonant (e.g. Ṣḥeri *ä-ġarb*, "the large well-bucket"; Mehri *a-ṣaar*, "the gazelle"). In Soqoṭri, however, it has apparently lost its spe-cific function and has become a constitutive part of a number of nouns, e.g. '*a'am* < *hā-'umm*, "mother". Similar examples are attested in

Mehri; e.g. *ḥayd*, "hand"; *ḥayb*, "father". However, it was also suggested that the *ḥa*-prefix in Mehri may go back to **ḥad*, "one", serving as an indefinite article, like *and* in Amharic (§33.18), with assimilation of *d* to the following consonant. This hypothesis is weakened by the fact that the Mehri numeral "one" is *ṭāṭ* (§35.3d).

33.9. Some particular points concerning the use of the article have to be mentioned. A peculiarity of the Mehri and Śḥeri definite article consists in being prefixed to nouns determined by personal suffixes; e.g. Mehri *bayt*, "house", *a-bətk*, "your house". The use of the definite article with place names, as Phoenician *h-Gdr*, "Gades", was originally limited to names originated from common nouns, as *gdr*, "wall, compound" (§67.10). This usage was later extended to some foreign place names, as Neo-Punic *h-Rm'*, "Rome", but this happened under Greek influence (e.g. ἡ Ῥώμη), as shown, for instance, by Aramaic *'ărōmā'ē*, "Romans", or Meroitic *Arome*, "Rome", i.e. in languages that have no article *h-/'-*. In Hebrew, the article is elided after the prepositions *b-*, *k-*, *l-*, contrary to Thamūdic and to Ṣafaitic where it is preserved; e.g. *l-h-mr't*, "for the lady"; *b-h-dr*, "in the camp"; *b-h-'bl*, "with the camels". However, the article is sometimes preserved in Late Biblical Hebrew as well; e.g. *lə-hā-'ām*, "for the people" (II Chr. 10,7).

33.10. Since the prefixed article is followed in Hebrew by the geminated initial consonant of the noun (e.g. *melek*, "king"; *ham-melek*, "the king"), it has long been assumed that its original form was *hn-*, found in Lihyānite before the consonants ' and ' (e.g. *hn-'ṣl*, "the socle"; *hn-'zy*, DN han-'Uzzay), — sometimes before other consonants as well (e.g. *hn-qbr*, "the grave"). This form *hn-* is already attested around 400 B.C., e.g. *hn-'lt*, "the goddess" (TSSI II,25). In Masoretic Hebrew, which does not geminate the gutturals, the gemination is compensated in similar cases by the lengthening of the vowel *a*, e.g. *hā'āreṣ*, "the land". These allomorphs parallel the Hebrew forms of the particle *min*, "from" (§48.12), and seem indeed to indicate that the original articulation of the article was *han-*, which should be related to the Arabic word *han*, "something", initially a deictic particle "this here, that here" (§49.6), as suggested by its demonstrative meaning in Pre-Islamic North Arabian (e.g. Thamūdic *hgml*, "this camel") and by some Hebrew expressions using the article: *hay-yōm*, "this day, today"; *hal-laylā*, "this night"; *haš-šānā*, "this year"; *hap-pa'am*, "this time". The weakening of the *h* led to the Punic spelling ' of the article (e.g. *'nsk*, "the smelter"), and to

its local forms *'an-* and probably younger *'am-* in ancient Yemenite colloquials (e.g. *'an-ḥulm*, "the dream"; *'am-raǧul* "the man"). The
Nabataean and later Arabic definite article *'al-* has also been regarded as
a variant form of *han-* > *'al-*, with the change *n* > *l* (§17.4). Although
there is no article *hl-* in Lihyānite (*hlḥm*... is the beginning of the
"South Arabian" and Ethiopic alphabet), this opinion is confirmed indirectly by the Mishnaic Hebrew demonstrative *hallāz* < **hal-'az*, "this
here", corresponding to Biblical Hebrew *hazze* < **han-ze* and to Neo-
Punic *h'z*, "this" (§36.38). Like the *n* of *hn-*, the *l* of the definite article
'al- is assimilated in Arabic to most initial consonants of the noun (e.g.
'aš-šams, "the sun"), although it is generally kept in writing. The (*'*)*a* is
commonly dropped after and before a vowel (e.g. *'alā l-'arḍi*, "on the
earth"; *əl-bēt l-əkbīr*, "the big house" in the Damascus colloquial). In
modern colloquials one encounters the pronunciations *al-*, *il-*, *əl-*.

33.11.　In Tigre, the particle *la-* is used as definite article and its
absence may signify indefiniteness; e.g. *la-gəndāb 'ənās*, "the old
man", with the word order: article + qualifier + qualified noun. Contrary
to other Semitic languages, the Tigre particle *la-* may be prefixed to a
noun qualified by a pronominal suffix (e.g. *la-bə'əs-a*, "her husband";
cf. §33.9) or by another noun (e.g. *la-wəlād la-dəgge*, the boys of the
village"). If it is prefixed only to the qualifying noun, it may imply the
indefiniteness of the qualified element; e.g. *fatāy wāldat la-walat*, "a
friend of the girl's parents"; *wəlād la-dəgge*, "(some) boys of the village", vs. *la-wəlād la-dəgge*, "the boys of the village".

33.12.　The determinate state of the noun was marked in Epigraphic
South Arabian by the morpheme *-n*, contrary to the situation reflected by
the modern South Arabian languages and by the ancient Yemenite colloquials (§33.8). This ending *-n* — or *-nhn* with duals and external masculine plurals — is attached in epigraphical texts to the singular (e.g.
ṣlmn, "the statue), to the broken plural (e.g. *'nḫln*, "the palmgroves"),
to the external plural (e.g. *'rb'tn m'nhn*, "the four hundred"), and to the
dual (e.g. *s²'bynhn*, "the two tribes").

　Since the Semitic article and the determinate state serve also to mark class
determination, two Gafat phrases mentioned by H. Ludolf in 1681 might belong
to a dialect still using the same morpheme *-n* to express determination, viz.
säbo-ň tälṣälam, "I don't molest a man" ("hominem non laedo"), *bäle-ň täl-
bälam*, "I don't eat millet" ("frumentum non edo"). The *-n* could alternatively
mark the accusative in Gafat (§32.28), but a pronominal suffix, attached to the
verb, should normally resume the preceding direct object and the postpositive

article -*əš* should be affixed to the nouns (§ 33.13). Similar cases occur in Harari where the suffix -*īn* expresses a strong determination, e.g. *aḥmara bäsär-īn tōlak̲ ?*, "do you eat (truly) Amharic meat?".

33.13. The determination may be expressed also by a demonstrative, as in Tigrinya (§36.36), or by a vocalic postposition which goes back to a suffixed pronominal element -(*h*)*u* functioning as demonstrative. This particular way of expressing determination occurs in Epigraphic South Arabian with the noun *wrḥ*, "month", followed by the pronominal suffix of the third person and by the name of the month. Thus, *wrḥ-h* is encountered frequently in Sabaic date formulas, while *wrḥ-s*[1] is used in Qatabanic (e.g. *wrḥ-s*[1] *d̲-tmnʿ*). This must be a fossilized structure going back to a period when the South Arabian languages had not yet developed the system of determination and indetermination based respectively on nunation and mimation (§33.17). That structure may explain the Aramaic emphatic state as well (§33.7) and it is paralleled in Indo-European by the suffixed -*s* (e.g. Latin *dominu-s*, "lord"), which has been explained by the demonstrative *so* (Greek ὁ). In the light of *wrḥ-h/s*[1], also the postpositive article -*əš*(*ä*) in Gafat (e.g. *gäg̲g̲-əš*(*ä*), "the house", vs. *gäg̲g̲ä*, "house") can best be explained as an unchangeable petrified pronominal suffix of the -*s*[1] type, despite the fact that the Gafat operative suffixes are of the -*h* type: -(*ə*)*ho*, "his", -(*ə*)*hä*, "her". Another related Semitic construction is attested in Amorite personal names ending in -*Cu-ú* (e.g. *I-la-kab-ka-bu-ú* /ʾIla-kabkabuhu/, "(T)his/ The star is the god", and with some Palaeosyrian divine names, as *A-dam-ma-sù*, "(T)his/The Adamma", [d]AMA-*ra-sù*, "(T)his/The AMA-*ra*", which are paralleled in the first millennium B.C. by North Arabian *hn-ʾlt*, *hn-ʿzy*, etc.

The use of the logogram TU, "to give birth", instead of AMA, "mother", in a parallel passage of the Ebla texts and the absence of the suffix -*sù* in similar sections are no sufficient reasons to postulate a new value for the sign AMA.

33.14. The related postpositive definite article -*u* (masc.) / -*wa* (fem.) of the Ethiopian languages evolved by elision of intervocalic *h* from suffixed third person pronouns like in **(bēt)u-hu* > (*bēt*)-*ū*, "his (house)", and **(bēt)u-ha* > (*bēt*)-*wa*, "her (house)", used as demonstratives (cf. §36.36). The article is thus -*u* in Geʿez (e.g. *dabru*, "the mountain"), in Amharic (e.g. *betu*, "the house"), and in Argobba (e.g. *bedu*, "the house") for the masculine and the plural, and -*wa* (or -*itu*) for the feminine singular (e.g. *ənəščawa*, "the woman"). One North Gurage dialect (Muher) uses the definite article -*we* regardless of the gender and of the number of the noun (e.g. *məssəwe*, "the man"; *məštəwe*, "the woman"; *gʷäbbabitwe*, "the brothers"). In other Gurage dialects, which preserve some archaic features, the postpositive definite article is -*i* after a consonant (e.g. *gari*, "the house"; *ätiti*, "the sister"; *bayočči*, "the children"), -*y* after a vowel (e.g. *gamelay*, "the camel"). The -*u* and -*wa* articles are identical with the Amharic third person possessive suffixes "his" and "her" so that sometimes there is ambiguity. However, the postpositive article in a noun phrase is suffixed to the modifier, not to the head (e.g. *tənnəšu bet*, "the small house"), while the possessive suffix is attached to the modified substantive (e.g. *tənnəš betu*, "his small house").

d) Indeterminate State

33.15. The indeterminate or "absolute" state is that of a noun which is neither construct, nor predicate, nor determinate in the sense described in §33.6-14. In principle, it corresponds to the bare stem form of the noun, with no additional affixes, as known to us best from various kinds of proper names, but also from some frozen expressions like *ul-tu re-eš a-di ki-id*, "from beginning to end" in Assyro-Babylonian. However, the appellation "absolute state" is likewise used in Semitics to designate the citation form of the noun, which may be identical with the predicative (§32.6), as well as the state of the undefined or indeterminate noun as opposed to the other states, and marked in consequence. Since nunation (-*n* ending) in Classical Arabic (e.g. *sāriqun*, "a thief") and mimation (-*m* ending) in ancient South Arabian (e.g. *ṣlmm*, "a statue") denote the undefined state of the noun, some scholars have assumed that mimation characterizes the indeterminate state of the noun also in East Semitic. However, there is no reason whatsoever to believe in the original determinate or indeterminate values of the mimation and nunation (§33.16). This is confirmed by early Liḥyānite forms like *h-ṣlmn*, "this statue", with the article and the North Arabian nunation, and by divine and personal names, like *Mlkm*, *'zzm*, etc., with the mimation.

33.16. The two endings -*m* and -*n* are allophones of the same original morpheme which initially characterized the non-construct state of the noun without denoting determination or indetermination. Most likely it was originally a masculine marker, only later used with feminines which already had their own marker -*t*. Some preserved pairs of divine names, like *'il-m* and *'il-t*, *b'l-m* and *b'l-t*, *'ttr-m* and *'ttr-t*, *mlk-m* and *mlk-t*, seem to confirm this explanation of the -*m/n* morpheme. Its earliest attestations in Palaeosyrian and in Old Akkadian already display the -*m* ending attached to the case vowels of the masculine singular and of the feminine, while the -*n* ending was used for the dual. However, the -*m* morpheme is missing in the masculine plural, and in Semitic loanwords borrowed by Sumerian with the case ending (e.g. n i - i s - k u = *nisqum*, a kind of servant; š e - e r - g u = *šerkum*, a quality of figs), and its use is inconsistent in Palaeosyrian. Besides, it can be omitted in Palaeosyrian, Old Akkadian, and Amorite proper names, which undoubtedly preserve archaic features. Its use is standardized, instead, in the Old Akkadian language and in Early Assyro-Babylonian dialects which regularly use the case endings -*um*, -*im*, -*am* with determinate and indeterminate nouns, but it becomes later a free variant of the case endings. In Amorite and in Ugaritic, an enclitic particle -*ma* may exceptionally occur with nouns in the construct state, but it is no mimation; e.g. Amorite *Ḫab-du-ma-ᵈDa-gan* next to *Ha-ab-du-ᵈDa-gan*, "Servant of Dagan"; Ugaritic *bnm 'il* next to *bn 'il*, "son of El". Instead, a "petrified" mimation and nunation seem to appear in adverbs ending in -*am* or -*an* (§47.2). Otherwise, the use of the -*m* ending is restricted in Ugaritic, Old Canaanite, Hebrew, and Phoenician to the absolute state of the dual and of the masculine plural, — contrary to East Semitic, — while Aramaic, Moabite, and Arabic employ the -*n* ending for the same purposes. Classical Arabic is adding -*n* also to the singular and to the feminine plural of the undefined state.

33.17. An innovation characterizes the ancient South Semitic languages represented by epigraphical South Arabian documents. Whereas mimation continues to be extensively used in proper names, just as in Palaeosyrian and in Old Akkadian, the language introduces a functional distinction between the mimation and the nunation. Henceforth, the mimation characterizes the absolute or non-construct state of the indeterminate noun (e.g. *ṣlmm*, "a statue"), while the nunation denotes the absolute or non-construct state of the determinate noun (e.g. *ṣlmn*, "the statue"). In consequence, the -*n* ending became the mark of the determinate state and the -*m* ending the mark of the undefined or indeterminate state of the common noun.

33.18. Another innovation, already encountered in Biblical Hebrew, appears regularly in some modern Semitic languages which have introduced a formal marking of the indeterminate state of the noun by means of a word functioning as indefinite article. It is obtained by a semantic weakening of the number "one", as in the Hebrew phrase *'īš 'eḥād*, "a (certain) man" (I Sam. 1,1). In Egyptian and Syrian Arabic, the numeral *wāḥid*, "one", is used alone for this purpose (e.g. *waḥda sitt*, "a woman"). It is combined with the article to *wāḥid əl-* in Moroccan Arabic (e.g. *wāḥd ərrāǧal*, "a man"), while the Algerian indefinite article *ḥa-l-* (e.g. *ḥə-rragəl*, "a man") goes probably back to *'aḥad.l-*, "someone". In Iraqi Arabic, instead, the noun *fard > fadd*, "single", is used for that purpose, and it is reduced to *fad > fa* in the Arabic of Uzbekistan (e.g. *fad ādami*, "a man"). A similar practice can be observed in modern Ethiopian languages, where the indefinite article can be expressed by *at* (< *ḥad*), "one"; e.g. *at ärč*, "a boy"; *attə gäräd* or *quna* (§36.28) *gäräd*, "a girl", in Gurage dialects. In Tigre, the numeral "one", masc. *woro(t)*, fem. *ḥatte*, is used in the same way; in Tigrinya, masc. *ḥadā*, fem. *ḥantit*; in Amharic, masc. *and*, fem. *andit*. The same usage has been assumed for Mehri forms like *ḥayd*, "hand" (§33.8).

e) Paradigms

33.19. It results from this investigation that the states of the noun influence the case inflection in the languages which have preserved the distinction of cases. Although the endings have various phonotactic variants, the following paradigm can be proposed for the triptotic inflection of Old Akkadian, Old Babylonian, and Old Assyrian nouns.

Construct State

	Singular		Plural		Dual	
	Masc.	Fem.	Masc.	Fem.	Masc.	Fem.
Nom.	*šar*	*šarrat*	*šarrū*	*šarrāt*	*šarrā*	*šarratā*
Gen.	*šarri*	*šarrati*	*šarrī/ē*	*šarrāti*	*šarrī*	*šarratī*
Acc.	*šar*	*šarrat*				

Determinate / Indeterminate State

	Singular		Plural		Dual	
	Masc.	Fem.	Masc.	Fem.	Masc.	Fem.
Nom.	*šarrum*	*šarratum*	*šarrū*	*šarrātum*	*šarrān*	*šarratān*
Gen.	*šarrim*	*šarratim*	*šarrī/ē*	*šarrātim*	*šarrīn*	*šarratīn*
Acc.	*šarram*	*šarratam*				

33.20. The syllabic writing of Ugaritic proper names and nouns, compared with the alphabetic spelling of nouns ending in *'u*, *'i*, *'a*, allows a reconstruction of a Ugaritic paradigm, probably identical to a great extent with an Old Canaanite paradigm that could be based on the glosses of the Amarna correspondence:

Construct State

| | Singular | | Plural | | Dual | |
	Masc.	Fem.	Masc.	Fem.	Masc.	Fem.
Nom.	*milku*	*milkat*	*milkū*	*milkāt*	*milkā*	*milkatā*
Gen.	*milki*	*milkati*	*milkī*	*milkāti*	*milkī*	*milkatī*
Acc.	*milka*	*milkat*				

Determinate / Indeterminate State

| | Singular | | Plural | | Dual | |
	Masc.	Fem.	Masc.	Fem.	Masc.	Fem.
Nom.	*milku*	*milkatu*	*milkūma*	*milkātu*	*milkām*	*milkatām*
Gen.	*milki*	*milkati*	*milkīma*	*milkāti*	*milkīm*	*milkatīm*
Acc.	*milka*	*milkata*				

33.21. Classical Arabic distinguishes the construct state, the determinate state, and the indeterminate state. Besides the use of the definite article *'al* in the determinate state, the difference between the determinate and the indeterminate states consists in adding the *-n* ending to the indeterminate singular and feminine plural. This distinction is not attested in Pre-Islamic and Pre-Classical Arabic. On the other hand, the nunation is known in the determinate state of ancient Yemenite and Eastern dialects, e.g. *mani ('a)m-qā'imun*, "who is the one who stands?". Here, we present the paradigm *sāriq*, "thief".

Construct State

| | Singular | | Plural | | Dual | |
	Masc.	Fem.	Masc.	Fem.	Masc.	Fem.
Nom.	*sāriqu*	*sāriqatu*	*sāriqū*	*sāriqātu*	*sāriqā*	*sāriqatā*
Gen.	*sāriqi*	*sāriqati*	*sāriqī*	*sāriqāti*	*sāriqay*	*sāriqatay*
Acc.	*sāriqa*	*sāriqata*				

Determinate State

	Singular		Plural		Dual	
	Masc.	Fem.	Masc.	Fem.	Masc.	Fem.
Nom.	'as-sāriqu	'as-sāriqatu	'as-sāriqūna	'as-sāriqātu	'as-sāriqāni	'as-sāriqatāni
Gen.	'as-sāriqi	'as-sāriqati	'as-sāriqīna	'as-sāriqāti	'as-sāriqayni	'as-sāriqatayni
Acc.	'as-sāriqa	'as-sāriqata				

Indeterminate State

	Singular		Plural		Dual	
	Masc.	Fem.	Masc.	Fem.	Masc.	Fem.
Nom.	sāriqun	sāriqatun	sāriqūna	sāriqātun	sāriqāni	sāriqatāni
Gen.	sāriqin	sāriqatin	sāriqīna	sāriqātin	sāriqayni	sāriqatayni
Acc.	sāriqan	sāriqatan				

33.22. The different states of the noun are clearly apparent in the Semitic languages without any case distinction, as Aramaic, Hebrew, Phoenician, Neo-Arabic. The most apparent differences are encountered in the Old Aramaic dialects that have the "emphatic" or determinate state:

Singular		Plural		Dual	
Masc.	Fem.	Masc.	Fem.	Masc.	Fem.

Construct State

Singular		Plural		Dual	
malk > melek	malkat	mal(ə)kē	malkəwāt	mal(ə)kē	-

Emphatic State

malkā(')	malkətā(')	mal(ə)kayyā(')	mal(ə)kātā(')	mal(ə)kayyā(')	-

Absolute State

malk > melek	malkā(h)	mal(ə)kīn	mal(ə)kān	mal(ə)kayin	malkətayin

33.23. The Hebrew paradigm can be considered as valid also for Phoenician with the exception of the feminine determinate and absolute states where the Phoenician noun preserves its original -*t* ending, at least in the writing.

Singular		Plural		Dual	
Masc.	Fem.	Masc.	Fem.	Masc.	Fem.

Construct State

malk > melek	*malkat*	*mal(ə)kē*	*mal(ə)kōt*	*malkē*	*malkətē*

Determinate State

ham-melek	*ham-malkā(h)*	*ham-məlākīm*	*ham-məlākōt*	*ham-malkayim*	*ham-malkātayim*

Absolute State

melek	*malkā(h)*	*məlākīm*	*məlākōt*	*malkayim*	*malkātayim*

33.24. In Neo-Arabic and in modern colloquials there are many dialectal and phonotactic variants. We give here a paradigm based on the Cairene pronunciation of the noun *mi'allim*, "teacher", although it is not used in the dual. One should add that the Maghrebine dialects employ the external masculine plural suffix -*īn* only with adjectives and participles, and that its ending -*n* is not dropped in the construct state of the modern colloquials, not even before a pronominal suffix, e.g. *mi'allimīnak*, "your teachers". The construct state of the feminine singular has the ending -*it* more often than -*at*.

	Singular		Plural	
	Masc.	Fem.	Masc.	Fem.

Construct State

| *miʿallim* | *miʿallimit* | *miʿallimīn* | *miʿallimāt* |

Determinate State

| *il-miʿallim* | *il-miʿallima* | *il-miʿallimīn* | *il-miʿallimāt* |

Absolute State

| *miʿallim* | *miʿallima* | *miʿallimīn* | *miʿallimāt* |

F. Adjectives

34.1. From the morphological point of view, the adjectives, participles, and verbal adjectives belong to the category of nouns. Some nominal patterns are used more often to form adjectives (cf. §29.35-36,41,44), but no strict rules can be established. The main difference between adjectives and substantives is rather of a semantic kind. When adjectives are not used as substantives (e.g. "the good", "the true"), they indicate the quality of another noun in a specific and concrete situation. And because they are referring to another noun, that can be either masculine or feminine, the adjectives have a proper basic characteristic which is gender inflection expressed by formal grammatical means.

34.2. As a rule, the adjectives agree with the substantive they modify in gender, number, and case. Their concord is in general plural *ad sensum*, even with collective nouns and with Arabic broken or internal plurals, which are grammatically singulars; e.g. Hebrew *hāʿām ha-holəkīm*, "the people who walk"; Classical Arabic *riǧālun ṣāliḥūna*, "pious men". Some Semitic nouns are plural in form though not plural in meaning, thus e.g. "God": Hebrew *ʾĕlohīm*, Phoenician *ʾēlīm*. In such cases, the adjective is more often in the singular (e.g. Hebrew *ʾĕlohīm* ḥay, "living God") than in the plural (e.g. *'ĕlohīm ḥayyīm*). On the opposite, there are adjectives belonging to some nominal patterns of Arabic that are not capable of concord; e.g. *bintun mulāḥun*, "a very pretty girl"; *nūqun hiǧānun*, "racing she-camels". In several languages, thus in Assyro-Babylonian, in Hebrew, in Aramaic, in modern Arabic colloquials, plural adjectives agree usually with dual substantives, e.g. Aramaic *šinnayin rabrabān*, "big teeth".

34.3. The concord of adjectives and substantives in modern Ethiopic frequently deviates from the common rule. In Tigrinya, adjectives agree in gender and number with the substantives they modify, except that inanimate plurals are treated as singulars. Besides, unlike Ge'ez, Tigrinya does not distinguish gender in plural adjectives; so we have, e.g. *ṣǝbbuqat 'awäddat*, "good-looking boys", and *ṣǝbbuqat 'awaləd*, "good-looking girls". Amharic adjectives only occasionally form plurals, and distinctive feminine forms are used optionally only in adjectives derived from Ge'ez. Interestingly, the definite article *-u* (§33.14) in an Amharic noun phrase is attached to the modifying adjective, not to the substantive, although the homophonous possessive suffix *-u* (§36.20) is attached to the substantive; e.g. *tǝnnǝš bet*, "a small house", *tǝnnǝš-u bet*, "the small house", *tǝnnǝš bet-u*, "his small house". In consequence, the *-n* marker of the definite direct object (§32.28) follows the same rule: *tǝnnǝš-un bet*, "the small house" (direct object), *tǝnnǝš bet-un*, "his small house" (direct object); in the latter case, however, the suffix can be added also to the adjective: *tǝnnǝš-un bet-un*, "his small house".

34.4. In other languages, the case inflection of the adjectives is in general the same as the declension of the substantives. However, the masculine plural of adjectives and participles ends in *-ūtu(m)*, *-ūti(m)* in Old Akkadian and in Assyro-Babylonian (§31.16), but its construct state ends in *-ū* in Old Akkadian, in contrast to the *-ūt* of Assyro-Babylonian; e.g. *māḥirū kaspim*, "the receivers of money".

34.5. The comparative degree of adjectives, called "elative", is formed in Arabic on the pattern *'afʿal*, thus *kabīr*, "great", *'akbar*, "greater". Traces of this formation are found in a few Hebrew adjectives, like *'akzār*, "cruel", *'akzāb*, "deceitful", *'ētān* < *'aytān*, "lasting". Classical Arabic has also feminine patterns for emphatic qualification, viz. *fiʿla, faʿla*, and *fuʿla*, e.g. *niʿma*, "how nice!", *ḥasna*, "how beautiful!", *'uẓma*, "how mighty!". These forms are no longer used in the colloquial speech. The comparative may be followed by *min* or, in the post-classical language, by *'an*, "from", which serve to express "than"; e.g. *'aṭwalu min naḫlatin*, "taller than a palm-tree". The same pattern *'af'al* is used for the superlative and may then take the article or be defined by a genitive; e.g. *'al-'akbar*, "the greatest"; *'afḍalu raǧulin*, "the most excellent man"; *'a'lā l-ǧibāli*, lit. "highest of mountains". The pattern *'f'l* appears in many South Arabian proper names, but its exact meaning and function are unknown. Instead, it has been borrowed into the Western Neo-Aramaic of Ma'lūla, where it was operative; e.g. *'awrab*, "greater", from *rab*, "great". Besides, a remnant of a larger use of this pattern in Semitic languages may be preserved by Hebrew *'almān* and Assyro-Babylonian *almānu*, "widower", a noun probably derived from *lemnu*, "bad", and meaning etymologically "worse".

34.6. An East Semitic elative is represented by a small number of adjectives with a prefix *ša-* / *šu*; e.g. *šalbabu* / *šalbubu*, "very violent"; *šanūdu*, "celebrated, famous"; *šūturu(m)*, "very large" (cf. §29.33).

G. Numerals

35.1. The numerals belong morphologically to the category of nouns. Beside the cardinals, Semitic languages possess derived forms or different stems to express ordinals, fractions, multiplicatives or iteratives, and distributives. The scribes have often represented the numerals logographically, writing them in cipher instead of spelling them out. This limits our knowledge of the numerals, especially in North and East Semitic languages using syllabic and logographic script. Most numerals have a Proto-Semitic origin, and they even exhibit close connections with Libyco-Berber and Egyptian. Cushitic and Chadic stand apart. The former, in particular Bedja, has cardinals based on the quinary Nilotic system and forms the numerals "six" to "nine" by composition: 6 = 5+1; 7 = 5+2; 8 = 5+3; 9 = 5+4.

a) Cardinals

35.2. The standard cardinal forms of the numerals in the principal Semitic languages are given below with reconstructed Proto-Semitic forms, as well as with Egyptian and selected Libyco-Berber numerals. Here, loanwords from Arabic may be deceitful. For instance, the

Ghadamsi numeral "one", *wayid*, is borrowed from Arabic, but South Moroccan Tachelhit *ya-n*, "one", derives from the same form **wa'(-n)* as ancient Egyptian *w'(y-w)* and must be considered as an authentic Libyco-Berber word. Tuareg forms are in general the most archaic ones. A selective approach is thus necessary, without pretending to go back to Proto-Berber numerals. Various phonetic developments occur in modern Aramaic, Arabic, South Arabian, and Ethiopic colloquials. They cannot be reported here.

35.3.   The numeral "one" is represented in Semitic by four different root morphemes, viz. *ḥad*, *'išt-*, *woro-*, and *ṭād*.

a) The best known numeral "one" is *ḥad*, the original form of which is preserved in Aramaic (*ḥad*), in some early Arabic vernaculars (*ḥad*), in Tigrinya (*ḥadä*), in Tigre (*ḥəd*, "about, some"; fem. *ḥatte*, "one"), and in South Ethiopic where Gurage *had*, *ad*, and *at(t)* must derive from *ḥad*, while Amharic *and* (fem. *andit*) and Tigrinya feminine *ḥantit* show an inserted *n* before the dental. Gafat *əǧǧä* (fem. *əǧǧät*), "one", goes back to **(ḥ)ənd*, but it shows an assimilation *nd > dd*, followed by the palatalisation *ədd > əǧǧ*. The forms with initial ', attested in Arabic (*'aḥad*), Hebrew (*'eḥād / 'aḥad*), Ugaritic (*'aḥd*), Epigraphic South Arabian (*'ḥd*), and Ge'ez (*'aḥadu*), use a secondary root morpheme brought into line with the triconsonantal system, as shown by other derivatives from *ḥad*, "one", viz. *waḥada*, "to be alone", *wāḥid*, "one, someone", in Arabic and in other Semitic languages; *wēdum*, "alone" in Assyro-Babylonian; *yaḥad*, "to be united" and "gathering" in Hebrew, also in Ugaritic (*yḥd*).

b) The second root is *'išt-*, with an allophone *'ašt-* in Hebrew which results from a change *i > a* occasioned by ' in a closed stressed syllable. It is the only numeral "one" attested in East Semitic where it is used with a suffix *-īn* (*ištīn*), *-ēn* (*ištēn*), or *-ān* (*ištiān-*, *ištān*), which is difficult to explain unless one considers *-n* as the masculine singular ending of the Afro-Asiatic pattern of agreement (cf. § 33.16), present also in the Libyco-Berber number "one": *yiw-ən / ya-n*. The feminine *ištiāt* and the Hebrew construct state *'aštē 'āśār*, "eleven", follow the declension of the plural, but a formal singular is implied by the Aramaic expression *b'št'*, "by the unit (of measure)". We do not know the vocalization of Ugaritic *'št 'šr(h)*, "eleven", and of Minaic *'s¹t*, "one", which is used next to *'ḥd*. The proposed etymologies of *'št* are highly conjectural, but the same numeral is attested by Libyco-Berber *iǧ*, feminine *išt*.

Cardinal Numerals

	Egyptian	Libyco-Berber	*Pr.-Sem.	O. Bab.	Ugar.
1 m.	wʿ(y-w)	yiwən/ya-n, iǧ	ḥad-, ʿišt-	ištēn	ʾaḥd
f.	wʿt	yiwət, išt		ištiāt	ʾaḥt
2 m.	śn-w(y)	sin, sən	ṯin-, kil'-	šinā	ṯn(m)
f.	śn-t(y)	snat, sənt		šittā	ṯt
3 m.	ḫmt-w	krad, šard	ślaṯ-	šalāšat	ṯlṯ(t)
f.		kratt, šarṭ		šalāš	ṯlṯ
4 m.	fd-w	kkuẓ	rbaʿ-	erbet(t)	ʾrbʿ(t)
f.		kkuẓt		erba	ʾrbʿ
5 m.	dỉ-w	səmmus, afus	ḥamš-	ḥamšat	ḥmš(t)
f.	dỉ-t	səmmust		ḥamiš	ḥmš
6 m.	śrś-w/śỉś-w	sḍis	šidṯ-	šiššet	ṯṯ(t)
f.		sḍist		šiš(š)	ṯṯ
7 m.	śfḫ-w	sa	šabʿ-	sebet(t)	šbʿ(t)
f.		sat		sebe	šbʿ
8 m.	ḫmn-w	tam	ṯmān-	samānāt	ṯmn(t)
f.		tamt		samānē	ṯmn
9 m.	psḏ-w	tẓa	tišʿ-	tišīt	tšʿ(t)
f.		tẓat		tiše	tšʿ
10 m.	mḏ-w	mraw	ʿaśr-	ešeret	ʿšr(t)
f.		mrawt		ešer	ʿšr
20	ḏwt	tə-mərwin		ešrā	ʿšrm
30	mʿb3	*tə-mərwin d mraw		šalāšā	ṯltm
40	ḥm	*sin-id tə-mərwin		erbā	ʾarbʿm
50	dỉyw	*sin-id tə-mərwin d mraw		ḥanšā < *ḥamšā	ḥmšm
60	iśś-	*krad-id tə-mərwin		šūš	ṯṯm
100	š(n)t	tə-meḏe	miʾt-	meʾat	mʾit
1000	ḫ3	a-žim/gim	liʾm-	līm	ʾalp
10.000	ḏbʿ		ribb-	ešeret līm	rbt

Cardinal Numerals

Hebrew	Aramaic	Arabic	Sabaic	Mehri	Geʿez	Tigre	Amharic
ʾeḥād, ʾaḥad	ḥad	wāḥid	ʾḥd	ṭāṭ	ʾaḥadu	woro(t)	and
ʾaḥat	ḥădā	wāḥida	ʾḥt	ṭayṭ	ʾaḥatti	ḥatte	
šnayim	trēn	ʾiṯnāni	tny	tərō	kəlʾe(tu)	kəlʾot	hulätt
štayim	tartēn	ʾiṯnatāni	tty	tərayt	kəlʾeti	kəlʾe	
šəlōšā	təlātā	ṯalāṯa	s²lṯt, ṯlṯt	śāṯayt	šalastu	salas	sost
šālōš	təlāt	ṯalāṯ	s²lṯ, ṯlṯ	śhəlēṯ	šalās, šəls		
ʾarbāʿā	ʾarbəʿā	ʾarbaʿa	ʾrbʿt	rəbōt	ʾarbāʿtu	ʾarbaʿ	aratt
ʾarbaʿ	ʾarbaʿ	ʾarbaʿ	ʾrbʿ	ʾarba	ʾarbāʿ, rəbʿ		
ḥămiššā	ḥamšā	ḥamsa	ḥms¹t	həmmōh	hamǝstu	ḥamǝs	ammǝst
ḥāmēš	ḥămēš	ḥams	ḥms¹	hayməh	hams, həms		
šiššā	šit	sitta	s¹dtt, s¹ṭt	yətēt	sədəstu	sǝs	sǝddǝst
šēš	šiš	sitt	s¹dt, s¹ṭ	hēt	səssu, səds		
šibʿā, šabʿā	šibʿā	sabʿa	s¹bʿt	yəbayt	sabʿatu	sabuʿ	säbatt
šebaʿ	šəbaʿ	sabʿ	s¹bʿ	hōba	sabʿu, səbʿ		
šəmōnā	təmanyā	ṯamāniya	tmn(y)t, ṯmt	təmənyīt	samāntu	samān	səmmǝnt
šəmōnē	təmānē	ṯamānin	ṯmny, ṯmn	təmōni	samāni, səmn		
tišʿā	tišʿā	tisʿa	ts¹ʿt	sāt	təsʿatu	sǝʿ	zäṭäňň
tēšaʿ	təšaʿ	tisʿ	ts¹ʿ	sā	təsʿu, təsʿ		
ʿăśārā	ʿaśrā	ʿašara	ʿs²rt	ʾāśərēt	ʿašartu	ʿasǝr	assǝr
ʿeśer, ʿaśar	ʿăśar	ʿašr	ʿs²r	ʾōśər	ʿašru, ʾəšr		
ʿeśrīm	ʿeśrīn	ʾišrūn	ʿs²ry		ʾəšrā	ʾəsra	haya
šəlōšīm	təlātīn	ṯalāṯūn	s²lty, ṯlty	(¹)	šalāsā	salāsa	sälasa
ʾarbāʿīm	ʾarbāʿīn	ʾarbaʿūn	ʾrbʿy		ʾarbəʿā	ʾarbəʿa	arba
ḥămiššīm	ḥamšīn	ḥamsūn	ḥms¹y		hamsā	həmsa	(h)amsa
šiššīm	šittīn	sittūn	s¹ty		səssā	sǝssa	sǝdsa, sǝlsa
mēʾā	məʾā	miʾat	mʾt		məʾət	məʾət	mäto
ʾelep	ʾălap	ʾalf	ʾlf		ʾašartū məʾət	šəḥ	ši(h)
ribbō	ribbō	ʿašara ʾālāf	śrt ʾʾlf		ʾəlf	ʾəlf	əlf

(¹) The series "twenty" – "ninety" is replaced by Coll. Arabic numerals.

c) Tigre *woro-* is apparently related to Tuareg *mraw*, "ten". The word might belong to the same root as Assyro-Babylonian *wurrū* or *murrū*, "to cut off", and originally designate a "bit" or a "bunch, cluster", as of dates, hence "ten". But, so far, this is just a guess.

d) The numeral "one" of Modern South Arabian, *ṭāṭ* in Mehri, *ṭād* in Ḥarsūsi, Śḥeri, and Soqoṭri, has an initial glottalized *ṭ* and goes back to Qatabanic *ṭd*, attested also in *ṭd 's²r*, "eleven". Its relation to *ḥad* is improbable, while there may be a link with the root **dad*, "someone", used in the Eastern "Sam" languages belonging to the Lowland East Cushitic group.

e) Another root is used by Egyptian *w'* and Libyco-Berber *yiw-ən* / *ya-n*, while Berber indefinite *ša*, "some", "something", goes back to Arabic *šay'*. To express the unit in the numeral "eleven" Gafat makes use of a derivative of **qənt-*, "single" (cf. §36.28): *asra qəmčättä*, lit. "ten-one".

35.4. The numeral "two" is represented by two different root morphemes, viz. *ṯin-* and *kil'-*.

a) The first one is employed in Old Akkadian and in Assyro-Babylonian with the dual ending -*ā* (*šinā*, *šenā*), to which the mimation is added in Ugaritic (*ṯnm*) and the nunation in Classical Arabic (*'iṯnāni*). The dual oblique case -*ay* is used in Sabaic and Minaic (*ṯny*), but one finds an ending -*w* in Qatabanic (*ṯnw*). The dual ending -*ay* appears with the mimation in Hebrew (*šnayim*) and in Phoenician (*šnm*, *'šnm*), and with the nunation in modern Arabic colloquials (*tnayn*, *tnēn*, *itnēn*). An early change *n > r*, which parallels the situation in Gurage where a non-geminated *n* becomes *r* in non-initial position (§17.6), explains the by-form *ṯir-* of *ṯin-* in Aramaic and in Modern South Arabian. This form is used in Aramaic with the dual ending of the oblique case followed by the nunation (*tryn > trēn*), while the South Arabian numeral *ṯərō* shows an ending -*ō* which is related to the Qatabanic ending -*w* of *ṯnw*. The Semitic verb **ṯanāyu(m)*, "to do (something) for the second time", "to repeat", derives from *ṯin-* either directly (§41.13) or through the ordinal **ṯāniy > ṯānī*, "second". The same numeral is attested in Egyptian (*śn-w*), with the dual form *śnwy*, and in Libyco-Berber (*sin*, *sən*); the substantive *śn* means "brother" in Egyptian (*śnt*, "sister"), as well as in Cushitic (e.g. Bedja *san*) and in Chadic (e.g. East Chadic *sin*, etc.).

b) The other numeral "two" is attested in Assyro-Babylonian under the form *kilallān / ūn* and, in the feminine, *kilaltān > kilattān*. The second liquid *l* corresponds to the glottal stop of the other Semitic languages (cf. §17.2); the noun has the dual ending with the nunation and it means "both". Its basis is probably related to Cushitic **kal-*, "one, alone" in the "Sam" languages. Only the feminine form *kl'at* is attested so far in Ugaritic and the masculine form *kil'ayim*, "of two kinds", in Hebrew and perhaps in Moabite (*kl'y*: Mesha 23), with the meaning "two" or "both". The Classical Arabic *kilā*, with the feminine *kiltā*, "both", is unchangeable when it is followed by a noun, but it has an oblique case *kilay-* / *kiltay-* when followed by a pronominal suffix. It is in reality a dual **kil'ā* which has lost its not pronounced ' like in ancient South Arabian where the archaic form *kl'y*, "both", is replaced in the mid-period by *kly*, next to a feminine *kl'ty*. In Geʿez, *kəl'e* < **kil'ay* is the normal numeral "two" for both genders, or *kəl'etu* may stand for the masculine and *kəl'eti* for the feminine. This noun "two" is used likewise in the modern Ethiopian languages where the phonetic development can lead to forms like *ḫʷet* in Gurage, where the labialized velar *kʷ* < *k* is spirantized into *ḫʷ* and the *l* reduced to the vowel *e*. Also Amharic *hulätt* and Gafat (*h*)*ələttä* > *ələč(čä)*, "two", go back to *kəl'et-*.

c) In Maghrebine Arabic, the noun *zawǧ*, "pair", is used as numeral "two", pronounced *žūz*, *zūz*, or *žuž*. Duality is also represented by *kpl*, "double", in Ugaritic, Aramaic, and Hebrew, but it may be expressed likewise without the numeral by using the sole dual formation of the noun.

35.5. The numerals "one" and "two" are either substantives (e.g. Assyro-Babylonian *ištēn ina libbišunu ul ūṣi*, "not one among them has escaped"; Hebrew *'al 'aḥad he-hārīm*, "on one of the mountains"; Arabic *'aḥaduhum*, "one of them") or adjectives which agree with the noun they determine in gender (e.g. Arabic *qaryatāni tnatāni*, "two villages"), case (e.g. Arabic *kulluhum li-'ummin wāḥidatin*, "they are all from one mother"), and the numeral "one" even in number (e.g. Hebrew *dəbārīm 'ăḥādīm*, "identical words").

35.6. The numerals "three" to "ten" are abstract or collective substantives marked by the suffix *-t* in historical times, and corresponding to ancient Egyptian collectives in *-t*, e.g. *dìw.t*, "a set of five" in Middle Egyptian. However, the bare root morpheme continued to be used with feminine nouns. This development, sometimes called "gender polarity", creates the false impression that cardinal numerals are used in the gender opposite to that of the noun which usually follows in the genitive plural, e.g. Classical Arabic *talātatu riğālin*, literally "a set of three men". However, this apparent inversion of gender seems to operate inconsistently in North Semitic, e.g. *er-bu u₄-mi*, "during four days", in the Babylonian dialect of Mari influenced by Amorite; *tlt sswm*, "three horses" in Ugaritic. Nevertheless, one might also surmise that certain nouns, for instance "day", are feminine instead of being masculine and that the lack of the ending *t* in Ugaritic results from its dropping in the spoken idiom (e.g. **talātat* > **talāta*). In later Semitic languages, however, the "gender polarity" tends to disappear. This grammatical principle is rarely or irregularly observed in Late Babylonian, in Syriac, and in Neo-Punic. In most modern languages, only one form is employed. Thus, Tigre uses the numerals "three" to "ten" without *-t*, while the opposite tendency can be observed in the other Ethiopian languages where the numerals with the ending *-t* are more frequently used, finally eliminating the distinction between masculine and feminine. A similar evolution is encountered in Neo-Aramaic, while most modern Arabic colloquials use the forms with the *-t* ending for independent numerals and those without *-t* in connection with plural nouns, regardless of their gender; e.g. in Damascus: *talāte*, "three", but *tlət banāt*, "three girls", and *tlət rğāl*, "three men". Chadic languages do not seem to distinguish the gender in numerals, while ancient Egyptian and Libyco-Berber add the mark *-t* to numerals qualifying feminine nouns, contrary to the common practice in "classical" Semitic languages.

35.7. The Proto-Semitic root morphemes of the numerals "three" to "ten" can be established as follows: *šlat-, rbaʿ-, ḥamš-, šidt-, šabʿ-, tmān-, tišʿ-, ʿašr*. The use of anaptyctic short vowels explains the vocalization attested in the "classical" languages with the exception of the numeral "four" where a prosthetic vowel was added to the root morpheme *rbaʿ*, still used without prothesis in the suffixed form *rəbōt* of the Mehri and Ḥarsūsi numeral, in the Mehri and Ḥarsūsi numeral *rība* for counting "four" days, also in the ordinals and in the fractions (§35.30).

35.8. The archaic and the modern South Arabian forms of the numeral "three" indicate that its original root morpheme had an initial lateral fricative *ś* (*ślat-*). This is confirmed by the Old Akkadian spelling *sa-li-iš-tim* of the ordinal (fem. genitive) with the sign SA used to express the syllable *ša/śa*, instead of ŠA which would indicate *ta* (§13.2). The later form *tlt* results from a regressive assimilation, as in the numeral *šidt-*, "six", especially in Ugaritic where two regressive assimilations took place (§35.11). The *l* of the numeral "three" is labialized in Gafat *sʷostä* and elided in Amharic *sost*. The numeral **ślaṭ-* had an allophone **śraṭ*, testifying to the change *l* > *r* in non initial position (§17.5). Its existence is confirmed by the Libyco-Berber numeral *kraḍ* / *šarḍ*, "three", which can easily be related to **śraṭ*. The change in question resulted from a dissimilation caused by the originally lateral character of *ś* (§16.1).

35.9. The Semitic numeral *rba'-*, "four", has an origin which is independent from the corresponding numeral in the other Afro-Asiatic language families. The Libyco-Berber numeral *kkuẓ* is related to Hebrew and Aramaic *qumṣ-*, "handful", and to Arabic *qamaza*, "to take with the fingertips". The word originally signified the bending of the four fingers over the hollow of the hand. A third Afro-Asiatic word meaning "four" is represented by Egyptian *fdw*, Bedja *fáḍig*, and Hausa *fu'du*.

35.10. The numeral *ḥamš-*, "five", signifies a hand (five fingers) and, as such, it is the basic unit of a quinary system. In fact, it must be related etymologically to Sabaic *ḥms*[1], "main army force", and to the Egyptian noun *ḥpš*, "strength" (*m* > *p*), originally "fist", also to the Bedja numeral *asa* < **assa* < **ḥassa* < **ḥamsa*, used in *asa-gwir*, "six" (5+1), *asa-rama*, "seven" (5+2), etc., and to Libyco-Berber *səmmus*, "five", which reflects a change *ḥ* > *s*, paralleled before front vowels in Slavic languages; e.g. *muḫa* vs. dative *musē* / *muše*, "fly". In the quinary system employed occasionally also in Libyco-Berber, the word *afus*, "hand", related directly to Egyptian *ḥpš*, may be used instead of *səmmus*.

35.11. The numeral *šidṭ-*, "six", is certainly related to Egyptian *śrś* / *śiš-w*, to Libyco-Berber *sḍis*, and to Hausa *šidda*. These forms testify to phonetic changes, attested also in Semitic languages, especially in Ugaritic where the form *ṯṯ* first implies the regressive assimilation *dṯ* > *ṯṯ*, attested also in other Semitic languages, and then a second regressive assimilation *šṯ* > *ṯṯ*.

35.12. The numeral *šab'-*, "seven", is certainly related to Egyptian *śfḫ-w* and to Libyco-Berber *sa*. The Old Akkadian mentions of the deified "Seven" (planets?) imply the initial *š* since the sign SI of *ᵈSi-bí* stands for *ši* / *še* (§13.2), and the *š* appears also in the Old Assyrian orthography *ša-be*, but later Assyro-Babylonian texts have *sebe* or *seba*, with the exception of spellings influenced by North Semitic, as *še-eb-i šanāti*, "seven years", at Alalakh. This shift *š* > *s* is paralleled by another shift in Mehri and Soqotri where the numerals "six" and "seven" appear with an initial *h* or *yh* instead of the expected palato-alveolar *š*: *hēt*, "six", and *hōba*, "seven", in Mehri, *yhaʿt* and *yhobə'* in Soqotri (cf. § 15.4; 36.10).

35.13. The numeral *ṯmān-*, "eight", is related to Egyptian *ḫmn-w* and to Libyco-Berber *tam*, but the phonetic differences are still in need of a consistent explanation of *ṯ* : *t* : *ḫ*. Also in East Semitic, the passage *ṯ* > *s* is not usual. In fact, the numeral "eight" is written *ša-ma-né* in Old Assyrian, a spelling which probably implies the pronunciation /*ṯamānē*/, but the later form is *samānē*. The original vocalization **ṯmān-t-* seems to be reflected by old Amharic *sant*.

35.14. The numeral *tišʿ-*, "nine", is related to Libyco-Berber *tẓa*, where the emphasis of *ẓ* is secondary. Attempts to relate this numeral to Egyptian *psḏ-w* should be abandoned. The Amharic numeral *zäṭäňň*, attested also in Gafat (*zäṭäňňä*), Gurage (*zäṭäň*), Argobba (*žäḫʷṭäňň*), and Harari (*zəḥṭän*), goes probably back to *zḥṭ* (*zḥẓ*), the same root as Old Akkadian *zuʾāzum* and Assyro-Babylonian *zāzu(m)*, "to divide", "to cut off", with a noun *zittu* (plur. *zīzātu*), "portion", "share". The final *ň* of the Ethiopic numeral is a suffix which is missing in most Gurage dialects (*zäṭä*, *ži'ä*). To judge also from the related Aramaic verb *zūḥ*, "to go away" or "to remove", and from Arabic *zaḥzaḥa*, "to displace", "to rip off", South Ethiopic **ziḥṭ* > **ziḥt*, "nine", is the portion or the amount that remains after one part has been removed, i.e. numbering one digit below a full ten or two hands.

35.15. The Semitic numeral *ʿaśr*, "ten", cannot be related to forms attested in other Afrasian language families. Its original meaning might be preserved by Arabic *ʿašīra(tun)*, "clan", and Epigraphic South Arabian *ʿs²rt*, "nomad group" (cf. §35.21). In Phoenician, the forms *ʿsr* and *ʿšrt* are attested for the numeral "ten"; they reflect different dialectal shifts of the original *ś* phoneme (§ 16.3).

35.16. The numerals from "eleven" to "nineteen" are normally formed by the juxtaposition of the unit-numbers or digits and of the numeral "ten". They appear in four variant forms:

a) Digits in the construct state, followed by "ten", are found in Assyro-Babylonian (e.g. *samānēšer*, "eighteen"), in Aramaic (e.g. *ḥamšat ʿăśar*, "fifteen"), and in Hebrew (e.g. *šənē ʿāśār*, "twelve").

b) Digits with the fixed ending -*a*, followed by "ten" with the same ending, are attested in Classical Arabic (e.g. *ṯalāṯata 'ašara*, "thirteen") and in ancient dialects (e.g. *'iḥdā 'ašrata / 'aširata / 'ašarata*, "eleven"); this form is developed into a compound in Neo-Arabic (e.g. *arba'ta'šar*, "fourteen"), it is reflected in modern colloquials (e.g. *tlətta'šar*, "thirteen"), and can perhaps be assumed in ancient South Arabian (e.g. *s¹dtt 's²r*, "sixteen"), although the lack of vocalization excludes any certitude and allows of an interpretation of the first type (a).

c) The mere asyndetic juxtaposition of digits and of "ten" occurs in Ugaritic (e.g. *'arb' 'šr*, "fourteen") and in Hebrew (e.g. *'arbā'ā 'āśār*, "fourteen"), also with inverted order (e.g. *'šr 'arb'*), which is usual in Tigre (e.g. *'asər 'arba'*, "fourteen"), in Tigrinya (e.g. *'asartä kələttə*, "twelve"; *'asartä šamante*, "eighteen"), in Gafat (e.g. *asra lättä*, "twelve"; *asra sʷostä*, "thirteen"), and in Amharic (e.g. *äsrand*, "eleven"; *äsrähulätt*, "twelve").

d) The component "ten" preceding digits and joined to them by *wa* or -*m*, "and", appears in Phoenician and Punic (e.g. *'sr w-ḥmš*, "fifteen"), in Nabataean (e.g. *'šr w-tlt*, "thirteen"; *'šrh w-šb'h*, "seventeen"), in Modern South Arabian (e.g. *'ōśər wə-śhəlēṯ*, "thirteen"), in Ge'ez (e.g. *'ašru wa-šalās*, "thirteen"), in modern Ethiopic (e.g. Tigre *'asər wa-səs*, "sixteen"; Gurage *asrə-m ḫʷet*, "twelve"), and exceptionally in Hebrew (*'ăśrā wa-ḥămiššā*, "fifteen").

35.17. In Aramaic, in Hebrew, in Arabic, and in ancient South Arabian, the digits of the numerals from "thirteen" to "nineteen" have the -*t* ending when used with masculine nouns, but only forms without -*t* are employed in Neo-Aramaic (e.g. *arbāsar*, "fourteen") and only forms with -*t* occur in modern Arabic colloquials (e.g. *arba'tāšar*, "fourteen"), regardless of the gender. In Ugaritic, in Modern South Arabian, and in Ge'ez, both components of the numeral have the -*t* ending when used with a masculine noun (e.g. Ugaritic *ṯmnt 'šrt*, "eighteen"; Mehri *'āśərēt wə-śāṯayt*, "thirteen"; Ge'ez *'ašartu wa-šalastu*, "thirteen"), but the practice of the Ugaritic scribes is not consistent. Besides, in Assyro-Babylonian, in Ugaritic, in Aramaic, and in Hebrew, the ending -*it* or -*ih* > -*ē* is added to the numeral "ten" when the teens are used with a feminine noun; e.g. Babylonian *ḥamiššerit*, "fifteen"; Ugaritic *šb' 'šrh*, "seventeen"; Syriac *'arba'sərē*, "fourteen"; Hebrew *šəlōš 'eśrē*, "thirteen".

35.18. Decade numerals have no gender differentiation, except in Late Babylonian where gender concord is attested with masculine and feminine plural endings (e.g. *erbē'*, "forty"; *ešrāt*, "twenty"), while *šūš*, "sixty", remains unchanged. Otherwise, the numeral "twenty" is expressed by the dual of "ten" in Assyro-Babylonian (*ešrā*), in South Arabian (*'s²ry*), in Ge'ez (*'əšrā*), in modern Ethiopian languages, probably in Libyco-Berber (Tuareg *tə-mərwin*; Tachelhit *mrawin*), where it is generally replaced by Arabic *'ašrin*, and perhaps in Ugaritic (*'šrm*). The dual afformative *-ā* spread analogically from "twenty" to the following tens, formed as duals of the numerals from "three" to "nine", e.g. *ḫanšā* < **ḫamšā*, "fifty" in Old Akkadian; *amsa* in Amharic. In other Semitic languages, thus in Hebrew, Phoenician, Aramaic, and Arabic, "twenty" is expressed by the plural of "ten" and the following tens are formed analogically by adding the plural ending to the numerals from "three" to "nine", thus e.g. Hebrew *šəlōšīm*, "thirty", Aramaic *təlātīn*, Neo-Aramaic *tlāy*, Classical Arabic *talātūna*, *tlātīn* in Damascene colloquial. This formation parallels the situation in ancient Egyptian where the tens, from fifty upwards, are plurals of the units. However, another system probably existed in Semitic languages, as suggested by the situation in South Ethiopic. In Argobba, Harari, and some Gurage dialects (Soddo and Gogot), the tens can be formed by compounding a unit with the numeral "ten", thus *sost assər*, "thirty"; *arbät assər*, "forty"; *ḥamməst assər*, "fifty"; *səddəst assər*, "sixty". This manner of expressing the tens is generally believed to have been taken from Cushitic, since "fifty" is *ontētonnēte* in Sidamo, literally "five tens"; "sixty" is *lētonnēte*, "six tens", etc. However, Modern South Arabian has preserved some numerals of a similar old series (e.g. Soqoṭri *śile 'eśarhin*, "thirty", literally "three tens"). Ge'ez forms the numeral "thousand" in this way (*'ašartu mə'ət*, literally "ten hundreds"), and the same system is used in other Semitic languages for hundreds and thousands (e.g. *talātu mi'atin*, "three hundred"; *talātatu 'alāfin*, "three thousand", in Classical Arabic). One may ask therefore whether Cushitic has not rather borrowed this use from the Semitic languages of Ethiopia or assume that this manner of expressing the tens is common to both language families, so much the more that a similar system is attested in Libyco-Berber with the numeral "twenty" as basis, unfortunately in its borrowed Arabic form *'ašrin*: *sin-id 'ašrin* (cf. §35.31), "twice twenty" = 40, *krad-id 'ašrin*, "three times twenty" = 60, *kkuz-id 'ašrin*, "four times twenty" = 80 (cf. French "quatre-vingt"), also *səmmus-id 'ašrin*, "five times twenty" = 100. The odd tens are formed by addition: *sin-id 'ašrin d* *mraw*, "twice twenty with ten" = 50, etc. The Semitic dual form for "20" seems to point to a former vigesimal system which is thus preserved in Libyco-Berber, where it is combined with the decimal system. The latter appears also in Indo-European (e.g. Latin *trī-gintā*, "thirty", literally "three tens").

35.19. Several systems are followed to join tens with the digits. The Assyro-Babylonian use is unknown, but two different systems are attested in Ugaritic: no conjunction is used to join tens with the digits that follow (e.g. *'šrm 'rb'*, "twenty four"), exactly as in Neo-Aramaic (e.g. *'esrī trē*, "twenty-two"), but an additive *l* precedes the "ten" when the digit stands first (e.g. *'rb' l-'šrm*, literally "four above twenty"). In Phoenician and Punic, the situation is opposite: no conjunction is needed to join tens with the digits that precede (e.g. *šlš ḥmšm*, "fifty-three"), but the conjunction *w-* is employed when the digits follow (e.g. *ḥmšm w-šnm*, "fifty-two"), like in modern Ethiopic using the conjunctions *wa-* or *-m* (e.g. *ḥamsa wa-'arba'*, "fifty-four" in Tigre; *ḥuʷya-m-at*, "twenty-one" in Gurage [Chaha]). This is also the most common construction in Hebrew, but the conjunction *wa-* joins the numerals also when the digits precede (e.g. *'eḥad wə-'eśrīm*, "twenty-one"). The latter scheme is the normal way of expressing the compound numerals in ancient South Arabian (e.g. *ḥms w-sˡty*, "sixty-five"), in Classical Arabic (e.g. *tamānin wa-'išrūna laylatan*, "twenty-eighth nights"), and in modern Arabic colloquials (e.g. *sab'ā w-'əšrīn*, "twenty-seven"). Schematically, the various systems can be presented as follows: 20+1, 1+20, 1-*l*-20, 1-*w*-20, 20-*w/m*-1.

35.20. The numeral "hundred" is derived from a common origin. It is attested in Palaeosyrian (*mi-at*, *me-at*), Old Akkadian (*mi-at*), Assyro-Babylonian (*me-at*, *ma-a-at*), indirectly in Amorite with the orthography *me-et* at Mari, which explains the Ugaritic singular *m'it* (**me'et* or **mēt*), while the plural is *m'at*. It is vocalized *mē(t)* in Late Babylonian, *mē'ā* in Hebrew, *mə'ā* in Aramaic, and *mā* in Syriac and in Neo-Aramaic, *mi'at* in Classical Arabic and *mīye* in the colloquial of Damascus. It is written *m't* in Phoenician and in ancient South Arabian, *mə'ət* in Ge'ez, *mäto* in Amharic. The numeral is attested also in Tuareg where *tə-mede*, "hundred", is related not to Egyptian *md-w*, "ten", but to Semitic *m't*, with an emphatic *ḍ* replacing the voiceless *t*, a change paralleled in *ḵraḍ* (§ 35.8), *sḍis* (§35.11), and *tẓa* (§35.14). It has a plural *ti-maḍ*. In South Ethiopic, besides, there is another term for "hundred", viz. *bäqər* or *bäqəl* in Gurage (*l/r*), *bäqlä* in Harari and in Gafat, and *baqol* in Somali, with variant forms in other Cushitic languages. The numeral may be related to the Ethiopic name of the "mule", in Ge'ez *baql* (cf. §35.21). The numeral "hundred" is used also in the dual (e.g. Aramaic *mā'tayin*) and in the plural (e.g. Arabic *mi'āt* and *mi'ūn*; Tigre *'am'āt*).

35.21.   There are five different ways of expressing the numeral "thousand". In Palaeosyrian, in Old Akkadian, and in Assyro-Babylonian one finds *li-im*, which is related to Ugaritic *l'im* and Hebrew *lə'ōm*, "people, clan", as well as to the divine name *Li'im*. Tuareg *a-žim*, "thousand" (plur. *i-žīm-ān*), might belong here too, since Libyco-Berber *ž* often derives from *l* (e.g. Tachelhit *alim* > Tamazight *ažim*, "straw"), but there is a dialectal variant *a-gim* that may suggest a link with Cushitic and South Ethiopic *kum*. In Ugaritic, in the West Semitic languages, and in South Arabian, instead, one encounters the noun *'alp-* which is related to the noun meaning either "clan" or "ox". The analogy with *li-im* is in favour of "clan", but the South Ethiopic *bäqər* may suggest "ox". In Ge'ez, *'əlf* is used for "ten thousand", while "one thousand" is expressed by *'ašartu mə'ət*, literally "ten hundreds" (cf. §35.18). Modern Ethiopic *šəḥ / ši(h)*, "thousand", used also in Cushitic (*ših*), suggests the notion of high number (root *šyḥ*), while the use of *'alf* with the meaning "thousand" in Tigre and in Harari is due to Arabic influence. In South Ethiopic, one also finds a noun "thousand" borrowed from Cushitic: *kum* in Harari, *kʷəm* and other forms in Gurage. It may be related to Tuareg *a-gim*, as just mentioned. The numeral "thousand" can be used in the dual and the plural.

35.22.   The numeral "ten thousand" has a special name in Palaeosyrian (*rí-ba₁₄?*), in Ugaritic (*rbt*), Aramaic (*rebbō*), and Hebrew (*ribbō*). It suggests the idea of "magnitude" and can be used in the dual and the plural. In Ge'ez, in Amharic, and in Tigre, *'əlf* has the meaning "ten thousand", with an internal plural *'a'lāf / 'ālāf*.

b) Ordinals

35.23.   The ordinals are adjectives and they follow the rules of the gender, number, and case. They generally derive from the cardinals by adding a suffix to the root morpheme or by adopting the *CāCiC* pattern. Since the ordinals are adjectives, they normally follow the substantive, except in East and North Semitic where they precede it.

35.24. With the exception of the rare Old Babylonian *ištiyūm* and of the South Ethiopic *atänä, andäňňa*, "first", the only known terms for the ordinal "first" derive from root morphemes different from the ones used for the cardinal "one". In Assyro-Babylonian, **maḫrīu(m)* > *maḫrū(m)* and *pānīu(m)* > *pānū(m)* are attested, both meaning literally "the one in front" or "former". The same basic meaning is attached to Aramaic *qadmāy*, to South Arabian *qdm*, and to Ge'ez *qadāmi*, as well as to Arabic *'awwal* or *'awwil*, which has been borrowed as *ḥāwīl* in Modern South Arabian and is suffixed into *awwalānī* in Syrian and Egyptian colloquials. Hebrew *rī'šōn* derives instead from the word "head", Gafat *mäžämmäryä*, "first", originates from the Ethiopic root *ğmr / žmr*, "to begin", while Tigrinya *fälämay* etymologically means "redeemed", probably by allusion to Ex. 13,13. The form of the ordinal "first" in Old Akkadian, Palaeosyrian, Amorite, and Ugaritic cannot as yet be ascertained.

35.25. The ordinal "second" is formed in general according to the same patterns as the ordinals 3-10 (§35.26-27). The ancient Aramaic ordinal *tinyān*, "second", does not reflect the change *n > r* of the cardinal, but the Neo-Aramaic form is *treyāna*. Ge'ez uses for "second" three different root morphemes, viz. *kālə', dāgəm*, and *kā'əb*, while Modern South Arabian employs *məšēġər* as ordinal "second".

35.26. The *CāCiC* pattern is used for the ordinals up to "tenth" in Old Akkadian (e.g. *sālištum*, "third" fem.), in Old Assyrian (e.g. *šādištum*, "sixth" fem.), in Arabic (e.g. *ṯāmin*, "eighth"), followed by Modern South Arabian (e.g. *ṯōmən*, "eighth"), also in Ge'ez (e.g. *sāmən*, "eighth"), in Tigre (e.g. *sāləs*, "third"), and probably in ancient South Arabian judging from Arabic and Ge'ez, from the absence of the *-y* suffix, and from the identity of the ordinal *s¹dṯ*, "sixth", with Mehri *sōdəs*, fem. *šədtēt*. This pattern can be assumed also in Ugaritic, where the suffix *-y* is likewise missing, while the ordinal *ṯdṯ* parallels the ordinal "sixth" in Old Assyrian (*šādiš*), Arabic (*sādis*), Ge'ez (*sādəs*), and South Arabian. The pattern *CāCiC* can therefore be regarded as Proto-Semitic, the more so if the later Assyro-Babylonian forms *šalšu*, "third", etc., result from the loss of the short *i* and from the subsequent shortening of *ā* to *a > e* in a close syllable (e.g. **šādišu > *šaššu > šeššu*). The alternative explanation for these Assyro-Babylonian forms would be a different pattern *CaCC* or *CiCC*, without any suffix.

35.27. Patterns with a suffix are attested in Middle Assyrian (e.g. *šalāšiyu*, "third"; *ḥamāšiyu*, "fifth"; *tišā'iyu*, "ninth"), in Hebrew (e.g. *ḥămīšī*, "fifth"; *təšī'ī*, "ninth"), in Phoenician and Punic (e.g. *'rb'y*, "fourth"; *ḥmšy*, "fifth"), in Aramaic (e.g. *təlītāy*, "third"; *rəbī'āy*, "fourth"), and in Ethiopic: there are parallel series with the endings *-āwi* and *-āy* in Ge'ez (e.g. *ḥamsāwi*, *ḥamsāy*, "fifth"; *sādsāwi*, *sādsāy*, "sixth"), *-āy* is used in Tigre (e.g. masc. *sālsāy*, fem. *sālsāyt*, "third"), and *-änä* in South Ethiopic (e.g. *ḫʷetänä*, "second"; *sostänä*, "third").

35.28. In Neo-Aramaic, ordinal numerals can also be formed by means of the determinative - relative particle *də* (§36.52) prefixed to the corresponding cardinal numeral, e.g. *dətre*, "second", from *tre*, "two"; *dətla*, "third", from *tla*, "three".

35.29. The ordinals above "tenth" occur in Assyro-Babylonian with a suffix *-ū* in the nominative, *-ī* in the genitive (e.g. *erbēšērī*, "fourteenth"; *ešrū*, "twentieth"). Above "tenth", no ordinals are attested in Ugaritic and in ancient South Arabian, and no special forms exist in Hebrew, Phoenician, and Aramaic: the cardinal numerals are used beyond "tenth". In Arabic, we have *ḥādiya 'ašara*, "eleventh", and further the ordinal followed by *'ašara*. In Ethiopic, likewise, the cardinal numeral "ten" is used with the ordinal of the digits; e.g. Tigre masc. *'asər wa-qadāmāy*, "eleventh", *'asər wa-kāl'āy*, "twelfth", *'asər wa-rāb'āy*, "fourteenth", etc. From "twentieth" onwards, the cardinal numerals are used, but endings of the ordinals may be applied in Ethiopic. In Ge'ez, either the cardinals or forms with the suffix *-āwi* can be used; e.g. *'əšrāwi*, "twentieth"; *šalāsāwi*, "thirtieth", etc. In Tigre, the ending *-āy* may be applied; e.g. *'əsrāy*, "twentieth", *mə'ətāy*, "hundredth", *mə'ətāy wa-qadāmāy*, "one hundred and first", *'asər šəḥāy*, "ten thousandth", etc.

c) Fractionals

35.30. The best proof that fractionals were initially derived from feminine ordinals can be deduced from the fact that *CāCiC* is the normal formation for fractionals as well as for ordinals in the early period of East Semitic and in Ge'ez (§35.26). In Old Babylonian, e.g., we encounter *šālištum*, "a third", *rābītum*, "a fourth"; *sā/sēbi'atum*, "a seventh". In Ge'ez, the ordinal is followed by *'əd*, "hand"; e.g. *rābə'ət 'əd*, "a quarter", literally "fourth part" (cf. §35.31). A related stem is

found also in Hebrew (e.g. *šəlīšīt*, "a third"). However, other patterns
are attested as well and the stem *CuCC* is widely used in West Semitic
languages, viz. in Aramaic (e.g. *ḥumš-*, "a fifth"), in Arabic (e.g. *ṯulṯ*, "a
third"), in Hebrew (e.g. *roba'*, "a fourth"), also in Late Babylonian
(*ḥunz*, "a fifth"), while the Phoenician and the South Arabian vocalizations are unknown. In Ugaritic, the attested fractions have prefixed
m- and suffixed *-t*, e.g. *mṯlṯt*, "a third"; *mrb't*, "a fourth". This pattern
is related to the feminine ordinal "second" in Mehri and Ḥarsūsi
(*məšəġərēt*), as well as to the plural fraction *mḫmsˡt*, "fifths", in Sabaic,
and to *masallas*, "third part", in Tigre. There are also forms which cannot readily be attached to common patterns, special words like *mišlu(m)*
in Assyro-Babylonian, *ḥṣt* in Ugaritic and in Hebrew, or *sar* in Tigre,
meaning "half", or *šinepiātum* > *šinepātu(m)* in Old Babylonian and
šnpt in Ugaritic, "two-thirds", and idiomatic ways of expressing fractions, e.g. *'ṣb'm bn ṯmny 'ṣb'* in Sabaic, "one finger from eight fingers",
i.e. "one eighth".

d) Multiplicatives

35.31. The meaning of multiplicatives or iteratives is not only "once",
"twice", "thrice", etc., but also "for the second time", "for the third
time", etc. These numerals are formed in East Semitic by adding *-išu* to
the stem of the cardinal numerals, often with the preposition *adi* or *ana*,
e.g. *adi / ana ḥamšišu*, "five times" or "for the fifth time". The vowel
-i- is dropped after *ištīn*, as shown by *ištiššu*, "once". This suffix *-išu*
goes back to *-*'iṭu* and corresponds to the South Arabian *-'ḏ* and to the
Ugaritic *-('i)d*, used to express the iterative, e.g. Sabaic *sˡdt'ḏ*, "for the
sixth time"; Ugaritic *šb''id* or *šb'd*, "seven times". The same formation
is preserved in some Libyco-Berber dialects, at least among the Igšan
(Tachelhit): *sin-iḏ*, "twice"; *kraḏ-iḏ*, "three times"; *kkuz-iḏ*, "four
times"; etc. An innovative Libyco-Berber use of the morpheme *iḏ* without preceding numeral aims at marking the plural of not-Berberized
loanwords borrowed in the singular; e.g. *iḏ ḫali* (< Arabic *ḫālī*, "my
maternal uncle"), "multiple maternal uncle(s)". A morpheme *-ad*
appears in Somali where it forms the ordinal numerals, e.g. *kōbá-ad*,
"first", *labá-ad*, "second", *saddeḥá-ad*, "third", etc.

35.32. From the Middle Assyrian and the Middle Babylonian periods
on, another method is attested for signifying that something happens
"for the first time" or "in the first place", "for the second time" or "in

the second place", viz. the ordinal with the suffix -ānu, e.g. šaniānu, šalšiānu, rabiānu, "for the second, third, fourth time". This formation is attested also in Arabic with the old ordinals of the pattern CāCiC: 'awwalan, tāniyan, tālitan, rābi'an, etc., "firstly, secondly, thirdly, fourthly". There are also forms specific to one language or idiomatic ways of expressing iteratives, e.g. the expressed or understood noun pa'am, "time", in Hebrew and in Phoenician with the cardinal (e.g. pa'am 'ahat, "once") or the ordinal (e.g. pa'am hămīšīt, "the fifth time"), or the numeral had, "one", used in Aramaic with a following cardinal (e.g. had šib'ā, "seven times").

e) Distributives

35.33. The distributive numerals have the characteristic formation CuCuCā' in East Semitic (ištinā', "one by one"; šinā', "two by two"; šulušā', "three by three"; rubu'ā', "four by four", etc.), but this pattern has not been identified as yet in other Semitic languages which usually express the distributive numerals by a repetition of the cardinals, e.g. talāta talāta, "three by three". In Arabic, however, there are also two patterns used to express the distributives, viz. fu'āl (e.g. tunā', "two by two"; tulāt, "three by three") and maf'al (e.g. matnā, "two by two"; matlat, "three by three").

f) Verbal Derivatives

35.34. The root morphemes of numerals are used in Semitic languages as base of verbal derivatives that sometimes have a particular meaning going beyond the basic acceptations "divide into x parts", "do for the x time", "make x-fold". E.g. the verb *tanāyu, "to repeat", derives from tin-, "two", to which a morpheme -y was added (§35.4; 41.13). Arabic Stem V tarabba'a, derived from Stem II rabba'a, "to quadruple", means "to sit cross-legged", and the phrase tarabba'a 'alā l-'arši has the specific meaning "he mounted the throne". Because of its use in spells and conjurations, the numeral šab'-, "seven", gave rise to different denominative formations. Although Arabic Stem II of sb' simply means "to make sevenfold", like other derivatives of the same type, the corresponding Palaeosyrian D-stem expresses the idea of adjuring, like the Hebrew and the Jewish Aramaic causative stem; e.g. Palaeosyrian si-ba /šibba'/ KI.KI, "adjure the lands!"; Hebrew hišbī'ekā, "he adjured you"; Aramaic mšby' 'ny 'lykm, "I am adjuring you". Instead,

the reflexive N-stem is used in Hebrew with the meaning "to swear",
e.g. *nišbaʿ*, "he swore".

3. PRONOUNS

36.1. Semitic languages have five types of pronouns besides the personal preformatives and afformatives of the verb inflection which will
be discussed in connection with the verb (§40). These five types are the
personal pronouns, the independent possessive pronouns, the demonstrative pronouns, the determinative-relative pronouns, and the indefinite
and interrogative pronouns. The personal pronouns are subdivided into
independent or separate pronouns and suffixed pronouns which can be
used with nouns, verbs, and prepositions, and may form reflexive pronouns. The system of the pronouns of the personal group can be said to
be genetically identical in all five branches of Afro-Asiatic, although full
sets of independent pronouns, dependent pronouns, and suffix-pronouns
are found only in Egyptian and in South Ethiopic, where the first set is
used as copula (§49.19). In Cushitic languages like Oromo, pronominal
suffixes are replaced by two sets of separate pronouns. One set is used
as isolated citation form, as predicate, and mainly as direct object preceding the verb, while the second set serves as possesssive pronoun following the noun. This leaves us in Oromo with three sets of personal
pronouns that correspond to an active or subject case (e.g. *inni*, "he"), a
non-active or non-subject case (e.g. *isā*, "him"), and a genitive or possessive (e.g. *kan* or *isā*, "his"). The Chadic branch, as usual, has the
greatest number of peculiarities, both morphological and morpho-syntactical. For example, the Hausa pronoun *mu* of the 1st pers. plur. may
be considered as the assimilated element *nu > mu* (cf. §11.7) of the corresponding pronoun in the other Afro-Asiatic branches, but the fact is
that it is identical with the West African pronoun of the Mandingo-
speaking Vai tribe (e.g. *mu-fa*, "our father"; *mu-ro*, "we say"). The personals are expressed in Hausa conjugation by separate pronouns that
precede the verb and are fused with morphemes indicating aspect and
tense, so that it is the pronoun which seems to be inflected; e.g. *su halbi*,
"they have hunted" (perfective), *su-na halbi*, "they were hunting"
(imperfective), *su-ka halbi*, "they hunted" (preterite), *s(u)-ā halbi*, "they
will hunt" (future). Such constructions do not occur with Semitic personal pronouns.

A. Independent Personal Pronouns

36.2. The following paradigm of the independent personal pronoun, free form, subject case, is limited to the principal Semitic languages and to *Proto-Semitic. Palaeosyrian is based on the Ebla texts. For comparison, a paradigm is added for Egyptian, for Rendille, a Lowland East Cushitic Language spoken in Kenya, and for Tuareg, which generally preserves archaic Libyco-Berber forms, although the existing pronouns

	Egyptian	Tuareg	Rendille	*Pr.-Sem.	P.Syr.	O.Bab.	Ugaritic	Hebrew	Aramaic
Sing.									
1	ỉn-k	n-ǝk	an(i)	'an-a	'anna	anāku	'an, 'ank	'ănī, 'ānōkī	'ănā
2 m.	nt-k	kay	at(i)	'an-ta/ka(?)	'anta	atta	'at	'attā	'anta, 'att
f.	nt-ṯ	kǝm		'an-ti/ki(?)	?	atti	'at	'att	'anti, 'att
3 m.	nt-f	nt-a	us(u)	šu-wa	šuwa	šū	hw	hū'(a)	hū(')
f.	nt-s		iče	ši-ya	šiya	šī	hy	hī'(a)	hī(')
Dual									
1				'an-kā					
2				'an-t/k(an)ā	*attunā				
3				š(u-n)ā	*šunā				
Plur.									
1 m.	ỉn-n	n-ǝkkǎ-ni	inno	niḥ-nu	?	nīnu		('ǎ)naḥnū, 'ānū	'ănaḥnā(n)
f.		n-ǝkkǎ-nǝti							
2 m.	nt-tn	kǎw-ni	atin	'an-ta-nu	'antanu	attunu		'attem(mā)	'antūn/m, 'att
f.		kǎmǎ-ti		'an-ti-na	?	attina		'attēn(ā)	*'antīn, 'attīn
3 m.	nt-sn	ǝntǎ-ni	ičo	šu-nu	šunu	šunu	hm	hēm(mā)	himmō(n), 'in
f.		ǝntǎ-nǝti		ši-na	?	šina	hn	hēn(nā)	hinnīn, 'innīn

seem to belong to a mixed paradigm, resulting from the contamination
of two older paradigms: one with the demonstrative element (*ə*)*nt-*, like
in Egyptian, used for the 1st and 3rd pers., the other without that element, attested with the 2nd pers. However, the element (*ə*)*nt-* is likely to
represent an expanded form of *-n*, and both elements form the basis of
South Ethiopic copulae (§49.19-20). It should be reminded that Old
Egyptian /k/ is palatalized into [č] = "ṯ" before the front vowel /i/ (*nt-k*,
masc.; *nt-ṯ* < **nt-**ki***, fem.; *nt-ṯn* < **nt-**kin***, plur.).

Arabic	Sabaic	Mehri	Ge'ez	Tigre	Tigrinya	Amharic
'anā, ana	'n	ho(h)	'ana	'ana	'anä	əne
'anta, inta	'(n)t	hēt	'anta	ənta	nəssəka ('anta)	antä
'anti, inti	't	hēt	'anti	ənti	nəssəki	anči
huwa, hū	h(w)'	ha(h)	wə'ətu	hətu	nəssu	əssu, ərsu
hiya, hī	hy'	sē(h)	yə'əti	həta	nəssa	əssʷa, ərsʷa
		əkəy				
'antumā		ətəy				
humā		həy				
naḥnu, (ni)ḥna		ənḥa	nəḥna	ḥəna	nəḥna, nəssatna	əňňa
'antum, intu	'ntmw	'ətēm	'antəmmu	əntum	nəssək(atk)um	əllantä, ənnantä
'antunna, intu		'ətēn	'antən	əntən	nəssək(atk)ən	
hum(ma)	hmw	hēm	wə'ətomu, 'əmuntu	hətom	nəss(at)om	ənnässu, ənnärsu
hunna, hin	hn	sēn	yə'əton, 'əmāntu	hətan	nəss(at)än	

36.3. The independent personal pronoun of Proto-Semitic most likely possessed at least one non-subject case. In fact, an oblique case is attested not only in East Semitic, from the Old Akkadian period downwards, but also in Palaeosyrian, in Ugaritic, and in South Arabian, while Phoenician (*hmt*), Hebrew (*hemmā*), and some Arabic vernaculars (*humā* denoting the plural and not the dual) probably preserve a trace of the oblique case in the third person plural. In the Ethiopian languages, its trace can be found in the personal pronouns of the third person singular and plural with an element *t* (§36.11), while Gafat has even a first person singular pronoun *anät(ti)*, to which Soddo *ädi*, "I", is probably related (< *äti*). An oblique case of the independent personal pronoun is attested also in Cushitic languages (§36.1); e.g. Oromo *ani* (subject), "I", *ana* (non-subject), "me"; Walamo *tani* (subject), "I", *tana* (non-subject), "me". Palaeosyrian, Old Akkadian, and Old Babylonian distinguish two oblique cases: the genitive/accusative and the dative. Fairly complete paradigms can be established only for East Semitic. The following paradigm gives the genitive/accusative form.

	Palaeo-syrian	Old Assyrian	Old Babylonian	Ugaritic	Sabaic	Qata-banic
Sing.						
1		*yāti*	*yāti*			
2	*kuwāti*	*ku(w)āti*	*kāti/a*			
3 m.	*šuwāti*	*šu(w)āti*	*šuāti/u, šāti/u*	*hwt*	*hwt*	*s¹wt*
f.		*šiāti*	*šuāti, šā/ēti*	*hyt*	*hyt*	*s¹yt*
Dual						
2		*kunīti*	*kunīti*			
3		*šunīti*	*šunīti*		*hmyt*	*s¹myt*
Plur.						
1	*ni(y)āti*	*niāti*	*nīāti, nēti*			
2 m.		*kunūti*	*kunūti*			
f.		*kināti*				
3 m.		*šunūti*	*šunūti*	*hmt*	*hmt*	*s¹mt*
f.	*šināt(i)*	*šināti*	*šināti*		*hnt*	

36.4. Dative forms are attested in Palaeosyrian, Old Akkadian, and Old Babylonian. The only distinct feminine form so far encountered is the third person singular *šiāšim* which occurs in Old Babylonian poetry.

	Palaeosyrian	Old Akkadian	Old Babylonian
Sing.			
1			*yāši(m)*
2	*kuwāši*	*kuāšim*	*kāši(m)*
3	*šuwāši*	*šuāšim*	*šuāšim, šāši(m)*
Plur.			
1	*ni(y)āši*		*niāšim*
2	*kanūši*		*kunūši(m)*
3	*šanūši*		*šunūši(m)*

36.5. The first and second persons singular and the second person plural of the subject case have a common element *'an-*, which appears as *in-* or *n-* in all persons of the Egyptian pronoun, as *n-* or *ən-* in the first and third persons of the Tuareg pronoun, and in several persons of the Cushitic pronouns; e.g. Qwara (Agaw) *an*, "I", *ənt*, "you", *ni*, "he", *anän*, "we", etc. The initial *'a-*, *i-*, *ə-*, *a-* seem to originate from a prosthetic vowel, as suggested also by the South Ethiopic copula *n-* which must go back to the same pronominal element (§49.20). In Semitic languages, *'an-* is followed by morphemes indicating the first person (*-a*), the second person masculine (*-ta*) and feminine (*-ti*), and the plural masculine (*-nu*) and feminine (*-na*). When compared with Cushitic (§36.3), the contrasting West Semitic forms *'ănī* vs. *'ănā* do raise the question whether *'ănā* wasn't once an oblique case, the use of which was generalized. An alternative explanation is suggested by the colloquial use of *'ana* for the masculine and of *'ani* for the feminine in the Djebel ed-Drūz (Syria) and in Yemen. The original form of the second person masculine plural is attested in Palaeosyrian, at Ebla (*an-tá-nu*). The second vowel *a* was subsequently dissimilated into *u* or *u > i* in all Semitic languages, but the original vowel did not disappear completely: it is still present in the Neo-Assyrian plural form *attanū-ni*. In most West Semitic and South Semitic languages, the *n* of the masculine pronoun changed into *m*, possibly under the influence of the preceding vowel *u*, a phenomenon attested sporadically also in East Semitic (e.g. Middle Assyrian *kunkā > kumkā*, "seal!") and in North Semitic (e.g. *Šadun-laba > Šadum-laba*, an Amorite personal name). There can be no doubt about the original nature of *n* since it is present not only in

Palaeosyrian, in East Semitic, and in Aramaic, but also in Egyptian (*nttn* < **ntkn*, "you", plur.). A morphological difference characterizes the Tuareg pronouns of the second person which are formed on the basis *k-* of the Semitic suffixed pronouns of the second person (§36.19, 22, 24).

36.6. The additional suffix *-ku* / *-ki* of the first person singular is attested in Old Akkadian (*a-na-ku*$_8$, *a-na-ku-ú*), Assyro-Babylonian, Ugaritic (*'ank*, *a-na-ku*), Old Canaanite (*a-nu-ki*), Hebrew, Phoenician (*'nk*), Moabite (*'nk*), Samalian (*'nk*), Tuareg (*nək*), and ancient Egyptian (*ink*), as well as with the first person dual in Mehri (*əkəy*) and Soqotri (*ki*). There is a probable relation between this suffix and the pronominal suffix of the second person singular (*-ka* / *-ki* / *-ku*) and plural (*-kun* / *-kin*) (§36.17). In fact, *k-* is the basis of the second person pronoun not only in Tuareg and in ancient Egyptian (§36.2), but also in some South Ethiopian languages: the singular pronoun "you" is *ank* in Argobba, *akāk* in Harari, *akä* (masc.) with variants in West and North Gurage dialects. These forms seem to imply a Proto-Semitic variant **'an-ka* / **'an-ki* of *'an-ta* / *'an-ti* for the second person singular and may suggest that the addition of *-ku* / *-ki* to the independent pronoun of the first person singular arose by analogy with the variant suffix of the second person.

The alternation *-ka* / *-ki* vs. *-ta* / *-ti* raises the problem of the alleged Afro-Asiatic opposition of masculine *k* vs. feminine *t*, as exemplified e.g. in the Oromo demonstratives (*kuni* / *tuni*, "this", etc.) and possessives (*kiyya* / *tiyya*, "my", etc.). Therefore, one might assume that once upon a time there had been an opposition of masculine **an-ka* vs. feminine **an-ti* (cf. §36.5), but that the Semitic languages have later used the forms with *-k-* or *-t-* for both genders (but cf. §12.4).

36.7. The ending of the first person pronoun *əkəy* of the Mehri dual corresponds to the dual *-ay* morpheme of the oblique case. For the Proto-Semitic dual, we assume a suffix *-kā* with the *-ā* of the subject case, like in the Arabic dual. In Arabic, this ending is added to the plural stems, exactly as in Old Egyptian where the suffixed dual pronouns are *-ny*, "of us two", *-tny* < **-kny*, "of you two", *-śny* = **-šny*, "of them two". Instead, the Modern South Arabian forms suggest that the dual morpheme was added to the singular stems of the pronoun. Since more and more Proto-Semitic features are being discovered in Semitic languages and dialects which are still spoken, these remote South Arabian idioms may represent the original situation of the dual.

36.8. For the first person plural of the subject case we may posit the Proto-Semitic form *niḥ-nu*, although Egyptian *inn*, vocalized *anon* or *anan* in Coptic, indicates that the element *'an-* was used also for the first person plural, while Cushitic *nu, nuni, nuna, inno* seem to indicate that *nu* is the only common element of Afro-Asiatic. The Semitic element *niḥ* is followed by this morpheme *-n-* which is used for the first person plural also in the suffixed personal pronouns, in Semitic, in Libyco-Berber, in Cushitic, and in Egyptian. The West Semitic vocalization *naḥ-* is probably due to the influence of the following pharyngal (§27.10), while the form *niḥ-* is implied by East Semitic (*nīnu*), colloquial Arabic (*niḥna*), and Geʻez (*nəḥna*). As for the variants in the final vowel, the *-a* of Aramaic, colloquial Arabic, Modern South Arabian, and all the Ethiopian languages is likely to be occasioned by a dissimilation of the final *-u* of *niḥnu* from *-i-*, since the opposition *i: u* is weak in Arabic and in South Semitic languages ($i > ə, u > ə$) This explanation is confirmed indirectly by the Assyro-Babylonian change *nīnu > nīni*, where the dissimilation did not take place; instead, the weakly opposed vowels *i* and *u* were harmonized.

36.9. The Proto-Semitic personal pronoun of the second person plural, attested in Geʻez, is replaced by secondary formations in most modern Ethiopian languages. It is still found in Tigre (*'əntum, 'əntən*), in Tigrinya only in the vocative "O you!" (*'antum, 'antən*), and in some East Gurage dialects (*atum*, masc. and fem.). Tigrinya uses the suffixed noun *näfs > nəss*, "person", thus *nəssəkum* for the masculine and *nəssəkən* for the feminine. Amharic prefixes the element *əllä / ənnä* of the plural demonstrative (§36.33, 41, 45) to the singular pronoun *antä*, thus *əllantä, ənnantä* for both genders, while Gafat prefixes it to the singular *antä* or to the plural *antum*, thus *ənnantä* or *ənnantum*. Argobba prefixes the same element *ənnä* to *ankum*, plural of the singular *ank*, "you" (§36.6), thus *ənnankum*. Harari adds the nominal plural ending *-ač* to the singular pronoun *akāk*, "you", thus *äkäkač*, while the Gurage dialects, other than East Gurage, use forms basically identical with the suffixed personal pronoun, e.g. in Chaha: *aku* (masc.), *akma* (fem.), etc. Instead, some Cushitic languages of Ethiopia preserve the original plural pronoun "you", like Walamo *inte* (subject), *intena* (non-subject).

36.10. For the third person singular and plural, as well as dual, we may posit a Proto-Semitic element *š-*, which changed into *h-* in several Semitic languages (§15.4), exactly as in the suffixed personal pronoun of the third person (§36.20), in the causative verbal stem (*š-* > *h-* > *'-*; cf. §41.11), and in the conditional particle (*š-m/n* > *h-m/n-* > *'-m/n*; cf. §61.2). The distinction between masculine and feminine was indicated by the suffixed morphemes -*wa* and -*ya*, which resulted in a masculine pronoun *šu-wa* and a feminine pronoun *ši-ya*, with a vowel corresponding qualitatively to the semivowels *w* and *y*. It is likely that this vowel was originally short. These forms are paralleled in Cushitic, e.g. Oromo *isā*, "him, his", *isī*, "her". The plural was marked by the addition of the morphemes -*nu* and -*na*, like for the second person plural, with parallel changes (§36.5). The same morpheme characterizes the plural in Cushitic, e.g. Oromo *isān*, "them", *isāni*, "they, their". Variant forms appear in Palaeosyrian (*su-u₉* /*šū*/, "he"; *si* /*šī*/, "she"), also in Old Assyrian and in later Assyro-Babylonian dialects, especially *šūt*, "he", and *šīt*, "she", which are used in Old Assyrian, in Middle Assyrian, and in the Western dialects, and derive from the oblique case (§36.3). As for the feminine *sē* of Modern South Arabian languages, it may have resulted from an early shift *šī* > *sī*, anterior to the change *ša* > *ha* of the masculine pronoun.

36.11.   In Ge'ez, the initial element *hu-* / *hi-* < *šu-* / *ši-* is omitted and the ending of the former oblique case of the independent personal pronoun is added to the elements *wa-* and *ya-*, that must be related to the Libyco-Berber determinatives *wa*, "this" (masc.), *ta*, "this" (fem.), *yi(n)*, "these" (masc.), *ti(n)*, "these" (fem.). The resulting forms are *wə'ətu* and *yə'əti* for the singular, *wə'ətomu* and *yə'əton* for the plural, thus with the addition of the plural morphemes -*mu* and -*n(a)*. In the variant form of the plural pronoun, these morphemes are placed before the ending of the former oblique case, thus *'əmuntu* and *'əmāntu*. Among the modern Ethiopian languages, Gafat comes closest to Ge'ez with the pronouns *wət*, "he", and *yət*, "she". In an early Ge'ez inscription, however, the independent personal pronouns are *h't* (**hə'tu*) for the 3rd pers. masc. sing. and *hmnt* (**həmuntu*) for the 3rd pers. masc. plur. These dialectal forms are obviously related to Tigre which has preserved the *hu-* > *hə-* of the masculine and the *hi-* > *hə-* of the feminine, as shown by *hətu*, "he", and *həta*, "she", with the *t* of the oblique case, the endings -*u* and -*a* being those of the suffixed pronouns of the third person masculine and feminine (§36.17). The *h* also survives or is reinforced to *ḫ* in the Gurage dialects, which likewise preserve the *t* or voice it to *d*, and they distinguish the masculine -*u* ending from the feminine -*i*, as in Ge'ez, e.g. *ḫut*, "he", *ḫit*, "she", or *ḫuda*, "he", *ḫida*, "she".

36.12. Other Ethiopian languages, viz. Tigrinya, Amharic, Argobba, and Harari, differ from Ge'ez, Gafat, Tigre, and Gurage in the formation of the personal pronoun of the third person. Tigrinya, Amharic, and Argobba express these pronouns by a noun with a suffixed pronoun of the third person. Tigrinya has *nəssu*, "he", *nəssa*, "she", from *näfsu*, "his person" > "he", and *näfsa*, "her person" > "she", like for the second person plural (§36.9). Amharic *əssu*, *ərsu* comes from **rə'su*, "his head" > "he", and *əss^wa*, *ərs^wa*, from **rə'sa*, "her head" > "she". Argobba has *kəssu*, probably from *kärsu*, "his belly" > "he", and *kəssa*, from *kärsa*, "her belly" > "she". These formations of the personal pronoun parallel an Aramaic use of the suffixed noun *npš* (e.g. *npšy l' td' 'rḥ'*, lit. "my person will not know the way": TAD III, C1.1,122) and they are closely related to the old use of the suffixed form of the same noun to express the reflexive pronoun (§36.28); e.g. Hebrew *'al tašši'ū napšotēkem*, "do not deceive yourselves"; Classical Arabic *qāla li-nafsihī*, "he said to himself".

36.13. Harari has for the masculine *azzo*, "he", for the feminine *azze*, "she", for the plural *azziyač*, "they". While the element *az-* is very likely related to the demonstrative *han-* (§36.32), with an assimilation *-nz-* > *-zz-* like in Hebrew *hazze*, the endings *-zo*, *-ze*, *-ziyač* are the respective suffixed personal pronouns of Harari. They obviously go back to the determinative-relative element *z* (§36.41).

36.14. The oblique case of the independent personal pronoun has a first element corresponding to the suffixed personal pronouns (§36.17) and a second element *-(w)āti / -ūti*, the final vowel of which is occasionally replaced by *a* or *u*. The vocalization of the South Arabian pronouns *hwt* and *hyt* of the third person singular is reflected in Andalusian forms transmitted by Pedro de Alcalá as *huet* and *hiet*. The element *ya-* of the first person singular apparently parallels the independent personal pronoun "I" in Argobba (*ay*) and in some Gurage dialects (Chaha and Ennemor *əya*; Masqan *əyya*; Zway *äyä*), but *y* results there from the palatalization *n* > *ň* > *y*. The form of the second and third persons singular can be traced back in the Egyptian language of the Pyramid texts and of the Old Kingdom (§2.2), when the corresponding masculine independent pronouns were *ṯwt* (i.e. **čuwāti < *kuwāti*), "you", and *śwt* (**šuwāti*), "he". The morpheme *-t(i)* characterizes the object-case of the personal pronoun also in Cushitic languages; e.g. *yət*, "me", *kut*, "you", *anät*, "us", in the Agaw dialects of the Qemant-Qwara group.

36.15. In the dative of the Palaeosyrian, Old Akkadian, and Old Baby-lonian independent personal pronoun, the second element is -(w)āši / -ūši instead of -(w)āti / -ūti; e.g. ana šu(w)āšim šaṭeršum, "it is ascribed to him". There is no evident connection between this element and the postpo-sition -iš / -eš of the so-called dative-adverbial case of the noun (§32.17).

B. Suffixed Personal Pronouns

36.16. The bound form of personal pronouns can be attached to nouns as possessive pronouns, to prepositions to express various relations, and to verbs both as direct and as indirect object, i.e. as accusative and as dative. The attachment of these suffixes to the noun may be effected either by means of case endings or glide vowels, or by way of assimila-tion or contraction. Allomorphs may occur after a verb, pending on the consonantal or vocalic ending of the verbal form. For details, grammars of the various languages and dialects should be consulted.

	Egyptian	Tuareg	Bedja	Hausa	*Proto-Semitic	Palaeosyrian	Old Babylonian
Sing.							
1 (noun)	-i	-i, -iyi	—	-na	-iy	-ī, -ya	-ī, -ya
(verb)					-ni	-ni	-(an)ni, [-a]
2 m.	-k	-k	-ka	-ka	-ka	-ka, [-kum]	-ka, [-ku]
f.	-ṯ	-m	-ki	-ki	-ki	-ki, -k	-ki
3 m.	-f	-s / -ṭ	-s	-sa	-šu	-šu, -š, [-šum]	-šu
f.	-ś	-s / -ṭ	-s	-ta	-ša	-ša, -š	-ša, [-ši]
Dual							
1	-ny				-nay(a)	-naya, -niya	
2	-ṯny				-k(un)ay(a)	-kumaya, -kumān	-kunī[ti/ši]
3	-śny				-š(un)ay(a)	-šumaya, -šumā	-šunī[ti/ši]
Plur.							
1	-n	-na, -nə	-n	-mu	-na	-na, -nu, -ni	-ni[āti/āši]
2 m.	-ṯn	-wəm	-kna	-ku(m)	-kun	-kunu	-kun(u)[/ūti/ūši]
f.		-wəmt			-kin	?	-kin(a)[/āti/āši]
3 m.	-śn	-sən / -ṭən	-sna	-su(m)	-šun	-šunu	-šun(u)[/ūti/ūši]
f.		-sənt / -ṭənt			-šin	-šini	-šin(a)[/āti/āši]

In some Cushitic languages, like the Agaw dialects of the Qemant-Qwara group, the pronouns are not suffixed but prefixed or placed before the noun in the possessive form and before the verb in the form of the object-case (§36.14); e.g. *yə-nkəra*, "my soul"; **ki**-*lämda*, "your shadow", **ni**-*səbra*, "his place"; **an**-*adära* or **anä** *adära*, "our God"; **nay**-*ki*, "all of them"; etc.

36.17. The following paradigm of the suffixed personal pronoun in the principal Semitic languages includes the East Semitic and Ugaritic suffixes of the verb, in the accusative and the dative for Palaeosyrian and East Semitic. The particular morphemes of these forms are placed between square brackets without the mimation which is often added to the dative ending *-ši(m)*, attested in Old Akkadian and in Old Babylonian, but not in Old Assyrian. Besides the paradigm for the main Semitic languages and for the reconstructed Proto-Semitic forms, a paradigm of Egyptian, Tuareg, Bedja, and Hausa suffix-pronouns is added for comparison.

Ugaritic	Hebrew	Aramaic	Classical Arabic	Sabaic	Mehri	Ge'ez	Tigre	Tigrinya	Amharic
	-ī	-ī	-ī, -ya	*-y	-i, -yä	-ya	-ye	-äy	-(ʸ)e
	-nī	-nī	-nī	*-n	-əy	-ni	-ni	. -ni	-ňň
	-kā	-k	-ka	-k	-k, kä	-ka	-ka	-ka	-h
	-k, -kī	-kī, -k	-ki	*-k	-š, -šä	-ki	-ki	-ki	-š
[-nh, -n, -nn]	-hū, -āw, -ō	-hī, -ih	-hu/i, -hū/ī	-hw	-h, -hä	-hu	-u, -o, -hu	-u, -o, -wo	-u, -o, -wo -u, -w, -t
[-nh, -n, -nn]	-hā, -ā(h)	-hā, -ah	-hā	-h, -hw	-s, -sä	-hā		-a, -wa	-wa, -at
y					-ki				
m			-kumā		-ki				
m			-humā, -himā	-hmy	-hi				
	-nū	-nā, -an	-nā		-n	-na	-na	-na	-(aččə)n
m	-kem(ā)	-kōn/m	-kum(ū)	-kmw	-kəm	-kəmmu	-kum	-kum	-aččəhu
n	-ken(ā)	-kēn	-kunna		-kən	-kən	-kən	-kən	
m	-hem(ā), ām(ō)	-hōn/m	-hum(ū), -him(ū)	-hmw	-həm	-(h)omu	-(h)om	-(w)om	-aččäw
n	-hen(ā), -ān(ā)	-hēn	-hunna, -hinna	-hn	-sən	-(h)on	-(h)an	-(w)än	

36.18.   The suffix of the first person singular, added to a noun or to a preposition, is *-iy* > *-ī* after a consonant or a short vowel, and *-ya* after a long vowel and after the originally short vowel *i* of the genitive (e.g. Assyro-Babylonian *be-el-ti-i-a*, "of my mistress"; Old Phoenician *'b*, "my father", but *'by*, "my father's"). It corresponds to the Egyptian suffixed pronoun *-i*. The form *-ay*, attested in Hebrew and in Aramaic, results from the adding of *-ī* to the ending of the masculine dual or plural construct state; e.g. **sūsay-ī* > *sūsāy*, "my horses". Perhaps by analogy with the suffix of the first person plural, the suffix of the verb is *-ni*, with the exception of Mehri *-əy*, but it is still *-əni* in the Ḥarsūsi dialect. Both forms *-y* and *-ň* occur as verbal suffixes also in Gafat (South Ethiopic).

The Hebrew nominal suffix *-nī* in *kāmō-nī*, "like me", and in *'ōdennī* <**'ōdē-nī* (cf. *'ōdē-nū/hū*), lit. "my time", is paralleled at sight by Mishnaic Hebrew *yeš-nō*, "he is", *yeš-nāh*, "she is", *yeš-nām*, "they are", but *yeš* is a frozen form of a verb (§49.23). Therefore, a better parallel is provided by the Phoenician and Punic suffix *-nm* of the 3rd pers. plur. This nominal *-n-* suffix is a probable transference from verb to noun or preposition, occurring first with the suffix of the first person after nominal forms terminating in long vowels to prevent hiatus, and spread later to other persons, regardless of the termination of the governing word.

36.19.   The second person singular suffixes *-ka*, *-ki*, and *-ku* for the masculine dative, correspond to Egyptian *-k* (masc.) and *-ṯ* (fem.). The latter derives from a palatalized *-ki* > *-č* ("ṯ") (§15.8), exactly as Modern South Arabian, colloquial Yemenite, Gafat *-č* / *-š* < *-ki*, and Amharic *-š* < *-k*. The vowel *i*, which causes palatalization, is usually absorbed in the palatal. Instead, the Amharic masculine suffix *-h* and the Gafat masculine suffix *-hä* have in reality a [x] derived from a spirantized *-k(a)*.

36.20.   The third person singular reflects the same changes *š* > *h* as the independent pronoun (§36.10) and corresponds exactly to the Egyptian "dependent" pronouns *św* (masc.) and *śy* (fem.) (§36.30). Palaeosyrian exhibits a shortened form *-š* of both the masculine (/*-šu*/) and the feminine (/*-ša*/) passessive suffixes (genitive). The feminine forms in *-s* of Modern South Arabian should be related to the *sē* of the independent pronoun (§36.10). The Amharic masculine object suffix *-(ä)w* and the Hebrew suffix *-āw* / *-ō* result from contractions of the type *-ahu* > *-au* > *-aw* > *-ō*, while Amharic *-t* of the masculine is an allomorph of *-u* / *-w* after the vowel *-u*, like in other South Ethiopian languages. The feminine suffix *-at* is the corresponding nominal ending (§30.1-3).

36.21. The Ugaritic object suffixes *-nh, -n, -nn* of the third person singular can be explained by the use of the energic endings *-anna* or *-an* of the prefix conjugation (§39.8-11). Since *-nh* alternates with *-n* in otherwise identical contexts, *-nh* represents the ending *-anna* + *hū* (e.g. *'aqbrnh*, "I shall bury him"), while *-n* stands for *-an* + *hū* > *-annū* (e.g. *'aqrbrn*, "I shall bury him"). As for the second *n* of the *-nn* suffix, often written as a separate word, it should be compared with the enclitic *-ən* which can be added in Gurage dialects to the object suffix of the main perfect or imperfect without an apparent change in meaning; e.g. *gäd-dälä-nnə-t-ən* < **gäddälä-nnu-u-ən*, "he killed him", with the allomorph *-t-* of *-u-* in the position *u-u*. The Ugaritic suffix *nn* of e.g. *yqbr.nn*, "he buried him", should then be explained as **-an+hū+un* > *-annūn*.

36.22. The dual forms of Proto-Semitic ended most likely in *-ay(a)* which is also the ending of dual nouns in the oblique case and which appears in Ugaritic *-ny*, in Old Egyptian *-ny, -tny* < **-kny, -śny* = *-šny*, in Palaeosyrian *-na-a* /*-naya*/ or *-ne-a* /*-niya*/, *gú-ma-a* /*-kumaya*/, *-su-ma-a* /*-šumaya*/, "of both", and it is implied by the Modern South Arabian *-ki* < *-kay* and *-hi* < *-hay*. The latter group of languages either did not preserve the plural morpheme *-n/m-* or reflects the Proto-Semitic situation (cf. §36.7).

36.23. The Proto-Semitic suffix of the first person plural was most likely *-na*, as suggested not only by Palaeosyrian, Aramaic, Arabic, Ge'ez, Tigre, Tigrinya (*-na*), Gafat (*-nä*), the Gurage dialects (*-na, -ñña, -ňňä*), Harari (*-zina*), and Tuareg, but also by the archaic or dialectal suffix *-na* in Old Akkadian (e.g. *A-bu-na*, "Our father"; *A-ḫu-na*, "Our brother"; *Sa-dú-na*, "Our mountain"), corroborated both by Amorite names (e.g. *Iš-ḫi-lu-na* /*Yiṭ'(u)-'iluna*/, "The Saviour is our god") and by the frequent form *-ne* of the suffix in the Mari documents, a spelling which seems to imply a colloquial reduction of an original Amorite *-na*, like in comparable cases at Mari (e.g. *in-ne-du-ú* for normal Babylonian *innadū*, "was given up"). The vocalization *-nu* of Palaeosyrian, Old Canaanite (*ti-mi-tu-na-nu*, "you make us die": EA 238,33), and Hebrew is most likely the result of analogy with the final vowel *-ū* of the independent pronoun (§36.2), while the suffix *-ni* of Old Akkadian, Assyro-Babylonian, and apparently Palaeosyrian (*-ne* /*-ni*/) results possibly from the generalized use of the old ending of the oblique case (?) *-ni*, *-kuni, -šuni*. In several languages, the suffix of the first person plural is attested also under the form *-(a)n*, without final vowel: Amharic *fäl-*

lägän, "he wanted us"; Neo-Aramaic *bētan*, "our house"; Mehri and Ḥarsūsi *-abyǝtiǝn*, "our houses". In Modern South Arabian, the personal suffixes are affixed to definite nouns (§33.9).

36.24.   For the second person plural, the observations on the independent pronoun (§36.5) have to be taken into account and Proto-Semitic forms *-kun* and *-kin* posited, without the final vowels which are unstable and which are missing or can be omitted in most Semitic languages. In Old Akkadian, the attested vowel is *-i* (in *qá-ti-ku-ni*, "in your hand"), and it is not certain that this is due to the oblique case, since the same text has *in na-ap-ḥa-rí-su-nu*, "in their total". In Old Babylonian, there is either no final vowel in poetry (*-kun*) or the vowel is *-u* (*-kunu*). The vowels marked by *h* in the suffixed pronouns of the Hebrew Qumrān scrolls (*-kmh, -knh, -hmh, -hnh*) may either be a trace of the Proto-Semitic oblique case in *-āt* (§36.26) or represent a late development by analogy with singular suffixes, while the Arabic forms *-kumū, -humū, -himū* are poetical and can alternate, e.g., with *-himi*.

36.25.   The observations made on the consonantal elements of the independent pronoun are relevant also for the suffixes of the third person plural (§36.5, 10). As for the final vowels, the situation is the same as for the second person (§36.24), with a great variety in their Old Akkadian use (*-šunu/i/a*) and a generally attested feminine *-šin* in that idiom, followed by the Old Babylonian poetry.

36.26.   With the exception of the accusative/dative pronoun *-ni(m)* of the first person singular, attested in all Semitic languages, only traces of the oblique case of the pronominal suffix are attested outside Palaeosyrian and East Semitic. The Old Akkadian and Assyro-Babylonian dative of the singular suffixes is characterized by the frequent use of the mimation (*-nim, -kum, -kim, -šum, -šim*), and there is an additional suffix *-a(m)* of the first person. The dative suffixes *-kum*, "to you", and *-šum*, "to him", are attested also in Palaeosyrian. The ending *-āt(i)* / *-ūti* is used for the plural suffixes of the Babylonian accusative and of the Assyrian dative, while the ending *-īši(m)* / *-ūši(m)* / *-āši(m)* is employed for the plural dative suffixes in Old Akkadian and Babylonian. Both types of endings correspond to those of the independent pronouns (§36.3-4). The suffixed pronouns sometimes have dative force in other Semitic languages as well, but there is no evidence to show that there was a formal distinction between accusative and dative suffixes.

36.27. Two suffixes can be added to a verb without intermediate preposition in Old Akkadian, Assyro-Babylonian, and Arabic, one acting as direct object, the other as indirect object; e.g. Old Babylonian *aṭrudakkuššu < *aṭrud-am-kum-šu*, "I sent it to you"; Classical Arabic *'a'ṭā-nī-hi*, "he gave it to me". The first person suffix precedes the second and third persons, the second precedes the third, regardless of their syntactical function.

C. Reflexive Pronoun

36.28. There is no distinct reflexive pronoun in the Semitic languages which can use, instead, the usual suffixed pronouns that are then referring to the subject of the sentence; e.g. Arabic *ba'aṯa 'ilā Marwāna fada'āhu 'ilayhi*, "he sent for Marwān and summoned him to himself"; Hebrew *wayy'aś lō 'Ēhūd ḥereb* (Judg. 3,16), "Ehud made a sword for himself". However, Semitic languages prefer to employ the noun *raman-*, "self", or *napš-*, "person", with the required pronominal suffix. In East Semitic, besides the generally recognized *ramanu* (e.g. *ana ramanišu*, "for himself"), one finds sometimes another noun, as *qaqqadu*, "head" (e.g. *qaqqassa ana šīmim iddin*, "she sold herself"), or *pagru*, "body" (e.g. *pagaršu ina šīmim iddin*, "he sold himself"). A similar use is attested in other Semitic languages, not only with *napš-* (e.g. Hebrew *nišba' bə-napšō*, "he swore by himself"), but also with nouns meaning "head", "belly" (cf. §36.12), "heart" (e.g. Hebrew *'āmar bə-libbō*, "he said to himself"), "bone" (e.g. Syriac *'al garmah*, "about herself", lit. "about her bone"; Sabaic *grmk*, "you yourself"). This construction is attested frequently in Ethiopic, especially with *nafs > nəss*, "soul", and *ra'as*, "head" (cf. also §36.12). Phoenician, Punic, Syriac, and Samaritan Aramaic use also the noun *qnūm-*, "person, being"; e.g. Neo-Punic *p'l mqr... l-qn'm*, "Maqer made it for himself"; Syriac *ba-qnūmeh*, "by himself". Christian Palestinian Aramaic has a word *qīqn-* functioning with a suffix as a kind of reflexive pronoun; e.g. *qīqnī*, "I myself". This word probably derives from the reduplicated root **qənqən*, the simple form of which is used in Gurage dialects with the sense of "single", "alone" (*quna > qura-*), while its derivative indicates the unit in the Gafat numeral "eleven": *asra qəmčättä* (*<qəmt < *qən-t + ättä*). It is likely that *qnūm-*, *quna*, and **qən* have the same origin and that Amharic *qəl*, "oneself" (e.g. *qəl-u*, "himself"; *qəl-eh*, "yourself"), is an allophone of *qən*, with the change *n > l*.

D. Independent Possessive Pronouns

36.29. Beside the suffixed personal pronouns of the noun which act as possessive pronouns (§36.17), East Semitic has two types of independent possessive pronouns which are formed on the same basic morphemes as the suffixed personal pronoun, and South Ethiopic, with the exception of Harari, has such a pronoun which is formed by the complement of appurtenance *yä-* combined with the personal pronoun. Semitic languages do not distinguish, in the way Latin does, between *suus* and *eius*.

36.30. In East Semitic, the independent possessive pronoun originally formed a separate inflectional class which is indicated by some Old Babylonian forms, while the process of its transfer into the adjectival category is already accomplished in Old Assyrian. There can be little doubt about the Proto-Semitic or even Afro-Asiatic origin of the posses-

Independent Possessive Pronouns

	Egyptian	Old Babylonian sing.
Sing.		
1 m.	*wỉ*	*ya'-um*
f.		*yattum < ya'-t-um*
2 m.	*ṯw < *kw*	*kūm < kuwa-um*
f.	*ṯn < *kn*	*kattum < kan(?)-t-um*
3 m.	*św*	*šūm < šuwa-um*
f.	*śy, śt*	*šattum < šan(?)-t-um*
Plur.		
1 m.	*n*	*nūm < ni-um*
f.		
2 m.	*ṯn < *kn*	**kunūm < kuni-um*
f.		
3 m.	*śn*	*šunūm < šuni-um*
f.		

sive with pronominal inflection, since it is paralleled by the Old Egyptian "dependent" pronoun. The following table shows the Egyptian dependent pronoun, the Old Babylonian forms attested with "pronominal" inflection, and the adjectival inflection of the mainly Assyrian forms of the possessive pronoun in the nominative case. The two sets "sing". and "plur." refer respectively to the singleness and the plurality of the items possessed, like Latin *meus, mei, mea, meae,* etc.

The "pronominal" inflection of the Old Babylonian pronoun is characterized by the plural ending *-un* which is considered as common to the Afro-Asiatic languages. This ending is added in the masculine forms to the abstract-collective morpheme *-ūt* (§29.48) in a pattern comparable with the Arabic collective ending *-atun* (e.g. *muslim-un*, "Moslem"; *muslim-atun*, "Moslems"). In the feminine forms, it is added to the feminine morpheme *-t*. This inflection probably reveals a Proto-Semitic or even Afro-Asiatic origin of this independent possessive pronoun.

Independent Possessive Pronouns

Old Babylonian plur.	Old Assyrian sing.	Old Assyrian plur.
yūtun < ya'-ūt-un	*ya'um*	*ya'ūtum*
yattun < ya'-t-un	*yātum*	*yātum*
kūtun < kuwa-ūt-un	*ku(w)a'um*	*ku(w)a'ūtum*
kattun < kan(?)-t-un	*ku(w)atum*	*ku(w)ātum*
šūtun < šuwa-ūt-un	*šu(w)a'um*	**šu(w)a'ūtum > šā'ūtum*
šattun < šan(?)-t-un	*šu(w)atum*	**šu(w)ātum*
nūtun < ni-ūt-un	*ni(y)a'um* *ni(y)atum*	*ni(y)a'ūtum* *ni(y)ātum*
*kunūtun < kuni-ūt-un	*kunu'um* *kunūtum*	**kunu'ūtum* *kunu(w)ātum*
*šunūtun < šuni-ūt-un	**šunu'um* *šunūtum*	**šunu'ūtum* **šunu(w)ātum*

36.31.   In the non literary language of the Middle Babylonian period appears a new type of independent possessive pronoun formed by addition of possessive suffixes to the complement of appurtenance *attu-* < **'aytu-*, which is to be identified with the Arabic particle *'iyyā* < *'iyyat-* introducing the suffixed pronominal object (*'iyyā-ya*, "me"; *'iyyā-ka* / *-ki*, "you"; etc.) and with the "accusative" particle *'yt* of Phoenician, *'ēt* of Hebrew, Edomite, and Moabite, *t* of Punic and Mishnaic Hebrew (Bar Kokhba letters), *'yt*, *wt*, and *yt* of Aramaic, which is an optional mark of the definite direct object, either noun or pronominal suffix (§52.10). The Middle Babylonian use of *attu-* parallels that of the Ethiopic complements of appurtenance *nāy-* and *yä-*, combined with the suffixed or independent personal pronouns. A similar formation is attested in Cushitic and in Egyptian, and it occurs also in Hausa (Chadic) with the complements of appurtenance *nā-*, when the object possessed is of the masculine gender (e.g. *nā-sa*, "his"), and *tā-* (< *ntā-*), when the object possessed is of the feminine gender (e.g. *tā-sa*, "his"). We give here the Middle Babylonian, the Tigre, and the Amharic paradigms in parallelism.

	Middle Babylonian	Tigre	Amharic	
Sing.				
1	*attu'a*	*nāye*	*yäna < yä-əne*	"mine"
2 m.	*attuka*	*nāyka*	*yantä < yä-antä*	"yours" masc.
f.	*attuki*	*nāyki*	*yanči < yä-anči*	"yours" fem.
3 m.	*attušu*	*nāyu*	*yässu < yä-əssu*	"his"
f.	*attuša*	*nāya*	*yäss^wa < yä-əss^wa*	"hers"
Plur.				
1	*attuni*	*nāyna*	*yäňňa < yä-əňňa*	"ours"
2 m.	*attukunu*	*nāykum*	*yännantä < yä-ənnantä*	"yours"
f.	*attukina*	*nāykən*		
3 m.	*attušunu*	*nāyom*	*yännässu < yä-ənnässu*	"theirs"
f.	*attušina*	*nāyan*		

E. Demonstrative Pronouns

36.32. Two series of demonstratives can be distinguished in the Semitic languages: demonstratives of remoter deixis or "far" demonstratives ("that, those"), and demonstratives of nearer deixis or "near" demonstratives ("this, these") (cf. §36.45). This distinction can be established for each language only on a contextual basis, because the same root morpheme, sometimes under a variant form or with affixes, can be used in both acceptations. However, the opposition *ə* : *a* distinguishes the "near" demonstrative in -*ə* / *ə*- from the "far" demonstrative in -*a* / *a*- in nearly all the South Ethiopian languages; e.g. Amharic *yə(h)*, "this", vs. *ya*, "that"; Gurage *zə*, "this", vs. *za*, "that"; Gafat *əňňə* < **hinni*, "this", vs. *aňňə* < **hanni*, "that" (§36.33-34). It does not yet appear clearly whether the same opposition exists in Palaeosyrian between *í-ne* /*hinni*/, "this$^{(?)}$", and *an-ne* /*hanni*/, "that$^{(?)}$". The demonstrative position of "previously mentioned" can be assumed by the definite article or its equivalent (§33.6 ff.). There is one Proto-Semitic root morpheme that functions essentially as demonstrative, viz. **hanni*- with its variants **halli*- and *'ulli*-, and with its later syncopated form *han*- > *hā*- of the West Semitic definite article. It is used also in Libyco-Berber (§36.34). Besides, the independent personal pronoun of the third person, placed before or after a substantive, and the determinative-relative pronoun have the value of a demonstrative in several Semitic languages.

36.33. The demonstrative **hanni*- appears in Old Akkadian and in Assyro-Babylonian under the form *anni-u(m)* > *annū(m)*, in Assyrian also *ammiu(m)* and *allū*, with a Babylonian variant *ullūm*. In South Ethiopic, *a/əňňə* (masc.), *ənna* (fem.), *a/ənnä* (plur.), are attested in Gafat, *ənne* or *ənnä*, and *annä* (plur.), are found in East Gurage, while *əňňə* occurs in various Amharic compounds, both literary and dialectal. The same demonstrative is composed in Ugaritic with the determinative-relative pronoun *ḏ* > *d*, thus *hn-d* (**hanni-dū* or **hinna-dū*), which formally corresponds to the later Hebrew *hazze*, Arabic *hāḏā* (§36.38), to Harari *azzo*, "he", *azze*, "she" (§36.13), to Gafat *ənnäz(əň)*, "these", *annäz*, "those", and to Amharic *ənnäzzih* or *əlläzzih*, "these" (§36.45), besides the Amharic base -*äzzih* preceded by various prepositions. The equivalent of *annium* in Mishnaic Hebrew is *hallā* and in Syriac *hānā*, with the same final vowel -*ā* as in Arabic plural *'ulā*, "these", while the North Ethiopic Tigre demonstrative is *'əlli* < **'ulli*, "this". The initial *h* was also preserved in the Aramaic dialect attested indirectly by the Neo-

Assyrian *ḫanniu*, in the Punic dialectal demonstrative *hnkt* (§36.35), and in the Sabaic indefinite pronoun *hn-mw* or *hl-mw*, "whatever". The change *h* > ' is otherwise widespread in the West and South Semitic languages which kept using the morpheme **hanni* to express the plural demonstrative: *'ēlle*, *'illēk*, *'illēn* in Aramaic, *'ēlle*, *'ēllū* in Hebrew, *'l* in Phoenician, -*'ulā-* in Classical Arabic, *'ln*, *'lt* in ancient South Arabian, *'əllū* in Geʿez. The change -*nn-* > -*ll-* reflected by all these forms parallels the shift *han-* > *'al-* of the definite article (§33.10), which is etymologically and functionally related to the demonstrative. This shift should be explained by the ancient tendency of the Semitic languages, best attested in the Gurage dialects (e.g. *wännät* and *wällät*, "forked digging pick"), to alternate the liquids *l* and *n* (§17.3-4).

The Ethiopic verb of presence *hallo* < **hallaw*, "he is (present)", goes probably back to the frozen demonstrative *halla* followed by the personal pronoun *hu*, preserved in Tigre *hə(tu)* and in the Gafat -*ho* suffix: **halla hu*, "here he is", > **hallau* > **hallaw*, a phrase comparable with ancient Ḥidjazi *huwa ḏā*, "there he is". Geʿez compound *hallo* is further inflected like a perfect notwithstanding its present meaning, and it is used in Tigrinya under the form *'allo*, while other Ethiopian languages adapt its final to the usual ending of the perfect, thus Tigre *halla*, Amharic and Argobba *allä*, some Gurage dialects *alä*, and Harari *ḥal*. Gafat and other Gurage dialects have forms based on *anä*, *enä*, that go back to the allophone **hanna* of the demonstrative. The latter is still attested in Gafat, in the 18th century, in the very compound *ən(n)aho* < **hanna-hu*, "here he is", with a variant *ən(n)ahuš*, where the fossilized pronominal suffix -*š* used as definite article (§33.13) is added to the demonstrative.

36.34. The principal forms of the Assyro-Babylonian demonstrative **(h)anni-* are given below in the non contracted form (-*ium* > -*ūm*). The demonstrative *annitān* at Mari is interpreted here as a frozen feminine dual originally meaning "this and that", thus "thing, matter". Related

Demonstrative Pronouns

	Assyro-Babylonian	Ugaritic
Sing. m.	*anniu(m)*	*hnd* = **hanni/a-dū*
f.	*annitu(m)*	*hnd(t)* = **hanni/a-dā(t)*
Dual m.	*anniān*	*hndn* = **hanni/a-dān*
f.	*annitān*	**hndtn* = **hanni/a-dātān*
Plur. m.	*anniūtu(m)*	**hndt* = **hanni/a-dūt*
f.	*anniātu(m)*	

demonstratives are selected only from Ugaritic, Syriac, Mandaic, Mishnaic Hebrew, Sabaic, and Tigre, although forms from other idioms could also be referred to.

The pronoun *anniu(m)* is used in Assyro-Babylonian as demonstrative of nearer deixis, while its variant forms, *ammiu(m)* and *allū* in Assyrian, and *ullūm* in Babylonian, are employed as "far" demonstratives. The demonstratives *hn-d* in Ugaritic, *hānā* in Syriac, *'ln/t* in Sabaic, and *'əlli* in Tigre are also used for the nearer deixis, while Mandaic *hānāt-* and Mishnaic Hebrew *hallā* appear to be "far" deictic pronouns. The Gafat "near" demonstrative is *əňňə* (masc.), *ənna* (fem.), *ənnä* (plur.), while the "far" demonstrative has an initial *a-* (§36.32): *aňňə* (masc.), *annä* (plur.). This demonstrative is attested also in Libyco-Berber where it is used as a "far" demonstrative. It is invariable and is suffixed to the noun; e.g. *a-ġyul-**inn***, "that jackass". A by-form ending in *-a* adds the nuance of "mentioned before"; e.g. *a-ham-**ənna***, "the tent (in question)".

36.35. The Neo-Babylonian and Late Babylonian "near" demonstrative *agā* (masc.), *agātu* (fem.), *agannūtu* (masc. plur.), *agannētu* or *agātu* (fem. plur.), possibly derives from **han-kā* with a partial progressive assimilation *nk > ng*, — frequent in Late Babylonian (§27.7), — followed by the complete regressive assimilation *ng > gg*. The plural was usually formed by adding the demonstrative *anniūtu > annūtu* (masc.) or *anniātu > annētu* (fem.) to the element *ag(g) < *ang < *hank*. A parallel "far" demonstrative was formed by adding the independent personal pronoun *šū* (masc.), *šī* (fem.), *šunu* (plur.), to the element *agā* (*agāšū / -šī / -šunu*). Also the Punic demonstrative *hnkt* combines *hn-* with the deictic element *-kō* (cf. Hebrew and Punic *kō < kā*, "here";

Demonstrative Pronouns

Syriac	Mandaic	Mishnaic Hebrew	Sabaic	Tigre
hānā	*h'n'th*	*hallā*	(*hn/l-mw*)	*'əlli*
hādē				*'əlla*
			'ln	
hallēn	*h'n'twn*	*ha'ēllū, hallālū*	*'ln*	*'əllom*
	h'n'tyn		*'lt*	*'əllan*

§49.9) followed by the ending *-t* which is suffixed in Phoenician-Punic also to other demonstratives (*hmt, st, 'st*). Since there is no assimilation of *n*, a form **ha/inni/akōt* has to be assumed, [*innokōt*] if the word appears in the "Poenulus" of Plautus. This demonstrative is used for both genders and appears to function as an adjective and as a pronoun of the nearer deixis; this results from the following examples: *n'pš š 'dyt hnkt 'bnt*, "the memorial of *'dyt* (PN) is this stele"; *hnkt qybr tḥt 'bn zt*, "this one (a man) is buried under this stele"; *hnkt n'bn'*, "this is her stele".

36.36. The independent personal pronoun of the third person is used as a demonstrative in East Semitic, Hebrew, Phoenician, Aramaic, ancient South Arabian, West Gurage. The distinction between the personal pronoun and the demonstrative is here not formal but functional, although the demonstrative employed as adjective has a case inflection in East

"Far" Demonstrative Pronouns

	Egyptian	Tuareg	East Semitic	Hebrew	Phoenician	Aramaic
Sing. m. nominative / oblique case	*pw*	*wu- / wa-*	*šū* / *šuā(ti/u)*	*(ha)hū'*	*h'*	*hw(')*
Sing. f. nominative / oblique case	*tw*	*tu- / ta-*	*šī* / *šiāti, šī*	*(ha)hī'*	*h', hy*	*hy*
Dual m.-f. nominative oblique case						
Plur. m. nominative / oblique case	*ipn*	*win-*	*šunu* / *šunūti, šunātunu*	*(hā)hēm(mā)*	*hmt*	*'innūn*
Plur. f. nominative / oblique case	*iptn*	*tin-*	*šina* / *šināti(na), šātina*	*(hā)hēnnā*	*hmt*	

Semitic and in Epigraphic South Arabian, viz. a nominative and one oblique case. The Tigre "far" demonstrative is also related to the independent personal pronoun, a shorter form of which is used with the definite article *la-*. As for Tigrinya, its "far" demonstrative goes back to an older form of the independent personal pronoun, replaced in the latter function by the suffixed noun *nəss-* < **näfs*, "soul / self" (§36.2,12), but used as definite article as well (§33.13). Also the suffixed personal pronoun was used as a kind of demonstrative and as definite article, at least in South Semitic and probably in North Semitic (§33.13-14).

For comparison, the Old Egyptian demonstratives, manifestly correlated, and the main variants of the Tuareg pronominal bases of demonstratives are added in the first and second columns of the paradigm. Their *p-* and *w-* elements are probably related to the demonstrative and pronominal *b-*prefix of Bedja and of West Cushitic (Omotic), but have no direct correspondent in Semitic.

"Far" Demonstrative Pronouns

Syriac	Neo-Aramaic	Sabaic	Qatabanic	Tigre	Tigrinya	West Gurage (Chaha)
hāw	*(h)ō*	*h', hw'* *hwt*	s^1w s^1wt	*lahay*	*'ətu*	*ḫuta*
hāy	*(h)ē*	*h', hy'* *hyt*	$*s^1y$ s^1yt	*laha*	*'əta*	*ḫita*
		hmy *hmyt*	$*s^1my$ s^1myt			
hānōn	*(')ān(i)*	*hmw* *hmt*	s^1m s^1mt	*lahom*	*'ətom*	*ḫəno*
hānēn	*(')ān(i)*	*hn* *hnt*	$*s^1n$ $*s^1nt$	*lahan*	*'ətän*	*ḫənäma*

The personal pronoun accompanying a substantive functions as demonstrative adjective. In South Arabian, it precedes the substantive, which shows the mark of determinate status (§33.12), e.g. Qatabanic *bs^lwt mhrmn*, "in that sanctuary". In other languages, it is generally placed after the substantive, e.g. Palaeosyrian *in* U_4 *su-wa-ti*, "on that day"; Aramaic *malkayyā 'innūn*, "those kings"; Chaha *ärč huta*, "that boy". In Hebrew, as a rule, the pronoun used adjectivally is preceded by the deictic element *hā-* < *han-* which is formally identical with the definite article (§33.8-10) but which is functionally the demonstrative particle employed also in Aramaic and in Arabic (§36.33,38). The personal pronoun can also function as isolable demonstrative pronoun, e.g. Aramaic *h' thwmwhy*, "that are its borders"; Hebrew *hū' 'ăšer dibbartī*, "that is what I said". It is generally used as demonstrative of remoter deixis.

36.37. In West and South Semitic languages, also the determinative-relative pronoun *du* (§36.46) is used as demonstrative, often with the addition of a variety of deictic affixes. The determinative-relative is employed for the singular demonstratives, while the plural is generally formed by the common Semitic demonstrative **hanni-/'ulli* or by its derivatives. Most languages distinguish demonstratives of nearer and of

"Near" Demonstrative Pronouns

	Hebrew	Phoenician	Aramaic	Arabic
Sing.				
m.	*(haz)ze, hallāz(e)*	*z('), (h)'z,*	*dǝnā, hādēn*	*(hā)dā*
		(')st, zn		
f.	*(haz)zot, hallēzū,*	*z('), 'z, st*	*dā(t), hādā*	*(hā)dihī, (hā)dī,*
	zō			*t(ih)ī, tā*
Dual				
m.				*(hā)dāni, dayni*
f.				*(hā)tāni, tayni*
Plur.				
m.	*(hā)'ēlle, 'ēl(lū)*	*'l*	*'ēllē, 'illēn,*	*(hā)'ulā'i, 'ulā*
			hā'ellayin	
f.				

remoter deixis by means of different affixes, but vocalic variations may play a role as well (§36.32). A comparable usage is attested in Libyco-Berber where an invariable near demonstrative -(a)ḏ may be suffixed to nouns (e.g. *a-rgaz-aḏ*, "this man") and to pronominal bases (e.g. *wa-ḏ*, "this one"). Besides, there is in Tamazight a suffixed form *ḏək > tək* which qualifies the person or thing present or visible (e.g. *a-rgaz-ad-ḏək*, "this here man"). The element -*k* seems to be related to the Semitic deictic particle -*k(a)* (§36.41-44; 49.9).

36.38. For the "near" demonstratives formed with the determinative-relative pronoun, mainly two affixes are employed in West and South Semitic, viz. the prefix *hā-* < *han-* < **ha/inni/a-*, like earlier in Ugaritic (§36.33), and the suffix -*n*. The prefix is used in Hebrew, in some Phoenician dialects, in Arabic, in Middle Aramaic dialects, in Tigrinya, and in South Ethiopic (§36.33), while the suffix appears in Aramaic, Thamūdic (masc. *ḏn*, fem. *ḏn* or *ḏt*), South Arabian, Ethiopic, and in the Phoenician dialect of Byblos (*zn*). Both the prefix and the suffix are used in the Gafat "near" demonstrative *ənnäzəň < *hinnazin*, "these". These demonstratives do not show case differentiation, with the exception of the Arabic dual attested in the oblique case also as *ḏayni* (masc.) and *tayni* (fem.).

"Near" Demonstrative Pronouns

Sabaic	Qatabanic	Šheri	Ge'ez	Tigrinya
ḏn	*ḏn*	*ḏänu*	*zə(ntu)*	*'əzu*
ḏt	*ḏt*	*ḏinu*	*zā(tti)*	*'əza*
ḏyn ?				
'ln	*ḏtn*	*iźänu*	*'əllu, 'əllo/āntu*	*'əzom*
'lt	?		*'əllā, 'əllo/āntā*	*'əzän*

36.39.   The Aramaic demonstrative is written *znh*, *z'/h*, and later *dnh*, *d'/h*, *hd(y)n*, *hd'/h*, a change which reflects the shift *ḏ > d* (§13.8). How-ever, Mandaic preserves the archaic spelling *h'zyn* (masc.) and *h'z'* (fem.). The *ź* of *iźänu* in Šḥeri is the palatalized *l* of *'ln*. The shift *ḏ > d* occurred also in many modern Arabic colloquials, also with new devel-opments in the form of the feminine *hāḏī*, where *hā-* changed locally into *hay-* (e.g. *haydi*, *hayye*), and especially in the plural demonstrative where *ḏ-* is added to Classical Arabic *(hā)'ulā('i)* or develops its own plural form and replaces the element *'ulā('i)*. The Yemenite colloquial of Ṣanʿa, e.g., presents the forms *hāḏawlā < *hā-ḏā-'ulā* and *ḏawlā'i < *ḏa-'ulā'i*, which is reduced to *ḏōl(a)* in the Meccan and Cairene collo-quials, while the Damascene form is *hadōle*. The determinative-relative develops its own plural form *ḏū*, "these", at Ḥassānīya (Mauritania); this plural is generally extended in the Maghrebine colloquials to *hāḏūma/na* with a feminine *hāḏāna*, "these".

36.40.   New forms are encountered likewise in the Modern South Ara-bian languages. The elements in the Mehri and Ḥarsūsi "near" demon-stratives are the base form, — used also independently as *ḏā* and *ḏī* in Ḥarsūsi, — and a -*məh* suffix which occurs as a deictic in other com-pounds, thus *ḏōməh* (masc.), *ḏīməh* (fem.), and *əlyōməh* (plur.) in Mehri, *ḏanəməh* (masc.), *ḏənəməh* (fem.), and *lən/ləməh* (plur.) in Ḥarsūsi. The Soqoṭri forms, — beside the basic *da* (masc.) and *dəš* (fem.), — are par-ticular in the sense that the deictic element *hā-* is placed after the base form: *dədha < *də-d-ha*, "this which (is) here" (masc.), *didha* (fem.), *əlha* (plur.). A similar "far" demonstrative occurs in Gafat: *az-əňňa*, "that".

36.41.   Beside Geʿez, the demonstrative element *z* is used in Tigrinya: *'əzu*, "this" (masc.), *'əzom*, "these" (masc.) (§36.38). Instead, Tigre has the demonstrative *'əlli*, "this" (§36.34). In South Ethiopic, the situation differs from one language to the other. In Amharic, the element *z* is pre-served only after preposition (e.g. *bä-(z)zih*, "in this") and in the plural *ənnäzzih* or *əlläzzih*, "these". The final -*h* derives from the spirantized deictic -*k* (cf. §49.9). The situation is similar in Gafat, with the exception of the demonstrative *az-əňňa* (§36.40). All North Gurage dialects and the West Gurage Chaha preserve *z* as demonstrative also in free position, as *zi* or *zə*, "this".

36.42.   The principal forms of the "far" demonstrative based on the determinative-relative *ḏ* are compounded with the deictic element -*k* (cf. §49.9). They are attested in Aramaic, Arabic, and in South Semitic languages, and they are also used with an additional suffix -*n*, which can change occasionally to -*m*, or with other extended suffixes. Classical Arabic preserved a dual with a subject case and an oblique case.

	Aramaic	Arabic	Mehri	Śheri	Ge'ez
Sing.					
m.	*dēk, denāk* ⎫ *dikkēn*	*dāka*	*dēk*	*ḏäku*	*zək(t)u*
f.	*ḏāk, ḏēkī* ⎭	*tāka, tīka*	*dayk*	*dikun*	*'əntəku, 'əntākti*
Plur.					
m.	*'illēk* ⎫ *'illēn, 'ellayin*	*'ulāka, 'ulā'ika*	*əlyēk*	*iźɔk*	*'əlləku*
f.	*'illēkī* ⎭				

The Aramaic demonstrative is written with *z* in the earlier periods, later with *d*, thus reflecting the shift *d̲* > *d* (§13.8), which occurred also in many modern Arabic colloquials. The lateral *ź* of *iźɔk* in Śheri is the palatalized *l* of *'lk* (§16.7).

36.43. Beside Ge'ez, the determinative-relative *z* forms "far" demonstratives in North Gurage dialects with the suffix -*k*, as *zak̲*, "that", or without, as *za*, "that". The "near" demonstrative is expressed by *zə*, "this". The opposition *ə : a* distinguishes the "near" demonstrative from the "far" demonstrative like in Gafat (§36.32,34).

36.44. Other "far" demonstratives are formed with suffixes -*lika* (Classical Arabic: *d̲alika, tilka, 'ulālika*), -*kəməh* (Mehri, Ḥarsūsi: *d̲ākəməh, d̲əkəməh, 'aləməh*), -*buk* (Soqoṭri: *dədbuk, didbuk, əlbuk*), or with the prefix *hā-* and the suffix -*k* (Arabic: *hād̲āk, hād̲īk, hā'ulāk / hawlāk*; Christian Palestinian Aramaic: *hdk, hlyk*). The element *hā-* is used as a suffix in the Arabic colloquial of Egypt (*dukha, dikha, dukham / dukhumma*; cf. §36.40).

36.45. Amharic has developed three degrees of the demonstrative pronoun, comparable with Latin *hic, iste, ille*. The demonstrative referring to an object near the speaker (first person) is *yəh* (masc.), *yəčč* (fem.), *annäzzih / alläzzih* (plur.). The demonstrative referring to an object near the addressee (second person) is the Amharic independent personal pronoun of the third person (§36.12): *ərsu / əssu* (masc.), *əssʷa / ərsʷa* (fem.), *annässu* (plur.). The demonstrative referring to an object near a third person is *ya* (masc.), *yəčč* (fem.), *annäzziya / alläzziya* (plur.).

F. Determinative-Relative Pronouns

36.46. The determinative-relative pronoun *ṯu* / *ḏu* introduces a determination which can consist either in a noun or proper name (e.g. ***ḏū***
l-qarnayn, "the two horned", lit. "the [man] of two horns", an epithet
given in Arabic to Alexander the Great), or in a relative sentence (e.g.
Ugaritic *rb ḥršm **d** šṣ'a ḥwyh*, "the chief of the craftsmen, who has carried out its repair": KTU 4.145, 9-10). In the first case, it functions in a
genitival structure (§51.18); in the second, it acts as a pronominal or
adjectival antecedent of a relative clause (§57.6).

36.47. The determinative-relative pronoun is written usually with the
signs ŠU, ŠÈ or ŠI, ŠA in Palaeosyrian at Ebla and at Tell Beydar, in Old
Akkadian, and partly in Amorite. This means that its original North and
East Semitic form was generally *ṯu*, paralleled in West and South
Semitic by *ḏu*, with the well-known opposition of voiced and unvoiced
consonants (§10.8). The subsequent change *ṯu* > *šu*, already noticeable
in some variants at Ebla and in the post-Ur III texts from Mari, accred-
ited the erroneous opinion that the determinative-relative pronoun of
East Semitic is formally connected with the independent personal pronoun *šū* (§36.2) and the related demonstrative (§36.36). The unvoiced
form *ṯu* existed also in West Semitic and it is attested by the Phoenician,
dialectal Hebrew (e.g. Judg. 5,7), and Mishnaic Hebrew relative pronoun
še-, while the voiced form *ḏu* appears also in Amorite dialects and at
Emar, *ca.* 1200 B.C., as shown by names like *Zu-ḫa-ad-ni* /*Ḏu-ġadni*/,
"The pleasant one", lit. "The (man) of pleasure", at Mari, or *Zu-Aš-tar-
ti*, "The (man) of Astarte", at Emar.

36.48. The determinative-relative pronoun was originally fully inflec-
tive, but it became indeclinable without gender, number, and case differentiation in practically all Semitic languages. The following paradigm
contains the fully or partly inflected forms of the pronoun. Further differentiations are hindered in Epigraphic South Arabian languages
because of the lack of vocalization. The vowels of the singular were initially short, but were lengthened in the course of time, already in Amorite (e.g. *Zu-ú-i-la* /*Ḏū-'ila*/) and in Ugaritic (*du-ú*).

	Old Akkadian & Palaeosyrian	Classical Arabic	Sabaic	Minaic	Qatabanic
Sing. masc.					
nominative	*ṭu*	*ḏū*			
genitive	*ṭi*	*ḏī*	*ḏ*	*ḏ*	*ḏ, ḏw*
accusative	*ṭa*	*ḏā*			
Sing. fem.					
nominative	*ṭat(u)*	*ḏātu*			
genitive	*ṭati*	*ḏāti*	*ḏt*	*ḏt*	*ḏt*
accusative	**ṭata*	*ḏāta*			
Dual masc.					
nominative	*ṭā*	*ḏawā*	*ḏy*	*ḏy*	*ḏw, ḏn*
obl. case		*ḏaway*			
Dual fem.					
nominative	*ṭā*	*ḏātā, ḏawātā*	*ḏty*	*ḏtyn*	?
obl. case		*ḏātay, ḏawātay*			
Plur. masc.					
nominative	*ṭūt(u)*	*ḏawū, 'ulū*	*'ly*	*'hl, ḏl*	*ḏtw, 'wlw*
obl. case	*ṭūt(i)*	*ḏawī, 'ulī*			
Plur. fem.					
nominative	*ṭāt(u)*	*ḏawātu, 'ulātu*	*'lt*		*ḏtw(?)*
obl. case	*ṭāt(i)*	*ḏawāti, 'ulāti*			

36.49. The Assyro-Babylonian determinative-relative pronoun appears from the end of the Old Akkadian period on under the indeclinable form *ša* of the accusative, which is in reality the old citation form (§32.6). Only in rare cases have *šūt* and *šāt* survived in the first centuries of the second millennium B.C. The Palaeosyrian determinative-relative pronoun is attested by the singular feminine oblique case *ša-ti* /ṭati/ rather than /ḏati/, since its variant spelling is *sa-ti* [šati]. In Amorite onomastics, the masculine forms *Zu(-ú)* /ḏū/ and *šu* /ṭu/ occur, as well as the feminine forms *ši* /ṭi/ and *si-i* /šī < ṭi/.

36.50. In Ugaritic, only $d < \underline{d}$ and $dt < \underline{d}t$ are attested, but they may be inflected according to number, gender, and case. Only the vocalization of d as du-$\acute{u}$ ($d\bar{u}$) is provided, but one can assume the existence of a genitive $*d\bar{\imath}$ and of an accusative $*d\bar{a}$. The form dt stands for the feminine singular ($*d\bar{a}t$-) and for the plural ($*d\bar{u}t$-). However, Ugaritic d appears sometimes in place of the expected dt, either because the pronoun was reduced to a single form or because the final $-t$ was dropped as in possibly similar cases (§35.6).

36.51. In Phoenician, the forms with $z < \underline{d}$ are used as demonstratives (§36.38), while those with $š < \underline{t}$ are employed as determinative-relative pronouns, often with a prefixed vowel ('š). In Hebrew, the archaic theonym $z\bar{u}$-$S\bar{\imath}nay$, "the (God) of Sinai", preserves the nominative of the pronoun $\underline{d}u$ used as determinative, while the masculine genitive $*\underline{d}i > ze$ and the feminine $*\underline{d}at > *zat > zot > z\bar{o}$ are employed as demonstratives (§36.38). The pronoun $z\bar{u}$ is attested as indeclinable relative in poetry, while the function of determinative-relative was usually taken by $še$-/$šə$- $< *\underline{t}i$, exactly as in Phoenician. However, the attestations of $še$ in Classical Hebrew are rather scarce owing to the widespread use of the noun $'ăšer$, "place", as relative pronoun (§36.56).

36.52. In Aramaic, the determinative-relative $\underline{d}i$ in the genitive case is used in its original function and as element of demonstratives (§36.38-39, 42). It is written z, zy, dy, and d with a very short vowel ($də$). Its old feminine $z't$ ($*\underline{d}āt$) is attested as demonstrative at Tell Fekherye (9th century B.C.).

36.53. The Classical fully declined Arabic pronoun reflects a systematic archaizing intervention, since the determinative-relative $\underline{d}\bar{u}$ was already indeclinable in the pre-classical poetry. Besides, Arabic developed an extended relative pronoun combining the deictic $'alla < *hanna$ with the determinative-relative: $'alla\underline{d}\bar{\imath}$ (sing. masc.), $'allat\bar{\imath}$ (sing. fem.), $'alla\underline{d}āni$ (dual masc.), $'allatāni$ (dual fem.), $'alla\underline{d}\bar{\imath}na$ (masc. plur.), $'allāti$ / $'allawāti$ (fem. plur.). There are many variants of this pronoun in the ancient dialects, which have used it also as an indeclinable $alla\underline{d}\bar{\imath}$, and the modern colloquials either reduce it to $il\underline{d}\bar{\imath}$, $i\underline{d}\underline{d}\bar{\imath}$, or derive $all\bar{\imath}$, $ill\bar{\imath}$, directly from a base $*'allay$, while simple $\underline{d}\bar{\imath}$ continues to be used in Yemen and in some Maghrebine colloquials.

36.54. Epigraphic South Arabian had most likely a fully inflected determinative-relative pronoun, also with some rarer forms as Sabaic feminine *t-* which corresponds to the *-tī* of Arabic *'alla-tī*, or Sabaic *hn-mw* and *hl-mw*, "whatever", where the older forms of Arabic *'alla-* appear. The Ḥasaean (§7.41) feminine determinative-relative *ḏ't* shows the use of *alif* as in Classical Arabic and in Old Aramaic *z't* (§36.52). The South Arabian determinative-relative antecedent is also employed in the sources as an indeclinable pronoun, as in other Semitic languages. In Modern South Arabian, Mehri uses *ḏi*, *ḏə* like the Arabic Yemenite colloquials.

36.55. The Geʻez relatival antecedent is *za* (masc.), *'ənta* (fem.), *'əlla* (plur.); *zə* is used in Tigrinya and *zi* in Harari (e.g. *zi-säbära*, "he who broke"). Instead, the Tigre relatival antecedent is *la-*, and the South Ethiopian languages, except Harari, use the element *yä-* for the relative pronoun. This particle, prefixed to the verb of the relative clause, has to be explained as a palatalized *lä-*, which was used first to express a genitival relation (§51.25) and then to introduce a relative clause (§57.9).

36.56. Semitic languages also use some nouns as relatival antecedents, regardless of their original meaning. The best known is the construct state *ašar* of the Assyro-Babylonian noun *ašru*, "place" (< *'aṯr-*), the Hebrew and Moabite *'ăšer*. Initially, this noun was simply followed by a relative asyndetic clause: e.g. Assyro-Babylonian *imtaši ašar iwwaldu*, "he forgot (the place) where he was born". Then it was used in apposition to another noun designating a place; e.g. Babylonian *eqelšu... ašar tattadnu*, "his field,... (place) which you have given"; Hebrew *habbayit 'ăšer bānītī*, "the house (place) which I have build". But since the meaning of *'ăšer* was forgotten in Hebrew, the word started soon to be employed with any qualified element, e.g. *Yaʻqob 'ăšer bəhartīkā*, "Jacob, (place) which I have chosen". In Neo-Assyrian, also the noun *bēt*, "house", is used in this way; e.g. *bēt šarru iqbūni lillikū*, "(the house) wherever the king will order, they shall go"; *šupru bēt šūtūni*, "write (the house) where he is". In several Semitic languages, an interrogative and indefinite pronoun can also be used as a relatival antecedent (§36.62).

G. Interrogative and Indefinite Pronouns

36.57.   The interrogative pronouns go back to a common Afro-Asiatic element transmitted in ancient Egyptian as *m*, "who?", "which?", "what?", in Tuareg as *ma*, "what?", and *mi*, "who?", in Hausa as *mèe*, "what?". Semitic languages provide here the only examples in which animate subjects are distinguished from inanimate subjects, like Latin *quis?* and *quid?* The pronoun referring to animate subjects is characterized by two different morphemes: *-an* in East Semitic, Amorite, Aramaic, Arabic, and South Semitic; *-iy(a)* in Palaeosyrian, Ugaritic, and in the "Canaanite" languages. The pronoun referring to inanimate subjects is likewise marked by two distinct morphemes: *-in* in East Semitic and Ethiopic; *-ah(a) > -ā* in the other Semitic languages. Tuareg *ma* and *mi* correspond to the situation in North Semitic and in "Canaanite" languages.

36.58.   The archaic forms *man* and *min*, attested in Old Akkadian, show neither case endings nor mimation, but these pronouns had already become *mannum* and *mīnum* in the Old Akkadian period. The Palaeosyrian pronoun *mī* appears at Ebla in the proper name *Mi-kà-il*, "Who is like Il?", and at Mari in the pre-Sargonic *Mí-ma-ḫir-sú*, "Who is his opponent?". In Amorite, *ma-an-na*, "who?", and *ma-a*, "what?", are both attested in proper names. The Old Canaanite form *mi-ia*, "who?", appears in several Amarna letters, as well as an extended form *mi-ia-ti* with the affix *-t* (cf. §36.35). Besides, there is an interrogative *ma-an-na* (EA 286,5), "what?", certainly related to Ugaritic *mn*, "what?", which can be explained in the light of Minaic *mhn*, "what?", as **mahna >* *manna*. In Arabic, *man* and *mā* are uninflected, but they have a masculine and a feminine form in Geʻez: *mannu* (masc.) and *manna* (fem.), "who?", *mənt* (masc.) and *mənta* (fem.), "what?". In colloquial Arabic, *min* has generally replaced *man* and its vowel is often lengthened, while *mā* is still used only in Yemen. In some Gurage dialects, the *n* of *mən* changes into *r* (§17.6).

36.59.   There is also an inflected Semitic interrogative *'ayyu*, "which?", derived from the interrogative particle *'ay*, "where?", which is attested in Old Akkadian, Old Babylonian, Amorite (/'ayya/, /'ayyāma/), Old Canaanite (/'ayyāmi/), Ugaritic (*'iy*), Hebrew (*'ayyē*). It is used as adjective in Assyro-Babylonian (e.g. *adi ayyim ūmim*, "until which day?") and as pronoun in Classical Arabic, followed by the genitive (*'ayyu raǧulin*, "which man?"). Its use is widespread in Arabic colloquials with an ending -*š* which goes back to classical *'ayyu šay'in*, "which thing?" Various reductions are attested, as *ayš*, *ēš* and *āš* with monophthongization, *wāš* and *wūš* with substitution of *w* for original ', or short forms as *əš*- and *š*- which often preserve the -*n* of *šay'in* when they are used with the agglutinated pronoun -*hu* employed as copula, e.g. *šenhu*, "who is...?" In Ugaritic and in Minaic, *'y* is encountered up to now only as an indefinite pronoun ("any"), while it is employed in Syriac, both as interrogative and as indefinite, with the affix -*nā*, the feminine *'aydā*, and the plural *'aylēn*. The indefinite use of *ay* is attested also in Libyco-Berber where this pronominal base combines with demonstrative suffixes: e.g. *ay-ad*, "this", *ay-inn*, "that", *ay-inna*, "that, in question", *ay-ad-dak*, "this here" (§36.37).

36.60. The forms assumed by the interrogative pronouns in the various languages are as follows:

	"Who?"	What?"	Which?"
Old Egyptian	*m*	*m*	
Tuareg	*mi*	*ma*	*ay*
Old Akkadian	*man*	*min*	
Assyro-Babylonian	*mannu(m)*	*mīnu(m)*	*ayyu*
Palaeosyrian	*mī*	?	
Amorite	*manna*	*mā*	
Ugaritic	*my*	*mh, mn*	*'ay*
Old Canaanite	*miya*	*manna*	
Phoenician	*my*	*m*	
Hebrew	*mī*	*mā*	
Aramaic	*man*	*mā*	
Syriac	*man*	*mā*	*'aynā*
Neo-Aramaic	*man, mānī*	*mā, mu*	*ēnī*
Classical Arabic	*man*	*mā*	*'ayy(un)*
Colloquial Arabic	*min*	*mā*	*ay-*
Minaic	*mn*	*mh(n)*	*'y*
Ge'ez	*mannu*	*mənt*	*'ayy(āt)*
Tigre	*man*	*mi*	*'ayi*
Tigrinya	*män*	*'əntay*	*'ayyänay*
Amharic	*man*	*mən*	*yätu*
Gurage	*m(ʷ)a(n)*	*mən/r*	*yitta, etäta*

Fig. 27. Aramaic ostracon from Elephantine, 5th century B.C.,
reverse with lines 10-17 of a letter (Bodleian Library, Oxford).

36.61. Indefinite pronouns, strictly speaking, do not exist in Semitic.
The forms used as a kind of indefinite pronouns are based on the interrogative pronoun. The pronouns *mn* in Ugaritic and *mā* in Arabic may
be placed in apposition to nouns with the meaning "any", "a certain";
e.g. Ugaritic *mn 'ib ypʿ lbʿl*, "did any foe rise against Baal?"; Arabic
raǧulun mā, "a certain man". More often a suffix is added to the interrogative, mainly *-ma* used in Old Akkadian, in Assyro-Babylonian
(*man-ma > mamma*, "whoever"; *min-ma > mimma*, "whatever"), in
Ugaritic (**mannama*, e.g. in the very same phrase: *mnm 'ib ypʿ lbʿl*), in
Poenician and Punic (*mnm*, "anything"), in Arabic (*'ayyumā*, "anyone"; *māmā*, "whatsoever"), in Ethiopian languages (e.g. Tigre *manma*,
"nobody"; Amharic *mannəm*, "whoever", *mənəm*, "whatever"; Gafat
manəm, "whoever", *mənəm* or *mənä*, "whatever"). Aramaic **manmi* or
*manma, "whoever", is preserved in Western Neo-Aramaic *mōnmi l-īṯ*
< *mōnmi ḏ-īṯ* or *mūnma l-īṯ*, "whoever he is". The indefinite pronoun
can also be formed with the deictic particle *-k* added to the interrogative,
as *mhk* and *mnk* in Ugaritic, or by reduplication of the interrogative, as
mamman < *man-man in Assyro-Babylonian and *mənəmən*, "whatever", in Amharic. Phoenician uses the reflexive pronoun *qnm-y*, lit. "he
himself" (§36.28), as indefinite in the clause *qnmy 't*, "whoever you
are".

36.62. The interrogative pronouns can be used also as relatival antecedents in several Semitic languages, as Aramaic, Liḥyānite, Arabic, South Arabian; e.g. Aramaic *mn yld šmy mn m'ny'*, "whoever removes my name from the objects…"; Sabaic *'l mn s²'r k-mhn h' ḥlṯhw*, "nobody knew what was his malady".

4. VERBS

A. Preliminaries

37.1. The verb is the grammatical category which inflects for tense, for aspect, for mood, for actor, for stem, and for voice. The problems raised by the verb are among the most difficult in Semitic linguistics and the varying terminology used in grammatical studies bearing on the single languages does not help in solving them. Authors call corresponding verbal forms, e.g., "subjunctive" in one language, "jussive" in another one, "cohortative" in a third one, or "modal" elsewhere. Also occasional confusions between "stative", "intransitive", and "passive", and fashionable resorting to modern linguistic analyses of Indo-European tenses may lead to a misinterpretation of the basic characteristics of the Semitic verbal system, as the distinction between the categories of transitive and intransitive, of active (event) and stative (state), and the Semitic aspects of action, considered either in a synchronic or in a diachronic perspective. Furthermore, the traditional explanation of Semitic verbal forms is based on the conception of a triconsonantal discontinuous morph or root, which is unpronounceable and did never exist in a spoken language. This artificial approach cannot lead to an understanding of the Semitic verbal system which was originally characterized by trimorphous *a*-class, *i*-class, and *u*-class roots, independently from the formal distinction between tenses and aspects (§38.1-14), and between transitive and the intransitive conjugations (§38.15-17), like in ergative languages. The primitive tenses, like the imperative and the jussive referring to futurity, and the preterite expressing a genuine past, derive from a "verbal" base of the types CvC, $C\bar{v}C$, $C_1vC_2C_2$ or $C_1C_2vC_3$, while the aspectual conjugation originates from a "nominal" base of the types CaC, $C\bar{a}C$, or $C_1aC_2C_3$ (cf. §28.7-12), the latter being further expanded to $CaCaC$, $CaCiC$, $CaCuC$. Important shifts from one group to the other occurred in the course of time, but both categories can be distinguished also in Libyco-Berber where they are represented, broadly speaking, by the proper verbal conjugation, on the one hand, and by the so-called "qualitative" which derives from a nominal base, on the other. Both types of conjugation occur in other Afro-Asiatic languages as well, for example in the "Sam" sub-group of Lowland East Cushitic (§2.11) with its prefix- and suffix-conjugation. — To avoid tedious repetitions or unwarranted hypotheses, we shall occasionally refer to Semitic roots or bases by designating them by the sole consonantal signs. Forms of the most ancient Semitic languages, attested in cuneiform script, are, as a rule, designated by the paradigmatic verb *parāsu*, "to separate", while the verb *fa'ala*, "he made", is generally used for Arabic, and *qatal*, "he killed", for the other languages.

37.2.   The essential function of the "verbal" base is to express, in grammatical categories, the distinction between a *future action* and a *past action*. In other words, it serves to form a kind of tenses which tell us something about the relative order of events, e.g. whether some event took place before the real or fictitious time of speaking or had not yet taken place at that moment. This bipartite distinction is the normal one in a wide range of languages, since the familiar tripartite division of time in "past", "present", and "future" is not a universal characteristic of temporal systems. The types CvC, $C\bar{v}C$, and $C_1vC_2C_2$ occur with biconsonantal roots, while the type $C_1C_2vC_3$ corresponds to those which are triconsonantal. Since the last group is more dominant in historically attested verbs than in any other part of speech, the pattern $C_1C_2vC_3$ will be followed in the general presentation, while the patterns CvC, $C\bar{v}C$, and $C_1vC_2C_2$ will be examined in a complementary section (§44).

37.3.   The essential function of the "nominal" base of verbal forms is to indicate a condition or a *situation* with respect to circumstances, viz. permanent or static, accomplished or perfected, and unaccomplished or not completely performed. In other words, it serves to express formally distinguished aspects which cannot be equated with telic and atelic situations. In fact, a telic situation involves a process that leads up to a well-defined terminal point (e.g. "John is making a chair"), while an atelic situation lacks such a determinate goal (e.g. "John is singing"). Now, the "telic/atelic" distinction is neutralized in the Semitic imperfective aspect, while the semantic feature of "accomplishment" replaces the "well-defined terminal point" in the perfective aspect. It means that the "telic/atelic" distinction is of no use in the analysis of Semitic aspects. As for the basic patterns of Semitic aspectual forms, the types CaC,

$C\bar{a}C$, and $C_1vC_2C_2$ are used for the biconsonantal bases, while the type $C_1aC_2C_3$ and its derivatives serve for the triconsonantal ones, and correspond to well-known patterns of verbal adjectives. The general presentation of the *Outline* will be referring to the triconsonantal pattern supplied by *parāsu, fa'ala*, and *qatal*, while the other types will be examined in §44.

37.4. The category of mood, as its name implies, denotes the manner in which the action or state is expressed. The moods of Semitic verbs, called indicative, subjunctive, jussive, ventive or allative, energic or energetic, etc., are thus purely grammatical-syntactic categories of coordination and subordination, unmarked or marked by affixes (§39). The indicative, broadly speaking, notifies a fact or what is alleged to be a fact. Besides the indicative, which is used essentially for statements expressed in main clauses, there are three basic moods in Semitic: 1° an unmarked jussive which derives from the imperative (§38.2), corresponds to the Indo-European injunctive, and is called "apocopate(d)" in grammars of Arabic (§39.14); 2° an East Semitic subjunctive marked by -u and used in all kinds of subordinate clauses (§39.3); 3° a West Semitic subjunctive marked by -a, having a final/consecutive function, and called "cohortative" in grammars of Hebrew (§39.5-6), while its suffixed variant in -n(na) is termed "energetic" or "energic" (§39.8-11). Both are probably related to the East Semitic ventive or allative mood which signifies a general movement of the action towards the speaker (§39.7) and which is expressed by the indicative with a suffixed "directive" morpheme. The imperative, the infinitive, and the participle are not considered as "modal" forms. In fact, the imperative, which denotes a command, is simply a base-form, while the infinitive and the participle belong, strictly speaking, to the category of nouns.

37.5. The actor affixes or personals specify person, gender, and number. They appear as both prefixes and suffixes. Their distribution depends on tense and aspect (§40). Despite some difficulties, a clear connection can be traced between the personals of the verb and the components of the personal pronoun.

37.6. The stem is a verbal pattern deriving from a root; it serves as the base of all the inflectional forms connected with a specific meaning. Each verbal root has a simple or basic stem — not always used in historically attested languages — and a varying number of derived stems.

In some languages, the stem can exhibit an active and a passive theme. By "voice" we intend these passive and active forms, showing vocalic differentiation, also in the derived stems which are formed from the root or from another stem, either with an affix or with lengthening. While some of these stems have an Afro-Asiatic origin, other seem to result from an internal evolution of a particular group of Semitic languages. The terminology and the symbols used in the grammars to denote the various stems are not identical for all the Semitic languages. Therefore, it is useful to present here a synoptic table of the main customary terms and symbols employed for East Semitic, Hebrew, Aramaic, Arabic, and Ethiopic. The symbols reported for Ethiopic, e.g. "Stem I.1/A", take two different usages into account, viz. I.1 and IA, which refer both to the same forms. The symbols will be explained in §41.

East Semitic	Hebrew	Aramaic	Arabic	Ethiopic
B/G-stem	pa'al/qal	pe'al	Stem I	Stem I.1/A
D-stem	pi'el	pa''el	Stem II	Stem I.2/B
(L-stem)	—	—	Stem III	Stem I.3/C
Š-stem	hif'il	haf'el	Stem IV	Stem II.1/A
ŠD-stem	—	—	—	Stem II.2/B
—	—	—	—	Stem II.3/C
N-stem	nif'al	—	Stem VII	—
B/Gt-stem	—	itpe'el	Stem VIII	Stem III.1/A
Dt-stem	hitpa'el	itpa''al	Stem V	Stem III.2/B
(tL-stem)	—	—	Stem VI	Stem III.3/C
Št-stem	—	ittaf'al	Stem X	Stem IV.1/A
ŠDt-stem	—	—	—	Stem IV.2/B
—	—	—	—	Stem IV.3/C

37.7. In the course of time, the Semitic verbal system underwent several important changes, noticeable either in a whole group of languages or in a particular idiom. Only a diachronic and comparative method can insert these changes in the wider context of the whole Semitic system. In order to illustrate the changes occurring in the verbal system, a morpho-syntactic approach is needed here. An exlusively morphological presentation is insufficient to explain the changes involved.

37.8. Tense, in the proper sense of the word, is far from being common to any type of Semitic verbal system, while European tense forms are, in many cases — also in the present *Outline* — the only available means of translating Semitic aspects in an intelligible manner (cf. §38.18). Thus, the so-called present-future (*iparras*) of the grammars of Akkadian, e.g., really is an imperfective aspect, indicating basically that a process has not reached completion at a certain moment of time. It may also indicate that an activity is in progress or a state is being entered upon under the influence of another activity or state. This formation can be translated in European languages by a present, a future, a future perfect, an imperfect, also by European subjunctives and other categories. The Semitic perfect may, for practical reasons, be rendered by a past tense of verbs which express action or by the present of verbs which express a state. Often however, in complex sentences, a present, a future, or a future perfect will be needed in translating. It is of the highest importance to distinguish these approximations from the real functions of Semitic verbal categories. Except for the imperative, the preterite, and certain modern innovations, Semitic languages have no tenses properly speaking, but only aspects. Each of the systems, the aspectual and the temporal, is clear in itself, but exact translation from the one to the other is very difficult, if not impossible. Therefore, the misuse of the translations in attributing, e.g., the functions of a future perfect or of a continuous present to the Assyro-Babylonian *iparras* results in a complete misunderstanding of the Semitic verbal system. A grammarian is not called upon to explain a function if it does not exist in a given language as a distinct form. That does not preclude the fact that most grammatical categories have a variety of meanings and thus may be ambiguous as long as a concrete context or life situation do not remove the ambiguity.

B. Tenses and Aspects

a) Fully Developed System

38.1. In the basic triconsonantal model $C_1C_2vC_3$, the simplest form morphologically is placed in the most unmarked category which is the imperative across the whole spread of Afro-Asiatic languages. The imperative stands outside any possible system of aspect; it refers by definition to futurity, i.e. to a future, as yet not performed action, e.g. *ktōb*, "write!", in the Arabic colloquial of Damascus. Paired with the imperative, there is another purely verbal form, outside the system of aspect, but referring to the past and signifying that an action has or has not been performed. It is characterized morphologically by the same basic model $C_1C_2vC_3$ as the imperative, exhibiting the same personal suffixes, but having besides personal prefixes, viz. the Assyro-Babylonian preterite, e.g. (*y*)*iprus* / *taprus*, "he / she separated". It is a narration oriented form, expressing a genuine past, which continued to be used by the West Semitic languages in a narrative context until the mid-first millennium B.C. and beyond, despite the changes that the verbal system had then undergone (§38.10-11). This form is attested also in Libyco-Berber, e.g. Tuareg *yə-krəs*, "he knotted". It occurs in Cushitic as well, e.g. Rendille *y-igis*, "he killed".

38.2.   Semitic imperative has no first and third persons, and it is not used in negative clauses. These cohortative (1st pers.), optative or precative (3rd pers.), and vetitive or prohibitive functions are assumed by the so-called "jussive", the simplest form of which would have been identical with the preterite if there were no differences in the stress, which was phonemic (§25.8). Therefore, one has to surmise that the stress rested in the preterite on the prefix (e.g. *yíprus*, *yáqtul*), while it rested in the jussive on the basic syllable of the imperative (e.g. *yiprús*, *yaqtúl*). This is confirmed by the stress of the prohibitive in modern Arabic colloquials and of the so-called subjunctive in Modern South Arabian; e.g. Mesopotamian *lā təbkáy*, "don't cry!" (fem.); Maghrebine *ma tal'ăbŭ̆š*, "don't play!" (plur.); Mehri *yəktéb*, "may he write"; Ḥarsūsi *yəlbéd*, "may he hit", Soqoṭri *liqbắr*, "may he bury". The very limited evidence provided by the Kabyle dialect of Libyco-Berber seems to go in the same direction, as shown by the quantitative vowel gradation, e.g. in *yərwəl* used as jussive in *yəsla yərwə́l* (60-90 msec.), "he heard, so that he ran away", and as subordinate past tense in *yəsla yə́rwəl* (80-70 msec.), "he heard that he had run away". Subsequent changes introduced special prefixes aimed at characterizing the cohortative, the optative or precative, and the vetitive or prohibitive, e.g. Assyro-Babylonian *luprus*, "may I separate"; *liprus*, "may he separate"; *ayiprus*, "may he not separate"; Aramaic *lhwy*, "may he be"; Arabic *li-yaktub*, "he should write"; *lā taqtul*, "you shall not kill". These proclitics express the expectation on the part of the speaker or active subject that the process will indeed take place, or not at all. The use of the jussive, called also "subjunctive", was extended to various subordinate verbal clauses, especially in Ethiopic.

38.3.   The aspectual category of the verbal system is based on the adjectival $C_1aC_2C_3$ pattern, represented e.g. by the Assyro-Babylonian verbal adjective *pars*(*um*), and developed to the stative / permansive forms, well-known in Old Akkadian and in Assyro-Babylonian: *CaCiC* (e.g. *damiq*, "he is good"), *CaCaC* (e.g. *rapaš*, "he is wide"), *CaCuC* (e.g. *qarub*, "he is near"). The anaptyctic vowel *a* / *i* / *u* should appear only when there is a two-consonant cluster (§27.19), i.e. in the 3rd pers. masc. sing., but its use was extended in several standard languages; e.g. Classical Arabic *malakat*, "she is the proprietress"; Geʻez *masalat*, "she is alike". Instead, many Arab vernaculars, in the East and especially in the West, have forms without anaptyxis; e.g. Damascene *katbet*, Maghrebine *katbat*, "she wrote". Despite relative distinctions made between an active pattern exhibiting *a* and stative patterns exhibiting *i* > *e* or *u* > *o*, the quality of the inserted vowel is not predictable (e.g. Assyro-Babylonian *rapaš*, "he is wide"), and the latter is not identical with the thematic vowel of the imperative-preterite (e.g. Assyro-Babylonian *ilmad*, "he learned", but *lamid*, "he is learned"). The Afro-Asiatic origin of this morphological category $C_1aC_2(v)C_3$ is demonstrated by the Egyptian old perfective, also called "pseudo-participle" (e.g. *hr-t/tì*, "you are content"), and by the Libyco-Berber suffix conjugation of stative verbs which express a quality, the so-called "qualitative"; e.g. Tuareg *măẓăg* or *məẓəg*, "he is deaf". The originally static aspect of this morphological category is opposed to the perfective and to the imperfective which express, in grammatical categories, the completed (perfect) and the incomplete (present-future) aspect of the action. This leaves us with one basically unmarked category, which is a stative or permansive form, and with two marked categories, which express the accomplished and the unaccomplished aspect of the action signified by the verb. These marked categories, which may function either as transitive or as intransitive forms, are conveniently termed "perfective" and "imperfective". They express a fundamental contrast between an event which is in the process of transpiring ("he is walking") and one that has already taken place and exists only as a resultant state or condition ("he is in a condition subsequent to walking"). It does not matter whether the process is continuous or repetitive, for this distinction results from the meaning of the verb; e.g. "he is walking" denotes a continuous process, while "he is striking" connotes a series of actions. Neither does it matter whether the action tends to a determinate goal ("telïc") or is simply considered as durative ("atelic").

The morphological categories *CaCiC*, *CaCaC*, *CaCuC* are disrupted in many Arabic colloquials following the elision of short vowels in open unstressed syllables or their qualitative change occasioned by vowel-harmony, vowel-opposition, influence of contiguous consonants. Thus in Mesopotamian *qəltu*-dialects (*qəltu*, "I said"), the basis is either *CaCaC* or *CəCəC*, while it is *CiCaC* or

CuCaC in the Mesopotamian *gǝlǝt*-dialects (*gǝlǝt*, "I said"). The base form shows the types *CaCaC*, *CiCiC*, and *CiCaC* in East Arabian, while the Maghrebine basis is *CCaC*, *CCiC*, or *CCǝC*, showing a shift from original pattern $C_1vC_2C_3$ to $C_1C_2vC_3$.

38.4. The perfective is formed with the *t*-infix, the basic function of which can be characterized as "effective" in the sense that a state is produced in someone or in something, whether it be caused by another or by himself / itself. This definition implies a functional congruence between the aspect-derivational -*t*- and the stem-derivational -*t*- (§41.20 ff.), notwithstanding their distinct structural planes. In other words, perfective originally conveys involvement of the acting subject, while preterite marks the simple past. Thus, e.g., the Neo-Babylonian preterite in PN$_1$ *ana* PN$_2$ *iddin* plainly means that "PN$_1$ has given to PN$_2$", but the perfective in ᶠPN$_3$ *kūm* ᶠPN$_4$ PN$_1$ *ana* PN$_2$ *ittadin* implies that "PN$_1$ has taken upon himself to give ᶠPN$_3$ instead of ᶠPN$_4$ to PN$_2$". Similarly, *mār šarri šipirti iltapra umma* means that "the king's son has issued the following writ", and not simply "has have it sent", *išpur*. Further synchronic and diachronic studies of verbal forms with infixed -*t*- are needed. The perfective is represented by the Assyro-Babylonian perfect (*y*)*iptaras*, "he has separated"; (*y*)*iptaqid*, "he has commanded"; (*y*)*irtapud*, "he has rushed". It is also attested in Palaeosyrian (e.g. *iš-tá-má* /*yištama'*/, "he has heard"), in Amorite (e.g. *ia-ab-ta-ḫa-ar-na* /*yabtaḫarna*/, "he has chosen us"), and in Ugaritic; e.g. *l'ištbm tnn*, "didn't I have muzzled the Dragon?" (KTU 1.3,III,40); *'imtḫṣ ksp 'itrṭ ḫrṣ*, "I have seized silver, acquired gold" (KTU 1.3,III, 46-47); *'an 'itlk*, "I myself have gone" (KTU 1.6,II,15).

As a rule, there is no formal difference in East and North Semitic between the preterite of the Gt-stem (§41.20) and the perfective of the basic stem. However, the distinction can be made on a contextual and syntagmatic basis. E.g. when the verb *maḫāṣu* governs a direct object, like in Old Assyrian *qātka imtaḫas*, "he has struck your hand", the form is an Assyro-Babylonian perfect, but when the same verb has a reciprocal connotation, as in the Old Akkadian dual *imtaḫṣā*, "they fought", the form can only be a preterite of the Gt-stem. The same analysis can be made in Ugaritic, where *'nt tmtḫṣ b-'mq*, "'Anat fought in the valley", contains a preterite of the Gt-stem, whereas *'imtḫṣ ksp* with a direct object means "I have seized / laid hands on silver", and obviously uses the perfective of the basic stem.

38.5. The imperfective is formed by a lengthened root, viz. by geminating the second consonant of a triconsonantal root. This aspect-derivational gemination signifies actuation in reference to the action, while the stem-derivational gemination expresses actuation in reference to the actor (§41.3: 2°). The imperfective is represented by the Old Akkadian and Assyro-Babylonian "present-future" *iparras, ipaqqid, irappud*, and by the Ethiopic *yəqattəl*, "he kills", "he will kill", a form which occurs not only in Ge'ez, but in modern Ethiopian languages as well. This imperfective is attested most likely also in Palaeosyrian, in Amorite, and in Ugaritic. Besides, its existence has to be assumed in Epigraphic South Arabian, since the imperfect of the Modern South Arabian goes apparently back to such a pattern (cf. §38.8); e.g. Mehri *yərōkəz* < *yarakkaz, "he stands upright"; Ḥarsūsi *yəlōbəd* < *yalabbad, "he shoots". Moreover, geminated imperfectives of the basic stem appear in early Andalusian Arabic, as reported by Pedro de Alcalá: *nihammí* [*niḥammī*] instead of *'aḥmī*, "I protect", *nixehéd* [*nišehhed*] instead of *'ašhad(u)*, "I certify", with the *ni*-prefix of the first person singular like in Maghrebine Arabic (§40.25). The source of such anomalous imperfective forms is to be looked for in South Arabian dialects brought to Spain in the 8th century A.D. by "Yemenite" tribesmen. This imperfective must have an Afro-Asiatic origin since its close cognate appears in Libyco-Berber (e.g. *yəlāmməd, ilāmməd*, or *irāmməd* with the change *l* > *r*, "he learns"), while the singular forms of the Bedja present seem to contain a dissimilated double consonant (e.g. *akantib* < *akattib, "I am writing").

38.6. The imperfective under consideration is documented in North Semitic. A Palaeosyrian incantation text from Ebla, e.g., has a form *i-ṭa-ḫa-ù* /*yiṭaḫḫawū*/, "they will come near", and Amorite proper names like *Ia-ma-at-ti-Èl* /*Yamatti'-'El*/, "El will protect", or *Ia-na-ab-bi-Èl* /*Yanabbi'-'El*/, "El will name", can hardly be explained without admitting the use of a *yaqattil* form, while the differences noticeable in Ugaritic verbs with first radical ' point to the use of a *yaqattul* (*iparras*) next to the *yaqtul* (*iprus*) and to the *yuqattil* (*uparris*) (§41.3). The available texts distinguish preterite forms like *y'iḫd* (*[*yīḫud*]) and *t'iḫd* (*[*tīḫud*]), "he/she took", or *y'uḫd* (*[*yuḫḫud*]) and *t'uḫd* (*[*tuḫḫud*]), "he/she held fast", from imperfectives like *y'aḫd* (*[*yaḫḫud*]) (KTU 4.44,28), "he takes", or *y'arš* (*[*yarriš*]) and *t'arš* (*[*tarriš*]), "he desires, you desire", or *t'asrn* (*[*tassirūn*]), "you will bind".

The frequent reference to the Ugaritic form *yqḥ* ("may he take"), allegedly incompatible with an imperfective corresponding to East Semitic *iparras*, fails distinguishing between a jussive *yiqqaḥ* and an imperfective *yilaqqaḥ, which influences the spelling of syllabic Ugaritian *i-le-qa-aš-šu-nu-ti*, "he will take them", instead of normal Babylonian *ilaqqē-šunūti*. One should refer also to fairly contemporaneous imperfectives from Emar which are clearly influenced by North Semitic; e.g. *e-ez-zi-ib-ka* /*e'ezzibka*/, "I shall dismiss you", instead of Middle Babylonian *ezzibka*, and occasional feminine forms like *te-er-ru-ub*, "she enters", *ta-al-la-ak*, "she goes", *tu-uš-ša-ab*, "she will stay", or *ki-i-me-e ... ta-lak*, "when ... she will go".

38.7.　While North Ethiopic — Ge'ez, Tigre, and Tigrinya — certainly uses the *yəqattəl* form with gemination of the second radical consonant, this consonant is generally not geminated in South Ethiopic which presents a pattern *yəqātəl*. However, despite the fact that some of these idioms, like East Gurage and Harari, are precisely languages of the non-geminating type, East Gurage dialects occasionally show the gemination of the second radical. Moreover, the South Ethiopic imperfect of Stem I.C/3 generally preserves the gemination of the second radical, contrary to the jussive where the gemination was not required by the system; e.g. Gafat *yədakkəm*, "he speaks", vs. *yädakəm*, "may he speak"; Amharic *yəmarrək*, "he takes prisoner", vs. *yəmark*, "may he take prisoner". Therefore, the South Ethiopic imperfect of Stems 1/A has very likely lost its gemination, so much the more so that North Ethiopic is, on the whole, closer to Proto-Ethiopic than the South Ethiopic group.

38.8.　The Modern South Arabian languages do not have the second radical consonant geminated in the imperfect. However, Śḥeri and Soqoṭri are again languages of the non-geminating type (cf. §41.4,6), while the non-gemination is compensated in Mehri and Ḥarsūsi by the lengthening of the preceding vowel (§38.5). In summing up the situation, one should say that the evidence points to an original imperfect *yəqattəl* / *yaqattal* in South Arabian, as well as in Ethiopic, although the close structural analogy between gemination and vowel lengthening allows of an allophone *yəqātəl* / *yaqātal*.

38.9.　Besides the *t*-infix and the lengthening of the root, the stative / permansive differs from the perfective and from the imperfective by the distribution of the actor affixes: they are all suffixed to the stative, while they appear as both prefixes and suffixes with the perfective and the imperfective.

b) Simplified Systems

38.10.　The purely "verbal" and aspectual categories were somewhat reduced in several Semitic languages, while changes in function and meaning also occurred. The perfective with *t*-infix is attested in East and

North Semitic, but it was supplanted in West Semitic by the preterite *yiqtul* / *yaqtul*, which in turn was superseded by the stative that acquired the meaning of a perfect without losing its original function. The perfective with *t*-infix has obviously appeared as redundant, since it referred to an action already accomplished and thus belonging to the past, expressed by the preterite. In fact, there is some parallelism between the "aspectual" notion of perfective and the "temporal" notion of past. And the difficulty of distinguishing past action and completion led to the disappearance of one of these categories. The second change was prompted by the parallelism between a situation existing at a determined moment and the situation resulting from an event anterior to the moment in question. This led to a further simplification of the verbal system. This last evolution was certainly on its way at the time of the Amarna correspondence and of the Ugaritic texts, in the 15th-13th centuries B.C. Although the old preterite was the regular narrative form in myths and epics, the stative appears already as a real perfect, at least sporadically (e.g. *'aḫd*, "he seized"; *'atwt*, "she came"). The question is whether this change goes back to Amorite or even to Palaeosyrian, as some authors believe. All Palaeosyrian cases cited refer to alleged perfect tenses of verbs *ultimae* or *mediae infirmae*, which can be explained in a different way; e.g. *Ba-na-a-ḫu* means "the brother is nice" rather than "the (divine) brother has created", and *Da-na*-LUGAL means "the king is powerful" rather than "the king has judged", with both *banā* and *danna* in the predicate state (§33.5; 40.3). The situation in Amorite is similar, and even *Ma-la-ak-ì-lí* can be interpreted either as a stative *malak*, "my god is king" (cf. Arabic *malaka*, "to be master"), or as a noun *mal'āk*, "messenger". There are, as it seems, no certain examples of the stative used as a real perfect before the later half of the second millennium B.C. As for East Semitic, only some Late Babylonian forms influenced by Aramaic may be considered as perfects; e.g. PN₁ *ma-ra-ṣu ḫal-liq ūmu 4* SÌLA ŠE.BAR *mandattašu* PN₂ *ušallam*, "(if) PN₁ (the pawned slave) will have fallen sick (or) will have escaped, PN₂ shall pay four litre of barley a day as his clearing". In Late Babylonian contracts, *ma-ḫi-ir* is often used in the sense "has received".

38.11. The old preterite preceded by *wa-*, "and", kept on acting as a narrative past tense, at least sporadically, in Hebrew (e.g. *way-yo'mer*, "and he said"), in Aramaic (e.g. *w-y'nny b'lšmyn*, "and Baalshamayn answered me"), in Moabite (e.g. *w-'š h-bmt z't*, "and I made this high place"), in Phoenician (e.g. *w-yp'l b-ḥlb [šl]m*, "and he made [pea]ce in

Aleppo"), in South Arabian (e.g. *w-yhtb mwy dhbhw*, "and he restored
the water-supply of his alluvial land"), and in Arabic (e.g. *darabahā ...
wa-yaqūlu*, "he struck her ... and said"). In Nabataean Arabic, the old
preterite is probably used also after *fa-*, as suggested by the Oboda
inscription: *fa-yaf'al lā fidā wa-lā 'atarā (p-yp'l l' pd' w-l' 'tr')*, "and
he acted neither for reward nor for favour". This narrative past tense
with the so-called "converted" imperfect was not used any more in
Mishnaic Hebrew, and biblical Dead Sea scrolls occasionally substitute
a suffixed form belonging to the contemporaneous spoken idiom.

38.12. The imperfective *iparras* / *yəqattəl* is not attested until now in
West Semitic languages, although an unconvincing attempt was made to
discover it in Hebrew on the basis of the orthography of the Qumrān
scrolls. This aspectual form was replaced by a new indicative *yaqtulu*,
developed from the jussive *yaqtúl* (§38.2) by adding an *-u*, which cannot
be completely independent from the *-u* of the Palaeosyrian and East
Semitic subjunctive (§39.2-3), and was already affixed at Mari to
preterite and imperfective forms without apparent change in their meaning and their function (§38.13). The development must have occurred
first in spoken dialects, in clauses where formal parataxis expressed logical hypotaxis (§55.1-8), thus justifying the hypercorrect use of a subjunctive marker, as examplified by the following sentence of a Byblos
letter: *a-na mi-nim qa-la-ta* (stative) *ù la-a ti-iq-bu* (jussive + *u*) *a-na
šàr-ri ù yu-wa-ši-ru-na* (jussive + *u* + energic *n*) *ṣāba pí-ṭá-ti*, "why do
you keep so silent that you do not say to the king that he should send the
bowmen?" (EA 71,10-14). This final vowel *-u* is preserved in Classical
Arabic, while its shedding is quite general in the other idioms, including
the Arabic vernaculars. However, the North Gurage dialects, which distinguish an imperfect for the main affirmative clause and an imperfect
for the subordinate clause, use a form of the *yəqat(tə)lu*-type in the main
clause , e.g. *yəsäbru*, "he breaks" or "he shall break", but *tisäbər < *tə-
yəsäbər*, "when he breaks".

38.13. The final *-u* added sometimes at Mari to verbs of main clauses
may result from an hypercorrect use of the subjunctive (e.g. ARM II,
136,23-26) but it most likely reflects occasional lapses of the scribes into
their native Amorite idiom in which the *-u* suffix must have taken root
(cf. §38.14). It certainly occurs with the preterite (e.g. *ú-ul aš-ku-un-nu*,
"I did not assign") and with the present-future (e.g. *be-lí i-ma-ar-ru-šu*,
"my lord will see it"). If so, we have evidence of the imperfective

yaqattalu and of the preterite *yaqtulu* in North Semitic. Further evidence is provided by Idrimi's autobiographical inscription from Alalakh (e.g. *ma-ti*[ki]*-ia u-ki-in-nu*, "I gave strength to my country") and by the Amarna correspondence with parallel examples of the preterite (*anumma iṣṣuru āl šarri*, "now, I did guard the king's city") and of the present-future (*anumma inaṣṣaru āla ša šarri*, "now, I shall guard the city of the king") in the same letter from Megiddo (EA 220,15-16.25-26). Besides, forms in *-u* are perhaps unveiled by Ugaritic literary texts where the final radical *'u* might characterize the singular preterite *yaqtulu* (e.g. *yml'u lbh bšmḫt*, "her heart was filled with joy"). However, this ending *-u* appears neither in proper names (e.g. *Ia-qub-Baʿal* /*Yaʿqub-Baʿal*/, "Baal has protected") nor in syllabic texts from Ugarit, and it seems therefore to have been an optional literary feature of the Ugaritic idiom, unless *yml'u*, e.g., stands simply for **yimlū* / **yamlū* (cf. §45.8).

38.14. The examples from Mari and from Alalakh, corroborated by the Amarna correspondence, by Classical Arabic, and by the Gurage dialects, testify nevertheless to the use of *-u* forms in main clauses. The bulk of the material is provided by Arabic that uses the indicative imperfect *yaqtulu* also in all kinds of subordinate clauses, except those that are final/consecutive or conditional. Besides, the situation in ancient Arabic dialects of the 6th - 7th centuries A.D., with Ḥidjazis using the indicative in *-u* where others employ the apocopate (cf. §39.14-18), suggests that the use of the marked indicative was dialectal or optional before the systematization introduced by Arab grammarians. The morpheme *-u* of the indicative may therefore be considered as a simple generalization of the *-u* suffix of subordinate clauses (§38.12; 39.3). This explanation is supported by the structural changes which had occurred in Semitic already in the third millennium B.C. By that time, a distinctive *-u* subjunctive had become superfluous, since its role was assumed by subordinate conjunctions that have developed in the course of time. As for the origin of the subjunctive in *-u* and of the Arabic subjunctive in *-a*, it has to be examined in the paragraphs dealing with moods (§39.4-6).

c) Transitivity — Intransitivity

38.15. A question related to aspects is the existence of certain morphological distinctions in the conjugation of active and stative, of transitive and intransitive verbs, especially in their basic stem since the meaning of the derived stems generally obliterates these fundamental semantic differences. The proper meaning of a transitive verb is "to perform an action" directly affecting another person or thing (e.g. "to kill"), whereas the intransitive verb either signifies an action which is complete in itself and affects the subject (e.g. "to lie"), or expresses the state of being in a certain condition (e.g. "to be pleased"). Authors often assume that this kind of distinction is indicated by the quality of the stem vowel which divides the Semitic verbs into three classes: the *a*-class, the *i*-class, and the *u*-class. This class distinction goes probably back to an Afro-Asiatic scheme, since it is attested also in Cushitic, e.g. in the prefix-conjugation of the "Sam" sub-group of Lowland East Cushitic (§2.11), especially in Rendille. The Semitic jussive is the verbal form which exhibits these differences at best; the "Sam" imperfect is added for comparison.

	a-Class	*i*-Class	*u*-Class
Ass.-Bab.	*ilmad*, "to learn"	*iqrib*, "to come near"	*irpud*, "to run"
Aramaic	*yilbaš*, "to dress"	*yiqrib*, "to come near"	*yiktub*, "to write"
Arabic	*yašrab*, "to drink"	*yaḥsib*, "to value"	*yanqud*, "to save"
Geʿez	*yəlbas*, "to dress"	*yəngər*, "to speak"	
"Sam"	*yaḥam*, "to eat"	*yagis*, "to kill"	*yamut*, "to die"

38.16.   In East Semitic and in West Semitic, most stative and intransitive verbs belong either to the *i*-class or to the *u*-class, but this distinction is not absolute and dialectal variants exhibit, e.g., *iqrab* next to *iqrib*, *islam* next to *islim* in Assyro-Babylonian, while intransitive verbs like Arabic *yaḏhab*, "to go away", or Hebrew *yigdal*, "to become great", always inflect like *a*-class verbs. Some verbs may be inflected according to two or even three classes without any semantic differences; e.g. Arabic *yadbaġ*, *yadbiġ*, *yadbuġ*, "to tan". In other cases, however, a change of class implies a modification in the meaning of the verb; e.g. Arabic *yafṣil*, "to separate"; *yafṣul*, "to depart". These class alternations must be distinguished from vocalic modifications resulting from the use of the passive voice, as in Arabic *yabtur*, "to cut", passive *yabtar*, "to be cut off"; *yanqud*, "to save", passive *yanqad*, "to be saved". The distinction of transitive and intransitive verbs is apparently somewhat clearer in Ethiopic, where the statistical data are inverted, viz. the *i*-class and *u*-class verbs came together in the mainly transitive *ə*-class, while the *a*-class consists of mainly intransitive verbs. The same situation occurs in some Chadic languages, as Migāma. However, there are Ethiopic verbs that are inflected according to two patterns. In conclusion, the stem vowel is neither predictable nor does it allow distinguishing transitive and intransitive verbs, although it introduces a relative morphological distinction between stative and active verbs. But this distinction has no direct bearing on the transitive or intransitive nature of active verbs. Its origin is not functional, as it seems: it is radicated in the $C_1C_2vC_3$ model of the root morphemes (§28.8).

38.17. Nevertheless, there is no doubt that the categories of transitive and intransitive are extremely important in any ergative language, and Semitic belonged originally to this linguistic type. In Semitic, this distinction was based mainly on the intransitive function of the basic stem (B/G), used with a subject in the non-active *a*-case, and the transitive function of the causative-factitive stems (D and/or Š), used with a subject in the ergative *u*-case (§40.16). However, a semantic development took place in an early phase of Proto-Semitic or even in Afro-Asiatic with the result that the basic stem of numerous Semitic verbs can be used both transitively and intransitively; e.g. Arabic *qariba r-raǧula*, "he approached the man", and *qariba r-raǧulu*, "the man came near". Similar cases occur also in other Afro-Asiatic languages, especially in Libyco-Berber; e.g. Tachelhit *imdl u-rgaz a-fruḫ*, "the man buried the child", and *imdl u-fruḫ*, "the child was buried". Besides, the basic stem of the historically attested languages contain exclusively transitive verbs as well. In consequence, the originally ergative character of Semitic was reduced mainly to the opposition of the active and non-active nominal components of the sentence (§32.1-4), since the predicate of a nominal clause — thus lacking any verbal form — may be inflected in -*a* under certain conditions like the object of a transitive verb. Therefore, the morphological distinction between transitive and intransitive verbs as such is no more essential in Semitic. It is the accomplished or unaccomplished aspect signified by the verbal form that is relevant.

38.18. Further changes in the West and South Semitic verbal system (§38.10) resulted in the course of the first millennium B.C. in a new scheme with two main morphological categories of the indicative: perfect and imperfect. There was no return to the basic "ergative" opposition of transitive to intransitive. The major distinction of category between the new perfect and the imperfect can be seen simply in terms of the aspectual contrast "accomplished" (perfect forms) / "unaccomplished" (imperfect forms). These categories imply a reference not to the absolute moment of speaking, but to any moment fixed in the utterance.

This is the main reason why these categories do not correspond to any particular tense of the temporal scheme which has been evolved in the Indo-European languages. Thus, e.g., perfect forms of verbs denoting feeling, thinking, speaking, acting must often be translated by a present, as Arabic *'alimtu*, "I know", *ḥalaftu*, "I swear". Instead, in a temporal clause introduced by *lammā* which in standard Arabic usage implies anteriority of the subordinate clause to the main sentence (§58.3), perfect forms may correspond to an English pluperfect, e.g. *fa-lammā qadima l-Ḥazraǧīyūna*, "when the Ḥazradjites had come". In temporal clauses referring to the future, like those introduced by *mā*, "as long as", the perfect should be translated by a future perfect; e.g. *mā dāma ḥayyan*, "as long as he will have been alive". Besides, the perfect preserved its original stative function, as in Arabic *'azza wa-ǧalla*, "he is mighty and great", or *laysa 'aḥadun 'afqara min ġaniyyin 'amina l-faqra*, "nobody is poorer than a rich man (if) he feels safe from poverty". As for the imperfect, it expresses unaccomplished actions in the past, present, and future. In the past, e.g., *fa-ṭālati š-šakwa wa-huwa yabkī 'aḥarra bukā'in*, "and the complaint took a long time, while he was crying bitterly". The imperfect is used naturally in clauses expressing finality and after verbs that denote setting in, discontinuing, wishing to, having power, being able to do, etc., e.g. *wa-ǧa'ala l-muslimūna ya'malūna*, "and the Moslems began working".

d) Modern Languages

38.19. While the "classical" verbal system of the Semitic languages is based on aspect, modern speech tends to found the verb inflection on the notion of time and to express it by means of "tenses". If we now turn to the tense formations which have been developed in some modern Semitic languages to express time relations in imitation of the western Indo-European tense scheme, we can see that these compound tenses are partly based an old formations which were used in the past to express particular aspects or situations and not time relations.

38.20. The pluperfect "he had written", etc., can be expressed in modern Arabic by using the perfect *kān*, "he was", with the perfect of another verb, e.g. *kān katab*, "he had written". This tense is related to Classical Arabic *kāna qad* or *qad kāna* followed by the perfect of another verb; e.g. *qad kāna ra'ā minka miṯla mā ra'aynā*, "he had already seen through you just as we have seen". As a matter of fact, *kāna* is a stative expressing a situation existing at the moment when "we saw" it and it does not shift the tense of the clause automatically to the pluperfect; thus: "he was already seeing through you just as we saw". A similar analysis explains the modern use of the perfect *kān* with the imperfect of another verb to express the European imperfect or past continuous "he was writing", *kān yəktub* (cf. §58.5). This compound tense goes back to Classical *kāna yafʿalu* which denotes a stable situation consisting in doing something; e.g. *kāna n-nabīyu yaʿūdu l-marīḍa*, "the prophet used to visit sick people". The duration in the past (past continuous) can be expressed also by the perfect of *kān* with the active participle, e.g. *kān kātib*, "he was writing" (§42.24). By using the imperfect *yəkūn* with the perfect of another verb, modern Arabic can express the future "he will write", *yəkūn katab*. This construction is used in Classical Arabic to signify a situation resulting from an action which will be accomplished in the future: e.g. *fa-nakūnu qad 'aḥaḏnā 'iwaḍan*, "then we shall already be in the situation of having taken an equivalent". The future sense can be expressed also by the participle *rāyiḥ*, "going", with the imperfect; e.g. *ana rāyiḥ asmaʿ*, "I am going to hear".

Authors generally assume that Syriac has created a pluperfect of the same type as Arabic by combining the auxiliary verb (*hǎ*)*wā*, "he was", with the preceding perfect of another verb; e.g. *de'mrēt* (*hǎ*)*wēt ləkōn*, "which I had said to you". In reality, however, the auxiliary does not alter the time reference of the verb in such constructions; e.g. *wīteb bāh wardā ʿamhōn bə-yammā wə-ʿal* (*hǎ*)*wā lə-Meṣrēn*, "and he boarded it (a ship) and sailed with them on the sea, and he entered Egypt". By using the imperfect *nehwē* with the participle of another verb, Syriac can express the future; e.g. *nehwē kāteb*, "he will write". These constructions are not operative in Neo-Aramaic (§42.18-22).

38.21. Additional morphs, other than verbs but acting as verb modifiers, are used in several modern Semitic colloquials to express time relations and aspects. In particular, various particles are prefixed or suffixed to verbal forms in order to express either the general present, or the continuous present denoting an action actually performed, or the future as opposed to the present. Only some examples can be given in the frame of this *Outline*.

38.22. In several Arabic dialects of the Arabian Peninsula and in Neo-Aramaic, a preverb *b(i)-* is employed to express the continuous present, but its use is extended to the general present in Syro-Palestinian and Cairene colloquials. In Eastern Arabian, instead, the imperfect with *b(i)-* indicates the future, usually with a volitive connotation; e.g. *bi-yruḥ*, "he will go", "he wants to go" (Kuwait). The same use is encountered in the Western Neo-Aramaic dialect of Ǧubb 'Adīn; e.g. *bi-yuḍmuḳ*, "he will sleep", "he wants to sleep". According to one opinion, the preverb *b(i)*- originated from the conjunction *baynā* which means "while" in Classical Arabic, but is used at Ṣan'a in phrases like *bayn-aktub*, "I am just writing". Another explanation considers *b(i)*- as the shortened form of *yibġi*, "he will", which is often used in Bedouin dialects and in Libya to signify an action that will be performed immediately. This construction parallels the Neo-Aramaic tense formed with the preverb *bit-* (§42.19) and the widespread Indo-European use of an auxiliary verb expressing desire to form a future tense (e.g. "he will do"), but it cannot serve as an explanation of the preverb *b(i)*- marking a present tense. Besides, both attempts to explain this *b(i)*- seem to be undermined by the regular use of a preverb *b*- in the Qatabanic indicative imperfect; e.g. *kḍm 'l s¹knw w'l bys¹knwn*, "because they did not decree and will not decree". Although the earliest Neo-Arabic instances of the *b*-imperfect date from the 9th century A.D., this formation must be linked to the earlier Qatabanic use which exactly parallels most Syro-Palestinian colloquials: the *b*- is prefixed to the indicative imperfect (§38.23), but not to the jussive or in some other way not-indicative; e.g. Qatabanic *wl ylṣq*, "let him prosecute"; Ḥawrāni vernacular *la teftaḥ(š)*, "don't open". An explanation based on the preposition *bi*- cannot be discarded if one takes some nominalizations into account, like Classical Arabic *'amara bi-qatlihī*, "he ordered his killing", that may have prompted, in turn, an innovation of the imperfect. In any case, the Neo-Aramaic preverb *bi*- is the common Semitic preposition *b*-, since it governs an original infinitive (§38.23; 42.21).

38.23. In Arabic colloquials, the preverb *b(i)*- is prefixed to the imperfect, e.g. Damascene *byəktob*, "he writes"; *btəktob*, "she writes"; *byəktbū*, "they write", etc., but *mnəktob*, "we write", with the partial assimilation *bn > mn*. In Eastern Neo-Aramaic, instead, the particle is prefixed to the infinitive followed by the preposition *l* with a pronominal suffix, in accordance with the Neo-Aramaic verbal system (§42.21), e.g. *bi-ptāḥā-lē*, "he is opening"; *bi-ptāḥā-lā*, "she is opening"; etc.

38.24. The particle *k*- is used in other dialects with the same function. It derives from the verb *kāna / kūn*, "to be", and is vocalized *kū-* (< *kūn*) in Anatolia, *kā-* (< *kān*) in the Maghrib, and *kī-* (< *kīn*) in Neo-Aramaic. In Arabic colloquials, it is used with the imperfect and serves to express the continuous present, e.g. *ka-niktib*, "I am writing". In Neo-Aramaic, instead, it is prefixed to the active participle, e.g. *ki-pātiḫ*, "he is open-ing"; *ki-pātḫā*, "she is opening"; *ki-pātḫī*, "they are opening". The place of the Arabic negative *mā* in Mesopotamian *qəltu*-dialects deserves a special mention. It may be placed either before or after the verb modifier *k-*; e.g. **mə**-*kišrab* in the Irbil dialect, but *kū-**mišrab*** at 'Aqra, "he is not drinking".

38.25. In most Ethiopian languages, the imperfect expresses the present and the future, thus in Ge'ez, in Tigre, in Amharic, in Argobba, in Harari, in Gafat, in East and North Gurage. Instead, in Tigrinya and in West Gurage dialects, the present is signified by the simple imperfect, while the future is expressed by the imperfect with various affixes. A similar development can be observed nowadays in the Mansa' dialect of Tigre. There is also a noticeable tendency, especially in Tigrinya and in Amharic, to establish tenses expressing continuous actions either in the present ("I am writing") or in the past ("I was writing").

38.26. The modern North Ethiopian languages have developed several compound tenses, especially in order to distinguish the present from the future, the simple present or past from the continuous present or past. In the Mansa' Tigre of today the future tense tends to be expressed more and more by the preposition *'əgəl*, "for, to", followed by the jussive and by the copulative pronoun *tu*, "he (is)" (§49.19); e.g. *fağər Baṣə' 'əgəl nigis tu*, "tomorrow we shall go to Massawa". Instead, the imperfect + *halla* expresses the present continuous; e.g. *ḥəna hədāy nətfarrar hallena*, "(only) we are going out to the wedding". In a past context, the imperfect + *'ala* expresses the past continuous; e.g. *kaləb 'əb gabay ləs'e 'ala*, "a dog was running on the road". Other compound tenses are used as well with the imperfect, the perfect, and the participle. Tigrinya exhibits a paral-lel development: whereas the old imperfect expresses the general present (e.g. *yəsäbbər*, "he breaks"), the future tense is formed by the particle *kə-*prefixed to the imperfect and by the copulative old pronoun *'əyyu*, "he (is)"; e.g. *kisäbbər* (< *kə-yəsäbbər*) *'əyyu*, "he will break". Instead, the imperfect + *allo* expresses the present continuous; e.g. *yəsäbbər-allo*, "he is breaking". In a past context, the imperfect + *näyru* or *näbärä* expresses the past continuous; e.g. *yəsäbbər näyru / näbärä*, "he was breaking". The gerund (§42.12) enters in the composition of other compound tenses.

38.27. In West Gurage dialects, there are two ways of expressing the future: either the imperfect is followed by *-te / -kʷe*, or the jussive/subjunctive is followed by *-šä* / *-se*. Thus, e.g., Chaha *yəräḵəb* means "he finds", whereas "he will find" is signified either by the suffixed imperfect *yəräḵəbte* or by the suffixed jussive *yənkäbšä*. It would appear that the jussive with *-šä* / *-se* expresses certainty, while the imperfect with *-te* / *-kʷe* implies doubt or simple intention.

38.28. Amharic uses the auxiliary verb *älla*, "he is", to form the imperfect of the main clause, and it combines it with the gerund to form the present perfect. Besides, Amharic developed a past continuous and a past perfect or pluperfect by using the verb *näbbär(ä)*, "he was", with the simple imperfect and with the gerund. This leaves Amharic with five tenses used in main positive clauses:

1° Imperfect. The simple imperfect expresses the present and the future in the main negative clause and in subordinate clauses, both affirmative and negative. The compound imperfect with the auxiliary verb *allä* > *all* expresses the present, the future, and the future perfect in the main affirmative clause: *yənägr* or *yənägər*, *yənägral*, "he speaks, he is speaking, he will speak".

2° Perfect. The perfect normally expresses the past and may also express the pluperfect. With certain verbs, the perfect may express the present, especially when the action occurs at the moment of speaking: *näggära*, "he spoke, he has spoken, he had spoken".

3° Past continuous. The simple imperfect followed by a frozen or a conjugated form of *näbbär(ä)* expresses a continuous, durative or habitual action in the past: *yənägər näbbär(ä)*, "he was speaking, he was used to speak".

4° Present perfect. The compound gerund, formed by the combination of the gerund (§42.12) with the auxiliary verb *allä* > *all*, expresses a past action the outcome of which continues into the present: *nägrʷall*, "he has spoken".

5° Past perfect. The combination of the gerund with *näbbär(ä)* expresses the pluperfect or past perfect: *nägro näbbär(ä)*, "he had spoken".

In main volitive and negative sentences, the jussive *yəngär* is used instead of form 1, and form 2 serves as the negative for tenses 2 and 4.

C. Moods

39.1.   One can distinguish five moods in Semitic languages: the indicative, which was initially unmarked, two types of the so-called subjunctive, the ventive or allative, the jussive with the energetic. Except for the jussive, to which the so-called apocopate or apocopated imperfect of Classical Arabic and of Hebrew is closely related, these moods are all characterized by suffixes. It is also possible to consider as moods the paradigm that comprises optative or precative forms, and the one which comprises the vetitive or prohibitive forms. These, however, are prefixed and hence structurally differ from the moods marked by a suffix.

39.2.   The indicative is unmarked in Palaeosyrian, in Old Akkadian, and in Assyro-Babylonian, but a suffix -*u* seems to appear in Amorite, in the Amarna correspondence, and perhaps in Ugaritic, at least with some prefix-conjugations (§38.13). The same suffix is attested in Classical Arabic and in North Gurage dialects (§38.12). There are good reasons to believe that this marked indicative originated from a generalization of the -*u* ending of the subjunctive which denoted subordinate clauses (§38.14; 39.3) and is functionally identical, to some extent, with the jussive.

39.3.   The subjunctive or "relative" is by definition the mood or form of verbs in clauses which are subordinate to another clause and introduced by a conjunction or a relatival antecedent. The subjunctive suffix is generally -*u* in Palaeosyrian, in Old Akkadian, and in Assyro-Babylonian, while the ending -*a*, which occurs in Old Akkadian and in Palaeosyrian subordinate clauses, may simply be the ventive suffix without mimation (§39.7), for a verb with a ventive suffix does not take the subjunctive suffix. The so-called "subjunctive" ending -*ni* occurring in the Assyrian dialect is not a mood ending, but an enclitic indicating the end of a dependent clause; it can be added to the subjunctive, to the ventive, and to the pronominal suffixes of a verb. The enclitic -*na* occurring in dialectal Old Babylonian may have the same grammatical function.

39.4.   We can assume that the -*u* suffix of the subjunctive derives from the -*u* ending of the ergative-instrumental case in nominal constructions (§32.1ff.) which historically preceded the appearance of formally subordinate clauses. The use of the same marking with the verb must imply that an analogy was perceived between the ergative and the subordinate clause. This is understandable if *-u* was suffixed at first to verbs of clauses which were situating the main action in operational circumstances of cause, space, and time (§57-58). It is remarkable, in any case, that Classical Arabic uses the *-u* imperfect precisely with these categories of subordinate clauses, whereas the apocopated imperfect, the *-a* subjunctive, and the energetic appear mainly in other subordinate clauses.

39.5. The Palaeosyrian and East Semitic subjunctive, which is the subordinate form of the preterite, of the stative, of the perfect, and of the present-future, cannot be equated with the Arabic subjunctive in *-a* which is a marked form of the jussive expressing wish, expectation, finality, or consequence after well determined conjunctions. It is used in the classical language after *fa-, kay-, li-*, "so that", *'aw*, "unless"; e.g. (*'i*)*ġfir lī yā Rabbi fa-'adhula l-ğannata*, "forgive me, O! my Lord, so that I may enter in the paradise!" The subjunctive is also used after *lan*, but phrases like *lan yaf'ala*, "he will not do", or *lan yazūraka 'abadan*, "he will never visit you", should not be understood as statements and negations, e.g., of (*sawfa*) *yaf'alu*, "he will do". They signify that one does not foresee, does not expect that "he will do" or "will pay a visit". Also other conjunctions, like *'an* (*'allā* < *'an-lā*) and *ḥattā*, "so that", may govern the subjunctive in certain circumstances, especially in the post-classical language; e.g. *wazannī yā bn-a l-'Arwā 'an ta'ūda*, "I presume, O! son of Arwa, that you will come back". Modern colloquials no longer distinguish the subjunctive. In the pre-classical language, instead, the subjunctive occurs sporadically also after *wa-*; e.g. *yā laytanā nuraddu wa-lā nukaḏḏiba bi-'āyāti Rabbinā*, "would God we were taken back (from hell), so that we might not contest the signs of our Lord".

39.6. Like in pre-Classical Arabic, this subjunctive in *-a* is used in Old Canaanite and in Hebrew after the conjunction *wa-* to express finality or consequence, but it is called "indirect cohortative" in the grammars of Hebrew; e.g. *yuballiṭ ardašu u anaṣṣara āl kittišu* (EA 74,55-56), "may he (the Pharaoh) keep his servant in life so that I may guard his faithful city"; *mī yittēn 'et- hā-'ām hazze bə-yādī wə-'āsīrā 'et-'Ăbīmelek*, (Judg. 9,29), "who will give this people in my hand that I might get rid of Abimelech?". This subjunctive in *-a* alternates in the Amarna correspondence with the East Semitic ventive, and its particular use with expressions of wish or expectation, especially in the first person singular, leaves little doubt that the West Semitic subjunctive in -*a* is but a ventive or allative, with some distinctive syntactical features. The directive *a*-morpheme is attested in Palaeosyrian (e.g. the Ur-III name *Tu-ra-*ᵈ*Da-gan /Tūr-a-Dagān/*, "Return, Dagan!", from Mari) and there is no need, therefore, to have recourse to an East Semitic borrowing to explain the -*a* suffix (§39.7).

39.7. If this interpretation is correct, the ventive or allative is not unique to East Semitic. This mood originally indicated motion toward the speaker or the focus of action, but very soon also signified a motion coming from the speaker or the focus of action. It is characterized by the afformative -*a* which is believed to have originated from the pronominal dative suffix of the first person singular, e.g. *illik*, "he came", *illikam*, "he came here". However, the historical process may have been in the contrary direction: it is the Afro-Asiatic directive morpheme, which indicates that action takes place in favour of someone or is directed toward a specific end, that probably gave rise to the dative suffix "to me", -*am*. The mimation can be missing, even in Old Akkadian, e.g. *šu a-na* PN *a-ti-na*, "(flour) that I gave away to PN". Since subjunctive and ventive suffixes are mutually exclusive, this verb *attina* with the ventive suffix -*a* does not take the subjunctive suffix, although it belongs to a subordinate relative clause.

There is a conspicuous analogy between the ventive/allative suffix -*a* and the "benefactive" suffix -*o* / -*oy* of Lowland East Cushitic, in particular of the "Sam" sub-group. This suffix probably derives from -**a*, since it appears as -*da* after verbs in plural, and it characterizes actions which profit to the logical subject or affect it in one or the other way. Boni has retained this suffix as a productive morpheme, the function of which appears e.g. in *fíl*, "to comb", and *fíl-o*, "to comb one's self"; *káàd*, "to buy", and *kád-o*, "to buy for one's self". However, the East Semitic suffix appears as -*im* after the -*í* ending of the 2nd pers. fem. sing. (e.g. *šūbilīm*, "send in!") and as -*nim* after the -*ū* termination of the plural (e.g. *ublūnim*, "they brought in"). This positional allomorph -*im* strengthens, in its turn, the similarity between the afformative of the ventive/allative and the "destinative" verbal extension -**in* reconstructed for Proto-Chadic. This morpheme, which is suffixed to the verbal stem, was used "to indicate that the action of a verb was destined for, done for the benefit of, or otherwise affected or pertained to someone"; it "would thus have been used with motion verbs to indicate simple action in the direction of the speaker" (P. Newman). In other words, a verb of motion with the "destinative" -**in* suffix would constitute a kind of pre-dative verb form, thus enhancing the proposed interpretation of the East Semitic ventive/allative, which is paralleled also in the Bantu languages by the verbal forms with the directive -*äl*- affix; e.g. Kwena *ḫu-rút-**äl**-á*, "to be teaching for", Sotho *ho-lúl-**äl**-á*, "to be sitting for someone, to be waiting".

39.8. The energetic denotes a strong wish rather than an emphatic asseveration or prohibition, and it is used in this way also in the protasis of conditional sentences and in interrogative sentences.. It is characterized in Classical Arabic by the endings *-anna*, *-an*, and *-ā* in pause: *yafaʿlanna / yafʿalan / yafʿalā*. These endings are all added to the "short" jussive and they are generally introduced by the optative proclitic *la-* (§39.13) in affirmative sentences; *ḥalafa la-yaqtulanna*, "he swore that he will try to kill"; *la-yaqūlunna*, "may they speak at last"; *la-tarawunna*, "you will well see". No proclitic is used in a sentence introduced either by the negative *lā* or by *wa-*, like *fa-lā taḥsabanna llāha muḥlifa waḥdihi rusulahu*, "so do not try to imagine God as a breaker of his promise concerning his envoys" (Qurʾān 14,48/47); *layta šiʿrī wa-ʾašʿuranna* …, "would I have known, and I shall well come to know …". These semantic connotations of the form appear also in conditional sentences introduced by *ʾimmā*, where the energetic signifies a desirable possibility and is thus comparable with forms in *-an* of Modern South Arabian (§39.9): *ʾimmā tarayanna mina l-bašari aḥadan fa-qūli* …, "if you happen to see a human being, say …"; *wa-ʾimmā taḥāfanna min qawmin ḥiyānatan* …, "if you should fear treason from people …". This mood, with its various functions, occurs already in Old Canaanite, where it is characterized, as a rule, by the ending *-un(n)a*; e.g. *ù yu-wa-ši-ru-na*, "that he should send" (EA 71,13). It corresponds exactly to the so-called "direct cohortative" of Biblical Hebrew, which uses the suffixes *-anna* (e.g. *ʾāsuranna*, written *ʾsrh-n*ʾ, "I should go across") or *-ā* (e.g. *ʾēləkā*, "I should go").

The energic in *-in* or *-ina* is the usual form of the jussive in the Agaw dialects of the Qemant-Qwara group; e.g. *wasin*, "let him hear!"; *anät alšina*, "may you sustain us!"

39.9. The suffix *-n* of the energetic is attested also in Phoenician (e.g. *yqṣn*, "may they perish"; *yšʿn*, "they shall draw") and in Aramaic (e.g. *ʾl tlqḥn*, "you may not take", in the 2nd pers. sing.: TAD III, C1.1,167), and *-ən* is the comparable suffix in Mehri and Śḥeri, used only in sentences involving unreal conditions (e.g. Mehri *yəslēmən*, "he would be safe"). The *-n* imperfect of ancient South Arabian occurs in jussive and subordinate clauses of all kinds (e.g. Sabaic *ʾl tʿyrn*, "don't abuse", sing.), including relative clauses (e.g. Minaic *wkl ḏ yqnyn*, "and all what he might acquire"), but there is a large number of controversial cases (e.g. Sabaic *wyḥmrhmw*, "and may he grant them"), which might indicate either that the use of *-n* was optional, or that *-n* could be assimilated to the consonant of the following pronominal suffix, or that -*an* was sometimes reduced to -*ā* like the Arabic pausal form and the Hebrew direct cohortative in -*ā*, and therefore had no graphic expression in these cases.

A particular problem is raised by the double -*nn* of the Sabaic dual and plural -*n* imperfect (e.g. *yqnynn*, "they may acquire"). Since the Qatabanic simple imperfect ends in -*wn* (*yf'lwn*, "they will make"), one can assume that -*n* was also the original ending of the Sabaic plural imperfect and that this -*n* was preserved before the energetic suffix -*an*(*na*), thus -*ūnan*(*na*).

39.10. The energetic is attested also in North Semitic. Its use in Ugaritic has long been recognized, although the interpretation of particular examples is sometimes open to question. The suffix -*an* or -*anna* is certainly used in "cohortative" cases like *'atbn 'ank w-'anhn* (KTU 1.17,II,12-13), "may I too sit down and be at ease", or *'iqr'an 'ilm n'mm* (KTU 1.23,23), "may I invoke the gracious gods". But the form in -*ā* is probably employed as well, as suggested by the parallel passage *'iqr'a 'ilm n'mm* (KTU 1.23,1) and by the phrase *yqr'a mt b-npš ystrn ydd b-gngnh* (KTU 1.4,VII,47-49), "may Mōt cry out from his throat, may the Beloved hide in his inwards", where the syntactic status of the two verbs *yqr'a* and *ystrn* is absolutely the same. Although the energetic does not appear in Amorite proper names, the Mari forms *iškunanna* and *imḫuranna* in subordinate clauses may reflect the native Amorite idiom of the scribes using the energetic ending -*anna*.

39.11. The origin of the energetic mood is linked to the element *n* of the suffix, to the alternate forms -*n* and -*a* in Ugaritic (§39.10), as well to the frequent use of this mood with verbs of motion (e.g. Hebrew *nēləkā*, "let us go!"). These convergent data seem to indicate that the energetic goes formally back to the ventive/allative, but semantically has optative or prospective connotations. It denotes especially either a strong desire of the speaker (e.g. Arabic *wa-'aš'uranna*, "I shall surely come to know"), or a desirable possibility (e.g. *'immā tarayanna*, "if you happen to see"), or even a predictable fatality (e.g. Hebrew *'āmūtā*, "I shall have to die").

39.12. Ethiopic and Modern South Arabian distinguish two moods: the indicative of the enunciative clause and the jussive or subjunctive of the volitive clause. The evidence of Mehri and Ḥarsūsi indicates that the subjunctive of Modern South Arabian formally corresponds to the ancient *yaqtúl* jussive (e.g. *hīs yərkēz*, "when he stands upright"), and the same usage is attested in Geʻez which has two jussive patterns: *yəqtəl* for the mainly transitive verbs and *yəqtal* for the intransitive ones (cf. §38.16). Only one jussive pattern occurs in Tigre, viz. *ləqtal*, which is used as a volitive mood; e.g. *barhat təgbaʼ*, "let there be light". It is found also in interrogative clauses, when the question is either rhetorical, or implying a doubt, or requiring an answer in the imperative; e.g. *mi ʼide*, "what should I do?". Besides, the jussive preceded by the conjunction *ʼəgəl*, "so that", appears in subordinate clauses; e.g. *ʼəgəl təššayam*, "so that you will be appointed"; *ʼəgəl ligis waggəbbo*, lit. "so that he should go, is his duty", i.e. "to go is his duty". Nowadays, the phrase *ʼəgəl* + jussive + *tu* is used in Mansaʻ Tigre as an expression of futurity without any modal connotation (§38.26). In most South Ethiopian languages, the simple imperfect (e.g. *yəqätl* or *yəqätəl* in Amharic) is used for the subordinate clause (and also for the negative clause), while the compound imperfect, composed of the simple imperfect and of a variable "auxiliary", is used for the main clause. Amharic does not use the jussive in subordinate clauses.

39.13.   In several languages, the volitive or injunctive forms of the verb are composed by prefixing a proclitic to the basic verbal pattern. The resulting paradigm can be considered as a kind of mood. Widespread is the use of the proclitic *lu-* / *li-* / *la-*, especially with the third person, to express the optative or precative (§38.2; 40.18,23,30). Prefixing of the proclitic *l-* to a verb occasionally entails graphic deletion of imperfect *y-*; e.g. Sabaic *lhṣlḥnn* < *l+yhṣlḥnn*, "may they grant prosperity". The vetitive or prohibitive is formed by prefixing *ay* or one of its derivatives (§38.2). There is no doubt that this prohibitive particle is originally identical with the interrogative *ʼay* (§36.59). The negative adverbs *lā*, *ʼal*, *ul* cannot be considered as proclitics (§47.8), even when they are attached to the verbal form. A similar construction of the volitive is attested in Libyco-Berber with the particle *ad-* / *at-* / *aḏ-* and the jussive; e.g. Tarifit *at-təksiḏ*, "you should take"; *aḏ-yəksi*, "one should draw"; *yəruḥ aḏ-yəġar*, "he left so that he might study".

39.14.   The so-called "apocopate" or "apocopated" imperfect in Classical Arabic and in Hebrew is a shortened form of the prefix-conjugation corresponding to East Semitic *iprus*. It is characterized by the absence of the indicative *-u* suffix in Arabic, and by the shortening or the loss of the final long vowel in verbs with a third weak radical, the so-called verbs *ultimae infirmae*. The historical appreciation of these peculiarities must reckon with the inflection of the verbs *ultimae infirmae* in Assyro-Baby-lonian. Now, their inflection precisely exhibits the phonotactic feature that length is dropped in absolute final position and that vocalic ending may drop altogether, as if the stem itself was shortened; e.g. preterite *ibni* instead of *ibnī*, "he built" (root *bny*); present-future *ibanni* instead of *ibannī*, "he will build"; *bān* instead of *bāni* < *bānī*, "building" (participle). The analogy suggests that Arabic and Hebrew apocopate reflects an earlier stage of West Semitic, documented already by the Amarna correspondence (e.g. *ia-aq-bi*, "may he speak") and traces of which were later systematized by the early Arab grammarians and by the Masoretes (cf. §43.12).

39.15. This interpretation is confirmed in Hebrew by the fact that apocopated forms are used as jussive and in *wayyiqṭol* (§38.11), i.e. when the original function of *yiqtul* is preserved. The variations in the spelling, e.g., of the verb *ṣwy*, "to order", — *yṣw* and *yṣwh*, *'ṣw* and *'ṣwh*, *ṣw* and *ṣwh*, — gave rise to different Masoretic vocalizations, — *yəṣaw* and *yəṣawwe*, *'ăṣaw* and *'ăṣawwe*, *ṣaw* and *ṣawwē*, — although the differences are purely graphic or dialectal. They reflect a spelling and a pronunciation either expressing the final short -*e* < -*i* (< *ī*) and indicating it by the vowel letter -*h*, or dropping it altogether.

39.16. The situation is similar in Classical Arabic where the jussive is operative only in determinate kinds of syntagms. It preserves the old volitive function of the *yaqtúl* after *li-* (inclusive *wal-*, *fal-*, *wa-li*, *fa-li*) and after the negative *lā*; e.g. *li-ya'ti*, "he should come!"; *li-yaf'al*, "he should do!"; *lā ya'ti*, "he should not come!"; *lā yaf'al*, "he should not do!". Besides, it preserves the old function of the jussive in asyndetic final / consecutive clauses following an imperative; e.g. *kallimī rasula llāhi yukallim*, "speak to God's envoy (in order that) he would speak"; *'irḥam turḥam*, "have pity (in order that) you will be pitied". As for the apocopate expressing negative statements after *lam*, "not", and *lammā*, "not yet", and real conditions after the particle *'in*, "if", its function exactly parallels the one of East Semitic preterite, and it is to be considered likewise as reflecting an earlier stage of the language. E.g. *lam ya'ti*, "he didn't come", and *lammā ya'ti*, "he didn't yet come" (cf. §58.4), parallel East Semitic *lā ibni*, "he didn't build"; *'in lam yabraḥ lam 'arḍa*, "if he does not depart, I shall not be satisfied", parallels Assyrian *šumma atta lā taqbi tamuat*, "if you do not tell, you will die".

39.17. In some ancient Arabic dialects, the apocopate was used also after *'an*, "that", and *lan* (< *lā-'an*) instead of the classical subjunctive, and after *law*, "if, when", instead of the indicative in *-u*. We can assume that those dialects didn't have the subjunctive and the indicative in *-u*. Thus in subordinate clauses they employed the jussive. On the other hand, in some categories of negative clauses, the old *lam-yaqtul* and *lammā-yaqtul* continued to be used to express the preterite, just like the *wayyiqṭol* in Hebrew. In Ḥidjazi dialects, instead, the indicative in *-u* was operational in cases where others used the apocopate. The grammatical analysis made by Arab philologists on a synchronic level should in fact be reinterpreted in both a diachronic and synchronic perspective.

39.18. In modern Arabic colloquials, the apocopated jussive is widely used without the particle *li-*; e.g. *Allah yarḍi 'alayk*, "Allah befriend you!"; *yuḫzi l-'ayn 'annak*, "may he put the (evil) eye to shame before you"; *Allah yakūn ma'ak wa-yaḥmīk*, "be Allah with you and may he protect you!".

39.19. The following branching diagram of tenses and aspects summarizes the presentation of the common Semitic development of basic verbal forms in the "classical" languages:

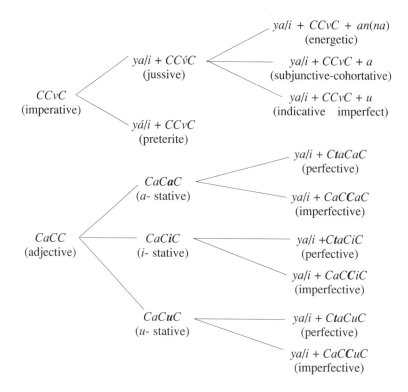

D. Actor Affixes

40.1. The actor affixes or personals specify person, gender, and number. They appear as suffixes with the stative and the imperative, both as prefixes and suffixes with the derived forms where person is designated by prefix morphs, gender and number by suffix morphs. In consequence, two types of paradigmatic sets determine the two types of conjugations: the suffix-conjugations and the prefix-suffix-conjugations, usually called prefix-conjugations. While the actor affixes of the suffix-conjugations go back basically to a form of pronominal suffixes of the noun, the prefixed personals are survivals of pronouns once separate, but later agglutinated to the verbal base. Remembering always the gaps in our knowledge and the dangers inherent in any argumentation from analogy, we can use the evidence supplied not only by important languages of the Niger-Congo family, but also by Hausa which expresses the personals by separate pronouns that precede the verb (§36.1). Whereas prefixed Semitic personals are not fused with morphemes indicating aspect and tense, like in Hausa, they preserve clear traces of case inflection (§40.16).

Fig. 28. The square of fountains at Ghadames, in 1845/6.

a) Suffix-Conjugation

40.2. In the paradigmatic set of the suffix-conjugation of the stative, the hyphen (—) indicates that there is no marking, as in the standard form of the third person masculine singular. The Ge'ez paradigm can serve also for Tigrinya. The following paragraphs (§40.3-12) will offer some observations on this table.

	*Proto-Semitic	East Semitic	Ugaritic	Hebrew	Aramaic
Sing.					
3 m.	—	—	—	—	—
f.	-at	-at	-t	-ā	-at
2 m.	-ka / -ta	-āt(a/i)	-t	-tā	-t
f.	-ki / -ti	-āti	-t	-t	-tī
1	-ku	-āk(u)	-t	-tī	-et
Dual					
3 m.	-ā	-ā	—		
f.	-atā	-tā	-t		
2	-kā (?) / -tanā (?)		-tm		
1	-kāya / -nāya		-ny		
Plur.					
3 m.	-ū	-ū	—	-ū	-ū
f.	-ā	-ā	—	-ū	-ū
2 m.	-kan(u) / tanu	-ātun(u)	-tm	-tem	-tūn
f.	-kin(a) /-tina	-ātin(a)	-tn	-ten	-tēn
1	-na	-ān(u/i)	?	-nū	-nā

40.3. The stative, which became also a perfect (§38.10), has a third person masculine singular in -a in Classical Arabic and in Ethiopic, also in some personal names occurring in Palaeosyrian (e.g. *Qá-ma-Da-mu*, "Damu is standing"), Old Akkadian (e.g. *Ìl-ba-na*, "the god is beautiful"), and Amorite (e.g. *Ṭa-ba-Èl*, "El is good"). Since the stative essentially represents the conjugation of a noun (§38.3), either substantive or adjective, this -a is the mark of the predicate state of the noun (§33.5), which became a mark of the perfect through the participial predicate as in *Qāma-Da'mu*. This may be the correct explanation of the few forms with final -a in the Amarna correspondence, as *damqa*, "is good", while the bulk of the material shows no -a; e.g. *ša-pár*, "he sent"; *du-ak*, "he killed". This suffix is generally believed to belong to the normal inflection of the Ugaritic stative/perfect because of forms like *nš'a* which are vocalized by some authors **naša'a*, "he lifted up". However, the syllabic spelling of Ugaritic proper names shows no -a ending in the stative/perfect (e.g. *Ba'al-ma-lak*, "Baal is king") and, in any case, the general trend in Semitic elides the final ' and lengthens the vowel (**našā*; cf. §27.24), which is indicated by '*a* (§19.8; 45.8). The assumption that the vowel *a/ā* linking the pronominal suffix to the stative/per-

Cl. Arabic	Coll. Arabic	Sabaic	Mehri	Ge'ez	Amharic
-a	—	—	—	-a	-ä
-at	-at / et	-t	-ōt	-at	-äčč
-ta	-t / -it	-k	-k	-ka	-h, -k
-ti	-ti	?	-š	-ki	-š
-tu	-t / -it	?	-k	-ku	-hu, -ku
-ā		-y	-ō		
-atā		-ty	-tō		
-tumā		?	-ki		
		?	-ki		
-ū	-u	-w	-aw-	-u	
-na	-in / -u	-n / -y	—	-ā	-u
-tum	-tu	?	-kəm	-kəmmu	
-tunna	-tin / -tu	?	-kən	-kən	-aččəhu
-nā	-na	?	-ən	-na	-(ə)n

fect in Hebrew (e.g. *qəṭālanī*, "he killed me") is a residue of the ancient
-*a* ending is also questionable, since the same vowel appears in Assyro-
Babylonian with the preterite (e.g. *iṣbatanni*, "he seized me"). Judging
from the Greek transcription of Pre-Islamic North Arabian names the
third person masculine singular of the Old Arabic perfect did not end in
-*a*, and the Classical form is therefore based on dialects having connections with South Semitic, where the -*a* predicative had become a firm
element of the stative/perfect, at least in Ethiopic. Only auxiliary verbs
and proper names may lack this -*a* or its equivalent -*o* (Soddo, Gogot);
e.g. Harari *ḥal*, "there is"; Amharic *näbbär*, "he was"; *Šäwa räggäd*,
"Shoa trembled".

Aramaic names in cuneiform script, like *Si-'-pa-rak-ka* /*Ši'-barak*/, "the
Moon-god has blessed", or ᵈIM-*ba-rak-ka* /*Hadad-barak*/, "Hadad has blessed",
do not exhibit a termination -*a*, as this can be seen in parallel names; e.g. *Še-er-*
ba-rak-ki /*Šehr-barak*/, "The Moon-god has blessed"; *Bé-il-ba-rak-ki* /*Be'əl-*
barak/, "Baal has blessed". The final signs -*ka* or -*ki* are phonetic complements
indicating that the penultimate sign is to be read *rak*, not *šal*, another value
attested in the same period.

40.4.   The feminine ending in *-t* corresponds to the feminine morpheme
of the noun (§30.1-2). In Hebrew and in Phoenician, the original ending
-t is preserved before pronominal suffixes, while the Amharic *-ačč*
results from the palatalization of *-ati*, a form with a final *-i* which
appears in some Gurage dialects (*-ätti* in main clauses of Soddo and
Gogot) and, as an euphonic vowel, in Harari. What is not generally
known is that a similar formation is encountered in dialectal Neo-Babylonian (e.g. *lu-ú ḫa-ma-ti*, "she can be confident"), possibly influenced
by the second person feminine singular. While the palatalization *-ati* > -
ač(č)- occurs also in some Gurage dialects (e.g. Chaha), Gafat is the
only language having an ending *-ättä* in *-ä*, perhaps under the influence
of the masculine *-a* termination (§40.3). In any case, the Egyptian
"pseudo-participle" *sḏm-tì*, "she heard", also indicates the presence of a
final vowel (cf. §33.5).

40.5.   The second person masculine and feminine is characterized by
the same morphemes as the personal pronoun of the second person,
either independent (§36.5: *-ta, -ti*) or suffixed (§36.6,19: *-ka, -ki*). It is
not possible to exclude the Proto-Semitic origin of the second one, so
much the less because it is used with the stative in Palaeosyrian (e.g. *a-
za-me-kà* or *a-zi-mi-kà* /*lazimika*/, "you are spell-bound), because the
Tuareg independent pronouns of the second person are formed on the
basis *k-*, and because the Old Egyptian suffix-pronouns of the second
person singular are *-k = -ka* for the masculine and *-ṯ < -*ki* for the feminine. They are suffixed as nominatives to the simple tenses of the verb
(e.g. masc. *śḏm-k*, fem. *śḏm-ṯ*, "you heard"), exactly in the same way as
the Semitic personals of the stative/perfect. Besides, the endings *-āka*
(masc.) and *-āki* (fem.) appear in dialectal Neo-Assyrian (e.g. *a-ta-a qa-
la-a-ka*, "why are you silent?"; *ka-aš-da-ki*, "you reach"), in Epigraphic South Arabian (e.g. Sabaic *'wdk*, "you brought back"; *s¹ṭrk*,
"you wrote"), and in Yemenite dialects of Arabic, both ancient (e.g.
'aṣayka, "you were disloyal") and modern (e.g. *kunk*, "you were"). The
survival of these variant forms, which later philologists explained saying
simply that "some Arabs occasionally substitute *k* for *t*" (*Lisān*
XX,330), is the strongest evidence for their use outside the proper realm
of South Semitic. The Gafat (*-ähä*), Masqan, Zway (*-hä*), and Amharic
masculine suffix in *-h* results from a spirantized *-ka*, while the Modern
South Arabian and Ethiopic feminine suffix *-š* (Argobba *-č*) originates
from a palatalized *-ki*. The Old Egyptian palatalized *-ki*, transcribed *-ṯ* by
Egyptologists, was written also *-t* in later periods, just as the plural suf-

fix *-tn* < -*kin was later indicated also by *-tn*. This might imply a phonetic change *-ki* > *-č* > *-t* through the depalatalization of *č* by the loss of
final *-i* (cf. Old Babylonian *-āt*) which usually finishes by being
absorbed in the palatal. If one assumes a similar evolution in Semitic,
the second person forms in *t* could have originated from Proto-Semitic
or Afro-Asiatic forms in *k* (§12.4).

40.6.   The first person singular suffix *-ku*, used both in East Semitic
and in South Semitic, can surely be considered as Proto-Semitic. It is
identical with the morpheme *-ku* of the independent personal pronoun
(§36.6) and it is attested also in Yemenite dialects of Arabic, both
ancient (e.g. *waladku*, "I bore"; *bahalku*, "I spoke") and modern (e.g.
kunk, "I was"; *katubk*, "I wrote"). The Amharic suffix *-hu* — attested
also in Gafat and in some Gurage dialects (*-hʷ*, *-uh*) — has a widespread allophone *-ku* and it results from the spirantization of *-ku*, like
the *-h* of the second person (§40.5). The intermediate spirantized form
-ḵu(m) occurs in Chaha, Muher, and Harari. Finally, the Libyco-Berber
suffix *-ġ* of the first person singular represents a pharyngalized velar
followed by a vowel, thus **-ku*. The suffix *-t* of North Semitic and
West Semitic languages is almost certainly to be explained by analogy
with the second person singular, and the additional ending *-ī* of Old
Canaanite (e.g. *ba-ni-ti*, "I built": EA 292,29), Phoenician and Punic
(e.g. *k'tbty*, "I wrote"), Hebrew (e.g. *'amartī*, "I spoke"), and Moabite
(e.g. *mlkty*, "I became king") derives from the possessive suffix *-ī*
(§36.18).

40.7.   The masculine ending *-ā* and the feminine ending *-tā* are attested
for the third person dual in East Semitic (used until the mid-second millennium B.C.), in Classical Arabic, and in Modern South Arabian with
-ō < **-ā* and *-tō* < **-tā*; these endings can therefore be considered as
Proto-Semitic. They correspond to the dual morpheme *-ā* of nouns in the
subject case, which seems logical (e.g. *marṣā*, "sick-we-two"), while
the endings *-y* (masc.) and *-ty* (fem.) of Sabaic are due probably to analogy with the oblique case (cf. §32.7). The Qatabanic masculine dual has
the ending *-w* and there is an alternative feminine dual ending *-tw* in
Sabaic. Although one must allow for the possibility of a pronunciation
-aw and *-taw*, there is certainly a relation to the Modern South Arabian
forms *-ō* and *-tō*.

40.8.   The second person dual raises the same questions as the personal pronouns (§36.7,22). While the dual ending -*ā* is added in Classical Arabic and probably in Ugaritic to the plural pronominal stem -*tum*-, the Modern South Arabian languages add the oblique ending -*ay* to the singular pronominal stem -*k*- (-*kay > -*ki* or -*ši* after palatalization, in Šḥeri). If one considers the -*ā* ending of the subject case as Proto-Semitic and the form -*tum*- as deriving from -*tan*- (§36.5), one may propose the alternative Proto-Semitic endings -*tanā and -*kā, which so far do not appear as such in any known language.

40.9.   The first person dual is attested only in Ugaritic (-*ny*) and in Modern South Arabian (-*ki*, -*ši* < -*ki), but it must have existed also in Palaeosyrian (§36.22). In Ugaritic, the dual morpheme -*ā*- is apparently added to the pronominal stem of the plural (-*n*-) and followed by the possessive suffix of the first person, resulting in -*nāya. The dual ending -*ay* of the oblique case would have been monophthongized in Ugaritic to -*ē* or -*ī* without being marked in writing. In South Arabian, as expected, the pronominal stem of the singular (-*k*-) is followed by the same elements -*ā-ya*, reduced to *ī* > *i*. The resulting form -*ki* is then identical with the suffix of the second person dual. It stands to reason therefore that the Proto-Semitic suffix was either -*nāya* or -*kāya*. The element -*ya* is the only one introducing a clear distinction either from the plural suffix of the first person (-*na* / -*nā*) or from the proposed dual suffix of the second person (-*kā*).

40.10.   For the third person plural of Proto-Semitic we may posit the endings -*ū* (masc.) and -*ā* (fem.) which appear as such in Palaeosyrian (e.g. *pá-na-ù* /*pānayū*/, "are clothed in", lit. "have a face of"; *ni-bù-ḫa* /*nibbūġā*/, "are outstanding"), in East Semitic, and in Geʿez. The same purely vocalic endings can perhaps be assumed for Ugaritic, but Hebrew, Aramaic, some Arabic colloquials, and Amharic use the ending -*ū*/-*u* for both genders. In Epigraphic South Arabian, in Classical Arabic, in several modern Arabic colloquials, and in Late Aramaic dialects, the feminine plural ending -*n* (§31.12) is added to the feminine suffix with various vocalizations (-*ūn*, -*ēn*, -*ayn*, -*ana*, -*an*). The Yemenite dialectal ending -*ayn* may be related to the Sabaic alternative feminine plural in -*y* which parallels the masculine -*w*. The latter should be compared with the colloquial Arabic -*aw* ending of the Persian Gulf region (e.g. *ktibaw*, "they wrote"), and with the metathetical Mehri pattern *kətawb*, "they wrote". Both Sabaic endings, masculine -*w* and feminine -*y*, are attested in

Tigre: masc. *fagr-aw*, fem. *fagr-aya*, "they went out". A masculine plural in *-m* is attested in the Western Ǧiblah dialect of the Arabian Peninsula (e.g. *katabum*, "they wrote") and in South Arabian Ḥarsūsi (e.g. *kətəbəm*). Instead, a feminine plural in *-m* is used in the West Gurage dialects which make a distinction of gender in the third person plural, e.g. Chaha masc. *näqär-o-m*, fem. *näqär-äma-m*, "they pulled out". The final *-m* is added to all the persons singular and plural in the positive main perfect of several Gurage dialects: it is an enclitic reinforcing the meaning of the word to which it is attached, and it has no connection with the actor suffix as such. Both the masculine and the feminine plural have a suffix in *-m* in Gafat and in Soddo (North Gurage). A common plural termination *-i^wm* < *-*um* occurs in Gafat, probably by analogy with the second person ending *-hu^wm* < *-*kumu*. As for Soddo, it distinguishes, e.g., masc. *säffär-əm*, fem. *säffär-ma*, "they measured", in a subordinate clause, and masc. *säffär-mu-n*, fem. *säffär-ma-n*, in a main clause. There is a relation between this element *-m* and the plural morphemes *-mu* and *-na* of the personal pronoun (§36.11), used for the third and second persons.

40.11. The second person plural of Proto-Semitic should be characterized by the same morphemes as the corresponding personal pronoun, either independent (§36.5: *-a-tanu*, *-a-tina*) or suffixed (§36.24: *-a-kun*, *-a-kin*). The passage from *-a-tanu* to *-a-tunu* and *-tum* has to be explained in the same way as in the case of the independent personal pronoun (§36.5). As for the problem concerning the consonants *t* and *k*, it is the same as in the case of the singular (§40.5). In fact, the suffixes in *-k-* appear not only in Modern South Arabian and in Ethiopic, but also in dialectal Neo-Assyrian with *-ākunu* (e.g. *at-tu-nu qa-la-ku-nu*, "you keep silent"), and in dialectal Yemenite Arabic with *-kum* for the masculine (e.g. *katabkum*, "you wrote"; cf. also *kunkū*, "you were") and *-kan* for the feminine (e.g. *katabkan*). Similar forms in *-k-* kan be assumed for Epigraphic South Arabian. The Proto-Semitic origin of *-kan(u)*, *-kin(a)* has to be taken seriously into account, since the same suffix-pronoun *-ṯn* < *-*kn* is attested in Old Egyptian for the second person plural, while the Tuareg independent pronouns of the second person plural are, e.g. masc. *kăw-ni* and fem. *kămă-ti*. The Amharic ending *-aččəhu* and its variants, used for both genders, indicate that the suffix originates from **-ātikum*, which adds the morpheme *-kum* > *-kəm* > *ku* to the nominal plural ending *-āti* (§31.17). This particular form is due to the fact that in some respects Amharic represents an innovated language type in the South Ethiopic group. Instead, East Gurage and Argobba preserve *-kum*, which is spirantized into *-ku̲m*, *-ku̲*, *-hum*, *-hu^wm*, or *-hu* in other South Ethiopian languages. Besides, the distinction of gender in the second person plural is preserved not only in North Ethiopic, as in Tigre (e.g. masc. *fagar-kum*, fem. *fagar-kən*, "you went out"), but also in some South Ethiopian languages, viz. in Soddo, a North Gurage dialect (e.g. masc. *säffär-kəmun*, fem. *säffär-kəman*, "you measured"), and in West Gurage (e.g. Chaha masc. *näqär-ku̲-m*, fem. *näqär-kəma-m*, "you pulled out").

40.12.   For the first person plural we may posit the Proto-Semitic actor affix *-na* which appears as such in Aramaic, Arabic, Ge'ez, and most South Ethiopian languages (e.g. Soddo *säffär-nä*, "we measured", in the subordinate clause). The final vowel is shedded in Modern South Arabian, in Argobba, and in Amharic, except in the northern Amharic dialects that preserve *-nä*. It appears as *-o* in Gogot and in Soddo, very likely as the result of a change *ä > ö > o*, and it is replaced by *-u* in Babylonian and in Hebrew, probably by analogy with the element *-nu* of the personal pronoun, while the Assyrian allomorph is *-āni* (§36.8, 23). In Late Aramaic dialects, a subsidiary *-n* is added to *-na* (> *nan*), obviously by analogy with the ending *-nan* of the independent personal pronoun (§36.2).

b) Imperative

40.13.   The conjugation of the imperative is likewise limited to the use of actor suffixes. In the paradigmatic set of the personals of the imperative, the hyphen (—) indicates that there is no marking. The following paragraphs will (§40.14-15) offer some observations on this table.

Actor Affixes of the Imperative

	*Pr.-Sem.	East Sem.	Ugaritic	Hebrew	Aramaic
Sing.					
2 m.	—	—	—	—	—
f.	*-i*	*-ī*	—	*-ī*	*-ī*
Dual	*-ā*	*-ā*			
Plur.					
2 m.	*-ū*	\}*-ā*	—	*-ū*	*-ū*
f.	*-ā*		—	*-nā*	*-ā*

40.14. The bare stem of the imperative is used for the second person masculine singular, and the feminine is formed with the suffix -*i* which characterizes the second person feminine singular of the stative/perfect (§40.5) and of the personal pronoun (§36.2,19). This -*i* may cause the palatalization of the preceding consonant, e.g. in the Chaha (Gurage) fem. *nəkaš* < *nəkəsi*, "bite!". The regular Sabaic ending -*n* of the masculine singular (e.g. *'wd-n*, "bring back!"; *s³ḥl-n*, "take care!"; *s¹ṭr-n*, "write!") goes back to the precative particle -*na* which is used with the imperative in Amorite (e.g. *šu-ub-na-*, "turn back, please!"), in Hebrew (e.g. *'ălē-nā*, "climb, please!"), and in Aramaic (e.g. *'zl n'*, "go, please!"), and might be related to the Amharic interjection *na*, "come!". Instead, there is probably no connection with the -*a* which can be added in Old Canaanite (*ku-na*, "be ready!": EA 147,36), in Hebrew (e.g. *qūmā*, "get up!": Ps. 82,8), and in Amharic to the imperative for emphasis (e.g. *səbär-a*, "break!"). This -*a* suffix may be related to the -*a* ending of the subjunctive (§39.5-6) and to the Assyro-Babylonian ventive/allative, which is used also with the imperative.

40.15. The dual ending -*ā* is employed as plural ending in East Semitic for both genders, and for the feminine in Aramaic and in Ge'ez. No particular ending can be proposed for the feminine plural in Proto-Semitic, since the -*na* suffix of Hebrew and Classical Arabic is most likely related to the precative particle -*na*, added to the imperative already in Amorite (§40.14). In some Late Aramaic dialects, in Neo-Aramaic, and in related Arabic colloquials, -*n* is added to a plural ending -*ū* (> -*ūn* / -*īn*) by analogy with the inflexion of the prefix conjugation. In other Arabic colloquials, the masculine ending -*ū* is used also for the feminine and this usage is implied likewise by the Aramaic suffix -*ūn* < -*ū* + *n*.

Actor Affixes of the Imperative

Cl. Arabic	Coll. Arabic	Sabaic	Mehri	Ge'ez	Amharic
—	—	-*n*	—	—	—
-*ī*	-*i*	?	-*i*	-*ī*	-*i*
-*ā*			-*ō*		
-*ū*	-*u*	-*w*	?	-*ū*	
-*na*	-*u* / -*in*	?	?	-*ā*	} -*u*

Also Amharic employs *-u* for both genders, but some South Ethiopian languages of the Gurage group distinguish the two genders, e.g. Chaha masc. *nəkso*, fem. *nəksäma*, "bite!"; Soddo masc. *galbəm*, fem. *galbəma*, "gallop!", with final vowel *-a < -ā* characterizing the feminine plural like in Ge'ez.

c) Prefix-Conjugation

40.16. The personals of the prefix-conjugations were represented originally by two paradigmatic sets characterized by the prefix vowels either *a/i* or *u*. These vowels are no "root-augments" but case endings of personals once separate, but later agglutinated to the base of the verbal stems (§40.1). This question brings us to the problem of the origin of personals and to the ergative foundations of Afro-Asiatic, where *u* characterizes the ergative case, while *a/i* marks the non-active case: *a* in the singular, *i* in the plural (§32.1-6). In Common Semitic, if we disregard the derived *t*-stems for the moment, the use of the *u*-set of personals characterizes the causative or factitive D-stem and Š-stem (§41.3,7 ff.), which by definition have a transitive meaning, hence a subject in the ergative case. The *a/i*-set is employed for the other stems, inclusive the basic stem which must be considered as originally intransitive, hence having a subject in the non-active case. This comes out very clearly in such examples as the following Assyro-Babylonian verb *qerēbu*, "to come near", *qurrubu*, "to bring near":

2 m. sing.	*ta-qrib*, "you came near"	*tu-qarrib*, "you brought near"
1 plur.	*ni-qrib*, "we came near"	*nu-qarrib*, "we brought near"

Barth's law stating that the prefix of the first set was vocalized with *i* when the thematic vowel was *a* (*yiqtal*), and with *a* when the thematic vowel was either *i* (*yaqtil*) or *u* (*yaqtul*), does apply only to a later stage of some Semitic languages. Instead, the vowel of the prefix is independent from the thematic vowel in East Semitic, in Palaeosyrian, in Amorite, in Hebrew, in Aramaic, in Modern South Arabian, in Ethiopic, and generally in Arabic, although the pair *fa'ila / yif'alu* is productive in Sibawayh's time (§40.24). The distinction of two sets of prefixes is lost in Neo-Arabic which mostly uses the *i*-vowel with all the stems, but *u* occurs when the basis of Stem I contains this vowel, e.g. *yuktub* besides *yiktub*, "he writes". There are also cases of vowel harmony. The Geez paradigm can serve also for Tigrinya.

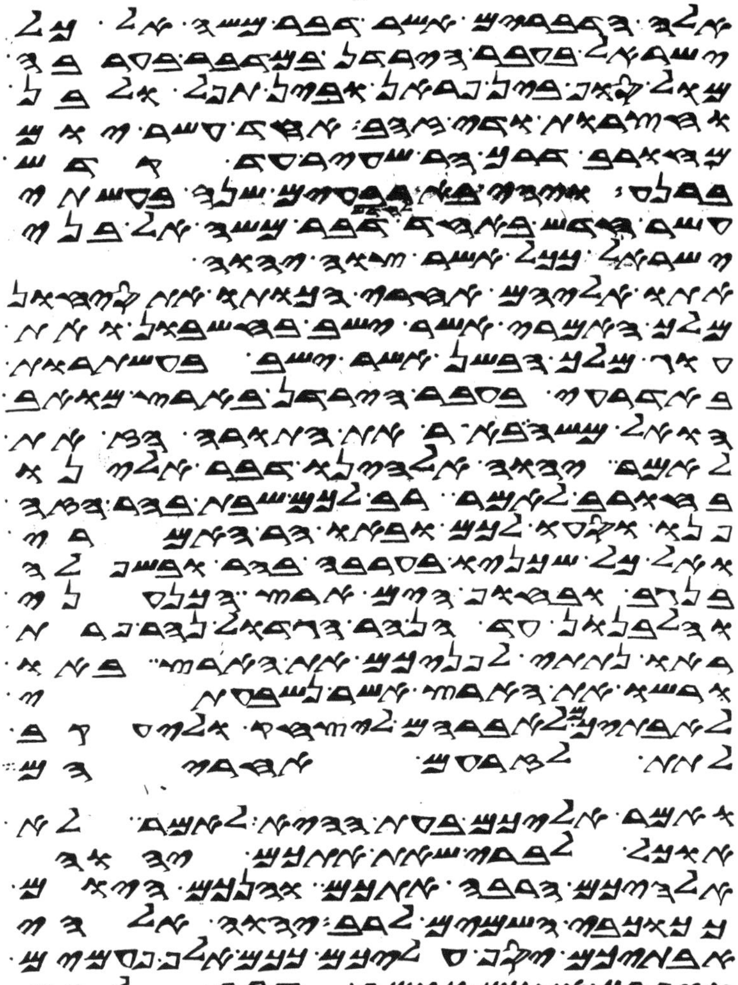

Fig. 29. Fol. 237ʳ of the Samaritan Pentateuch from the collection of Pietro della
Valle (1586-1652) in the Vatican Library. Text of Deut. 1,1-11.

Set I

40.17. The first set of the prefix and suffix elements is shown in the
following table. It will be commented in §40.18-31.

	*Pr.-Sem.	O.Akk.	O.Bab.	Ugaritic	Hebrew	Aramaic
Sing.						
3 m.	*ya-*	*(y)i-*	*i-*	*y-*	*yi-/ya-*	*yi-*
f.	*ta-*	*ta-*	*i-*	*t-*	*ti-/ta-*	*ti-*
2 m.	*ta-*	*ta-*	*ta-*	*t-*	*ti-/ta-*	*ti-*
f.	*ta-...-ī*	*ta-...-ī*	*ta-...-ī*	*t-...-n*	*ti-/ta-...-ī*	*ti-...-īn*
1	*'a-*	*(')a-*	*'a-*	*'a/'i-*	*'e-/'a-*	*'i-*
Dual						
3 m.	*ya-...-ā*	*(y)i-...-ā*	*i-...-ā*	?		
f.	*ta-...-ā*			**ta-...-ā*		
2	*ta-...-ā*	**ta-...-ā*				
1						
Plur.						
3 m.	*yi-...-ū*	*(y)i-...-ū*	*i-...-ū*	*y/t-...-(-n)*	*yi-/ya-...-ū*	*yi-...-ūn*
f.	*yi-...-ā*	*(y)i-...-ū*	*i-...-ā*	*t-...-n*	*ti-/ta-...-nā*	*yi-...-ān*
2 m.	*ti-...-ū*	**ti-/ta-...-ā*	*ta-...-ā*	*t-...*	*ti-/ta-...-ū*	*ti-...-ūn*
f.	*ti-...-ā*	**ti-/ta-...-ā*	*ta-...-ā*	*t-...-n*	*ti-/ta-...-nā*	*ti-...-ān*
1	*ni-*	*ni-*	*ni-*	*n-*	*ni-/na-*	*ni-*

40.18. Palaeosyrian and Amorite are not included in this table because a full paradigm cannot be established as yet on the basis of the available evidence and because this evidence points to important dialectal variations. Ebla texts provide examples of affixes which are identical with those of Old Akkadian: third person singular masculine (e.g. *Iš-má-Il* /Yišma'-'Il/, "Il heard") and feminine (e.g. *Tàš-má-*ᵈUTU /Tašma'-Šepeš/, "The Sun-goddess heard"), first person singular (e.g. *an-na áš-tá-ma* /'anna 'aštama'/, "I heard myself") and plural (e.g. *ne-'à-la-a* /niḥallal/, "we purify"), third person plural masculine (e.g. *i-ṭa-ḥa-ù* /yiṭaḥḥawū/, "they will come near"). However, prefixes of a Western type occur as well. Thus, there is a distinct dual feminine (e.g. ᵈ*Ba-li-ḥa-a* ᵈSIG.AMA *tá-ṣa-a* /taṣṣa'ā/, "DN DN₂ will go out"). A prefix *ti-* of the third person feminine singular appears in some names (e.g. *Ti-iš-te-Da-mu*, "Damu has drunk", fem. because of the sex of the name bearer) and texts (e.g. ᵈUTU *ti-a-ba-an* /tilabban/ SIG₄GAR, "the Sun-goddess will dry bricks"). Besides, Mari tablets use the form *tiqtulū* for the third person masculine plural (e.g. *timḥaṣū ... tikkulū ... tištayū ... tiltaptū*, "they have hammered ..., eaten ..., drunk ..., rubbed themselves ..."), and this form occurs at Ebla as well (e.g. *na-ṭì-lu ti-na-ṭa-ú* /nāṭilū tinaṭṭalū/, "the wailers strike up"), like in Ugaritic and in Old Canaanite texts from the later

Cl. Arabic	Coll. Arabic	Sabaic	Mehri	Ge'ez	Amharic
ya-	yi-/ya-/i-	y-	yə-	yə-	yə-
ta-	ti-/ta-/tu-/tə-	t-	tə-	tə-	tə-
ta-	ti-/ta-/tu-/tə-	t-	tə-	tə-	tə-
ta-...-ī	ti-/ta-/tu-/tə-...(-i/-īn)	?	tə-...-i	tə-...-i	tə-...-i
'a-	a-/ni-/nə-	?	ə-	'ə-	ə-
ya-...-ā		y-...-y	yə-...-ō		
ta-...-ā		t-...-y	tə-...-ō		
ta-...-ā		?	tə-...-ō		
		?	ə-...-ō		
ya-...-ū	yi-/ya-/yu-/ī...-u(m/n)	y-...-w	yə-...-əm	yə-...-u	yə-...-u
ya-...-na	yi-/ya-/yu-/ī-...-u/-ayn/-ēn/-an	y-...-n	tə-...-ən	yə-...-ā	
ta-...-ū	ti-/ta-/tu-/t-...-u(m/n)	t-	tə-...-əm	tə-...-u	tə-...-u
ta-...-na	ti-/ta-/tu-/t-...-u/-ayn/-ēn/-an	?	tə-...-ən	tə-...-ā	
na-	ni-/na-/nu-/n-...-u	?	nə-	nə-	ənnə-

half of the second millennium B.C. (§40.21). Finally, there are Ebla texts with verbal forms having *a*-prefixes of the first person plural, as *na-na-ṣa-ab* /nanaṣṣab/, "we are staying", and of the third person, indicated by *a*- /ya-/ or rather precative-optative /la-/ (§38.2; 39.13; 40.23,30), just like the *yi*-prefix may be expressed by *i*- /yi-/; e.g. *a-a-tá-qá*- /laltaqqaḥ/, "he should take"; *a-na-pá-ap* /lanappap/, "he should besprinkle"; *a-pá-kà-ru₁₂* /lapakkarū/, "they should join"; *a-pá-kà-ra* /lapakkarā/, "they should join" (dual). These variations and the probable precative-optative use of the imperfective — a construction which would be unusual in East Semitic — obviously reflect the intrusion of local forms into a text written originally in another language (§4.2). As a matter of fact, *liqattal* is encountered later in the precative-optative function at Alalakh (e.g. *li-na-ṣa-ru-šu*, "may they protect him"), in Amurru (e.g. *li-na-ṣa-ṣár*, "may he protect": EA 169,15), and in Canaan (*li-ba-lu-uṭ-ni*, "may he give me life": EA 198,20). As for Amorite, important dialectal variations are shown by third person forms like *Ia-am-ru-uṣ-Èl*, *Ia-am-ra-aṣ-Èl*, and *Iu-um-ra-aṣ-Èl*, "El did care", or *Ia-ás-ma-aḫ-*ᵈIM, *Ia-ás-mi-iḫ-*ᵈIM, and *Iš-ma-*ᵈIM, "Haddu did hear". Some of these examples seem to favour Barth's law (§40.16), like all the names in *I-ba-al-* /Yib'al/, *-ti-ba-al* /tib'al/, but most cases do decidedly not conform to this principle.

40.19. The Old Akkadian prefix *yi-* is never indicated as such, but spellings like *i-ig-mu-ur*, "he conquered", or *i-ik-mi*, "he captured", suggest that the prefix may have been *yi-* in the Sargonic period. The personals of Set I are used for the basic stem (§41.2), for the stem with prefix *n-*, and for the *-t-* and *-tan-* infixed stems which secondarily derive from the two above-mentioned stems. All the other stems take actor-affixes of Set II.

40.20. The distinction of the third person singular masculine *i-* and feminine *ta-* may occur in Assyrian and in archaizing or poetical Babylonian, as well as in Late Babylonian which happens to reflect the spoken Aramaic language. Besides, it occurs occasionally in the 13th-12th centuries B.C. in texts from Emar where it reveals an influence of the local North Semitic idiom. Dual forms are rarely encountered in Old Assyrian and in Old Babylonian, but they are attested at Emar (§40.21), obviously under North Semitic influence. The distribution of the two sets of Assyro-Babylonian dual personals is the same as in Old Akkadian, but the dual is normally replaced by the plural.

40.21. Barth's law seems to be generally operative in Ugaritic, as it appears from the sequence *'i - 'a* of prefixed and thematic vowels in forms of the first person singular (e.g. *'il'ak*, "I shall dispatch"; *'iš'al*, "I shall ask"), and from personal names in syllabic script (e.g. *Ig-ma-ra-*^dIM */Yigmar-Haddu/*, "Haddu has completed"; *Iš-la-ma-na /Yišlam-ānu/*, "He kept peace..."). However, one must reckon with exceptions, as shown e.g. by *Ia-an-ḫa-mu /Yanḫamu/*, "He comforted...". The third masculine plural form is either *yqtl(n)* or *tqtl(n)*. The form *tiqtulū(na)* occurs along with the usual *yiqtulū(na)* also in Palaeosyrian documents (§40.18) and in Old Canaanite as reflected in the Amarna correspondence, especially the one from Byblos, and in texts from Kāmid el-Lōz; e.g. *tilqūna ... u tidūkūna*, "they will take ... and they will kill" (EA 104,32-34); *ilānu tiddinū bāštaka*, "may the gods give you influence" (Kāmid el-Lōz 6,18-19). The Ugaritic feminine dual is reconstructed in the paradigm (§40.17) according to two nearly contemporaneous North Semitic forms from Emar: *lu-ú ta-aṣ-bu-ta₅*, "may they both take possession", and *lu-ú ta-ad-di-na*, "may they both give".

40.22. The variation of vowel pattern *i/a* in Hebrew prefixes is independent from the thematic vowel. The vowel of the prefix is generally *i* (*yi-/ti-*), except in the first person singular where the laryngal occasions the change $i > a$; the usual '*e*- is an allophone of '*a*-, as shown by the Jewish Babylonian vocalization and by the Jewish Yemenite traditional pronunciation. The vowel of the prefix is likewise *a* or its allophone *e* before a guttural (§27.10), and it is generally $a > \bar{a}$ before monosyllabic verbal roots of the type *Cv̄C* (e.g. *yāqūm*, "he will get up").

40.23. The vowel of the prefixes is generally *i* in Aramaic, but it can change into *a* before a guttural (e.g. *yaḥləpūn*, "they will pass over") and be reduced to a short *ə* in open unstressed syllables before a monosyllabic radical *Cv̄C* (e.g. *yəqūm*, "he will get up"). However, the vowel *e* attested in Galilean Aramaic and in Syriac (e.g. *tektōb*, "she will write") goes very likely back to an original *a* and implies a variant set of *a*- prefixes *ya*-, *ta*-, '*a*-, *na*-, like in Classical Arabic. There are third person forms with preformatives *l*- or *n*- which originated from the precative or optative (§39.13). In Syriac, *ne*- became the standard prefix of the third person masculine singular, as well as masculine and feminine plural, but the imperfect prefix *y*- is still preserved in early Syriac inscriptions (e.g. *yḥz'*, "he sees"), while the Middle Aramaic of Hatra and Ashur prefixes *l*- to the third person in the imperfect (e.g. *lnsb*, "he takes away").

40.24. The *a*-prefixes are used in Classical Arabic for the active conjugation of the basic stem (I) and of Stems V-XV, regardless of the thematic vowel, and only *a*-prefixes are found in the canonical readings of the Qur'ān. However, among the non-canonical or *šādd*-readings some *i*-prefixes occur in verbal forms with the thematic vowel *a*, e.g. *lā tiqrabā hāḏī š-šiǧra*, "do not go near this tree" (Qur'ān 2,33/35). According to Sibawayh and other early philologists, Ḥedjaz was the only region where the prefixes of the *a*-imperfect had not the vowel *i*, i.e. *yif'alu* (*yiqtal*) in conformity with Barth's law. There is reason to believe therefore that the *i*-prefixes were old-inherited in Arabic and that the choice of the *a*-prefix for the *a*-imperfects in Classical Arabic results from a systematization of the language.

40.25. In modern Arabic colloquials, the *a*-prefixes are restricted to the Dōsiri dialect as spoken in Kuwait and to other colloquials of the Persian Gulf region. However, the latter follow a contrasting vocalization, e.g. *yaktib*, "he will write", but *yišrab*, "he will drink". In general, the *i*-prefix is used when the thematic vowel is *i* or *a*, and the *u*- or *i*-prefix appears when the thematic vowel is *u*, e.g. *yuktub* or *yiktub*, "he will write". The prefix vowel can also be reduced to *ə*. The vowel *a* is characteristic of the prefix of the first person singular (e.g. *aktub, aktib*, "I shall write"), except in Maghrebine Arabic where this prefix is *ni-* (e.g. *niktib, nəktəb*, "I shall write"), like for the first person plural which ends in *-u* (e.g. *nikitbu, nkətbu*, "we shall write"). This *ni*-prefix of the singular is already attested in early Andalusian Arabic as transmitted by Pedro de Alcalá; e.g. *niçéh* [*niṣēḥ*], "I shall cry", next to *çayaht* [*ṣayaḥt*], "I have cried". It is attested also in Western Neo-Aramaic with new formations based on old participles; e.g. *nsōfar*, "I travel"; *niḏmek*, "I had slept". The distinction between the second person singular masculine and feminine has disappeared in several Arabic colloquials.

A characteristic feature of Mesopotamian vernaculars, shared by Bedouin dialects in North and Central Arabia, and by dialects spoken along the Persian Gulf and in Ḏofār, is the ending *-īn, -ūn* of the second person feminine singular and of the second and third persons plural. This form is common in Ugaritic and in West Semitic (cf. §40.17), but its persistence in Mesopotamia, despite the contrary use of Classical Arabic, is probably due to the Aramaic substratum, as suggested by the following examples taken from Syriac, from the Mardin dialect in Anatolia, from the Moslem dialect of Baghdad, and from the dialects of the Persian Gulf (*ktb*, "to write"):

	Syriac	Mardin	Baghdad	Persian Gulf
2 pers. fem. sing.	*tektəbīn*	*təktəbīn*	*tkitbīn*	*taktəbīn*
2 pers. m. plur.	*tektəbūn*	*təktəbūn*	*tkitbūn*	*taktəbūn*

40.26. The paradigm of the Sabaic simple imperfect (without the *-n* or *-nn* ending) is incomplete and the feminine plural is only dubiously attested. In Minaic there seems not to be any graphic differentiation between masculine singular and plural, while the Qatabanic masculine plural is *yf'lwn*.

40.27. The affixes of the prefix-conjugation are the same in all the Modern South Arabian languages. However, the second person singular feminine is characterized in Śḥeri and in Soqoṭri by an internal vowel change which appears instead of the *-i* suffix. Depending on the type of verb, this morphological feature may occur also in Mehri, but many verbs display the internal vowel change and the *-i* suffix.

40.28. The Ge'ez *yə-, tə-, 'ə-* prefixes go most likely back to *i-* prefixes, since the vowel *ə* in Ge'ez originates either from *i* or from *u*. However, *a-* prefixes are found in the affirmative jussive in Gurage, Harari, and Gafat. Thus in Gurage: *yäsbär*, "let him break"; *yäskär*, "let him be drunk"; in Harari: *yäsbär*, "let him break"; in Gafat: *yältäm*, "let him arrive". In Selṭi, an East Gurage dialect, and in Harari, the vowel of the prefix is *ä* after any consonant, and it is also *ä* in Soddo (North Gurage) in the first person singular after the *n-* prefix (e.g. *näšäkkət*, "let me make"). Besides, the prefix of the first person singular of the imperfect is also *ä* in various Gurage dialects (e.g. Chaha *äräk̲əb*, "I find"). The vowel *ə* instead of *ä* after the prefixes *t-* and *n-* in the jussive (e.g. *təsbär*, "let her break") of the languages using the *yä-* prefix is therefore to be explained by analogy with the vowel *ə* of the imperfect. The *a*-prefixes were thus used at least in some of the South Ethiopian languages and their preservation marks an archaic state which parallels the North Ethiopic *i-* prefixes underlying the Ge'ez set of *ə-* prefixes.

40.29. Modern North Ethiopic makes a distinction in gender, like Ge'ez, in the second and third persons plural, as shown e.g. by Tigre imperfect plural forms masc. *təfagro*, fem. *təfagra*, "you go out", and masc. *ləfagro*, fem. *ləfagra*, "they go out". In South Ethiopic, the distinction is lost not only in Amharic, but also in Argobba, Harari, Gafat, and in East Gurage. The distinction is kept instead in West and North Gurage, as indicated e.g. by Chaha imperfect plural forms masc. *təräk̲bo*, fem. *təräk̲bäma*, "you find", and masc. *yəräk̲bo*, fem. *yəräk̲bäma*, "they find".

40.30. The jussive prefix of the first person singular is *l-* in Amharic (e.g. *ləsbär*, "let me break"), in Gafat (e.g. *ləltäm*, "let me arrive"), in East Gurage (e.g. Selṭi *läsbär*, "let me break"), while it is *n-* in Harari (e.g. *näsbär*, "let me break") and in other Gurage dialects (e.g. *näsbər*, "let me break"). These prefixes are precative or optative preformatives (§39.13) and their use was extended to the imperfect, like in Aramaic (§40.23), especially in North Ethiopic Tigre (e.g. *ləfagro*, "they go out") and perhaps in some Gurage dialects, like Chaha, where the *n-* prefix appears in the first person when the verb is introduced by a conjunction (e.g. *tənräk̲ʸəm*, "while I find"). In Modern South Arabian, *l-* is prefixed to subjunctive forms of the verb which begin with a vowel, after elision of the glottal stop or of the initial *y-*; e.g. Mehri *lərkēz*, "may I stand up"; Soqoṭri *liqbər*, "may they bury".

40.31. The expected vowels of the prefixed Proto-Semitic personals in Set I are *a* in the singular and *i* in the plural (§40.16), but the assimilatory effect of *y*- on the following vowel occasioned the change of *a* into the homorganic *i* in most languages (§22.14), while a harmonizing tendency obliterated the difference between singular and plural. Therefore, the reconstruction of Proto-Semitic affixes is not based, as a rule, on their most ancient attestations. In particular, the *yi*-prefix occurs in Palaeosyrian, in Old Akkadian, in Aramaic, in a large area of Arabic, and in North Ethiopic, regardless of the thematic vowel of the verb. However, the original use of *ya*- in the singular is confirmed by the second and first persons where *a* is employed with the prefixes *ta*- and *'a*- even in Palaeosyrian, in Old Akkadian, and in Assyro-Babylonian, despite their use of the suffix *yi*-. The vowel *i* is, very rightly, the best attested for the prefix of the first person plural, while the plural *ti*- forms in North Semitic and in Old Canaanite (§40.18,21) confirm the antiquity of the *i*-vowel in the plural prefixe. The complete harmonization of the prefix vowels or the alternative contrasting vocalization, as formulated in Barth's law, are to be considered as results of later developments. Instead, distinctive suffixes have to be posited for the genders of the third and the second persons plural: -*ū* for the masculine and -*ā* for the feminine, endings which are broadly reflected in Old Babylonian and in Ge'ez. The feminine ending -*ā* is identical with that of the dual and it is used in Assyro-Babylonian for the second person plural of both genders.

Set II

40.32. The second set of the prefix and suffix elements of the prefix-conjugations is characterized by the vowel *u* in the prefix, but this assumed *u* is reduced to *ə* in Hebrew, Aramaic, South Arabian, and Ethiopic, while *i* is predominant in the Amarna correspondence and in modern Arabic colloquials. Besides, the first person singular, which is the unique form in Ugaritic where the vowel *u* would be recognizable, has *'a*- instead of the expected *'u*-, exactly as in modern Arabic colloquials. Since no distinctive pattern is recognizable for Set II in Sabaic, Mehri, Ge'ez, and Amharic, these languages are omitted in the following table. Palaeosyrian and Amorite are not included because only some forms can be established on the basis of the available evidence. Additional comments will be found in §40.33-36.

	*Pr.-Sem.	O.Akk.	O.Bab.	Ugaritic	Hebrew	Aramaic	Cl. Arabic	Coll. Arabic
Sing.								
3 m.	yu-	(y)u-	u-	y-	yə-	yə-	yu-	(y)i-
f.	tu-	tu-	u-	t-	tə-	tə-	tu-	t(i)-
2 m.	tu-	tu-	tu-	t-	tə-	tə-	tu-	t(i)-
f.	tu-...-ī	tu-...-ī	tu-...-ī	t-	tə-...-ī	tə-...-īn	tu-...-ī	t(i)-...-i
1	'u-	(')u-	u-	'a-	'ă-	'ă-	'u-	'a-
Dual								
3 m.	yu-...-ā	(y)u-...-ā	u-...-ā				yu-...-ā	
f.	tu-...-ā						tu-...-ā	
2	tu-...-ā	*tu-..-ā					tu-...-ā	
Plur.								
3 m.	yu-...-ū	(y)u-...-ū	u-...-ū	y/t-...(-n)	yə-...-ū	yə-...-ūn	yu-...-ū	(y)i-...-u
f.	yu-...-ā	*(y)u-...-ū	u-...-ā	t-...-n	tə-...-nā	yə-...-ān	yu-...-na	(y)i-...-en
2 m.	tu-...-ū	*tu-...-ā	tu-...-ā	t-	tə-...-ū	tə-...-ūn	tu-...-ū	t(i)-...-u
f.	tu-...-ā	*tu-...-ā	tu-...-ā	t-...-n	tə-...-nā	tə-...-ān	tu-...-na	t(i)-...-en
1	nu-	nu-	nu-	n-	nə-	nə-	nu-	n(i)-

40.33. Despite the incomplete evidence, the use of the characteristic vowel *u* is nevertheless well attested both in Palaeosyrian (e.g. *tù-a-ba-áš* /tulabbaš/, "she puts on"; *nu-wa-sa-ra-si* /nuwaššaraši/, "we let her go", *u₉-qá-ṭa-ra-* /yuqaṭṭarā/, "they will burn incense") and in Amorite (e.g. *Uš-taš-ni-Èl* /Yuštaṯnī-'El/, "El acted for the second time"). The reconstructed Old Akkadian forms parallel those of Set I (§40.16).

40.34. In Ugaritic, the prefix of the first person singular in Set II is vocalized with *a*, e.g. *'aqrb*, "I shall bring near"; *'ašhlk*, "I shall cause to flow". Here Ugaritic agrees with Hebrew, Aramaic, and Colloquial Arabic against East Semitic and Classical Arabic.

40.35. The vowel *u* is reduced in Hebrew and in Aramaic to *ə*, but the *'ă* of the first person singular does not reflect *'u*, which should appear in this position as *'ŏ*. In Syriac, the prefix of the third person is *nə*, with *n-* like in Set I (§40.23).

40.36. Set II is used in Classical Arabic for the active forms of Stems II, III, and IV, and for the passive forms of all the stems (§41.43-47). In Colloquial Arabic, there is an overwhelming use of the vowel *i* with the exception of the prefix *'a-* of the first person singular.

E. Stems and Voices

41.1. Besides moods, tenses, and aspects, the Semitic verb has a set of stems or themes in which formal changes correspond to certain semantic variations. In West Semitic and in Modern South Arabian, different vowel patterns can also determine an active and a passive voice of the stem or theme (§41.43-47). This additional vowel variation should be distinguished from the stem-vowel or thematic vowel of the verb, which belongs to the root. The triconsonantal verbs are divided into three classes characterized by the vowels *a*, *i*, or *u*. The biconsonantal verbs, which will be examined in a separate section (§44), generally have or initially had either a long thematic vowel *ā*, *ī*, or *ū*, or a short vowel and a geminated second radical consonant. There are traces of some other patterns as well.

a) Basic Stem

41.2. The simple or basic stem is either called Stem I or it is designated by the symbols B(asic) or G(rundstamm, in German). It shows the three consonants of the root with the thematic vowel, and inflects for

Suffix-Conjugation

	Libyco-Berber ("qualitative")	Egyptian (old perfective)	Old Babylonian (stative)	Neo-Assyrian (stative)	Ugaritic (perfect)	Mishnaic Hebrew (perfect)
Sing.						
3 m.	ḫnin	sḏm(w)	lamad	lamad	katab	kātab
f.	ḫninət	sḏm-t(ỉ)	lamdat	lamdat	katbat	kātəbā
2 m.	ḫninəd	sḏm-t(ỉ)	lamdāt(a)	lamdāt(i)/āk(a)	katabta	kātabtā
f.	ḫninəd		lamdāti	lamdāt(i)	katabti	kātabt
1	ḫninəġ	sḏm-kwỉ / kỉ / k	lamdāku	lamdāk(a/u)	katabtu	kātabtī
Dual						
3 m.		sḏm-wy	(lamdā)		katbā	
f.		sḏm-ty			katabtā	
2					?	
1					ktbny	
Plur.						
3 m.	ḫninit	sḏm(w/y)	lamdū	lamdū	katbū	kātəbū
f.		sḏm-tỉ	lamdā	lamdā	*katbā (?)	
2 m.		sḏm-tỉwny	lamdātunu	lamdātun(u) / ākun(u)	katabtum	kətabtem
f.			lamdātina	lamdātin(a)	katabtin	kətabten
1		sḏm-wyn	lamdānu	lamdān(i)	*katbān (?)	kātabnū

tense, for mood, and for actor. The threefold vocalic scheme is attested in East Semitic (e.g. Assyro-Babylonian *i-lmad*, "he learned"; *i-pqid*, "he delegated"; *i-prus*, "he separated"), in North Semitic (e.g. Amorite *ya-bḫar*, "he chose"; *ya-ntin*, "he gave"; *ya-ḏkur-*, "he remembered"), and in West Semitic (e.g. Classical Arabic *ya-ḏhab-u*, "he goes away"; *ya-ḍrib-u*, "he strikes"; *ya-qtul-u*, "he kills"), while the change $i > ə$ and $u > ə$ led to a twofold scheme in Ethiopic (e.g. Ge'ez *yə-ngər*, "may he speak"; *yə-lbas*, "may he dress"), but South Semitic certainly had a threefold vocalic scheme at an earlier stage. Dialectal differences may affect the stem-vowel; e.g. *i-qrab* or *i-qrib*, "he approached", in Assyro-Babylonian; *ya-ḥsab-u* or *ya-ḥsib-u*, "he considers", and even *ya-dbuġ-u*, *ya-dbiġ-u*, *ya-dbaġ-u*, "he tans", both verbs in Arabic. Sometimes the vocalic variation has semantic implications, e.g. in Arabic *ya-fṣil-u*, "he separates", and *ya-fṣul-u*, "he moves away". As suggested by the vowel *a/i* of the prefixed personals, Stem I probably represented the conjugation of intransitive verbs (§38.17; 40.16), in functional opposition to Stem II, before it became the basic stem of the entire system. A formal trace of this shift is preserved by the gemination of the second radical consonant in the positive suffix-conjugation of several South Ethiopian languages, viz. Amharic, Argobba, Gafat, and some Gurage dialects

Suffix-Conjugation

Old Aramaic (perfect)	Syriac (perfect)	Cl. Ar. (perfect)	Damascene Coll. (perfect)	Maghrebine Coll. (perfect)	Mehri (perfect)	Ge'ez (perfect)	Tigre (perfect)	Amharic (perfect)
katab	ktab	kataba	katab	ktəb	kətōb	nagara	nagra	näggärä
katbat	ketbat	katabat	katbet	kətbət	kətəbōt	nagarat	nagrat	näggäräčč
katabta	ktabt	katabta	katabt	ktəbti	kətəbk	nagarka	nagarka	näggärh/k
katabti	ktabt	katabti	katabti	ktəbti	kətəbš	nagarki	nagarki	näggärš
katabtu/i	ketbet	katabtu	katabt	ktəbt	kətəbk	nagarku	nagarko	näggärhu/ku
		katabā			kətəbō			
		katabatā			kətəbtō			
		katabtumā			kətəbki			
					kətəbki			
katabū	ktabūn	katabtū	katabu	kətbu	kətowb	nagaru	nagraw	näggäru
katabā	ktabēn	katabna	katabu	kətbu	kətōb	nagarā	nagraya	näggäru
katabtūn	ktabtōn	katabtum	katabtu	ktəbtīw	kətəbkəm	nagarkəmmu	nagarkum	näggäräččəhu
katabtīn	ktabtēn	katabtunna	katabtu	ktəbtīw	kətəbkən	nagarkən	nagarkən	näggäräččəhu
katabnā	ktabn(an)	katabnā	katabna	ktəbna	kətōbən	nagarna	nagarna	näggärn

(§41.53). This gemination, extended from the positive perfect to the perfect throughout, was most likely produced by analogy with the perfect of Stem II or Ethiopic I.2/B (§41.3) when Stem I was developing into a transitive conjugation form. Other signs of this functional shift can still be traced back in the passage of some particular verbs from Stem II to Stem I (§63.2), in the synonymy of Stems I and II in numerous other cases (e.g. East Semitic *gamāru* and *gummuru*, "to achieve"), or in the lack of finite forms of Stem I in the conjugation of a number of transitive verbs (e.g. East Semitic *qu''ū*, *quwwū*, "to expect"; Hebrew *dibber*, "he said").

Prefix-Conjugation: *iprus*-Type

	Bedja		Libyco-Berber		Old Babylonian	Neo-Assyrian	Ugaritic	Mishnaic Hebrew
	(past)	("conditional")	(preterite / perfective)	(jussive)	(preterite)	(preterite)	(perfective)	(imperfect)
Sing.								
3 m.	*yi-dbil*	*yī-dbil*	*i-lkăm*	*yə-lkəm*	*ilmad*	*ilmad*	*yaktub*	*yiktob*
f.	*ti-dbil*	*tī-dbil*	*tə-lkăm*	*tə-lkəm*	*ilmad*	*talmad*	*taktub*	*tiktob*
2 m.	*ti-dbil-a*	*tī-dbil-a*	*tə-lkăm-əd*	*tə-lkəm-əd*	*talmad*	*talmad*	*taktub*	*tiktob*
f.	*ti-dbil-i*	*tī-dbil-i*	*tə-lkăm-əd*	*tə-lkăm-əd*	*talmadī*	*talmidī*	*taktubin*	*tiktəbī*
1	*'a-dbil*	*'ī-dbil*	*lkăm-əġ*	*əlkəm-əġ*	*almad*	*almad*	*'aktub*	*'ektob*
Dual.								
3 m.					*ilmadā*			
f.								
2								
1								
Plur.								
3 m.	*yi-dbil-na*	*yī-dbil-na*	*lkăm-ən*	*əlkəm-ən*	*ilmadū*	*ilmudū*	*yaktubū(na)*	*yiktəbū*
f.			*lkăm-ənt*	*əlkəm-ənt*	*ilmadā*	*ilmadā*	*taktubna*	*yiktəbū*
2 m.	*ti-dbil-na*	*tī-dbil-na*	*tə-lkăm-əm*	*tə-lkəm-əm*	*talmadā*	*talmadā*	*taktubū(na)*	*tiktəbū*
f.			*tə-lkăm-əmt*	*tə-lkəm-əmt*	*talmadā*	*talmadā*	**taktubā(?)*	*tiktəbū*
1	*ni-dbil*	*nī-dbil*	*nə-lkăm*	*nə-lkəm*	*nilmad*	*nilmad*	*naktub*	*niktob*

The suffix- and prefix-conjugation of the basic stem is inflected in the principal Semitic languages as shown in the following tables where paradigms of the Egyptian old perfective or "pseudo-participle" (*sḏm*, "to hear"), of the Bedja conjugation (*-dbil-*, "to collect"), and of the Libyco-Berber verb, as inflected in Kabyle (*ḥnin*, "to be gracious") and in Tuareg (*-əlkem-*, "to follow"), are added for comparison. The Libyco-Berber emphatics *-ḍ* and *-ġ* represent Afro-Asiatic pharyngalized stops followed by a vowel, thus *-ta* / *-ti* and *ku*; the *ṯ* is a spirantized final *t*. The vocalization of Ugaritic and of Old Aramaic is based on analogy with vocalized proper names. Only attested Semitic verbs are used in this paragraph, viz. *lamādu*, "to learn", *ktb*, "to write", *nagara*, "to speak".

Prefix-Conjugation: *iprus*-Type

Old Aramaic (imperfect)	Syriac (imperfect)	Cl. Arabic (jussive)	Damascene Coll. (imperfect)	Maghrebine Coll. (imperfect)	Mehri (subj.)	Ge'ez (subj.)	Tigre (jussive)	Amharic (subj.)
iktub	nektob	yaktub	byəktob	iktəb	yəktēb	yəngər	ləngar	yəngär
tktub	tektob	taktub	btəktob	təktəb	təktēb	təngər	təngar	təngär
tktub	tektob	taktub	btəktob	təktəb	təktēb	təngər	təngar	təngär
tktubīn	tektəbīn	taktubī	btəktbi	təktəb	təktēbi	təngəri	təngari	təngäri
aktub	'ektob	'aktub	bəktob	nəktəb	ləktēb	'əngər	'əngar	ləngär
		yaktubā			yəktəbō			
		taktubā			təktəbō			
		taktubā			təktəbō			
					ləktəbō			
iktubūn	nektəbūn	yaktubū	byəktbu	īkətbu	yəktēbəm	yəngəru	ləngaro	yəngäru
iktubān	nektəbān	yaktubna	byəktbu	īkətbu	təktəban	yəngərā	ləngara	yəngäru
tktubūn	tektəbūn	taktubū	btəktbu	tkətbu	təktēbəm	təngəru	təngaro	təngäru
iktubān	tektəbān	taktubna	btəktbu	tkətbu	təktəban	təngərā	təngara	təngäru
iktub	nektob	naktub	mnəktob	nkətbu	nəktēb	nəngər	nəngar	ənnəngär

Prefix-Conjugation: *iparras*-Type

	Bedja (imperfective)	Libyco-Berber (imperfective)	Old Babylonian (present-future)	Neo-Assyrian (present-future)
Sing.				
3 m.	(*yi-*)*danbīl*	*i-lākkəm*	*ilammad*	*ilammad*
f.	(*ti-*)*danbīl*	*ti-lākkəm*	*ilammad*	*talammad*
2 m.	(*ti-*)*danbīl-a*	*ti-lākkəm-əd*	*talammad*	*talammad*
f.	(*ti-*)*danbīl-i*	*ti-lākkəm-əd*	*talammadī*	*talammidī*
1	*'a-danbīl*	*lākkem-əġ*	*alammad*	*alammad*
Dual				
3 m.			} *ilammadā*	
f.				
2				
1				
Plur.				
3 m.	*nē-dbīl*	*lākkəm-ən*	*ilammadū*	*ilammudū*
f.		*lākkəm-ənt*	*ilammadā*	*ilammadā*
2 m.	*tē-dbīl-na*	*tə-lākkəm-əm*	*talammadā*	*talammadā*
f.		*tə-lākkəm-əmt*	*talammadā*	*talammadā*
1		*'ē-dbīl-na nə-lākkəm*	*nilammad*	*nilammad*

b) *Stem with Geminated Second Radical Consonant*

41.3. Stem II with geminated or lengthened second radical consonant is attested over the whole Semitic area. It is generally designated by the symbol D(oubled or "Doppelungsstamm" in German) which alludes to the "doubling" of the second radical. Considering the function of Stem II and the vowel *u* of the prefixed personals, it is likely that this stem originally represented the conjugation of transitive verbs (§38.17; 40.16), in functional opposition to Stem I (§41.2); this characteristic of Stem II is well preserved in the historically attested languages (2°). As result of particular developments, however, some Semitic languages, as Modern South Arabian, Harari, and most Gurage dialects, are of a non-geminating type, just as Cushitic Bedja, for instance, which exhibits verbal formations with vocalic modifications alone that nevertheless match the two main functions of Stem II in Semitic.

1° Stem II is called also "intensive" in consideration of its function in expressing repetition or spatial dispersion, and in indicating plurality of the object in the transitive verbs and plurality of the subject in the intran-

Prefix-Conjugation: *iparras*-Type

Ugaritic (imperfective)	Mehri (imperfect)	Ge'ez (imperfect)	Tigre (imperfect)	Amharic (imperfect)
*yakattub	yəkōtəb	yənaggər	lənaggər	yənägr
*takattub	təkōtəb	tənaggər	tənaggər	tənägr
*takattub	təkotəb	tanaggər	tənaggər	tənägr
*takattubin	təkētəb	tənagri	tənagri	tənägri
*'akattub	əkōtəb	'ənaggər	'ənaggər	ənägr
	yəktəbō			
	təktəbō			
	təktəbō			
	əktəbō			
*yakattabū	yəkatbəm	yənagru	lənagro	yənägru
takattubna	təkatbən	yənagrā	lənagra	yənägru
*takattabū(na)	təkatbəm	tənagru	tənagro	tənägru
*takattabā(?)	təkatbən	tənagrā	tənagra	tənägru
*nakattab	nəkōtəb	nənaggər	'ənnaggər	ənnənägr

sitive ones. Thus, it denotes intensity, both of qualitative result (e.g. Arabic *qaṭa'a*, "he cut off", but *qaṭṭa'a*, "he cut into pieces") and particularly of quantity (e.g. Old Babylonian *butuqtam ibattaq*, "he will open a breach", but *butuqātim ubattaq*, "he will open breaches"; Hebrew *bātar*, "he cut" one thing, but *bittēr*, "he cut" several things). There is a parallel rule in Bedja that the verb must be in the intensive stem when the subject or the direct object are in plural, but this stem is formed in Bedja by modifications of the stem vowel; e.g. intransitive *kitim*, "to arrive", *kātim*, "to arrive repeatedly"; transitive *dir*, "to kill", *dar*, "to cause carnage", "to massacre".

2° When inflecting intransitive verbs of Stem I, Stem II gives them a causative and transitive sense (e.g. Arabic *ṯabata*, "he was firm", but *ṯabbata*, "he made fast"); then it is used also as a factitive of transitive verbs (e.g. Hebrew *šāma'*, "he heard", but *šimma'*, "he gave to hear"), thus approximating the stem with preformatives *š-* / *h-* / *'-* / *y-* in sense (§41.7). Here too, Bedja offers parallels like *ginaf*, "to kneel down", *ginif*, "to make kneel down"; *sikal*, "to be choking", *sikil*, "to choke"; *rimad*, "to avenge one's self", *rimid*, "to avenge"; *šibab*, "to see one's self", *šibib*, "to see"; *fal*, "to overflow", *fil*, "to pour out". The causative form of these intransitive verbs is characterized by the vowel *i* like the Semitic D-stem (*uparris*; *yəqattil*, *yufaʿʿil*).

3° In Semitic, the D-stem can have two supplementary functions related to the causative: it can be declarative (e.g. Arabic *kaḏaba*, "he lied", but *kaḏḏaba*, "he accused of lying"), and it is quite often denominative (e.g. Hebrew *qiṭṭēr*, "he made sacrificial smoke", from *qəṭoret*, "smoke of sacrifice").

4° The corresponding Stem I.2/B of Ethiopic is no longer a derived stem, but a basic stem. There are very few exceptions; e.g. Geʿez *qarba*, "he was near", and *qarraba*, "he brought near". Whether a verb is of Stem I.1/A or Stem I.2/B is then a question of vocabulary and of usage in the language. A particular feature is the vowel *e* in the Geʿez imperfect *yəqettəl* of Stem I.2/B. This is a replacive vowel aimed at distinguishing the imperfect from the jussive *yəqattəl*. It had to be *e* < *ē* in order to avoid its reducing to *ə* in a form which already contained two *ə*. In consequence, this much discussed *e* does not result from the monophthongization of a diphthong *ay* which would have been morphologically and phonologically unexplainable.

It should be noticed that some Stem II verbs in dictionaries of Classical Arabic probably not hark back to historically "intensive" forms, but owe their present shape to a misinterpretation of South Arabian imperfective forms of Stem I metanalyzed as Stem II verbs.

The following table is limited to the forms of the third person masculine singular in the Semitic languages presented in §41.2, except Mehri which is a language of a non-geminating type (cf. §41.4). Only one Assyro-Babylonian paradigm is given below for East Semitic, and the usual paradigmatic verbs are being used for the sake of clarity. The three forms shown below belong to the suffix-conjugation (**1**), to the East and South Semitic imperfective (**2**), and to the preterite, jussive, and West Semitic imperfect (**3**):

	1	**2**	**3**
Assyro-Babylonian	*purrus*	*uparras*	*uparris*
Ugaritic	*qtl*	*yqtl*	*yqtl*
Hebrew	*qittēl*		*yəqattēl*
Old Aramaic	*qtl*		*yqtl*
Syriac	*qattel*		*nəqattel*
Classical Arabic	*faʿʿala*		*yufaʿʿilu*
Damascene Coll.	*faʿʿal*		*bīfaʿʿel*
Maghrebine Coll.	*fəʿʿəl*		*yifəʿʿəl*
Geʿez	*qattala*	*yəqettəl*	*yəqattəl*
Tigre	*qattala*	*yəqattəl*	*yəqattəl*
Amharic	*qättälä*	*yəqättəl*	*yəqättəl*

c) Stem with Lengthened First Vowel

41.4. Stem III with lengthened first vowel may be designated by the symbol L(engthening), already used in some grammars. This stem is attested in Arabic (*fā'ala*, *yufā'ilu*) and in Ethiopic (e.g. Ge'ez *šāqaya*, "he tormented"; Tigre *gādala*, "he rang"; *kāfala*, "he dissected, cut in many pieces"; Chaha *yəbanər*, "he demolishes"), but Stem III of Ethiopic (I.3/C) is no longer felt by native speakers as a derived stem, but as a basic stem, except in Tigre. Besides, a stem with lengthened first vowel appears in Modern South Arabian; e.g. Mehri *arōkəb*, "he put (a pot) on the fire" (with a vowel prefixed to a voiced or glottalized first radical). However, given that internal gemination is not a feature of derived verbal stems in Modern South Arabian, the long vowel may also replace the gemination of the second radical; in consequence, this derived stem, e.g. Mehri *(a)CōCəC*, represents not only the so-called third stem of Arabic (*fā'ala*), but also the second stem (*fa''ala*), as confirmed by its either conative (Stem III) or intensive (Stem II) meaning. Stem III of Arabic indicates an action directed towards an object, i.e. either an attempt to accomplish something (conative, e.g. *qātala*, "he tried to kill", i.e. "he fought") or a correlative motion towards someone (e.g. *kātaba*, "he corresponded"; *lāyana*, "he treated with kindness"; *zāmala*, "he kept company").

The following table is limited to Arabic, South Arabian, and Ethiopic. The presentation is the same as in §41.3:

	1	2	3
Classical Arabic	*fā'ala*		*yufā'ilu*
Damascene Coll.	*fā'al*		*bīfā'el*
Maghrebine Coll.	*fā'al*		*yifā'al*
Mehri	*fō'əl*	*yafa'lən*	*yafō'əl*
Geez	*qātala*	*yəqāttəl*	*yəqātəl*
Tigre	*qātala*	*yəqāttəl*	*yəqātəl*
Amharic	*qattälä*	*yəqattəl*	*yəqatl*

41.5. A variant of Stem III with a diphthong derived from the long vowel, but often reduced to *ō* or *ē*, is attested in Arabic (e.g. *ğawraba*, "he put on socks"; *ḥōrab*, "he song war songs"), in Ethiopic (e.g. Ge'ez *degana*, "he pursued"), and in Syriac (e.g. *gawzel*, "he set fire to"). It must be distinguished from the Ethiopic verbs with the vowel *o* after the first radical which was originally a labiovelar *gʷ*, *kʷ*, *qʷ* or a rounded consonant *bʷ*, *fʷ*, *mʷ*; e.g. Amharic *qʷättärä* > *qottärä*, "he cut". The examples of authentic variants *-aw-* > *-ō-* of Stem III are rare in Ethiopic and in Syriac, where they practically became basic stems. However, some South Ethiopic verbs generally classified as Stem I.2/B may have belonged here, in particular the Gafat, Harari, Soddo, and East Gurage verbs with vowel *e* or *i* after the first radical consonant; e.g. Gafat *kimmärä* < **kaymara*[(?)] < **kāmara*[(?)], "he piled up"; Harari *bētäna* and East Gurage *betänä* or *bītänä* < **baytana*[(?)] < **bātala*[(?)], "he dispersed" (cf. Arabic *battala*, "he cut off"). This interpretation is supported by the use of these verbs with the causative reflexive affix *at-* (§41.14) which is normally prefixed to Ethiopic verbs with lengthened first vowel (I.3/C); e.g. Gafat *at-kimmärä*, "he caused to pile up". In Arabic, especially in modern colloquials, this variant stem appears mainly in denominative verbs; e.g. *baytara*, "to practice as veterinary" (from Greek ἱππίατρος, "veterinary"); *sawǧar*, "he collared" (a dog).

41.6. Since the stem with lengthened first vowel has not been identified hitherto in North and East Semitic, it is generally considered as a secondary development in West and South Semitic languages. More precisely, it would have resulted from a specialization of functions originally attached to a single Stem II-III. This opinion is confirmed by the situation in Modern South Arabian, by the intensive meaning of Stem III of many Arabic and Ethiopic verbs, and by the parallel cases of the Bedja "intensive" (cf. §41.3) and of the Libyco-Berber "intensive" perfective, which are both formed by quantitative or qualitative modifications of the stem vowel; e.g. Tuareg *ilkăm*, "he followed, *ur ilkim*, "he didn't follow", but *ilkām*, "he followed with result"; *ikkərăḍ*, "he behaved violently", but *yăkkīrăḍ*, "he behaved violently to the end"; Bedja *kitim*, "to arrive", but *kātim*, "to arrive repeatedly". The Libyco-Berber "intensive" imperfective has probably merged with the imperfective of the basic stem which is characterized by both vowel lengthening and gemination, as *ilākkəm*, "he follows" (§2.14). Like in Modern South Arabian, there is no verbal class with gemination in Cushitic, and the Bedja "intensive" forms with *-ā-* may testify to a phonological equivalence of *-v̄C-* and *-vCC-*. This leads to the hypothesis that the alternation *-v̄C-* and *-vCC-* was originally a phonotactic free variation in the realization of the "intensive" stem *faʿʿala / fāʿala* (Stems II-III) and of its reflexive correspondent *tafaʿʿala / tafāʿala* (Stems V-VI: §41.20 ff.). In fact, the conative or reciprocal acceptation of Stems III and VI implies repetition, as Stems II and V do, and this may indicate that originally there was only one intensive stem with lengthening either of the consonant (-*vCC*-) or of the vowel (-*v̄C*-), and with a secondary conative or reciprocal meaning which led finally to a semantic opposition between *fā'ala* and *fa''ala* in certain Arabic and Ethiopic verbs. Early Arab grammarians established then *fā'ala* as a distinct derived stem, basing themselves on the contrasting use of *fā'ala* and *fa''ala* in a number of verbs. Owing to the lack of internal gemination in the South Arabian verbal system, the *fā'ala* type was instead entrenched there as the sole intensive/conative stem, while Ethiopic Stems II (I.2/B) and III (I.3/C) were no longer felt by native speakers as derived stems, and the two forms with -*vCC*- and with -*v̄C*- could thus coexist perfectly as basic stems of different verbal roots.

d) "Causative" Stem

41.7. Stem IV with *š*-affix is attested in all the Afro-Asiatic language families, all sharing a causative connotation. It is well-known that Egyptian has a verbal form with *ś*-prefix — later also *s* — cognate with the Semitic causative (e.g. *ś'nḫ*, "to make to live", "to nourish", from *'nḫ*, "to live"), and there is likewise an *s*-causative in Berber, used with words borrowed from Arabic (e.g. Tamazight *ssbəddəl*, "to cause to change", from *bəddəl*, "to change") and with authentic Libyco-Berber verbs; e.g. *yəssəzdəġ*, "he lodged", vs. *yəzdəġ*, "he settled"; *yəssird*, "he clothed", vs. *yird*, "he dressed himself", both examples in Tarifit. In Cushitic and Chadic languages, as well as in Bantu (§1.2), a morpheme -*s* or -*š* is suffixed to the causative form of the verb (e.g. Highland East Cushitic *imm-is-*, "cause to give", from *imm-*, "give"; Agaw *šäy-š*, "cause to take", from *šäy-*, "to take"; Oromo *dammaq-s*, "to awaken", from *dammaq*, "to wake up"), but Bedja has a stem with the *s*-prefix; e.g. *yisodir*, "he ordered to kill". The *š*-suffix is attested also in Semitic, but only as a morpheme deriving verbs from nouns; e.g. Hebrew *pū-š*, "to blow", from *pe < pū*, "mouth"; *ḥāla-š*, "to weaken", from *ḥŏlī*, "weakness"; *rā'a-š*, "to shake", from *ra'*, "evil"; *ḥāra-š*, "to cut in, to engrave", from *ḥor*, "hole". These formations have exact parallels in Libyco-Berber and in Cushitic; e.g. Tachelhit *s-ġyul*, "to behave like a donkey", from *a-ġyul*, "donkey"; West Cushitic (Walamo) *ord-es*, "to grow fat", from *ord-iya*, "fat"; Oromo *hark-is-u*, "to pull, draw", from *hark-a*, "hand".

41.8. In Semitic, the uses of the causative extend beyond the one usually viewed as central, namely that in which someone causes a certain action to be performed or a certain state to be produced, e.g. Assyro-Babylonian *ušalbiš*, "he clothed", from *labāšu*, "to be clothed". The factitive use ("to have something done by another") is also widespread; e.g. Ugaritic *'šspr-k*, "I shall make you count". Besides, the adjutative acceptation ("to help to do something") and the use as causative of reciprocity ("to cause to do something one against another") are encountered likewise, as well as intransitive and denominative uses; e.g. Hebrew *he'ĕšîr*, "he grew rich"; Assyro-Babylonian *šumšū*, "to spend the night" (from *mūšu*, "night"), paralleled by Libyco-Berber (Tamazight) *ssəns*, "to spend the night", with the frequent allophone *n* of *m*. Such denominative formations are not exceptional in Tamazight; e.g. *s-mi'iw*, "to mew"; *s-udəm*, "to kiss", from *udəm*, "face" (cf. Arabic *'udn-*, "ear"). These examples show that Afro-Asiatic *š*-causative performs the same functions as Stem II in historically attested Semitic languages. The coexistence of the two stems is nevertheless explainable in a diachronic perspective, if Stem II originally was the conjugation of transitive verbs in opposition to Stem I (§41.3), which was acting as intransitive inflection, and to Stem IV, which had a causative and factitive function.

41.9. In Semitic, the *š*-prefix occurs in Palaeosyrian (e.g. *uš-tá-si-ir* /yuštāšir/, "he has released", at Ebla; *ú-ša-dì-ú-šu* /yušādi'ūšu/, "they let him know", at Mari), probably in Amorite (e.g. *ia-ás-ki-in* /yaškīn/, "he caused to be"), certainly in Ugaritic (e.g. *'ašhlk*, "I shall cause to flow"), in Old Akkadian (e.g. *ú-ša-ak-lí-il*, "he completed"), in Assyro-Babylonian (e.g. *ušamqit*, "he caused to fall"), in Minaic (e.g. *ys¹'lyns¹*, "they bring him up"), in Qatabanic (e.g. *s¹hdt*, "he inaugurated"), in Hadramitic (e.g. *s¹qny*, "he offered"), in Amharic (e.g. *asnäggärä*, "he let speak"; *asattärä*, "he made short"; *ašqädaddämä*, "he put ahead", from *qäddämä*, "he was ahead of"), in Gafat (*asdänäbbäta*, "he frightened"), and in Argobba (e.g. *asmelläsa*, "he let answer"), while its traces are encountered in North Ethiopic (cf. §41.14). Besides, the *š*-prefix is preserved in the causative-reflexive Stem X or Št (§41.29) in Aramaic (e.g. Syriac *'eštawdī*, "he confessed", from *yidā*), in Hebrew (*hištaḥªwā*, "he prostrated himself"), in Arabic (e.g. *'istakbara*, "he held himself for great", "he displayed arrogance"), in Sabaic (e.g. *s¹tqr'*, "he was convened"), in Modern South Arabian (e.g. Ḥarsūsi *šəlbōd*, "he was hit"), in Ge'ez (e.g. *'astamhara*, "he showed himself merciful"). The preservation of the sibilant before *t* also characterizes Slavic languages where *s* does not change into *ḥ* before a consonant, in particular *t*; e.g. *byste*, "you were" (plur.), vs. *byḫu*, "I was"; *prusti* vs. *praḫu*, "dust". In East Semitic and in Ethiopic, the causative morpheme *š* > *s* may be prefixed not only to the basic stem and to the reflexive-passive stems with *t*-affix (e.g. Amharic *astamammänä*, "he inspired confidence", "he convinced"), but also to the stem with geminated second radical consonant, and in Ethiopic, besides, to the stem with lengthened first vowel.

41.10. Due to Assyro-Babylonian influence, the *š*-prefix is attested also in loanwords borrowed by Aramaic (e.g. *šēzib*, "he saved"; *šaklilū*, "they completed") and in some derived verbal forms of Eastern Late Aramaic (e.g. *ša'bēd*, "he enslaved", from *'ăbed*, "slave"). In its turn, Mishnaic Hebrew borrowed this prefix from Aramaic (e.g. *šiklēl*, "he completed"; *ši'bēd*, "he enslaved"). Traces of a *š*-causative have been detected also in Arabic (e.g. *sa-baqa*, "he left behind", from *baqiya*, "he remained", "he was left behind"), in Ethiopic (§41.14), and in Neo-Aramaic (e.g. *šaḫlep*, "changing", from Syriac *šaḫlep*, "he changed"), but the preformative *š*- / *s*- is not productive in these languages.

41.11. Instead of the *š*-prefix, a *h*-prefix — later weakened to ' — is used in Old Canaanite (*ḫi-iḫ-bi-e* /hiḫbī'/, "he has hidden": EA 256,7), in Aramaic (e.g. *hanpēq*, "he caused to go out"; *'a'bēd*, "he caused to produce"), in Hebrew (e.g. *hiqdīš*, "he consecrated"), in Moabite (e.g. *hr'ny*, "he let me see"), in North Arabian (e.g. Liḥyānite *hmt'*, "he worked out his salvation"; *hqny*, "he offered"; Thamūdic *hyd'*, "he made known"; Ṣafaitic *'s²rq*, "he went eastward"), in Arabic (e.g. *'aḏhaba*, "he caused to go away"), in Sabaic (e.g. *hqny*, "he offered"), in Modern South Arabian (e.g. Mehri *hənsōm*, Ḥarsūsi *ansōm*, "he breathed"), and in Ethiopic (e.g. Ge'ez *'aqtala*, "he caused to kill"; Tigre *'asbara* and Tigrinya *'asbärä*, "he caused to break"; Gafat *alättämä*, "he caused to happen"; Amharic *aqärräbä*, "he caused to be near", "he brought"). Its alleged use in Amorite is questionable. In Ethiopic, the *'a*- / *a*- morpheme may be added to the basic stem (I.1/A > II.1/A), to the stem with geminated second radical consonant (I.2/B > II.2/B), to the stem with lengthened first vowel (I.3/C > II.3/C), and to the stem with *t*-affix (IV, cf. §41.14,28). In the prefix-conjugation, the stem preformative *h* > ' is usually elided in Old Canaanite, in Hebrew, in Moabite, in some Aramaic dialects, in Arabic, and in Ethiopic. E.g. Old Canaanite *ti-mi-tu-na-nu* [timītūnanū], "you (plur.) make us die" (EA 238,33); Hebrew *yaqṭīl* < **yahaqṭīl*, "he will cause to kill";

Moabite *w'šb*, "and I brought back". This is the rule in Arabic, e.g. *yuḥibbu*, "he will love", but even Classical Arabic has instances of *h* retained, e.g. *yuharīqu*, "he will pour out", from *rāqa*, "to be clear" (liquid). In Geʻez, the vowel is lengthened; e.g. *yānakkər*, "he will wonder". Modern Arabic colloquials have lost Stem IV with the exception of Eastern Bedouin dialects and of same forms of speech at the rand of the Syrian desert, in Saudi Arabia, and in Yemen; e.g. *iḥrab, yiḥrib*, "to destroy", vs. *ḥirib, yiḥrab*, "to go to ruin", at Dēr ez-Zōr (Syria). The apparent mediaeval use of Stem IV instead of Stem I, especially in Iraq and in Palestine, in reality exhibits forms with prosthetic ' developed from e.g. *ẓhar* (*ẓahar*) > *'aẓhar*, "he appeared", next to *ẓuhar* (!), with an anaptyctic *u* (9th century A.D.).

41.12.   The use of the *š*-prefix in the causative stem (IV) goes together with the *š*-base of the third person independent and suffixed pronouns, except in Ugaritic, while the use of the *h* / '- prefix parallels the one of the pronominal *h*- base (§36.10, 20). The connection between the verbal affixes and the pronouns is generally accepted, but the question is whether the elements *š*- and *h*- are only morphologically equivalent or etymologically identical, the difference resulting from a simple phonological development *š* > *h*, which is known from Modern South Arabian (§15.4). The preservation of reflexive *št*-forms and traces of *š*-causatives in languages which otherwise have an *h* / '- causative (§41.9-11) indicate that these languages have lost the *š*-causative. Whether this loss was the result of a non-universal prevocalic change *š* > *h* — also attested for the conditional particle "if", *šum-ma* in East Semitic but *hm/n* > *'m/n* in the other Semitic languages (§61.2) — or was based instead on the analogy of the use of *h*-pronouns is hard to determine. Given the fact that the change *š* > *h* is attested in Semitic and that this change concerns the third person pronouns, the causative stem, and the conditional particle, it seems reasonable to assume a phonological development, although its conditions remain obscure.

41.13.   Phoenician is the only Semitic language having a *y*-prefix of the causative (e.g. *yqdšt*, "I consecrated") and a pronominal third person *y*-suffix (e.g. *'dny*, "his Lord"). However, their origin is different. In the verbal stem, the prepalatal *y*- can be an on-glide before the vocalic initial *i*- resulting from the dropping of the laryngeal *h* in the causative *h*-prefix, originally pronounced **hi*- like in Hebrew. Both the loss of initial *h* and the use of *y* as an on-glide are paralleled in Ethiopic. This on-glide *yi-* was then replaced in Punic by '*ī-*; e.g. '*yqdš*, "he consecrated". An alternative explanation would consist in viewing *y* as an old causal morpheme used also to form verbs by suffixing it to a monosyllabic nominal base; e.g. *ṯn-y*, "to make another", from *ṯn-*, "two"; *bn-y*, "to make a son", from *bn*, "son"; *ḥṭ-y*, "to make an arrow", hence "to cut", from *ḥṭ*, "arrow"; *bk-y*, "to make *bk*", an onomatopoeia that denotes weeping (§62.2); *ḥm-y*, "to act as a father-in-law", hence "to protect", from *ḥm*, "father-in-law"; *rb-y*, "to increase", from *rb*, "great". A similar process is operative in Central Somali (Cushitic) with an *-ōy* extension suffixed to nouns to form a related verb; e.g. *biōy*, "to water", from *biyǝ*, "water"; *sokorōy*, "to sugar", from *sokor*, "sugar"; *usbōy*, "to salt", from *usbǝ*, "salt". Besides, there is in Somali an *-i* suffix that has a causative function, e.g. *warāb*, "to drink", vs. *warābi*, "to water (animals)"; *kah*, "to rise", vs. *kahi*, "to raise". Further research, based on Afro-Asiatic, is needed here. As for the pronominal suffix *-y*, it can best be explained as derived from a masculine suffix *-hi*, such as occurs in Aramaic. After a vowel the *h* was elided, giving raise to a diphthong *-*ay < -*ahī*, *-*ēyī < -*ēhī*, or *-*ūyī < -*ūhī*.

41.14. Two causative preformatives occur in modern Ethiopian languages, viz. *as-* or *aš-*, and '*a-* / *a-*. The widespread use of the first one in South Ethiopic (§41.9) confirms the latter's archaic features, since the morpheme *as-* / *aš-* very likely preserves the original *š- > -s-* prefix of the causative with a prosthetic *a-* (like in *astä-*), explainable in the light of Libyco-Berber where the causative morpheme can be prefixed directly to the first radical consonant (e.g. *s-qas*, "cause to taste"). The prefix *as-*, perhaps borrowed from Amharic, is used in Geʿez in isolated verbs without any definite value, and traces of its use are encountered in Tigre and Tigrinya; e.g. Tigre '*asqamqama*, "he groaned".

1° Apart from these cases, the North Ethiopian languages of Tigre and Tigrinya form the causative either with the prefixed morpheme '*a-* (§41.11) or with '*at-*, the latter being a combination of the causative '*a-* morpheme and of the reflexive-passive (§41.28) or frequentative (§41.34) *t-*affix. While the simple causative function of '*a-* appears, e.g., in Tigre '*azmata*, "he caused to raid", from the transitive verb *zamta*, "he raided", the complex role of '*at-* is evidenced, e.g., in Tigre '*atḥādaga*, "he caused to leave", from *ḥadga*, "he left". The latter (I.1/A) is actually converted into a verb of type III.3/C with lengthened first vowel (**ta-ḥādaga*) and with a passive meaning ("he was induced to leave"), which is changed into a causative one by the *'a-* morpheme: "he induced to leave". The prefix *'at-* can apparently be added also to the old reflexive/passive form **ta-qatala* > **taqtala* of the basic stem, which was replaced by *təqattala*, the corresponding form of the D-stem; e.g. Tigre **'attaqtala**, "he caused to be killed"; **'attabala**, "he caused to be said". However, the geminated *tt* should be explained by a phonetic gemination of an intervocalic *t*, not by the addition of the composite morpheme *'at*: from the strictly morphological point of view, only *'a-* is prefixed to **taqtala*. Ge'ez, which does not use the prefix *'at-*, is generally believed to represent the situation of ancient Ethiopic, what would imply that this composite prefix is an innovation in Tigre and Tigrinya.

2° However, the prefix *at-* is used in all the South Ethiopian languages, except in Argobba. Also in South Ethiopic, the *at-* morpheme expresses the causative of intransitive verbs as well as the causative of the reflexive/passive, thus in Amharic *abbazza*, "multiply", from the causative prefix *a* + *tä-bazza*, "become multiple", with a complete assimilation of *t* to the following consonant; Soddo **atkiddänä**, "he caused to cover" or "he caused to be covered", from the causative prefix *a* + the reflexive/passive prefix *tä-* + *käddänä*, "he covered". Similarly, Gafat **atkimmärä**, "he caused to pile up", "he got it piled up", prefixes the causative morpheme *a-* to the passive *tä-kimmärä*, "it was piled up". The *at-* morpheme can also express the factitive when referring to an action that one does habitually or frequently, as being in the habit of preparing meat; e.g. Chaha **atbäsäräm**, "he made someone cook", from *bäsär*, "meat". Further, it can express the adjutative and the causative of reciprocity, e.g. in Soddo **atgaddälä**, "he helped to kill" or "he caused to kill one another". In short, while *-t-* is a reflexive/passive or frequentative morpheme, *a-* is the causative prefix which performs the same functions as those attested in Amharic for the *as*-prefix, e.g. *asnäggärä*, "he let speak".

This leaves us with a variegated conspectus of causative stems with prefixed morphemes *š-, h-, 'a-, y-*, as well as with a series of composite prefixes *'an- / an-* (§41.17-18), *št-, st-, ht-, 'at-, -tt-* (§41.28-32). A recapitulative table will be offered in §41.54. Contrary to the Bantu languages, Semitic does not possess a causative of the N-stem which is not attested, besides, over the entire Semitic area (§41.15-17). Thus, forms corresponding to Swahili *pat* ("obtain") *-an* ("from each other") *-iš* ("cause to") *-a*, i.e. "to unite", do not occur in Semitic.

e) Stem with n-Prefix

41.15. As a rule, the N-stem or Arabic Stem VII corresponds in Semitic to the basic stem, denoting its reflexive (e.g. Hebrew *niptaḥ*, "it got open", from *pātaḥ*, "to open"), reciprocal (e.g. Old Assyrian *naṣbutū*, "they hold each other fast", from *ṣabātu*, "to seize"), and passive (e.g. Arabic *'inhazama*, "he was put to flight", from *hazama*). Therefore this stem is also called "medio-passive". It occurs likewise in Libyco-Berber where it gives a reflexive or reciprocal meaning to transitive verbs, and where it coexists with an M-stem that exercises the same function; e.g. Tarifit *yəmmarni ġar-s u-symi*, "a he-baby (< *šim + ī) added himself to her", i.e. "she got a baby" (cf. *yarni a-ġi*, "he added milk"). The M-stem replaces the N-stem in some Cushitic languages, as prefix (e.g. Bedja *amodārna*, "kill each other!") or suffix (e.g. Highland East Cushitic *mōgam*, "to be buried", from *mōg-*, "to bury"; Oromo *bēkam*, "to be known", from *bēka*, "to know"), but *n-* is preserved in the western Boni area of Lowland East Cushitic (*n-d'el-*, "to be born", from *d'el*, "to give birth"), whereas it is replaced by *l-* in the eastern Boni area (*l-d'el*) and in Rendille (*lá-ḍel*). In all likelihood, *l-*, *m-*, and *n-* are just allophones of the same Afro-Asiatic affix. A reciprocal verb suffix *-án-* occurs also in Bantu languages (§1.2), and reciprocity may inded have been the original semantic value of the N-stem.

41.16. The N-stem is not attested over the entire Semitic area, perhaps partly because the vowelless *n* was totally assimilated to the first consonant of the verbal root and cannot be recognized. Thus, there are so far no certain attestations of this stem in Palaeosyrian, in Amorite, and not even in Ugaritic, since the Ugaritic form *tntkn* (KTU 1.14,I,28), from *ntk*, "to pour", is apparently an imperfective *tanattukna*, "(his tears) pour down", while *nlqḥt* in broken context (KTU 4.659,1) could be a noun meaning something like "drawings" (otherwise one would expect *nqḥt*). Besides, no reliable attestation of the N-stem was encountered so far in both Epigraphic South Arabian and the Aramaic group of languages, though scholars have tried to find remnants of such forms. Some Neo-Aramaic dialects have derived stems with an *n*-prefix, but these forms are either borrowed from Arabic or result from a change *m > n*.

41.17. Ethiopic and Modern South Arabian do not have an N-stem deriving from the basic stem, but there is a series of Ethiopic verbs that have either the prefix *'an-* / *an-*, or the prefix *ən-* / *tän-*, or both, while an *ən*-prefix is encountered in Modern South Arabian. These prefixes are not productive in the sense that they cannot derive a verb with these prefixes from the basic stem. The verbs under consideration are lexical items and mainly express sound, movement, or light, usually by means of quadriconsonantal reduplicated stems of the pattern $C_1C_2C_1C_2$, e.g. Śḥeri *əndəbdəb*, "he dragged behind"; Tigre *'anqaṭqaṭa*, "he was shaken"; Amharic *anqäsaqqäsä*, "he moved". Quadriconsonantal verbs with a *na*-prefix, originally expressing movement, are attested also in East Semitic, e.g. *nabalkutu(m)*, "to transgress"; *naparqudu(m)*, "to fall backwards". In Egyptian, there is an *n*-prefix used likewise with quadriconsonantal reduplicated stems, e.g. *ngsgs*, "to overflow". The "mediopassive" function of the N-stem cannot be equated with the meaning of these "expressive" verbs, the *n*-preformative of which has formed triconsonantal verbs as well, as shown e.g. by a comparison of *napāšu* with *pūš*, "to blow", and of *nawāru* with *'ūr*, "to shine". The function of this verbal *n*-preformative can be compared with that of a *na*-suffix in Margi, a language of the Biu-Mandara branch of the Chadic family; e.g. *ndàlnà*, "to throw away", from *ndàl*, "to throw". This suffix "mainly seems to indicate that the action is done in the direction 'away'" (P. Newman). Its general acceptation thus described suits quite well the Semitic verbs having the prefixes *'an-* / *an-*, *ən-* / *tän-*; e.g. Amharic *ankäbällälä*, "throw someone down in wrestling"; *tänkärättätä*, "wander from place to place".

41.18. In Ethiopic, whenever there is a concurrence of a form with *'an-* / *an-* and *ən-* / *tän-*, the form with (*'*)*an-* has a transitive or a causative meaning; e.g. Amharic *anqäsaqqäsä*, "he moved (someone or something)"; Soddo (Gurage) *anqəlaqqälä*, "he made wander here and there". Instead, the form with *ən-* or *tän-* is either intransitive, or used as a verb of state, or as a passive; e.g. Amharic *tänqäsaqqäsä*, "he moved (himself)"; Muher (Gurage) *ənkrättätä*, "he was bent"; Soddo *tänqälaqqälä*, "he wandered from place to place". This evidence leads to the conclusion that the (*'*)*an*-preformative combines the causative (*'*)*a*-prefix with the *n*-prefix, while the intransitive is then formed with the sole *ən-* < *$(i)n$- or with *tän-* which combines the reflexive-passive morpheme *t* with *n*-. This explanation is strengthened by the parallel existence of a *š*-causative of the East Semitic quadriconsonantal verbs with the *n*-preformative; e.g. *nabalkutu(m)*, "to transgress", and *šubalkitu*, "to bring over". However, a verb that occurs only with (*'*)*an-* in Ethiopic can be either transitive (e.g. Amharic *ankäbällälä*, "he threw someone down") or intransitive (e.g. Ge'ez *'anfar'aṣa*, "he jumped"). Some verbs have an only apparent *an-* prefix, as Amharic *anqaqqa*, "he dried", which is a verb formed by reduplication: **anq-anq-a*. The allomorphs *am-* and *täm-* before *b* (e.g. Amharic *amb^wattärä*, "he bragged"; *tämbäräkkäkä*, "he knelt down") do not create any particular problem: they simply result from a partial assimilation *nb* > *mb*.

41.19. The *n*-prefix of the N-stem does not seem to be connected to any particular vowel. In the imperative, which is morphologically the simplest form of a "verbal" base (§37.2; 38.1), it is vocalized *na-* in East Semitic (e.g. *napqid*, "be entrusted!"), and this was also the case in Old Canaanite, since the stative has there a *na-*prefix (e.g. *na-aq-ṣa-pu*, "they are irritated": EA 82,51), but *in-* appears in later West Semitic, also in the Hebrew imperative (e.g. *hiqqāṭəlū* < **hinqāṭəlū*, "be killed!"). The attested vocalization *na-* probably reflects the contrasting patterns *i* - *a* (e.g. Old Akkadian *tikal* next to *takal*, "trust!"), *a* - *i* (e.g. *naplis*, "look upon!"), like in modern Arabic colloquials of the Persian Gulf (e.g. *yaktib*, "he writes", but *yišrab*, "he drinks"), while the *i* of Arabic *in-* is the most common prosthetic vowel (§27.16) and it also contrasts with the vowel *a*. Therefore, no firm conclusion can be drawn from these vocalizations with regard to an original vowel of the *n*-prefix. As for its assumed connection with the Egyptian, Berber, and Chadic prepositional or pronominal morpheme *n*, it is by no means certain (cf. §41.15).

The following table is presented in the same way as the tables in §41.3-4:

	1	2	3
Assyro-Babylonian	*naprus*	*ipparras*	*ipparis*
Hebrew	*niqtal*		*yiqqātel*
Classical Arabic	*'infa'ala*		*yunfa'ilu*
Damascene Coll.	*nfa'al*		*byenfa'el*
Maghrebine Coll.	*nfə'əl*		*yinfə'əl*

f) Stems with t-*Affix*

41.20. Stems with a *t*-affix are widely used in Afro-Asiatic, especially in Semitic. Two T-stems occur frequently in Libyco-Berber, where they are operative nowadays. However, the forms with the simple *t*-prefix have a frequentative function and are obviously related to the East Semitic infix *-tan-* (§41.33), while the stem with the *ttwa*-prefix, the

so-called "agentless passive", is probably akin to the Cushitic (*a*)*to*-stem
(e.g. Bedja **atomān**, "to be shaved") and to the Egyptian "pseudo-passive" form *sḏm-tw* where *tw* is the indefinite pronoun "(some)one".
Since Libyco-Berber is an ergative language, a pro form of the non-active
subject had to be used instead of the passive; e.g. Tarifit *yəttwašš u-
ġrum*, "the bread has been eaten"(by someone), lit. "someone has eaten
by means of bread", contrasting *yəšša u-fġaḥ a-ġrum*, "the countryman
has eaten bread". The Semitic *t*-affix does not have the same origin. It is
basically a morpheme expressing an effective involvement, like in the
perfective *iptaras* aspect (§38.4); its original function was also reflexive
and frequentative (§41.34-35), regardless of its use as infix, prefix, or
suffix. In the Chadic branch and in some Cushitic languages, the T-stem
is formed by suffixation instead of prefixation. Its reflexive function may
be prominent, as in Oromo, e.g. *bit-at-a*, "(he) buys for himself", vs. *bit-
a*, "(he) buys"; *fid-at-e*, "(he) brought for himself". Allophones of -*at*-
may occur, as -*aḍ*- in Rendille. The widespread use of the morpheme in
combination with various verbal stems contributed to the widening of its
functions. In Semitic, stems with a *t*-affix can be formed from the basic
stem (B/Gt; Stem VIII *'ifta'ala* in Arabic; Stem III.1/A in Ethiopic),
from the stem with doubled second radical consonant (Dt; Stem V
tafa''ala in Arabic; Stem III.2/B in Ethiopic), from the stem with lengthened first vowel (Lt; Stem VI *tafā'ala* in Arabic; Stem III.3/C in
Ethiopic), from the causative stem (Št; Stem X *'istaf'ala* in Arabic; Stem
IV and stem *'at*- / *at*- in Ethiopic), and from the Ethiopic "frequentative"
stem (§41.36). The principal function of the Semitic *t*-stems can be characterized as reflexive; e.g. *ištaknu*, "he set up for himself" (subjunctive),
Old Babylonian Stem Gt from *šakānu*; *mn dy ytptḥ yth*, "whoever opens
it for himself", in Nabataean Aramaic; *'ittaḥaḍa*, "he took for himself",
Arabic Stem VIII from *'aḥaḍa*, "to take". But they have also a passive
and a reciprocal meaning, especially in languages such as Aramaic and
Ethiopic, where there is no N-stem; e.g. Old Aramaic *ytšm'*, "it will be
heard"; Tigre *təgādabaw*, "they fought each other"; Tigrinya *täsäbrä* or
täsäbärä, "it was broken"; Amharic *tägäddälä*, "he was killed"; Gafat
tädär(r)äsä, "he was found"; Chaha (Gurage) *tärakäsom*, "they quarrelled with one another". From the semantic point of view, the stems
with *t*-affix, especially the one corresponding to the basic stem, approximately cover the same field as the N-stem.

41.21.   The *t*-affix can be put in Semitic before or after the first consonant
of the verbal stem to which it is added. Its position can be questioned in

some cases because of phonological factors which occasion the assimilation of *t* to the first radical (§41.25,32), and it can change in consequence of a widespread tendency in Semitic languages to restrict the use of stems with infixed *t* and sometimes to create new stems with prefixed *t* or (*i*)*sta-* (Stem X in Arabic).

41.22. The original situation of the *t*-affix after the first radical of the basic stem is preserved in Palaeosyrian (e.g. *ti-il-tap-tu*, "they rubbed themselves", from *lapātu*), in Amorite (e.g. the proper name *Ia-an-ta-qí-im*, "he was avenged", from *naqāmu*), in Ugaritic (e.g. *yrtḥṣ*, "he washed himself", from *rḥṣ*), in Old Akkadian (e.g. *imtaḫṣā*, "they fought with each other", from *maḫāṣu*), in Assyro-Babylonian (e.g. *mitlik*, "take advice!", from *malāku*), in Moabite (e.g. *w'ltḥm*, "and I fought", from *lḥm*), in Old Phoenician (e.g. *thtpk*, "it will be overturned", from *hpk*), in Old Aramaic (e.g. *ygtzr*, "it will be cut off", from *gzr*), in Arabic (e.g. *'irtafa'a*, "he rose", from *rafa'a*, "to lift"), in Epigraphic South Arabian (e.g. *ḍtrrn*, "to wage war against each other", from *ḍrr*, "to wage war"), and in Modern South Arabian (e.g. Mehri and Ḥarsūsi *əktəlōf*, "he was troubled", from *klf*).

41.23. The tendency to drop the stem with infixed *t* appears in standard Phoenician, where *qttl* is not attested, as against the early Byblos dialect (*thtsp*, "it will be torn away"; *thtpk*, "it will be overturned"). Only possible traces of this stem survive in Biblical Hebrew (*štn*, "to urinate", from *šyn*; *htl*, "to mock", from *hll*), and the original *t*-infix is generally replaced in Aramaic from the 8th century B.C. on by a *t*-prefix (e.g. *ytšm'*, "it will be heard"). In Sabaic, *ts²(y)m*, "he appointed for his sake", from the root *s²ym*, can only be interpreted as *tafa'la*, despite the *t*-infix of the form *ḍtrrn*.

41.24. A new basic stem with prefixed *t* and a passive meaning was created also in Arabic colloquials, especially in Egypt and in the Maghrib; e.g. Cairene *it'add*, "it was counted", from *'add*, "to count"; *itfataḥ*, "it was opened", from *fataḥ*, "to open"; *itmisik*, "he was seized", from *misik*, "to seize"; Maghrebine *tfa'al* or *tfa'il*, "it was made". These formations go back to old colloquials, since the secondary stem *taḫiḏa*, "he took for himself", is quoted from an ancient Ḥidjazi dialect, *tabanī* (*tbny*), "he consummated the marriage", occurs in a South-Palestinian text from the 9th century A.D., and similar forms are encountered elsewhere. The reflexive-passive *t*-prefix is used with the basic stem in Aramaic from the 8th century B.C. on (e.g. Old Aramaic *ytšm'*, "it will be heard"; Syriac *'etqǝṭel*, "he was killed") and in all the Ethiopian languages (e.g. Geʿez *taqatla*, "he was killed"). However, the affix can preserve its original place in Aramaic whenever it follows a sibilant, exactly as in the cluster *-št-* / *-st-* of the Semitic reflexive causative stem (§41.28), thus *hištǝkah*, "he was found", from the root *škḥ*.

41.25. The Dt-stem derived from Stem II with doubled second radical consonant has not been identified so far in Palaeosyrian, in Amorite, and in Ugaritic, but it is amply attested in the other branches of Semitic.

1° The *t* is certainly infixed in East Semitic, e.g. Old Babylonian *uštallamū*, "they will be kept safe". It preserved its original place also in Hebrew, in Phoenician, and in Aramaic when it follows a sibilant, exactly as in the cluster *-št-* / *-st-* of the reflexive causative; e.g. *hištappēk*, "to be poured out", from the root *špk*; *ysthyalm* in Poenulus 931 = **'št'lm*, "I beg you", from the root *š'l*; *yištammǝ'ūn*, "they will obey", from the root *šm'*. In post-classical Hebrew, however, the *t* can be prefixed to a sibilant, e.g. *htš'š'w* (1QIsᵃ) instead of *hišta'ašǝ'ū*, "enjoy yourselves" (Is. 29,9). The reflexive stem of the Modern South Arabian intensive-conative, which corresponds to Arabic Stems V and VI (cf. §41.4), is formed with the *t*-infix; e.g. Mehri and Ḥarsūsi *yǝftǝgōr*, "he will burst".

2° Instead, there is no hard evidence as yet that this has been the case also in Stem V (and VI) of Pre-Classical Arabic and that the forms with *t*-affixes assimilated to the first radical bear witness to an Old Arabic assimilation of the *t*-infix to the preceding sibilant or dental, like in Arabic Stem VIII; e.g. *yaṭṭahharu < *yaṭtahharu*, "he will perform an ablution"; *yaṣṣaddaqu < *yaṣtaddaqu*, "he gives alms", to compare with Hebrew *yiṣṭaddāq*, with partial assimilation of *t*, instead of Classical Arabic *yataṣaddaqu*. This assumption is nevertheless supported by the parallel situation in Stem VIII and by the prosthetic vowel in perfect forms, like ˙ *'izzayyana < *ztayyana* (Stem V), "he was adorned", *'iṯṯāqala < *ṯtāqala* (Stem VI), "he became heavy". In fact, neither the prosthesis nor the assimilation do appear in North Arabian inscriptions showing the *t* prefixed to the root, e.g. Ṣafaitic *ts²wq*, "he longed"; *trwḥ*, "he was rushed up". These formations, which antedate the 4th/5th century A.D., obviously parallel the "innovative" forms used in Classical Arabic *tafaʿʿala* (e.g. *taʿallama*, "he learned") and *tafāʿala*, also in the

Central-Arabian colloquials, and in the camel-bedouin dialects spoken by the Shammar and the Rwāla, with forms as *teḥedder*, "he discarded", *iteḥedder*, "he will discard".

3° The elision of the vowel of reflexive *ta-* is, instead, the rule in the vernaculars of the settled Arab population, with the consequence that mediaeval and modern colloquials prefix the *t* with the prosthetic vowel *a-*, like in Andalusian *atfaʻʻal*, or with *i-*, like in modern colloquials, e.g. Cairene *itgawwiz*, "he was married", from *gawwiz*, "he married".

4° Besides the cases mentioned under 1°, the *t* is prefixed in Hebrew (e.g. *hitqaddeš*, "he sanctified himself"), in Phoenician (e.g. *htqdš*), in Aramaic (e.g. Syriac *ʾethassan*, "he was fortified"), in Geʻez (e.g. *taqaddasa*, "he was sanctified"), in Tigre (e.g. *təmazzana*, "he was weighed"), in Amharic (e.g. *täfällägä*, "he was wanted"), and in the other Ethiopian languages (e.g. Soddo *täzibbärä*, "he returned" [intransitive], from *zibbärä*, "he returned" [transitive]; L-stem if the *i* derives from *ay < ā*, cf. §41.5). The initial *h / ʾ* of the forms of the suffix-conjugation is simply introducing the prosthetic vowel (§27.16) and has no phonemic function.

41.26. Mishnaic Hebrew has a form *nitpaʻʻal* or *niptaʻʻal* (with a sibilant as first radical) which combines the N-stem with the tD/Dt-stem and is used as a reflexive (e.g. *nistappag*, "he dried himself"), also as an intransitive (e.g. *ništaṭṭā*, "he went made"), a reciprocal (e.g. *ništattāpū*, "they became partners"), and very often as a passive (e.g. *nitgallā*, "it became uncovered"). A similar evolution is attested in various Arabic colloquials of the Maghrib, especially in Algeria, where the passive-reflexive meaning of a *t*-stem is underscored by the addition of a prefix *n-* leading to a form *ntafʻal* or, with assimilation, *ttafʻal*; e.g. *ntədrəb*, *ttədrəb*, and even *ttəndrəb*, "he was beaten". In Morocco, the *nt*-stem is restricted to verbs with initial radical *w*; e.g. *ntqud*, "it took fire", from *waqada*.

41.27. The *t*-affix produces a new stem also when joined to the theme with first vowel lengthened (§41.4), viz. Stem VI *tafāʻala* of Classical Arabic, which has a reflexive or reciprocal meaning. The Modern South Arabian reflexive intensive-conative of the pattern *CātCəC* and the assimilated Pre-Classical Arabic forms of the type *ʾiffāʻala / yaffāʻalu* (cf. §41.25) seem to indicate that the *t* was originally infixed, but prefixed forms are attested in Classical Arabic (e.g. *taqātalū*, "they fought together"), in Mediaeval Arabic (e.g. Andalusian *atfāʿal*), in Geʿez (e.g. *tamāsalū*, "they resembled each other"), in Tigre *təšārama*, "he was cut into strips"), in Amharic (e.g. *tämarräkä*, "he was taken prisoner"), in Gafat (*täqaṭṭälä*, "it was burnt"), and in the other Ethiopian languages (e.g. Chaha *tärakäsom*, "they quarrelled with one another"). The *t* is also prefixed in modern Arabic colloquials (e.g. Cairene *itgāwib*, "he was answered", from *gāwib*, "to answer").

41.28.   The reflexive morpheme *t* of the *š*-causative and of the Ethiopic *ʾa*-causative is always infixed and follows the causative morphemes *š-* / *s-* and *ʾa-* / *a-* (§41.9, 14). This would also be the case of the unique Old Aramaic form *htn'bw*, "they were withered", if this is a Ht-stem with the causative prefix *h-* replacing the original Št-stem of **n'p* / *na'ābu*, "to dry", and not a tD-stem with *h-* simply introducing the prosthetic vowel *i* instead of the usual Aramaic ʾ. In any case, the *ʾat-* / *at*-stem of the modern Ethiopian languages (§41.14) offers an exact parallel to the possible Old Aramaic Ht-stem. In general, the Št-stem and the Ethiopic *ʾat*-stem have either a causative-passive / reflexive meaning or a causative-reciprocal or adjutative connotation. The corresponding Cushitic stem signifies that something is being done by oneself or for oneself; e.g. Oromo *bā-sat-a*, "(he) causes to get out (*bah-*) by himself", i.e. "(he) himself takes out"; Rendille *golol-saḍ-*, "cause to feed (*golol-*) oneself", i.e. "eat".

41.29.   The Št-stem, Arabic Stem X, is well attested in all Semitic languages families: in Palaeosyrian (e.g. *uš-tá-si-ir* /*yuštāšir*/, "he has released", from the root *wšr*), in Amorite proper names (e.g. *Uš-ta-aš-ni-Èl* /*Yuštatnī-'El*/, "El acted for the second time", from the root *tny*), in Ugaritic (e.g. *tštḥwy*, "she prostrated herself", from *ḥwy*), in Old Akkadian (e.g. *uš-tá-za-kà-ar-si* /*yuštazakkarši*/, "he will swear on it", i.e. on a sheep to be sacrificed, from *zakāru*), in Assyro-Babylonian (e.g. *uštalpit*, "it was destroyed", from *lapātu*), in Hebrew (e.g. *hištaḥ°wā*, "he prostrated himself", from *ḥwy*), in Aramaic (e.g. Syriac *'eštawdī*, "he confessed", from *wdy*), in Arabic (e.g. *'istakbara*, "he deemed great", from *kabara*), in Epigraphic South Arabian (e.g. Sabaic *s¹ts¹'l*, "he put forward a request", from *s¹'l*), in North Ethiopic (e.g. Geʿez *'astamḥara*, "he showed himself merciful", from *mḥr*), and in South Ethiopic (e.g. Amharic *astämammänä*, "he inspired confidence", "he convinced", from *'mn*). The absence of the morpheme *t* in the Modern South Arabian forms of the causative reflexive (e.g. Ḥarsūsi *šəlbōd*, "he was hit", from *lbd*) and of the intensive-conative reflexive (e.g. Ḥarsūsi *šələbəd*, "he hit back") is to be explained by the total assimilation of *t* to the preceding *š*: **štalbad > šəlbōd* and **štalabbad > šələbəd*. The existence of these two forms parallels the two types of the East Semitic Št-stem recognizable by the imperfectives (present-future) *uštapras*, which is the passive of the Š-stem, and *uštaparras*, which has a reciprocal connotation (e.g. *uštamaḫḫar*, "she makes herself equal to"). There is a clear correspondence between the Modern South Arabian and the East Semitic forms, both from the morphological and from the semantic points of view.

41.30. The tendency to drop or to restrict the use of the stems with *t*-infix is also manifest in the case of the Št-stem. The latter is not attested in Phoenician and its use in Hebrew is restricted to one verb. In Aramaic, it tends to be replaced by a Th-stem, the passive-reflexive of the *h*-causative (§41.11); e.g. Official Aramaic *'thḥsynn*, "they refrained", from *ḥsn*. Following the change *h > '* it became a T'-stem (e.g. participle *mt''l*, "brought in", from *'ll*) and finally a Tt-stem with the assimilation *t' > tt*; e.g. Syriac *'ettrīm*, "he was raised", from *rwm*. Instead, Moroccan Arabic prefixes *t* to the *s*, thus creating a stem *tsəf'al*.

41.31. In modern Arabic colloquials, the prefix (*i*)*sta-* of Stem X is sometimes extended to other stems; e.g. Palestinian *istarayyaḥ*, "he found rest", combines Stems II and X of *rāḥa*; Tunisian *st'āhid*, "he agreed with", and Damascene *stnāwal*, "he packed with", combine Stems III and X respectively of *waḥada* and of *nāla*.

41.32. Beside the South Arabian total assimilation *št > š* (§41.29) and the Aramaic assimilation *t' > tt* (§41.30), other changes related to the *t*-affix can be observed. Thus, the morpheme *št* can change in Assyro-Babylonian into *lt* and become *ss* in the Neo-Assyrian orthography, which conceals a pronounced *śś > šš* (§15.2; 27.5). Moreover, the *t*-affix is assimilated in various languages to the first consonant of the verbal root. In Arabic, the *t*-infix of Stem VIII is totally or partially assimilated to the preceding interdental (*t, d, ḍ, ṭ*) and dental plosive (*d, ṭ*) or fricative (*z, ṣ*); e.g. *'iṭṭa'ara < *ṭta'ara*, "he was avenged"; *'izdaḥama < *ztaḥama*, "it was crowded". In Pre-Classical Arabic, the original *t*-infix rather than prefix of Stems V and VI (§41.25) is likewise assimilated to the interdentals (*t, d*), dental plosives (*d, ṭ*) or fricatives (*s, z, ṣ*), and to the palato-alveolar *š* (< *ś*); e.g. *'izzayyana < *ztayyana*, "he was adorned"; *yaddaṭṭaru* < **yadtaṭṭaru*, "he covers himself". In Hebrew, a partial assimilation of the *t*-infix of the Dt-stem (corresponding to Arabic Stem V) is attested when the preceding consonant is *ṣ* (e.g. *hiṣṭaddēq* < **hiṣtaddēq*, "he justified himself"), and the assimilation is total when this consonant is *d* or *ṭ* (e.g. *yiddakkǝ'ū* < **yidtakkǝ'ū*, "they will be crushed"; *yiṭṭammā* < **yiṭtammā*, "he defiles himself"). In Aramaic, the assimilation can be total when the preceding consonant is *z* (e.g. *hzmntwn* < **'iztǝmintūn*, "you have agreed"). In the North Ethiopian languages of Geʻez and Tigre the *t*-affix of the reflexive-passive stem is assimilated to the contiguous dental or sibilant (e.g. Geʻez *yǝssabbar* < **yǝtsabbar* and Tigre *lǝssabar* < **lǝtsabar*, "it is broken"), but in Tigrinya it is assimilated to any contiguous radical which, however, is not geminated (e.g. *yǝkǝffät* < **yǝtkǝffät*, "it is opened"). In the South Ethiopian languages of Amharic and Argobba the *t*-affix is assimilated to any first radical, in Argobba also in the perfect (e.g. Amharic *yǝnnäggär-all*, "it is said"; Argobba *ǝnnekkäsa*, "he was bitten"; *yǝnnekkäsäl*, "he will be bitten"). Besides, a total assimilation of *t* occurs in the Amharic forms *aqqattälä* < **atqattälä* < **'a-tä-qātala* and *aqqätattälä* < **atqätattäla* < **'a-tä-qatātala* with the causative reflexive prefix *at-* (§41.14), except in verbs beginning with *a*, where the weakened original guttural is assimilated to the preceding *t* giving rise to a geminated *tt* (< *t'*), as in *attäsassäbä*, "he caused to settle financial accounts", from the reciprocal stem *täsassäbu*, "they settled accounts", formed from *assäbä*, "he calculated" (root *ḥšb*). In Harari, Gafat, and Gurage, the *t* is assimilated only to a contiguous dental or sibilant (e.g. Gafat *yǝssikkäm* for **yǝtsikkäm*, "he carries a burden"), but it can optionally be maintained in some of the Gurage dialects (e.g. Ennemor *yǝtsädäb* or *yǝssädäb*, "he is offended"). This optional usage clearly indicates that the assimilation takes place with a prefixed *t*, contrary to the situation in Arabic (§41.25).

Considering the various combinations of prefixed and infixed *t*-stems with other stems, a recapitulative table will be offered in §41.55.

g) Frequentative Stems

41.33. The frequentative or iterative meaning is expressed in Palaeosyrian, in Old Akkadian, and in Assyro-Babylonian by an infix *-tana-* in the imperfective (present-future) and *-tan-* in the other "tenses", where the *n* is assimilated to the following consonant; e.g. Palaeosyrian preterite *iš-ta-pá-ru* /yištapparū/ < **yištanparū*, "they sent continuously", but

Old Akkadian imperfective *aš-tá-na-pá-ra* /(')*aštanappara*/, "I send continuously". This infix can be inserted in all the forms of the basic stem (B/Gtn: *iptanarras*), of the stem with lengthened or geminated second radical consonant (Dtn: *uptanarras*), of the causative stem (Štn: *uštanapras*), and of the passive-reflexive stem (Ntn: *ittanapras*). Some Canaanized verbal forms of the Amarna correspondence use the infix *-tan(a)-* as well; e.g. *iš-te-nem-mu* (with an indicative *u*-suffix), "I am always heeding" (EA 261,10); *u lāmi tittaṣṣūna* (with the plural *-ūna* termination) *ṣābu piṭṭātu*, "and lest the bowmen continue to come forth ..." (EA 244,19-20). It is not clear as yet whether these forms are hybrid or belong to an authentic West Semitic conjugation. Since the assimilation of *-n-* has to be assumed in most cases, while the gemination is not indicated, the frequentative or durative meaning may also be explained by the use of a *ta*-infix, attested in Assyro-Babylonian (e.g. *aštammar*, "I praise continuously"). The latter is sometimes combined with the reflexive *t*-affix (§41.35), and it is paralleled by the Ethiopic and Libyco-Berber *ta*-prefix (§41.34). Further research is needed. In any case, the infix *-tan(a)-* is not related to the Ethiopic *tän*-prefix (§41.17-18).

41.34. The frequentative stem with the *ta(n)*-affix, which was believed to be unique to the ancient Syro-Mesopotamian Semitic, corresponds instead to the Libyco-Berber *t*-prefix, which has to be distinguished from the *ttwa*-prefix (§41.20), and to the Ethiopic *ta*-prefix when the latter is added to the stem of some verbs with lengthened first vowel (I.3/C). In Libyco-Berber, this morpheme can denote a frequentative, habitual, or continuous action; e.g. *yətəffəġ*, "he often goes out" (vs. *yəffəġ*, "he went out"), *yətətt a-ḏir*, "he usually eats grapes" (vs. *yəšša*, "he ate"); *träžiġ*, "I keep on waiting" (vs. *ražiġ*, "I waited"); *tməttən*, "they die one after the other" (vs. *yəmmut*, "he died"); *itākārāḏ*, "he keeps on behaving violently", *ur itəkəriḏ*, "he doesn't keep on behaving violently" (vs. *ikkərāḏ*, "he behaved violently"). In Ethiopic, this stem may express an action that one does habitually or normally; e.g. Amharic *yəh wəšša tänakaš näw*, "this dog is likely to bite" or "is in the habit of biting". It may also assume the various meanings of the "reduplicative" or "frequentative" stem (§41.36). If the original prefix was **tan-*, the *n* has been lost completely in Libyco-Berber and in Ethiopic. However, the existence of a simple *t*-affix with the same functions in Syro-Mesopotamian Semitic seems to suggest a different answer (§41.35).

41.35. Ugaritic and Assyro-Babylonian happen to use a double *t*-affix in reflexive conjugations, where the second -*t*- denotes a progressive or frequentative action, although there is no trace of *n* (cf. §41.33). The clearest case occurs in Ugaritic with a tB/Gt infinitive followed by a feminine pronominal suffix: *wl šb't tmtḫṣh b'mq*, "and she was not sated with her habit of fighting in the valley" (KTU 1.3,II,19). Since the form is an infinitive, no perfect of the *iptaras* type may enter here into account. A similar example is found in a syllabic text from Ugarit, where the restitution is based on a parallel passage from Boghazköy: [*šumma... lā tanta*]*tḫaṣ* (< *tamtatḫaṣ*), "if ... you do not fight over and over again". The context requires the imperfective *iparras* where the gemination of the second radical is supplanted by the -*t*- infix: *imtatḫaṣ* < **imtatḫḫaṣ*, comparable with *uptarris* < **uptanrris*. Similar cases occur in temporal clauses at Boghazköy; e.g. *abūya itti nakrīšu kī intatḫaṣṣu*, "when my father was fighting over and over again with his enemies". In these temporal clauses using the frequentative, the imperfective *iparras* is employed instead of the *iprus*, like in Old Assyrian, e.g. *inūmi ... taštanapparanni ... aqbī-šum*, "when you were writing to me over and over again, I told you ...". Comparable forms without *n* are found in other Assyro-Babylonian texts with a B/Gtt-form, e.g. *lū terēq lū tenessī lū tatatlak*, "may you recede, may you disappear, may you go further and further away!"; with a Dtt-form, e.g. [...] *īrub ištiššu šinīšu šalšīšu rigimšu iddi-ma uteteṭṭi*, "[when Adad] enters, darts his roar once, twice, three times, and it darkens more and more ..."; with a Štt-form, e.g. *libittašu ina ramānišu uštatalpit*, "its brickwork crumbles more and more by itself". In the last three examples, the imperfective *iparras* denotes a progressive situation, rather than an iterative one. This leaves us with a strong analogy to the Libyco-Berber usage of the *t*-affix (§41.34). The forms in question continued to be used in Late Babylonian, as shown by the Štt- imperfective in the Aramaizing asyndetic construction of a perfective followed by an imperfective in *upattā nērbēti mālak erinē uštetešer*, "I opened up passes (so that) the road of the cedars will be practicable on and on". The paradigm of the East Semitic imperfective (*iparras*) of these reflexive-frequentative stems can be presented as follows:

B/Gtt	Dtt	Štt
imtatḫaṣ	*uptat(ar)ras*	*uštatapras*

41.36. A "frequentative" stem with repeated second radical consonant is very common in modern Ethiopic. It is usually called either "redu-plicative" or "frequentative" in consideration of its main semantic

function. In fact, this stem mostly expresses an intensive or a frequentative action; e.g. Tigre *kadādama*, "he worked on and off"; *sabābara*,
"he broke thoroughly"; Amharic *säbabärä*, "he smashed"; Tigrinya
qätatälä, Soddo (Gurage) *gədaddälä*, "he slaughtered" (root ·*qtl*); Chaha
(Gurage) *bənanäräm* or *bənänäräm*, "he went on demolishing", from
banäräm, "he demolished". Also the biconsonantal verbs can form a
reduplicative stem; e.g. Chaha *səmamäm*, "he went on kissing", from
samäm, "he kissed" (root *s'm*). There are verbs whose basic meaning is
expressed only by the reduplicative stem; e.g. Muher (Gurage) *tä-blal-
läqäm*, "he was joyful". The reduplicative may often be rendered by
"completely, constantly, thoroughly, all over, on and on".

41.37.   There exist in Hebrew some related cases where the second and
third radicals are repeated; e.g. *səharhar*, "he continuously turned
about", from *shr*, "to go about"; *hŏmarmar*, "it was continuously foaming", from the root *hmr*. The same formation is attested in Ethiopic with
verbs possessing a meaning which implies iterative connotations; e.g.
Ge'ez *'ahmalmala*, "it became green"; *'arsāhsəha*, "he sullied";
Amharic *bäläqälläqä*, "he became clumsy".

h) Reduplicated Biconsonantal Stems

41.38.   Originally biconsonantal roots of the type CvC give rise by
reduplication to quadriconsonantal themes of the type $C_1vC_2C_1vC_2$, e.g.
Ugaritic *ykrkr*, "he snapped"; Hebrew *gilgēl*, "he rolled"; Aramaic and
Mishnaic Hebrew *balbēl*, "he confused"; Arabic *zalzala*, "he shook";
la'la'a, "it glittered"; Ge'ez *badbada*, "he devastated"; *'an-safsafa*, "it
dripped"; Amharic *gʷänäggʷänä*, "he wove"; *lalla*, "he is loose", from
Ge'ez *lahləha* with loss of the pharyngals; Chaha (Gurage) *qəraqäräm*,
"he mixed". Some of these verbs give rise by dissimilation to quadriconsonantal verbs with three different consonants, e.g. Aramaic *qašqēš*
> *qarqēš*, "he knocked"; Arabic *tabtaba* > *tartaba*, "he gurgled". Both
examples show the dissimilatory function or *r* (cf. §23.9). It is noteworthy that reduplicated biconsonantal stems frequently occur in Libyco-
Berber; e.g. Tamazight *bəgbəg*, "to overfill", *barbar*, "to drink hard";
s-tartar, "to make the milk boil". A dissimilation may occur in the same
conditions as in Semitic; e.g. *krkb* < **kbkb*, "to roll".

i) Stems with Geminated or Reduplicated Last Radical Consonant

41.39. Certain secondary and rarer themes with geminated or reduplicated last radical consonant occur in various languages. In Arabic, the stem *'if'alla*, classified as Stem IX, is used for denominative verbs related to adjectives of the pattern *'af'alu* and indicates colours or physical features; e.g. *'iṣfarra*, "he became yellow", from *'aṣfaru*, "yellow"; *'izwarra*, "he became bent", from *'azwaru*, "bent". In Libyco-Berber, the last radical consonant is reduplicated in similar cases (cf. §41.38); e.g. Tamazight *šəmrər*, "to become white". A variant of Arabic Stem IX is Stem XI (*'if'ālla*), which replaces Stem IX in West Arabian dialects and is inflected in modern colloquials in three different ways: e.g. *smānt*, or *smənt*, or *smānayt*, "I became fat". A formation apparently corresponding to Arabic Stem IX is attested in Ethiopic, but it is not considered as a derived stem and the verbs belonging to this category go back historically to quadriconsonantal patterns formed often by dissimilation from triconsonnantal roots (§41.42); e.g. Amharic *bärätta* < **bärättä'ä*, "he became strong", from the root *bt'* (cf. Arabic *bāti'*, "strong"); *aräǧǧä* < **'ärässäyä*, "he grew old", from the root *'sy* (cf. dialectal Arabic *'asiya*, "he became big" [*Lisān*]), where the radical *s* was palatalized by *y* into *ǧǧ*. In both examples, the dissimilatory con­sonant is *r* (**batta'a* > **barta'a* [Tigrinya *bärtə'e*] > **bärättä'ä*; **'assaya* > **'arsaya* > **'ärässäyä*).

41.40. Stems with reduplicated last radical consonant occur in various Semitic languages. From the semantic and the morphological points of view, they are often related to Stem II or D (§41.3). In Hebrew, such a stem (*pōlēl*) occurs mainly with biconsonantal verbal roots (§44); e.g. *rōmēm*, "he set up", from *rūm*; *sōbēb*, "he enclosed", from *sobb*. As in Hebrew, a stem *pll* is used in Ugaritic with biconsonantal roots; e.g. *trmm*, "they set up"; *ykllnh*, "let him complete it". The stem *pa'lal* appears in Hebrew with denominative verbs, derived from an adjective; e.g. *ra'ănan*, "it grew luxuriant", from *ra'ănān*, "luxuriant". The East Semitic verbs *šu-ḥarrurum* and *šu-qammunu*, "to be dead-silent", belong to the same category. In Ugaritic, in Aramaic, and in Ethiopic, a corresponding stem can derive also from substantives; e.g. Ugaritic *šḥrrt*, "she was heating", from *šḥr*, "heat"; Syriac *'abded*, "he enslaved"; Ge'ez *bardada*, "he covered with stones"; Arabic *ǧalbaba* and Ge'ez *galbaba*, "he wrapped", derived from *ǧilbāb*, "garment".

j) Other Stems

41.41. There is a residue of rarer stems which occur in one or another language, e.g. Arabic Stems XII (*'if'aw'ala*), XIII (*'if'awwala*), XIV (*'if'anlala*), and XV (*'if'anlā*), where almost each case requires a particular examination. These stems cannot be treated here in the framework of an outline of comparative grammar. Besides, the combination of two stems is widely attested in modern Arabic colloquials and in Ethiopian languages (§41.26, 31), and there are verbs with more than three radical consonants (§41.42).

k) Verbs with Four Radical Consonants

41.42. Semitic languages possess a certain number of verbs with four radical consonants which do not result from the reduplication, either of one or two radicals, or of the whole biconsonantal root, as mentioned above (§41.36-40). They are then borrowed from a foreign language or originate, as a rule, by dissimilation, diphthongization, etc., from originally triconsonantal roots, or are simply denominative verbs. Their origin can still be established in several cases. E.g. the Babylonian verb *naḥarmumu*, "to decay", is related to Arabic *ḥamma*, "putrid smell", while *na-šarbuṭu*, "to carry by storm", derives from the same root as South Arabian *s¹bṭ*, "to defeat". The Arabic verb *'iḥranṭama* (with *n*-infix: §17.8), "he looked sulky", derives from the noun *ḥurṭūm*, "proboscis", borrowed through Aramaic from Babylonian *ḥuṭṭimmu* or by dissimilation *ḥulṭimmu*, "snout". In any case, the dissimilatory consonant of the East Semitic verbs with four radicals is always *l* or *r*, a feature which confirms their derivation from triconsonantal roots (cf. §41.39). Amharic *sänäbbätä*, "he spent the week", is a denominative verb deriving from the noun *sanbat*, borrowed with the dissimilation *nb* < *bb* from Hebrew *šabbāt*, "Sabbath", while *täräggʷämä*, "he translated", derives from the West Semitic noun *targūm*, "translation" (root *rgm*). *Bäräkkätä*, "he abounded", is related to Ge'ez *barakat*, "blessing", and Arabic *basmala*, "he said *bismillāhi*", is based on the whole expression "in the name of God". In some Maghrebine colloquials, the nominal pattern of diminutives is applied also to verbs which are thus diphthongized and get a pejorative or ironic meaning; e.g. *yakaytib*, "he writes"; *staygbal*, "he turned his face towards the Qibla". The examples fit some patterns, but they should be examined one by one.

l) Passive Voice

41.43. Internal passives are known in West Semitic languages and in Modern South Arabian. Their existence cannot be proved convincingly in Amorite, in Ugaritic, and in Epigraphic South Arabian, while they do not occur in Palaeosyrian, East Semitic, and Ethiopic. Therefore, they are probably to be regarded as a secondary development of West Semitic, that spread to South Arabia. The passive is already attested in Old Canaanite by a Taanach letter dating from the 15th century B.C.: *lū tuddanūna*, "let (the copper arrows) be given". Several examples occur in the Amarna correspondence, both in the prefix and the suffix conjugation. The basic pattern is *yuqtal* for the preterite, as in *tuddanūna*, and *yuqattal* for the imperfective, as in *ú-na-ṣár* /yunaṣṣar/, "(he) will be protected" (EA 327,5), and *tu-ṣa-bat* /tuṣabbat/, "(she) will be seized" (EA 85,46). The stative is represented e.g. by the Amarna gloss *ṣí-ir-ti*, "I am besieged" (EA 127,34), where the form *ṣīrti* exactly parallels the Aramaic and Pre-Classical Arabic passive of the *CūC* verbs, always spelled with *ī* in the Qur'ān. Also the passive of the D-stem appears in a letter from Kāmid el-Lōz (*lū tuwaššarūna*, "may they be despatched") and in a letter from Byblos (EA 126,19.40), where the Old Canaanite form *iú-ša-ru* /yuššarū/, "they are despatched" (from *yšr < wšr*), parallels the Hebrew *quṭṭal* (§41.45).

41.44. Internal passives are in full use in Classical Arabic where the suffix conjugation is formed on the vowel pattern *u-i* instead of *a-a* or *a-i* (e.g. *kutiba*, "it was written"; *tukūtiba*, "the correspondence was kept"), while the prefix conjugation follows the vowel pattern *u-a* (e.g. *yuktabu*, "it will be written"; *yutakātabu*, "the correspondence will be kept"). Arabic makes use of a variation in vowel pattern to express the distinction between active and passive voices not only for Stems I-IV, but even for Stems V-VIII and X, although these stems usually have a passive-reflexive or a reflexive-intransitive meaning. In these cases, however, a distinctive passive acceptation is only realized when the "active" vocalization of the stem concerned does not express a passive meaning. The internal passive existed probably in North Arabian, as suggested e.g. by the following Ṣafaitic sentence: *mt' s¹tt 's²hr f-ḥwr*, "he was taken away (**muti'*) for six months and he returned". Instead, it has disappeared in most modern Arabic colloquials. It is still used in the Ristāq dialect of ʿOmān and in Bedouin dialects of Central and Eastern Maghrib. A new passive form with an *u*-prefix appears in the Ḥassānīya dialect spoken in Mauritania; e.g. *ubaḫḫaṛ, yubaḫḫaṛ*, "to be fumigated", vs. *baḥḥaṛ, ibaḥḥaṛ* "to fumigate". A periphrastic passive formed with *tamma*, "to be done", + verbal noun is used in Modern Arabic to report durative actions.

41.45. In vocalized Biblical Hebrew, the passive of the basic stem has, as a rule, been superseded by the N-stem, since Mishnaic Hebrew had no passive of the B/G-stem. Generally, the Masoretes preserved it only when the consonantal skeleton did not render possible its vocalization as an N-stem; they had then recourse to the paradigms *quttal* and *yuqtal* (e.g. *luqqaḥ*, "he was taken"; *yuqqaḥ*, "he will be taken"). In reality, however, *quttal* was the passive of the D-stem (e.g. *quddaš*, "he was made hallowed"), with an imperfect *yəquttal* (e.g. *yəšullaḥ*, "he will be sent off"), which is secondary as shown by the Old Canaanite *yuqattal* pattern. There was also a passive of the causative stem, vocalized *hoqtal* (e.g. *hošlak*, "he was thrown") and *yoqtal* in the imperfect.

41.46. In Official Aramaic, the passive of the basic stem is often written *ktyb*, "it is written", *yhybw*, "they were delivered", with an internal vowel letter *y*, which suggests an original pattern *qutil, like in Arabic, subsequently changed into *qətīl* as a consequence of the lengthening of the stressed vowel *í*: *qutíl > *qətīl*. Old Aramaic examples of the imperfect (e.g. *ygzr*, "he will be cut") should probably be vocalized *yuqtal*, also like in Arabic. The passive of the Aramaic D-stem and of the causative stem has practically disappeared, with only a few examples left of a vocalized *huqtal* form (e.g. *hūbad*, "he was destroyed", from the root *'bd*), instead of the expected *huqtil.

41.47. Passive forms occur in Modern South Arabian, at least in the basic stem, although there are also clear examples from the causative stem. The original pattern of the perfect may have been *qutil, like in Arabic, since the Śḥeri and Soqoṭri forms follow the pattern *CəCiC* for the perfect; e.g. Śḥeri *rəfis*, "he was kicked"; Mehri shows a change *i* > *ē*, e.g. *ərfēs*, parallel to Aramaic *kətīb*. The original pattern of the imperfect does not result clearly from Śḥeri *yərfös* and Mehri *yarfös*, "he will be kicked", while Soqoṭri has a passive imperfect *yiqətol*. The passive causative, e.g. Mehri *əglēl*, "it was boiled", may derive from a *huqtil pattern.

m) Recapitulation of Stems

41.48. The following paradigmatic tables aim at presenting a synoptic view of the main verb-stems in Semitic languages. A table is offered also for North Semitic, although the available evidence for Palaeosyrian and Amorite is incomplete, while the graphically distinguishable verb-stems of Ugaritic do certainly not represent the entire system. In fact, there is a strong presumption that stems existed which were character-ized by gemination or vocalic lengthening, unmarked in the script. Addi-tional recapitulative tables are offered for the causative stems (§41.54) and the stems with *t*-infix (§41.55). The tables refer to triconsonantal verbal roots, while the biconsonantal ones will be examined in a further section (§44). Most Semitic verbs possess only a part of the stems and forms attested in the entire system.

41.49. The paradigm of Old Babylonian verb-stems can be considered as representative for all the Assyro-Babylonian dialects, as well as for Old Akkadian. Besides, it may coincide to a large extent with the situa-tion in Palaeosyrian. The paradigmatic verb *parāsu*, "to separate", is used in this table.

	Preterite	Present-Future	Perfect	Stative
B/G-stem	*iprus*	*iparras*	*iptaras*	*paris*
B/Gt-stem	*iptaras*	*iptarras*	*iptatras*	*pitrus*
B/Gtn-stem	*iptarras*	*iptanarras*	*iptatarras*	*pitarrus*
D-stem	*uparris*	*uparras*	*uptarris*	*purrus*
Dt-stem	*uptarris*	*uptarras*	*uptatarris*	—
Dtn-stem	*uptarris*	*uptanarras*	*uptatarris*	*putarrus*
Š-stem	*ušapris*	*ušapras*	*uštapris*	*šuprus*
Št-stem	*uštapris*	*uštap(ar)ras*	*uštatapris*	*šutaprus*
Štn-stem	*uštapris*	*uštanapras*	*uštatapris*	*šutaprus*
N-stem	*ipparis*	*ipparras*	*ittapras*	*naprus*
Ntn-stem	*ittapras*	*ittanapras*	*ittatapras*	*itaprus*

41.50. Despite its unvocalized script, Ugaritic offers the largest num-ber of North Semitic verbal forms which can lead to a provisional and partial reconstruction of the verb-stems. The paradigmatic verb *qatal*, "to kill", will be used in this table. We assume that the verb belongs to the *u*-class, like Arabic *qatala*, and we apply Barth's law (§40.16,21).

	*Preterite	*Imperfective	*Perfective	*Stative-Perfect
B/G-stem	*yaqtul*	*yaqattul*	*yaqtatul*	*qatal*
B/Gt-stem	*yaqtatul*	*yaqtattul*	*yaqtattul*	*qittul*
D-stem	*yuqattil*	*yuqattal*	*yuqtattil*	*quttul*
Dt-stem	*yuqtattil*	*yuqtattal*	*yuqtatattil*	—
Š-stem	*yašaqtil*	*yašaqtal*	*yaštaqtil*	*šaqtil*
Št-stem	*yaštaqtil*	*yaštaq(at)tal*	*yaštataqtil*	*šataqtil*

41.51. For the West Semitic languages the system of Classical Arabic has been chosen. This is the only language which makes use of the entire system and has a consistent vocalization of all the stems, including their passive voice. The paradigmatic verb *fa'ala*, "to make", is used in this table, which only represents the main Stems I-VIII and X.

	Perfect active	Perfect passive	Imperfect active	Imperfect passive
Stem I (B/G)	*fa'ala*	*fu'ila*	*yaf'ulu*	*yuf'alu*
Stem II (D)	*fa''ala*	*fu''ila*	*yufa''ilu*	*yufa''alu*
Stem III (L)	*fā'ala*	*fū'ila*	*yufā'ilu*	*yufā'alu*
Stem IV (Š/H/')	*'af'ala*	*'uf'ila*	*yuf'ilu*	*yuf'alu*
Stem V (tD)	*tafa''ala*	*tufu''ila*	*yatafa''alu*	*yutafa''alu*
Stem VI (tL)	*tafā'ala*	*tufū'ila*	*yatafā'alu*	*yutafā'alu*
Stem VII (N)	*'infa'ala*	*'unfu'ila*	*yanfa'ilu*	*yunfa'alu*
Stem VIII (B/Gt)	*'ifta'ala*	*'uftu'ila*	*yafta'ilu*	*yufta'alu*
Stem X (Št)	*'istaf'ala*	*'ustuf'ila*	*yastaf'ilu*	*yustaf'alu*

41.52. South Semitic can best be represented by the entire system of Ge'ez, the traditional presentation of which distinguishes four fundamental stems — the basic stem, the stem with prefix *'a-*, the stem with prefix *ta-*, and the stem with prefix *'asta-* —, each subdivided into three themes: the basic one, the theme with lengthened or geminated second radical consonant, and the theme with lengthened first thematic vowel. The paradigmatic verb *qatala*, "to kill", is used in this table. The Ethiopic imperfect corresponds morphologically and semantically to the East Semitic present-future (§38.5-7), while the Ethiopic jussive/subjunctive corresponds morphologically to the East Semitic preterite (§38.2).

	Perfect	Imperfect	Jussive/Subjunctive
Stem I. 1/A (B/G)	*qatala*	*yəqattəl*	*yəqtəl*
2/B (D)	*qattala*	*yəqettəl*	*yəqattəl*
3/C (L)	*qātala*	*yəqāttəl*	*yəqātəl*
Stem II. 1/A (Š/H/')	*'aqtala*	*yāqattəl*	*yāqtəl*
2/B (Š/H/'D)	*'aqattala*	*yāqettəl*	*yāqattəl*
3/C (Š/H/'L)	*'aqātala*	*yāqāttəl*	*yāqātəl*
Stem III. 1/A (tB/G)	*taqat(a)la*	*yətqattal*	*yətqatal*
2/B (tD)	*taqattala*	*yətqettal*	*yətqattal*
3/C (tL)	*taqātala*	*yətqāttal*	*yətqātal*

	Perfect	Imperfect	Jussive/Subjunctive
Stem IV. 1/A (Št)	*'astaqtala*	*yāstaqattəl*	*yāstaqtəl*
2/B (ŠDt)	*'astaqattala*	*yāstaqettəl*	*yāstaqattəl*
3/C (ŠtL)	*'astaqātala*	*yāstaqāttəl*	*yāstaqātəl*

41.53. The second radical consonant of the stative or perfect of the basic stem (I.1/A) is not geminated or lengthened in the Semitic languages with the exception of South Ethiopic, where Amharic (e.g. *näg-gärä*, "he spoke"), Argobba (e.g. *säddäba*, "he offended"), and Gafat (e.g. *gällädä*, "he girded himself") have a secondary gemination by analogy with the verbs used in the D-stem or Ethiopic type 2/B (§41.2). In fact, this type 2/B of Ethiopic is no longer, with very few exceptions, a derived stem but a basic stem, just as the verbs used in form 1/A. However, the geminating Gurage dialects, viz. Soddo and Muher-Gogot-Masqan, preserve the archaic not-geminated form in the negative, but use the innovated type with gemination in the positive forms, e.g. Soddo *säffäräm*, "he camped", but *al-säfärä*, "he did not camp". The other South Ethiopic idioms belong to a non-geminating language group; therefore, the not-geminated second radical consonant of the perfect cannot be explained as preservation of the archaic type of the basic stem.

41.54. The recapitulative table of the causative stems is limited to the third person masculine singular of the suffix-conjugation (**1**) and of the two prefix-conjugations, respectively expressing the imperfective (**2**) and the preterite, jussive, or West Semitic imperfect (**3**). The paradigmatic verbs *parāsu*, *qtl* and *f'l* are being used:

		1	**2**	**3**
Assyro-Babylonian	Š	*šuprus*	*ušapras*	*ušapris*
	ŠD		*ušparras*	*ušparris*
	Št	*šutaprus*	*uštap(ar)ras*	*uštapris*
Ugaritic	Š	*šqtl*	*yšqtl*	*yšqtl*
	Št	*štqtl*	*yštqtl*	*yštqtl*
Hebrew	H	*hiqtīl*		*yaqtīl*
	Št	*hištaqtal*		*yištaqtel*
Old Aramaic	H	*hqtl*		*y(h)qtl*
	Ht?	*htqtl*		**y(h)tqtl*
Syriac	ᵓ	*'aqtel*		*naqtel*
	Tt	*'ettaqtal*		*nettaqtal*
Classical Arabic	ᵓ	*'af'ala*		*yuf'ilu*
	St	*'istaf'ala*		*yastaf'ilu*

		1	**2**	**3**
Damascene Coll.	'	*af'al*		*byəf'el*
	St	*staf'al*		*byəstaf'el*
	StL	*stfā'al*		*byəstfā'el*
Magrebine Coll.	'	—		
	St	*staf'el*		*yistaf'el*
	StL	*stfā'il*		*yistfā'il*
	tS	*tsəf'al*		*yitsəf'al*
Mehri	h	*həf'ōl*	*yəhəf'ōl*	*yəhaf'əl*
	Š(t)	*šəf'ōl*	*yəšəf'ōl*	*yəšaf'əl*
	Š(t)L	*šəfē'əl*	*yəšfa'lən*	*yəšfē'əl*
Ge'ez	II.1/A	*'aqtala*	*yāqattəl*	*yāqtəl*
	2/B	*'aqattala*	*yāqettəl*	*yāqattəl*
	3/C	*'aqātala*	*yāqāttəl*	*yāqātəl*
	IV.1/A	*'astaqtala*	*yāstaqattəl*	*yāstaqtəl*
	2/B	*'astaqattala*	*yāstaqettəl*	*yāstaqattəl*
	3/C	*'astaqātala*	*yāstaqāttəl*	*yāstaqātəl*
Tigre	II.1/A	*'aqtala*	*yāqattəl*	*yāqtəl*
	2/B	*'aqattala*	*yāqettəl*	*yāqattəl*
	3/C	*'aqātala*	*yāqāttəl*	*yāqātəl*
	'at-	*'atqātala*	*yātqāttəl*	*yātqātəl*
Amharic	II.1/A	*aqättälä*	*yaqätl*	*yaqtəl*
	2/B	*aqättäla*	*yaqättəl*	*yaqättəl*
	3/C	*aqattälä*	*yaqattəl*	*yaqatəl*
	as- 1/A-2B	*asqättälä*	*yasqättəl*	*yasqättəl*
	3/C	*asqattälä*	*yasqattəl*	*yasqatl*
	at-	*aqqattälä*	*yaqqattəl*	*yaqqatl*
	astä- IV.3/C	*astäqattälä*	*yastäqattəl*	*yastäqatl*

41.55. The recapitulative table of the stems with *t*-affix is presented like the causative stems (§41.54):

		1	**2**	**3**
Assyro-Babylonian	B/Gt	*pitrus*	*iptarras*	*iptaras*
	Dt	*putarrus*	*uptarras*	*uptarris*
	Št	*šutaprus*	*uštap(ar)ras*	*uštapris*
Ugaritic	B/Gt	**qttl*	*yqttl*	*yqttl*
	Št	**štqtl*	*yštqtl*	*yštqtl*
Hebrew	tD	*hitqattēl*		*yitqattēl*
	NtD	*nitqattēl*		
Old Aramaic	B/Gt	**qttl*		*yqttl*
	tG-tD	*'tqtl*		*ytqtl*
	Ht?	*htqtl*		**yhtqtl*
Syriac	B/Gt	*'etqətel*		*netqətel*

		1	**2**	**3**
	Dt	*'etqattal*		*netqattal*
	Tt	*'ettaqtal*		*nettaqtal*
Classical Arabic	B/Gt	*'iftaʻala*		*yaftaʻilu*
	tD	*tafaʻʻala*		*yatafaʻʻalu*
	tL	*tafāʻala*		*yatafāʻalu*
	St	*'istafʻala*		*yastafiʻlu*
Damascene Coll.	B/Gt	*ftaʻal*		*byəftaʻel*
	tD	*tfaʻʻal*		*byətfaʻʻal*
	tL	*tfāʻal*		*byətfāʻal*
	St	*stafʻal*		*byəstafʻel*
	StL	*stfāʻal*		*byəstfāʻel*
Maghrebine Coll.	tB/G	*tfaʻal, tfaʻil*		*yitfaʻal, yitfaʻil*
	tD	*tfeʻʻəl*		*yitfeʻʻəl*
	Nt	*ntafʻal*		*yintafʻal*
	tL	*tfāʻal*		*yitfāʻal*
	St	*stafʻel*		*yistafʻel*
	tS	*tsəfʻal*		*yitsəfʻal*
Mehri	B/Gt	*əftaʻōl*	*yəftaʻēlən*	*yəftaʻōl*
	Lt	*fataʻəl*	*yəftaʻōl*	*yəftēʻel*
	Š(t)	*šəfʻōl*	*yəšəfʻōl*	*yəšafʻəl*
	Š(t)L	*šəfēʻəl*	*yəšfaʻlən*	*yəšfēʻəl*
Ge'ez	III.1/A	*taqat(a)la*	*yətqattal*	*yətqatal*
	2/B	*taqattala*	*yətqettal*	*yətqattal*
	3/C	*taqātala*	*yətqāttal*	*yətqātal*
	IV.1/A	*'astaqtala*	*yāstaqattəl*	*yāstaqtəl*
	2/B	*'astaqattala*	*yāstaqettəl*	*yāstaqattəl*
	3/C	*'astaqātala*	*yāstaqāttəl*	*yāstaqātəl*
Tigre	III.1/A-2/B	*təqattala*	*lətqattal*	*lətqattal*
	3/C	*təqātala*	*lətqātal*	*lətqātal*
	at- 2/B	*'atqattala*	*latqattəl*	*latqattəl*
	3/C	*'atqātala*	*latqātəl*	*latqātəl*
Amharic	III.1/A-2B	*täqättälä*	*yəqqättäl*	*yəqqätäl*
	3/C	*täqattälä*	*yəqqattäl*	*yəqqatäl*
	at-	*aqqattälä*	*yaqqattəl*	*yaqqatl*
	astä- IV.3/C	*astäqattälä*	*yastäqattəl*	*yastäqatl*

41.56. The reconstruction of Proto-Semitic verb-stems is based on the assumption that the stem with lengthened first vowel does not belong to the common Semitic system, but that the N-stem, traces of which are found also in the other Afro-Asiatic language families, should be considered as Proto-Semitic. The whole reconstruction is of course hypothetic. The thematic vowel of the prefix-conjugations is supposed to be *a*, regardless of the real *u*-class of the Arabic verb *qatala* (§41.50).

	*Preterite	*Imperfective	*Perfective	*Stative
B/G-stem	*yaqtal*	*yaqattal*	*yaqtatal*	*qata/i/ul*
B/Gt-stem	*yaqtatal*	*yaqtattal*	*yaqtattal*	*qittul*
D-stem	*yuqattil*	*yuqattal*	*yuqtattil*	*quttul*
Dt-stem	*yaqtattil*	*yaqtattal*	*yaqtatattal*	—
Š-stem	*yušaqtil*	*yušaqtal*	*yuštaqtil*	*šuqtul*
Št-stem	*yaštaqtil*	*yaštaq(at)tal*	*yaštataqtil*	*šataqtul*
N-stem	*yanqatil*	*yanqattal*	*yantaqtal*	*naqtul*

F. Infinitive and Participle

42.1. The infinitive and the participle are two morphological categories of the verb lacking the indications of tense, aspect, mood, and actor that characterize the verbal inflection. This is the reason why they are rightly considered as nominal forms of the verb, the infinitive being a verbal noun, used also in construct state, and the participle a kind of verbal adjective. They are both subject to nominal inflection, govern pronominal suffixes, may be introduced by prepositions, and can be used with or without an added *-m* (mimation) or *-n* (nunation), as nouns. However, both the infinitive and the participle occur not only in the basic theme, but also in a varying number of derived verbal stems. Besides, the participle can be used both in an active and in a passive sense, with distinct vocalizations, and it may exercise functions comparable to those of finite verbal forms; e.g. Arabic *kullu nafsin ḏa'iqatu l-mawti*, "every soul experiences death"; *wa-ǧā'anī Ǧibrilu wa-'anā nā'imun* "and Gabriel came to me when I was sleeping". The active and passive participles, as well as the infinitive, furnish the basis for the verbal inflection in Neo-Aramaic (§42.18-22); they serve also to form tenses in Mishnaic and Modern Hebrew, in Modern Arabic and Ethiopic (§42.23-25).

a) Infinitive

42.2. The infinitive of the basic stem was formed in older phases of Semitic on the pattern *CaCāC*, attested in Palaeosyrian, in Old Akkadian, in Assyro-Babylonian, in syllabically written Ugaritic, in Aramaic, and in Arabic. Forms in other languages clearly demonstrate the same origin, as Hebrew *qāṭōl* < **qaṭāl*, with the change *ā* > *ō*, and its construct state *qəṭol* with shortened vowels. A vowel reduction *a* > *e* or *a* > *ə* seems to occur also in Palaeosyrian infinitives followed by an objective complement (§21.6).

42.3. Vocalic changes occur in some Assyro-Babylonian verbs for reasons which have not been explained in a satisfactory way, although the influence of velar fricatives and of the liquid *r* certainly plays a role (§19.10; 21.10). E.g. Babylonian *šebēru(m)*, "to break", corresponds to Old Akkadian and Assyrian *šabāru(m)*, while *šapāru(m)*, "to send", remains unchanged. In Classical Arabic, the pattern *CiCāC* or *fi'āl(un)* (e.g. *ḥisābun*, "to count"; *šifā'un*, "to heal") appears next to *CaCāC* (e.g. *halākun*, "to perish"; *fasādun*, "to be rotten"), but both can be replaced by a wide range of other nominal patterns. One of the patterns used in North Ethiopic to form the infinitive is *CaCīC*, well attested in Ge'ez (*qatil*, "to kill") and in Tigre (*qatil*).

42.4. Among the nominal types used to form the verbal noun of the basic stem occur patterns with the *ma-* / *mi-* prefix (§29.19-26). They are encountered in Arabic (e.g. *maḥmalun*, "to carry"), and they became the usual form of the infinitive of the basic stem in Official and Standard Literary Aramaic (e.g. *mišbaq*, "to leave"), and later in Middle and Late Aramaic (e.g. Syriac *meqṭal*, "to kill"; Galilean Aramaic *mektōb*, "to write"), but the Early Aramaic infinitive *qatāl* continued to be used in Syriac as a substantive (e.g. *'əbādā*, "acting"; *qərābā*, "fight"), and it appears in Neo-Aramaic as the regular form of the infinitive (e.g. *ptāḫā*, "to open"). The pattern with the *mi-* prefix is rarely encountered in Hebrew (e.g. *miqrā'*, "to call"), but the infinitive *məqtāl* / *məqtal* (<**miqtāl*) is used regularly in Tigre and Tigrinya, while a *maqtal* type appears in the South Ethiopian languages of Amharic, Argobba, and Harari (e.g. *mängär*, "to speak"). The morpheme *mä-*, that is used in the formation of the infinitive, became *wä-* in Gafat and in all the Gurage dialects. In Soddo, the prefix is either *wo-* or *o-*.

42.5. In Ge'ez, the infinitive of the type *qatilot* predominates, and it is still in use in ancient Harari (e.g. *limadot*, "to learn") and in some Gurage dialects, especially in Ennemor that has only forms with *-ot*. Tigre has *qətlat* beside other forms, and a given verb may have more than one infinitive form; e.g. *nadiq* (§42.3), *nədqat*, *nədqo*, *məndāq* (§42.4), "building" (*nadqa*, "to build", in the absolute state). The infinitive with the ending -*at* in the construct state and -*ā* in the absolute state is encountered also in Hebrew (e.g. *'ahăbā*, "to love").

42.6. The infinitives of the derived stems often follow the vocalic structure either of the imperative or of the suffix conjugation. Particular features appear in each language and we must confine ourselves to the observation of certain common elements. However, there is as yet insufficient evidence for Palaeosyrian and Amorite, while the unvocalized Ugaritic, Phoenician, and Epigraphic South Arabian texts limit the weight of the available information.

42.7. In Old Akkadian and in Assyro-Babylonian the infinitive coincides with the third person masculine singular of the stative, followed by the nominal morpheme -*u(m)*, etc. E.g. the Babylonian infinitive *šuprusu(m)* of the Š-stem corresponds to the Š-stative *šuprus*, while Assyrian *šaprusu(m)* is related to the Assyrian Š-stative *šaprus*. Old Akkadian follows the Babylonian pattern, while Assyrian has a particular vocalization of the B/Gt-infinitives, e.g. *mitalku(m)*, "to consider", instead of Babylonian *mitluku(m)*.

42.8. In Hebrew, the infinitive of the derived stems coincides with the second person masculine singular of the imperative. However, the absolute infinitives may also be formed on the pattern of their basic stem with the vowel *ō* < *ā* (e.g. *qaṭṭōl*, *niqṭōl*), but these forms are rarely used in Hebrew.

42.9. In Aramaic, the situation is rather complex and implies a morphological distinction in Early Aramaic between absolute infinitives — without any recognizable suffix — and construct infinitives ending in -*t*. However, this suffix -*ūt* / -*at* was later extended to the absolute infinitive of the derived stems (-*h* < -*t*), while the *m*- morpheme could be prefixed to all the infinitives by analogy with the basic stem, as early as the 6th/5th century B.C. (e.g. D-stem *mšlmwth*, "its repaying": TAD III, C1.1,131; *lmḥwh*, "to explain": RÉS 1792B,8). This formation is generalized in Late Aramaic, in Western Aramaic (e.g. Galilean Aramaic D-stem *məkattābā* instead of *kattābā*, "cause to write") as in Eastern Aramaic (e.g. Syriac causative stem *maktābū*[*t*] instead of *'aktābū*[*t*], "cause to write").

42.10. Classical Arabic follows, as a rule, the main pattern *fiʿāl(un)* of Stem I (§42.3), thus *fiʿʿāl(un)* (Stem II), *fiʿāl(un)* (Stem III = I),

'if'āl(un) (Stem IV), *'infi'āl(un)* (Stem VII), *'ifti'āl(un)* (Stem VIII),
'istif'āl(un) (Stem X), but *tafa''ul(un)* (Stem V) and *tafā'ul(un)* (Stem
VI), with a vocalic qualitative change. A form *taf'īl(un)* with *ta*-prefix is
usually employed also for Stem II instead of *fi''āl(un)*, while the feminine of the passive participle is generally used as the infinitive of Stem
III, e.g. *muḥāṭabat(un)*, "to address". Some ancient and modern colloquials have *fi'āl* for Stem III — without the vocalic shortening seen in
Classical Arabic — and *tifi''āl* for Stem V.

42.11.   In Ge'ez, the infinitives of the derived stems are formed on the
same pattern as the imperative with the addition of the ending *-o(t)*. Thus
fassəmo(t), "to complete", in the D-stem (I.2/B), *bārəko(t)*, "to bless",
in the stem with lengthened first vowel (I.3/C), *talabso(t)*, "to dress", in
the reflexive-passive stem (III.1/A), etc. This formation is attested also
in Tigre, except in stems which have the prefix *t-*; e.g. *'allabot*, "counting" (*'allaba*, "he counted"; Stem I.2/B = D), *ḥābarot*, "joining" (*ḥābara*,
"he joined"; Stem I.3/C = L), etc. Besides, it occurs in ancient Harari and
in some of the Gurage dialects. The other North and South Ethiopian
languages use infinitives with the prefix *mə-/mä- > wä- > o* (cf. §29.19),
e.g. Soddo D-stem (I.2/B) *wäšäkkət*, "to make"; stem with lengthened
first vowel (I.3/C) *wogalb* or *ogalb*, "to gallop". Tigre uses the *ma*-form
with stems having the prefix *t-*; e.g. *matqallā'*, "appearing" (but
təqallə'a; "to appear"; Stem III.2/B = tD).

42.12.   The Ethiopian languages of Ge'ez, Tigrinya, Amharic,
Argobba, and West Gurage have a form called "(pseudo-)gerund",
"gerundive", or "coverb" which mainly signifies an action related to the
action expressed by the verb of the following main clause; e.g. Ge'ez
nabiro (gerund) *'Iyasus nagaromu* (main verb), "having sat down, Jesus
said to them"; Amharic *mäsobun käfto* (gerund) *dabbowən wässädä*
(main verb), "having uncovered the basket, he took the bread". The
bases of the gerund, which morphologically originates from infinitives
(*CaCīC* and perhaps *CaCiCot*), are *qatila-* in Ge'ez, *qätil-* in Tigrinya,
qätlä- in Amharic, *qätlət-* in Argobba, and *qətlətä-* in West Gurage, all
of them followed by pronominal suffixes of the noun. This formation is
paralleled by the Hebrew construction using the infinitive with a
pronominal suffix and continued by a finite verb, e.g. *hărīmī qōlī
wā'eqrā'*, "lifting up my voice, I cried". A variant or earlier form of the
"gerund" syntagm is attested in Phoenician with the absolute infinitive
followed by the independent personal pronoun; e.g. *p'l 'nk ... lrbty ...*

wšm' ql, "I having made (this) ... for my Lady ..., she heard my voice" (§53.5).

It is noteworthy that Isidorus Hispalensis (Berne Latin Codex 123, f° 7a) tells of twelve parts of speech in Phoenician, viz. the classical eight with the addition of the article, of the "impersonal mode" (participle?), of the infinitive, and of the "gerund" mentioned immediately after the infinitive.

b) Participle

42.13. The active participle of the basic stem goes back to a Proto-Semitic pattern *CāCiC* which appears as such in Palaeosyrian, in Amorite names, in syllabically spelt Ugaritic proper names, in Old Akkadian, in Assyro-Babylonian, in Aramaic, in Arabic, while the Hebrew and Phoenician form *qōtēl* results from the changes $ā > ō$ (§21.12-13,20) and $i > ē$ (§21.1), the latter characterizing also the Late Aramaic participle *kātēb / kāteb*, "writing". The Ethiopic pattern *CāCəC* reflects the general change $i > ə$, but it is not productive and subsists only in some nouns (e.g. Ge'ez *wārəs*, "heir"; *ṣādəq*, "just"; Tigre *qābəl*, "former"). A new participial form *qatāli / qätali* appears in North Ethiopic, and in Harari, Amharic, and Argobba, in the south. The other South Ethiopian languages have only traces of this form. The vowel *i* generally causes palatalization of a final radical dental, sibilant, or liquid, and is usually absorbed in the palatal; e.g. Amharic *käfač < *käfati*, "who opens". The forms *qātlāy* and *qatāl* occur in Tigre with a meaning similar to that of *qatāli*; e.g. *qatāli / qātlāy / qatāl*, "killer, murderer".

42.14. The passive participle of the basic stem goes back to the nominal patterns *CaCīC* and *CaCūC*. The Palaeosyrian, Amorite, and Ugaritic evidence is as yet either insufficient or unclear, while Old Akkadian and Assyro-Babylonian exhibit both forms, though rarely, since the function of the passive participle is normally assumed in East Semitic by the verbal adjective of the *parsu(m)* type. Besides, cuneiform spelling as such does often not allow distinguishing the active participle (e.g. *ma-ḫi-iṣ /māḫiṣ/*, "striking"), the passive participle in -*ī*- (e.g. *na-ti-in /natīn/*, "given"), and the stative (e.g. *da-mi-iq /damiq/*, "he is good"). The context and the usage have to be taken into account in each particular case. Old Canaanite *ḫa-mu-du* (EA 138,126), "desired", Neo-Punic *ḥlwṣ*, "saved", and Hebrew *qāṭūl*, "killed", presuppose an original *CaCūC* form, while Aramaic *kətīb*, "written", goes back to the *CaCīC* pattern, attested as such by cuneiform transliterations of Aramaic names (e.g. *Za-bi-i-ni*, "bought", "redeemed"). In Arabic, the adjectival pattern *fa'īl* can be used with a passive meaning (e.g. *kaḥīl*, "darkened with kohl", "dyed black"), while *fa'ūl* can have either an active or a passive value (e.g. *kaḏūb*, "deceiving"; *rasūl*, "envoy" = "sent"), but the proper passive participle is formed with the prefix *ma-* on the theme *maf'ūl* (e.g. *maqtūl*, "killed"), probably by analogy with the participial forms of the derived stems. This seems to have been already the case in North Arabian, as suggested by Nabataean passive participles like *mdkwr*, "remembered" (instead of Aramaic *dkyr*), and also in South Arabian, where both participial *f'l* and *mf'l* forms of the basic stem occur in a passive sense. North Ethiopic can form a passive participle *qǝtul* from every transitive verb, and Tigre has occasionally a feminine form *qǝtǝl* as well (e.g. *bǝšǝl*, "cooked"). In South Ethiopic, there are several adjectives with passive meaning of the type *qǝtul*, but a passive participle of this type cannot be formed automatically from the verb, except in Harari and in Soddo (North Gurage) where, e.g., the passive participle "broken" from *säbära / säbbärä*, "he broke", is *sǔbur* in Harari and *sǝbur* in Soddo. All these forms probably derive from an original *qatūl* type. In the 18th century, the passive participle seems to have been still operational in Gafat, as suggested by the unique example *ǝ-squli*, "hung up, suspended", with a final *-i* like the active participle and without palatalization (§42.13).

42.15.   The participles of the derived stems go back to Proto-Semitic patterns with the prefix *mu-* which appears as such in Palaeosyrian, in Amorite and Ugaritic proper names spelt syllabically, in Old Akkadian, in Assyro-Babylonian, in Old Aramaic names transliterated in cuneiform script, and in Arabic. The original form of a dialectal Phoenician causative participle can be reconstructed tentatively as **muyaqtil* (cf. §21.8; 41.13), as suggested by Late Punic *myšql*, "honouring", and *myskr*, "making known". Considering the usual change *uy > iy > ī / ē*, this could explain the Amorite proper names of the *mēqtil* type, which does not appear to represent a Proto-Semitic possibility. As for the *ma-* prefix of the Ethiopic participle of the derived stems, and of the causative participle in Hebrew (*maqtīl*) and in Aramaic (e.g. *mašpīl* "humiliating"), it is not relevant for Proto-Semitic since the vowel *a* in the prefix originally belonged to the syncopated *h > '*, as is proved in Biblical Aramaic. Thus, the following evolution has to be assumed in accordance with the principles governing the reduction of short vowels in open unstressed syllables (§21.1), like *mu-*: **muhaqtil > *mǝhaqtil >*

maqtil. The resulting *ma-* was generalized by analogy in Ethiopic, but the *ma-* participles became, in fact, lexical items, used often as substantives; e.g. Tigre *ma'amrāy* (Stem I.2/B = D), "scientist"; *malāṣyāy* (Stem I.3/C = L), "barber". A similar change *mu-* > *mə-* has to be assumed for the other Hebrew and Aramaic participial forms, as well as a subsequent contraction with the prefixes of the various stems, e.g. Aramaic **muhitqətēl* > **məhitqetēl* > *mitqətēl* > *mētqətēl*.

42.16. Apart from the *mu-*prefix, the participles of the derived stems are characterized by the vowels *a - i* in the active and *a - a* in the passive; e.g. Assyro-Babylonian active *mušaprisu* (Š-stem); Arabic passive *mufaʻʻal(un)* (Stem II = D). In Assyro-Babylonian, the vowel *i* of the active participle is dropped in the B/Gt-stem and in the N-stem because of the succession of short syllables. There are no passive forms in *mu-* in East Semitic which uses instead verbal adjectives of the types *purrus* (D-stem) and *šuprus* (Š-stem) in Old Akkadian and Babylonian, while the types *parrus* and *šaprus* are employed in Assyrian; e.g. *šubburum* (D-stem), "broken into pieces", *šūṣūm* (Š-stem), "thrown away" (from the root *wṣ'*). A similar situation is attested in Ethiopic where the *qətul* type of the basic stem gave rise to analogous formations in the derived stems, e.g. Tigre *gərrum* (Stem I.2/B = D), "beautiful"; Soddo *təkkul* (Stem I.2/B = D), "boiled in water".

42.17. A particular form of participle occurs in Phoenician and in Hebrew in the N-stem where the sole *n*-prefix is used; e.g. Phoenician *nšt'm*, "dreaded" (plural), with unknown vocalization; Hebrew *niqṭāl*, "killed". In Ethiopic, the active form *qatāli* of the basic stem gave rise to analogical formations in the derived stems; e.g. Ge'ez *rawwaṣi*, "runner"; *ḥarrasi*, "ploughman" (Stem I.2/B = D); *nāzazi*, "comforter"; *nāfaqi*, "unbeliever" (Stem I.3/C = L); *'ašgāri*, "fisherman"; *'anbābi*, "reader" (causative Stem II.1/A); *'assassāli*, "expeller" (Stem II.2/B = ŠD); *tašayami*, "decided" (reflexive-passive Stem III.1/A); *tafannāwi*, "envoy" (Stem III.2/B = tD); *tasālaqi*, "ridiculous" (reflexive-passive Stem III.3/C = tL).

c) Neo-Aramaic Verbal System

42.18. The Semitic verbal inflection has undergone considerable changes in Neo-Aramaic. Although Western Neo-Aramaic continues to use prefixed imperfect forms as subjunctive and suffixed perfect forms

to express the preterite, it also formed new tenses based on the old active
and passive participles in order to indicate the present and the pluperfect; e.g. *ṭō'nin*, "they carry" (masc.), *ṭ'īnin*, "they had carried"
(masc.). *Ṭūrōyo* bases the whole system — with the exception of the
imperative — on old participles, while Eastern Neo-Aramaic uses both
verbal nouns: the participles and the infinitive. Eastern Neo-Aramaic
was greatly influenced by the neighbouring non-Semitic languages,
especially by Kurdish which is an Iranian language and to which authors
attribute the changes in the Neo-Aramaic verbal system. Another innovated conjugation consists of forms of the verb *(h)wayā*, "to be", used
with nouns; e.g. *wewā nḥitā*, "he came down". Leaving aside this colloquial development, we shall point out some fundamental characteristics of the Neo-Aramaic paradigmatic system. The verbal forms, which
are really syntagms, fall into three groups: Group I is based on the active
participle *qātil*; Group II, on the passive participle *qtīl*; Group III, on the
infinitive *qtālā*. Pronominal enclitics and special preverbs (*ki-*, *bit-*, *qam-*:
§42.19) are affixed to these basic forms in order to build the various
tenses and moods which replace the two aspects of ancient Aramaic —
perfect and imperfect. The whole system cannot be presented here,
since it is peculiar to one Semitic language. Aside from distinctions of
person, number, and gender, it presents thirty-three different formal
categories indicating tenses, aspects, moods, transitivity and intransitivity, active and passive voices. We limit ourselves to some typical
examples.

42.19.   Group I is based on the active participle *qātil* which refers to
the actor and is conjugated by adding enclitic pronouns. The person or
object acted upon is indicated by the preposition *l-* plus pronominal
suffixes. Group I comprises the subjunctive, the conditional, and
indicative tenses. In the indicative, e.g., the preverb *ki* < **kīn*, "being"
(cf. §38.24), is prefixed to the participle to form the continuous present; e.g. *ki-pātiḥ*, "he is opening". The future requires the preverb *bit*
< **b'ē + d*, "(it is to be) wished that" (cf. §38.22), placed before the
participle; e.g. *bit-pātḥā*, etymologically "(it is to be) wished that she
(well be) opening", i.e. "she will open"; the preverb *qam* < ** qā(d)m*,
"before", is used to form the preterite; e.g. *qam-pātḥin*, "I have
opened".

General Present

Sing. 3 m.	*pātiḫ*	"he opens"
f.	*pātiḫ + ā > pātḫa*	"she opens"
2 m.	*pātiḫ + it > pātḫit*	"you open"
f.	*pātiḫ + at > pātḫat*	"you open"
1 m.	*pātiḫ + in > pātḫin*	"I open"
f.	*pātiḫ + ān > pātḫan*	"I open"
Plur. 3	*pātiḫ + ī > pātḫī*	"they open"
2	*pātiḫ + ītu(n) > pātḫītu(n)*	"you open"
1	*pātiḫ + aḫ(n) > pātḫaḫ(n)*	"we open"

Other tenses are formed from the general present by prefixing one of the above-mentioned particles or/and adding the frozen form (*h*)*wā*, "he was", of the auxiliary verb "to be":

Continuous present:	*ki-pātiḫ*	"he is opening", etc.
Future:	*bit-pātiḫ*	"he will open", etc.
Preterite:	*qam-pātiḫ*	"he has opened", etc.
Imperfect:	*pātiḫ-wā*	"he opened", etc.
Continuous past:	*ki-pātiḫ-wā*	"he was opening", etc.
Conditional:	*bit-pātiḫ-wā*	"(if) he will have opened", etc.

42.20. Group II comprises indicative and conditional tenses. It is based on the passive participle *qtīl* which refers to the person or object acted upon and is conjugated according to gender and number by adding enclitic pronouns, while the actor is indicated by the preposition -*l*- plus pronominal suffixes; e.g. preterite *ptīḫ-lē*, etymologically "opened by him", i.e. "he has opened"; *ptīḫā-lē*, "it (fem.) is opened by him", i.e. "he has opened it"; *ptīḫē-lā*, "they are opened by her", i.e. "she has opened them"; etc. This syntagm is a development of the impersonal passive attested already in the Achaemenian period when the Aramaic construction *'byd ly*, meaning "I have done", was directly borrowed from Old Persian *manā* ("by me") *kṛtam* ("done") (§65.4). It continued to be used in Eastern Late Aramaic; e.g. *ḥazī lī*, "I have seen", in Jewish Babylonian Aramaic; *kniš-lia u-zlih-lia*, "I swept and I cleaned", in Mandaic.

42.21. Group III is based on the infinitive *qtālā* and includes indicative tenses formed by prefixing the preposition *bi-* / *be-* and by appending the preposition -*l*- with pronominal suffixes; e.g. the continuous present *bi-ptāḫā-lē*, etymologically "in opening by him", i.e. "he is opening". By adding the enclitic *-wā < (h)wā*, "was", every tense is cast into the past, thus the continuous past *bi-ptāḫā-wā*, "in opening (he) was", i.e. "(he) was opening".

42.22. There are only three stems in Neo-Aramaic: they parallel the basic stem, the D-stem, and the causative stem. Their conjugation is based on the corresponding participles and infinitives, with the addition of the imperative. The reflexive-passive stems with the *t*-affix and the passive voice of the basic stems are not encountered in Neo-Aramaic which expresses the passive by means of the auxiliary verb *pā'iš*, "remaining", the conjugated forms of which are followed by the invariable passive participle of the given verb in the emphatic state; e.g. *ki-pā'iš škīla*, "he remains taken", i.e. "he is taken".

d) Participial Tense Forms in Other Languages

42.23. The speakers of Semitic languages, in course of time, came to feel a need for tense as distinguished from aspect (§38.19). This was accomplished in Neo-Aramaic thanks to the new verbal system (§42.18-22). Also the Hebrew verbal categories underwent a profound change that is clearly visible in Mishnaic and Modern Hebrew, but was already prepared to a certain extent in Biblical Hebrew. To express the present tense Hebrew used the active participle in a nominal clause; e.g. *hā-'ārōn wə-Yiśrā'ēl w-Īhūdā yōšəbīm bas-sukkōt*, "the ark, and Israel, and Judah (are) abiding in booths" (II Sam. 11,11). This became the normal mood of denoting a present tense in Modern Hebrew, while the perfect serves as a preterite to denote past tense, and the imperfect may function as a volitive mood. The participle may be used with the personal pronoun (e.g. *'attā hōlēk*, "you are going") and with inflected forms of the verb *hāyā*, "to be", in the perfect (e.g. *hāyā qōṭēl*, "he killed" or "he was killing"), and in the imperfect (e.g. *yihye nākōn*, "he will be established").

42.24. A similar development took place in Arabic and the resulting compound tenses have a certain vogue in colloquial Arabic, being employed in the expression of time. Thus, the perfect *kān*, "he was", with the active participle may express the European imperfect (e.g. *kān kātib*, "he was writing"), while the independent personal pronoun with the active participle may express the present tense (e.g. *huwa kātib*, "he is writing"). The future can be expressed by the participle *rāyiḥ*, "going", with the imperfect; e.g. *ana rāyiḥ aktəb*, "I am going to write". In Maghrebine Arabic, one can also use the participle *māši* in the same way, e.g. *māši yəsmaʿ*, "he is going to hear".

42.25. Comparable developments occurred in modern Ethiopian languages. Thus, compound tenses consisting of a participle and of one of the auxiliary verbs *halla*, *ʿala*, or *ṣanḥa*, "to be", are used in Tigre to express the perfective present or the perfective past. The perfective present is formed by the participle followed by *halla*; e.g. *nəgus Kabasa māṣəʾ* (active participle) *halla*, "the king of Kabasa has arrived (and he is present)"; *həta kəbub qobəʿ lābsat* (fem. active participle) *hallet*, "she has put on a round hat (and she is wearing it)". To form the perfective past, Tigre can use the participle with *ʿala* or *ṣanḥa*; e.g. *qadam bəzuḥ ʿāmotāt ʾət ʾətyopya māṣəʾ* (active participle) *ʿalko*, "many years ago I had come to Ethiopia"; *radʾit lanəwāy ḥālfat* (fem. active participle) *ʾəlu ṣanḥat*, "the raid on the cattle had passed him by". In Amharic, instead, the participle with the copula *näw*, "he is, it is" (§49.20), expresses an event that will happen or is likely to happen; e.g. *säw mʷač näw*, "man is mortal"; from Stem III.1/A, *säw täsäbari näw*, "man is fragile", lit. "breakable".

G. Particular Types of Verbs

43.1. The following sections will deal with some types of verbs the inflection of which differs in certain forms from the most common triconsonantal pattern. These verbs are traditionally examined under the general title of "weak" verbs, but this appellation is subject to serious reserves.

a) "Weak" Verbs

43.2. In fact, "weak" verbs is a denomination used in traditional grammars of Semitic languages to designate certain categories of verbs which exhibit only one or two consonants in some of their basic forms. This appellation implies that these verbs are nevertheless triconsonantal, but that one or two of their radicals are "weak" and subject either to reduction to long vowels or to assimilation. More advanced linguistic study has shown, however, that a large part of these verbs are originally monosyllabic and that additional morphemes, secondary diphthongization, nasalization, or morpho-phonemic glides are responsible for the emergence of a supplementary consonant with the consequent inclusion of these verbs into the triconsonantal system.

43.3. Because of the development of laryngals and pharyngals in Assyro-Babylonian and in Libyco-Berber (§43.23) also the verbs containing these consonants are often regarded as "weak", but they should be considered as a subdivision of originally strong verbs and examined separately (§45). Some verbs with the laryngal ' belong nevertheless to the group of originally monosyllabic roots (§44.5), in particular the verbs with first radical ' which usually have a biconsonantal imperative. This is a general rule in Arabic, e.g. *ḥuḏ*, "seize!"; *kul*, "eat!"; *mur*, "order!". A confirmation may be found in other branches of Afro-Asiatic; e.g. Tuareg *yəkša* < **yikla*, Tarifit *yəšša*, Tamazight *ičča*, Hausa *ci*, "he has eaten". Further researches are needed in this comparative lexical field.

43.4. Verbs with identical second and third radical are commonly called *mediae geminatae*. They are traditionally considered as a subdivision of the "weak" verbs, because they do not follow the triconsonantal pattern in many forms. However, it stands to reason that this verbal class originates in monosyllabic roots, which were partly expanded to triliterals by disjoining the long consonant by means of an inserted vowel (§44.10-11). The number of verbs with an originally long second radical consonant was probably greater, since a long consonant can be dissimilated through the glottal stop or through one of the liquids *l*, *n*, *r*. This question requires a thorough investigation. It has long been recognized that there existed a semantic correlation between verbs *mediae geminatae* and corresponding "weak" verbs with third radical *w* or *y* (§43.11); e.g. Hebrew *šgg* and *šgy*, "to err".

43.5. Also verbs with first radical *n* are generally considered as "weak" because the vowelless *n* is often assimilated to the following consonant. However, on the one hand, this assimilation is operative neither in all the Semitic languages, nor with all the verbs of the languages where such assimilation occurs, and, on the other hand, some inflected forms of the same verbs have no *n* in the position of the first radical; e.g. Old Akkadian *uṣur*, "watch!"; Assyrian *din*, "give!"; Hebrew *gaš*, "approach!"; Aramaic *śē'*, "carry away!". Since the imperative is the most elementary inflected form from which many prefix-conjugations are likely to derive (§38.1), the appearance of a first radical *n* should be considered in such verbs as a secondary phenomenon. It could be explained in two different ways. The Old Akkadian and Assyro-Babylonian imperative forms with a prosthetic vowel *u* or *i* (e.g. *uqur*, "break!"; *ikis*, "cut!") may suggest that the first radical of these monosyllabic verbs was originally long (e.g. **qqur*, **kkis*). The appearance of *n* in some of the inflected forms may then be interpreted as resulting from the dissimilation of the long phoneme in certain circumstances with a consequent generalization of the use of *n*. Another explanation may simply refer to the large number of roots in South Ethiopic, especially in Gurage (at least 120 examples), with a non-etymological *n* inserted in roots before velars (e.g. *əngər*, "foot", vs. *ägər* < *ragl*), dentals (e.g. *əndät*, "mother", vs. *adot*), labials (e.g. *ənbərbäya*, "butterfly", vs. Amharic *birrabirro*), sibilants (e.g. *ənzən*, "ear", vs. *əzən* < *'uḏn*), palatals (e.g. *ənǧ*, "hand", vs. *äǧ* < *yad*). This development still perceptible in Gurage dialects may have been operative in Proto-Semitic as well. In this hypothesis, the initial vowels of Old Akkadian and Assyro-Babylonian ought to be regarded as a secondary development, the more so that forms without prosthesis do occur.

43.6. Verbs with first radical *w* or *y* constitute a mixed category with originally monosyllabic roots, without initial *w* / *y*, and with roots comprising three consonants. The distinction can best be made on the basis of the imperative, but forms from the prefix conjugations and the infinitive confirm the results of this analysis. Thus, in Arabic, the initial *w* of most verbs with first radical *w* does not appear in the imperative and the imperfect of Stem I; e.g. *ya-ǧid-u*, "he will find", *hab*, "give!". This is already the case in Pre-Islamic North Arabian (e.g. Thamūdic *hb*, "give!") and, e.g., over the entire Semitic area initial *w* is absent in the imperative "give birth!" of the verb mentioned in dictionaries under *walada > yālad* (cf. §43.7): Assyro-Babylonian *lidī*, Ugaritic *ld*, Hebrew *lədī*, Arabic *lidī*, Ge'ez *ladi*, Tigre *ladi*. Instead, other verbs are triconsonantal even in the imperative; e.g. Assyro-Babylonian *eniq*, "suck!"; Hebrew *yərā'*, "fear!"; Arabic *'īqaẓ*, "watch!"; Ge'ez *wəṭən*, "begin!". The first group is by far the largest and contains roots attested in most Semitic languages. However, under the influence of the triconsonantal system and by analogy with the second group, exceptional forms may occur in the first group, like the Syriac imperative *yiladī* and Harari *wŭläǧi*, "give birth!". Also variants are attested in the same language, like Ge'ez imperatives *wəgər* and *gar* / *gər*, "stone!".

43.7.   No satisfactory explanation has been given as yet to the development $C_1vC_2 > wa\text{-}C_1vC_2$ and — where initial w had shifted to y — also $ya\text{-}C_1vC_2$, although the same phenomenon is attested in ancient Egyptian where, e.g., the noun *'bw*, "purification", is certainly related to the verb *w'b*, "to be pure", while *wdi*, "to thrust", seems to be a derivative of *di*, "to give". The possible recourse to an on-glide *w* in initial position (§22.18) would not be convincing in front of a consonant, e.g. *l* in *lidī*, but a vowel may form in front of a monosyllabic verbal radical, as in the Gafat perfect **ahorä** and infinitive **wähor**, "to go", of the verb corresponding to Ge'ez *hora* and to Sabaic *ḥwr*. The same tendency appears in the Gafat perfect *wabä < *wa-haba*, "he gave", although the jussive *yab* and the imperative *ab* do not show any trace of *wa-* and correspond to the usual Ethiopic form *haba* of this verb. Also Gafat *waššä*, "he wanted", vs. Amharic *ša* and Gurage *šä*, *se'ä*, *šä'ä*, should be explained in such a way, since the Semitic root is *ṯ'y*, "to look for". Now, the clearest and earliest attestations of the syllable *wa-* in the East Semitic verb "to bear" occur especially in the stative, e.g. *walid*, "he is born", *waldāku*, "I am born", i.e. in forms morphologically identical to the perfect in Gafat. The derivation of the *wa-* forms from a monosyllabic verbal root, e.g. *lid*, might thus be explained tentatively by the prefixing of an element *wa-*. This hypothesis would explain the remarkable fact that the element *wa-* is missing, e.g., in the Tigre verb *haba* and in the Tigrinya verb *habä*, both meaning "to give" and obviously related to Ge'ez *wahaba*. Besides, Tigre has the variant forms *hada*, "to be little", and *haṭa*, "to devour", next to *wahada* and to *wahaṭa*. In any case, in this hypothesis, the verbs with an original first radical *y* would belong to the triconsonantal group. This is confirmed by East Semitic, Arabic, and Ethiopic where verbs having a first radical *y* are inflected as strong verbs, although the rules of diphthong contractions apply to them as well (§22). The originally monosyllabic verbs of the type CvC, developed to verbs of class $wa\text{-}CvC$, will be examined briefly in the next section (§44.4).

43.8.   This assumed origin of the verbs with first radical *w* does not contradict the fact that this *w* can be elided in some inflected forms of the root already adapted to the triconsonantal pattern, especially after a prefix. In Hebrew, e.g., the causative stem of the verb *wtb > yšb* exhibits the form *hōšēb / hōšīb < *hawšib*, "he caused to sit / dwell". In Harari, the verbs that begin with *w* show contraction wherever *w* is preceded by an element. In particular, the sequence *awä-* of the causative stem is contracted into *ā-*; e.g. *ādāqa*, "he caused to fall", from *wädāqa*; *ārāda*, "he brought down", from *wärāda*; *āsāda*, "he caused to take", from *wäsāda*, etc. As for the Palaeosyrian orthography of forms derived from the D-stem and the Š-stem, it does not imply the presence of the initial syllable *wa-* in the verbs *wld*, "to bear", *wdʿ*, "to know", and *wṣʾ*, "to go out". However, the reduction of the diphthong *aw > ā* must be taken into account (§22.3) in the case of the causative infinitive *sa-da-um*, "to let know", which can be read *šadaʿum* or *šādaʿum / ša(w)daʿum*. An alternative interpretation is possible also in the case of the noun *sa-zu-wa-tum*, "dismissal", that can be interpreted as *šaṣu(ʾ)watum* or *šāṣu(ʾ)atum / ša(w)ṣu(ʾ)atum*. Instead, the feminine D-participle *mu-li-tum*, "midwife", must be read *mullittum*, while an initial radical *w* would have normally required a form **muwallittu*.

43.9. The verbs with supposed medial radical *w* or *y*, called also "hollow verbs", as well as a few verbs exhibiting ' as medial radical, have forms which cannot derive from triconsonantal patterns, in particular the imperative and the prefix-conjugation. It stands to reason that these verbs originate in monosyllabic roots of the type *Cv̄C* (§28.9) and that forms corresponding to those with long second radical (e.g. *iparras*) result from the disjunction of the long vowel through the insertion of the glottal stop in case the stem-vowel is *ā*; e.g. Assyro-Babylonian present-future *išaʾal*, "he asks", as against preterite *išāl*. The phonetic reason for the rise of the glottal stop is a two-peak syllable which arose through the difficulty of pronouncing a very long vowel in a closed syllable. The vocalic clusters *ūa* and *īa* explain the rise of *w* and *y* in the following cases. Thus, the semivowel *w* is inserted in case the stem-vowel is *ū*, as in Assyrian *ikūwan*, "he is true", as against preterite *ikūn*, and the semivowel *y* is produced in case the stem-vowel is *ī*; e.g. Assyro-Babylonian *iqīyaš*, "he offers", as against preterite *iqīš*. Similar phenomena occur in West Semitic and South Semitic languages, e.g. Arabic Stem II *qawwama* as against Stem I *qāma*, "to get up", Geʿez *qawwama* as against *qōma < *qāma*. Some languages may exhibit *ī > ay* instead of the *ū > aw* of other languages, e.g. Aramaic *qayyēm*, while Hebrew has formations on the pattern of verbs with doubled second radical (*qōmēm*).

43.10. There are also verbs with a "weak" *l*, especially in Aramaic: *ʾzl*, "to go"; *hlk*, "to go"; *lqḥ*, "to take"; *slq*, "to go up". The Syriac first person singular perfect of *ʾzl* is *ʾezzet*, while the "walker" is called in Neo-Aramaic *azāna < ʾāzālnā*. The Aramaic imperfect of *hlk* is *yəhāk*; *ysq* is the imperfect of *slq*, and *yqḥ* the imperfect of *lqḥ*. The real weakness of the liquid *l*, attested already in Palaeosyrian (§17.2), explains this development which is largely paralleled in Gurage where medial and final *l* can be lost or reduced to a vowel. The West Semitic imperative *lk* and infinitive *lkt* of *hlk* present a different development which probably reveals the originally monosyllabic root **lik* of the verb *hlk*. This is confirmed apparently by Libyco-Berber *llukk* < **hlukk*, "to tread on", with its causative *slukk* (cf. §27.25). As for *'zl*, the imperative of which is usually *zīl*, the Libyco-Berber *azəll*, "to run", seems to contradict such assumption. There is a strong, tense *ll* in both Libyco-Berber verbs.

43.11. The verbs with third radical *w* or *y* are traditionally called *ultimae infirmae*. In reality, however, they are "strong" triconsonantal verbs and only syncope of intervocalic *w* / *y*, contraction of diphthongs, and elision of final *w* / *y* must be taken into account in languages and dialects where these changes occur. Verbs with final radical *y* are well represented in Libyco-Berber, as shown e.g. by the unmarked imperative forms *aləy*, "go up!"; *zrəy*, "pass!"; *fsəy*, "melt!", in Tamazight. Such a Libyco-Berber imperative may be found already in the verb *nby*, attested also in Bedja (*nifi*) and in Coptic (*nibe, nibi, nifi*), and used frequently in Numidic funerary inscriptions: *nby b'* [**nbəy i-bba'*], "sigh for my father!". These "strong" features do not mean that the original root of all the verbs in question was triconsonantal. In fact, some of them seem to derive from nouns to which a causative affix *-y* was added (§41.13).

43.12. Old Babylonian stative forms like *ra-bi-ia$_8$-ku* /rabiyāku/, "I am great", or *ra-bi-(a-)at* /rabiyāt/, *ra-bi-e-et* /rabiyēt/, "she is great", still testify to a "strong" inflection, while a Middle Babylonian form like *ra-bat* /rabāt/ indicates the syncope of *y* between vowels and the subsequent contraction *iā* > *ā*. Imperfective forms like *i-ra-ab-bi*, "he becomes great", may be interpreted as *irabbiy*, or *irabbī* with the contraction *iy* > *ī*, or *irabbi* with a subsequent shortening of the final vowel. In Semitic languages, also in the Qur'ān and the Ḥadīth, one finds frequently forms in which a long final *ī* is shortened or sometimes elided altogether (§39.14). Even the suffix of the first person singular could be affected by this tendency. Analogous dialectal differences can be observed in verbs with third radical *w*. E.g. Middle Assyrian stative *za-ku-a-at* /zakuwāt/, "she is pure", still testifies to a "strong" inflection, while Middle Babylonian *za-ka-at* /*zakāt*/ implies the syncope of *w* between vowels and the subsequent contraction *uā* > *ā*. Old Assyrian imperfective forms like *i-za-ku-wa* /*izakkuw*/ clearly indicate the "strong" inflection, but the latter can be implied as well by the spelling *i-za-ku* /*izakkuw*/, although an interpretation *izakkū* and *izakku* is also possible, since shortening and even elision of final long *ū* is attested in Semitic.

43.13. Verbal forms in Palaeosyrian and Amorite names show that different languages are involved. Thus, Eblaite names like *Ib-na-Il* /*Yibnā-'Il*/, "Il has created", and *Iq-na-Da-mu* /*Yiqnā-Da'mu*/, "Damu has begotten", seem to indicate that the final diphthong *-ay* was reduced to *ā*, although it is preserved in the infinitive *qá-na-(u₉-)um* /*qanāyum*/, "to beget". Instead, Amorite names like *Ia-ab-ni-ᵈDa-gan* and *Ia-aq-ni-Ìl* show a change *iy* > *ī* > *i*. In Ugaritic, the last radical *y* is written in some cases (e.g. *wy'ny Krt*, "and Keret answered"), while it is not preserved in other passages (e.g. *wy'n*, "and he answered"). The few examples with *w* suggest that the third radical *w* was to some extent treated like *y*. A thorough investigation is needed, although the spelling of the suffixed perfect stative without *y* (e.g. *'lt*, "she is up"; *mġt*, "I came") indicates that the syncope of *y* and the subsequent contraction have already occurred in Ugaritic. Spellings like *y'ny* may reflect an archaic pronunciation in *-iy* or a simple use of *y* as *mater lectionis* for *-ī*.

43.14. In Hebrew, the forms of the suffix-conjugation terminate in *-ā* and therefore imply the monophthongization *-ay* > *-ā* and *-aw* > *ā*; e.g. *bākā* < **bakay*, "he cried". The forms of the prefix-conjugation terminate in *-ē* / *e*, an ending resulting from the reduction of *-iy*. As for verbs with third radical *w*, they have been assimilated to those with final *y*. In Early Phoenician, the final consonant of these verbs was still indicated in the perfect; e.g. *bny*, "he built". In Moabite, instead, the final *w* was preserved, as shown by *wy'nw*, "and he oppressed", and by *''nw*, "I shall oppress", but the third radical *y* was reduced to a vowel, as appears e.g. from *bnty* and *w'bn*, "and I built".

43.15. The Aramaic verbs with third radical *w* have been absorbed by those ending in *y*. In Early Aramaic, the concomitant use of *'l yrwh* and *'l yrwy*, "let it not be sated", shows that *yrwh* and *yrwy* may be regarded as orthographic variants of the same verbal form in which either *-h* or *-y* is used as a vowel letter marking the contracted diphthong *-ē* < *-ay*

(but cf. §22.9). As for the perfect, the third person singular terminates in
-ā < -ay; e.g. bə'ā < *baġay, "he requested". Instead, the third person
plural exhibits endings -ō (e.g. bənō < *banayū, "they built") and -īw (e.g.
'ištīw < 'ištiyū, "they drank"). Like in Arabic (§43.17), not contracted
forms occur before the consonant of a personal, at least in the singular;
e.g. na-šá-a-a-tu = našayt(u), "I took"; ḥǎzaytā, "you saw". They should
also occur in the plural (e.g. rmyn' /*ramaynā/, "we threw"; ḥzytwn
/*ḥazaytūn/, "you saw"), although contracted vocalizations ay > ē / ī are
attested in manuscripts. Besides, non contracted forms of the participle
plural, vocalized bānayīn, "who build", are found in Galilean Aramaic.
While contraction is the rule in Syriac (e.g. bəkā, nebkē, "to cry"; dəlā,
nedlē, "to draw out"), the third radical y is preserved in Neo-Aramaic
when it is followed by the vowel a, like in Arabic (§43.17); e.g. the infinitive štāyā, "to drink". In the other cases, y is either contracted to ī or
elided altogether; e.g. šātī, "they drink"; šātaḥ, "we drink".

43.16. In North Arabian languages, viz. Thamūdic, Liḥyānite, and
Ṣafaitic, the monophthongization in verbs with third "weak" radical
seems to be restricted to proper names where the theophorous element
-'il is attached to the verbal form. In other cases, the spellings 'ty /'atay/,
"he came", bny /banay/, "he built", r'y /ra'ay/, "he pastured", bky
/bakay/, "he wept", hqny, "he offered", b'yt, "she overcame", show the
preservation of the diphthong like in Epigraphic South Arabian (§43.19)
and in Ethiopic (§43.20). Proper names derived from such roots, like
M'wy /Mu'āwiy/ and Ġzy /Ġazzay/, have conserved the diphthong as
well, as shown by Greek transcriptions Μοοααυιος, Μαυια, Αζζαιος.

43.17. In Classical Arabic, instead, the monophthongization occurs in
the verbs of the a-class, i.e. fa'ala; e.g. bakā < *bakaya, "he cried";
da'ā < *da'awa, "he called". For the verbs of the i-class and the u-class,
i.e. fa'ila and fa'ula, there is a difference between the perfect, which
preserves the third radical (e.g. laqiya, "he found"; waliya, "he was
near"; saruwa, "he was noble"), and the imperfect where monophthongization does occur (e.g. yalqā, "he will find"; yalī, "he will be near";
yasrū, "he will be noble"). As a rule, the radical w / y is preserved
before the consonant of a personal (e.g. ramayta, "you threw";
da'awna, "we called") and, in some cases, before the vowel a (e.g.
yarmiya, "he would throw"; saruwat, "she was noble"). On the other
hand, there were ancient dialects saying, e.g., baqā, "he remained", for
baqiya; fanā, "he passed away", for faniya, thus changing iya in ā. The

same monophthongization occurred in passive forms, e.g. *ruḍā* for *ruḍiya*, "he was well received"; *nuhā* for *nuhiya*, "he was prohibited". New diphthongs appear when the personals *-ū*, *-ī*, *-ūna*, *-īna* are added: *-ā-ū* > *aw* (e.g. *ramaw*, "they threw"), *-ā-ī* > *-ay* (e.g. *talqayna*, "you [fem.] will find"). There was a quite common confusion of third radicals *w* and *y* in Arabic, resulting in parallel dialectal forms as *'aṣawtu* and *'aṣaytu*, "I struck with a stick", and several other dialectal sound-changes have been reported in ancient dialects, e.g. *laqayat* instead of *laqiyat*, "she found"; *baqīta* instead of *baqayta*, "you remained", etc.

43.18. In modern Arabic colloquials, the distinction of the ancient endings *-ā* and *-ī* is largely obliterated, while an ending *-u* occurs only in the third person masculine plural. Some colloquials tend to generalize the use of *-ā*, while *-ī* is preferred, e.g., in the Cairene dialect, as in *banit* instead of *banat*, "she built". The dialects of the Bedouin are more conservative.

43.19. In Epigraphic South Arabian, the lack of vocalization hinders the analysis of inflectional forms in the "weak" verbs. However, there is one feature that seems strongly marked in roots with *w* / *y* as third consonant, namely that the singular of the basic stem retains the *w* / *y*, as in *bny*, "he built", *'dw*, "he moved". In the plural, and in derivative stems, there is some variation. While the full causative form *hqnyw*, "they dedicated", is very common indeed in Sabaic, there is one example of *hqnw*, without *y*, and some instances where *'dw* appears to be a plural, which is normally written *'dww*. It seems therefore that dialectal monophthongization did occur. Also the dialectal confusion of third radicals *w* and *y* may occur in the latest period, as shown by *'dyw* instead of *'dww*. As for *yhrḍyn* and *yhrḍwn*, "he will satisfy", these forms result from the parallel use of the variants *rḍw* and *rḍy*.

43.20. As a rule, Ge'ez preserves the final radicals *w* / *y*, but there is an optional contraction *aw* > *ō* > *o* and, rarely, *ay* > *ē* > *e* when *-aw-* and *-ay-* form closed syllables in the suffix-conjugation; e.g. *bakayka* > *bakeka*, "I cried"; *fannawka* > *fannoka*, "I sent". In the prefix-conjugation and in the imperative, a reduction *-aw* > *-ū* > *-u* and *-iy* > *-ī* > *-i* occurs usually when no affix beginning with a vowel is added; e.g. *yəbakki* < **yibakkiy*, "he will cry"; *yə'tu* < *yə'taw*, "may he go home". Tigrinya shows a few changes in comparison to Ge'ez, although contracted forms do appear (e.g. *tälo* < *täläwä*, "he found"), as well as forms articulated -*y*e; e.g. *bän*y*e*, "he built". In Tigre, instead, the monophthongization is virtually complete; e.g. in the case of *y*: *bakā* vs. Ge'ez *bakaya*, "he cried"; *ra'ā* vs. Ge'ez *rə'əya*, "he saw". The situation is the same with the third radical *w*, as in *'aṣā*, "he fenced in", vs. Ge'ez *'aṣawa*, "he closed"; *naqe* vs. Ge'ez *naqawa*, "he shouted"; *ka'ā* vs. Ge'ez *ka'awa*, "he spilled".

43.21.   In South Ethiopic, traces of the third radicals *w* and *y* appear often in qualitative changes of the final vowel occasioned by the reduction; e.g. Amharic *näkka* < **näkkäyä*, "he touched"; East Gurage *qäre* < **qäräyä*, "he remained behind". Consonantal traces subsist in verbs of several Gurage dialects, e.g. in Chaha *ḵ*w*ä-m* vs. Ge'ez *ka'awa*, "he spilled"; *näq*w*ä-m* vs. Ge'ez *naqawa*, "he shouted"; *bäk*y*ä-m* vs. Ge'ez *bakaya*, "he cried"; *aq*y*ä-m* vs. Ge'ez *ḥaqaya*, "he craunched". This is not the case, instead, in other South Ethiopian languages, except some particular occurrences like Harari verbal adjective *wəy*, "hot", related to Ge'ez *wə'ya*, "he was burnt". Gurage and Harari are precisely South Ethiopian languages with several features in common with North Ethiopic.

43.22.   There is a residue of so-called irregular verbs, i.e. of verbs which combine two of the aforementioned categories of "weak" verbs, e.g. East Semitic *ewū* < **hawāyu*, "to become", as well as a number of defective verbs which are not attested in a sufficient number of inflected forms in any one dialect. The inflection of the "doubly weak" verbs takes account of both categories concerned, while the scanty attested defective verbs ought to be analyzed one by one, inasmuch as a reliable philological analysis and hence their assignment to a root are possible. Such verbs cannot be treated in the framework of a general outline of comparative grammar, and the reader is thus referred to the grammars of single languages and dialects. Nevertheless, it may be posited as a rule that these verbs will be found to belong to one or the other pattern discussed under verb inflection. If their root cannot be attached to the Semitic core, their origin has to be checked and sorted out according to dialect distribution, as in the case, e.g., of Cushitic loanwords in Gurage.

43.23.   "Weak" verbs constitute an important chapter in the comparative study of Afro-Asiatic. The question is whether the Cushitic and the Libyco-Berber biradicals and monoradicals still reflect an early stage of Afro-Asiatic, anterior to the development of the Semitic triconsonantal pattern. In our opinion, some verbs preserve an ancient biconsonantal pattern, not yet "squeezed" into a triconsonantal system, but a large number of Cushitic and especially Libyco-Berber verbs have, instead, lost one or two of their radical consonants after the separation of the various branches of the Afro-Asiatic language family, i.e. not earlier than *ca*. 3000 B.C. This loss of radical semivowels and gutturals, comparable with the situation in South Ethiopic, is to be explained not only by elision, but also by monophonemization in monosyllabic root morphemes. That problem cannot be discussed here in the framework of an outline of Semitic comparative grammar, but a few examples ought to be given in order to illustrate the questions involved. Thus, the absence of a "weak" third radical can be exemplified by the Libyco-Berber (Tamazight) verbs *ġr*, "to call", *nġ*, "to kill", and *ns*, "to spend the night", which belong to the same root morphemes as Semitic *qr'*, *nky*, and *mśy*. The absence or loss of a "weak" radical can be accompanied by the spirantization of *b* > *ḇ* > *w*, as in *sw*, "to drink", and *wt*, "to strike", corresponding to Semitic *šb'* and *ḫbṭ*. The absence of the "weak" first radical can be observed, e.g. in *wš*, "to give", and *žn*, "to sleep", related respectively to Semitic *'wš* and *wšn*. The "weak" middle radical is apparently lost in Libyco-Berber *ddr*, "to live", and *zr*, "to see", to be linked respectively with Semitic *dūr* / *dry* and *zhr*. Both the first and the third radicals are missing in *af*, "to find", *as*, "to go towards, to gather", *ddu*, "to go", *ž*, "to make", *ini*, "to say", and *aġ*, "to befall, to happen", that belong to the same root morphemes as Semitic *yp'*, *wṣ'*, *wdw* or *'dw*, *'śy*, *'ny*, and *wq'*. A somewhat different problem may occur in the class of $C_1vC_2C_2$ verbs when the Semitic gemination of the second radical, as in *rśś* (*rḍḍ*), does not correspond to a "tense" consonant in Libyco-Berber *rz*, "to break". Finally, also the Libyco-Berber *b* is considered as a "weak" consonant because its spirantization to *ḇ* > *w* may lead to its further reduction to the vowel *u*, as in *sku*, "to bury", and *rnu*, "to prevail", where the Ghadamsi dialect still preserves a pronunciation *rnaḇ*. Now, *sku* corresponds to Semitic *škb*, "lay down", and *rnu* is apparently related to ancient Egyptian *rnpi*, "recover one's strength". The Libyco-Berber verbs mentioned in this paragraph are not borrowed from Arabic, as indicated in several cases by their semantic value or by their absence from the Arabic vocabulary. Besides, their phonology implies a development the basis of which was not Arabic, but a language phonetically close to a form of Proto-Semitic, deprived of its gutturals already in Antiquity, — at least in the northern Berber dialects, — and characterized later by a secondary tendency to pharyngalize or to voice the consonants. It is extremely hazardous, at present, to attempt an approximate dating of the loss of the gutturals that took place at some time between 3000 and the mid-first millennium B.C. Only slight changes occurred, instead, since the Numidian and Roman times, as suggested by some probable identifications, e.g. of present-day -*səggan*, "black", with ancient *Suggan, Suggen, Sucan*; of present-day *məllul*, "he is white", with ancient *MLL'*, Μαλλυλα(s); of present-day -*mawal*, "shepherd", with ancient *MUL'*.

b) Biconsonantal Verbs

44.1. This chapter deals with the three types CvC, $C\bar{v}C$, and $C_1vC_2C_2$ of originally biconsonantal verbal roots the inflection of which differs to some extent from the regular conjugation, but most likely preserves an older verbal pattern. Their forms have been regarded in the past — and by some authors even today — as explainable on a basis of triconsonantal verbs, by means of phonetic changes which sometimes characterize "weak" or geminated consonants. More recent studies have shown, however, that the roots which have *w* as first radical in certain forms (§43.7) or which contain length — both the "hollow roots" of the type $C\bar{v}C$ and the roots *mediae geminatae* of the type $C_1vC_2C_2$ — have to be described and analyzed on their own merits, without recourse to a triconsonantal proto-form and without inventing *ad hoc* phonetic laws devised uniquely to explain the divergent forms in accordance with the patterns of the triconsonantal verbs.

44.2. Several Semitic languages possess verb-stems which exhibit only two radical consonants, or even only one consonant, in most of their inflected forms, although these forms appear as triconsonantal in the periods earlier than the dialect under consideration (e.g. Ge'ez *sam'a*; Amharic *sämma*, "to hear") or in related languages (e.g. Old Akkadian *banāyum*; Old Babylonian *banūm*, "to build"). In these cases, we deal with verbs that have lost a consonant, either between Proto-Semitic and the dialect under investigation, or during the historical evolution of the language. These verbs are not taken here into account because, as a rule, they follow the regular pattern. Instead, the problem arises with roots the basic forms of which never had more than two consonants. On the other hand, there are verbs containing three radical consonants in most of their inflected forms (e.g. *ntn*, "to give"), except the imperative (e.g. *tn*) and occasionally some other "tense" of the basic stem (§43.5-9). Since these forms are the simplest of the verbal system, they are rightly regarded as exhibiting the primary elements of the root. These biconsonantal forms of the type CvC probably belong to the same (pre)historical phase of Semitic as the verbs of the type $wa + CvC$ and as the types $C\bar{v}C$ and $C_1vC_2C_2$ (cf. §44.1).

44.3. Before analyzing the monosyllabic roots and illustrating their inflection, a further element, the thematic vowel has to be introduced. This feature is normally treated in the grammars in relation to the pharyngals and laryngals characterized by their tendency to change the quality of the contiguous vowels (§45), e.g. Hebrew *yišloḥ > yišlaḥ, "he sends". However, the distinction in vocalism is not restricted to these phonetically explainable cases, because specific vowels belong to determined triconsonantal and biconsonantal roots. Among the verbs of the type CvC, the stem vowel of the verb *hab*, "give!", is *a*, while the one of the verb *ṭib*, "sit!", is *i*, and *u* is the stem vowel of the verb *ḫuḏ*, "seize!".

44.4. Various categories of the "so-called" weak verbs go back to an original monosyllabic root of the type CvC, in some cases perhaps $C_1C_1vC_2$. There are such verbs at least in the groups with first radical *n* (§43.5), *w* (§43.6-7), *h* (§43.10), and ' (§43.3). The problem involved is presented in the respective paragraphs and we limit ourselves here to a common "classical" paradigm of the originally monosyllabic verbs of the type CvC with vocalized samples of prefix-conjugations, of the imperative, and of the infinitive or verbal noun of the basic stem. Examples are taken from the verb *waṯaba*, "to sit", or *wahaba*, "to give". The East Semitic "preterite" corresponds formally to the West Semitic imperfect and to the Ethiopic jussive/subjunctive; the "imperfective" is the East Semitic present-future and the Ethiopic imperfect.

		Old Babylonian	Hebrew	Aramaic	Arabic	Ge'ez
Preterite	3 m. sing.	*ušib*	*yēšēb*	*yittib*	*yaṭibu*	*yahab*
	plur.	*uš(i)bū*	*yēš(ē)bū*	*yittəbū*	*yaṭibū*	*yahabu*
Imperfective	3 m. sing.	*uššab*				*yəhub*
	plur.	*uššabū*				*yəhubu*
Imperative	2 m. sing.	*šib*	*šēb*	*tib*	*ṭib*	*hab*
	plur.	*šibā*	*šəbū*	*təbū*	*ṭibū*	*habu*
Verbal noun / Infinitive		*šubtu/šubat*	*šebet/šābet*	*mittab*	*ṭibatun*	*habt*

44.5. In the stems which include length, especially those of the type
$C\bar{v}C$, the stem vowel plays an important role because it determinates, to
a great extent, which of the three consonants w, y, $'$ will appear as
medial radical in some forms of the basic stem and in derived stems.

1° Specific vowels belong thus to specific biconsonantal roots (e.g.
qūm, "to stand"; *šīm*, "to place"; *subb*, "to turn"), although a replacive
vowel can be used in the inflection in order to distinguish different verbal forms which otherwise would be homophonous. The Libyco-Berber
conjugation preserves remarkable traces of this replacive system, e.g. in
the imperfective *iraḥ*, "he will leave" (root *rūḥ*), vs. the perfective *iruḥ*,
"he left" (Tarifit), or in the imperfective *yəmmət*, "he will die" (root
mūt), vs. the perfective *yəmmut*, "he died" (Tarifit, Tuareg), thus pointing to an Afro-Asiatic origin of inflections based on vocalic alternations
(cf. §41.3). In Semitic, e.g. Babylonian present-future *ikān* has to be distinguished from the preterite *ikūn* (from the root *kūn*, "to be [firm,
true]") in the singular, but the replacive vowel is not required in the
plural, since the preterite appears to be *ikūnū*, while the present-future is
inflected *ikunnū*. The same explanation is valid in the case, e.g., of the
West Semitic stative *qām*, "he stood", which has to be distinguished
from the imperative *qūm*, "stand!". The inflection of the roots $C\bar{\imath}C$ and
$C\bar{u}C$ shows that the vocalic replacive provides sufficient tense contrast.
However, the replacive vowel did not provide an adequate contrast
between imperative and stative of the roots $C\bar{a}C$, at least in some languages. Therefore, certain forms of this numerically small group of verbs
can be characterized by a glottal stop which serves for the disjunction of
the long vowel (e.g. Arabic *sāla* and *sa'ala*, "he asked"), like in some
modern Ethiopic and Cushitic dialects, or for its splitting into two different vowels a - i (e.g. Neo-Babylonian *šá-'-il*; Late Aramaic *š'yl*; early
Arabic *s'yl* [*sa'il*]). In the latter case, a y-glide can occasionally replace
the glottal stop (e.g. Neo-Babylonian *šá-a-a-il*; Late Aramaic *šyyl*).

2° There are Palaeosyrian (e.g. *i-tù-wa-ar* /yituwwar/, "he comes
back"), Old Akkadian (e.g. *in tù-a-rí-su*, "on his return"), and Old
Assyrian forms (e.g. *adi tù-wa-ar*, "until the return of PN") of the basic
stem that are nevertheless conform to a triconsonantal conjugation which
undoubtedly goes back to prehistoric times. Much later, Ṣafaitic full
spellings of Stem I, like in *ṣyr m-mdbr*, "he came back from the steppe",
and in *mt' s¹tt 's²hr f-ḥwr*, "he was taken away for six months and he
returned", also point to a North Arabian conjugation based on the triconsonantal pattern, viz. **ṣayar* and **ḥawar*. The distribution of full and

defective spellings in Epigraphic South Arabian (e.g. *ṣyd* and *ṣd*, "he hunted") does not respond to easy analysis of principle, but early Andalusian Arabic, as reported by Pedro de Alcalá, preserves an internal *y* between identical vowels in perfect forms which go probably back to South Arabian, but also parallel Ṣafaitic; e.g. *çayáht* [*ṣayaḥt*], "I cried", instead of Classical *ṣiḥtu*. It is very likely, therefore, that the coexistence of forms like *ṣayad(a)* and *ṣīd(a)* has to be assumed in ancient South Semitic. However, since the oldest Sabaic inscriptions use the form *ṣd*, "he hunted", it is reasonable to surmise that *ṣyd*, e.g., reflects the steady development leading to the assimilation of the verbal type *CV̄C* to triconsonantal verbs.

3° Future research dealing with these questions should also consider the hypothesis of Proto-Afro-Asiatic rounded and palatalized radicals, e.g. in *mʷut*, "to die", *qʸim*, "to stay, to stand" (cf. §28.9). They might help explaining forms like Libyco-Berber *mmut* and *qqim*, the dialectal Tuareg variant *ġaym*, "to stay", Old Akkadian *muātu* [*mwātu*], or Aramaic *qyāmā*, "statute". The problem affects the phonology of the whole Afro-Asiatic area, as shown e.g. by the Logone (Chadic) noun ***ngun***, "belly", with a plural ***ngwaren***.

44.6. The verbs chosen to illustrate the inflection of the *CV̄C* roots are *kūn*, "to be (firm)", and *qūm*, "to stand", for the *CūC* type, *śīm*, "to place", and *ṣīr*, "to begin", for the *CīC* type, and *šāl*, "to ask", for the *CāC* type. Only "classical" languages are presented in the table, viz. Old Babylonian, completed when necessary by Neo-Babylonian forms between brackets, Biblical Hebrew, Aramaic, Classical Arabic, and Ge'ez. The paradigm is restricted to the basic stem, third person masculine singular and plural, or second person for the imperative. The names given in the table to the tenses reflect the analysis presented in §38. The "preterite" corresponds to the Hebrew, Aramaic, and Arabic imperfect, and to the Ge'ez jussive/subjunctive. The "imperfective" is the Old Babylonian present-future and the Ge'ez imperfect. The "perfective" is the perfect of Old Babylonian, while the "stative" corresponds to the West and South Semitic perfect. Paragraphs §44.12-14, which follow the tables, will offer some comments.

44.7. Basic stem of the roots of the *CūC* type.

		Old Babylonian	Hebrew	Aramaic	Arabic	Ge'ez
Preterite	3 m. sing.	*ikūn*	*yāqūm*	*yəqūm*	*yaqūmu*	*yəqum*
	plur.	*ikūnū*	*yāqūmū*	*yəqūmūn*	*yaqūmū*	*yəqumu*
Imperfective	3 m. sing.	*ikān*	—	—	—	*yəqawwəm*
	plur.	*ikunnū*	—	—	—	*yəqawwəmu*
Perfective	3 m. sing.	*iktūn*	—	—	—	—
	plur.	*iktūnū*	—	—	—	—
Imperative	2 m. sing.	*kūn*	*qūm*	*qūm*	*qum*	*qum*
	plur.	*kunnā*	*qūmū*	*qūmū*	*qūmū*	*qumu*
Stative	3 m. sing.	*kīn*	*qām*	*qām*	*qāma*	*qoma*
	plur.	*kīnū*	*qāmū*	*qāmū*	*qāmū*	*qomu*

44.8. Basic stem of the roots of the *CīC* type.

		Old Babylonian	Hebrew	Aramaic	Arabic	Ge'ez
Preterite	3 m. sing.	*išīm*	*yāśīm*	*yəśīm*	*yaṣīru*	*yəšim*
	plur.	*išīmū*	*yāśīmū*	*yəśīmūn*	*yaṣīrū*	*yəšimu*
Imperfective	3 m. sing.	*išām*	—	—	—	*yəšayyəm*
	plur.	*išimmū*	—	—	—	*yəšayyəmu*
Perfective	3 m. sing.	*ištīm*	—	—	—	—
	plur.	*ištīmū*	—	—	—	—
Imperative	2 m. sing.	*šīm*	*śīm*	*śīm*	*ṣir*	*šim*
	plur.	*šīmā*	*śīmū*	*śīmū*	*ṣīrū*	*šimu*
Stative	3 m. sing.	*šīm*	*śām*	*śām*	*ṣāra*	*šema*
	plur.	*šīmū*	*śāmū*	*śāmū*	*ṣārū*	*šemu*

44.9. Basic stem of the roots of *CāC* type.

		Old Babylonian	Hebrew	Aramaic	Arabic	Ge'ez
Preterite	3 m. sing.	*išāl*	*yiš'āl*	*yiš'al*	*yasalu*	*yəs'al*
	plur.	*išālū*	*yiš'ālū*	*yiš'ălūn*	*yasalū*	*yəs'alu*

		Old Babylonian	Hebrew	Aramaic	Arabic	Geʿez
Imperfective	3 m. sing.	*iša'al*	—	—	—	*yəsə'(')l*
	plur.	*išallū*	—	—	—	*yəsə'(')lu*
Perfective	3 m. sing.	*ištāl*	—	—	—	—
	plur.	*ištālū*	—	—	—	—
Imperative	2 m. sing.	*šāl*	*šə'al*	*šə'al*	*sal*	*sa'al*
	plur.	*šālā*	*ša'ălū*	*šə'alū*	*salū*	*sa'alu*
Stative	3 m. sing.	(*ša'il*)	*šā'al*	*šə'ēl / šā'ēl*	*sāla*	*sa'ala*
	plur.	(*ša'ilā*)	*šā'ălū*	**šə'ēlū / *šā'ēlū*	*sālū*	*sa'alu*

44.10. Verbs with second and third identical consonants are tradition-ally called *mediae geminatae*. Although these verbs are almost com-pletely adapted to the triconsonantal pattern in East Semitic, the mono-syllabic origin of the type $C_1vC_2C_2$ is particularly evident in West Semitic languages. The difference results basically from a double artic-ulation of the geminated consonant in East Semitic, while it is often pro-nounced continuously or tensely in West Semitic (§23.1). In order to present, as far as possible, attested verbal forms which are built accord-ing to the pattern of biconsonantal stems involving length, the following paradigm is based on the verb *danānu*, "to be strong", for Old Babylon-ian, *sabba*, "to turn", "to abuse", for Hebrew and Arabic, *'al(l)*, "to enter", for Aramaic, and *ḥamama*, "to be ill", for Ethiopic. The forms are selected and designated like in the preceding paragraphs (cf. §44.6).

		Old Babylonian	Hebrew	Aramaic	Arabic	Geʿez
Preterite	3 m. sing.	*idnin*	*yāsob*	*yēʿōl*	*yasubbu*	*yəḥmam / yəḥməm*
	plur.	*idninū*	*yāsobbū*	*yēʿlūn*	*yasubbū*	*yəḥmamu / yəḥməmu*
Imperfective	3 m. sing.	*idannin*	—	—	—	*yəḥamməm*
	plur.	*idanninū*	—	—	—	*yəḥammu / yəḥamməmu*
Perfective	3 m. sing.	*iddanin*	—	—	—	—
	plur.	*iddannu*	—	—	—	—
Imperative	2 m. sing.	—	*sob*	*ʿōl*	(*'u*)*sbub / subb-i(-a/u)*	*ḥəmam*
	plur.	—	*sobbū*	*'ullū*	*subbū*	*ḥəmmu / ḥəmamu*

		Old Babylonian	Hebrew	Aramaic	Arabic	Ge'ez
Stative	3 m. sing.	*dān*	*sābab*	*'al*	*sabba*	*ḥamma* / *ḥamama*
	plur.	*dannū*	*sabăbū*	*'allū* / *'ālū*	*sabbū*	*ḥammu* / *ḥamamu*

44.11. These examples do not give a complete picture of the attested verbal forms of the group concerned. In fact, also North Semitic attests singular stative forms of the monosyllabic *dān* / *dann* type; e.g. Eblaite *Da-na*-LUGAL /*Danna-śarrum*/, "the king is powerful"; *En-na-Il* /*Ḥenna-'Il*/, "Il is merciful". In Amorite occur names like *Ia-ḫu-un-Èl* /*Yaḫūn-'El*/, "El did favour", with the preterite of the same verb *ḥanna*. Some monosyllabic stems seem to appear in Ugaritic, but the prefix-conjugations are mostly adapted to the triconsonantal pattern. In Hebrew, also perfect forms like *qal*, *qallā*, "he / she is small", are attested, but only in verbs denoting state. This is also the case of the Assyro-Babylonian *dān* and of the Ge'ez *ḥamma*. In Ge'ez, however, the imperfect forms ending in a vowel preserve the shorter pattern which can be used optionally with verbs expressing action as well, e.g. *yənabbu* or *yənab-bəbu*, "they speak". Also the Assyro-Babylonian imperative has this shorter pattern when the form ends in a vowel; e.g. *dubub*, "speak!", but feminine *dubbī* and plural *dubbā*. Instead, Ethiopic examples taken from Stem III.A/1 (Gt), like *tanabba*, "he was read", *tasadda*, "he was expelled", do not prove that the biconsonantal pattern is used since the second and third radical are always juxtaposited in this *taqatla* stem.

44.12. The inflection of monosyllabic roots, both $C\bar{v}C$ and $C_1vC_2C_2$, exhibits two parallel sets of allophones: the first one concerns the quality of the long vowel, the second one shows the phonetic alternation -$\bar{v}C$ / -vC_2C_2 and thus bears on the place of length.

44.13. There are some variants among the attested verbal forms of the $C\bar{v}C$ type which reflect dialectal alternations $\bar{\imath}$ / $\bar{u}$ and thus seem to relativize the distinction of the three sub-classes $C\bar{u}C$, $C\bar{\imath}C$, and $C\bar{a}C$. In Amorite anthroponomy, e.g., one finds names with *Ia-ki-in-* and *Ia-ku-un-*, with *Ia-ši-ib-* and *Ia-šu-ub-*. Statistics indicates however that *Ia-ki-in-* and *Ia-ši-ib-* are exceptional forms which ought to be considered as dialectal variants. They are easily explainable in the light of the common Semitic weakness of the opposition $i : u$ which may affect long vowels, as well. For example, long $\bar{\imath}$ may in some cases stand in place of an $\bar{u}$ of some older stage of Arabic. In particular, the forms of the passive perfect of *CūC* verbs with vocalic affixes were pronounced either with *ī* or with *ū* in Pre-Classical Arabic, thus *qīla* or *qūla*, "(it) was said", *sīṭa* or *sūṭa*, "(it) was whipped together". In the Qur'ān, all cases of passive *CūC* verbs are spelled with *ī*, and the spelling with *ū* was later considered unclassical. A similar situation, with divergent "standardized" solutions, must be assumed in other Semitic languages. It affects also derivatives, as shown by Assyro-Babylonian *kayyānu* when compared with Palaeosyrian *kà-wa-nu* /*kawwānu*/, "stable", "permanent".

44.14. The alternation $-\bar{v}C$ / $-vC_2C_2$ characterizes already the Old Babylonian singular stative *da-a-an*, "(he) is strong", when compared with the plural *da-an-nu*, "(they) are strong". A comparable alternation gave probably rise to distinctive Stems II and III in Arabic (§41.6), and it occurs sometimes in modern Arabic dialects, e.g. in Ḥawrāni *šaršubba* and *šaršūba*, "tassel". These differences are purely phonetical and not phonemic. They ought to be considered as free variations, in particular when a final long consonant (e.g. *dann*) loses its length in favour of the preceding vowel (e.g. *dān*). The only situation where such free variation cannot be operative is the case when the place of length has a functional load and serves to differentiate two morphs, as in *ikūnū* and *ikunnū* (§44.5). This does not obtain in the inflection of the $C_1vC_2C_2$ verbs, where the place of length does not serve to differentiate tenses.

44.15. The derived stems of the verbs *mediae geminatae* are generally adapted to the pattern of triconsonantal verbs. In Arabic, however, the integration is by far not complete and many forms preserve the biconsonantal character of the root, especially in Stems III, IV, VI, VII, VIII, and X. However, triradical variants are attested; e.g. the participle *fārir(un)* next to *fārr(un)*, "runnig away", in Stem III; the Pre-Islamic North Arabian imperfect *yhbrr* /*yuhabrir*/ instead of Classical Arabic *yubirru* and of Sabaic *yhbr* /*yuhabbir*/, "he fulfils", and the Liḥyānite perfect *'ṭll* /*'aṭlal*/ next to *'ṭl* /*'aṭall*/, "he hollowed out", all in Stem IV; the perfect *tašādada* next to *tašādda*, "he argued with somebody", in Stem VI; etc. The triradical variants proceed basically from a different articulation of the geminated consonants, viz. pronounced doubly instead of being articulated continuously or tensely (§23.1).

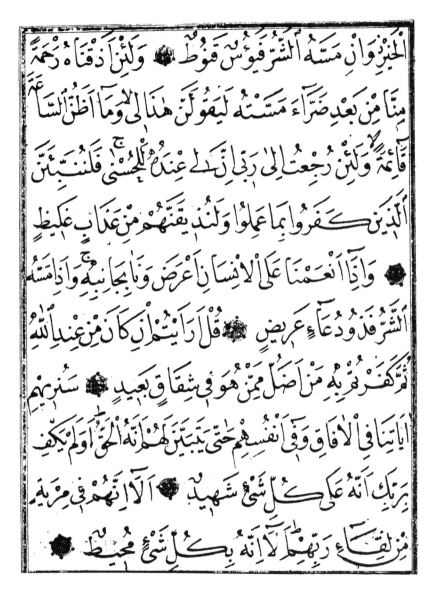

Fig. 30. Page of a Qur'ān manuscript in bold *nasḫi*-script,
copied by Ḥalīl ibn Zain ad-Dīn in A.H. 1084 = *ca.* A.D. 1672.

c) Verbs with Pharyngals, Laryngals, Velar Fricatives

45.1. The verbs with gutturals, i.e. pharyngals, laryngals, and velar fricatives, and to a certain extent also those with *r*, which will be referred to collectively as gutturals, exhibit certain peculiarities due to the phonetic changes that accompany these consonants (§27.10). Besides, syllabic cuneiform script is unable to indicate all these phonemes in an adequate way, and reduces some of them to glottal stop or signifies their presence by the vocalic change *a > e* (§19.5; 21.6-7). The scribal usages related to these consonants create supplementary problems.

45.2. In syllabic cuneiform script, both velar fricatives *ḫ* and *ġ* are in general indicated by signs with *ḫ* (§19.6,11) and no particular phonetic changes are observed in the conjugation of verbs having these consonants. Instead, the pharyngals and laryngals are reduced to glottal stop or to zero, and very often there is no graphic notation of the assumed glottal stop (§19.5,7,9-10). The original syllables *ḫa*, *'a*, in some cases also *'a* and *ha*, appear graphically as *e*, but *'a* and *ha* preserve, as a rule, their original vowel, like in *akālu* (< *'*akālu), "to eat", and *alāku* (< *halāku*), "to go". In consequence, there is no sure way to predict the form a verbal root with an original pharyngal, laryngal, or velar fricative will assume in a determinate period and in a determinate East Semitic dialect.

45.3. As a rule, the first characteristic of Assyro-Babylonian verbs with first radical ' is the elision of postvocalic ', with an assumed lengthening of the preceding vowel: *i' > ī* in Babylonian, *i' > ē* in Assyrian. Examples will be taken from Old Babylonian forms of the verbs *akālu* (< *'*akālu), "to eat", *emēdu* (< *'*amādu), "to lean", and *erēbu* (< *'*arābu), "to enter", with original first laryngal (') and first pharyngal ('):

Preterite	Perfect
īkul (< *yi'kul*)	*ītakal* (< *yi'takal*)
īmid (< *yi'mid*)	*ītemid* (< *yi'tamid*)
īrub (< *yi'rub*)	*īterub* (< *yi'tarub*)

45.4. The second characteristic of these verbs is the syncope of intervocalic ', followed by contraction in which the vowel of the prefix prevails. This phenomenon occurs in the present-future, although spellings like *i-ik-ka-al*, *i-im-mi-id*, *i-ir-ru-ub* indicate that this characteristic is not

general, because the cuneiform system never uses an initial vowel syllable, as *i*, to indicate the length of the vowel. Thus, these spellings point
to some other phonetic feature and, since the signs *ik*, *im*, *ir*, etc., mark
also *ek*, *em*, *er*, etc., they must indicate the presence of the glottal stop
followed by the vowel *e*, thus *'e < 'a*. It seems therefore that there were
forms with and without syncope of intervocalic ', although the scribal
writing habits do not allow us to distinguish clearly cut dialects. The two
sets of present-future forms will then appear as follows:

ikkal	*i'ekkal*	< **yi'akkal*
immid	*i'emmid*	< **yi'ammid*
irrub	*i'errub*	< **yi'arrub*

45.5. East Semitic verbs *mediae aleph* are usually considered as having a consonantal middle radical, namely a glottal stop. Only in a few
verbs, however, is the glottal stop written, and then only in a limited
number of forms. The etymological explanation is that there are forms
where no consonant occurs in the middle, like in the preterite, because
the glottal stop assimilates to the following vowel, with the latter's consequent lengthening; e.g. Old Akkadian *e-be-el* /ebēl/ < /*yib'al/, "he
became master", and Babylonian *i-be-lu* /ibēlu/, "(who) became master". In other forms, like the present-future, the glottal stop subsists in
the middle, like in Old Akkadian *i-be-al* < /yibe''al/, "he is master", "he
rules", and it is implied likewise by spellings as Old Babylonian *i-bé-el*
/ibe'el/ and not /ibēl/ or /ibêl/.

45.6. In Assyro-Babylonian, some verbs with third radical ' are
inflected like verbs with final *w / y* (§43.12), while another group shows
a "strong aleph". Both groups contain verbs with original third pharyngal, like *šemū*, "to hear" (< **šamā'u*), and *mašā'u*, "to wipe away"
(< **mašāḫu*), but a complete reduction affected the pharyngal of *šemū*,
which was still pronounced in Old Akkadian as shown by the spelling *iš-
má* /yišma'/ instead of the later *iš-me*, "he heard", while the glottal stop
derived from *ḫ* subsisted in *mašā'u*. It is impossible to predict which
forms are contrasting in one and the same dialect.

45.7. The situation in Palaeosyrian is similar to the one in East Semitic
with the phonetic change *a > e* after the pharyngals ' and *ḫ*. The vowel
remains unchanged when it occurs before the pharyngal; e.g. *áš-tá-ma*
/'aštama'/, "I heard". In Amorite, the pharyngal ' contiguous to a labial
tends to assimilate either to this consonant or to the adjacent vowel *a*

(§19.7), with their assumed lengthening; e.g. *ia-mu-ud* < **ya'mud*, "he propped"; *ia-mu-ur* < **ya'mur*, "he made prosperous"; *i-ba-al* < **yib'al*, "he made". These examples concord with Barth's law according to which **yaqtal* became *yiqtal*, while *yaqtul* and *yaqtil* remained unchanged.

45.8. Barth's law is applied also at Ugarit and at Emar, where verbal elements of proper names generally concord with this rule, while no vocalic changes seem to occur near gutturals; e.g. *ir-am* /*yir'am*/, "he thundered", *iš-ma-aḫ* /*yišma'*/, "he heard", *ib-ḫar* /*yibḫar*/, "he choosed", *iz-ra-'* /*yizra'*/, "he sowed", but *ia-mu-ud* /*ya'mud*/, "he propped". However, the use of the prefix *yi-* is attested at Emar also with radical vowels *i* and *u*, as shown e.g. by *im-lik* /*yimlik*/ and *i-mu-ud* /*yi'mud*/, while *ya-* can be found at Ugarit with the radical vowel *a* (§40.21). Concerning the pharyngal ', there are examples of a reduction of the ' contiguous to a labial (§19.7; 45.7). Besides, one encounters at Ugarit some instances of *'ain* becoming *aleph* in the beginning of a name. Whether this de-pharyngalized *'ain* was pronounced as a glottal stop or simply disappeared depends on the fate of original *aleph* in Ugaritic. Now, there are examples of laryngal ' reduced to zero (§19.8), and the *aleph* closing a syllable of a verbal form was most likely elided and reduced to a vocalic sign, while the preceding vowel was compensatorily lengthened; e.g. *yṣ'a* = **yaṣā*, "he went out", *qr'itm* = **qarētumu*, "you called"; *nš'u* = **našū*, "they lifted up". In fact, syllabic spellings of verbal forms (e.g. *ma-lak*) indicate that the Ugaritic suffix-conjugation had forms of the *qatal*-type, not *qatala*; e.g. *Ba'al-ma-lak*, "Baal is king"; *Ia-pa-milku* /*Yapa'-milku*/, "Splendid is the king", *Na-qa-ma-du* /*Naqam-(H)addu*/, "Avenging is Haddu", *Ga-mi-rad-du* /*Gamir-(H)addu*/, "Perfect is Haddu". Consequently, *yṣ'a* is to be interpreted **yaṣā*, not **yaṣa'a*, and *yṣ'at* is **yaṣāt* or **yaṣ'at* not **yaṣa'at*; cf. *'n-qp't* = ᵘʳᵘIGI-*qáp-at* /*'īnu-qap'at*/, "the source is buoyant". The morpho-graphemic spelling *yṣ'a* reflects not only the underlying root-morpheme *yṣ'*, but also the actual pronunciation of the final syllable indicated by the *mater lectionis* '*a*; hence this type of spelling might be termed "morpho-phonemic".

45.9. A characteristic feature of Hebrew and Biblical Aramaic, as presented by the Masoretic tradition, is their inability to geminate laryngals (', *h*), pharyngals (', *ḥ*), and *r*, with consequent lengthening of the preceding vowel. This inability, shared by the modern pronunciation of

Ge'ez, is paralleled to a certain extent by the possible non-gemination of medial *r* in the conjugation of some Gafat verbs (e.g. *däräsä*, "he met", vs. Amharic and Argobba *därräsä*). It has consequences for the inflection of the D-stem (§41.3); e.g. Hebrew *bērak* instead of **birrēk*, "he blessed". However, there are indications (§19.21) that these consonants were geminated in an earlier period, and there is no reason to suppose that they were an exception in the classical languages. The particular treatment of the gutturals in the Masoretic tradition is a legacy from the Roman period when the back-of-the-throat sounds could be reduced to zero, like in the Samaritan pronunciation of Hebrew and Aramaic. The phonetic notation of the Masoretes aimed at insuring the pronunciation of the pharyngals and laryngals by providing them with artificial short vowels (e.g. *ya'ᵃqob* instead of normal *ya'qob*; §27.10), but it failed in restoring their original geminated or tense articulation.

45.10. Hebrew, Biblical Aramaic, and Syriac verbs with gutturals are characterized by the tendency to change into *a* vowels contiguous to these consonants, obviously as a kind of assimilation (§27.10); e.g. Hebrew *yišlaḥ* instead of *yišloḥ*, "he sends". This tendency, which is not general in Syriac, has to be considered as a dialectal innovation, like in Arabic (§45.14). In fact, the Hebrew of the Qumrān scrolls (e.g. *šlwḥ* /*šᵊloḥ*/ instead of Masoretic *šᵊlaḥ*, "send!") and Mishnaic Hebrew (e.g. *yšḥwṭ* /*yišḥoṭ*/ instead of Masoretic *yišḥaṭ*, "he shall slaughter") still preserve the normal vocalization of the verbs with gutturals. As for Aramaic, this trend does not even appear in Galilean Aramaic, in Christian Palestinian Aramaic, and in Neo-Aramaic at Ma'lūla, where the imperative, the imperfect, and the infinitive are pronounced with *ō*, even when the third radical is a guttural; e.g. *zrw'*, "seed!", *mymwr*, "to say". Instead, the change *a > e* before a pharyngal is sometimes attested in Galilean Aramaic; e.g. *mišme'* < *mišma'*, "to hear".

45.11. The elision of postvocalic ', with consequent lengthening of the preceding vowel, is a characteristic of the verbal inflection in Masoretic Hebrew and in Late Aramaic; e.g. Hebrew *māṣā*, "he found"; Syriac *neḥod*, "he will seize". The same phenomenon is attested in East Semitic (§45.3-6), in Ugaritic (§45.8), in Phoenician and Punic (§45.13), and in Neo-Arabic. The spelling does not reveal this phenomenon to its full extent, because this *aleph* belongs to the "image" of the root and the scribal practice tends to preserve it, also because it serves as a *mater lectionis*.

45.12. In Late Aramaic, especially in Jewish Babylonian Aramaic and in Mandaic, the laryngals and pharyngals were weakened or reduced to zero altogether. Also in Neo-Aramaic, the laryngals and the pharyngal ' are not pronounced, except in the Ṭūr 'Abdīn dialect which preserves '. This phonetic evolution led to an extension of the "weak" conjugations; e.g. Jewish Aramaic *yymr* [*yīmar*], "he will speak"; Neo-Aramaic [*šmilan*], "we heard"; [*ki-bayī*], "they want".

45.13. The weakening of Phoenician pharyngals and laryngals increased considerably in Punic (§19.16), leaving some rare traces in verbal forms attested in inscriptions (e.g. *ṭn* for *ṭn'*, "to erect") or in Latin transcription (e.g. *nasot* for *nš't*, "I brought"). They all testify to the elision of postvocalic '.

45.14. The influence of gutturals on adjoining vowels was stronger in East Arabian than in the Ḥidjazi dialect. Several cases have been observed where the Eastern dialects have an *a* against a Ḥidjazi *u*; e.g. *yafraġu*, "he is at rest", for *yafruġu*; *yaǧnaḥu*, "he inclines", for *yaǧnuḥu*. On the other hand, the elision of postvocalic radical ' with consequent lengthening of the preceding vowel occurs in Classical Arabic in initial syllables beginning with another ', thus in the first person singular of the imperfect of Stems I and IV, as well as in the perfect and in the infinitive of Stem IV; e.g. *'āḏanu* < **'a'ḏanu*, "I shall allow"; *'īmānun* < *'i'mānun*, "to believe".

45.15. In the non-classical language, the verbs with final radical ' are conjugated like verbs with final *w* / *y*; e.g. *nabbā* for classical *nabba'a*, *yunabbī* for *yunabbi'u*, "to announce". Besides, some old forms are preserved from originally biconsonantal verbs, to which ' was later added, like the imperatives *ḫuḏ*, "seize!", *kul*, "eat!", *mur*, "speak!", *sal*, "ask!", as well as a few imperfect forms, like *yasal*, "he will ask", *yarā*, "he will see" (cf. §44.9). In modern colloquials, which go obviously back to an old phase of the spoken language, more forms without ' are used in the imperfect (e.g. *yāḫuḏ* or *yūḫuḏ*, "he will seize"; *yākul* or *yūkil*, "he will eat"), and even in the perfect (*ḫāḏ*, *ḫḏā*, "he seized"; *kāl*, *klā*, "he ate"). There are also participial forms with *w* replacing ', as *wāḫid*, *wākil*, next to *ḫādi*, *kāli*, "seizing", "eating".

45.16. In Epigraphic South Arabian, there is a series of random instances where one of the laryngals ' and *h* or the pharyngal ' are missing from a word in which they would normally have occurred. This fact is the graphic result of a phonetic trend towards reduction of these consonants to zero. Thus, e.g., the occurrence of a Sabaic imperfect *ts²r*, "she will be aware", against perfect *s²'rt* immediately before, indicates that the pharyngal was not always pronounced in determinate positions (probably **tiś'ar*). One can assume that vocalic changes accompanied the reduction of the concerned consonants. These back-of-the-throat laryngal and pharyngal sounds are instable also in the Modern South Arabian languages.

45.17.   In Ge'ez, the vowel *ə* may occur in certain circumstances before and after a guttural radical instead of the expected *a*; e.g. *kəhədka*, "you denied"; *nassəha*, "he repented". On the contrary, when the first radical is a guttural followed by *a*, the prefixes of the imperfect have -*a*- instead of -*ə*-; e.g. *yaḥabbər*, "he will join". Besides, Ge'ez may lengthen *a* before a vowelless etymological guttural; e.g. *nassāḥna*, "we repented". In Tigrinya, the vowel following an initial radical guttural is pronounced *a* instead of *ä*; e.g. *ḥaräsä*, "he ploughed", vs. *säbärä*, "he broke". As a result of the disappearance of gutturals in South Ethiopic, the verbs with an original laryngal or pharyngal as first radical, have an initial vowel *a*, remaining also after the prefixes of the imperfect, like Amharic *alläfä*, *yalf*, "to go by" (root *ḫlp*), vs. *näggärä*, *yənägr*, "to speak". The verbs with an original guttural as second radical, like *la'aka*, "to send", or *məhra*, "to have pity", are pronounced *lakä*, *marä* in the perfect, *yəlak*, *yəmar* in the jussive. The verbs with an original guttural as third radical, like *šm'*, "to listen", have a final vowel *a*; e.g. Amharic *sämma* (perfect), *yəsäma* (imperfect), *yəsma* (jussive), *səma* (imperative).

H. Verbs with Pronominal Suffixes

46.1.   The verbal form to which a pronominal suffix is attached may itself undergo changes. There are three main categories of changes in question. Firstly, the verbal form preserves its archaic ending, "protected" by the pronominal suffix, in cases where original endings are otherwise shortened. Secondly, the stress often shifts because of the addition of the pronominal suffix, with consequent reduction of vowels in determinate syllabic positions. Thirdly, certain assimilatory phenomena may occur between the final phoneme of the verbal form and the pronominal suffix.

46.2. In East and North Semitic, the pronominal suffixes are appended to verbal forms which have preserved their archaic ending. In East Semitic, pronouns are suffixed in some circumstances to the ventive / allative morpheme *-am* after a consonantal verbal ending, as in **iṣbat-am-ni > iṣbatanni*, "he seized me", *-im* after *-ī*, as in **taṣbatī-im-ni > taṣbatīnni*, "you (fem.) seized me", and *-nim* after *-ū* of plural, as in **iṣbatū-nim-ni > iṣbatūninni*, "they seized me". The Ugaritic object suffixes *-nh*, *-n*, *-nn* of the third person singular should rather be explained by the use of the energic endings *-anna* or *-an* of the prefix conjugation (§36.21; 39.10), since this ending appears also in Hebrew and in Arabic (§39.8). Besides the regressive assimilation of the East Semitic ventive / allative phoneme *m* to pronominal suffixes, reciprocal assimilations occur when a third person suffix is appended to a verbal form ending in *-t*; e.g. **iṣbat-šu > iṣbassu*, "he seized him" (§27.5).

46.3. In Hebrew and in Phoenician, the archaic endings of the perfect reappear before suffixes; e.g. Hebrew *qǝṭālātam*, "she killed them", as against *qāṭǝlā*; Phoenician *p'ltn*, "she made me", as against *p'l*. Important changes occur at the same time in the vocalization, which also approaches the archaic one (**qatalat*). If the verbal form preceding the pronominal suffix terminates in a consonant, the suffix is generally "linked" to the verb by means of a vowel, *a* / *ā* being the favourite vowel after Hebrew perfect, *ē* or *e < a* after imperfect and imperative. Since the same "connecting" vowels occur with nouns and prepositions, they cannot be considered as a residue of an ancient *-a* ending of the perfect, like Arabic *fa'ala*. While the "connecting" vowels used with nouns might be regarded as the residue of a case inflection, they are just anaptyctic vowels (§27.19) when they are attached to verbal forms. Both in Hebrew and in Phoenician, the suffixes are sometimes appended to an ending *-n* which is added to forms of the prefix-conjugation; e.g. Hebrew *yiqqāḥennū*, "he will take him", with assimilation of the suffix *-hū* to *-n*; *'ăromǝmenhū*, "I will exalt him", without such assimilation; Phoenician *ydbrnk*, "they will speak to you". However, there is a difference between Phoenician and Hebrew: the final *-n* characterizes the Phoenician indicative after forms ending in a long vowel, while the Hebrew usage seems to go back to an "energic" form, similar to the one of Arabic (§39.8-9). This final *-n* was preserved only in some cases, when it was "protected" by the suffix.

46.4. In Aramaic, a "connecting" vowel is generally inserted between the verbal form terminating in a consonant and the pronominal suffix.

The latter's affixing occasions a shifting of the stress and some changes in the vocalization of the verbal form; e.g. *qaṭlēh*, "he killed him", as against *qəṭal*. Old Aramaic and Imperial Aramaic may also insert the energic morpheme *-(i)n / -(i)nna* before the suffixes of the imperfect, e.g. *yqtlnh*, "he shall kill him"; *yədahălinnanī*, "he terrifies me"; *yəhōdə'unnanī*, "they shall explain to me". This morpheme is distinct from the imperfect ending *-n* of the third and second persons plural. In Neo-Aramaic (§42.18-22) suffixes are attached to verbal forms by means of the preposition *l- / el-*; e.g. *ptuḥ-lē*, "open it (masc.)!". The *l-* is completely assimilated to the preceding liquids *l*, *n*, *r*; e.g. *āmērā < *āmēr-lā*, "he should say it (fem.)". When attached to the preposition *el-*, which is a dialectal variant of *-l*, the suffixes can be written separately from the verbs; e.g. *bit-pātiḥ elē*, "he will open it (masc.)".

46.5. In Arabic, the adding of pronominal suffixes occasions facultative lengthenings or shortenings of actor affixes; e.g. *ḍarabtī-nī* instead of *ḍarabti-nī*, "you (fem.) beat me"; *taḍribīnī* instead *taḍribīna-nī*, "you (fem.) will beat me"; *yaḍribūnā* instead of *yaḍribūna-nā*, "they will beat us", with a clear example of haplology (§27.15). Also facultative contractions may occur; e.g. *šānīki* for *šāni'uki*, "who hates you". In Neo-Arabic, like in Hebrew and in Aramaic, a connecting vowel *u*, *a*, *i*, *ə* is inserted between the verbal form terminating in a consonant and the pronominal suffix; e.g. *ḍarabək*, "he beat you"; *ḍarabtuhum*, "I beat them".

46.6. In Ge'ez, the attachment of pronominal suffixes shows some changes in the actor affixes of the verb, thus *-at* becoming *-ata-* (e.g. *sam'atani*, "she heard me"), *-ki* becoming *-kə* (e.g. *sam'akəni*, "you [fem.] heard me"), *-kən* becoming *-kən(n)ā* or *-kā* (e.g. *sam'akənāni* or *sam'akāni*, "you [fem. plur.] heard me"), and *-na* becoming *-nā* (e.g. *sam'anāka*, "we heard you"). The attachment of the third person suffixes occasions different alterations in the actor affixes, *-u-* changing to *-əww-* (e.g. *sam'əwwo*, "they heard him"), *-i-* changing to *-əyy-* (e.g. *sam'akəyyo*, "you [fem. sing.] heard him"), and *-a-* being assimilated to the suffix altogether (e.g. *sam'o*, "he heard him"). The original *-h-* of the third person suffixes subsists only after the actor ending of the third person feminine plural (e.g. *sam'āhu*, "they [fem.] heard him"). In South Ethiopian dialects, the suffixed pronouns may occasion various alterations in the verbal root itself. In Chaha e.g., the suffix of the third person masculine singular, added to the third person singular form of the verb, changes any velar of the root in labiovelar (e.g. *näkʷäsä-nə-m*, "he bit him", as against *näkäsä-m*), while *b* becomes *w* (e.g. *näkäwä-nə-m*, "he found him", as against *näkäbä-m*) and the other labials *m*, *f*, *p* are rounded (e.g. *qäpʷärä-nə-m*, "he buried him", as against *qäpärä-m*). Indirect pronominal suffixes can be attached to the verb by means of the prepositions *l-* and *b-*. The suffix pronouns of the verb and the changes they cause require a thorough investigation. For detailed information about developments in the various Ethiopian languages the reader is referred to the relevant grammars and studies.

5. ADVERBS

47.1. The adverb is, by definition, an indeclinable part of speech, modifying verbs, adjectives, or other adverbs for the purpose of limiting or extending their signification. This part of speech usually expresses time, place, manner, condition, cause, result, degree, means, etc. In Semitic languages, there are adverbs of nominal origin and others which have a different common Semitic basis.

A. Adverbs of Nominal Origin

47.2. Many adverbs of nominal origin derive from an adverbial accusative in *-a* (cf. §52.5-9) and often seem to preserve the mimation or nunation of the noun. E.g. Babylonian *imittam*, "right", *šumēlam*, "left", *umām*, "by day"; Hebrew *ḥinnām*, "in vain", *rēqām*, "empty-handed", *yōmām*, "by day"; Arabic *'abadan*, "always", *yawman*, "by day", *ǧiddan*, "very", "much". However, a number of adverbs end in *-a* without any mimation, as early as the Palaeosyrian, the Old Babylonian, and the Old Assyrian periods; e.g. Palaeosyrian *am-sa-a* /'amšala/, "yesterday", "last evening"; Assyro-Babylonian *maḫra*, "before", *warka*, "behind", *pāna*, "earlier"; Aramaic *ḥerbā*, "badly", *'elāyā*, "upstairs", *rābā*, "very", "much"; Hebrew *ri'šonā*, "first"; Arabic *ṣabāḥa masā'a*, "mornings and evenings", γεδδα for *ǧiddan*, "much"; Ge'ez *nagha*, "in the morning", *ṭəqqa*, "very", "extremely", *tāḥta*, "beneath".

47.3. Other adverbs end in *-um* like Babylonian *aḫarrum*, "later", and *pānānum(ma)*, "earlier", "formerly", or Hebrew *pit'om*, "suddenly".

This ending seems to correspond to adverbial formations in *-u* which are encountered in other languages; e.g. Arabic *ba'du*, "later", *taḥtu*, "beneath", *fawqu*, "above", *qablu*, "earlier". Ge'ez adverbs in *-u*, like *kantu*, "gratuitously", *qadimu*, "previously", *lā'lu*, "above", had initially a final long *-ū* which may derive from an original *-um* > *-əm*. Some Amharic adverbs in *-o*, like *zändəro*, "this year", *dəro*, "previously", etc., may belong to this group, while others, like *wätro*, "continuously", *dägmo*, "again", are rather frozen forms of gerund (§42.12). In some cases, like *qädmo*, "first" (cf. Ge'ez *qadimu*), both interpretations are possible.

47.4. There are adverbial endings characterized by *-t*, but different vocalizations indicate that these formations do not constitute a homogeneous group. E.g. Assyro-Babylonian *timāliattam*, "yesterday", *emūqattam*, "violently"; Hebrew *yəhūdīt*, "in Hebrew", *šēnīt*, "a second time", *qāšōt*, "roughly"; Palmyrene Aramaic *škytyt*, "honourably", related morphologically to Syriac *rāḥūmā'īt*, "kindly", *ṭābā'īt*, "well", *məganbā'īt*, "by stealth".

47.5. East Semitic also uses the postposition *-iš* (§32.17; 48.10) for the formation of adverbs; e.g. *arkāniš*, *arkiš*, or *urkiš*, "back", "later", *maḥriš*, "before", *eliš*, "above".

B. Adverbs of Place and Negatives

47.6. Apart from the adverbs of obviously nominal origin, there are others of major importance which have a common basis in Semitic, in particular adverbs of place and negatives.

47.7. Adverbs of place answer the question "where?", formulated in Semitic by adverbs deriving from the interrogative pronoun *'ayyu* (§36.59) with addition of various morphemes; e.g. Old Assyrian *ayyakam*, Hebrew *'ēkā*, Syriac *'aykā*, Arabic *'ayna*, Ge'ez *'ayte*. The answers "here", "there", are expressed in East Semitic by derivatives of the demonstrative pronouns (§36.32-36); e.g. Old Babylonian *annīkī'am*, "here", *ullīkī'am*, "there". Instead, distinctive words are used in West Semitic languages: Hebrew *hēnnā*, Aramaic *tanā*, Arabic *hunā*, "here"; Ugaritic *ṯmt*, Hebrew, Phoenician, Moabite *šam(mā)*, Aramaic *ṯam*, Syriac *tammān*, Arabic *ṯamma*, Ge'ez *həyya*, "there".

Other locative adverbs are of nominal origin, as e.g. Assyro-Babylonian *ašrānu(m)*, "there".

47.8. The main Semitic negatives are *lā*, *'l*, *'ay*, and *'in*, but *lā* and *'l* are to be considered as two variant forms of originally the very same negative adverb. The universal negative particle in Old Akkadian and in Assyro-Babylonian is *lā*, while *'l* is the usual negative in Epigraphic South Arabian. Old Akkadian, Old Assyrian, and Babylonian use also *ula* / *ul* which corresponds to *'l*, but *ula* / *ul* does not seem to have there any specific functions different from those of *lā*. This form of the negative is related directly to Libyco-Berber *ur* < *war*, "not", exhibiting the well-known alternations of initial *'* / *w* and of *l* / *r*: *'al* / *war* > *ul* / *ur*. Suffixed to the conditional particle *m-*, the Libyco-Berber negative *ur* introduces unreal conditions (§61.2) and, precisely, there is an Old Babylonian standard use of *ul* in unreal conditional clauses, while this negative does not seem to appear in prohibitive sentences. The negative *'l* does not occur in Arabic, while *lā* is unattested in the Ethiopian languages, most of which use the negative element *al-* with the negative perfect. This particle changes into *an-* in Gurage dialects having *l* only in specific cases. As for Geʿez which uses the negative particle *'i-*, it preserves *'al-* in the negative forms of the pseudoverb *ba-*, i.e. the preposition *b-* with pronominal suffix; e.g. *'al-bena māya*, "we have no water". Verbs and, optionally, nouns are negated in Tigrinya by prefixing *'ay-* and suffixing *-ən*; e.g. *'ay-ḥaddis-ən*, "not new". The Amharic negative marker consists of the prefix *al-* and of the suffix *-m(m)*, which is omitted in subordinate clauses; e.g. *al-näggärä-m(m)*, "he didn't speak". In Modern South Arabian, Mehri negates with *əl...la'*, but its Ḥarsūsi dialect does it normally with *la'* alone; e.g. Mehri *əl ha gīd əla'*, as against Ḥarsūsi *ha gəd əla'*, "he is not good". The Kurdish negative *čū* is used besides *lā* in Eastern and even in Western Neo-Aramaic (e.g. Maʿlūla *čū ndōmek*, "I do not sleep"). The Gafat negative morpheme *tä...m*, encountered e.g. in the negative copula *tä-däbəlla-m*, "he is not" (§49.21), deserves a special consideration in the field of Afro-Asiatic because it must be related to the Egyptian negative *tm* which seems to result from a coalescence of *tä...m* and which is conjugated, while the verb is not; e.g. *iḫ tm-ì sbḫ*, "then will I not cry out".

The Hebrew spelling *l'* of the negative goes back to an allophone *ló'* of *lō* < *lā*, which is attested in Ṭūrōyo and paralleled by *la'* in Modern South Arabian.

47.9.   To deny a notion is different either from denying a fact or from prohibiting an action, and this semantic difference may lead to specialization of negatives. Thus, in Ugaritic, Hebrew, Phoenician, and Aramaic, a functional distinction was made between *lā > lo'* and *'al*, the second form being used in volitive, i.e. prohibitive, optative, and cohortative sentences; e.g. Hebrew *'al-teḥeṭ'ū*, "do not sin". However, no distinction was introduced between the denial of a notion (e.g. Hebrew *'am nābāl wə-**lo'** ḥākām*, "a people brutish and not wise") and the denial of a fact (e.g. Hebrew *lo' yādə'ū*, "they don't know"). Also East Semitic used special forms of negatives for prohibitions, viz. the particle *ay > ē* (§47.11) and, in Neo-Assyrian, the compound form *lū lā*; e.g. *ana* PN *šarru lū lā išappara*, "the king should not write to PN".

47.10.   Derivatives of *lā / 'al* appear in some languages. Thus, the negative particle *lam < lā-ma* with the enclitic morpheme *-ma*, followed by an imperfect or an apocopate verbal form is found in the particular Sabaic dialect of the Haram area, in Minaic (*lhm*) which does not use *'l*, and in Classical Arabic; e.g. Sabaic *lm yġts¹l*, "he had not washed". Arabic *lan* with following subjunctive derives from **lā-'an < *lā-han*, *'an < han* being a presentative (§49.6); e.g. *lan yunǧiḥū*, "they will not succeed". As for *laysa*, it is the negative *lā* followed by the Semitic particle of existence **yṯ* (§49.23).

47.11.   The prohibitive particle *ay > ē* is widely employed in Old Akkadian and in Assyro-Babylonian verbal sentences. Its use is extended to negative indicative clauses in Ge'ez (*'i-*), in Tigre (*'i-*), and in Tigrinya (*'ay-*); e.g. *'i-rakaba ḥaba nabarna*, "he did not find the place where we had settled". The negation *'y* occurs likewise in Phoenician indicative clauses; e.g. *k 'y šm bn mnm*, "for they did not lay anything in it". Since Old Akkadian names like *A-a-bí*, "Where is my father?", clearly have a negative meaning, the particle *'ay* must be related to the interrogative *'ay*, "where?".

47.12.   The suffixed form *ayyānu* of the same interrogative is related, in turn, to the Semitic particle of non-existence *'in* which was originally used in nominal clauses. This link is strongly supported by the Hebrew pausal form *'ayin*, comparable with the Arabic interrogatives *'ayyun*, "which?", and *'ayna*, "where?", and by the Middle and Late Babylonian particle *yānu*, which occurs in a similar function; e.g. *yānu mē*, "there is no water". The particle *'in* of non-existence is probably a compound *'ay*

+ *n*-copula (§49.20) and it may be used in Hebrew with pronominal suffixes (e.g. *'ēnēk*, "you are not"). It is attested in Ugaritic (*'in*), in
Hebrew (*'ēn, 'ayin*), in Moabite (*'n*), probably in Punic (*ynny / ennu*), in
Arabic (*'in*), and in various Ethiopian languages (*'an, ən*); e.g. Arabic
'in 'aḥadun ḫayran min 'aḥadin 'illā bil-'āfiya, "no one is better than
another, if not by Grace". The Arabic negation *'in* has a completely different origin than the conditional particle *'in* which is used here in *'illā*
< *'in-lā*, "if not", but confusions occur, especially when *'in* is preceded
by the indefinite-interrogative pronoun *mā*, "what?", as in rhetorical
questions, e.g. *mā 'in 'atayta bišay 'in 'anta takrahuhu*, "what if you had
accomplished something you yourself dislike?"; *mā 'in ǧazi'tu*, "what
if I was worried?". In Gurage dialects, *ən-* with the perfect may be used
to express prohibition (e.g. Chaha *ən-käfätkä*, "don't open"), while the
negative *an-* < *al-* is employed in forming the negative perfect (e.g.
Chaha *an-käfätkä*, "you didn't open").

47.13. Various compounds with the particle of non-existence occur in
Ethiopian languages. Thus, Ge'ez *'əndaʻi*, "I don't know", must be analyzed as *'ən-* and *-daʻi*, from the root *ydʻ*, "to know". The same
idiomatic phrase occurs in Tigrinya *'əndəʻi* and in Amharic *ənǧa*, with
palatalization of *d* to *ǧ*. Ge'ez *'ənbi, 'ənbəyā*, "no!", combines *'ən-* with
bi < *bəyā*, "in me"; the same word appears in Tigrinya as *'əmbi* and in
Amharic as *əmbi*, "no!", with the assimilation *nb* > *mb* (§27.6). This
assimilation occurs also in Amharic *əmbəzam*, "not much", deriving
from the negative element *ən-* and from *bäzza*, "to be much". Amharic
ənkʷan, "no!", is explained as resulting from *ən* and from a form *kʷan*
of the verb *konä*, "to be". Tigre *'ifālu*, "no!", consists of the negative
particle *'i-*, plus *fāl* with the pronominal suffix of the third person masculine singular which is used for all persons.

47.14. The use of other negatives is restricted to a few languages or
dialects. Thus Ugaritic, Hebrew, and Phoenician *bal*, which is used in prohibitive sentences like *'al*, goes back to the preposition *bal(um)*, "without",
attested in Old Akkadian, Old Assyrian, Babylonian, Ugaritic, and
Hebrew; e.g. Old Akkadian *Ma-an-ba-lum-ᵈDa-gan*, "Who-(does-exist-)
without-Dagan?". In Classical Arabic, *bal* is, properly speaking, not a
negative particle since it means "rather"; e.g. *'aʻṭani dirhaman bal
dirhamayni*, "he gave me one dirham, rather two dirhams", or in the
answer to an alternative question: *qāla 'a-ḏakarun 'am 'untā fa-qultu bal
'untā*, "he said: man or woman? And I answered: rather woman".

47.15. The interrogative pronoun *mā*, "what?", is used in Hebrew and in Arabic as a negative particle, first in nominal clauses, later even in prohibitive ones. The passage from an interrogative *mā* to a negative one can best be seen in clauses like Hebrew *ma-bə-yādī rā'ā*, "what is in my hand as evil?", i.e. "there is no evil in my hand" (I Sam. 26,18), and Arabic *mā hunna 'ummahātihim*, "what are they as their mothers?" (Qur'ān 68,2), i.e. "they are not their mothers". The use of *mā* in prohibitive clauses is already attested in Biblical Hebrew; e.g. *ma-taggīdū lō šə-ḥolat 'ahăbā 'ānī*, "don't tell him that I am faint with love" (Cant. 5,8). Examples in volitive clauses are found in Classical Arabic (e.g. *mā yarāka*, "he doesn't want to see you") and formal prohibitions may occur in modern colloquials which widely use *mā* as negative, the more so that *mā* has lost its original interrogative function nowadays, except in Yemen; e.g. *ma tidḫulš*, "don't go inside!" (Cairo); *ma tal'ăbūš*, "don't play" (Tripoli). In both examples, an ending -*š* is added to the verbal form, a usage best attested in Egypt and in Syria. This element -*š* is a corruption of *šay'*, "thing", "something", and it can be added to any negatived word, e.g. to a personal pronoun as in *mā aniš rāyiḥ*, "I am not going". This ending does not appear either in the classical or in the literary language; e.g. *mā ġu'tu*, "I didn't hunger".

47.16. The adverbially used adjective *ġayru*, "different", negatives adjectives in Sabaic (e.g. *ġyr ṭhr*, "not pure") and in Classical Arabic (e.g. *raġulun ġayru malūmin*, "a man not reprehensible"). There is, finally, a negative *d'* occurring in a few Sabaic texts of the most recent period (6th century A.D.) and recorded as *dū* or *da'* near Ta'izz, in the southernmost part of Yemen. This particle may be related to the High-land East Cushitic negative *di* linked to the verb *did-*, "to refuse", and there is perhaps a connection with the Tigrinya interrogative enclitic -*do* (§54.5), used in a way comparable with Latin -*ne*.

C. Adverbs of Time

47.17. The common Semitic interrogative adverb of time *matay*, "when?", is attested from the third millennium on in East Semitic (*mati*, *mat*), in West Semitic (*mātay*, *matā*), in South Arabian (*mty*, *mt*), and in South Ethiopic (*mäčä*, *mäči*). It is often combined with a preposition, like East Semitic *adi mati* and Hebrew *'ad-mātay*, "until when?, how long?", East Semitic *immati < in(a) mati*, Aramaic *'mt(y)*, Hebrew *lə-mātay*, "when?, until when?", Amharic *əskä mäčä*, "until when?, how long?", etc. Used as subordinate conjunction, it may introduce an indirect question; e.g. Gafat *mäčä əndisälä tilšəlam*, "I don't know when he will come". Like *mā* in Arabic and in Hebrew (§47.15), *mäčä* with an affirmative verb may sometimes express a negative in Amharic; e.g. *mäčä hakim yadənäwall?*, "a doctor will never cure him" (lit. "when will a doctor cure him?").

47.18. A particular category of adverbs is formed by verb modifiers specifying the temporal sphere of the action. However, their use is generally restricted to one or two languages. One of the best known is the Arabic particle *qad* employed in the pre-classical language to indicate the past; e.g. *qad 'arā ġawāyatahum*, "at that time I have seen your error". The particle must derive from *qdm*, which is used as adverb and preposition "before" in various West Semitic languages, in Epigraphic South Arabian, and in Ethiopic (§47.3). In Classical Arabic, *qad* with the perfect refers to a past action the effects of which are perceivable, and it sometimes corresponds to English "already"; e.g. *qad māta*, "he was already dead"; *qad ġu'tu*, "I got hungry already". Instead, its use with the imperfect adds a nuance of probability; e.g. *qad 'aktubu*, "I might write". In Mehri, the particle *ber / bər* has a similar function; it is employed as an auxiliary verb in Śḥeri and Soqoṭri.

6. PREPOSITIONS

48.1. Prepositions are words functioning to indicate the relation of a part of speech — noun, suffixed pronoun, infinitive — to another part of speech, viz. a substantive, an adjective, or a verb. A preposition is usually placed before its object (whence its name), although Semitic languages also provide examples of postpositive prepositions, suffixed to their logical object; they may then be called "postpositions". The use of postpositions is general in Cushitic languages, also when the same particle is used as in Semitic, e.g. *b* (§48.5), and South Ethiopic may use some prepositions as postpositions; e.g. Harari *bād-be*, "in the city" (cf. §48.5); *Alla-le ḥamdi*, "praise to Allah" (cf. §48.6). A comparable situation occurs in Palaeo-syrian and in Old Akkadian in the case of the particle *iš* (§48.10). The preposition or postposition with its object constitute a prepositional phrase which serves as an adjectival or adverbial modifier, but may also function as the predicate of a nominal clause (§50.7).

48.2. In Semitic languages preserving a case system, the object governed by a preposition is in the genitive, and several prepositions assume the form of a construct state before pronominal suffixes. Thus, the relation between a preposition and its object belongs clearly to the category of genitival relations. In Libyco-Berber instead, the prepositions — like the *nomen regens* (§51.9) — govern the noun complement in the locative/instrumental case which is formally identical with the ergative (§32.3); e.g. *yəhwa **ġar u**-ḇriḏ*, "he went down to the road"; *yəwṯa w-ma-s **s u**-kššuḏ*, "he struck his brother (lit."his mother's son") with a stick". The exceptions occurring with the old prepositions *s* and *ar*, when indicating direction (e.g. *s aman*, "towards the water"; *ar aḫḫam*, "up to the house"), can be explained by an older phase of the language in which the non-active case was governed directly by a verb denoting motion, later complemented by a preposition, exactly as in Semitic (§52.3).

48.3. There is a close relationship between certain prepositions and adverbs or subordinate conjunctions, and the same word may have two or even three functions, depending on the context. While the most part of Semitic prepositions is of demonstrably nominal origin, a few are deictic particles or morphemes the original function of which consisted in indicating position, direction, or concomitance, and in establishing relations between parts of speech. Only the more important prepositions, attested in several Semitic languages, can be presented here and briefly discussed. A preliminary observation might be useful. In fact, quite often the same preposition is said to mean e.g. "down, under, after, behind, beyond". These meanings, resulting partly from the requirements of the English translation, cannot be separated in an etymological investigation and depend often either on the immediate context or on an idiomatic use with specific verbs. The alleged polysemy of Semitic prepositions is based to a certain extent on their rendering into English, not on their use in Semitic speech or in Semitic texts.

A. Primary Prepositions

48.4. In early Semitic, there are three primary prepositions which respectively indicate position, direction, and concomitance, in a general way, both locally and temporally. It should by stressed here that there is a sharp distinction in Semitic between concomitance and coordination.

For the preposition indicating position, the main lines of development are "in", "from". The original signification of the particle expressing direction is "to", "towards", and the attested meaning of the third one is "with", "near", "in connection with". Position is indicated by *b-* in most Semitic languages, but *in* is used in Palaeosyrian and in Old Akkadian. Direction is indicated by *l-*, but *ana* occurs instead in Palaeosyrian and in East Semitic. Concomitance is expressed by *iš*, very likely *iš*, which is largely replaced by the particle indicating position.

	Position	Direction	Concomitance
East/North Semitic	*in(a)*	*an(a)*	*iš*
West/South Semitic	*'ib/bi*	*'il/li*	*'əs(ka)/s²k*
Old Egyptian	*im/m*	*ir/r*	*is(k)/sk*
Libyco-Berber	*f*	*i*	*is/s*

48.5. The primary preposition *b-* and its dialectal variants, *'b-* in Phoenician, *'əb-* in Tigre, *'ab-* in Tigrinya, indicate position generally, either locally or temporally. They correspond to ancient Egyptian *m*, before suffixes *im*. Their Palaeosyrian and Old Akkadian equivalent is *in*, later *ina* in Assyro-Babylonian. However, texts from Ebla use also *b-* with the augmentative *-n* and the consequent partial assimilation **bi-in > mi-in* or **bi-nu > mi-nu* (§27.8). Since both alternations *m / b* and *m / n* occur in Semitic languages (§11.6-7), the Hamito-Semitic form of the preposition is likely to have been **im / *m-*, with allophones. The North Arabian and Arabic preposition *fī-*, "in", "at", "on", "by", is probably a devoiced variant **pi > fī* of the preposition *b-* which covers its semantic range not only in other West Semitic languages and in South Arabian, but even in some Nadjdi dialects.

The postposition *-eb* in Bedja is related to this primary preposition, as shown by the following examples: *ē-yām-eb*, "into the water", *ō-hawād-eb*, "in the night"; *tē-'ar-t-eb*, "concerning the girls". The same can be said of the Oromo postposition *-fi, -fa, -fu, -f*, which has several uses, including cause, scope, and termination. It can be suffixed also to a verb, like in *kenne-f*, "he gave to" (cf. *kenne*, "he gave").

48.6. The primary preposition *l-* indicates direction generally, either locally or temporally. It corresponds to ancient Egyptian *r* and it is originally identical with the West Semitic preposition *'l*, just as Neo-Aramaic *el-* and Tigre *'əl-* are variants of *l-*, and as Egyptian *ir* is believed to be the primitive form of the preposition *r*. Its Palaeosyrian and East Semitic equivalent is *ana*, sometimes shortened to *an*, but *lina*, an

expanded form of *l-*, probably occurs in Palaeosyrian as well (§48.9).
The well-known alternation of liquids *l* / *n* / *r* (§17.3-5) does not allow
us at first sight to decide which is the basic form of the preposition.
However, although ancient Egyptian distinguishes *l* / *r* from *n*, — a fact
which would favour an original form in *l* / *r*, — there is also a preposition *in* or *n* in Egyptian, which covers the semantic range of Semitic
l- and *ana*, and most likely derives from the same common Hamito-
Semitic preposition, just as Tigrinya *nə-* is related to Geʿez *la-*. All these
forms are best explained by a basic *'in/l-* preposition, with dialectal variants. In fact, Egyptian *ir* might be considered as resulting from *in*, if a
Hamito-Semitic non-geminated liquid *n* could become *r* in non-initial
position, like in modern Gurage and in Margi, a language of the Chadic
family. The South Ethiopic preposition *yä-*, attested in all the South
Ethiopian languages except in Harari, is a palatalized **lä-* as well. It is
used with nouns to indicate a genitival relation (e.g. Amharic *yä-säw*,
"of a man"; cf. §51.25.) and with verbs to introduce a relative clause
(e.g. Amharic *yä-qärräwən*, "what remained").

Also the Libyco-Berber preposition *n* indicates the genitival relation; e.g.
awal n u-maziġ, "the Berber's word", instead of *awal u-maziġ*.

48.7.   The distinction between the prepositions *ina* and *ana* is obliterated already in the Middle Babylonian period, at least in the so-called
peripheral regions, especially in the West. Later, in the Neo-Assyrian
period, a similar confusion seems to occur between *ana* and *ina*, both
being indicated by the logogram AŠ. On the other hand, a Middle Babylonian deed from Emar, dated to the 13th-12th century B.C., uses *la* in
the phrases *la* AN.TA (*elīti*), "at the upper end", and *la* KI.TA (*šaplīti*), "at
the lower end", i.e. in formulations that reappear in Imperial Aramaic as
l-ʿly' and *l-tḥty'*. Also Neo-Assyrian borrows the Aramaic particle *la-*
which it uses to indicate direction "from" a place; e.g. ***la** qātē šarre
bēliya lā elli*, "may I not slip out from the hands of the king, my lord!"
The same usage is attested with the stereotyped phrases *la qātē* and *la
pān* in Neo-Babylonian and in Late Babylonian.

48.8.   The alleged *lam(ed) auctoris*, often translated "by" in some
prepositional phrases of the Bible (e.g. *barūk lə-Yhwh, lə-Dāwid*) and in
North Arabian inscriptions (e.g. *l-Zbd bn Hn'*), expresses direction, as
usual: "recommended be to Yahwe"; "(belonging) to David";
"(belonging) to Zabdu, son of Hāni'u". The person whose name is introduced by *l-* can obviously be the owner of the object or piece of work

under consideration because of its authorship. On the other hand, a prepositional phrase governed by *l-* can replace the accusative (§52.4,11). This use of *l-* appears however as a later development.

48.9. The Epigraphic South Arabian preposition *ln* occurs especially with following *'d / 'dy* (§48.17) in archaic and middle period texts; e.g. Sabaic *ln 'wdn d̠-s¹ṭrn 'dy s²qrm*, "from the level of the inscription up to the summit". It is not attested in recent texts which instead use the preposition *bn < mn* (§48.12) for the same purpose. The particle *ln* is attested also in Ugaritic, where it parallels the simple *l-* in identical phrases: *l-k̠ḫt zblhm / ln k̠ḫt zblkm*, "to their / your princely seats" (KTU 1.2,I,23-24//29). Besides, the Palaeosyrian directional preposition NI-*na* should most likely be read *lí-na* as well, rather than *ì-na* or *'a₅-na*. Therefore, it seems highly probable that Sabaic has preserved the preposition *l-* with the augmentative *-n*, which is attested also with *b-* at Ebla (§48.5) and with *'m / 'mn* in Ugaritic and in Sabaic (§48.13), but the obsolescent use of *ln* was restricted already in the Sabaic archaic period to indicate direction from a place or from a given moment. Thamūdic and the dialect of the Book of Job (27,14; 29,21) use the preposition *l* with the augmentative *-m* (*lm*, *ləmō*), which often nasalizes the Thamūdic *lm* into *nm /nimā/*.

48.10. The primary preposition *iš* (**iš?*) indicates concomitance or connection generally, also in Old Egyptian and in Libyco-Berber. It occurs commonly in the oldest Egyptian texts as postposition *is* with the meaning "like, as"; e.g. *ìr-n-ì n-f m mtt nt ìb nsw is n ntr nb*, "I acted for him in loyalty of heart, as a king (does) for every god". Its derivatives *isk* and *sk*, which are archaic variants of later *ìst* and *st̠*, introduce a concomitant fact; e.g. **isk** *ḥmt-s m ìnpw*, "when Her Majesty was a child"; **sk** *wì m šmsw-f*, "when I was in his following". Its meaning and functions in Libyco-Berber are closer to Semitic, although the Berber use of *s/is* in the sense "near", "to" (e.g. Tamazight *s-Azru*, "to Azru") is being replaced by *ġar*, sometimes with a combination of both prepositions (e.g. *ġar-s-Azru*). E.g. Berber *iša sksu s-imkli*, "he ate couscous for breakfast"; *nəbənna tiddar s-uzru*, "we are building houses in stone"; *utġ asrudun s-ukuray*, "I struck the mule with a stick". The preposition occurs in Palaeosyrian and, occasionally, in Old Akkadian; e.g. 5 GÍN URUDU **iš** *sá-né-en sá* SAGINA, "5 shekels of copper in connection with / for a pair of shoes of the governor" (Mari); ŠE KÚ ANŠE **iš** KASKAL, "barley of the donkey-fodder for the journey"; EN **iš** ᵈ*Ša-ma-gán* BA.GIN, "the king went to Šamagan" (Tell Beydar). This preposition is obviously the same as the postposition -*iš* used likewise in Palaeosyrian and in Old Akkadian (e.g. in *e-ra-si-iš*, "for tilling"), and as the ending of adverbs formed with the element -*iš*, as in *arḫiš*, "with speed", "quickly" (cf. §47.5). Its allophone -(*i*)*č* is attested in Cushitic; e.g. Kafa *bušēč*, "for the woman", *šowōič*, "on earth", *qētōč*, "towards the house". Besides, the preposition must be related to the Minaic morpheme *s*^{2} prefixed to *k*- in the various presentative and conjunctional usages of the latter, and thus forming a compound particle which reappears with another significance in Ethiopic *'əska*, "up to", "until" (§48.17). Contrary to previously held opinions, there is no comparable Palaeosyrian preposition *iš*$_{11}$-*ki* at Ebla, since this is a Sumerogram. In Tigrinya *əs* is combined with *m*- (§48.12) into a preposition *məs*, "with"; e.g. *məs ḥawwu*, "with his brother". In Amharic, instead, *əs* may be prefixed to *kä* and to *kännä*, "with", while its variant *sə* marks the concomitance when it is used as conjunction, and it may be prefixed to *lä*, "to"; e.g. *əskahun mən təsära näbbär?*, "what have you been doing *up to* now?"; *maretun əs-kännä-zafoččú gäztänali*, "we bought the land, *including* the trees"; *simäṭu əhedalläᵂh*, "I will go *when* they come"; *səläne mənəm attəččäyyär*, "don't go to any trouble *because of* me".

48.11. The particle *k*- is generally considered as a primary preposition equivalent to "as", "like". However, *k*- is in reality a deictic and asseverative particle (§49.9), used also as a subordinate conjunction (§49.14). Its prepositional usage is partly based on an augmented form *kīma* in Assyro-Babylonian, *kəmō* in Hebrew, and *kama* / *kəm* / *käm* in Ethiopic. Besides, in Minaic *k*- normally indicates direction, "to", "for", and it is used instead of *l*-, a fact which confirms its originally deictic character. In Amharic, *kä*- generally expresses centrifugal direction, but it may also mean "to", as in Minaic; e.g. *kä-kätäma yəmäṭall*, "he is coming from the town"; *kä-šumät täšarä*, "he was dismissed from the office"; *kä-yuniversiti gäbba*, "he went to the university". In Amharic colloquial of Šäwa, *tä*- is used instead of *kä*-, with the same meaning (§48.18). Ḥaḍramitic *h*- and Modern South Arabian *h*-, used instead of *l*-, are variants of a spirantized *k*- (§18.5).

B. Prepositions of Nominal Origin

48.12. Since the primary preposition *b-* and *l-* indicated, respectively, position and direction only in general, the need was felt for a particle having the specific meaning "from" or "away from", both locally and temporally. Thus, in the first millennium B.C., a new preposition *min* appears in West Semitic and in South Semitic with a centrifugal meaning. It is found in Hebrew (*min*, *mē-*, *minnē-*), in Aramaic (*min*), rarely in Phoenician, in North Arabian (Safaitic *mn*, *m-*), in Arabic (*min*, *mini*, *mil-* < *min-a l-*), in South Arabian mainly under the dissimilated form *bn*, in Modern South Arabian (*mən*), and in Ethiopic (Ge'ez *'əm-*, *'əmənna*; Tigre *mən*; Gafat *mä*, *əmmä*). Its variant forms *minnē-* in Hebrew and *mini* in Arabic, as well as its frequent Arabic use in the sense "a certain amount of", "a part of" (e.g. *šaribtu min-a l-mā'i*, "I drunk a part of the water"), indicate that it originated from a noun **minī*, "measure" (cf. Assyro-Babylonian *minītu*), related to the verbal root *mny*, "to count", "to measure". In the mid-first millennium A.D. *min* begins to mark the agent of the passive in Aramaic and in Arabic; e.g. Jewish Babylonian Aramaic *minnī u-minnēh yitqallēs*, "he is praised by myself and by himself"; Neo-Arabic *ḫuliq min 'al-ḫallāq*, "he was created by the Creator". The synonymous Arabic preposition *'an* apparently derives from another verbal root, viz. *'anna*, "to take shape", "to arise", "to spring up"; e.g. *kāna ḏālika 'an 'amrika*, "this occurred as a result of your order", where another vocalization (*'anna 'amruka*) would lead to a paratactic construction meaning lit. "this occurred, your order took shape". The preposition *'an*, "from", is attested also in Śḥeri and in Soqoṭri, but does not occur in Mehri.

48.13. The Semitic preposition *'amm-*, which means primarily "together with", has, instead, a centripetal function. It is obviously related to the noun *'am(m)*, "people", and to the verb *'amma*, "to be common". It is attested only in the central area of Semitic languages. While most Aramaic dialects preserve its original vocalization in *-a-*, Hebrew changes it in *'imm-*. These functionally determined variants represent a general linguistic phenomenon. In fact, individual lexical items are susceptible to change in their phonological representations, e.g. in order to form sufficient contrast with a similar form of a functionally different item. In the present case, the change aims at preventing that the preposition *'m* would be homophonous with the substantive *'m*. This results in Hebrew in the replacement of the vowel *a* (*'am*) by *i* (*'im*). The vocalization of the Ugaritic and of the South Arabian preposition is unknown, but the suffixed form *'mn* is often employed in these languages, while Sabaic also uses the combined form *b-'m, b-'mn*.

48.14. North Arabian and Arabic use the preposition *ma'* / *ma'a*, "with", which is related to *ma'īya*, "company". There is little doubt that *ma'(a)* and *'am(m)* go back to the same root, dissimilated by metathesis. The preposition might appear already in Palaeosyrian, although the use of the sign *má* instead of *ma* would have been more appropriate: *wa-ma-sa* /*wa-ma'ša*/, "and with it", "and besides that". Since Arabic *ma'-an* is used adverbially, "together", it might be related also to Ugaritic *m'*; e.g. *šm' m'*, "listen, at once".

48.15. The nominal origin of other prepositions may easily be detected. Thus, East Semitic *eli*, Palaeosyrian *al* at Tell Beydar and *al₆* or *al₆-a* /*'alay*/ at Ebla, perhaps also *a* /*'al*/, Ugaritic *'l*, Hebrew, Phoenician, Aramaic *'l* / *'ly*, Arabic *'alā* / *'al*, South Arabian *'l* / *'lw* / *'ly*, Ethiopic *lā'la*, all meaning "over", "above", originate from a noun *'ly*, "upper part", which is related to the verbal root *'ly*, "to go up". When governing some specific nouns, this preposition forms phrases which are employed in turn as a kind of expanded prepositions with a characteristic meaning; e.g. Hebrew *'al-pī*, "according to", lit. "on the word of"; Aramaic *'al dibr(at)*, "because of", lit. "on the course of"; Arabic *'alā ḥasabi*, "according to", lit. "on the measure of".

48.16. The antithetical preposition *tḥt*, "under", "below", also "instead of", "on the authority of", must be of nominal origin as well, considering its Arabic and Ge'ez ending in *-a* which is related to the construct state. However, this nominal origin is not demonstrable at present, since it is a derivative *tḥty > tačč* that must appear in phrases like Amharic *kä-lay əskä tačč*, "from top to bottom". Thus, one can just speculate that the noun from which *tḥt* derives must mean something like "bottom", "underneath". Instead, there are two nouns deriving from the preposition, viz. *tḥty*, "lower", "lower part", known in Hebrew, Aramaic, and South Arabian, and *taḥtān*, used in Amorite (*taḥ-tu-un, ta-aḥ-ti-in*), in Arabic (*taḥtāni*), and in Hebrew (*taḥtōn*); e.g. Amorite *Bu-nu-taḥ-tu-un-i-la*, "Son-of-god's-underbelly"; *Ša-ta-aḥ-ti-in*-DINGIR, "That-of-god's-underbelly"; Old Aramaic *'ly 'rm wtḥtḥ* (**taḥtāh < *taḥtayha*), "the upper part of Aram and its lower part", i.e. respectively "north" and "south". The preposition *tḥt* is attested in

Amorite (*Ta-aḫ-ta-ḫu-um*, "(Given-)instead-of-the-brother"; *Ta-aḫ-tu-pí-il*, "(Born-)by-order-of-god's-mouth"), in Ugaritic (*tḥt*), in Old Canaanite (EA 252,26: *ta-aḫ-ta-mu*, "under them"), in Hebrew (*taḥat*), in Phoenician (*tḥt*), in Aramaic (*tḥt, təḥōt, ti-ḥu-ú-tú, tḥeyt*), in Arabic (*taḥta*), in South Arabian (*tḥt*), in Soqotri (*nḥaṭ*), and in all the Ethiopian languages: Ge'ez (*taḥta*), Tigre (*taḥat*), Tigrinya (*taḥti*), Harari (*taḥay*), Amharic (*tačč*), Gafat (*tačča*), Gurage (*tatä, ta'ačä, tätte, tät, tat*).

48.17. The preposition *'ad* is attested in Palaeosyrian as *a-dì* (Tell Beydar) and *a-dì-ma* (Ebla), used both in the local sense "to(wards)" and the temporal sense "until". Besides, the short form *a-dè* is attested at Ebla with the meaning "corresponding to", like Sabaic *k-'d*, e.g. *k'd h' ṯhrn*, "according to this document". The preposition appears in Old Akkadian under the forms *adi, adīna, adīni, adum*, in Assyro-Babylonian as *adi*; it means "up to", "until", "as long as", "as much as". It is found in Ugaritic (*'d*), in Hebrew (*'ad, 'ădē*), in Phoenician (*'d*), in Aramaic (*'ad*), in Epigraphic South Arabian (*'d, 'dy, 'dn*), in Modern South Arabian ([*'ə]d-, wdə-*), and it survives in Ge'ez as an adverb *'ādi*, "still more". Its augmented form *'dky* occurs in Liḥyānite. There is no doubt that this preposition is related to the Hebrew substantives *'ad*, "lasting future", and *'ōd*, "duration", and probably to the South Arabian verb *'dw/y*, "to march", and to its Arabic equivalent *'adā ('dw)*, "to speed". However, the preposition *'ad* is not attested in Arabic where its function may be exercised by *ḥattā* (cf. §59.2). It is replaced by *'əska* in Ge'ez, *'asək* in Tigre, *əskä* in Amharic, a preposition which is etymologically related to the Minaic particle *s²k* (§48.10).

48.18. The old preposition **'tt* and its variant **wtt* — paralleled by the pairs *'aḥad / wāḥid*, "one", *'aḫārum / waḫārum*, "to be behind", *'ayna / wayn*, "where", *'udun / widn*, "ear", etc. (§19.24) — derive from a noun used in ancient Egyptian as *išt*, "belongings", and they are probably related to Arabic *'atta*, "to be abundant"; *'atāt*, "furnishings". The preposition is first attested in Palaeosyrian, at Ebla (*áš-tu, áš-tù, áš-tù-ma, áš-tá, áš-ti*, i.e. /'att-/) and at Tell Beydar (*áš-te₄, áš-tum*), likewise in Old Akkadian (*iš-tum, iš-tu, iš-te₄*, i.e. /'itt-/), which also uses the form *itti* resulting from the assimilation *'itt- > 'itt-*. The usual translation of this particle is "from", "since", "with", although its Ge'ez equivalent *wəsta* (< **witta*) clearly means "in", "into", preserving the original acceptation "within", "next to". One should stress here that, e.g. English syntagms like "to escape *from*" or "to take *from*" cannot give any

clue as to the meaning of Semitic prepositions translated by "from". The
action of escaping or taking something away starts *within* a place and the
Semitic particle, either *ʾṭṭ or *b- (§48.5), expresses the relation between
that action and its location by a word meaning "within". In Assyro-
Babylonian, the preposition *ʾ/wṭṭ is later attested also under the forms
uštu, ultu, iltu, ilte, issu, issi, ittu, itte, itti, while Canaanite languages
— Amarna correspondence, Hebrew, Phoenician — use the form *itta-,
ʾitt-* resulting from the assimilation *ʾiṭt-* > *ʾitt-*. An assimilated form of
the preposition is probably preserved also in South Ethiopic as *tä-*,
"from", "in", "with", attested in Amharic, in Argobba, and in most
Gurage dialects; e.g. Amharic *let tä-qän tägʷazən*, "we traveled day and
night", lit. "night with day" (the Semitic day commences at *ca.* 6 p.m.).
The preposition "with", "and", may appear as *ət* in Tuareg, but it is
usually voiced into *d* in the Libyco-Berber dialects. It is used as a postposition *(i)tti*, "to, at, in", in Cushitic; e.g. Oromo *inni Gobātti auto-
busarrā buʾe*, "he got off the bus at Goba".

48.19. The preposition *ʾ/wṭṭ must be distinguished from the Arabic
preposition *wasṭa*, "among", "within", which derives from the substantive *wasaṭ, wasṭ < wšṭ*, "midst", known also from South Arabian *(ws¹ṭ)*,
from Geʿez *(wəsṭ, wəsāṭe)*, from Amharic *(wəsṭ)*, and from the other
Ethiopian languages. Its verbal root, with derivatives, is attested likewise
in East Semitic, in Hebrew, and in Aramaic, but with different semantic
connotations. In certain Gurage dialects, there are adverbs derived from
the same root, but meaning "under", "downwards". The Amharic,
Argobba, Gafat, Soddo, Ennemor, and Gogot noun *wašša*, "cellar",
"cave", may have the same origin *(*wašṭa > wašša)* and be borrowed
into Agaw *(waša, waši)*.

48.20. The Palaeosyrian directional preposition *si-in* has apparently
the same meaning as *ana / lí-na*. It is attested also in Epigraphic South
Arabian under the forms *s¹n* and *s¹wn*, as well as *s³n*. This preposition is
related to the East and South Semitic verbal root *šanānu*, and probably
to the West Semitic **šawiya* as well, both meaning "to come up to" or
"with", "to vie"; e.g. Babylonian *išibbāma išannanā ilšin*, "when
replete, they come up with their god"; Geʿez *tasannana*, "to vie with
each other". The idea of motion "up to", of coming "next to", should
thus correspond to the first meaning of the preposition which in fact is
used in this way; e.g. Palaeosyrian *si-in Gub-lu*[ki], "up to Byblos";
Sabaic *ḏ-s¹n ms³wdn*, "which is next to the hall". However, *si-in* is also

employed in the dative sense "to", "for"; e.g. Palaeosyrian *en-ma A-bu si-in Ṭū-bù-ḫu-*^d*'À-da*, "thus (speaks) Abu to Ṭubbūḫu-Hadda"; *si-in I-li-lu*, "for Enlil".

48.21. The preposition *byn*, "between", is a noun meaning "separation", "interval", like Arabic *bayn*, derived from the verbal root **bīn*, "to discern", "to distinguish". The preposition is attested in Ugaritic (*bn*), in Hebrew (*bēn*), in Phoenician (*bn*), in Aramaic (*byn, baynay, baynat*), in Arabic (*bayna*), in Epigraphic South Arabian (*byn, bn, bynn*), in Modern South Arabian (*bīn, mbīn, mun*), in Ge'ez (*babaynāti-*).

48.22. The Hebrew preposition *'immād*, "with", the widely used Arabic preposition *'inda*, "with, upon, in the opinion of", and the Amharic, Argobba, and Gafat preposition *əndä*, "such as, according to", derive from a noun *'umd-* / *'imd-* / *'omed*, "support", attested also in Assyro-Babylonian (*imdu > indu*). In Biblical Hebrew, it is attested only in the frequent phrase *'immādī*, "with me", but its Arabic and South Ethiopic use is variegated. The same meaning as in Hebrew occurs, e.g., in Arabic *šufa'ā'unā 'inda llāhī*, "he is our advocate with God", but a widely attested acceptation is represented by a clause like *kāna 'indāna mayyitan*, "he was dead according to us", or Amharic *əndä səraw kəfäläw*, "pay him according to his work". The meaning "such as, like" occurs often in Ethiopic; e.g. Gafat *anät əndäwət gäddärmanä*, "I am as big as he"; Amharic *lekk əndabbatu näw*, "he is exactly like his father".

48.23. When prepositions of nominal origin are used with pronominal suffixes, a vowel, mostly *-ē-*, may be added to the preposition in Hebrew (e.g. *'ălēhem*, "on/against them"), in Aramaic (e.g. *qŏdāmēhon*, "before them"), and in Ge'ez (e.g. *tāḥteka*, "under you"). This vowel seems to go back to the ending of the plural construct state, as also suggested by the Ge'ez particle *wəsta* which apparently gets a plural *-āt > -et* ending: *wəstetəya*, "to me".

C. Compound Prepositions

48.24. In the domain of the prepositions it is a characteristic feature of the Semitic languages, in particular of Phoenician, South Arabian, and Ethiopic, that various particles are often combined together, sometimes without preserving their original meaning. It will be sufficient to mention the Phoenician preposition *b-*, "in", in the combinations *l-m-b-ḥwy*, "still during my life", and *l-b-hr*, "against the mountain". The latter combination occurs also in Ugaritic: *'im ht l-b-mṣqt yṯbt qrt*, "if now it replunges the city into grief" (KTU 2.72,17-19). The Sabaic preposition *'m*, "with", in the frequent combination *b-'m* likewise means "together with". The Ge'ez preposition *lā'la*, "upon", "over", "above", which already agglutinates the preposition *l-* to the common Semitic *'al / 'alā*, "on", "upon", is used in the combinations *ba-lā'la* and *'əm-lā'la* which have more or less the same meaning.

48.25. In South Ethiopian languages, relations are often expressed by a combination of prepositions and postpositions. In Chaha, e.g., *bä..fʷär* indicates the positional relation "on", "above": *bä-bet-fʷär*, "on the house"; *bä...mädär* means "instead", lit. "in the place of". The elements *yä...e* indicate the directional relation "to": *yä-dəbr-e bäsäno anqʸä*, "after they arrived to the forest", where *anqʸä* (< *ḥaqʷe*, "loins" in Ge'ez) is the postpositive subordinate conjunction (§49.17). In Amharic, e.g., *kä... bähʷala* means "after" with either nouns or verbs. This combination of prepositions and postpositions occurs also in modern North Ethiopic, viz. in Tigrinya; e.g. *bə... gəze*, "at the time, when".

7. CONNECTIVE AND DEICTIC PARTICLES

A. Conjunctions

49.1. The common Semitic particle of simple coordination is *wa-*, "and", attested also in Bedja as enclitic added to all enumerated elements (e.g. *ləhắwēt-wa káray-wa*, "and a jackal and a hyena"), while the Semitic enclitic *-ma* is very likely its phonetic nasalized variant *-ma* < *-wa*. The double prefixed and suffixed use of the conjunction is paralleled, e.g., by the preposition *iš* and the postposition *-iš* (§48.10). Both *wa-* > *u-* and *-ma* are used in East Semitic and in some Ethiopian languages. Harari frequently employs *-ma* as conjunction coordinating clauses which express a succession of actions, while *-ma* serves in Tigre to connect alternatives; e.g. *'Aksum nə'iš ta-ma 'abbāy*, "is Aksum small or big?". Besides, *-(ə)m(mə)* is attested in Amharic, Gafat, and in some Gurage dialects, as Chaha and Muher, where *-m* can be suffixed to one or to all enumerated elements; e.g. Chaha *dangʸam grädəm yət-fäqʸär*, "the boys and the girls are playing". In the same Gurage dialects, however, the preposition *tä-*, also meaning "and", "with" (cf. §48.18), can be prefixed to the second element alone; e.g. *däng^ya tägräd*, "boys and girls", lit. "boys with girls". In other Gurage dialects, in Amharic, and in Argobba, the usual conjunction of coordination "and" is -(ə)nna or -n, which is probably borrowed from Highland East Cushitic -nna, "and". It might seem therefore that the South Ethiopic -(ə)m(ma) conjunction is a phonetic variant of -nna.

The hypothetically reconstructed form *wan- of the Hebrew conjunction used in the *wayyiqtol* tense is never attested as such. The doubling of the consonants *y, t, n* which follow *wa-* is a secondary phenomenon. It results probably from a pronunciation of *way-* that aimed at avoiding the monophthongization of *ay* which might easily occur if the *y* was not geminated. The gemination was then extended to *t* and to *n*. As for Ugaritic *wn*, it results from the elision of intervocalic *h* in *wa-hanna/u*, "and behold" (§27.25). In the occasional spelling *wa-a* at Ebla, the *-a* is a phonetic complement specifying the vowel of the sign that may be read *wa / we / wi / wu*.

49.2. Coordinative *pa- > fa-*, linking two clauses of equal syntactic status, occurs in Ugaritic, in Aramaic dialects, especially in Samalian, in Nabataean, in North Arabian, in Arabic sequential narrative, and in the Sabaic dialect of the Haram area. It is attested also in Hebrew under the form *pen-*, with a suffixed *n*; *pen-* serves there to introduce consecutive clauses which parallel Classical Arabic sentences with *fa-* and the subjunctive (§59.3). In standard Sabaic, *pa- > fa-* introduces the conditional apodosis. Although both *'ap* and *pa-* occur in Ugaritic and in Aramaic, it is probable that they go back to the same particle *p* which seems to be related to the Libyco-Berber *f*, "thereupon", and to Cushitic *fi*, "and" (e.g. Oromo *dīmā fi gurrāčča*, "red and black"). The conjunction *'ap*, "also", is attested in Palaeosyrian, in Ugaritic, in Hebrew, in Phoenician, and in Aramaic; it is pronounced *up* in Neo-Aramaic.

49.3. The particle of simple coordination is often omitted in Semitic languages, for linking can be expressed by direct juxtaposition. On the other hand, *wa-* covers also adversative coordination "but", and disjunctive "or". Besides, it can have the sense "comprising", "consisting of", "with", and it may also be used with some sort of deictic force. In other words, *wa-* does not fix the precise relation between the elements and the sentences thus linked.

49.4. Yet the disjunction can be expressed explicitly by *'aw*, "or". Only the context allows distinguishing *ū < 'aw* from *u < wa* in

cuneiform texts, except in Ugaritic alphabetic script where *'u* corresponds to *'aw*, while *w* represents *wa-*. The particle *'m*, "or", is likely to
go back to a phonetic variant of *'aw* (§11.8). It a attested in Phoenician
(e.g. *kl 'dm 'š ypth ... 'm 'š yš' ... 'm 'š y'msn*, "every man who will
open ... or who will lift up ... or who will remove..."), in Punic (e.g. *dl
mqn' 'm dl ṣpr*, "devoid of cattle or devoid of birds"), in Hebrew (e.g.
hă-lānū 'attā 'im lə-ṣārēnū, "are you for us or for our enemies?"), and
in Arabic (e.g. *min ḏahab 'am fiḍḍa*, "from gold or silver"). In Classical
Arabic and in modern literary Arabic, *'m* introduces the second member
of an alternative question or condition. It is probable that *'am* had disap-
peard from living speech before the 9th century A.D. and that Arabic
'ammā, "if" (§50.6,8; 61.2), and Hebrew *'im*, "or", have developed by
blend between the conditional particle *'immā / 'im* (§61.2) and the disjunction *'am*. In modern literary Arabic, the second member of a disjunctive question may be introduced also by *kam*. The disjunctive particle appears as *wäy* in South Ethiopic and in Tigrinya. An augmentative
-əmm, *-əss*, *-əš* may be added in most Ethiopian languages, while a
monophthongization > *we* occurs in some Gurage dialects. This form
appears as *wa* in Tigre (cf. §49.1: *-ma*), while Tigrinya *wäy* may be contracted to *u*.

B. Presentatives

49.5.   Presentatives are particles the basic use of which aims at alerting
the hearer or drawing his attention. They may constitute minor clauses
(§50.3-4) or introduce whole sentences, direct speeches, sometimes smaller
parts of a sentence. Their general meaning is "behold", "see", "thus".

49.6.   One of the oldest and most important presentatives is **han*,
attested in Palaeosyrian and in Old Akkadian as *en-ma*, later *umma* by
assimilation. It is found in Ugaritic (*hn*), in Old Canaanite (*a-nu, a-nu-ú,
an-nu, an-nu-ú*), in Hebrew (*hinnē*), in Arabic (*'inna*), in Ge'ez (*'ən-ka*);
e.g. Arabic *'inna llāha 'alā kulli šay'in qadīrun*, "behold, God has
power over everything". It should be identified with the West Semitic
article *han-* (§33.10), but carefully distinguished from the conditional
particle *hn > 'n* (§61.2).

49.7.   Another presentative is *lū*, used in Old Akkadian and in Assyro-
Babylonian to emphasize the sentence it introduces; e.g. *lū ēpuš*, "see, I

did (it)". It is widely employed to express the precative, may introduce conditional and temporal/causal clauses (§61.6,8-9), and it is related to the North and West Semitic asseverative particle *la-* / *li-*, which is also used to form the precative (§38.2; 49.12).

49.8. The two particles are combined in the *allū* (< *han-lū*), *alla* (< *han-la*) or *alli* (< *han-li*) of the Amarna correspondence and often strengthened by the enclitic particle *-mi* which is a variant of *-ma*. The same compound presentative appears later in Aramaic under the form *hlw* > *'lw* with variants *'r(h/w)* and *hry* showing a change *l* > *r* (§17.5). It is uncertain, instead, whether Ugaritic *hl* has to be explained in the same way or be rather related to Hebrew *hǎlō'* and Arabic *hal* / *hallā* that combine the interrogative particle *ha-* > *'a-* with the negative *lā* in the sense of the rhetoric question *nonne?*, "didn't?". E.g. Hebrew *hǎlō' 'āmartī 'ǎlēkem*, "didn't I tell you?"; Arabic *hal taḏkurunī*, "don't you remember me?"

49.9. The deictic and asseverative particle *ka-*, "thus", "so", "truly", is common to Semitic languages and to ancient Egyptian (*k3*); e.g. Tigre *'arwe 'ashattenni kabal'ako*, "the serpent enticed me, so I ate". The originally long *ā* of Hebrew and Phoenician **kā* gave rise to the form *kō* (*kh, k'*), "so, here". The particle plays an important role in the formation of demonstratives (§36.35,42-44) and developed from a presentative into a subordinating conjunction with various functions ("that", "because", "when", "for"), and also into a comparative preposition "like", "as". It is often enlarged by suffixed elements, e.g. *-y* (*kay* > *kī*), *-ma* (*kama* > *kəmō*), *-n* (*kn, kēn*). The affinity of the diverse functions of *ka-* appears not only in its use as conjunction (§49.14), but also when it is employed as a comparative particle, e.g. Arabic *riǧālun ka-'usūdi l-ġābati*, "men like lions of the thicket" or "men, truly lions of the thicket". It preserved its asseverative function with nouns in Hebrew, Aramaic, and Arabic, as the so called *kaph veritatis*. E.g. Hebrew *kī hū' kə-'īš 'emet*, "for he was a *really* trustworthy man"; Aramaic *'l kbdl*, "I shall bring *proper* tin"; Arabic *'al-'alwānu kal-ḥumrati waṣ-ṣufrati*, "the *proper* red and yellow colours". Under the strengthened forms *ki'ām, kēm, kām, kā*, it often introduces the direct speech in Assyro-Babylonian; e.g. *ki'ām tašpuram umma attama*, "thus you wrote to me as follows".

49.10. The presentative *ha-* is common to Semitic, ancient Egyptian (*h3*), and Libyco-Berber (*ha*). It subsists in Arabic as *hā-* with personal pronouns (e.g. *hā-'anā-ḏā*, "here I am"), and perhaps as interjection *'a-* (e.g. *'a-rākiban kamīyan*, "ho! valiant rider!"), but Libyco-Berber distinguishes *ha* from *a*, "ho!".

49.11.   The conditional particles, which will be examined in the frame of conditional clauses (§61.2), are presentatives introducing the protasis, which may be expressed as well without any introductory formula. Their nature appears clearly in East Semitic, since the verb of the protasis introduced by the conditional particle *šumma*, "if", is not used in the subjunctive, as verbs of subordinate clauses.

49.12.   The particle *l-* used to introduce volitive clauses (cf. §38.2) is also a presentative (§49.7). Originally, it was phonetically different from the primary preposition *l-* which goes probably back to *n-* (§48.6).

C. Subordinate Conjunctions

49.13.   Semitic languages have no primary subordinate conjunctions or subjunctions, as they are called nowadays. In fact, Semitic is characterized by a remarkable preference for paratactic constructions, either asyndetic or syndetic (§55). However, changes in the syntactic system led to the use of presentatives, of nouns in the construct state, of prepositions, and of prepositions combined with presentatives, with nouns or with determinative-relative pronouns as subordinate conjunctions introducing temporal / causal, final / consecutive, substantival, and conditional clauses (§56-61).

49.14.   A specially frequent marker of subordinate clauses is the presentative *k-* with a series of affixes which are not used in any discernible correspondence with the nature of the subordinate clause; e.g. Ge'ez *'əressəyakkəmu kama təḥuru*, "I shall you shape so that you may walk". It may be governed by a preposition; e.g. Hebrew *'ad kī-ḥādal lispor*, "till he ceased numbering". It is sometimes found before the determinative-relative *ḏ*; e.g. Sabaic *hwry ... kḏ 'l s¹'l ḥdrn*, "they made (it) clear... that they lay no claim to the grave chamber". Combined with the construct state *'ăšer* which was employed as a relative pronoun (§57.5), the presentative *k-* is often used in Hebrew in the sense of "when"; e.g. *ka'ăšer-bā' Yōsēp*, "when Joseph had come". Various temporal subjunctions are formed in Amharic by combining *kä* with a postposition (cf. §48.25; 49.17); e.g. *gänzäbun* **kä**-*käffälhu* **bäh*ʷ*ala** *mäṣhafun wässädhu*, "after having paid the sum, I took the book", lit. "the-sum-that-I-have-paid after the-book I-took".

49.15. The construct state of the noun *yawm*, "day", functions in several Semitic languages as a subordinate conjunction in the temporal / causal sense "when", "as soon as". E.g. Old Babylonian *ūm tašapparī šuprim*, "as soon as you can write to me, write to me!"; Sabaic *ym s¹tyfꜥ T'lb*, "as soon as Ta'lab has declared his will". One should also mention Cushitic *yōm(i)*, "when", in Oromo. This prepositional function of *yawm* is paralleled by the use of the same noun with a local preposition, as in Old Assyrian *inūmi < in(a) ūmi* and in Hebrew *bə-yōm*, "when". Several other nouns have evolved into a virtual subordinate conjunction followed by a relative clause.

49.16. Prepositions and presentatives are often made to function as subordinate conjunctions by the addition of the determinative-relative pronoun, followed by a relative clause (cf. §57.6). E.g. Aramaic *b-zy l' šbqn ln lmbnyh*, "since they do not let us (re)build it"; Sabaic *b-ḏt hwpyhmw bkl 'ml' štml'w*, "because he granted them every help they have sought for"; Geʽez *wa-'ənza (< *hin-za) 'i-rakaba māya ḫalafa*, "and since he didn't find any water, he went on". Most Neo-Aramaic subordinate clauses, except the conditional ones, are formed in such a way with the demonstrative-relative *d-*; e.g. *mbater d-muḫkēlay kalbā mǧuweble(h)*, "after they have spoken, the dog answered".

49.17. South Ethiopian languages use conjunctions of subordination that are placed either before the verb or after it; e.g. Amharic *gänzäb agaňň zänd*, "that I may make money" (*zänd*, "so that"). Others consist of one element preceding the verb and another following it; e.g. Chaha *tämatäm ḵäma*, "as soon as he died" (*tä... ḵäma*, "as soon as"). The position of conjunctions after the verb is a feature borrowed from Highland East Cushitic, but it parallels the use of postpositions.

D. Copulae

49.18. The copula merely connects the subject and the predicate of a sentence without asserting action, but occasionally it also signifies presence. That link between subject and predicate was originally expressed

in Semitic by the predicate state (§33.5). Later it is often left unexpressed in a formal manner, but various Semitic languages employ the
personal pronoun as a kind of substitute for copulae (§50.9), while South
Ethiopic and Tigre make use of two particles, viz. *n* and *nt* > *tt* > *t*, both
of which have an Afro-Asiatic background. A different particle (**yṭ* or
'iṭ), derived from a verb (§49.23), is used in other Semitic languages.

49.19. The fullest form of the South Ethiopic *t*-copula appears in
Harari as *int-* with pronominal suffixes of the verb: *int-äň*, "I am";
int-ak, "you are" (masc.); etc. The assimilated form *tt* without prosthetic
vowel occurs in Gafat, likewise with pronominal suffixes of the verb:
tt-äy, "I am"; *tt-ähä*, "you are" (masc.); *tt-äš*, "you are" (fem.), etc.;
e.g. *wət al-əǧǧä-tt-o*, "he is (*tt-o*) my brother". The copula is used in the
same way in Soddo (Gurage), e.g. *uha abbo-t-ah*, "he is (*t-ah*) his
father". The geminated *tt* is reduced here to a simple *t* like in the other
Gurage dialects, in Tigre (*t-u*, "he is"; *t-a*, "she is"; *t-om*, "they are";
etc.), and also in Harari that uses the *t-* form besides *int-*: *t-aň*, "I am";
t-ak, "you are"; etc. Now, the element *-nt-* and its construction with
pronominal suffixes are exactly paralleled by Egyptian and Tuareg independent pronouns (§36.2), e.g.:

Egyptian	Tuareg	Harari	Gafat	Tigre	
nt-s	*nt-a*	*int-a*	*tt-a*	*t-a*	"she is"

The Egyptian independent pronoun is used as subject of sentences
with directly juxtaposed nominal or adjectival predicate (e.g. *nt-f s3-s*,
"he is her son"). There is little doubt therefore that the South Ethiopic
copula *t* < *tt* < *nt* is an Afro-Asiatic independent pronoun, the use of
which was replaced in other Semitic languages by forms corresponding
to the Egyptian "dependent pronoun", at least for the third person singular and plural (Egyptian *św*, *śy*, *śn*). A further question concerns the
possible relation of the pronominal base *-nt-* to the Bantu basis *-ntu* of
nouns designating persons and things (e.g. *mu-ntu*, "man"; *ka-ntu*,
"something").

49.20. The *n-* copula is used with pronominal suffixes of the verb in all
the South Ethiopian languages, except Harari. This copula is related to
the Tuareg and Cushitic pronominal element *n-* (e.g. Tuareg *n-ək*, "I"),
to the Egyptian *n-* (e.g. *n3y-s*, "hers") and *ìn-* (*ìn-k*, "I"), and to the general Semitic *'an-* (§36.5), where the initial *ì/'a* seems to have originated

from a prosthetic vowel while an anaptyctic vowel appears in Tuareg and in the South Ethiopic copula. Thus, the latter uses a Proto-Semitic pronominal basis *'an/na* with personal suffixes:

	Suffixes	*Proto-Copula	Gafat	Amharic
Sing.				
1 pers.	*-ni*	*na-ni*	*näy*	*naňň*
2 pers. m.	*-ka*	*na-ka*	*nähä*	*näh*
f.	*-ki*	*na-ki*	*näš*	*näš*
3 pers. m.	*-hu*	*na-hu*	*no*	*näw*
f.	*-ha*	*na-ha*	*na*	*näčč*
Plur.				
1 pers.	*-na*	*na-na*	*nänä*	*nän(nä)*
2 pers.	*-kum*	*na-kum*	*nähum*	*naččəhu*
3 pers.	*-hum*	*na-hum*	*näwm*	*naččäw*

49.21. The South Ethiopic copulae *t* and *n* are, in reality, personal pronouns. Therefore, they cannot be used either as negative copulae or as copulae referring to the past, except in particular contexts. The negative of the copula is thus expressed by inflected negative forms of the verb *-däbəl-* (Gafat) > *-däll-* (Amharic), which probably means "to fulfil" in Sabaic, "to repeat" or "to add" in Gafat, in Gurage dialects, in Amharic, and in Harari, "to collect" in Arabic and in Bedja. E.g. Gafat *wət ənd-antä gäddärmä tädäbəllam*, "he is not as big as you", lit. "he as-you big he-is-not"; Amharic *əssu bätam tänkarra aydällämm*, "he is not very strong", lit. "he very big he-is-not". In Amharic relative clauses, the negative copula is expressed mainly by the negative perfect of *honä* (root *kūn*); e.g. *təru yalhonä mäshaf alfälləgəmm*, "I don't want a book that is not good", lit. "good that-it-is-not a-book I-don't-want". The copula in the past is expressed in Amharic by *näbbärä*, "he was", *alnäbbärä*, "he wasn't", conjugated as a regular triconsonantal verb.

49.22. Besides the copulae, Ethiopic also possesses some "existential" verbs which express presence, accessorily existence. The most common verb of presence is **hallaw*, "he is present", "there is". It goes back to the frozen demonstrative *halla* followed by the personal pronoun *hu* (§36.33), and it may be replaced in Amharic by the copula *n-* wherever the idea of "being present" is expressed. There is a second "existential" verb *yən-*, used in Gafat and in North Gurage. This verb is related to Cushitic *wan-* (e.g. Qemant-Qwara *wanäk*[w], "I am") and to ancient

Egyptian *wn(-n)*, "to be", used with verbal personals and still attested in Coptic as an indefinite pronoun *won/wan*, "someone". In Egyptian, only the long form *wn-n* is common in main clauses, and an *-n* is suffixed in Gafat to forms of the main clauses alone; e.g. Egyptian *wn-n-ṯ*, Gafat *yǝn-čǝ-n*, "you (fem.) are/will be present". The opposition *w* : *y* in the on-glide may result from a different radical vowel: *w-an/on* vs. **y-in* (cf. *t-ini*, "when he is").

49.23.   The East, North, and West Semitic languages make use, to a various extent, of the copula **yṯ* which is a frozen form of a verb **yṯw*, "to be (present)", attested in Palaeosyrian. It appears as *'iṯ* in Ugaritic, *i-šu* in Old Canaanite, *yēš* in Hebrew, *'īt(ay)* in Aramaic, *iš*(+ *šū/šī*, "he/she is") in Late Babylonian, and only with a negative as **lā-išu* > *laššu* in Assyrian and **lā-'īṯ* > *laysa* (also *lāta*) in Arabic. It is a fossilized form of a verb attested at Ebla as *i-ša-wu* [*yiṯāwu*] and considered in lexical lists as a synonym of *ba-ša-um* /*baṯāyum*/, known as *bašū(m)*, "to be (present)", in East Semitic. This copula may be employed either impersonally in its bare form, or be inflected with personal suffixes or with enclitic personal pronouns.

1°   The bare **yṯ* is real predicate in sentences stressing that someone or something is present, available, or simply exists; e.g. Ugaritic *rgm 'iṯ ly* (KTU 1.3,III,20-21), "I have a message", lit. "there is a message with me"; *bl 'iṯ bn lh* (KTU 1.17,I,21), "he has no son", lit. "there isn't any son for him"; Old Canaanite *rabiṣ šarri ša i-šu-ú ina Ṣumur* (EA 68,19-20), "the king's commissioner who is in Ṣumur"; Assyrian *tibnu ana aṣappē laššu*, "there is no straw for the pack-animals"; Syriac *lǝ-ta'lē neq'ē 'it lǝ-hon*, "there are holes for foxes". Although the Old Akkadian and Assyro-Babylonian verb *išū* < **yaṯāwu(m)* means "to have", the acceptation "to be" probably occurs in Old Akkadian anthroponomy, e.g. *I-su-a-ḫu*, "There is a brother", *I-su*-DINGIR, "There is a god".

2°   When **yṯ* is suffixed, it functions as a genuine copula; e.g. Hebrew *'im yešǝkā mǝšalleᵃḥ 'et-'āḥīnū*, "if you are sending our brother" (Gen. 43.4), where the predicate is *mǝšalleᵃḥ*; Aramaic *ha-'ītāyk kāhēl lǝhōdā'utanī ḥelmā*, "are you able to let me know the dream?"; Syriac *'ellā 'itēh lan ḥērutā ba-qnoman*, "but there is freedom for us in ourselves", where the predicate is constituted by the prepositional phrase *lan*, "for us"; Arabic *lastu baḥīlan*, "I am not greedy", with the predicate in the accusative (non-active *a*-case), or *lastu bi-baḥīlin*, lit. "I am not as a greedy one". The Arabic forms *laysa* and *lāta* seem to imply borrowing; e.g. pre-classical Arabic *lāta ḥīna manāṣin*, "it is not the right time for escaping". At least *lāta*, "not to be", appears to be borrowed from Late Aramaic *layt* used as a negative copula and followed by an independent personal pronoun; e.g. *layt 'ennon nəbiyē*, "they are not prophets".

3° The semantic relation between *yaṯāwu* "to be", and East Semitic *išū*, "to have" (§49.25), may imply that the verb "to have" could either function as an "agentless passive" like Libyco-Berber *ili*, "to have" or "to be", or govern a reflexive pronoun like Latin *se habere* and the innovated Libyco-Berber *ill-e*, lit. "to have one's self". In Tuareg, e.g. *ila a-zgar* means "he had an ox", but the imperfective *ill-e-ttu ə-zgar* (< *u-zgar*) means "there is an ox", lit. "one has him (by) an ox", where the direct object is represented by the pronominal suffix *-e-*. The plural suffix occurs e.g. in *ill-ān-(t)tu middən əššin*, "there are two men", lit. "one has them (by) two men". A construction which must be innovative omits the indefinite pronoun *-ttu*, e.g. *ill-e ə-zgar de*, "there is an ox here", lit. "an ox has himself here".

The construction with a suffixed direct object still occurs apparently in Hebrew *'im yešənō bā'āreṣ*, "if he is in the country", lit. "if (one) has him in the country" or "if (he) has himself in the country" (I Sam. 23,23; cf. §36.18). If this interpretation is correct, *yṯw* was used also in some West Semitic languages with the meaning "to have", like *išū* in East Semitic.

49.24. The particle *yṯw*, used either as copula or as "existential" verb, was unfit to express aspect or time, although *yaṯāwu* was a real verb. In fact, while the idea of becoming was deeply rooted in the Semitic verbal system, the idea of being was late and therefore the verbs used for this purpose differ in the various Semitic languages and have a different basic meaning. E.g. the Arabic verb *kāna* means "to occur", but its perfect is used in the Classical language to express a situation in the past (e.g. *kāna lī 'aḫun*, "there was a brother to me", i.e. "I had a brother"), while its imperfect fulfils the same function in the future (e.g. *yakūnu lī 'aḫun*, "there will be a brother to me", i.e. "I shall have a brother"). Hebrew can use the verb *hāyā*, "to become, to occur", in the same way, e.g. *lo' hāyū 'ăbādēkā məraggəlīm*, "your servants have not been spies". In modern Ethiopian languages, the existence is expressed in the present by *halla* in Tigre, *'allo* or *'allä* in Tigrinya, *allä* in Amharic, *ḥal* in Harari, *anä* in West Gurage. All these forms are related to Ge'ez *hallaw* (§36.33; 49.22). This is the reason why the existence in the past and in the future has to be expressed by other means. E.g. Tigre uses 'ala for the past and the imperfect of gab'a for the future, while Tigrinya has *näbärä* or the gerundive *näyru* for the past, and the imperfect of *konä*, "to become", for the future (cf. §42.25). The latter is also used as negative, e.g. *'ay-konän*, "he isn't".

The Libyco-Berber copula -*ga*- might be borrowed from Arabic *ǧā'*, "he came", that often implies "become", "be", as in *lammā ǧēt arūḥ*, lit. "when I came to go", i.e. "as I was about to go". E.g. Kabyle *amkiga?*, "how is he getting on?"

E. Expression of Possession

49.25.   East Semitic has a verb *išū*, "to have" (§49.23:3°), that signifies actual possession; e.g. Old Akkadian *la ti-su*, "you don't have"; Old Babylonian *Aḫam-ni-šu*, "we have a brother"; Middle Babylonian stative *i-ša-a-ku*, "I have". In the other Semitic languages, possession is usually expressed by various particles or by verbs of presence combined with prepositional phrases or personal affixes (§49.23). Some languages use prepositional phrases like Ugaritic *yt ly*, "I have"; Aramaic *'yt lk*, "you have"; Mishnaic Hebrew *š-yš ly*, "what I have"; Western Neo-Aramaic (Maʻlūla) *īle* (< *īt le*), "he has"; Arabic *kūn l-* (§49.24); Tigre *halla 'əl* (e.g. *halla 'əlka*, lit. "it is yours"). In other languages, the personals referring to the possessor are suffixed to the verbal form; e.g. Tigrinya *'allonni* or Amharic *allaňň*, "I have", lit. "there is to me". The personal suffix attached to the verb of presence is an object suffix, while the item possessed is the subject of the verb; e.g. Amharic *bet alläňň*, lit. "a house is-to-me". A frozen form of the Semitic verb (')*ḥd*, "to seize", is employed in Gafat with actor suffixes to express the possession (e.g. *əzz-it*, "he has", lit. "he seized"), and East Semitic uses *rašā'u(m)* / *rašū*, "to acquire", in a similar way, since *išū* can express a static condition only; e.g. *mešrā irašši*, "he will have wealth", lit. "he will acquire wealth". This is also the reason why South Ethiopian languages make use of the verbs *näbbärä*, "to be", *nāra / norä*, "to be", *agäňňä*, "to find", to express possession in the past or in the future; e.g. Gafat *näbbäräy*, "I had", lit. "there was to me"; Amharic *yənoräňňall*, "I shall have", lit. "there will be to me".

IV

SYNTAX

50.1. The words of a language having been analyzed and their constituent morphemes determined, the next step in grammatical analysis is to consider the relation of words to each other in sentences expressing mental concepts and to find out the kinds of constructions in which the words occur. Although most Semitic languages and dialects have been submitted to such analysis, this area has not yet been sufficiently investigated and no systematic attempt was made to synthesize the results of these studies in the frame of a comparative grammar since the publication of Vol. II of C. Brockelmann's *Grundriss* in 1913. Yet, a broadly based historical analysis of Semitic syntax with a diachronic orientation is a major desideratum, even if it is difficult to discuss syntax with the accuracy feasible in phonology, morphology, and etymology. Since the languages concerned have a long history and since syntax, unlike morphology, can undergo radical change, it is not surprising that the syntax of modern Semitic languages differs more or less from that of earlier periods, but the recent periods are seldom fully intelligible without knowledge of earlier stages, and the syntax of older languages can only rarely receive satisfactory explanation without examining the syntax of cognate languages. It is true that some ancient Semitic languages present serious problems in respect to syntax. The wide use of logograms in Palaeosyrian, the shortness and the simplicity of the clauses forming Amorite personal names, the lack of vocalization in Ugaritic and in Epigraphic South Arabian inscriptions impose us limits, and only a partial picture of Semitic syntax can therefore be gained. On the whole, however, the syntax of the languages just mentioned is very similar to the one of the "Classical" languages, which form the backbone of our synthesis, and we can, with fair certainty, lay down general principles with which most Semitic languages will be found to agree.

Sentences placed in wider contexts may appear as the best way of illustrating complex syntactical relations, but they would often require lengthy annotations that might veil the very points in question. Therefore preference was given to short, simple sentences, clauses, or phrases. Translations are kept as literal as possible so that the reader can clearly see the syntactical structure.

Fig. 31. Old Assyrian envelop with tablet from Kültepe
(Ankara Archaeological Museum).

1. Classes of Sentences

50.2. We can first distinguish between major or two-term sentences, containing subject and predicate at least, and minor or one-term sentences, in which no such analysis is possible. However, one should not consider as real one-term sentences those in which the subject, the predicate, and even a direct or indirect object are expressed by a single word. In Semitic, as in many inflected languages, a sentence can consist of a verb phrase alone, e.g. Old Babylonian *uštābilakkum*, "I sent (it) to you", or Classical Arabic *ḍarabtumūnī*, "you have beaten me". The sentence may also consist entirely of a noun phrase, e.g. Babylonian *šarrāq*, "he is a thief", or Arabic *ḥasbuka*, "it is enough for you". There are also apparent one-term sentences which in reality are shortened two-term clauses, the second term of which has to be completed from the context; e.g. Hebrew *bǝ-'amtaḥtī*, "(the money is) in my sack"; Arabic *ḥadītaka*, "(tell) your story!"; *'al-'asada*, "(beware of) the lion!" Such clauses are, properly speaking, two-term sentences.

A. Minor Clauses

50.3. Many exclamatory sentences have the form of minor clauses. Thus, the vocative can generally be considered as a minor clause evoking the hearer, e.g. *il(u)*, "god!", *ilī*, "my god!", *mārū'a*, "my sons!", in Old Babylonian. The Tigre interjections *yǝbba*, "father!", and *yǝmma*, "mother!", are used regularly by children when addressing one of their parents; they consist of the particle *yǝ and of the nouns "father" and "mother". In Arabic, such clauses are often introduced by the same particle *yā* or *'ayyuhā* (e.g. *yā ġulāmu*, "oh! boy!"), but this particle is not necessary and it does not affect the nature of the minor clause. Another frequent interjection is *hā*, that is already attested in Thamūdic; e.g. *h'lh bk wdd w'n*, "Oh! God! There is love and rest with you!", where a nominal sentence (§50.6) follows immediately upon the introductory minor clause.

50.4. Interjections constitute minor clauses as well. Besides the particles meaning "yes" or "no" (e.g. Babylonian *anna* or Hebrew *kēn*, "yes"; Arabic *'alā*, *'amā*, "indeed"), one could refer here to presentatives (e.g. Old Akkadian *enma*, Hebrew *hinnē*, "behold!"), to expressions of emotion, amazement or grief (e.g. Babylonian *aḫulāp* or Aramaic *ḥăbal*, "woe!"; Arabic *hayhāta*, "wrong!"; *yā salām*, "what a pity!"), to particles signifying summons (e.g. Babylonian *gana* or *agana*, "well!"; Arabic *hāka*, "here, take it!"; *haygā*, "let's go!"), and to salutations like *salām* in Arabic or *šālōm* in Hebrew, which are in reality shortened two-term nominal clauses to be completed from the context. The Arabic presentative *'inna*, "behold!" (§49.6), is often followed by an archaic one-term nominal clause with the case ending *-a* which was marking the non-active subject in ergative Semitic; e.g. *'inna Zaydan wa-'inna 'Amran*, "here's Zayd and here's 'Amr!". The same use is attested with *hāka*; e.g. *hāka naẓmān*, "here's a poem for you!" These idioms might be interpreted also as two-term nominal clauses.

B. Major Clauses

50.5. Two-term sentences having a finite verb as predicate are called verbal clauses, while those having other predicates — substantives, adjectives, participles, adverbs, prepositional phrases — are as a rule called nominal clauses, although "non-verbal" or "verbless" clauses would be a more convenient class-name for all those sentences which either have no finite verb as predicate, or else have an anaphoric pronoun as copula, i.e. as "link" between subject and predicate. Sentences containing a noun conjugated as a stative (§38.3) are generally considered as verbal clauses, although the East Semitic stative may also be interpreted as a nominal sentence (but cf. §50.6).

C. Nominal Clauses

50.6. Nominal clauses signify an existing or a desirable situation or condition. They correspond roughly to English sentences containing "is", but they often do not use any copula and express the situation by direct juxtaposition of subject and predicate. Because of this absence of any copula, a nominal sentence may consist of two noun phrases only, e.g. Babylonian *abūbu rūbšu*, "his anger is a flood". However, although the predicate *abūbu* is a nominal form morphologically, syntactically it assumes a quasi-verbal function, for predication is basically a function exercised by a verb. This particular syntactical status of the nominal predicate is underscored in the oldest historically known phases of Semitic by the predicate state of the noun characterized by the morpheme *-a*

(§33.5), the use of which is still attested in Classical Arabic in certain cases; e.g. *'ammā 'anta barran fa-qtarib*, "if you are pious, approach"; *'immā 'aqamta wa-'ammā 'anta murtaḥilan fa-llāhu yakla'u mā ta'tī wa-mā tadharu*, "whether you remain or are departing, Allah guards what you do and what you forgo" (cf. §61.2). Nevertheless, there are differences. Since the predicate of these clauses is not a finite verb, nominal clauses do not specify by themselves whether the situation is permanent, or resulting from a completed action, or only expected to be realized. Of course, they are also extra-temporal or timeless, unless the wider context or an adverb of time specify the present, past, or future temporal sphere; e.g. Cairene Arabic *fī əs-sana di iḥna saymīn*, "this year we are fasting!" It seems that Proto-Semitic did not possess the possibility of expressing aspect or time by a verb meaning "to be", although it had an existential verb **yaṯāwu* (§49.23). However, verbal forms may be used as copula in some forms of speech, specially in modern languages (§49.24), but such phrases are no longer real nominal clauses, since they have a finite verb as predicate (i.e. *kāna, yakūnu, hāyā, 'alla, ləgabbə', näbärä, norä*).

50.7. The predicate of a nominal clause generally follows the subject, e.g. Old Babylonian *Adad šarrum*, "Adad (is) king"; Hebrew *Yhwh ro'ī*, "Yahwe (is) my shepherd"; Arabic *salām 'alaykum*, "(may) peace (be) upon you!", *'al-ǧāriyatu fī l-bayti*, "the slave-girl (is) in the house"; Mehri *nha 'aytōm*, "we are orphans"; Geʻez *Yoḥannəs makʷannən*, "John is a / the judge". However, to express emphasis on the predicate, the word order can be inverted and the predicate placed in front of the sentence, e.g. Hebrew *'āpār 'attā*, "dust you (are)"; Aramaic *rəḥīqān 'ănaḥnā minnāk*, "withdrawn we (are) from you"; Assyrian *ilāni rabûti attunū-ma*, "the great gods you (are)"; Geʻez *kama ḥoṣā bāḥər bəzəḥomu*, "as the sand of the sea (is) their multitude". In particular, there is a tendency to invert the order when the subject is not determined (e.g. Arabic *fī l-bayti ǧāriyatun*, "there is a slave-girl in the house"), unless it answers a question and therefore is emphasized; e.g. Arabic *man fī l-bayti*, "Who is in the house?"; answer: *ǧāriyatun fī l-bayti*, "It is a slave-girl that is in the house".

50.8. A special type of nominal clauses enables the Semitic languages to take any term out of an ordinary nominal or verbal sentence and to place it in its front as an isolated subject, — also called *casus pendens* or "suspended subject", — while the rest of the sentence, with a pronoun representing the term taken out, functions as a kind of predicate. The extra-posed or "topicalized" noun, i.e. the *casus pendens*, is in the nominative, regardless of the function the resumptive pronoun exercises in the sentence; e.g. Old Babylonian *ṣuḫaru ... ṭāti alaktim šutaṣbitaššu*, "the servant, ... provide *him* with a present for the journey"; Hebrew *Yhwh baššāmayim kis'ō*, "Yahwe, in the heaven is *his* throne"; Arabic *Zaydun māta 'abūhu*, "Zayd, *his* father died"; *kullu n-nāsi 'aqdiru 'urḍihim*, "all people, I cannot satisfy *them*". In Assyro-Babylonian poetry, the determinative *ša* followed by the *nomen rectum* may occur as a *casus pendens*, while the *nomen regens* is determined in the sentence by a pronominal suffix; e.g. *ša āliya Zabban šitta abullātišu*, lit. "of my city Zabban, two are *its* gates". Similar topicalizations occur often in Libyco-Berber with the difference that the topicalized noun, — even if it is the logical subject of the sentence, — is used not in the ergative *u*-case, but in the non-active *a*-case; e.g. *a-ġbar yu'ra*, "the fence, it became high", or *a-rgaz idda ġar ssuq*, "the man, he went to the market", to compare with *idda u-rgaz ġar ssuq*, "the man went to the market", where the normal construction verb-subject is followed. This use of the *a*-case is paralleled in Classical Arabic when the extra-posed indeterminate verbal noun follows *'inna*, *'anna*, also *'ammā*, which is usually translated "as far, concerning", although it goes back to a form of the conditional particle "if ever" (cf. Ḥarsūsi *'am*, "if"), used to introduce a nominal clause; e.g. *'ammā 'ilman fa'ālimun*, "if ever (there was) knowledge, he is knowledgeable", *'ammā qatlan fa-lastu qātilan*, "if ever (there was) killing, I am not a killer", where the predicate following *lastu* is also in the accusative (§49.23). There are other cases as well, often with variant readings in the nominative and the accusative.

50.9. Topicalization or extraposition is probably the construction that gave rise to three-term nominal clauses using a third person personal pronoun as a kind of copula. This personal pronoun generally agrees with the subject in gender and number. As to its position in the sentence, it follows the logical predicate and therefore stands either between the predicate and the subject or at the end of the clause. E.g. Neo-Assyrian *Iyyāru urḫu ṭābu šū*, "Iyyar is a good month", lit. "Iyyar, *it* (is) a good month"; Hebrew *wə-Yōsēp hū' haššallīṭ*, "and the governor was Joseph", lit. "Joseph, *he* (was) the governor"; Syriac *šemšā šrāgan-ū*, "the sun is our lamp", lit. "the sun, *it* (is) our lamp"; Arabic *'ulālika humū 'al-kāfirūna*, "the unbelievers are those", lit. "those, *they* (are) the unbelievers"; Ge'ez *Yoḥannəs wə'ətu mak"annən*, "the judge was

John", or *Yoḥannəs makʷannən **wə'ətu***, "John was a/the judge". The logical predicate may also be a personal pronoun, e.g. Hebrew *'attā **hū'** malkī*, "you are my king"; Colloquial Arabic *anā **huwa** t-tāǧir*, "I am the merchant". This construction with the anaphoric pronoun used as a copula does not seem to occur in Assyro-Babylonian texts before the first millennium B.C., but it is paralleled in Old Egyptian by the use of the demonstrative pronoun *pw*, e.g. *dmi **pw** 'Imnt*, "the West is an abode", lit. "an abode, *this* (is) the West". A similar construction occurs also in Libyco-Berber with the so-called predicative particle *d*, e.g. *Muḥnd ḏ a-mqqran*, "Muhend is great/tall". In Tigre, the copula-pronoun must intervene, but it generally agrees in person, gender, and number with the subject; e.g. *'ənta wa-'ana ṣar **ḥəna***, "you and I, *we* (are) friends". A shortened form of the third person copula-pronouns is used (*tu*, "he"; *ta*, "she"; *tom, tan*, "they": §49.19), and *tu* is encountered also with subjects in other persons than the third, like in other Semitic languages. The substitution of this construction for the original method of direct juxtaposition of subject and predicate was obviously due to the desire to indicate the logical predicate more clearly than could be done by a simple juxtaposition, in connection with which inversions were frequent. The intercalation or addition of a pronoun aims at marking the preceding noun as the logical predicate, although the latter may often be viewed as the grammatical subject. The effect of such a construction will be felt by comparing French *le roi, c'est lui* with *il est le roi*, where the use of *ce*, just like that of a pronoun in the Semitic languages, in Libyco-Berber, and in Egyptian, points unmistakably to *lui* as the logical predicate.

50.10. Another type of three-term nominal clauses attested in several Semitic languages is characterized by the use of the existential particle **yṯ* (§49.23). The particle means "there is / are" and it can be employed with actor suffixes of the verbal conjugation or with pronominal suffixes expressing the subject of the clause.

D. Verbal Clauses

50.11. The main function of verbal clauses is to express an action that either has taken place once and is accomplished, or is not accomplished because it is still going on or is supposed to take place in the future. The predicate of a verbal clause is, of course, a finite form of a verb either

perfective or imperfective, imperative, jussive, or stative. The participial
predicate is used, instead, in nominal clauses. When the verb is transitive, the verbal clause generally contains also a direct object and often
prepositional phrases, as well as adverbial modifiers. The adverbials
may complement the predicate, but they often add details to the contents
of the sentence as a whole.

50.12.   The pronominal subject of a Semitic verbal clause is generally
expressed only by the actor affixes of the verb, like in Latin and in
Slavic languages. Its independent occurrence in classical languages has
emphatic value in most cases and it is mainly aimed at contrasting the
behaviour or the situation of two persons; e.g. Old Babylonian *wardīka
attā tīde*, "it is you who know your servants"; Hebrew *'ānokī
'e'ərbennū*, "it is I who shall go surety for him"; Arabic *kāna huwa
s-sāriqa*, "it is he who was the thief". The independent pronominal subject can also be used when the word order subject-predicate is desirable
for contrast, instead of the normal order predicate-subject in verbal
clauses; e.g. Hebrew *gādal Šēlā wə-hī' lo'-nittənā lō lə-'iššā*, "Shelah
had grown up, but she had not been given to him as a wife"; Arabic
marra bī wa-'anā 'anzuru 'ilayhi, "he passed next to me, when I paid
attention to him".

50.13.   The usual word order in a Semitic verbal sentence is predicate-
subject, e.g. Palaeosyrian *uš-tá-si-ir ^dKà-mi-iš*, "Kamiš has heard";
Amorite *Ia-as-ma-aḫ-^dAddu*, "Haddu has heard"; Hebrew *bā' 'āḫīkā*,
"your brother arrived"; Samalian Aramaic *qāmū 'immī 'ilāhū*, "the
gods stood with me"; Arabic *ṭala'at aš-šamsu*, "the sun has risen"
("sun" fem.); Ge'ez *takala bə'si 'əḍa*, "the man planted a tree". The
same word order is followed in Libyco-Berber; e.g. Tarifit *ṭuru tə-mġart
a-hram*, "the woman bore a boy"; Tachelhit *imdl u-rgaz a-fruḫ*, "the
man buried the child". However, this order is inverted when the speaker
or the writer wants for some reason to attract attention upon the subject.
In consequence, there is no rigid word order in a sentence and the most
important term is usually placed in front. In a verbal clause, the action
expressed by the verb is generally considered as the main point of the
utterance, and this is the reason why the predicate is often placed before
the subject. Instead, the subject is usually the focal term of the nominal
clause, hence it generally precedes the predicate. However, various
influences and reasons have led to a different word order in particular
Semitic languages or idioms. Generally speaking, languages lacking a

case inflection, like modern Arabic or Ethiopic, make greater use of word order than highly inflected ones.

50.14. Syntax is much more subject than either phonology or morphology to influence from other languages and Semitic texts written in cuneiform script — especially deeds, letters, legal stipulations — are influenced to a great extent by the Sumerian syntax with the verb at the end of the sentence. This sequence is already followed in Eblaite administrative texts and in Old Akkadian, then in Assyro-Babylonian. Later, the East Semitic word order occurs also in the so-called Imperial Aramaic (§7.12), especially in Biblical Aramaic. The initial Sumerian impact results not only from the frequent use of Sumerograms to indicate verbal forms, regularly placed at the end of the sentence in the oldest Semitic texts (e.g. at Tell Beydar: EN *iš* ^{d}*Ša-ma-gán* BA.GIN, "the king went to Šamagan"), but also from the counter-check provided by Palaeosyrian and Old Akkadian personal names in which the verbal predicate precedes the subject, while the stative or the nominal predicate follow it (§50.7). Proper names frequently preserve archaic features which elsewhere have disappeared, and the word order they attest is thus pointing very likely to old constructions; e.g. *I-ku-un-sar-su* /*Yikūn-šaršu*/, "His king became firm", but *Sar-ru-*GI /*Šarru-kīn*/, "The king is firm"; *Im-lik-É-a* /*Yimlik-Ea*/, "Ea counselled", but *É-a-ma-lik* /*Ea-malik*/, "Ea is a counsellor".

50.15. On the opposite spectrum of the Semitic area, a similar situation occurs in modern Ethiopian languages. The verb, or a syntactically equivalent word, is placed at the end of the sentence and the word order is the same as in Sumerian: subject - direct or indirect object - verb; e.g. Tigre *Rabbi 'astar wa-mədər faṭra*, "God created heaven and earth"; *worot 'ənās 'ət qišot 'ala*, "A man was (living) in a hamlet"; Amharic *direktäru betun* (the house) *bäsost ših bərr* (for 3000 dollars) *šäṭṭä* (has sold), "the director has sold the house for 3000 dollars". A pronoun suffixed to the verb is often resuming the preceding direct object, as in Gafat *əňňə kab-əš təlšəl-y-am*, "I don't know this village". In Amharic, this rule is applied when the determined direct object precedes the subject; e.g. *bäqlo-wa-n wəšša näkkäsä-t* vs. *wəšša bäqlo-wa-n näkkäsä*, "a dog bit the mule". This structure of the Ethiopic sentence is completely independent from the impact of Sumerian on East Semitic; it is due to the Cushitic substratum the influence of which was stronger in the south than in the north. North Ethiopic was affected to a certain degree by the Bedja and Agaw syntax, while South Ethiopic was mainly influenced by the Sidamo group of languages, now called Highland East Cushitic. However, even in South Ethiopic, the verb-subject order may occur in proverbs and in petrified phrases which witness to the old Semitic free word order; e.g. Amharic *mən yəsäma ǧoro, mən yəwəṭ gʷərroro*, "what did the ear hear?! what did the throat swallow?!"; *zännäbä wärq*, "gold rained". The explanation referring to the Cushitic substratum is most likely correct, but it raises in turn the question of how the Cushitic languages came to place the verb at the end of the sentence although they belong to the same Afro-Asiatic language family. The question is left open here, since we are not dealing directly with Cushitic.

50.16. Despite the use of case inflection, the older Semitic free word order was submitted in Classical Arabic to rather strict regulations. The reason was probably the loss of the case system in the spoken language, while the rules of Classical Arabic obviously aimed at preserving a traditional sentence structure. However, these rules are not followed in Neo-Arabic and in Colloquial Arabic, where the subject simply precedes the verbal predicate; e.g. *er-raǧul amsiknī bi-yadih*, "the man seized me with his hand".

50.17. Any major clause can be extended by adding direct or indirect objects, prepositional phrases, adverbs, etc. In general, the word order of the nominal clause is then: subject - predicate - prepositional phrase. In the verbal clause, instead, the typically Semitic sequence is the following: predicate - subject - object and/or prepositional phrase. This seems to be the normal word order of the Afro-Asiatic verbal clause, since it characterizes also Egyptian (e.g. *wbn Rʿ m pt*, "the Sun rises in the sky") and Libyco-Berber (e.g. Tarifit *yəššur u-fǧah a-ġarraf s waman*, "the countryman filled the jar with water"). However, due to the relatively free word order in the Semitic sentence other sequences occur as well, viz. subject - predicate - object or prepositional phrase - predicate. The latter sequence is usual in Assyro-Babylonian and it appears also in Aramaic (§50.14) and in modern Ethiopic (§50.15).

50.18. Particular reasons may suggest a different word order. Thus, for the sake of euphony or clarity a short prepositional phrase — generally consisting of a preposition with a pronominal suffix — stands often between the verbal predicate and the subject; e.g. Old Aramaic *hwḥd ʿly*

Brhdd ... š[št] 'šr mlkn, "Bar-Hadad assembled against me sixteen kings"; Safaitic *f-wgmt* **mnh** *nkht*, "and the bride went into mourning because of him". Examples occur also with a preposition followed by a substantive; e.g. Arabic *kāna* **lil-'abdi** *himārun*, "the servant had a donkey", lit. "a donkey was (belonging) to the servant".

50.19. For emphasis, any part of the sentence other than the subject and the predicate can be placed in front. The predicate, in this case, may both precede or follow the subject, although the finite verbal predicate generally precedes the subject, except in East Semitic, in Imperial Aramaic (§50.14), and in modern Ethiopic (§50.15). E.g. the Hebrew nominal clause *'et-'ahay 'ānokī mabaqqēš*, "it is for my brothers that I am looking"; the Arabic verbal clause *wa-fīhi qāla š-šā'iru*, "and about him the poet said ..."; the Old Babylonian verbal clause *šeriktaša mārū ... izuzzū*, "her dowry, the sons ... shall divide". Time determinations are usually placed in front, e.g. in the Aramaic verbal clause *'ədayin Dānī'ēl lə-baytēh 'ăzal*, "then Daniel went to his house"; in Tigre *hatte dol 'əllom hames nafar 'aha bəzhət 'alat 'əllom*, "once upon a time, much cattle belonged to these five persons".

50.20. There is also emphasis in the case of the so-called *casus pendens*, as explained above (§50.8), when a noun is placed in "isolation" at the beginning of the sentence. In the rest of the sentence, which has the form of a full clause, a pronoun refers back to that "isolated" noun, acting as subject (e.g. Hebrew *Yhwh* **hū'** *yišlah*, "Yahwe, he shall send"), as direct object (e.g. Old Babylonian *mātam ilūša izzibūši*, "the country, its gods will abandon it"), as complement of a noun (e.g. Hebrew *Yhwh baššāmayim kis'ō*, "Yahwe, his throne is in heaven"; Tigre *'əssit hilata hawānit ta*, "a woman, her strength is weakness"), or as object of a prepositional phrase (e.g. Hebrew *Yərušalayim hārīm sābīb lah*, "Jerusalem, there are mountains around it"; Arabic colloquial of Tunis *il-'ayd l-ikbīr hādāya yidbhu fīh l-akbāš*, "this great feast, they slaughter rams for it").

E. Concord of Subject and Predicate

50.21. The predicate agrees generally with its subject in gender and number. However, if the plural subject is definitely expressed and follows the verb, it is optional in Arabic whether the verb is in the plural or singular; e.g. *qad ǧā'akum rusulun*, "messengers arrived for you", with the verb in the singular. Such a lack of grammatical concord sporadically occurs also in other Semitic languages, but its frequency in old Arabic texts must result from a particular usage which did not take root in Neo-Arabic; e.g. *it'allamū l-wilād*, "the children did learn". The general validity of this Neo-Arabic feature is confirmed by a South-Palestinian work from the 9th century A.D. in which verbs in the singular occurring in quotations from the Qur'ān are automatically changed into the plural whenever the following subjects denote several persons. Contrary to Classical Arabic, the finite verb of South Arabian inscriptions shows strict concord in gender and number with its subject, irrespective of whether the subject precedes or follows the verb, and irrespective of whether a plural subject denotes persons or non-persons. Elsewhere, only the progressive. disuse of the dual deserves special consideration. When the subject is a dual, the predicate can be a plural; e.g. Hebrew *'ēnē Lē'ā rakkōt*, "Leah's eyes were dull". Yet, in older phases of a language and in more conservative idioms the predicate is used in the dual form as well, also when there are two parallel subjects, both singular in form; e.g. Old Akkadian *Enlil u Šamaš ... lissuḫā*, "May Enlil and Shamash tear out ...".

50.22. When the subject consists of nouns of different gender, then is the predicate treated as a masculine plural. However, it can also agree with the nearest feminine noun, as in this Old Babylonian example from Mari: *ilānu u ilātum ištē*, "the gods and the goddesses have drunk". Similarly, if the first of two parallel nouns forming the subject is a singular, — also a feminine singular, — the preceding verb very often agrees with the nearest noun and takes, accordingly, a singular form, eventually a feminine one; e.g. Hebrew *wattašar Dəbōrā ū-Bārāq*, "and Debora and Baraq sang". If the subject consists of nouns which are singular in form and which are related to each other by a disjunctive particle meaning "or", the verb is usually treated as a singular; e.g. Arabic *ḍaraba 'imru'un 'aw-i mra'atun ḥaddāmī*, "did a man or a woman beat my servant?".

50.23. Collective nouns may be treated either as singulars or as plurals (*constructio ad sensum*); e.g. Ge'ez *maṣ'a ḥəzb* or *maṣ'u ḥəzb*, "the people came"; Tigre *Rabbi 'əgəl 'addām bellom*, "God said to the mankind", lit. "God, to the mankind (collective), said to them (masc. plur.)". However, the choice is not entirely arbitrary: it depends on the usage of each language. Thus, Hebrew *'am(m)*, "people", is generally used with the predicate in plural, while Old Babylonian *ṣābûm*, "men", is usually treated as a singular. In Hebrew, the name of a country may be used with the verbal predicate in plural (e.g. *wayyišmə'ū Miṣrayim*, "and Egypt heard"), while Arabic treats such names as feminine singulars (e.g. *qālat-i l-Yahūdu*, "the Jews said"). The latter usage is comparable with the Indo-European neuter plural governing a verb in the singular, notably in Greek, in Avestan, and in Modern Persian. In Neo-Arabic, broken plurals are treated *ad sensum* as real plurals, even if they follow the verbal predicate (§50.21); e.g. *itlammu il-awlād*, "the children gather" (Tunis).

50.24. The "plural of majesty", like *'ĕlohīm* in Hebrew, *'elīm* in Phoenician, *ilāni* in Assyro-Babylonian, can be treated syntactically as a singular or a plural (cf. §51.5); e.g., the predicate is plural in Hebrew *hit'ū 'otī 'ĕlohīm* (Gen. 20,13), "God set me wandering". In modern Ethiopian languages, especially in Tigre, Tigrinya, and Amharic, the plural personal pronouns of the second and third persons may be used as polite forms of address or reference. They are grammatically plural forms and require a plural predicate; e.g. Tigre *wa-'əntum 'abuye sema 'ərəf 'itərakbo*, "and you (masc. plur.), my father, never find rest". A plural verb is used also with subjects designating respected personalities; e.g. Amharic *nəgūs Tewodərosəm wada Lagā Gʷarā hedu*, "king Theodoros went to Laga Gʷara" (cf. also §31.34).

50.25. Particular concord rules may govern the verbal predicates of proper names, viz. the gender of the verbal form can be derived from the sex of the name bearer, regardless of the gender of the theophorous element which is the grammatical subject of the verb. E.g. the third feminine singular form occurs in the Palaeosyrian feminine name *Ti-iš-te-Da-mu*, "Damu has drunk", although Damu is a masculine deity. Instead, the third masculine form is used in the Old Akkadian masculine name *I-din-Eš₄-tár*, "Ishtar has given", although Ishtar is a goddess, but a nearly contemporaneous feminine name with the same theophorous element has the third feminine form *Tá-din-Eš₄-tár*. The third feminine singular form occurs in the Old Babylonian feminine name *Ta-ra-am-ᵈIM*, "Adad loves" (present future) or "fell in love" (preterite) although the storm-god Adad is undoubtedly a masculine deity. This particular concord rules are attested also in later periods, generally with feminine theophorous elements governing a masculine verbal predicate, because the name bearer is a man. Examples are found in Aramaic as late as the Roman period; e.g. *'tntn*, "'Atta has given".

2. Nominal Phrases

A. Attribute

51.1. Any substantive can be modified by an attribute, i.e. an adjective, a participle, a demonstrative pronoun used adjectivally, or a numeral. The attribute in general follows its head, — as a rule, immediately, e.g. Palaeosyrian *sa-ma-nu ṭa-bù*, "good oil"; Old Akkadian *qurādum azzum*, "fierce warrior"; Liḥyānite *h-sfr dh*, "this inscription"; Hebrew *'īš ṭōb*, "a good man"; Old Babylonian *šarrum dannum*, "a mighty king"; Geʿez *nəguš-ṣādəq*, "a just king"; Tigre *la-bāb ʿali*, "the big gate". If, however, the head is a construct, the genitive or *nomen rectum* intervenes between the head and the attribute, e.g. Arabic *sayfu l-fārisi l-battāru*, "the knight's sharp sword"; Geʿez *nəguša Ḥamer sə'ur*, "the deposed king of Ḥimyar". The rule is the same, of course, when a pronominal suffix is attached to the substantive, e.g. Arabic *rabbuka l-'akramu*, "your most noble lord". It is rarely extended to prepositional phrases used instead of a *nomen rectum*, e.g. Aramaic *melek lə-Yiśrā'ēl rab*, "a great king of Israel". The attribute sometimes precedes its head, but this usage is attested mainly with the demonstrative pronoun used adjectivally, e.g. Aramaic *sb dn lwḥ' mn yd[y]*, "take this tablet from [my] hand"; Geʿez *ba-zā hagar*, "in this city". In Classical Arabic, demonstrative pronouns only precede nouns determined by the definite article, but in Neo-Arabic they may precede nouns in the construct state as well. Also attributes like "other", "numerous", may precede their head. This inverted order occurs likewise in Hebrew, Syriac, North Ethiopic, and in Arabic colloquials when the head of the attribute is semantically unimportant or functions as an apposition (§51.7); e.g. Hebrew *mēt 'ādām*, "dead man"; *kəsīl 'ādām*, "foolish man"; Syriac *bīšē bnaynāšā*, "bad men"; *ḥakkīmē nāšā*, "wise men"; Tigre *la-ṣəgub 'ənās*, "the rich man"; Tigrinya *ṭə'əmti qal*, "sweet voice"; Syriac *sābā mār Ewgēn*, "the old Father Eugène"; Arabic *eš-šāṭir Məḥamməd*, "the clever Mohammed".

51.2. South Ethiopic, strongly influenced by Highland East Cushitic, has a different word order, in which the qualifier is placed before the qualified element. Thus, as a rule, the adjectival attribute is placed before the substantive; e.g. Amharic *adaddis betočč*, "new houses"; Chaha (Gurage) *nəq säb*, "a big man".

51.3. As a rule, the adjectival or participial attribute and the demonstrative pronouns used as attributes agree with their head in gender, number, determination, and case; e.g. Arabic *'imāmun 'ādilun*, "a honest imam", both indeterminate and in the nominative; *'al-'imāmi l-'ādili*, "of the honest imam", both determinate and in the genitive. Even if the feminine plural substantive terminates in a "masculine" plural morpheme or the masculine plural substantive has a "feminine" plural ending, the adjectival attribute terminates in the usual, respectively feminine or masculine ending; e.g. Hebrew *šeba' šānīm bā'ōt*, "seven forthcoming years"; *məqomōt ḥădāšīm*, "new places". The broken plurals are generally treated in Arabic as feminine singulars, no doubt because they were originally collectives (§31.23); e.g. *ǧibālun rāsiyatun*, "unshakeable mountains". Those, however, which denote human beings may be considered as plurals; e.g. *riǧālun ṣāliḥūna*, "pious men"; *nisā'un ṣāliḥātun*, "pious women". Also other broken plurals are sometimes treated as plural; e.g. *dumū'un ḏārifatun* or *ḏārifātun*, "trickling tears".

51.4. An adjective qualifying a dual is often treated as a plural; e.g. Assyro-Babylonian *šēpēya allakāti*, "my fast feet"; Hebrew *yādayim rāpōt*, "slack hands". However, strict concord is followed in Classical Arabic; e.g. masculine *raǧulāni ṣāliḥāni*, "two pious men"; feminine *laylatāni bāridatāni*, "two chilly nights".

51.5. The *constructio ad sensum* is used often for attributes qualifying collective substantives, e.g. Hebrew *ṣo'n rabbōt*, "a great flock"; Arabic *qawmum ṣāliḥūna*, "pious people". The nouns plural in form though not plural in meaning, like Phoenician *'lm*, "god", or Hebrew *ḥayyīm*, "life", are most often treated as singulars; e.g. Punic *l'lm hqydš*, "to the holy God"; Hebrew *'ĕlōhīm ḥay*, "living God" (cf. §50.24).

51.6. The numerals "one" and "two" are adjectives and agree with their head in gender and case; e.g. Arabic *qaryatun wāḥidatun*, "one village"; *qaryatāni ṯnatāni*, "two villages". However, they may also govern the counted noun that can remain in the singular; e.g. Hebrew *šənē ha-'omer*, "two omers" (Ex. 16,22); Late Babylonian *šitt kusīt*, "two

garments". The other cardinal numbers are substantives and, in consequence, they are not used as adjectival attributes but either as appositions (§51.8) or as constructs followed by the item numbered (§51.14).

B. Apposition

51.7. Appositions are substantives used to modify another substantive
which does not stand in the construct state and, as a rule, precedes the
apposition; e.g. Hebrew *hammelek Šəlomō*, "king Solomon"; *haṣṣəbī
Yiśrā'ēl*, "the gazelle Israel" (II Sam. 1,19); Old Assyrian *ālum Aššur*,
"the city of Ashur". A proper name can modify a common noun, as in
the three examples just quoted, and it can also be modified by an apposition; e.g. Arabic *Zaydun 'aḫūka*, "Zayd, your brother". The head of an
apposition may also be a pronoun, as well as a pronominal suffix or a
subject pronoun contained in a finite verb; e.g. Phoenician *bšnt ... 14
lmlky mlk 'šmn'zr*, "in the 14th year of his reign, (viz.) king Eshmuna-
zor's"; Hebrew *'al-tōnū 'īš 'et-'āḥīw*, "you shall not cheat, one
another". In such cases, the apposition itself may consist of a resumptive
independent pronoun used either for emphasis (e.g. Aramaic *w-šbyqt
'nh*, "and I myself was spared"; Arabic *nubāyi'uka 'anta*, "we will
acknowledge you yourself as leader") or for grammatical coordination
(e.g. Hebrew *pen tiwwārēš 'attā ū-bētəkā*, "lest you are reduced to
poverty, you and your household"; Arabic *ba'aṯanī 'anā wa-'anta*, "he
sent me, me and you"). As a rule, appositions agree with their head in
determination and case; e.g. Arabic *ṯawbun ḏirā'un*, "a cubital garment",
lit. "a garment a cubit", both indeterminate; *'al-ḫātamu l-ḥadīdu*, "the
iron ring", lit. "the ring the iron", both determinate. Note that with
nouns in apposition the preposition may be repeated; e.g. Punic *l-'dn
l-b'l ḥmn*, "to the Lord, to Baal Hamon".

51.8. The most frequent appositions are personal names and geographic names (§51.7), nouns expressing material (e.g. Old Babylonian
kilīlum kaspum, "a silver necklace", lit. "a necklace a [piece of] silver";
Arabic *'al-bābu 'al-ḫašabu*, "the wooden door", lit. "the door the [piece
of] wood"; cf. §51.7), items which are measured or counted (e.g.
Hebrew *šibə'ā 'ănāšīm*, "seven men"; *'ēpā śə'orīm*, "an ephah of
barley"), as well as numerals and measures (e.g. Arabic *riǧālun
ṯamāniyatun*, "eight men"; *'al yawmu kulluhū*, "the whole day", lit.
"the day its entirety"). The items, either measured or counted, may

stand in the singular; e.g. Hebrew *šəloš mē'ōt hā-'īš*, "the three hundred men"; Late Babylonian *20 dannu rīqu*, "20 empty jars"; Tigre *samān mə'ət walat*, "eight hundred girls"; Harari *hammisti bäri*, "five gates". According to the typically Semitic and certainly older usage, the head of the apposition is the numeral or the measure, while the items, either counted or measured, are considered as expressing the material. However, the material could also be expressed by the formal genitive or *nomen rectum* (§51.14) and by a prepositional phrase (§51.26). Both constructions occur in Libyco-Berber; e.g. the apposition *ḳraḍ i-rigazn* (plur.), "three men"; the genitival phrase *sin d mraw (n) u-rgaz* (sing.), "twelve (lit."two with ten") men". In Arabic, also the accusative of the quantified stuff can be used (§52.9).

C. Genitival or Subjoining Relation

51.9. A substantive can be added to another substantive standing in the construct state in the same way as a suffixed pronoun is attached to a noun. The relation of the subjoined substantive or *nomen rectum* to the head of such a nominal phrase or *nomen regens* is about that of a genitival qualifier to the noun governing it in languages with case inflection. Therefore, grammarians generally use the term "genitive" to signify the *nomen rectum*, although case distinctions in nouns were lost or no longer fully functioning in most Semitic languages from the first millennium B.C. on (§32.21,24-27). Also adjectives and participles may function as *nomen regens*. In Libyco-Berber, the *nomen rectum* is in the locative/instrumental case, which is formally identical with the ergative (§32.3); e.g. *a-ḫḫam u-rgaz*, "the tent of the man"; *ṭa-ḍuṭṭ wulli* (< *u-ulli*), "the wool of the sheep"; *a-zzar yiḫf* (< *u-iḫf*), "the hair of the head". The last two examples explain the use of the locative ("the wool **on** the sheep", "the hair **on** the head"), which expanded to all similar constructions, as e.g. "the master **in** the house" (§51.12).

51.10. The logical genitive causes the head of the nominal phrase to be defined by indicating its possessor, master, principal, or the like; e.g. Old Babylonian *bīt awīlim*, "the freeman's house" or "a freeman's house"; Arabic *kitābu l-walīdi*, "the boy's book"; Ge'ez *walda nəguš*, "a/the king's son". Besides the logical genitive conveying a possessive meaning, Semitic languages use the formal genitive, which does not denote author or possessor but merely describes or qualifies the *nomen* *regens*. The use of the formal genitive is widespread and its shades of meaning are multiple.

51.11. A kind of genitive called *genetivus subiectivus* defines the *nomen rectum* as author, source, origin, or the like. E.g. Palaeosyrian *ba-tá-qí i-dim* /*batāq yidim*/, "cutting by hand"; Old Babylonian *errēt ilī*, "the curses of the gods"; Arabic *maṭaru š-šitā'i*, "the winter rain", lit. "the rain of the winter"; Geʿez *qāla nabiy*, "the prophet's voice". Passive verbal adjectives and participles are used with this genitive; e.g. Hebrew *mukkē 'ĕlohīm*, "smitten by God"; Arabic *qatīlu l-ǧū'i*, "killed by starvation".

51.12. The genitive can also be used as a kind of *genetivus obiectivus* to express the object which is possessed, ruled, made, or aimed by the *nomen regens*; e.g. Old Akkadian *abarak ti'amtim*, "the superintendent of the sea"; Old Babylonian *bēl bītim*, "the master of the house"; *šar Anunnaki*, "the king of the underworld gods"; Hebrew *melek Yiśrā'ēl*, "the king of Israel"; *yir'at 'ĕlohīm*, "the fear of God"; Arabic *ṭarīqu l-Šāmi*, "the road to Syria"; Geʿez *nəguša hagar*, "the king of the city". The active participle can be used with this genitive; e.g. Arabic *qātilu 'aḫī*, "the killer of my brother".

51.13. The partitive genitive expresses the relation of a part to a whole, as Old Babylonian *warkat bītim*, "the rear of the house"; *ušumgal šarrī*, "the dragon amongst kings". Notions denoting quantity are related to this kind of genitive, e.g. Hebrew *rob dāgōn*, "an abundance of grain"; Arabic *ba'ḍu l-kāfirīna*, "some of the unbelievers"; *'aǧmalu n-nisā'i*, "the most beautiful of women". In particular, the words meaning "all" or "every" — *kullatu(m)* in East Semitic, *kull(u)* in West Semitic — are used with the genitive; e.g. Old Babylonian *kullatu ilātim*, "all the goddesses"; Hebrew *kŏl-bānāyw*, "all his sons"; Arabic *kullu l-madīnati*, "all the city", *kullu madīnatin*, with an indeterminate *nomen rectum*, "every city"; Geʿez *kʷəllā hagar*, "all the city" or "every city".

51.14. Genitive can be used to express material, instead of an apposition (§51.8), of a prepositional phrase (§51.26), or of the accusative (§52.9); e.g. Old Babylonian *ṣalam ṭīṭim*, "a statue from clay"; Hebrew *ləšōn zāhāb*, "a golden tongue"; Arabic *bābu ḫašabin*, "a wooden door". The items counted, measured, or weighed may also be considered as material and be used in the genitive with numerals acting as *nomen* *regens*; e.g. Old Assyrian *arbē manēm*, "forty minas"; *sebet dayyānim*, "seven judges"; Hebrew *'ăśeret haššəbāṭīm*, "the ten tribes"; Arabic *sab'atu sāriqīna*, "seven thieves"; *ḫamsu nisā'in*, "five women".

51.15. Genitive can also express contents; e.g. Old Babylonian *bīt šurīpim*, "ice-house"; Hebrew *no'd yayin*, "a skin of wine"; Arabic *ka'su ḥamrin*, "a cup of wine".

51.16. The so-called *genetivus epexegeticus* is used to specify the *nomen regens*, often by indicating its use, its location, or the like; e.g. Old Babylonian *erṣet Sippar*, "the territory of Sippar"; Arabic *sūqu 'Ukāẓin*, "the market of Ukāẓ"; Hebrew *'ereṣ Yiśrā'ēl*, "the land of Israel"; *śārē qōdeš*, "temple officers"; Ge'ez *fəlsata Bābilon*, "the Babylonian exile". The formal genitive governed by an adjective or its equivalent belongs to the same category since it specifies the domain concerned; e.g. Assyro-Babylonian *ṣalmāt qaqqadim*, "the dark-headed ones"; Hebrew *yəpē to'ar*, "handsome", lit. "beautiful of aspect"; Aramaic *'attīq yōmayyā'*, "the ancient in days"; Arabic *ḥasanu l-waǧhi*, lit. "handsome of face"; *qalīlu l-'aqli*, "scanty in intelligence".

In Arabic, however, the adjective governing the genitive may be used with the article; e.g. *'al-ḥasanu l-waǧhi*. This irregular construction probably implies a syntactical shift from a pre-classical explicative accusative *'al-waǧha* (cf. §52.9), used with the article like in Hebrew (e.g. *raq* **hakkissē'** *'egdal mimmeka* [Gen. 41,40], "I shall be greater than you only by the throne"), to the genitive *'al-waǧhi*. This shift may be considered as a hypercorrection dictated by the absence of a determinate explicative accusative in Classical Arabic.

51.17. Semitic languages often use the genitive instead of an adjective to express a quality of the thing named, something attributed to it, or to specify and describe a thing as distinct from something else, and so to limit and define it. E.g. Old Babylonian *dayyān kittim*, "a just judge", lit. "a judge of rectitude", *šar tašimtim*, "an intelligent king", lit. "a king of intelligence"; Phoenician *bn ṣdq*, "a legitimate son", lit. "a son of lawfulness"; Ge'ez *ma'āra gadām*, "wild honey", lit. "honey of the wilderness".

51.18. The genitive may be governed by a determinative-relative pronoun (§36.46). This construction occurs frequently in Old Akkadian and in Assyro-Babylonian, e.g. *ši* (genitive) *atānim*, "of the (man) of the she-ass", *šūt* (plural) *Ibalpēl*, "the (men) of Ibalpēl". However, it is attested also in ancient Hebrew (e.g. *ze-Sīnay*, "the [god] of Sinai"), in

Nabataean (e.g. *ḏū-Šarā*, "the [god] of [mount] Šarā", i.e. Dusares), in Liḥyānite (e.g. *ḏū-Ġabat*, "the [god] of the Thicket"), in Classical Arabic (e.g. *ḏū l-qarnayn*, "the two-horned", an epithet given to Alexander the Great), in Colloquial Arabic (e.g. *ḏū ʻilm*, "the [man] of learning"), in Sabaic (e.g. *ḏāt-ḥamīm*, "the [goddess] of the heat", i.e. the Sun-goddess).

51.19.   The determinative-relative pronoun followed by a *nomen rectum* can be used also in apposition to the true *nomen regens* which in this case, however, is not a construct. This construction is often called "periphrastic genitive". E.g. the Babylonian phrase *mimma lemnu ša šīrēya*, "every pain of my body", can be expressed without the pronoun *ša* as well: **mimma lemnu šīrēya*. The same usage is attested in Aramaic (e.g. *gappīn dī-nəšar*, "eagle's wings") and in Neo-Aramaic (e.g. *ktāḇā d-ʼeskōlāyā*, "a pupil's book"), in Phoenician (e.g. *khn š-Bʻlšmm*, "priest of the Baal of Heavens"), in Epigraphic South Arabian (e.g. *ṣlmn ḏ-ḏhbn*, "the golden statue"), in Geʻez, and in modern Arabic colloquials. In Geez, the determinative-relative *za-* is used mainly to express determination, especially of material (§51.14); e.g. *bet za-nəguš*, "king's house"; *bet za-ʼəbn*, "house in stone" (cf. §51.23). The modern Arabic vernaculars use the ancient determinative-relative *dī*, *d-*, etc., with the shortened relative pronoun *əlli* < *ʼallāḏi*, especially in North Africa; e.g. *ən-nās əlli d-dowwār*, "the people of the village". Besides, several other words are employed as markers of the genitive, thus *šīt*, *šīyāt* (< **šayʼat-*, "something") in Damascus, *bitāʻ* (< *matāʻ*, "property") in Egypt, etc.; e.g. *haššabāb šīyāt əš-Šam*, "the youths of Damascus"; *il-bāb bitāʻ il-bēt*, "the door of the house". Under the probable influence of the short Aramaic nominal clauses of the type *zy ly*, "what (belongs) to me", the determinative-relative *š-* (§36.51) is combined in Mishnaic Hebrew with the preposition *l-* (cf. §51.23) to form a genitival particle *šel*, which is already separated from the *nomen rectum* in the Bar Kokhba letters (132-134 A.D.); e.g. *hprnsyn šl Byt Mškw*, "the officials of Bet-Maševo"; *nipšeret šellazzāhāb*, "the golden candlestick", where the vocalization includes the definite article (< **šel-han-zāhāb*).

51.20.   The use of the determinative-relative pronoun to introduce the *nomen rectum* after the *nomen regens* gave rise in Assyro-Babylonian and in Aramaic to a construction with a proleptic suffix announcing the *nomen rectum*; e.g. Babylonian *mār aḫātišu ša* PN, "the son of **his** sister, that of PN"; Aramaic *šəmēh dī ʼĕlāhāʼ*, "**his** name, that of God".

The same construction occurs in Hebrew with *šel* (cf. §51.19): *miṭṭatō šelli-Šəlomō* (Cant. 3,7), "**his** litter, that of Solomon"; *karmī šellī* (Cant. 1,6), "**my** vineyard, that of myself". This usage appears also in colloquial Arabic and in Modern South Arabian. The preposition *l-* is used, e.g., in Iraqi Arabic *fallšuha lil-madrasa*, "they demolished **it**, the school", and in Palestinian and Lebanese Arabic *qāl-lu lə-l-ḥkīm*, "he spoke to **him**, to the physician". Various syntactic devices are used in South Arabian after the proleptic suffix; e.g. Śḥeri *həs lə-'əmi*, "for **her**, for my mother"; Soqoṭri *re'iš dsə bīoh*, "ask **her**, her mother". The same construction is attested in Libyco-Berber with the preposition *n*; e.g. *baba-s n ṭṭalb*, "**his** father, (that) of the school-master".

51.21. The determinative-relative pronoun used in apposition to a noun can be followed also by a subordinate clause, which is then called "syndetic relative clause" (§57.2,6). When such a clause follows immediately upon the construct *nomen regens*, it is called "asyndetic relative clause" (§57.3,5).

51.22. It is characteristic of the Semitic languages to use such words as "master", "father", "son", etc., with various nouns as descriptives. E.g. Hebrew *ba'al ha-ḥălomōt*, lit. "the master of the dreams", means "the dreamer", and *ben šəba'-'eśrē šānā*, lit. "son of twenty-seven years", means "twenty-seven years old". In Arabic, *'abū šawārib*, lit. "father of mustaches", designates a man with a long mustache, while *'abū l-yaqẓān*, "the father of the vigilant", is the rooster, the cock. This usage is widespread in Amharic where such expressions form the so-called "adjectival syntagms", used mainly as attributes or appositions; e.g. *balä arat əgər*, "four-footed", lit. "master of four feet"; *näfsä bis*, "evil-minded", lit. "spirit of evil".

51.23. The determination of the construct — e.g. *bīt* in Old Babylonian *bīt awīlim*, "the freeman's house" or "a freeman's house", and *kitābu* in Arabic *kitābu l-walīdi*, "the boy's book" — is a function of the *nomen rectum*, i.e. *awīlim* and *('a)l-walīdi* in the examples quoted: a definite *nomen rectum* implies a definite construct and an indefinite *nomen rectum* an indefinite construct. However, in languages which do not possess any formal expression of definiteness or indefiniteness, like the North and East Semitic languages, or Ge'ez, it is not possible to decide whether the construct is fully defined or no without recurring to the context. This is why *bīt awīlim* can mean either "the freeman's house" or "a freeman's house". In Arabic instead, the article *'al-* used with the *nomen rectum* indicates that the construct is fully defined: "**the** book of the boy". But this construction cannot be used to express directly "**a** book of the boy", for the following genitive (*'a)l-walīdi* would fully define the book. So one should employ a prepositional phrase with *l-*: *kitābun lil-walīdi*, "a book (belonging) to the boy". The same phrase or an equivalent one is used in other Semitic languages; e.g. Hebrew *bēn lə-Yišay*, "a son of Jesse"; Aramaic *melek lə-Yiśrā'ēl*, "a king of Israel"; Ge'ez *waldu la-nəguš*, "the king's son". This construction is generalized in Tigrinya, as well as in Libyco-Berber and in Egyptian. In Tigrinya, any genitive relation can be expressed by the use of the preposition *nay* followed by the modifying noun which may be placed either before or after the head; e.g. *mäṣḥaf nay tämähari* or *nay tämähari mäṣḥaf*, "a student's book". Libyco-Berber and ancient Egyptian use the preposition *n-* which originally is an allophone of *l-* (§48.6); e.g. Tamazight *baḇ n-taddart̠*, "the father (master) of the house"; Numidic *nbb-n n-šqr'*, "cutters of wood"; *nbt-n n-zl'*, "splitters of iron" (Dougga, 2nd century B.C.); Middle Egyptian *nsw n-Kmt*, "the king of Egypt". This use of *n-* as a "connective" particle between a noun and a following dependent genitive is attested also in Chadic languages. In modern colloquial Arabic, one of the nouns employed as markers of the genitive (§51.19) can be inserted in the phrase and then it is this inserted word which is defined by the *nomen rectum*, while the preceding noun, i.e. the logical *nomen regens*, may or may not have the article; thus, e.g. *əl-kitāb bitā' əl-walad*, "the boy's book", lit. "the book, property of the boy"; *kitāb bitā' əl-walad*, "a book of the boy", lit. "a book, property of the boy".

51.24. Nothing must break the connection between the construct and the *nomen rectum*. Accordingly, even an adjectival attribute of the construct has to come after the genitive, as Middle Assyrian *mār bīte rabû*, "the eldest son of the house"; Hebrew *yeled zəqunīm qāṭān*, "a small child of (his) old age"; Arabic *kitābu r-raġuli l-kabīru*, "the man's large book". However, enclitics may be added to the construct, e.g. Amorite *Ḥabdu-**ma**-Dagan* /*'Abdu-**ma**-Dagan*/, "Servant of Dagan"; Hebrew *'arṣāh Kənā'an*, "unto the land of Canaan"; Arabic *yā ṭūla **mā** šawqin*, "Oh! what a tediousness of longing!". Also a negation considered as forming one word with the *nomen rectum* can intervene between the latter and the construct; e.g. Old Babylonian *kasap **lā** kanīkim*, "silver without a sealed tablet", i.e. without guaranty; Arabic *ḫāṭī'atu **lā**-dīnīyatin*, "a crime of irreligion".

51.25.   South Ethiopic follows Highland East Cushitic also with regard to the genitival relation (cf. §51.2). Thus the modifier precedes the modified element in this case as well; e.g. Amharic *yä-kätäma näwari*, "the population of the city", where *yä-* is the particle of appurtenance of Amharic and of the other South Ethiopian languages. It is the palatalized preposition *lä-* which is occasionally used in Ge'ez and in some Tigrinya dialects (cf. §48.6). This periphrastic construction allows a grammatical distinction between possessivity (logical genitive) and qualification (formal genitive). In the possessive complex, the Amharic definite article *-u* and the accusative marker *-n* are suffixed to the qualifier; e.g. *yä-hakim-u mäṣhaf*, "the doctor's book"; *yä-hakim-u-n mäṣhaf amṭu*, "bring the doctor's book". Besides, the pronominal suffix *-u*, "his", and the accusative marker *-n* may be attached to the *nomen regens*; e.g. *yä-hakim-u-n mäṣhaf-u-n amṭu*, lit. "the-doctor's his-book bring". In the qualifying complex, the article and the accusative marker are often attached to the qualified noun; e.g. *yä-warq säat-u*, "the golden watch"; *yä-warq säat-u-n amṭu*, "bring the golden watch". They cannot be affixed to both elements of the genitival phrase. Also the relative clause qualifying the noun is placed in South Ethiopic before the noun; e.g. Muher (Gurage) *yä-mʷätä säb yəqäbrəmʷət*, "they bury the dead man", lit. "who-died (the-)man they bury". In Harari, a resumptive pronoun is suffixed to the *nomen regens*; e.g. *mäḥawa qïmo-zo*, "the price of the goods", lit. "(of)-the-merchandise its-price"; *wäḥačäč adäb-ziyu*, "the manner of the girls", lit. "(of)-the-girls their-manner". The same structure occurs with the postposition *-le*, "to", used in Harari instead of a preposition (§51.23); e.g. *nädäba-le qäñït gäräb-dä-le*, "to the right side of the seat", lit. "to-the-seat right to-its-side".

51.26.   In Semitic languages preserving a case inflection, the genitive is used also with prepositions (§48.2). In fact, most of them are of nominal origin. Prepositional phrases have a very wide range of functions. They may act as predicate in nominal clauses (§50.7), and they may replace a logical genitive (§51.23) and a genitive expressing material or quality (§51.14); e.g. Arabic *libāsun min-a l-ḥarīri*, "a silken dress"; *'al-kitābu bi-l-ḥaqqi*, "the book with the truth", i.e. "telling the truth". They can be used instead of an accusative with verbs denoting motion, fullness, dressing, etc. (§52.3), especially when a verb governs a double accusative (§52.4). They may also replace an accusative of time and of place (§52.6-7). Their use increases in languages lacking case distinctions (§52.11), thus widening the original semantic field of the prepositions (cf. §48). Prepositional phrases may also form adverbs (e.g. Hebrew *bazze*, "here"; *mizze*, "hence"; Amharic *bähayl*, "strongly"; *bäqällal*, "easily") and subordinate conjunctions (§49.15-16). The South Ethiopic preposition *yä-* (§51.25) can be prefixed to substantives in order to use them as a kind of adjectives; e.g. *yä-säw*, "human", lit. "(proper) to a man"; *yä-krəstiyan*, "Christian", lit."(proper) to a Christian".

3. Verbal Phrases

52.1. A verbal phrase is built around a verb and consists at least of a subject and of a verbal predicate. While their presence is essential, it is by no means necessary that these be separate words, for the same word may contain the two components (§50.2). When the sentence is more complex, it often contains a direct or internal object. The accusative is the case of direct objects of verbal action and of internal objects denoting the content of such action. The Proto-Semitic accusative seems to have originated from the so-called "patient" or non-active case in an ergative language structure and, therefore, this case is used not only with direct objects of transitive verbs, but also with Arabic and Ethiopic intransitive verbs meaning "to be" (§52.8), and in Arabic negative nominal clauses (§54.3). These morpho-syntactic features most likely preserve a case function going back to prehistoric times. Grammarians often use the term "accusative" to signify the direct or the internal object of verbal action also when describing languages in which case distinctions were lost or no longer fully functioning. A verbal phrase can also contain an infinitive which is a verbal noun (§53).

A. Accusative

52.2. As a rule, stative verbs and passive or reflexive verbal stems have no direct or internal object, but passive forms of verbs or stems used with double objects (§52.4) can govern one accusative, and verbs expressing a circumstantial situation, like Babylonian *zunnu(m) izannun*, "the rain rains", *berqu(m) ibarriq*, "the lightning lights", or Ugaritic *mṭr B'l*, "Baal is raining", also occur with the accusative, e.g. Babylonian *Adad ... māssu libriq*, "may Adad strike his land by lightning". Besides, both transitive and intransitive verbs can govern internal objects, e.g. Hebrew *way-yaḥălom Yōsēp ḥălōm*, "and Joseph dreamed a dream".

52.3. The range of transitive verbs is wider in Semitic than in most Indo-European languages. Besides verbs expressing an action referring directly to an object like "to strike" or "to send", also verbs denoting motion, fullness, dressing, etc., may be used in a transitive way with a direct object; e.g. Babylonian *ḫarrāna illak*, "he will go on a journey"; Arabic *nahaba š-Šāma*, "he went to Syria"; Ge'ez *bo'a hagara*, "he entered the city"; Gafat *gäbäyä əhur*, "I shall go to the market", lit. "market I-shall-go". However, a prepositional phrase can be used instead of the accusative; e.g. Babylonian *ana ḫarrāni lā illak*, "he will not go on a journey"; Arabic *nahaba 'ilā š-Šāmi*, "he went to Syria". The same constructions are used with verbs denoting fullness; e.g. Babylonian *akālam ula ešebbi*, "I am not getting satiate with food"; Hebrew *wan-niśba' leḥem*, "and we were satiated with food". But the accusative can be replaced in Hebrew and in Arabic by a prepositional phrase; e.g. Hebrew *yiśba' bə-ḥerpā*, "may he be satiated with disgrace"; Arabic *šabi'a min laḥm(in)*, "he was satiated with meat".

52.4. Double accusatives may be governed by the causative and factitive stems of verbs which normally govern one direct object in the basic stem. E.g. Babylonian *iṣṣurātim šūbilaššu*, "let him bring the birds"; *mahrêm-ma ... ṣubātam lubbiš*, "dress the first one with a garment"; Hebrew *way-yapšīṭū 'et-Yōsēp kuttāntō*, "and they stripped Joseph of his tunic"; Arabic *'a'ṭā bnatahū niṭāqan*, "he gave his daughter a girdle". Besides, verbs denoting making or forming into anything, appointing to an office, feeding, burning, washing, etc., take a second accusative of product, office, stuff, etc. E.g. Babylonian *mê egubbê tasallaḥšu*, "you will besprinkle him with lustral water"; Hebrew *way-yiqrā' šəmō Pāreṣ*, "and (people) called his name Parez"; Arabic *mala'a d-dalwa mā'an*, "he filled the bucket with water". In a passive construction, the first accusative becomes subject, while the second one is preserved; e.g. Babylonian *šū išātam liqqali*, "may he be burnt with fire"; Arabic *mali'a d-dalwu mā'an*, "the bucket was filled with water". In Hebrew and in Aramaic, one of the two accusatives may be replaced by a prepositional phrase introduced by *lə*: e.g. Hebrew *wa-yəśīmēnī lə-'āb*, "and he made me a father"; Aramaic *halbišū lə-Dāniyyēl 'argəwānā*, "rob Daniel in purple".

52.5. The so-called "adverbial" accusative is used with verbal predicates to express different circumstances, mainly of time, place, manner, cause, result, degree, means, etc. These uses of the accusative were the starting-point of adverbs of nominal origin (§47.1-5).

52.6. The accusative expressing time denotes the duration, sometimes the moment as well. E.g. Babylonian *ūma u mūša*, "through day and night"; Arabic *laylan*, "by night"; Ge'ez *ṣabāḥa*, "in the morning". In languages lacking a case inflection, this accusative of time is often considered as an adverb not introduced by a preposition, e.g. Hebrew *yāmīm rabbīm*, "for many days". However, a comparison between e.g. Hebrew *hayyōm* and Classical Arabic *'al-yawma*, "to-day", shows beyond any doubt that this temporal use of certain phrases originates from the "adverbial" accusative. The latter may be replaced by a prepositional phrase; e.g. Babylonian *ūm* or *ina ūm(i)*, "on the day that…"; Arabic *ġadan*, or *min ġad(in)*, or *fī ġad(in)*, "to-morrow"; Ge'ez *məseta* or *ba-məset*, "in the evening".

52.7. The accusative can also denote the place in which something happens. E.g. Babylonian *māssunu … uššabū*, "they live in their country"; Hebrew *šəkon 'ereṣ*, "dwell in the land!"; Arabic *nazala makānahū*, "he settled down in his place"; Ge'ez *nabara gadāma*, "he dwelt in the wilderness". In some case, this accusative can hardly be distinguished from the direct object of verbs of motion; e.g. Hebrew *'ŏniyyā bā'ā Taršīš*, "a ship was going to Tarshish". With the same verbs, the accusative may be replaced by a prepositional phrase; e.g. Old Assyrian *ina ālim wašab*, "he is living in the city"; Hebrew *haš-šokənīm bam-midbār*, "those who dwell in the steppe"; Arabic *'inzil 'ilā l-bustāni*, "go down to the garden!".

52.8. The so-called "predicative" accusative denotes a concomitant circumstance. It can be a substantive, an adjective, or a nominal phrase. E.g. Babylonian *šalmam … išaqqal*, "in perfect condition it weighs"; Hebrew *qāhāl gādōl yāšūbū*, "they will return a mighty throng"; Arabic *ǧā'a rākiban*, "he arrived riding". The particular nature of this construction may be exemplified by *hāḏā Zaydun munṭaliqun* (nominative), "this is Zayd departing", as opposed to *hāḏā Zaydun munṭaliqan* (accusative), "this is Zayd (as the) departing one". The "predicative" accusative occurs regularly in the Canaanized Amarna correspondence with the particle *yānu* of non-existence (§47.12); e.g. *yānu ḫazanna ina arkitiya*, "there is no mayor behind me" (EA 117,9-10). It may be used in Arabic with the verb *kāna*, "to be"; e.g. *kāna 'aḫān lī*, "he was a brother to me". This is also the case when *kāna* is employed impersonally; e.g. *'iḏā kāna ḥīna l-'aṣri*, "when it was the time of the evening prayer". This use of the accusative is understandable if the *-a* ending goes in reality back to the -*a* case of the non-active subject or predicate used in an ergative language with intransitive verbs or in equivalent constructions. This explanation can be applied also to the examples quoted above, since all the verbs are intransitive; thus "the perfect condition weighs", "a mighty throng will return", "a rider arrived".

52.9. A kind of explicatory accusative aims at better determining the contents of the phrase, at indicating its more specific subject or object. E.g. Middle Assyrian *qāta miṯḫār*, "as for the share, it is equivalent"; Hebrew *lō' nakkennū nāpeš*, "let us not smite him as far as life is concerned"; Arabic *'ammā ṣādiran fa-wasīquhu ǧamīlun*, "as for one who returns from battle, his booty is fine"; *da'awtu llāha samī'an*, "I call upon Allah as the one who hears". The indeterminate accusative can assume a similar function in Classical Arabic with the elative (§34.5); e.g. *'ašadduhum tawāḍu'an*, lit. "the strongest among them as for humbleness", i.e. "the humblest of them". Used with nouns designating objects or with quantitative expressions, the accusative may specify the material or the quantified item (cf. §51.8,14,26); e.g. *ǧubbatuka ḫazzan*, "your silken jacket"; *ṯalāṯata 'arṭālin nabīḏan*, "three *raṭl* (measure unit) of date-wine".

52.10. In West Semitic languages lacking case distinctions, the particle **'iyyat* optionally precedes the determinate direct object; it is generally called *nota accusativi*. It is attested in Phoenician and Punic (*'yt* > *'t* > *t*), in Hebrew (*'t* > *t*), in Moabite and Edomite (*'t*), and in Aramaic (*'yt* > *yt*, *wt*). In Classical Arabic, instead, — where the final -*t* was lost, — the use of the particle is reduced to pronominal suffixes when the pronominal object has to be stressed (e.g. *'iyyāka na'budu wa-'iyyāka nasta'īnu*, "You do we worship and You do we ask for help"), or when two pronominal suffixes should be used (e.g. *'a'ṭāhā 'iyyāya*, "he gave her to me", instead of *'a'ṭānīhā*). A similar usage is attested in Neo-Aramaic with a resumptive pronominal suffix; e.g. **yātē marī bid mnāḥimlī**, "in my own person will the Lord resuscitate me". In Modern South Arabian, *t(ə)*- is the accusative marker of personal pronouns. Cf. also §36.31.

52.11. A prepositional phrase governed by *ana* or *l*- may replace the accusative in languages lacking case distinctions. This construction occurs with *ana* in Neo-Assyrian texts of the 8th-7th centuries B.C.; e.g. **ana šarre bēliya usaḥsis**, "I have reminded the king, my lord". It is attested likewise in Neo-Babylonian and in Late Babylonian; e.g. *adduku **ana** Gūmātu*, "I killed Gaumāta". A similar use of *l-* is encountered at that time in West Semitic, not only with verbs governing a double accusative (§52.4), but also with other verbs. Its earliest attestations are found in Biblical Hebrew; e.g. *yāda'tā **lə-**'iwwaltī* (Ps. 69,6), "you know my foolishness". Authors often assume an Aramaic influence since most Hebrew occurrences are roughly contemporaneous with the Aramaic texts of the Achaemenian period when this construction is attested for the first time in Aramaic; e.g. *'nh yhbt l-ky l-byt'*, "I have given you the house". As a matter of fact, no such examples with *l-* are known from earlier times, neither in Aramaic inscriptions nor in cuneiform texts (§48.7). This new function of the particles *ana* and *l-* is just an extension of their syntagmatic use with various verbs; e.g. Western Middle Babylonian *kīmē anāku **ana** šarri bēliya araḫḫam*, "as I have an affection for the king, my lord"; Aramaic *rhnw l-PN*, "they vouched for PN". Since there was no longer a fully functioning case system in Pre-Classical Arabic, it is not surprising that the preposition *li-* is used in a similar way in the Qur'ān; e.g. *'in kuntum **lir**-ru'yā ta'burūna*, "if you can interpret the dream". This construction occurs frequently in Neo-Arabic. It is found also in Ge'ez which may then anticipate the accusative by adding a proleptic pronominal suffix to the verb, e.g. *rəinā**hu** la-'əgzi'əna*, "we saw our Lord". This use of a prepositional phrase to express a direct object is paralleled in other Ethiopian languages, e.g. Tigrinya *nə-'arkäy rə'iyä*, "I have seen my friend".

B. Infinitive

53.1. The infinitive is a verb form lacking the indications of person, tense, and mood that characterize the finite verb. It has two distinct usages. It may function as a verbal noun introduced by prepositions and used in the oblique cases of the singular. In the second usage, however, the morphological infinitive may be semantically equivalent to a finite verb, being able to take a subject, an object or an adverbial modifier, and expressing purpose or other functions related to the action signified by the finite verb of the clause. Both usages can occur in the same phrase. The subject of an infinitive, if expressed, is most often a suffixed pronoun or a substantive in genitival position, i.e. immediately following the verb; e.g. Hebrew *bə-yōm* (*nomen regens*) *'ăśōt* (infinitive in the genitive) *Yhwh 'ĕlohīm* (subject) *'ereṣ wə-šāmāyim* (direct object), "on the day that God made earth and heaven". But the subject can appear separated from the infinitive, and in that case it has nominative status; e.g. Old Assyrian *adi* (preposition) *nēmal kaspiya* (direct object) *tamkārī* (subject) *lā ṣabātim* (infinitive in the genitive), "as long as my merchant did not collect the profit of my money"; Sabaic *bn* (preposition) *hyʿ* (infinitive) *lhmw* (indirect object) *hʾ fnwtn* (subject), "from the flowing, for them, of that canal".

53.2. The infinitive called "construct" in Hebrew grammars has usual infinitive functions, as Babylonian *nadānam* (infinitive in the accusative) *iqbû*, "(what) he ordered to give"; Hebrew *mēṭib naggēn*, "he who excels in playing" (Ez. 33,32); Sabaic *ḫmr ʿbdyhw … tʾwln bwfym*, "he vouchsafed to his two servants … to return in safety"; Geʿez *kalʾani waḍiʾa*, "he prevented me from leaving". But the infinitive dependent on a governing verb is frequently preceded by a preposition, very often by *ana* in Assyro-Babylonian and by *l-* in Hebrew and in Aramaic (§48.4), even when it does not express purpose; e.g. Aramaic *lā ʾărīk lanā lə-meḥzē*, "it is not convenient for us to see …". The postposition *-iš* occurs with the infinitive in Old Akkadian (e.g. *nadāniš qabi*, "he was ordered to give"), and rarely in Old Babylonian and in Old Assyrian (e.g. *muwātiš illikā*, "they went to die").

53.3. Auxiliary verbs, which syntactically occupy the position of the main verb in the clause, may be followed by an infinitive; e.g. Aramaic *yūkal lə-haḥăwāyā*, "he is able to explain"; Hebrew *ḥāpēṣ … la-hămītēnū*, "he wanted to kill us"; Sabaic *wl-wzʾ… hwfyn ʿbdhw*, "and may he keep granting to his servant …"; Geʿez *ʾi-kəhəlna bawiʾa*, "we were not able to enter". The infinitive precedes the auxiliary verb in Tigre: *naqila* (infinitive with a feminine pronominal suffix) *tahallaw*, "they were unable to uproot it" (i.e. the bush). However, the infinitive may be replaced by an asyndetic finite verb, used in the same person and the same tense; e.g. Aramaic *tkln thytn ln tqm*, "you will be able to procure us castor oil"; Sabaic *w-wzʾw s²rʾw bythmw*, "and they added to the equipment of their house …"; Arabic *ʾaqdar(u) ʾaḍrab(u)*, "I am able to beat". In Arabic, the asyndetic construction is widely used instead of the infinitive also in other cases; e.g. *ǧaʿaltu* (perfect) *ʾuḥaḏḏiruhum* (imperfect), "I began to warn them". It occurs in Geʿez as well; e.g. *nabara* (perfect) *yənabbəle* (imperfect), "he sat to speak".

53.4. The so-called "infinitive absolute" — so named because it does not stand in the construct state nor is it governed by a preposition — is mainly used as the internal object of its cognate finite verb in order to add emphasis or specification. It often precedes the finite verb and is usually translated adverbially in European languages. E.g. Palaeosyrian *pá-kà-ru₁₂ a-pá-kà-ru₁₂* /pakāru lapakkarū/, "they should join firmly"; Babylonian *šuggušu ušaggaš*, "he slaughters ruthlessly"; Old Aramaic *nkh tkwh*, "you will strike it pitilessly"; Arabic *ḍarabahū ḍarban*, "he beat him severely"; Ge'ez *zabṭəwwo zəbṭata*, "they whipped him heavily". In Assyro-Babylonian, the particle *-ma* is frequently added to the infinitive; e.g. *pašārum-ma apaššar*, "surely I shall release". This construction is widely used in negative sentences with the negative placed before the finite verb; e.g. Babylonian *šālu ul išālanni*, "he did not ask me at all"; Hebrew *hāmēt 'al-təmītuhū*, "anyway do not kill him". The same construction is attested in Libyco-Berber and in ancient Egyptian. Thus, it must go back to Proto-Afro-Asiatic. The usual Semitic word order is encountered in Libyco-Berber; e.g. Kabyle *učči ičča*, "he has surely eaten"; *tuffġa iffeġ*, "he surely went out". The complementary infinitive follows the finite verb in Egyptian; e.g. *wbn-k wbnt*, lit. "you rise a rising"; *ḫnn-sn ḫnt*, lit. "they row a rowing". This word order occurs also in Semitic, e.g. in Palaeosyrian *i-na-'à-áš na-'à-su* /yinaḥḥaš naḥāšu/, "he will certainly recover".

53.5. The infinitive may be used as some sort of gerund in various constructions. It follows the finite verb and is preceded by the preposition *l-* in Hebrew (e.g. *lāmā ḥărē'otem lī lə-haggīd lā-'īš*, "why did you hurt me by telling the man?") and in Aramaic (e.g. *ḥătībūnā lə-mē'mar*, "they answered us, saying"). In Sabaic, it is linked to the preceding finite verb by the conjunction *w-*; e.g. *b'dw whb'ln ... wmtlyn*, "they carried off, having seized ... and looted"; *tnḥyt wtnḍrn*, "she confessed, having done penance". In the Ethiopian languages of Ge'ez, Tigrinya, Amharic, Argobba, and West Gurage, instead, the so-called "(pseudo-) gerund", "gerundive", or "converb", which originates from the infinitive as well (§42.12), precedes the main clause with the finite verb; e.g. Ge'ez *qatiləya* (gerund) *bə'se gʷayayku* (main verb), "having slain the man, I fled"; Amharic *mäsobun käfto* (gerund) *dabbowən wässädä* (main verb), "having uncovered the basket, he took the bread". This construction is paralleled in Old Canaanite, as appears from some passages in the Amarna correspondence; e.g. *allu paṭārima awīlut ḫupši u ṣabtū Ḥapirū āla* (EA 118,36-39), "behold! the serfs having deserted,

the 'Apiru have seized a city". It is attested later by the Hebrew use of
the infinitive with a pronominal suffix, continued by a finite verb; e.g.
(*ba*-)*ḥălotō wa-yəḥī mē-ḥolyō* (Is. 38,9), "(when) having been ill, he
recovered from his illness" (cf. §42.12). In Phoenician, instead, the
infinitive absolute is followed by the independent personal pronoun and
it is continued by the main sentence with the finite verb; e.g. *w-p'l 'nk
ss 'l ss ... w-šbrt mlṣm*, "and having added horse to horse, ... I broke the
wicked ones" (cf. §42.12).

53.6. There is a tendency in modern Amharic to replace constructions
with finite verbal forms by infinitives in the accusative; e.g. *lä-mäššom
mist magbatun əṭṭäraṭṭärallähu*, "I doubt that he married a woman in
order to be appointed", lit. "to be-appointed a-woman his-marrying
(infinitive) I-doubt".

4. CLAUSES

A. Particular Types of Main Clauses

54.1. The question as to how many kinds of utterances there are in any
language was variously answered by grammarians depending upon how
close they stood under the influence of a determinate language family. In
addition to declaration or statement, a typical list should include negations, denials and refusals, questions, as well as various types of volitive
and interjectional utterances. The particular types of main clauses that
may require special attention in Semitics are the negative, interrogative,
and hortatory, imperative, vetitive, optative or precative clauses.

54.2. In Semitic languages, as a rule, the negatives neither cause a
change in the word order of the sentence, nor influence the use of verbal
forms and of cases in nouns, as it happens in some Indo-European forms
of speech. However, verbs of negative clauses have a different vocalic pattern in most South Ethiopian languages, especially in the Gurage group.
One cannot dismiss this fact as a simple secondary feature of these
dialects, since a similar situation is attested by the Libyco-Berber perfect
negative (e.g. Tamazight *išəmməl*, "he finished"; *ur išəmmil*, "he didn't
finish"), by Cushitic conjugations, e.g. in Southern Agaw or Awngi (e.g.
desé, "he studies"; *desá-la*, "he doesn't study"), and in Bedja (e.g. *tamáni*, "I am eating"; *ka-tam-an*, "I am not eating"), as well as in Chadic

languages. In general, negative clauses seem to have preserved old patterns better than the positive ones. This does not imply that the differentiation is a secondary one. The overall picture rather gives the impression that Semitic has generally lost this morphological distinction.

54.3. Another question bears on the case system, since negatives are often followed by the accusative in Arabic nominal clauses, e.g. *lā šakka*, "there is no doubt"; *lā 'abā laka*, "may there be no father to you"; *lā 'ilāha 'illā llāh*, "there is no god but Allah". One might assume that this usage arose when *lā* still had its original exclamatory function "no!" (§47.8), while the accusative was felt as adverbial: *lā raǧula*, "no! as for a man", i.e. "there is no man". Also *mā* is employed with the accusative (e.g. Qur'ān 69,47: *mā minkum min 'aḥadin 'anhu ḥāǧizīna*, "not one of you serves as shields against him"), but it can be followed by the nominative as well. As for *laysa*, which governs the accusative, it is a compound negative with particular features (§47.10; 49.23). The analysis of these and some related syntactical questions pertains to the comparative study of ancient Arabic dialects, but the fundamental question is whether the *-a* denotes a true accusative, which normally should not appear in an intransitive nominal clause. Very likely that *-a* goes back to the "patient" or non-active *-a* case denoting the predicate in an intransitive clause of an ergative language, as Semitic appears to have been in an early phase (§32.1-12; 52.1).

54.4. In modern Arabic colloquials, especially in Egypt, Palestine, and Syria, a *-š* may be added to the word negatived; e.g. *ma tegiš*, "do not come"; *ma anīš rāyiḥ*, "I am not going". When *-š* precedes a consonant, it may be pronounced *-šə*. This element is a corruption of the noun *šay'*, "thing", "something". The latter was borrowed into Berber dialects as an indefinite pronoun *ša*, "something", and it is used likewise in Tamazight negative sentences, e.g. *ur inžiḥ ša*, "he did not succed". The function of *-š* / *ša* presents some analogy with the Amharic enclitic *-ssa* which simply reinforces a question.

54.5. Any sort of statement in Semitic languages can be turned into a question in any of the three ways: it may be spoken in an interrogative tone of voice, and this rising tone is sometimes indicated by a complementary sign in cuneiform script; e.g. Babylonian *šarrānu... islimū (is-li-mu-ú)*, "did the kings make peace?", while the answer is *islimū (is-li-mu)* (cf. §10.6). Otherwise, either an interrogative pronoun (§36.57-60) or an interrogative particle (§47.7) may be used before the sentence. Besides, in modern Arabic colloquials, an element -š or -əš may be added to the word which is the subject of question, like in negative clauses (§54.4); e.g. 'ənta 'əṭšānəš, "are you thirsty?", from 'aṭšān, "thirsty". It may be added also to the interrogative pronoun; e.g. 'ayš ḍarabaha, "why did he beat her?" (cf. §36.59). A similar usage is attested in Ethiopic when no interrogative pronoun or adverb is employed. The question is indicated then by the interrogative marker -nu in Ge'ez, -do in Tigrinya, wäy or -(ə)nə in Amharic, which are suffixed to the word emphasized in North Ethiopic (e.g. 'adgi-do 'alläka, "do you have a donkey?) and to the last word of the Amharic sentence (usually a verb), with rising intonation. While -nu or -(ə)nə is likely to be an expressive particle, -do goes probably back to a negative (§47.16) and wäy, used also as disjunctive particle (§49.4), is related to the interrogative pronoun 'ayyu (§36.59).

54.6. There are different ways of formulating a hortatory, imperative, or vetitive clause. The imperative has only the second person and this can be employed positively only (§38.2). In the negative, a form of a prefix-conjugation must be used in its place; e.g. Old Akkadian vetitive ā taqbi, "don't say!"; Assyro-Babylonian vetitive ē-taprus, "don't separate!"; Old Babylonian (Mari) and Late Babylonian imperfective lā taqabbi, "you will not speak!"; Hebrew jussive 'al ta'aś, "don't doe!", or imperfect lo' tirṣaḥ, "don't commit murder!"; Arabic jussive lā taqal, "don't say!", in the classical language, but e.g. mā tašrab, "don't drink!", in modern colloquials; Tigre 'i-təbkay, "don't cry!". The intimate interrelationship between aspect and modality explains why the forms of the imperfective, which denote unaccomplished actions, may be substituted for the imperative in the positive command as well; e.g. *iparras* forms in Assyro-Babylonian, as *ana Zimri-Lim kīam taqabbi*, "to Zimri-Lim you will speak as follows"; imperfect forms in Hebrew, as *šēšet yāmīm ta'ᵃbod*, "you will labour for six days"; in colloquial Arabic, as *taktub ğawāb lī*, "write me a letter"; in Aramaic, as *tippəlūn wə-tisgədūn*, "you will prostrate yourselves and you will worship" (Dan. 3,5). Under influence of Aramaic, *iprus* forms are used in the same way in Late Babylonian; e.g. *ana pānīya tašpur*, "may you send to me!" An indirect command or an exhortation in the first or third person necessarily use jussive, cohortative, or imperfective forms. The positive form is preceded by the particle *l-* in East Semitic, in Aramaic, in Classical Arabic, and optionally in Ethiopic. As a rule, only a negative is

used in vetitive or prohibitive forms, except in Middle and Neo-Assyrian
(*lū lā*). E.g. Assyro-Babylonian *l-iprus*, "may he separate"; *ay-iprus*,
"may he not separate", *l-uprus*, "may I separate", *ay-aprus*, "may I not
separate"; (*i*) *nillik*, "let us go!"; *ul inaddin*, "he may not give";
Samalian Aramaic *'l ytn lh*, "may he not give to him!"; Hebrew *'al-nā
no'bədā*, "let us not perish!"; Arabic *li-ya'ti*, "he should come!"; *lā
yuḥzinkum-u llāhu*, "may God not grieve you!"; Ge'ez *la-yəqrab*, "let
him approach!"; *'əngər*, "let me speak!", without particle; Tigre
barhat təgba', "let there be light!". Again under Aramaic influence,
iprus forms are used in the same way in Late Babylonian, without any
particle; e.g. *kapdu ikšud*, "may he arrive quickly!".

54.7.   Optative or precative clauses can also assume the form of a nominal sentence, as e.g. Old Akkadian *anākū lū amtum*, "let me be a maid-
servant!"; Hebrew *šālōm ləkā* or Arabic *salām 'alaykum*, "peace be
with you!". The use of the optative particle *lū* with the stative in Old
Akkadian and in Assyro-Babylonian is related to this construction; e.g.
lū dari, "long live!". Since the stative, like nominal clauses, was not
expressing *per se* either the accomplished or the unaccomplished aspect
of an action, it could easily be used as a precative. Also the West
Semitic perfect, which derives from the stative (§38.10), originally had
an optative or precative function (e.g. *ḥay Yhwh*, "long live Yahwe!"),
which favoured the development of the so-called "*waw*-conversive"
with the perfect in Hebrew (§54.8).

54.8.   The copulative *waw* with the so-called "converted" perfect *wə-
qaṭal* is frequent in Classical Hebrew, and it is supposed to refer to a
future action which will continue another action. In reality, the alleged
examples of this construction in the Bible are either clauses signifying a
desirable or expected situation, like the Old Canaanite optative/precative
and the perfect in Classical Arabic, or sentences simply ascertaining a
fact, like number of proverbs and stereotyped expressions inherited by
Arab writers from pre-classical times. Some examples of this optative
construction occur in the Amarna correspondence from Byblos; e.g.
*dūkūmi eṭlakunu u ibaššātunu kīma yātinu **u pašḫātunu*** (EA 74,25-27),
"kill your man and you will be like us, and may you then have peace!".
Well attested is the use of the optative perfect in Classical Arabic; e.g.
raḥimahū llāhu, "may God have mercy upon him!"; *ḥalaftu wallāhi lā
fa'altu hāḏa*, "I swear: By God! May I not do this!", i.e. "I shall never
do this". The Hebrew usage parallels the Old Canaanite one; e.g.

'ăḥappēś ū-ləqaḥtīm (Am. 9,3), "I will search and may I then seize them!"; *wə-hārīt wə-yāladtə bēn* (Judg. 13,3), "and you have conceived and may you then give birth to a son!", where the first perfect ascertains a new fact, while the second one expresses a wish or signifies the forthcoming desirable situation. A similar case occurs, e.g., on the ostracon from Meṣad Ḥashavyahu: *wyqṣr 'bdk wykl w'sm* (TSSI I,10,4-5), "and your servant reaped and measured, and intended storing".

54.9. The "converted" perfect is not alien to the prohibitive use of the stative in Old Babylonian, in Old Assyrian, and possibly in Sabaic. In Old Assyrian, the negative $ē < ay$ occurs with the stative (e.g. *ē naš'āti*, "you may not bring"), while the negative *lā* is used in Old Babylonian (e.g. *lā wašbat*, "she may not sit"). Sabaic inscriptions with juridical contents employ various prohibitive phrases with the negative *'l* and the stative/perfect, like *'l s¹'l*, "let nobody lay claim", *'l hs¹'l*, "let nobody forward a request". However, these phrases may be shortened forms of clauses in which the existential negative *'l* immediately precedes a noun in the construct state (e.g. *'l 's¹ s¹'l*, "let there be no man who laid claim") or a pronoun (e.g. *'l ḏ-s¹'l*, "let there be nobody who laid claim"). There are also formally declarative sentences in Sabaic with a prohibitive sense, like *w'l s³n hrg bnthw*, "and the killing of his own daughter is not lawful".

B. Parallel Clauses

55.1. There is a variety of ways in which sentences can be conjoined and embedded. The mechanism of conjoining sentences produces paratactic constructions on the surface, while their embedding by various devices is productive of hypotactic structures. One of the main traits of Semitic syntax is the preference given to paratactic or coordinate constructions over hypotactic or subordinate ones. E.g. the English hypotactically build sentence "I saw him **as** I was walking in the street" will be expressed by two parallel clauses in Arabic: *šuftuh(ū)* **wa-**'*anā rā'iḥ fī s-sikka(ti)*, "I saw him **and** I was walking in the street". To say that "the mother brings up her children **by** working" Harari uses a paratactic construction with *-ma* (§49.1): *āy tidälgi-**ma** wäldāč-zew tälīqat*, lit. "the mother works **and** brings up her children". By saying *tiṭṭam liddinam**ma** anāku lupuš*, "let him give me the clay **and** may I make (the mankind)", the Babylonian birth-goddess signifies: "let him give me the clay **so**

that I can make (it)". The parataxis can be either syndetic, like in the examples just mentioned with a copulative *wa-* or *-ma*, or asyndetic, i.e. without a conjunction connecting the parallel clauses, like in Ugaritic *rḥt[h] yml'u n'm rṯ ṯ['iṯ] yqrṣ dt b-pḫr*, "they filled [his] hands with the best m[uddy] clay so that he might knead that one in the assembly" (KTU 1.16,V,28-30). Asyndetic parataxis occurs similarly in Arabic *qatalū 'Abdallah(i) ḏabaḥūhu ḏabḥan*, "they killed Abdallah as they did really butcher him". Also in this case, the two substructures seem to be on a par with one another, like in the first Arabic example, since they are seemingly identical on the surface to their manifestation in isolation. Yet, the second clause (*ḏabaḥūhu...*) appears as some reduced version of the corresponding independent sentence "they really butchered Abdallah", because the pronominal suffix *-hu* is all that is left of the constituent otherwise manifested as *'Abdallah(i)*'s name. Therefore, the asyndetic parataxis hides, at least in this example, a complex conceptual structure in which the second clause is logically embedded as a constituent in the former. One should thus bear in mind, especially when dealing with parataxis, that the surface structure of a sentence represents only one facet of its syntactic organization. Every surface structure is derived from an underlying conceptual structure, which may imply subordination, also when the construction is paratactic.

55.2. Every language has syntactic reduction rules which, under certain conditions, allow constituents to be deleted from a sentence when identical constituents occur elsewhere within the same sentence. In Semitic languages, rules such as subject and object deletion are very common. When two or more parallel clauses have the same subject, the latter does not need to be repeated, being already represented by the actor affixes of the verbal forms; e.g. Babylonian *imērū ... ilūnim-ma... izzazzū*, "the donkeys ... came up and... they stand". The same applies to the direct object; e.g. Hebrew *wayyiqəḥū 'et-'aṣmōtēhem wayyiqbərū*, "and they took his bones and buried (them)". The reduction of duplicated elements thus eliminates a great deal of potential repetition without a loss of semantic content. However, reduction does not always mean full deletion, since a remnant is frequently left when a repeated constituent is erased. Oftentimes such a remnant, called a "pro form", is a suffixed pronoun, but there are numerous others as well. Thus, a pronominal suffix referring to the object is often attached to the second verb and eventually to the following ones. E.g., the pausal suffix pronoun *-ah* of the 3rd pers. fem. sing. is the placeholder for the accusative ḥubāsata, "injustice", in the following Arabic sentence: *fa-lam 'ara miṭlahā ḥubāsata wāḥidin wa-nahnahtu nafsī ba'da mā kidtu 'af'alah*, "Never have I seen someone's injustice like this, but I checked myself when I had nearly committed **it**".

55.3. The syndetic parataxis plays an important role in the Semitic "sequence of tenses". Thus, in Old Babylonian and occasionally in Old Assyrian a perfect *iptaras* may follow after a preterite *iprus* in a series of narrative forms; e.g. *kaspam aknukam* (preterite ventive) *-ma uštābilakkum* (perfect with a dative suffix), "I sealed the silver **and** I sent (it) to you". The choice of a perfect form for *uštābil-*, that follows after the preterite *aknuk-*, indicates not only that the action of "sending" is chronologically posterior to the one of "sealing", but probably that *uštābil-* expresses the immediate purpose of "sealing the silver", as well. However, this modal nuance does not appear everywhere and it is missing, e.g., in the following Late Babylonian relative clause where the same sequence of tenses occurs: *kī mimma ṭuppi u nēpešu ša anāku lā ašpurakkunušu u tātamrama* ..., "if any tablet or utensil, about which I myself didn't write to you but which you would have noticed (subsequently by yourself), ...". The use of the perfect in the second clause is nevertheless justified not only in consideration of the "sequence of tenses", but also as means of underlying the personal involvement of the subject (§38.4), a nuance expressed in the first clause by the emphatic use of the personal pronoun *anāku* (§50.12).

55.4. In West Semitic languages the imperfect *yqtl* may follow after the perfect *qtl* in a series of narrative clauses (cf. §38.11); e.g. Hebrew *hammayim gābərū* (perfect) *mə'od mə'od 'al-hā-'āreṣ wa-yəkussū* (imperfect) *kol-he-hārīm* (Gen. 7,19), "the waters increased more and more over the earth **and** all the mountains were covered". Here too, the imperfect *yəkussū* ("were covered") denotes an event chronologically posterior to the swelling (*gābərū*) of the waters, but it also expresses its immediate consequence. In Old Aramaic, the asyndetic parataxis with the old preterite (§38.11) in the first clause and the imperfect/jussive in the second one can express the consequence, e.g. *wyškb 'by yhk 'l*[...]*h*, lit. "and my father lay down, (so that) he would go to his [fate?]". The asyndetic parataxis occurs e.g. in Arabic *'inna zayannā s-samā'a ... lā yassama'ūna*, "indeed, we adorned the sky ... (so that) they should not listen" (Qur'ān 37, 6-8). The purpose is meant in the following syndetic sentence with a perfect followed by an imperfect: *kataba bi-ḏālika 'ilā*

Hišāmin wa-yasta'ḏinuhu fīhi, "he wrote about this to Hišām **and** he will ask him permission in the matter", i.e. "in order to ask him permission". However, the tense of the second clause does not need to be changed in Arabic when the conjunction *fa-* is used in comparable cases. In fact, *fa-* implies by itself that the second action results from the first one or follows after it; e.g. *ḍarabtuhū fa-bakā*, lit. "I beat him **and** he cried", i.e. "I beat him so that he cried". The same construction occurs after verbs of wishing and commanding, e.g. Arabic *'amarahu fa-faʿala*, lit. "he told him **and** he did (it)", i.e. "he told him to do (it)".

55.5. Parataxis can be used to express purpose or consequence also after an imperative or a nominal clause. Because the same surface structure corresponds to both conceptual structures, it is often difficult to see which of the two modalities is intended, e.g. in Babylonian *petā bābkā-ma lūruba anāku*, "open the door to me **and** may I enter"; Hebrew *šallaḥ 'et-ʿammī wə-yaʿabdunī*, "let my people go **and** they will worship me". In Arabic, one could also use an asyndetic object clause with the imperfect either apocopated or indicative; e.g. *qul ... yaġfirū(na)*, "tell... (that) they should forgive". The asyndetic construction was most likely the older one in Arabic. The consequence is intended, e.g., in Babylonian *ul qaqqaru qerbum-ma aḫūka isemmē-ma šulma išapparakku*, lit. "the ground-plot is not near **and** your brothers will hear **and** send you greetings", which means that "the ground-plot is not so near **that** ...". The content resulting from the choice of lexical items resolves the ambiguity. A similar case occurs, e.g., in Hebrew *lō' 'īš 'ēl wīkazzēb*, lit. "God is not a man **and** he will lie", which obviously means that "God is not a man **that** he should lie". The first clause is negative in both cases.

55.6. Formal parataxis expresses logical hypotaxis also in circumstantial clauses, either nominal or verbal. E.g. Hebrew *wayyābō' 'Elīšaʿ Dammeśeq ū-melek 'Arām hōle*, "Elisha came to Damascus **and** the king of Aram was ill", i.e. "when the king of Aram was ill". The preterite *īpuš-* is followed by the present-future *izakkar-* in the Old Babylonian sentence *pīšu īpušam-ma izakkaram ana* PN, "he opened his mouth **and** he was speaking to PN", i.e. "while he was speaking to PN" (cf. §55.1). Comparable cases can be found in Classical Arabic with a perfect followed by an indicative imperfect: *ḫaraǧa hāriban wa-'aṣḥābu l-qatīli yaṭlubūnahu*, "he went out fleeing **and** the companions of the killed (man) were searching for him", i.e. "while they were searching for him"; *'aqbalat 'īrun wa-naḥnu nuṣallī*, "a caravan approached **and** we were praying", i.e. "while we were praying".

55.7. Formal parataxis is used frequently to express logical hypotaxis in conditional sentences which often exhibit the protasis and the apodosis as parallel syndetic or asyndetic clauses. In Old Babylonian, as a rule, the present-future is used in both clauses, connected by the conjunction *-ma*; e.g. *tubbab-šunūti-ma aḫḫū-šunu ... išemmū*, "(if) you prove them clear, their brothers will hear (of it)". Instead, no conjunction is used in the following Hebrew example: *tiptaḥ yādəkā yiśbə'ūn ṭōb*, "(if) you open your hand, they will be satiated with goods". Conditional asyndetic clauses may occur in Arabic even with an imperative as protasis, e.g. *wa-d'u 'ibāda llāhi ya'tū(na) madadan*, "and (if you) call on the servants of God, they will come to help". The nature of such conditional sentences results from their context, but conditional particles may be used as well (§61.2-3). In both constructions, the protasis may be interpreted also as a temporal clause, and thus be translated with an introductory "when" instead of "if".

55.8. North Arabian inscriptions regularly use formal syndetic parataxis instead of relative clauses. They introduce the explicative verbal clause by the conjunction *w-*; e.g. Safaitic *l-S¹wd bn Mḥlm bn Rb'l w-r'y h'bl*, "(belonging) to Šuwādu, son of Muḥallimu, son of Rabb'il, who pastured these camels". There are also examples of a chain of such clauses; e.g. Safaitic *l-'d bn 'd w-wgd spr 'bh w-wlh kbr 'l 'bh w-'l ddh*, "(belonging) to 'Ōdu, son of 'Ōdu, who found the inscription of his father and was very much grieved on account of his father and on account of his uncle".

C. Subordinate Clauses

56.1. Subordinate clauses perform a function within a complex sentence. Semitic subordinate clauses belong to three categories: the relative clauses, the adverbial clauses, and the conditional clauses. The second category is generally subdivided in substantival or object clauses, in temporal clauses, in causal clauses, in final and consecutive clauses. However, there is no discernible correspondence between these conceptual structures and the surface structures which are not characterized by distinctive markers of subordinate clauses, other than the relative ones.

In the modern Ethiopian languages as Amharic and Tigrinya, the subordinate clauses are "encased" and precede the main clause. This structure result in long and complex periods, without adequate marks of segmentation and ponctuation. In the ordinary conversation, however, such complex structures are relatively rare.

56.2. The main Semitic subordinate conjunction is *k-* with a series of complex forms having that element as core. Now, *k-* is basically an asseverative particle (§48.11; 49.14) and its original function as marker of adverbial clauses was presentative, i.e. "indeed"; e.g. Sabaic *s²'r k-mhn h' ḥlṯhw*, "he knew indeed what was his malady". But the particle exercises manifold functions, — even in the same language, — and it may be strengthened by enclitics or constitute the core of complex forms.

56.3. As a rule, after verbs expressing perception or command, the subordinate clause introduced by *k-* is felt as a substantival or object clause; e.g. Ugaritic *td' ky 'rbt lpn špš*, "you may know that I entered into the presence of the Sun", i.e. of the Great King. The particle *ky* represents nothing in the conceptual structure underlying these two sentences, but it is inserted by a syntactic rule in order to formalize their link, to manifest their embedding in the surface structure. Other adverbial clauses may be broadly categorized as either temporal / causal, "when / because", — often with a perfective verbal form in the clause, — or final / consecutive, "in order that / so that", — usually with an imperfective verbal form in the adverbial clause.

56.4. In general, no morphological or syntactical feature allows distinguishing a causal clause from a temporal one, such distinction being mainly the result of our feeling. E.g. Moabite *wy'nw 't M'b ymn rbn ky y'np Kmš b'rṣh*, "and he had oppressed Moab many days, when Kamosh was angry with his land". Strictly speaking, *ky* might still be a presentative here ("... indeed, Kamosh was angry with his land"), but the preceding words "many days" (*ymn rbn*) support a temporal interpretation, although authors generally attribute a causal function to *ky* in the Mesha inscription.

56.5. Similarly, no morphological or syntactical peculiarities distinguish a final clause from a consecutive one. E.g. Arabic *'ismā ḥadīṯan ka-mā yawman yuḥaddiṯahū*, "listen to a story so that / in order that some day you may tell it". With a perfect in the adverbial clause, a final / consecutive interpretation is also possible, although a temporal function would suit *k-* better in such a case; e.g. Hebrew *lō'-'āśītī mə'ūmā kī śāmū 'otī babbōr*, "I had done nothing when they have / that they should have placed me in the dungeon" (Gen. 40,15).

56.6. Many allegedly adverbial clauses are governed by a noun or the determinative relative pronoun. Despite their usual interpretation as temporal / causal or final / consecutive clauses, from the syntactical point of view they ought to be regarded as relative clauses.

56.7. In South Ethiopic, strongly influenced by the Highland East Cushitic substratum and adstratum, the subordinate clause precedes the main verb; e.g. Muher (Gurage) *tawät bä-gäbba-gi deng^yä bä-färäz g^yäbbät yəgäbo*, "when the ark has entered (the church), the boys race on horses", lit. "(the-)ark when-it-has-entered (the-)boys on-horses a-race are-racing" ("when" is expressed by *bä* + perfect + *gi*).

56.8. In other Semitic languages, the subordinate clause may also precede the main one. This occurs generally with conditional sentences and often with temporal ones. There is an increasing tendency in these cases to connect the main clause with the preceding subordinate one by a conjunction, viz. *fa-* in Classical Arabic (e.g. *fa-lammā ra'aytu l-ḫayla...fa-ǧāšat 'ilayya n-nafsu*, "and when I saw the riders ..., the soul boiled in me"), *wa-* in Arabic colloquials (e.g. *wə-lammā əl-walad širib min əl-ibrīq wə-nizil əl-ǧirḏōn fī baṭnuh*, "and when the boy drank from the jug, the field mouse went down into his stomach"), in Hebrew (e.g. *bə-ṭerem yābō' ḥēbel lāh wə-himlīṭā zākār*, "before the onset of her labour she gave birth to a boy"), and in Aramaic (e.g. *wkzy ṣyd' 'bd 'nh tnh wb'tr' znh mštrh 'nh*, "and when I was hunting here, I was used to encamp in this place"). The main clause may be introduced also by "then", *'iḏ* or *'iḏā* in Arabic, *'āz* in Hebrew.

a) Relative Clauses

57.1. Semitic relative clauses are subjoining clauses which are linked to an antecedent substantive either asyndetically or by means of a determinative-relative pronoun which is generally used in apposition to a substantive, exactly as in the case of a periphrastic genitive (§51.19). Where there is no antecedent substantive, the pronominal antecedent has the value of "he who" / "what" (e.g. Ge'ez *za-mota*, "he who died"). The relative clause is syntactically equivalent to a genitive or a *nomen rectum*, while the nominal or pronominal antecedent exercises the function of a *nomen regens* (cf. §51.9).

57.2.   Semitic languages do not have any real relative pronoun. This is by no means an isolated case since relative pronouns are missing from many languages, even from Homeric Greek where they are still properly demonstratives. In the Semitic languages, their function may be attributed either to a determinative (e.g. Aramaic *zī / dī*) or indefinite pronoun (e.g. Arabic *man, mā*), or to a substantive in the construct state (e.g. Hebrew *'ăšer*), generally used in apposition to the logical antecedent which, in such cases, is in the absolute or determinate state. Other words may be used as well, e.g. Assyro-Babylonian *mala*, "as much as", "as many as": *mārū mala waldū*, "the children, as many as you have given birth to"; *kaspam mala ilaqqi'u*, "silver, as much as he is used to take".

57.3.   Relative clauses linked asyndetically to an antecedent substantive, like a *nomen rectum* is linked to the *nomen regens* in the construct state, represent the older usage of the Semitic languages and go back to Afro-Asiatic since this construction is currently used in Cushitic and in Libyco-Berber. In Somali, e.g., there are no words corresponding in their function to a relative pronoun and the antecedent is followed immediately by the dependent verbal clause; e.g. *wìilkíi yimí*, "the boy who came", to compare with *wìilkíi-bàa yimí*, "the boy came". The Libyco-Berber construction is similar, and no resumptive pronominal suffix is used in the relative clause, except when there is an Arabic influence, but a particle, either definite (*lli*) or indefinite (*nna*), may optionally determinate the antecedent; e.g. *a-kuray lli s* (with) *utġ a-srdun*, "the stick with (which) I struck the mule". This asyndetic construction is attested in Assyro-Babylonian, e.g. *bīt īpušu imqut*, "the house which he build, collapsed", where the construct state *bīt* is followed by the relative clause *īpušu* with the verb in the subjunctive like in any subordinate clause, while the verb *imqut* of the main clause stands at the end of the sentence. In Ugaritic, the same construction occurs, e.g. in KTU 1.15,II,22-23: *ġlmt tš'rb ḥtrk tld šb' bnm lk*, "the lass whom you introduce to your court, shall bear you seven sons". It is not frequent in Hebrew, but one finds it, e.g., in *'ereṣ lō' lāhem*, "the land which does not belong to them", with the construct state *'ereṣ* followed by a nominal asyndetical relative clause. It occurs in Gen. 1,1 when the Masoretic vocalization *bərē'šīt* of the construct state is followed, contrary to the Samaritan reading *bará'šīt* (§25.3), thus: "in the beginning of God's creating heaven and earth". In Arabic, this construction occurs fre- quently with an antecedent in the construct state, i.e. without definite article; e.g. *marrat(u) bi-raǧul(i) 'abūh(u) nā'im(un)*, "I passed by the man whose father was asleep". In this case, the relative clause is a nom- inal one, with a resumptive pronominal suffix attached to its subject and referring to the antecedent *raǧuli*. The same usage is widely attested in North Arabian and in Epigraphic South Arabian; e.g. Safaitic *s¹nt ngy qṣr h-mdnt*, "(in) the year (in which) he has rescued the compound of the province"; *s¹nt b'yt Ḥwlt M'ṣ*, "(in) the year (in which) Ḥawlat has overcome Ma'aṣ"; Minaic *b-kbwdt dyns¹ 'ttr*, "from the taxes which 'Attar laid upon him". However, one finds a suffixed antecedent as well; e.g. Safaic *w-wgm 'l 'bh qtl*, "and he mourned for his father who was killed". In Ge'ez, this construction is restricted mainly to short non- verbal clauses; e.g. *bə'si səmu Yoḥannəs*, "a man whose name is/was John". Nevertheless, it occurs also in verbal sentences; e.g. *'atfə' šəgā 'amə'ataka* (I En. 84,6), "exterminate the flesh which exasperated you".

57.4. Instead of a construct noun, a mimated antecedent substantive may be linked asyndetically in Sabaic and in Qatabanic; e.g. Sabaic *'hgrm w-'bḍ'm gn' w-hfṭn … l-'lmqh wl S²b'*, "towns and territories which he walled and assigned to Almaqah (or Ilmuqah) and to Saba"; Qatabanic *b-ḍrm tns²' Yd''l*, "in a war which Yada''el waged". Like- wise, a nunated antecedent may be linked asyndetically to a relative clause in Classical and modern literary Arabic; e.g. *raǧulun qad ḍara- banī*, "a man that has beaten me"; *'anā raǧulun lā māla lī*, "I am a man who has money". Indefinite antecedents in the absolute state might appear also in Hebrew, in Deut. 32,17, if we change the vocalization: *yizbəḥū *lə-Šaddayīm lo' 'ĕlōᵃh 'ĕlohīm lo' yədā'ūm*, "they sacrificed to Shaddayīm that are not a god, (to) gods which they do not know". This use of the absolute state has a clearly defined grammatical function: it distinguishes the indeterminate antecedent from the determinate one which is characterized by its construct state. A syntactically different sit- uation occurs in Arabic when the head of an asyndetical relative clause denotes a category and has a definite article which, accordingly, is said to be used *li-ta'rīfi l-ǧins*, "for the definiteness of the category"; e.g. *'anta l-wazīru lā yu'ṣā*, lit. "you are the vizier whom one does not defy", i.e. "you are the kind of vizier whom …". In such sentences, the definite article bears on the whole clause *wazīru lā yu'ṣā*, and not on the sole noun *wazīru* which can be considered as construct. This interpretation may be applied also to cases in Hebrew where nouns with the definite article would be linked asyndetically with a relative clause. If the texts in question are not corrupt, the same explanation ought to be proposed; e.g. *'ayyē **hā***'*ēder nittan lāk* (Jer. 13,20), "Where is the flock which was entrusted to you?". In such a case, the definite article refers to the whole clause *'ēder nittan lāk*, and not to the sole noun *'ēder* which should be analyzed as a construct.

57.5. Relative clauses may be introduced in Assyro-Babylonian, in Hebrew, in Epigraphic South Arabian, and probably in Ge'ez, by a substantive in the construct state which acts as a pro form for the real antecedent. In Assyro-Babylonian, the construct state *ašar* of the noun *ašru* (< *aṯru), "place", is thus used in cases in which the antecedent designates a place; e.g. *eqelšu... **ašar** tattadnu lū nadin*, "may his field..., which you have given, be given"; *imtaši **ašar** iwwaldu*, "he forgot where he was born". The same substantive *'ăšer* was employed in Hebrew in analogous circumstances; e.g. *hā'āreṣ **'ăšer** yāṣā'tā miššām*, "the land from which you came out", lit. "the land: place you came out from there"; *habbayit **'ăšer** bānītī*, "the house which I build", lit. "the house: place I build". A peculiar feature of the Masoretes consists in vocalizing the synonymous antecedent *māqōm* as a construct state as well; e.g. *məqōm **'ăšer** 'ăsīrē hammelek 'ăsūrīm*, "the place where the king's prisoners were imprisoned". Since the word *'šr < 'ṯr* was fallen out of the usage in Hebrew as a substantive, its construct state became a generalized "relative pronoun" introducing any relative clause regardless of its antecedent; e.g. *hayyōm **'ăšer** nātan Yhwh*, "the day which Yahwe gave". Neo-Assyrian also uses the construct state *bēt* of *bētu*, "house", to introduce relative clauses; e.g. *ina libbi bēt abīka **bēt** atta kammusākāni*, "in the midst of your father's house where you yourself are living". In Sabaic, the word *brṯ*, attested as a substantive meaning "place", may function in the construct state as a relative pronoun in the sense "where"; e.g. *hqdmw brdnn **brṯ** ydnn 'rbn*, "they sent the courier (to the place) where the Bedouin will submit". Similarly, the Sabaic construct state *ywm, ym*, "day", and Babylonian *ūm* may be followed by a relative clause; e.g. Babylonian *ūm PN išpuram ... uštābil*, "as soon as PN wrote to me,... I sent (it)"; Sabaic *ym s¹tyf' T'lb*, "when Ta'lab has declared his will" (cf. §58.14). The oldest, so far, attestation of this construction is encountered at Ebla where the noun "day" (u_4-*bu*; §11.6) introduces a subordinate clause with the verb in the subjunctive:

qu_6-*ra-dum* ᵈUTU u_4-*bu* AN.AN *ti-da-ḫu-ru*$_{12}$ (/*tidaḫḫulu*/), "the heroic Sun-goddess, when she enters upon the skies". It can be preceded by a preposition, e.g. in order to signify "since" or "after", as in *áš-tù-ma* U$_4$ IN.NA.SUM, "since/after he has given". Because of the noun "day", these relative clauses have a temporal connotation. In Geʿez, a word *ḫaba* or *ḫabba*, probably related to Sabaic *ḫbb*, "recess$^{(?)}$", and to Ugaritic *ḫabbu* that qualifies ground-plots, functions as a relative pronoun with nouns of place, which may be omitted; e.g. *makān* **ḫab(b)a** *nabarku*, "the place where I sat down", or *'i-rakaba* **ḫab(b)a** *nabarna*, "he did not find where we had settled". The final *-a* of *ḫab(b)a* is the ending *-a* of the construct state in Geʿez (§33.4).

57.6. Most relative clauses are introduced by the determinative-relative pronoun. The pronoun *ṯū*, written *šu*, is fully inflected in Palaeosyrian and in Old Akkadian (§36.48). Its nominative form introduces relative clauses, e.g., in Palaeosyrian PNs **šu** *sí-kà-tim tim-ḫa-ṣú*, "PNs who have driven the nails", and in Old Akkadian *ḫu-bu-lum* **šu** *al* PN *i-ba-šè-ù*, "the debt which is upon PN". The accusative or "absolute" (§32.6) form *ša* was used later for all cases, numbers, and genders; e.g. Old Babylonian *ana māriša ša irammu*, "for her son whom she loves". The same pronoun is attested with various vocalizations in Phoenician, Punic, and Mishnaic Hebrew (§36.51); e.g. Punic *'bn* **'š** *ṭ'n l*-PN, "the stone which was erected for PN"; Hebrew *hkhn ... š 'śh hpsypws*, "the priest... who made the mosaic". The determinative-relative *ḏū* (§36.50) is used in Ugaritic; e.g. *w mnm rgm d tšm'*, "and every rumour which you hear" (KTU 2.10,16-17). In Epigraphic South Arabian, it is either declinable or indeclinable without gender and number differentiation; e.g. Sabaic *hqnythw* **ḏ**-*s²fthw*, "his offering which he had promised him". Its originally genitive form *ḏī* > *dī* is typical of the Aramaic; e.g. *nṣb' zy šm Br-Hdd*, "the stele which Bar-Hadad placed"; *kə-ḥokmat 'ĕlāhāk* **dī** *bīdāk*, "according to your God's wisdom which is in your hand" (Esd. 7,25). In Pre-Classical Arabic, the nominative form *ḏū* was used in some dialects for all numbers, genders, and cases, but it was inflected partly in other idioms, as shown by the Ḥegrā' inscription from 267 A.D. (§7.38): *mn y'yr* **ḏ'** *'ly mnh* /*man yuġayyir* **ḏā**(*t*) *'aliya minhu*/, "whoever changes what is above it". In Ṣafaitic, the constant spelling is *ḏ*; e.g. *w-wgd sfr M'r ḏ 'wq*, "and he found the inscription of Mō'aru, who was imprisoned". The relative pronoun in Classical Arabic is the expanded demonstrative *'allaḏī* (§36.53); e.g. *'al-raǧulu* **llaḏī** *ša'ru 'abyaḍ*, "the man whose hair is white". The common colloquial *allī, illī,* *əlli*, etc., is no reduced form of *'alladī* (§36.53), but a direct derivative of the base **'allay* of the plural demonstrative *'ul(l)ā, 'ul(l)ā'i*, "these", which could be used in Classical Arabic for the singular according to the grammarians; e.g. colloquial *əl-kitāb* **illī** *kətəbtuh*, "the book which I wrote". The originally oblique case *za-* of the pronoun is used in Geʿez; e.g. *bə'si* **za**-*maṣ'a*, "the man who came".

The Libyco-Berber inflected determinative *wa* cannot be used in the same way as the Semitic determinative-relative; e.g. Tuareg *aret wa d-ewəya*, "the thing (that) I-brought-here", where *wa* does correspond to a definite article and not to a relative pronoun.

57.7. The indefinite-interrogative pronouns *man*, "who", *mā*, "what", and their derivatives (§36.57-62), may also be used to introduce relative clauses. This usage is well-known from Arabic (e.g. *'allama l-'insāna* **mā** *lam yaʿlam*, "he taught people what they did not know"), and it is already attested in Old Akkadian; e.g. **mammāna** *ṣalmam šu(w)a (y)u(w)aḫḫaru*, "whoever removes this statue". Many examples occur later in Assyro-Babylonian with *mimma*, but the Neo-Babylonian use of *mannu* without *ša* (e.g. *manna atta*, "however you are") is probably influenced by Early Aramaic, e.g. **mn** *yld šmy*, "whoever removes my name".

57.8. No peculiar features characterize relative clauses when their antecedent is the subject of the relative clause; e.g. Babylonian *aššat awīlim ša zikaram lā īdū*, "a citizen's wife who has not known a man"; Arabic *raǧulu ǧā'a*, "the man who came". However, a pronominal suffix in the relative clause refers back to the antecedent when the latter is either the direct object of the verb of the relative clause, or a *nomen rectum* governed by a noun in the relative clause. The resumptive pronoun is obligatory, if the antecedent is governed by a noun or a preposition; e.g. Babylonian *Ninlil ummum rabītum ša qibissa ... kabtat*, "Ninlil, the great mother whose word (*qibit-ša*) carries weight"; Hebrew *ḥastā 'al haqqīqāyōn 'ăšer lo'-'āmaltā bō*, "you had pity on the ricinus, for which you have not laboured"; Geʿez *bə'si za-qataləwwo la-waldu*, "the man whose son they killed". When the antecedent is the direct object of the verb in the relative clause, the resumptive pronoun is optional; e.g. Babylonian *eleppam ... ša ummidū-ši-ma ... libnātim izbilu*, "the ship which they put ashore and ... loaded with bricks", where the pronominal suffix is attached only to the first verb; Arabic *'ar-raǧulu lladī ḍarab-tuhū*, "the man whom I have beaten", with the resumptive pronoun, but

Hebrew *haḥălōm hazze 'ăšer ḥālāmtī*, "this dream which I have dreamed", without such a pronoun.

57.9. Under the influence of the Highland East Cushitic substratum, the relative clause precedes the qualified noun in South Ethiopic (§56.7) and this position is sufficient to indicate its subordinate nature; e.g. Muher (Gurage) *bä-gʷa yənäbrəmʷ säb äḫi yəzärämʷət*, "people who live in the highland sow cereals", lit. "in-(the-)highland who-live people cereals sow". This construction occurs also in North Ethiopic; e.g. Tigrinya *zə-qʷädälä fəqru*, "the love that died off". The main difference consists in the South Ethiopic use of the palatalized preposition *yä-* < *lä-* to introduce the relative clause, assimilated to a prepositional phrase with *l-* (§51.23); e.g. Amharic **yä-*mäṭṭa-w säwəyye wändəmme näw*, "the man who came is my brother", lit. "who-came-the (the)-man my-brother is".

b) Temporal / Causal Clauses

58.1. Various subordinate conjunctions are governing temporal / causal clauses. In reality, these conjunctions are either prepositions followed by a relative clause, comparable to a genitive (§51.26; 58.10-11,14-16), or adverbs of time (§58.12-13), or nouns followed by an asyndetic relative clause (§58.9), or lastly combinations of a preposition with a noun (§58.14,16) or a determinative-relative pronoun (§58.14-15). In other words, the surface structure of the temporal / causal clauses does not constitute any particular syntactical category in the Semitic languages. These clauses denote time inasmuch as the prepositions, the nouns, or the adverbs introducing them have temporal connotations. As for their causal interpretation, it is based mainly on the context and on the conceptual structure we attribute to the complex sentence.

58.2. The main temporal / causal conjunction is the preposition or rather deictic particle *k-*, with a series of complex forms having that element as core (§56.2). Again, *k-* has no independent semantic content, but the conceptual structure effecting its insertion into the surface structure endows it with a particular function. It occurs frequently in Old Akkadian and in Assyro-Babylonian as *kī* or *kīma*, "as", "when", *kī* being interpreted also as a causal conjunction in Middle and Late Babylonian texts; e.g. *kī ašmū taqabbi* …, "as I heard, you were telling …". The same conjunction is widely used in Ugaritic (*k-*, *ky*), in Hebrew (*kī*), in Phoenician and Punic (*k-*), in Moabite (*ky*), in Aramaic (*ky*), in Arabic (*ka-*, *kay-*), in South Arabian (*k-*), and in Ethiopic; e.g. Tigre *'ət 'Adigrat kəm baṣḥaka salf mi wadeka*, "when you arrived at Adigrat, what did you do first?". The temporal function of the conjunction is well represented in "Canaanite" languages; e.g. Hebrew *kī-bā'nū 'el hammālōn*, "when we entered the dormitory"; Phoenician *k-bn Bd'štrt... 'yt šrn*, "when Bodashtart has build... the esplanade". Its temporal or causal function appears clearly, e.g., in the Moabite Mesha inscription (cf. §56.4) and in the stereotyped Phoenician and Punic formula *k-šmʿ ql('),* "when / because he has listened to his voice", but *kay*, *kay-mā*, and *ka-mā* are used in Arabic to express purpose or consequence with the subordinate verb in the subjunctive or the indicative imperfect (§59.4).

58.3. Some obscurity surrounds the conjunction *lammā*, "when", which in standard Arabic usage implies anteriority of the subordinate clause to the main sentence, and not simultaneity, and therefore means "after (that)"; e.g. *lammā ramatnī 'aqṣadatnī bi-sahmihī*, "when she shot at me, she hit me with her arrow". In Assyro-Babylonian, instead, *lāma* implies posteriority of the subordinate clause to the main one, and in consequence means "before" or "lest"; e.g. *lāma ṣābum ... ikaššadam* (imperfective) *māssu ṣallat*, "lest troops ... arrive, his land was quiet". The conjunction seems to occur with the same meaning in Ugaritic, in Old Canaanite, in Hebrew, in Phoenician, and in Punic; e.g. Ugaritic *'išttk lm ttkn* (KTU 1.12,II,57), "I have installed you lest you assert yourself"; Old Canaanite *palḥati anāku lāmi udāka*, "I am afraid lest I be killed" (EA 131,27-28); Hebrew *šalləḥinī lāmā 'ămītēk*, "send me away before I kill you"; Phoenician *'l yš' 'yt ḥlt mškby lm ysgrnm 'lnm hqdšm 'l* (TSSI III, 28,21-22), "they should not lift up the sarcophagus of my couch, lest these holy gods deliver them up"; Punic *'š ndr* PN *lm yʿms 'm Qrtḥdšt*, "what PN dedicated, lest the people of Carthage carries (him) away". We might either suppose that we have to do with different conjunctions or look for an explanation of this apparent contradiction in the tenses used by the various languages in the temporal clause. The first solution seems the best. Thus, one conjunction derives from the augmented negative *lā-ma/mi*, "not yet" (§58.4,6). The other one is based on the preposition *l-* used temporally or causally and enlarged by the addition of *-amma* (§58.5,7-8). And there is a third conjunction with the preposition *l-* followed by the indefinite pronoun *mā*, "for what", hence "why?" in an interrogative sentence, as Ugaritic *lm*, Arabic *lima*, and Hebrew *lāmā*; e.g. Hebrew *lāmā 'ăzabtānī* (Ps. 22,2), "why did you forsake me?".

58.4. Old Akkadian and Old Babylonian use the negative *lā-ma*, "not yet"; e.g. *lāma ikkanik*, "it was not yet sealed". The same negative is widely employed in Arabic with the apocopate; e.g. *lammā ya'ti*, "he didn't yet come" / "before he comes"; *lammā yamut*, "he wasn't yet dead" / "before he dies". In Assyro-Babylonian, this adverb became a preposition "before" (e.g. *lāmika*, "before you"), as well as a conjunction (§58.3). A parallel development seems to have taken place in Ugaritic, in Old Canaanite, in Phoenician, and in Hebrew (§58.3); e.g. *sūr ləkā mē'aḥărāy lāmmā 'akkekkā 'arṣāh*, "for your sake stop following me before / lest I smite you to the ground" (II Sam. 2,22).

58.5. The Arabic conjunction *lammā* frequently has a causal connotation which may be original, since the particle borrowed into Late Biblical Hebrew already implies this nuance: *kī **lm** bā-ri'šōnā lo' 'attem pāraṣ Yhwh 'ĕlohēnū bānū*, "For, **since** you were not (present) the first time, Yahwe our God broke out upon us" (I Chr. 15,13). In Arabic, this causal feature appears clearly, e.g. *fa-lammā 'ayqanū bil-halakati sa'alūhu 'an yusayyirahum*, "and since they were convinced of the danger, they asked him to free them". It also colours the following Neo-Arabic example (9th century A.D.) where *lammā* introduces durative *kān* with the imperfect (§38.20): *fa-lammā kunnā naḏhab 'ilā bayt 'aṣ-ṣalāḥ ṣārafnā* (Act. 16,16), "and as we were going to the prayer house, we met".

58.6. The first conjunction, used likewise with the perfect, is attested in Arabic as well (cf. §58.4), but might have been pronounced once in a different way (*lā-ma, lā-mā?*). In Syrian colloquial, e.g., the *lammā* of the following sentence can only mean "before": *lammā ridnā nəsäfir dafa'nā*, "before we set out upon the journey, we paid". In the "Thousand and One Nights" I,263,3, one reads *fa-lammā kāna ṣ-ṣubḥu qarubnā min-a l-ǧabali*, where *lammā* may also mean "before": "and before it was daylight, we got close to the mountain". Both interpretations are perhaps possible in some classical texts, e.g. *fa-lammā kānat sanatu ṯamānin waǧǧaha rasūlu llāhi l-'Alā'a 'ilā l-Ǧayrūni*, "and before/when the eighth year came, God's messenger sent 'Alā' to Djayrūn". We might even assume that this construction occurs also in Pre-Classical Arabic; e.g. *'uqsimu 'alayka lammā fa'alta ḏālika*, "I adjure you before you do this", and *'as'alka lammā 'aḫbartanī*, "I implore you before you inform me", with the subordinate verbs in the perfect, and with a subordinate nominal clause in *'in kullu nafsin lammā* *'alayhi ḥāfiẓun*, "there was not a soul before there was a guardian (looking) after her".

58.7. If this interpretation is correct, a clear distinction should be made between *lammā* < *lā-ma*, "not yet" > "before" (§58.3-4,6), *lammā* < *la-mā*, "for what (purpose)", which corresponds exactly to Old Egyptian *r m*, and *lammā*, "when", "after", "since", which is the preposition *l-* used temporally or causally (§48.6) with a suffixed *-m* in Arabic (§58.3,5,8) and a suffixed *-n* in South-Arabian (§48.9); e.g. Sabaic *ln s¹tyfʻ*, "when he has declared his will", parallel with *ym s¹tyfʻ*, "on the day that he has declared his will" (cf. §57.5).

58.8. The conjunction *lammā* is frequently strengthened in Arabic by the particle *'an* (§60.2); e.g. *fa-lammā 'an taḥammala 'ālu Laylā*, "and when Layla's family set out". The two particles are contracted into *lammān* in various dialects; e.g. *lammān eṣ-ṣulṭān 'arā*, "when the sultan saw".

58.9. An excellent example of a noun governing temporal clauses is provided by the frequent Assyro-Babylonian conjunction *inūma / enūma*, "when", which corresponds to Old Akkadian *īnu*. Now, *īnu(m)* is originally a noun "time", as best evidenced by *i-nu ᵈNa-ra-am-ᵈEN.ZU da-nim*, "at the time of Narām-Sîn, the mighty". This noun is identical with Arabic *ḥīn(un)*, "time", the adverbial accusative of which, *ḥīna*, may introduce a relative clause in Classical Arabic; e.g. *'aḥṭa'ahu sahmī ḥīna ramaytu*, "my arrow missed him when I shot". In post-classical language, the enclitic *-mā* is often added to the noun, *ḥīna-mā*, exactly like *-ma* is suffixed to *īnu* in Assyro-Babylonian *inūma*; e.g. Old Babylonian *inūma ītaplūninni* (perfect)... *ašapparakkim*, "when they will have paid me, I shall write to you"; Arabic *ḥīnamā hum yaz'umūna*, "while they themselves are claiming". The enclitic *-ma / -mā* must not be regarded as a conjunction, not even as an adverbial morpheme, but probably as a mark of construct noun, similar to the enclitic *-ma* attached mainly to monosyllabic nominal roots in the construct state (§33.16).

58.10. *Ištu, uštu, ultu, issi*, etc., "after", "since", is another East Semitic conjunction widely used to introduce subordinate temporal and causal clauses, either nominal or verbal, with the verb in the subjunctive of the stative, perfect, preterite, or present-future, e.g. Old Babylonian *ištu mārīša urtabbū* (perfect)... *inaddinū-šim*, "after she will have brought up her sons, they shall give her…". Now, this subordinate conjunction isn't anything but the Semitic preposition "with", "from", originally *'*ṯṯ* / *wṯṯ* (§48.18). Instead of governing only nouns in the genitive, it may also introduce relative clauses in Palaeosyrian (§57.5), in Old Akkadian, and in Assyro-Babylonian. In the first millennium B.C., it is often replaced by *issi bēt* or *issi mar* (< *mala*?) in Neo-Assyrian (cf. §57.2,5), followed by a relative clause in the subjunctive; e.g. *issi bēt pān* PN *iḫliqanni*, "since he fled to PN".

58.11. We find a comparable situation in the case of other East Semitic temporal conjunctions as *adi* or *qadu(m)*, both of which are prepositions: *adi*, "until", "as long as", *qadu(m)*, "faced with", "alongside" (§48.17,23). These prepositions are used in various Semitic languages to introduce subordinate temporal clauses; e.g. Late Babylonian **adi** *muḫḫi* PN *ana ṭubšarrē ša šarri iqabbūma*, "until PN will speak to the king's scribes"; **adi lā** *ana gizzi allaka šupraš*, "so long as I do not come for the sheepshearing, send him to me"; Ugaritic '*d tšb' tmtḫṣ b-bt*, "until she was sated, she fought in the house" (KTU 1.3,II,29); Ge'ez *'i-hallona 'əm-**qədma** yəftərana*, "we did not exist till he created us".

58.12. Several other prepositions govern temporal clauses, some of which are attested in only one or two languages. E.g. the Arabic conjunction *'iḏ* or *'iḏā*, "when", is also an adverb, identical with Hebrew *'āz*, *'əzay*, "then". Even if it introduces a verbal clause, — e.g. *'innī la-'indahum* **'iḏ** *'aqbala 'īrun*, "I was with them when a caravan approached", — in reality it remains an adverb: "I was with them: then a caravan approached". The same use of *'ḏ* is attested in Sabaic; e.g. *'l hwfyhw mṭrdhw b-ḏ-Mwṣb^m* **'ḏ** *ṯ'nw l-Yṯl*, "they didn't offer him his game in (the month of) *ḏū-Mwṣb^m*, when they moved to Yaṯil". Also Hebrew *'āz* may be used as conjunction; e.g. *hălō'… 'āśā mišpāṭ ū-ṣədāqā **'āz** ṭōb lō*, "Wasn't he doing justice and right when it was going well for him?".

58.13. Several other nouns, used as adverbs, appear also as temporal conjunctions. Babylonian *warka* and *warki*, "after (that)", are, respectively, the substantive *warku(m)*, "back", "rear" — in the adverbial accusative *warka* — and the adjective *warkiyu(m)*, "later"; both are employed adverbially with the same meaning "afterwards" and both occur as conjunctions; e.g. *warka abum ana šīmtim ittalku … ul izāz*, "after the father has gone to (his) fate, … he shall not share". Also

Ugaritic *'aḫr*, "afterwards", derives from a noun meaning "rear", "posterity", or the like, and it is used as a temporal conjunction "after (that)"; e.g. *'aḫr mġy Ktr-w-Ḫss št 'alp qdmh* (KTU 1.4,V, 44-45), "after Kotar-and-Ḫasis did arrive, they did set an ox before him". The same use of *'aḥar* is attested in Hebrew; e.g. *'aḥar dibber Yhwh ... 'el-'Iyyōb wayyo'mer...*, "after Yahwe had spoken ... to Job, he said ...".

58.14.   Another group of temporal conjunctions consists of prepositions governing either a noun or the determinative-relative pronoun. Thus Old Assyrian *inūmi* is not related to *inūma* (§58.9), but results from the contraction of *in(a) ūmi*, "on the day that"; e.g. *inūmi mer'assu mētatni ... ušēbil*, "when his daughter was dead, I sent ...". Various prepositional phrases are used in Hebrew as temporal conjunctions: *'ad 'ăšer*, "until", *'aḥărē 'ăšer*, "after (that)", *ka-'ăšer*, "when", *bə-ṭerem*, "before (that)". The preposition always governs a noun in the construct state which is followed in reality by a relative asyndetic clause. In Aramaic, instead, the preposition governs the determinative-relative pronoun *dī*, e.g. *'ad dī*, "until"; *min dī*, "after (that)"; *kə-dī*, "when"; e.g. Syriac *kad* (< *kə-dī*) *šəma' (hă)wā 'Abgar henēn hālēn*, "when Abgar heard these things". The same usage is attested in Assyro-Babylonian by *ana ša >ašša*, "as soon as", and also in Phoenician as shown by the Punic example *'ḥr 'š*, "after (that)". The temporal clauses thus introduced are formally relative clauses governed by a determinative-relative pronoun or by a noun in the construct state. E.g. Old Assyrian *ana ša lā ḫabbulākū-šunni-ma kaspam ilqi'u ṣabtā-šu*, "as soon as I am no longer his debtor and as he has taken the silver, seize him!"; Hebrew *bə-ṭerem yiqrab 'ălēhem wayyitnakkəlū 'otō la-hămītō*, "before he came near unto them, they plotted against him to kill him" (Gen. 37,18); Aramaic *'ad dī 'iddānā' yištannē'*, "until the time changes" (Dan. 2,9).

58.15.   The same usage persists in Neo-Aramaic which employs various compound conjunctions, always with the determinative-relative *d-*. The main conjunctions governing a subordinate temporal clause are *'dāna d- > 'dant*, "when", lit. "at the time (*'edānā*) that"; *mən bā(t)r d- > mbār d-*, "after (that)", lit. "from behind that"; *hal d-*, "till"; *mən d-*, "since"; *qa(d)m d-*, "before"; *ka-d*, "while", "when". E.g. *kad mšīḥā mūqīminnē*, "when the Messias resuscitated me". Other conjunctions govern a causal clause: *sābāb d-*, "because", borrowed from Arabic *bi-sababi*, "on account of"; *čunkē d-*, "because", "as", borrowed from Persian.

58.16. Babylonian frequently uses a special causal conjunction *aššu(m)*, "because"; e.g. *tamkārum aššum šamallāšu ikkiru ... inaddin*, "the merchant, because he has called his agent in question, shall give ...". The Old Assyrian form *aššumi* clearly indicates that the conjunction derives from *ana šumi > an-šumi > aššumi*, lit. "in the name of", and that the subordinate clause is a relative asyndetic sentence governed by the noun *šumi* in the genitive of the construct state. An identical use of the noun *sem*, "name", occurs in Ge'ez where the subordinate conjunction *'əsma*, "because", derives from *'əm*, "from", and *sema*, "name" in the construct state, i.e. "from the name of". As for the Neo-Assyrian conjunction *nēmel*, "since", "because", it is the construct state of a noun meaning "profit" and followed by an asyndetic relative clause.

c) Final / Consecutive Clauses

59.1. A final / consecutive clause can generally be distinguished from a temporal / causal clause by the use of an imperfective verbal form. E.g. the Sabaic conjunction *b-k-n* used with the perfect means "when / because", but employed with the imperfect signifies "so that / in order that"; e.g. *bkn mt'hw*, "when he had delivered him", but *bkn yfqln*, "so that he may gather the crops". Also the simple conjunction *kī* may introduce a final / consecutive clause in Hebrew; e.g. *mā-'ĕnōš kī-tizkərennū*, "what is man in order that you should remember him?".

59.2. Ambivalence is found also in the Arabic subordinate conjunction *ḥattā*, "until", "so that", which is a preposition with the temporal sense "until" or with the local meaning "as far as"; e.g. *ḥattā l-mamāti*, "until the death"; *ḥattā l-baḥri*, "as far as the sea". *Ḥattā* may be used also as an adverb; e.g. *qad ǧā'a kullu n-nāsi ḥattā 'anta*, "everybody has come, even you". As conjunction introducing consecutive clauses *ḥatta* is employed in post-classical Arabic with the subjunctive, but the indicative is attested in the classical language, reflecting the adverbial origin of the word; e.g. *mariḍa ḥattā lā yarǧūnahū*, "he is so ill that they have no hope for him", lit. "he is ill: they don't even have a hope for him". The purely temporal function of *ḥattā* is attested as well, especially in the combination *ḥattā 'iḏā*; e.g. *ḥattā 'iḏā 'aṣbaḥat*, "at last when the day broke"; *fa-hum yūza'ūna ḥattā 'iḏā 'ataw 'alā wādī n-namli qālat namlatun* (Qur'ān 27,18), "thus did they hurry; at last when they reached the valley of the ants, an ant spoke".

59.3. The various Hebrew conjunctions considered as final or consecutive derive from nouns in the construct state, as *ʿăbūr, "effect", *maʿan, "intention", etc. The subordinate clauses thus introduced belong therefore to the category of asyndetic relative clauses. E.g. *tiqqaḥ miyyādī ba-ʿăbūr tihye-llī lə-ʿēdā* (Gen. 21,30), lit. "you should take (it) from my hands to the effect (that) it may become for me a token"; *nišmaʿ lə-maʿan ʾăšer yīṭab-lānū* (Jer. 42,6), lit. "we shall listen with the intention that it may be well with us". The particle *pen* is often considered as derived from the noun "face", but it is the conjunction *p-* strengthened by *-n* (§49.2). This is evident in the light of the parallel use of *pen* and of Arabic *fa-*; e.g. Hebrew *loʾ tiggəʿū bō* **pen**-*təmutūn* (Gen. 3,3), "you will not touch it, lest you die"; Arabic *lā taṭlub-i l-fasāda fī d-dunyā* **fa**-*takūna qad nasīta naṣībaka min-a l-ʾāḫirati*, "don't be in quest of evil in the world, lest you lose your share in the hereafter". In a few cases *pen* seems to be employed in the absolute beginning of the sentence, but another division of the text may give a different picture; e.g. *ʾēl qannā hūʾ* **pen**-*tikrot bərīt lə-yōšēb hā-ʾāreṣ* (Ex. 34,14-15), "he is a jealous god, lest you make a covenant with the inhabitant of the land".

59.4. In Arabic, final / consecutive clauses are often introduced by the simple prepositions *li-* and *kay*, or by a series of complex forms having these elements as core: *li-ʾan, kay-mā, ka-mā, li-kay, li-kay-mā*, "so that", "in order to". E.g. *fa-ltaqaṭahū ʾālu Firʿawna* **li**-*yakūna lahum ʿadūwan*, "Faraoh's people picked him up, so that he would become a foe to them" (Qurʾān 28,7/8); *wa-ʾašrikhu fī ʾamrī* **kay** *nusabbiḥaka kaṯiran*, "and let him participate in my business, so that we may praise you much"; *ḥāwalā* **li-kay** *yunzilāhā*, "they tried to get it out"; *ʾarādū* **li-kay-mā** *yastabīḥū qibābanā*, "they wanted to take possession of our tents". These particles are used with the subjunctive, which indicates the final / consecutive character of the clauses, but *kay-mā* and *ka-mā* were employed in the pre-classical language also with the imperfect of the indicative. This construction occurs already in Ṣafaitic, e.g. *w-trwḥ l-ys²rq l-mdbr*, "and he set out in the evening, so that he would go eastward into the desert". As said above, no morphological or syntactical feature allows discerning purpose from consequence; e.g. *yatūqu qalbī ʾilaykum* **kay** *yulāqiyakum*, "my heart aspires to you so that / in order that it may come to meet you".

59.5. Neo-Aramaic uses two conjunctions to introduce subordinate final or consecutive clauses: *qā d- > qat*, "in order to", "so that", and *d-lā*, "lest"; e.g. *qat māḫē l-dibā*, "in order to strike a bear"; *dlā* (*y*)*waḥ beḥzāyā*, "lest we see".

59.6. In North Ethiopic, *kama* (Geʿez), *kəm* (Tigre), and *kə* (Tigrinya) may introduce final / consecutive and substantival clauses. The particle *kə* is mostly used in Tigrinya to express purpose; e.g. *säʿamənni kəqʷərräṣu käbdom*, "kiss me, so that their belly would shrivel"; *yəfätəwū kizoru*, "they like to walk up and down".

d) Substantival Clauses

60.1. In most Semitic languages the conjunction *kī* may introduce substantival clauses after verbs which generally express command, perception, etc., the expanded form *kīma* being probably better attested than *kī* in East Semitic. These clauses may be either subject clauses or object clauses; e.g. the Hebrew subject clause *mabbeṣaʿ **kī** nahᵃrog ʾet-ʾāḥīnū*, "what profit is it that we kill our brother?", and the Middle Babylonian object clause *altapra **kī** qanū nadū*, "I wrote that the reed is laid out". Geʿez uses *kama* to introduce, e.g., the following subject clause: *ba-ʾəntazə taʿawwaqa **kama** Māryām walatta Dāwīt yəʾətī*, "in that way one recognized that Mary was the daughter of David". Similar clauses may be introduced in Tigre by *kəm*, with the conjunction generally placed immediately before the verb, and in Tigrinya by *käm* or *kämäzə*; e.g. Tigre *kaʾasʾalatto Kantebāy Ṣallim **kəm** ʾabdayom*, "then she told him that Kantebay Ṣallim had annihilated them"; Tigrinya *təʾämnu **käm** ʾäne ʾiye*, "believe that I am it" (John 13,19).

60.2. In Arabic, the conjunctions introducing substantival clauses are *ʾan* / *ʾanna* and *mā*. Now, *ʾan* is followed several times in the Qurʾān by a quotation; e.g. *ʾāḫiru daʿwahum **ʾan**-i l-ḥamdu li-llāhi*, "their last cry is thus: Praise be to God!" (Qurʾān 10,11/10; cf. 4,139/140; 27,8). This indicates that *ʾan*, from which *ʾanna* probably developed under certain conditions, goes back to the presentative **han*, "thus" (§49.6). The latter is already attested in Old Akkadian as *en-ma*, which became *umma* by assimilation, and it occurs in Ugaritic as *hn*, with unknown vocalization. Babylonian *anna*, Hebrew *hinnē*, and Classical Arabic *ʾinna* have the same origin. As for *mā*, it is the indefinite-interrogative pronoun "(that) what" (§36.58), which may be used also as a relative pronoun. Actually, substantival clauses introduced by *mā* are relative clauses; e.g. *šafā n-nafsa **mā** ḫubirtu Murrāna ʾuzhifat*, lit. "it healed the soul, what I got to know: Murrana was exhausted".

60.3.   Relative clauses are used as substantival clauses also in other
Semitic languages. In Assyro-Babylonian, the determinative-relative
pronoun *ša* may introduce such a clause; e.g. *tammar ša … lā errubu*,
"you will see that he will not enter". In Hebrew, *'ăšer* can be used to the
same purpose; e.g. *higgīd lāhem 'ăšer hū' Yəhūdī*, "he had told them
that he was a Jew". In Tigrinya, the determinative-relative *zə* may govern substantival clauses, e.g. the following object clause: *mäsälätom
zebəzəhu məwsad*, "it seemed to them that they will receive something
extra". A similar use of *dī, də* occurs in Aramaic, e.g. *yədī' lehwē'-lāk
malkā **dī** lē'lāhāyk lā-'ītaynā pālḥīn*, "be it known to you, O king, that
we are not serving your god" (Dan. 3,18). This usage continues in
Neo-Aramaic, mostly with object clauses; e.g. *gelā ğūweblē d-'am buta
d-miḥāğē ḥōra (h)wī īwen (h)wā*, "the grass replied that it had been
friendly with a cluster of pinks".

e) Conditional Clauses

61.1.   Conditional sentences usually comprise two clauses: the protasis
and the apodosis. The apodosis, if self evident, may be omitted, especially for the expression of a hope or wish, as Arabic *'in ra'ā l-maliku
'an yaf'ala*, "if (only) the king would see fit to do (so)", Ge'ez *'əm-
nassāḥku*, "if (only) I had repented!". As a rule, the apodosis is omitted
when it should contain a formula of imprecation, like in oaths (§61.4-5).
The paratactic construction, either syndetic or asyndetic, is used frequently for conditional sentences (§55.7), but the protasis can also be
introduced by a particle. Besides the specifically conditional conjunctions (§61.2), also the temporal particle *kī* can be used, especially in
Neo-Babylonian, in Late Babylonian, and in Biblical Hebrew.

61.2.   At first sight, there is a great variety in the particles used by
Semitic languages to express real conditions. Actually, the specific conjunctions go all back to a Proto-Semitic morpheme *š / h*, used also for
the personal pronouns of the third person (§36.10,20) and for the
causative stem of the verb (§41.11), and to an enclitic *-m / -n*, diversified
phonetically for reasons which were originally dialectal. The following
scheme shows the evolution of the conditional particle:

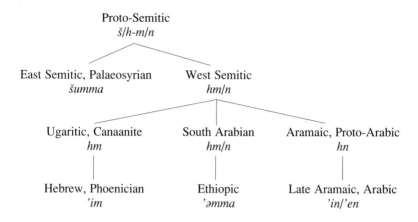

The vowel *u* of the first morpheme in East Semitic and in Palaeo-syrian results from the rounding of the original *i* under influence of following *m* (§27.10). As for the *a* of the conditional particle *ham* in Mehri and *'am* in Ḥarsūsi, it should be explained by the vowel harmony which occurred in **himmā > *hammā* and *'immā > 'ammā*. The latter form is preserved in Pre-Classical and Classical Arabic where it appears as a variant of *'immā*, "if", in formally nominal clauses which are followed by a verbal clause introduced by *fa-*; e.g. *fa-'ammā l-yatīma fa-lā taḥqar* (Qur'ān 93,9), "and if it is an orphan, do not wrong!"; *'ammā Ṯamūdan fa-hadaynāhum* (Qur'ān 41,16/17), "if it is Thamūd, we guided them aright" (cf. §50.6,8). The Šḥeri forms *hél* and *hér*, "if", represent dialectal allomorphs of *hin* which go back to variations of liquids *n > l* and *n > r* (§17.4-6). As for the second morpheme *-ma* of the East Semitic conditional particle *šumma*, it appears not only in Ethiopic *'əmma*, but also in the Sabaic occasional variant *hmy /*himmay/*, perhaps in the Qatabanic particle *hmw*, "if", and in Arabic *'immā* and *'ammā* that served as simple "if" besides *'in*. The examples collected in various grammars are exclusively West Arabian. Hence it is uncertain whether *'immā* is based on the allophone *'im < him* or implies the assimilation *'in-mā > 'immā*. The form *hin*, presented in the figure as Aramaic and Proto-Arabic, is still attested as such by Nabataean Arabic *hinna* (*hn'*, "if"), and in the ancient Ṭayyi' dialect, spoken in the region of present-day Ḥā'il, where also the *h-* of the presentative *hinna > 'inna* was preserved (§49.6).

The Libyco-Berber conditional conjunction *mš*, "if", does not seem to be related directly to the Semitic one, because *-š* most likely corresponds to the Semitic deictic particle *k-* (§49.9), while the negative *ur* is suffixed to *m-* (*mur*) when it introduces unreal conditions. Instead, *m-* may be related to the second component -*ma* of the Semitic conditional particle and to the Egyptian preposition *m* used with the tense *śdm-f*; e.g. *m mrr-tn 'nḫ*, "if you love life". Further research is needed.

61.3. If the condition is negative, the conditional particle is followed by a negative, "if not": *šumma lā* in East Semitic, *hm l* in Ugaritic, *'im lo'* in Hebrew, *hēn lā* in Aramaic > *'ellā* in Syriac, *'in lā* > *'illā* in Arabic, *hm lm* in a Sabaic text from the Haram area; e.g. Arabic *'in-i l-ḥukmu 'illā li-llāhi*, "there is no judgement, if not God's". In Neo-Aramaic, the Persian-Turkish loanword *māgār* is used in the sense "if not". In the case of a disjunctive condition, "if ... if", "whether ... or", the conditional particle is normally repeated with or without a conjunction: *šumma ... šumma*, *'im ... (wə-)'im*, *hēn ... hēn*, *'in ... wa-'in*.

61.4. In an oath, the formula of imprecation, i.e. the apodosis, is generally omitted because of the belief in the effectiveness of one's words and of the fear that a self-curse made in conditional form might go into effect if the condition was fulfilled. It is a typical language taboo. The full conditional sentence, including the curse, is therefore rarely found and the condition or protasis alone appears in oath statements, the self-curse being omitted for superstitious reasons. Thus a positive oath normally is framed as a negative conditional statement; e.g. Babylonian *šumma lā iqbianni*, "if he didn't tell me (that), (may I die!)"; Hebrew *'im lo' neḥzaq mīhem*, "if we shall not be stronger than they, (may I die!)"; Arabic *bi-ḥayātī 'illā 'anšadtanī l-bayta*, "by my life, if you don't recite me the verse, (may I die!)". In such a context, which implies opposition between form and content, the negative conditional particles *šummā lā*, *'im lo'*, *'illā* may be felt by the speaker as an emphatic affirmation.

61.5. When the oath has a negative meaning, instead, the protasis is a positive conditional clause; e.g. Old Assyrian *šumma mimma kaspam... ilqe'u*, "if he has taken any silver, (may I die!)"; Hebrew *'im yəkuppar*, "if he will be exculpated, (may I die!)"; Arabic *našadtuka llāha 'in rimta hādā l-makāna 'abadan*, "I adjure you by God: if you ever leave this place, (may I die!)". Again, since this usage implies opposition between positive form and negative content, the particles *šumma*, *'im*, *'in* may be felt by the speaker as an emphatic negation. The same usage is attested in Libyco-Berber; e.g. Tamazight *ullah mš žriḫ*, "by Allah, if I have thrown (it, may I die!)".

61.6. Unfulfilled, unreal, or contrary-to-fact conditions are introduced in Babylonian by *šumma-man* > *šumman*, and in Old Assyrian by *šumma-min*; e.g. *šumma-min šēpē mamman ikbus*, "if he had stepped on somebody's feet ...". The particle *-man* / *-min* derives from the indefinite-interrogative pronouns *mannu(m)* / *mīnu(m)* (§36.57-62). Hebrew, Mehri, and Arabic use the particle *lw* in such cases, — *lū* in Hebrew and in Mehri, *law* in Arabic, — although its original sense is precative. In negative clauses, *lw* is linked with the negative particle: *lūlē'* in Hebrew, *lu-(ə)l ... əla'* in Mehri, *lawlā* in Arabic; e.g. Hebrew *lūlē' hitmahmāhnū*, "if we had not lingered"; Mehri *lu-(ə)l əmzōz əla' yak'ān šəy dərēhəm*, "if I had not smoked, I would have money". The distinction between *ləw* and *'in* tends to be blurred in modern Arabic colloquials which may use *law* to express a real condition. In Hebrew and in Syriac, instead, *'im* and *'en* may introduce also unreal conditions, while *lū* disappears in Mandaic and in Neo-Aramaic.

61.7. A split protasis expressing a condition and a subcondition may be indicated in Old Babylonian by *šumma ... inūma*; e.g. *šumma warad ekallim ū lū warad muškēnim mārat awīlim iḫḫuzma inūma iḫḫuzuši ... mārat awīlim šeriktaša iliqqī*, "if a slave of the palace or a slave of a villein has married a freeman's daughter, when he has married her ..., the freeman's daughter shall take her dowry". In the Middle Babylonian of Emar, *šumma kī* is used in the same way, e.g. *šumma kī anāku allaka mimma iqabbā balṭa lū e'ezzibka*, "If, when I come myself, he tells me something, I shall surely dismiss you all alive!". In Hebrew, this kind of protasis may be used with *kī ... 'im*, e.g. *nepeš kī-teḥĕṭā' bi-šəgāgā ... 'im hakkohēn hammāšī'ḥ yeḥĕṭā' ... wə-hiqrib ...*, "Somebody, in case he sins by inadvertence ..., if it is an anointed priest who sins ..., he shall offer ...". The same construction may occur in Ugaritic: **ky tdbr 'umy** *l-pn qrt* **'im** *ht l-b-mṣqt ytbt qrt p-mn l'ikt 'ank lḥt*, "in case my mother heads for the city (council), if now it replunges the city into grief, what is the use of my sending a tablet...?" (KTU 2.72,15-20). The subcondition can be introduced also by a simple *wa-*, "and".

61.8. These examples of *inūma* and of *kī* introducing a protasis reflect the logical link existing between conditional and temporal / causal clauses. In New and Late Babylonian *šumma* is even replaced by *kī*; e.g. *kī šarru ana emūqišu iltapru ...*, "if the king has written to his army ...". This link appears also in the complex Aramaic use of *lw*, first as a temporal / causal conjunction; e.g. *p-lw ntn Hdd mt l[yr]ty*, "and when /

since Hadad gave the land as my [heri]tage"; *k'n lw l' šbw lntn tmh ynpq 'ly*, "Now, since they did not capture Natan there, let him go forth to me". A similar usage of *lū* is attested in Babylonian, in Old Canaanite, and in Punic, where the shift *ū > ı* takes place; e.g. Babylonian *lū marṣum iballuṭ*, "when it is a sick man, he will live"; Old Canaanite *lu-ú Yanḥama yānu ina* [*šat*]*ti annīte*, [*ḥ*]*alqātma gabbi mātāti ina ḥapirī* (EA 215,9-15), "when / since Yanḥamu will be absent this year, all the lands will be lost to the 'Apirū"; Punic *l(y)-šm' ('t) q(')l'*, "since he heard his voice"; *li pho caneth yth bynuthi* (Poenulus 932), "when / since I have recovered my daughters here".

61.9. In conditional clauses, Aramaic combines *hn* and *lw* in *hnlw >* *'ellū*; e.g. *hnlw glyn 'npyn* (TAD I, A4.2,8), "if we had revealed our presence", and Syriac *'āflā 'ellū nehwē*, "not even if he would be". The conditional particle *hn l*, "if", is attested also in a Sabaic text from the Haram area. In Aramaic, however, *hn(w) lw*, written in two words, seems to correspond to Babylonian *šumma ... inūma, šumma ... šumma, šumma kī*, and to Hebrew *kī ... 'im*, used in a split protasis expressing a condition and a subcondition (§61.7); e.g. Samalian Aramaic *whnw lw šḥṭ b-'šrh w-tl'y 'ynk*, "but if, when there was rape in her place, your eye pities ..."; Imperial Aramaic *'l thḥšk brk mn ḥṭr hn lw l' tkhl thnṣlnh*[*y* ...] (TAD III, C1.1,176), "do not withhold your son from a rod if, when you are not able to save him, ...".

61.10. An expanded form of frequentative conditional sentences occurs in Hebrew phrases like *wa-yǝhī 'im ..., wǝ-hāyā 'im ...*, or *wǝ-hāyā kī ...*, "and it happened, if / when ..., that ..."; e.g. *wǝ-hāyā 'im nāšak han-nāḥāš 'et-'īš wǝ-hibbīṭ 'el-nǝḥaš han-nǝḥošet wā-ḥāy* (Nb. 21,9), "and it happened, if a snake had bitten a man and he looked at the bronze serpent, that he recovered". The same construction occurs in the Arabic portion of the Nabataean inscription from Oboda, where the verb *kān(a)* is used instead of Hebrew *hāyā* (cf. §50.6): *fa-kān(a) hinna yabġīna 'al-mawtu lā 'abġāh(u) fa-kān(a) hinna 'arād(a) ǧurḥu lā yurdīna* (*p-kn hn' yb'n' 'l-mwtw l' 'b'h p-kn hn' 'rd grḥw l' yrdn'*), "and it happened, if Death was to claim us, that He did not let it claim (us), and it happened, if an injury moved closer, that He was not letting us perish". In Classical Arabic, *kāna 'in* occurs in similar sentences with conditional implications.

61.11. Unfulfilled conditions, i.e. unreal hypothetical clauses, are introduced in Ge'ez with *soba*, "when", which semantically corresponds to Aramaic *lū*. The verb of the apodosis is preceded by the shorter form of the conditional particle *'əm-*; e.g. *soba rakabkəwwo 'əm-'aḥazkəwwo*, "if I had found him, I would have seized him".

61.12. Conditional apodoses may be marked off from the protasis by a conjunction "and" (*-ma*, *wa-*, *fa-*), but the opposite usage is attested as well. It depends mainly on the writer's or speaker's discretion and on the common usage of any particular language (cf. §56.8).

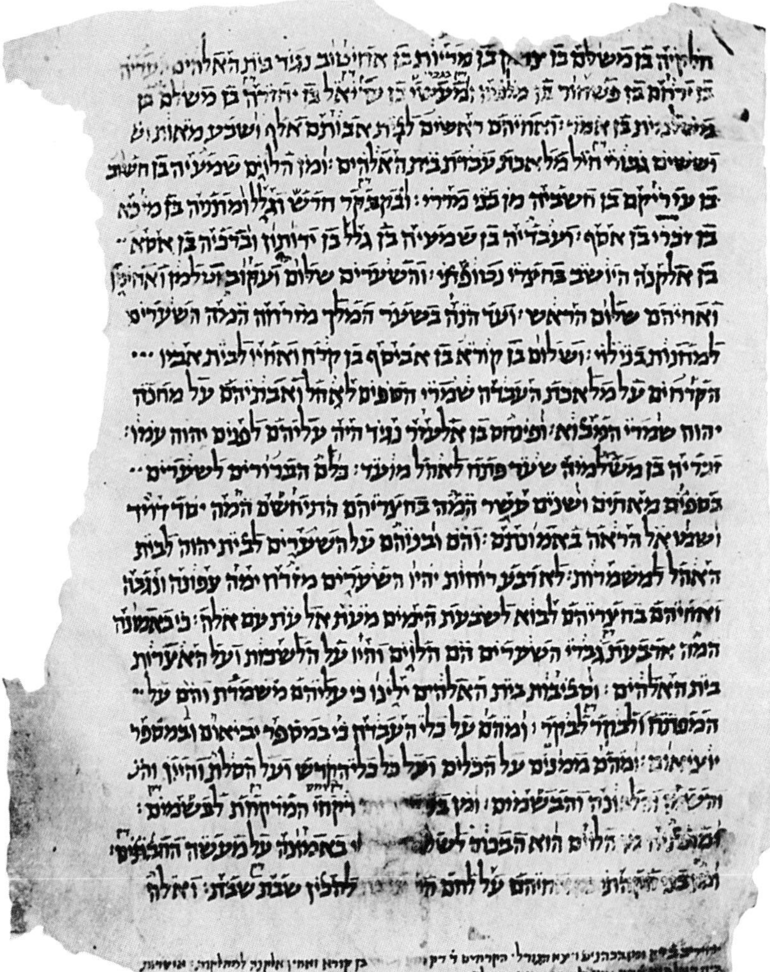

Fig. 32. Page from the Codex Berlin Or. Qu. 680 + New York J.T.S. 510: text of I Chron. 9,11-13 with Babylonian vocalization.

V

LEXICON

62.1. Part Five of our grammatical outline does not aim at comparing the use and the meaning of roots in the different Semitic languages. This is done in D. Cohen's *Dictionnaire des racines sémitiques ou attestées dans les langues sémitiques* (Louvain 1994 ff.). Our purpose is rather to present some fundamental insights about lexicographical analysis without entering into the discussion of modern linguistic systems and concepts related to semantics. Consequently, we abstain from examining and contrasting the views of competing linguistic schools and we avoid introducing their arsenals of technical terminology. We prefer instead referring to concrete examples. Following questions will be taken into account: etymology, derivatives, languages in contact, internal change, proper names.

62.2. The relation between a word and its meaning is in general quite arbitrary, at least if we remain in the realm of an observable development. There is no apparent reason, for example, why a dog should be designated in Semitic languages by the word *kalb* instead of by some other word. That the word *kalb* is used in this way by Semitic speakers over the whole Semitic area during five thousand years, or more, is merely a fact of linguistic history. There happens to be a word *kalb* also in German, but it means "calf", not "dog". It is a generally valid principle, therefore, that the relation between a historically attested word and its historically attested meaning cannot be explained by some inherent reason. However, this principle requires qualification, because many words are clearly onomatopoeic, that is, imitative of non-linguistic sounds. Besides, easily articulated nursery words are found consistently among the first sounds that a child learns to produce deliberately. The first definite syllables come at about eight months, and they begin with *m*, *p/b*, or *n*, *t/d*. Thus we hear *mama*, *papa*, *baba*, *nana*, *tata*, *dada*, *me*, *ni*, and *tu/ta*, "thou", "that", referring to a second person and to the background objects. We should be careful not to underestimate the importance of these onomatopoeic and nursery words for the development of elementary linguistic sounds, although they don't acquire the same meaning in all the languages. E.g. the sounds *adda*, *dada* may have a feminine function, as *dāda*, "mother" in Fulani and Ewe (Niger-Congo family), *adda*, "eldest sister" in Fulani, but "mother" in Highland East Cushitic, in Tigrinya (*'adde*), in Gurage (*adde, adot*), and "paternal aunt" in Rendille and in some Gurage dialects (*adda, adāda*), contrary to usual Semitic *dād-*, "paternal uncle". *Bāba*, instead, means "mother" in Luba (Niger-Congo), but "father" in Fulani, Hausa, Libyco-Berber, etc. The nursery and imitative words are to a large degree conventionalized and even adapted to the Semitic triconsonantal system of roots. Thus, the first nursery sounds, that coincide with the first meaningful things, are conventionalized in Semitic into *'imm-*, "mother", *'ab-*, "father", *dād-*, "paternal uncle", *nīn-*, "child, offspring", while *tu/ta* becomes the pronominal morpheme *-tu/-ti* of the second person (§36.5; 40.5), as well as the determinative-relative pronoun *ṯu/ḏu* (masc.), *ṯa/ḏa* (fem.) (§36.46). As for the onomatopoeic words, e.g. Hebrew *tāqaʿ*, "he beat", does sound something like the sound made by beating (cf. Italian *tocco*, from *tocc-*, "beat"). Assyro-Babylonian *alālu, elēlu*, Arabic *hallala*, etc., "to jubilate", is not a bad imitation of the trills expressing joy in the Middle East. The common Semitic verb *bakaya, bakā, bakū*, "to cry", "to weep", is formed from the sound of cries, just as the English verb "to beg" or the Polish noun *bek-sa*, "weeper".

62.3.   The relation between a word and its actual use in a given idiom is another unforeseeable element, depending on fashion, on partly unconscious selection, on written practice of influential schools or writers, etc. E.g. why do the D-stem *rāwa*, "he showed", and the noun *riya*, "eyesight", occur in the northeastern Arabian dialect of the Ḍafīr tribe, while the basic stem of the verb *raʾā* is replaced there by *rāʿā*, "he observed, he saw"? Why is there a preference for *'atā*, "he came", in elevated style of Classical Arabic, although the homonymous verb *ğāʾa* is also known to the writers? Which are the dialectal or diachronic implications of the Syriac substitution of *šaddar* to an earlier *šəlaḥ* when the latter verb means "to send" a person? Such questions cannot be answered by simply collecting the various roots used in a given language. They require complementary studies of the standardizing procedures, of the style either of a writer or of a school, of the literary forms and genres, etc. The study of such problems is of interest also for lexicography, and it goes far beyond an investigation of synonyms.

62.4.   Another general problem concerning the Semitic lexicon is its translation in categories of another culture. Persons engaged in translating from one language into another ought to be constantly aware of the contrast in the entire range of culture represented by the two languages. Nevertheless, the problems of translation have seldom been examined from this point of view and a too frequent recourse to an alleged polysemy of the words used in Semitic languages tries to conceal the real difficulties of the translation task. The kinship terminology and the vocabulary expressing social relations show, for instance, that certain words have to be analyzed in terms of human interrelationships. The West Semitic noun ʿabd-, e.g., can designate a slave, a servant, a king's minister, a god's worshipper, because its conceptual content is not a social rank, but a relation created by a dependent activity. As a result, when one is translating the Bible, e.g., into some European language, the problems of equivalence can be acute. It is easier to translate the noun in question by "servant" and to have recourse to the polysemy of the English word, but ʿabd- really does not mean "servant" and the corresponding polysemy does not exist in Semitic. Neither "dependent" would fit the case, because ʿabd- is etymologically related to the verb ʿbd which suggests some form of performed activity. Besides, diachronic aspects should not be forgotten. E.g. if the Hebrew word šipḥā is often translated by "slave-girl", — probably under influence of Arabic sifāḥ, "concubinage by capture", "cohabitation by force", — one cannot forget that mišpaḥā was a clan or a larger family in biblical times, and that špḥ means "posterity" in Ugaritic and "family" in Punic. One can assume therefore that šipḥā was originally a house-born girl who was not a legal daughter of the paterfamilias, probably because she was born from a kind of sifāḥ. Now, these social implications are missing in a translation like "slave-girl". These examples show that languages are basically a part of culture, and that words cannot be understood correctly apart from the local cultural phenomena for which they are symbols.

1. ETYMOLOGY

63.1. Etymological semantics will always play an important role in the study of Semitic languages, despite diachronic and geographical differences, i.e. in time and place. However, the reconstruction of an "original" meaning of a nominal or verbal root is not always feasible and, in any case, several factors have to be taken into account, as shifts in verbal stems (§63.2), social and economic environment (§63.3), very general basic meaning (§63.4), use of the same roots in other branches of

Fig. 34. Commemorative medal of Abu Naṣr al-Fārābi (A.D. 872-950),
author of *'Iḥṣā' 'al-'ulūm*, a survey of philosophical knowledge
and of specific Islamic sciences of his time.

the Afro-Asiatic family (§63.5-6), evolution of ideas and euphemisms (§63.7), phonetic changes (§63.8), impact of other languages (§63.9-12), apparent borrowings inside the Afro-Asiatic language family (§63.13), etc. Besides, etymological semantics has limits which can be often transcended by an investigation of syntagmatic relations (§63.14).

63.2. It has long been noticed that Hebrew *'āmar* means "to say" and Arabic *'amara*, "to command", while East Semitic *amāru(m)* signifies "to see". An allegedly Proto-Semitic sense "to be clear" has been proposed in order to conciliate these divergent acceptations and to find a kind of common ground or common "denominator". It is useless to say that such purely conceptual procedure has nothing to do with sound etymological semantics. Now, in Ge'ez, Stem I.B/2 (D) *'ammara* means "to make known", "to show", and this causative acceptation corresponds to the general meaning of Hebrew *'āmar* and Arabic *'amara*. There is little doubt therefore that East Semitic preserves the original meaning of the basic stem, while the signification "to make known", "to say", is the one of the D-stem, but *'ammar(a)* shifted in West Semitic from the D-stem to the basic stem *'amar(a)*. This is confirmed by the lack of a D-stem in the inflection of the Hebrew verb *'mr* and by the denominative acceptation of the Arabic D-stem *'ammara*, "to make an emir", from the noun *'amīr*. Similar shifts from one stem to another, especially between the D-stem and the basic stem, can be observed even in closely related languages and in various dialects of the same language (§41.2). Thus the D-stem of the Arabic and of the Hebrew verb *ḫlṣ / ḥlṣ* means "to save", but the basic stem of this verb is used with the same meaning in Phoenician and in Punic, as shown by several vocalized forms of the perfect *ḥalōṣ* (e.g. *Ba-al-ḥa-lu-ṣu*) and of the passive participle *ḥalūṣ* (e.g. *Ḥa-lu-ṣu*, *ḥlwṣ*). In Arabic and in Masoretic Hebrew, the D-stem of the verb *brk* means "to invoke a blessing", "to bless", but the Hebrew passive participle *bārūk*, "blessed", and vocalized names like *Ba-ra-ki-Ìl*, "God has blessed", Βαραχια, "Yahu has blessed", indicate that the basic stem was used likewise in the very sense "to bless". In Arabic, also Stem III *bāraka* means "to bless".

63.3. Another factor determining the meaning of a word are social and economic circumstances. E.g. the same noun *laḥm* which signifies "meat" for the Arab pastoralists, hence in Arabic, designates the "bread" among countrymen cultivating barley and wheat, hence in Hebrew, while it means "fish" among the islanders of Soqotra. The

original sense of the word was most likely "food", which is not a simple hypothesis since Old Akkadian *la'āmu* /*laḥāmu*/ means "to consume" or "to taste" food and beverage, and Lowland East Cushitic
aḥam (Rendille) signifies "to eat". A similar example is provided by
Ge'ez *ḥamar*, "boat", in plural *'aḥmār*. This word seems to be the common Semitic name of the "donkey", *ḥimār* in Arabic, but *emāru* <
*ḥamāru in Assyrian. It is not used otherwise in Ethiopian languages,
except in the Gurage dialects which have the word *əmar*, *umar*, *ämar*,
äwän, "donkey". The latter is perhaps borrowed from Arabic *ḥimār*, but
it could also be the Proto-Semitic noun preserved in Gurage with its
original meaning, while Ge'ez transferred it to other means of con-
veyance. Another example is provided by the verb *ṣada'*. Its material
sense in Arabic is "to break", but the etymologically corresponding
Libyco-Berber verb *zḍəġ* has the special "nomadic" meaning "to
camp", i.e. to interrupt a journey, "to break". This acceptation had probably existed in Semitic as well, since the Assyro-Babylonian D-stem of
the same verbal root, viz. *ṣuddū*, means "to supply with food". One can
compare the semantic development implied by this meaning with that of
the Libyco-Berber causative stem *ss-əns* of *əns*, "to spend the night",
which in Tamazight may signify "to have to dinner".

63.4. The use of cognate languages to discover the exact sense of a
word is often helpful, but it may result in the discovery of a very general
basic sense, valid mainly for the prehistoric period. For example, the
Arabic noun *markab*, "ship", borrowed with the same meaning into
Amharic, Gurage, and Harari (*märkäb*), is certainly identical from the
etymological point of view with Hebrew *merkab* and *merkābā*, "chariot". Instead, Syriac distinguishes *markəbā*, "ship", from *markabtā*,
"chariot", while East Semitic has a noun *narkabtu(m)*, "chariot", next
to *narkabu(m)*, "upper mill-stone", so called metaphorically because of
the oscillating movement impressed upon the stone in grinding. The
Assyro-Babylonian verb *rakābu* means "to ride" as well as "to sail",
which signifies that its basic meaning is quite general: "to set out". This
is confirmed by the Aramaic use of its causative stem in the sense of
"shooting" an arrow at somebody: *'l thrkb ḥtk lṣdyq*, "you will not
shoot your arrow at a righteous man". The common Semitic noun
*'arwiy-, with a prosthetic *'a-*, preserves its general meaning "wild animal" in Ge'ez (*'arwe*) and in South Ethiopic (*awre* with metathesis), but
it means "serpent" in Tigrinya (*'arawit*) and in Tigre (*'arwe*), "lion" in
Hebrew and in Aramaic (*'aryē*), "gazelle" in Old Akkadian (*arwiyum*)

and in Amorite (*arwûm*), "ibex" in Arabic (*'urwīya*) and in Sabaic (*'rwy*), but "eagle" in Babylonian (*arû, erû*). Sometimes, chronologically and geographically distant languages preserve the same basic meaning of the root, as Assyro-Babylonian *birtu*, "stronghold", and South Ethiopic *bərtu*, "strong", *bärätta, bərätä*, "to be strong", which seem to go all back to **birtu' < *bittu'* (§41.39).

63.5. The cognate languages of the other Afro-Asiatic branches, in particular Libyco-Berber, may also be helpful in etymological and semantic researches. For example, the Bedja (Cushitic) word for "water" is *yām* in the singular and *yam* in the plural, while Berber dialects use the plural **am-an*, "waters", *yam-an < *ī-am-an* in the "patient" case, and *wam-an < *ū-am-an* in the ergative case. There is little doubt that this word is identical with West Semitic *yam-*, "sea", although *may-/maw-* means "water" in Semitic and in Egyptian. It stands to reason that both *yam-* and *may/w-* go back to the same root-morpheme *m* or to its allophone *n* which is represented in Egyptian hieroglyphs by one ripple of water. Different realizations of this mono-syllabic word gave rise to two nouns, semantically distinguished in a later phase of Afro-Asiatic, except in Chadic where "water" is called *iyam* in Sukur and *amay* in Dangla. Another example is provided by the Tuareg verb *-kkərăḍ-*, "to have recourse to violence". This verb is etymologically related to Assyro-Babylonian *qarādu*, that has the same meaning. While the East Semitic verb is often understood in the sense of "pulling" hair, etc., and distinguished from a presumed *qarādu* II attested in the D-stem with the meaning "to make strong", the Tuareg verb *-kkərăḍ-* indicates that there is only one root which may occasionally refer to pulling somebody's hair, but which is used in a very proper sense when a Babylonian magical text mentions pigs that "assail the brick-work of a citizen's house", *libitti bīt amēli iqarradū*. A further example is provided by the Assyro-Babylonian lexical equation *perḫu = māru*, "son", when compared with Libyco-Berber *fruḫ*, "child"; e.g. Tachelhit *imdl u-rgaz a-fruḫ*, "the man buried the child". Also the Libyco-Berber word *symi < *šim+ī*, "baby", clears up the Amorite use of the noun *šum- < *šim-*, "name", in the general sense of "posterity". Further, the Tachelhit verb *-mərz-* or Tarifit *-marz-*, "to hit on the head", gives a concrete sense to Neo-Assyrian *marāsu*, translated usually by "to squash". Another Libyco-Berber word, viz. "speech", *awal* in Tachelhit, *awaž* in Tamazight with the dialectal change *l > ž*, and *awar* in Tarifit with the regular allophone *r // l*, reveals the etymological link between the East Semitic verb *awū- < *awālu(m) (cf. §17.2), "to speak", and the substantive awīl-, "citizen", etymologically and originally "speaker" in an assembly. In the light of Libyco-Berber ižžar < *iggar, "field", of Agaw agär, "country", and of the Gurage verb taggärä, "cultivate the field for the first time" (with agglutinated t of the tä-stem), one may doubt that North and East Semitic ugār-, "field", was borrowed from Sumerian a - g àr, "water meadow". On the other hand, the differences do not favour a link with Latin ager, Umbrian ager, Greek ἀγρ-ós, Gothic akr-s, etc., since the Indo-European root is *agr-, without any vowel between g and r.

63.6.   Cushitic and Chadic languages may be helpful also in other cases. For instance, Greek and Latin sources give caesar / καίσαρ as the Punic name of the elephant, used probably as personal name under the form Kyšr(m). Now, the elephant is called cuwar in Bura, a sub-group of Chadic languages belonging to the Biu-Mandara branch, and *gaisar is the name of another large animal, the buffalo, in the "Sam" languages of Lowland East Cushitic. A relation to kyšr seems evident. The same languages have a noun kor, "camel bell", and a verb kor, "to climb" e.g. a camel, which are most likely related to the Hebrew noun *kōrkōrōt (1QIsᵃ 66,20), translated by Saadia Gaon (882-942 A.D.) in Arabic ʾal-ʿammārīyāt, "camel-borne sedans". The Arabic noun ġulām, "boy", in plural ġilmān or ġilma, is related to Libyco-Berber hram, "boy" (Tarifit), to Highland East Cushitic (Burǧi) haläm, "boy", and to Oromo ilm, "son", while Oromo mot-, "chief", is etymologically linked with Semitic mut-, "man", Hausa mutum, "man", and perphaps Tuareg tamtut / tamṭat (cf. Tachelhit təməṭṭut), "woman". Instead, the noun gabr, which means "man" in Aramaic, designates the "slave" in Oromo, but gurbā is a "boy". Semitic tillu can hardly be separated from Cushitic tullū, "hill", and from the Cushitic verb tūl-, "to pile up" (Oromo). South Ethiopic kʷara, "sun", is directly borrowed from Cushitic, but this noun is related etymologically to Arabic kūra, "ball", and originally it designated the round-shaped sun "disk". These examples show that an etymological research based exclusively on Semitic can hardly be considered nowadays as complete and fully satisfactory.

63.7.   The evolution of ideas, especially of religious beliefs, can influence the meaning of certain lexemes. The paradigmatic example is the noun nafs which in Geʿez may designate the "soul", the "spirit", like in Arabic, although the verb nafsa signifies that the wind "has blown", while the noun *nəfās* means "wind", like Arabic *nafas*, "breath", "draught". These acceptations correspond to the original meaning of the root, as confirmed by the Old Akkadian use of the verb *napāšum* in the sense "to breathe". Hence the physical meanings of Hebrew *nepeš* and of Assyro-Babylonian *napištu*, like "throat" and "neck", result from a semantic development just as "soul" and "spirit". The throat was experienced as the breathing organ, hence its appellation *nepeš*, *napištu*. These nouns have still other senses, but the main point lies now in understanding that there was no diachronic shift of meaning from "throat" to "soul". Both acceptations are synchronic results of a development which started with the experience of "breath", which is the sign of life, while the last breath signifies the end of the life, the departure of the soul or spirit. Social conventions rather than religious conceptions preside over the wide field of euphemism, where words of unpleasant or obscene connotation are replaced by other terms that acquire a new meaning. Thus, e.g., the Hebrew noun *regel* and the Phoenician noun *p'm*, both meaning "foot", are being used to designate the penis.

63.8. Old phonetic changes probably explain the various forms of the word "son", *māru* in East Semitic, *bar* / *bir* in Aramaic, *bin* / *'ibn* in North Semitic, in most West Semitic languages, and in South Arabian (§11.6), as well as the existence of the corresponding verbs *bānā* and *bārā'*. Another example is provided by *ġzr* and *'dr*, both written *'zr* in Hebrew. It is not always easy to distinguish the derivatives of these two roots, although the first one expresses the idea of copiousness, while the second one means "help". Important factors are the numerous variations in the use of voiced and unvoiced consonants in the same Semitic root (§10.8), shifts in the place of an emphatic phoneme (§10.9), and metatheses (§27.12). Also diachronic and synchronic passages from interdentals to dentals are very common (§13.8-9), and shifts from emphatic to non-emphatic consonants occur dialectally (e.g. §16.9). Etymological semantics has to take all these facts into account.

63.9. Impact of foreign languages and lexical borrowings are other important factors in etymological semantics. Borrowing is a widespread linguistic phenomenon, but the actual pronunciation and spelling of a word borrowed into one language from another can differ considerably, and differences of meaning also occur. E.g. the Arabic noun *bāliġ*, "adult", is borrowed into South Ethiopic either with the same meaning or in the sense "old man", as in Gurage. Now, this word "old man" is pronounced *bariq* in West Gurage, with the change *l* > *r* (§17.5). Aramaic borrowed from Babylonian, e.g., the noun *kimaḫḫu*, "tomb", and the verb *maḫāru*, "to receive". Phonetic changes obliterate these borrowings, since Neo-Babylonian *m* became *w* in intervocalic position, while the Aramaic spirantization of *k* made this letter suitable for indicating Babylonian *ḫ*. Thus, *kimaḫḫu* appears in Jewish Aramaic as *kwk* < [*kiwaḫ*], transcribed κοκχος in Greek, and *maḫāru* is attested in Syriac as *məkar* < [*maḫar*] with the sense "to acquire", "to buy". But the Babylonian allophone *gimāḫu*, "grave", was borrowed in other Aramaic dialects as *gwḥ* (Nabataean) or *gwmḥ* (Palmyrene), with the meaning "burial niche" or "burial site". The Hebrew word *pesaḥ*, "passover", is borrowed into Syriac through Greek πάσχα under the rare form *psk*, but the classical Syriac spelling is *psḥ'*.

63.10. Differences may even be bigger when a word is borrowed from a non-Semitic language (cf. §65.4ff.). Normally, it is made to fit the phonological system of the borrowing Semitic language. The Aramaic and Arabic word *qaṣr*, for example, was taken from the Latin word *castrum*, but it appears from the oldest attestations that it found its way into Semitic through its plural, under the forms **k/qaṣərīn* (κασερειν), *kṣry'*, *qṣry'*, from which originated the singular *qaṣr*. It is pronounced with the Semitic *ṣ*, not the Latin *st*. Because of the spirantization of *k* in Middle and Late Aramaic, Greek and Latin *k* is more often transcribed by *q*, as in *qṣry'*, *qpyls* < κάπηλος, "retailer", and *'yqwn'* < εἰκών, "image". The Greek noun πανδοκεῖον, "inn", was borrowed in Arabic as *funduq* with the change *p* > *f* (§11.1) and with its adaptation to the pattern *fu'lul* (e.g. *ǧundub*, "grasshopper") suggested by the form πονδόχιον, which is attested in Syria. Greek κλίμα with its meanings "climate" and "region" entered Arabic as *'iqlīm*, with a prosthetic vowel (§27.17) and the rendering of Greek κ by *q*. Besides, Arabic developed a denominative verb *'aqlama*, "to acclimate", with a reflexive *ta'aqlama*. Tigrinya *gäza* and Gafat *gäǧǧä*, "house", related to Ge'ez *gaza*, "store-room", go back to Old Persian **ganda-*, "store-room", borrowed in Aramaic and Syriac as *ganzā* > *gazzā*, and in Greek as γάζα. The word probably entered Ethiopic when Greek-speaking Syrian monks arrived in Ethiopia toward the end of the 5th century A.D.

63.11. Beside the assimilation of the borrowed word to the Semitic phonological system, phonetic criteria and dialectal peculiarities have to be taken into account also on the side of the non-Semitic language lending the lexeme. E.g. Aramaic borrowed the noun *kārōz*, "herald", from Hellenistic Greek, apparently not from Attic κῆρυξ but from Dorian κᾶρυξ. In Mishnaic Hebrew and in Jewish Late Aramaic occurs the title *'ămarkāl* or *markōl* of an official superintending the Temple cashiers. This word is obviously identical with Late Babylonian *am-mar-kar-ra*, which is a Persian loanword, in Middle Persian *āmārkār / aḥmarkār*, "accountant". Yet, the Hebrew and Aramaic noun shows the grapheme *l* where an etymological *r* is expected. Since the existence of an Old Persian *l*-dialect is as yet uncertain, while Middle Persian spellings with *l* instead of *r* are well attested, it is likely that Late Aramaic borrowed *'ămarkāl* in Babylonia from Middle Persian. At Paikuli, in an inscription dating from 293 A.D., this title is written *'ḥmrkr* in the Parthian version, but *'m'lkry* in Pahlavi, thus with a spelling that shows the alternation *l / r*.

63.12. An interesting variant of lexical borrowing is a phenomenon known as loan translation. E.g. Arabic borrowed *ṯāwulūǧiya*, "theology", from Greek and this word is still attested in 960 A.D., but its Greek components were also translated into *'ilm 'al-'ilāhīyāt*, lit. "the knowledge of divine matters". In recent times, European phrases happen to be literally transposed into Arabic; e.g. "in the full sense of the term", *bi-kull ma'nā l-kalima*. Similar cases occur in Modern Hebrew or *ivrīt* where the compound *tapuᵃḥ-'ădāmā*, "potato", for example, is a literal translation of French *pomme de terre*, while *gan yəlādīm*, "infant-school", is a literal translation of German *Kindergarten*. What Hebrew speakers borrowed, in both cases, were not actual lexical items, but rather a pattern for combining them figuratively to express a certain notion, new in their own social and economic environment.

63.13. There is a danger in Afro-Asiatic that in listing forms claimed as loanwords from one language of the family in other languages of the group we sometimes lose sight of the fact that forms of both languages under consideration could show exact or very close correspondence to each other. For example, it may be risky to argue that Tuareg *isəm*, "name", is a loan from Arabic *'ism* simply because they are so similar. In fact, Bedja *sim*, "name", does not reveal any Arabic impact, Hausa *súù-n-áa*, "name", goes most likely back to **sum-n-áa* without showing any Arabic influence, and Tarifit *symi*, "baby", must be considered as a derivative of **šim+ī* used in an acceptation similar to that of "name" in Amorite onomastics (§63.5). A confirmation is provided, e.g., by animal names appearing with a different meaning in various languages belonging to the Afro-Asiatic group, as Semitic *ḏi'b* (broken plur. *ḏu'b-ān*), "wolf", and Cushitic *zobbä-* or *dōbbi-*, "lion", borrowed in Gafat as *zibbä*. Not infrequently, of course, the origin of particular forms is altogether uncertain. We could cite for instance, the word "iron": Arabic *firzil*, with variant forms in other Semitic languages, Somali *bir*, Latin *ferr-um*, Numidic *zl'*, and Tuareg *uzzal*. Do these nouns have something in common etymologically with Semitic *firzil* which apparently combines *fir+zil*?

63.14.   In all Semitic languages we find a number of verbs, the actual meaning of which depends not merely on their context, but also on the prepositions and prepositional phrases which they govern. Such combinations based on sequentiality of verb and preposition create syntagmatic relations which give a new dimension to the semantic load of the verbs in question. In Arabic, for example, intransitive verbs denoting movement acquire a factitive meaning when they are used with the preposition *bi-*; e.g. *'atāhu bi-kitābin*, "he came to him with a book", means that "he brought him a book"; *qāma bi-ġāratin*, "he got up with a raid", means that "he launched a raid". The Aramaic verb *'yr < ġyr* used in the D-stem with the preposition *l-* does not mean "to alter, to modify", like in Arabic, but "to transfer, to alienate"; e.g. Nabataean *wl' y'yrwn mn wgr' dnh l'nwš klh*, "they shall not transfer anything from this rock-tomb to any man, whoever he be"; Old Aramaic *'yr ksp l-Ḥdy*, "he transferred silver to Ḥaddiy". The Hebrew verb *'āmar* used with the prepositional phrase *bə-libbō*, lit. "in his heart", means "to think". Syntagmatic relations are formed not only by combinations of verb and preposition, but this particular type of connection brings about semantic shifts more often than others.

2. DERIVATIVES

64.1.   The relation between derivatives and the root to which they obviously belong is an important question of semantic analysis. Semitic languages do not have compound verbs, formed by combining a simple verbal root with different prepositional elements. Syntagms consisting in a verb used with a determinate preposition replace this feature of Indo-European languages to a certain extent. Instead, Semitic languages have a large number of nouns etymologically attached to a verbal root or to a simple nominal root, e.g. Arabic *maqām(un)*, "place", related to the verb *qāma*, "he stood"; Assyro-Babylonian *abbūtu*, "paternity", derived from *abu*, "father". The real significance of the derivatives is often very different from their theoretical "etymological" meaning and, in many cases, it is not predictable.

64.2. The example of Arabic *maqām(un)* is apparently simple since the preformative *ma-* is generally used to form nouns designating a site, a location, while the verb *qūm* means "to stand". The sense "place", which the noun often has, corresponds thus to the results of a simple etymological analysis. However, the noun in question is used also with several specialized acceptations which cannot be attached etymologically to the verbal root. Hebrew *māqōm* may signify "shrine", "sanctuary", and Arabic *maqam* is used in the same way but it designates, especially, the tomb of a saint. In Samalian Aramaic, *mqm* may be a "tomb", and "tomb" or "necropolis" is a frequent meaning of *mqm* in Phoenician and Punic, beside the acceptation "locality", "town", attested by several toponyms **Maqōm ḥadaš*, "New town". A completely different meaning of *mqm* occurs in Epigraphic South Arabian where this word signifies "might", "power", but may also be used in the sense "position". We do not know whether the same vocalization corresponds to these different meanings, but it is evident that the conceptual link between *mqm*, "might", and the verb *qūm*, "to stand", is different from the one resulting in the acceptation "site" or the like. It is probably related to the idea of standing somebody off, but it is not predictable from a purely etymological point of view.

64.3. A similar example is provided by Arabic *'al-manāḫ* or *'al-munāḫ*, which nowadays means either "halting place" or "climate". This noun, likewise with the preformative *ma- / mu-*, is certainly related to the verb *nawwaḫa*, "to halt for a rest" (Stem II), and *'anāḫa*, "to make (a camel) kneel down" (Stem IV). Its meaning was extended by metonymy from "halting place" of caravans to astronomic tables containing a calendar of the days, weeks, and months of the year, and a record of various astronomical phenomena. This word, used in Hispano-Arabic, entered with the article, *'al-manāḫ*, into various non-Semitic languages and it is already quoted as *almanac* by Roger Bacon in the 13th century. Since such an astronomic table described seasonal patterns as well, it came to be used in a later period, first in Syria as it seems, in the sense "climate". It is obvious that this acceptation, as well as "almanac", cannot be explained etymologically without knowing the history of the word.

64.4.   Social-economic experience, for example, may occasion important shifts in the meaning of a verb and its derivatives. Words, in fact, like human beings who use them, sometimes manifest an unfortunate tendency to "go to the bad". Their "pejoration" is often due to a selection and a specialization of some ethically lower connotation which may be implied in them. Thus *makara* means in Arabic and in Ethiopic "to deceive" and the *makkār* or *mākir* is an "impostor", a "swindler". Still in Sabaic the collective noun *mkr* designated "traders", like Ugaritic and Hebrew *mkr*, and East Semitic *tamkāru*, which derives from the same verb *makāru*, "to deliver goods", "to sell". The semantic shift of *mkr* in Arabic opened the door to a new term designating "trade" and "traders" which was borrowed as *taǧara*, "to trade", and *tuǧǧār*, "traders", from Aramaic / Syriac *taggārā*, "trader", itself derived through **tangār* from Assyro-Babylonian *tamkār(u)*. The paths of lexical borrowing reflect, to a certain extent, the paths of cultural and economic influence. Hence, this borrowing, which came to Arabic through Late Aramaic, attest Aramaean or Syro-Mesopotamian influence in trade during Late Antiquity. From the verb *taǧara*, the participle *tāǧir* was coined in Arabic, and it is used as the singular of *tuǧǧār*.

64.5.   An interesting variant of derivatives are genitival compounds as Aramaic *byt spynt'*, "ship-yard", lit. "house of boats", borrowed into Neo-Babylonian as *bīt sa-pi-na-a-tú*. In the same semantic field, one can mention Arabic *dār 'aṣ-ṣinā'a*, lit. "the house of handicraft", which was used in the Middle Ages to designate a ship-yard. This compound noun was borrowed into Italian as *darsena* and later into French as *darsine*, *darse*. The Romance word was borrowed in turn by Modern Arabic in the forms *tarsāna* and *tarsḫāna*, "ship-yard". Assyro-Babylonian *qaqqad kaspi(m)*, lit. "head of the silver", designates the "capital", the amount of silver invested or deposited, without its expected yield. This expression appears already in the reduced form *qaqqadu(m)*, without the genitive "silver", in Old Assyrian deeds, and it was borrowed about the fifth century B.C. into Greek as κεφάλαιον, later into Latin as *caput*. Modern Arabic uses *i'āda*, "handing back", + *nomen rectum* for English "re-" (e.g. *i'ādat an-naẓar*, "re-examination"), and *muta'addid*, "manifold", for "multi-" (e.g. *muta'addid al-ḫalāyā*, "multicellular"). No conceptual etymology can explain the meaning of such words and phrases without taking their concrete usage into account. Now, similar usages are based on professional language which must be distinguished from the standard language, in Antiquity as well as nowadays.

64.6. Legal terminology, both ancient and modern, is an important source of semantic developments that are apparent in determinate phrases and even in isolated words when employed in legal contexts. Thus, Early Aramaic *gzr 'dy'*, lit. "to cut the treaty", means "to conclude a treaty", while *mḥ' yd*, lit. "to strike the hand", signifies "to pledge", "to give security", by reference to symbolic gestures. In Phoenician, an official seal with the inscription *ḥn šlmt b'rb' l'm ṣr* signifies an "acknowledgment of full payment in (year) four of the people of Tyre", while the usual meaning of the noun *ḥn* is "token of favour", "grace", i.e. thing given or done in return for a service, a prayer, etc. In Islamic Law, e.g., the legal principle of "public advantage" or *'istiṣlāḥ* is expressed by a term derived from Stem X of the verb *ṣalaḥa*, "to be good". This stem expresses the idea of deeming something good, but its legal significance cannot be established by pure etymology since it implies that a rule causing a general injury is to be set aside.

3. LANGUAGES IN CONTACT

65.1. Living languages never hold still and one way languages change is through the influence of other languages. This problem was already discussed by Sibawayh (?-793 A.D.) in his *Kitāb*, where he deals with Persian loanwords in Arabic, and Abū Manṣūr al-Ǧawālīqī (1072-1145 A.D.) handled the subject in his treatise *Kitāb 'al-Mu'arrab min 'al-kalām 'al-'a'ǧamī*. Much attention was paid to this question also by modern scholars. However, the study of language contact in the Near East, for all the attention it has already received, is beset with many difficulties, and some of the work that has already been done in this field is vitiated by the urge to draw conclusions from inadequate, and sometimes inadmissible, evidence. However, there is also an increasing amount of solid evidence and we have already referred several times to examples of lexical borrowing; it may take place between Semitic languages, and between a Semitic and a non-Semitic language, in either direction. Also changes in the syntax or phonology of a language may result from borrowing, but somewhat less frequently. There are cases in Semitic languages that demonstrate the existence of this kind of influence. Besides, it is proper to include in this problematics some reference to discussion of contact with both known and unknown non-Semitic and pre-Semitic substrata.

65.2. The linguistic substratum of an area in which a new language is introduced plays an important role in lexical, syntactical, and phonological borrowing. Its impact is even greater if the substratum exercises a cultural influence as well, and if there is a certain amount of bilingualism. Now, there can be little or no doubt that there was in Mesopotamia a Sumero-Semitic bilingualism from the mid-third millennium B.C. on. And since persons with a command of two languages are more likely to accept new words because they have an insight, to a certain extent, into two cultures, there is no need for a particular justification of the large number of Sumerian loanwords in East Semitic. Many borrowings go back not to single Sumerian morphemes, but to compounds like, e.g., in the case of East Semitic *malāḫu(m)*, "sailor", borrowed from Sumerian m á, "ship", and l a ḫ₄, "to transport". These borrowings include words which the Sumerians have received from the previous inhabitants of Mesopotamia, but these "Proto-Euphratic" words, as they are called, have entered into Semitic through Sumerian. There are also a few words which were originally Semitic, borrowed into Sumerian and then borrowed from Sumerian back into East Semitic after having undergone phonological and semantic changes; e.g. *šakkanakkum*, "viceroy", from Sumerian šakkana with the genitival postposition *-k*, coined in turn from a derivative of Semitic *šakānum*, "to appoint". In the consideration of the extent of linguistic interference in Mesopotamia too little attention is sometimes paid to the influence of Sumerian on Old Akkadian and Assyro-Babylonian in spheres other than that of the lexicon. Phonemic and grammatical interference should receive equal attention. The impact of the Sumerian language was felt, no doubt, also in phonology and syntax. Thus, the early disappearance of laryngals and pharyngals in East Semitic is most likely due to Sumerian influence, as well as the usual place of the verb at the end of the phrase (§50.14). The Cushitic substratum exercised a similar influence on the Ethiopian languages, especially on South Ethiopic which borrowed a large number of Highland East Cushitic words and was also affected by Cushitic syntax and phonology. A similar situation occurs nowadays in North Africa and in the Middle East where Berber or Neo-Aramaic dialects and Arabic colloquials are used side by side throughout a speech community, each with a clearly defined role (§65.10). This leads, e.g., to the frequent use of the Berber feminine noun pattern *ta-...-ət* in combination with the pattern *faʿʿāl* of names of professions (§29.11); e.g. *ṭā-ḥaddād-əṭ*, "smithery";

ṭā-fəndāq-ət, "funduq-keeping". The particular Berbero-Arabic bilingualism is widespread in Morocco and in Algeria, although it is rarely described in a satisfactory way. A full analysis of this phenomenon can be of considerable help in dealing with problems in linguistic description and in historical linguistics.

65.3. After the Assyrian and Babylonian conquest of regions inhabited by Aramaeans, a great number of loanwords came into Aramaic from Assyro-Babylonian. Included among these borrowed words are terms in such areas as government (e.g. *sāgān* < *šakan* < *šaknu*, "governor", "official"), the military (e.g. *'abūlā* < *abullu*, "city gate"), law (e.g. *giṭṭā* < *giṭṭu*, "document"), and religion (e.g. *'egūrā* < *ekurru*, "temple"). The influx of Assyro-Babylonian borrowings into Aramaic was not matched by any comparable flow of loanwords from Aramaic into Assyro-Babylonian, except Late Babylonian (§6.6). At that time, Babylonian was no longer a spoken language and the scribes were obviously influenced by their native idiom. However, the Aramaizing process started earlier, probably at a period prior to the Neo-Babylonian dynasty, and it certainly continued apace in the 6th century B.C. and in various ways, but it reached a peak in the following period, at the time of the Achaemenids. Many Aramaic words thought to have been borrowed into Assyro-Babylonian have been collected, but they still need to be classified according to their semantic categories and fields. Attempts at demonstrating Aramaic interference beyond the lexical level have been somewhat tentative and sporadic, and the question of dating such interferences to the Neo-Assyrian, Neo-Babylonian or Late Babylonian period has hardly been faced at all so that the relevance of certain suggestions for the consideration of language contact is uncertain, e.g. in the case of the allegedly Aramaic origin of the Late Babylonian formula PN[1] *mār-šu ša* PN[2], lit. "PN[1], his son, that of PN[2]" (§51.20).

65.4. Aramaic was an official language of the great Near Eastern empires of the first millennium B.C. This is noticeable particularly in the Achaemenian period when Aramaic was the main idiom used by the Imperial administration. Number of Old Persian words entered then into Aramaic, mainly in such areas as government and administration, e.g. *gizzabrā / ganzibrā* < **ganza-bara-*, "treasurer". The Persian word *karš-*, originally "weight", was first borrowed into Aramaic and it was later used with the meaning "coin" in Arabic (*qirš, ġirš, ġurš*), in Soqoṭri (*qerš*), and in Ethiopian languages (*qərš, qərši, qarš, qärši*). Besides, the influence of Old Persian upon Aramaic is perceptible in syntax, especially in the formally passive syntagm *'ăbīd lī*, "I have done", which has no Semitic background but exactly parallels the Old Persian construction *manā kṛtam*. Yet this phrase, in which only the third person singular of the verb is used, is clearly impersonal in origin, so that it really means "there is a making by me". Some authors have sought Persian influence also in the Aramaic use of *šmh*, "his name", following personal names, but Old and Late Babylonian "PN *šumšu*", Hebrew "PN *šmw*" (Job 1,1), and Tigrinya "PN *zə-səm-u'*", are the most precise equivalents of Aramaic *šmh*, all having the pronominal element (-*šu*, -*w*, -*u*), contrary to Old Persian *nama*. In Roman times, many Greek and Latin terms referring to institutions, law, and army were borrowed into Aramaic and early Rabbinic Hebrew, e.g. *bwl'* < βουλή, "Senate", *liblar* < *libellarius*, "clerk". The influence of Rome in Syro-Phoenicia and in Palestine was usually at its strongest and most obvious in towns, and it has been reflected in language. But here the problems which confront us in trying to understand what happened in regard to language contact and language shift or transference are exceedingly difficult. The intrusion of Rome in the Middle East did cause a disturbance in linguistic patterns that have been quite complex already before the Latin language first began to leave its indelible mark on Aramaic and Mishnaic Hebrew. Higher classes of the Levantine society were predominantly Greek speaking by the time of the Roman conquest, although the country and lower classes were largely using Aramaic, while Hebrew was still spoken in the Judaean hills, and North Arabian idioms in the Transjordanian countryside and in Idumaea. Greek influence increased again, as it seems, in the period of the Late Roman Empire and in Early Byzantine times. A new period of intense borrowings coincides with the first centuries of the Islam, as rightly seen by the Arab lexicographer Abū Bakr ibn Durayd (?-933 A.D.): *wa-qad daḥala fī 'arabīyati 'ahli š-ša'mi kaṯīrun mina s-suryānīyati kamā sta'mala 'arabu l-'irāqi 'ašyā'a mina l-fārisīya*, "A great deal of Syriac has pervaded the Arabic of the population of Syria, just as the Arabs of Iraq make use of Persian borrowings". Literary and contemporary primary sources to aid us in an attempt to understand various situations of language contact in the region during all these centuries are not sparse, but they are one-sided and tell us too little about social gradations in language, about the mixing of languages and bilingualism. What is needed above all, it is a study of language contact, based on new information and new approaches.

65.5. A few Semitic terms belong to the category of old culture words the origin of which cannot be assigned to any particular language. The most conspicuous case is provided by *wayn, "wine", attested in Semitic languages spoken along the East Mediterranean coast, i.e. in Ugaritic (yn), Old Canaanite (ye-nu; ye-ni: EA 84,44), Hebrew (yāyin, yn), Phoenician (yn), and also Ammonite (yn), everywhere with the shift w > y. The word appears also in Sabaic inscriptions as wyn or yyn, with a plural 'wyn or 'ywn, and the meaning "vineyard". It has most likely been borrowed into South Arabian from a Syro-Palestinian idiom and thereafter entered Arabic as wayn(un) and Ge'ez as wayən. This word is certainly identical with Hittite and Luwian wa-ia-na-, with Greek Ϝοῖν(ος), Latin uīn(um), Umbrian uin(u), Armenian gini, Albanian vēne. Another noun belonging to this category is ṯawr, "ox", "bull", attested in East Semitic (šūru), in Ugaritic (ṯr), Hebrew (šōr), Aramaic (šwr, swr, twr, tōrā), Arabic (ṯawr), and Ethiopic (sor), and obviously identical with Greek ταῦρ(ος), Latin taur(us), Lithuanian taúr(as), Polish tur, etc. The Semitic name for "rose", Arabic ward, warda, Mishnaic Hebrew wered, and Late Aramaic wardā, is generally considered as a Persian loanword, attested in Avestan as varəδa-. However, this is a common Mediterranean or Near Eastern noun which is already attested in Mycenaean Greek *Ϝορδο-, a variant of *Ϝροδο- that appears as βρόδον in the Aeolian dialect of the 7th century B.C. It is used in ancient North Arabian anthroponomy, viz. in Nabataean (Wrdw and its diminutive Wrydw), in Ṣafaitic (Wrdn, Wrd, Ουαρδα, Ουαρδης), in Palmyrene (Wrdn), and it gave rise in Arabic to the denominative verb warrada, "to blossom" or "to dye red". The assumed Persian provenance of the Semitic noun is therefore questionable, although the fact that it begins with w- points to its non-Aramaic and non-Hebrew origin. Another culture word of the Mediterranean world is the name of the juniper, called ba-ra-su-um /barāšum/ in Palaeosyrian, burāšu(m) in Old Akkadian and in Assyro-Babylonian, bərōš in Hebrew, bərāt(ā) in Aramaic, βράθυ in Greek, and iuni-perus in Latin. It should not be confused with the birch, which does not occur in southern regions and is called brēza in Slavic, bérža-s in Baltic.

65.6. Trade brings languages together and it is a cause of lexical borrowing when it creates the need to find words for new objects and goods. In fact, it is easier to borrow an existing term from another language than to make one up. The Greek word χρῡσός, "gold", attested already in Mycenaean documents (ku-ru-so), is borrowed from Canaanite ḥarūṣ(u), as shown by the long ū in χρῡσός, not from Assyro-Babylonian ḫurāṣu. The words μύρρα, κασία, λίβανος, λιβανωτός, found in

Sappho's poems, were borrowed from Phoenician at the time when these goods started to be imported by sea. This does not imply that all these names are of Semitic origin; cassia, for instance, is believed to have come from India. The Indian word "lac, sealing wax", Sanskrit *lakṣaṇa-*, entered Sabaic as *lk-m* and then Arabic as *lakk* or *lukk*, most likely through Middle Persian *lāk*. The Persian word *musk*, "musk", was borrowed by Sabaic as *ms¹k* and by Arabic as *misk*. The Arabic noun *sukkar*, "sugar", is borrowed from Sanskrit *çarkara-* > **çakkara-*, probably through Tocharian *çakkār*, but the word is completely assimilated to the phonological and morphological system of Arabic, being adapted to the nominal pattern *fuʻʻal* which is used for names of plants. As a matter of fact, the name "sugar" was originally applied only to the sucrose derived from the sugar-cane plant. A denominative verb *sakkara*, "to sugar", was coined in Arabic from *sukkar*, which was borrowed into Spanish as *azúcar* < *'as-sukkar* and came to other European languages through Spanish. Instead, the Greek word σάκχαρ has only been used to create the name of saccharin. Borrowings through trade are important not only for linguistics but also for economic history.

65.7. Also social relations bring languages together and may be a cause of lexical borrowing. E.g. the Hebrew word *pilegeš* (*pylgš*, *plgš*) and the later Jewish Aramaic noun *pillaqtā*, "concubine", are certainly related to Greek πάλλαξ, παλλακίς, πάλλας, and to Latin *paelex*, *pelex*, "young lady". They probably imply a particular form of cohabitation which justified the borrowing of a foreign word. Another Semitic word borrowed from an Indo-European language is Ugaritic and Hebrew *msk*, Aramaic *mzg*, and Arabic *mašaǧa* or *mazaǧa*, "to mix". Its oldest attestations clearly show that it was used in the sense of diluting wine with water, which means that it was borrowed together with that practice. The verb is certainly related to Greek μίσγω and to Latin *misceo*.

65.8. Many linguists have stressed the cultural aspect of lexical borrowing. The urge to adopt new words for new objects and new concepts is a universal one. In general, the prestige factor and science are here very common causes of lexical borrowing. This explains why words of Canaanite origin, testifying to the higher Semitic culture and inventiveness, are frequent in Egyptian texts, e.g. *mrkbt* for "chariot" (cf. §63.4) and *mktr* for "tower". Many of them describe materials and technical innovations brought from Western Asia. Their meaning was well understood in Egypt, as often shown by appropriate determinatives. Many of them unveil their foreign origin by their consonantic structure alien to Egyptian or by being written in the alphabetic or syllabic orthography (§2.4). A similar situation occurred in North Africa where Libyco-Berber borrowed Punic words and continues to use them nowadays. Thus, Phoenician-Punic *gdr*, "wall", but also "compound" as it appears from the name of Gadir (Cádiz), was borrowed as *a-gadir* with the meaning either "wall" in Tamazight, or "fortified granary" in Tachelhit. The Punic substantive *sḥrt*, related to Assyro-Babylonian *sāḥertu*, "witch", may have given rise to a denominative verb of the D-stem (§41.3) which appears in Tarifit as *-səḥḥar-* with the meaning "to bewitch", but the Arabic verb *saḥḥara* has the same meaning. Tuareg *a-ẓrəf*, "silver", appearing in Hausa as *azùrfā*, is certainly related to Assyro-Babylonian *ṣarpu*, "silver", generally called *ṣurpu* in ancient Syria. The word may have been borrowed through Punic, but it is not attested so far in this language. Mishnaic Hebrew *nəyār*, "paper, parchment, papyrus", is borrowed from Assyro-Babylonian *niāru* or *nayāru*, "papyrus", which in turn goes back to Neo-Egyptian or Demotic *n-yr* < *ny ỉtrw*, "belonging to the Nile". A new period of borrowings occurs much later in Europe, where the great prestige of Arab science and mathematics during the mediaeval period occasioned an influx of Arabic words into English and other European languages through the medium of Spanish. These borrowings pertain to the realm of science and their use shows that there was a great measure of understanding of their technical acceptation. However, the meaning of a borrowed term does not always correspond exactly to its original significance in Arabic. Thus, both "zero" and "cipher" go back to Arabic *ṣifr*, "zero", "nothing", but the original sense of this word is "empty", "void". Similarly, "algebra" is borrowed from Arabic (*'ilm*) *'al-ǧabr*, lit. "(the knowledge of) the coercion" or "inevitability", with an adjective *ǧabrī* meaning either "algebraic" or "compulsory". Original and technical meaning have to be distinguished in any case.

65.9. The semantic analysis of some other scientific terms requires an even greater cautiousness, because they have been borrowed from Greek into Arabic and from Arabic into West European languages, with consecutive semantic changes. E.g., Arabic *'al-kīmiyā'*, which nowadays signifies "chemistry", meant "alchemy" in the early mediaeval period. The word was borrowed from Byzantine Greek χυμεία, "fluid", and it came to Spanish under the from *alquímia* already in the 13th century. Another term related to alchemy was *elixir*, borrowed likewise from

Byzantine Greek ξηρόν, "dry stuff", through Arabic *'al-'iksīr*, which underwent a semantic evolution as well. Thus borrowing may be combined with semantic changes which are sometimes very important.

65.10. A particular aspect of language contact is represented by the so-called "diglossia", i.e. the use of two or more varieties of the same language throughout the community under different conditions (§65.2). Perhaps the most familiar example is the standard language and regional dialect as used, say, in Arabic, where many people speak their local dialect at home or among family and friends of the same dialect area, but use the standard language in communicating with speakers of other dialects or in public occasions. There are, however, quite different examples of the use of two varieties of a language in the same speech community. In Baghdad, e.g., the Christian Arabs speak a "Christian Arabic" among themselves, but speak the general Baghdad dialect, "Muslim Arabic", when talking in a mixed group. Arabic diglossia reaches almost as far back as our knowledge of Arabic goes, with the "Classical" or standard language (*'al-fuṣḥā*) and the colloquials (*'al-'ammīya*), but a semiformal kind of spoken Arabic, with a generous admixture of colloquial vocabulary, is much used on public occasions instead of the *'al-fuṣḥā* language. In general, the grammatical structure of any colloquial is simpler than that of its corresponding standard form, but a striking feature of diglossia is the existence of many paired lexemes, one standard, one colloquial. For example, in Arabic the classical verb for "to see" is *ra'ā*, but the widespread colloquial word is *šāf*, which is hardly used in written Arabic. The range of meaning of the two items is roughly the same, but they belong to two varieties of the language, to two different speech levels. This is a research subject that requires further study and assembling of much descriptive and historical data.

4. INTERNAL CHANGE

66.1. Not all changes in semantic systems are brought about by the influence of other languages. Internal changes occur as well and can be discerned at all levels of linguistic structure. They affect individual lexical items as well as general rules, and they occur in phonology (§10-27), morphology (§28-49), syntax (§50-61), and semantics alike. That is an exceedingly treacherous field when we approach ancient languages. A number of scholars have argued, in fact, that only a very small percentage of the population would have been able to read and write, especially perhaps in areas far removed from the influence of the towns. The written documentation at our disposal would therefore reflect the language and the vocabulary of an educated minority. True, within any recognizable speech community, variations are normally found on all levels of linguistic structure — phonological, grammatical, and lexical. Some of these variations are correlated with location, other depend on the identity of the speaker, of the person spoken to or spoken about. This type of variation may be termed sociolinguistic. However, we should not let this fact of linguistic variation carry too much weight in societies using an alphabetic script, with a reduced number of signs. The thousands of Ṣafaitic inscriptions engraved on stones in areas far removed from towns and the symbols of the Tuareg script, known to many members of the clans, indicate that we should not be at all surprised to find that people were able to write and read in the country and among Bedouin tribes. Therefore, observable changes do not concern the sole urban and educated society. In this chapter, we are dealing only with semantics.

66.2. The simplest form of internal change is probably the loss and addition of lexical items. Since every language loses a percentage of its vocabulary in the course of time, it is highly pertinent to trace such words and to ascertain their meaning, as well as to attempt to determine why a certain word or group is lost or replaced by new words incorporated into a language. There used to be, e.g., a North Arabian noun *nq't* that must mean "clearing" (cf. Aramaic and Hebrew *nāqī'*, "clear") and occurs in Ṣafaitic inscriptions; e.g. *s¹lm w-nq't b-nfs wdd l-ḏ y'wr h-s¹fr*, "well-being and clearing away by any friendly person upon anyone who would blind the inscription!"; *ṣm wnq't mqbr l-ḏ y'wrnh*, "deafness and clearing out of the tomb upon those who would blind it!". This word became obsolete and does not appear later in Arabic, so that even its meaning is now somewhat uncertain. What this example shows, of course, is that words can drop out of common use into oblivion. Were it not for written records, we would have no knowledge at all of a word like *nq't*.

66.3. In every society, on the other hand, there is a constant need for new lexical items. Where borrowing does not suggest itself as a way of obtaining a new term, alternative methods are available. A new term can be obtained by extending the use of an old one, making it applicable to new situations. Another possibility is to combine existing lexical items to form more complex ones that are in some way descriptive or appropriate. In Semitic languages, this can be realized with the help of genitival compounds. Still a third way to obtain a new term is to make it up from an existing root, to coin it just to meet the new need.

66.4. The extension of existing lexical items to new situations involves both semantic change and the metaphorical side of language. E.g. the Arabic noun *maḥzan*, related to the verb *ḥazana*, "to store", basically means "storeroom", borrowed into English as "magazine". In Morocco, however, it came to designate the governmental finance department and finally the Makhzan, *'al-maḥzan*, the Moroccan government. In the older Islamic administration, the *dīwān* was an account book of the treasury and this noun was the basis from which the denominative verb *dawwana*, "to write down", "to register", was coined. The initial acceptation of *dīwān* was extended to "office", "board", "court of justice", and the word was borrowed with the article into Spanish as *aduana* < *'ad-dīwān*, "custom office". On the other hand, *dīwān* was used metaphorically to designate a collection of poems written by one author. The noun *ḥāl*, fem. *ḥāla(t)*, designates in Arabic and in other Semitic languages the "maternal uncle" or the "mother's brother", respectively the "maternal aunt" or the "mother's sister". Its meaning is somewhat different in Gafat where *alä* simply means "brother" and *alət*, "sister".

66.5. The creation of complex lexical items is a frequent means of obtaining new terms. In Old Assyrian, e.g., *bīt ālim*, lit. "house of the town", is the "town-hall" also in an administrative sense, while *bīt ili(m)*, lit. "god's house", means "temple" in Assyro-Babylonian. In Classical Hebrew, *śar hā-'īr*, lit. "prince of the city", is the "burgomaster", the "mayor", while the *'ăšer 'al-hab-bayit*, lit. "who is over the house", was "the mayor of the palace". Arabic had no appropriate architectural term to name the capital. Thus the compound *rās 'al-'amūd* was coined to designate "the head of a column", i.e. a "capital". In Tigre, the "cousin" is called *wad ḥal*, lit. "son of the mother's sister", — a designation comparable with Libyco-Berber *u-ma*, "brother", lit. "the mother's son" —, and the Tigre name of the "school" is *bet məhro*, lit. "house of gaining skill".

66.6. New coinages from existing nominal and verbal roots are frequent in Semitic languages (§64.1-6). E.g. the Arabic noun *kuḥl*, "antimony", also designated a preparation of pulverized antimony used for darkening the eyelids, and its use was extended to any preparation for colouring the eyelids. From this noun a denominative verb *kaḥḥala* (Stem II), *takaḥḥala* (Stem V), and *'iktaḥala* (Stem VIII) was coined to signify the colouring of the eyelids with kohl. On the other hand, the nominal pattern *fa''āl* of professional names served to coin the noun *kaḥḥāl*, which has designated the "eye doctor", the "oculist", while the adjectival pattern *fa'īl* gave rise to *kaḥīl*, "darkened with kohl" as well as metaphorical appellation of horses of noblest breed, called also *kuḥaylī* or *kuḥaylān*. The name of "alcohol", *kuḥūl*, derives historically from the same root, but its meaning and its vocalization are borrowed from the European term adopted in the 16th century by Paracelsus from Arabic *'al-kuḥl* to designate his *alcool vini*, "wine spirit".

66.7. Individual lexical items are also susceptible to change in their phonological representations. One can refer here to the description of phonetic changes in Part Two of the present *Outline* (§10-27).

5. PROPER NAMES

67.1. A proper name may be defined, broadly, as a word or a small group of words indicating a particular entity in its entirety without necessarily or essentially signifying any special quality of the entity. Nevertheless, it must be originally meaningful as name of a concrete entity that belongs to a well defined category; e.g. the name of a person cannot mean "fields". In practice, a particular entity will be named only if it is important enough to make a name for it useful. This, in human society, includes all human beings, which receive each a *personal name*, and a vast number of items in their environment, as towns, rivers, mountains, houses, etc., which receive each a *place name*. Hence the subdivision of the present section into two parts, viz. anthroponomy and toponymy. Still other classes of proper names may be distinguished, but they are related, broadly, to the two above-mentioned categories. A special observation should nevertheless be added concerning the divine names that may be the object of a linguistic tabu. In some religions, in fact, the real name of the deity had to be kept secret with the result that the divinity was called only by some descriptive epithet. The reason for such substitution, not rare in the Semitic world, must be sought in the widespread belief in the power of the Name, made known to the initiate alone.

A. Anthroponomy

67.2. Semitic personal names are derived regularly from ordinary words or consist either in short verbal and nominal sentences, or in genitive compounds. Frequently they represent an abbreviated form of names belonging to the preceding categories with only one of the elements preserved, to which a suffix is normally added. These names are called "hypocoristica". In most societies, bestowal of proper names has a religious and a legal significance, hence their study has wider implications than the very linguistic ones. This problem was already dealt with explicitly by Ibn Qayyim al-Ǧawzīya (?-1350 A.D.) in his treatise *Tuḥfat 'al-mawdūd bi-'aḥkām 'al-mawlūd*, where he examines the attitude of the Islamic law and religion to the bestowal of personal names.

67.3. In general, every human being receives a name shortly after birth. This name is necessarily given by others than the individual receiving it, and these others are usually a parent or both parents, or at least some member or members of the family or group. Since these are well-wishers of the child, the name in any society will ordinarily be a "good" one, *nomen omen*, whether chosen because of religious feeling, as happens often among Semites, or inspired by family pride, fashion, or mere practicality. Although a newly born child possesses only a minimal number of individual traits, also descriptive names, as "strong", "beautiful", may be applied. In some cases, Semites have resorted to numbering their children, especially when the number is a "lucky" one, as "third". Incident names are common. These are suggested by the time or circumstances of birth, or sometimes of pregnancy. Incident-names may refer to a feast-day, like *Šabbatay*, or to the recent death of a member of the family, whose place will be taken by the newly born child. Names that dedicate a child to some god, or in some way connect him with the god, are extremely common among Semites, e.g. "Servant of God". These names are called "theophoric". Plant and animal names also occur, e.g. "Wolf", "Gazelle", and these may originally have put the baby into what was conceived to be a proper relationship with the tribal totem. Others, however, are just referring to plants and flowers as, e.g., the name *Ḥbdrt* or *Ḥmdrt* borne by the Canaanite mother-in-law of Ramses III; it simply corresponds to Hebrew *ḥăbaṣṣelet* and Syriac *ḥamṣalaytā*, the "stalk" of a plant or flower.

67.4. Inevitably, after the passage of a few generations, names lose touch with their origins, but they tend to be repeated either because of the common practice of naming a child "after" someone, usually some member of the family, or because the use of an established "good" name seems safer and more suitable. With the continuation of this practice, a name, which is by nature conservative, which aims at preserving the "name" of the family, and is less subject to linguistic change, may therefore reflect earlier stages of the language and deserves a special consideration in linguistic studies. For example, David's patronymic *Yeššay* (Greek Ιεσσαι) probably preserves an old Afro-Asiatic noun attested in Amharic as *wašša*, "dog", in East Cushitic as *wišš-*, "dog", in Tuareg as *uššən*, "jackal", in Egyptian as *wnš*, "wolf". Of course, the name may also become meaningless to later generations and degenerate into a mere label or tag. This loss of lexical meaning affects especially names borrowed from one language into another. A name may also be reinterpreted and receive a new meaning; e.g. the name of Jehu's grandfather *Nmšy*, certainly related to Amorite *Na-am-se-e-*ᵈIM /*Namšē-Hadda*/, was vocalized *Nimšī* by the Masoretes who thought of Arabic *nims*, "ichneumon", while it was pronounced Ναμεσσι in the Hellenistic period, what shows a connection with Babylonian *nammaššū*, "beast".

67.5. The original name, even if its bestowal had been a solemn occasion and a ritual, may be replaced either by a surname or nickname, used for practical purposes and sometimes even officially, or by a new name or "to-name" chosen at some definite time or on the occasion of some event. Again, a "good" name is sought and it can now be chosen by the individual himself. We can rarely ascertain the existence of such practices among the ancient Semites, but certain cases decidedly suggest it, as some of the so-called "officials' names", especially those containing the name of the reigning king, e.g. /*'Ammurāpi'-'ilī*/, "Hammurabi is my god". In later periods, the custom of changing the name or giving an additional name is well attested in the Bible and in the Jewish tradition as symbolic of a new status or destiny.

67.6. The inherited family name is a recent development in the Semitic world, in which families and individuals traditionally identify themselves by the patronymic of a real or reputed ancestor. Among Carthaginians we find cases of high officials identifying themselves by the names of their sixteen ancestors, and comparable numbers of forefathers occur in Ṣafaitic genealogies.

67.7. Most scholarship upon Semitic personal names has concentrated upon their etymology, categories, manners of origin, and method of development. Statistical and historical study of naming as a social phenomenon is little advanced. The main classes of names comprehend verbal sentence names as Phoenician /Yatan-'El/, "God has given", nominal sentence names as Amorite /Šamaš-ġazzīr/, "the Sun-god is a hero", genitive compound names as Arabic 'Abdu-llāhi, "Servant of God", hypocoristica as Aramaic 'Abday, "Servant (of)", one-word names, either augmented as Hebrew Šabbatay, "(Born on) Sabbath", or not-augmented as Aramaic Ša'īl, "Requested", finally plant and animal names as Arabic 'Arnabu, "Hare".

B. Toponymy

67.8. The giving of place names depends, much like that of personal names, upon a sense that a place is an entity which possesses an individuality differentiating it from other places, and a recognition that a place is useful and therefore worth naming. From the linguistic and historical points of view, however, there is a basic difference between place names and personal names. Personal names are borne by living people and reflect therefore, at least to a certain extent, the linguistic situation of the area with which they are connected at the time either of the concerned written sources or of the surveys of spoken idioms. Geographical names, instead, with the exception of newly founded settlements, in general reflect an old and inherited linguistic tradition of the specific areas and may yield information about their protopopulation.

67.9. Notable periods of naming occur only when an uninhabited country is being populated and developed, or when the speakers of a new language expel the former inhabitants and impose themselves upon a country. In historical times, such situations have rarely occurred in countries inhabited by speakers of Semitic languages, although many settlements have been abandoned in the course of time and their names forgotten. Elsewhere the place names were firmly established and clung with great pertinacity even in cities whose names had been changed by Greeks which used them officially during centuries, e.g. Λαοδίκεια for Beirut or Πτολεμαΐς for Acre. Though suffering great change of form, also Libyco-Berber place names survived in North Africa through periods of shift in population and language. Thus, most of the Maghrebine toponyms in *ta-* / *ti-*, like *Tanǧa* (Tangier), *Tipasa*, etc., can safely be considered as Libyco-Berber, not as Phoenician, Latin, or Arabic. Other toponyms, like *Tasigda*, present Skikda (Algeria), are Berberized forms of Latin or Punic names. This may be the case also of *Rās 'Adar*, at the north-eastern corner of Cap Bon, in Tunisia. This name seems to go back to Punic **Ruš 'Addīr*, "Cape of the Mighty One", but its actual form, attested already in the 11th century by el-Bekri, is likely to reproduce a Libyco-Berber word that appears in North-African proper names of the Roman period; e.g. *U-adar-ius*, *I-adar*, Neo-Punic *Y'dr*, Numidic *IDR*. It is etymologically related to East Semitic *adāru*, "to fear", but also to Agaw *adära*, "God", perhaps "Lord" as suggested by the regular translation "lady" of its feminine derivative *tadära* in the Qemant-Qwara dialects. For the Libyco-Berber population of ancient Tunisia, *Rās 'Adar* seems therefore to have been a God's Cape or a Tremendous Cape, while personal names like *Uadarius* and *Iadar* would mean "Son of God" and "(Belonging) to God", etymologically "the Tremendous one", as confirmed by West Semitic *'addīr*, "mighty". In other words, when analyzing toponyms, all the available evidence should be taken into account.

67.10. Originally place names need not to have been fully differentiated from common nouns. Just as people now living near a large river say ordinarily "the river", so the population of Upper Mesopotamia and Northern Syria called Euphrates *nāru* or *nahrā*, "the river". Place naming in a fuller sense begins when people recognize two examples of the same class, and distinguish, e.g., "the white cape", *Rās 'al-'Abyaḍ*, from "the red cape", *Rās 'al-'Aḥmar*, whence White cape and Red cape. In this example, Arabic *rās* is the "generic" element of the place name and *'abyaḍ* / *'aḥmar* is called its "specific". Practice may permit the combination of both elements into one "word", e.g. *Qarthadašt*, Carthage, i.e. "Newtown".

67.11. The etymology of many place names occurring in Semitic sources or attested in areas inhabited by populations speaking a Semitic language is unknown, because these names are either altered or going back to a protopopulation of unknown or insufficiently known linguistic affiliation. However, number of place names consist in a simple Semitic generic, e.g. Beirut < *Bī'rōt*, "Wells", Byblos < *Gublu*, "Mount", Tyre < *Ṣūr*, "Rock", Acre < *'Akkā*, "Mooring-post", Medina < *'al-Madīna*, "the City", Gades < *ha-Gadīr*, "the Compound", Alcalá < *'al-Qal'a*, "the Castle", *Ma'īn*, "Spring", *Timna'*, "Stronghold", *Miṣpā*, "Watch-tower", *'an-Naḫl*, "the Palmgrove", *'al-'Uyūn*, "the Sources", *'Aynān*, "Two sources" (but cf. §67.16), *'Ugārat / 'Ugārit*, "Fields, Plain", etc.

67.12.   Other names are descriptive and employ a specific element indi-cating a long-enduring quality of the generic; e.g. Guadalquivir < *Wād(i) 'al-kabīr*, "the Big river", Caltagirone < *Qal'at 'al-ġīrān*, "the Castle of the caves", Caltabellotta < *Qal'at 'al-ballūṭ*, "the Castle of the oaks". Sometimes the generic can be omitted, as in Hadrumetum (Sousse) < *ha-Dărōmīt*, "the Southern (town)", in Ḥadattu (Arslan Tash) < *Ḥadattu*, "New (town)", in Judah < *Yahūdā*, "Low(land)" or "Hallow (land)" (cf. *wahda*, "lowland", "depression").

67.13.   Incident names arise from an incident occurring at the place and making it memorable. Names of persons are often applied to natural fea-tures for this reason, as are names of animals. E.g. Gibraltar < Old Span-ish *Gebaltari* derives from Arabic *Ǧabal Ṭāriq*, "Mount of Ṭāriq" ibn Zayd, the Arab chieftain who crossed into Spain and conquered Andalu-sia in 711 with an army of 12.000 Arabs and Berbers. The feminine *nisba*-form *'Abbāsīya*, "Abbasid", designates a settlement established by 'Abbās. *Rās 'al-Kalb*, "the Peak of the Dog", and *Rās 'al-Ḥimār*, "the Peak of the Donkey", lay both in Lebanon and contain an allusion to a local incident.

67.14.   Possessive names spring from the idea of ownership, whether legal or informal, though the possessive form of the noun need not be maintained; e.g. *Dūr-Kurigalzu*, "Residence of Kurigalzu (I)", *Dūr-Šarrukēn*, "Residence of Sargon (II)". Such place names mostly occur with the name of a deity considered as owner of the site, e.g. *Bēt Šemeš*, "House of the Sun-god", *Bēt 'Anāt*, "House of Anat", etc.

67.15.   Folk-etymologies, though they may be said to transform old names, really produce semantically new names through the mishearing and misinterpretation of unintelligible toponyms. E.g. Babylon, whose name goes probably back to a Proto-Euphratic *Babil-*, was reinterpreted in Semitic as *Bāb-ilī*, "the Gate of the gods". Irbil, with its Pre-Semitic name *Urbīl-*, was explained in Assyrian as *Arba-ilī*, "the Four gods", while the name of Jerusalem (<*Warúšalim?*) was reinterpreted as "Peaceful city" (*'īr šālēm*). The Aramaic place name *Qšt*, meaning "hamlet" like Tigre *qišot* (plural *qawašši*), is indicated in Neo-Assyrian by the logogram ᵘʳᵘBAN which was read *qaštu*, "bow". Sometimes the old name is preserved with the addition of a new generic, like in Caltanissetta < *Qal'at 'an-nisā'*, "the Castle of the women", which reflects the misinterpretation of the old Siciliote name *Nissa* of the site. The local name Mongibello of Mount Etna combines Romance *mons* with Arabic *ǧabal*, "mount".

67.16. Several Semitic toponyms end in *-ām / -ayim* or *-ān / -ayin* without being grammatical duals (§29.54). E.g. *Nahᵃray(i)m* is the region of the Middle Euphrates, "the River", *nāhār*, *'Epray(i)m* is the central highland of Palestine, so-called because it was one of the most fertile areas in Palestine, and is planted at present with such fruit as trees of vine, olive, pomegranate, carob, etc.; therefore, its name is likely to derive from a variant form *'pr* (cf. *'ăpar*, *'eprā*, "meadow") of the root *wpr* (cf. §19.24), which produces *wafr*, "wealth" in Arabic, "farmland" in Geez, and is related to *p(ə)rī*, "fruit".

67.17. Several Semitic place names, in particular number of present Arab toponyms of Syria-Palestine and North Africa, are misheard and misformed Greek and Latin names. E.g. *Ṭarābulus* in Lebanon and *Ṭarābulus 'al-Ġarb* in Libya go back to Greek Τρίπολις, "Triple city". The Syrian seaport *'al-Lāḏiqīya* transcribes Greek Λαοδίκεια, while Palestinian *Nablūs* and Tunisian *Nabewl* go back to Νεάπολις, "New city". *Saraqusṭa*, which became Zaragoza in Spanish, is a shortened form of the Latin name *Caesar Augusta*.

67.18. The tenacity of the place names (§67.8-9) render them valuable to the study of history and prehistory, and necessitates careful study of the alterations to which they are subject. In general, being a part of the language, place names change pronunciation along with the rest of the language. E.g., when the Phoenician glottal stop was elided in certain positions and when the pronunciation of the Punic vowel *o* shifted to *u*, this change occurred in place names as in other words. Thus, the frequent generic element "head" used in the sense "cape" was transcribed *ra-'-si* in 9th-century B.C. cuneiforms, but it could be written *r's* or *rš* in Punic inscriptions of the 3rd century B.C., while later Greek and Latin authors transcribed it Ρουσ-, Ρυσ-, *Rus-*. The same change *ā > ō > ū* is attested in the North African place names *A-megdul* and *Meǧdul* attested in the 11th century A.D. by el-Bekri. Both go back to Phonician-Punic **magdāl*, "tower", but the Libyco-Berber case marker *a-* is prefixed to the first one. Dialectal variations are common and place names, through constant use, may be shortened (e.g. §67.17); originally foreign toponyms are subject to greater alterations. However, a trained linguist is able to penetrate most of the disguises, insofar as the original language in which the toponym was coined is sufficiently known.

67.19. In fact, there is a high number of place names of unknown origin in areas inhabited by populations speaking Semitic languages. Attempts have been made in the past to elucidate some of these names attested in Mediterranean areas by assigning them to an otherwise non recorded language of a very remote period. Thus a basic root *kal- (e.g. Calahorra, ancient Calagurris), also supposed to exist in numerous variants, such as *kar- (e.g. Carcassonne), has been isolated in a large number of toponyms, and the meaning "rock" has been postulated, extended in one direction to mean "mountain" and in another to include "fortress". Such conclusions must, however, be viewed as highly hypothetical despite the existence of some widespread culture words as "wine" and "bull" (§65.5). In particular, the discovery of the Ebla writings confirms a long-suggested association of the name of *Karkamiš* with the Semitic god Kamosh and the Sumerian loanword k a r > *kār(um)*, "quay". The name in its earliest attestations may thus be analyzed as *Kār-ᵈKamit̠*, "Quay of (the god) Kamit̠", but this meaning might be based on folk-etymology (§67.15). As for Mount Carmel, having the same name as a city in Southern Palestine, the linguistic affiliation of this toponym is unknown. The recent tendency of connecting North Syrian place names with Hurrian should also be viewed with great caution. Anyhow, individual names, i.e. not belonging to a whole "pattern", may show close resemblance or even be identical as the result of coincidence, as Maqueda in Castile and Maqqeda in Palestine, the resemblance of which has led some Jewish commentators to assert that the Spanish city had been founded by Jews from Maqqeda who had been exiled by Nebuchadnezzar. In examining place names, history must always be consulted as far as possible. Caution is required even with regard to modern toponyms. The name of Tel Aviv, Israel, e.g., refers superficially to a "tell", i.e. an artificial mound resulting from the accumulation of debris of successive settlements. In reality, the city name is not derived from the name of an existing Palestinian "tell", but it was taken in 1910 from Ez. 3,15 where this name designates a place in Babylonia where Judaean exiles were settled in the 6th century B.C.

GLOSSARY OF SELECTED LINGUISTIC TERMS

absolute state: basic form of the noun, neither construct, nor suffixed.

abstract noun: noun indicating a quality considered apart from concrete beings, in opposition to "concrete".

accent: a stress of voice on a particular syllable in pronouncing a word; a mark used to indicate such stress or to distinguish homophonous cuneiform signs, as *šá*, *šà*.

accusative: case denoting, in inflected languages, the function of direct object, internal object, or certain categories of circumstantial relations.

acrophonic principle: attribution of a phonetic value to a pictogram in such a way that it would symbolize the initial phoneme of the name of the object it represents, as /b/ symbolized by a house which is called ***baytu*** in Semitic.

actor: subject.

actor affixes: verbal affixes, called also personals, that refer to the subject of the verb and specify person, gender, and number.

acute accent: mark used in tone languages to indicate a high tone, as *á*.

adjutative: verbal form expressing assistance or help given in an action.

adnominal: an adjective, especially when used as a noun.

adverbial: used as an adverb.

adverbial accusative: the accusative of a noun indicating a circumstance.

adversative: expressing opposition or antithesis, especially a conjunction as "but", "or".

affix: a non-separable morpheme added to the beginning or to the end of a word, base, or root, producing a derivative or a compound, prefix or suffix.

afformative: morpheme suffixed to a root or a basis.

affricate, affricative: complex sound consisting of a stop followed immediately by a fricative in the same position of the vocal organs, as [tʃ], [tʒ].

Afrasian: pertaining to Afro-Asiatic.

agentless passive: derived Berber verbal stem with a *ttwa*-prefix, which is a pro form of a non-active subject.

agglutinative, agglutinating: language which loosely combines radicals and relational suffixes; e.g. Sumerian, Turkish.

agreement: concord.

'al-'ammīya: Arabic designation of the colloquial language, as distinguished from *'al-fuṣḥā*.

'al-fā'il: "the actor", name given by Arab grammarians to the subject of a verbal clause.

'al-fuṣḥā: Arabic designation of the Classical or standard literary language, as distinguished from *'al-'ammīya*.

'alif 'al-waṣl: *'alif*-sign not pronounced as glottal stop in Classical Arabic.

'alif mamdūda: name given by Arab grammarians to a final *-ā'u(n)* indicated by *'alif* and the *hamza*.

'alif maqṣūra: name given by Arab grammarians to a final long -*ā* which is indicated by a written *y*.

allative: grammatical form indicating a movement towards a person, an object, or a time limit.

allograph: variant of a grapheme.

allomorph: a positional or free variant of a morpheme.

allophone: a variant realization of a phoneme.

'al-mubtada' bihi: "one starts off with him", name given by Arab grammarians to the subject of a nominal clause.

alternation: occurrence of different phonemes or forms in comparable circumstances.

alternative: affording a choice between two or more possibilities.

amorphous: qualification used mainly in Russian to designate an agglutinating language the words of which do not suffer any change of form, but are associated with auxiliaries and placed in a significant order.

anaphora: repetition of a word in the same sentence or context.

anaphoric: pertaining to an anaphora.

anaptyctic: qualification of a vowel inserted in the body of a word for articulatory reasons.

anaptyxis: insertion of a vowel in the body of a word for articulatory reasons.

antecedent: nominal head to which a relative clause is attached.

anthroponomy: nomenclature of personal names, science or study of personal names.

apex: the tip of the tongue.

apheresis, aphesis: the dropping of an unaccented syllable or sound from the beginning of a word.

apocopate(d): the shortened form of the Arabic imperfect; jussive.

apophony: vowel alternation denoting different forms and functions.

apposition: substantive placed beside another to add to or to explain the first.

article: auxiliary morpheme added to a noun in order to specify its definite or indefinite character.

articulation: movements of the organs of speech in producing an articulate sound.

aspect: a grammatical categorizing of the verb aimed at indicating the degree to which or the manner in which the action is performed.

aspectual: pertaining to grammatical aspects.

asseverative: affirmative.

assimilation: articulatory joining of adjacent sounds into one sound or adaptation of a sound to a neighbouring one.

asyndetic: not connected by a conjunction.

atelic situation: situation that involves a process that does not lead up to a well-defined terminal point (cf. telic action); e.g. Arabic *'at-timsāḫu yaʿīšu fī l-māʾi*, "the crocodile lives in water".

attribute: a word used to qualify the main element of a sentence.

augmentative: semantic class denoting greater size or intensity, as Tigre *garhāy*, "large field", against *garhat*, "field".

back-formation: alteration of a basic form under the influence of a form which is historically derived from it.

basic: pertaining to original and simple forms or stems, without derivational affixes or infixes; unmarked.

basis: verbal type, pattern, principal constituent.

biconsonantal, biradical: root consisting of two radical consonants.

bilabial: articulated with both lips, as [b], [p], [m], [w].

binyān: Hebrew name for "verb pattern" or "conjugation".

bound form: said of a noun in the construct state and of a suffixed pronoun, as opposed to "free" form.

boustrophedon: "as the ox ploughs", name given to script running from right to left and from left to right, in alternate lines.

"broken" plural: plural of nouns, formed by internal change, such as Arabic *kitāb*, "book", *kutub*, "books".

cardinal number: basic form of the number, as "one", "two", "three", etc.

case: nominal or pronominal form characterized by declensional endings and indicating, in inflected languages, the syntactical relationship of a noun, pronoun, or adjective to other words in a sentence.

casus agens: active subject in an ergative language, also called "ergative case".

casus patiens: non-active subject in an ergative language, also called "patient case" or "non-active case".

casus pendens: isolated element of a sentence, placed afore and resumed in the sentence itself by a pronominal morpheme; extraposition.

category: class, one of the several forms.

causal clause: expressing cause, origin, agency.

causative: verbal form indicating that the subject causes the action.

citation form: form of the noun given in answer to a question like: "what is the Arabic word for...?"

clause: a group of words containing a subject and a predicate, but forming a subordinate part of a compound or complex sentence.

cluster: a group, especially of consonants.

cohortative: the verbal mood expressing will, exhortation, or order in the first person singular or plural.

collective noun: noun expressing a plurality of individuals under a singular form, as "army", "people", etc.

common noun: the name an individual object has in common with others of its class, as "man", "city", etc.

complex sentence: a sentence consisting of a principal clause and of one or more subordinate clauses.

componential analysis: method consisting in the analysis of the semantic components or features of the word.

compound: consisting of two or more elements.

compound sentence: a sentence consisting of more than one independent clause.

conative: verbal form expressing endeavour or effort.

concord: agreement of words grammatically connected, as in gender, number, case, or person.

concrete noun: designating concrete persons or objects.

conditional clause: expressing or implying a condition.

conjugation: inflection of verbs.

conjunction: a word used to connect words, phrases, clauses, or sentences.

consecutio temporum: sequence of tenses.

consecutive clause: expressing result, consequence.

consonant: sound produced by a contact or constriction of the speech organs which results in complete or partial blockage of the breath stream; a letter representing such a sound (e.g. *b*, *d*, *k*).

construct state: form of the noun governing, in Semitic languages, another noun or a relative asyndetic clause.

constructio ad sensum: Latin expression meaning that the concord is not based on the grammatical gender or number of a noun, but on its real significa-tion.

continuant, continuous: consonant that is articulated without complete closure of the speech organs and therefore can be uttered continuously, without changing quality, as [m], [f]; opposed to "stop".

contraction: the shortening of a syllable, a word, or words by monophthongiza-tion or by the omission of one or more letters or syllables, as in "don't" for "do not".

co(n)verb: verbal form not expressing time or aspect, but serving to correlate two or more utterances.

copula: morpheme which expresses the relation between the subject and the predicate in a nominal sentence, especially a form of a verb meaning "to be".

crasis: the coalescence of two vowels into one long vowel.

cuneiform writing: characterized by the wedge shape of the characters or "signs", which nevertheless derive from schematized pictograms.

dageš dirimens: a *dageš forte* which is explained traditionally as serving to sep-arate (Latin *dirimere*) syllables.

dageš forte: Tiberian Masoretic diacritical dot indicating the gemination of a consonant.

dageš lene: Tiberian Masoretic diacritical dot indicating the plosive pronuncia-tion of *b*, *g*, *d*, *k*, *p*, *t*.

ḍamma: Arabic vowel sign for the short vowel *u*, called *ḍamm*.

dative: case denoting, in inflected languages, the function of indirect object.

declension: inflection of nouns, pronouns, and adjectives.

defective: verb or noun lacking one more of the inflectional forms normal for its class; word lacking one or more vowel letters normal for its spelling.

deglottalization: disappearance of the glottal closure in the articulation of a speech sound.

deictic: demonstrative, drawing attention to a situation or a context.

delocutive verb: verb which derives from a locution, a phrase, as Arabic *bas-mala*, coined from the invocation *bi-smi-llah*, "in the name of God…"

demonstrative: pronoun or adjective that directly points out its antecedent, as "this", "that".

denominative: derived from a noun.

dental: articulated with the tip of the tongue against or near the upper front teeth, as [d], [t].

depalatalization: disappearance of the palatal articulation of a speech sound.

descriptive linguistics: the branch of linguistics which studies the characteristics of language systems or dialects at given points in their histories; synchronic linguistics.

detensing: process by which a tense consonant becomes lax.

determinant: an element affixed to a base which modifies or determines its meaning, as *'ā* or *-al* in Hebrew *'āmal* : *mālal*, "to languish", from a base **mal*.

determinative: cuneiform or hieroglyphic graph specifying the semantic field to which a word belongs, as in ^d*Adad* where ^d indicates that *Adad* is a divine name.

determinative-relative pronoun: pronoun functioning as a kind of demonstrative and of relative.

develarization: disappearance of velar features of a speech sound.

deverbal: derived from a verb.

devoiced, unvoiced: rendered voiceless, as in the change [d] > [t].

diachronic: pertaining to the study of language changes over a period of time, historical.

diacritic, diacritical mark/sign: mark, point, or sign added to a letter to indicate its exact phonetic value or to distinguish it from another letter.

dialectology: the linguistic study of the dialects of a language.

diaphone: phoneme overlapping the boundaries of other phonemes.

diglossia: the use of two or more varieties of the same language throughout the community under different conditions; e.g. literary and colloquial Arabic.

diminutive: a word formed from another to express diminished size, or familiarity, affection, etc.

diphonemization: phonemic change from a single phoneme into a cluster of two phonemes, e.g. [s:] > [rs].

diphthong: a continuous monosyllabic speech sound combining a vowel with one of the semivowels [w] and [y].

diptotic: qualification of a declension system limited to two cases.

disjunctive: expressing an alternative, as "either... or", or a separation.

dissimilation: articulatory differentiation either introduced into one long or geminated sound, or produced between two identical or similar neighbouring sounds.

distributive: referring singly to the persons or things of a group, as "each one", "each two", etc.

dual: the form of the noun, pronoun, or verb indicating its application to two persons or things.

ejective: emphatic, glottalized.

elative: superlative, said of a form of comparison of adjectives.

elision: the suppression of a part of a word.

ellipsis: the omission of a word or words which are necessary to complete a sentence or phrase, but which the hearer or reader may easily supply.

elliptical: pertaining to ellipsis.

emphatic: glottalized or pharyngalized consonants; definite state of the noun in Aramaic.

enclitic: monosyllabic particle attached to a preceding word.

energetic, energic: a strengthened expression of wish or intention, formed from
    the jussive.
epenthesis: anaptyxis.
ergative: pertaining to languages like Sumerian, Hurrian, Urartian, and many
    of the Caucasian languages, where the basic finite verbal form is doubly
    oriented, with an active subject (ergative case, *casus agens*) and a non-
    active subject (non-active case, *casus patiens*), without any distinctive
    grammatical category of direct object.
exhortative: verbal mood expressing wish, exhortation.
extraposition: placing as *casus pendens*.

factitive: verbal form indicating that the subject produces a new condition in the
    object of a transitive verb which takes a second objective complement, e.g.
    Hebrew *šimmaʻ*, "he gave (him) to hear (the news)"; causative.
fatḥa: Arabic vowel sign for the short vowel *a*, called *fatḥ*.
final clause: expressing aim, purpose.
finite: said of inflected verb forms that can serve as predicates in sentences, dis-
    tinguished from infinitives, participles, and gerunds.
formation: derivation.
fortis: a consonant, usually a voiceless stop, pronounced with tension of the
    speech organs or with strong plosion.
free form: said of a noun in the absolute state and of an independent pronoun.
frequentative: verbal form denoting repeated or habitual action.
fricative: articulated with a forced escape and friction of the breath through a
    narrow aperture.
fricativization: spirantization.
function: the role of a linguistic element in a form or grammatical structure.
future: a verb tense denoting action that will take place at some time posterior
    to a determinate moment.

ǧazma: Arabic diacritical sign used at the end of a word to indicate that the final
    consonant is not followed by a vowel.
gemination: lengthening or doubling of a consonant, e.g. Amharic *boqqollo*,
    "corn", to be clearly distinguished from the reduplication (e.g. Amharic
    bəlul, "turtle"), which is called "gemination" by Egyptologists.
gender: grammatical category having a partial correspondence to sex for ani-
    mate beings, while sexless objects can be of any gender.
genitive: case denoting, in inflected languages, a noun or pronoun that qualifies
    another nominal element of the sentence by indicating possession, origin,
    source, appurtenance, etc.
gentilitial: said of a noun or an adjective denoting tribal, racial, national, or
    local extraction, and often characterized in Semitic by the ending *-ī < -iy*,
    called in Arabic *nisba*; e.g. *Qāhirī*, "Cairene".
gerund, gerundive: a verbal noun expressing correlation between two actions or
    utterances, as in "having written (gerundive) the letter, I sent it".
glide: transitional sound made in passing from the articulatory position of one
    sound to that of another, especially a semivowel or a glottal stop articulated
    between two vowels.

glottal stop: sound produced in the larynx by an instantaneous closure of the glottis; *hamz(a)*.

glottalized: said of consonants articulated with a glottal closure of the sound, indicated in script either by a dot under the letter ([p̣]) or by an accent placed higher on its right ([p']).

glottis: Adam's apple.

glottochronology: statistical technique which attempts to provide dates for the earlier stages of languages by comparing the basic core vocabulary of cognate languages.

glottography: a description of the tongue and of its movements.

graph: realization of a grapheme.

grapheme: graphic distinctive features representing a phoneme.

graphemic: pertaining to a graph or grapheme.

grave accent: mark used in tone languages to indicate a low tone as *à*, or a lowering of the tone from a higher pitch, as *áà*.

guttural: generic designation of laryngals, pharyngals, velar fricatives ([x], [γ]), and of the uvular [R].

Ḥadīth: compilation of traditions referring to the teachings and the life of the prophet Mohammed, an important source for ancient Arabic dialects.

hamza: Arabic vowel sign of the glottal stop, called *hamz*.

hamzat 'al-waṣl: *'alif*-sign introducing the prosthetic vowel which is required in Classical Arabic to avoid consonant clusters in initial position.

haplology: omission of one of two contiguous identical or similar syllables or sounds, resulting in the contraction of a word.

haplography: the unintentional omission of one or more repeated letters, words, or parts of a text in writing or copying.

ḥaraka, plur. *ḥarakāt*: Arabic name of the three short vowels *a*, *i*, *u* indicated by diacritical signs.

ḥarf, plur. *ḥurūf*: Arabic name of the letters of the alphabet.

head: main nominal element to which the secondary elements refer.

Hexapla: Origen's edition of the Bible containing six Hebrew and Greek versions in parallel columns, the second one giving the Hebrew text in Greek vocalized transcription (3rd century A.D.).

hieratic: cursive form of ancient Egyptian hieroglyphs.

hieroglyphs: picture writing of ancient Egyptians.

ḥireq: Tiberian Masoretic vowel sign for *i*.

hiss: sibilant, fricative.

historical and comparative linguistics: the branch of linguistics which describes changes in language systems over periods of time and considers the interrelationships of languages; diachronic linguistics.

ḥolem: Tiberian Masoretic vowel sign for the vowel *o*.

homonymy: identity of sound or name with diversity of meaning.

homorganic: said of speech sounds which are produced in a similar position of the speech organs, as [p] and [b].

hypocoristic: pertaining to or characterizing a hypocoristicon.

hypocoristicon: shortened name, pet name, endearing diminutive.

hypothetical conditional clause: unfulfilled conditional clause.

'ibdāl luġawī: name given by Arab grammarians to pairs of words which mutually correspond in meaning but differ from each other by one consonant; e.g. *ǧadaṯ* and *ǧadaf*, "grave". In reality, this phenomenon is not lexical (*luġawī*) but phonetic, and it goes back to a shift in the articulation of some consonants, in certain conditions.

'ibdāl naḥwī or *ṣarfī*: name given by Arab grammarians to morpho-phonological changes, such as the substitution of the glide *y* by the glottal stop.

'imāla: palatalized articulation of vowels in the terminology of Arab grammarians.

'imāla šadīda: "strong palatalization", change of [a:] into [e:] or [i:] in the terminology of Arab grammarians.

imperative: mood of the verb which expresses command.

imperfect: tense of the verb that indicates action as unaccomplished, incomplete, being performed.

imperfective: verbal aspect denoting incompletion.

indefinite: said of noun, pronoun, article that does not specify the person or object.

indefinite pronoun: a pronoun that represents an object indefinitely or generally, as "any", "each".

indicative: mood of the verb in which an act or condition are stated, negated, or questioned as actual facts.

infinitive: mood of the verb which expresses action or condition without specifying the person, the gender, the number, the time, the aspect, etc., and which may function as a noun.

infix: a grammatical morpheme inserted in the body of a word.

infixed plural: broken plural.

inflected: said of a language modifying radicals by affixes or internal changes to show the syntactic relation of one word to other words in a sentence.

inflection: a pattern of changes undergone by words to express grammatical and syntactical relations, as of case, number, gender, person, tense, mood, voice, etc. The inflection of nouns, adjectives, and pronouns is called "declension"; that of verbs, "conjugation".

instrumental: the case of the noun indicating the means or instrument by or with which an action is performed.

intensive: verbal form expressing action performed with intensity, by several subjects, or on a plurality of objects.

interdental: articulated with the tip of the tongue between the teeth, as [θ], [δ].

interjection: one-term sentence expressing emotion or simple exclamation, as "oh!"

international phonetic alphabet: alphabet drawn by the International Phonetic Association, designed to be applicable to all languages, and consisting, as a rule, of single characters of the Roman alphabet, with diacritical marks if necessary, and supplemented by italics and by Greek letters when occasion demands.

interrogative: a word, phrase, or sentence used to ask a question.

interrupted: kinetic.

intransitive verb: verb whose action is not transferred to an object but terminates in the subject or doer, patient or agent.

isogloss: the geographical boundary of a linguistic trait.
iterative: frequentative, repetitive.

jussive: mood expressing command, exhortation, wish, also finality or consequence.

kasra: Arabic vowel sign for the short vowel *i*, called *kasr*.
kinetic: consonant that cannot be uttered continuously without changing quality, as [p], [b], [t], [d], [k], [g]; stop.

labial: articulated chiefly by the lips, bilabial as [p], [b], [m], [w], or rounded vowel as [ö].
labialization: articulation characterized by the rounding of the lips, a slight narrowing of the pharynx, and a concomitant velarization; labialized consonants are indicated by an exponent w, e.g. [tʷ], [sʷ].
labialize: to modify a sound by rounding the lips.
labiodental: articulated with the lower lip and the upper front teeth, as [f].
laryngal, laryngeal: said of speech sound originating in the larynx, as [ʔ], [h].
laryngography: description of the larynx based on its examination by means of a laryngoscope.
laryngo-pharyngoscope: device showing action by the uvula and the glottis.
lateral: articulated with the tongue making an alveolar closure in the centre of the mouth, while breath escapes on the side or sides, in Latin *latera*, hence "lateral", as [l].
lax consonant/vowel: formed with a relatively relaxed tongue and jaw; opposed to "tense".
length: period required for the articulation of a sound, vowel or consonant.
lenis: a consonant, usually a voiced stop, weakly articulated; in Greek grammar, *spiritus lenis*.
lexeme: lexical distinctive features of a word or phrase, expressing its meaning in a given language, as distinguished from its syntactical function.
lexicography: description of the meaning of the words of a language.
lexicostatistics: glottochronology.
linguistic geography: the branch of linguistics which studies the characteristics and the geographic diffusion patterns of the various dialects of a language system.
liquid: articulated with a smoothly flowing sound, as [l], [r].
lisping: pronouncing a sibilant with the tongue between the teeth so that the sound produced is like [θ].
loanword: a word adopted from another language.
locative: case of the noun denoting, in inflected languages, place where or time at which.
logogram: cuneiform word sign.

madda: Arabic diacritical sign placed above the *'alif* to signify the syllable *'ā* and, in an earlier orthography, to indicate *ā'*, *ī'*, *ū'*.
maǧhūra: "fortis" in Sibawayh's terminology, often explained erroneously as "voiced".

mahmūsa: "lenis" in Sibawayh's terminology, often explained erroneously as "voiceless".

marked: said of forms derived from an unmarked basis or stem by means of additional morphemes.

mater lectionis: Latin expression indicating a Semitic consonantal character used as vowel letter.

metanalyze: analyze one form as another one, despite their different nature or origin.

metaphor: figurative meaning of a word implying a tacit comparison; kind of polysemy.

metaplasm: a change in a word or sentence by adding, transposing, or removing a syllable, letter, or word.

metaplastic: pertaining to metaplasm.

metathesis: transposition of letters, syllables, or sounds in a word.

metathetical: pertaining to a metathesis.

metonymy: a figure of speech that consists in the naming of a person or thing by one of its attributes, as Arabic *ḏū l-qarnayn*, "the two-horned", for Alexander the Great.

mimation: an -*m* ending added to nouns.

modal: denoting a mood of grammar.

monophonemization: phonemic change from a cluster to a single phoneme, e.g. [st] > [ʃ:].

monophthongization: changing of a diphthong into a long vowel.

monosemy: uniqueness of sense attached to a lexeme, rare, except in scientific terminology.

monosyllabic: consisting of a single syllable.

mood, mode: particular manner in which the action or condition expressed by a verb is stated, whether as actual (indicative), desirable (jussive), commanded (imperative), subordinate (subjunctive), etc.

morph: realization of a morpheme.

morpheme: the smallest meaningful unit in the language, such as a stem, a root, an affix.

morphology: the branch of linguistics which deals with morphemes, their arrangement in words, the inflection, and the changes the words undergo in various grammatical structures.

morpho-phonemic: indicating both a phoneme and a morpheme.

morpho-syntactic(al): pertaining to morpho-syntaxis.

morpho-syntaxis: branch of linguistics dealing with morphological data related to syntaxis.

multiplicative: a numeral indicating multiplication, as "twice", "three times", or "double", "triple", etc.

nasal: articulated with the voiced breath passing partially or wholly through the nose, as in [m], [n], [ñ].

nasalize: to modify a sound by articulating it in the manner of nasals, as in the change [b] > [m].

negative: to express refusal or denial; a word, phrase, clause, or sentence expressing refusal or denial.

nisba: Arabic appellation of an adjective or a name denoting descent or origin, ending in -*ī*(*y*).

nomen rectum: Latin name of the noun governed by another noun and being, in inflected languages, in the genitive case.

nomen regens: Latin name of the noun governing another noun or an asyndetic relative clause, and being, in Semitic languages, in the construct state.

nomen unitatis: Latin appellation of a singulative.

nominal: pertaining to nouns or functioning as nouns.

nominalization: the transformation of verbally expressible content, of a predication, of a sentence, into a noun or a nominal phrase, like Hebrew *bā'al hab-bayit*, "he owns the house", into *ba'al hab-bayit*, "the owner of the house".

nominalizer: morpheme affixed to a noun or to a verbal form, and thus producing a nominal pattern.

nominative: case denoting, in inflected languages, the subject of a finite verb, or a word agreeing with, or in apposition to the subject.

noun: a word used as the name of a thing, quality, or action; a substantive, an adjective, a participle, an infinitive (verbal noun).

noun of agent: noun designating an actor, doer, performer.

numeral: a word that expresses a number.

nunation: an -*n* ending added to nouns.

object: a noun or pronoun to which the action of a verb is directed, or which receives the effect of this action.

occlusive: articulated with a total blockage of the breath stream followed by an explosive release, as [p], [t].

on-glide: initial sound made in articulating a vowel standing at the beginning of a word.

onomatopoeia: word imitating natural sounds, as Hebrew *tāqa'*, "to beat" (cf. "tick-tack").

onset: beginning of a consonant articulation, as opposed to "wipe-off".

operative: used to produce new words, new forms; productive.

optative: the mood which expresses wish, desire, or entreaty.

ordinal number: a numeral that shows the order of a unit in a given series, as "first", "second", etc.

orthography: system of written symbols to represent language sounds; art of writing with the correct spelling; the part of grammar which treats of writing systems and of spelling.

palatal: articulated by placing the front of the tongue near or against the hard palate, as in [j].

palatalize: to modify a sound by articulating it in the manner of palatals, as in the change [k] > [č].

palato-alveolar: articulated with the front of the tongue touching the hard palate near the alveolar ridge, as [ʃ], [ʒ].

paradigm: pattern of nominal, pronominal, and verbal inflection.

paragogic: qualification of an inorganic sound or syllable added at the end of a word without a change in meaning, as in Hebrew *bənō Ṣippōr*, "son of Ṣippōr".

parallelism: correspondence or similarity of construction in successive passages or clauses, especially in Semitic poetry.

paroxytone: having the stress or accent on the penultimate syllable.

participle: verbal derivative that may function as both a verb and a noun.

particle: a short, uninflected part of speech, as a preposition, an interjection, an article, a conjunction, a subjunction.

passive: nominal or verbal form indicating that the subject is being acted upon.

pataḥ: Tiberian Masoretic vowel sign for the vowel *a*.

patronymic: the name derived from the father, from an ancestor, and sometimes becoming a family name.

pattern: a combination of phonemes according to a general design corresponding to a semantic category of words.

paucative: grammatical category expressing smallness of number or quantity, as Tigre *wa'āt*, "a few cows".

pausal form: particular word-form occurring at the end of an utterance, especially in Classical Arabic and in Biblical Hebrew.

pejorative: semantic class denoting a deteriorating meaning, as Tigre *waletāy*, "bad girl", against *walat*, "girl".

penult, penultimate: the syllable next to the last in a word.

perfect: tense of the verb that indicates action as accomplished, completed.

perfective: verbal aspect denoting completion.

permansive: stative.

person: grammatical inflected category of pronouns and verbs that distinguishes the speaker (first person), the addressee (second person), and the person or thing spoken of (third person).

personal: actor affix denoting or indicating the person, as the personal pronoun.

pharyngal, pharyngeal: said of speech sound originating in the pharynx, as [ħ], [ʕ].

pharyngalized, pharyngealized: said of consonants articulated with the contraction of the upper pharynx, accompanied by a velarization; these consonants are indicated in script by a dot under the letter ([ḍ]) or by a tilde in the centre of the letter ([ɫ]).

phone: realization of a phoneme.

phonematics: phonemics.

phoneme: bundle of concurrent distinctive acoustic features which serves primarily to differentiate morphemes and whole words (from Greek φώνημα, "speech-sound"); the phonemes are usually represented between slant lines (e.g. /p/, /u/) and their actual realization is variable. One or more phonemes may constitute one morpheme.

phonemics: study of the distinctive function of speech sounds.

phonetic complement, phonetic indicator: cuneiform graphic affix which specifies the Semitic ending of a word represented by a Sumerogram or logogram, as ĸɪ-*tim* that indicates the reading of the genitive *erṣetim*, "of the earth". Hence it is a graphic affix with morpho-phonemic reference.

phonetics: the branch of linguistics which deals with the analysis, description, and classification of speech sounds.

phonology: phonemics.

phonotactics: the branch of linguistic which deals with questions related to the order and arrangement of phonemes.

phrase: a group of two or more associate words, not containing a subject and predicate, but forming a distinctive part of a sentence.

pictogram: pictorial graph.

pitch: the acuteness or gravity of the tones of a language.

"plene" spelling/writing: orthography characterized by the use of vowel letters or signs which, as a rule, indicate length, sometimes high stress or pitch.

plosive: occlusive.

plural: the form of the noun, pronoun, or verb indicating its application either to more than one person or thing, or, in idioms using the dual, to more than two.

plus-vocalic: a consonant possessing vocalic qualities in addition, as the sonorants.

polysemantic: having several meanings.

polysemous: pertaining to polysemy.

polysemy: diversity of sense resulting from the various usage of the same lexeme.

postposition: postpositive preposition.

pragmalinguistics: the study of linguistic acts or utterances, and of the contexts in which they are performed.

precative: optative.

predicate: the word or words in a sentence that express what is stated of a subject.

predication: saying something about the subject.

prefix: a non-separable morpheme affixed to the beginning of a word to modify its meaning, to specify its function, etc.

preformative: morpheme prefixed to a root or a basis.

pre-glottalized emphatic: pronounced with a closed and stationary glottis in the initial phase of the articulation.

prepalatal: palatal.

preposition: particle functioning to indicate the relation of a noun or pronoun to another element of the sentence.

prepositional phrase: phrase governed by a preposition.

present: tense of the verb that indicates action being performed or condition being in existence.

preterite: tense of the verb that indicates past time or completed past action.

preverb: a verbal prefix, usually marking an aspectual or temporal feature; e.g. Damascene Arabic *byəktob*, "he writes" (present).

proclitic: monosyllabic particle attached to a following word.

productive: used to produce new words, new forms; operative.

pro form: short word, often a pronoun, replacing a logical constituent of the clause.

progressive assimilation: partial or total assimilation of a sound to a preceding one.

prohibitive: the mood which expresses the interdiction.

prolepsis: anaphoric anticipation of a word in a clause.

proleptic: pertaining to prolepsis.

pronominal suffix: a pronoun suffixed to a noun, a verb, or a preposition.

pronominalization: process by which a noun is replaced by a pronoun.

pronoun: a word used as a substitute for a noun.

proper name: the distinctive appellation by which a person, a place, or a thing is known.

prosthesis, prothesis: addition of a vowel or syllable at the beginning of a word for articulatory reasons.

prosthetic, prothetic: qualification of a vowel or syllable added at the beginning of a word for articulatory reasons.

qameṣ: Tiberian Masoretic vowel sign interpreted in Modern Hebrew as a long vowel *ā*.

qibbuṣ: Tiberian Masoretic vowel sign for *u*.

qualitative: class of denominative verbs, generally expressing a quality; used especially in the grammar of Libyco-Berber as an equivalent of "stative".

quantitative vowel gradation: the quantity or acoustic duration of the vowels in a word as conditioned by the presence or absence of stress accent; it is usually expressed in milliseconds ($^1/_{1000}$ of a second).

radical: consonant or vowel belonging to the root.

realization: actual phonetic value or pronunciation of consonantal and vocalic phonemes or written letters, signs, and characters of a language.

reciprocal: mutual, especially in relation to assimilation.

reduction: shortening of a vowel or monophthongization of a diphthong.

reduplication: repetition of an element, as a syllable, in a word; e.g. Tigrinya *bäsbäsä*, "to be rotten".

reflex: adaptation from another language or dialect, seen in a synchronic or diachronic perspective.

reflexive: action referring to its subject, tense expressing such an action.

reflexive pronoun: a pronoun or its substitute referring back to the subject of a clause.

regressive assimilation: retroactive assimilation causing the partial or total change of a sound in the following one.

relative clause: qualifying an antecedent term.

relative pronoun: a pronoun or its substitute that relates a subordinate relative clause to an antecedent.

rhino-pharyngoscope: laryngo-pharyngoscope.

root: morpheme serving as the basic constituent element of a related group of forms or words.

rounding: uttering of a vowel with the lips in a rounded position; labializing.

šadda: Arabic diacritical sign indicating the *tašdīd*, i.e. the gemination of a consonant.

sandhi: the assimilative changes produced in combined sounds of neighbouring words in consecutive speech and the subsequent changes occurring sometimes in their spelling.

secondary: produced in a subsequent phase, resulting from an influence.

segol: Tiberian Masoretic diacritical sign for the vowel *e*.

segolate: Hebrew noun type characterized by *segol* (*e*) vowels in the singular absolute state.

semantic: pertaining to meaning.

semantic field: a group of words that share one or more semantic components, as "white", "black", "blue", etc., or "sell*ing*", "buy*ing*", "walk*ing*", etc.

semantics: the study of the development and changes in meaning of words and syntagms, considered both in a diachronic and in a synchronic perspectives.

semiotic: pertaining to semantics.

semiotics: semantics.

semivowel: a vowellike sound used as a consonant and as a glide, as [w] and [y].

sentence: a word or a related group of words expressing a complete thought.

sequence of tenses: normal choice of tense for a verb that follows another in a sentence; *consecutio temporum*.

ṣere: Tiberian Masoretic vowel sign for *ē*.

šəwa mobile: Masoretic diacritical sign borrowed from the Syriac *šəwayyā* and having the same shape as the *šəwa quiescens*, but indicating a very short vowel of the *ə* type; it is called *mobile* (Latin), i.e. pronounceable, in contrast with the *šəwa quiescens*.

šəwa quiescens: Masoretic diacritical sign indicating that a consonant is not followed by a vowel; it is called *quiescens* (Latin), i.e. "quite", in contrast with the *šəwa mobile*.

šəwayyā: Syriac name of an accent sign consisting of two dots, one being placed above the other, and marking the end of a syntactic unit.

simple sentence: a sentence consisting of one independent clause.

singular: denoting one person, thing, or class.

singulative: singular derived from a collective noun by means of an afformative; e.g. Classical Arabic *dam'atun*, "tear", from *dam'un*, "tears".

sonorant: voiced consonant of relatively high resonance, as [l], [m], [n], [r], capable of constituting a syllable and therefore said to be "plus-vocalic"; liquid.

"sound" plural: plural of nouns, formed by adding a plural ending to the stem.

sound spectrography: method used in acoustic phonetics to record, by means of an electronic instrument, the frequencies and the amplitude of speech sounds.

speech strecher: device playing back a sample of speech at some rate other than that at which it was originally uttered, but still retaining the original pitch of the utterance and making it possible to analyze new and unrecorded languages.

spelling: formation of words by using written symbols; orthography.

spirant: fricative.

spirantization: fricative articulation of plosives, producing the changes [b] > [β], [p] > [φ], [t] > [θ], [d] > [ð], [k] > [x], [g] > [γ].

spiritus asper: in Greek grammar, the rough breathing indicated by ʻ, as ἁ, ῥ, etc.

spiritus lenis: in Greek grammar, the smoot breathing indicated by ʼ, as ἀ, ἰ, etc.

state: nominal form depending on its function in the phrase.

stative: inflected verbal or nominal form expressing the condition or state in which the subject exists; it does not imply a preceding change, contrary to the perfect or perfective, nor does it signify a process of change, contrary to the imperfect or imperfective.

stem: element common to all the members of a given inflection, in particular of a verbal type.

stop: consonant articulated with complete closure of the speech organs, as [p], [b], [t], [d], [k], [g], opposed to continuant.

stress: the relative force with which a sound, a syllable, or a word is uttered.

strong plural: "sound" plural.

stylistics: study of literary expression, such as vocabulary, sound, form, order, etc.

subject: the constituent of a sentence about which something is stated or asked in the predicate.

subjoining: placing in immediate sequence or juxtaposition to another element of the sentence, as the *nomen rectum* subjoined to the *nomen regens*.

subjunction: a word used to connect a subordinate clause with the main clause of a sentence; subordinate conjunction.

subjunctive: mood of the finite verb that is used to express the subordinate function of the clause, a future contingency, a mere supposition, a wish, a desire, etc.

subordinate conjunction: subjunction.

substantival clause: expressing the object of the action, utterance, etc.

substantival, substantivized: used as a substantive.

substantive: noun as distinguished from the adjective, the participle, and the infinitive or verbal noun.

suffix: a non-separable morpheme affixed at the end of a word to modify its meaning, to specify its function, etc.

sukūn: Arabic diacritical sign indicating that a consonant is not followed by a vowel.

Sumerogram: cuneiform sign or group of signs corresponding to a Sumerian word, but legible also in other languages, as Palaeosyrian, Old Akkadian, Assyro-Babylonian.

superlative: said of a form of comparison of adjectives or adverbs expressing or involving the highest or utmost degree.

surface structure: linguistic organization of morphemes that constitutes a sentence and aims at formulating a thought that a speaker wants to express.

suspended subject: *casus pendens*.

syllabary: a list of characters representing syllables.

syllable: a word or part of a word uttered in a single vocal impulse, and consisting of a vowel, a diphthong, or a vowel with one or more consonants.

syllabogram: cuneiform syllabic sign.

synchronic: pertaining to the study of some aspect of a language at a given stage in its development.

syncope: elision of a sound or syllable in the middle part of a word.

syndetic: connected by a conjunction.

syntactic: pertaining to syntax.

syntagm(a): linear organization of two or more consecutive units in a sentence.

syntagmatic: pertaining to a syntagm(a).

syntax: arrangement and interrelationship of words in grammatical structures; the branch of linguistics dealing with this.

tafḫīm: velarized articulation in the terminology of Arab grammarians.

Talmud: compilation of Jewish civil and religious laws, with related commentaries and discussion, not comprised in the Bible; it is extant in a Babylonian and in a Palestinian tradition, both with sections written either in Mishnaic Hebrew or in Jewish Aramaic.

tā' marbūṭa: Arabic diacritical sign indicating that the classical feminine endings *-atun*, *-atin*, *-atan* should be restored where the final vowel letter *-h* marks the non-classical feminine ending *-a*.

tanwīn: affixing a final *nūn* to noun forms as an indefinite marker, i.e. nunation in the terminology of Arab grammarians.

tarḫīm: apheresis of the final syllable in an Arabic word introduced by the exclamatory particles *'a* and *yā*, according to the terminology of Arab grammarians.

Targum: Aramaic translation of the Hebrew Bible.

tarqīq: lack of velarized articulation in the terminalogy of Arab grammarians.

tašdīd: gemination of consonants in the terminology of Arab grammarians.

telic situation: situation that involves a process that leads up to a well-defined terminal point (in Greek τέλος, "result, achievement"), beyond which the process cannot continue; e.g. Arabic *tasīrūna 'ilā l-ǧibāli*, "you march to the mountains", involves a telic process that ends when the mountains are reached (cf. atelic action).

temporal clause: expressing time.

tense: a form of the verb that relates it either to time, — past, present, future, — or to aspect, — accomplished, unaccomplished.

tense consonant/vowel: pronounced with the tongue and its muscles taut, so that it may be amplified up to its double; opposed to "lax"; voiced sounds, as [b], [g], [d], are reckoned less tense than voiceless, e.g. [p], [k], [t].

tensing: amplifying a consonant or a vowel by its lengthening or by a sharper onset and/or wipe-off.

textology: explication of texts, text analysis.

theonym: divine name.

theophoric, theophorous: pertaining to proper names containing a divine name, e.g. Arabic *'Abd-Allāh*, *'Abdu-llāhi*.

toneme: a phoneme in which the pitch of utterance is a necessary characteristic, especially in tone languages.

topicalization: placing as *casus pendens*, extraposition.

toponym: place name.

toponymy: nomenclature of place names; science or study of place names.

transcription: transfer of a text written in one script into a continuous text expressed in the alphabetic characters of another script.

transitive verb: expressing an action that terminates upon a direct object, that passes from one party to another.

transliteration: transfer of a sequence of graphemes in a corresponding sequence of their values expressed in the alphabetic characters of another script, letter by letter, sign by sign.

triconsonantal, triradical: root consisting of there radical consonants.

ultima: the last syllable in a word.

unmarked: basic.

unrounding: uttering of a vowel without rounding the lips, as [ū-ī] > [ī].
unvoiced: voiceless.
uvular: articulated by vibration of the uvula, as [R], or with the back of the
    tongue near or against the uvula, as [q], [χ].

value: the value of a cuneiform sign or of a grapheme, in general, is a phoneme
    or a sequence of phonemes represented by the sign or grapheme.
variant: showing variation in articulation, morphology, syntax, or spelling; dif-
    fering from a standard form.
velar: articulated with the back of the tongue touching or near the soft palate, as
    [k], [g].
velarization: articulation characterized by a raising of the back part of the
    tongue in the region of the velum; it accompanies pharyngalization as well
    as labialization.
velarized: said of consonants characterized by velarization.
ventive: allative.
verb: the part of speech which predicates something, expressing existence,
    action, or occurrence.
verbal noun: infinitive.
verbalization: formation of denominative verbs.
vetitive: prohibitive.
vibrant: a speech sound made with vibration of the vocal cords, as [R].
voiced: articulated with vibration of the vocal cords, as [b], [d], [z].
voiceless, unvoiced: articulated without voiced breath, as [p], [t], [s].
volitive: verbal form or clause expressing a will or a permission.
vowel: sound produced by a relatively unimpeded passage of air through the
    mouth, as [a], [i], [u]; distinguished from "consonant".
vowel harmony: mutual assimilation of vowels in a word, especially assimila-
    tion of unstressed short vowels to the stressed ones.

waṣla: name of the 'alif-sign used as hamzat 'al-waṣl and not pronounced as
    glottal stop in Classical Arabic.
wāw compaginis: Latin phrase designating a paragogic -ū / -ō.
wipe-off: end of a consonant articulation, as opposed to "onset".
word: a complex of phonemes, which has come to signify and communicate a
    particular idea or thought and which functions as the smallest meaningful
    unit of a language when used in isolation.

yōd compaginis: Latin phrase designating a paragogic -ī.

zero phoneme: phoneme lacking distinctive consonantic or vocalic features.

BIBLIOGRAPHY

The following bibliography includes works published up to 1997. It is a selective bibliography and, except in cases of special importance, it does not include either works on Semitic published before C. Brockelmann's *Grundriss* or articles dealing with particular questions. However, more articles are quoted in sections 9 and 10.

1. Semitic Languages in General

ARO, J., *Die Vokalisierung des Grundstammes im semitischen Verbum*, Helsinki 1964.

ASPESI, F., *La distinzione dei generi nel nome antico-egiziano e semitico*, Firenze 1977.

BÄR, E., *Bibliographie deutschsprachiger Islamwissenschaftler und Semitisten vom Anfang des 19. Jahrhunderts bis 1985*, 2 vols., Wiesbaden 1985-91.

BARTH, J., *Die Nominalbildung in den semitischen Sprachen*, 2nd ed., Leipzig 1894 (reprint: 1967).

BARTH, J., *Sprachwissenschaftliche Untersuchungen zum Semitischen*, Leipzig 1907-11 (reprint: 1972).

BARTH, J., *Die Pronominalbildung in den semitischen Sprachen*, Leipzig 1913 (reprint: 1967).

BAUER, H., *Die Tempora im Semitischen. Ihre Entstehung und ihre Ausgestaltung in den Einzelsprachen* (Beiträge zur Assyriologie 8/1), Leipzig 1910 (reprint: 1968).

BERGSTRÄSSER, G., *Einführung in die semitischen Sprachen*, München 1928 (reprint: 1975 & 1989). English ed. by P.T. Daniels: *Introduction to the Semitic Languages*, Winona Lake 1983 (reprint: 1994).

BLAU, J., *On Pseudo-Corrections in Some Semitic Languages*, Leiden 1970.

BOTTERWECK, G.J., *Der Triliterismus im Semitischen*, Bonn 1952.

BRAVMANN, M.M., *Studies in Semitic Philology*, Leiden 1977.

BROCKELMANN, C., *Grundriss der vergleichenden Grammatik der semitischen Sprachen*, 2 vols., Berlin 1908-13 (reprint: 1982).

BRUGNATELLI, V., *Questioni di morfologia e sintassi dei numerali cardinali semitici*, Firenze 1982.

BYNON, J. & T., *Hamito-Semitica* (Janua linguarum, Series practica 200), The Hague 1975.

CAQUOT, A. & D. COHEN (eds.), *Actes du Premier Congrès International de Linguistique Sémitique et Chamito-Sémitique*, The Hague 1974.

CASTELLINO, G.R., *The Akkadian Personal Pronouns and Verbal System in the Light of Semitic and Hamitic*, Leiden 1962.

COHEN, D., *La phrase nominale et l'évolution du système verbal en sémitique*, Paris 1984.

COHEN, D. (ed.), *Les langues chamito-sémitiques*, Paris 1988.

COHEN, D. (ed.), *Dictionnaire des racines sémitiques ou attestées dans les langues sémitiques*, Leuven 1993 ff.

COHEN, M., *Le système verbal sémitique et l'expression du temps*, Paris 1924.

COHEN, M., *Essai comparatif sur le vocabulaire et la phonétique du chamito-sémitique*, Paris 1947 (reprint: 1969).

COHEN, D., *Études de linguistique sémitique*, The Hague 1970.

CONTI, G., *Studi sul bilitterismo in semitico e in egiziano. 1. Il tema verbale* (Quaderni di semitistica 9), Firenze 1980.

CORRIENTE, F., *Problemática de la pluralidad en semítico: el plural fracto*, Madrid 1971.

DIAKONOFF, I.M., *Semito-Hamitic Languages. An Essay in Classification*, Moscow 1965.

DIAKONOFF, I.M., *Afrasian Languages*, Moscow 1988.

DIEM, W., *Die Entwicklung des Derivationsmorphems der t-Stämme im Semitischen*, in *Zeitschrift der Deutschen Morgenländischen Gesellschaft* 132 (1982), p. 29-84.

FEGHALI, M. & A. CUNY, *Du genre grammatical en sémitique*, Paris 1924.

FLEISCH, H., *Les verbes à allongement vocalique interne en sémitique*, Paris 1944.

FONTINOY, C., *Le duel dans les langues sémitiques*, Paris 1969.

FRONZAROLI, P., *Studi sul lessico comune semitico*, in *Rendiconti dell'Accademia Nazionale dei Lincei. Classe di scienze morali, storiche e filologiche*, 8th ser., 19 (1964), p. 155-172, 245-280; 20 (1965), p. 135-150, 246-269; 23 (1968), p. 267-303; 24 (1969), p. 285-320; 26 (1971), p. 603-642.

FRONZAROLI, P. (ed.), *Studies on Semitic Lexicography* (Quaderni di Semitistica 2), Firenze 1973.

FRONZAROLI, P. (ed.), *Atti del Secondo Congresso Internazionale di Linguistica Camito-Semitica* (Quaderni di Semitistica 5), Firenze 1978.

GAI, A., *The Category 'Adjective' in Semitic Languages*, in *Journal of Semitic Studies* 40 (1995), p. 1-9.

GARR, W.R., *The* Niphal *Derivational Prefix*, in *Orientalia*, n.s. 62 (1993), p. 142-162.

GELB, I.J., *A Study of Writing*, 2nd ed., Chicago 1963.

GOLDENBERG, G. & S. RAZ, *Semitic and Cushitic Studies*, Wiesbaden 1994.

GRANDE, B.M., Введение в сравнительное изучение семитских языков, Moscow 1972.

GRAY, L.H., *Introduction to Semitic Comparative Linguistics*, New York 1934 (reprint: 1971).

GREENBERG, J., *Studies in African Linguistic Classification*, New Haven 1955.

GREENBERG, J., *The Languages of Africa*, The Hague 1963 (reprint: 1966, 1970).

HEINE, B., Th. C. SCHADEBERG & E. WOLFF (eds.), *Die Sprachen Afrikas. Ein Handbuch*, Hamburg 1981.

HETZRON, R., *The Evidence for Perfect* *y'aqtul *and Jussive* *yaqt'ul *in Proto-Semitic*, in *Journal of Semitic Studies* 14 (1969), p. 1-21.

HETZRON, R. (ed.), *The Semitic Languages*, London 1997.

HODGE, C.T. (ed.), *Afroasiatic: A Survey*, The Hague 1971.

HOSPERS, J.H. (ed.), *A Basic Bibliography for the Study of the Semitic Languages*, 2 vols., Leiden 1973-74.

HURWITZ, S.T.H., *Root-Determinatives in Semitic Speech*, New York 1913.

IZRE'EL Sh. & Sh. RAZ (eds.), *Studies in Modern Semitic Languages* (Israel Oriental Studies 16), Leiden 1996.

JANSSENS, G., *Contribution to the Verbal System in Old Egyptian. A New Approach to the Reconstruction of the Hamito-Semitic Verbal System* (Orientalia Gandensia 6), Leuven 1972.

JUNGRAITHMAYR, H. & W.W. MÜLLER (eds.), *Proceedings of the 4th International Hamito-Semitic Congress* (Current Issues in Linguistic Theory 44), Amsterdam-Philadelphia 1987.

KAMIL, M., *Beiträge zur Entstehung der vierradikaligen Verben in den gesprochenen semitischen Sprachen*, Le Caire 1963.

KAYE, A.S. (ed.), *Semitic Studies in Honor of Wolf Leslau*, 2 vols., Wiesbaden 1991.

KHAN, G., *Studies in Semitic Syntax* (London Oriental Series 38), Oxford 1988.

KRAMERS, J.H., *De Semietische talen*, Leiden 1949.

KURYŁOWICZ, J., *L'apophonie en sémitique*, Wrocław-Kraków 1961.

KURYŁOWICZ, J., *Studies in Semitic Grammar and Metrics*, Kraków 1972.

LEVI DELLA VIDA, G. (ed.), *Linguistica semitica: presente e futuro* (Studi semitici 4), Roma 1961.

LIEBERMAN, S.J., *The Afro-Asiatic Background of the Semitic N-Stem*, in *Bibliotheca Orientalis* 43 (1986), col. 577-628.

LINDBERG, O.E., *Vergleichende Grammatik der semitischen Sprachen I. Lautlehre*, Göteborg 1897.

LOPRIENO, A., *Das Verbalsystem im Ägyptischen und im Semitischen*, Wiesbaden 1986.

MEILLET, A. & M. COHEN (eds.), *Les langues du monde*, 2nd ed., Paris 1952, p. 81-181.

MOSCATI, S., *An Introduction to the Comparative Grammar of the Semitic Languages*, Wiesbaden 1964 (reprint: 1969 & 1980).

MUKAROVSKY, H.G. (ed.), *Proceedings of the Fifth International Hamito-Semitic Congress* (Beiträge zur Afrikanistik 40-41), 2 vols., Wien 1990-91.

NAVEH, J., *Early History of the Alphabet*, 2nd ed., Jerusalem 1987.

NÖLDEKE, T., *Beiträge und Neue Beiträge zur semitischen Sprachwissenschaft*, Strassburg 1904-10 (reprint: 1982).

O'LEARY, DE LACY, *Comparative Grammar of the Semitic Languages*, London 1923 (reprint: 1969).

OREL, V.E. & O.V. STOLBOVA, *Hamito-Semitic Etymological Dictionary. Materials for a Reconstruction*, Leiden 1995.

PENNACCHIETTI, F.A., *Studi sui pronomi determinativi semitici*, Napoli 1968.

PENNACCHIETTI, F.A., *Appunti per una storia comparata dei sistemi preposizionali semitici*, in *Annali dell'Istituto Orientale di Napoli* 34 (1974), p. 161-208, pl. I-VII.

PETRÁČEK, K., *Die innere Flexion in den semitischen Sprachen*, in *Archiv Orientální* 28 (1960), p. 547-606; 29 (1961), p. 513-545; 30 (1962), p. 361-408; 31 (1963), p. 577-624; 32 (1964), p. 185-222.

PETRÁČEK, K., *Altägyptisch, Hamitosemitisch und ihre Beziehungen zu einigen Sprachfamilien in Afrika und Asien*, Praha 1988.

Proceedings of the International Conference on Semitic Studies, Jerusalem 1969.

REINISCH, L., *Das persönliche Fürwort und die Verbalflexion in den chamito-semitischen Sprachen*, Wien 1909.

RETSÖ, J., *Diathesis in the Semitic Languages: A Comparative Morphological Study*, Leiden 1989.

RÖSSLER, O., *Verbalbau und Verbalflexion in den semito-hamitischen Sprachen*, in *Zeitschrift der Deutschen Morgenländischen Gesellschaft* 100 (1950), p. 461-514; English ed.: *The Structure and Inflexion of the Verb in the Semito-Hamitic Languages*, in Y.L. Arbeitman & A.R. Bomhard (eds.), *Bono Homini Donum* (Current Issues in Linguistic Theory 16), Amsterdam 1981, p. 679-748.

RUNDGREN, F., *Über Bildungen mit š- und n-t- Demonstrativen im Semitischen. Beiträge zur vergleichenden Grammatik der semitischen Sprachen*, Uppsala 1955.

RUNDGREN, F., *Intensiv und Aspekt-Korrelation. Studien zur äthiopischen und akkadischen Verbalstammbildung*, Uppsala 1959.

RUNDGREN, F., *Erneuerung des Verbalaspekts im Semitischen. Funktionell - diachronische Studien zur semitischen Verblehre*, Uppsala 1963.

RŮŽIČKA, R., *Konsonantische Dissimilation in den semitischen Sprachen* (Beiträge zur Assyriologie 6/4), Leipzig 1909 (reprint: 1968).

SARAUW, C., *Über Akzent und Silbenbildung in den älteren semitischen Sprachen* (Det Kgl. Danske Videnskabernes Selskab, Hist.-fil. Meddelelser 26/8), København 1939.

SEBEOK, A.T. (ed.), *Current Trends in Linguistics* VI. *Linguistics in South West Asia and North Africa*, The Hague 1970.

SHILO, V., *Hebrew-Aramaic-Assyrian Dictionary*, 2 vols., Jerusalem 1994.

SIEDL, S.H., *Gedanken zum Tempussystem im Hebräischen und Akkadischen*, Wiesbaden 1971.

SODEN, W. VON, *Tempus und Modus im älteren Semitischen*, in H.-P. Müller (ed.), *Babylonien und Israel*, Darmstadt 1991, p. 463-493.

SOLÁ-SOLÉ, J.M., *L'infinitif sémitique*, Paris 1961.

SPEISER, E.A., *Oriental and Biblical Studies*, Philadelphia 1967.

SPULER, B. (ed.), *Handbuch der Orientalistik. Band III. Semitistik*, Leiden 1952-54 (reprint: 1964).

STARININ, V.P., Структура семитского слова, Moscow 1963.

STEINER, R.C., *The Case for Fricative Laterals in Proto-Semitic* (American Oriental Series 59), New Haven 1977.

THACKER, T.W., *The Relationship of the Semitic and Egyptian Verbal Systems*, Oxford 1954.

VERGOTE, J., *De verhouding van het Egyptisch tot de Semietische talen* (Mededelingen van de Koninklijke Vlaamse Academie voor Wetenschappen, Letteren en Schone Kunsten von België, Kl. der Letteren 27/4), Brussel 1965.

WRIGHT, W., *Lectures on the Comparative Grammar of the Semitic Languages* (ed. by W.R. Smith), Cambridge 1890 (reprint: 1966 & 1981).

ZABORSKI, A., *Biconsonantal Verbal Roots in Semitic*, in *Zeszyty naukowe Uniwersytetu Jagiellońskiego* 269 (1971), p. 51-98.

ZEMÁNEK, P., *The Origin of Pharyngealization in Semitic*, Praha 1996.

ZEMÁNEK, P. (ed.), *Studies in Near Eastern Languages and Literatures. Memorial Volume of Karel Petráček*, Praha 1996.

ZETTERSTÉEN, K.V., *De semitiska Språken*, Uppsala 1914.

ZIMMERN, H., *Vergleichende Grammatik der semitischen Sprachen*, Berlin 1898.

2. NORTH SEMITIC

AARTUN, K. *Die Partikeln des Ugaritischen* (Alter Orient und Altes Testament 21), 2 vols., Kevelaer-Neukirchen-Vluyn 1974-78.

AARTUN, K., *Studien zur ugaritischen Lexikographie* I, Wiesbaden 1991.

AISTLEITNER, J., *Untersuchungen zur Grammatik des Ugaritischen*, Berlin 1954.

AISTLEITNER, J., *Wörterbuch der ugaritischen Sprache*, 4th ed., Berlin 1974.

CAGNI, L. (ed.), *La lingua di Ebla*, Napoli 1981.

CAGNI, L. (ed.), *Il bilinguismo a Ebla*, Napoli 1984.

CAGNI, L. (ed.), *Ebla 1975-1985. Dieci anni di studi linguistici e filologici*, Napoli 1987.

CUNCHILLOS, J.-L. & J.-P. VITA, *Concordancia de palabras ugaríticas en morfología desplegada*, 3 vols., Madrid-Zaragoza 1995.

DEL OLMO LETE, G. & J. SANMARTÍN, *Diccionario de la lengua ugarítica* I, *A/L*, Sabadell 1996.

DIETRICH, M. & O. LORETZ, *A Word-List of the Cuneiform Alphabetic Texts from Ugarit, Ras Ibn Hani and Other Places (KTU: second, enlarged edition)*, Münster 1996.

FISHER, L.R. (S. Rummel) (ed.), *Ras Shamra Parallels*, 3 vols., Rome 1972-81.

FRONZAROLI, P., *La fonetica ugaritica*, Roma 1955.

FRONZAROLI, P. (ed.), *Studies on the Language of Ebla* (Quaderni di Semitistica 13), Firenze 1984.

FRONZAROLI, P. (ed.), *Miscellanea Eblaitica* (Quaderni di Semitistica 15-17), 3 vols., Firenze 1988-90.

GELB, I.J., *La lingua degli Amoriti*, in *Accademia Nazionale dei Lincei. Rendiconti della Classe di Scienze morali, storiche e filologiche*, 8th ser., 13 (1958), p. 143-164.

GELB, I.J., *Thoughts about Ibla. A Preliminary Evaluation* (Syro-Mesopotamian Studies I/1), Malibu 1977.

GELB, I.J., *Computer-Aided Analysis of Amorite*, Chicago 1980.

GELB, I.J., *Ebla and the Kish Civilization*, in L. Cagni (ed.), *La lingua di Ebla*, Napoli 1981, p. 9-73.

GELB, I.J., *Mari and the Kish Civilization*, in G.D. Young (ed.), *Mari in Retrospect*, Winona Lake 1992, p. 121-202.

GORDON, C.H., *Ugaritic Textbook*, 3 vols., Rome 1965 (reprint: 1967).

GORDON, C.H. & G. RENDSBURG (eds.), *Eblaitica* 1-3, Winona Lake 1987-92.

HAMMADE, H., F. ISMAIL, M. LEBEAU, I. POINOT, W. SALLABERGER, P. TALON & K. VAN LERBERGHE, *Administrative Documents from Tell Beydar* (Subartu II), Turnhout 1996.

HUEHNERGARD, J., *Ugaritic Vocabulary in Syllabic Transcription* (Harvard Semitic Studies 34), Atlanta 1987.

HUFFMON, H.B., *Amorite Personal Names in the Mari Texts*, Baltimore 1965.

PARDEE, D. & R.M. WHITING, *Aspects of Epistolary Verbal Usage in Ugaritic and Akkadian*, in *Bulletin of the School of Oriental and African Studies* 50 (1987), p. 1-31.

PETTINATO, G. (ed.), *Thesaurus inscriptionum Eblaicarum*, Roma 1995 [1996] ff.

PETTINATO, G., *I pronomi personali indipendenti e suffissi in eblaita*, in *Festschrift S. Moscati*, Roma 1996.

RENFROE, F., *Arabic-Ugaritic Lexical Studies*, Münster 1992.

SEGERT, St., Угаритский язык, Moscow 1965.

SEGERT, St., *A Basic Grammar of the Ugaritic Language*, Berkeley-London 1984.

SIVAN, D., *Ugaritic Grammar* (in Hebrew), Jerusalem 1993. English ed.: *A Grammar of the Ugaritic Language*, Leiden 1997.

TROPPER, J., *Der ugaritische Kausativstamm und die Kausativbildungen des Semitischen*, Münster 1990.

VERREET, E., *Modi Ugaritici*, Leuven 1988.

ZEMÁNEK, P., *Ugaritischer Wortformenindex* (Lexicographia Orientalis 4), Hamburg 1995.

3. EAST SEMITIC

ADLER, H.-P., *Das Akkadische des Königs Tušratta von Mitanni* (Alter Orient und Altes Testament 201), Kevelaer-Neukirchen-Vluyn 1976.

ARO, J., *Abnormal Plene Writings in Akkadian Texts* (Studia Orientalia 19/1), Helsinki 1953.

ARO, J., *Studien zur mittelbabylonischen Grammatik* (Studia Orientalia 20), Helsinki 1955.

ARO, J., *Glossar zu den mittelbabylonischen Briefen* (Studia Orientalia 22), Helsinki 1957.

ARO, J., *Die akkadischen Infinitivkonstruktionen* (Studia Orientalia 26), Helsinki 1961.

BERKOOZ, M., *The Nuzi Dialect of Akkadian. Orthography and Phonology*, Philadelphia 1937 (reprint: 1966).

BORGER, R., *Assyrisch-babylonische Zeichenliste* (Alter Orient und Altes Testament 33), Kevelaer-Neukirchen-Vluyn 1978 (reprint: 1981, with *Ergänzungsheft*).

BUCCELLATI, G., *An Interpretation of the Akkadian Stative as a Nominal Sentence*, in *Journal of Near Eastern Studies* 27 (1968), p. 1-12.

BUCCELLATI, G., *The Case against the Alleged Akkadian Plural Morpheme* -ānū, in *Afroasiatic Linguistics* 3 (1976), p. 19-27.

BUCCELLATI, G., *The State of the "Stative"*, in Y.L. Arbeitman (ed.), *Fucus* (Current Issues in Linguistic Theory 58), Amsterdam-Philadelphia 1988, p. 153-189.

BUCCELLATI, G., *A Structural Grammar of Babylonian*, Wiesbaden 1996.

DE MEYER, L., *L'accadien des contrats de Suse*, Leiden 1962.

EHELOLF, H., *Ein Wortfolgeprinzip im Assyrisch-Babylonischen* (Leipziger semitistische Studien 6/3), Leipzig 1916.

FINET, A., *L'accadien des lettres de Mari*, Bruxelles / Brussel 1956.

GELB, I.J., *Glossary of Old Akkadian* (Materials for the Assyrian Dictionary 3), Chicago 1957 (reprint: 1973).

GELB, I.J., *Old Akkadian Writing and Grammar* (Materials for the Assyrian Dictionary 2), 2nd ed., Chicago 1961 (reprint: 1973).

GELB, I.J., *Sequential Reconstruction of Proto-Akkadian* (Assyriological Studies 18), Chicago 1969.

GIACUMAKIS, G., *The Akkadian of Alalaḫ*, The Hague 1970.

GRONEBERG, R.M., *Syntax, Morphologie und Stil der jungbabylonischen "hymnischen" Literatur*, 2 vols., Stuttgart 1987.

HECKER, K., *Grammatik der Kültepe - Texte*, Rom 1968.

HECKER, K., *Rückläufiges Wörterbuch des Akkadischen*, Wiesbaden 1990.

HUEHNERGARD, J., *On Verbless Clauses in Akkadian*, in *Zeitschrift für Assyriologie* 76 (1986), p. 218-249.

HUEHNERGARD, J., *"Stative", Predicative Form, Pseudo-Verb*, in *Journal of Near Eastern Studies* 46 (1987), p. 215-232.

HUEHNERGARD, J., *The Akkadian of Ugarit* (Harvard Semitic Studies 34), Atlanta 1989.

HYATT, J.Ph., *The Treatment of Final Vowels in Early Neo-Babylonian*, New Haven 1941 (reprint: 1980).

IKEDA, J., *Syntax & Paradigmatic of Emar Akkadian*, in T. Mikasa (ed.), *Essays on Ancient Anatolia and Syria in the Second and Third Millennium B.C.*, Wiesbaden 1996, p. 241-257.

IZRE'EL, Sh., *Amurru Akkadian: A Linguistic Study* (Harvard Semitic Studies 40-41), 2 vols., Atlanta 1991.

JUCQUOIS, G., *Phonétique comparée des dialectes moyen-babyloniens du nord et de l'ouest*, Louvain 1966.

KIENAST, B., *Glossar zu den altakkadischen Königsinschriften*, Stuttgart 1994.

KRAUS, F.R., *Nominalsätze in altbabylonischen Briefen und der Stativ*, Amsterdam 1984.

KRAUS, F.R., *Sonderformen akkadischer Parataxe*, Amsterdam 1987.

LABAT, R., *L'akkadien de Boghaz-Köi*, Bordeaux 1932.

LABAT, R., *Manuel d'épigraphie akkadienne*, new ed. by Fl. Malbran-Labat, Paris 1976.

LESLAU, W., *Vocabulary Common to Akkadian and South-East Semitic (Ethiopic and South-Arabic)*, in *Journal of the American Oriental Society* 64 (1944), p. 53-58.

LESLAU, W., *Southeast Semitic Cognates to the Akkadian Vocabulary*, in *Journal of the American Oriental Society* 82 (1962), p. 1-4; 84 (1964), p. 115-118; 89 (1969), p. 18-22.

LIEBERMAN, S.J., *The Sumerian Loanwords in Old-Babylonian Akkadian* (Harvard Semitic Studies 22), Missoula 1977.

LIPIN, A.A., *The Akkadian Language*, Moscow 1973.

MEYER, W., *Untersuchungen zur Grammatik des Mittelassyrischen*, Kevelaer-Neukirchen-Vluyn 1971.

POEBEL, A., *Studies in Akkadian Grammar* (Assyriological Studies 9), Chicago 1939.

RAVN, O.E., *The So-Called Relative Clauses in Accadian, or the Accadian Particle* ša, Kjøbenhavn 1941.

REINER, E., *A Linguistic Analysis of Akkadian*, The Hague 1966.

RIEMSCHNEIDER, K.K., *Lehrbuch des Akkadischen*, Leipzig 1969 (5th reprint: 1988); English ed. by T.A. Caldwell, J.N. Oswalt & J.F.X. Sheehan: *An Akkadian Grammar*, Milwaukee 1978 (reprint: 1990).

ROWTON, M.B., *The Use of the Permansive in Classic Babylonian*, in *Journal of Near Eastern Studies* 21 (1962), p. 233-303.

RYCKMANS, G., *Les formes nominales en babylonien*, Paris 1919.

RYCKMANS, G., *Grammaire accadienne*, 4th ed. by P. Naster, Louvain 1960.

SALONEN, E., *Untersuchungen zur Schrift und Sprache des Altbabylonischen von Susa*, Helsinki 1962.

SODEN, W. VON, *Der hymnisch-epische Dialekt des Akkadischen*, in *Zeitschrift für Assyriologie* 40 (1932), p. 163-227; 41 (1933), p. 9-183 and 236.

SODEN, W. VON, *Grundriss der akkadischen Grammatik*, Roma 1952; *Ergänzungsheft*, Roma 1969 (3rd ed. with W.R. Mayer, Roma 1995).

SODEN, W. VON, *Akkadisches Handwörterbuch*, 3 vols., Wiesbaden 1965-81.

SODEN, W. VON & W. RÖLLIG, *Das akkadische Syllabar*, 4th ed., Roma 1991.

STRECK, M.P., *Funktionsanalyse des akkadischen $Št_2$-Stamms*, in *Zeitschrift für Assyriologie* 84 (1994), p. 161-197.

STRECK, M.P., *Zahl und Zeit. Grammatik der Numeralia und des Verbalsystems im Spätbabylonischen* (Cuneiform Monographs 5), Groningen 1995.

The Assyrian Dictionary of the Oriental Institute of the University of Chicago, Chicago-Glückstadt 1956 ff.

UNGNAD, A. & L. MATOUŠ, *Grammatik des Akkadischen*, München 1969 (reprint: 1979). English ed. by H.A. Hoffner, *Akkadian Grammar*, Atlanta 1992.

VAN SOLDT, W.H., *Studies in the Akkadian of Ugarit: Dating and Grammar* (Alter Orient und Altes Testament 40), Kevelaer-Neukirchen-Vluyn 1991.

WILHELM, G., *Untersuchungen zum Ḫurro - Akkadischen von Nuzi* (Alter Orient und Altes Testament 9), Kevelaer-Neukirchen-Vluyn 1970.

4. WEST SEMITIC

BANGE, L.A., *A Study of the Use of Vowel-Letters in Alphabetic Consonantal Writing*, München 1971.

COOK, E.M. (ed.), *Sopher Mahir. Northwest Semitic Studies Presented to St. Segert* (= *Maarav* 5-6), Winona Lake 1990.

FREEDMAN, D.N., A.D. FORBES & F.I. ANDERSEN, *Studies in Hebrew and Aramaic Orthography*, Winona Lake 1992.

GUILLAUME, A., *Hebrew and Arabic Lexicography. A Comparative Study*, Leiden 1965.

HOFTIJZER, J. & K. JONGELING, *Dictionary of the North-West Semitic Inscriptions*, 2 vols., Leiden 1995.

JASTROW, M., *A Dictionary of the Targumim, the Talmud Babli and Yerushalmi, and the Midrashic Literature*, 2 vols., New York 1886-1903 (reprint: 1950 & 1967).

JEAN, Ch.-F. & J. HOFTIJZER, *Dictionnaire des inscriptions sémitiques de l'Ouest*, Leiden 1965.

KUTSCHER, E.Y., *Studies in Hebrew and Semitic Languages*, Ramat-Gan 1980.

LAGARDE, P. DE, *Uebersicht über die im Aramäischen, Arabischen und Hebräischen übliche Bildung der Nomina*, Göttingen 1889-91.

MORAG, S., *The Vocalization System of Arabic, Hebrew, and Aramaic. Their Phonetic and Phonemic Principles*, s' Gravenhage 1962 (reprint: 1972).

A. "Canaanite"

ALBRECHT, K., *Neuhebräische Grammatik auf Grund der Mišna bearbeitet*, München 1913.

ANDERSEN, F.I., *Moabite Syntax*, in *Orientalia*, n.s., 35 (1966), p. 81-120.

ANDERSEN, F.I., *The Hebrew Verbless Clause in the Pentateuch*, Nashville - New York 1970.

ANDERSEN, F.I., *The Sentence in Biblical Hebrew*, The Hague 1974.

AZAR, M., *The Syntax of Mishnaic Hebrew* (in Hebrew), Jerusalem 1994.

BARTH, J., *Etymologische Studien zum Semitischen, insbesondere zum hebräischen Lexicon*, Leipzig 1893.

BAUER, H. & P. LEANDER, *Historische Grammatik der hebräischen Sprache des Alten Testaments* I. *Einleitung, Schriftlehre, Laut- und Formenlehre*, Halle 1918-22 (reprint: 1965 & 1991).

BEN-ḤAYYIM, Z., *The Literary and Oral Tradition of Hebrew and Aramaic amongst the Samaritans* (in Hebrew), 4 vols., Jerusalem 1957-67.

BEN-ḤAYYIM, Z. & U. ORNAN, *Hebrew Grammar*, in *Encyclopaedia Judaica*, vol. 8, Jerusalem 1971, col. 77-175.

BEN-YEHŪDĀ, E., *Ha-Millōn ha-'Ibrī ha-yāšēn wə-he-ḥādāš*, 16 vols., Jerusalem 1908-58 (reprint: New York 1960).

BERGSTRÄSSER, G., *Hebräische Grammatik I-II*, Leipzig 1918-29 (reprint: 1985 & 1991).

BEYER, K., *Althebräische Grammatik. Laut- und Formenlehre*, Göttingen 1969.

BIRKELAND, H., *Akzent und Vokalismus im Althebräischen*, Oslo 1940.

BLAU, J., *On Polyphony in Biblical Hebrew*, Jerusalem 1982.

BLAU, J., *A Grammar of Biblical Hebrew*, 2nd ed., Wiesbaden 1993.

BODINE, W.R. (ed.), *Linguistics and Biblical Hebrew*, Winona Lake 1992.

BÖHL, F.M.Th., *Die Sprache der Amarnabriefe mit besonderer Berücksichtigung der Kanaanismen*, Leipzig 1909 (reprint: 1977).

BOMBECK, St., *Das althebräische Verbalsystem aus aramäischer Sicht: Masoretische Text, Targume und Peschitta*, Frankfurt a/M 1997.

BOTTERWECK, G.J., H. RINGGREN & H.-J. FABRY (eds.), *Theologisches Wörterbuch zum Alten Testament*, 8 vols., Stuttgart 1973-95.

BROCKELMANN, C., *Hebräische Syntax*, Neukirchen 1956.

BRØNNO, E., *Studien über hebräische Morphologie und Vokalismus auf Grundlage der Mercatischen Fragmente der zweiten Kolumne der Hexapla des Origenes*, Leipzig 1943.

BROWN, F., S.R. DRIVER & C.A. BRIGGS, *A Hebrew and English Lexicon of the Old Testament, with an appendix containing the Biblical Aramaic*, Oxford 1906 (reprint: 1972).

CHOMSKY, W., *David Ḳimḥi's Hebrew Grammar (Mikhlol) systematically presented and critically annotated*, New York 1952.

CLINES, D.J.A. (ed.), *The Dictionary of Classical Hebrew*, 8 vols., Sheffield 1993 ff.

COHEN, D. & H. ZAFRANI, *Grammaire de l'hébreu vivant*, Paris 1968.

CONTINI, R., *Tipologia della frase nominale nel semitico nordoccidentale del I millennio a.C.*, Pisa 1982.

DAVIDSON, A.B., *Hebrew Syntax*, 3rd ed., Edinburgh 1901 (reprint: 1964).

DHORME, É., *La langue de Canaan*, in *Revue Biblique* 22 (1913), p. 369-393; 23 (1914), p. 37-59, 344-372 = *Recueil Édouard Dhorme*, Paris 1951, p. 405-487.

DONIACH, N.S. & A. KAHANE, *The Oxford English-Hebrew Dictionary*, Oxford-New York 1996.

DRIVER, G.R., *Problems of the Hebrew Verbal System*, Edinburgh 1936.

DRIVER, S.R., *A Treatise on the Use of Tenses in Hebrew*, 3rd ed., Oxford 1892.

EBELING, E., *Das Verbum der El-Amarna Briefe*, Leipzig 1910.

EBEN-ŠŌŠĀN, A., *Ha-Millōn he-Ḥādāš*, 7 vols., Jerusalem 1966-70.

EHLICH, K., *Verwendungen der Deixis beim sprachlichen Handeln. Linguistisch-philologische Untersuchungen zum hebräischen deiktischem System*, 2 vols., Frankfurt a/M 1979.

Encyclopaedia Judaica, Jerusalem 1971, vol. 8, col. 9-17 and 77-175; vol. 13, col. 1120-1145; vol. 16, col. 1352-1482 and 1560-1662.

ENDO, Y., *The Verbal System of Classical Hebrew in the Joseph Story* (Studia Semitica Neerlandica 32), Assen 1996.

ESKHULT, M., *Studies in Verbal Aspect and Narrative Technique in Biblical Hebrew Prose* (Studia Semitica Upsaliensia 12), Stockholm 1990.

FRIEDRICH, J. & W. RÖLLIG, *Phönizisch-punische Grammatik*, 2nd ed., Roma 1970.

FRITZ, W., *Die Wortbildung der hebräischen Adjektiva*, Wiesbaden 1983.

FUENTES ESTAÑOL, M.-J., *Vocabulario fenicio*, Barcelona 1980.

FUENTES ESTAÑOL, M.J., *Manual di gramática fenicia*, Barcelona 1995.

GARR, W.R., *Dialect Geography of Syria-Palestine, 1000-586 B.C.E.*, Philadelphia 1985.

GESENIUS, W., *Thesaurus philologicus criticus linguae Hebraeae et Chaldaeae Veteris Testamenti*, 3 vols., Leipzig 1829-58.

GESENIUS, W. & F. BUHL, *Hebräisches und aramäisches Handwörterbuch über das Alte Testament*, 17th ed., Leipzig 1915 (reprint: 1921 & 1962).

GESENIUS, W., *Hebräisches und aramäisches Handwörterbuch über das Alte Testament*, 18th ed. by R. Meyer, H. Donner & U. Rüterswörden, Berlin 1987 ff.

GESENIUS, W. & E. KAUTZSCH, *Hebräische Grammatik*, 28th ed., Leipzig 1909 (reprint: 1985 & 1991). English ed.: *Hebrew Grammar*, 2nd ed. by A.E. Cowley, Oxford 1910 (reprint: 1974).

GIBSON, J.C.L., *Davidson's Introductory Hebrew Grammar. Syntax*, Edinburgh 1994.

GORDON, A., *The Development of the Participle in Biblical, Mishnaic and Modern Hebrew* (Afro-Asiatic Linguistics 8/3), Malibu 1982.

GROSS, W., *Verbform und Funktion*: wayyiqtol *für die Gegenwart? Ein Beitrag zur Syntax poetischer althebräischer Schriften*, St. Ottilien 1976.

HADAS-LEBEL, M., *Histoire de la langue hébraïque des origines à l'époque de la Mishna*, new ed., Leuven 1995.

HARRIS, Z.S., *A Grammar of the Phoenician Language* (American Oriental Series 8), New Haven 1936 (reprint: 1977 & 1990).

HARRIS, Z.S., *Development of the Canaanite Dialects* (American Oriental Series 16), New Haven 1939.

HOFTIJZER, J., *The Function and Use of the Imperfect Forms with Nun Paragogicum in Classical Hebrew*, Assen 1985.

JACKSON, K.P., *The Ammonite Language of the Iron Age*, Chico 1983.

JACKSON, K.P., *The Language of the Mesha Inscription*, in A. Dearman (ed.), *Studies in the Mesha Inscription and Moab*, Atlanta 1989, p. 96-130.

JANSSENS, G., *Studies in Hebrew Historical Linguistics Based on Origen's Secunda* (Orientalia Gandensia 9), Leuven 1982.

JENNI, E., *Das hebräische Pi'el*, Zürich 1968.

JENNI, E., *Die hebräischen Präpositionen*, 2 vols., Stuttgart 1992-94.

JOHNSON, B., *Hebräisches Perfekt und Imperfekt mit vorangehendem w^e*, Lund 1979.

JOÜON, P., *Grammaire de l'hébreu biblique*, Roma 1923 (reprint: 1965).

JOÜON, P. & T. MURAOKA, *A Grammar of Biblical Hebrew*, 2 vols., 2nd ed., Rome 1993.

KOEHLER, L., W. BAUMGARTNER, B. HARTMANN, E.Y. KUTSCHER & J.J. STAMM, *Hebräisches und aramäisches Lexikon zum Alten Testament*, 5 vols., Leiden 1967-95. English ed. by M.E.J. Richardson: *The Hebrew and Aramaic Lexicon of the Old Testament*, 4 vols., Leiden 1994 ff.

KÖNIG, F.E., *Historisch-kritisches Lehrgebäude der hebräischen Sprache*, 3 vols., Leipzig 1881-97 (reprint: 1979).

KOSKINEN, K., *Kompatibilität in den dreikonsonantigen hebräischen Wurzeln*, in *Zeitschrift der Deutschen Morgenländischen Gesellschaft* 114 (1964), p. 16-58.

KUTSCHER, E.Y., *The Language and Linguistic Background of the Isaiah Scroll (1QIsa^a)*, Leiden 1974; *Indices and Corrections* by E. Qimron, Leiden 1979.

KUTSCHER, E.Y., *A History of the Hebrew Language*, Jerusalem 1982.

LAMBERT, M., *Traité de grammaire hébraïque*, Paris 1938.

LETTINGA, J.P., *Grammatica van het bijbels Hebreeuws*, 8th ed., Leiden 1976; German ed.: *Grammatik des biblischen Hebräisch*, Basel 1992.

MACUCH, R., *Grammatik des samaritanischen Hebräisch*, Berlin 1969.

MALONE, J.L., *Tiberian Hebrew Phonology*, Winona Lake 1993.

McFALL, L., *The Enigma of the Hebrew Verbal System: Solutions from Ewald to the Present Day* (Historical Texts and Interpreters in Biblical Scholarship 2), Sheffield 1982.

MEYER, R., *Hebräische Grammatik*, 4 vols., 3rd ed., Berlin 1969-82; *Mit einem bibliographischen Nachwort* by U. Rüterswörden, Berlin 1992.

MORAN, W.L., *A Syntactical Study of the Dialect of Byblos as Reflected in the Amarna Tablets*, PhD John Hopkins University, Baltimore 1950.

MORAN, W.L., *Early Canaanite yaqtula*, in *Orientalia*, n.s., 29 (1960), p. 1-19.

MORAN, W.L., *The Hebrew Language in its Northwest Semitic Background*, in G.E. Wright (ed.), *The Bible and the Ancient Near East*, Garden City - London 1961, p. 54-72.

MURTONEN, A., *A Grammar of the Samaritan Dialect of Hebrew*, Helsinki 1964.

MURTONEN, A., *Hebrew in Its West Semitic Setting* (Studies in Semitic Languages and Linguistics 13 & 16), 2 vols., Leiden 1988-90.

NEBE, G.W., *Text und Sprache der hebräischen Weisheitsschrift aus der Kairoer Geniza* (Heidelberger Orientalistische Studien 25), Frankfurt a/M 1993.

NICCACCI, A., *The Syntax of the Verb in Classical Hebrew Prose*, Sheffield 1990.

POLZIN, R., *Late Biblical Hebrew. Toward an Historical Typology of Hebrew Prose*, Missoula 1976.

PRIJS, L., *Die grammatikalische Terminologie des Abraham ibn Esra*, Basel 1950.

QIMRON, *The Hebrew of the Dead Sea Scrolls*, Atlanta 1986.

RABIN, C., *A Short History of the Hebrew Language*, Jerusalem 1973. German ed.: *Die Entwicklung der hebräischen Sprache*, Wiesbaden 1988.

RAINEY, A.F., *Morphology and the Prefix-Tenses of West Semitized El-'Amarna Tablets*, in *Ugarit-Forschungen* 7 (1975), p. 395-426.

RAINEY, A.F., *Is there really a* yaqtula *Conjugation Pattern in the Canaanite Amarna Tablets?*, in *Journal of Cuneiform Studies* 43-45 (1991-93), p. 107-118.

RAINEY, A.F., *Canaanite in the Amarna Tablets. A Linguistic Analysis of the Mixed Dialect used by Scribes from Canaan*, 4 vols., Leiden 1996.

RENDSBURG, G.A., *Diglossia in Ancient Hebrew* (American Oriental Series 72), New Haven 1990.

RICHTER, W., *Grundlagen einer althebräischen Grammatik*, 3 vols., St. Ottilien 1978-80.

RIDZEWSKI, B., *Neuhebräische Grammatik auf Grund der ältesten Handschriften und Inschriften* (Heidelberger Orientalistische Studien 21), Bern 1992.

ROSÉN, H.B., *A Textbook of Israeli Hebrew*, Chicago-London 1966.

ROSÉN, H.B., *Contemporary Hebrew*, The Hague 1977.

RUNDGREN, F., *Das althebräische Verbum. Abriss der Aspektlehre*, Stockholm 1961.

SAENZ-BADILLOS, A., *A History of the Hebrew Language* (transl. by J. Elwolde), Cambridge 1993.

SCHOORS, A., *The Preacher Sought to Find Pleasing Words. A Study of the Language of Qoheleth* (Orientalia Lovaniensia Analecta 41), Leuven 1992.

SCHRÖDER, P., *Die phönizische Sprache. Entwurf einer Grammatik nebst Sprach- und Schriftproben. Mit einem Anhang, enthaltend eine Erklärung der punischen Stellen im Pönulus des Plautus*, Halle 1869 (reprint: 1979).

SEGAL, M.H., *A Grammar of Mishnaic Hebrew*, Oxford 1927 (reprint: 1958 & 1986).

SEGERT, St., *Die Sprache der moabitischen Königsinschrift*, in *Archiv Orientální* 29 (1961), p. 197-267.

SEGERT, St., *A Grammar of Phoenician and Punic*, München 1976.

SHIFMAN, I.Sh., Финикийский язык, Moscow 1963.

SIEBESMA, P.A., *The Function of Niph'al in Biblical Hebrew*, Assen 1991.

SIMON, H., *Lehrbuch der modernen hebräischen Sprache*, Leipzig 1970; 3rd ed., München 1975.

SIVAN, D., *Grammatical Analysis and Glossary of the Northwest Semitic Vocables in Akkadian Texts of the 15th-13th C.B.C. from Canaan and Syria* (Alter Orient und Altes Testament 214), Kevelaer-Neukirchen-Vluyn 1984.

SPERBER, A., *A Historical Grammar of Biblical Hebrew*, Leiden 1966.

TOMBACK, R.S., *A Comparative Semitic Lexicon of the Phoenician and Punic Languages*, Missoula 1978.

VAN DEN BRANDEN, A., *Grammaire phénicienne*, Beyrouth 1969.

WALDMAN, N.M., *The Recent Study of Hebrew. A Survey of the Literature with Selected Bibliography*, Winona Lake 1989.

WALTKE, B.K. & M. O'CONNOR, *An Introduction to Biblical Hebrew Syntax*, Winona Lake 1990.

WILLIAMS, R.J., *Hebrew Syntax. An Outline*, 2nd ed., Toronto 1980.

Zeitschrift für Althebraistik 1 (1988) ff.

ZORELL, Fr., *Lexicon Hebraicum et Aramaicum Veteris Testamenti*, Roma 1957.

ZUBER, B., *Das Tempussystem des biblischen Hebräisch, eine Untersuchung am Text* (Beihefte zur Zeitschrift für die alttestamentliche Wissenschaft 164), Berlin 1986.

B. Aramaic

ALTHEIM, F. & R. STIEHL, *Die aramäische Sprache unter den Achaimeniden* I, Frankfurt a/M 1963.

ARNOLD, W., *Lehrbuch des Neuwestaramäischen* (Semitica Viva: Series Didactica 1), Wiesbaden 1989.

ARNOLD, W., *Das Neuwestaramäische* (Semitica Viva 4), 5 vols., Wiesbaden 1989-91.

ATTO, S., *Nederlands-Suryoyo woordenboek*, Enschede 1986.

BAR-ASHER, M., *Palestinian Syriac Studies* (in Hebrew), Jerusalem 1977.

BAR-ASHER, M., *Le syro-palestinien - Études grammaticales*, in *Journal Asiatique* 276 (1989), p. 27-59.

BAUER, H. & P. LEANDER, *Grammatik des Biblisch-Aramäischen*, Halle 1927 (reprint: 1969).

BEN-ḤAYYIM, Z., *The Literary and Oral Tradition of Hebrew and Aramaic amongst the Samaritans* (in Hebrew), 4 vols., Jerusalem 1957-67.

BERGSTRÄSSER, G., *Glossar des neuaramäischen Dialekts von Ma'lula*, Leipzig 1921 (reprint: 1966).

BEYER, K., *Die aramäischen Texten vom Toten Meer*, Göttingen 1984; *Ergänzungsband*, Göttingen 1994.

BEYER, K., *The Aramaic Language. Its Distribution and Subdivisions*, Göttingen 1986.

BLACK, M., *A Christian Palestinian Syriac Horologion*, Cambridge 1954 (reprint: 1978), p. 52-72 (glossary).

BROCKELMANN, C., *Lexicon Syriacum*, 2nd ed., Halle 1928 (reprint: 1966, 1982 & 1995).

BROCKELMANN, C., *Das Aramäische, einschliesslich des Syrischen*, in *Handbuch der Orientalistik* III 2/3, Leiden 1954, p. 135-162.

BROCKELMANN, C., *Syrische Grammatik*, 12th ed., Leipzig 1976.

CANTARINO, V., *Der neuaramäische Dialekt von Ǧubb 'Adīn*, Chapel Hill, N.Y., 1961.

CANTINEAU, J., *Le Nabatéen*, 2 vols., Paris 1930-32 (reprint: 1978).

CANTINEAU, J., *Grammaire du palmyrénien épigraphique*, Le Caire 1935 (reprint: 1987).

CAQUOT, A., *L'araméen de Hatra*, in *GLECS* 9 (1960-63), p. 87-89.

COHEN, D., *Neo-Aramaic*, in *Encyclopaedia Judaica*, Jerusalem 1971, vol. 12, col. 948-951.

COHEN, D., *Sur le système verbal du néo-araméen de Maʿlûla*, in *Journal of Semitic Studies* 24 (1979), p. 219-239.

CORRELL, C., *Untersuchungen zur Syntax der neuwestaramäischen Dialekte des Antilibanon (Maʿlūla, Baḥʿa, Ǧubb ʿAdīn)*, Wiesbaden 1978.

COSTAZ, L., *Dictionnaire syriaque - français / Syriac - English Dictionary*, Beyrouth 1963.

COSTAZ, L., *Grammaire syriaque*, 2nd ed., Beyrouth 1964.

DALMAN, G., *Grammatik des jüdisch-palästinischen Aramäisch*, 2nd ed., Leipzig 1905 (reprint: 1981).

DALMAN, G., *Aramäisch-neuhebräisches Handwörterbuch zu Targum, Talmud und Midrasch*, 2nd ed., Frankfurt a/M 1922; 3rd ed., Göttingen 1938 (reprint: 1967 & 1987).

DEGEN, R., *Altaramäische Grammatik der Inschriften des 10.- 8. Jh. v. Chr.*, Wiesbaden 1969 (reprint: 1978).

DION, P.-E., *La langue de Yaʾudi*, Waterloo (Canada) 1974.

DROWER, E.S. & R. MACUCH, *A Mandaic Dictionary*, Oxford 1963.

DUVAL, P.R., *Traité de grammaire syriaque*, Paris 1881 (reprint: 1969).

DUVAL, P.R., *Les dialects néo-araméens de Salamas*, Paris 1883.

EPSTEIN, J.N., *Diqduq ʾAramīt Bablīt*, Jerusalem 1960; cf. E.Y. Kutscher, in *Lešonénu* 26 (1961-62), p. 149-183.

EPSTEIN, J.N., *Studies in Aramaic Philology*, ed. by D. Boyarin, New York 1978.

FASSBERG, S.E., *A Grammar of the Palestinian Targum Fragments from the Cairo Genizah* (Harvard Semitic Studies 38), Atlanta 1990.

FITZMYER, J.A. & S.A. KAUFMAN, *An Aramaic Bibliography I. Old, Official, and Biblical Aramaic*, Baltimore 1991.

FOLMER, M., *The Aramaic Language in the Achaemenid Period. A Study in Linguistic Variation* (Orientalia Lovaniensia Analecta 68), Leuven 1995.

FOX, S.E., *The Neo-Aramaic Dialect of Jilu* (Semitica Viva 16), Wiesbaden 1997.

FRANK, Y., *Grammar for Gemara. An Introduction to Babylonian Aramaic*, new ed., Jerusalem 1995.

GARBELL, I., *The Jewish Neo-Aramaic Dialect of Persian Azerbaijan. Linguistic Analysis and Folkloristic Texts*, The Hague 1965.

GELLER, M.J., J.C. GREENFIELD & M.P. WEITZMAN (eds.), *Studia Aramaica: New Sources and New Approaches* (Journal of Semitic Studies, Supplement 4), Oxford 1995.

GIGNOUX, P., *Glossaire des inscriptions pehlevies et parthes*, London 1972.

GOLDENBERG, G., *On Syriac Sentence Structure*, in M. Sokoloff (ed.), *Aramaic and the Aramaic Literary Tradition*, Ramat-Gan 1983, p. 97-140.

GOLOMB, D.M., *A Grammar of Targum Neofiti* (Harvard Semitic Monographs 34), Chico 1985.

GOTTHEIL, R., *The Judaeo-Aramaean Dialect of Salamas*, in *Journal of the American Oriental Society* 15 (1893).

HEINRICHS, W. (ed.), *Studies in Neo-Aramaic*, Atlanta 1990.

HOBERMAN, R.D., *The Syntax and Semantics of Verb Morphology in Modern Aramaic. A Jewish Dialect of Iraqi Kurdistan* (American Oriental Series 69), New Haven 1989.

HUG, V., *Altaramäische Grammatik der Texte des 7. und 6. Jh.s v. Chr.* (Heidelberger Studien zum Alten Orient 4), Heidelberg 1993.

JACOBI, H., *Grammatik des Thumischen Neuaramäisch (Nordostsyrien)*, Wiesbaden 1973.

JASTROW, O., *Laut- und Formenlehre des neuaramäischen Dialekts von Miḏin in Ṭūr-'Abdīn*, Bamberg 1967; 4th ed. (Semitica Viva 9), Wiesbaden 1993.

JASTROW, O., *Der neuaramäische Dialekt von Hertevin (Provinz Sürt)* (Semitica Viva 3), Wiesbaden 1988.

JASTROW, O., *Lehrbuch der Ṭuroyo-Sprache* (Semitica Viva: Series Didactica 2), Wiesbaden 1992.

JASTROW, O., *Der neuaramäische Dialekt von Mlaḥsô* (Semitica Viva 14), Wiesbaden 1994.

JOOSTEN, J., *The Syriac Language of the Peshitta and Old Syriac Versions of Matthew: Syntactic Structure, Inner-Syriac Developments, and Translation Technique* (Studies in Semitic Languages and Linguistics 22), Leiden 1995.

KAUFMAN, S.A., *The Akkadian Influences on Aramaic* (Assyriological Studies 19), Chicago 1974.

KRAUSS, S., *Griechische und lateinische Lehnwörter im Talmud, Midrasch und Targum*, 2 vols., Berlin 1898-99 (reprint: 1966).

KOTTSIEPER, I., *Die Sprache der Aḥiqarsprüche* (Beihefte zur Zeitschrift für die alttestamentliche Wissenschaft 194), Berlin 1990.

KROTKOFF, G., *A Neo-Aramaic Dialect of Kurdistan* (American Oriental Series 64), New Haven 1982.

KUTSCHER, E.Y., *Aramaic*, in *Encyclopaedia Judaica*, Jerusalem 1971, vol. 3, col. 259-287.

KUTSCHER, E.Y., *Aramaic*, in Th. Sebeok (ed.), *Current Trends in Linguistics VI. Linguistics in South West Asia and North Africa*, The Hague 1970, p. 347-412.

KUTSCHER, E.Y., *Studies in Galilean Aramaic*, Ramat-Gan 1976.

LEANDER, P., *Laut- und Formenlehre des Ägyptisch-Aramäischen*, Göteborg 1928 (reprint: 1966).

LEVIAS, C., *A Grammar of the Aramaic Idiom Contained in the Babylonian Talmud*, Cincinnati 1900 (reprint from *The American Journal of Semitic Languages and Literatures* 13-16 [1897-1900]).

LEWY, J., *Wörterbuch über die Talmudim und Midraschim*, 4 vols., Leipzig 1876-89; 2nd ed., Berlin-Wien 1924 (reprint: 1963).

LIPIŃSKI, E., *Studies in Aramaic Inscriptions and Onomastics* (Orientalia Lovaniensia Analecta 1 & 57), 2 vols., Leuven 1974-94.

LIPIŃSKI, E., *L'araméen d'Empire*, in *Le langage dans l'Antiquité*, Leuven-Paris 1990, p. 94-133.

LÖW, I., *Aramäische Pflanzennamen*, Leipzig 1881.

MACLEAN, A.J., *Grammar of the Dialects of Vernacular Syriac as spoken by the Eastern Syrians of Kurdistan, North-West Persia, and the Plain of Mosul*, Cambridge 1895 (reprint: 1971).

MACLEAN, A.J., *Dictionary of the Dialects of Vernacular Syriac as spoken by the Eastern Syrians of Kurdistan, North-West Persia, and the Plain of Mosul*, Oxford 1901 (reprint: 1972).

MACUCH, R., *Handbook of Classical and Modern Mandaic*, Berlin 1965.

MACUCH, R., & E. PANOUSSI, *Neusyrische Chrestomathie*, Wiesbaden 1974.

MACUCH, R., *Zur Sprache und Literatur der Mandäer*, Berlin 1976.

MACUCH, R., *Grammatik des samaritanischen Aramäisch*, Berlin 1982.

MACUCH, R., *Neumandäische Chrestomathie mit grammatischer Skizze, kommentierter Übersetzung und Glossar*, Wiesbaden 1989.

MACUCH, R., *Neumandäische Texte im Dialekt von Ahwāz* (Semitica Viva 12), Wiesbaden 1993.

MARCUS, D., *A Manual of Babylonian Jewish Aramaic*, Washington 1981.

MARGOLIOUTH, J., *A Compendious Syriac Dictionary founded upon the Thesaurus Syriacus of R. Payne Smith*, Oxford 1903 (reprint: 1967).

MARGOLIOUTH, J.P., *Supplement to the Thesaurus Syriacus of R. Payne Smith*, Oxford 1927 (reprint: 1981).

MARGOLIS, M.L., *Lehrbuch der aramäischen Sprache des babylonischen Talmuds*, München 1910.

MAROGULOV, Q.I., *Grammaire néo-syriaque pour écoles d'adultes* (*dialecte d'Urmia*), Paris 1976.

MARSHALL, J.T., *Manual of the Aramaic Language of the Palestinian Talmud*, Leiden 1929.

MURAOKA, T. (ed.), *Studies in Qumran Aramaic* (Supplements to Abr-Nahrain 3), Leuven 1992.

MURAOKA, T., *Classical Syriac. A Basic Grammar*, Wiesbaden 1997.

MÜLLER-KESSLER, Chr., *Grammatik des Christlich-Palästinisch-Aramäischen I. Schriftlehre, Lautlehre, Formenlehre*, Hildesheim 1991.

NÖLDEKE, T., *Grammatik der neusyrischen Sprache am Urmia-See und in Kurdistan*, Leipzig 1868 (reprint: 1974).

NÖLDEKE, T., *Mandäische Grammatik*, Halle 1875 (reprint: 1964).

NÖLDEKE, T., *Kurzgefasste syrische Grammatik*, 2nd ed., Leipzig 1898 (reprint: 1977); English ed. by J.A. Crichton: *Compendious Syriac Grammar*, London 1904 (reprint: 1970).

NYBERG, H.S., B. UTAS & C. TOLL, *Frahang i Pahlavīk*, Wiesbaden 1988.

ODISHO, E.Y., *The Sound System of Modern Assyrian* (*Neo-Aramaic*) (Semitica Viva 2), Wiesbaden 1988.

ODDO, M.T., *Assyrian Dictionary*, Mosul 1897 (reprint: 1978).

ORAHAM, A.J., *Dictionary of the Stabilized and Enriched Assyrian Language and English*, Chicago 1943.

PARISOT, M., *Le dialecte de Ma'lula. Grammaire, vocabulaire et textes*, Paris 1898 = *Journal Asiatique*, 9th ser., 11 (1898), p. 239-312; 12 (1898), p. 124-176.

PAYNE SMITH, R., *Thesaurus Syriacus*, 2 vols., Oxford 1879-1901 (reprint: 1981).

POIZAT, B., *Une bibliographie commentée pour le néo-araméen*, in *GLECS* 18-23 (1973-79), p. 347-414.

POLOTSKY, H.J., *Studies in Modern Syriac*, in *Journal of Semitic Studies* 6 (1961), p. 1-32.

PRYM, E. & A. SOCIN, *Der neu-aramäische Dialekt des Ṭūr-'Abdīn*, 2 vols., Göttingen 1881-83.

QIMRON, E., *Biblical Aramaic* (in Hebrew), Jerusalem 1993.

RHÉTORÉ, J., *Grammaire de la langue soureth ou chaldéen vulgaire selon le dialecte de la plaine de Mossoul et des pays adjacents*, Mossoul 1912.

RITTER, H., *Ṭurōyō. Die Volkssprache der syrischen Christen des Ṭūr 'Abdīn*, 4 vols., Beirut - Wiesbaden 1967-79.

ROSENBERG, I., *Lehrbuch der neusyrischen Schrift- und Umgangssprache*, Wien 1903.

ROSENTHAL, F., *Die Sprache der palmyrenischen Inschriften und ihre Stellung innerhalb des Aramäischen*, Leipzig 1936.

ROSENTHAL, F., *Die aramaistische Forschung seit Th. Nöldeke's Veröffentlichungen*, Leiden 1939 (reprint: 1964).

ROSENTHAL, F. (ed.), *An Aramaic Handbook*, 4 vols., Wiesbaden 1967.

ROSENTHAL, F., *A Grammar of Biblical Aramaic*, 6th rev. ed., Wiesbaden 1995.

ROSSELL, W.H., *A Handbook of Aramaic Magical Texts*, Astoria (New Jersey) 1953.

ROWLEY, H.H., *The Aramaic of the Old Testament. A Grammatical and Lexical Study of its Relations with Other Early Aramaic Dialects*, Oxford 1929.

SACHAU, E., *Skizze des Fellichi-Dialekts von Mosul* (Abhandlungen der Königlich-Preussischen Akademie der Wissenschaften zu Berlin 80. Phil.-hist. Cl. 1), Berlin 1895.

SARA, S.I., *A Description of Modern Chaldean*, The Hague 1974.

SCHLESINGER, M., *Satzlehre der aramäischen Sprache des babylonischen Talmuds*, Leipzig 1928 (reprint: 1995).

SCHULTHESS, F., *Lexicon Syropalaestinum*, Berlin 1903 (reprint: 1979).

SCHULTHESS, F., *Grammatik des christlich-palästinischen Aramäisch*, ed. by E. Littmann, Tübingen 1924 (reprint: 1965 & 1983).

SEGAL, J.B., *The Diacritical Point and the Accents in Syriac*, London 1953.

SEGERT, S., *Altaramäische Grammatik*, Leipzig 1975 (reprint: 1983 & 1990).

SEIDEL, U., *Studien zum Vokabular der Landwirtschaft im Syrischen*, in *Altorientalische Forschungen* 15 (1988), p. 133-173; 16 (1989), p. 89-139.

SIEGEL, A., *Laut- und Formenlehre des neuaramäischen Dialekts des Ṭūr 'Abdīn*, Hannover 1923 (reprint: 1968).

SODEN VON, W., *Aramäische Wörter in neuassyrischen und neu- und spätbabylonischen Texten*, in *Orientalia*, n.s., 35 (1966), p. 1-20; 37 (1968), p. 261-271; 46 (1977), p. 183-197.

SOKOLOFF, M., *A Dictionary of Jewish Palestinian Aramaic of the Byzantine Period*, Ramat-Gan 1990 (reprint: 1991).

SPITALER, A., *Grammatik des neuaramäischen Dialekts von Ma'lula (Antilibanon)*, Leipzig 1938 (reprint: 1966).

STEFANOVIC, Z., *The Aramaic of Daniel in the Light of Old Aramaic*, Sheffield 1992.

STEVENSON, W.B., *Grammar of Palestinian Jewish Aramaic*, Oxford 1924; 2nd ed., 1962 (reprint: 1974).

STODDARD, D.T., *Grammar of the Modern Syriac Language, as spoken in Oroomiah, Persia, and Koordistan*, in *Journal of the American Oriental Society* 5/1 (1855), p. 1-180.

TAL, A., *The Language of the Targum of the Former Prophets and Its Position within the Aramaic Dialects* (in Hebrew), Tel Aviv 1975.

TROPPER, J., *Die Inschriften von Zincirli*, Münster 1993.

TSERETELI, K.G., *The Modern Assyrian Language*, Moscow 1978.

TSERETELI, K.G., Сирийский язык, Moscow 1979.

TSERETELI, K.G., *Grammatica generale dell'aramaico*, in *Henoch* 17 (1995), p. 3-102.

UNGNAD, A., *Syrische Grammatik*, 3rd ed., München 1913 (reprint: 1992).

VILSKER, L.H., *Manuel d'araméen samaritain* (French ed. by J. Margain), Paris 1981.

VINNIKOV, I.N., Словарь арамейских надписи, in *Palestinskiy Sbornik* 3 (1958), p. 171-216; 4 (1959), p. 196-240; 7 (1962), p. 192-237; 9 (1962), p. 141-158; 11 (1964), p. 189-232; 13 (1965), p. 217-262.

VIVIAN, A., *Studi di sintassi contrastiva: dialetti aramaici*, Firenze 1981.

VOGT, E., *Lexicon linguae Aramaicae Veteris Testamenti documentis antiquis illustratum*, Roma 1971.

C. Arabic

AARTUN, K., *Zur Frage altarabischer Tempora*, Oslo 1963.

ABDEL-MASSIH, E.T., *An Introduction to Moroccan Arabic*, Ann Arbor 1973.

ABDEL-MASSIH, E.T., *Advanced Moroccan Arabic*, Ann Arbor 1974.

ABOU-FETOUH, H.M., *A Morphological Study of Egyptian Colloquial Arabic*, The Hague 1969.

ABU-HAIDAR, F., *A Study of the Spoken Arabic of Baskinto*, Leiden - London 1979.

ABU-HAIDAR, F., *Christian Arabic of Baghdad* (Semitica Viva 7), Wiesbaden 1991.

AGIUS, D.A., *Siculo-Arabic* (Library of Arabic Linguistics 12), London 1996.

AL-NASSIR, A.A., *Sibawayh the Phonologist* (Library of Arabic Linguistics 10), London 1993.

AL-TĀJIR, M.A., *Language and Linguistic Origins in Baḥrain*, London 1982.

AL-TONSI, A., *Egyptian Colloquial Arabic: A Structure Review*, Cairo 1982.

AMBROS, A., *Damascus Arabic* (Afroasiatic Dialects 3), Malibu 1977.

AQUILINA, J., *The Structure of Maltese. A Study in Mixed Grammar and Vocabulary*, La Valetta 1959.

AQUILINA, J., *Papers in Maltese Linguistics*, La Valetta 1961 (reprint: 1970).

BAALBAKI, R., *Reclassification in Arab Grammatical Theory*, in *Journal of Near Eastern Studies* 54 (1995), p. 1-13.

BAKALLA, M.H., *Bibliography of Arabic Linguistics*, London 1975.

BAKALLA, M.H., *The Morphological and Phonological Components of the Arabic Verb (Meccan Arabic)*, London 1979.

BAKIR, M.J., *Aspects of Clause Structure in Arabic: A Study of Word Order Variation in Literary Arabic*, Bloomington 1980.

BARTHÉLEMY, A., *Dictionnaire arabe-français. Dialectes de Syrie*: *Alep, Damas, Liban, Jérusalem*, Paris 1935-60.

BAUER, L., *Das palästinische Arabisch*, Leipzig 1926 (reprint: 1970).

BEESTON, A.F.L., *Written Arabic. An Approach to the Basic Structures*, Cambridge 1968.

BEESTON, A.F.L., *The Arabic Language Today*, London 1970.

BEHNSTEDT, P., *Die Dialekte der Gegend von Ṣaʿdah, Nord-Jemen* (Semitica Viva 1), Wiesbaden 1987.

BEHNSTEDT, P., *Der arabische Dialekt von Soukhne* (*Syrien*) (Semitica Viva 15), 2 vols., Wiesbaden 1994.

BEHNSTEDT, P. & M. WOIDICH, *Die ägyptisch-arabischen Dialekte*, 4 vols., Wiesbaden 1985-88; *Glossar: Arabisch-Deutsch*, Wiesbaden 1994.

BERGSTRÄSSER, G., *Zum arabischen Dialekt von Damaskus*, Hannover 1924 (reprint: 1968).

BIRKELAND, H., *Altarabische Pausalformen*, Oslo 1940.

BIRLELAND, H., *Growth and Structure of the Egyptian Arabic Dialect*, Oslo 1950.

BIRKELAND, H., *Stress Patterns in Arabic*, Oslo 1954.

BLACHÈRE, R. & M. GAUDEFROY-DEMOMBYNES, *Grammaire de l'arabe classique* (*morphologie et syntaxe*), 3rd ed., Paris 1952 (reprint: 1975).

BLACHÈRE, R., C. PELLAT, M. CHOUÉMI & C. DENIZEAU, *Dictionnaire arabe-français-anglais* (*langues classique et moderne*), 5 vols., Paris 1963 ff.

BLANC, H., *Studies in North Palestinian Arabic: Linguistic Inquiries among the Druzes of Western Galilee and Mt. Carmel*, Jerusalem 1953.

BLANC, H., *Communal Dialects in Baghdad*, Cambridge, Mass., 1964.

BLANC, H., *The Arabic Dialect of the Negev Bedouins*, in *The Israel Academy of Sciences and Humanities. Proceedings* 4/7, Jerusalem 1970, p. 112-150.

BLAU, J., *Syntax des palästinensischen Bauerndialektes von Bīr-Zēt*, Walldorf 1960.

BLAU, J., *A Grammar of Christian Arabic, Based mainly on South-Palestinian Texts from the First Millennium*, Leuven 1966-67.

BLAU, J., *The Emergence and Linguistic Background of Judaeo-Arabic. A Study of the Origins of Middle Arabic*, 2nd ed., Oxford 1981.

BLAU, J., *Studies in Middle Arabic and Its Judaeo-Arabic Variety*, Jerusalem 1988.

BLOCH, A.A., *Studies in Arabic Syntax and Semantics*, Wiesbaden 1986.

BOHAS, G. & J.-P. GUILLAUME, *Étude des théories des grammairiens arabes* I. *Morphologie et phonologie*, Damas 1984.

BOHAS, G., J.-P. GUILLAUME & D.E. KOULOUGHLI, *The Arabic Linguistic Tradition*, London 1990.

BOHAS, G. (ed.), *Développements récents en linguistique arabe et sémitique*, Damas 1993.

BORG, A., *Cypriot Arabic*, Stuttgart 1985.

BORG, A. & M. AZZOPARDI-ALEXANDER, *Maltese* (Descriptive Grammars), London 1996.

BORIS, G., *Lexique du parler arabe des Marazig*, Paris 1958.

BRAVMANN, M.M., *Materialien und Untersuchungen zu den phonetischen Lehren der Araber*, Göttingen 1934.

BRAVMANN, M.M., *Studies in Arabic and General Syntax*, Cairo 1953.

BRAVMANN, M.M., *The Arabic Elative* (Studies in Semitic Languages and Linguistics 2), Leiden 1968.

BROCKELMANN, C., *Arabische Grammatik*, 21st ed. by M. Fleischhammer, Leipzig 1982 (reprint: 1992).

BROCKETT, A.A., *The Spoken Arabic of Khābūra on the Bāṭina of Oman*, Manchester 1985.

CANTARINO, V., *Syntax of Modern Arabic Prose*, 3 vols., Bloomington 1974-75.

CANTINEAU, J., *Le dialecte arabe de Palmyre*, Beyrouth 1934.

CANTINEAU, J., *Études sur quelques parlers de nomades arabes d'Orient*, in *Annales de l'Institut d'Études Orientales, Alger* 2 (1936), p. 1-118; 3 (1937), p. 119-237.

CANTINEAU, J., *Les parlers arabes du Ḥōrān*, 2 vols., Paris 1940-46.

CANTINEAU, J., *Études de linguistique arabe*, Paris 1960.

CANTINEAU, J., *Cours de phonétique arabe*, Paris 1960.

CASKEL, W., *Liḥyan und Liḥyanisch*, Köln-Opladen 1954.

CASPARI, C.P., *Arabische Grammatik*, 5th ed. by A. Müller, Halle a/S 1887.

CAUBET, D., *L'arabe marocain*, 2 vols., Leuven 1993.

CHEJNE, A.G., *The Arabic Language: Its Role in History*, Minneapolis 1969.

COHEN, D., *Le dialecte arabe Ḥassānīya de Mauritanie. Parler de la Gebla*, Paris 1963.

COHEN, D., *Le parler arabe des Juifs de Tunis*, 2 vols., La Haye 1964-75.

COHEN, M., *Le parler arabe des Juifs d'Alger*, Paris 1912.

CORRIENTE, F., *A Grammatical Sketch of the Spanish Arabic Dialect Bundle*, Madrid 1977.

CORRIENTE, F., *El lexico árabe andalusí según P. de Alcalá*, Madrid 1988.

COWELL, M., *A Reference Grammar of Syrian Arabic*, Washington 1964.

DENIZEAU, C., *Dictionnaire des parlers arabes de Syrie, Liban et Palestine (Supplément au Dictionnaire arabe-français de A. Barthélemy)*, Paris 1960.

DENZ, A., *Die Verbalsyntax des neuarabischen Dialekts von Kwayriš (Irak)*, Wiesbaden 1971.

DERENBOURG, H. (ed.), *Le livre de Sibawaihi, traité de grammaire arabe*, 2 vols., Paris 1881-89 (reprint: 1970).

DÉVÉNYI, K. & T. IVANYI (eds.), *Proceedings of the Colloquium on Arabic Grammar*, Budapest 1991.

Dialectologia Arabica. A Collection of Articles in Honour of... H. Palva (Studia Orientalia 75), Helsinki 1995.

DIEM, W., *Die nabatäischen Inschriften und die Frage der Kasusflexion im Altarabischen*, in *Zeitschrift der Deutschen Morgenländischen Gesellschaft* 123 (1973), p. 227-237.

DIEM, W., *Skizze jemenitischer Dialekte*, Beirut 1973.

DIEM, W., *Hochsprache und Dialekt im Arabischen. Untersuchungen zur heutigen arabischen Zweisprachigkeit*, Wiesbaden 1974.

DIEM, W., *Untersuchungen zur frühen Geschichte der arabischen Orthographie*, in *Orientalia*, n.s., 48 (1979), p. 207-257; 49 (1980), p. 67-106; 50 (1981), p. 332-383; 52 (1983), p. 357-404.

DOZY, R., *Supplément aux dictionnaires arabes*, 2 vols., Leiden 1881 (reprint: 1927).

Du dictionnaire historique de la langue arabe (Études et recherches 15), Carthage 1991.

DURAND, O., *Introduzione ai dialetti arabi*, Milano 1995.

EKSELL HARNING, K., *The Analytic Genitive in the Modern Arabic Dialects*, Göteborg 1980.

FAGNAN, E., *Additions aux dictionnaires arabes*, Alger 1923.

FAURE, P., *Introduction au parler arabe de l'est du Tchad*, Lyon-Fort Lamy 1969.

FÉGHALI, M., *Syntaxe des parlers arabes actuels du Liban*, Paris 1928.

FISCHER, W., *Die demonstrativen Bildungen der neuarabischen Dialekte. Ein Beitrag zur historischen Grammatik des Arabischen*, 's Gravenhage 1959.

FISCHER, W. (ed.), *Grundriss der arabischen Philologie. Band I: Sprachwissenschaft*, Wiesbaden 1982.

FISCHER, W., *Grammatik des klassischen Arabisch* (Porta Linguarum Orientalium, n.s., 11), 2nd ed., Wiesbaden 1987.

FISCHER, W. & O. JASTROW (eds.), *Handbuch der arabischen Dialekte* (Porta Linguarum Orientalium, n.s., 16), Wiesbaden 1980.

FISCHER, W. & O. JASTROW, *Lehrgang für die Arabische Schriftsprache der Gegenwart*, 2 vols., 3rd ed., Wiesbaden 1982-86.

FLEISCH, H., *Traité de philologie arabe*, 2 vols., Beyrouth 1961-79.

FLEISCH, H., *L'arabe classique. Esquisse d'une structure linguistique*, 2nd ed., Beyrouth 1968.

FLEISCH, H., *Études d'arabe dialectal*, Beyrouth 1974.

FRAYHA, A., *A Dictionary of Non-Classical Vocables in the Spoken Arabic of Lebanon*, Beirut 1973.

FREYTAG, G.W., *Lexicon Arabico-Latinum*, 4 vols., Halle 1830-37 (reprint: 1975).

FRIEDLÄNDER, I., *Der Sprachgebrauch des Maimonides* I., Frankfurt a/M 1902.

FÜCK, J., *Arabiya. Untersuchungen zur arabischen Sprach- und Stilgeschichte*, Berlin 1950.

GAIRDNER, W.H.T., *Phonetics of Arabic*, Oxford 1925.

GAMAL-EL-DIN, S.M., *A Syntactic Study of Egyptian Colloquial Arabic*, The Hague 1967.

GOLDZIHER, I., *Abhandlungen zur arabischen Philologie*, 2 vols., Leiden 1896-99 (reprint: 1982).

GOLDZIHER, I., *On the History of Grammar among the Arabs*, English ed. by K. Dévényi & T. Iványi, Amsterdam 1994.

GRAF, G., *Der Sprachgebrauch der ältesten christlich-arabischen Literatur*, Leipzig 1905.

GRANDE, B.M., Курс арабской грамматики в сравнительно-историческом освещении, Moscow 1963.

GRAND'HENRY, J., *Le parler arabe de Cherchell (Algérie)*, Louvain 1972.

GRAND'HENRY, J., *Les parlers de la région du Mzāb (Sahara algérien)*, Leiden 1976.

GROTZFELD, H., *Laut- und Formenlehre des Damaszenisch-Arabischen*, Wiesbaden 1964.

GROTZFELD, H., *Syrish-arabische Grammatik: Dialekt von Damaskus* (Porta Linguarum Orientalium, n.s., 8), Wiesbaden 1965.

GRUENDLER, B., *The Development of the Arabic Scripts* (Harvard Semitic Studies 43), Cambridge, Mass., 1993.

HAGÈGE, Cl., *Profil d'un parler arabe du Tchad*, Paris 1974.

HAJJÉ, H. EL-, *Le parler arabe de Tripoli (Liban)*, Paris 1954.

HALLOUN, M., *Cours d'arabe parlé palestinien. Le dialecte de Jérusalem avec des références à d'autres dialectes palestiniens* I, Paris 1995.

HÄMEEN-ANTILLA, J., *Lexical Ibdāl* I (Studia Orientalia 71), Helsinki 1993.

HAMZAOUI, M.R., *À propos du dictionnaire de langue arabe: problématiques et approches* (Études et recherches 16), Carthage 1991.

HARNING, K.E., *The Analytic Genitive in the Modern Arabic Dialects*, Göteborg 1980.

HARRELL, R.S., *The Phonology of Colloquial Egyptian Arabic*, New York 1957.

HARRELL, R.S., *A Basic Course in Moroccan Arabic*, Georgetown 1965.

HARTMANN, R., *Untersuchungen zur Syntax der arabischen Schriftsprache. Eine generativ-transformationelle Darstellung*, Wiesbaden 1974.

HARVEY, L.P., *The Arab Dialect of Valencia in 1595*, in *Al-Andalus* 36 (1971), p. 81-115.

HOLES, C., *Language Variation and Change in a Modernising Arab State*, London 1987.

HOLES, C., *Modern Arabic: Structures, Functions and Varieties*, Harlow 1995.

HOPKINS, S., *Studies in the Grammar of Early Arabic, Based upon Papyri datable to before A.H. 300 / A.D. 912*, London 1984.

HOWELL, M.S., *A Grammar of the Classical Arabic Language*, 4 vols., Allahabad 1883-1911 (reprint: 1986).

HUMBERT, G., *Les voies de la transmission du Kitāb de Sībawayhi* (Studies in Semitic Languages and Linguistics 20), Leiden 1995.

IBN MUKARRAM B. AL-MANẓŪR, MḤ. (1232-1311), *Lisān al-'arab*, 15 vols., Beirut 1955-56 (reprint: 1970).

INGHAM, B., *North East Arabian Dialects* (Library of Arabic Linguistics 3), London 1982.

INGHAM, B., *Najdi Arabic. Central Arabian* (London Oriental and African Language Library 1), Amsterdam 1994.

JAHN, G., *Sibawaihi's Buch über die Grammatik, übersetzt und erläutert*, 4 vols., Berlin 1894-1900 (reprint: 1969).

JAKOBSON, R., *Mufaxxama — The 'Emphatic' Phonemes in Arabic*, in E. Pulgram (ed.), *Studies Presented to Joshua Whatmough*, 's-Gravenhage 1957, p. 105-115.

JANSSENS, G., *Stress in Arabic and Word Structure in the Modern Arabic* (Orientalia Gandensia 5), Leuven 1972.

JASTROW, O., *Daragözü, eine arabische Mundart der Kozluk-Sason-Gruppe (Südostanatolien). Grammatik und Texte*, Nürnberg 1973.

JASTROW, O., *Die mesopotamisch-arabischen* qeltu-*Dialekte. Band I. Phonologie und Morphologie*, Wiesbaden 1978.

JASTROW, O., *Der arabische Dialekt der Juden von 'Aqra und Arbīl* (Semitica Viva 5), Wiesbaden 1989.

JIHA, M., *Der arabische Dialekt von Bišmizzīn*, Beirut 1964.

JOHNSTONE, T.M., *Eastern Arabic Dialect Studies*, London 1967.

JOMIER, J., *Manuel d'arabe égyptien (parler du Caire)*, Paris 1964.

Journal of Arabic Linguistics 1 (1978) ff.

JUSTICE, D., *The Semantics of Form in Arabic*, Amsterdam 1987.

KAHLE, E., *Studien zur Syntax des Adjektivs im vorklassischen Arabisch*, Erlangen 1975.

KAYE, A.S., *Chadian and Sudanese Arabic in the Light of Comparative Arabic Dialectology*, The Hague 1976.

KAYE, A.S., *Dictionary of Nigerian Arabic*, Malibu 1982.

KAZIMIRSKI, A. DE BIBERSTEIN., *Dictionnaire arabe-français*, 2 vols., Paris 1860 (reprint: 1970).

KOFLER, H., *Reste altarabischer Dialekte*, in *Wiener Zeitschrift für die Kunde des Morgenlandes* 47 (1940), p. 61-130, 233-262; 48 (1941), p. 52-88, 247-274; 49 (1942), p. 15-30, 234-256.

KYAMILEV, S. Kh., Марокканский диалект арабского языка, Moscow 1968.

LANDBERG, C. DE, *Études sur les dialectes de l'Arabie méridionale*, 4 vols., Leiden 1901-13.

LANDBERG, C. DE, *La langue arabe et ses dialectes*, Leiden 1905.

LANDBERG, C. DE, *Glossaire datînois*, 3 vols., Leiden 1920-42.

LANDBERG, C. DE, *Glossaire de la langue des bédouins 'Anazeh*, Uppsala-Leipzig 1940.

LANE, E.W., *Arabic-English Lexicon*, 8 vols., London-Edinburgh 1863-93 (reprint: 1968 & 1980).

LEBEDEV, V.V., Поздний средне-арабский язык (XIII-XVIII вв.), Moscow 1977.

LEVIN, A., *Sībawayhi's Attitude to the Spoken Language*, in *Jerusalem Studies in Arabic and Islam* 17 (1994), p. 204-243.

LITTMANN, E., *Zur Entzifferung der Ṣafā - Inschriften*, Leipzig 1901.

LITTMANN, E., *Survivals of the Arabic Dialects in the Arabic Literature*, in *Bulletin of the Faculty of Arts. University of Cairo* 10 (1948), p. 1-58.

LITTMANN, E., *Thamūd und Ṣafā*, Leipzig 1940 (reprint: 1966).

MALAIKA, N., *Grundzügen der Grammatik des arabischen Dialekts von Baghdad*, Wiesbaden 1963.

MANSOUR, J., *The Judaeo-Arabic Dialect of Baghdad* (in Hebrew), 3 vols., Haifa 1974-83.

MANSOUR, J., *The Jewish Baghdadi Dialect - Studies and Texts*, Or-Yehuda 1991.

MARÇAIS, P., *Le parler arabe de Dijdjelli* (*Nord - Constantinois, Algérie*), Paris [1956].

MARÇAIS, P., *Esquisse grammaticale de l'arabe maghrébin*, Paris 1977.

MISHKUROV, E.N., Алжирский диалект арабского языка, Moscow 1982.

MITCHELL, T.F. & S.A. AL-HASSAN, *Modality, Mood and Aspect in Spoken Arabic, with special reference to Egypt and the Levant* (Library of Arab Linguistics 11), London 1994.

MOSEL, U., *Die syntaktische Terminologie bei Sībawayh*, München 1975.

NEBES, N., *Funktionsanalyse von* kāna yafʻalu. *Ein Beitrag zur Verbalsyntax des Althocharabischen mit besonderer Berücksichtigung der Tempus- und Aspektproblematik* (Studien zur Sprachwissenschaft 1), Hildesheim 1982.

NÖLDEKE, T., *Zur Grammatik des klassischen Arabisch*, Wien 1896 (reprint: 1963).

OWENS, J., *The Foundations of Grammar: An Introduction to Medieval Arabic Grammatical Theory*, Amsterdam 1987.

OWENS, J., *A Grammar of Nigerian Arabic* (Semitica Viva 10), Wiesbaden 1993.

PALVA, H., *Linguistic Sketch of the Arabic Dialect of El-Karak*, in P. Wexler, A. Borg & S. Samekh (eds.), *Studia linguistica et orientalia memoriae Haim Blanc dedicata*, Wiesbaden 1989, p. 225-251.

PELED, Y., *Conditional Structures in Classical Arabic* (Studies in Arabic Language and Literature 2), Wiesbaden 1992.

PELLAT, CH., *Introduction à l'arabe moderne*, Paris 1956 (reprint: 1985).

PIAMENTA, M., *Studies in the Syntax of Palestinian Arabic*, Jerusalem 1966.

PIAMENTA, M., *Dictionary of Post-Classical Yemeni Arabic*, 2 vols., Leiden 1990-91.

PROCHAZKA, T., *Saudi Arabian Dialects* (Library of Arab Linguistics), London 1988.

RABIN, Ch., *Ancient West-Arabian*, London 1951.

RECKENDORF, H., *Die syntaktischen Verhältnisse des Arabischen*, Leiden 1895-98 (reprint: 1967).

RECKENDORF, H., *Arabische Syntax*, Heidelberg 1921 (reprint: 1977).

REICHMUTH, S., *Der arabische Dialekt der Sukriyya im Ostsudan* (Studien zur Sprachwissenschaft 2), Hildesheim 1983.

RHODOKANAKIS, N., *Der vulgärarabische Dialekt im Dofâr (Ẓfâr)*, 2 vols., Wien 1908-11.

ROMAN, A., *Étude de la phonologie et de la morphologie de la koinè arabe*, Aix-en-Provence 1983.

ROTH-LALY, A., *Lexique des parlers arabes tchado-soudanais*, Paris 1969-72.

SABUNI, A., *Laut- und Formenlehre des arabischen Dialekts von Aleppo* (Heidelberger Orientalistische Studien 2), Frankfurt a/M 1980.

SACY, A.S. DE, *Grammaire arabe*, 2 vols., Paris 1831.

SCHAADE, A., *Sībawaihi's Lautlehre*, Leiden 1911.

SCHABERT, P., *Laut- und Formenlehre des Maltesischen anhand zweier Mundarten*, Erlangen 1976.

SCHALL, A., *Elementa Arabica. Einführung in die klassische arabische Sprache*, Wiesbaden 1988.

SEZGIN, F., *Geschichte des arabischen Schrifttums* IX. *Grammatik*, Leiden 1984.

SIENY, M.E., *The Syntax of Urban Hijazi Arabic (Sa'udi Arabia)*, Beirut 1978.

SOBELMAN, H. (ed.), *Arabic Dialect Studies*, Washington D.C. 1962.

SOMEKH, S., *Genre and Language in Modern Arabic Literature* (Studies in Arabic Language and Literature 1), Wiesbaden 1991.

SPENCER TRIMINGHAM, J., *Sudan Colloquial Arabic*, 2nd ed., London 1946.

STETKEVYCH, J., *The Modern Arabic Literary Language. Lexical and Stylistic Developments* (Publications of the Center for Middle Eastern Studies 6), Chicago-London 1970.

SULEIMAN, S., *Jordanian Arabic between Diglossia and Bilingualism: Linguistic Analysis*, Amsterdam 1986.

TALMOUDI, F., *The Arabic Dialect of Sūsa*, Göteborg 1980.

TAINE-CHEIKH, C., *Dictionnaire ḥassāniyya - français*, 6 vols., Paris 1988-90.

TAINE-CHEIKH, C., *Lexique français - ḥassāniyya*, Nouakchott 1990.

TOMICHE, N., *Le parler arabe du Caire*, The Hague 1964.

ULLMANN, M. (ed.), *Wörterbuch der klassischen arabischen Sprache*, vol. I (*Kāf*), Wiesbaden 1970; vol. II (*Lām*), Wiesbaden 1983-94.

VANHOVE, M., *La langue maltaise. Études syntaxiques d'un dialecte arabe "périphérique"* (Semitica Viva 11), Wiesbaden 1993.

VERSTEEGH, C.H.M., *Arabic Grammar and Qur'ânic Exegesis in Early Islam*, Leiden 1993.

VIOLET, B., *Ein zweisprachiges Psalmfragment aus Damaskus*, in *Orientalisti-sche Literaturzeitung* 4 (1901), col. 384-403, 425-441, 475-488 (reprint: 1902).

VOCKE, S. & W. WALDNER, *Der Wortschatz des anatolischen Arabisch*, Erlangen 1982.

VOIGT, R.M., *Die infirmen Verbaltypen des Arabischen und das Biradikalismus-Problem*, Wiesbaden 1988.

VOLLERS, K., *Volkssprache und Schriftsprache im alten Arabien*, Strassburg 1906.

WATSON, J.C.E., *A Syntax of Ṣanʿānī Arabic* (Semitica Viva 13), Wiesbaden 1993.

WEHR, H., *Der arabische Elativ*, Wiesbaden 1953.

WEHR, H., *A Dictionary of Modern Written Arabic. Arabic-English*, ed. by J.M. Cowan, 4th ed., Wiesbaden 1979.

WEHR, H., *Arabisches Wörterbuch für die Schriftsprache der Gegenwart. Arabisch - Deutsch*, 5nd ed., Wiesbaden 1985.

WORSLEY, A., *Sudanese Grammar*, London 1925.

WRIGHT, W., *A Grammar of the Arabic Language*, 3rd ed., 2 vols., Cambridge 1896-98 (reprint: 1975 & 1986).

YUSHMANOV, N.V., Грамматика литературного арабского языка, Leningrad 1928.

YUSHMANOV, N.V., Строй арабского языка, Leningrad 1938. English ed. by M. Perlmann, *The Structure of the Arab Language*, Washington 1961.

ZAWADOWSKI, Yu. N., *The Maghreb Arabic Dialects*, Moscow 1978.

ZAWADOWSKIY, Yu. N., Тунисский диалект арабского языка, Moscow 1979.

ZAWADOWSKIY, Yu. N., Мавританский диалект арабского языка (Хасания), Moscow 1981.

ZEMÁNEK, P., *Korelace emfáze v arabštině*, Praha 1991.

ZWETTLER, M., *The Oral Tradition of Classical Arabic Poetry. Its Character and Implications*, Columbus, Ohio, 1978.

5. SOUTH SEMITIC

A. South Arabian

AVANZINI, A., *Glossaire des inscriptions de l'Arabie du Sud, 1950-1973* (Quaderni di Semitistica 3), 2 vols., Firenze 1977-80.

BEESTON, A.F.L., *Phonology of the Epigraphic South-Arabian Unvoiced Sibilants*, in *Transactions of the Philological Society* 1951, p. 1-26.

BEESTON, A.F.L., *Arabian Sibilants*, in *Journal of Semitic Studies* 7 (1962), p. 222-233.

BEESTON, A.F.L., *Sabaic Grammar*, Manchester 1984.

BEESTON, A.F.L., M.A. GHUL, W.W. MÜLLER & J. RYCKMANS, *Sabaic Dictionary (English-French-Arabic)*, Louvain-la-Neuve - Beyrouth 1982.

BIELLA, J.C., *Dictionary of Old South Arabic: Sabaean Dialect*, Chico 1982.

BITTNER, M., *Studien zur Laut- und Formenlehre der Mehri - Sprache in Südarabien*, 5 vols., Wien 1909-15.

BITTNER, M., *Vorstudien zur Grammatik und zum Wörterbuche der Soqoṭri-Sprache*, 3 vols., Wien 1913-18.

BITTNER, M., *Studien zur Šḫauri-Sprache in den Bergen von Ḍofar am Persischen Meerbusen*, 4 vols., Wien 1915-17.

CONTI ROSSINI, K., *Chrestomathia Arabica Meridionalis Epigraphica, edita et glossario instructa*, Roma 1931 (reprint: 1958), p. 99-261 (glossary).

CORRIENTE, F., *South Arabian Features in Andalusí Arabic*, in P. Wexler, A. Borg & S. Somekh (eds.), *Studia Linguistica et Orientalia memoriae Haim Blanc dedicata*, Wiesbaden 1989, p. 94-109.

HÖFNER, M., *Altsüdarabische Grammatik*, Leipzig 1943 (reprint: 1976).

JAHN, A., *Die Mehri-Sprache in Südarabien. Texte und Wörterbuch*, Wien 1902.

JAHN, A., *Grammatik der Mehri-Sprache in Südarabien*, Wien 1905.

JOHNSTONE, T.M., *A Definite Article in the Modern South Arabian Languages*, in *Bulletin of the School of Oriental and African Studies* 33 (1970), p. 295-307.

JOHNSTONE, T.M., *Dual Forms in Mehri and Ḥarsūsi*, in *Bulletin of the School of Oriental and African Studies* 33 (1970), p. 501-512.

JOHNSTONE, T.M., *The Modern South Arabian Languages* (Afroasiatic Linguistics I/5), Malibu 1975.

JOHNSTONE, T.M., *Ḥarsūsi Lexicon and English-Ḥarsūsi Word-List*, London 1977.

JOHNSTONE, T.M., *Jibbāli Lexicon*, Oxford 1981.

JOHNSTONE, T.M., *Mehri Lexicon and English-Mehri Word-List*, London 1987.

KOROTAYEV, A., *Ancient Yemen. Some General Trends of Evolution of the Sabaic Language and Sabaean Culture* (Journal of Semitic Studies, Supplement 5), Oxford 1995.

LESLAU, W., *Lexique soqotri (sudarabique moderne) avec comparaisons et explications étymologiques* (Collection de la Société de Linguistique de Paris 41), Paris 1938.

MÜLLER, D.H., *Die Mehri- und Soqotri-Sprache*, 3 vols., Wien 1902-07.

MÜLLER, W.M., *Die Wurzeln* mediae *und* tertiae y/w *im Altsüdarabischen*, Tübingen 1972.

NAKANO, A., *Comparative Vocabulary of Southern Arabic: Mahri, Gibbali and Soqotri* (Studia Culturae Islamicae 29), Tokyo 1986.

NAUMKIN, V. & V.Ia. PARKHOMOVSKIY, Очерки по этнолингвистике Сокотры, Moscow 1981.

NEBES, N., *Syntaktische und epigraphische Untersuchungen zur Verwendung des Partikels* fa- *im Altsüdarabischen* (Veröffentlichungen der Orientalischen Kommission der Akademie der Wissenschaften und der Literatur zu Mainz 40), Wiesbaden 1994.

NEBES, N. (ed.), *Arabia Felix*, Wiesbaden 1994.

RHODOKANAKIS, N., *Zur Formenlehre des Mehri*, Wien 1910.

RICKS, ST.D., *Lexicon of Inscriptional Qatabanian* (Studia Pohl 14), Rome 1989.

RYCKMANS, J., W.W. MÜLLER & Y.H. ABDALLAH, *Textes du Yémen antique inscrits sur bois*, Louvain-la-Neuve 1994.

WAGNER, E., *Syntax der Mehri-Sprache, unter Berücksichtigung auch der anderen neusüdarabischen Sprachen*, Berlin 1953.

B. Ethiopic

ABBADIE, A. D', *Dictionnaire de la langue amariñña* (Actes de la société philologique 10), Paris 1881.

ABRAHAM, R.C., *The Principles of Amharic*, London 1942.

AFEVORK, G.J., *Grammatica della lingua amarica*, Roma 1905 (reprint: 1981).

AFEVORK, G.J., *Il verbo amarico*, Roma 1911.

AFERVOK, G.J., *Grammatica della lingua amarica*, Roma 1905 (reprint: 1981).

AMSALU, A., *Etymologischer Beitrag zur A. Dillmanns 'Lexicon linguae Aethiopicae'*, Tübingen 1962.

AMSALU, A. & G.P. MOSBACK, *English-Amharic Dictionary*, Addis Ababa 1973.

AMSALU, A., *Amharic-English Dictionary*, Addis Ababa 1979 [1986].

APPLEYARD, D.L., *A Comparative Approach to the Amharic Lexicon*, in *Afroasiatic Linguistics* 5 (1977-78), p. 43-110.

APPLEYARD, D.L., *Colloquial Amharic*, London 1995.

ARGAW, M., *La prononciation traditionnelle du guèze*, Paris 1973.

ARMBRUSTER, Ch.H., *Initia Amharica. An Introduction to Spoken Amharic*, 3 vols., Cambridge 1908-20.

BAETEMAN, J., *Grammaire amarigna*, Addis Ababa 1923.

BAETEMAN, J., *Dictionnaire amarigna - français suivi d'un vocabulaire français - amarigna*, Dire Daoua 1929.

BEATON, A.C. & A. PAUL, *A Grammar and Vocabulary of the Tigre Language, as spoken by the Beni Amer*, Khartoum 1954.

BENDER, M.L., *The Languages of Ethiopia. A New Lexicostatistic Classification and Some Problems of Diffusion*, in *Anthropological Linguistics* 13 (1971), p. 165-288; 14 (1972), p. 196-203.

BENDER, M.L., J.D. BOWEN, R.L. COOPER & C.A. FERGUSON, *Language in Ethiopia*, London 1976.

BENDER, M.L. & H. FULASS, *Amharic Verb Morphology: A Generative Approach*, East Lansing 1978.

BRZUSKI, W.K., *Gramatyka języka gyyz (etiopskiego klasycznego)*, Warszawa 1972.

CERULLI, E., *Studi etiopici I. La lingua e la storia di Harar*, Roma 1936.

CHAINE, M., *Grammaire éthiopienne*, Beyrouth 1907 (reprint: 1938).

COHEN, D., *Le vocabulaire de base sémitique et le classement des dialectes du sud*, in D. Cohen, *Études de linguistique sémitique et arabe*, The Hague 1970, p. 7-30.

COHEN, M., *Études d'éthiopien méridional*, Paris 1931.

COHEN, M., *Nouvelles études d'éthiopien méridional*, Paris 1939.

COHEN, M., *Traité de langue amharique (Abyssinie)*, Paris 1936 (reprint: 1970).

CONTI ROSSINI, C., *Lingua tigrina I*, Milano 1940.

COULBEAUX, P.S. & J. SCHREIBER, *Dictionnaire de la langue tigraï*, Wien 1915 (letters *h* to *n* only).

DA BASSANO, F., *Vocabolario tigray-italiano e repertorio italiano-tigray*, Roma 1918.

DA LEONESSA, M., *Grammatica analitica della lingua tigray*, Roma 1928.

DA MAGGIORA, G., *Vocabolario etiopico-italiano-latino*, Asmara 1953.

DA OFFEIO, A., *Grammatica della lingua tigrai*, 3rd ed., Asmara 1935.

DA RONCIGLIONE, A., *Manuale tigray-italiano-francese*, Roma 1912.

DILLMANN, A., *Lexicon linguae Aethiopicae cum indice Latino*, Leipzig 1865 (reprint: 1955 &1970).

DILLMANN, A., *Grammatik der äthiopischen Sprache*, 2nd ed. by C. Bezold, Leipzig 1899 (reprint: 1959 & 1967). English ed.: *Ethiopic Grammar*, 2nd ed., London 1907 (reprint: 1974).

GANKIN, E.B., Амхарско-русский словарь, Moscow 1969.

GOLDENBERG, G., *The Amharic Tense System* (in Hebrew), Jerusalem 1966.

GOLDENBERG, G., *Kəstanəñña: Studies in a Northern Gurage Language of Christians*, in *Orientalia Suecana* 17 (1968), p. 61-102.

GRÉBAUT, S., *Les pluriels brisés des formations éthiopiennes* qetl, qatl, qatal (*classement et tables*), Paris 1947.

GRÉBAUT, S., *Supplément au Lexicon linguae Aethiopicae de A. Dillmann (1865) et édition du lexique de J. d'Urbin (1850-55)*, Paris 1952.

GUIDI, I., *Vocabolario amarico-italiano*, Roma 1901 (reprint: 1953); *Supplemento*, Roma 1940.

GUIDI, I., *Grammatica elementare della lingua amarica*, 3rd ed., Napoli 1924 (reprint: 1952).

HARTMANN, J., *Amharische Grammatik* (Äthiopistische Forschungen 3), Wiesbaden 1980.

HETZRON, R., *Ethiopian Semitic. Studies in Classification*, Manchester 1972.

HETZRON, R., *The Gunnän-Gurage Languages*, Napoli 1977.

HOUGHTON, H.P., *Aspects of the Amharic Verb in Comparison with Ethiopic*, Northfield 1948.

KANE, T.L., *Amharic - English Dictionary*, 2 vols., Wiesbaden 1990.

KAPELIUK, O., *Problems of the Comparative Grammar of Hebrew, Amharic, and Tigrinya* (in Hebrew), Jerusalem 1983.

KAPELIUK, O., *Nominalization in Amharic* (Äthiopistische Forschungen 23), Stuttgart 1988.

KAPELIUK, O., *Syntax of the Noun in Amharic* (Äthiopistische Forschungen 37), Wiesbaden 1994.

KRAČKOVSKIY, I.Iu., Введение в эфиопскую филологию, Leningrad 1955.

LAMBDIN, T.O., *Introduction to Classical Ethiopic (Ge'ez)* (Harvard Semitic Studies 24), Ann Arbor 1978.

LESLAU, W., *Contributions à l'étude du harari*, in *Journal Asiatique* 229 (1937), p. 431-479, 529-606 = *Contributions à l'étude du harari* (*Abyssinie méridionale*), Paris 1938.

LESLAU, W., *Documents tigrigna (éthiopien septentrional). Grammaire et textes* (Collection de la Société de Linguistique de Paris 48), Paris 1941.

LESLAU, W., *Short Grammar of Tigré (North Ethiopic). Dialect of Mensa'*, New Haven 1945.

LESLAU, W., *Gafat Documents. Records of a South-Ethiopic Language. Grammar, Text and Comparative Vocabulary* (American Oriental Series 28), New Haven 1945.

LESLAU, W., *Ethiopic Documents: Gurage*, New York 1950.

LESLAU, W., *Étude descriptive et comparative du Gafat (éthiopien méridional)* (Collection de la Société de Linguistique de Paris 57), Paris 1956.

LESLAU, W., *The Verb in Harari (South Ethiopic)* (University of California Publications in Semitic Philology 21), Berkeley - Los Angeles 1958.

LESLAU, W., *A Preliminary Description of Argobba*, in *Annales d'Éthiopie* 3 (1959), p. 251-273.

LESLAU, W., *Etymological Dictionary of Harari* (University of California Publications in Near Eastern Studies 1), Berkeley - Los Angeles 1961.

LESLAU, W., *An Annotated Bibliography of the Semitic Languages of Ethiopia*, The Hague 1965.

LESLAU, W., *Amharic Textbook*, Wiesbaden 1968.

LESLAU, W., *Hebrew Cognates in Amharic*, Wiesbaden 1969.

LESLAU, W., *English-Amharic Context Dictionary*, Wiesbaden 1973.

LESLAU, W., *Concise Amharic Dictionary. Amharic-English / English-Amharic*, Wiesbaden 1976.

LESLAU, W., *Etymological Dictionary of Gurage*, 3 vols., Wiesbaden 1979.

LESLAU, W., *North Ethiopic and Amharic Cognates in Tigre*, Napoli 1982.

LESLAU, W., *Comparative Dictionary of Ge'ez (Classical Ethiopic)*, Wiesbaden 1987 (reprint: 1991).

LESLAU, W., *Fifty Years of Research. Selection of Articles on Semitic, Ethiopian Semitic and Cushitic*, Wiesbaden 1988.

LESLAU, W., *Arabic Loanwords in Ethiopian Semitic*, Wiesbaden 1990.

LESLAU, W., *Gurage Studies. Collected Articles*, Wiesbaden 1992.

LESLAU, W., *Reference Grammar of Amharic*, Wiesbaden 1995.

LITTMANN, E. & M. HÖFNER, *Wörterbuch der Tigrē-Sprache. Tigrē-Deutsch-Englisch*, Wiesbaden 1956-62.

LOCKOT, H.W., *Bibliographia Aethiopica. Literature in English on the Horn of Africa* (Äthiopistische Forschungen 41), 2 vols., Wiesbaden 1995.

LUDOLF, H., *Lexicon Aethiopico-Latinum*, London 1661 (2nd ed. 1699).

LUDOLF, H., *Grammatica linguae Amharicae*, Frankfurt a/M 1698 (reprint: 1986).

LUDOLF, H., *Lexicon Amharico-Latinum*, Frankfurt a/M 1698.

MITTWOCH, E., *Die traditionelle Aussprache des Äthiopischen*, Berlin 1926.

MONDON-VIDAILHET, F.M.C., *Grammaire de la langue abyssine (amharique)*, Paris 1898.

MONDON-VIDAILHET, F.M.C., *La langue harari et les dialects éthiopiens du gouraghê*, Paris 1902.

MONDON-VIDAILHET, F.M.C., *Études sur le guragiè* (ed. by E. Weinzinger), Wien 1913.

MURTONEN, A., *Early Semitic. A Diachronical Inquiry into the Relationship of Ethiopic to the Other So-Called South-East Semitic Languages* (Studies in Semitic Languages and Linguistics 1), Leiden 1967.

PALMER, F.R., *The Morphology of the Tigre Noun* (London Oriental Series 13), London 1962.

PODOLSKY, B., *Historical Phonetics of Amharic*, Tel Aviv 1991.

POLOTSKY, H.J., *Collected Papers*, Jerusalem 1971, p. 477-573.

PRAETORIUS, F., *Grammatik der Tigriñasprache in Abessinien, hauptsächlich in der Gegend von Aksum und Adoa*, Halle 1871-72 (reprint: 1974).

PRAETORIUS, F., *Die amharische Sprache*, 2 vols., Halle 1878-79 (reprint: 1970).

PRAETORIUS, F., *Äthiopische Grammatik mit Paradigmen, Literatur, Chrestomathie und Glossar*, Karlsruhe - Leipzig 1886 (reprint: 1955).

RAZ, S., *Tigre Grammar and Texts* (Afroasiatic Dialects 4), Malibu 1983.

RICHTER, R., *Lehrbuch der amharischen Sprache*, Leipzig 1987.

SAHLE, A., *Tigrigna Grammar. An Outline*, in *Ethiopian Journal of African Studies* 1 (1981), p. 19-62.

SCHNEIDER, R., *L'expression des compléments de verbe et de nom et la place de l'adjectif épithète en guèze*, Paris 1959.

SEGERT, St. & A.J.E. BODROGLIGETI (eds.), *Ethiopian Studies dedicated to Wolf Leslau*, Wiesbaden 1983.

STARININ, V.P., Эфиопский язык, Moscow 1967.

TITOV, E.G., *The Modern Amharic Language*, Moscow 1976.

ULLENDORFF, E., *The Semitic Languages of Ethiopia. A Comparative Phonology*, London 1955.

ULLENDORFF, E., *An Amharic Chrestomathy*, Oxford 1965 (reprint: 1978).

ULLENDORFF, E., *A Tigrinya (Təgrəñña). Chrestomathy* (Äthiopistische Forschungen 19), Stuttgart 1985.

ULLENDORFF, E., *Studia Aethiopica et Semitica* (Äthiopistische Forschungen 24), Stuttgart 1987.

VOIGT, R.M., *Das tigrinische Verbalsystem* (Marburger Studien zur Afrika- und Asienkunde 10), Berlin 1977.

YUSHMANOV, N.V., Строй амхарского языка, Leningrad 1936.

YUSHMANOV, N.V., Амхарский язык, Moscow 1959.

6. LIBYCO-BERBER

ABDEL-MASSIH, E.T., *Tamazight Verb Structure. A Generative Approach*, The Hague 1968.

ABDEL-MASSIH, E.T., *A Course in Spoken Tamazight (Middle Atlas Berber)*, Ann Arbor 1971.

ABDEL-MASSIH, E.T., *A Reference Grammar of Tamazight*, Ann Arbor 1971.

ALOJALY, Gh., *Lexique touareg-français*, Copenhague 1980.

APPLEGATE, J.R., *An Outline of the Structure of Shilha*, New York 1958.

APPLEGATE, J.R., *The Berber Languages*, in Th. Sebeok (ed.), *Current Trends in Linguistics* VI. *Linguistics in South West Asia and North Africa*, The Hague 1970, p. 586-661.

ASPINION, R., *Apprenons le berbère. Initiation aux dialects chleuhs*, Rabat 1953.

BASSET, A., *La langue berbère. Morphologie. Le verbe - étude de thèmes*, Paris 1929.

BASSET, A. & J. CROUZET, *Cours de berbère (parlers de la Kabylie)* I. *Exposé grammatical*, Alger 1937.

BASSET, A. & A. PICARD, *Éléments de grammaire berbère. Kabylie, Irjen*, Alger 1948.

BASSET, A., *La langue berbère* (Handbook of African Languages 1), London 1952 (reprint: 1969).

BASSET, A., *Articles de dialectologie berbère* (Collection de la Société de Linguistique de Paris 58), Paris 1959.

BÉGUINOT, F., *Il berbero nefûsi di Fassâṭo*, 2nd ed., Roma 1942.

BENTOLILA, F., *Grammaire fonctionnelle d'un parler berbère: Aït Seghrouchen d'Oum Jeniba (Maroc)*, Paris 1981.

Biarnay, S., *Étude sur les dialectes berbères du Rif*, Paris 1917.

Cadi, K., *Système verbal rifain: forme et sens* (Études ethno-linguistiques Maghreb-Sahara 6), Paris 1987.

Chaker, S., *Un parler berbère d'Algérie (Kabylie): Syntaxe*, Lille 1983.

Chaker, S., *Textes en linguistique berbère: introduction au domaine berbère*, Paris 1984.

Chaker, S., *Une décennie d'études berbères (1980-1990). Bibliographie critique*, Alger 1992.

Chaker, S., *Linguistique berbère. Études de syntaxe et de diachronie*, Paris-Louvain 1995.

Cidkaoui, S., *Dictionnaire français-tachelh'it et tamazir't (dialectes berbères du Maroc)*, Paris 1907.

Cortade, J.-M. & M. Mammert, *Lexique français-touareg*, Paris 1967.

Cortade, J.-M., *Essai de grammaire touarègue (dialecte de l'Ahaggar)*, Alger 1969.

Dallet, J.M., *Le verbe kabyle I. Formes simples*, Alger 1953.

Dallet, J.M., *Initiation à la langue berbère (Kabylie). Grammaire*, Fort-National 1960.

Dallet, J.M., *Berbère de l'Oued-Mzab: le verbe, glossaire, classification*, Fort-National 1970.

Dallet, J.M., *Dictionnaire kabyle-français — Dictionnaire français-kabyle. Parler des Aït Mangellat, Algérie*, 2 vols. (Études ethno-linguistiques Maghreb-Sahara 1 & 3), Paris 1982-85.

Delheure, J., *Dictionnaire mozabite-français. Index récapitulatif français-mozabite* (Études ethno-linguistiques Maghreb-Sahara 2), Paris 1984.

Delheure, J., *Dictionnaire ouargli-français. Index récapitulatif français-ouargli* (Études ethno-linguistiques Maghreb-Sahara 5), Paris 1987.

Destaing, E., *Études sur le dialecte berbère des Beni Snous*, 2 vols., Paris 1907-11.

Destaing, E., *Dictionnaire français-berbère (dialecte des Beni Snous)*, Paris 1914.

Destaing, E., *Étude sur le dialecte berbère des Aït Seghrouchen (Moyen Atlas marocain)*, Paris 1920.

Destaing, E., *Étude sur le tachelhît du Soûs. Vocabulaire français-berbère*, Paris 1938.

Foucauld, Ch. de, *Dictionnaire touareg-français, dialecte de l'Ahaggar*, 4 vols., Paris 1951-52.

Galand, L., *Langue et littérature berbères. Vingt-cinq ans d'études*, Paris 1979.

Guerssel, M. & K. Hale (eds.), *Studies in Berber Syntax*, Cambridge 1987.

Hanoteau, A., *Essai de grammaire kabyle*, Alger 1858 (reprint: 1976).

Hanoteau, A., *Essai de grammaire de la langue tamachek'*, 2nd ed., Alger 1896 (reprint: 1976).

Jordan, A., *Dictionnaire berbère-français*, Rabat 1934.

Kossmann, M.G., *Grammaire du berbère de Figuig (Maroc oriental)*, Leuven 1996.

Lanfry, J., *Ghadamès*, 2 vols., Fort-National - Alger 1968-73.

Laoust, É., *Étude sur le dialecte berbère des Ntifa*, Paris 1918.

Laoust, É., *Siwa I. Son parler*, Paris 1932.

LAOUST, É., *Cours de berbère marocain*, 3rd ed., Paris 1939.

LEGUIL, A., *Structures prédicatives en berbère. Bilan et perspectives*, Paris 1992.

LOUBIGNAC, V., *Étude sur le dialecte berbère des Zaïan et Aït Sgougou*, 2 vols., Paris 1924-25.

MAMMERI, M., *L'Ahellil du Gourara*, Paris 1984.

MERCIER, H., *Vocabulaire et textes berbères dans le dialecte berbère des Aït Izdeĝ*, Rabat 1937.

PENCHOEN, T.G., *Étude syntaxique d'un parler berbère (Aït Frah de l'Aurès)* (Studi Magrebini 5), Napoli 1973.

PENCHOEN, T.G., *Tamazight of the Ayt Ndhir* (Afroasiatic Dialects 1), Malibu 1973.

PETITES SOEURS DE JÉSUS, *Initiation à la langue des Touaregs de l'Aïr*, Agadès 1968.

PETITES SOEURS DE JÉSUS, *Contes touaregs de l'Aïr. Introduction linguistique* by L. Galand; *Commentaires* by G. Calame-Griaule, Paris 1974 (reprint: 1991).

PICARD, A., *De quelques faits de stylistique dans le parler berbère des Irjen (Kabylie, Algérie). De la phrase inorganique à la phrase organisée*, Alger 1960.

PRASSE, K.G., *Manuel de grammaire touarègue (tăhăggart)*, 3 vols., Copenhague 1972-74.

RENISIO, A., *Étude sur les dialectes berbères des Beni Iznassen, du Rif et des Senhaja de Srair. Grammaire, textes et lexique*, Paris 1932.

RÖSSLER, O., *Die Sprache Numidiens*, in *Sybaris. Festschrift Hans Krahe*, Wiesbaden 1958, p. 94-120.

RÖSSLER, O., *Libyen von der Cyrenaica bis zur Mauretania Tingitana*, in *Die Sprachen im römischen Reich der Kaiserzeit* (Bonner Jahrbücher, Beiheft 40), Bonn 1980, p. 267-284.

SADIQI, F., *Studies in Berber Syntax. The Complex Sentence*, Würzburg 1986.

SARRIONANDIA, P., *Gramática de la lengua rifina*, Tanger 1905.

STUMME, H., *Handbuch des Schilḥischen von Tazerwalt*, Leipzig 1899.

TAIFI, M., *Dictionnaire tamazight-français (parlers du Maroc central)*, Paris 1992.

WILLMS, A., *Grammatik der südlichen Berberdialekte (Südmarokko)* (Afrikanistische Forschungen 6), Hamburg 1972.

WILLMS, A., *Die dialektale Differenzierung des Berberischen* (Afrika und Übersee, Beiheft 31), Berlin 1980.

ZAWADOWSKIY, Yu. N., Берберский язык, Moscow 1967.

7. CUSHITIC

ABRAHAM, R.C., *Somali-English Dictionary*, London 1962 (reprint: 1964) (with an outline of grammar, p. 258-332).

ABRAHAM, R.C., *English-Somali Dictionary*, London 1962 (reprint: 1967).

ALI, M. & A. ZABORSKI, *Handbook of the Oromo Language* (Äthiopistische Forschungen 30), Stuttgart-Wrocław 1990.

ALMKVIST, H., *Die Bischari-Sprache (Tū-Beḍāwie) in Nordost-Afrika*, 2 vols., Uppsala 1881-85.

AMBORN, H., G. MINKER & H.-J. SASSE, *Das Dullay. Materialien zu einer ostkuschitischen Sprachgruppe* (Kölner Beiträge zur Afrikanistik 6), Berlin 1980.

AMSTRONG, L.E., *The Phonetic Structure of Somali*, Berlin 1934.

ANDRZEJEWSKI, B.W., *Declensions of Somali Nouns*, London 1964.

BELL, C., *The Somali Language*, London 1953 (reprint: 1968).

BENDER, M.L. (ed.), *The Non-Semitic Languages of Ethiopia*, Ann Arbor 1976.

BENDER, M.L., J.D. BOWEN, R.L. COOPER & C.A. FERGUSON, *Language in Ethiopia*, London 1976.

BLIESE, L., *A Generative Grammar of Afar*, Arlington 1981.

BORELLO, M.P., *Grammatica di lingua galla*, Torino 1939.

BORELLO, M.P., *Dizionario Oromo-Italiano / Oromo-Italian Dictionary*, ed. by H.J. Sasse & P. Tablino (Kuschitische Sprachstudien 10), Hamburg 1995.

BRYAN, M., *The Distribution of the Semitic and Cushitic Languages*, London 1947.

CERULLI, E., *Studi etiopici* II. *La lingua e la storia dei Sidamo*, Roma 1938; III. *Il linguaggio dei Giangerò ed alcune lingue sidama dell'Omo*, Roma 1938 (reprint: 1963); IV. *La lingua caffina*, Roma 1951.

CHIOMO, G., *Lingua uollamo*, Torino 1938.

COLIZZA, G., *Lingua 'afar nel nord-est dell'Africa*, Wien 1887.

CONTI ROSSINI, C., *La langue des Kemant en Abyssinie*, Wien 1912.

DA LUCHON, P., *Grammatica della lingua wallamo*, Roma 1938.

DA THIENE, G., *Dizionario della lingua galla*, Harar 1939.

DOLGOPOLSKIY, A.B., Сравнительно-историческая фонетика кушитских языков, Moscow 1973.

EHRET, C., *The Historical Reconstruction of Southern Cushitic Phonology and Vocabulary* (Kölner Beiträge zur Afrikanistik 5), Berlin 1980.

FARAH, M.A. & D. HECK, *Somali Wörterbuch*, Hamburg 1990.

FLEMING, H.C., *Baiso and Rendille: Somali Outliers*, in *Rassegna di Studi Etiopici* 20 (1964), p. 35-96.

FOOT, E.C., *A Galla-English, English-Galla Dictionary*, Cambridge 1913 (reprint: 1968).

GREENBERG, J., *Studies in African Linguistic Classification*, New Haven 1955.

GREENBERG, J., *The Languages of Africa*, The Hague 1963 (reprint: 1966, 1970).

HABERLAND, E., *Die Galla Süd-Äthiopiens*, Stuttgart 1963.

HABERLAND, E. & M. LAMBERTI, *Ibaaddo ka-Ba'iso. Culture and Language of the Ba'iso* (Studia linguarum Africae orientalis 2), Heidelberg 1988.

HEINE, B., *A Typology of African Languages Based on the Order of Meaningful Elements* (Kölner Beiträge zur Afrikanistik 4), Berlin 1976.

HEINE, B., *Bemerkungen zur Boni-Sprache*, in *Afrika und Übersee* 60 (1977), p. 242-295.

HEINE, B., *The Sam Languages — A History of Rendille, Boni and Somali*, in *Afroasiatic Linguistics* 6 (1978-79), p. 23-115.

HEINE, B., *Language and Dialect Atlas of Kenya*, 2 vols., Berlin 1980.

HETZRON, R., *The Verbal System of Southern Agaw*, Berkeley-Los Angeles 1969.

HETZRON, R., *The Agaw Languages*, in *Afroasiatic Linguistic* 3 (1976-77), p. 31-45.

HODGE, C.T. (ed.), *Afroasiatic. A Survey*, The Hague 1971.

HODSON, A.W. & C.H. WALKER, *An Elementary and Practical Grammar of the Galla or Oromo Language*, London 1922.

HUDSON, G., *Highland East Cushitic Dictionary* (Kuschitische Sprachstudien 7), Hamburg 1989.

Journal of African Languages 1 (1962) ff.

Journal of African Languages and Linguistics 1 (1979) ff.

KIRK, J.W.C., *A Grammar of the Somali Language*, Cambridge 1905.

LAMBERTI, M., *Die Somali-Dialekte. Vergleichende Untersuchung* (Kuschitische Sprachstudien 5), Hamburg 1986.

LAMBERTI, M., *Die Nordsomali-Dialekte. Synchronische Beschreibung* (Studia linguarum Africae orientalis 1), Heidelbeg 1988.

LAMBERTI, M., *Kuliak and Cushitic. Comparative Study* (Studia linguarum Africae orientalis 3), Heidelberg 1988.

LAUNHARDT, J., *Guide to Learning the Oromo Language*, Addis Ababa 1973.

LESLAU, W., *A Dictionary of Moča* (*Southwestern Ethiopia*) (University of California Publications in Linguistics 18), Berkeley-Los Angeles 1959.

Linguistique africaine 1 (1988) ff.

MASERA, C., *Primi elementi di grammatica caffina e dizionario*, Roma 1936.

MINOZZI, M.T. & C. POLETTI-TURRINI, *Dizionario italiano-somalo*, Milano 1961.

MINOZZI, M.T. & C. POLETTI-TURRINI, *Dizionario somalo-italiano, migiurtino-italiano*, Milano 1962.

MORENO, M.M., *Introduzione alla lingua ometo*, Milano 1938.

MORENO, M.M., *Grammatica teoretico-pratica della lingua galla*, Milano 1939 (reprint: 1964).

MORENO, M.M., *Manuale di Sidamo*, Milano 1940.

MORENO, M.M., *Il somalo della Somalia*, Roma 1955.

MOUS, M., *A Grammar of Iraqw* (Kuschitische Sprachstudien 9), Hamburg 1993.

OOMEN, A., *Gender and Plurality in Rendille*, in *Afroasiatic Linguistics* 8 (1981-82), p. 33-75.

ORWIN, M., *Colloquial Somali*, London 1995.

OWENS, J., *Grammar of Harar Oromo, Northeastern Ethiopia* (Kuschitische Sprachstudien 4), Hamburg 1985.

PARKER, E.M. & R.J. HAYWARD, *An Afar-English-French Dictionary*, London 1985.

PRAETORIUS, F., *Zur Grammatik der Galla-Sprache*, Berlin 1893 (reprint: 1978).

REINISCH, L., *Die Sprache der Irob-Saho in Abessinien*, in *Sitzungsberichte der Kaiserlischen Akademie der Wissenschaften. Phil.-hist. Classe* 90 (1878), p. 89-142.

REINISCH, L., *Die Bilīn-Sprache*, 2 vols., Wien 1883-87 (reprint: 1986).

REINISCH, L., *Die Chamir-Sprache in Abessinien*, 2 vols., Wien 1884.

REINISCH, L., *Die Quara-Sprache in Abessinien*, 3 vols., Wien 1885-87.

REINISCH, L., *Die 'Afar-Sprache*, 3 vols., Wien 1886-87.

REINISCH, L., *Die Kafa-Sprache in Nordost-Afrika*, Wien 1888.

REINISCH, L., *Die Saho-Sprache*, 2 vols., Wien 1889-90 (reprint: 1986).

REINISCH, L., *Die Beḍauye-Sprache in Nordost-Afrika*, 4 vols., Wien 1893-94.

REINISCH, L., *Wörterbuch der Beḍauye-Sprache*, Wien 1895.

REINISCH, L., *Die Somali-Sprache*, 3 vols., Wien 1900-03.
REINISCH, L., *Der Dschäbbärti-Dialekt der Somali-Sprache*, Wien 1904.
ROPER, E.M., *Tu Bedawie: Grammar, Texts, and Vocabulary*, Hertford 1928.
SAEED, J.T., *Central Somali — A Grammatical Outline*, in *Afroasiatic Linguistics* 8 (1981-82), p. 77-119.
SAEED, J.I., *The Syntax of Focus and Topic of Somali* (Kuschitische Sprachstudien 3), Hamburg 1984.
SAEED, J.I., *Somali Reference Grammar*, Wheaton 1987.
SASSE, H.-J., *The Consonant Phonemes of Proto-East-Cushitic (PEC): A First Approximation*, in *Afroasiatic Linguistics* 7 (1979-80), p. 1-67.
SCHLEE, G., *Sprachliche Studien zum Rendille*, Hamburg 1978.
SIM, R.J., *Morphophonemics of the Verb in Rendille*, in *Afroasiatic Linguistics* 8 (1981-82), p. 1-33.
STROOMER, H., *Comparative Study of Three Southern Oromo Dialects in Kenya: Phonology, Morphology, and Vocabulary* (Kuschitische Sprachstudien 6), Hamburg 1987.
TOSELLI, Fr.G., *Elementi di lingua magi*, Torino 1939.
TUCKER, A.N. & BRYAN, M.A., *The Non-Bantu Languages of North-Eastern Africa* (Handbook of African Languages 3), 2nd ed., London 1966.
TUTSCHEK, Ch., *Lexicon der Galla-Sprache*, München 1844.
TUTSCHEK, Ch., *A Grammar of the Galla Language*, München 1845.
VITERBO, E., *Vocabolario della lingua oromonica (lingua galla)*, Milano 1892; 2nd ed., Milano 1938.
WEDEKIND, Kl., *Generating Narratives, Interrelations of Knowledge, Text Variants, and Cushitic Focus Strategies*, Berlin 1990.
WHITELEY, W.H., *Studies in Iraqw. An Introduction*, Kampala 1953.
WHITELEY, W.H., *A Short Description of Item Categories in Iraqw*, Kampala 1958.
ZABORSKI, A., *Studies in Hamito-Semitic* I. *The Verb in Cushitic*, Kraków 1975.
ŽOLKOVSKIY, A.K., Синтаксис Сомалии, Moscow 1971.

8. CHADIC

ABRAHAM, R.C., *The Language of the Hausa People*, London 1959.
ALIO, K. & H. JUNGRAITHMAYR, *Lexique bidiya*, Frankfurt a/M 1989.
BARGERY, G.P., *A Hausa-English Dictionary*, London 1934.
CAPRILE, J.-P. & H. JUNGRAITHMAYR (eds.), *Préalables à la reconstruction du Proto-Tchadique*, Paris 1978.
EBERT, K., *Sprache und Tradition der Kera (Tschad)* II. *Lexikon/Lexique*, Berlin 1976.
ÉBOBISSÉ, C., *Die Morphologie des Verbs im Ost-Dangaleat (Guera, Tschad)*, Berlin 1979.
FÉDRY, J., *Dictionnaire dangoléat (Tchad)*, Lyon 1971.
GREENBERG, J., *Studies in African Linguistic Classification*, New Haven 1955.
GREENBERG, J., *The Languages of Africa*, The Hague 1963 (reprint: 1966, 1970).
HEINE, B., *A Typology of African Languages Based on the Order of Meaningful Elements* (Kölner Beiträge zur Afrikanistik 4), Berlin 1976.

HEINE, B., Th. C. SCHADEBERG & E. WOLFF (eds.), *Die Sprache Afrikas*, Hamburg 1981.

HOFFMANN, C., *A Grammar of the Margi Language*, London 1963.

Journal of African Languages 1 (1962) ff.

Journal of African Languages and Linguistics 1 (1979) ff.

JUNGRAITHMAYR, H., *Die Ron-Sprachen*: *Tschado-hamitische Studien in Nordnigerien* (Afrikanistische Forschungen 3), Glückstadt 1970.

JUNGRAITHMAYR, H. & K. SHIMIZU, *Chadic Lexical Roots* II, Berlin 1981.

JUNGRAITHMAYR, H. (ed.), *The Chad Languages in the Hamitosemitic-Nigritic Border Area*, Berlin 1982.

JUNGRAITHMAYR, H. & W. MÖHLIG (eds.), *Lexikon der Afrikanistik*, Berlin 1983.

JUNGRAITHMAYR, H. (ed.), *Contacts de langues et contacts de culture* V. *Langues tchadiques et langues non tchadiques en contact en Afrique Centrale*, Paris 1987.

JUNGRAITHMAYR, H., *Lexique mokilko*, Berlin 1990.

JUNGRAITHMAYR, H. & A. ADAMS, *Lexique migama*, Berlin 1992.

KRAFT, Ch. H., *Chadic Word-Lists*, 3 vols., Berlin 1981.

Linguistique africaine 1 (1988) ff.

LUKAS, J., *Die Logone-Sprache im Zentralen Sudan*, Leipzig 1936 (reprint: 1966).

LUKAS, J., *Zentralsudanische Studien*, Hamburg 1937.

LUKAS, J., *Studien zur Sprache der Gisiga (Nordkamerun)*, Glückstadt 1970.

MEYER-BAHLBURG, H., *Studien zur Morphologie und Syntax des Musgu*, Hamburg 1972.

MOHRLANG, R., *Higi Phonology* (Studies in Nigerian Languages 2), Zaria-Kano 1972.

NEWMAN, P. & R. MA, *Comparative Chadic: Phonology and Lexicon*, in *Journal of African Languages* 5 (1966), p. 218-251.

NEWMAN, P., *A Grammar of Tera: Transformational Syntax and Texts*, Berkeley-Los Angeles 1970.

NEWMAN, P., *The Kanakurn Language* (West African Language Monograph Series 9), Leeds 1974.

NEWMAN, P. & R.G. SCHUH, *The Hausa Aspect System*, in *Afroasiatic Linguistic* 1 (1974-75), p. 1-39.

NEWMAN, P., *Chadic Classification and Reconstruction*, in *Afroasiatic Linguistics* 5 (1977-78), p. 1-42.

NEWMAN, P., *The Classification of Chadic within Afroasiatic*, Leiden 1980.

RAPP, E.L. & B. BENZING, *Dictionary of the Glavdá Language*, 2 vols., Frankfurt a/M 1968-69.

SACHNINE, M., *Le lamé, un parler zimé du Nord-Cameroun (langue tchadique)*, 2 vols., Paris 1982.

SCHUBERT, K., *Zur Bedeutung und Anwendung der Verbalparadigmen in Hausa und Kanuri*, Hamburg 1972.

SCHUH, R.G., *The Chadic Verbal System and Its Afroasiatic Nature*, in *Afroasiatic Linguistics* 3 (1976-77), p. 1-14.

SCHUH, R.G., *Bole-Tangale Languages of the Bauchi Area (Northern Nigeria)*, Berlin 1978.

SHIMIZU, K., *Boghom and Zaar: Vocabulary and Notes*, Kano 1975.

SHIMIZU, K., *The Southern Bauchi Group of Chadic Languages* (Africana Marburgensia, Sonderheft 2), Marburg 1978.

Studies in African Linguistics 1 (1970) ff.

TOURNEUX, H., *Le mulwi ou vulum de Mogroum (Tchad), langue du groupe musgu — famille tchadique: phonologie, éléments de grammaire*, Paris 1978.

WESTERMANN, D., & M.A. BRYAN, *The Languages of West Africa* (Handbook of African Languages 2), London 1952.

WOLFF, H.E., *Die Verbalphrase des Laamang*, Hamburg 1972.

WOLFF, H.E., *Grammatical Categories of Verb Stems and the Marking of Mood, Aktionsart, and Aspect in Chadic*, in *Afroasiatic Linguistics* 6 (1978-79), p. 161-208.

9. LANGUAGES IN CONTACT

ALI, A.S.M., *A Linguistic Study of the Development of Scientific Vocabulary in Standard Arabic* (Library of Arabic Linguistics), London 1987.

AL-SELWI, I., *Jemenitische Wörter in den Werken von al-Hamdānī und Našwān und ihre Parallelen in den semitischen Sprachen*, Berlin 1987.

ARNOLD, W. & P. BEHNSTEDT, *Arabisch - Aramäische Sprachbeziehungen im Qalamūn (Syrien)* (Semitica Viva 8), Wiesbaden 1993.

ASHAGHI, A., *Die semantische Entwicklung arabischer Wörter im Persischen*, Wiesbaden 1987.

ASHAGHI, A., *Persische Lehnwörter im Arabischen*, Wiesbaden 1988.

BECHHAUS-GERST, M., *Nubier und Kuschiten im Niltal. Sprach- und Kulturkontakte im 'no man's land'*, Köln 1989.

BEESTON, A.F.L., *Foreign Loanwords in Sabaic*, in N. Nebes (ed.), *Arabia Felix*, Wiesbaden 1994, p. 39-45.

BEHNSTEDT, P., *Weitere koptische Lehnwörter im Ägyptisch-Arabischen*, in *Die Welt des Orients* 12 (1981), p. 81-98.

BISHAI, W.B., *Coptical Influence on Egyptian Arabic*, in *Journal of Near Eastern Studies* 23 (1964), p. 34-47.

BROWN, J.P., *Israel and Hellas* (Beihefte zur Zeitschrift für die alttestamentliche Wissenschaft 231), Berlin 1995.

CAMPS, G., *Comment la Berbérie est devenue le Maghreb arabe*, in *Revue de l'Occident musulman et de la Méditerranée* 35 (1983), p. 7-23.

COHEN, D., *A Dictionary of Latin and Greek Legal Terms in Rabbinic Literature*, Ramat-Gan 1984.

CONTI, G., *Rapporti tra egiziano e semitico nel lessico egiziano dell'agricoltura* (Quaderni di Semitistica 6), Firenze 1978.

DOZY, R. & W.H. ENGELMANN, *Glossaire des mots espagnols et portugais dérivés de l'arabe*, 2nd ed., Leyde 1896 (reprint: 1974).

DVOŘÁK, *Über die Fremdwörter im Koran*, Wien 1885.

EGUILAZ Y YANGUAS, L. DE, *Glosario etimológico de las palabras españolas de origen oriental*, Granada 1886 (reprint: 1970).

EHRET, Chr., *Ethiopians and East Africans. The Problem of Contacts*, Nairobi 1974.

EILERS, W., *Iranisches Lehngut im arabischen Lexikon: Über einige Berufsnamen und Titel*, in *Indo-Iranian Journal* 5 (1962), p. 203-232, 308-309.

ENDRESS, G. & D. GUTAS, *A Greek and Arabic Lexicon*, Leiden 1992 ff.

FÉGHALI, M.F., *Études sur les emprunts syriaques dans les parlers arabes du Liban*, Paris 1918.

FRAENKEL, S., *De vocabulis in antiquis Arabum carminibus et in Corano peregrinis*, Leiden 1880.

FRAENKEL, S., *Die aramäischen Fremdwörter im Arabischen*, Leiden 1886 (reprint: 1982).

GARULO, T., *Los arabismos en el léxico andaluz*, Madrid 1983.

GHŪL, M.A., *Early Southern Arabian Languages and Classical Arabic Sources*, Irbid 1993.

GREENBERG, J.H., *Arabic Loan-Words in Hausa*, in *Word* 3 (1947), p. 85-97.

GREGORIO, G. DE & CHR. SEYBOLD, *Glossario delle voci siciliane di origine araba*, in *Studi glottologici italiani* 3 (1903), p. 225-251.

GRIFFIN, D.A., *Los mozarabismos del "Vocabulista" atribuido a Ramón Marti*, in *Al-Andalus* 23 (1958), p. 251-337; 24 (1959), p. 333-380; 25 (1960), p. 93-169.

GRIMME, H., *Über einige Klassen südarabischer Lehnwörter im Koran*, in *Zeitschrift für Assyriologie* 20 (1912), p. 158-168.

GROHMANN, A., *Griechische und lateinische Verwaltungstermini im arabischen Aegypten*, in *Chronique d'Égypte* 7 (1932), p. 275-284.

GRÜNEBAUM, G. VON, *Persische Wörter in arabischen Gedichten*, in *Le Monde Oriental* 31 (1937), p. 18-22.

HOCH, J.E., *Semitic Words in Egyptian Texts of the New Kingdom and Third Intermediate Period*, Princeton 1994.

HÜSING, G., *Semitische Lehnwörter im Elamischen*, in *Beiträge zur Assyriologie* 5 (1906), p. 405-412.

ISSAWI, Ch., *European Loanwords in Contemporary Arabic Writing. A Case Study of Modernization*, in *Middle Eastern Studies* 3 (1966-67), p. 110-133.

JEFFERY, A., *The Foreign Vocabulary of the Qur'ān*, Baroda 1938.

KAMIL, M., *Persian Words in Ancient Arabic*, in *Bulletin of the Faculty of Arts. University of Cairo* 19 (1957), p. 55-67.

KAUFMAN, S.A., *The Akkadian Influences on Aramaic* (Assyriological Studies 19), Chicago 1974.

KOPF, L., *The Treatment of Foreign Words in Mediaeval Arabic Lexicology*, in *Studies in Islamic History and Civilization* (Scripta Hierosolymitana 9), Jerusalem 1960, p. 191-205 = L. Kopf, *Studies in Arabic and Hebrew Lexicography*, Jerusalem 1976, p. 247-261.

KRAUSS, S., *Griechische und lateinische Lehnwörter im Talmud, Midrasch und Targum*, 2 vols., Berlin 1898-99 (reprint: 1966).

LAGARDE, P. DE, *Gesammelte Abhandlungen*, Leipzig 1866, p. 1-84.

LAMBDIN, Th.O., *Egyptian Loanwords in the Old Testament*, in *Journal of the American Oriental Society* 73 (1953), p. 145-155.

LESLAU, W., *Ethiopic and South Arabic Contributions to the Hebrew Lexicon* (University of California Publications in Semitic Philology 29), Berkeley-Los Angeles 1958.

LESLAU, W., *Arabic Loanwords in Ethiopian Semitic*, Wiesbaden 1990.

LEVIN, S., *The Indo-European and Semitic Languages: An Exploration of Structural Similarities Related to Accent, chiefly in Greek, Sanskrit and Hebrew*, New York 1971.

LEVIN, S., *Semitic and Indo-European: The Principal Etymologies, with Observations on Afro-Asiatic*, Amsterdam-Philadelphia 1995.

LEWY, H., *Die semitischen Fremdwörter im Griechischen*, Berlin 1895.

LIEBERMAN, S.J., *The Sumerian Loanwords in Old-Babylonian Akkadian*, Missoula 1977.

LIPIŃSKI, E., *Emprunts suméro-akkadiens en hébreu biblique*, in *Zeitschrift für Althebraistik* 1 (1988), p. 61-73.

LITTMANN, E., *Koptischer Einfluss im Ägyptisch-Arabischen*, in *Zeitschrift der Deutschen Morgenländischen Gesellschaft* 56 (1902), p. 566-576.

LITTMANN, E., *Türkisches Sprachgut im Ägyptisch-Arabischen*, in *Westöstliche Abhandlungen*, Wiesbaden 1954, p. 107-127.

LOKOTSCH, K., *Etymologisches Wörterbuch der europäischen ... Wörter orientalischen Ursprungs*, Heidelberg 1927.

MARÇAIS, W., *Articles et conférences*, Paris 1961, p. 171-192.

MARGOLIOUTH, D.S., *Some Additions to Professor Jeffery's Foreign Vocabulary of the Qur'ān*, in *Journal of the Royal Asiatic Society* 1939, p. 53-61.

MARTÍNEZ RUIZ, J., *Languages in Contact in Morisco Granada (XVI Century)*, in *Actas del Congreso Internacional sobre Interferencias Lingüísticas Arabo-Romances y Paralelos Extra-Iberos*, Zaragoza 1994, p. 141-156.

MASSON, E., *Recherches sur les plus anciens emprunts sémitiques en grec*, Paris 1967.

MEEKS, D., *Les emprunts égyptiens aux langues sémitiques durant le Nouvel Empire et la Troisième Période Intermédiaire. Les aléas du comparatisme*, in *Bibliotheca Orientalis* 54 (1997), col. 32-61.

NEUVONEN, E.K., *Los arabismos del español en el siglo XIII*, Helsinki 1941.

NIEHOFF-PANAGIOTIDIS, J., *Koine und Diglossie*, Wiesbaden 1994.

NÖLDEKE, TH., *Neue Beiträge zur semitischen Sprachwissenschaft*, Strassburg 1910, p. 23-66.

NYBERG, H.S., B. UTAS & CHR. TOLL, *Frahang i Pahlavīk*, Wiesbaden 1988.

O'CONNOR, M., *The Arabic Loanwords in Nabatean Arabic*, in *Journal of Near Eastern Studies* 45 (1986), p. 213-229.

OSMAN, N., *Kleines Lexikon deutscher Wörter arabischer Herkunft*, 4th ed., München 1993.

PELLEGRINI, G.B., *Terminologia geografica araba in Sicilia*, in *Annali dell'Istituto Orientale di Napoli. Sezione di Linguistica* 3 (1961), p. 109-201.

PELLEGRINI G.B., *Gli arabismi nelle lingue neolatine con speciale riguardo all'Italia*, 2 vols., Brescia 1972.

POWELS, S., *Indische Lehnwörter in der Bibel*, in *Zeitschrift für Althebraistik* 5 (1992), p. 186-200.

PROKOSCH, E., *Arabische Kontaktsprachen (Pidgin- und Kreolsprachen) in Afrika* (Grazer linguistische Monographien 2), Graz 1986.

RABIN, Ch., *Hittite Words in Hebrew*, in *Orientalia*, n.s., 32 (1963), p. 113-139.

ROSÉN, H.B., *Hebrew at the Crossroads of Cultures from outgoing Antiquity to the Middle Ages* (Orbis supplementa 3), Leuven 1995.

RUNDGREN, F., *Semitische Wortstudien*, in *Orientalia Suecana* 10 (1961), p. 99-136.

SAʿID, M.F., *Lexical Innovation through Borrowing in Modern Standard Arabic* (Princeton Near Eastern Papers 6), Princeton 1967.

SALGADO, F.M., *Los arabismos del castellano en la baja Edad Media* (*Consideraciones históricas y filológicas*), Salamanca 1983.

SALONEN, A., *Alte Substrat- und Kulturwörter im Arabischen* (Studia Orientalia 17/2), Helsinki 1952.

SALONEN, E., *Alte Substrat- und Kulturwörter im Arabischen* (Studia Orientalia 51/7), Helsinki 1979.

SCHALL, A., *Studien über griechische Fremdwörter im Syrischen*, Darmstadt 1960.

SCHALL, A., *Geschichte des arabischen Wortschatzes — Lehn- und Fremdwörter im klassischen Arabisch*, in W. Fischer (ed.), *Grundriss der arabischen Philologie. Band I: Sprachwissenschaft*, Wiesbaden 1982, p. 142-153.

SCHOLTZ, A., *Gli arabismi siciliani: prospetto riassuntivo dei principali studi*, in J. Lüdtke (ed.), *Romania Arabica. Festschrift für R. Kontzi zum 70. Geburtstag*, Tübingen 1996, p. 169-189.

SHIRR, A., *Persian Arabicised Words in Arabic* (in Arabic), Beirut 1908 (reprint: 1965).

SIDDIQI, A., *Studien über die persischen Fremdwörter im Klassischen Arabisch*, Göttingen 1919.

SIDDIQI, A., *Ibn Duraid and His Treatment of Loan-Words*, in *The Allahabad University Studies* 6 (1930), p. 669-750.

SIMONET, F.J., *Glosario de voces ibéricas y latinas usadas entre los Mozárabes. Precedido de un estudio del dialecto hispano-mozárabe*, Madrid 1888 (reprint: 1967).

SIVAN, D., *Grammatical Analysis and Glossary of the Northwest Semitic Vocables in Akkadian Texts of the 15th-13th c. B.C. from Canaan and Syria* (Alter Orient und Altes Testament 214), Kevelaer-Neukirchen-Vluyn 1984.

SIVAN, D. & Z. COCHAVI-RAINEY, *West Semitic Vocabulary in Egyptian Script of the 14th to the 10th Centuries B.C.E.* (Beer-Sheva 6), Beer-Sheva 1992.

SOBHY, G., *Common Words in the Spoken Arabic of Egypt of Greek or Coptic Origin*, Cairo 1950.

SODEN VON, W., *Aramäische Wörter in neuassyrischen und neu- und spätbabylonischen Texten*, in *Orientalia*, n.s., 35 (1966), p. 1-20; 37 (1968), p. 261-271; 46 (1977), p. 183-197.

SOUSA, F.J. DE, *Vestigios da lingua arabica em Portugal*, Lisboa 1788 (reprint: 1995).

SPITALER, A., *Materialien zur Erklärung von Fremdwörter im Arabischen durch retrograde Ableitung*, in *Corolla Linguistica. Festschrift Ferdinand Sommer*, Wiesbaden 1955, p. 211-220.

SPITTA, W., *Die Lücken in Ǧawâlîqî's Mu'arrab*, in *Zeitschrift der Deutschen Morgenländischen Gesellschaft* 33 (1879), p. 208-224.

STACHOWSKI, S., *Studien über die arabischen Lehnwörter im Osmanisch-Türkischen*, 4 vols., Wrocław 1975-86.

STEIGER, A., *Contribución a la fonética del hispano-árabe y de los arabismos en el ibero-románico y el siciliano*, Madrid 1932.

VOLLERS, K., *Beiträge zur Kenntnis der lebenden arabischen Sprache in Aegypten. II. Über Lehnwörter, Fremdes und Eigenes*, in *Zeitschrift der Deutschen Morgenländischen Gesellschaft* 50 (1896), p. 607-657; 51 (1897), p. 291-326, 343-364.

WAGNER, M., *Die lexikalischen und grammatikalischen Aramaismen im alttestamentlichen Hebräisch* (Beihefte zur Zeitschrift für die alttestamentliche Wissenschaft 96), Berlin 1966.

WARDINI, E., *Neologisms in Modern Literary Syriac: Some Preliminary Results*, Dissert. Univ. of Oslo 1995.

WEXLER, P., *The Schizoid Nature of Modern Hebrew. A Slavic Language in Search of a Semitic Past*, Wiesbaden 1990.

ZABORSKI, A., *Arabic Loan-Words in Somali: Preliminary Survey*, in *Folia Orientalia* 8 (1967), p. 125-175.

ZIMMERN, H., *Akkadische Fremdwörter als Beweis für babylonischen Kultureinfluss*, 2nd ed., Leipzig 1917.

10. ANTHROPONOMY AND TOPONYMY

ABBADI, S., *Die Personennamen der Inschriften aus Hatra* (Texte und Studien zur Orientalistik 1), Hildesheim 1983.

AGUILAR, V., *Antroponimia tribal árabe en el Mágreb en los siglos XII-XIII*, in *Estudios Onomástico-Biográficos de al-Andalus* 6 (1994), p. 19-53.

AHITUV, S., *Canaanite Toponyms in Ancient Egyptian Documents*, Jerusalem 1984.

AL-KHRAYSHEH, F., *Die Personennamen in den nabatäischen Inschriften des Corpus Inscriptionum Semiticarum*, Marburg 1986.

AL-MA'ANI, S., *Nordjordanische Ortsnamen* (Texte und Studien zur Orientalistik 7), Hildesheim 1992.

AL-SAID, S.F., *Die Personennamen in den minäischen Inschriften* (Veröffentlichungen der Orientalischen Kommission 41), Wiesbaden 1995.

AL-SHEIBA, Ah., *Die Ortsnamen in den altsüdarabischen Inschriften*, in *Archäologische Berichte aus dem Yemen* 4 (1987), p. 1-62.

AL-ZUBAIR, M. (ed.), *Dictionary of Arab Names*, 2 vols., Muscat 1991.

ARCHI, A. (ed.), *Eblaite Personal Names and Semitic Name-Giving*, Roma 1983.

ARCHI, A., P. PIACENTINI & F. POMPONIO, *I nomi di luogo nei testi di Ebla* (Archivi Reali di Ebla. Studi 2), Roma 1993.

AVANZINI, A. (ed.), *Problemi di onomastica semitica meridionale*, Pisa 1989.

AVI-YONAH, M., *Gazetteer of Roman Palestine* (Qedem 5), Jerusalem 1976.

BAUER, Th., *Die Ostkanaanäer*, Leipzig 1926.

BENZ, F.L., *Personal Names in the Phoenician and Punic Inscriptions* (Studia Pohl 8), Rome 1972.

BIGGS, R.D., *Semitic Names in the Fara Period*, in *Orientalia*, n.s., 36 (1967), p. 55-66.

BIROT, M., *Noms de personnes*, in *Archives royales de Mari* XVI/1, Paris 1979, p. 43-249.

BORG, A., *Some Maltese Toponyms in Historical and Comparative Perspective*, in P. Wexler, A. Borg & S. Somekh (eds.), *Studia linguistica et orientalia memoriae Haim Blanc dedicata*, Wiesbaden 1989, p. 62-85.

BORGER, R., *Einige westsemitische Personennamen aus mesopotamischen Quellen*, in *Texte aus der Umwelt des Alten Testaments* I, Gütersloh 1982-85, p. 411-418.

BRÄU, H.H., *Die altnordarabischen kultischen Personennamen*, in *Wiener*

Zeitschrift für die Kunde des Morgenlandes 32 (1925), p. 31-59, 85-115.

BRON, F., *Remarques sur l'onomastique sudarabique archaïque*, in N. Nebes (ed.), *Arabia Felix*, Wiesbaden 1994, p. 62-66.

BURCHARDT, M., *Die altkanaanäischen Fremdworte und Eigennamen im Ägyptischen*, Leipzig 1909-10 (reprint: 1988).

CAETANI, L. & G. GABRIELI, *Onomasticon Arabicum* I, Roma 1915.

Cahiers d'Onomastique Arabe, Paris 1979 ff.

CAMPS, G., *Liste onomastique libyque d'après les sources latines*, in *Reppal* 7-8 (1992-93), p. 39-73.

CARACAUSI, G., *Onomastica araba in Sicilia*, in *Zeitschrift für romanische Philologie* 109 (1993), p. 349-380.

CASKEL, W., *Ǧamharat an-nasab. Das genealogische Werk des Hišām ibn Muḥammad al-Kalbi*, 2 vols., Leiden 1966.

CHIERA, E., *Lists of Personal Names from the Temple School of Nippur*, 3 vols., Philadelphia 1916.

CLAY, A.T., *Personal Names from Cuneiform Inscriptions of the Cassite Period*, New Haven 1922 (reprint: 1980).

COOGAN, M.D., *West Semitic Personal Names in the Murašû Documents*, Missoula 1976.

DELLER, K., *Neuassyrisches aus Sultantepe*, in *Orientalia*, n.s., 34 (1965), p. 457-477.

DE SIMONE, A., *La kunyah negli antroponimi arabi di Sicilia*, in *Studi linguistici e filologici offerti a G. Caracausi*, Palermo 1992, p. 77-98.

DIB, F., *Les prénoms arabes*, Paris 1995.

DIETRICH, A., *Phönizische Ortsnamen in Spanien*, Leipzig 1936 (reprint: 1966).

DURAND, J.-M., *L'emploi des toponymes dans l'onomastique d'époque amorrite 1*, in *Studi epigrafici e linguistici* 8 (1991), p. 81-97.

EBELING, E., *Die Eigennamen der mittelassyrischen Rechts- und Geschäftsurkunden*, Leipzig 1939 (reprint: 1972).

EDEL, E., *Neue Deutungen keilschriftlicher Umschreibungen ägyptischer Wörter und Personennamen*, Wien 1980.

Elementi per la toponomastica etiopica, Roma 1937.

FALES, F.M., *West Semitic Names from the Governor's Palace*, in *Annali di Ca'Foscari* 13 (1974), p. 179-188.

FALES, F.M., *On Aramaic Onomastics in the Neo-Assyrian Period*, in *Oriens Antiquus* 16 (1977), p. 41-68.

FALES, F.M., *L'onomastica aramaica in età neo-assira*, in *Atti del I Convegno Italiano sul Vicino Oriente Antico* (Orientis Antiqui Collectio 13), Roma 1978, p. 199-229.

FALES, F.M., *A List of Assyrian and West Semitic Women's Names*, in *Iraq* 41 (1979), p. 55-73.

FISCHER, W., *Der Beitrag der Araber zur Ortsnamengebung im Vorderen Orient*, in *Beiträge zur Namenforschung*, n.s., 18 (1980), p. 27-31.

FOWLER, J.D., *Theophoric Personal Names in Ancient Hebrew* (Journal for the Study of the Old Testament, Suppl. Ser. 49), Sheffield 1988.

FRANCHINI, V., *Contributo alla toponomastica dell'Eritrea tigrina*, in *Quaderni di Studi Etiopici* 3-4 (1982-83), p. 163-175.

FREYDANK, H. & C. SAPORETTI, *Nuove attestazioni dell'onomastica medio-assira*, Roma 1979.

GELB, I.J., P.M. PURVES & A.A. MCRAE, *Nuzi Personal Names*, Chicago 1943.

GELB, I.J., *Computer-Aided Analysis of Amorite* (Assyriological Studies 21), Chicago 1980.

GEMSER, B., *De beteekenis der persoonsnamen voor onze kennis van het leven en denken der oude Babyloniërs en Assyriërs*, Wageningen 1924.

GOLDMANN, W., *Die palmyrenischen Personennamen*, Leipzig 1935.

GRATZL, E., *Die altarabischen Frauennamen*, Leipzig 1906.

GRAY, G.B., *Studies in Hebrew Proper Names*, London 1896.

GREGORIO, G. DE & CHR. SEYBOLD, *Sugli elementi arabi nel dialetto e nella toponomastica dell'isola di Pantelleria*, in *Studi glottologici italiani* 2 (1901), p. 225-237.

GRÖNDAHL, F., *Die Personennamen der Texte aus Ugarit* (Studia Pohl 1), Rom 1967.

GUSTAVS, A., *Die Personennamen in den Tontafeln von Tell Taʿannek*, in *Zeitschrift des Deutschen Palästina-Vereins* 51 (1928), p. 169-218.

HALFF, G., *L'onomastique punique de Carthage*, in *Karthago* 12 (1965), p. 61-146.

HAZIM, R., *Die safaitischen theophoren Namen im Rahmen der gemeinsemitischen Namengebung*, Marburg / Lahn 1986.

HAZIM, R., *Ein Typus altsüdarabischer theophorer Namen*, in N. Nebes (ed.), *Arabia Felix*, Wiesbaden 1994, p. 95-101.

HESS, J.J., *Beduinennamen aus Zentralarabien*, Heidelberg 1912.

HESS, R.S., *Amarna Personal Names*, Winona Lake 1993.

HESS, R.S., *Studies in the Personal Names of Genesis* (Alter Orient und Altes Testament 234), Kevelaer-Neukirchen-Vluyn 1993.

HÖLSCHER, M., *Die Personennamen der Kassitenzeitlichen Texte aus Nippur*, Münster 1996.

HOROVITZ, J., *Jewish Proper Names and Derivations in the Koran*, in *Hebrew Union College Annual* 2 (1925), p. 145-227 (reprint: 1964).

HUBER, E., *Die Personennamen in den Keilschrifturkunden aus der Zeit der Könige von Ur und Nisin*, Leipzig 1907.

HUFFMON, H.B., *Amorite Personal Names in the Mari Texts. A Structural and Lexical Study*, Baltimore 1965.

JONGELING, K., *Names in Neo-Punic Inscriptions*, Groningen 1983.

JONGELING, K., *North African Names from Latin Sources*, Leiden 1994.

KLINGBELL, G.A., *The Onomasticon of the Aramaic Inscriptions of Syro-Palestine during the Persian Period*, in *Journal of Northwest Semitic Languages* 18 (1992), p. 67-94.

KORNFELD, W., *Onomastica Aramaica aus Ägypten*, Wien 1978.

KOSOWSKY, B., *Concordance of Names in the Babylonian Talmud*, 5 vols., Jerusalem 1976-82.

KREBERNIK, M., *Die Personennamen der Ebla-Texte. Eine Zwischenbilanz* (Berliner Beiträge zum Vorderen Orient 7), Berlin 1988.

KUPPER, J.-R., *Noms géographiques*, in *Archives royales de Mari* XVI/1, Paris 1979, p. 1-42.

LANFRANCO, R., *Nomi personali fra genti a lingua tigrina*, in *Rassegna di Studi Etiopici* 21 (1965), p. 111-161.

LANKESTER HARDING, G., *An Index and Concordance of Pre-Islamic Arabian Names and Inscriptions*, Toronto 1971.

La toponymie antique, Leiden 1977.

LAYTON, S.C., *Archaic Features of Canaanite Personal Names in the Hebrew Bible* (Harvard Semitic Monographs 47), Atlanta 1990.

LEDRAIN, E., *Dictionnaire des noms propres palmyréniens*, Paris 1886.

LIPIŃSKI, E., *Studies in Aramaic Inscriptions and Onomastics* (Orientalia Lovaniensia Analecta 1 & 57), 2 vols., Leuven 1975-94.

MARAQTEN, M., *Die semitischen Personennamen in den alt- und reichsaramäischen Inschriften aus Vorderasien* (Texte und Studien zur Orientalistik 5), Hildesheim 1988.

MEOUAK, M., *Rapport bibliographique sur l'onomastique arabo-sémitique*, in *Onoma* 32 (1994-95), p. 52-61.

MERLINI, C.G., *Analisi lessico-semantica dell'onomastica femminile ebraico-biblica*, in *Rivista Biblica* 43 (1995), p. 449-466.

NAIMUR-RAHMAN, M., *The Kunya-Names in Arabic*, in *Allahabad University Studies* 5 (1929), p. 341-442; 6 (1930), p. 751-883.

NEGEV, A., *Personal Names in the Nabatean Realm* (Qedem 32), Jerusalem 1991.

NOTH, M., *Die israelitischen Personennamen im Rahmen der gemeinsemitischen Namengebung*, Stuttgart 1928 (reprint: 1966).

OWEN, D.I., *Syrians in Sumerian Sources from the Ur III Period*, in M.W. Chavalas & J.L. Hayes, *New Horizons in the Study of Ancient Syria* (Bibliotheca Mesopotamica 25), Malibu 1992, p. 107-176.

PREISIGKE, F., *Namenbuch*, Heidelberg 1922.

RANKE, H., *Early Babylonian Personal Names*, Philadelphia 1905.

REEG, G., *Die Ortsnamen Israels nach der rabbinischen Literatur*, Wiesbaden 1989.

Répertoire géographique des textes cunéiformes, 12 vols., Wiesbaden 1974 ff.

RINGEL, H., *Die Frauennamen in der arabisch-islamischen Liebesdichtung*, Leipzig 1938.

RÖLLIG, W., *Griechische Eigennamen in Texten der babylonischen Spätzeit*, in *Orientalia*, n.s., 29 (1960), p. 376-391.

RYCKMANS, G., *Les noms propres sud-sémitiques*, 3 vols., Louvain 1934-35.

SAPORETTI, C., *Onomastica medio-assira* (Studia Pohl 6), 2 vols., Roma 1970.

SARKISIAN, G., *Greek Personal Names in Uruk and the Graeco-Babyloniaca Problem,* in *Drevniy Vostok* 2 (1976), p. 181-217 & 304-309.

SCHALIT, A., *Namenwörterbuch zu Flavius Josephus*, Leiden 1968.

SCHIMMEL, A.-M., *Islamic Names*, Edinburgh 1989.

SCHNEIDER, Th., *Asiatische Personennamen in ägyptischen Quellen des Neuen Reiches* (Orbis Biblicus et Orientalis 114), Fribourg-Göttingen 1992.

SILVERMAN, M.H., *Religious Values in the Jewish Proper Names at Elephantine* (Alter Orient und Altes Testament 217), Kevelaer-Neukirchen-Vluyn 1985.

SINGER, H.-R., *Ortsnamenkunde und Dialektologie im Muslimischen Spanien*, in *Journal of Arabic Linguistics* 5 (1980), p. 137-157.

SINGER, H.-R., *Conquista und Reconquista im Spiegel spanisch-arabischer Ortsnamen*, in *Beiträge zur Namenforschung*, n.s., 18 (1980), p. 119-130.

SOCIN, A., *Die arabischen Eigennamen in Algier,* in *Zeitschrift der Deutschen Morgenländischen Gesellschaft* 53 (1899), p. 471-500.

SOLIN, H., *Juden und Syrer im westlichen Teil der römischen Welt. Eine ethnisch-demographische Studie mit besonderer Berücksichtigung der sprachlichen Zustände*, in W. Haase (ed.), *Aufstieg und Niedergang der römischen Welt* II/29, 2, Berlin - New York 1983, p. 587-789, 1222-1249.

SPITALER, A., *Beiträge zur Kunya-Namengebung*, in E. Gräf (ed.), *Festschrift Werner Caskel*, Leiden 1968, p. 336-350.

STAMM, J.J., *Die akkadische Namengebung*, Leipzig 1939 (reprint: 1968).

STAMM, J.J., *Beiträge zur hebräischen und altorientalischen Namenkunde* (Orbis Biblicus et Orientalis 30), Fribourg-Göttingen 1980.

STARK, J.K., *Personal Names in Palmyrene Inscriptions*, Oxford 1971.

STEPHENS, F.J., *Personal Names of Cappadocia*, New Haven 1928 (reprint: 1982).

STOWASSER-FREYER, B., *Formen der geselligen Umgangs und Eigentümlichkeiten des Sprachgebrauchs in der frühislamischen städtischen Gesellschaft Arabiens* (*nach Ibn Saʿd und Buḫārī*), in *Der Islam* 38 (1962), p. 51-105; 42 (1965), p. 25-57, 179-234.

SUBLET, J., *Le voile du nom. Essai sur le nom propre arabe*, Paris 1991.

TAIRAN, S.A., *Die Personennamen in den altsabäischen Inschriften* (Texte und Studien zur Orientalistik 8), Hildesheim 1992.

TALLQVIST, K.L., *Neubabylonisches Namenbuch*, Helsingfors 1905.

TALLQVIST, K.L., *Assyrian Personal Names*, Helsingfors 1914 (reprint: 1966).

THILO, U., *Die Ortsnamen in der altarabischen Poesie* (Schriften der Max Freiherr von Oppenheim-Stiftung 3), Wiesbaden 1958.

VATTIONI, Fr., *Antroponimi fenicio-punici nell'epigrafia greca e latina del Nordafrica*, in *Archeologia e Storia Antica* 1 (1979), p. 153-191.

VATTIONI, Fr., *Per una ricerca dell'antroponimia fenicia e punica*, in *Studi Magrebini* 11 (1979), p. 43-123; 12 (1980), p. 1-82; 14 (1982), p. 1-65.

WILD, S., *Libanesische Ortsnamen*, Beirut 1973.

WILD, S., *Arabische Eigennamen*, in W. Fischer (ed.), *Grundriss der arabischen Philologie. Band I: Sprachwissenschaft*, Wiesbaden 1982, p. 154-164.

WUTHNOW, H., *Die semitischen Menschennamen in griechischer Inschriften und Papyri des Vorderen Orients*, Leipzig 1930.

ZADOK, R., *On West Semites in Babylonia during the Chaldean and Achaemenian Periods*, 2nd ed., Jerusalem 1978.

ZADOK, R., *The Jews in Babylonia during the Chaldean and Achaemenian Periods according to the Babylonian Sources*, Haifa 1979.

ZADOK, R., *Arabians in Mesopotamia during the Late-Assyrian, Chaldean, Achaemenian and Hellenistic Periods, chiefly according to the Cuneiform Sources*, in *Zeitschrift der Deutschen Morgenländischen Gesellschaft* 131 (1981), p. 42-84.

ZADOK, R., *The Pre-Hellenistic Israelite Anthroponomy and Prosopography*, Leuven 1988.

ZADOK, R., *On the Onomasticon of the Old Aramaic Sources*, in *Bibliotheca Orientalis* 48 (1991), col. 25-40.

ZADOK, R., *A Prosopography and Ethno-Linguistic Characterization of Southern Canaan in the Second Millennium BCE*, in *Michmanim* 9 (1996), p. 97-145.

GENERAL INDEX

References are to paragraphs.

', first radical, *19*.24; *44*.4; *45*.3,15
   its dissimilatory function, *43*.4
' < ', *10*.10; *19*.9-10,15-20; *45*.8
' < h, *19*.9-10,13,17; *36*.10,33; *41*.11,30; *42*.15; *61*.2
' < ḥ, *19*.9-10
' < ḫ, *19*.9
' < m, *11*.8
' < n, *17*.2
' < q, *10*.10; *18*.8
' < ṭ, *13*.12
' < w, *27*.11
' < y, *19*.17
' < ', *27*.8
' < ġ, *19*.15,17,19-20
' < q, *16*.7; *18*.8
-a < -at, *27*.28; *30*.4
a < ā, *21*.30; *27*.11,24; *29*.42; *35*.26; *40*.15
a < ə, *45*.17
a < ə+a, *22*.15
a < i, *35*.3; *61*.2
a < o, *27*.10
a < u, *27*.10
a < ha, *27*.25
ä < a, *21*.30
ä < ə+a, *22*.15
ā < a, *27*.28; *40*.22
ā < a', *21*.13; *27*.24
ā < a', *21*.13
ā < aw, *11*.11; *22*.1,3-4; *27*.23-24; *43*.8,14,20
ā < ay, *22*.1,3-5,7-9; *27*.24; *29*.42,54; *31*.3-5; *43*.14-15
ā < āy, *22*.15
ā < ī, *27*.11
ā < iy(a), *27*.24; *43*.17
ā < uā, *43*.12
ā̄ < ay, *22*.11
ā' < āw, *11*.14

ā' < āy, *11*.14
Abaya, Lake, *2*.11
Abbasid period, *7*.43; *32*.25
'Abbasīya, town, *67*.13
Abdada, Bedja tribe, *2*.9
absolute state of the noun, *30*.4; *33*.5,15-24; *57*.4
abstract nouns, *29*.25,37,46-48,50,52; *30*.1-2; *31*.16; *35*.6; *36*.30
Abū Bakr ibn Durayd, *65*.4
Abū Manṣūr al-Ǧawālīqī, *65*.1
accent, *24*.10; *25*.1-8; *26*.5; *38*.2
Accius, *21*.13
accusative case, *32*.1-5,13,15-16,20-24,27-28; *33*.12; *34*.3; *36*.3,16-17, 26,48-50; *51*.8,16,25; *52*.1-11; *54*.3
   adverbial, *52*.5-6; *54*.3
   double accusative, *52*.4
   explicatory, *52*.9
   of place, *52*.7
   of time, *52*.6
   predicative, *52*.8
   see also: oblique case, "patient" case
Achaemenian period, *7*.12-13; *42*.20; *52*.11; *65*.3-4
action, noun of, *29*.30
actor affixes, *37*.5,9; *40*.1-36; *50*.12
   imperative, *40*.13-15
   prefix-conjugation, *38*.17; *40*.16-36; *41*.2-3
   suffix-conjugation, *40*.2-12
Addis Ababa, *8*.15,17
adjectival syntagm, *51*.22,26
adjective, *29*.1,6,8,11,16,32,35-36,41, 44,48,52; *30*.1; *31*.12,14-16; *32*.17; *34*.1-6; *35*.23; *51*.11,26
adstratum, *3*.5; *21*.27; *50*.14; *56*.7
adverbs, *29*.54; *32*.17-19; *33*.16; *47*.1-18; *48*.3; *52*.5-6; *58*.12-13

Aeolian dialect (Greek), *65*.5

'*af'al*, *29*.16; *31*.26; *32*.8; *34*.5; see also: elative

'*af'āl*, *29*.16; *31*.26,28-29,36

'*af'ala*, *41*.11

Afar, *2*.13; *8*.19; *30*.10; *31*.24

affixes, *28*.16-19
   actor affixes, *37*.5,9; *40*.1-36; *50*.12
   demonstrative -*t* affix, *36*.35,58
   nominal patterns, *29*.15-53
   pronominal affixes, *36*.16-27

affricates, *12*.3; *14*.7; *18*.6; *23*.1

Afghanistan, *7*.14

'*af'ila*(*t*), *29*.16; *31*.36

'*af'ilā*(')*u*, *29*.16; *31*.36

Africa, *1*.1-2; *2*.11; *3*.2-3; *21*.1; *28*.8; *30*.9
   Central Africa, *1*.2; *2*.16; *7*.46
   Horn of Africa, *1*.2; *2*.8; *3*.2-4
   North Africa, *1*.2; *2*.14-15; *3*.3-4; *7*.6; *12*.2; *14*.6; *17*.1; *22*.7; *24*.10; *51*.19; *62*.2,8; *67*.9,17
   West Africa, *2*.16; *36*.1
   East Africa, *8*.5

Afro-Asiatic, preface; *1*.1-3; *2*.1,8,12, 14,16-17; *3*.1-5; *10*.11-12; *11*.7; *12*.4; *14*.10; *15*.18; *17*.1,4; *19*.15, 23-24; *27*.12; *28*.7,9,19; *29*.20; *30*.1,10; *31*.24; *32*.3,6-7,17; *33*.5; *35*.3,9,15; *36*.1,6,8,30,57; *37*.1,6; *38*.1,3,5,15,17; *39*.7; *40*.31; *41*.2,7, 13,15,56; *43*.23; *44*.5; *47*.8; *53*.4; *57*.3; *63*.1,5,13; *67*.4

'*af'ul*, *29*.16; *31*.26,36

'*af'ūl*, *29*.16; *31*.26,29

Agades (Niger), *2*.14

Agaw, *2*.10; *8*.9,12-13; *15*.18; *28*.13; *30*.11; *32*.1; *36*.5,14,16; *39*.8; *41*.7; *48*.19; *50*.15; *54*.2; *63*.5; *67*.9

agent case (*casus agens*), *32*.1-3,7; *40*.16; see also: ergative, instrumental, locative, nominative case

agentless passive, *2*.14; *41*.20; *49*.23

agent nouns, *11*.7; *29*.7,11,35,39,52

Ahaggar dialect (Tuareg), *14*.10

Ahiqar, Story of, *7*.13

aḫlāmu, *31*.26

Air, oasis, dialect (Tuareg), *2*.14; *14*.10

Akkad, Agade, *6*.1
   see: Old Akkadian

Akkadian(s), preface; *3*.1,3; *4*.1; *6*.1,4; *10*.6; *21*.11; *37*.8
   see: Assyrian, Assyro-Babylonian, Babylonian, East Semitic, Old Akkadian

Aksum, *2*.9; *8*.11-12; *11*.2; *13*.10; *16*.7

Alaba (Cushitic), *2*.11

Alalakh, *13*.4; *35*.12; *38*.13-14; *40*.18

Albanian, *65*.5

Aleppo, *7*.46; *11*.6; *27*.8

Aleppo Codex, *21*.19

Algeria, *2*.14; *3*.3; *10*.10; *12*.2-3; *13*.9; *18*.6,8-9; *21*.27; *33*.18; *41*.26; *65*.2

Algiers, *21*.27

Algonquian languages, *30*.9

Alhambra, *11*.9

al-Ḥidjr, see: Ḥegrā'

allative/ventive, *39*.3,6-7; *40*.14; *46*.2

allophones, *21*.18; *44*.12
   b/*m*, *11*.6
   b/*p*, *11*.4
   -*ē*/-*ī*, *31*.11-12
   ī/*ū*, *44*.13

alphabet, alphabetic script, *2*.6; *5*.4; *9*.2,4-11; *13*.6-7; *19*.3,12-13; *33*.10, 20; *66*.1

"alphabetic" hieroglyphs, *2*.4

alternation: '/*w*, *11*.11,14; *19*.17,24; *36*.59; *47*.8; *54*.5
   '/*g*, *19*.23
   a/*i*, *21*.10; *22*.14; *43*.12
   a/*u*, *21*.8,10; *45*.14
   d/*l*, *17*.7; *36*.61
   d/*r*, *12*.4; *17*.7
   ḍ/*ẓ*, *7*.45
   e/*i*, *21*.8
   ə/zero, *21*.31
   i/*u*, *21*.8
   k/*q*, *18*.2
   l/*n*, *17*.3-4; *36*.33
   l/*n*/*r*, *17*.1,3-5; *48*.6

l/r, 2.4,6; *17*.1,5; *30*.10; *35*.20; 47.8;*63*.11

m/b, 11.6; *48*.5

m/n, 11.7; *48*.5; *61*.2

n/r, 17.6

ō/ū, 21.27

ś/š, 16.9

t/k, 12.4; *36*.6; *40*.5,11

w/m, 32.17

y/w, 11.13; *43*.17

-v̄C/-vC$_2$C$_2$, 44.14

al-ʿUlā, 7.37; *8*.4

Amarar, a Bedja tribe, 2.9

Amarna, correspondence, 2.5; *6*.3; 7.4; *11*.13; *15*.2; *16*.2; *19*.12; *21*.5,12; *29*.54; *32*.23; *33*.20; *36*.58; *38*.10,13-14; *39*.2,6,14; *40*.3,21,32; *41*.33,43; *48*.18; *49*.8; *52*.8; *53*.5; *54*.8

American Indians, 30.9

Amharic, 2.10; *8*.8-9,11,13-15,18; *9*.7

adjectival syntagm, 51.22

adjectives, 34.3

adverbs, 47.3,8,17; *51*.26

articles, 32.28; *33*.8,14

case inflection, 32.5,28

conjugation, 38.25,28; *39*.12; *40*.2-6,10-15,17,29-30,32; *41*.2-5,9, 11,14,17-18,20,25,27,32,34,36-39, 42,53-55; *42*.4,12-13,25; *43*.7, 21; *44*.2; *45*.9,17

conjunctions, 49.1,14,17

construct state, 33.4

copulae, 49.20-21

"existential" verbs, 49.22,24

expression of possession, 49.25

genitival relation, 51.25

gerund, 42.12; *53*.5

infinitive, 53.6

noun gender, 30.6,8,11

noun number, 31.15,17,22,26,34

noun patterns, 29.14,21-22,25-27,30, 37,44,47,49-50,52,55

numerals, 35.2-4,8,13-14,16,18,20, 22

phonology, 11.5,9,15; *13*.12; *14*.3,7, 9; *15*.6; *17*.6-9; *18*.5-6; *19*.1,20; *22*.15; *23*.2,8; *27*.3,19

"plural of majesty", 31.34; *50*.24

prepositions, 48.6,10-11,16-19,22, 25

pronouns, 36.2,9,12,17,19-20,23,28, 31-33,41,45,60-61

questions, 54.4-5

subordinate clause, 56.1

syllabary, 9.7

syllable, 24.8-9

word accent, 25.1

word order, 50.15; *51*.2; *57*.9

words cited, 8.18; *43*.5; *63*.4; *67*.4

see also: Ethiopic, South Ethiopic

Ammān, 7.7

Ammonite, 4.5; *7*.2,7; *13*.7; *27*.3; *31*.10,14; *33*.8; *65*.5

Amorite, 4.1-2,5; *5*.3; *7*.1; *50*.1

case inflection, 32.4,8,11-12

conjugation, 38.4-6,10,13; *39*.2,10; *40*.3,14-16,18,33; *41*.2,9,11,16, 22,25,29,43,48; *42*.6,13-15; *43*.13; *44*.11,13; *45*.7

genitival relation, 51.24

lexicography, 63.4

noun gender, 30.11

noun patterns, 29.9,13,32,36,41

numerals, 35.6,20,24

phonology, 11.4,6,13; *13*.3-4; *19*.7, 9; *21*.8; *22*.14; *23*.7; *25*.5; *27*.11

prepositions, 48.16

pronouns, 36.5,23,47-49,57-60

"states" of nouns, 33.5-6,13,16

word order, 50.13

words or names cited, 63.5,13; *67*.4,7; see also p. 684-685.

Amorites, 3.3

Amratian culture, 3.4

Amurru, 21.5; *40*.18

ʿAnan ben David, 7.29

anaptyctic vowel, 17.9; *24*.5,8,10; *26*.2; *27*.16,19; *28*.8; *29*.5-6; *35*.7; *38*.3; *41*.11; *49*.20

Anatolia, 7.6; *12*.4; *38*.24; *40*.25

ʿAnaze bedouin dialect, 7.46

Andalus, al-, Andalusian Arabic, 7.46; *8*.2; *11*.6,9,13; *13*.9; *16*.8; *18*.6; *19*.24; *27*.3; *29*.9; *36*.14; *38*.5; *40*.25; *41*.25,27; *44*.5; *64*.3

animal names, *17*.1; *27*.16; *29*.16-18,28; *30*.5,8,10; *31*.38; *63*.13; *67*.3
antecedent of relative clauses, *57*.8
anthropological evidence, *3*.4
Anyuk, Nilotic language, *2*.2
apocopate(d), *26*.4; *38*.14; *39*.14-18; *58*.4
applicative, *2*.2
apposition, *51*.7-8,19,21
aqqätattälä, aqqattälä (Amharic), *41*.32
'Aqra dialect, *38*.24
Arab conquests, *2*.9; *7*.44; *67*.13
Arab philologists, *7*.42-43; *11*.15; *21*.26-27; *22*.4,15; *25*.1,15; *38*.14; *39*.14,17; *40*.5,24; *41*.6; *57*.6; see also: Sibawayh
Arab science, *65*.8-9
Arabia, *2*.11; *3*.2,4; *4*.4; *7*.39,46; *30*.10; *32*.25; *38*.22
   Central Arabia, *7*.43; *18*.6; *27*.20; *32*.25; *40*.25; *41*.25; see also: 'Omān, Persian Gulf
   North Arabia, *7*.1,16,35,39-40,41, 46; *11*.6; *22*.7; *32*.25; *40*.25; *41*.25; see also: Transjordan
   South Arabia, *8*.1-2,7; *41*.43; see also: Yemen
   West Arabia, *40*.10; see also: Ḥedjaz
Arabic, preface; *1*.1; *2*.11; *3*.5; *4*.1,3,5; *7*.1,35-46; *8*.13; *43*.23
   accusative, *52*.3-4,6-11
   adjectives, *34*.2,5
   adverbs, *47*.2-3,7-8,10,12,14-18
   Algerian dialects, *12*.2-3; *13*.9; *18*.6,8-9; *21*.27; *33*.18; *41*.26
   Andalusian, *7*.46; *8*.2; *11*.6,9,13; *13*.9; *16*.8; *18*.6; *19*.24; *27*.3; *29*.9; *36*.14; *38*.5; *40*.25; *41*.25,27; *44*.5; *64*.3
   and Libyco-Berber, *2*.14-15; *65*.2
   apposition, *51*.7-8
   article, *33*.10,18
   attribute, *51*.1,3-4,6
   Baghdadi dialect, *31*.4,6,12; *40*.25; *65*.10

Bedouin dialects, *7*.35,42,46; *18*.6; *32*.25; *38*.22; *40*.25; *41*.11,25, 44; *43*.17; *66*.1
Cairene dialect, *18*.6; *27*.10; *29*.8; *33*.24; *36*.39; *38*.22; *41*.24-25, 27; *43*.17; *47*.15; *50*.6
case inflection, *32*.4-5,8,11,15,18, 20,25
classical, preface; *7*.43,46; *9*.9-10; *10*.1; *13*.9; *18*.6; *19*.17,24; *21*.1-2,24,26-27; *22*.4,15,17; *24*.4,10; *26*.4; *27*.3,5,9; *28*.10; *31*.10-11,25,28; *32*.4-5,8,11,25; *33*.2-3,5,15-16,21; *34*.2,5; *35*.2,4,6, 16,18-20; *36*.17,27,33,39,42, 44, 46,48,53-54,59-60; *38*.3,12,14, 17,20,22; *39*.1-2,4,8,14,16; *40*.2-3,7-8,10,13,15,17,23-24,32,34, 36; *41*.2-4,11,19,25,27,44,51, 54-55; *42*.3,10,17; *44*.5-10,15; *45*.14; *47*.10,14-16,18; *49*.2,4, 24; *50*.2,6,8,16,21; *51*.1,4,16,18; *52*.6,9-10; *54*.6,8; *55*.6; *56*.8; *57*.4,6; *58*.9; *60*.2; *61*.2,10; *62*.3; *65*.10
colloquial and modern, *7*.32,46; *12*.2; *13*.9; *14*.5-6; *17*.1,4,8-9; *18*.2,6-7,9; *21*.27,30; *22*.7,15, 17; *23*.11; *24*.9-10; *25*.1-3,7; *26*.2; *27*.6,8,17,19,22,24; *29*.8, 40-41,45,47; *31*.4,11,19,28; *32*.5; *33*.10, 18; *34*.2; *35*.2-4,6,16-17, 19-20,24; *36*.3,8,27-28,30-31,39, 53,58-60; *38*.1-2,12,20,22-24; *39*.5,18; *40*.2,5-6,10-11,13, 15,17, 25,32,34,36; *41*.2-4,9,11,19, 24-27,30-31,39,44,54-55; *42*.1,4,10, 24; *43*.17; *45*.15; *47*.15; *50*.6, 9,13,16,20-21; *51*.1,18-20; *54*.4-6; *56*.8; *57*.4; *61*.6; *64*.5; *65*.2,9
concord of subject and predicate, *50*.21-23
conditional clause, *49*.4; *61*.1-6,10
conjugation, *35*.34; *37*.1,4,6; *38*.1-3,11-12,14-18,20,22-24; *39*.1-2, 4-5,8-9,14,16-18; *40*.2-3,5-8,10-13,15-17,23-25,31-32,34,36; *41*.2-9,11,15-16,19-20,22,24-

27,29-32,38-44,46-47,50-51, 54-56; *42*.1-4,10,13-14,16-17, 24; *43*.3, 6-7,9, 15,17; *44*.4-10,13-15; *45*.10,14-15; *46*.2-3,5

conjunctions, *38*.14; *49*.2,4,13-17; *58*.2-9,12,15; *59*.2-4; *60*.2; *61*.1-6,10

copulae, *36*.59; *49*.23-24

Damascene dialect, *21*.27; *29*.8; *31*.4,6; *33*.10; *35*.6,18,20; *36*.39; *38*.1,3,23; *41*.2-4,19,54-55; *51*.19

Datīna dialect, *16*.7-8; *17*.4

Dēr ez-Zōr dialect, *41*.11

Dafīr dialect, *62*.3

Dofār dialect, *18*.8; *25*.7; *40*.25

Eastern Arabic, *7*.46; *11*.2; *18*.8-9; *22*.7; *27*.10; *33*.21; *38*.3,22; *45*.14; *62*.2

Egyptian dialects, *25*.4; *26*.2; *27*.10 ,17; *33*.18; *35*.24; *36*.44; *41*.24; *47*.15; *51*.19; *54*.4

expression of possession, *49*.25

final/consecutive clause, *59*.2-4

genitival relation, *51*.10-16,18-20, 22-24,26; *64*.5

Ḥassānīya dialect, *13*.9; *36*.39; *41*.44

Ḥidjazi dialects, *7*.46; *11*.13-14; *21*.9; *27*.20; *36*.33; *38*.14; *39*.17; *41*.24; *45*.14

hypotaxis, *56*.5-8

influence on Hausa, *2*.16

influence on Samaritan Hebrew, *7*.5

language of Palmyra, *7*.17; *18*.6; *27*.28; *65*.5

lexicography, *35*.14; *49*.21; *62*.2-4; *63*.2-4,6-7,9-10,12-14; *64*.1-5; *65*.1-2, 4-10; *66*.4-6

Maghrebine dialects, *7*.46; *11*.6; *12*.2-3; *17*.4; *18*.6-8; *19*.17; *22*.7, 15; *24*.9; *25*.2-3; *27*.6,8,19; *33*.18,24; *35*.4; *36*.39,53; *38*.2-3,5,24; *40*.25; *41*.2-4,19,24,26, 30,42,44, 54-55; *47*.15; *65*.2; *66*.4

Middle Arabic, *7*.44-45; *21*.25; *24*.10; *32*.25; *41*.27

Nabataean Arabic, *7*.16,36,38,40;

9.12; *21*.24; *22*.4; *32*.5; *33*.10; *38*.11; *49*.2; *51*.18; *61*.2,10; *65*.5

Neo-Arabic, *4*.5; *7*.27,44-46; *19*.17; *21*.25; *23*.6; *29*.36; *30*.6; *31*.4; *32*.25; *33*.22,24; *35*.16; *38*.22; *40*.16; *41*.11,24; *45*.11; *46*.5; *48*.12; *50*.16,21,23; *51*.1; *52*.11; *58*.5

nominal clause, *50*.6-10

North Arabian ("Mesopotamian") dialects in Iraq and Anatolia, *7*.46; *17*.1; *18*.6,8; *29*.8; *33*.18; *38*.2-3; *41*.11; *51*.20; *65*.4

noun gender, *30*.4-5,10-11

noun number, *31*.1-2,4-6,9-13,18-19,24-26,28-30,35-36,38,41-42

noun patterns, *29*.1-3,5-14,16-18, 21-25,30,36-38,40-42,44-48,51, 54

numerals, *35*.2-6,15-21,24,26,29-34

'Omānī dialects, *7*.46; *15*.7; *27*.13; *41*.44

one-term sentence, *50*.2-4

parataxis, *55*.1-2,4-7

periphrastic passive, *41*.44

phonology, *10*.1,3,7,9; *11*.1-3,6,9-11,13-15; *12*.1-3; *13*.1,9,12; *14*.1-6,10; *15*.3,7; *16*.5-9; *17*.1-2,4-5,8-9; *18*.2,6-9; *19*.14-15,17, 21,24; *20*; *21*.1-2,15,23-27,30; *22*.2-4,7,13,15-17; *23*.1-2,4,8-9, 11; *27*.3-11,13,15-17,20,22,24, 28

Post-Classical, *29*.36; *31*.40

Pre-Classical, *7*.42,44; *9*.6; *13*.9; *21*.25; *22*.4,15; *27*.14,24,28; *32*.25; *33*.21; *39*.5-6; *41*.25, 27,32,43; *44*.13; *51*.16; *52*.11; *54*.8; *57*.6; *58*.6; *61*.2

prepositions, *48*.5,12,14-19,21-22

presentatives, *49*.6,8-10

pronouns, *28*.13; *36*.2-3,7-8,17,23-24,27-28,30-31,33,36,38-39,42, 44,46,48,53-54,57-62

proper names, *67*.4,7,9,15,17

Proto-Arabic, *7*.35; *61*.2

questions, *49*.4; *54*.3-5

relative clause, *57*.2-4,6-8

root morpheme, *28*.1,3-4,6,8-10,13
sentence stress, *26*.2,4
"states" of nouns, *33*.2-3,5-6,8,10,
　15-16,18,21,24
substantival clause, *60*.2
syllable, *24*.4-6,8-10
Syro-Palestinian dialects, *7*.46;
　13.9; *14*.6; *17*.8; *22*.4,7,15,17;
　25.1; *26*.2; *27*.20; *33*.18; *35*.24;
　36.5; *38*.22; *41*.11,24,31; *47*.15;
　50.21; *51*.20; *54*.4; *58*.6; *65*.4
Tamīm dialect, *22*.7; *27*.20
temporal/causal clause, *58*.2-9,12, 15
Tunisian dialects, *12*.3; *22*.4; *41*.31;
　50.20,23; *67*.9
verbal clause and phrase, *50*.12-
　13,16-20; *52*.1
volitive clause, *54*.6-8
West Arabian, *61*.2
word accent, *25*.1-4,8
word order, *50*.7-9,13,16-20; *56*.8
Yemenite, *7*.46; *16*.8; *17*.4; *18*.6;
　26.2; *31*.28-29; *32*.25; *33*.10,12,
　21; *36*.5,19,39,53-54,58; *38*.22;
　40.5-6,10-11; *41*.11; *47*.15-16
Arabic script, *7*.42-43; *8*.16; *9*.5,9-10;
　10.1; *13*.9; *14*.3; *19*.3; *21*.15,26
used for Hausa, *2*.16
used for Libyco-Berber, *2*.14
garšūnī, *9*.13
Judaeo-Arabic, *9*.13
Aramaeans, *31*.26; *65*.3
Aramaic, preface; *1*.1; *4*.1,3,5; *6*.3;
　7.1,10-36
accusative, *52*.4,10-11
adjectives, *34*.2
adverbs, *32*.19; *47*.2,4,7-9,17
apposition, *51*.7
attribute, *51*.1
concord of subject and predicate,
　50.25
conditional clause, *61*.2-3,6,8-9,11
conjugation, *37*.6; *38*.2,5,10-11,15;
　39.9; *40*.2-3,10,12-17,22-23,25,
　30-32,34-35; *41*.9-11,16,20,23-
　25,29-30,32,35,38,40,42-43,46;
　42.2,4,9,13-15,18,20; *43*.5,9-10,
　15; *44*.4,6-10; *45*.9-10,12; *46*.4-5

conjunctions, *49*.2,16; *58*.2,14; *60*.3;
　61.2-3,8-9,11-12
copula, *49*.23
Early Aramaic, *4*.3; *7*.11; *9*.10; *13*.8;
　21.15; *22*.8-10; *27*.12,25; *33*.22;
　36.54; *41*.2-3,11,20,22,24,28,46,
　54,55; *42*.9,15; *43*.15; *46*.4;
　48.16; *50*.18; *53*.4; *55*.4; *57*.7;
　63.14
Eastern Aramaic, *7*.17-20,26-30;
　17.4; *42*.9,20
emphatic state, *28*.13; *32*.15; *33*.7,13
expression of possession, *49*.25
genitival relation, *51*.16,19-20,23
infinitive, *53*.2-5
influence on Arabic, *7*.42,44; *9*.5-6
influence on Hebrew, *7*.5; *28*.13
influence on Late Babylonian, *6*.6
influence on Neo-Assyrian, *6*.5
Jewish Aramaic, *7*.23,26,29,34;
　9.9; *11*.7-8; *16*.5; *17*.1-2; *35*.34;
　40.22; *45*.12; *63*.9,11; *65*.6
Late Aramaic, *7*.22-30; *9*.5; *21*.21-
　22; *40*.10,12,15; *41*.10; *42*.4,9,
　13, 20; *44*.5; *45*.10-12; *49*.23;
　61.2; *63*.10-11; *64*.4; *65*.5
lexicography, *14*.3; *35*.14; *63*.4-
　5,8-11,14; *64*.2,4; *65*.3-5,7; *66*.2
Mandaic, *7*.26,28,34; *18*.7; *21*.21;
　36.34,39; *42*.20; *45*.12; *61*.6
Middle Aramaic, *7*.14-21; *19*.14;
　27.27; *33*.7; *36*.38; *40*.23; *42*.4;
　63.10
Nabataean, *7*.16,38,40; *11*.4; *17*.4;
　21.24; *27*.24; *29*.16; *35*.16;
　42.14; *49*.2; *63*.14
negatives, *47*.8-9
no case inflection, *32*.24
nominal clauses, *50*.7,9
nota accusativi, *52*.10
noun gender, *30*.4,6,11
noun number, *31*.4,10-14,18-19,21,
　26-28
noun patterns, *29*.3,5,7-8,10-14,16-
　18,21,25-26,30,33,36-37,41,48-
　49,54
numerals, *35*.2-4,9,16-18,20,22,24-
　25,27,29-30,32,34

one-term sentence, *50*.4
Palmyrene, *7*.17,20; *9*.10; *13*.9;
    14.3; *27*.3; *29*.31; *47*.4; *65*.4
phonology, *11*.4,6-8,10,13; *12*.3;
    13.6-9; *14*.1-2; *15*.2; *16*.4-5;
    17.2, 5-6,8; *18*.4-5,7-8; *19*.9,13-
    14,21,23; *21*.21-25; *22*.8-10,15-
    16; *23*.3,5,7, 9; *27*.3,7,10-11,13-
    14,16-17,20,25-28
prepositions, *48*.2,13-13,15-17,19,
    21,23
prepositional phrase, *52*.4,11
presentatives, *49*.8-9
pronouns, *36*.2,5-6,8,12,17-18,23,
    28,31,33-34,36,38-39,42,52,57,
    60-62
proper names, *33*.9; *50*.25; *67*.7,15
relative clause, *57*.2,6
root morpheme, *44*.5
states of nouns, *33*.3,6-7,16,22
subordinate clause, *56*.8
substantival clause, *60*.3
syllable, *24*.7
temporal/causal clause, *58*.2,14
verbal clause, *50*.13-14,17,19
volitive clause, *54*.6
Western Aramaic, *7*.17,20,22-25;
    36.61; *42*.9; *49*.25
word accent, *25*.1,3
word order, *50*.13-14,17,19; *56*.8
see also: Mandaic, Neo-Aramaic,
    Samaritan Aramaic, Syriac
Aramaic script, *9*.5-6,10-11; *10*.3,9
    used for Ammonite, *7*.7
    used for Arabic, *7*.42; *9*.5-6
    used for Nabataean, *7*.42; *9*.10; *14*.3
Argobba, *8*.8,15
    conjunctions, *49*.1
    gerund, *42*.12; *53*.5
    nouns, *30*.10-11; *31*.17; *32*.28;
        33.14
    numerals, *35*.14,18
    phonology, *11*.9,15; *12*.2; *13*.12;
        14.7; *17*.7; *19*.20
    prepositions, *48*.18-19,22
    pronouns, *36*.9,12,14,33
    verbs, *38*.25; *40*.5,11-12,29; *41*.2,
        9, 14,32,53; *42*.4,12-13; *45*.9

Armenia(n), *7*.34; *14*.10; *65*.5
Arsacid period, *6*.6
article, definite, *2*.2; *32*.27; *33*.3,12;
    36.36
    a-/ä-, *33*.8
    'al-, *17*.4; *33*.1,10,21; *51*.16; *57*.4
    'an-/'am-, *33*.7,10
    ha-/han-, *17*.4; *33*.1,8-10
    *hal-, *33*.10
    ḥa-, *33*.8
    'ī-, *33*.7
    la-, *33*.11
    'ū-, *33*.7
article, definite, postpositive:
    -ā, *33*.7
    -(ə)š, *33*.13; *36*.33
    -i, -y, *32*.28; *33*.14
    -itu, *32*.28; *33*.14
    -u, *32*.28; *33*.13-14; *34*.3; *51*.25
    -wa, -we, *32*.28; *33*.14
    -y, *33*.14
article, indefinite, *2*.2
    and, andit, *33*.8,18; *35*.3
    at, attə, *33*.8
    'əḥād, *33*.18
    fad, fa, *38*.18
    fard, fadd, *38*.18
    ḥa-, *33*.18
    ḥadä, *33*.18
    ḥa-l-, *33*.18
    ḥantit, *33*.18
    ḥatte, *33*.18
    waḥd əl-, *33*.18
    wāḥid, waḥda, *33*.18
    woro(t), *33*.18
article *li-ta'rīfi l-ğins*, *57*.4
Arunta language, *21*.1
Asaṭir, *7*.24
aspect, in Chadic, *2*.16-17; *36*.1
    in Cushitic, *2*.8,11
    in Libyco-Berber, *2*.14
    in Semitic, *37*.3,8; *38*.3-14,17-18
assimilation, *23*.6; *27*.1-10
    between consonants, *24*.2; *27*.3-8,
        20
    between consonant and vowel,
        27.10; *45*.10
    between vowels, *27*.9

contiguous, *10*.12; *24*.2; *27*.3-7,20, 25,27; *29*.13; *33*.10; *35*.3,11; *38*.23; *39*.9; *41*.29-30,32-33; *43*.5; *45*.10; *46*.2
  in Berber dialects, *2*.15
  non-contiguous, *27*.8-9; *35*.8; *48*.5
  partial, *27*.6-9; *38*.23
  progressive, *27*.4,7,9-10; *41*.29-30, 32
  reciprocal, *2*.15; *10*.12; *15*.2; *27*.5; *46*.2
  regressive, *10*.12; *24*.2; *27*.3,6,8-10,20,25,27; *29*.13; *33*.10; *35*.3, 8,11; *38*.23; *39*.9; *41*.32-33; *43*.5; *45*.10; *46*.2
  total, *10*.12; *15*.2; *27*.3-5,9,25,27; *29*.13; *33*.10; *35*.3,8,11; *39*.9; *41*.29-30,32-33; *43*.5; *46*.2
Assyria, *6*.4; *7*.11; *65*.3
Assyrian, *6*.5; *15*.3; *21*.5; *27*.9; *36*.26, 33; *39*.3,16; *40*.12,20; *42*.3,7,16; *43*.5,9; *45*.3; *49*.23; *50*.7
  designation of Neo-Aramaic, *7*.34
  Middle Assyrian, *4*.6; *6*.5; *11*.6, 8,12; *15*.2; *17*.2; *19*.9; *23*.10; *29*.41; *35*.27,32; *36*.5,10; *43*.12; *51*.23; *52*.9; *54*.6
  Neo-Assyrian, *4*.6; *6*.5; *7*.35; *10*.8-9; *11*.4,6,8,12; *14*.2; *15*.2; *16*.3-4; *17*.2,6; *18*.4; *19*.9,11,17; *23*.7,10; *27*.5,7,28; *30*.4-5; *32*.21; *36*.5, 33,56; *40*.5,11; *41*.2,32; *47*.9; *48*.7; *50*.9; *52*.11; *53*.5; *54*.6; *57*.5; *58*.10,16; *63*.5; *65*.3; *67*.15
  Old Assyrian, *4*.6; *6*.5; *9*.2,11; *11*.6,12; *13*.3; *17*.4; *19*.9; *22*.14; *29*.41; *30*.1; *31*.11,25; *32*.17,19; *35*.12-13,26; *36*.3,10,17,30; *38*.4; *40*.20; *41*.15,35; *43*.12; *44*.5; *47*.2,7-8,14; *49*.15; *51*.7,14; *52*.7; *53*.1-2; *54*.9; *55*.3; *58*.14,16; *61*.5-6; *64*.5; *66*.5
  see: Assyro-Babylonian, East Semitic
Assyro-Babylonian (East Semitic), preface, *4*.5; *6*.1,3
  accusative, *52*.2-4,6-9,11
  adjectives, *34*.2,4-6
  adverbs, *47*.2-5,7-9,11-12,14,17

apposition, *51*.7-8
attribute, *51*.1,4,6
case inflection, *32*.5,17-19,21
concord of subject and predicate, *50*.22,25
conditional clause, *61*.1-9
conjunctions, *49*.1,15; *58*.2-4,9-11, 13-14,16; *60*.1,3; *61*.1-9
conjugation, *37*.4,6,8; *38*.2-6,10, 12,15-16; *39*.2-4,6-7,14,16; *40*.2-7, 10-17,20,31-32,34; *41*.2-3,6,8-10,12,15,17-20,22,25,29,32-33,35,40,42-43,49,52,54-55; *42*.2-3,7,13-16; *43*.3,5-7,9,11-12, 22; *44*.2,4-10,13-14; *45*.2-3,5-7, 11; *46*.2
copula, *49*.23
expression of possession, *49*.25
genitival relation, *51*.10-20,23-24
infinitive, *53*.1-2,4-5
lexicography, *35*.14; *63*.2-5,7-9,11; *64*.1,4-5; *65*.2-6,8; *66*.5
nominal clause, *50*.5-9
noun gender, *30*.1-7
noun number, *31*.7,10-12,14-16,20-21,25-26
noun patterns, *29*.2,5-8,11-14,16, 21,23,25-26,28-33,36-39,41,46-48,51,55
numerals, *35*.1-6,12-13,16-21,23-24,26-27,29-32
one-term sentence, *50*.2-4
parataxis, *55*.1-3,5-6
phonology, *10*.8-9,12; *11*.4,6-12; *13*.3-4; *14*.2; *15*.2-3,6,8; *16*.2-4,7; *17*.2,4-6; *18*.3-5; *19*.6,9-11,13,17,21,24; *21*.3-5,9-13; *22*.5,13-15; *23*.7-10; *27*.3-5,7,9-10,13-14,17,19, 23,28
"plural of majesty", *50*.24
prepositional phrase, *52*.11
prepositions, *48*.4,6-7,11-12,15,17-20,22
presentatives, *49*.7,9
pronouns, *36*.2-6,8,10,15,17-18,23-31,33-36,47,49,56-57,59-61; *46*.2
proper names, *50*.25; *67*.4,9,15

questions, *10.6; 54.5*
relative clause, *57*.2-3,5-8
root morpheme, *28*.3-4,6-9,12,18-19; *44*.5
sentence stress, *10.6; 26.3; 54.5*
states of nouns, *33*.3,5-6,15-16,19
substantival clause, *60*.1,3
syllable, *24*.2,8
temporal/causal clause, *58*.2-4,9-11,13-14,16
verbal clause, *50*.5,12,14-15,17,19-20
volitive clause, *54*.6-7,9
word accent, *25*.2,5,8
word order, *32*.21; *50*.7-9,14,17,19-20
Asyût (Egypt), *2.7*
Atlantic coast, *2.14; 7.6*
Atlas, Mounts, *2.14*
Attic, *63.11*
attribute, *51*.1-6
augmentatives in Ethiopic, *29.43*
Aurès (Algeria), *2.14*
Austronesian, *12.4*
auxiliary verbs,
    to form tenses, *38*.20,26-28
    to introduce an infinitive, *53.3*
    used as copula, *36.33; 49.22-24; 50.6*
    used asyndetically with a finite verb, *53.3*
Avaro-Andi (Caucasian), *30.9*
Avestan, *50.23; 65.5*
Avroman parchment, *7.21*
aw < ā, 22.17
aw < ā + ū, 43.17
Awngi (Agaw), *2.10; 32.1; 54.2*
Awsān, *8.5*
ay < ā + ī, 43.17
Aymallal (Gurage), *8.17-18;* see: Soddo
'ayn, influence of, *27.8*
'Azd dialect, *18.6*

Bab el-Mandeb, Straits of, *3.4*
Babylonia, *3.3; 5.2; 67.15,19*
Babylonian, *4.5; 6.1,3-4,6; 7.4; 11.6-8; 21.5; 22.15; 23.7; 25.5; 27.13;*
    29.6; 32.5,18; 35.17; 36.23,26,33,56; 40.12,20; 41.42; 42.3,7,16; 44.5-6; 45.3,5; 47.2-3,8,14; 48.20; 50.2,4,6; 51.19-20; 52.2-4,6-8; 53.2,4; 54.5; 55.1-2,5; 57.5,8; 58.13,16; 60.2; 61.4,6,8-9; 63.4-5,9; 65.3; 67.4
Late Babylonian, *4.5; 6.1,5; 16.4; 18.5; 19.21; 21.3,11; 24.2; 27.3,7,17; 29.46; 31.10; 35.6, 18,20,30; 36.35; 38.10; 40.20; 47.12; 48.7; 49.23; 51.6,8,24; 52.11; 54.6; 55.3; 58.2,11; 61.1,8; 63.11; 65.3-4*
Middle Babylonian, *6.4; 15.2; 19.9; 25.5; 32.21; 35.32; 36.31; 43.12; 47.12; 48.7; 49.25; 52.11; 58.2; 60.1; 61.7*
Neo-Babylonian, *6.4; 11.8; 16.4; 27.3,7; 32.21; 36.35; 38.4; 40.4; 41.35; 44.5-6; 48.7; 52.11; 57.7; 61.1,8; 63.9; 64.5; 65.3*
Old Babylonian, *5.3; 6.4; 7.3; 10.6; 11.9,12; 13.3-4; 18.3; 19.6,24; 21.12; 23.9; 24.2; 25.5; 26.3; 29.41; 30.1,6; 31.7,11-12,26; 32.5,17-18; 33.19; 35.2, 6,24,30; 36.2-4,15,17,24-25,27, 30,59; 40.5,17,20,31-32; 41.2-3, 20,25,49; 43.12; 44.2,4,6-10,14; 45.3; 47.2,7-8; 49.15,25; 50.2-3,7-8,12,19-20,22,25; 51.1,8,10-17,23-24; 53.2; 54.6,9; 55.3,6; 57.6; 58.4,9-10; 61.7; 65.4*
    see: Assyro-Babylonian, East Semitic
Bacon, Roger, *64.3*
Baghdad, *31.4,6,12; 40.25; 65.10*
Baḥ'ā (Syria), *7.32*
Baḥrain, *7.46; 18.9*
Ba'iso (Cushitic), *2.11*
Bakr dialect, *11.6*
Baltic languages, *65.5*
Bantu languages, *1.2; 2.13; 3.3; 10.6; 12.3; 17.7; 21.1; 28.7; 30.9; 31.1; 39.7; 41.7,14-15; 49.19*
Bar Kokhba letters, *7.15; 36.31; 51.19*
Bar Punesh, *7.13*

Barth's law, *40*.16,18,21,23,31,50; *45*.7-8
Baṣrā' (Iraq), *7*.43
Baṭhari dialect, *8*.7
Bayuda desert (Sudan), *2*.9
bb < mb, *27*.3
Bedawi (To), see: Bedja
Bedja, *2*.9; *3*.4; *8*.9,12; *30*.10; *31*.21, 24; *32*.1; *35*.1,4,9-10; *36*.17,36; *38*.5; *41*.2-3,6,15,20; *43*.11; *48*.5; *49*.1,21; *50*.15; *54*.2; *63*.5,13
Bedouin, *3*.4; *7*.35,42,46; *18*.6; *32*.25; *38*.22; *40*.25; *41*.11,25,44; *43*.17; *66*.1
Bedyat of Ennedi, *2*.9
Beeston, A.F.L., preface
Ben-Asher, *7*.5; *21*.19
Benfey, Th., *1*.1
Beni 'Amar, *2*.9
Beni Omayya, *2*.9
Benjamin of Tudela, *7*.34
Ben Naphtali, *21*.19
Berber, *1*.1; *2*.14-15,17; *3*.4; *9*.13; *17*.7; *22*.18; *31*.9; *35*.3; *41*.7,19; *48*.10; *63*.5; *65*.2; *67*.13
Proto-Berber, *35*.2
b g d k p t, *11*.10; *23*.4; *27*.20
Bible, *2*.7,10; *7*.5,12-13,25; *8*.11; *11*.10; *17*.1; *19*.15; *21*.15,20,22; *23*.3,8; *26*.2; *48*.8; *62*.4; *67*.5
biconsonantal verbal roots, *41*.1,38, 40,44
Bidiya (Chadic), *2*.16
bilingualism, *7*.43; *65*.2,10
Bisharin, Bedja tribe, *2*.9
Bisherla, *2*.9
Biu-Mandara (Chadic), *41*.17; *63*.6
Blemmyes, *2*.9
blending, *29*.54
bn < mn, *48*.9
Boghazköy, *21*.5; *41*.35
Bohairic (Coptic), *2*.7
Boni (Cushitic), *2*.11,16; *11*.9; *30*.10; *39*.7; *41*.15
br < bb, *23*.9
Brockelmann, C., preface, *50*.1
Bruce, James, *2*.10; *8*.18
Bura (Chadic), *63*.6

Burǧi (Cushitic), *2*.11; *63*.6
Byblos, *7*.3,6; *10*.8; *15*.2; *21*.12; *36*.38; *38*.12; *41*.23,43; *54*.8
Byzantine period, *2*.7; *7*.23,39; *65*.4,9
č < ǧ < g, *15*.8; *18*.6
č < k, *15*.8; *18*.6; *27*.10; *36*.2,19
č < t, *12*.3; *15*.8; *31*.7
č < q, *15*.8
č < ṭ, *12*.3
Cairo, *18*.6; *27*.10; *33*.24,39; *38*.22; *41*.24-25,27; *43*.17; *47*.15; *50*.6
Cairo Genizah, *7*.23
Calahorra, Calagurris, *67*.19
Cameroon, *2*.16; *3*.3
Canaan, *7*.2; *9*.4; *40*.18
Canaanite, *4*.1,3,5; *7*.1-9; *9*.10; *11*.13; *13*.7; *19*.12; *21*.9,20; *27*.13; *31*.11; *32*.24; *33*.8; *36*.57; *48*.18; *58*.2; *61*.2; *65*.6,8; *67*.3
"East Canaanite", *5*.3
Proto-Canaanite, *7*.3; *13*.7
Old Canaanite, *7*.3-4; *16*.2; *21*.12-13; *22*.6; *32*.23; *33*.16,20; *36*.6,23,58-60; *39*.6,8; *40*.6,14, 18,21,31; *41*.11,19,33,43,45; *42*.14; *48*.16,18; *49*.6,23; *52*.8; *53*.5; *54*.8; *58*.3-4; *61*.8; *65*.5; see also: Amarna correspondence
Canary Islands, *2*.14
Cantineau, J., preface
Carcassonne, *67*.19
Cap Bon, *67*.9
Carthage, Carthaginians, *7*.6; *67*.6
case inflection, *17*.9; *26*.2; *27*.19,47; *31*.3-5; *32*.1-28; *33*.3,16; *34*.4; *40*.1,16; *50*.16; *51*.9; *52*.1,6,10-11
Cassite, *27*.13
casus pendens, *50*.8,20
Caucasian languages, *1*.2; *7*.14; *30*.9; *32*.3
causal *y* morpheme, *28*.13; *41*.13; *43*.11
causative verbal stem, *1*.2; *2*.1; *14*.10; *15*.10; *41*.7-14
Chad, *2*.16; *18*.8
Chadic, preface; *1*.1; *2*.16,17; *3*.3; *17*.1,6; *30*.11; *31*.12,21-22; *35*.1, 4,6; *36*.1,31; *38*.16; *41*.7,17,19-20; *44*.5; *48*.6; *51*.23; *54*.2; *63*.5-6

Chadic-Berber equations, *30*.11; *35*.4; *63*.5-6

Chadic-Cushitic equations, *17*.1; *35*.4; *63*.5

Chadic-Egyptian equations, *2*.16; *30*.11; *35*.4; *63*.5

Chadic-Mandingo equation, *36*.1

Chadic-Semitic equations, *2*.16; *17*.1; *30*.11; *35*.4; *36*.31; *41*.17; *63*.5-6

Proto-Chadic, *3*.3; *39*.7

Chaha (Gurage), *8*.17,18; *11*.2,6; *17*.9; *29*.19,27; *35*.19; *36*.9,14,36, 41; *38*.27; *40*.4,6,10-11,14-15,28-30; *41*.4,14,20,27,36,38; *43*.21; *46*.6; *47*.12; *48*.25; *49*.1,17; *51*.2

Chalcolithic period, *3*.5

Chaldaean, *6*.6; *7*.18,41

Chaldaeans (Christians), *7*.34

Chaouia (Tachaouit), *2*.14

Chechen (Causasian), *30*.9; *32*.3

Cherchel, *12*.2; *21*.27

Chinese, *10*.6,8; *28*.3

Christian Palestinian Aramaic, *7*.25; *9*.5; *30*.6; *36*.28,44; *45*.10

citation form, *32*.6; *36*.49

Clause, *50*.2-20; *54*.1-*61*.12
  circumstantial, *55*.6
  conditional, *38*.14; *39*.8,16; *49*.47; *55*.7; *56*.8; *61*.1-12
  final/consecutive, *38*.14,16; *55*.5; *56*.3,5-6; *59*.1-6
  interrogative, *49*.4; *54*.5
  main, *54*.1
  major, *50*.5,17
  minor, *50*.2-4
  negative, *52*.1; *53*.4; *54*.2-4,6,9; *55*.5
  nominal, *33*.5; *50*.6-10; *54*.3,7
  relative, *39*.9; *49*.15-16; *55*.8; *56*.6; *57*.1-9; *58*.1,10-11,14-16; *59*.3,9,14,16; *60*.2-3
  relative asyndetic, *33*.2; *51*.21; *57*.1,3-4; *58*.1; *59*.3,9,14,16
  relative syndetic, *36*.46,55; *51*.21; *57*.1,5-6; *58*.1,10-11,14-16
  subordinate, *38*.14; *39*.2-5,9; *56*.1-*61*.12
  substantival, *56*.3; *60*.1-3
  temporal/causal, *49*.7; *56*.3-4,6,8; *58*.1-16; *61*.8

verbal, *50*.11-20; *54*.1-2
volitive, *54*.6-9

Cohen, D., *62*.1

cohortative, *38*.2; *39*.6,8-10; *54*.6

collective nouns, *29*.46-47; *30*.1-2; *31*.1,15,23,38-39; *34*.2; *50*.23; *51*.5

colour names, *29*.14,16

comparative, *34*.5-6

compensatory lengthening, *17*.2; *23*.1, 5; *32*.19

concord, *30*.5; *31*.14,16-17,23; *32*.3; *34*.2-3; *35*.5,18,23
  apposition, *51*.7
  attribute, *35*.5; *51*.3-6
  subject and predicate, *50*.21-25

condition,
  frequentative, *61*.10
  negative, *61*.3
  real, *55*.7; *61*.2
  split, *61*.7,9
  unreal, *47*.8; *61*.2,6,11

conditional particle, *14*.10; *41*.12; *47*.8; *49*.6,11; *61*.2-3,6-11

conditioned sound changes, *27*.1-30

conjunctions, *49*.1-4,13-17; *61*.12
  conditional, *61*.1-11
  disjunctive, *49*.3-4
  enclitic copulative:
    -(ə)m(ma), *49*.1
    -(ə)nna, -n, *49*.1
    -ma, *32*.17; *49*.1; *61*.12
  proclitic copulative:
    'ap, *49*.2
    fa-, f-, *38*.11; *49*.2; *61*.12
    pa-, *49*.2
    wa-, *11*.13; *32*.27; *38*.11; *49*.1,3; *53*.5; *61*.12
  subordinate, *38*.14; *48*.3,25; *49*.13-17; *58*.1-*60*.3

consecutio temporum, *55*.3-4; see: sequence of tenses

consonant cluster, *17*.9; *24*.2-3,8-9; *27*.16-19; *28*.4,8,10,12; *30*.3

consonantal length, *23*.1; *24*.2,4,7-9

consonants, *9*.3; *10*.2-4,11; *11*.1-20; *24*.1-11; *27*.1-8,10-14,16-29

construct state, *27*.19; *30*.4; *32*.2,5, 14,26; *33*.2-5,19-24; *34*.4; *51*.1, 9,23; *57*.2,4-5 continuants, *10*.4; *23*.1

continuous
past, *38*.20,25-26,28; *42*.19,21,24; *58*.5
present, *38*.22-26; *42*.19,21

contraction, *18*.9; *24*.11; *31*.5; *43*.8,19; *46*.5; *49*.4

"converted" imperfect, *38*.11

"converted" perfect, *54*.8-9

Coptic, *2*.1,6-7; *8*.18; *17*.4; *23*.7; *31*.24; *36*.8; *43*.11; *49*.22

copula, *36*.1-2,5,59; *42*.25; *47*.12; *49*.18-25; *50*.6,9-10

Cosmas Indicopleutes, *2*.9

coverb, *42*.12

crasis, *22*.15

culture words, *30*.10

cuneiform script, *5*.2,4; *6*.1-2; *9*.2-3,10; *11*.12-13; *12*.1; *13*.2-4,9; *14*.2; *15*.2,6; *16*.2; *18*.3,5; *19*.3-7,13; *21*.4-5; *22*.14-15; *24*.2,6; *27*.19; *29*.5; *30*.4; *32*.21; *35*.1; *45*.1-2,4; *50*.14; *54*.5

Cushitic, preface; *1*.1; *2*.8-13,16-17; *3*.2,4; *8*.1,9,12,14-15; *10*.10; *11*.3; *12*.4; *14*.7; *17*.2; *18*.6-7; *19*.23; *22*.16; *29*.20,46; *30*.10-11; *31*.15, 17,21-22,24; *32*.1,5-7; *35*.1,4,18, 20-21; *36*.1,3,5,8-10,14,16,31; *38*.1 15; *41*.3,6-7,13,15,20,28; *43*.22; *44*.5; *48*.1,10,18; *49*.2,15,17,20,22; *50*.15; *54*.2; *57*.3; *63*.5-6,13; *65*.2
Central Cushitic, see: Agaw
East Cushitic, *2*.11; *8*.9; *10*.6; *27*.12; *67*.4
Highland, *2*.11; *17*.7; *30*.8,10; *31*.15; *32*.7; *35*.3d; *41*.7,15; *43*.23; *47*.16; *49*.1; *50*.15; *51*.2,25; *56*.7; *57*.9; *63*.6; *65*.2; see also:Hadiyya, Sidamo
Lowland, *2*.11; *30*.7,10; *36*.2; *37*.1; *38*.15; *39*.7; *41*.15; *63*.3,6; see also: Afar, Ba'iso, Boni, Galaboid, Galla, Konso, Oromo, Rendille, Saho, "Sam" languages, Somali
North Cushitic, see: Bedja
South Cushitic, *2*.13.

West Cushitic, *2*.12; *15*.8; *17*.1; *36*.36; *41*.7; see also: Kafa, Omotic, Walamo

Cyprus, *10*.8; *13*.10; *17*.4

d < ḏ, *13*.6,8,11; *36*.33,50

d < ḏ, *13*.9

d < l, *17*.7

d < r, *17*.7

d < t, *27*.8

d < ṭ, *27*.11

ḏ < d, *13*.11

ḏ < ḏ, *13*.9

ḍ < d, *27*.8

ḍ < ṣ́, *10*.9,12; *16*.7-8

ḍ < ṭ, *13*.11

Ḍafīr tribe, *62*.3

dageš, *10*.3; *23*.4; *31*.25

Dahalo (Cushitic), *2*.13

Damascus, *7*.32,40,44; *13*.9; *19*.17; *21*.27; *29*.8; *31*.4,6; *33*.10; *35*.6, 18,20; *36*.39; *38*.1,23; *51*.19

Dangla (Chadic), *63*.5

Darasa (Cushitic), *2*.11

Darghi (Caucasian), *30*.9

Datīna dialect, *16*.7-8; *17*.4

dative, *36*.3-4,15-17,26

dative-adverbial, *32*.17; *36*.15

dd < dt, *41*.32

dd < ḏt, *10*.12; *27*.5

dd < nd, *27*.3; *35*.3

dd < rd, *27*.3

dd < td, *27*.3

Dead Sea scrolls, *7*.5,8; *21*.20; *23*.8; *25*.3; *27*.10; *38*.11-12; *45*.10

Dedān(ite), *7*.37; *8*.4

definiteness, *2*.2; *33*.6-14,19-24; *51*.23

deglottalization, *27*.11

deictic particles, *48*.3; *56*.2-5; *58*.2

Deir 'Allā, *7*.11

demonstratives, *13*.2; *14*.2; *33*.10,13-14

Demotic, *2*.6-7; *11*.10; *14*.7; *17*.4; *27*.3; *65*.8

denominative verbs, *23*.9; *41*.3,8,40, 42

dental fricatives, *13*.2; *14*.1-10

dental laterals, see: laterals

dental liquids, see: liquids
dental nasal, see: nasals
dental plosives, *10*.4; *11*.10; *12*.1-4
Dēr ez-Zōr (Syria), *41*.11
derivatives, *44*.13; *64*.1-5; *66*.6
determinants
 grammatical genders, *30*.10-11
 -b, *17*.1; *30*.10
 -l/r, *30*.10
 -n, *30*.11
 -t, *29*.46-49; *30*.3,10
 verbs, *28*.2
determinate state, *33*.6-14,17,19-24
develarization, *14*.6; *27*.11
devoicing, *10*.8; *14*.2; *15*.8; *26*.2; *27*.11
Dhinka (Nilotic), *2*.2
diacritic signs, *9*.10
Diakonoff, I.M., preface; *1*.2
dialect, *4*.6
diglossia, *7*.43; *65*.2,10
diminutives, *29*.10,14,35-36,38,42,49, 53; *31*.37
Dioscorides, Island of, *8*.7
diphonemization, *10*.12; *23*.6; *27*.11
diphthongization, *11*.11; *22*.2,9,15-18; *26*.2; *43*.17
diphthongs, *11*.14; *21*.20; *22*.1-18; *29*.9-11; *31*.5,28,32; *43*.17
diptotic declension, *31*.3,10; *32*.1-2,7-8,12
directive morpheme, *37*.4; *39*.7
dissimilation, *23*.6-11; *27*.11
 contiguous, *10*.12; *14*.6; *17*.8; *23*.6-11; *38*.5; *41*.38,42
 non-contiguous, *27*.11; *29*.9,13; *35*.8
 of gemination, *10*.12; *17*.8; *23*.6-11; *38*.5; *41*.38,42
 of vowels, *27*.11; *29*.13
 progressive, *23*.9; *27*.11
distributive, *31*.21; *35*.22
divine names, *29*.55; *32*.6,8,10; *33*.16; *67*.1
Diyala region, *6*.4
Diyarbakır (Turkey), *7*.33
Djandjero, *2*.12
Djawf (Yemen), *8*.2,4

Djebel ed-Drūz, *36*.5
Djibbāli, *8*.7; see: Śḥeri
Djibouti, *2*.11
Djidjelli (Algeria), *21*.27
Ḏofār (Oman), *8*.7; *18*.8; *25*.7; *40*.25
domestication of animals, *30*.10
Doric, *63*.11
Dōziri dialect, *7*.46; *40*.25
doubling of consonants, *24*.7
Dougga bilinguals, *2*.15; *29*.26; *31*.12,28; *51*.23
dual, *11*.6; *29*.54; *31*.1-8,12; *32*.8,23; *33*.3,16; *34*.2; *35*.4,18,20-21; *36*.6-7; *40*.2,7-9,15,18,20-21,31; *50*.21; *51*.4; *67*.15

e < a, *19*.5-6,10; *21*.6-7,10,24,32; *27*.9-10; *35*.26; *42*.2; *45*.1,10; *46*.3
e < ā, *27*.9,11,24
e < ay, *21*.30; *22*.12,17
e < äy, *49*.4
e < ē, *22*.12; *43*.20
e < i, *21*.7,10,13,24,27
e < l, *35*.4
ē < ā, *21*.10,27; *27*.9
ē < ay, *21*.6-7,9-10,12-13,24; *22*.1,5-9,12; *29*.31; *31*.3-4; *40*.9; *43*.15, 20; *47*.9,11
ē < āy, *22*.15
ē < ayī, *27*.23
-ē < -ēt, *27*.28
ē < 'i, *45*.3
ē < i, *21*.1; *29*.7-8; *42*.13
ē < ī, *21*.7; *22*.8; *43*.14
ē < ih, *35*.17
ē < -iye- < -uya- < -uha-, *21*.8; *42*.15
ē < ō, *27*.11
ə < a, *21*.27,30,32; *42*.2; *45*.17
ə < i, *21*.27,30; *27*.19; *29*.8; *36*.8
ə < u, *21*.27,30; *27*.9,19; *36*.8
Ea, *27*.16
Early Bronze Age, *3*.5
Early Dynastic III, *6*.2
East Arabian, Epigraphic, *7*.36,41
East Semitic, *4*.1-2,5; *6*.1-6; *9*.2-3; *10*.9; *11*.7,12; *15*.8; *16*.2,7; *21*.3-4; *25*.5; *27*.10; *28*.3,7,18-19; *29*.26,32-33,48,51; *30*.3; *31*.12;

32.5,17,21; 33.5-6,15-16; 34.6; 35.1,3,13-14,23,30-32; 36.3,5,8, 17,26,28-30,36,47,57; 37.4,6; 38.6, 10,12,16; 39.4,6-7,14,16; 40.2,6- 7,10,13,15-16,18,34; 41.2-3,6,9,12, 17-20,25,29,35,40,42-43,52; 42.14,16; 43.7,22; 44.4,10; 45.2,5, 7,11; 46.2; 47.5,7,9,17; 48.4,6,15, 19-20; 49.1,23,25; 50.5,14-15,19; 51.13,23; 54.6; 58.10-11; 60.1; 61.2- 3; 63.2,4-5,8; 65.2,5; 67.9; see: Assyro-Babylonian, Old Akkadian

Ebla, Eblaite, 5.2; 9.3; 11.9; 13.2; 17.1-2,5; 19.5; 21.6,32; 22.3; 24.2; 27.19,28-29; 28.13; 29.29,41,54; 31.3,21; 32.17-18; 33.13; 36.5,47, 58; 38.6; 40.18; 41.9; 44.11; 48.5,10,15,17-18; 49.1,23; 50.14; 57.5; 67.19

Edessa, 7.20,27

Edomite, 7.2,9; 22.14; 27.10; 33.8; 36.31; 52.10

Egypte, Egyptian, preface; 1.2; 2.1- 7,9,14,16,17; 3.3-4; 5.3; 7.3- 4,12,16,46; 8.18; 10.8,12; 11.15; 12.1; 13.7; 14.2; 15.8; 16.2; 17.1- 2,4-5; 19.7,12,24; 27.28; 29.20, 41,44,46,54; 30.1,4,10; 31.21,24; 32.1; 33.5; 35.1-4,6,9-14,18,20; 36.2,5-8,14,17-20,30-31,36,57,60; 38.3; 40.4-5,11; 41.2,7,17,19-20; 43.7,23; 48.4-6,10,18; 47.8; 49.9- 10,19-20,22; 50.9,17; 51.23; 53.2; 58.7; 61.2; 63.5; 65.8; 67.3-4
Egypto-Berber equations, 43.23; 53.2; 63.5; 67.4
Egypto-Chadic equations, 2.16; 30.11; 35.4; 63.5
Egypto-Cushitic equations, 8.18; 29.20
Egypto-Nubian equations, 2.2
Egypto-Semitic equations, 1.3; 2.1, 4-5; 10.12; 13.7; 17.2; 19.24; 47.8; 63.5; 65.8; 67.3-4
relation to Nilotic, 2.2

Egyptian Arabic, 25.4; 27.10; 33.18; 35.24; 36.44; 41.24; 47.15; 51.19; 54.4; see also: Arabic, Cairo

Egyptian hieroglyphs, 2.2,4-5,7; 9.4- 5,10; 31.21; 63.5
consonantal correspondences with Semitic, 2.4-6; 13.7; 19.12
source of the Semitic alphabet, 9.4- 5

Eichhorn, J.G., 1.1

ejectives, 10.9

Elam, Elamite, 6.4; 16.4

elative, 29.9,16,33; 34.5-6; 52.9

el-Bekri, 67.9,18

Elijah Levita, 7.5

elision, 24.11; 25.5; 26.2,4; 27.21- 29; 33.9
of ', 27.24; 41.11; 45.3-4,8,11,13- 16
of ', 45.16
of final d or t, 27.28-29; 30.4
of final k, 27.29
of final r, 27.29
of h, 27.25; 33.9,14; 36.20; 41.11, 13; 45.16; 49.1
of initial 'a, 27.26
of l and n, 27.27,29; 35.8
of short vowel, 27.17
of w, 43.8
of y, 43.15

Emar, 21.9; 27.29; 32.21; 36.47; 38.6; 40.20-21; 45.8; 48.7; 61.7

emphatic consonants, 2.8; 10.3,9-10; 11.3; 12.1-3; 13.1,6; 14.1,6; 16.1, 7-10; 18.1-3; 27.11

emphatic state, 29.51; 31.13; 32.15; 33.7,22

enclitics, 51.24
-a, 28.13; 40.14
-ah, 51.24
-do, 54.5
-(ə)m(ma), 49.1
-(ə)na, 54.5
-(ə)nna, 49.1
-m, 40.10
-ma, -mā, 49.1,8; 51.24; 53.4; 58.9
-mi, 49.8
-n, 49.1
-na, 39.3
-ni, 39.3
-nu, 54.5

-*š(ə)*, -*(ə)š*, *54*.4-5
-*ssa*, *54*.4
-*wa*, *49*.1
Endegeň (Gurage), *8*.17; *11*.2; see: Gurage
energic, *36*.21; *38*.12; *46*.2
English, *11*.2; *14*.1; *19*.9; *27*.30; *28*.3; *29*.55; *38*.18; *48*.3,18; *50*.6; *55*.1; *62*.2,4; *63*.12; *65*.8; *66*.4
Ennemor (Gurage), *8*.17; *11*.26; *36*.14; *41*.32; *42*.5; *48*.19; see also: Gurage
ergative, *1*.2; *2*.8,14,17; *22*.18; *29*.20; *32*.1-3,6-7,18; *33*.5; *38*.17; *39*.4; *40*.16; *48*.2; *50*.4,8-9; *52*.1,8; *54*.3; *63*.5,13; see also: agent case, instrumental, locative, nominative case
Eritrea, preface; *2*.10-11; *8*.1,8-10,12-13
Eshmun, *28*.8
Eshnunna, *18*.3
Essaouira, *27*.8
esṭrangelō, *7*.27
Ethiopia, preface; *1*.1; *2*.10-11; *3*.3; *4*.4; *8*.1,3,8-10,13-14,16; *12*.2, *18*.8; *19*.18; *36*.9; *63*.10; *64*.4
Ethiopic, *1*.3; *3*.1; *4*.1-3,5; *8*.1,3,7-18; *9*.7,11
  accusative, *32*.27-28; *52*.1,3,6-7,11
  adjectival syntagm, *51*.22
  adjectives, *34*.3
  adverbs, *47*.2-3,7-8,11-12,17-18; *51*.26
  apposition, *51*.8
  articles, *32*.28; *33*.8,14
  attribute, *51*.1-2
  case inflection, *32*.4-6,8,11,13,15, 18,20,27-28
  concord of subject and predicate, *50*.23
  conditional clause, *61*.1-2,11
  conjugation, *37*.6; *38*.2-3,5,7-8,12, 14-15,25-28; *39*.2,12; *40*.2-6,10-17,27-32; *41*.2-6,9-11,13-14,17-18,20,24-25,27-29,32-34, 36-43,52-55; *42*.1,3-5,11-17,25; *43*.5-10,16,20-22; *44*.2,4-11; *45*.9,17; *46*.6

conjunctions, *32*.17; *49*.1,4,9,14, 16-17; *58*.2,11,16; *59*.6; *60*.1; *61*.2
copula, *49*.17-22,24
expression of possession, *49*.25
final/consecutive clause, *59*.6
genitival relation, *51*.10-13,16-17, 19,23,25
gerund, *42*.12; *53*.5
infinitive, *53*.2-5
lexicography, *63*.2-4,6-7,9-10,13; *64*.4; *65*.2,4-5; *67*.4
negative clause, *54*.2
nominal clause, *50*.7-9
North Ethiopic, *8*.8,11-13,16-17; *13*.12; *23*.1; *29*.16,47,50; *30*.11; *31*.12,15,17-18,26,31-33; *36*.33; *38*.7,26; *40*.11,28-31; *41*.9-10, 14,29,32; *42*.3,11,13-14; *43*.21; *48*.25; *50*.15; *51*.1; *54*.5; *57*.9; *59*.6; see also: Geʿez, South Semitic, Tigre, Tigrinya
noun gender, *30*.2-3,5-8,10-11
noun number, *31*.1,9,12,15-20,22, 24-26,29-35,37-41
noun patterns, *29*.8-9,11,13-14,16-17,19,21-22,25-27,30,37,41-45, 47-52,55
numerals, *35*.2-4,6,8,13-14,16-22,24-27,29-30
one-term sentence, *50*.3
parataxis, *55*.1
phonology, *10*.9-10; *11*.1-3,5-6,8-11,15; *12*.1-4; *13*.10,12; *14*.2-3,7,9; *15*.3,5-6; *16*.6-7; *17*.1-9; *18*.2,5-8; *19*.1,20-21; *20*; *21*.2, 17,30-31; *22*.12-13,15-18; *23*.1-2,5,7-10; *27*.3-4,6,8-13,15-20,25, 27; *43*.23
"plural of majesty", *50*.24
prepositional phrase, *52*.11
prepositions, *48*.1,5-6,10-12,15-25
presentatives, *49*.6
pronouns, *36*.1-3,5-6,8-9,11-14,17-21,28-29,31-34,36,38,40-43, 45,55,57-58,60-61
proper names, *67*.15
Proto-Ethiopic, *8*.8; *21*.30; *38*.7

questions, *47*.16; *54*.4-5
relative clause, *57*.1,3,5,8-9; *60*.3
South Ethiopic, *2*.11; *8*.8,14-18;
    11.6; *12*.3-4; *13*.12; *17*.4,8;
    18.6; *19*.20; *22*.15,18; *23*.1;
    25.8; *29*.19,26,45,50; *30*.8,10;
    31.15,17,22; *32*.11,17,20,27-28;
    35.3,14,18,20-21,24,27; *36*.1-
    2,5-6,18,20,29,32-33,38,41,55;
    38.7,28; *39*.12; *40*.11-12,15,28-
    29; *41*.2,5,14,29,32,53; *42*.4,11,
    13-14; *43*.5,21,23; *45*.17; *47*.17;
    48.6,18,22,25; *49*.1,4,17-21,25;
    50.15; *51*.2,25; *54*.2; *56*.7; *57*.9;
    63.4,6,9; *65*.2; see also: Am-
    haric, Argobba, Gafat, Gurage,
    Harari, South Semitic
states of nouns, *33*.3-5,8,11-14,18
subordinate clause, *56*.7
substantival clause, *59*.6; *60*.1,3
syllabary, *2*.11; *9*.7; *21*.30; *27*,19;
    33.10
syllable, *24*.5,8-10
temporal/causal clause, *58*.2,11,16
verbal clause, *50*.13,15,17,19-20
volitive clause, *54*.6
word accent, *25*.1,3,7-8
word order, *50*.7,9,13,15,17,19-20;
    51.2; *56*.7; *57*.9
Ethiopic syllabary, *2*.11; *9*.7; *21*.30;
    27.19; *33*.10
Ethio-Semitic, *8*.1
etymology, *63*.1-14; *67*.10
euphemism, *63*.7
Ewe, *62*.2
exclamations, *26*.4; *32*.5; *50*.3
execration texts, *5*.3; *19*.7; *21*.24;
    29.54
"existential" verb, *49*.23-25; *50*.6,10
extraposition, *50*.8,20
-*ey* < -*ē*, *22*.9
Eža (Gurage), *8*.17; *11*.2,6; see:
    Gurage
Ezana, *2*.9

f < *ff* < *nf*, *27*.3
f < *p*, *11*.4
f < *š*/*s*, *11*.15

fa'al, *29*.5; *31*.42
fa'ala, *31*.36; *32*.15
fa'ālil, *31*.28; *32*.8
fa'ālīl, *31*.28
fa''āl, *66*.6
Fabre d'Olivet, Antoine, *9*.1
fa'il, *18*.6; *27*.22; *29*.5
fa'īl, *31*.28; *66*.6
fa'ila, *27*.22
fa'l, *27*.22; *29*.5; *31*.42
fa'la, *27*.22; *34*.5
fa'lān, *32*.8
f'āl, *31*.28
Falasha, *2*.10
family-tree theory, *3*.1
Fāra (Iraq), *4*.2
fa'ul, *27*.22
fawa'l, *22*.16
fawl, *22*.16; *29*.9
fay'al, *22*.16
fay'āl, *22*.16
fayl, *22*.16; *29*.9
fay'ūl, *22*.16
feminine endings/morphemes, *26*.2;
    29.42,46-47,49; *30*.1-5; *31*.6,12,
    14-15; *32*.1; *33*.16,23; *34*.3; *35*.6;
    36.20,30; *40*.4
    gender, categories, *30*.6-8
fi'al, *31*.25
fi'āl, *31*.28,36
fi'ala, *31*.36
fi''awl, *22*.16; *29*.10
fi'il, *27*.22
fi'l, *27*.22
fi'la, *34*.5
fi'lān, *31*.12
Fischer, W., preface
fortis consonant, *18*.2; *19*.2
Frahang i Pahlavīk, *7*.30
France, French, *11*.9-10; *35*.18; *63*.12;
    64.5
frequentative, *41*.20,33-37; *61*.10
fricative, *10*.4; *13*.1; *23*.1
fricative palatal, *14*.4
fu'al, *31*.25; *32*.8
fu'āl, *31*.25; *32*.8; *35*.33
fu'alā', *31*.28
fu'ayl, *22*.16

fu"al, *31*.25; *65*.6
fu"āl, *31*.25
fu"ayl, *22*.16
fu'l, *27*.22; *31*.25
fu'la, *34*.5
fu'lān, *31*.12
fu'lul, *63*.10
fu'lun, *31*.25
fu'ul, *27*.22; *31*.36
Fulani, *12*.4; *62*.2

g < k, *18*.4
g < q, *18*.2,8
ǧ < d, *12*.3; *15*.5; *35*.3
ǧ < g, *18*.6
ǧ < ll, *2*.15; *15*.8
ǧ < q, *18*.6
ġ < ', *27*.8
ġ < g, *30*.10
ġ < r, *17*.1
ġ < ṭ, *10*.10; *13*.6
Gafat, *8*.8-9,18
    accusative, *52*.3
    adverbs, *47*.8,17
    case inflection, *32*.6,28
    conjugation, *38*.7,25; *40*.4-
        6,10,27,29-30; *41*.2,5,8,11,14,20,
        27,32,53; *42*.4,14; *43*.7; *45*.9
    conjunctions, *49*.1
    copulae, *49*.19-22
    expression of possession, *49*.25
    lexicography, *30*.10; *63*.10,13; *66*.4
    noun gender, *30*.2,8,10-11
    noun number, *31*.17
    noun patterns, *29*.55
    numerals, *35*.3-4,8,14,16,20,24
    phonology, *14*.7; *15*.5; *17*.1,5,7;
        22.16; *27*.3
    prepositions, *48*.12,16,19,22
    pronouns, *36*.3,9,11-12,18,19,23,
        28, 32-33,38,40-41,43,61
    states of nouns, *33*.12-13
    verbal clause, *50*.15
    word order, *50*.15
    see also: Ethiopic, South Semitic
Galaboid (Cushitic), *2*.11
Galilean Aramaic, *7*.23; *40*.23; *42*.4,9;
    43.15; *45*.10

Galilee, *7*.23
Galla, Galləňňa, *2*.11; *8*.9; see:
    Oromo
garšūnī, *9*.13
ǧazma, *10*.3
Ge'ez, preface; *1*.3; *8*.1,8-9,11-13
    accusative, *52*.3,6-7,11
    adjectives, *34*.3
    adverbs, *47*.2-3,7-8,11
    attribute, *51*.1
    case inflection, *32*.4-5,8,11,13,18,
        20,27
    concord, *50*.23
    conditional clause, *61*.1-2,11
    conjugation, *38*.3,5,7,15,25; *40*.2,
        10,12-13,15,17,28-29,31-32;
        41.2-5,9,11,14,18,24-25,27,29,
        32,37-38,40,42,52,54-55;
        42.3,5,11-13,17; *43*.6-7,9,20-21;
        44.2,4,6-11; *45*.9,17; *46*.6
    conjunctions, *49*.14,16; *58*.11,16;
        59.6; *60*.1
    final/consecutive clause, *59*.6
    genitival construction, *51*.10-13,16-
        17,19,23,25
    gerund, *42*.12; *53*.5
    infinitive, *53*.2-5
    lexicography, *30*.11; *63*.2-3,7,10;
        64.4; *65*.5
    nominal clause, *50*.7,9
    noun gender, *30*.3,11
    noun number, *31*.9,12,15,17,20,
        26,31,34
    noun patterns, *29*.8,11,13-14,21-22,
        30,37,41,44,47-50
    numerals, *35*.2-4,16-18,20-22,24-
        27,29-30
    phonology, *11*.2,5,8; *13*.12; *14*.3,9;
        16.6; *17*.7-8; *18*.7-8; *19*.20;
        21.30; *22*.12; *27*.3,6,12-13,25,27
    prepositional phrase, *52*.11
    prepositions, *48*.6,12,16-21,23-25
    presentatives, *49*.6
    pronouns, *36*.2,8-9,11-12,17,23,33,
        38,41-43,55,58,60
    questions, *54*.5
    relative clause, *57*.1,3,5,8
    states of nouns, *33*.4,14

substantival clause, *59*.6
temporal/causal clause, *58*.11,16
verbal clause, *50*.13
volitive clause, *54*.6
word accent, *25*.1,3
word order, *50*.7,9,13
see also: Ethiopic, South Semitic
Gelb, I.J., preface
gələt-dialects, *38*.3
gemination, non-gemination, *17*.1,3,5,
  8; *19*.21; *21*.5; *23*.1-11; *24*.2-
  3,5,7-9; *27*.11,16; *28*.11; *29*.3,11-
  12,51; *31*.28; *33*.10; *38*.5-8; *41*.2-
  4,25-26,28,31,33,39,53; *45*.9; *49*.1
gender, *10*.6; *28*.4; *30*.1-11; *31*.38;
  34.1; *36*.6,58
  animals, *30*.8,10
  gender-number relation, *30*.6
  gender polarity, *35*.6,17
  grammatical, *28*.4; *30*.9-11
  variation, *30*.5-6; *31*.38
Genesis Rabba, *7*.23
genitival compounds, *29*.55; *64*.5; *66*.5
genitive, *29*.54; *31*.3; *32*.1,7,12-14,
  16,21-25,27; *36*.3,48,50,52,55; *48*.2;
  51.8-26; *53*.1
  after determinative-relative pronoun,
    51.18-21
  descriptive, *51*.22
  epexegeticus, *51*.16
  logical, *51*.10,25
  obiectivus, *32*.7; *51*.12
  of contents, *51*.15
  of material, *51*.14
  of quality, *51*.17
  partitive, *51*.13
  periphrastic, *36*.46; *51*.19,25; *57*.1
  subiectivus, *51*.11
gentiles, *29*.36,41,44,49,54; *31*.29,40;
  32.7
Geonic texts, *7*.29
Georgia, Georgian, *7*.34; *10*.10
German, Germanic, *1*.2; *10*.8; *62*.2;
  63.12
gerund, *42*.12; *47*.3; *53*.5
Gerzean culture, *3*.4
Gezer calendar, *7*.3; *31*.11
gg < ng, *27*.3; *36*.35

Ghadamsi (Tuareg), *35*.2; *43*.23
Ghassulian culture, *3*.3
Ghat dialect (Tuareg), *14*.10
Ğiblah dialect, *40*.10
glide, *11*.11; *15*.7; *22*.15; *27*.23;
  28.13; *31*.19; *36*.16
glottalization, *2*.8; *10*.9-10; *11*.3;
  15.5; *23*.6; *26*.2; *33*.8
glottal stop, *18*.2; *19*.1-22; *21*.1,26;
  22.15; *24*.11; *43*.3-4; *45*.3-6,8;
  67.18
Gogot (Gurage), *8*.17; *11*.8-9; *35*.18;
  40.3-4,12; *41*.53; *48*.19
Gothic, *63*.5
Gozo, island, *17*.7
Grande, B.M., preface
Greece, *7*.16
Greek, *2*.7,9,15; *7*.25,39,44; *8*.11;
  9.5; *10*.8; *11*.1-4,8-10,15; *12*.4;
  13.7,9; *14*.4,7,10; *15*.3; *16*.3; *17*.4-
  5; *19*.2,12,17,21; *21*.3,11,13,16,
  20, 22,24-25; *22*.4,10; *23*.7; *25*.1,
  3; *27*.7,11,28; *28*.10; *30*.1,27; *32*.5;
  33.9,13; *40*.3; *41*.5; *43*.16; *50*.23;
  57.2; *63*.5-6,9-12; *64*.5; *65*.4-7,9;
  67.4,9,17-18
Greek sibilants in Semitic, *13*.10
Greenberg, J.H., *1*.1
group-writing, *2*.4
Guanches, *2*.14
Ğubb 'Adīn (Syria), *7*.32; *23*.1;
  27.10; *38*.22
Gurage, *8*.8,17-18
  adverbs, *47*.8,12
  article, *32*.28
  attribute, *51*.2
  case inflection, *32*.4,6,11,20,27
  conjugation, *38*.7,12,14,25,27; *39*.2;
    40.4-6,10-11,14-15,28-30; *41*.2-
    3,5,18,20,32,36,38,53; *42*.4-5,11-
    12,14; *43*.5,7,10,21-22
  conjunctions, *49*.1,4
  copula, *49*.19,21-22,24
  East Gurage, *8*.17; *11*.3,9; *15*.5;
    17.5, *31*.17; *32*.4,11,20,27; *36*.9,
    33; *38*.7,25; *40*.11,28-30; *41*.5;
    43.21; see also: Selṭi, Wolane,
    Zway

genitival construction, *51*.25
gerund, *42*.12; *53*.5
infinitive, *53*.5
lexicography, *62*.2; *63*.3-4,9
negative clause, *54*.2
North(east) Gurage, *8*.17-18; *18*.6;
 27.25; *33*.14; *35*.18; *36*.41,43;
 38.12,25; *39*.2; *40*.10-11,28-29;
 42.14; *49*.22; see also: Gogot,
 Masqan, Muher, Soddo
noun gender, *30*.2,8,10-11
noun number, *31*.17,22
noun patterns, *29*.19,27,45,50-51
numerals, *35*.3-4,14,16,18-21
phonology, *11*.2-3,5-6,8-9,11; *12*.2;
 13.12; *14*.3,7; *15*.5; *17*.1-3,5-
 6,9; *18*.6-8; *19*.20; *22*.15,18;
 23.1,5,7-10; *27*.3-4,8-9,11-12,15,
 17-18,25
prepositions, *48*.6,16,18-19
pronouns, *36*.3,9,11-12,14,21,23,
 28, 32-33,41,43,58,60
relative clause, *57*.9
states of nouns, *33*.14,18
subordinate clause, *56*.7
syllable, *24*.5
West Gurage, *8*.17; *11*.2; *12*.2;
 17.5-6; *23*.10; *25*.7-8; *27*.3;
 31.17; *32*.6; *36*.41; *38*.25,27;
 40.10-11,29; *42*.12; *49*.24; *53*.5;
 63.9; see also: Chaha, Ennemor
gutturals, *19*.1-22; *27*.10; *40*.22-23
Gyeto (Gurage), *8*.17; *11*.2,6; see:
 Gurage

ḥ, first radical, *43*.9; *44*.4
ḥ < ḫ, *19*.7
ḥ < h, *19*.20
ḥ < k, *18*.5; *36*.19,41
ḥ < s < š, *14*.10; *15*.4; *35*.12;
 36.10,20; *41*.12; *61*.2
ḥ < z/s, *14*.10
ḥ < ', *19*.17
ḫ < ḥ, *19*.15,19-20
ḫ < ḥ, *7*.33; *19*.11,14-15
ḫ < k, *35*.4
Hadendowa, Bedja tribe, *2*.9
Ḥadīth, *21*.26; *43*.12

Hadiyya (Cushitic), *2*.11; *32*.7
Ḥaḍramawt, *3*.3; *8*.3,6; *18*.8; *22*.11;
 27.8; *31*.4
Ḥaḍramitic, *8*.2,6; *13*.10; *18*.5; *19*.18;
 31.19; *41*.9; *48*.11; see: South
 Arabian, Epigraphic
Hamath, *33*.7
Hamito-Semitic, preface, *1*.1; *3*.3;
 48.5-6; see: Afro-Asiatic
hamza, *10*.3
Hanish islands, *3*.4
haplology, *27*.15
Haram (Sabaic), *13*.10; *14*.3; *47*.10;
 49.2; *61*.3,9; see: Sabaic, South
 Arabian, Epigraphic
Harari, *8*.8,15-17
apposition, *51*.8
case inflection, *32*.28
conjugation, *38*.7,25; *40*.3-4,6,28,
 30; *41*.3,5,32; *42*.4,11,13-14;
 43.6,8,21
conjunctions, *49*.1
copula, *49*.19-21,24
genitival construction, *51*.25
lexicography, *30*.11; *63*.4
noun gender, *30*.10
noun number, *31*.17
numerals, *35*.14,18,20-21
parataxis, *55*.1
phonology, *11*.5,9,15; *13*.12; *14*.3,
 7; *15*.5; *17*.5; *18*.7; *19*.20; *27*.12,
 16,18,27
prepositions, *48*.1,6,16
pronouns, *36*.9,12-13,23,29,33,55
states of nouns, *33*.12
word accent, *25*.3
see also: Ethiopic, South Semitic
Harran (Turkey), *7*.28
Harris, Z.S., preface
Ḥarsūsi, *8*.7; *35*.3,7,30; *36*.18,23,40,
 44; *38*.2,5,8; *39*.12; *40*.10; *41*.9,
 11,22,25,29; *47*.8; *50*.8; *61*.2; see:
 Mehri, South Arabian, Modern
Ḥāsa', al- (Saudi Arabia), *7*.41
Ḥasaean, *7*.41; *36*.54
Ḥassānīya, *13*.9; *36*.39; *41*.44
Hatra, Hatraean, *7*.19; *11*.7
Hausa, *1*.1; *2*.11,16; *28*.7; *29*.20;

31.21-22; *35*.9,11; *36*.1,17,31,57;
  40.1; *43*.3; *62*.2; *63*.6,13; *65*.8; see
  also: Chadic
Ḥawrān colloquial, *13*.9; *16*.7; *25*.2-
  3; *31*.19; *32*.5; *38*.22; *44*.14
Ḥayyudj of Fez, *28*.1
Hazor, *7*.3; *21*.12
Hebrew, preface; *1*.1; *2*.15; *3*.5;
  4.3,5; *7*.1-2,5,7-8,25; *9*.1,5
  accusative, *52*.2-4,6-11
  adjectives, *34*.2,5
  adverbs, *47*.2-4,7,9,12,14-15,17
  apposition, *51*.7-8
  article, *33*.10,18
  attribute, *51*.1,3-6
  case inflection, *32*.19-20,24
  concord of subject and predicate,
    50.21-23
  conditional clause, *61*.1-7,9-10
  conjugation, *35*.34; *37*.4,6,11-12;
    38.11,16; *39*.1,6,8-9,14-15,17;
    40.2-4,6,10,12-17,22,32,34-35;
    41.2-3,7-11,13,15,19,23,25-
    26,29-30,32,37-38,40,42-
    43,45,54-55; *42*.1-2,4-5,8,12-15,
    17,23; *43*.5-6,8-9,14; *44*.4,6-11;
    45.9-11; *46*.2-3,5
  conjunctions, *49*.1-2,4,14-15; *58*.2-
    5,7,12-14; *59*.1,3; *60*.1-3; *61*.1-
    7,9-10
  copula, *49*.23-24
  expression of possession, *49*.25
  final/consecutive clause, *59*.1,3
  genitival relation, *51*.11-16,18-20,
    22-24,26
  hypotaxis, *56*.5,8
  infinitive, *53*.1-5
  lexicography, *62*.4; *63*.2-4,6-9,11,
    14; *64*.2,4; *65*.4-5,7-8; *66*.2,5
  Mishnaic Hebrew, *7*.5,25; *9*.5;
    11.7; *17*.8; *19*.15; *21*.15; *23*.9;
    27.26,30; *28*.13; *29*.13,39; *33*.10;
    36.18,31,33-34,47; *38*.11; *41*.2,
    10,26,38,45; *42*.1; *45*.10; *49*.25;
    51.19; *57*.6; *63*.11; *65*.4-5,8
  Modern Hebrew, *29*.38,49,53; *42*.1,
    23; *63*.12
  nominal clause, *50*.7-9
  noun gender, *30*.1,3-6,11
  noun number, *31*.4,8,10,13-14,19-
    21,26,28,38,41
  noun patterns, *29*.5,7-9,11,13-14,
    16-18,21-22,24-25,30,33,35-
    39,41-42,47-49,55
  numerals, *35*.2-5,9,16-22,24,27,29-
    30,32,34
  one-term sentence, *50*.2,4
  parataxis, *55*.2,4-6
  phonology, *10*.1,3,7,10; *11*.5-7,9-
    10,13; *12*.1-2; *13*.7-8; *14*.5,7;
    15.2; *16*.5,7; *17*.1-2,4-5,8; *18*.4-
    5,8; *19*.12,15,20-21,24; 20;
    21.2,15-20,22; *22*.6,13,15; *23*.1-
    5,8-9; *27*.3-4,7-17,19-20,25-26,
    28,30
  "plural of majesty", *50*.24
  prepositions, *48*.11-13,15-19,21-23
  presentatives, *49*.6,8-9
  pronouns, *36*.2-3,6,13,17-18,20,23-
    24,28,31,33-36,38,47,51,56,59-
    60
  pronunciation, *10*.1; *11*.10; *19*.20;
    25.3,6
  European, *14*.7; *17*.1; *19*.15
  Moroccan, *14*.5; *18*.8
  Oriental, *17*.8; *18*.8; *21*.16; *40*.22
  Sephardi, *12*.2; *21*.19
  proper names, *67*.3-4,7
  questions, *49*.4
  relative clause, *57*.2-6,8; *60*.1
  root morpheme, *28*.2,7-8,13
  sentence stress, *26*.2
  states of nouns, *33*.6,8-10,16,18,22-
    23
  substantival clause, *60*.1-3
  syllable, *24*.5-9
  temporal/causal clause, *58*.2-5,7,
    12-14
  verbal clause, *50*.12-13,19-20
  volitive clause, *54*.6-8
  word accent, *25*.1,3,6,8
  word order, *50*.7-9,13,19-20; *56*.8
  writing, *9*.1,9-11,13
  see also: West Semitic
Ḥedjaz (Saudi Arabia), *7*.39; *27*.20;
  40.23

Ḥegrā' (Saudi Arabia), *7.37-38; 57.6*
Hellenistic period, *8.7; 9.6; 13.8; 19.12-13; 21.21; 25.1; 63.10; 67.4*
Herakles statue (Parthian), *7.21*
Hexapla, *9.13; 21.19; 24.9; 27.19*
h-glide, *28.13; 31.19*
Ḥidjazi, *7.46; 11.13-14; 21.9; 27.20; 36.33; 38.14; 39.17; 41.24; 45.14;* see also: Arabic
hieroglyphic script; see Egyptian hieroglyphs
hif'il, *27.16; 41.11*; see: causative verbal stem
Ḥimyar, *8.3; 51.1*
Hindus, *8.7*
Hispano-Arabic, see: Andalus, al-
hitpa'el, *27.16; 41.25*
Hittite, *14.1; 27.29; 65.5*
"hollow" roots, *43.9; 44.1,5-9*
homophones, *19.5*
homorganic sounds, *17.1; 27.11*
Horn of Africa, *1.2; 2.8,11; 3.2-4*
Hudhail, *11.14*
Hurrian, *9.5; 19.8; 22.3; 27.16; 67.19*
hypercorrection, *11.8; 27.30; 38.12-13; 51.16*
hypocoristic suffix, *27.29,41; 67.2*
hypotaxis, *38.12; 55.1; 56.2-61.12*

i < *a*, *21.32; 27.9*
i < *ay*, *36.22*
i < *əy*, *22.8*
i < *ī*, *21.30; 22.12; 29.42; 31.4; 40.9; 43.13,20*
i < *u*, *27.9; 36.5*
i- < *wi-*, *11.14*
i- < *ya-*, *22.14*
i- < *yi-*, *15.6; 22.14*
ī < *ay*, *21.9-10,13; 22.1,5-8; 29.42, 54; 31.3-4; 40.9*
ī < *āya*, *40.9*
ī < *ē*, *21.23; 22.8*
ī < *'i*, *45.3*
-ī < *-iy*, *22.9,13,36,41; 36.18; 42.15; 43.12-14,20*
ī < *iya*, *21.9; 22.13*
ī < *ū*, *27.9*
-ī- < *-iyi-*, *29.54*

ī < *ū* + *ī*, *22.15*
'ī < *yī*, *41.13*
Iberian peninsula, *3.4*
'ibdāl, *11.15; 22.15*
Ibn al-Mudǧāwir, *8.7*
Ibn Khaldun, *2.14*
Ibn Qayyim al-Ǧawzīya, *67.2*
Idumaea, *65.4*
Iġšan (Tachelhit), *35.31*
imāla, *21.27; 22.7*
imperative, *24.8-9; 38.1-2; 40.13-15; 43.3,6; 54.6*
imperfect, *2.11; 7.32; 28.16; 38.5,7-8,14,18,22,24-28; 39.9; 54.6*
imperfective, *17.4; 38.3,5-9,12; 40.18; 54.6*
indefiniteness, indeterminate state, *33.5-6,13,15-24; 51.23*
indicative, *28.16; 38.14,18,22; 39.2, 12,14*
Indian, *65.6*
Indo-European, *1.2; 10.8; 11.9; 12.4; 19.1; 28.3; 33.6,13; 35.18; 37.1,4; 38.2,18-19; 50.23; 52.3; 63.5; 64.1*
infa'ala, *24.8; 41.15,19*
infinitive, *29.25,32; 32.27; 38.22; 42.1-12; 53.1-6*
   absolute, *53.4*
   basic stem, *42.2-5,21; 43.8*
   construct, *53.2*
   derived stems, *42.6-11,22*
   gerund, *42.12; 53.5*
infix, *28.16,18; 38.4*
   -t-, *38.4,9-10*
instrumental, *29.20; 32.1-4,18; 39.4; 48.2; 51.9*
interdentals, *10.4; 11.15; 13.1-12*
interjection, *40.14; 50.4*
international phonetic alphabet, *10.1-2*
interrogative particle, *47.7; 54.5*
"interrupted" consonant, *23.1*
intonation, *10.6,11; 26.1-4; 54.5*
intransitive, *32.2-3,15; 38.3,15-17; 39.12; 41.2,8; 52.1-2,8; 54.3; 63.14*
Iran, *7.28,34,46*
Iranian, *7.21,26,30; 42.18*
Iraq, *4.2; 7.18,28,34,46; 17.1; 18.6; 41.11; 65.4*

Iraqw (Cushitic), 2.13; *10*.3
Irbil (Iraq), *38*.24
Isaac of Antioch, 22.4
Isidorus Hispalensis, *42*.12
Islam, 2.9; *7*.43; *66*.4; *64*.6; *67*.2
Israel, 2.10; *7*.11,46; *21*.19; *67*.19
Israelite Hebrew, *7*.5
Italy, Italian, *7*.16; *12*.2; *62*.2; *64*.5
i : *u* opposition, *36*.8
ivrīt, *7*.5
-iy < *-iw*, 22.13
-iy < *-uw*, 22.13
iy < *uy*, *42*.15

Jacob of Edessa, *7*.27
Jacobites, *7*.27,34; *21*.22
Jerome, Saint, *19*.12; *29*.5
Jerusalem, *21*.12
Jewish Babylonian Aramaic, *7*.26, 29,34; *9*.9; *16*.5; *17*.2; *40*.22; *42*.20; *45*.12; *48*.12; *63*.9,11
Jewish Palestinian Aramaic, *7*.23; *9*.9; *11*.7; *16*.5; *17*.1; *65*.6
Job, language of the Book of, *48*.9
Johnstone, T.M., preface
Jordan, *7*.7,40,46; *13*.9; *14*.6; *18*.6; *21*.12
Judaea, *7*.5,15,25; *65*.4
Judaean Desert, *7*.5,15,16
Judaeo-Arabic, *9*.13
Judaeo-Spanish, *29*.53
Judahite Hebrew, *7*.5
Judah ibn Quraysh, *1*.1
jussive, *10*.6; *17*.4; *25*.8; *26*.4; *38*.2, 6-7,12,15,22,26-28; *39*.5,9,12,15-18; *40*.30; *54*.6

Kabyle, Kabylia, 2.14-15; *38*.2; *41*.2; *49*.24; *53*.4; see: Libyco-Berber
Kafa (Cushitic), 2.12; *31*.22; *48*.10
Kambata (Cushitic), 2.11
Kāmid el-Lōz (Libanon), *7*.4; *40*.21; *41*.43
kaph veritatis, *49*.9
Karaites, *7*.29; *21*.19
Kassala (Sudan), 2.9
Kenya, 2.13; *36*.2
Kera (Chadic), 2.16
Keren (Eritrea), 2.10

Khamir (Agaw), 2.10
Khamta (Agaw), 2.10
Khamtanga (Agaw), 2.10
Khirbet Barāqish (Yemen), *8*.4
Khirbet Ma'in (Yemen), *8*.4
Khor Rori ('Omān), *8*.6
Khuzistan (Iran), *7*.46
Khwarezmian (Iranian), *7*.21
"kinetic" sounds, *23*.1
Kish, *3*.3; *4*.2; *5*.2; *6*.2; *32*.19
kk < *bk*, *27*.3
kk < *lk*, *27*.3
kk < *rk*, *27*.3
Konso (Cushitic), 2.13
Kordofan hills, 2.8
Krzyżaniak, L., *3*.3
Kūfa, al-, Kufic, *7*.43; *21*.26; *22*.7
Kurdish, Kurdistan, *7*.34; *42*.18; *47*.8
Kutscher, E.Y., preface
Kuwait, *7*.46; *18*.9; *38*.22; *40*.25
Kwang (Chadic), 2.16
Kwena (Bantu), *1*.2; *39*.7

l, its dissimilatory function, *23*.8; *41*.42; *43*.4
   weak consonant, *17*.2; *24*.2; *43*.10
l < *d*, *36*.61
l < *n*, *17*.4; *36*.28; *61*.2
labialization, *9*.7; *10*.3; *11*.11; *12*.3; *27*.10; *35*.4,8; *36*.5; *61*.2
labials, *10*.4; *11*.1-14; *19*.7; *29*.26
labiodental, *11*.1,10,15; *29*.26
labiovelars, *11*.11; *18*.7; *28*.8-9; *41*.5
Lachish, *9*.11
Ladino, *29*.53
lam(*ed*) *auctoris*, *48*.8
languages in contact, *65*.1-10
Lapethos (Cyprus), *13*.10
laryngals, *7*.33; *10*.4; *13*.6; *17*.8; *19*.1-22; *43*.3; *45*.2-17; *65*.2
laterals, latelarized, *13*.2; *15*.2; *16*.1-11; *23*.1; *35*.8
Latin, 2.15; *3*.1; *10*.8; *11*.9; *14*.2,6; *19*.16; *21*.13,20; *27*.3,23,28; *29*.5, 20,44; *30*.1; *32*.24; *33*.13; *36*.29-30,57; *45*.13; *47*.16; *49*.23; *50*.12; *63*.5-6,10; *64*.5; *65*.4-5,7; *67*.9,17-18

Latino-Punic inscriptions, *7*.6; *15*.3
Lebanon, *7*.46; *23*.6,11; *51*.20; *67*.13
legal terminology, *64*.6
lengthening of vowels, *24*.6; *26*.2;
   29.47; *38*.8-9; *45*.3-6,8-9,11,13
lenis consonant, *19*.2
Leslau, W., preface; *8*.18
Leviticus Rabba, *7*.23
lexicon, *15*.8; *28*.1-2,14-19; *31*.7-8;
   62-67
Libya, *7*.6; *38*.22
Libyco-Berber, preface; *1*.1,3; *2*.2,14-
   15,17; *3*.3-5
   case inflection, *32*.1-7,10
   conditional clause, *61*.2
   conjugation, *2*.14; *37*.1; *38*.1-3,5,
      17; *40*.6; *41*.2,6-8,14-15,19-20,
      33-35, 38-39; *43*.10-11; *44*.5;
      49.23
   conjunctions, *49*.2
   copula, *49*.23
   ergative language, *2*.14; *21*.30;
      32.1-7; *33*.5
   genitival relation, *51*.8-9,20,23
   infinitive, *53*.4
   lexicography, *30*.10; *43*.3,10; *62*.2;
      63.3,5-6; *65*.8; *66*.5; *67*.9
   negatives, *47*.8; *54*.2,4
   nominal clause, *50*.8-9
   noun gender, *30*.1,10-11
   noun number, *28*.13; *31*.12,24,28
   noun patterns, *29*.11,13,20,26,28,
      30,33,35,42,46
   numerals, *35*.1-4,6,8-14,18,21,31
   phonology, *2*.15; *10*.3,9; *11*.7; *15*.8;
      17.5,7; *21*.1,27; *27*.8,25
   prepositions, *48*.2,4,10,18
   presentative, *49*.10
   pronouns, *36*.2,8,11,32,37,59
   relative clause, *57*.3,6
   root morpheme, *28*.7,9,13; *43*.23;
      44.5
   toponymy, *67*.18
   word order, *50*.13,17
   writing, *2*.15
   see also: Kabyle, Numidic, Ta-
      chaouit, Tachelhit, Tamazight,
      Tarifit, Tuareg

Liḥyān, Liḥyānite, *4*.5; *7*.37; *9*.6;
   11.15; *14*.3; *17*.5; *19*.24; *27*.3,28;
   29.16; *31*.10; *33*.8,10,15; *36*.62;
   41.11; *43*.16; *44*.15; *48*.17;
   51.1,18; see also: North Arabian
linguistic expansion, *3*.5
liquids, *13*.6; *17*.1-9; *23*.3; *24*.2,9;
   27.13,19,27; *35*.4; *43*.4-5; *46*.4
lisping, *11*.15; *13*.10
literacy, its extent, *66*.1
Lithuanian, *65*.5
Littmann, E., preface
loan translation, *63*.12
loanwords, *2*.14,16; *7*.4; *10*.12; *11*.2-
   3; *14*.3; *16*.3; *21*.11; *29*.12,26,
   39,47-48,51; *31*.34; *32*.6,9,10;
   33.16; *35*.31; *41*.7,10; *43*.22-23;
   49.23; *58*.15; *61*.3; *63*.3,9-12;
   65.1-10; *66*.3-4
locative, *29*.20; *32*.2,18; *48*.2; *51*.9;
   63.5
logograms, Aramaic, *7*.21,26,30
   Sumerian, *5*.2; *9*.2; *50*.14
Logone (Chadic), *17*.6; *31*.12; *44*.5
loss of vowels, *21*.10,21; *24*.10; *26*.2
lt < št, *41*.32
Luba, *62*.2
Ludolf, H., *33*.12
Luwian, *14*.10; *17*.7; *65*.5
Lycian, *12*.4; *14*.10; *17*.7

m < b, *27*.8; *38*.23; *48*.5
m < n, *11*.7; *31*.12; *36*.1,5
m < w, *49*.1
Maʿān (Jordan), *13*.9; *18*.6
Macro-Sudanic, *2*.2,8
Macuch, R., preface
Madji (Cushitic), *2*.12
mafʿal pattern, *32*.8
Maghrib, *7*.46; *12*.3; *19*.17; *22*.11;
   38.24; *41*.44; *67*.9
maġhūra, *18*.2
"magic" bowls, *7*.29
Mahra tribe, *8*.7; *15*.5; see also:
   Mehri
Maʿin (Yemen), *8*.4,6
Malayo-Polynesian, *12*.4
Mali, *2*.14-15

Malta, Maltese, 7.46; *18.9*
Ma'lūla (Syria), *7.32; 18.6; 21.23;
    27.20; 33.7; 34.5; 45.10; 47.8;
    49.25*
Maman (Sudan), *2.9*
Mandaic, *7.26,28,34; 18.7; 21.21;
    36.34,39; 42.20; 45.12; 61.6*
Mandingo, *36.1*
Mansaʻ (Tigre), *8.12; 38.25-26; 39.12*
mappiq, *10.3*
Maqrizi, *2.7,9*
Mardin (Turkey), *7.33; 40.25*
Margi (Chadic), *41.17; 48.6*
Mari, *4.2; 5.2,3; 6.4; 13.3; 18.3;
    19.5; 21.12; 24.2; 25.5; 26.3;
    29.41,54; 30.6; 32.17; 35.6,20,
    23,34; 36.47,58; 38.12-14; 39.7,
    10; 40.18; 41.8; 50.22; 54.6*
Masoretes, *7.5; 9.11; 11.5; 16.5;
    19.15,21; 21.15-19; 22.6; 23.2,5;
    24.9; 25.1,3,8; 26.2; 27.10-11,19;
    29.5; 31.25; 39.14-15; 41.45; 45.9-
    11; 57.3,5; 63.2; 67.4*
    Babylonian tradition, *21.16-18;
        29.5; 40.22*
    Palestinian tradition, *21.16,18*
    Tiberian tradition, *7.5; 21.16,19;
        29.5*
Masqan (Gurage), *8.17; 36.14; 40.5;
    41.53*
Masʻūdī, *15.5*
matres lectionis, *7.28,42; 9.5-6,8-9;
    10.3; 21.14-15,20-22,24-26,28; 22.10,
    13,15; 24.10; 27.28; 30.4; 33.7;
    39.15; 43.13; 45.8,11*
Mauritania, *2.14; 13.9; 36.39; 41.44*
Mazigh, *2.14*
mb < b, *11.9*
mb < m, *10.12; 11.9; 29.5*
mb < nb, *27.6*
Mbugu (Cushitic), *2.13*
Mecca, *7.39,42; 36.39*
mediae geminatae, *43.4,10-11; 44.1,
    10-15*
Medina, *7.42*
Mediterranean, *2.14; 3.4; 7.6; 17.7;
    65.5; 67.19*
Medju, *2.9*

Megillat Taʻanit, *7.13*
Mehri, *8.7*
    adverbs, *47.8,18*
    article, *33.8-9,18*
    conditional clause, *61.2,6*
    conjugation, *38.2,5,8; 39.9,12; 40.2,
        10,13,17,27,30,32; 41.2,4,11,22,
        25,47,54-55*
    nominal clause, *50.7*
    numerals, *35.2-3,7,12,17,26,30*
    phonology, *13.11; 14.8; 15.4; 18.6-7;
        19.18; 21.29; 27.8*
    prepositions, *48.12*
    pronouns, *36.2,6-7,17-18,23,40,42,
        44,54*
Melchite liturgy, *7.25*
Memar Marqah, *7.24*
Meroitic, *2.8; 33.9*
Meṣad Ḥashavyahu ostracon, *54.8*
Mesopotamia, *1.2; 3.2-3; 4.2,4; 5.3;
    6.6; 7.11,28,44; 13.3; 29.54; 41.34;
    64.4; 65.2; 67.10*
metathesis, *2.16; 27.1,12-14; 30.11;
    63.4*
Middle East, *65.2,4*
Midrash, *7.23*
Migāma (Chadic), *2.16; 38.16*
mimation, *29.54; 31.3-5,10,27; 32.9;
    33.3,6,12-13,15-17; 35.4; 36.26,58;
    57.4*
Minaic, Minaeans, *7.37; 8.2,4; 13.10;
    19.12; 31.19,27; 35.3-4; 36.48,58-
    60; 39.9; 40.26; 41.9; 47.10; 48.11,
    17; 57.3*; see: South Arabian, Epi-
    graphic
Mishnah, *7.5*
Mishnaic Hebrew, *7.5,25; 9.5; 11.7;
    17.8; 19.15; 21.15; 23.9; 27.26,30;
    28.13; 29.13,39; 33.10; 36.18,33-
    34,47; 38.11; 41.2,10,26,38,45;
    42.1; 45.10; 49.25; 51.19; 57.6;
    63.11; 65.4-5,8*; see: Hebrew
Mlaḥsố (Turkey), *7.33*
Moabite, *4.5; 7.2,8; 9.5,11; 16.3;
    27.28; 29.49,54; 31.10; 33.8,16;
    35.4; 36.6,31,56; 38.11; 40.6;
    41.11,22; 43.14; 47.7,12; 52.10;
    56.4; 58.2*

Moča (Cushitic), *2.12*
Mohammed, *7.42*
monophonemization, *10.12*; *27.2*
monophthongization, see: contraction
Monophysites, *21.22*
monosyllabic verbal roots, *22.17*; *40.23*; *43.4-7,9-15*
mood, *37.4*; *38.2,14*; *39.1-19*
  apocopate, *38.14*; *39.14-18*
  direct cohortative, *39.8-9*
  energetic, *39.8-11*
  indicative, *28.16*; *38.14,18*; *39.2, 14,17*
  indirect cohortative, *39.6*
  jussive, *10.6*; *17.4*; *25.8*; *26.4*; *38.2, 6-7,12,15,22,26-28*; *39.5,9,12,15-18*; *40.30*; *54.6*
  optative / precative, *39.13*; *40.30*
  prohibitive / vetitive, *39.13*
  subjunctive, *39.2-6,12,17*
  ventive / allative, *39.3,6-7*
Morocco, *2.14*; *7.6*; *10.10*; *12.3*; *17.4*; *18.6-8*; *27.8*; *33.18*; *35.2*; *41.26,30*; *65.2*; *66.4*
morpheme,
  "bound", *28.15*
  "empty", *28.15,18*
  "free", *28.14*
  "full", *28.14,18*
  grammatical, *28.1,4,15*
  lexical, *28.1,4,14-15*
  root, *28.1-19*
Mosul, *7.19,34*
mp < m, *10.12*; *11.9*
Mubi (Chadic), *2.16*
Muher (Gurage), *8.17-18*; *11.8*; *33.14*; *40.6*; *41.18,36,53*; *49.1*; *51.25*; *56.7*; *57.9*; see: Gurage
Müller, Fr., *1.1*
Mycenaean Greek, *10.8*; *17.5*; *65.5-6*

n, ablative morpheme, *41.17*
  augmentative, *48.5-6,9*
  first radical, *41.17*; *43.5*; *44.4*
  its dissimilatory function, *23.7*; *43.4*
n < l, *17.3-4*; *21.13*; *27.11-13*; *29.13*; *36.33*
n < ll, *29.27*

n < m, *11.7*; *27.30*; *29.26*; *41.35*
n < r, *17.6*
ñ < n, *17.1*
Nabataean Arabic, *7.16,36,38,40*; *9.12*; *21.24*; *22.4*; *32.5*; *33.10*; *38.11*; *49.2*; *51.18*; *61.2,10*; *65.5*
Nabataean Aramaic, *7.16,38,40*; *11.4*; *17.4*; *21.24*; *27.24*; *29.16*; *35.16*; *41.20*; *42.14*; *49.2*; *63.9,14*
Nabataeans, *7.37,39*; *11.8*; *17.2*; *23.7-8*; *32.25*
Nabataean script, *7.42*; *9.10*; *14.3*
Nadjd (Saudi Arabia), *7.43*; *48.5*
Nadjrān, *7.42*
Namāra, an-, inscription, *7.38*; *9.12*
Naqāda culture, *3.4*
narrative "tense", *38.10-11*
nasalization, *17.8*; *21.31*; *26.2*; *27.8*; *35.3*
nasals, *10.4*; *11.1*; *17.1-9*; *23.1,3*; *27.27*
nb < bb, *41.42*
nd < dd, *10.12*
negative clause, *38.24*; *52.1*; *53.4*; *54.2-4,6,9*; *58.4*; *61.3-6*
negatives, *36.28*; *38.24*; *39.13*; *47.8-16*; *54.9*; *58.3-4*; *61.3-4,6*
Negev, *7.9,16*
Neo-Aramaic, *3.5*; *7.31-34*
  accusative, *52.10*
  adjectives, *34.5*
  article, *33.7*
  conditional clause, *61.3,6*
  conjugation, *38.2,22-24*; *40.15,25*; *41.10,16*; *42.1,4,18-23*; *43.10*; *45.10,12*; *46.4*
  conjunctions, *49.2,16*
  expression of possession, *49.25*
  final / consecutive clause, *59.5*
  genitival relation, *51.19*
  lexicography, *65.2*
  negatives, *47.8*
  noun gender, *30.5*; *31.14*
  noun number, *31.10-12,14*
  noun patterns, *29.6,8,11,13,25,30, 35-36,38-39,49,53,55*
  numerals, *35.2,6,17-20,25,28*
  phonology, *10.8,12*; *11.5,10*; *12.3*;

15.5,7; *17*.9; *18*.5-6; *11*.11,14,
   21; *21*.23; 22.8; *23*.1,5; 27.10,
   12,17,20
prepositions, *48*.6
pronouns, *36*.23,36,60-61
root morpheme, 28.8
script, *9*.10
states of nouns, *33*.7
substantival clause, *60*.3
syllable, *24*.9
temporal / causal clause, 58.15
word accent, 25.8
   see also: Aramaic, Maʿlūla
Neofiti I, 7.23
Neolithic, *3*.3-4
Nestorians, 7.27,34; *21*.22
Newman, P., 2.16; *39*.7; *41*.17
Newman, T.N., *1*.1
ng < nk, 27.7; *36*.35
nifʿal, 24.8; 27.19; *41*.15,19
New Testament, 27.26
Niger, 2.14-16
Niger-Congo language family, *3*.3;
   12.4; *40*.1; *62*.2
Nigeria, 2.16; *3*.3
Nile, 2.1-2,8,10; *3*.3-4; *8*.18
Nilotic languages, 2.2; *35*.1
Nippur, 7.29
Nisa, 7.21
nisba, 29.41; *31*.29,40; *67*.13
nm < lm, 48.9
nn < dn, 27.3
nn < ln, 27.3
nn < nh, 27.4
nn < rn, 29.16
nomen rectum, 28.18; *32*.5,14; *51*.8-
   26; *57*.1,3,8
nomen regens, 28.18; *32*.5,14; *48*.2;
   51.9-26; *57*.1,3
nominal clause, *33*.5; *54*.3
nominal compounds, 29.54; *66*.5
nominalization, *32*.7; *38*.22
nominal patterns, diphthongized
   CawC, 22.16; *29*.9
   CawCaC, 29.9
   CayC, 22.16; *29*.9
   CayCaC, 29.9
   CvCayC, 29.10

geminating:
   $C_1aC_2C_2\bar{a}C_3$, 29.11; *64*.4; *65*.2
   $C_1\partial C_2C_2\bar{a}C_3$, 29.11
   $C_1iC_2C_2\bar{u}C_3$, 29.11
   $C_1vC_2C_2vC_3$, 29.11
   $C_1vC_2C_2\bar{v}C_3$, 29.11
   infixed *-t-*, 29.32
   prefixed, 29.15-33
   ʼ-, 29.16; *34*.5
   ʿ-, 29.17
   ən-, 29.27
   ma- / mi- / mu-, *1*.2; *11*.7; *22*.4;
     28.15; 29.3,19-26; *35*.3,30,33;
     64.2-3
   n-, *11*.7; 29.26
   nä-, 29.27
   ša- / šu-, 29.33; *34*.6
   ta- / ti- / tu-, 29.28-31
   tā-...-ət, *65*.2
   wä-, 29.19,26,45
   reduplicated:
   $C_1vC_2C_1vC_2$, 29.13
   $C_1vC_2vC_2vC_3$, 29.14
   $C_1vC_2C_3vC_3$, 29.14
   simple:
   C$\bar{v}$, 28.6; *29*.4
   CvC, 28.7; *29*.4
   $C_1vC_2C_2$, 28.11; *29*.4
   $C_1vC_2C_3$, 28.12; *29*.5
   CvCvC, 29.6
   C$\bar{v}$CvC, 29.7
   CvC$\bar{v}$C, 29.8; *35*.33
   $C_1C_2\bar{v}C_3$, 28.10; *29*.8
   C$\bar{a}$CiC, 35.23,26,30,32
   CaCC, 35.26
   CiCC, 35.26
   CuCC, 35.30
   CuCuCāʼ, 35.33
   C$\bar{a}$C, 22.16
   C$\bar{\imath}$C, 22.16
   C$\bar{u}$C, 22.16
   suffixed, 29.34-54
   -ad, 35.31
   -akku, ikku, 29.12,51
   -an, 35.32
   -ān > -ōn > -ūn, 29.35-40; *31*.28;
     32.8; *35*.32
   -änä, 35.27

*-ānay, -ānī, 29.*36,41
*-äňňä, -äňňa, 29.*51-52
*-at, -it, -ut, 28.*17; *29.*42-43,46-49;
    *30.*3; *36.*20
*-āt > -ōt > -ūt, 29.*47-48
*-ā'um > -ūm, -ā'u, 29.*51
*-āwī, -āwi, -awi, 29.*44; *35.*27,29
*-ay, 29.*36,41-42,54
*-āy, 29.*42-43; *35.*27,29
*-ayim, -īm, -ām, 29.*54; *67.*16
*-ayin, -īn, -ān, 29.*54; *67.*16
*-čik, 29.*53
*-ənna, -ənnat, 29.*52
*-(ə)nnät, 29.*52
*-i, 29.*22
*-'id, -id̠, -'d̠, 35.*31
*-ik-, 29.*53
*-iko, 29.*53
*-išu, 35.*31
*-ít, 29.*49
*-ī'u(m) > -ū(m), 29.*51; *35.*29
*-iy > -ī, 29.*36,41,54; *35.*26-27,29
*-iyya, 29.*45
*-(iy)ān(u), 29.*30,36,39
*-le, 29.*53
*-när, 29.*50
*-o, 29.*50
*-ón, -ónet, 29.*38
*-ot, 29.*47
*-t, 35.*30
*-ūn, 29.*38
*-ya, 29.*19,45
nominative case, *29.*54; *31.*3-5,9-11;
    *32.*1-5,13,15,21-24,27; *33.*5; *36.*36,
    48; *53.*1; *54.*3; see also: agent
    case, ergative, instrumental, loca-
    tive
non-active case (*casus patiens*), *2.*14;
    *32.*1,7; *48.*2; *50.*8
North Africa, see: Africa, Maghrib
North Arabian, *4.*3,5; *7.*1,16,35-40,46
    article, *33.*8-10
    attribute, *51.*1
    case inflection, *32.*5,25
    conditional clause, *61.*2,10
    conjugation, *38.*11; *40.*3; *41.*11,
        25,44; *42.*14; *43.*6,16; *44.*5,15
    conjunctions, *49.*2

final / consecutive clause, *59.*4
    genitival relation, *51.*18
    lexicography, *65.*4-5; *66.*1-2
    noun number, *31.*3,10,13
    noun patterns, *29.*16,44
    one-term sentence, *50.*3
    parataxis, *55.*8
    phonology, *11.*15; *13.*9; *14.*3; *16.*7;
        *17.*4-5; *18.*6; *19.*17,24; *21.*24;
        *22.*4,7,15; *23.*3,7-8; *27.*3,23,25, 28
    prepositions, *48.*5,8-9,12,14,17
    pronouns, *36.*38,62
    proper names, *67.*6
    relative clause, *55.*8; *57.*3,6
    script, writing, *9.*6,12
    states of nouns, *33.*2,6,8-10,13,15,
        21
    word order, *50.*18
    see also: Liḥyān, Nabataean, Ara-
        bic, Ṣafaitic, Thamūdic
*nota accusativi, 52.*10
noun, *29-35*
    adjectives, *34.*1-6
    case inflection, *32.*1-27
    gender, *30.*1-11
    number, *31.*1-42
    numeral, *35.*1-33
    patterns, *29.*1-54
    states, *33.*1-24
Nubian, Old Nubian, *2.*2,8
numerals, *28.*10; *29.*54; *30.*1; *35.*1
    cardinals, *33.*8,18; *35.*2-22,32-33;
        *51.*6,8,14
    decimal system, *35.*18
    distributives, *35.*33
    fractionals, *35.*30
    multiplicatives, *35.*31-32
    ordinals, *35.*23-29,31-32
    quinary system, *35.*1,10
    verbal derivatives, *35.*34
    vigesimal system, *35.*18
Numidia, Numidic, *2.*15; *7.*6; *11.*5;
    *17.*7; *29.*26,46; *31.*12,28; *43.*11,
    23; *51.*23; *63.*13; *67.*9; see also:
    Libyco-Berber
nunation, *21.*26; *29.*54; *31.*3-4,10;
    *32.*28; *33.*3,12-13,15-17,21; *35.*4;
    *57.*4

nursery words, *29*.53; *62*.2
Nusayris, *22*.4

o < *a*, *21*.24,32
o < *aw*, *21*.30; *22*.12,17
o < *ō*, *22*.12; *43*.20
o < *ö* < *ä*, *40*.12
o < *u*, *21*.24,27
o < *wä*, *42*.11
ō < *a*, *21*.1
ō < *ā*, *7*.32-33; *21*.9,12-13,20,27; *24*.6; *25*.6; *27*.24,28; *29*.7-8,11,35-40,47; *42*.2,8,13; *67*.18
-*ō* < -*ahu*, *21*.27; *27*.25
ō < *aw*, *21*.9,13,24; *22*.1,6-7,10-12; *29*.13; *36*.20
ō < *aw* < *ab*, *11*.5; *22*.10; *29*.39
oath formula, *61*.4-5
object, *32*.1,5,27; *34*.3
oblique case, *31*.3-5,10-12,15; *32*.1, 22,27; *36*.36; *40*.7-9; see also: accusative, genitive, non-active case, "patient" case
Oboda bilingual, *7*.38; *9*.12; *38*.11
occlusive, see: plosive
Old Akkadian (East Semitic), preface; *2*.16; *3*.2; *4*.2,4-5; *6*.1-2
adjectives, *34*.4,6
adverbs, *47*.5,7-9,11,14,17
attribute, *51*.1
case inflection, *32*.3-6,9,11,13,17-19,21
concord of subject and predicate, *50*.21,25
conditional clause, *61*.2-3
conjugation, *37*.4,6; *38*.3-6,10,12, 16; *39*.2-4,6-7,14,16; *40*.2-3,6-7,10,13,15-20,31-34; *41*.2-3,6, 9,17-20,22,25,29,33,35,40,42-43,49,52; *42*.2-3,7,13-16; *43*.5, 7,22; *44*.2,4-5,10; *45*.2,5-7,11; *46*.2
conjunctions, *49*.1,6-7; *58*.2,4,9-11; *60*.1-2; *61*.2-3
copula, *49*.23
expression of possession, *49*.25
genitival relation, *51*.12-13,18,23
infinitive, *53*.2

lexicography, *35*.14; *63*.2-5,7-8; *65*.2,5
nominal clause, *50*.5
noun gender, *30*.3
noun number, *31*.2-3,10-12,25,38
noun patterns, *29*.12,21,26,29-30, 32-33,41,48,51
numerals, *35*.1,3-4,8,12-13,18,20-21,23-24,26,30-32
one-term sentence, *50*.4
phonology, *10*.9; *11*.12; *13*.2; *15*.6, 8; *16*.2,7; *19*.4-6; *21*.3-4,7; *22*.5, 14; *23*.7; *27*.3,10
prepositions, *48*.1,4-6,10,15,17-20
pronouns, *36*.3-6,8,15,17,23-30,33, 36,47-49,57-61
proper nouns, *50*.25; *67*.9
relative clause, *57*.6-7
root morpheme, *28*.3,6,18-19; *44*.5
states of nouns, *33*.5-6,15-17,19
substantival clause, *60*.1-2
syllable, *24*.2
temporal / causal clause, *58*.2,4,9-11
verbal clause, *50*.14-15,19
volitive clause, *54*.6-7
word accent, *25*.5
word order, *50*.14-15,19
writing, *9*.2-3
see also: East Semitic
old perfective, see: pseudo-participle
'Omān, *7*.41,46; *8*.6; *10*.1; *15*.7; *27*.13; *41*.44
Omdurman (Sudan), *2*.9
Omo river, *2*.12
Omotic (Cushitic), *2*.12-13; *15*.8; *17*.1; *30*.11; *36*.36
on-glide, *15*.7; *19*.24; *22*.18; *41*.13; *43*.7; *49*.22
onomatopoeia, *62*.2
opposition voiced-unvoiced, *10*.8; *36*.47
optative, *38*.2; *39*.13; *40*.18,23,30; *54*.7
Origen, *9*.13; *21*.20; *24*.9; *27*.19; *29*.5
Oromo (Cushitic), *2*.11; *8*.9,15,18; *10*.3,6; *17*.7; *22*.16; *27*.12; *29*.20, 46; *30*.11; *32*.1,4-7; *36*.1,3,6,10;

*41.*7,15,20,28; *48.*5,18; *49.*2,15; *63.*6

p < b, 27.6,8
Pahlavi, *7.*21,26,30; *63.*11
Paikuli, *63.*11
Pakistan, *7.*14
Palaeo-Hebrew script, *7.*24
Palaeosyrian, preface; *3.*2; *4.*4-5; *5.*2-3
  adverbs, *47.*2
  attribute, *51.*1
  case inflection, *32.*3-4,6,9,11,13,17-18
  concord of subject and predicate, *50.*25
  conditional clause, *61.*2
  conjugation, *35.*34; *38.*4-6,10,12; *39.*2-3,6; *40.*3,5,9-10,16,18,21, 31,33; *41.*9,16,22,25,29,33,43, 48-49; *42.*2,6,13-15; *43.*8,10,12; *44.*5,11,13; *45.*7
  conjunctions, *49.*1-2; *61.*2
  copula, *49.*23
  genitival relation, *51.*11
  infinitive, *53.*4
  lexicography, *35.*34; *65.*5
  noun gender, *30.*2
  noun number, *31.*2-3,19,21,25-28
  noun patterns, *29.*6-7,11,21-22,26, 28-30,33,37,41,48-49,51
  numerals, *35.*20-22,24,34
  phonology, *11.*6-7,9; *13.*2; *17.*1-2,5; *19.*4-6; *21.*6-7; *22.*3,13-14; *23.*7; *27.*3,9,17,19,28
  prepositions, *48.*1,4-6,9-10,14,17-18, 20
  presentative, *49.*6
  pronouns, *36.*2-5,15,17,20,22-23, 26,32,36,47,57-58,60
  proper names, *50.*25
  relative clause, *57.*5-6; *58.*10
  root morpheme, *28.*13
  states of nouns, *33.*3,5-6,13,16-17
  syllable, *24.*2
  temporal clause, *57.*5; *58.*10
  verbal clause, *50.*13-14
  word order, *50.*13-14

  writing, *5.*2; *50.*1
  see also: Ebla, North Semitic, Tell Beydar
palatals, *10.*4; *15.*1,6-7; *17.*1
palatalization, *8.*14; *12.*3; *14.*2-3,9; *15.*3,5-6,8; *17.*1; *18.*6; *27.*10; *29.*51; *31.*15; *35.*3; *36.*2,5,14,19, 39; *40.*4-5,14; *41.*39; *42.*13-14; *57.*9
palato-alveolar fricative, *10.*4; *13.*2; *15.*1-5; *24.*9
Palestine, *3.*3; *4.*4; *5.*4; *6.*3; *7.*1-2,5,22,32,44,46; *13.*9; *14.*1; *19.*17; *21.*12; *23.*7; *27.*20,26; *29.*47,54; *41.*11,24; *50.*21; *54.*4; *65.*4-5; *67.*16-17,19
Palestinian Syriac, *7.*25
Palmyra, Palmyrene Aramaic, *7.*17, 20; *9.*10; *13.*9; *27.*3; *29.*31; *47.*4; *63.*9; *65.*4
Palmyrene Arabic, *13.*9; *14.*3; *18.*6; *27.*28; *65.*5
Paracelsus, *66.*6
paragogic vowel, *32.*5,24; *33.*4
parataxis, *38.*12; *55.*1,3-8
  asyndetic, *55.*4-5,7
  syndetic, *38.*12; *55.*3-8
Parthian, *7.*19,21; *63.*11
participle, *29.*25,32; *30.*1; *31.*12,15; *32.*17; *38.*26; *42.*1,13-17; *51.*11-12
  B/G-stem, active, *29.*7,39; *38.*24; *42.*13,19
  B/G-stem, passive, *29.*8; *42.*14,20
  derived stems, *42.*15-17,22; *43.*8
  "participial" tenses, *42.*18-25
parts of speech, *28.*19
passive, *32.*2; *38.*16; *41.*43-47; *52.*2,4
past tense, *38.*28
  past continuous, *38.*20,25-26,28; *42.*19,21,24; *58.*5
  past perfect, *38.*28
pataḥ, "furtive", *10.*3
"patient" case (*casus patiens*), *32.*1,7; *50.*8; *52.*1; *54.*3; *63.*5; see also: accusative, non-active case
paucative, *31.*1,35-37
pausal forms, *24.*4; *26.*2,4; *29.*5; *39.*9
Pedro de Alcalá, *36.*14; *38.*5; *40.*25; *44.*5

pejoratives, *29*.43
Pella, *21*.12
perfect, *2*.11; *24*.9-10; *32*.4,15; *33*.5;
   38.3,10,18,26,28; *40*.3; *54*.7-9
perfective, *38*.3-4,9-10
Periplus of the Erythraean Sea, *8*.5,7
permansive, *38*.3,9
Persepolis, *7*.12
Persian, *6*.6; *7*.12,14,37,42; *11*.2;
   14.10; *27*.13,17; *42*.20; *50*.23;
   58.15; *61*.3; *63*.10-11; *65*.1,4-6
Persian Gulf region, *40*.10,25; *41*.19
personal names, *5*.3; *7*.35; *10*.1;
   15.3; *17*.2; *27*.20; *29*.32-33,35-
   36,41,53; *30*.8; *32*.3-5,8-12,17-
   18,21; *33*.13,16; *34*.5; *36*.49,58;
   38.6; *40*.3; *42*.14-15; *45*.8; *50*.14,
   25; *51*.7-8; *65*.4; *67*.1-7,9
personals, see: actor affixes
Petra, *7*.16
pharyngalization, *2*.15; *10*.9-10; *11*.3;
   12.3; *19*.2
pharyngal fricatives, *2*.8; *7*.33; *10*.4;
   19.1-23; *43*.3; *45*.2-3,7-10,12-14,
   16-17; *65*.2
Phoenician and Punic, preface, *2*.15;
   4.5; *7*.2-3,6
   accusative, *52*.10
   adjectives, *34*.2
   adverbs, *47*.7,9,11-12,14
   apposition, *51*.7
   article, *33*.10
   attribute, *51*.5,7
   concord of subject and predicate,
      50.24
   conditional clause, *61*.2,8
   conjugation, *38*.11; *39*.9; *40*.4,6;
      41.13,22-23,25,30; *42*.6,12-15,
      17; *43*.14; *45*.11,13; *46*.3
   conjunctions, *49*.2,4; *58*.2-3,14;
      61.2,8
   genitival relation, *51*.17,19
   gerund, *42*.12; *53*.5
   infinitive, *53*.5
   lexicography, *62*.4; *63*.2,5,7; *64*.2;
      65.5-6,8
   noun gender, *30*.3
   noun number, *31*.4,8,10-12,14,19,28

   noun patterns, *29*.7,11,13,21,26,30,
      35-37,46-49
   numerals, *35*.4,6,15-16,18-20,27, 29-
      30,32
   phonology, *11*.5; *13*.2,7,10; *14*.2;
      15.3; *16*.2-3,7; *17*.4,7,9; *19*.3,
      12-13,16; *21*.9,13-14; *22*.6,13;
      27.3,12,17,19-20,23-24,26-28
   "plural of majesty", *50*.24
   prepositions, *48*.5,12,15-18,21,24
   presentatives, *49*.9
   pronouns, *36*.3,6,18,28,31,33,35-36,
      38,47,51,60-61
   proper names, *67*.7,9,18
   relative clause, *57*.6
   root morpheme, *28*.8
   script, *9*.4-5,8,10
   states of nouns, *33*.3,8-10,16,22-23
   syllable, *24*.6,10
   temporal / causal clause, *58*.2-4,14
   word accent, *25*.6
   see also: Punic
phoneme, *10*.7,11-12
phonemic changes, *10*.12-13; *27*.2
phonemics, *10*.2
phonemic shift, *10*.12
phonemic word stress, *25*.8
phonetic zero < ', *13*.12; *19*.9,15-
   18,20
phonetic zero < ', *19*.15-16,18,20
phonetic zero < *h*, *19*.15-16,18,20
phonetic zero < *ḥ*, *19*.15-16,20
phonetic zero < *k/q*, *18*.8
phonetic zero < *l*, *21*.6
phonetics, *10*.2
phonology, *9*.3; *10*.1-27.30
pitch, *26*.1-5
place, nouns of, *29*.21,24,31
place names, *10*.1; *29*.31,44,47,54;
   32.8-10; *33*.9; *51*.7-8; *67*.1,8-17
   their gender, *30*.6
Plautus, *9*.13; *19*.12; *21*.13; *36*.35;
   41.25; *61*.8
Pliny, *11*.1
plosives, *10*.4,8; *23*.1,4
pluperfect, *38*.20,28; *42*.18
plural, *31*.1-2,6-7,9-34; *32*.8,22-23;
   33.3; *34*.2-3

broken / internal, *11*.9; *19*.17; *29*.6,8,10,16,35,40; *31*.1,9,23-37; *34*.2; *50*.23; *51*.3
by reduplication, *31*.9,21-22
double, *31*.9
external, *29*.40,47-48; *31*.1,9-20
plural endings / morphemes
  -ač, äč, *31*.15,17; *32*.28
  -ām, *31*.12,37
  -an, *31*.12
  -ān, *31*.9,12,14-15
  -ān + (y)āt, *31*.10
  -at, -āt, -ōt, *31*.9-10,12-15,17-18,20, 25,33,37,39; *32*.28
  -atāt, -otāt, *31*.20
  -čä, -əččä, *31*.17
  -h, *31*.9,19
  -ht, *31*.19
  -ī, -ē, *31*.10-12,14,25
  -īm, *28*.16
  -īn, *31*.12,14
  -očč, *29*.54; *31*.15,17,22; *32*.28
  -ōtən, *31*.12
  -t-, *31*.15,18,22
  -tat, *31*.15,20
  -ū, *28*.15
  -ūt, *31*.16,25; *34*.4
  -yāt(i), *36*.10
plurale maiestatis, *31*.34; *34*.2; *50*.24
Polish, *62*.2; *65*.5
Polynesian, *14*.10
polysemy, *48*.3; *62*.4
possession, expression of, *49*.25
post-palatal *ñ*, *17*.1
postpositions, *2*.8; *32*.1,7,17; *48*.1; *49*.17
  -ah, *32*.20
  -be, *48*.1
  -iš, *32*.17,19; *47*.5; *48*.1,10; *53*.2
  -(i)tti, *48*.18
  -le, *48*.1; *51*.25
  -uš, *32*.17
postpositive auxiliary vowel, *27*.16
precative, *38*.2; *39*.13; *40*.18,23,30; *54*.7
predicative, predicate state, *32*.1-4,7,11,15; *33*.5-7,14; *38*.10; *49*.18; *50*.6; see also: accusative, non-active case, "patient" case

prefix-conjugation, *2*.11; *7*.32; *17*.4; *36*.21; *39*.14-19; *40*.16-36; see also: stems
pre-glottalized emphatics, *10*.9
prepositions, *1*.2; *11*.15; *32*.14,17-18; *33*.9-10; *35*.31; *46*.4,6; *48*.1-25; *49*.9,12; *51*.26; *58*.1-11,14; *59*.2-4
compound, *48*.24-25
with pronominal suffix, *48*.23
prepositional phrase, *32*.18-19; *36*.28; *52*.3-4,6-7,11; *57*.9; *63*.14; *64*.1
Pre-Sargonic period, *5*.2; *6*.2; *36*.58
Pre-Semitic, *3*.3; *67*.15
present
  general present, *38*.24-26
  present continuous, *38*.22-26; *42*.19, 21
  present perfect, *38*.26
presentatives, *27*.25; *49*.5-12; *50*.4
present-future, *38*.3,5-6,13,25
Pre-Sumerian, *3*.3; *5*.2; *6*.1; *9*.3; *10*.6; *11*.12
preterite, *10*.6; *25*.8; *38*.1-2,10-13
Prichard, J.C., *1*.1
primitive languages, *21*.1
proclitics
  at- / ad-, *39*.13
  ay-, *38*.2; *39*.13
  lu- / li- / la-, *38*.2; *39*.8,13; *40*.23, 30
professions, names of, *29*.11,29,44, 52; *64*.4
prohibitive, *38*.2; *39*.13; *54*.6,9
pronominal affixes, *27*.25; *28*.13; *30*.6; *32*.2; *33*.7,9,11,14; *34*.3; *36*.5-6,16-27,33,35; *41*.12-13; *62*.2
proleptic suffix, *33*.7; *51*.20
pronouns, *30*.1,6; *36*.1-62; *40*.1,16; *55*.2
  demonstrative, *36*.32-45,47,51
  determinative-relative, *32*.14; *35*.28; *36*.37,42,46-56,62; *49*.16; *51*.18-21; *57*.2,6; *58*.1,14; *60*.3; *62*.2
  indefinite, *36*.56,61; *57*.2,6; *60*.2
  independent personal, *14*.10; *28*.13; *36*.2-15,36,47; *40*.5; *41*.12; *49*.18; *50*.9
  independent possessive, *36*.29-31
  interrogative, *36*.56-60,62; *47*.7,15; *54*.5; *57*.6; *60*.2

oblique case, *36*.3-5,14-15,36,38,48
reflexive, *36*.28
"relative", *57*.5
subject case, *36*.2,5-13,36,48
suffixed personal, *33*.13; *36*.5-6,16-
   27,33,35; *40*.5; *41*.12-13; *46*.1-
   6; *57*.8
prosthetic vowel, *17*.9; *19*.24; *21*.26;
   24.8-10; *27*.16-18; *28*.8; *29*.15-17;
   35.7; *36*.5; *41*.11,14,19; *43*.5;
   49.20; *63*.4
Proto-Euphratic, *65*.2; *67*.15
Proto-Sinaitic, *7*.3; *13*.7
Proto-Sumerians, *4*.2
pseudo-hieroglyphic script of Byblos,
   7.3
pseudo-participle, *2*.1; *33*.5; *38*.3;
   41.2
pseudo-passive, *2*.14; *41*.20
punctuation marks, *9*.11; *10*.6
Punic, Neo-Punic, *2*.15; *3*.5; *7*.6; *9*.8;
   11.5; *14*.2; *15*.3; *19*.12,16; *21*.9,
   13-14; *22*.6; *24*.10; *27*.17,24,27-
   28; *29*.21,26,47; *31*.8,12,28; *33*.9-
   10; *35*.6,16,19,27; *36*.18,28,31,33,
   35,61; *40*.6; *42*.14-15; *45*.11,13;
   47.12; *49*.4; *51*.5,7; *52*.10; *57*.6;
   58.2-3,14; *61*.8; *62*.4; *63*.2,5;
   64.2,5; *65*.8; *67*.9,18; see: Phoenician and Punic
purussā', *29*.51
Pyramid texts, *2*.2; *36*.14

q < kq, *27*.3
q < ś, *16*.7
Qabenna (Cushitic), *2*.11
Qarnāwu, *8*.4
Qaryat al-Fāw (Saudi Arabia), *7*.42;
   8.4; *9*.6
Qatabān, Qatabanic, *8*.2-3,5-6; *13*.2;
   31.19; *33*.13; *35*.3-4; *36*.3,36,
   38,48; *38*.22; *39*.9; *40*.7,26;
   41.9; *57*.4; *61*.2; see: South
   Arabian, Epigraphic
Qaṭar, *7*.46
Qaṭara, *13*.3
Qaynu, *7*.16
Qedar, *7*.16

qəltu-dialects, *38*.3
Qemant (Agaw), *2*.10; *29*.20; *30*.11;
   36.14,16; *39*.8; *49*.22; *67*.9
qq < lq, *27*.3
qṭ < qt, *27*.7
quadriconsonantal verbs, *41*.39,42
qualitative, *2*.2
questions, *10*.6; *54*.5
Qumrān, *7*.13; *22*.6; *36*.24; *38*.12;
   45.10
Qur'ān, *7*.39,42-44; *13*.9; *21*.15,25-
   26; *22*.7,15; *25*.4; *26*.2; *27*.20,28;
   29.37; *40*.24; *41*.43; *43*.12; *44*.13;
   50.21; *52*.11; *54*.3; *59*.1; *60*.2;
   61.2
Qwara dialects (Agaw), *2*.10; *29*.20;
   30.11; *36*.5,14,16; *39*.8; *49*.22;
   67.9

r, influence of, *27*.8; *29*.17; *42*.3
   its dissimilatory function, *23*.9;
      41.38,39,42; *43*.4
   non-gemination, *17*.1; *19*.21; *45*.9
r < l, *15*.8; *17*.3,5; *35*.8; *63*.9
r < n, *17*.6; *35*.4,25; *36*.58; *61*.2
Rabbath-Ammon, *7*.7
Ras Ibn Hani, *5*.4
Ras Shamra, *5*.4
rb < bb, *23*.9
rd < dd, *23*.9
Red Sea, *2*.8-9; *3*.4
reduplicated stems, *29*.13-14; *31*.21-
   22; *36*.28; *41*.36-40
   partial reduplication, *29*.14; *31*.22;
      41.36-40
   total reduplication, *29*.13; *31*.21;
      36.28
relative pronoun, *36*.46-56,62; *49*.14;
   57.1-2
Rendille (Cushitic), *2*.11; *10*.3,6;
   11.9; *17*.2; *19*.23; *30*.10; *36*.2;
   38.1,15; *41*.15,20,28; *62*.2; *63*.3
replacive vowel, *41*.3; *44*.5
results of actions, *29*.11
resumptive pronoun, *50*.8,15; *51*.7,
   25; *52*.10; *57*.8
Rifan, *2*.14; *30*.10; see: Tarifit
Ripoll Ms., *29*.5

Ristāq (ʿOmān), *41*.44
rolled consonant, *23*.1; see also: liquids
Roman period, *2*.6-7,9,14-15; *43*.23; *45*.9; *50*.25; *65*.4
Romance languages, *1*.2; *3*.1; *30*.1; *64*.5; *67*.15
Rome, *65*.4
root, *28*.1-19; *29*.1,3
   biconsonantal, *28*.2-3,13; *29*.4
   monoconsonantal, *28*.5-6; *29*.4
   monosyllabic, *28*.4-12; *29*.4-5
   triconsonantal, *28*.2-3,9,13; *29*.5-8
rounded phonemes, *11*.11; *41*.5
rr < *lr*, 27.20
rs < *ss*, *10*.12; *23*.9
Rudolf, Lake, *2*.11
Russia, Russian, *7*.5,34; *14*.1; *27*.17
Rwāla bedouin dialect, *7*.46; *41*.25

š / *s*, first radical, *41*.10
   third radical, *41*.7
s < *ḫ*, *35*.10
s < *ṣ*, *14*.6
s < *ś*, *16*.3-6; *35*.15
s < *š*, *14*.3-5,9-10; *15*.2-3; *35*.12; *41*.9,14
s < *ṯ*, *13*.12; *35*.13
s³ < *ṯ*, *13*.10
s < *z*, *14*.2,6
ṣ < *ś*, *16*.7
ṣ < *ṯ̣*, *13*.10,12
ś < *ṣ́*, *16*.9
š < *ç* < *ś*, *14*.4; *16*.5
š < *k*, *15*.5; *18*.6; *36*.19
š < *q*, *15*.5
š < *s*, *14*.2-5,9
s¹ < *s³*, *14*.3
š < *ṣ*, *14*.8
š < *ś*, *13*.2-4; *16*.2-3,9; *35*.15
š < *št*, *41*.29,32
š < *ṯ*, *10*.8; *13*.3-4,6; *27*.13; *36*.47
Saadia Gaon, *63*.6
Saba, Sabaic, *8*.2-3,6; *11*.13; *13*.10; *14*.3; *16*.4; *17*.2,5; *19*.18,23; *27*.3, 12; *29*.9-10,17; *30*.5; *31*.19,21; *33*.3,13; *35*.2,4,10,30-31; *36*.2-3,17,28,33-34,36,38,48,54,62; *39*.9,13; *40*.2,5,7,10,13-14,17,

26,32; *41*.9,11,23,29; *43*.7,19; *44*.5,15; *45*.16; *47*.10,16; *48*.9, 17,20,24; *49*.2,14-16,21; *51*.18; *53*.1-3,5; *54*.9; 56.2; *57*.4-6; *58*.7,12; *59*.1; *61*.2-3,9; *63*.4; *64*.4; *65*.5-6; see: South Arabian, Epigraphic
šadda, *10*.3; *23*.4
Ṣafā, *7*.40; *29*.44
Ṣafaitic, *4*.5; *7*.40; *19*.17; *21*.24; *22*.4,15; *23*.3,7; *27*.3,25,28; *29*.44; *31*.3,13; *33*.2,6,8-9; *41*.11,25,44; *43*.16; *44*.5; *48*.12; *50*.18; *55*.8; *57*.3,6; *59*.4; *65*.5; *66*.1-2; *67*.6; see: North Arabian
šafʿel, *29*.33
Sahara, *2*.14; *3*.3
Saho-Afar (Cushitic), *2*.13; *8*.9; *30*.10-11; *31*.24
Salālah (ʿOmān), *8*.6
Ṣalṭ, eṣ- (Jordan), *14*.6
"Sam" languages (Cushitic), *2*.11; *10*.6; *27*.12; *30*.7; *35*.3-4; *37*.1; *38*.15; *39*.7; *63*.6
Samalian, *7*.11; *31*.10-11; *36*.6; *48*.2; *50*.13; *54*.6; *61*.9; *64*.2; see: Aramaic
Samaria, *7*.12; *22*.6
Samaritan Aramaic, *7*.24; *19*.14; *21*.21, 23; *25*.3; *29*.11; *31*.28; *36*.28; *45*.9; see: Aramaic
Samaritan Hebrew, *7*.5; *16*.5; *19*.15, 21; *25*.3; *45*.9; *57*.3; see: Hebrew
Samaritans, *7*.24; *11*.10; *21*.16,18
Samhar (ʿOmān), *8*.6
Samoan, *12*.4
Ṣanʿa (Yemen), *36*.39; *38*.22
sandhi, *27*.20
Sanskrit, *27*.20; *30*.1; *65*.6
Sappho, *65*.6
Sarda (Eritrea) code, *8*.13
Sargon of Agade, Sargonic, *6*.1; *40*.19
Sassanid, *7*.21
Saudi Arabia, *7*.41; *13*.9; *18*.6; *32*.25; *41*.11
Šäwa (Ethiopia), *48*.11
Schloezer, A.L., *1*.1
Schön, J.F., *1*.1

Sheikh el-Faḍl (Egypt), 7.13
scribal conservatism, 10.1
Scroll of Antiochus, 7.13
Segert, S., preface
segolate noun, 25.6; 27.19; 29.5; 30.3; 31.28
Seleucid period, 6.6; 21.3
Selṭi, (Gurage), 8.17; 11.3; 40.28,30; see: Gurage
Sem, Semites, 1.1; 3.3
semantic fields,
    action, 29.30
    animals, 17.1; 27.16; 29.16-18,28; 30.5,8,10; 31.38; 63.13; 67.3
    army, 65.3-4
    divinities, 32.6,8,10; 33.16
    body, 29.4,16; 30.6; 31.2,6
    colours, 29.14,16
    extension, 29.23
    government, 65.3-4
    kinship, 29.4; 62.4
    law, 64.6; 65.3-4
    metals, 30.6
    meteorological phenomena, 30.6
    months, 30.6; 32.8,10
    numerals, 29.4
    places, 29.21,24,31
    plants, 29.18; 65.6; 67.3
    professions, 29.11,29,35,39,52; 64.4; 65.2
    religion, 65.3
    rivers, 30.6
    stars, 30.6
    time, 29.23
    tools, 29.11,19-20,22-24
    weapons, 30.6
semantics, preface; 62.1-67.19
Semitic, passim
    classification, 4.1-6
    homeland, 32.5
    North Semitic, 4.5; 5.1-4; 7.1; 9.2; 16.2,7; 21.3-4,12; 22.5; 27.3, 10,16; 29.2,32; 31.10,26; 32.22; 33.5-7; 35.1,12,23; 36.5,36,47, 57; 38.6,10; 39.10; 40.6,20-21, 31; 41.26,48; 44.11; 46.2; 48.4, 7; 49.23; 51.23; 63.5,8; see: Amorite, Palaeosyrian, Ugaritic

Northwest Semitic, 4.1,3
Proto-Semitic, 3.1-3; 10.8,11-12; 11.1; 12.1; 13.1-2,4; 14.1,10; 16.11; 19.2; 21.9-10,18,26; 25.1,8; 28.4; 30.11; 31.10,24; 32.18; 35.1-2,7,26; 36.2-3,7-10,17,21-24,30,32; 38.17; 40.2,5-13,17,31-32,56; 42.13,15; 43.5; 44.2; 50.6; 61.2; 63.2-3
South Semitic, see: Ethiopic, South Arabian, Epigraphic and Modern, South Semitic
Southwest Semitic, 4.1,3
West Semitic, see: Ammonite, Arabic, Aramaic, Edomite, Hebrew, Phoenician and Punic, West Semitic
semivowels, 11.1,11; 15.1,6-7; 24.11
sentence,
    classes, 50.2
    nominal, 33.5; 50.6-10
    one-term, 50.2-4
    pitch, stress, 26.1-5
    two-term, 50.2,5
    verbal, 50.11-20
Sephardi Hebrew, 12.2
Septuagint, 11.10; 17.1
sequence of tenses, 55.3-4
    iprus-iptaras, 55.3
    qatal-wayyiqtol, 55.4
serṭō, 7.27
šǝwa, 10.3; 24.9
sex gender, 10.6; 30.1-8
Shabwa, 8.6
Shammar bedouin dialect, 7.46; 41.25
Ŝḥeri, 8.7; 11.10; 14.4,8; 15.4-5; 18.6; 19.19; 21.29; 27.8; 33.8-9; 35.3; 36.38-39,42; 38.8; 39.9; 40.8,27; 41.17,47; 47.18; 48.12; 51.20; 61.2; see: South Arabian, Modern
shibbolet, 13.7
Shilluk (Nilotic), 2.2
Shleuh, 2.14; see: Tachelhit
shortening of consonants, 24.5
shortening of vowels, 24.4
Sibawayh, 10.1; 14.3-4; 16.5; 18.2; 27.20,22; 40.16,24; 65.1

sibilants, *13*.10; *14*.1; *27*.14; see: dental fricatives, interdentals, palato-alveolar

Siciliote, *67*.15

Sicily, *7*.46

Sidamo, *2*.11,13; *8*.9; *35*.18; *50*.15

Sidon, *7*.6

Sinai, *7*.3

singulative, *29*.49; *31*.1,39-42

Siwa Oasis, *2*.14

Slavic languages, *1*.2; *7*.5; *30*.1; *35*.10; *41*.9; *50*.12; *65*.5

Soddo (Gurage), *8*.17-18; *11*.6; *18*.6; *30*.2; *31*.17; *35*.18; *36*.3; *40*.3-4,10-12,15,28; *41*.5,14,18,25,36,53; *42*.4,11,14,16; *48*.19; *49*.19; see: Gurage

Soden, W. von, preface

Somali, Somalia, *2*.11,13; *8*.9; *11*.9; *19*.23; *28*.19; *30*.10-11; *31*.22; *35*.20,31; *41*.13; *57*.3

Songhai, *2*.14

Soqoṭra, Soqoṭri *8*.5,7; *10*.1; *13*.11; *14*.8; *15*.4; *18*.6; *19*.19; *21*.29; *25*.7; *33*.8; *35*.3,12,18; *36*.6,40,44; *38*.2,8; *40*.27,30; *41*.47; *47*.18; *48*.12,16; *51*.20; *63*.3; *65*.4; see: South Arabian, Modern

Sotho (Bantu), *1*.2; *39*.7

South Arabian, Epigraphic, preface; *4*.1-2,5; *7*.37-38; *8*.1-7,9-10

  adjectives, *34*.5

  adverbs, *47*.8,10,16-18

  case inflection, *7*.38; *32*.24-25,28

  concord of subject and predicate, *50*.21

  conditional clause, *61*.2-3,9

  conjugation, *38*.5,8,11,22; *39*.9,13; *40*.2,5,7,10-11,13-14,17,26,32; *41*.3,9,11,16,23,29,42-43; *42*.6,14; *43*.7,16,19; *44*.5,15; *45*.16

  conjunctions, *49*.2,14-16

  final/consecutive clause, *59*.1

  genitival relation, *51*.18-19

  infinitive, *53*.1-3,5

  lexicography, *49*.21; *63*.4,8; *64*.2,4; *65*.5-6

negative clause, *54*.9

noun number, *29*.16; *31*.11,19,21, 24,26-27,29,31-32

noun patterns, *29*.3,9-10,16-17,20-21,30,36,40

numerals, *35*.2-4,8,10,15-21,24,26, 29-31

phonology, *11*.1,6,13; *13*.1-2,5,10; *14*.3; *16*.2,4,6-7; *17*.2,5; *18*.5; *19*.3,12,18,23; *20*; *21*.28,30; *22*.11, 15; *27*.3,8,12,29

prepositions, *48*.5,9,11-13,15-17, 19-21,24

pronouns, *36*.2-3,14,17,28,33-34,36, 38,48,54,58-60,62

relative clause, *54*.9; *57*.3-6

script, *7*.36,41-42; *9*.4,6-7,10-11; *32*.25; *50*.1

states of nouns, *33*.3,10,12-13, 15,17

temporal/causal clause, *58*.2,7,12

volitive clause, *38*.22; *54*.9

see also: Ḥaḍramitic, Minaic, Qatabanic, Sabaic

South Arabian, Modern, *4*.1-2,5; *8*.2,7

  accusative, *52*.10

  adverbs, *47*.8,10,18

  article, *33*.3,8-9,12,18

  case inflection, *32*.25

  conditional clause, *61*.2,6

  conjugation, *38*.2,5,8; *39*.8-9,12; *40*.2,5,7-13,16-17,27,30,32; *41*.1-4,6,9,11-12,17,22,25,27,29, 32,43,47,54-55; *45*.16

  genitival relation, *51*.20

  lexicography, *63*.3; *65*.4

  nominal clause, *50*.7-8

  noun number, *29*.16; *31*.2,4,6,12,30

  noun patterns, *29*.16

  numerals, *35*.2-4,7-8,12,16-18,24-26,30

  phonology, *9*.10; *10*.1,9-10; *11*.1, 5,10; *12*.2; *13*.11; *14*.4,8; *15*.4-5; *16*.2,7; *18*.5-7; *19*.18-19; *21*.29; *27*.8

  prepositions, *48*.11-12,16-17,21

  pronouns, *36*.2,6-8,10,17-20,22-23, 38-40,42,44,54

word accent, *25.7*
see also: Ḥarsūsi, Mehri, Šḥeri, Soqoṭri, South Semitic
South Semitic, *4.1,3,5; 8.1-18; 9.4; 11.1; 18.5; 29.41; 33.6-7,17; 36.5, 33,36-38,42,47,57; 38.18; 40.3,5-6,10; 41.2-3,6,22,52; 43.9; 44.5-6; 48.4,12,20;* see also: Ethiopic, South Arabian, Epigraphic and Modern
Spain, Spanish, *7.6,46; 8.2; 11.10; 16.8; 38.5; 65.6,8-9; 66.4; 67.13, 17*
speech levels, *65.10; 66.1*
speech sounds, analysis, *10.2*
spirantization, *2.15; 10.3; 11.1,8,10; 13.7; 18.5; 23.6; 27.10-11,20; 35.4; 36.19,41; 40.5-6; 63.13*
split protasis, *61.7,9*
ss < dš, 9.3
ss < lt, 27.5; 41.32
ss < sf, 27.4
ss < ts, 41.32
ṣṣ < nṣ, 27.3
ṣṣ < ṣf, 27.4
ṣṣ < ṣt, 27.4
šš < lš, 27.3
šš < śś, 41.32
šš < tš, 27.3
st < zt, 27.6
ṣt < ṣt, 27.7; 41.32
standard language, *4.3; 6.4; 7.13-14; 62.3*
states of nouns, *33.1-24*
stative, *28.12; 30.3; 32.4; 33.5; 38.3,9-10; 40.3; 50.5; 54.7,9*
stem vowel, *44.3*
stems of verbs, see: verb-stems
stops, *10.4*
St. Petersburg Codex, *21.19*
strees, *10.2; 24.4,6,10; 25.1-8; 26.1-5; 38.2; 40.23*
subject, *32.1,3-5,22-24,27; 40.7-8; 50.12*
subjoining (genitival) relation, *51.9-26*
subjunctive, *38.2,12-14,27; 57.3,5*
substratum, *3.5; 21.27; 25.5; 40.25; 50.14-15; 51.2,25; 56.7; 57.9; 65.1-2; 67.8*

Sudan, *2.2,8-9; 7.46; 18.8*
sukūn, 10.3
Sukur (Chadic), *63.5*
Sulayyil (Saudi Arabia), *7.42*
Šumaliya, *27.13*
Sumerian, *3.5; 4.2; 5.2; 6.1; 9.3; 10.6,8; 11.12; 24.2; 27.16; 28.3; 29.9,12,39,51; 30.9-10; 31.21; 32.6,9-10; 33.16; 48.10; 50.14-15; 63.5; 65.2; 67.19*
Sumerogram, see logogram
Surt (Libya), *7.6*
Susa, *6.4*
Swahili (Bantu), *1.2; 2.11; 41.14*
syllabic signs, *2.4*
syllable, *22.4,8; 24.1-11; 25.1-8; 26.2-3; 27.9,15-17; 28.4*
syntactic reduction, *55.2*
syntax, preface; *50-61*
Syria, *1.2; 3.2-3; 4.2,4; 5.2-3; 6.3; 7.1-2,11,40,44,46; 11.15; 13.9; 14.6; 17.4; 22.4; 29.54; 41.34; 47.15; 54.4; 63.10-11; 64.3-4; 65.4-5,8; 67.10,17,19*
Syriac, preface; *4.3; 7.1,20,26-27,34*
adverbs, *47.4,7*
attribute, *51.1*
case inflection, *32.18*
conditional clause, *61.3,6,9*
conjugation, *38.20; 40.23,25,35; 41.2-3,5,9-10,24-25,29-30,40,54-55; 42.4,9; 43.6,10,15; 45.10-11*
lexicography, *62.3; 63.4,9-10; 64.4; 65.4*
Modern Syriac, *7.34;* see: Neo-Aramaic
nominal clause, *50.9*
noun gender, *30.11*
noun number, *31.21*
noun patterns, *29.6,11,14,30,38*
numerals, *35.6,17,20*
phonology, *10.8; 11.5-6,10; 16.4; 17.2; 18.5,8; 19.11,14,17,23; 21.15-16,21-23,26; 22.7-8,10,17; 27.3,11,15*
pronouns, *36.28,33-34,36,59-60*
proper names, *67.3*
syllable, *24.9*

temporal clause, 58.14
word accent, 25.3
writing, 7.27; 9.9-10,13; 10.3
see also: Aramaic

t < *d*, 10.8; 27.11
t < *ṭ*, 13.8,11; 27.13
ṭ < *d*, 27.8
ṭ < *ḏ*, 13.11
ṭ < *ṣ*, 14.7
ṭ < *ṯ*, 13.6,8,12
ṭ < *ḏ*, 13.9
ṭ < *t*, 13.11
ṭ, indicated by "s", 13.8
ṯ < *š*, 16.7
Taanach letters, 41.43
Tabūk (Saudi Arabia), 13.9; 18.6
Tachaouit, 2.14-15
Tachelhit, 2.14-15; 17.5; 29.33; 30.11;
  32.4,7; 35.2,18,21,31; 38.17; 41.7;
  50.13; 63.5-6; 65.8
tafḫīm, 10.9; 21.27
Taʿizz, 47.16
Talḥayum, 29.54
Talmud, 7.23,29; 11.8
Tamazight, 2.14-15; 15.8; 30.11;
  35.21; 36.37; 41.7-8,38; 43.3,11,
  23; 48.10; 51.23; 54.2,4; 61.5;
  63.3,5; 65.8
Tamīm dialect, 22.7; 27.20
-*tan*(*a*)-infix, 41.20
Tana, Lake, 2.10
Tana river (Kenya), 2.11
tanwīn, 21.26
Tanzania, 2.13
Targum, 7.13,23,24; 17.1; 21.22
Tarifit, 2.14-15; 15.8; 17.5; 30.10;
  32.1,3-4,6; 33.5; 39.13; 41.7,15,
  20; 43.3; 44.5; 49.22; 50.13,17;
  63.5-6,13; 65.8
Taymaʾ (Saudi Arabia), 7.16,39,42
Ṭayyiʾ, 11.6
Tell Abū Ṣalābīkh (Iraq), 4.2
Tell ar-Rimaḥ, 13.3
Tell Beydar, 4.2; 5.2; 27.28; 36.47;
  48.10,15,17-18; 50.14
Tell el-Maskhūta, 7.16
Tell el-Qāḍi (Tel Dan), 7.11

Tell Fekherye, 7.11; 9.10-11; 13.8;
  22.8-9; 27.25; 31.26-27; 36.52
Tell Ḥalaf, 7.11
Tell Mardikh, 5.2; see also: Ebla
Ṭembaro (Cushitic), 2.11
tense consonants, 10.4; 23.1
terminative-adverbial, 32.17
Thadj, 9.12
Thamūd(ic), 4.5; 7.39; 21.24; 27.3,
  28; 31.3; 33.8-10; 36.38; 41.11;
  43.6,16; 48.9; 50.3; see: North
  Arabian
tematic vowel, 38.3
Tiberias, 7.5; 21.16,19; 29.5
Tiberian vowel signs, 10.3
tifīnaǧ, 2.15
Tigray, 8.13
Tigre, 8.8-9,12
  adverbs, 47.11
  apposition, 51.8
  article, 33.11
  attribute, 51.1
  concord of subject and predicate,
    50.23
  conjugation, 38.7,25-26; 39.12;
    40.10-11,29-30; 41.2-4,11,14,17,
    20,25,27,32,36,54-55; 42.3-5,11,
    13-16,25; 43.6-7,20
  conjunctions, 49.1,4,9; 58.2; 59.6;
    60.1
  copula, 49.18-19,24
  expression of possession, 49.25
  final/consecutive clause, 59.6
  infinitive, 53.3
  lexicography, 63.4; 66.5
  nominal clause, 50.9
  noun gender, 30.5-7
  noun number, 31.12,15,19-20,26,
    31-33,37-41
  noun patterns, 29.11,14,21-22,42-
    43,50,52
  numerals, 35.2-3,6,16,19-22,26-27,
    29-30
  one-term sentence, 50.3
  phonology, 10.10; 11.6,11; 13.12;
    18.7-8; 19.20; 21.17,30; 27.3,6,
    10,12-13,20
  "plural of majesty", 50.24

prepositions, *48*.5-6,12,16-17
proper names, *67*.15
pronouns, *36*.2,9,11-12,17,23,31,33-34,36,41,55,60-61
states of nouns, *33*.3,8,11,18
substantival clause, *60*.1
temporal/causal clause, *58*.2
verbal clause, *50*.15,19-20
volitive clause, *54*.6
word accent, *25*.7
word order, *50*.9,15,19-20
see also: Ethiopic, South Semitic
Tigre province (Ethiopia), *8*.11,13
Tigrinya, *2*.10; *8*.8-9,13
   accusative, *52*.11
   adjectives, *34*.3
   adverbs, *47*.8,11
   attribute, *51*.1
   conjugation, *38*.7,25-26; *40*.2,16; *41*.11,14,20,32,36,39; *42*.4,12; *43*.7,20; *45*.17
   conjunctions, *59*.6; *60*.1
   copula, *49*.24
   expression of possession, *49*.25
   final/consecutive clause, *59*.6
   genitival relation, *51*.23,25
   gerund, *42*.12; *53*.5
   infinitive, *53*.5
   lexicography, *62*.2; *63*.4,10; *65*.4
   noun number, *31*.12,15,18,20,26,31,33
   noun patterns, *29*.14,27,44,50
   numerals, *35*.3,16,24
   phonology, *13*.12; *14*.3,9; *17*.4; *19*.20; *22*.15; *23*.1; *27*.9,16
   "plural of majesty", *50*.24
   prepositions, *48*.5-6,16,25
   pronouns, *36*.2,9,12,17,23,33,36,38,41,55,60
   questions, *47*.16; *54*.5
   relative clause, *57*.9; *60*.3
   states of nouns, *33*.13,18
   subordinate clause, *56*.1
   substantival clause, *59*.6; *60*.3
   syllable, *24*.8
   word accent, *25*.7
   word order, *57*.9
   see also: Ethiopic, South Semitic

Tigris, *7*.19
time, nouns of, *29*.23
Tipasa, *67*.9
Tocharian, *65*.6
Tombouctou, *2*.14
tone languages, *10*.6
tone, *10*.2,6; *25*.1; *26*.3; *29*.47
tonemes, *25*.8
tools, instruments, names of, *29*.11,19-20,22-24
topicalization, *50*.8,20
Toprak-kale, *7*.21
Tosefta, *7*.5
transcription, *9*.12-13; *10*.12
transitive verbs, *32*.15,24; *38*.3,15-17; *39*.12; *41*.2-3; *52*.2-4
Transjordan, *7*.9,11,16; *9*.10; *13*.7; *65*.4
translation, *8*.8; *38*.18; *53*.4; *62*.4; *63*.12
transliteration, *9*.12; *10*.3
Tripoli, Tripolitania, *18*.7; *47*.15
tt < *dt*, *27*.3
tt < *lt*, *35*.4
tt < *nt*, *10*.12; *27*.3; *28*.7
tt < *t'*, *41*.30,32
tt < *th*, *27*.4
tt < *ṭṭ*, *13*.8; *27*.3; *41*.32
ṭṭ < *ṭṭ*, *27*.4; *41*.32
ṭṭ < *dṭ*, *35*.11
ṭṭ < *nṭ*, *27*.3
ṭṭ < *šṭ*, *35*.11
Tuareg, *2*.14-15; *10*.3; *11*.7; *29*.11,13,46; *30*.10; *32*.1,6; *35*.2-3,18,20-21; *36*.2,5-6,17,23,36,57,60; *38*.1,3; *40*.5,11; *41*.2,6; *43*.3; *44*.5; *48*.18; *49*.19-20; *57*.6; *63*.5-6,13; *65*.8; *66*.1; *67*.4; see also: Libyco-Berber
Tunisian Arabic, *12*.3; *22*.4; *41*.31; *50*.20,23; *67*.9
Ṭūr ʿAbdīn, *7*.33; *33*.7; *45*.12
Turkana, Lake, *2*.11
Turkey, *7*.33,34,46
Turkish, *10*.12; *61*.3
Turkmenistan, *7*.14,21
Ṭūrōyo, *7*.33; *11*.10; *22*.8,10; *23*.1; *33*.7; *42*.18; *45*.12; *47*.8
Tyre, *7*.6; *13*.7; *21*.12

u < *a*, *10*.9; *27*.9; *28*.13
u < *əw*, *22*.10
u < *hu*, *27*.25
u < *i*, *21*.7,10; *61*.2
u < *o*, *67*.18
u < *ū*, *21*.30; *31*.26; *43*.20
u < *wa*, *49*.1,4
u- < *wu-*, *11*.14
u- < *yu-*, *15*.6; *22*.14
ū < *ă*, *21*.27
ū < *ā'u*, *45*.6
ū < *aw*, *21*.9,13; *22*.1,5-7,10-11; *43*.20; *49*.4
ū < *iū*, *27*.23
ū < *ī* + *ū*, *22*.15
ū < *iw*, *22*.13
ū < *iyu*, *25*.2
ū < *ō*, *21*.13,23; *22*.10; *29*.7,35,47; *67*.18
ū < *uw*, *22*.13
ū < *uy*, *22*.13
ū < *w* < *b*, *11*.5
Ugaritic, *4*.1-2,5; *5*.4; *7*.1
    accusative, *52*.2
    adverbs, *47*.7,9,12,14
    case inflection, *32*.8,12,18,20,22
    conditional clause, *61*.2-3,7
    conjugation, *38*.4-6,10,13; *39*.2,10; *40*.2-3,8-10,13,17-18,21,32,34; *41*.2-3,8-9,12,16,22,25,29,35,38, 40,43,48,50,54-55; *42*.2,6,13-15; *43*.6,12; *44*.11; *45*.8,11; *46*.2
    conjunctions, *49*.1-2,4; *56*.3
    copula, *49*.23
    expression of possession, *49*.25
    lexicography, *62*.4; *64*.4; *65*.5,7
    noun gender, *30*.11
    noun number, *31*.2,5-6,10,14-15, 19-20,26-27
    noun patterns, *29*.3,16-18,20-21,26, 29-31,33,36-37,41,54
    numerals, *35*.2-4,6,11,16-22,24,26, 29-31
    parataxis, *55*.1
    phonology, *10*.9; *11*.4,6,9,13; *13*.1, 4-6; *16*.7; *19*.7-8; *21*.1,3,5,9,12, 32; *22*.3,5; *27*.8-9,13,17,24-25,28
    prepositions, *48*.9,13-17,21,24
    presentatives, *49*.1,6
    pronouns, *36*.2-3,6,17,21-22,33-34, 38,46,48-49,57-61
    relative clause, *57*.3,5-6
    script, *9*.2,4-5,11; *50*.1
    states of nouns, *33*.16,20
    subordinate clause, *56*.3
    substantival clause, *60*.2
    temporal/causal clause, *58*.2-4,11, 13
    see also: Semitic. North Semitic
'Ulā, al- (Saudi Arabia), *7*.37; *8*.4
ultimae infirmae verbs, *43*.11-22
Umbrian, *63*.5; *65*.5
United Arab Emirates, *7*.46
unvoiced, voiceless consonants, *10*.4,8; *11*.1; *12*.1-2; *13*.1; *14*.1; *15*.1; *16*.1; *18*.1; *19*.2; *23*.1
Ur III period, *5*.2; *36*.47; *39*.7
Urfa (Turkey), *7*.20
Urmia, *7*.34
Uruk incantation, *7*.18
uvular, *17*.1
Uzbekistan, Uzbeks, *7*.21,46; *12*.3; *33*.18

Vai tribe, *36*.1
Vatican Library, *7*.23
velar fricatives, *2*.8; *19*.1-22; *42*.3; *45*.2
velarization, *10*.9-10; *13*.6; *27*.10
velars, velar plosives, *10*.4; *11*.10; *15*.5; *17*.1; *18*.1-9
ventive/allative, *39*.3,6-7; *40*.14; *46*.2
verb, *37*.1; *46*.6
    active/stative, *38*.15-16
    actor, *37*.5,9; *40*.1-36
    aspect, *37*.3,8; *38*.3-10,12-14,17-18
    changes in the system, *37*.1,7; *38*.10-14,18
    irregular, *43*.22
    mood, *37*.4; *38*.2,14; *39*.1-19
    "nominal" base, *37*.1,3
    stem, *37*.6; *38*.4,15; *40*.24; *41*.1-56
    telic/atelic situation, *37*.3
    tense, *37*.2,8; *38*.1-2,10-11,19-28
    transitive/intransitive, *32*.2-3,15; *38*.3,15-17; *39*.12
    translation, *38*.18

"verbal" base, *37*.1-2
voice, *37*.6; *38*.16; *41*.1,43-47
"weak" verbs, *22*.18; *28*.9; *38*.10;
 39.14; *43*.1-23; *44*.1-*45*.17
with pharyngals, laryngals and
 velar fricatives, *45*.1-17
with pronominal suffixes, *46*.1-6
verbal classes, *28*.3; *37*.1; *38*.15-16;
 41.1-2; *44*.3
verbal nouns, *7*.33; *29*.19,25,30,32,
 35,37; *53*.1-6
verbal phrases, *52*.1-*53*.6
verbal *t*-infix/prefix, *27*.14; see: stems
 of verbs
verbs of motion, *48*.2; *52*.3
verb-stems, '*at*-, *at*-, *41*.28
 B/G, basic, *38*.4; *40*.16; *41*.2
 B/Gt, *38*.4; *41*.22-23,55; *42*.2-5
 B/Gtn, *41*.33
 B/Gtt, *41*.35
 causative, *40*.16; *41*.7-14,28-32,54
 D, *40*.16; *41*.3,45
 Dt, *41*.25-26
 Dtn, *41*.33
 Dtt, *41*.35
 frequentative, *41*.33-36
 Ht, *41*.28
 L, *41*.4-6
 Lt, *41*.25,27
 M, *41*.15
 N, *1*.2; *41*.14-19,45
 NDt, NtD, *41*.26
 Ntn, *41*.33
 Š/S, *1*.2; *40*.16; *41*.7-14,54
 Št/St, *41*.28-32,54
 StD, *41*.31,54
 StL, *41*.31
 Štn, *41*.33
 Štt, *41*.35
 T, *41*.20-32,55
 T' > Tt, *41*.30
 Th, *41*.30
 tB/G, *41*.23
 tB/Gt, *41*.35
 tD, *41*.25-26,28
 tL, *41*.27,34
 Ts, *41*.30
vetitive, *38*.2; *39*.13; *54*.6

vocative, *26*.4; *32*.5-6,10; *50*.3
voiced consonant, *10*.4,8; *11*.1; *12*.1-
 2; *13*.1; *14*.1; *18*.1-2; *19*.2; *23*.1
voiceless, see: unvoiced
voicing, *12*.2; *13*.9; *27*.11
vowel(s), *9*.3,5; *10*.2-3,5,11; *21*.1-32;
 24.1-11
 as case markers, *32*.1-26
 assimilation, *27*.9-10
 changes, *26*.2; *29*.13; *45*.17
 dissimilation, *27*.11
 elision, *27*.21-23
 harmony, *27*.9; *40*.16,31; *61*.2
 indicated by diacritics or vowel
  signs, *21*.15-19,22,26; *29*.3
 matres lectionis, *7*.28,42; *9*.5-6,8-
  9; *10*.3; *21*.14-15,20-22,24-26,
  28; *22*.10,13,15; *24*.10; *27*.28;
  30.4; *39*.15; *43*.13; *45*.8,11
 not represented, *2*.2; *9*.5; *50*.1
 rôle of, in noun patterns, *29*.3,6-8
 rôle of, in root morphemes, *28*.3-12

w, first radical, *41*.26; *43*.6-8; *44*.4
 medial radical, *44*.5
 third radical, *43*.11-21
w < ', *19*.17
w < *ḇ* (< *m*), *11*.6,9; *27*.11
w < *m̠* < *m*, *11*.6,8; *29*.19,26; *42*.11
Wadi Bayḥān, *8*.5
Wadi Dāliyeh, *7*.12
Wadi Ḥarīb, *8*.5
Wadi Sirḥān, *7*.40
Walamo (Cushitic), *2*.12; *36*.3,9; *41*.7
wave-theory, *3*.1
waw-conversive, *54*.7-8
wayyiqtol, *38*.11; *39*.15,17
"weak" consonants, *27*.21,24; *43*.23
"weak" verbs, *22*.18; *28*.9; *38*.10;
 39.14; *43*.1-23; *44*.1-*45*.17
Wello province (Ethiopia), *2*.10
Western Asia, *1*.2; *3*.3,5; *30*.11; *48*.7;
 65.8
West Semitic, *4*.2,5; *7*.1-46; *9*.4,8,11;
 11.4,6; *15*.2; *16*.2; *19*.12; *24*.6;
 27.3,8,16,24; *29*.2,9,41; *31*.26;
 32.23; *35*.21,30; *36*.5,32-33,37-
 38,47; *37*.4; *38*.1,10,16,18; *39*.14;

40.6; *41*.1-3,6,11,19,33,43,51; *43*.9-
10; *44*.4-6,10; *47*.7,17-18; *48*.4-
6,12,20; *49*.6-7,23; *51*.13; *52*.10-
11; *54*.7; *61*.2; *63*.2,5; *67*.9
w-glide, *11*.11; *22*.15; *27*.23; *28*.13
Wolane (Gurage), *8*.17; see: Gurage
word accent, *25*.1-8
word dividers, *9*.2,11
word order, *32*.1,21,24; *33*.11; *36*.36;
50.7-9,12-20; *51*.1-2,25; *53*.3-5;
56.7-8; *57*.9; *65*.2
writing and speech, *9*.1

y, first radical, *43*.6-7
    medial radical, *44*.5
    third radical, *41*.13; *43*.11-21
y < *ǧ* < *g*, *18*.9
y < *l*, *15*.6; *17*.1
y < *ň* < *n*, *36*.14
y < *w*, *11*.13
Yaṭil, *8*.4
Yemen, *3*.3; *7*.46; *8*.2-3,9-10; *12*.2;
16.8; *17*.4; *18*.6; *31*.28; *36*.5,53,
58; *38*.5; *41*.11; *47*.16

Yeshaq I, *2*.11
y-glide, *15*.7; *22*.15; *27*.23
yi < *ya*, *22*.14
Yiddish, *7*.5; *29*.53
yifʿalu, *40*.16

z < *ḏ*, *13*.10,12; *14*.2
ź < *ś*, *16*.7
ž < *g*, *2*.15; *18*.6
ž < *l*, *15*.8; *30*.10; *35*.21,39
ž < *š*, *15*.5
ž < *z*, *27*.10
Ẓafar, *8*.3
Zainīya, *2*.7
Zanzibar, *7*.46
zd < *zt*, *41*.32
Zenaga, *2*.14
Zimmern, H., preface
Zincirli, *7*.11
Zway (Gurage), *8*.17; *36*.14; *40*.5;
    see: Gurage
zz < *nz*, *27*.3
zz < *zt*, *41*.32
z < *zz* < *rz*, *27*.3

INDEX OF WORDS AND FORMS

References are to paragraphs. The index mentions only words and forms somehow analyzed or commented.

The following alphabetic order is followed:
ʾ, a (ʾa, a, ā, ä, ă, ᵃ), ʿ, ʿa, ʿi, ʿu, b (b, ḇ, ḅ), c, č, (č̣, c̣), d, ḏ, ḍ (ḍ, d', ḑ), e, (ʾe, e, ē), ə (ʾə, ə), f, g (g, ǧ), ġ, h, ḥ, ḫ, ḥ, i (ʾi, i, ī), j, k (k, ḵ, ḳ), l (l, ḷ), m (m, ṃ), n (n, ň, ñ), o (ʾo, o, ō, ŏ, ö, ɔ), p, (p, ṗ, p̄), q, r (r, ṛ), s, ṣ, ś, ṡ, š, ṧ, t (t, ṭ), ṯ, ṱ, u, (ʾu, u, ū, ŭ), w, y, z, ẓ, ž (ž, ż). Thus, ʿain is treated as second letter of the alphabet.

AGAW

adära "God", 67.9
agär "country", 63.5
alšina "may you sustain", 39.8
an, ana "I", 28.13; 36.5
anä, anän "we", "our", 36.5,16
an-adära "our God", 36.16
anät "us", 36.14; 39.8
desá-la "he doesn't study", 54.2
desé "he studies", 54.2
ənt "you", 36.5
əzän "heart", 30.11
käzär(ä) "ear", 30.11
ki-lämda "your shadow", 36.16
kut "you", "thee", 36.14
kʷara "sun", 63.6
maḥdär "dwelling", 29.20

nay-ki "all of them", 36.16
ni "he", 36.5
ni-səbra "his place", 36.16
nkəra "soul", "spirit", 15.18; 36.16
šäy(š) "(cause to) take", 41.7
tadära "lady", 67.9
wanäkʷ "I am", 49.22
wasin "let him hear", 39.8
waša, waši "cellar", 48.19
yage "he brings", 2.10
yaġe "he is", "he becomes", 2.10
yaqe "he knows", 2.10
yə-nkəra "my soul", 36.16
yət "me", 36.14
yigʷe "he remains", 2.10
yinte "he comes", 2.10

AMHARIC

abbazza "he multiplied", 41.14
adbar "mountains", 31.26
aga'əzt "sovereigns", 31.34
agäňňä "he found", 49.25
al-...-(m)m "not", 47.8
allä "he is", 36.33; 38.28; 49.24-25
alläfä "he went by", 45.17
alläňň "I have", 49.25
amaləkt "gods", 31.34

ambʷattärä "he bragged", 41.18
amlak "God", 31.34
ämləkot "domination", 29.47
amsal "parables", 31.26
anabəst "lions", 31.34
anbäsa "lion", 31.34
and, andit "one", "a", 33.8,18; 35.3
andäňňa "first", 35.24

anəst ṭəǧǧa "she-calf", 30.8

ankäbällälä "he throw (someone) down", 41.17-18

anqaqqa "he dried", 41.18

anqäsaqqäsä "he moved", 41.17-18

antä "you" (sing.), 36.9

aqärräbä "he brought", 41.11

*aqqätattälä, *aqqattälä "cause to combat each other", 41.32

aräǧǧä "he grew old", 41.39

arat "four", 11.5

asaṭṭärä "he made short", 41.9

asnäggärä "he let speak", 41.9,14

assäbä "he calculated", 41.32

astämammänä "he convinced", 41.9,29

ašqädaddämä "he put ahead", 41.9

attäsassäbä "he caused to settle accounts", 41.32

awre "wild animal", 65.4

bähayl "strongly", 51.26

balä arat əgar "four-footed", 51.22

balä betočč "owners", 29.55

bäläqälläqä "he became clumsy", 41.37

balənna mistočč "married couple", 29.55

bäqällal "easily", 51.26

bäräkkätä "he abounded", 41.42

bärätta "he became strong", 41.39; 63.4

bäzza "it was much", 47.13

bäzzih "in this", 36.41

bet, betočč "house", "houses", 31.17

betu "the house", 32.28

birrabirro "butterfly", 43.5

bosta "post office", 11.3

čən "thigh", 30.11

däbbälä "he added", 49.21

dägmo "again", 47.3

däll "isn't", 49.21

därräsä "he found", "he met", 45.9

dəro "previously", 47.3

əbab, əmbab "snake", 30.10

əgər "foot", 24.8

əgərañña "pedestrian", 29.52

əgzi'ə "sovereign", 31.34

əllä "these", 29.27; 36.9

əllantä "you" (plur.), 36.9

əlläzzih "these", 36.33,41,45

əlläziya "those", 36.45

əmbəzam "not much", 47.13

əmbi "no!", 47.13

-(ə)mm "and", 49.1

əndä "such as", "according to", 48.22

-(ə)nə interrogative, 54.5

ənǧa "I don't know", 47.13

ənkʷan "no!", 47.13

-(ə)nna "and", 49.1

ənnä "these", 29.27; 36.9

ənnantä "you" (plur.), 36.9

ənnäzzih "these", 36.33,41,45

ənnäziya "those", 36.45

əññə "these", 36.33

ənqəfat "obstacle", 17.8

ənqʷərarit "frog", 29.27

ərsu, ərsʷa "he", "she", 36.12,45

əs "with", 48.10

əskä, 'əskännä "with", "up to", 48.10,17

əskä mäčä "until when?", "how long?", 47.17

əsport "sport", 27.17; 29.52

əsportañña "sportsman", 29.52

əssu, əssʷa "he", "she", 36.12,45

fällägän "he wanted us", 36.23

fəyyäl "goat", 30.10

gazeṭa "newspaper", 29.52

gazeṭañña "correspondent", 29.52

gädamat "convents", 31.15

ǧəb "hyena", 18.6

Goǧǧam "Gojjam", 11.11

grañ "left-handed", 17.9

Gʷaǧǧam "Gojjam", 11.11

gʷänäggʷänä "he wove", 41.38

gʷädən "rib", 30.11

hawaryat "apostles", 31.15

haya "twenty", 15.6

honä "he is", 49.21

hulätt "two", 35.4

kä- "from", "to", "with", 48.10-11; 49.14

kä-... bähʷala "after that", 48.25; 49.14

käbäro "tambourine", *29.50*
käfač "who opens", *42.13*
käfto "having uncovered", *42.12*
kännä "with", *48.10*
kərämt "rainy season", *27.19*
konä "to be", *47.13*
krämt "rainy season", *17.9; 27.19*
*kʷan "is", *47.13*
lalla "he is loose", *41.38*
ləsanat "languages", *31.15*
ləsbär "let me break", *40.30*
liq(awənt) "learned man (men)", *31.34*
mäčä "never", *47.17*
malik "king", *31.34*
mädhanit "medicine", *29.49*
mäkina nägiwočč "car drivers", *29.55*
mälhəq "anchor", *29.22*
mänbär, mänabərt "seat", "seats", *31.34*
mängär "to speak", *42.4*
mängəst "kingdom", "government", "state", *17.9; 27.19; 29.21,44*
mängəstawi "official", *29.44*
mänka "spoon", *29.22*
mannəm "whoever", *36.61*
mäqdäs "sanctuary", *29.21*
märkäb "ship", *63.4*
mäṣhaf, mäṣahəft "book", "books", *30.6; 31.34*
mäto "hundred", *35.20*
məgbar "action", *29.25*
məhrät "mercy", *29.25*
mənəm, mənəmən "whatever", *36.61*
mərfaq "dining-room", *29.21*
məsraq "east", *29.21*
mossa "child", *8.18*
muziqa, muziqäñña "music", "musician", *29.52*
na "come!", *40.14*
näbbär(ä) "he was", *38.28; 40.3; 49.21,25*
näbər "leopard", *24.8*
nafqot "longing", *29.47*
näfs "soul", "person", *17.9*
näfsä bis "evil-minded", *51.22*
nägäst "kings", *31.34*

näkka "he touched", *43.21*
näggärä "he spoke", *41.53; 45.17; 47.8*
näw "he is, it is", *41.34; 42.25; 49.20*
nəgus "king", *31.34*
norä "he was", *49.25*
posta "post office", *11.3*
prezident(ənnät) "president", "presidency", *29.52*
qäddämä "he was ahead of", *41.9*
qädmo "first", *47.3*
qänd "horn", *17.7*
qämbär "yoke", *11.9*
qəl "oneself", *36.28*
qərš "piaster", *65.4*
qoṭṭärä "he cut", *41.5*
qurä "crow, raven", *30.10*
qʷättärä "he cut", *41.5*
qwənṭan "stomach-ache", *29.37*
räggäd "he trembled", *40.3*
säbabärä "he smashed", *41.36*
sämma "he listened", *44.2; 45.17*
samənt "week", *27.3*
sänäbbätä "he spent the weak", *41.42*
sant "eight", *35.13*
säw "man", *11.5*
set ləǧ "girl", *30.8*
sə "when", *48.10*
səbära "break!", *40.14*
sədsa, səlsa "sixty", *17.7; 23.8*
sälä "to", "because of", *48.10*
sälṭan "authority", *29.37*
səma "listen!", *45.17*
sənde "wheat", *17.7*
sərqot "theft", *29.47*
-ssa interrogative, *54.4*
ša "he wanted", *43.7*
ši(h) "thousand", *35.21*
tä- "from", "to", "with", *48.11,18*
täbat ṭäǧǧa "he-calf", *30.8*
täbazza "it became multiple", *41.14*
tačč "under", *11.15; 48.16*
täfällägä "he was wanted", *41.25*
tägäddälä "he was killed", *41.20*
tägbar "work", *29.30*
talallaq "great", *29.14*

tämarräka "he was taken prisoner", *41.27*

tämbäräkkäkä "he knelt down", *41.18*

tänakaš "is in the habit of biting", *41.34*

tänkärättätä "he wandered from place to place", *41*, 17

tänqässaqqäsa "he moved (himself)", *41.18*

täräggʷämä "he translated", *41.42*

täräkäz "heel", *29.30*

täsassäbu "they settled accounts", *41.32*

təmhərt "teaching", *29.30*

ṭamma "be thirsty", *13.12*

ṭəqit "few", *18.8*

wämbar "chair", *29.26*

wändəmm, wändəmamočč "brother", "brothers", *31.22*

wänd ləǧ "boy", *30.8*

wänfit "sieve", *29.26*

wänz "river", *17.9*

wäsfe "awl", *23.5*

wašša "cellar", *48.19*

wätro "continuously", *47.3*

wättaddär "soldier", *29.26,44*

wättaddärawi "military", *29.44*

wäy "or", interrogative *49.4; 54.5*

wäyəmm "or", *49.4*

wäyəss "or", *49.4*

wäyzäro, wäyzazər "lady", "ladies", *31.22*

wəsṭ "midst", *48.19*

wəšša "dog", *41.34; 67.4*

wof "bird", *11.11*

ya "that" (masc.), *36.32,45*

yä- "(belonging) to", *36.31,55; 48.6; 51.25-26; 57.9*

yäkrəstiyan "Christian", *51.26*

yäsäw "human", *51.26*

yačč "that" (fem.), *36.45*

yalf "he will go by", *45.17*

yəčč "this" (fem.), *36.45*

yəh "this" (masc.), *36.32,45*

yəmark "may he take prisoner", *38.7*

yəmarrək "he takes prisoner", *38.7*

yənägr "he will speak", *45.17*

yənnäggär-all "it is said", *41.32*

yənoräññall "I shall have", *49.25*

yəsäma "he will listen", *45.17*

yəsma "may he listen", *45.17*

zäḥəṭäň "smaller", *35.14*

zänd "so that", *49.17*

zändəro "this year", *47.3*

zändo "python", *29.50*

zäṭäňň "nine", *35.14*

žəb "hyena", *18.6*

AMMONITE

ʾnk "I", *36.6*

yn "wine", *65.5*

ywmt rbm "many days", *31.14*

AMORITE

abbūtu "elders", *29.46*

ayya, ayyāma "where", *36.59*

ʿAmmurāpiʾ-ʾilī "Hammurabi is my god", *67.5*

arwûm "gazelle", *63.4*

*Ba-aḥ-la-*DINGIR "El is lord", *32.11*

Bataḥra "chosen" (fem.), *29.32*

Bataḥrum "chosen" (masc.), *29.32*

bin- "son of", *63.8*

Bu-nu-taḥ-tu-un-i-la "son of god's underbelly", *48.16*

Ekallātayum "man from Ekallātu", *29.41*

Elaḥutayum "man from Elaḥutu", *29.41*

E-lu-ra-ma "El is high", *32.4*

Ḫa-ab-du-A-šu-ra "servant of Ashur", *32.12*

Ḫa-ab-du-Ba-aḫ-la "servant of Baal", *32.12*

Ḫab-du-(ma-)ᵈDa-gan "servant of Dagan", *33.16; 51.24*

Ia-ab-ni-ᵈDa-gan "Dagan has created", *43.13*

ia-ab-ta-ḫa-ar-na "he has chosen us", *38.4*

Ia-am-ra-aṣ-Èl "El did care", *40.18*

Ia-am-ru-uṣ-Èl "El did care", *40.18*

Ia-an-ta-qí-im "he was avenged", *41.22*

Ia-aq-ni-Ìl "Il has acquired", *43.13*

ia-ás-ki-in "he caused to be", *41.9*

Ia-ás-ma-aḫ-ᵈIM "Haddu did hear", *40.18*

Ia-ás-mi-iḫ-ᵈIM "Haddu did hear", *40.18*

Ia-ḫu-un-Èl "El did favour", *44.11*

Ia-ki-in- "he is firm", *44.13*

Ia-ku-un- "he is firm", *44.13*

Ia-ma-at-ti-Èl "El will protect", *38.6*

ia-mu-ud "he propped", *45.7-8*

ia-mu-ur "he made prosperous", *45.7*

Ia-na-ab-bi-Èl "El will name", *38.6*

Ia-qub-Baʿal "Baal has protected", *38.13*

Ia-ši-ib- "he turned back", *44.13*

Ia-šu-ub- "he turned back", *44.13*

i-ba-al- "he made", *11.4; 19.7; 40.18; 45.7*

I-ba-al-pi-El "the mouth/word of El has made", *19.7*

I-la-kab-ka-bu-ú "(t)his star is the god", *33.13*

Iš-ḫi-lu-na "the Saviour is our god", *36.23*

Iš-ma-ᵈIM "Haddu did hear", *40.18*

iš-ma-aḫ "he did hear", *45.8*

Iu-um-ra-aṣ-Èl "El did care", *40.18*

kawkab-u "star", *29.13*

ma-a "what?", *36.58*

ma-an-na "who?", *36.58*

Ma-la-ak-ì-lí "my god is king / messenger", *38.10*

Na-am-se-e-ᵈIM "beast? of Haddu", *67.4*

si-i "the (woman) of", *36.49*

Ṣú-ra-Ḫa-am-mu-ú "his ancestor is a rock", *32.11*

Šadum/n-lab(w)a "(milked at) the teat of a lioness", *36.5*

ša-du-un "teat", "udder", *30,11*

Šamaš-ġazzīr "the Sun-god is a hero", *67.7*

*Ša-ta-aḫ-ti-in-*DINGIR "that of god's underbelly", *48.16*

ši "the (woman) of", *36.49*

šu-ub-na- "turn back, please!", *40.14*

šum- "name", *63.5*

Ta-aḫ-ta-ḫu-um "instead of the brother", *48.16*

Ta-aḫ-tu-pí-ìl "by order of god's mouth", *48.16*

-ti-ba-al "she made", *40.18*

Ṭa-ba-Èl "El is good", *40.3*

Uš-ta-aš-ni- / Uš-taš-ni-Èl "El acted for the second time", *40.33; 41.29*

yabamu "brother-in-law", *11.6*

yamamu "brother-in-law", *11.6*

Yamlikān "... became king", *29.36*

zu(-ú)- "the (man) of", *36.47,49*

ARABIC

The feminine ending *-t* and the nunation are not indicated.

ʾa- "ho!", *49.10*

ʾaʿmūm "uncles", *31.29*

ʾaʿraǧ "lame", *29.16*

ʾaʿṭānīhi "he gave it to me", *36.27*

ʾab "father", 29.1
ʾabā "(my) father", 28.13
ʾabadan "always", 47.2
ʾabʾār, ʾābār "some wells", 31.36
ʾabbahāt "fathers", 31.19
ʾabū l-yaqẓān "roaster, cock", 51.22
ʾabū šawārib "man with long mustache", 51.22
ʾabyaḍ "white", 16.7; 67.10
abyaḷ "white", 16.7
ʾabnāʾ "sons", 28.13
ʾāḏanu "I shall allow", 45.14
ʾaḏhaba "he caused to go away", 41.11
ʾAflāṭūnu "Plato", 27.17
ʾafsal "he abhorred", 14.4
ʾaǧāra "he granted asylum", 24.2
ʾaǧbāl "mountains", 31.28
ʾaǧā "agha", 31.18
ʾaǧral "sluggish", 27.13
ʾaḥad "one", 19.24; 35.3; 48.18
ʾaḥmar "red", 27.10; 29.16; 67.10
ʾaḥā "(my) brother", 28.13
ʾakbar "greater", "very great", 34.5
ʾakkil "he fed", 11.11
ʾakram "nobler", "very noble", 29.16
aktib, aktub "I shall write", 40.25
ʾal- "the", 51.23
ʾalā "indeed", 50.4
ʾal-ḥāṣilu "briefly", 17.4
ʾalifa "he is familiar", 19.24
ʾāliha "some gods", 31.36
ʾallā "that... not", 39.5
ʾallaḏāni "who" (m. dual) 36.53
ʾallaḏī "who" (m. sing.), 36.53; 57.6
ʾallaḏīna "who" (m. plur.), 36.53
ʾAllāh "God", 17.1
ʾallatāni "who" (f. dual), 36.53
ʾallatī "who" (f. sing.), 36.53-54
ʾallāti, ʾallawāti "who" (f. plur.), 36.53
ʾallī "who", 36.53; 57.6
ʾal-Madīna "the City", 67.11
ʾal-Qalʿa "the Castle", 67.11
ʾal-ʿUyūn "the Sources", 67.11
ʾal-yawma "to-day", 52.6

ʾam "or", 49.4
ʾamā "indeed", 50.4
ʾamara "he ordered", 63.2
ʾamīr "emir", 63.2
ʾammā "if (ever)", 49.4; 50.6,8; 61.2
ʾammara "he made an emir", 63.2
ʾamrāḍ "ilnesses", 31.28
ʾamwāh, ʾamyāh "waters", 19.17
ʾan "that", 39.5,17; 47.10; 60.2
ʾanā "languid woman", 19.24
anāya "I", 28.13
ʾanf "nose", 30.11
ʾanāḥa "he made (a camel) kneel down", 64.3
ʾanhur "some rivers", 31.36
ʾanna "thus", "that", 60.2
ʾan-Naḥl "the Palm-trees", 67.11
ʾaqāwil "ensembles of sayings", 31.9
ʾaqlama "he acclimated", 63.10
ʾaqribā "some relatives", 31.36
ʾaqwāl "sayings", 31.9
arbaʿtaʿšar "fourteen", 35.16
ʾarǧal "sluggish", 27.13
ʾarnabu "hare", 29.16; 67.7
ʾasmāʾ "names", 28.13
ʾasmāʾ "the beautiful one", 19.24
ʾaṣdaq "the most reliable", 29.16
ʾaṣfaru "yellow", 41.39
āš "which", 36.59
ʾašall "withered?", 29.16
ʾatā "he came", 62.3
atfāʿal "he combined with", 41.27
atfaʿʿal "(the verse) was scanned", 41.25
ʾatāt "furnishings", 48.18
ʾattā "it was abundant", 48.18
att "you", 27.3
ʾaw "unless", 39.5
ʾawfar "more abounding", 29.9
ʾawnuq "she-camels", 29.9
ʾawwal, ʾawwil, ʾawwalāni "first", 35.24
ʾayādin "hands", 31.6
ʾayna "where?", 47.7,12; 48.18
ʾaynuq "she-camels", 29.9
ayš "which", 36.59; 54.5

ʾayyuhā "oh!", *50.3*

ʾayyumā "anyone", *36.61*

ʾayyun "which?", *47.12*

ʾayyu šayʾin "which thing?", *36.59*

ʾazwaru "bent", *41.39*

ʾaẓhar "he appeared", *41.11*

ʿabīd "slaves", *31.28*

ʿAbbāsīya "Abbasiya", *67.13*

ʿAbdu-llāhi "servant of God", *67.7*

ʿadā "he speeded", *48.17*

ʿal, ʿalā "over", "above", *48.15*

ʿalā ḥasabi "according to", *48.15*

ʿalimtu "I know", *38.18*

ʿallim "he taught", *27.10*

ʿamara "he lived long", *10.7*

ʿambar "ambergris", *27.6*

ʿamm "uncle", *31, 29*

ʿammārīyāt "camel-borne sedans", *63.6*

ʿan "from", *48.12*

ʿanbar "ambergris", *27.6*

ʿankabūt "spider", *30.10*

ʿanna "it took shape", *48.12*

ʿaqrab "scorpion", *29.17*

ʿaqrabān "small scorpion", *29.38*

ʿaraǧ "lameness", *29.16*

ʿarakrak "thick", *29.14*

ʿasiya "he became big", *41.39*

ʿaskar, ʿaskarī "army", "soldier", *31.40*

ʿaṣawtu "I struck with a stick", *43.17*

ʿaṣayka "you were disloyal", *40.5*

ʿaṣaytu "I struck with a stick", *43.17*

ʿašīra "clan", *35.15*

ʿAynān "Two sources", *67.11*

ʿazza wa-ǧalla "he is mighty and great", *38.18*

ʿēnēn, ʿentēn "eyes", "two eyes", *31.4,6*

ʾIblīn "Iblin", *29.54*

ʾiǧǧawl "small calf", *29.10*

ʿilm ʾal-ʾilāhīyāt "theology", *63.12*

ʿimd- "support", *48.22*

ʿinda "with", "upon", "in the opinion of", *48.22*

ʿiẓam "greatness", *29.8*

ʿumd- "support", *48.22*

ʿurf "mane (of a horse)", *27.8*

ʿuṣfūr "birds", *29.17*

ʿuẓma "how mighty!", *34.5*

b- "in", "by", *48.5*

baʿdu "later", *32.18; 47.3*

bāba "its door", *11.3*

ḅāḅa "father", *11.3*

badenǧāl, badinǧān "aubergine", *17.4*

baḍā́ "white", *22.4*

baǧaḥa "he rejoiced", *11.6*

bahalku "I spoke", *40.6*

baḫḫara "to fumigate", *41.44*

bakā "he wept", "he cried", *22.4; 43.17; 62.2*

bal "but", "rather", *17.4; 47.14*

bāliġ "adult", *63.9*

ban "but", *17.4*

banā "he built", *63.8*

banat, banit "she built", *43.18*

baqā "he remained", *43.17*

baqar "cattle", *31.38*

baqara "cow", *18.8*

baqayta "you remained", *43.17*

baqīta "you remained", *43.17*

baqiya "he remained", *41.10; 43.17*

bāraka, barraka "he blessed", *63.2*

bā smuk "what is your name", *11.6*

basmala "he said *bismillāhi*", *41.42*

bāšā "pasha", *31.18*

bāt "house", *22.4*

batara "he cut off", *23.9*

bātiʿ "strong", *41.39*

batta "he cut off", *23.9*

bat(t)ala "he cut off", *23.9; 41.5*

baṭan "serpent", *29.6*

bayāḍ "white", *16.8*

bayn "separation", "interval", *48.21*

bayn-aktub "I am just writing", *38.22*

bayna "between", *48.21*

bayt(u) "(a) house", *22.16; 29.9; 32.25*

bayṭara "he practiced as veterinary", *41.5*

bgara "cow", *18.8*

b(i)- "in", prefix of the imperfect *38.22-23; 63.14*

biʾār, *biʾr* "wells", "well", *31*.36

biḥār "seas", *29*.8

bi-kull maʿnā l-kalima "in the full sense of the term", *63*.12

bīn "between", *22*.7

birind "sword", *11*.2

bi-sobabi "on account of", *58*.15

bismillāhi "in the name of God", *41*.42

bitāʿ "of", *51*.19,23

bi-yruḥ "he will go", *38*.22

btektob "she writes", *38*.23

buhhal "free men", *31*.25

byəktob, *byəktbū* "he writes", "they write", *38*.23

d- "of", *51*.19

dʾ "what", *57*.6

daʾ "not", *47*.16

daʿā "he called", *43*.17

daʿawnā "we called", *43*.17

dabala "he collected", *49*.21

dabara "he passed", *27*.12

dalmasa "he hid", *23*.8

damā, *damawīy* "blood", "bloody", *28*.13

damara "he perished", *10*.7

damʿ "tears", *31*.38

dammasa "he hid", *23*.8

dār ʾaṣ-ṣināʿa "ship-yard", *64*.5

darbane "our road", *32*.5

dawbal "young ass", *30*.10

dawwana "he registered", *66*.4

darbin "a road", *32*.25

dī "of", *51*.19

dikha "that", *36*.44

dīwān "account book", "office", "collection", *66*.4

dmʾrnʾ "our hearts", *13*.9

dōl(a) "these", *36*.39

dū "not", *47*.16

dukha, *dukham(ma)* "that", *36*.44

dunyāwī "earthly", "wordly", *29*.44

dalika "that" (m.), *36*.44

dā(t) "what", *57*.6

diʾb "wolf", *30*.10; *63*.13

dū "this", "who", *10*.8; *36*.39,53; *57*.6

duʾbān "wolfs", *63*.13

dū l-qarnayin "the (man) of two horns", *36*.46

ḍāʿ "he was lost", *16*.7

ḍaḥika "he laughed" *10*.9

ḍamāʾirunā "our hearts", *13*.9

ḍarabək "he beat you", *46*.5

ḍarabtīnī "you (fem.) beat me", *46*.5

ḍarabtuhum "I beat them", *46*.5

ēš "which", *36*.59

əlli "who", *51*.19; *57*.6

əntāya "you", *28*.13

əš- "which", *36*.59

-(ə)š interrogative particle, *54*.5

fa- "so that", "and", *38*.11; *39*.5; *49*.2; *55*.4; *56*.8; *59*.3

faḥd "clan", "tribe", *13*.9

fa-kān(a) "and it happened", *61*.10

falṭaha "he made broad", *23*.8

fanā "he passed away", *43*.17

faniya "he passed away", *43*.17

faras "mare", "horse", *30*.5

fārir, *farr* "running away", *44*.15

fasād "to be rotten", *42*.3

faṭṭaha "he made broad", *23*.8

fawḥa "fragrant emanation", *11*.13

fawqu "above", *32*.18; *47*.3

fa-yafʿal "and he acted", *38*.11

fayḥa "fragrant emanation", *11*.13

fayṣal "arbiter", *29*.9

fenğāl, *finğān* "cup", *17*.4

fī- "in", "at", "on", "by", *48*.5

fī ġad(in) "to-morrow", *52*.6

filizz "(non-precious) metal", *29*.12

firind "sword", *11*.2

firzil "iron", *63*.13

fū "mouth", *28*.6

funduq "inn", *63*.10; *65*.2

ğāʾa "he came", "he was about", *49*.24; *62*.3

ğabal "mountain", "mount", *31*.28; *67*.15

Ğabal Ṭāriq "Gibraltar", *67*.13

ğabr "coercion", "algebra", *65*.8

ğabrī "compulsory", "algebraic", *65*.8

ğadaf, *ğadaṭ* "grave", *11*.15

ğady "young goat", *2*.15; *29*.42

ǧafā   "he treated harshly", 22.4
ǧā'iz   "lawful", 11.14
ǧalbaba   "he wrapped", 41.40
ǧalǧala   "skull", 29.13
ǧawraba   "he put on socks", 41.5
gawwiz   "he married", 41.25
ǧawzal   "young pigeon", 30.10
ǧbāl   "mountains", 31.28
gbīr   "great", 29.8
gələt   "I said", 18.8; 38.3
ǧibāl   "mountains", 31.28
ǧiddan   "very", "much", 47.2
ǧilbāb   "garment", 41.40
ǧīr   "lime-plaster", 29.9
ǧišmāni   "corpulent", 29.36
ǧundub   "grasshopper", 63.10
ġadan   "to-morrow", 52.6
ġamada   "he shut the eyes", 27.12
ġanam   "sheep", 17.4
ġanība, ġanīma   "booty", 11.6
ġarmaš   "he scratched", 23.6
ġayru   "different", 47.16
ġazāl   "gazelle", 29.40; 31.12,28
ġilma, ġilmān   "boys", 63.6
ġirš   "piaster", 65.4
ġiṭamm   "vast (ocean)", 29.12
ġizlān   "gazelles", 29.40; 31.12,28
ġlem   "sheep", 17.4
ġulām   "boy", 63.6
ġurš   "piaster", 65.4
ġyr   "to modify", 63.14
hā   "oh!", 50.3
hā-'anā-ḏā   "here I am", 49.10
hab   "give", 43.6; 44.3
hadōle   "these", 36.39
hāḏā   "this" (m.), 36.33
hāḏāk   "that" (m.), 36.44
hāḏāna   "these" (f.), 36.39
hāḏawlā   "these", 36.39
hāḏī   "this" (f.), 36.39
hāḏīk   "that" (f.), 36.44
hāḏūma/na   "these" (m.), 36.39
hāka   "here, take it!", 50.4
hal   "didn't?", 49.8
halāk   "to perish", 42.3
hallā   "didn't?", 49.8
hallala   "he jubilated", 62.2
han   "the", "something", 33.10

(hā)'ulā('i)   "these", 36.39
hā'ulāk   "those", 36.44
hawba   "gravity", 11.13
hawlāk   "those", 36.44
hawr   "lake", 29.9
hayba   "gravity", 11.13
haydi   "this" (f.), 36.39
haygā   "let's go!", 50.4
hayhāta   "wrong!", 50.4
hayye   "this" (f.), 36.39
hiet   "she", 36.14
hiǧān   "racing (camel)", 34.2
hinna   "if", 61.2
huet   "he", 36.14
humā   "them", "their", 36.3
hunā   "here", 47.7
huwa ḏā   "there he is", 36.33
huwa kātib   "he is writing", 42.24
ḥabál   "pregnancy", 25.7
ḥabaltu   "I carried", 11.6
ḥad   "one", 35.3
ḥaddādīn   "smiths", 31.11
ḥadīd, ḥadīda   "iron", "a piece of
    iron", 31.41
ḥaǧar   "stone", 18.9
ḥāla   "mother's sister", 30.4
ḥalaftu   "I swear", 38.18
ḥamaltu   "I carried", 11.6
ḥamām, ḥamāma   "pigeons", "sin-
    gle pigeon", 31.41
ḥamar   "red", 27.10
ḥamīr   "donkeys", 31.28
ḥasna   "how beautiful", 34.5
ḥattā   "so that", "even", "until",
    39.5; 48.17; 59.2
ḥayar   "stone", 18.9
ḥaydar   "small", 29.9
ḥazara   "he fenced in", 13.12
ḥimār   "donkey", 31.38; 63.3
ḥīn, ḥīna   "time", "when", 29.9; 58.9
ḥīnamā   "when", 58.9
ḥinnawṣ   "piglet", 29.10
ḥiṣāb   "to count", 42.3
ḥōrab   "he song war songs", 41.5
ḥulm   "dream", 29.9
ḫab'   "hidden thing", 31.21
ḫabbaṣa   "he mixed", 23.8
ḫādi   "seizing", 45.15

ḥāḏ "he seized", *45*.15

ḥafaqān "heartbeat", "fluttering", *29*.37

ḫāl "maternal uncle", *66*.4

ḫāla "maternal aunt", *66*.4

ḥalbaṣa "he mixed", *23*.8

Ḫaldūn "Khaldun", *29*.38

Ḫalfūn "Khalfun", *29*.38

ḫalīfa "deputy", "successor", *29*.46; *30*.1

ḫallaṣa "he saved", *63*.2

ḥamma "putrid smell", *41*.42

ḫarāf "lamb", *31*.28

ḫariba "he went to ruin", *41*.11

ḫāṭiʾatu lā-dīmīyatin "crime of irreligion", *51*.24

ḥazana "he stared", *66*.4

ḥdā "he seized", *45*.15

ḥirāf "lambs", *31*.28

ḥirbāʾu "chameleon", *29*.51

ḫörfān "lambs", *29*.40

ḫrāf "lambs", *31*.28

ḫubz "bread", *14*.4

ḥuḏ "seize!", *43*.3; *43*.6; *45*.15

ḥumra "date", *27*.13

ḥurṭum "proboscis", *41*.42

iʿādat an-naẓar "re-examination", *64*.5

ibg "stay!", *18*.8

ʾibn "son", *27*.17; *63*.8

ʾibrīq "pitcher", *28*.10

ʾiḏ, ʾiḏā "then", *56*.8; *58*.12

ʾiddī "who", *36*.53

ʾiftaʿala "it was fabricated", *27*.16

ʾiḡrāʾ "enforcement", *11*.14

ʾiḥranṭama "he looked sulky", *41*.42

ʾikdīš "jade", *28*.10

ʾiksīr "elixir", *65*.9

ʾiktaḥala "he coloured with kohl", *66*.6

ʾilāh "God", *31*.36

ildī "who", *36*.53

ʾillā "if not", *47*.12; *61*.3-4

illī "who", *36*.53; *57*.6

ʾīmānum, ʾiʾmānum "to believe", *45*.14

ʾimmā "if", *39*.8; *49*.4; *61*.2

ʾin "isn't", "if", *39*.16; *47*.12; *49*.6; *61*.1-2,5-6

ʾin lā "if not", *61*.3-4

ʾinna "behold", *49*.6; *50*.4; *60*.2; *61*.2

ʾirtafaʿa "he rose", *41*.22

ʾīqaẓ "watch!", *43*.6

ʾiqlīm "climate", *63*.10

ʾirṯ "inheritance", *11*.14

ʾism "name", *63*.13

ʾistakbara "he deemed great", *41*.9,29

ʾistiṣlāḥ "public advantage", *64*.6

ʾiṣfarra "he became yellow", *41*.39

itʿadd "it was counted", *41*.24

iteḥedder "he will discard", *41*.25

itfataḥ "it was opened", *41*.24

itgāwib "he was answered", *41*.27

itgawwiz "he was married", *41*.25

itmisik "it was seized", *41*.24

ʾiṭṭalaba "he sought", *27*.4

iṭnāni, iṭnēn "two", *35*.4

ʾittaʾara "he was avenged", *41*.32

ʾittāqala "he became heavy", *41*.25

ʾiyyā particle of pronominal objects, *36*.31; *52*.10

ʾizdaḥama "it was crowded", *41*.32

ʾizwarra "he became bent", *41*.39

ʾizzayyana "he was adorned", *41*.25,32

ka(-mā) "so that", "in order to", *49*.9; *58*.2; *59*.4

kā- "prefix of the imperfect", *38*.24

kabīr "great", *29*.6,8

kaddān "harness collar", *29*.11

kadīš "jade", *28*.10

kaḏūb "deceiving", *42*.14

kaff "palm of the hand", *30*.6

kaḥḥaba "he struck", *23*.8

kaḥḥāl "eye doctor", "oculist", *66*.6

kaḥḥala "he rubbed with kohl", *66*.6

kaḥīl "darkened with kohl", *42*.14; *66*.6

kāl "he ate", *45*.15

kalḥaba "he struck", *23*.8

kāli "eating", *45*.15

kam "or", *49*.4

kamā "so that", "in order to", *49*.9; *58*.2; *59*.4

kān(a) "he was", "it happened", *38*.20,24; *42*.24; *58*.5; *61*.10

kāna qad "he was already", *38*.20

kāna yafʿalu "he used to do", *38*.20

ka-niktib "I am writing", *38*.24

kān yəktub, kān kātib "he was writing", *38*.20; *42*.24

karīm "noble", *29*.16

kaslān "lazy", *29*.36

katabkan, katabkum "you wrote" (f., m. plur.), *40*.11

katabum "they wrote", *40*.10

kātib "scribe", *28*.1; *29*.7; *31*.28

katubk "I wrote", *40*.6

kawākib, kawkab "stars", "star", *31*.28

kawṭar "generous", *29*.9

kay(-mā) "so that", "in order to", *39*.5; *58*.2; *59*.4

kibar "greatness", *29*.6

kibīr "great", *29*.8

kilā, kiltā "both", *35*.4

killim "he spoke", *27*.10

kīmiyā "alchemy", "chemistry", *65*.9

kirkira "callous protuberance", *27*.3

kittarā "you would see", *27*.3

klā "he ate", *45*.15

kpr' "the tomb", *11*.4

ktibaw "they wrote", *40*.10

kū- "he is", *38*.24

kuḥaylān, kuḥaylī "horse of noblest breed", *66*.6

kuḥl "antimony", *66*.6

kuḥūl "alcohol", *66*.6

kūmišrab "he is not drinking", *38*.24

kul "eat!", *43*.3; *45*.15

kulayb "small dog", *29*.10

kunk "I was", "you were" (sing.), *40*.5-6

kunkū "you were" (plur.), *40*.11

kūn l- "to belong to", *49*.25

kūra "ball", *63*.6

kuttāb "scribes", *31*.28

l- "belonging to", *51*.20; *54*.6

la- proclitic of the optative, *39*.8,13

lā "not", *39*.16; *47*.10; *54*.3,6

lāʿ "he was lost", *16*.7

laʿall(a) "perhaps", *19*.17

labin, labina "bricks", "single brick", *31*.41

la'la'a "it glittered", *41*.38

Lāḏiqīya "Latakia", *67*.17

laḥm "meat", *63*.3

lakk "lac", *65*.6

lam, lā-ma "not", *39*.16-17; *47*.10

lammā "not yet", "when", *38*.18; *39*.16-17; *58*.3-8

lammān "when", *58*.8

lan "not", *39*.5,17; *47*.10

laqayat "she found", *43*.17

laqiya, laqiyat "he / she found", *43*.17

lastu "I am not", *49*.23

lā taqtul "you shall not kill", *38*.2

law, ləw "if", "when", *39*.17; *61*.6

lawbān "olibanum", *29*.9

lawlā "if not", *61*.6

laylan "by night", *52*.6

laysa "he is not", *47*.10; *54*.3

layt "lion", *17*.4

lbən "for whom?", *11*.6

l-ḥāṣōn "briefly", *17*.4

li- "to", "for", "so that", *39*.5,16, 18; *49*.7; *54*.6; *59*.4

li-'an "so that, "in order tò", *59*.4

lidī "give birth!", *43*.6-7

li-kay, li-kay-mā "so that", "in order to", *59*.4

lima "why?", *58*.3

lisān "language", "tongue", *27*.12

li-yaktub "he should write", *38*.2

lizām "duty", *17*.5

lmən "for whom?", *11*.6

lubān "olibanum", *29*.9

luḥūm "meat" (plur.), *14*.4

lukk "lac", *65*.6

mā, ma "what?", "as long as", "not", *36*.58,61; *38*.18,24; *47*.12,15,17; *54*.3, 6; *57*.2,7; *60*.2

mā' "water", *19*.17; *63*.5

maʿ, maʿa "with", *48*.14

maʿan "together", *48*.14

maʿīya "company", *48*.14

maġaḥa "he rejoiced", *11*.6

maǧlis "conference room", "court", 29.3,21

maġrib "evening", 27.10

maġzal "spindle", 29.24

maḥmal "to carry", 42.4

maḥzan "storeroom", 66.4

makara "he deceived", 64.4

mākir "impostor", "swindler", 64.4

makkār "impostor", "swindler", 64.4

Makkāwī, Makkī "Meccan", 29.44

maktaba "library", 28.1,16-17

malaka "he is the owner", "he took possession", 33.5

malakat "she is the proprietress", 38.3

malakūt "kingship", 29.48

malik, malika "king", "queen", 30.1

māmā "whatsoever", 36.61

man "who?", 36.58; 57.2

manāḥ "halting place", "climate", 29.20; 64.3

maqam "place", 64.1-2

maqraba "closeness", 29.25

maqrūwa "being read", 11.11

maqtūl "killed", 42.14

marad "illness", 31.28

markab "ship", 63.4

marṣā "we are both sick", 40.7

masǧid "mosque", 18.9

mā smuk "what is your name?", 11.6

maṣḥaf "book", "codex", 29.24

mašaġa "he mixed", 65.7

māši "he is going to hear", 42.24

matā "when?", 47.17

mataʿ "property", 51.19

maṭaru š-šitāʾi "the winter rain", 51.11

mazaġa "he mixed", 65.7

məkišrab "he is not drinking", 38.24

mġarib "evening", 27.10

miʿar "provisions", 22.15

miʾat, miʾāt "hundred", "hundreds", 35.20

miftāḥ "key", 29.22

miġzal "spindle", 29.24

miḥrāb "prayer niche", 29.21

mil- "from", 48.12

mimbar, minbar "pulpit", 27.6

min ġad(in) "to-morrow", 52.6

min(i) "from", "by", 11.6; 36.58; 48.12

misk "musk", 65.6

miṣdāqiyya "credibility", 29.45

miṣḥaf "book", "codex", 29.24

miʾūn "hundreds", 35.20

miyar "provisions", 22.15

mīye "hundred", 35.20

mizān "scale", 29.22

mizlaġ "skate, ski", 29.22

mnəktob "we write", 38.23

msīd "masque", 18.9

muʾassasāt "institutions", 29.47

muġzal "spindle", 29.24

muḥāṭaba "to address", 42.10

mulāḥ "very pretty", 34.2

munāḥ "halting place", "climate", 64.3

munhal, munhul "sieve", 29.23

mur "order!", "speak!", 43.3; 45.15

muṣḥaf "book", "codex", 29.24

mutaʿaddid al-ḫalāyā "multicellular", 64.5

nabbā, nabbaʾa "he announced", 45.15

Nabewl "Nabeul", 67.17

Nablūs "Nablus", 67.17

nafas "breath", "draught", 63.7

nafs "soul", "spirit", 36.12; 63.7

naǧǧār "carpenter", 29.11

nahar "river", 29.5

nahr "river", 29.5; 31.36

nāqa "she-camel", 29.9; 34.2

nasr "eagle", 31.38

naṭaqa "he spoke", 12.2

nawwaḥa "he halted for a rest", 64.3

ndaq "he spoke", 12.2

nə "for", 17.4

nəktəb "I shall write", 40.25

nəṣṣ "half", 27.4

niʿma "how nice!", 34.5

niḥammī "I protect", 38.5

niḥna "we", *36*.8
nikitbu "we shall write", *40*.25
niktib "I shall write", *40*.25
nims "ichneumon", *67*.4
niṣēh "I shall cry", *40*.25
niṣf "half", *27*.4
nišehhed "I certify", *38*.5
niṭāq "belt", *29*.8
nkətbu "we shall write", *40*.25
ntəḍrəb "he was beaten", *41*.26
ntqud "it took fire", *41*.26
nuhā "he was prohibited", *43*.17
nuhiya "he was prohibited", *43*.17
nuhur "rivers", *31*.36
parda "curtain", *11*.2
pēp "pipe", *11*.2
qablu "earlier", *47*.3
qad "already", *47*.18
qaddūs "most holy", *29*.11
qad kāna "he was already", *38*.20
qāḍi "judge", *16*.8
Qalʿat ʾal-ballūṭ "Caltabellotta", *67*.12
Qalʿat ʾal-ġirān "Caltagirone", *67*.12
Qalʿat ʾan-nisāʾ "Caltanissetta", *67*.15
qāma "he stood", *43*.9; *64*.1
qamaza "he took with the finger-tips", *35*.9
qaraʾa, *qarā* "he recited", "he read", *27*.8; *29*.37
qarīb "relative", *31*.36
qaṣr "castle", *63*.10
qatala "he killed", *10*.9
qatīl "killed", *29*.8
qatīlu l-ǧuʿi "killed by starvation", *51*.11
qawl "saying", *31*.9
qawwama "het set upright", *43*.9
qīla "(it) was said", *44*.13
qinnab, qinnam "hemp", *11*.6
qirš "piaster", *65*.4
qišr "slough", *29*.17
qlam "sheep", *17*.4
quddūs "most holy", *29*.11
quds "holiness", *29*.5
qūla "(it) was said", *44*.13
qultu "I said", *18*.8
qūm "to stand", *44*.5-6; *64*.2
qunwān "bunch of dates", *29*.40

qurʾān "Coran", *29*.37
qwly "tell me!", *27*.20
raʾā "he saw", *62*.3; *65*.10
rāʾā "he observed", "he saw", *62*.3
rabaḍ "suburb", *16*.8
rabbaʿa "he quadrupled", *35*.34
rabbanā "our Lord!", *32*.5
raġul "man", *18*.9
rāḥ "he went", *17*.1
ramaw "they threw", *43*.17
ramayta "you (sing.) threw", *43*.17
Rās ʾAdar "Ras Addar", *67*.9
Rās ʾal-ʾAbyaḍ "Ras el-Abyad", *67*.10
Rās ʾal-ʾAḥmar "Ras el-Aḥmar", *67*.10
rās ʾal-ʿamūd "capital", *66*.5
Rās ʾal-Ḥimār "Ras el-Ḥimar", *67*.13
Rās ʾal-Kalb "Ras el-Kalb", *67*.13
rasūl "sent", "envoy", *42*.14
rāwa "he showed", *62*.3
rawz "rice", *29*.9
rāyiḥ "going", *38*.20; *42*.24
rayyis "head", *19*.17
riʾa, riʾā "lung", "lungs", *31*.13
riǧāl "men", *29*.8
riǧl "foot", *18*.9; *30*.6
riǧlēnāt "pairs of paws", *31*.12
riʾūna "lungs", *31*.13
rīl "man", *18*.9
riya "eyesight", *62*.3
ruḍā "he was well received", *43*.17
Ruḍā "Ruḍā" (deity), *16*.8
ruḍiya "he was well received", *43*.17
ruḥānī "spiritual", *29*.36
ruzz "rice", *29*.9
saʾala, sāla, sʾyl "he asked", *44*.5
saʿīd "lucky", *14*.3
sabaqa "he left behind", *41*.10
sabba "he abused", *44*.10
sahm "arrow", *14*.3
saḥḥara "he bewitched", *65*.8
sakkara "he sugared", *65*.6
sal "ask!", *45*.15
salām "peace", *50*.4
samāʾ "heaven", *19*.7

sami‛ "he heard", *14*.4

sana, sanawāt "year", "years", *31*.13

sāraḥa "he dispatched", *17*.5

Saraqusṭa "Zaragoza", *67*.17

sāriqūna/īna "thieves", *31*.11

saruwa, saruwat "he / she was noble", *43*.17

sarw "cypress", *11*.6

sawǧar "he collared (a dog)", *41*.5

sifāḥ "concubinage by capture", *62*.4

sīgān, sīǧān "legs", *18*.6; *29*.40

sinūna "years", *31*.3

sīqān "legs", *18*.6; *29*.40

sīṭa "(it) was whipped together", *44*.13

smānayt "I became fat", *41*.39

smānt, smənt "I became fat", *41*.39

staygbal "he turned his face towards the Qibla", *41*.42

st‛āhid "he agreed with", *41*.31

stnāwal "he packed with", *41*.31

suhaym "little arrow", *14*.3

sukkar "sugar", *65*.6

sūṭa "(it) was whipped together", *44*.13

ṣa‛id "it came up", *14*.4

ṣabāḥa masā’a "mornings and evenings", *47*.2

ṣada‛ "he broke", *63*.3

Ṣafāwī "man from Ṣafā", *29*.44

ṣalaḥa "he was good", *64*.6

ṣawf "wool", *29*.9

ṣayaḥt "I cried", *40*.25; *44*.5

ṣifr "zero", *65*.8

ṣiǧar "smallness", *29*.8

ṣiḥtu "I cried", *44*.5

ṣubyān "boys", *29*.40

ṣūf "wool", *29*.9

ṣūra "image", *29*.9

š- "which", *36*.59

ša‛ar, ša‛r "hair", *29*.5

šā‛ir "poet", *31*.28

šāf "he saw", *65*.10

šaḥḥāḍ, šaḥḥāṭ "beggar", *13*.9

šākir "thankful", "rewarding", *14*.3

šabi‛ū "they were sated", *14*.4

šanīkī "who hates you", *46*.5

šarb, šārib "drinkers' company", "drinker", *31*.42

šarqan wa-ǧarban "eastward and westward", *32*.20

šaršūba, šaršubba "tassel", *44*.14

šay’ "thing", "something", *35*.3; *47*.15; *54*.4

šayāṭīn, šayṭān "devils", "devil", *31*.28

šayham "hedgehog", *29*.9

šenhu "who is …?", *36*.59

-š(ə) negative particle, *54*.4

šifā’ "to heal", *42*.3

šifāh "lips", *31*.19

šīt, šīyāt "of", *51*.19

šrabt, šrapt "I drink", *27*.6

šu‛arā’ "poets", *31*.28

šumlūl "small amount", *29*.14

ta’aqlama "he was acclimated", *63*.10

ta‛allama "he learned", *41*.25

taḍribīnī "you (fem.) will beat me", *46*.5

ṭāfəndāqəṭ "*funduq*-keeping", *65*.2

tafrīq "partition", *29*.30

taǧara "he traded", *64*.4

tāǧir "trader", *64*.4

ṭāhaddādəṭ "smithery", *65*.2

taḥta "under", *48*.16

taḥtāni "lower", *48*.16

taḥtu "below", "beneath", *32*.18; *47*.3

taḥiḍa "he took for himself", *41*.24

takaḥḥala "he coloured with kohl", *66*.6

tal‛a "water-course", *27*.12

talqayna "you (fem.) will find", *43*.17

tamma "it was done", *41*.44

Tanǧa "Tangier", *67*.9

taqallubāt "fluctuations", *29*.47

taqātalū "they fought together" *27*.15

taqātalū(na) "you fight together", *41*.27

tarabba‛a "he sat cross-legged", *35*.34

tarabūt "trained", "manageable", 29.48

tarawwas "he became chief", 19.17

tarsāna "ship-yard", 64.5

taršhāna "ship-yard", 64.5

tašādada, tašādda "he argued with somebody", 44.15

tbny "he consummated the marriage", 41.24

teḥedder "he discarded", 41.25

tfaʿal, tfaʿil "it was made", 41.24

tilka "that" (f.), 36.44

tlāt- "three", 29.8

tmān- "eight", 29.8

tnayn, tnēn "two", 35.4

tsəfʿal "he was moved to act", 41.30

ttəḍrəb "he was beaten", 41.26

ttənḍrəb "he was beaten", 41.26

tuǧǧār "traders", 64.4

ṭabṭaba "he gurgled", 41.38

ṭallaʿ "he brought up", 23.11

Ṭarābulus "Tripoli", 67.16

ṭarad, ṭard "hunt", 29.5

ṭarṭaba "he gurgled", 41.38

ṭaylaʿ "he brought up", 23.11

ṭayr "birds", 31.38

ṭīb "scent", 29.9

ṭaʿlab "fox", "she-fox", 30.5

ṭadan "teat", "udder", 30.11

ṭalāṭāʾu, ʾaṭ- "Tuesday", 29.51

ṭamma "there", 47.7

ṭaqīl "heavy", 29.6

ṭawm "garlic", 29.9

ṭawr "bull", 65.5

ṭāwulūǧiya "theology", 63.12

ṭiqal "heaviness", 29.6

ubaḥḥar "it was fumigated", 41.44

ʾubūwa "fatherhood", 29.1

ʾudn- "ear", 41.8

ʾuḏun "ear", 48.18

ʾulā(ʾi) "these", 36.33,39; 57.6

ʾulālika "those", 36.44

ʾummahāt "mothers", 31.19

ʾummane "our mother", 32.5

ʾurwīya "ibex", 63.4

ʾustāḏ "master", 31.18

ʾuṣūliyya "fundamentalism", 29.45

wa- "and", 39.5; 56.8

Wād(i) ʾal-kabīr "Guadalquivir", 67.12

wafara "he abounded", 29.9

wafr "wealth", 67.16

waǧh "face", 18.9

waḥda "lowland", 67.12

waḥada, wāḥid "to be alone", "one", 19.24; 33.5; 48.18

wāḥid "seizing", 45.15

wākil "eating", 45.15

wakkil "he fed", 11.11

waladku "I bore", 40.6

walifa "he is familiar", 19.24

waliya "he was near", 43.17

wanā "he languished", 19.24

waqaʿa "it befell", "it happened", 43.23

ward, warda "rose", 65.5

wariq "green", 27.8

wariṯa "he inherited" 11.14

warrada "it blossomed", "he dyed red", 65.5

wasaṭ, wasṭ "midst", 48.19

wasmāʾ "the beautiful one", 19.24

wasṭa "among", "within", 48.19

waṣada "he stood firm", 10.8

wāš "which", 36.59

wa-yaqūlu "and he said", 38.11

wayn "where", 48.18

wayn "vineyard", 65.5

wēh "face", 18.9

widn "ear", 48.18

wūš "which", 36.59

yā "oh!", 50.3

yabrūḥ "mandrake", 29.18

yabtar "may he be cut off", 38.16

yabtur "may he cut", 38.16

yad, yadā "band", 28.13; 30.6

yadāni "two hands", 31.6

yadbaǧ, yadbiǧ, yadbuǧ "may he tan", 38.16

yaddaṯṯaru "he covers himself", 41.32

yaḍribūnā "they will beat us", 46.5

yafraǧu, yafruǧu "he is at rest", 45.14

yafṣil "may he separate", 38.16

yafṣul "may he depart", 38.16

yaǧidu "he will find", 43.6

yaǧnaḥu, yaǧnuḥu "he inclines", 45.14

yaḥmūr "deer", *29.18*
yaḥsib "may he value", *38.15*
yāḥud̠, ya'ḥud̠u "he will seize", *28.4; 45.15*
yakaytib "he writes", *41.42*
yaktib "he will write", *40.25; 41.19*
yākul "he will eat", *45.15*
yalī "he will be near", *43.17*
yalqā "he will find", *43.17*
yanqad "may he be saved", *38.16*
yanqud "may he save", *38.15-16*
yarā "he will see", *45.15*
yarmiya "he would throw", *43.17*
Yarmūk "Yarmouk", *29.18*
yasal "he will ask", *45.15*
yā salām "what a pity!", *50.4*
yasrū "he will be noble", *43.17*
yaṣṣadaq "he will prove his righteousness", *27.14*
yaṣṣaddaqu "he gives alms", *41.25*
yašrab "may he drink", *38.15*
yataṣaddaqu "he gives alms", *41.25*
yaṭṭahharu "he will perform an ablution", *41.25*
Yat̠rib "Medina", *29.18*
yawm "day", *29.9*
yawman "by day", *47.2*
yəkūn katab "he will write", *38.20*

yibġi "he will", *38.22*
yifassaḥ "he takes out for a walk", *27.10*
yikammil "he achieves", *27.10*
yiktub "he will write", *40.25*
yišrab "he will drink", *40.25; 41.19*
yubaḥḥar "it will be fumigated", *41.44*
yubirru "he fulfills", *44.15*
yudīyun "hands", *31.6*
yuharīqu "he will pour out", *41.11*
yuḥibbu "he will love", *41.11*
yūḥud̠ "he will seize", *45.15*
yūkil "he will eat", *45.15*
yuktub "he will write", *40.25*
yūm "day", *22.7*
yunabbī, yunabbi'u "he will announce", *45.15*
zahara "he shone", *43.23*
zaḥzaḥa "he displaced", "he ripped off", *35.14*
zalzala "he shook", *41.38*
zammām "bolt", *29.11*
zātūn "olives", *22.4*
zawǧ "pair", "two", *35.4*
ẓaltu, ẓiltu "I became", *24.5*
ẓami'a "he was thirsty", *13.12*
ẓuhar "he appeared", *41.11*

ARAMAIC
MANDAIC, NEO-ARAMAIC, SYRIAC

'a'bēd "he caused to produce", *41.11*
'ăbāhātōk "your fathers", *31.19*
'abūlā "city gate", *65.3*
'aḥărīt "future", *29.49*
'aḥūnā "brother", *29.38*
'aktābū(t) "cause to write", *42.9*
'al "not", *47.9*
'ămarkāl "accountant", *63.11*
amelə̄l, amell "he said to them", *23.1*
amērā "he should say it", *46.4*
'ănā "I", *36.5*
'ap "also", *49.2*
'ar'ā "on the ground", "below", *32.19*

'ărōmā'ē "Romans", *33.9*
'aryā, 'aryē "(the) lion", *11.13; 27.15; 31.18; 63.4*
'āsē "doctor", *31.18*
'awrab "greater", *34.5*
'aydā "which?", "any" (fem.), *36.59*
'aykā "where?", *47.7*
'aylēn "which?", "any" (plur.), *36.59*
'aynā "which?", "any" (masc.), *36.59*
'āzālnā, azāna "walker", *43.10*
'dqr "jugs", *31.26*
'dr' "arm", *30.6*
'glh "Ekallāte", *27.28*
'lwr "Ilu-Wēr", *11.8*
'm', 'mr "to say", *17.2*

ʾl "not", *54*.6
ʾl smk "God is my support", *11*.7
ʾlw "behold", "see", *49*.8
ʾmt(y) "when?", "until when?", *47*.17
ʾnk "I", *36*.6
ʾpyn "face", *30*.6
ʾrʿm "he raised", *17*.1
ʾr(h/w) "behold", "see", 49.8
ʾṣdq "executor", *29*.16
ʾthḥsynn "they refrained", *41*.30
ʾusṭol "table", *27*.17
ʾyqwnʾ "image", *63*.10
ʾyt "accusative" marker, *36*.31; *52*.10
ʾyt lk "you have", *49*,25
ʾzl "to go", *43*.10
ʾzlh "he went away", *27*.20
ʾzl nʾ "go, please!", *40*.14
ʿAbday "servant (of)", *67*.7
ʿabded "he enslaved", *41*.40
ʿAbdūn "servant (of)", *29*.38
ʿăbīd lī "I have done", *42*.20; *65*.4
ʿabrānā, orāna "passer-by", *29*.39
ʿad "up to", "until", *48*.17
ʿad dī "until", *58*.14
ʿal dibr(at) "because of", *27*.13; *48*.15
ʿall "he entered", *19*.23; *44*.10
ʿam(m-) "together with", *48*.13
ʿanbītā "a grape", *29*.49
ʿaqrab "scorpion", *29*.17
ʿbyd ly "I have done", *42*.20; *65*.4
ʿdant "when", *58*.15
ʿdbr "because of", *27*.13
ʿtntn "Atta has given", *50*.25
ʿelāyā "upstairs", *47*.2
ʿəbādā "acting", *42*.4
ʿl, ʿly "over", "above", *48*.15
ʿmbrʾ "sheep", *11*.9
ʿmmʾ "the people", *23*.3
ʿštʾ "the unit (of measure)", *35*.3
ʿulaym "young boy", *29*.10
ʿyn "eye", *30*.6
ʿyr "to transfer", "to alienate", *63*.14
Bʿšm(y)n "Baal of the skies", *27*.27
balbēl "he confused", *41*.38

bānayīn "who build", "builders", *43*.15
bar, bir "son", *11*.6; *63*.8
bārā "outside", *32*.19
baynay, baynat "between", *48*.21
berča "daughter", *12*.3
bētan "our house", *36*.23
bəʾā "he requested", *43*.15
bəkā "he cried", *43*.15
bənō "they built", *43*.15
bərāt(ā) "juniper", *65*.5
b(i)- "in", *38*.22
bi-ptāḫā-lē/ā "he / she is opening", *38*.23; *42*.21
bi-ptāḫā-wā "he was opening", *42*.21
birānyāt "strongholds", *31*.10
birtā "stronghold", *31*.10
bit-pātḥā "she will open", *42*.19
bit-pātiḥ elē "he will open it", *46*.4
bi-yuḏmuk "he will sleep", *38*.22
brūnā "son", *29*.38
bwlʾ "Senate", *65*.4
byn "between", *48*.21
byt spyntʾ "ship-yard", *64*.5
b-zy "since", "as", *49*.16
čū "not", *47*.8
čunkē d- "because", "as", *58*.15
d- "which", "of", "that", *60*.3
dʾ, dh "this", *36*.39
dābāšā, dabbāšā "bee", *23*.1
dabbūḥā "sacrificer" *29*.11
dabr- "pasture", *31*.25
Dahabān "golden", *29*.36
daqdəqē "little ones", *31*.21
Darmeśeq "Damascus", *23*.9
dbhh "she-bear", *28*.13
deqlā "palm-tree", *27*.30
də "which", "of", "that", *36*.52; *60*.3
dəlā "he drew out", *43*.15
dəmā "blood", *27*.30
dī "which", "of", "that", *36*.52; *57*.2,6; *60*.3
dkyr "remembered", *42*.14
dlā "lest", *59*.5
dnh "this", *36*.39
dqr "jug", *31*.26
dššn "doors", *23*.3

dy "which", "of", *36.52; 57.2,6; 60.3*

ebra "son", *24.9*

ʾegūrā "temple", *65.3*

el- "to", "of", "by", *46.4; 48.6*

ʾellā "if not", *61.3*

ʾēlle "these", *36.33*

ʾellū "if", *61.9*

ʾen "if", *61.2,9*

ʾeprā "meadow", *67.16*

ʾestəmek "he leaned", *27.14*

ʾeštawdī "he confessed", *41.9,29*

ʾethassan "he was fortified", *41.25*

ʾetkālā "the grapes", *31.26*

ʾetkəteb "it was written", *27.16*

ʾetqəṭel "he was killed", *41.24*

ʾettrīm "he was raised", *41.30*

ʾezzet "I went", *43.10*

gʾyṭʾ "summer", *18.8*

gabr "man", *63.6*

galgal "wheel", "globe", *29.13*

ganzā "store-room", *63.10*

ganzibrā "treasurer", *65.4*

garm- "bone", "person", *36.28*

gawzel "he set fire to", *41.5*

gazzā "store-room", *63.10*

gazzūrā "butcher", *29.11*

gazzūzā "shearer", *29.11*

ginnā, ginnāta "garden", "the gardens", *31.13*

ginnīn, ginnayyā "gardens", "the gardens", *31.13*

giṭṭā "document", *65.3*

gizzabrā "treasurer", *65.4*

gizzūr "piece", *29.11*

ġlabtā "victory", *10.8; 19.14*

gōra "man", "husband", *11.5*

grb, grībā "bushel", *27.17*

gulgultā "skull", *29.13*

gwḥ, gwmḥ "burial niche/site", *63.9*

gzr ʿdyʾ "to conclude a treaty", *64.6*

hʾzʾ, hʾzyn "this" (fem., masc.), *36.39*

hal d- "till", *58.15*

hānā, hānāt- "this", "that", *36.33-34*

hanʿālā "he brought in", *17.8*

hanpēq "he cause to go out", *41.11*

hansāqā "he brought up", *17.8*

(hǎ)wā "(he) was", *38.20*

hdʾ, hdh "this", *36.39*

hdk "that", *36.44*

hd(y)n "this", *36.39*

hēn, hēn lā "if", "if not", *61.2-3*

hištəkah "he was found", *41.24*

hlk "to go", *43.10*

hlw "behold", "see", *49.8*

hlyk "that", *36.44*

hn "if", *61.2*

hnlw "if", *61.9*

hn(w) lw "if ... when", *61.9*

hrkb "to shoot", *63.4*

hry "behold", "see", *49.8*

htnʾbw "they were withered", *41.28*

hūbad "he was destroyed", *41.46*

hussaq "he was brought up", *17.2*

hzmntwn "you have agreed", *41.32*

ḥǎbal "woe!", *50.4*

ḥad "one", *27.26; 35.3,32*

Ḥadattu "Ḥadattu", *67.12*

ḥadhədānē "certain ones", *31.21*

ḥamṣalaytā "stalk", *67.3*

ḥašbānā "bill", *15.5*

ḥaylānā "strong", *29.36*

ḥǎzaytā "you saw", *43.15*

ḥazī lī "I have seen", *42.20*

ḥerbā "badly", *47.2*

ḥimār, ḥmāra "donkey", *29.8*

ḥiṭīṭā "a grain of wheat", *29.49*

ḥsl "to save", *27.12*

ḥyyʾ "life", *9.5*

ḥzytwn "you saw", *43.15*

iftaḥ "he opened", *24.9*

īle "he has", *49.25*

ʾillēk, ʾillēn "those", *36.33*

ʾimməhātā "the mothers", *31.19*

ʾištīw, ʾištīyū "they drank", *43.15*

ʾit, ʾīt "there is", *49.23*

k- "as", "like", "truly", *48.11; 49.9*

kad, kaḏ "while", "when", *58.15*

kaddū "sufficiently", "enough", *32.18*

karmā "vineyard", *29.53*

karmiktā "small vineyard", *29.53*

kārōz "herald", *63.11*

katbānā "writer", *29.39*

kāteb, kātēb "writing", *42.13*
kattābā "cause to write", *42.9*
kēᵃfa "stone", *27.10*
kə-dī "when", *58.14*
kəlakkā "raft", *29.12*
kətīb "written", *29.8*; *42.14*
kī- "(he) is", *38.24*
ki-bayī "they want", *45.12*
kīfiš "your (fem.) stone", *18.6*
ki-pāʾiš škīla "he is taken", *42.22*
kinā "companion", *31.18*
ki-pātiḥ, ki-pāṯḥā/ī "he / she is open-
    ing", "they are opening", *38.24*;
    42.19
klm, kln "all of them", *27.25*
kniš-lia "I swept", *42.20*
knkr "talent", *23.7*
korsē, kursiʾ "seat", "throne", *23.9*;
    31.18
kpl "double", *35.4*
krš "weight", "coin", *65.4*
ktúli "I wrote", *22.10*
ktyb "it is written", *41.46*
kṭl "to kill", *10.9*; *27.11*
ky "as", "when", *58.2*
kwk "grave", *18.5*; *63.9*
l- "to", "for", "of", "by", *46.4*;
    48.6; *51.23*; *52.11*; *53.2,5*; *54.6*
lā "not", *47.9*
laytā "lion", *17.4*
l-ʿlyʾ "at the upper end", *48.7*
Lʿš "Luġaṯ", *17.4*
lhwy "may he be", *38.2*
lmḥwh "to explain", *42.9*
lnsb "he takes away", *40.23*
lō, lóʾ "not", *47.8*
lqḥ "to take", *43.10*
l-tḥtyʾ "at the lower end", *48.7*
lū "if", *61.6,11*
lw "if", *61.8-9*
lyb "heart", *30.6*
mā "hundred", *35.20*
madbaḥ, madbəḥā "altar", *11.7*;
    29.21
māgār "if not", *61.3*
maktābū(t) "cause to write", *42.9*
malkān "queens", *31.12*
malkū, malkūt "kingship", *29.48*; *30.4*

mallāḥ "sailor", *29.11*
manbig "spring site", *11.4*
*manmi, *manma "whoever", *36.61*
māra "owner", *31.14*
markabtā "chariot", *63.4*
markəbā "ship", *63.4*
markōl "accountant", *63.11*
maršema "famous", *29.55*
marṭūṭ "lint", *29.14*
mārwātā "known owners", *31.14*
masgad "house of prayer", *14.3*
mašpīl "humiliating", *42.15*
māʾtayin "two hundred", *35.20*
mayyā "water", *63.5*
mbār d- "after (that)", *58.15*
mbater d- "after (that)", *49.16*
mdkwr "remembered", *42.14*
mektōb "to write", *42.4*
meqṭal "to kill", *42.4*
məʾā "hundred", *35.20*
məganbāʾīt "by stealth", *47.4*
məkar "he bought", *18.5*; *63.9*
məkattābā "cause to write", *42.9*
mən d- "since", *58.15*
*mht "lands", *31.27*
mḥʾ yd "to pledge", *64.6*
mílef "it is learned", *22,8*
millā, millīn "word", "words",
    30.4; *31.10*
min "from", "by", *11.6*; *48.12*
min dī "after (that)", *58.14*
mišbaq "to leave", *42.4*
miškab "bed", "grave", *29.3,21*
mišmeʿ "to hear", *45.10*
mīta, mitta "dead" (masc., fem.),
    23.5
mkr "to buy", *18.5*; *63.9*
mlkw, mlky "kings", *31.11*
mn "whoever", *36.62*; *57.7*
-mnkw "king", *17.4*
mōnmi ḏīṯ / līṯ "whoever he is",
    36.61
mqm "tomb", *64.2*
mqrh "bales (of straw)", *27.28*
mšbyʿ ʾny "I am adjuring", *35.34*
mšlmwth "its repaying", *42.9*
mšn "treasurer", *14.2*
mšqy "watering-place", *30.4*

mt'l "brought in", *41*.30

mt kln "all the lands", *31*.27

mūnma līṭ "whoever he is", *36*.61

mymwr "to say", *45*.10

mzg "to mix", *65*.7

nahrā "the river", *67*.10

Nahrīn "North Mesopotamia", *29*.54

nāqī' "clear", *66*.2

na-šá-a-a-tu "I took", *43*.15

našūnā "little fellow", *29*.38

n'bs "bowl-like leg", *11*.7

nbš "breath", *10*.8; *11*.5

ndbkh "the altar", *11*.7

nebkā "well", *10*.8

nebkē "he cries", *43*.15

nedlē "he draws out", *43*.15

nehod "he will seize", *45*.11

nhwy' "may he be" (?), *17*.4

nidmek "I had slept", *40*.25

nōša "person", "soul", *11*.5

nphr "sum", *29*.26

npš "breath", *10*.8; *36*.12

nqdš' "the sanctuary", *11*.7

nsōfar "I travel", *40*.25

nšpṭ "judgement", *11*.7; *29*.26

nwṭy "Nabataean", *11*.8

pa- "and so", *49*.2

pā'iš "remaining", *42*.22

palāha, pallāha "worker", *29*.11

parhalēle "bat", *29*.55

pehā "governor", *31*.18

pərakkā "altar", *29*.12

phd, phz "clan", "tribe", *13*.9

pillaqtā "concubine", *65*.7

pirpira "butterfly", *29*.13

pndšw Nabataean PN, *23*.8

psh' "Easter", *63*.9

psk "Easter", *63*.9

ptāhā "to open", *42*.4

ptīh-lī, ptīhā-lē, ptīhē-lā "he / she has opened (it/them)", *42*.20

ptuh-lē "open it", *46*.4

ptwr "interpreter (of dreams)", *29*.11

pṭ'sy Egyptian PN, *27*.28

puqdānā "order", *29*.37

qadmāy "first", "former", *35*.24

qa(d)m d- "before", *58*.15

qam-pāthin "I have opened", *42*.19

qarnayin "horns", *31*.4

qarqēš "he knocked", *41*.38

qaṣr "castle", "compound", *63*.10

qašqēš "he knocked", *41*.38

qat "in order to", "so that", *59*.5

qaṭlēh "he killed him", *46*.4

qayṭā "summer", *18*.8

qayyēm "he caused to stand", *43*.9

qbāltā "complaint", *11*.5

qeštīmāran "rainbow", *29*.55

qərābā "fight", *42*.4

qəṭal "he killed", *46*.3

qilqiltā, qīqiltā "rubbish dump", *17*.2

qīqn- "single", *36*.28

qnūm- "person", "being", *36*.28

qŏdāmēhon "before them", *48*.23

qpyls "retailer", *63*.10

Qšt "hamlet", *67*.15

qulqālā "disgrace", *17*.2

qumṣ- "handful", *35*.9

qwaltā "complaint", *11*.5

qwaz "he leapt" *11*.5

qyāmā "statute", *44*.5

rab "great", *31*.21; *34*.5

rābā "very", "much", *47*.2

rahmān "merciful", *29*.36

rāhūmā'īt "kindly", *47*.4

rebbō "ten thousand", *35*.22

rēgālen "feet", *31*.28

rgl "foot", *30*.6

rmyn "we threw", *43*.15

rsh "first-fruits", *27*.28; *30*.4

sābāb d- "because", *58*.15

sāgān "governor", "official", *65*.3

sāhid "to harvest", *27*.12

sirsur "broker", *29*.13

skr "rewarding", *14*.3

slq "to go up", *17*.2; *43*.10

smk, snk "to support", *11*.7

ss "sun", *11*.8

swr "ox", "bull", *65*.5

ṣabbā "wagon", *23*.7

ṣiyyūd "game", *29*,11

ṣln, ṣnm "statue", *17*.4

śē' "carry away!", *43*.5

š'yl "he asked", *44*.5

šaʿbēd "he enslaved", *41*.10

Šabbatay "(born on) sabbath", *67*.3

šaddar "he sent", *62*.3

šaḥlep, šaḥlep "he changed", "changing", *41*.10

Šaʾīl "requested", *67*.7

šaklēl, šaklilū "he / they completed", *29*.33; *41*.10

šalhēb, šalhēbītā "he kindled", "flame", *29*.33

šappīr "beautiful", *29*.11

šarbīṭ "staff", "sceptre", *23*.9

šarwaynā "cypress", *11*.6

šātaḥ "we drink", *43*.15

šātī "they drink", *43*.15

šʿd "lucky", *14*.3

šəlaḥ "he sent", *62*.3

šəlamləmā "complete", *29*.14

šəmāhāt "names", *31*.19

šəparpārā "lightness", "morning light", *29*.14

šēzib "he saved", *41*.10

šh(y)mw "(little) arrow", *14*.3

šimšā "sun", *30*.5

šišiltā "chain", *31*.10

škr "rewarding", *14*.3

škytyt "honourably", *47*.4

šlḥ "to send", *17*.5

šmh "his name", *65*.4

šmhʾ "the memorial", *28*.13

šmilan "we heard", *45*.12

šolṭān "power", *29*.37

štāyā "to drink", *43*.15

šuklālā "completion", *29*.33

šurbīnā "cypress", *11*.6

šwr "ox", "bull", *65*.5

šwš "sun", *11*.8

šyyl "he asked", *44*.5

taʿdīrā "help", *29*.30

taggārā "trader", *64*.4

takrīk "covering", "garment", *29*.30

tām, tammān "there", *47*.7

tanā "here", *47*.7

tarʿā "gate", "door", *27*.13

tarbūt "training", *29*.48

targūm "translation", *29*.30; *41*.42

taymān, tēmān "south", *29*.31

tešmeštā "service", *29*.30

tədā "breast", *30*.11

təḥōt, theyt, tḥt "under", "below", *48*.16

tḥty "lower part", *48*.16

ti-ḥu-ú-tú "under", "below", *48*.16

tinyān "second", *35*.25

tmk "to seize", *18*.5

tōrā "ox", "bull", *65*.5

tōrī/ē "bulls", *31*.11

tryn, trēn "two", *35*.4

treyāna "second", *35*.25

tṣlwth "praying to him", *27*.28

twr "ox", "bull", *65*.5

ṭābāʾīt "well", *47*.4

ṭʿīnin "they had carried", *42*.18

ṭbh "sweet" (fem.), *27*.28

ṭōʿnin "they carry", *42*.18

ṭuranāyā "mountaineer", *29*.36

ṭam "there", *47*.7

up "also", *49*.2

wardā "rose", *65*.5

wt "accusative" particle, *36*.31; *52*.10

yabrūḥ "mandrake", *29*.18

yaḥmūr "deer", *29*.18

yalūnā "youngster", *29*.38

yāma, yammā "sea", *23*.5, *63*.5

yədaḥălinnanī "he terrifies me", *46*.4

yəhāk "he goes", "he shall go", *17*.2; *43*.10

yəhōdəʿunnanī "they shall explain to me", *46*.4

ygtzr "it will be cut off", *41*.22

ygzr "he will be cut", *41*.46

yhybw "they were delivered, given", *41*.46

yhzʾ "he sees", *40*.23

*yidā *"he shall pay blood money", *41*.9

yiktub "he writes", *38*.15

yiladī "give birth!", *43*.6

yilbaš "he dresses", *38*.15

yiqrib "he comes near", *38*.15

yištamməʿūn "they will obey", *41*.25

yqtlnh "he shall kill him", *46*.4

yqḥ "he takes", *43*.10

yrwh, *yrwy* "let it be sated", *22.9*; *43.15*

ysq "he goes up", *43.10*

yt "accusative" marker, *36.31*; *52.10*

ytšmʿ "it will be heard", *41.20,23-24*

yymr "he will speak", *45.12*

z "which", "of", *36.52*

zʾ, *zh* "this", *36.39*

Za-bi-i-ni "bought", "redeemed", *42.14*

zʾt "this" (fem.), *36.52,54*

zeqlā "palm-tree", *27.30*

zəmā "blood", *27.30*

zī "which", "of", *36.52*; *57.2,6*

zīl "go!", *43.10*

zlih-lia "I cleaned", *42.20*

znh "this", *36.39*

zrwʿ "seed!", *45.10*

zūḥ "to go away", "to remove", *35.14*

zy "which", "of", *36.52*; *57.2,6*

zy ly "of mine", *51.19*

ARGOBBA

allä "he is", *36.33*

ank "you (sing.)", *36.6,9*

ankum "you (plur.)", *36.9*

asmelläsa "he let (somebody) answer", *41.9*

awre "wild animal", *63.4*

ay "I", *36.14*

bärätta "he became strong", *41.39*; *63.4*

bedač "houses", *31.17*

bedu "the house", *32.28*

čən "thigh", *30.11*

därräsä "he found", "he met", *45.9*

əndä "such as", "according to", *48.22*

-(ə)nna "and", *49.1*

ənnä *"these", *36.9*

ənnankum "you" (plur.), *36.9*

ənnekkäsa "he was bitten", *41.32*

fəyyäl "goat", *30.10*

hansia "donkey", *30.10*

haṭṭära "he fenced in", *13.12*

həwaw "snake", *11.9*

kärsa/u "her / his belly", *36.12*

kəssa/u "she", "he", *36.12*

lef "on", *11.15*

-n "and", *49.1*

qänd "horn", *17.7*

qärš "piaster", *65.4*

qurä "crow", "raven", *30.10*

säddäba "he offended", *41.53*

tä- "from", "in", "with", *48.18*

tef "under", *11.15*

ṭamma- "be thirsty", *13.12*

wäsfe "awl", *23.5*

wašša "cellar", *48.19*

wäyəš "or", *49.4*

wəfč "inside", *11.15*

wof "bird", *11.11*

yä- "of", *36.31,55*; *48.6*

yənnekkäsäl "he will be bitten", *41.32*

žäḥʷṭäňň "nine", *35.14*

ASSYRO-BABYLONIAN
LATE BABYLONIAN, OLD AKKADIAN

The mimation is not indicated; EA is the marker of Canaanisms in the Amarna correspondence.

ā "not", *54.6*

A-a-bi "where is my father?", *47.11*

A-ba-Il "Il / God is (the) father", *32.11*; *33.6*

abātu "to perish", *10.8*

Abba "Father" (DN), *32.6*

abbū "fathers", *31.25*

abbūtu "fatherhood", "paternity", *28.4*; *64.1*

A-bi₄-i-lí "my god is my father", *33.6*

abu "father", *64.1*
abullu "city gate", *31.*15; *65.*3
A-bu-na "our father", *36.23*
adāru "to fear", *67.9*
adi, adīna, adīni "up to", "until", *35.*31; *48.*17; *58.*11
adi mati "until when?", "how long?", *47.17*
adum "up to", "until", *48.17*
agā, agātu "this", "these", *36.35*
agana "well!", *50.4*
agannētu, agannūtu "these", *36.35*
agāšu "that", *36.35*
aḫāru "to be behind", *19.*24; *48.18*
aḫarrum "later", *47.3*
aḫāzu "to seize", *19.6*
aḫlāmu "boys", "lads", *31.26*
aḫḫū "brothers", *31.25*
aḫulāp "woe!", *50.4*
A-ḫu-na "our brother", *36.23*
aḫuzzatu "marriage", *29.12*
a it-ti-in "may he not give", *22.5*
akālu "to eat", *45.2-3*
alāku "to go", *45.2*
a-la-ni-i-ka, a-la-nu-ú "your cities", "cities", *31.12*
āliku "going", "envoy", *29.7*
alkakātu "ways", *31.25*
alla, alli, allū (EA) "behold", *49.8*
allū "that", *36.33-34*
almānu "widower", *34.5*
al-Na-šuḫ "Nusku", *17.4*
ālu "city", *30.6*
amāru "to see", *63.2*
amēlūtu "mankind", *31.16*
am-mar-kar-ra "accountant", *63.11*
ammiu "that", *36.33-34*
an(a) "to", *35.*31; *39.*7; *48.*4,6-7; *52.*11; *53.*2
a-na-ku₈, a-na-ku-ú "I", *36.*6; *55.*3
anamziq "I am angry", *23.7*
ana ša "as soon as", *58.14*
anna "yes", *50.*4; *60.*2
annabu "hare", *29.16*
annīkī'am "here", *47.7*
annitān "this and that", *36.34*
anniu, annū "this", *19.*9; *36.33-35*
an-nu(-ú) (EA) "behold", "yes", *49.6*

anṣabtu "ear-ring", "ring", *29.16*
a-nu-ki (EA) "I", *36.6*
a-nu(-ú) (EA) "behold", "yes", *49.6*
A-pìl-ki-in "the heir is firm", *32.10*
aqṭirib "I approached", *27.7*
arammu "wharf", "ramp", *29.12*
Arba-ilī "Irbil", *67.15*
arḫiš "with speed", "quickly", *48.10*
āribu "crow", "raven", *30.10*
arkāniš, arkiš "back", "later", *47.5*
Ar-pa-a-a "Arab", *11.4*
arrakūtu "long" (plur.), *31.25*
arû "eagle", *63.4*
arwiyu "gazelle", *63.4*
ašar "place of", "where", *28.*17; *36.*56; *57.*5
aš-ku-un-nu "I assigned", *38.13*
ašrānu "there", *47.7*
ašša "as soon as", *58.14*
aššu(mi) "because", *28.*18; *58.*16
aštammar "I praise continuously", *41.33*
aš-tá-na-pá-ra "I send continuously", *41.33*
attanūni "you" (plur.), *36.5*
attina "I gave away", *39.7*
attu'a "mine", *36.31*
aṭrudakkuššu "I sent it to you", *36.27*
aṭṭarad "I sent", *27.4*
a-wi-li-e "men", *31.11*
awīlu "citizen", *21.*10; *63.*5
awū "to speak", *63.5*
ay "not", *47.9,11*
ayaprus "may I not release", *54.6*
ayiprus "may he not separate", *38.*2; *54.*6
ayya, ayyān "where?", "which?", *36.*59; *47.*10,12
ayyābu "enemy", *22.5*
ayyakam "where?", *47.7*
ayyāmi (EA) "where?", *36.59*
aznu "ear", *21.10*
azzu "fierce", *19.*5; *51.*1
Bāb-ilī "Babylon", *67.15*
bābu, bābāni, bābāti "gate", "gates", *31.14*

bakkarī "young camels", *31.25*

bakū "to cry", "to weep", *62.2*

baluḫḫu "galbanum", *29.12*

balum "without", *32.18; 47.14*

banāyu "to build", *44.2*

ba-ni-ti (EA) "I built", *40.6*

banū "to build", *39.14,16; 44.2*

baqāmu, baqānu "to pull away", *11.7*

Ba-ra-ki-Ìl "God has blessed", *63.2*

bašmu "serpent", *29.6*

bašū "to be present", *49.23*

be-el-ti-i-a "of my mistress", *36.18*

Bé-il-ba-rak-ki "Baal has blessed", *40.3*

bēlān, bēlīn "two masters", *31.3*

be-lí "my lord", *21.7*

bēltu "lady", *30.3*

bēlān, bēltīn "two mistresses", *31.3*

bēt "house of", "where", *28.17; 36.56; 57.5*

biblu, biblāni, biblāti "gift", "gifts", *31.14*

bīranātu "strongholds", *31.10*

birbirrū "glare", *31.21*

birtu "stronghold", *63.4*

bīt āli "town-hall", *66.5*

bi-ʾ-ti "daughter", *23.10*

bi-ti-e "houses", *31.11*

bīt ili "temple", *66.5*

bīt sa-pi-na-a-tú "ship-yard", *64.5*

bītu "house", *22.5*

burāšu "juniper", *65.5*

da-a-an "(he) is strong", *44.14*

da-ak (EA) "he killed", *40.3*

da-an-nu "(they) are strong", *44.14*

daʾānu "might", *17.2*

damiq "he is good", *11.8; 38.3; 42.14*

dammaqūtu "good" (plur.), *31.25*

damqa (EA) "is good", *40.3*

damqu "good", *31.25*

dān "he is strong", *44.11,14*

danānu "might", *17.2*

danānu "to be strong", *44.10*

da-ni-iš "strongly", *32.17*

dannu, dannūtu "strong", "power-ful", *29.48*

daqqaqūtu "fine" (plur.), *31.25*

darū "to live", "to last", *43.23*

dayyān kittim "a just judge", *51.17*

dēq "he is good", *11.8*

dibbē "words", *23.9*

din "give!", *43.5*

dubbā, dubbī "speak!" (plur., fem. sing.), *21.5; 44.11*

dubub "speak!" (masc. sing.), *44.11*

Dūr-Kurigalzu "Aqarquf", *67.14*

Dūr-Šarrukēn "Khorsabad", *67.14*

dumqu "goodness", *31.25*

ē "not", *47.9,11; 54.6,9*

Ea-ra-bí "Ea is great", *33.5*

E-eb-la-a- "Ebla", *22.3*

e-ez-zi-ib-ka "I shall dismiss you", *38.6*

ebbarūtu "friends", *31.25*

e-eb-el "he became master", *45.5*

e-ḫi-il-tum "debt", *19.9*

Ekallāte "Ekallatu", *27.28*

ekurru "temple", *65.3*

Ela "God" (DN), *32.6*

eleppu "ship", *31.15*

eli "over", "above", *48.15*

eliš "above", *47.5*

elmešu "precious stone", *23.8*

emāru "donkey", *63.3*

emēdu "to lean", *45.3*

emūqattam "violently", *47.4*

eniq "suck!", *43.6*

en-ma "behold", *49.6; 50.4; 60.2*

En-num-ì-lí "by the grace of my god", *32.3,18*

ēnu "eye", *21.10; 22.5*

enūma "when", *58.9*

epinnu "plough", *31.15*

epru "dust", *19.10*

eqlu "field", *31.15*

e-ra-si-iš "for tilling", *48.10*

erbē "forty", *35.18*

erbēšēri "fourteenth", *35.29*

erēbu "to enter", *21.10; 45.3*

errēt ilī "the curses of the gods", *51.11*

ersetu "earth", *30.2*

erû "eagle", *63.4*

eṣādu, eṣēdu "to reap", *19.10*

-eš/-iš "to", "with", "for", *32*.16;
36.15

ešrā(t) "twenty", *35*.18

ešrū "twentieth", *35*.29

Eštar-ra-bí-at "Ishtar is great", *33*.5

ewū "to be", "to become", *19*.10;
43.22

gallābu "barber", *29*.11

gamāru "to achieve", *41*.2

gamru "expenditure", *21*.10

gana "well!", *50*.4

gimāḫu "grave", *63*.9

gimru "expenditure", *21*.10

girru "road", "march", *30*.7

gitmālu "perfect", *29*.32

giṭṭu "document", *65*.3

gulgull(at)u "skull", *29*.13

gummuru "to achieve", *41*.2

gursidakku "flour basket", *29*.12

ḫa-an-ni-e "this", *19*.9

ḫakāmu "to understand", *19*.11

ḫal-liq "is fugitive", "has escaped",
38.10

Ḫalmān "Aleppo", *11*.6

ḫaluppu "oak", *29*.12

ḫamāšiyu "fifth", *35*.27

ḫa-ma-ti "she is confident", *40*.4

ḫamiššerit "fifteen", *35*.17

ḫamištu "five", *30*.3

ḫamšišu "(for) the fifth time", "five
times", *35*.31

ḫamšu "five", *30*.3

ḫa-mu-du (EA) "desired", *42*.14

ḫanāmu "to grow rich", *19*.11

ḫanāšu "to bow", "to bend", *18*.5;
19.11

ḫannabātu "voluptuous" (plur.), *31*.25

ḫanniu "this", *36*.33

ḫapāru "to dig", *19*.9

ḫanšā "fifty", *35*.18

ḫarā'u "to empty", *19*.6

ḫaṣṣīnu "axe", *29*.11

ḫerū "to empty", *19*.6

ḫiblātu, ḫiblētu "damage", *27*.9

ḫi-iḫ-bi-e (EA) "he has hidden",
41.11

ḫi-na-ia (EA) "my eyes", *32*.33

ḫulmiṭṭu "a reptile", *23*.8

ḫulṭimmu "snout", *41*.42

ḫuluqqā'u "destruction", *29*.51

Ḫumbaba "Humbaba", *11*.9

ḫunzu "a fifth", *35*.30

ḫurāṣu "gold", *65*.6

ḫuṭṭimmu "snout", *41*.42

Ḫuwawa "Humbaba", *11*.9

i deprecative particle, *54*.6

ia-aq-bi (EA) "may he speak",
39.14

i-be-al, i-bé-el "he is master", "he
rules", *45*.5

i-be-lu "(who) became master",
45.5

I-bi-ì-lum "God has named", *32*.3

ib-ḫar "he choosed", *45*.8

idāti "hands", *31*.14

iddin "he gave", *27*.3; *38*.4

īde "he knows", *22*.13

Idiglateš "into the Tigris", *32*.17

I-din-Eš₄-tár "Ishtar has given",
50.25

idu, idū "hand", "hands", *31*.14

I-dum-be-lí "by the hand of my
lord", *32*.18

I-ib-la-a "Ebla", *22*.3

i-ig-mu-ur "he conquered", *15*.16;
40.19

i-ik-ka-al "he eats", *45*.4

i-ik-mi "he captured", *15*.16; *22*.14;
40.19

i-im-mi-id "he leans", *45*.4

i-ir-ru-ub "he enters", *45*.4

i-iš-e "he searched", *22*.14

i-ìš-qú-ul "he weighed out", *22*.14

ikān "he is true", *44*.5

ikis "cut!", *43*.5

ikkaru "peasant", *31*.15

ikribu "prayer", *27*.17; *29*.16

Ik-se-nu-nu "Xenon" (PN), *27*.17

ikūn(u) "he was true", *43*.9; *44*.5

ikunnu "they are true", *44*.5,14

ikūnū "they were true", *44*.5,14

ikūwan "he is true", *43*.9

ilāni "gods", "God", "divinity",
31.12; *50*.24

ilaqqēšunūti "he will take them",
38.6

Ìl-ba-na "God is beautiful", *40.3*

i-le-qa-aš-šu-nu-ti "he will take them", *38.6*

ilī "my god!", *50.3*

ilkamma "he came here", *24.2*

ilku "they went", *25.5*

illikam(ma) "he came here", *24.2; 39.7*

ilmad "he learned", *38.3,15; 41.2*

Ìl-pa-rak-ka "God has blessed", *11.4*

ilte, iltu "from", "since", "with", *48.18*

ilteqe "he took", *27.5*

Ilū-da-nu "the gods are powerful", *33.5*

I-lu-Me-er "Ilu-Mēr", *11.8*

Ì-lum-i-bí "God has named", *32.3*

i-ma-ar-ru-šu "he will see it", *38.13*

ᵈIM-ba-rak-ka "Hadad has blessed", *40.3*

imdu "support", *48.22*

imḫuranna "may he receive", *39.10*

imittam "right", *47.2*

imittu "right hand", *30.2*

im-lik "he became king", *45.8*

immati "when?", "until when?", *47.17*

imtaḫṣā "they fought with each other", *38.4; 41.22*

imtatḫaṣ "he is fighting over and over again", *41.35*

i-mu-ud "he propped", *45.8*

in(a) "in", *36.24; 48.4-5,7*

in(a) mati "when?", "until when?", *47.17*

inanandin "he gives", *23.7*

inaṣṣar, inaṣṣur "he guards", *10.9*

in(a) ūmi "when", *49.15; 52.6; 58.14*

indu "support", *48.22*

innadū "was given up", *36.23*

in-ne-du-ú "was given up", *36.23*

inṣabtu "ear-ring", "ring", *29.16*

intatḫaṣṣu "(when) he was fighting over and over again", *41.35*

i-nu (EA) "wine", *21.9*

īnu "eye", *21.10*

īnu "when", *58.9*

inūma "when", *58.9,14*

inūmi "when", *41.35; 49.15; 58.14*

ipqid "he delegated", *41.2*

iprus "he separated", *41.2*

ip-te "he opened", *21.7*

ipṭeru "ransom", *29.16*

iqīš "he offered", *43.9*

iqīyaš "he offers", *43.9*

iqrab, iqrib "he came near", *38.15-16; 41.2*

i-ra-ab-bi "he becomes great", *43.12*

i-rak-ka-si "he ties", *21.11*

ir-am "he thundered", *45.18*

irpud "he ran", *38.15*

Ìr-ra-na-da "Irra is exalted", *32.11*

islam, islim "he made peace", *10.6; 38.16*

isseqe "he took", *27.5*

issi, issu "from", "since", "with", "after", *15.2; 48.18; 58.10*

issi bēt "since", *58.10*

issi mar "since", *58.10*

issu "foundation", *15.2*

I-su-a-ḫu "there is a brother", *49.23*

I-su-DINGIR "there is a god", *49.23*

iṣbassu "he seized him", *46.2*

iṣbatanni "he seized me", *40.3; 46.2*

iṣbatūninni "they seized me", *46.2*

iš, -iš "to", "with", "near", "for", *32.17; 48.1,4; 49.1; 53.2*

iša'al "he asks", *43.9*

išāl "he asked", *43.9*

išātu "fire", *31.20*

išdiḫu "profit", *29.16*

išdu "foundation", *15.2*

iškunanna "may he place", *39.10*

iš-má, iš-me "he heard", *19.5; 45.6*

išši'akku "city ruler", *29.12,51*

iššū, iššī "he is", "she is", *49.23*

iš-te₄ "from", "since", "with", *48.18*

iš-te-nem-mu "I am always heeding", *41.33*

ištenšeret "eleven", *29.55*

ištēn/īn/ān "one", *35.3,5,31*

ištiāt "one" (fem.), *35.3*

ištinā' "one by one", *35.33*

ištiššu "once", *35.31*

ištiyū "first", *35.24*

iš-tu(m) "from", "since", "with", "after", *15.2; 21.7; 48.18; 58.10*

išū "to have", *49.23,25*

i-šu-ú (EA) "he is", *49.23*

itta- (EA) "with", *48.18*

itte, itti, ittu "from", "since", "with", *48.18*

iu-se-bi-la (EA) "he has sent", *15.2*

iú-ša-ru (EA) "they are despatched", *41.43*

i-za-ku-(-wa) "he becomes pure", "he will be cleared", *43.12*

iz-ra-' "he sowed", *45.8*

kā "thus", *49.9*

ka-a-nu "to be stable", *21.4*

ka-aš-da-ki "you reach", *40.5*

kabātu "to be heavy", *10.8*

kakkaru "round disk", "round loaf", *27.3*

kalbu, kalbatu "dog", "bitch", *21.10; 29.5; 31.10-11*

Kaldaya "Chaldaean", *16.4*

kalmatu "parasite", "louse", *11.7*

kām "thus", *49.9*

Ka-[ma-]as-ḫal-ta-a "Kamosh-ʿaśā", *16.3*

kanāšu "to bow", "to bend", *18.5; 19.11*

kangu, kanku "sealed", *27.7*

karānu "vineyard", *32.10*

kāru "quay", *67.19*

karūbu "blessed", *29.8*

kasap lā kanīkim "silver without guaranty", *51.24*

kayyānu "stable", "permanent", *44.13*

kēm "thus", *49.9*

kī "as", "when", "that", *41.35; 58.2; 60.1; 61.1,8*

ki'ām "thus", *49.9*

kilallān/ūn, kilaltān/ttān "two", *35.4*

kīma "as", "when", "like", *48.11; 58.2; 60.1*

kimaḫḫu "tomb", "grave", *18.5; 63.9*

ki-rí-šum "to the orchard", *32.19*

kīru "oven", *28.9*

kulbābu "ant", *29.14*

kulda "come here!", *15.2*

kulkā, kumkā, kunkā "seal!", *17.4; 36.5*

ku-na (EA) "be ready!", *40.14*

kunukku "seal", *29.12*

kussī'u "throne", *29.51*

kušda "come here!", *15.2*

la "at", "from", *48.7*

lā "not", *47.8; 54.6,9*

la'āmu "to consume", "to taste", *63.3*

Labba "Lion" (DN), *32.6*

labāšu "to be clothed", *41.8*

la elīti "at the upper end", *48.7*

lāma "not yet", "before", "lest", *58.3-4*

lamādu "to learn", *28.8*

la-mar-sú-[u]m "guardian she-angel", *23.9*

lāmi (EA) "before", "lest", *41.33; 58.3*

lamid "he is learned", *38.3*

lamṣatu "fly", *17.4*

la pān "from the presence", *48.7*

la qātē "from the hands", *48.7*

laqlaqqu "stork", *17.5*

la šapliti "at the lower end", *48.7*

laššu "he is not", *49.23*

lemnu "bad", *34.5*

li-ba-lu-uṭ-ni (EA) "may he give me life", *40.18*

libbātu "heartstirings", "anger", *30.7*

libbu "(in the) heart (of)", "within", *30.7; 32.18*

Li-da-at-GI "the progeny is firm", *32.10*

lidī "give birth!", *43.6*

li-im "thousand", *35.21*

lillika(m) "may he come", "reach me", *21.5; 32.5*

li-na-aṣ-ṣár (EA) "may he protect", *40.18*

li-na-ṣu-ru-šu "may they protect him", *40.18*

liprus "may he separate", *38.2; 54.6*

li-qí-bu-ni "may they speak", *21.11*

lū (EA) "when", "since", *61.8*

lū "see", "behold", *49.7*; *54.7*

Luḫuti "Luġaṭ", *17.4*

lū lā "not", *47.9*; *54.6*

luprus "may I separate", *38.2*; *54.6*

lū tuddanūna "may they be given", *41.43*

lū tuwaššarūna "may they be despatched", *41.43*

lu-ú precative particle, 40.21

-ma enclitic, "and", *49.1,8*; *53.4*; *55.7*

ma-a-al-tum "height", "step", 29.21

ma-a-at "hundred", *35.20*

ma-aḫ-ḫa-du "city", 29.21

Ma-an-ba-lum-ᵈDa-gan "who (does exist) without Dagan?", *47.14*

ma-a-ni "who", 25.5

ma-an-na (EA) "what", 36.58

ma-aṭ-ni-a (EA) "supply", 32.23

maḫāru "to equalize in value", "to receive", *18.5*; *19.6*; *63.9*

ma-ḫi-ir "receiver", "has received", *34.4*; *38.10*

māḫiṣ "striking", 42.14

maḫra "before", *47.2*

maḫ-ri-iš "in front of", "before", *32.14*; *47.5*

maḫrū "former", "first", *35.24*

makāru "to deliver goods", "to sell", *29.29*

mala "as much as", "as many as", *57.2*

malāḫu "sailor", *65.2*

mamma, mamman, mammāna "whoever", *36.61*; *57.7*

man, mannu "who", *36.58*; *57.7*

maqarrāt(e) "bales (of straw)", 27.28

maqlū "burning", 29.25

marāsu "to squash", *63.5*

ma-ra-ṣu "is sick", "has fallen sick", *38.10*

māru, marʾu "son", *11.6*; *63.8*

mārūʾa "my sons", 50.3

masennu "treasurer", *14.2*

māssu "his country", *33.3*

mašāʾu "to wipe away", *45.6*

maškanu "settlement", 29.21

mat, mati "when?", *47.17*

mātu "country", *32.6*

me-at, me-et "hundred", *35.20*

mé-e-ma (EA) "water", *21.12*

mērānu "whelp", 29.38

merʾu "son", *11.6*

me-sar "right", 22.5

-mi enclitic, *49.8*

mi-at "hundred", *35.20*

mi-ia, mi-ia-ti (EA) "who?", *36.58*

mimma, minma "whatever", *36.61*

min, mīnu "what", *36.58*

minītu "measure", 48.12

mišlu "half", *35.30*

mitalku "to consider", *42.7*

mitlik "take advice!", *41.22*

mitluku "to consider", *42.7*

muātu "to die", *2.16*; *44.5*

murrū "to cut off", *35.3*

muṣlālu "midday", 29.23

mūšabu "dwelling", 29.21

mušaḫḫinu "stove", *30.5*

mušpalu "depth", 29.23

mūšu "night", *41.8*

mutu "man", *2.16*; *28.7*

na-ap-ḫa-ri-su-nu "their total", 36.24

na-aq-ṣa-pu (EA) "they are irritated", *41.19*

nabalkutu "to transgress", *41.17-18*

na-da-ni-iš "to give", 32.17

nadānu "to give", *10.8*

nadāru "to be wild", 29.26

nādinānu "seller", 29.39

naḫarmumu "to decay", *41.42*

nāḫiru "narwhal", 29.16

Na(ḫ)rīmaḷi (EA) "North Mesopotamia", 29.54

nammaššū "beast", *67.4*

Nam-pi-gi "Manbiğ", *11.4*

namṣatu "fly", *17.4*

nanduru "fearful", 29.26

naparqudu "to fall backwards", *41.17*

napāšu "to blow", *41.17*; *63.7*

napḫaru "total", "sum", *11.7*; *29.26*; *36.24*

napištu "throat", "neck", "breath", *30.2*; *63.7*

naplaqtu "battle-axe", *29.26*
naplis "look upon!", *41.19*
napqid "be entrusted!", *41.19*
narkabtu "chariot", *63.4*
narkabu "upper mill-stone", *63.4*
nāru "river", *30.5*; *67.*10
nasīku, nasīkāni/āti "sheikh", "sheikhs", *31.*14
naṣbutū "they hold each other fast", *41.*15
našāpu "to breath", *2.*16
našarbuṭu "to carry by storm", *41.*42
nāš(ī) "holder", *21.*10
natīn "given", *42.*14
nawāru "to shine", *41.*17
nayāru "papyrus", *65.*8
nēmel "since", "because", *58.*16
nešakku "a priest", *29.*12
nēšu "lion", *17.*4
niāru "papyrus", *65.*8
nibu "shellfish" (?), *29.*16
nīnu, nīni "we", *36.*8
nisqu "a servant", *33.*16
nīšu "people", *31.*38
Nuḫašše "Luġat", *17.*4
Nu-ri-a-na/nu "Nūriānu" (PN), *32.*12
Nušḫu "Nusku" (DN), *11.*10
pagru "body", *36.*28
pāḫātu "governor", *29.*46
pāna "earlier", *47.*2
pānānum(ma) "earlier", "formerly", *47.*3
pānīu, pānū "former", "first", *35.*24
panū'a, panūwa "my face", *11.*11
pasāmu, pasānu "to hide", *11.*7
pe-'-ta "charcoal", *23.*10
pelludû, pilludû "cult", 11.4
perḫu "son", *65.*3
pitluḫu "awful", *29.*32
pū "mouth", *28.*6
Pu-lu-zi-na/nu PN, *32.*12
pu-ru-su-tat-te-su "prostates", "chief", *21.*11
qā "gauge", *28.*6
qá-a-ab-la-at ta-am-ti "the middle of the sea", *25.*5
qabāru "to bury", *21.*10

qadu "alongside", "as long as", *58.*11
qa-la-a-ka "you are silent" (sing.), *40.*5
qa-la-ku-nu "you are silent" (plur.), *40.*11
qanṭuppi "stylus", *17.*6
qaqqadu "head", *29.*13; *31.*15; *36.*28; *64.5*
qaqqad kaspi "capital", *64.5*
qarābu "to approach", *21.*10
qarādu "to have recourse to violence", *63.5*
qarbu "near", *10.*9; *21.*3
qarnāt nāli "horns of roebuck", *30.*6
qarṭuppi "stylus", *17.*6
qarub "he is near", *38.*3
qaštu "bow", *67.*15
qātā(n), qātāti "hands", "shares", *31.*7
qá-ti-ku-ni "(in) your hand", *36.*24
qātka imtaḫaṣ "he has struck your hand", *38.*4
qattanu "very small", *29.*11
qātu "hand", *15.*8; *28.*19; *36.*24
qebēru "to bury", *21.*10
qè-e-ṣí (EA) "summer", *21.*12
qerēbu "to approach", *21.*10; *40.*16
qināzu "whip", *29.*8
qirbu, qurbu "near", *10.*9; *21.*3
qu''ū "to expect", *41.*2
qurrubu "to bring near", *40.*16
quwwū "to expect", *41.*2
ra-bat "she is great", *43.*12
rab(ī) "chief", *21.*10
ra-bi-(a-)at "she is great", *43.*12
rabiānu "for the forth time", *35.*32
ra-bi-e-et "she is great", *43.*12
ra-bi-ia₈-ku "I am great", *43.*12
rābītu "a fourth", *35.*30
rabiu "great", *31.*16
raḫābu "to be terrified", *19.*9
Ra-ḫi-a-nu "Raḍyān", *10.*9
rakābu "to ride", "to sail", *63.4*
ramanu "person", *36.*28
ramānga, ramānka "you yourself", *27.*7

rapaš "he is wide", *38.3*

rapaštu "wide" (fem.), *30.3*

rapšu "wide", *30.3*

Ra-qi-a-nu "Radyān", *10.9*

raqraqqu "stork", *17.5*

rašā'u, rašū "to acquire", *49.25*

rēmē'ū, rēmēnū "merciful", *17.2*

rēšāti "first fruits", *27.28; 30.4*

rigmu "voice", *27.19*

rittū'a "in my fingers", *32.18*

rubu'ā' "four by four", *35.33*

Ru-ul-da-a-a-ú "Ruḍā" (DN), *16.8*

sā/sēbi'atu "a seventh", *35.30*

sa-du-na "our mountain", *36.23*

sāḫertu "witch", *65.8*

sà-ki-ni "prefect", *21.12*

sa-li-iš-tim "of the third (one)" (fem.), *35.8,26*

Samun- "Eshmun" (DN), *28.8*

samānē(šer) "eight(een)", *35.13,16*

sá-pu-wa-an "flexible (shoes)", *11.12*

Sar-ri-iš-da-gal "rely upon the king!", *32.17*

sa-'-te "morning dawn", *23.10*

sebe, seba "seven", *35.12*

ᵈ*Si-bí* "Seven (planets?)", *35.12*

sikkūru "bolt", *29.11*

simmiltu "ladder", *27.13*

Si-'-pa-rak-ka "The Moon-god has blessed" *40.3*

Su₄-be-la, Su₄-be-lí "he is the / my lord", *33.6*

sú-ki-ni (EA) "prefect", "governor", *21.12; 32.33*

su-ru-uš "foundation", *13.2*

ṣabū "people", "workmen", *31.38*

ṣaḫāru "to be small", *19.6*

ṣaḫḫārū "small" (plur.), *31.25*

ṣaḫru "small", *31.25*

ṣarpu "silver", *65.8*

ṣeḫēru "to be small", *19.6,1*

ṣeḫḫerūtu "small" (plur.), *31.25*

ṣí-īr-ti (EA) "I am besieged", *41.43*

ṣubbu "wagon", *23.7*

ṣuddū "to supply with food", *63.3*

ṣuḫartu "girl", *31.20*

ṣuḫru "the small ones", *31.25*

ṣumbu "wagon", *23.7*

ṣuprānuššu "with his claws", *32.18*

ṣurpu "silver", *65.8*

ṣú-ú-nu (EA) "small cattle", *32.23*

ša "who", "what", "that", *57.6; 60.3*

ša-a-a-il "he has asked", *44.5*

ša-('-)a-le "ask!", *19.9*

ša-aḫ-ri (EA) "gate", *16.2*

šá-'-il "he has asked", *44.5*

šabāru "to break", *42.3*

šabbiṭu "staff", "sceptre", *23.9*

ša-be "seven", *35.12*

šādiš(tu) "sixth" (fem.), *35.26*

šadū "mountain", *32.10*

šagapūru "very strong", *29.33*

šakan "governor", "official", *27.19; 65.3*

šakānu "to appoint", *65.2*

šakkanakku "viceroy", *65.2*

šakkūru "drunkard", *29.11*

šaknu "governor", "official", *27.19; 65.3*

šalāšiyu "third", *35.27*

šalbabu, šalbubu "very violent", *34.6*

šālištu "a third", *35.30*

šalšiānu "for the third time", *35.32*

šalšu "third", *35.26*

ša-ma-né "eight", *35.13*

šamaš "sun(-god)", *11.8*

ša-me-ma (EA) "heaven", *16.2; 21.12; 32.23*

šamnu "oil", *30.7*

ša-mu-ma (EA) "heaven", *16.2; 32.23*

šanānu "to come up with", *48.20*

šaniānu "for the second time", *35.32*

šanūdu "celebrated", "famous", *34.6*

ša-pár (EA) "he sent", *40.3*

šapāru "to send", *42.3*

šapattu "full moon", *10.8*

ša-qu-u "to drink", *21.4*

šarrānu "kings", *31.12*

šarraqānu "thief", *29.39*

šarratu "queen", *29.47; 30.3; 33.19*

šarru "king", *29.47; 33.19*

šarrūtu "kingship", *21*.5; *29*.48; *30*.1; *31*.16

šar tašimtim "an intelligent king", *51*.17

šāt "the one", "who", "what", *36*.49

ša-te-e (EA) "field", *16*.2

šebēru "to break", *21*.10; *42*.3

še-eb-i "seven", *35*.12

še-e-mi-šu "his hearing", *25*.3

Še-er-ba-rak-ki "The Moon-god has blessed", *40*.3

šemū "to hear", *45*.6

šenā, šinā "two", *35*.4

šēpū'a "at my feet", *32*.18

šerku "a quality of figs", *33*.16

šeššu "sixth", *35*.26

šībūtu "elders", *3*.16

šinā' "two by two", *35*.33

šinepiātu, šinepātu "two-thirds", *35*.30

Šinnānu "toothed", *29*.36

ši'mu "price", *21*.7

šīt "she", *36*.10

šu, šū "this", "who", "that", *10*.8; *36*.47,49; *39*.7; *57*.6

šubalkitu "to bring over", *41*.18

šubburu "broken into pieces", *42*.16

šūbil "send!", *22*.13; *39*.7

šūbultu "present", *29*.33

šuharruru "to be dead-silent", *41*.40

šulmānu "greeting", "present", "bribe", *29*.37

šulmu "well-being", "peace", *10*.5; *29*.5

šulušā' "three by three", *35*.33

šumēlam "left", *47*.2

šumma "if", *41*.12; *49*.11; *61*.2,5,8

šumma ... inūma "if ... when", *61*.7,9

šumma kī "if ... when", *61*.7,9

šumma lā "if not", *61*.7,9

šumma-man, šumman "if", *61*.6

šumma-min "if", *61*.6

šumma ... šumma "if ... if", "whether ... or", *61*.3,9

šumšu "his name", *65*.4

šumšū "to spend the night", *41*.8

šūmu "garlic", *32*.10

šuqammunu "to be dead-silent", *41*.40

šurmīnu "cypress", *11*.6

šūru "ox", "bull", *65*.5

Šu-ru-uš-ki-in "the root is firm", *32*.10

šūṣū "thrown away", *42*.16

šūš "sixty", *35*.18

šūšur "is kept in order", *22*.13

šūt "he", "the one", "who", *36*.10,49

šutābultu "interpretation", *29*.33

šūturu "very large", *34*.6

ta-ad-di-na "they both gave", *40*.21

ta-ah-ta-mu (EA) "under them", *48*.16

ta-al-la-ak "she goes", *38*.6

ta-aṣ-bu-ta₅ "they both took possession", *40*.21

Tá-din-Eš₄-tár "Ishtar has given", *50*.25

takal "trust!", *41*.19

takbaru "fattened sheep", *29*.28

takšītu "large profit", *30*.1

ta-lak "she goes", *38*.6

tallaktu "going", *29*.30

talmīdu "disciple", *29*.29

tamāhu "to seize", *18*.5

tamāku "to seize", *18*.5

tamhāru "battle", *29*.30; *32*.6

tamkāru "supplier", "merchant", *29*.29; *32*.10; *64*.4

tamlāku "counsellor", *29*.29

tamšīlu "image", *29*.30

tanamdina "you give me", *23*.7

tananziq "you are angry", *23*.7

tantathaṣ "you fight over and over again", *41*.35

tappā'u "partner", *29*.51

tapšahu "resting-place", *29*.31

Ta-ra-am-ᵈIM "Adad loves", *50*.25

tarbāṣu "fold", *29*.31

tarbū "pupil", *29*.29

targīgu "evil-doer", *29*.29

targumānu "interpreter", *29*.30

tarmiktu "layerage", "soakage", *29*.30

taṣbatīnni "you (fem.) seized me", *46*.2

taštanapparanni "you are writing to me over and over again", *41*.35

tatatlak "you go further and further away", *41*.35

te-er-ru-ub "she enters", *38*.6

tešemma "you will hear", *25*.5

tidūkūna (EA) "they will kill", *40*.21

tikal "trust!", *41*.19

tillu "hill", *63*.6

tilqūna (EA) "they will take", *40*.21

timāliattam "yesterday", *47*.4

ti-mi-tu-na-nu (EA) "you (plur.) make us die", *36*.23; *41*.11

tiṣbutu "to grasp", *27*.14

tišā'iyu "ninth", *35*.27

tittaṣṣūna ṣābu "the troops continue to come forth", *41*.33

tizqāru "eminent", *27*.14

tū'amu "twin", *29*.29

tu-ṣa-bat (EA) "(she) will be seized", *41*.43

tu-uš-ša-ab "she will stay", *38*.6

ṭuppu "tablet", *30*.7

u- "and", *49*.1

ū- "or", *49*.4

ūbil "he brought", *22*.13; *39*.7

ugāru "field", *63*.5

uḫappi, uḫeppi "he struck", *27*.9

u-ki-in-nu "I gave strength", *38*.13

ul, ula "not", *38*.13; *47*.8; *54*.6

ullīkī'am "there", *47*.7

ullū "that", *36*.33-34

ultu "from", "since", "with", "after", *48*.18; *58*.10

ūm "when", "as soon as", *49*.15; *52*.6; *57*.5

umām "by day", *47*.2

ūma u mūša "through day and night", *52*. 6

umīšam "daily", *32*.19

umma "behold", *49*.6

ummānu "army", *31*.38

ummatu "tribe", "people", *29*.46

ummiānu "master", *29*.39

ummu "mother", *21*.10

ūmu "day", *21*.3; *22*.5

ú-na-ṣár "(he) will be protected", *41*.43

unqu "signet ring", *30*.5

uqur "break", *43*.5

urkiš "back", "later", *47*.5

u-su-zi "he led on", *22*.5

uṣāru "court", *21*.7

uṣṣabbit "he imprisoned", *27*.4

uṣṣu "arrow", *21*.10

uṣur "watch!", *43*.5

ú-ša-ak-lí-il "he completed", *41*.9

ušalbiš "he clothed", *41*.8

ušallim "he made good", *13*.2

ušamqit "he caused to fall", *41*.9

uštābilakkum "I sent (it) to you", *50*.2

uštallamū "they will be kept safe", *41*.25

uštalpit "it was destroyed", *41*.29

uštamaḫḫar "she makes herself equal to", *41*.29

uštatalpit "it crumbles more and more", *41*.35

uš-tá-za-kà-ar-si "he will swear on it", *41*.29

uštetešser "it will be practicable on and on", *41*.35

uštu "from", "since", "with", "after", *21*.7; *48*.18; *58*.10

utetetti "it darkens more and more", *41*.35

u-ub-lam "he brought", *22*.14

ú-ub-lu "they brought", *22*.14

u-ur-da-ni "it went down on me", *22*.14

uznu "ear", *21*.3,10-11

wa- "and", *49*.1

wabālu "to bring", "to transport", *11*.12; *29*.33

waḫāru "to be behind", *19*.24; *48*.18

waldāku "I am born", *43*.7

walid "he is born", *43*.7

waqru "precious", "excellent", *19*.24

warka "after (that)", "behind", *47*.2; *58*.13

warki "after (that)", *58*.13

warqu "yellow-green", *30*.3

waruqtu "yellow-green" (fem.), *30*.3

wasāmu "to be fit, skilled", *11*.7

wēdu "alone", *35.3*
wurrū "to cut off", *35.3*
yānu "there is no …", *47.12; 52.8*
ye-nu, ye-ni (EA) "wine", *65.5*
yu-wa-ši-ru-na (EA) "(that) he should send", *39.8*
Za-bi-i-ni "Zabīn" (PN), *42.14*
za-ka-at "she is pure", *43.12*
za-ku-a-at "she is pure", *43.12*

zamāru "song", *31.28*
zāzu "to divide", *35.14*
zikkarū "men", *31.25*
zikru "mention", *27.19*
zittu "portion", "share", *35.14*
zu- "the (man) of", *36.47-49*
zuʾāzu "to divide", *13.2; 35.14*
zuqaqīpu "scorpion", *29.14*

BANTU

ba-ntu "men", *31.1*
fung-iš-a "to cause to shut", *1.2*
ho-lúl-ǎl-á "to be waiting", *39.7*
ho-óp-án-á "to be striking one another", *1.2*
ḥu-rút-ǎl-á "to be teaching for", *39.7*
ḥu-rút-ís-á "to cause to teach", *1.2*

ka-ntu "little man", *31.1; 49.19*
mu-ntu "man", *31.1*
mu-rút-i "teacher", *1.2*
pat-an-iš-a "to unite", *41.14*
patiliz-an-a "to vex one another", *1.2*
-tund- "teach", *17.7*
tu-ntu "little men", *31.1*

BEDJA

akantib "I am writing", *38.5*
asa "five", *35.10*
atkehan "to be loved", *2.9*
atomān "to be shaved", *41.20*
b- demonstrative and pronominal prefix, *36.36*
dar "to cause carnage", *41.3*
dbil "to collect", *2.9; 41.2; 49.21*
dir "to kill", *2.9; 41.3*
-eb "into", "in", "concerning", *48.5*
fáḍig "four", *35.9*
fal, fil "to overflow", "to pour out", *41.3*
ginaf, ginif "to kneel down", "to make kneel down", *41.3*
gumad "to be long", *2.9*
kām, kam "dromedary" (sing., plur.), *30.10*
ka-taman "I am not eating", *54.2*

kātim "to arrive repeatedly", *41.3,6*
kehan "to love", *2.9*
kitim "to arrive", *41.3,6*
mdedar "to kill each other", *2.9*
nifi "to sigh", *43.11*
rimad, rimid "to avenge one's self", "to avenge", *41.3*
san "brother", *31.21; 35.24*
sikal, sikil "to be choking", "choke", *41.3*
sim "name", *63.13*
sugumād "to lengthen", *2.9*
šibab, šibib "to see one's self", "to see", *41.3*
tamáni "I am eating", *54.2*
-wa "and", *49.1*
yām, yam "water" (sing., plur.), *63.5*
yisodir "he ordered to kill", *41.7*

Chadic

amay (Dangla) "water", *63*.5
bēni (Mubi) "he built", *2*.16
binnáa (Mubi) "he is building", *2*.16
cuwar (Bura) "elephant", *63*.6
iyam (Sukur) "water", *63*.5
kar- "dog", *17*.1
**lš-* "tongue", *30*.11
náàsò (Migama) "to breath", *2*.16

ndàl (Margi) "to throw", *41*.17
ndàlnà (Margi) "to throw away", *41*.17
ngun (Logone) "belly", *17*.6; *31*.12; *44*.5
sin (East Chadic) "brother", *35*.4
sín (Migama) "brother", *2*.16
See also Hausa.

Coptic

anan, anon "we", *36*.8
ğinğōr, ğinğor "talent (weight)", *23*.7
las "tongue", *17*.4

mase "calf", *8*.18
nibe, nibi, nifi "to sigh", *43*.11
wan, won "someone", *49*.22

East and West Cushitic

adda (Highland) "mother", *62*.2
bakál (Afar) "kid", *30*.10
bākik-ō (Kafa) "cocks", *31*.22
bāk-ō (Kafa) "cock", *31*.22
*dad ("Sam") "someone", *35*.3
dábel (Saho) "goat", *30*.10
ḍal, ḍel ("Sam", Saho) "to give birth", *27*.12; *41*.15
di (Highland) "not", *47*.16
dōbbi-ččo (Highland) "lion", *63*.13
fíl (Boni) "to comb", *39*.7
fíl-o (Boni) "to comb one's self", *39*.7
*gaisar ("Sam") "buffalo", *63*.6
gāl (Boni) "dromedary", *30*.10
gʷidin (Highland) "rib", *30*.11
haläm (Burji) "boy", *63*.6
-(i)č (Kafa) "for", "on", "towards", *48*.10
imm- (Highland) "to give", *41*.7
immis- (Highland) "cause to give", *41*.7
inte, intena (Walamo) "you" (plur.), *36*.9
káàd (Boni) "to buy", *39*.7
kád-o (Boni) "to buy for one's

self", *39*.7
**kal-* ("Sam") "one", "alone", *35*.4
kan- (Omotic) "dog", *17*.1
kis- (Omotic) "hand", "arm", *15*.8
kor ("Sam") "camel bell", *63*.6
kor ("Sam") "to climb", *63*.6
kuč- (Omotic) "hand", "arm", *15*.8
lóba- (Highland) "hippopotamus", *30*.10
nēfso (Boni) "to breath", *2*.16
-nna (Highland) "and", *49*.1
nu, nuna, nuni "we", *36*.8
ordes (Walamo) "to grow fat", *41*.7
ordiya (Walamo) "fat", *41*.7
qaro (Omotic) "horn", *30*.11
qura, ġura "crow", "raven", *30*.10
sənde (Highland) "wheat", *17*.7
ših "thousand", *35*.21
šimir (Boni) "bird", *11*.9
tana, tani (Walamo) "me", "I", *36*.3
wazana (Saho) "heart", *30*.11
*waž "ear", *30*.11
wišš- (Highland) "dog", *41*.34; *67*.4
yagis ("Sam") "he kills", *38*.15
yaḥam ("Sam") "he eats", *38*.15

yamut ("Sam") "he dies", *38*.15

zobbä- (Kambata) "lion", *30*.10; *63*.13

See also Oromo, Rendille, Somali.

EGYPTIAN

ȝbw "elephant", *30*.10

ȝby "lioness", *17*.2

ʿbw "purification", *43*.7

ʿkȝ, ʿky "Akko, Acre", *19*.12; *29*.54

ʿnḫ "to live", *41*.7

db "hippopotamus", *30*.10

dbḫ "Ṭubiḫi", *12*.1

dỉ "to give", *43*.7

dỉwt "a set of five", *35*.6

ḏbʿ "finger", *2*.5

ḏr "Tyre", *13*.7

-f "his", *11*.15

fdw "four", *35*.9

gḏt "Gaza", *19*.12

hȝ "ho!", *49*.10

ḥrt(ỉ) "you are content", *38*.3

ḥbḏrt "stalk" (Canaanite), *67*.3

ḥkȝ, ḥkȝw "magic", "magician", *29*.41

ḥkȝ "to rule", *10*.12

ḥm, ḥmy "to steer", "steersman", *29*.41

ḥmḏrt "stalk" (Canaanite), *67*.3

ḥmt "craft", *29*.44

ḥmww "craftsman", *29*.44

ḥsw "singer", *29*.44

ḥśỉ "to sing", *29*.44

ḫm "not to know", *2*.2

ḫmnw "eight", *35*.13

ḫpš "strength", *35*.10

ḫnỉ "to row", *29*.20

-ỉ "me", "mine", *36*.18

ỉȝw.t "old age", *29*.46

ỉȝḥbwm "Rehob", *17*.2

ỉb "heart", *17*.2

ỉbỉȝfỉ "Yib(')al-pī" (Amorite), *19*.7

ỉkȝ "souls", *31*.24

ỉḳr "excellent", *19*.24

ỉm "in", *48*.4-5

ỉn "to", "for", "by", *48*.6

ỉnk "I", *36*.6; *49*.20

ỉnn "we", *36*.8

ỉpn, ỉpw "these", *31*.24

ỉr "(as) to", *48*.4,6

ỉrp "wine", *2*.2

ỉs(k) "as", "when", *48*.4,10

ỉśḳȝn "Ashkelon", *2*.4; *17*.2

ỉšt "belongings", *48*.18

ỉyr "deer", *30*.10

-k "you", *36*.19

kȝ "thus", "so", *49*.9

kȝ, kȝw "soul", "souls", *31*.24

kȝỉ "to think out", "to plan", *2*.2

kȝm "vineyard", *17*.2

kbn, kpn "Byblos", *2*.4; *10*.8

krkr "talent" (weight), *27*.3

ktt "little one", *8*.18

ḳȝb "intestines", *17*.2

ḳḏt "Gaza", *19*.12

m "who?", "which?", "what?", *36*.57

m "not", *2*.2

m "in", "from", "if" *48*.4-5; *61*.2

mȝw.t "mother", *29*.46

mḏw "ten", *35*.20

mḫȝ.t "balance", *29*.46

mḫnt "ferry-boat", *29*.20

mktr "tower", *65*.8

mktry "Magdali", *19*.7; *22*.3; *29*.54

mnḫt "clothing", *29*.20

mnw "halting place", *29*.20

mrḥt "fat", *29*.20

mrkbt "chariot", *65*.8

mś, mśỉ "child", "to give birth", *8*.18

n "to", "for", *48*.6; *49*.20; *51*.23; *63*.5

nbty "the Ombite", *29*.41

nȝy-s "hers", *49*.20

ngsgs "to overflow", *41*.17

ngś "Luǵat", *17*.4

nhrn "North Mesopotamia", *29*.54

nḫny "of Nḫn", *29*.41

ns "tongue", *17.4; 30.11*

nšp "to breath", 2.16

nt- base of independent pronouns, *49.19*

ntk, ntṯ, nttn "you", *36.2,5*

nṯr "god", *15.8*

-ny "of us two", *36.7,22*

ny ìtrw, n-yr "belonging to the Nile", *65.8*

p3-dì-3ś.t "whom Isis has given", *27.28*

pn "this", *31.24*

pśḏw "nine", *35.14*

pw "this", *31.24; 50.9*

qḏt "Gaza", *19.2*

r "(as) to", *48.4,6*

rḫ "to know", *2.2*

rḫt, rḫty "to wash", "washerman", *29.41*

r m "for what (purpose)", *58.7*

rnpì "to recover one's strength", *43.23*

sḏm-k/ṯ "you heard", *40.5*

sḏm-tì "she heard", *40.4*

sḏm-tw-f "he was heard", *41.20*

sk "when", *48.4,10*

snb "to be healthy", *10.12*

srw "sheep", *30.10*

ś'nḫ "to make to life", "to nourish", *41.7*

śfḫw "seven", *35.12*

śìšw "six", *35.11*

śn(t) "brother", "sister", *2.16; 35.4*

śnw(y) "two", *35.4*

-śny "of them two", *36.7,22*

śrśw "six", *35.11*

św "he", *36.20*

śwt "he", *36.14*

śy "she", *36.20*

šmšwìpìrìm "the sun is God's face" (Amorite PN), *22.3*

tw "is not", *47.8*

tw sḏm-f "one heard it", *41.20*

-ṯ "you", *15.8; 36.19*

-ṯny "of you two", *36.7,22*

ṯwf.y "papyrus plant", *2.5*

ṯwt "you", *36.14*

w' "one", *35.3*

w'b "to be pure", *43.7*

wdì "to thrust", *43.7*

wdn "to be heavy", *10.12*

whr "dog", *30.10*

wnḫ "to clothe one's self", *29.20*

wn(n) "to be", *49.22*

wnš "wolf", *67.4*

wrḫ "to anoint", *29.20*

yb3y "Ebla", *22.3; 29.54*

GAFAT

ab "give!", *43.7*

abälam^wä "shepherd", *29.55*

afärä "earth", "dust", *32.6*

ahorä "he went", *43.7*

al- "not", *47.8*

alä "brother", *66.4*

älam^wä "cow", *29.55; 30.10*

alättäma "he caused to happen", *41.11*

alət "sister", *66.4*

anä "he is", *36.33*

anät(ti) "I", *36.3*

annä, aňňə "those", "this" (masc.), *36.33-34*

annäz "those", *36.33*

ansətä bušä "girl", *30.8*

anšəlä "donkey", *30.10*

antä "you" (sing.), *36.9*

antum "you" (plur.), *36.9*

asdänäbbäṭä "he frightened", *41.9*

asra qəmčättä "eleven", *35.3; 36.28*

atkimmärä "he caused to pile up", *41.5,14*

awre "wild animal", *63.4*

bäqlä "hundred", *35.20*

bäsärä "meat", *32.6*

bati "roof", *22.16*

čən "thigh", *30.11*

däbbälä "he repeated", *29.29; 49.21*

där(r)äsä "he met", *45.9*

əǧǧä(t) "one", 35.3

ələč(čä) "two", 35.4

-(ə)mma "and", 49.1

əmmä "from", 48.12

əmmäǧätit "lady", 29.55

əmʷit "mother", 30.2

əndä "such as", "according to", 48.22

ənna, ənnä, əňňə "this" (fem.), "these", "this" (masc.), 36.33-34

ən(n)aho, ən(n)ahuš "here he is", 36.33

ənnantä "you" (sing.), 36.9

ənnantum "you" (plur.), 36.9

ənnäz(əň) "these", 36.33,38

əsquli "hung up", "suspended", 42.14

-(ə)š "the", 33.13,33

əzz- "to have", "to seize", 49.25

fəǧǧälä "goat", 30.10

gäddärä "he is big", 17.5

gäǧǧä "house", 33.13; 63.10

gäǧǧaš "your (fem.) house" 15.5

gäǧǧəš "the house", 33.13

gällädä "he girded himself", 41.53

gʷönä "rib", 30.11

gʷöräbetä "neighbour", 29.55

(h)ələttä "two", 35.4

kimmärä "he piled up", 41.5

kitač "children", 8.8

kʷara "sun", 63.6

ləltäm "let me arrive", 40.30

mä "from", 48.12

mäčä "when", 47.17

manəm "whoever", 36.61

mənä, mənəm "whatever", 36.61

mäžämmäryä "first", 35.24

mossay "child", 8.18

näbbärä "he had", 49.25

qändä "horn", 17.7

qəmčättä "one" (in "eleven"), 35.3; 36.28

qurä "crow", "raven", 30.10

samət, saməttä "week", 27.3

səndä "wheat", 17.7

-š "the", 33.13,33

ši "thousand", 35.21

täbat bušä "boy", 30.8

taččä "under", "below", 48.16

tädäbəllam "he does not repeat" > "he is not", 47.8; 49.21

tädär(r)äsä "he was found", 41.20

täkimmärä "it was piled up", 41.14

tä ... m "not", 47.8

täqattälä "it was burnt", 41.27

təgäldi, təgälǧi "you gird yourself" (fem.), 15.5

tt- "is", 49.19

wabä "he gave", 43.7

wähor "to go", 43.7

wašša "cellar", 48.19

waššä "he wanted", 43.7

wäy "or", 49.4

wət "he", 36.11

yä- "of", "who", "that", "which", 36.55

yab "may he give", 43.7

yädakəm "may he speak", 38.7

yältäm "let him arrive", 40.28

yədakkəm "he speaks", 38.7

yən- "to be", 49.22

yəssikkäm "he carries a burden", 41.32

yət "she", 36.11

zätäňňä "nine", 35.14

zibbä "lion", 30.10; 63.13

GE'EZ

'abhərt "seas", 31.31

'abqəl "mules", 31.31

'adbār "mountains", 27.19; 31.31

'af "mouth", 30.11

'ahgur "towns", 31.26,31

'ahadu "one", 35.3

'ahmalmala "it became green", 41.37

'ahmār "boats", 63.3

'ahqul "fields", 31.26,31

'a'läf, 'āläf "tens of thousands", 35.22

'al-ba- "there is no(t)", 47.8

'albās "dresses", 31.31

'ammara "he made known", "he showed", 63.2

'amsāl(āt) "proverbs", 31.9

'anbābi "reader", 42.17

'anf "nose", 30.11

'anfarʻaṣa "he jumped", 41.18

'ansərt "eagles", 31.31

'anṣafṣafa "it dripped", 41.38

'aqtala "he caused to kill", 41.11

'arbaʻt "four", 11.5

'arsāḥsəha "he sullied", 41.37

'arwe "wild animal", 63.4

'assassāli "expeller", 42.17

'astamḥara "he showed himself merciful", 41.29

'aṣhəl "chalices", 31.31

'ašgāri "fisherman", 42.17

'aydug "ass", 29.9

'ayte "where?", 47.7

'aznāb "tails", 31.31

ʻādi "still more", 48.17

ʻaqrab "scorpion", 27.13; 29.17; 30.10

ʻaṣawa "he closed", 43.20

babaynāti- "between", 48.21

badbada "he devastated", 41.38

baḥr "sea", 31.31

baḥrāwi "maritime", 29.44

bakaya "he cried", 43.20-21; 62.2

bakayka, bakeka "I cried", 43.20

ba-lāʻla "on", "upon", 48.24

ba-məset "in the evening", 52.6

baql "mule", 31.31

barakat(āt) "blessing(s)", 31.20; 41.42

bardada "he covered with stones", 41.40

bārəko(t) "to bless", 42.11

baʾəsit "woman", 30.3

dabr "mountain", 31.25,31

dāgəm "second", 35.25

danāgəl "girls", 31.31

degana "he pursued", 41.5

dəngəl "girl", 31.31

ḍabsa "he was weak", 11.5

ḍawasa "he was weak", 11.5

'əd "hand", 35.30

'əlf "ten thousand", 35.21,22

'əlla "who" (plur.), 36.55

'əllū "these", 36.33

'əm-, 'əmənna "from", 48.12

'əm, 'əmma "if", 61.1-2,11

'əmāntu, 'əmuntu "they" (fem., masc.), 36.11

'əm-lāʻla "on", "upon", 48.24

'ən "no(t)", 47.12-13

'ənbi, 'ənbəyā "no!", 47.13

'əndaʻi "I don't know", 47.13

'ənka "behold", 49.6

'ənta "who" (fem.), 36.55

'ənza "since", 49.16

'əska "up to", "until", 48.10,17

'əsma "because", 58.16

'əzn, 'əzan "ear", "ears", 31.31

fannawka, fannoka "I sent", 43.20

fassəmo(t) "to complete", 42.11

fətlo "spinning", 29.50

gabbār "workman", 29.11

galbaba "he wrapped", 41.40

gar, gər "stone!", 43.6

gaza "store-room", 63.10

gʷadən "rib", 30.11

hagar "town", 31.26,31

hallo, *hallaw "he is", 36.33; 49.22,24

h't "he", 36.11

həyya "there", 47.7

hmnt "they (masc.)", 36.11

ḥadis "new", 31.15

ḥamalmāl "green", 29.14

ḥamama "he was ill", 43.10

ḥamar "boat", 63.3

ḥamma "he was ill", 44.11

ḥaqaya "he craunched", 43.21

ḥaql "field", 31.26,31

ḥaqʷe "loins", 48.25

ḥarrasi "ploughman", 29.41; 42.17

ḥaṣara "he fenced in", 13.12

ḥəṣn "lap", 30.11

ḥirut "goodness", 29.48

ḥora "he went", 43.7

ḥab(b)a "where", 57.5

'i- "not", 47.8,11

kaʻawa "he spilled", 43.20-21

kā'əb "second", *35.25*
kahənāt "priests", *31.12*
kālə' "second", *35.25*
kama "as", "like", "so that", *48.11; 49.14; 59.6; 60.1*
kantu "gratuitously", *47.3*
kəhədka "you denied", *45.17*
kəl'e(tu/i) "two", *35.4*
krəstiyanāwi "Christian", *29.44*
la "to", "for", "of", *48.6; 51.23; 52.11; 54.6*
la'aka "he sent", *45.17*
lā'la "upon", "over", "above", *48.15,24*
lā'lu "above", *32.18; 47.3*
ladī "give birth!", *43.6*
lahləha "he is loose", *41.38*
ləbs "dress", *31.31*
liq, liqān(āt) "elder", "elders", *31.9*
ma'āra gadām "wild honey", *51.17*
mahfad "tower", *29.21*
mal'ak, malā'əkt "messenger", "messengers", *31.31*
malbas "dress", *29.22*
manna, mannu "who?" (fem., masc.), *36.58*
marir "bitter", *29.8*
masalat "she is alike", *38.3*
masih(ān) "Messiah(s)", *31.12*
māy(āt) "water(s)", *31.15*
mə'ət "hundred", *35.20,21*
məhra "he had pity", *45.17*
mənt, mənta "what?" (masc., fem.), *36.58*
məsāle "proverb", *31.9*
məseta "in the evening", *52.6*
məšrāq "east", *29.21*
na'asāt "youth", *29.47*
nabiro "having sat down", *42.12*
nāfaqi "unbeliever", *42.17*
nafs "soul", "spirit", *36.28; 63.7*
nafsa "he has blown", *63.7*
nagha "in the morning", *47.2*
nakasa "he bit", *27.12*
naqawa "he shouted", *43.20-21*
nasaka "he bit", *27.12*
nassāhna "we repented", *45.17*
nassəha "he repented", *45.17*

nāzazi "comforter", *42.17*
nəfās "wind", *63.7*
nəhəb "bee", *30.10*
nəhna "we", *36.8*
nəsr "eagle", *31.31*
-nu interrogative, *54.5*
parāqlitos "Paraclete", *11.3*
qadāmit "beginning", *29.49*
qadimu "previously", *47.3*
qarn "horn", *17.7*
qatala "he killed", *33.5*
qawwama "he set up", *43.9*
qədma "until", *58.11*
qədsāt "holiness", *29.47*
qənāt "belt", *29.8*
qōma "he got up", *43.9*
qʷəyṣ, qʷəyāṣ "shin", "shins", *31.31*
ra'as "head", *36.28*
rawwaṣi "runner", *29.41; 42.17*
rə'əya "he saw", *43.20*
rəš'ān "growing old", *29.37*
sab' "man", *11.5*
sam'a "he heard", *44.2*
sam'o, etc. "he heard him", etc., *46.6*
sanbat "Sabbath", *41.42*
sanbatāwi "Sabbatical", *29.44*
sansal "chain", *29.13*
soba "when", *61.11*
sor "ox", "bull", *65.5*
ṣādəq "just", *42.13*
ṣahāfi, ṣahaft "writer", "writers", *31.31*
ṣāhl "chalice", *31.31*
ṣam'a "he was thirsty", *13.12*
ṣəbāha "in the morning", *52.6*
tafannāwi "envoy", *42.17*
tafṣām "completing", *29.30*
tahta "under", *48.16*
tāhta "beneath", *47.2*
tāhteka "under you", *48.23*
talabso(t) "to dress", *42.11*
tamāsalū "they resembled each other", *41.27*
tanabba "he was read", *44.11*
taqaddasa "he was sanctified", *41.25*
taqatla "he was killed", *41.24; 44.11*

tasadda "he was expelled", *44*.11

tasālaqi "ridiculous", *42*.17

tasannana "he vied with somebody", *48*.20

tašayami "decided", *42*.17

ṭarappeza "table", *11*.3

ṭəqqa "very", *47*.2

wafr "farmland", *67*.16

wahaba "he gave", *43*.7

wārəs "heir", *42*.13

wayən "vineyard", *65*.5

wəʾətu "he", *36*.11

wəʾətomu "they" (masc.), *36*.11

wəʿya "he was burnt", *43*.21

wəgər "stone!", *43*.6

wəsāṭe, wəsṭ "interior", "inside", *48*.19

wəsta "in", "into", "to", *48*.18,23

wəstetəya "to me", *48*.23

wəṭən "begin!", *43*.6

yaḥabbər "he will join", *45*.17

yānaqqər "he will wonder", *41*.11

yəʾati "she", *36*.11

yəʾəton "they" (fem.), *36*.11

yəbakki "he will cry", *43*.20

yəlbas "may he dress", *38*.15

yənabbəbu "they speak", *44*.11

yənabbu "they speak", *44*.11

yəngər "may he speak", *38*.15

yəssabbar "it is broken", *41*.32

yəʿtu "may he go home", *43*.20

za- "who" (masc.), *36*.55; *51*.19; *57*.6

zanab "tail", *31*.31

GREEK

The order of the Greek alphabet is followed.

Αβδαδουσαρος "servant of Dusares", *32*.5

Αβδαγης "Abdalga", *17*.2

Αβιλαας "'Ab'ilaha'", *21*.25

ἀγρός "field", *63*.5

Αζζαιος "Ġazzay", *43*.16

'Ακχώ "Acre", *23*.1

Αμβρι "Omri", *11*.9

ἄμβροτος "immortal", *11*.9

Αννω "Hanno", *21*.13

'Ασθήρ, 'Αστήρ "Esther", *21*.16

Αυσαλλας "Awsallah", *21*.24

αφ.σελ 'afsal ("he abhorred"), *14*.4

βάλσαμον "balsam", *16*.3

βανι "sons of", *21*.25

Βαραχια "Yahu has blessed", *63*.2

Βεγά "Bedja", *2*.9

βεν "son", *21*.25

Βιθια "House of the Spring", *21*.9,13

Βιλλοδω "cult", *11*.4

Βουγαειτοι "Bedja", *2*.9

βράθυ "juniper", *65*.5

βουλή "Senate", *65*.4

βρόδον "rose", *65*.5

βροτός "mortal", *11*.9

Βυτυλλιον "House of El", *21*.9

γάζα "store-room", "treasure", *63*.10

γεδδα ğiddan ("much"), *47*.2

Γερ- "devotee", *21*.13

Γολγοθά "skull", *29*.13

Γόμορρα "Gomorrah", *17*.1

εἰκών "image", *63*.10

Ελιουν "Most High", *29*.35,36

ἐργάτης "worker", *32*.1

Εσμουν "Eshmun", *28*.8

Ϝοῖνος "wine", *65*.5

*Ϝορδο-, Ϝροδο- "rose", *65*.5

θέρμος "hot", *11*.15

Ιαμβλιχος "Iamblichus", *11*.9

Ιαμνια "Yabneh / Yavneh", *11*.6

ιβωρθ "through the cistern", *27*.3

Ιεσσαι "Jesse", *67*.4

Ιεσχωρ "Yeshŏr", *21*.25

ἱππίατρος "veterinary", *41*.5

καίσαρ "elephant", *63*.6

κάπηλος "retailer", *63*.10

κᾶρυξ "herald", *63*.11

κασερειν "castles", *63.10*
κασία "cassia", *65.6*
Κεειλος "Kahīl", *21.24*
κεφάλαιον "capital", *64.5*
κῆρυξ "herald", *63.11*
κίνχαρες "talents" (weights), *23.7*
κλίμα "climate", "region", *63.10*
κλωβός "cage", *28.10*
κοκχος "grave", *63.9*
Κοσιδη "Qōs recognized" (*Qwsyd*ʿ),
   22,14; 27.10
ku-ru-so "gold", *65.6*
Λάζαρος "Lazarus", *27.26*
λάμβδα "lām(ed)", *11.9*
Λαοδίκεια "Laodicea", *67.9,17*
λίβανος "incense", *65.6*
λιβανωτός "incense", *65.6*
λῖς "lion", *17.4*
λυχουμ *luḥūm* ("meat"), *14.4*
Μάζικες Berber tribes, *2.14*
Μαίφα "Maifaʿat", *29.21*
Μασαχηλος "Masak-ʾEl", *22.4*
Μάριαβα "Marib", *29.21*
Ματθαθίας "Mattathias", *23.1*
Μαυια "Muʿāwiy", *43.16*
Μελκ-, Μιλκ- "king", *21.13*
μίσγω "I mix", *65.7*
Μολαιχος "Mulaiḥ", *21.24*
Μολεχη "Mulaiḥa", *21.24*
Μοοααυιος "Muʿāwiy", *43.16*
μορτός "mortal", *11.9*
Μουθ "Death", *21.9,13*
μύρρα "myrrh", *65.6*
Μωδαδ "Mōdad", *22.11*
Ναμεσσι "Nimshi", *67.4*
Νεάπολις "New town", *67.17*
Νοτερος "Noṭayru", *21.24*
ξηρόν "dry stuff", *65.9*
Οβαιδαλλα "ʿAbdallah", *21.25*
οζον "ear", *21.3*

Ολεμος "ʿUlaym", *21.24*
Οσεδος "ʾAwsad", *21.24*
Ουαρδα, Ουαρδης "Warda", *65.5*
ὀφθαλμός "eye", *9.5*
παλλάδ(ες) "tetradrachm(s)", *11.1*
παλλακίς, πάλλαξ, πάλλας "young
   lady", *65.7*
πανδοκεῖον "inn", *63.10*
παράκλητος "Paraclete", *11.3*
πάσχα "Easter", *63.9*
πονδόχιον "inn", *63.10*
προστάτης "chief", *21.11*
Πτολεμαΐς "Acre", *67.9*
Πτολεμαῖος "Ptolemy", *27.17*
πῦρ "fire", *19.1*
Ροσαουαθος "Raḍawat", *21.24*
Ρουσ-, Ρυσ- "Cape", *67.18*
σάκχαρ "sugar", *65.6*
σαγ[ιδ] *ṣaʿid* ("it came up"), *14.4*
Σαμαχηλος "Samak-ʾEl", *22.4*
Σαμιψαι "Šamšay", *11.9*
Σαος "Šamaš", *11.8*
Σάρρα "Sara", *17.1*
σεμιγ *samiʿ* ("he heard"), *14.4*
Σεπφώρα "Sipporah", *23.1*
Σοββαθο(ς) "Shabbat(ay)", *21.32*
Σο(υ)ρ "Tyre", *13.7*
ταῦρος "ox", "bull", *65.5*
τράπεζα "table", *11.3*
Τρίπολις "Tripoli", *67.17*
Τύρος "Tyre", *13.7*
φοῖνικ- "Phoenician", *2.15*
Χαρράν "Harran", *17.1*
Χαττεσος "Ḥaṭṭash", *23.7*
χεβιγοῦ *šabiʿū* ("they were sated"),
   14.4
χουβζ *ḥubz* ("bread"), *14.4*
χρῦσος "gold", *65.6*
χυμεία "fluid", *65.9*
ωει "days", *21.3*

GURAGE

ad, at "one", *35.3*
adāda, adda "paternal aunt", *62.2*
adde "mother", *62.2*
ädi "I", *36.3*

adot "mother", *43.5; 62.2*
āfuna "nose", *30.11*
äǧ "hand", *43.5*
ägər "foot", *43.5*

aḵä, aḵu "you" (sing., plur. masc.), 36.6,9

aḵma "you" (plur. fem.), 36.9

al- "not", 41.53; 47.8,12

alä "there is", 36.33

al-säfärä "he did not camp", 41.53

äm "female", 30.8

amänägä "he escaped", 11.6

ämar "donkey", 31.22; 63.3

ämararä "donkeys", 31.22

ammärä "he believed", 17.6

an- "not", 47.8,12

anä "there is", 36.33; 49.24

anqəlaqqälä "he made wander here and there", 41.18

anqᵞä "back of body", "after", 48.25

agᵞäm "he craunched", 43.21

äräkəb "I find", 40.28

ärč "boy", 30.8

arəst "female", 30.8

ärkus "impure", 27.17

äsok "thorn", 27.18

ast, āst "female", 30.8

atänä "first", 35.24

atbäsäräm "he made (someone) cook", 41.14

atgaddälä "he helped to kill", "he caused to kill one another", 41.14

atkiddänä "he caused to cover / to be covered", 41.14

at(t) "one", 35.3

attəlännä "first", 35.24

atum "you" (plur.), 36.9

aṭara "he fenced in", 13.12

äwän "donkey", 63.3

awänägä "he escaped", 11.6

awre "wild animal", 63.4

äyä "I", 36.14

bäče "he cried", "he wept", 15.5

bä..fʷär "on", "over", 48.25

bakᵞäm "he cried", 43.21

baliq "adult", "old man", 63.9

banäräm "he demolished", 41.36

bäqəl, bäqər "hundred", 35.20-21

bariq "adult", "old man", 63.9

bäsär "meat", "flesh", 41.14

bäššä "he cried", 18.6

bet "house(s)", 31.17

betänä, bītänä "he dispersed", 41.5

bənanäräm, bənänäräm "he went on demolishing", 41.36

bərätä, bərätta "he became strong", 63.4

bərtu "strong", 63.4

bʷäz "slave", 11.11

čən "thigh", 30.11

čulo, čulalo "baby", "babies", 31.17,22

dabäna dämmäna "cloud", 11.6

däbbälä, däbbärä "he repeated", "he added", 11.2; 29.29; 49.21

dām, dāw, "master", 11.6

dänägäm "he hit", 29.19

däp(p)ärä "he added", 11.2

ebäryä(t) "so-and-so", 30.8

enä "there is not", 36.33

əbab "snake", 43.5

-(ə)m "and", 49.1

əmar "donkey", 63.3

əmbab, əmbāb "snake", 11.9; 30.10

əmmit "mother", 30.2

ən "don't", 47.12

ənbərbäya "butterfly", 43.5

əndät "mother", 43.5

əngər "foot", 43.5

ənǧ, ənǧəččä "hand", "hands", 31.17; 43.5

ənkrättätä "he was bent", 41.18

-ənna "and", 49.1

ənnä, ənne "this", "these", 36.33

ənqolo "roasted grain", 29.27

əntəlfit "(kind of) hawk", 29.27

ərkus "impure", 27.17

əya, əyya "I", 36.14

ənzən, əzən "ear", 43.5

färäz "horse(s)", 31.17

gädärä "he is big", 17.5

galbəm, galbəma "he / she galloped", 40.15

gamela(lo) "camel(s)", 31.17

gamēra, gamera "camel", 17.5

gäräd "girl", 30.8

gari "the house", 32.28

gədaddälä "he slaughtered", 41.36

gərd "misery", 23.9

godärä "he is tall", *17.5*
gregät "women of the same clan", *30.8*
gudärä "he is tall", *17.5*
gum'a, gumma "club", *23.10*
gun'är, gunnan "head", *23.10*
gʷäbbe, gʷäbbabit "brother(s)", *31.22*
gʷädin "rib", *30.11*
gʸäbbätä "race", *56.7*
had "one", *35.3*
hağis "new", *29.11*
ḥida, ḥuda "she", "he", *36.11*
ḥit, ḥut "she", "he", *36.11*
ḫʷet "two", *35.4*
irda "carding bow", *23.9*
käbäzä "he lied", *27.12*
käddänä "he covered", *41.14*
käzäbä "he lied", *27.12*
kətabäňňä "teacher", *29.51*
korda "water bottle", *23.9*
kutara, kut(t)ära "poultry", *30.8,10*
k̲ʷäm "he spilled", *43.21*
k̲ʷəm "thousand", *35.21*
lä- "for", "to", *36.55; 48.6*
läsbär "let me break", *40.30*
mäčä "when", *47.17*
märkäb "boat", *63.4*
mässē, mäzässē "sieve", *27.15*
mən, mər "whatever", *36.58*
mossa "calf", *8.18*
mʷäs(s)a "calf", *8.18*
-n "and", *49.1*
nä- marker of plural, *29.27*
näkäbäm "he found", *46.6*
näkäsäm "he bit", *46.6*
näkäwänəm "he found him", *46.6*
näkʷäsänəm "he bit him", *46.6*
näqärkum/kəmam "you pulled out" (plur. masc., fem.), *40.11*
näqärom, näqärämam "they pulled out" (masc., fem.), *40.10*
näqəb "a great quantity of butter", *29.27*
näqʷäm "he shouted", *43.21*
närä "he was", *49.25*
näsbər "let me break", *40.30*
näšäkkət "let me make", *40.28*
näṭäräm "it melted", *29.19*

nazäm "it was heavy", *29.50*
näžnär "heaviness", *29.50*
nəb "bee", *30.10*
nəḇ "charm", *11.6*
nəkəš "bite!" (fem.), *40.14*
nəkso, nəksäma "he / she bit", *40.15*
nəm, nəṃ "charm", *11.6*
of "bird", *11.11*
ogalb "to gallop", *42.11*
qän(n) "horn", *17.6*
qäpäräm "he burried", *46.6*
qäp̲ʷäränəm "he buried him", *46.6*
qär "horn", *17.6*
qäre "he remained behind", *43.21*
qärši "piaster", *65.4*
qəraqäräm "he mixed", *41.38*
qʸənn "buttocks", *30.11*
qollä "he roasted", *29.27*
quna, qura- "single", "alone", *33.18; 36.28*
qurä/e/i "crow", "raven", *30.10*
qurər "basket", *24.5*
räk(k)äsä "he was impure", *27.17*
säbbärä "he broke", *42.14*
säffäräm "he camped", *41.53*
säffärəm, säffärma "they measured" (masc., fem.), *40.10*
säffärkəmun/man "you measured" (plur. masc., fem.), *40.11*
säffärmun/man "they measured" (masc., fem.), *40.10*
säffärnä "we measured", *40.12*
samäm "he kissed", *41.36*
se'ä "look for", "want", *43.7*
səbur "broken", *42.14*
sədsa, səlsa "sixty", *23.8*
səmamäm "he went on kissing", *41.36*
šä, šä'ä "look for", "want", *43.7*
ši "thousand", *35.21*
-t- "he is", "it is", *49.19*
tä- "with", "and", *48.18; 49.1*
ta'ačä "under", *48.16*
täbət "male", *30.8*
täblalläqäm "he was joyful", *41.36*
täggärä "he cultivated the field for the first time", *63.5*
tä...k̲äma "as soon as", *49.17*
tambuyä, tamuyä "orphan", *11.9*

tänqälaqqälä "he wandered from place to place", *41.18*

tärakäsom "they quarelled with one another", *41.20,27*

tat, tät, tatä, tätte "under", *48.16*

täzibbärä "he returned" (intr.), *41.25*

tə- "when", "while", *38.12; 40.30*

təkkul "boiled in water", *42.16*

tənräkʸəm "while I find", *40.30*

təräk̠bo/bäma "you find" (masc., fem.), *40.29*

təsbär "let her break", *40.28*

tisäbər "when he breaks", *38.12*

ṭama- "be thirsty", *13.12*

ṭäpäbä "it was narrow", *27.8*

ṭəlfit "(kind of) hawk", *29.27*

ṭit "few", *18.8*

umar, umär "donkey", *63.3*

ūn "stone", *11.5*

urāba "hyena", *30.10*

wädrägya "hammer", *29.19,45*

waği(ğo) "elder brother(s)", *31.17*

wällät, wännät "forked digging pick", *36.33*

wänṭiya "filter", *29.19*

wärabä, wärābä "hyena", *30.10*

wässe "awl", *23.5*

wäšäkkət "to make", *42.11*

wašša "cellar", "cave", *48.19*

wäz "slave", *11.11*

we "or", *49.4*

wər "male", *30.8*

wogalb "to gallop", *42.11*

wolla(lu) "neighbour(s)", *31.22*

yä- "of", "to", "who", *36.55; 48.6*

yä...e "to", "toward", *48.25*

yäsbär "let him break", *40.28*

yäskär "let him be drunk", *40.28*

yən- "he is", "it is", *49.22*

yəräk̠bo/bäma "they find" (masc., fem.), *40.29*

yəsäbər "(when) he breaks", *38.12*

yəsäbru "he breaks", *38.12*

yəssädäb "he is offended", *41.32*

yətsädäb "he is offended", *41.32*

za "that", *36.32,43*

zak̠ "that", *36.43*

zak̠it "this one", *30.8*

zäṭäň "nine", *35.14*

zə- "this", *36.32,41,43*

zi "this", *36.41*

zibbärä "he returned" (trans.), *41.25*

žäṭä "nine", *35.14*

ži'ä "nine", *35.14*

HARARI

ādäqa "he caused to fall", *43.8*

af "mouth", *30.11*

akāk̠ "you" (sing.), *36.6,9*

äk̠äk̠ač "you" (plur.), *36.9*

al- "not", *47.8*

alf "thousand", *35.21*

āräda "he brought down", *43.8*

āsäda "he caused to take", *43.8*

azze, azzo "she", "he", *36.13,33*

bād "city", "country", *48.1*

azziyač "they", *36.13*

bäqlä "hundred", *35.20*

-be "in", *48.1*

bētäna "he dispersed", *41.5*

däbäla "he added", *49.21*

gädära "he became great", *17.5*

gōdära "he is tall", *17.5*

ḥal "there is", *36.33; 40.3; 49.24*

ḥamdi "praise", *48.1*

ḥēṭära "he fenced in", *13.12*

ḥubāb "snake", *11.9; 30.10*

int- "he is", "it is", *49.19*

kūd "liver", *11.5*

kum "thousand", *35.21*

kura "crow", "raven", *30.10*

-le "to", "for", *48.1*

limadot "to learn", *42.5*

-ma "and", *49.1*

mäči "when", *47.17*

märkäb "boat", *63.4*

nāra "he was", *49.25*

näsbär "let me break", *40.30*

qäbri "cemetery", *27.16*

qärši "piaster", *65.4*

säbri "endurance", *27.16*
sinān "language", *27.12*
sŭbur "broken", *42.14*
t- "he is", "it is", *49.19*
taḥay "under", *48.16*
tisäbraš "you (fem.) break", *27.27*
urūs "head", *27.18*
usṭu "inside", *11.15*
wädäqa "he fell", *43.8*

wärāba "hyena", *30.10*
wäräda "he went down", *43.8*
wäsäda "he took", *43.8*
wəyi "hot", *43.21*
wŭläǧi "give birth!", *15.5; 43.6*
yäsbär "let him break", *40.28*
zəḥtän "nine", *35.14*
zi "who", *36.55*

HAUSA

azùrfā "silver", *65.8*
bāba "father", *62.2*
ci "he has eaten", *43.3*
dambe "struggle", *31.21*
fu'du "four", *35.9*
kas- "to kill", *29.20*
kofa "door", *31.22*
magana "ward", *31.22*
mákásáa "site of killing", *29.20*
mákáshíi "weapon", *29.20*
mákàshíi "killer", *29.20*
mèe "what?", *36.57*

mu "we", *36.1*
mutu "to die", *2.16*
mutum "man", *2.16; 28.7; 63.6*
nā-sa "his", *36.31*
su halbi, etc. "they have hunted", *36.1*
súù-n-áa "name", *63.13*
šidda "six", *35.11*
tā-sa "his", *36.31*
tazo "she came", *2.16*
yazo "he came", *2.16*

HEBREW

As a rule, the spirantization of *b g d k p t* is not taken into account.

'ābad "he perished", *10.8*
'ábale "little father", *29.53*
'abbā "(my) father", *28.13*
'ābōt "fathers", *30.1*
'Abrām, 'Abrāhām "Abra(ha)m", *28.13*
'ādām, 'ādān "man", "men", *11.7; 27.30*
'ădamdām "reddish", *29.14*
'addīr "powerful", "mighty", *29.11; 67.9*
'ahăbā "to love", *42.5*
'aḥad "one", *35.3*
'aḥar "after", *58.13*
'aḥărē 'ăšer "after (that)", *58.14*
'aḥeret "other" (fem.), *30.3*
'akzāb "deceitful", *34.5*

'akzār "cruel", *29.16; 34.5*
'l "to", "towards", *48.6*
'al "not", *47.9; 54.6*
'almān "widower", *34.5*
'ămāhōt "handmaids", *31.19*
'āmar "he said", *63.2*
'āmar bə-libbō "he thought", *36.28; 63.14*
'ămarkāl "accountant", *63.11*
'amartī "I said", *40.6*
'ānā "I", *19.24*
'anī "I", *36.5*
'ap "also", *49.2*
'ăpar "meadow", *67.16*
'ăroməmenhū "I will exalt him", *46.3*
'aryē "lion", *11.13; 63.4*

ʾăšer "who", "what", "which", 36.51,56; 49.14; 57.2,5; 60.3

ʾăšērā, ʾăšērīm, ʾăšērōt "sanctuary", "sanctuaries", 31.13

ʾăšer ʿal-habbayit "mayor of the palace", 66.5

ʾaškāl "grapes", 31.26

ʾašmoret "night-watch", 27.17

ʾayil "large tree", 29.37

ʾayin "there is no...", 47.12

ʾāz, ʾăzay "then", 56.8; 58.12

ʾbṭlmys, ʾpṭlmys "Ptolemy", 27.17

ʿAbdī-ʾĒl "servant of God", 32.24

ʿad "lasting future", 48.17

ʿad, ʿădē "up to", "until", 48.17

ʿad ʾăšer "until", 58.14

ʿad kī "til", 49.14

ʿad-mātay "until when?", "how long?", 47.17

ʿAkkō "Acre", 23.1

ʿal-dibrat "because of", 48.15

ʿălēhem "on/against them", 48.23

ʿălē-nā "climb, please!", 40.14

ʿal-pī "according to", 48.15

ʿammūd "column", "pillar", 29.11

ʿAnātōt "Anatot", 29.47

ʿăqalqallōt "crooked paths", 29.14

ʿāqēb "heel", 31.25

ʿaqrab "scorpion", 29.17

ʿāṣam "he shut the eyes", 27.12

ʿăṣeret, ʿaṣṣərōt "crowd", "crowds", 31.25

ʿāṣūm "strong", 29.8

ʿAštārōt "Ashtarot", 29.47

ʿaštē ʿăśār "eleven", 35.3

ʿebed "servant", 10.7

ʿēnāb "grape", 31.25

ʿĒnayim/ām "Enayim", 29.54

ʿereb "evening", 19.23

ʿēṣ "tree", 19.23

ʿēśeb "herb", 31.25

ʿim(m-) "with", 48.13

ʿimmād "with", 48.22

ʿinnəbē "grapes", 31.25

ʿiqqəbē/ōt "heels", 31.25

ʿīr šālēm "peaceful city", 67.15

ʿiṣṣəbōt "herbs", 31.25

ʿl, ʿly "over", "above", 48.15

ʿōd "duration", 48.17

ʿōdennī "as yet" ("my time"), 36.18

ʿomed "support", 48.22

ʿorep "base of neck", 27.8

ʿzr "to be copious", "to help", 63.8

ba-ʿăbūr "to the effect (that)", 59.3

baʿal ha-ḥălomōt "dreamer", 51.22

Bābēlāh "to Babylon", 32.20

baḥúrčik "little lad", 29.53

bākā "he cried", 43.14; 62.2

bal "not", 47.14

balbēl "he confused", 41.38

bānā "he built", "he made", 63.8

baqbūq "flask", 29.13

bārāʾ "he created", "he made", 11.6; 63.8

bārūk "blessed", 63.2

bat "daughter", 10.7

bayit "house", 30.6

bazze "here", 51.26

bēn "between", 48.21; 63.8

ben šabaʿ-ʿeśrē šānā "twenty-seven years old", 51.22

bērak "he blessed", 45.9; 63.2

bēt "house of", 27.15

Bēt ʿAnāt "House of Anat", 67.14

Bēt Šemeš "House of the Sun-god", 67.14

bəkīt "crying", 29.49

bənō Bəʿor "son of Beʿor", 32.24

bərōš "juniper", 65.5

bə-ṭerem "before (that)", 58.14

bə-yōm "when", 49.15

delet "door", 31.20

dəbārāk "your word", 27.30

dibber "he spoke", 23.9; 41.2

dibrē "words", 23.9

Dotān/ayin "Dothan", 29.54

drwm/n "south", 11.7

ʾēber "pinions", 31.41

ʾebrā "pinion", 31.41

ʾeḥād "one", 33.18; 35.3

ʾēkā "where?", 47.7

ʾelle, ʾellū "these", 36.33

ʾēn "there is no...", 47.12

ʾēnēk "you are not", 47.12

ʾEprayim "Ephraim", 67.16

'eškōl "grapes", *31.26*
'ēt "accusative marker", *36.31; 52.10*
'ētān "lasting", *34.5*
'ēzōr "belt", *29.8*
gādal "he became big", *17.5*
galgal "wheel", "globe", *29.13*
galmūd "sterile", *23.8*
gan yəlādīm "infant-school", *63.12*
gaš "approach!", *43.5*
gəbəret "lady", *30.3*
gədī "young goat", *2.15; 29.42*
gəmallīm "camels", *23.1*
gilgēl "he rolled", *41.38*
gozlān "robber", *29.39*
gulgolet "skull", *29.13*
hallā(z) "this", *33.10; 36.33-34*
hallaylā "this night", *33.10*
hălō' "didn't?", *49.8*
han- "the", *33.9-10; 49.6*
happa'am "this time", *33.10*
harərē "mountains", *23.3*
haššānā "this year", *33.10*
hāyā "he was", "he became", *49.24*
hayyōm "today", *33.10; 52.6*
hazze "this", *36.13,33*
he'ešīr "he grew rich", *41.8*
hēkāl "temple", *27.16; 29.9*
hēnnā "here", *47.7*
hennē "behold", *49.6; 50.4; 60.2*
hiqdīš "he consecrated", *41.11*
hiqqāṭəlū "be killed!" (plur.), *41.19*
hiṣṭaddēq "he justified himself", *41.32*
hišbī'ekā "he adjured you", *35.34*
hišta'ašə'ū "enjoy yourselves", *41.25*
hištaḥawā "he prostrated himself", *41.9,29*
hištappēk "it was poured out", *41.25*
hitqaddeš "he sanctified himself", *41.25*
hōšēb, hōšīb "he caused to sit / dwell", *43.8*
hošlak "he was thrown", *41.45*
htl "to mock", *41.23*
htš'š'w "enjoy yourselves", *41.25*
ḥăbaṣṣelet "stalk", *67.3*
ḥabbūrā "contusion", *29.11*

habériko "comrade", *29.53*
ḥālaš "he weakened", *41.7*
ḥallāmīš "a precious stone", *23.8*
ḥămēšet "five", *30.3*
ḥamórčık "little donkey", *29.53*
ḥāraš "he cut in", "he engraved", *41.7*
ḥarṭom "nose", *17.8*
ḥārūṣ "gold", *65.6*
ḥăṣōṣərā "clarion", *17.2*
ḥillēṣ "he saved", *63.2*
ḥinnām "in vain", *47.2*
ḥkym, ḥkyn "wise person", *11.7*
ḥokmōt "Wisdom", *29.47*
ḥŏlī "weakness", *41.7*
ḥor "hole", *41.7*
ḥŏmarmar "it was continuously foaming", *41.37*
ḥomeṭ "kind of reptile", *23.8*
Ḥoronayim "Horonayim", *29.54*
ḥṣt "half", *35.30*
ḥyhwh "Yahwe is alive", *27.20*
'Iblayim "Iblayim", *29.54*
'im "or", *49.4*
'im "if", *49.4; 61.2,5-6*
'ímale "little mama", *29.53*
'im lo' "if not", *61.3-4*
'immā "(my) mother", *28.13*
'īš "man", *29.9*
'iššā(h) "woman", *30.4*
'it(t-) "with", *48.18*
ka'ăšer "when", *49.14; 58.14*
kābēd "he is heavy", *10.8*
kadít "little pitcher", *29.49*
kalbón "small dog", *29.38*
kāmōnī "like me", *36.18*
Karmel "Carmel", *67.19*
kasít "little glass", *29.49*
kebeś "lamb", *27.12*
kēn "yes", "so", *49.9; 50.4*
kepel "double", *35.4*
kerem "vineyard", *29.5; 30.5*
keśeb "lamb", *27.12*
kə, kəmō "like", "that", "because", "when", *48.11; 49.9*
kənāpayim, kənāpōt "wings", "extremities", *31.8*
kəsūt "covering", *29.48*

kh "so", "here", *49.9*

kī "because", "for", "really", *49.9,14; 58.2; 59.1; 60.1; 61.1*

kī ...'im "when ... if", "if ... when", *61.7,9*

kikkār "round disk", "round loaf", *27.3*

kil'ayim "two", "both", *35.4*

kō "so", "here", *36.35; 49.9*

kōkāb "star", *11.5; 29.13*

*kōrkōrōt "camel-borne   sedans", *63.6*

l' "not", *47.8*

lām(m)ā "before", "since", "why?", *58.3-5,7*

layiš "lion", *17.4*

leḥem "bread", *63.2*

lǝ- "(belonging) to", "for", *48.6,8; 51.23; 52.11; 53.2,5*

lǝdī "give birth!", *43.6*

lǝ-ma'an "with the intention (that)", *59.3*

lǝ-mātay "when?", "until when?", *47.17*

lǝmō "to", "for", *48.9*

lǝ'ōm "people", "clan", *35.21*

libb- "heart", *17.2; 36.28*

liblar "clerk", *65.4*

lk, lkt "go!", "to go", *27.25; 28.7; 43.10*

lo' "not", *47.9; 54.6*

lšm, lšn "tongue", "language", *11.7*

lūlē' "if ... not", *61.6*

luqqaḥ "he was taken", *41.45*

mā "what?", *47.15,17*

ma'ǝrāb "west", *29.19*

ma'gāl "encampment", *29.20*

maḥzīt "mirror", *29.24*

mākar "he sold", *64.4*

malkut/ūt "kingship", *29.48; 30.3*

mānōᵃḥ "resting place", *29.20*

maptēᵃḥ "key", *29.22*

māqōm "place", *57.5*

Maqqēdā "Maqqeda", *67.19*

maqṭīl "causing to kill", *42.15*

markōl "accountant", *63.11*

māṣā "he found", *45.11*

mātay "when?", *47.17*

Mattityā "Mattathias", *23.1*

may "water", *63.5*

mazlēg "fork", *29.22*

mē- "from", *48.12*

mē'ā "hundred", *35.20*

mēmē "waters", *31.21*

merkab "chariot", *63.4*

merkābā "chariot", *29.24; 63.4*

mǝbaqǝšīm "seeking" (plur.), *23.2*

mǝkubbāl, mǝkurbāl "wrapped", *23.9*

m(ǝ)lākīm "kings", *31.28*

mǝtīm "men", *28.7*

midbār "desert", "steppe", *29.21*

migdalor "lighthouse", *29.55*

migdōl "tower", *29.24*

min(nē-) "from", *11.6; 33.10; 48.12*

miqdāš "sanctuary", *31.25*

miqqǝdāš "sanctuaries", *31.25*

miqrā' "to call", *42.4*

mismār "nail", *29.22*

Miṣpā "Watch-tower", *67.11*

mišpaḥā "clan", *62.4*

mišpāṭ "judgement", *29.25*

mišqāl "weight", *29.22*

mizrāḥ "east", *29.21*

mizze "hence", *51.26*

Mō'ābīt, Mō'ǎbiyyā "Moabite" (fem.), *29.49*

msk "to mix", *65.7*

mukkē 'ĕlohīm "smitten by God", *51.11*

nāhār "river", *67.16*

Naḥᵃrayim "Upper Mesopotamia", *29.54; 67.16*

nāqī' "clear", *66.2*

nātan "he gave", *10.8*

nepeš "breath", "soul", "throat", *36.12,28; 63.7*

nǝyār "papyrus",   "parchment", "paper", *65.8*

Nimšī "Nimshi", *67.4*

nistappag "he dried himself", *41.26*

nišba' "he swore", *35.34*

ništattāpū "they became partners", *41.26*

ništattā "he became made", *41.26*

nitgallā "it became uncovered", *41.26*

Nmšy "Nimshi", *67.4*

'ŏnī, 'ŏniyyā "ships", "fleet", "ship", *31.41*

'ōr "light", *29.55*

pā'al "he made", *10.8; 11.4*

pa'am "foot", *33.10; 35.32*

pat "bit", *10.7*

pe "mouth", *31.21; 41.7*

pen- "lest", *49.2; 59.3*

Pənū-'Ēl "Face of God", *32.24*

pərī "fruit", *67.16*

pilegeš "concubine", *65.7*

pilpēl "pepper", *29.13*

pīpiyyōt "cutting edges", *31.21*

pit'ōm "on a sudden", *32.18; 47.3*

pldš "Faddās" (PN), *23.8*

plṭyš "forge hammer", *23.8*

*pū "mouth", *41.7*

pūš "to blow", *41.7,17*

qadmōn(ī) "oriental", *29.36*

qal, qallā "he / she is small", *44.11*

qām, qūm "he stood", "stand!", *44.5*

qāšōt "roughly", *47.4*

qaššətōt "bows", *31.25*

qāṭal "he killed", *10.9*

qāṭəlā "she killed", *46.3*

qāṭūl "killed", *29.8; 42.14*

qešet "bow", *31.20,25*

qəṭālātam "she killed them", *46.3*

qīqālōn "disgrace", *17.2*

qōmēm "he raised up", *43.9*

qomeṣ "handful", *35.9*

qorbān "offering", *29.35,37*

quddaš "he was made hallowed", *41.45*

qūmā "get up!", *40.14*

ra' "evil", *41.7*

ra'ănan "it grew luxuriant", *41.40*

ra'ănān "green", *29.14; 41.40*

rā'aš "he shook", *41.7*

rabbīm "many", *10.7*

raglayim "feet", "paws", *31.4*

rakkāb "horseman", *29.11*

Rāmōt "Ramot", *29.47*

regel "foot", "penis", *63.7*

rēqām "empty-handed", *32.19; 47.2*

rē'šīt "beginning", *29.49*

ribbō "ten thousand", *35.22*

ri'šōn "first", *35.24*

ri'šōnā "first", *47.2*

rōmēm "he set up", *41.40*

roshān "murderer", *29.39*

sabab "he turned", *44.10*

salsillōt "shoots", *27.3*

sar'appā "palm leaf", *17.8*

səbak "thicket", *31.25*

səharhar "he continuously turned about", *41.37*

siprón "booklet", *29.38*

sirsur "braker", *29.13*

sōbēb "he enclosed", *41.40*

subbəkō "his thickets", *31.25*

sullām "ladder", *27.13*

sūp "papyrus plant", *2.5*

sūsāy "my horses", *36.18*

sūsīm "horses", *31.11*

ṣabbīm "wagons", *23.7*

ṣāḥaq "he laughed", *10.9*

ṣāpōn "north", *10.7*

ṣby "splendour", *23.7*

ṣippōr, Ṣippōrā "birds", "bird", *10.7; 23.1; 29.17*

ṣo'n "small cattle", *31.38*

ṣwy "to order", *39.15*

śa'ărā "single hair", *31.41*

śāḥaq "he laughed", *10.9*

śahărōn "little-moon" (amulet), *29.38*

śalmā "coat", *27.12*

śar'appīm "anxieties", *17.8*

śar hā-'īr "burgomaster", "mayor", *66.5*

śē'ār "hair", *31.41*

śə'ippīm "anxieties", *17.8*

śimlā "coat", *27.12*

śṭm, śṭn "to accuse", *11.7*

š "who", "what", "which" (cf. *še*), *57.6*

ša'ar "gate", *27.13*

šabbāt "sabbath", *10.8; 41.42*

Šabbatay "born on the sabbath-day", *67.3,7*

šad "breast", *30.11*

šalhebet "flame", *29.33*

šālōm "peace", "well-being", 50.4

šāmar "he guarded", 10.8

šam(mā) "there", 47.7

šānā, šānīm "year", "years", 31.13

šarbīṭ "staff", "sceptre", 23.9

šblt "stream", "flood", 13.7

šēnīt "a second time", 47.4

še, šə "who", "what", "which", 36.47,51; 51.19

šel "of", 51.19-20

šəharhar "blackish", 29.14

šəlah "send!", 45.10

šənōt "years", 31.13

šgg, šgy "to err", 43.4

ši'bēd "he enslaved", 41.10

šiklēl "he completed", 41.10

šilšōm "the day before yesterday", 29.55; 32.18

Šimšōn "sunny", "small sun", 29.36

šiphā "house-born (slave-)girl", 62.4

šīr, šīrā "songs", "single song", 31.41

škb "lie down", "be buried", 63.13

šlwh "send", 45.10

šmarṭaf "babysitter", 29.55

šmw "his name", "whose name is", 65.4

šnayim "two", 35.4

šōpēṭ "judge", 29.7

šōr "ox", "bull", 30.5; 65.5

štē "two", 27.170

štn "to urinate", 41.23

šulḥān "table", 29.35,37

šwh "to come up to", 48.20

š-yš ly "what I have", 49.25

t "accusative" particle, 36.31; 52.10

taḥat, taḥtī "under", "lower", 48.16

taḥtōn "lower part", 48.16

talmīd "disciple", 29.29

tapuᵃḥ 'ădāmā "potato", 63.12

tāqaʿ "he beat", 62.2

tarbīt "increase", 30.1

targūm "translation", 29.30; 41.42

Tēl 'Abīb "Tel Aviv", 67.19

tə'ālā "water-course", 27.12

təhillā "praise", 29.30

tipe'ret "ornament", 29.30

tō'ām "twin", 29.29

tōšāb "resident", "metic", 29.29

ṭōṭapot "frontlet between the eyes", 11.5

'ūr "to shine", 41.17

wa- "and", 11.13; 39.6; 61.7

*wan- "and", 49.1

wāw "hook", 11.13

wa-yəhī 'im "and it happened, if / when …", 61.10

wayyo'mer "and he said", 38.11

wə-hāyā 'im/kī "and it happened, if / when …", 61.10

wered "rose", 65.5

yaʿaqob "Jacob", 45.9

yabrūḥ "mandrake", 29.18

yad "hand", 30.6

Yahūdā "Judah", 67.12

yaḥad "he was united", "gathering", 35.3

yaḥmūr "deer", 29.18

yām "sea", 63.5

yāmīm "days", 31.14

yāmīm rabbīm "for many days", 52.6

yāmīn "right hand", 30.6

yaqṭīl "he will cause to kill", 41.11

yāyin "wine", 65.5

ybnh "Yabneh / Yavneh", 9.5; 11.6

yeš "is", 49.23

yešnāh, yešnām, yešnō "she is", "they are", "he is", 36.18

Yeššay "Jesse", 67.4

yədabber "he speaks", 23.9

yəhūdīt "in Hebrew", 47.4

yəkarsəmennā "it gnaws it", 23.9

yəmōt "days", 31.14

yərā' "fear", 43.6

yəraqraq "yellowish", "greenish", 29.14

yəšullaḥ "he will be sent off", 41.45

yiddakkə'ū "they will be crushed", 41.32

yigdal "he becomes great", 38.16

yiqqāḥennū "he will take him", 46.3

yiṣṭaddāq "he will justify himself", 41.25

yišḥaṭ "he shall slaughter", 45.10

yišlaḥ, yišloḥ "he sends", *45.*10
yištammer "he is on his guard", *27.*14
yiṭṭammā "he defiles himself", *41.*32
yn "wine", *65.*5
yōmām "by day", *32.*19; *47.*2
yrḥw ᵓsp "months of ingathering", *31.*11

yšḥwṭ "he shall slaughter", *45.*10
yukkaḥ "he will be taken", *41.*45
ywwny "Yabneh / Yavneh", *9.*5
zalʿāpōt "deadliness", *23.*8
zikkārōn "remembrance", *29.*37
zū-Sīnay "the (God) of Sinai", *36.*51

HITTITE

ku-ni-ir-ša "who owns the earth", *14.*1
ma-li malik ("is king"), *27.*29

paḥḥur "fire", *19.*1
tà-ka "Dagan", *27.*29
wa-ia-na- "wine", *65.*5

LATIN

ager "field", *63.*5
alcool vini "wine spirit", *66.*6
alonuth "goddesses", *29.*47
Anna "Hanna", *27.*28
Bathillo "God's house", *22.*8
caesar "elephant", *63.*6
Caesar Augusta "Zaragoza", *67.*17
caput "capital", *64.*5
carfiathum "autumnal", *11.*1
castrum "fortified camp", *63.*10
charm "vineyard", *29.*5
ferrum "iron", *63.*13
formus "hot", *11.*15
hic "this here", *36.*45
Iadar "Iadar", *67.*9
ille "that", *36.*45
iste "this there", *36.*45

iuniperus "juniper", *63.*5
libellarius "clerk", *65.*4
magalia maʿgal ("enclosure"), *29.*20
Mazices Berber tribes, *2.*14
misceo "I mix", *65.*7
mons "mount", *67.*15
-ne, nonne "didn't?" *47.*16; *49.*8
Otthara "ʿAttara", *29.*44
paelex, pelex "young lady", *65.*7
quid?, quis? "what?", "who?", *36.*57
Rus- "cape", *67.*18
se habere "to be", *49.*23
strata "way", *14.*6
taurus "ox", "bull", *63.*5
Uadarius "Vadarius", *67.*9
vīnum "wine", *63.*5
zambr "kind of gazelle", *29.*5

LIBYCO-BERBER
NUMIDIC, TUAREG

a "ho!", *49.*10
ăbəggi "fox", *2.*14
a-bərkan "black", *29.*35
*adar "tremendous", "God", *67.*9
af "to find", *43.*23
a-fərrad "sweeper", *29.*11
a-fǧaḥ "peasant", *15.*8

a-funas "bull", *32.*16
afus "hand", *35.*10
a-gadir "wall", "fortified granary", *65.*8
a-gim "thousand", *35.*21
a-gʸānba "crocodile", *30.*10
a-ġarraf "jar", *32.*3

aġ "to befall", "to happen"; *43.23*
a-ġyul(-inn) "donkey", "ass", "(that) jackass", *30.10; 36.34; 41.7*
a-ham-ənna "the tent in question", *36.34*
aləy "go up!", *43.11*
alam "camel", *30.10*
alġʷm "camel", *30.10*
alim "straw", *35.21*
a-maddaz "mallet", *29.22*
a-maziġ "Berber", *2.14*
a-məllal "white", *29.11; 43.23*
a-mnukal "king", *17.7; 21.30*
a-mūssen "skilled man", *11.7*
a-nəbbal "grave-digger", *29.11*
ar "up to", *48.2*
a-rgaz-ad(-dək) "this (here) man", *36.37*
arġəm "camel", *30.10*
as "to go towards", "to gather", *43.23*
a-šiban "bald", *29.35*
atbir "pigeon", *30.10*
awal, awar, awaž "word", *17.5; 63.5*
ˀwdštr "servant of Astarte", *11.5*
a-wəssar "old", *29.11*
ay expressive particle, *28.13*
ay-ad(-dək) "this (here)", *36.59*
ay-inn(a) "that (in question)", *36.59*
azəll "to run", *43.10*
a-ẓrəf "silver", *65.8*
ažġəm "camel", *30.10*
ažim "thousand", "straw", *35.21*
bāba "father", *62.2*
barbar "to drink hard", *41.38*
bbəy "cut", *29.26*
bdu "divide", *29.26*
bəddəl "to change", *41.7*
bəgbəg "to overfill", *41.38*
bəṭṭu "divide", *29.26*
d "with", *48.18; 50.9*
ddəhhašt "laughing", *2.15*
ddr "to live", *43.23*
ddu "to go", *43.23*
ekahi "cock", *29.46*
əlkasən "gourds", *21.30*
-əlkəm- "follow", *2.14; 41.2,6*

əns "to spend the night", *43.23; 63.3*
ət "with", *48.18*
əwl "heart", *2.14*
əzzəht "oil", *2.15*
f "thereupon", *48.4; 49.2*
fad "thirst", *32.10*
fruh "child", *63.5*
fsəy "melt!", *43.11*
-ga- "to be", *49.24*
gld, gldt "king", *2.15; 29.46*
ġar "to", "by", *48.2,10*
ġaym "to stay", *44.5*
ġbalu, ġbula "spring", "springs", *31.28*
-ġəṭṭ- "goat", *29.42*
ġr "to call", *27.8; 43.23*
-ġra- "to read", "to study", *27.8*
ha "behold", *49.10*
hik "make haste!", *14.10*
hram "boy", *63.6*
hnin "be gracious", *2.14; 41.2*
i "to", "for", *41.11; 48.4; 67.9*
ičča "he has eaten", *43.3*
IDR "Iadar", *67.9*
id multiplicative and plural marker, *35.31*
id hali "maternal uncles", *35.31*
iġ "one", *35.3*
*iggar "field", *63.5*
ikkərăd "he behaved violently", *41.6,34*
ilākkəm "he follows", *41.6*
ilāmməd "he learns", *38.5*
ili "to have", "to be", *49.23*
ils, ilsawən "tongue", "tongues", *28.13; 30.11*
ini "to say", *43.23*
irah, iruh "he will leave", "he left", *44.5*
irāmməd "he learns", *38.5*
is "towards", "with", *48.4,10*
ism, isəm, ismawən "name", "names", *28.13; 63.13*
išəmməl "he finished", *54.2*
išt "one", *35.3*
itākărăd "he keeps on behaving violently", *41.34*

itəkərid̦ "he (doesn't) keep on behaving violently", *41*.34

izimmər "ram", "lamb", *30*.10

ižīmān "thousands", *35*.21

ižžar, "field", *63*.5

kămă-tid̦ "you" (fem. plur.), *40*.11

kašaf "to guess", *19*.23

kăwă-nid̦ "you" (fem. plur.), *40*.11

-kərz- "to plough", *19*.23; *29*.33

-kkərăd̦- "behave violently", *41*.6,34; *63*.5

kkuz̦ "four", *35*.9

kra "something", *32*.10

k̲rad̦ "three", *35*.8,20

krkb "to roll", *41*.38

laz̦ "hunger", *32*.10

lukk "to tread on", *27*.25; *28*.7; *43*.10

ma "what?", *36*.57

-mawal "shepherd", *43*.23

măz̦ăg, məz̦əg "he is deaf", *38*.3

məllul "he / it is white", *43*.23

-mətrəg- "be freed", *2*.14

mi "who", *36*.57

middən, məddən "people", "men", *28*.7

mmut "die", *44*.5

mnkd "king", *17*.7

mraw "ten", *35*.3

Mrič "Melilla", *15*.8

mš "if", *61*.2,5

mur "if", *47*.8; *61*.2

mwsn "skilled man", *11*.7

n- "of", *48*.6; *51*.20,23

-naz̦um "fastener", *29*.26

-nbarš "blessed", *29*.26

nbbn "cutters", *2*.15; *29*.26; *31*.12; *51*.23

nbt̲n "splitters", *29*.26; *31*.12; *51*.23

nby b' "sigh for my father!", *41*.11

-nəfsad̦ "roper", *29*.26

-nəġmar "hunter", *29*.26

-nəhšam "judge", *29*.26

nək "I", *36*.6; *49*.20

-nəsləm "Moslim", *21*.30

-nəz̦dam "woodcutter", *29*.26

nġ "to kill", *43*.23

nšqr' "of wood", *2*.15

nt- "there is", *49*.19

qqim "stay!", *28*.9; *44*.5

ražiġ "I waited", *41*.34

rnəb̲, rnu "to prevail", *43*.23

s "towards", "with", *32*.3; *48*.2,4, 10

sa "seven", *35*.12

sd̦is "six", *35*.11,20

-səġəm- "to great", *15*.8

-səggan "black", *43*.23

-səhhar- "to bewitch", *65*.8

səmmus "five", *35*.10

-sərtək- "cause to fall", *2*.14

sġyul "to behave like a donkey", *41*.7

sin, sən "two", *35*.4

sku "to bury", *43*.23

skərz "plough", "ploughshare", *29*.33

slukk "cause to walk on", *43*.10

smi'iw "to mew", *41*.8

sqas "cause to taste", *41*.14

ssbəddəl "cause to change", *41*.7

ssəns "to spend the night", *41*.8; *63*.3

s-t̲art̲ar "to make the milk boil", *41*.38

sud̦əm "to kiss", *41*.8

sw "to drink", *43*.23

symi "baby", *63*.5,13

ša "some", "something", *35*.3; *54*.4

šard̦ "three", *35*.8

šəmrər "to become white", *41*.39

šqr' "wood", *31*.28; *51*.23

ta "this" (fem.), *36*.11

ta-bəġlit̲, ta-bəġliht̲ "mule", *2*.15

ta-funast "cow", *32*.1

tă-kəlkəbba "occiput", *29*.13

tă-kərkort "skull", *29*.13

takerza "ploughing", *29*.30

tam "eight", *35*.13

ta-maziġ-t "Berber language", *2*.14

tamed̦e "hundred", *35*.20

tamġart "elderly woman", *30*.1

tamtut, tamt̲ət "woman", *63*.6

tekahit "hen", *29*.46

tə-barart "girl", *21*.30

təmət̲t̲ut "woman", *63*.6

tifīnaġ "Tuareg writing", *2.15*

tiġəṭṭən "she-goats", *2.15*

tiləft "wild sow", *30.1*

timaḍ "hundreds", *35.20*

ti(n) "these" (fem.), *36.11*

tməttən "they die one after the other", *41.34*

träžiġ "I keep on waiting", *41.34*

-ttu "one", *49.23*

-ttwaddəz- "be crushed", *2.14*

tuššənt "she-jackal", *30.1*

tẓa "nine", *35.14,20*

udəm "face", *41.8*

ul "heart", *2.14; 15.8*

u-ma "brother", *66.5*

ur "not", *41.34; 47.8; 54.2; 61.2*

ur "heart", *2.14*

u-rgaz "man", *32.3*

ur išəmmil "he didn't finish", *54.2*

ur ... ša "not", *54.4*

uššən "fox", "jackal", *2.14; 67.4*

uzzal "iron", *63.13*

už "heart", *2.14; 15.8*

w "son of", "that of", *67.9*

wa-(ḏ) "this (one)" (masc.), *36.11, 37; 57.6*

waman "water", *32.1,3; 63.5*

war "not", *47.8*

-warġ- "yellow", *27.8*

wsm "to be skilled", *11.7*

wš "to give", *43.23*

wt "to strike", *43.23*

yaman "water", *32.1; 63.5*

yan "one", *35.3*

yəffəġ "he went out", *41.34*

yəkrəs "he draws", *38.1*

yəksi "he knotted", *32.1*

yəkša "he has eaten", *43.3*

yəlämməd "he learns", *38.5*

yəmmət "he will die", *44.5*

yəmmut "he died", *41.34; 44.5*

yərwəl "he ran away", *38.2*

yəssəzdəġ "he lodged", *41.7*

yəssird "he clothed", *41.7*

yəšša "he ate", "he has eaten", *2.15; 41.34; 43.3*

yəššur "he filled", *32.1,8*

yətəffəġ "he often goes out", *2.14; 41.34*

yətətt "he usually eats", *41.34*

yəzdəġ "he settled", *41.7*

yi(n) "these" (masc.), *36.11*

yird "he dressed himself", *41.7*

yiwən "one", *35.3*

zḍəġ "to camp", *63.3*

zik "make haste!", *14.10*

zl' "iron", *31.28; 51.23; 63.13*

-zlaf "rush", *31.28*

zlufa "rushes", *31.28*

zrəy "pass!", *43.11*

ẓr "to see", *43.23*

ž "to make", *43.23*

žəġid "king", *2.15*

žn "to sleep", *43.23*

MOABITE

ʿnw "I shall oppress", *43.14*

'n "there isn't", *47.12*

't "accusative" particle, *52.10*

bnty "I built", *43.14*

hr'ny "he let me see", *41.11*

Ḥwrnn "Hawrānān", *29.54*

*Kamōš-ʿaśā "Kamosh has made", *16.3*

kl'y "two", "both", *35.4*

ky "when", "because", "indeed", *56.4; 58.2*

Mhdbh "Medeba", *27.28*

mlkty "I became king", *40.6*

w''š "there", *38.11*

šm "and I made", *47.7*

w'bn "and I built", *43.14*

w'ltḥm "and I fought", *41.22*

w'šb "and I brought back", *41.11*

wyʿnw "and he oppressed", *43.14*

North Arabian

'<u>d</u>h "while", 27.28

'āfaqū "they agreed", 19.24

'ṣdq "executor", 29.16

's²ll "withered" (?), 29.16

's²rq "he went eastward", 41.11

'ty "he came", 43.16

'z̧l, 'z̧ll "he hollowed out", 44.15

'dky "up to", "until", 48.17

'mt "folk", 27.28

'trw "(man) from 'Aṯṯara", 29.44

b'yt "she overcame", 43.16

bkrt "young she-camel", 27.28

bky "he wept", 43.16

bnw, bny "sons of", 31.10-11

bny "he built", 43.16

bqrtn "two young she-camels", 31.3

<u>d</u>n, <u>d</u>t "this", 36.38

f- "and", 9.12; 38.11; 49.2; 61.10

f- "in", "at", 48.5

Ġzy "Gazzay", 43.16

h- "oh!", 50.3

hb "give!", 31.3; 43.6

hmt' "he worked out his salvation",
   41.11

hn- "the", 33.9; 49.6

hn' "if", 61.2

hqny "he offered", 41.11; 43.16

hyd' "he made known", 41.11

ḥdṣ "he made anew", 13.9

ḥwr "he returned", 44.5

kllhm "all of them", 23.3

kn "it happened", 61.10

l- "to", "for", 48.8

lm "to", "for", 48.9

m' "with", 48.14

M'wy "Mu'āwiy", 43.16

m- "from", 44.5; 48.12

mh "what(?)", 27.28

mn "from", 48.12

n'mtn "two ostriches", 31.3

nm "to", "for", 48.9

nqt "she-camel", 27.28

nq't "clearing", 66.2

r'y "he pastured", 43.16

s¹'d "lucky", 14.3

s¹nn "years", 31.13

s¹nt "year", 27.28

s²kr "rewarding", 14.3

ṣyr "he came back", 44.5

ṣ̌yt "sheepfold", 13.9

ṯnn'l "God has considered", 23.3

wgm, wṯm "he was mourning", 18.6

Wrd(n/w), Wrydw "rose", "little
   rose", 65.5

yhbrr "he fulfills", 44.15

Oromo

abbōtī "elders", 29.46

afān "mouth", 30.11

ana, ani "I", 36.3

bah- "to get out", 41.28

bara "year", 10.6

bará "learner", 10.6

bās- "to take out", 41.28

bati "roof", 22.16

bēk- "to know", 10.3; 41.15

bit- "to buy", 41.20

činā "side", 30.11

dammaq- "to wake up", 41.7

dabra "he passes", 27.12

darba "he passes", 27.12

did- "to refuse", 47.16

d'al- "to give birth", 27.12

-f, -fa, -fi, -fu "on", "by", "to",
   48.5

fi "and", 49.2

fid- "to bring", 41.20

fuňňān "nose", 30.11

gabra "slave", 63.6

gara "towards", 10.6

gará "stomach", 10.6

gurbā "boy", 63.6

hama "bad", 32.1

harka(n) "hand", 32.1; 41.7

harkisu "to pull", "to draw", 41.7

ilm "son", *63.6*
inni "he", *36.1*
isā "him", "his", *36.1,10*
isān "them", *36.10*
isāni "they", "their", *36.10*
isī "her", *36.10*
(i)tti "to", "at", "in", *48.18*
kan "his", *36.1*
kenne(f) "he gave (to)", *48.5*
kiyya "my" (masc.), *36.6*
kuni "this" (masc.), *36.6*
magālā "market place", *29.20*

mana "home", "house", *29.20*
mot "chief", *63.6*
mučā "child", *8.18*
nama "the man", *32.1*
namni "the man", *32.1*
sinra "wheat", *17.7*
tiyya "my" (fem.), *36.6*
tūl "to pile up", *63.6*
tullū "hill", *63.6*
tuni "this" (fem.), *36.6*
ummata "people", *29.46*
yōm(i) "when", *49.15*

PALAEOSYRIAN

a "on" (?), *48.15*
ʾà-a-gú-um "to go", *17.2*
a-a-tá-qá- "he should take", *40.18*
ʾÀ-da "Hadda", *32.6*
Adamma(ʾum) "Adamma", *29.51; 32.6*
A-dam-ma-sù "(t)his / the Adamma", *33.13*
a-dè "corresponding to", *48.17*
a-dì "to(wards)", "until", *48.17*
a-dì-ma "until", *48.17*
al, al$_6$, al$_6$-a "on", *48.15*
a-li-iš "instead of", *32.17*
^{d}*AMA-ra-sù* "(t)his / the AMA-ra", *33.13*
A-mi-ì, A-mi-du "Amidu", *27.29*
am-sa-a "yesterday", "last evening", *47.2*
an(a), a$_5$-na "to", "towards", *48.4, 6,9,20*
a-na-pá-ap "he should besprinkle", *40.18*
an-na "I", *40.18*
an-ne "that?", *36.32*
an-tá-nu "you" (masc. plur.), *36.5*
ap "also", *49.2*
a-pa-kà-ra "they should join" (dual), *40.18*
a-pá-kà-ru$_{12}$ "they should join", *40.18; 53.4*
ʾà-rí-tum "pregnant", *29.49*
ar-ša-lu "despicable (men)", *31.26*

A-ru$_{12}$-ga-tù "Larugatu", *17.2*
a-sa-lu "rush", *31.26*
áš-kà-lum "grapes", *31.26*
áš-tá "within", "in", *48.18*
áš-tá-ma "I heard", *40.18; 45.7*
áš-te$_4$, áš-ti, áš-tu, áš-tum, áš-tù(-ma) "from", "since", "within", *48.18; 54.5*
a-za-me-kà, a-zi-mi-kà "you are spell-bound", *40.5*
a-za-me-tù "coercion", "spell-binding", *29.45; 33.3*
ba "water", *11.6; 32.4*
Ba-na-a-ḫu "the brother is nice", *38.10*
ba-ra-su-um "juniper", *65.5*
ba-ša-um "to be (present)", *49.23*
ba-ša-nu(-um) "serpent", *29.6*
ba-ta-a "two houses", *31.3*
ba-tá-qi i-dim "cutting by hand", *51.11*
Da-mu "Damu", *24.2; 40.18*
Da-na-LUGAL "the king is powerful", *38.10; 44.11*
da-nu-nu "(are) very strong", *29.11*
du-ba-lu "pastures", *31.25*
du-ḫu-rí (gen.) "inner part", "rear", *33.3*
Eb-la "Ebla", *22.3*
en-ma "behold!", *49.6*
En-na-Il "Il is merciful", *44.11*
éš "with", "near", "for", *32.17*

gú-a-tum "hands", *31.27*

gu-la-'à-tum "cups", *31.19*

ha-ba-ha-bí (gen.) "hidden things", *31.21*

Ha-lam^{ki} "Aleppo", *11.6*

ì-a-la-nu "a large tree", *22.13*

Ib-na-Il "Il has created", *43.13*

Íl-'à-aq-Da-mu "Damu caught up", *17.5*

ì-la-nu-um, ì-la-num "a large tree", *22.13*

I-li-lu "Enlil", *32.4*

ì-ma-tum "mother", "woman", *30.2*

in, ì-na "in", *48.4,9*

í-ne "this?", *36.32*

Iq-na-Da-mu "Damu has begotten", *43.13*

Ìr-'à-aq-Da-mu "Damu caught up", *17.5*

íṣ-ba-um "finger", *27.17*

iš "with", "near", "for", *32.17; 48.1,4,10; 49.1*

i-ša-wu "to be (present)", *49.23-24; 50.6*

Iš-má-Il "Il heard", *40.18*

iš-tá-má "he has heard", *38.4*

i-tù-wa-ar, "he comes back", *44.5*

i-ṭa-ha-ù "they will come near", *38.6*

kà-ma-tum "parasite", "louse", *11.7; 24.2*

kà-na-na-um/im "Canaanite", *29.41*

kà-na-tù-um "parasite", "louse", *11.7*

Kār-^d*Kāmiṭ* "quay of Kamosh", *67.19*

kà-ši-bù(-um) "liar", *29.7*

kà-wa-nu "stable", "permanent", *44.13*

-kum "to you", *36.26*

Ku-ra "Kura" (DN), *32.6*

li-im "thousand", *35.21*

lí-na "to", "towards", *48.6,9,20*

ma-pá-hu(-um) "bellows", *29.26*

ma-qar-tum "chisel", *29.22*

mar-a-tum "pasture-land", *29.21*

ma-sa-gàr-tù-um, mas-gàr-tum "asylum", *24.2*

ma-ša-ba-tum "dam structures", *29.21*

ma-za-lum-sù "for/with its/his messenger", *32.18*

ma-za-ri-gú "set of javelins", *29.22*

me-at, mi-at "hundred", *35.20*

mi-in "in", *48.5*

Mi-kà-Il "who is like Il?", *36.58*

Mí-ma-hir-su "who is his opponent?", *36.58*

mi-nu "in", *48.5*

mu-da-bil sí-kà-ri "story-teller", *13.2; 31.28*

Mug-rí-i, Mug-rí-du "Mugridu", *27.29*

mu-li-tum "midwife", *43.8*

mu-lu-iš "in addition to", *32.17*

na-'à-su "to recover", *32.4; 53.4*

na-na-ṣa-ab "we are staying", *40.18*

na-pá-hu-um "bellows", *29.26*

na-ṭì-lu "wailers", *40.18*

ne-'à-la-a "we purify", *40.18*

ni-bù-ha "are outstanding" (fem.), *40.10*

ni-bù-hu "(are) outstanding", *29.11*

nu-wa-sa-ra-si "we let her go", *40.33*

*pá-kà-ru*₁₂ "to join", *53.4*

pá-na-ù "are clothed in", *40.10*

Qá-ma-Da-mu "Damu is standing", *32.15; 40.3*

*qá-na-(u*₉*-)um* "to beget", *43.13*

*ri-ba*₁₄ "ten thousand?", *35.22*

sa-a-dum "a kind of barley", *31.27*

sa-da-bí-iš "on behalf of", *32.17*

sa-da-um "to let know", *43.8*

sa-i-lum "barley", *31.28*

sa-ì-lu-um "barley", *31.28*

sa-ma-nu "oil", *29.5*

^d*Sa-mu-ga-ru*₁₂ "Moon-god", "Djebel Sindjar", *27.17*

sa-ti "the one" (fem.), *36.49*

sa-zu-wa-tum "dismissal", *28.13, 33; 43.8*

si "she", *36.10*

Si-a-ha "she is a sister? / brother", *27.28*

si-ba "adjure!", *35.34*

si-in "up to", "next to", "to", "for", *32.3; 48.20*

si-ne-mu "of the teeth", *39.3*

sí-piš "Sun-goddess", *11.9; 13.2*

su-lu-la-a "of the two (moon's) horns", *27.3*; *31.3*

su-ma "if", *61.2*

-*su-ma-a* "of both of them", *36.22*

su-u₉ "he", *36.10*

su-wa-ti "him", "that", *36.3,36*

ṣí-na-ba-ti (gen.) "sunbeams", *23.7*

-*š* "his", "her", *36.20*

ša-mi-na "cypress", *17.2*

šar-mi-na "of two cypresses", *11.6*; *17.2*

ša-ti "the one" (fem.), *36.49*

šu "that", "who", *36.48*; *57.6*

-*šum* "to him", *36.26*

tá-aš-tá-me-lum "the man of the mourners", *29.29*

tá-da-bí-lu "interpreter", *29.29*

tá-er-iš-tù-um "ploughing", *29.30*

tá-ṣa-a "they will go out" (dual), *40.18*

Tàš-má-ᵈUTU "the Sun-goddess heard", *40.18*

ti-a-ba-a "she dries (bricks)", *40.18*

ti-ʾà-ma-tù "sea", *32.4*

ti-da-ḫu-ru₁₂ "she enters" (subjunctive), *57.5*

Ti-iš-te-Da-mu "Damu has drunk", *21.6*; *40.18*; *50.25*

tikkulū "they have eaten", *40.18*

tiltaptū "they have rubbed themselves", *40.18*; *41.22*

timḫaṣū "they have hammered", *40.18*

ti-na-ṭa-ú "they strike up", *36.36*; *40.18*

tištayū "they have drunk", *40.18*

tù-a-ba-áš "she puts on", *40.33*

tù-la-dì "new-born crop", *29.28*

Tu-ra-ᵈDa-gan "return, Dagan!", *39.7*

tù-bù-a-tum "goodness", *28.13*

Ṭù-bù-ḫu-ᵈʾÀ-da "very slaughterous is Hadda", *29.11*; *48.20*

u₄-bu "day", "when", *11.6*; *57.5*

ù-ḫu-wa-tum "fraternity", *28.13*

ù-mu-tum "fattening", *29.48*

u₉-qá-ṭa-ra- "they will burn incense", *40.33*

ú-ša-dì-ú-šu "they let him know", *41.9*

uš-tá-si-ir "he has released", *41.9, 29*

wa-a "and", *49.1*

wa-ma-sa "and with it", "and besides that", *48.14*

wa-zi-um "quitter", *29.7*

zu-mu-ba-ru₁₂ "songs", *11.9*; *31.28*

PERSIAN

aḥmarkār "accountant", *63.11*

āmārkār "accountant", *63.11*

ganza- "store-room", *63.10*

ganza-bāra "treasurer", *65.4*

ḫurma "date", *27.13*

karš- "weight", *65.4*

lāk "lac", *65.6*

māgār "if not", *61.3*

manā kṛtam "I made", *42.20*; *65.4*

musk "musk", *65.6*

nama "name", *65.4*

parde "curtain", *11.2*

pirind "sword", *11.2*

varəδa- "rose", *65.5*

PHOENICIAN AND PUNIC

ʾb, ʾby "my father('s)", *36.18*

ʾb "in", *48.5*

Abaddir (Latin) "stone of the Mighty one", *27.27*

ʾaddīr "mighty", *29.11*; *67.9*

ʾdny "his Lord", *41.13*

ʾḥr ʾš "after (that)", *58.14*

ʾḥym "two brothers", *31.4*

ʾklyn "Cleon", 27.17
ʾl "these", 36.33
ʾlk "I", 17.4
ʾln "god", 29.37
ʾm "if", 61.2
ʾm "or", 49.4
ʾmt "maid", 29.47
ʾnk "I", 17.4; 36.6
ʾp "also", 49.2
ʾst "this", 36.35
ʾš "who", "which", "what", 36.51; 57.6
ʾšmn "Eshmun", 27.17
ʾšnm "two", 35.4
* ʾštʾlm "I beg you", 41.25
ʾt "with", 48.18
ʾt "accusative" marker, 52.10
ʾy "not", 47.11
ʾyqdš "he consecrated", 41.13
ʾyt "accusative" particle, 52.10
ʿAkkā "mooring-post", 67.11
ʿd "up to", "until", 48.17
ʿl "over", "above", 48.15
ʿlyn "Most High", 29.36
ʿsʿr "ten", 24.10
ʿsr, ʿšrt "ten", 16.3; 35.15
ʿštrʾsy "Astarte-Isis", 29.55
ʿštrny "(man) of Astarte", 29.36
Ba-al-ḥa-lu-ṣu "Baal saved", 63.2
Bīʾrōt "wells", 67.11
bl "son", 17.4; 47.14
bn "between", 48.21
bn ṣdq "legitimate son", 51.17
bny "he built", 43.14
byrm "son of Yarīm", 27.20
dlht "doors", 31.19
ennu (Latin) "no", 47.12
gdr "wall", "compound", 65.8
glgl "wheel", "globe", 29.13
Gublu "mount", 67.11
*ha-Dărōmīt "Hadrumetum", 67.12
ha-Gadīr "the compound", 33.9; 67.11
hbrk "steward", 27.16
hmt "those", 36.35
hnkt "this", 36.33,35
htqdš "he sanctified himself", 41.25
h-Rmʾ "Rome", 33.9

Ḥa-lu-ṣu "saved", 63.2
ḥlṣ "to save", 27.12; 63.2
ḥlwṣ "saved", 42.14; 63.2
ḥn šlmt "acknowledgment of full payment", 64.6
Ḥnt "Anna", 27.28
k- "when", "as", 58.2
kʾ "here", 36.35; 49.9
kʿtbty "I wrote", 40.6
kkr "talent" (weight), 27.3
Kyšr(m) "elephant", 63.6
l-b- "against", 48.24
lm "lest", 58.3
l-m-b- "still during", 48.24
*maʿgal "enclosure", 29.20
*magdāl, magdōl "tower", 29.24; 67.18
maqōm "place", 29.21
*Maqōm ḥadaš "new town", 64.2
mʾt "hundred", 35.20
milk "king", 10.5; 27.19
mlkty "king of Kition", 27.20
Mlqrt "Melqart" 27.20; 29.55
mmlkt "king", 29.46,48
m(n) "from", 48.12
mnm "anything", 36.61
mqm "place", 64.2
mtl "gift", 17.4
myqdš "temple", 29.21
myskr "making known", 42.15
myšql "honouring", 42.15
nasot (Latin) "I brought", 45.13
ndʿr "vow", 24.10
nšʾt "I brought", 45.13
nštʾm "dreaded" (plur.), 42.17
pʿl "he / she did", 27.28; 46.3
pʿl ʾnk "I having done", 42.12; 53.5
pʿltn "she made me", 46.3
pʿm "foot", "penis", "time", 35.32; 63.7
pʿmm, pʿmt "feet", "paws", "times", 31.8
qart "city", 27.19; 30.3
Qartḥadašt "Carthage", 67.10
qbcr "tomb", 24.10
qnm, qnʾm "one's self", 36.28
qnmy "whoever", 36.61
ra-ʾ-si, rʾš, rš "head", "cape", 67.18

*Ruš ʾAddīr "cape of the Mighty one", 67.9

šḥrt "witch", 65.8

skʿr "memory", 24.10

skr "to remember", 13.2; 14.2

srsr "broker", 29.13

st "this", 36.35

ṣdyqʾ "just" (fem.), 27.28

Ṣūr "rock", 67.11

škb "to lie down", "to be buried", 63.13

šm "there", 47.7

šmʿ "she heard", 42.12

šmr (ΣVMAR) "guardian", 15.3

šnm "two", 35.4

špḥ "family", 62.4

št "year", 27.3

šūfēṭ "judge", "suffete", 29.7

t "accusative" marker, 36.31; 52.10

thtpk "it will be overturned", 41.22-23

tḥt "under", "below", 48.16

tḥtsp "it will be torn away", 41.23

tklt "summing up", 29.30

tmʾ "perfect" (fem.), 27.28

ṭn, ṭnʾ "to erect", 45.13

wypʾl "and he made", 38.11

Yʾdr "Yadar", 67.9

Yatan-ʾEl "God has given", 67.7

ydbrnk "they will speak to you", 46.3

ymm, ymt "days", 31.14

yn "wine", 65.5

ynny (Latin) "no", 47.12

yqdšt "I consecrated", 41.13

zn "this", 36.38

RENDILLE

ada "paternal aunt", 62.2

aham "to eat", 17.2; 63.3

čimbir "bird", 11.9

gāl "camel", 30.10

géèl "to enter", 10.3; 19.23

geléb "evening", 19.23

gololsaḏ "eat", 41.28

ínàm "boy", 10.6

ìnám "girl", 10.6

laḥ "ewe", 30.10

yigis "he killed", 38.1.

SEMITIC, COMMON

ʾab- "father", 30.1; 62.2

ʾabn- "stone", 30.6

ʾanp "nose", 30.11

ʾarnab- "hare", 29.16; 30.10

ʾarṣ- "earth", 30.2

ʾarwiy "wild animal", 63.4

ʾatan- "she-ass", 30.1

ʾty "to come", 2.10

ʾaw "or", 49.4

ʾwš "to give", 43.23

ʾayyal- "deer", 30.10

ʾzn / wzn "to be heavy", 10.12

ʿabd- "to serve", 62.4

ʿagal- "calf", 30.10

ʿaqrab- "scorpion", 30.10

ʿayn- "eye", 9.5; 30.6,11

ʿayr- "ass-foal", 30.10

ʿdw "to go", 43.23

ʿdr "to help", 63.8

ʿigl- "calf", 30.10

ʿly "upper part", "over", "above", 48.15

ʿny "to answer", 43.23

ʿsy "big", 41.39

ʿśy "to make", 43.23

b- "in", "from", 48.4

baqar- "cattle", 30.10

baṭn- "stomach", 30.11

bayt "house", 22.16; 29.9

bīr "well", 28.9

bky "to cry", "to weep", 41.13; 62.2

bny "to make a son", *41.13*
bśm "balsam-oil", *16.3*
btʿ "strong", *41.39*
būr "well", *28.9*
dād- "paternal uncle", *62.2*
dry "to last", *43.23*
dubb- "bear", *30.10*
dūr "to last", *43.23*
ḍabb- "lizard", *30.10*
ḍiʾb- "wolf", *30.10*
ḍu, ḍū "that (one)", *28.5-6; 62.2*
ḍubb-, ḍubāb "flies", *30.10*
gaḥān- "belly", *30.11*
gamal- "camel", "dromedary", *30.10*
gbr, gpr "strong", *29.33*
ġzr "copious", *63.8*
ha- "behold!", *49.10*
habb- "elephant", *30.10*
ḥamār-, ḥimār- "ass", *30.1,10*
ḥarb- "sword", *30.6*
ḥiśn "lap", "bosom", *30.11*
ḥmy "to protect", *41.13*
ḥqq "to be right", *10.12*
ḥrt "to plough", *19.23*
ḥšb "to assume", *41.32*
ḥty "to make an arrow", *19.23; 41.13*
ḫbṭ "to strike", *43.23*
ḫizzīr-, ḫuzzīr- "swine", "pig", *30.10*
ḫlp "to go by", "to follow", *45.17*
ʾimm- "mother", *30.1-2; 62.2*
ʾimmar- "ram", "lamb", *30.10*
ʾiṣbaʿ- "finger", *2.5*
k- "as", "like", *48.11; 49.9,14; 56.2-5; 58.2*
kalb "dog", *17.1; 27.19; 29.5; 30.10; 62.2*
kās- "bowl", *30.6*
kirr- "lamb", *30.10*
kkr "round disk", *23.7; 27.3*
krkr "round disk", *23.7; 27.3*
kūn "to be (firm)", *28.9; 44.5-7*
kūr "oven", *28.9*
l- "to", "for", *48.4,6; 49.12*
laḥām- "to eat", *17.2*
laḫr- "ewe", *30.10*

lašān, lišān "tongue", *27.12; 30.11*
lbʾ/b/w "lioness", "lion", *17.2*
lmd "to learn", *29.29*
milḥ- "salt", *30.6*
mny "to count", "to measure", *48.12*
mśy "to walk (by night)", *43.23*
mut- "man", *63.6*
naml- "ant", *30.10*
napš- "breath", *30.2,6*
nayyal- "goat", "roebuck", *30.10*
nbʿ "spring", "source", *63.13*
niḥnu "we", *36.8*
nīn- "child", "offspring", *62.2*
nkr "strange(r)", *15.8*
nky "to kill", *43.23*
paʿn- "foot", *30.11*
pan- "face", *30.11*
qarn- "horn", *30.6,11*
qrʾ "to call", *43.23*
qūm "to stay", "to stand", *2.10; 28.9; 44.5-7*
quṭn- "small finger", *30.11*
raḫl- "ewe", *30.10*
rb "great", *41.13*
rby "to increase", *41.13*
rgm "to speak", "to utter", *29.30*
rigl- "foot", *30.6*
rśś "to break", *43.23*
rūḥ- "breath", *30.6*
sbʾ "to drink", *43.23*
subb "to turn", *44.5*
ṣīr "to begin", *44.6,8*
śīm "to place", *44.5-6,8*
šabʿ "seven", *15.4*
šāl "to ask", *44.6,9*
šinn- "tooth", *30.6*
škb "to lie down", "be buried", *63.13*
šlm "to be healthy", *10.12*
šmʿ "to hear", *45.17*
Tadmer, Tadmor "Palmyra", *29.31*
tḥt "under", "below", *48.16*
tillu "hill", *63.6*
ṯaʿlab- "fox", "jackal", *30.10*
ṯʿy "to look for", *43.7*
*ṯanāyu "to repeat", *35.4,34*
ṯānī "second", *35.4*

ṭawr- "ox", _30_.10
ṯin- "two", _28_.14; _35_.4,34
ṯniy- "double", _28_.14
ṯny "to make another", _41_.13
_ṯu, ṯū_ "that (one)", _28_.5-6; _62_.2
ʾuḏn- "ever", _30_.6,11
_wa-_ "and", _11_.13; _49_.1,3
wʾm "agree", _29_.29
wdʿ "to know", _43_.8
wdw "to flow", "to run", _43_.23
wgʿ "to labour", _2_.10
wld "to bear", _43_.8

wqʿ "to befall", "to happen", _2_.10; _43_.23
wqr "to be excellent", _19_.24; _63_.13
wqy "to keep", _2_.10
_wṣ́_ "to go out", _28_.13; _42_.16; _43_.8
wšn "to sleep", _43_.23
wṯb "to sit", _29_.29
yad- "hand", _30_.6
yaman- "right hand", _30_.2,11
ypʿ "to become visible", _43_.23
zhr "to shine", _43_.23

SOMALI

_-ad_ "afformative of ordinals", _35_.31
biōy "to water", _41_.13
bir "iron", _63_.13 ·
biyə "water", _41_.13
boqol "hundred", _35_.20
gal "to enter", _19_.23
galab "evening", _19_.23
gargar "to help", "help", _28_.19
geid "tree", "wood", _19_.23
gēla "camels", _30_.10
habār "to curse", "curse", _28_.19
hal "one", _35_.4
kah "to rise", _41_.13
kahi "to raise", _41_.13

keli "alone", _35_.4
kor "to climb", "camel bell", _63_.6
laḥ "ewe", _30_.10
qād "to take", _28_.19
qufaʿ "to cough", "cough", _28_.19
san(an) "nose(s)", _31_.22
sukor "sugar", _41_.13
sokorōy "to sugar", _41_.13
šimbirta "bird", _11_.9
usbə "salt", _41_.13
usbōy "to salt", _41_.13
wadne "heart", _30_.11
warāb "to drink", _41_.13
warābi "to water (animals)", _41_.13

SOUTH ARABIAN
EPIGRAPHIC

ʾbh "fathers", _31_.19
ʾbhty "fathers", _31_.19
_ʾd̲_ "when", _58_.12
_-ʾd̲_ afformative of multiplicatives, _35_.31
ʾhlht "clans", _31_.19
ʾḥd "one", _35_.3
ʾḥdr "Ḥaḍramites", _31_.29
ʾḥh "brothers", _31_.19
_ʾl_ "not", _47_.8; _54_.9
ʾlʾlt "gods", _31_.21
ʾlf "thousand", _35_.21
ʾln, ʾlt "these", _36_.33-34

ʾlwny "(man) of Alw", _29_.36
ʾmh "female clients", "handmaids", _31_.19
ʾmht "mothers", _31_.19
ʾmt "female client", "handmaid", _31_.19
ʾnfs¹ "souls", "persons", _31_.29
ʾnṯht "women", _31_.19
ʾrwy "ibex", _63_.4
ʾwyn "vineyards", _65_.5
_ʾy_ "which?", _36_.59
ʾys¹ "man", _29_.9
ʾywn "vineyards", _65_.5

ʿd, ʿdn "up to", "until", *48*.9,17

ʿdw, ʿdww, ʿdy, ʿdyw "to march", "to move", *43*.19,23; *48*.17

ʿdy "up to", "until", *48*.9,17

ʾl, ʾlw, ʾly "over", "above", *48*.15

ʿm, ʿmn "with", *48*.9,13,24

ʿrgl "locust", *29*.17

ʿs¹t "one", *35*.3

ʿs²rt "nomad group", *35*.15

ʿttr "ʿAttar", *29*.17

ʿwdk "you brought back", *40*.5

ʿwdn "bring back!", *40*.14

b- "in", *48*.24

b-ʿm(n) "with", *48*.13,24

b-dt "because", *49*.16

bhn(t) "sons", "daughters", *31*.27

bkn "when", "because", *59*.1

bn "between", *48*.21

bn "from", *11*.6; *48*.9,12

bn, bnw, bny "son", "sons", *31*.11; *32*.26; *63*.8

bny "he built", *43*.19

brṭ "place", "where", *57*.5

byn, bynn "between", *48*.21

dʾ "not", *47*.16

dbl "to fulfil", *49*.21

ḏ "which", "who", *57*.6

ḏʾt "that", "who" (fem.), *36*.54

ḏmr "to protect", *10*.8

ḏtrrn "to wage war against each other", *41*.22-23

f "and", *49*.2

gr "enter (a sanctuary)", *24*.2

grm "body", "one's self", *36*.28

gyr "lime-plaster", *29*.9

ġyr "not", *47*.16

h- "to", "for", *48*.11

hlmw, hnmw "whatever", *36*.33,54

hm, hn "if", *61*.2

hm lm "if not", *61*.3

hmw, hmy "if", *61*.2

hn l "if", *61*.9

hqny "he offered", *41*.11

hqnyw, hqnw "they dedicated", *43*.19

hwry "to make clear", *49*.14

hwt "he", *36*.14

hykl "palace", *29*.9

hyt "she", *36*.14

ḥrf "autumn", *11*.1

ḥwlm "dream", *29*.9

ḥwr "to go to", "to settle in", *43*.7

ḥykl "palace", *29*.9

ḥyn "time", *29*.9

ḥbb "recess" (?), *57*.5

ḥms¹ "main army force", *35*.10

k- "to", "for", "when", "that", *48*.11; *58*.2

kʿd "according to", *48*.17

kd "that", *49*.14

kl'y, kl'ty, kly "both", *35*.4

krkr "talent" (weight), *27*.3

l- "to", "for", *48*.11

lb' "lion", "lioness", *30*.5

lhm "not", *47*.10

lhṣlḥnn "may they grant prosperity", *39*.13

lk "lac", *65*.6

lm "not", *47*.10

ln "from", *48*.9; *58*.7

m't "hundred", *35*.20

Ma'in "spring", *67*.11

mdwr "territories", *29*.10

mḏ'w "they reached", *13*.10

mhn "what", *36*.58

mhrb "prayer niche", *29*.21

mhms¹t "fifths", *35*.30

mkr "traders", *64*.4

mn "who?", "someone", *36*.62

mqm "might", "power", *64*.2

Mryb "place of contests", *29*.21

ms¹gd "house of prayer", *14*.3

ms¹k "musk", *65*.6

mṭ'w "they reached", *13*.10

Myf't "visible site", *29*.21

nfs¹ "soul", "person", *31*.29

nhl "palmgrove", *30*.5

qdm "first", *35*.24

rḍw, rḍy "goodwill", *11*.13; *43*.19

rzm "land-tax", *17*.5

s¹bṭ "to defeat", *41*.42

s¹dt'd "for the sixth time", *35*.31

s¹hdṭ "he inaugurated", *41*.9

s¹n "towards", "next to", *48*.20

s¹qny "he offered", *41*.9

s¹tqr' "he was convened", *41*.9

s^1ts^1ʾ*l* "he put forward a request", *41.29*

tnw/y "two", *35.4*

$s^1ṭrk$ "you wrote", *40.5*

w- "and", *53.5*

$s^1ṭrn$ "write!", *40.14*

wdw "to flow", *43.23*

s^1wn "towards", "next to", *48.20*

wdʾ "to go out", *43.23*

$s^2ʿrt$ "she was aware", *45.16*

whbʿtt "gift of ʿAttar", *17.2*

s^2k "thus", "that", *48.10,17*

wrḫḫ "the mouth", *33.13*

$s^3ḫln$ "take care!", *40.14*

$wrḫs^1$ "the mouth", *33.13*

s^3n "towards", "next to", *48.20*

$ws^1ṭ$ "midst", *48.19*

ṣd "he hunted", *44.5*

wṣṭ "to be established", *10.8*

ṣlym "statuette", *29.10*

wyhṯb "and he restored", *38.11*

ṣwr "image", *29.9*

wyn "vineyard", *65.5*

ṣyd "he hunted", *44.5*

yfʿlwn "they will make", *40.26*

tḥt, *tḥty* "under", "below", *48.16*

yhbr "he fulfils", *44.15*

Timnaʿ "stronghold", *67.11*

yhrḍwn, *yhrḍyn* "he will satisfy", *43.19*

tnḥyt "confession of sin", *29.30*

ts^2r "she will be aware", *45.16*

ym "day", "when", *22.11*; *49.15*; *57.5*

$ts^2(y)m$ "he appointed for his sake", *41.23*

ys^1ʿ$lyns^1$ "they bring him up", *41.9*

ṭd "one", *35.3*

ywm "day", "when", *22.11*; *57.5*

ṭyb "scent", *29.9*

yyn "vineyard", *65.5*

SOUTH ARABIAN
MODERN

ʾ*aʾam* "mother", *33.8*

dōmǝh "this" (masc.), *36.40*

a-bǝtk "your house", *33.9*

(ʾǝ)*d-* "up to", "until", *48.17*

-abyǝtiǝn "our houses", *36.23*

ǝglēl "it was boiled", *41.47*

aġā, *aġayw* "brother", "brothers", *31.30*

ǝkǝy "both of us", *36.6-7*

ä-ġarb "the large well-bucket", *33.8*

ǝktǝlōf "he was troubled", *41.22*

ʾ*am* "if", *50.8*; *61.2*

(ǝ)*laʾ* "not", *47.8*

ansōm "he breathed", *41.11*

ǝlbuk "those", *36.44*

a-ṣaar "the gazelle", *33.8*

ǝl...(ǝ)*laʾ* "not", *47.8*

bayt "house", *33.9*

ʾ*ǝlǝmǝh* "those", *36.44*

ber, *bǝr* auxiliary word, *47.18*

ǝlha "these here", *36.40*

bīn "between", *48.21*

ǝlyōmǝh "these", *36.40*

da "this" (masc.), *36.40*

ǝndǝbḍǝb "he dragged behind", *41.17*

dǝš "this" (fem.), *36.40*

dǝdbuk, *didbuk* "that", *36.44*

ǝrfēs "he was kicked", *41.47*

dǝdha, *didha* "this here", *36.40*

ʾ*ǝṣbaʿ* "finger", *14.8*

ḍā "this" (masc.), *36.40*

fǝlhi, *fǝlho* "foal", "foals", *31.30*

ḍākǝmǝh, *ḍǝkǝmǝh* "that", *36.44*

gǝfnīn "eyebrows", *31.12*

ḍanǝmǝh, *ḍǝnǝmǝh* "this", *36.40*

gǝrēt "slave-girl", *18.6*

ḍǝ, *ḍi* "who", "which", *36.54*

gǝwf, *gǝwǝft* "chest", "chests", *31.30*

ḍī "this" (fem.), *36.40*

ġarb "base of neck", *27.8*

ḍīmǝh "this" (fem.), *36.40*

ġǝgōtǝn "girls", *31.12*

ġōreb "base of neck", 27.8
ha "he", 36.10
ham "name", 15.4
ham "if", 61.2
hāwil "first", 35.24
hél, hér "if", 61.2
hēt "six", 35.12
hežə "he watered", 15.4
hənsōm "he breathed", 41.11
həqu "he watered", 15.4
hīma "he heard", 15.4
hōba "seven", 15.4; 35.12
hʸemah "he heard", 15.4
hamoš "five", 15.4
hayb "father", 33.8
hayd "hand", 33.8,18
hīš "five", 15.4
hayməh "five", 15.4
iźänu "these", 36.39
iźɔk "those", 36.42
kətawb "they wrote", 40.10
kətabəm "they wrote", 40.10
ki "both of us", 36.6
lahm "fish", 63.2
lən/məh "these", 36.40
lərkēz "may I stand up", 40.30
liqbär "may he bury", 38.2
liqbər "may they bury", 40.30
lū "if", 61.6
lu-(ə)l...əlaʾ "if not", 61.6
lūn "white", 11.5
mbīn "between", 48.21
mən "from", 48.12
məšēġər, məšəġərēt "second", 35.25, 30

mun "between", 48.21
nasf, nasfi "half", "halves", 31.6
nənhən, nənyhon "younger brother / brothers", 31.30
nhat "under", "below", 48.16
qerš "piaster", 65.4
rəbōt "four", 35.7
rəfis "he was kicked", 41.47
rība "four (days)", 35.7
sē "she", 36.10
šem "name", 15.4
šeqe "he watered", 15.4
šəlbōd "he was hit", 41.9,29
šələbəd "he hit back", 41.29
šīʿ "he heard", 15.4
šōʿ, šbaʿət "seven", 15.4
šubdet "liver", 18.6
šum "name", 15.4
šəbaʿ "finger", 14.8
t(ə) "accusative" marker, 52.10
tərō "two", 35.4
tād, tāt "one", 33.3,8; 35.3
wdə- "up to", "until", 48.17
yarfōs "he will be kicked", 41.47
yəftəgōr "he will burst", 41.25
yəktēb "may he write", 38.2
yəlbēd "may he hit", 38.2
yəlōbəd "he shoots", 38.5
yərfōs "he will be kicked", 41.47
yərōkəz "he stands upright", 38.5
yhaʿt "six", 35.12
yhobəʾ "seven", 15.4; 35.12
žirit "slave-girl", 18.6

SUMERIAN

a-gàr "water meadow", 63.5
anše "donkey", 30.10
dam-gàr "supplier", "tradesman", 32.10
dam-ha-ra "battle", 32.6
ensí "city ruler", 29.51
ga-ra-an "vineyard", 32.10
guzi "throne", 29.51
kar "quay", 67.19

ku₄ "to enter", 24.2
kur-kur "mountains", 31.21
lah₄ "to transport", 65.2
má "ship", 65.2
ma-da "country", 32.6
ni-is-ku "a kind of servant", 33.16
sa-tu "mountain", 32.10
šakkana "governor", "viceroy", 65.2

še-er-gu "a quality of figs", *33*.16
šúm "garlic", *32*.10

taba "partner", *29*.51
ummia "master", *29*.39

Tigre

'abayt "fathers", *31*.19
'ab'ərat "oxen", *31*.33
'abra'āt, 'abrə'at "pens", *31*.33
'abyāt "houses", *31*.32
'adbər "mountains", *31*.31
'addām(ātāt) "people", "men", "crowds", *31*.39
'adgām(āt) "tales", *31*.33
'adqul "masts", *31*.31
'afayt "mouths", *31*.19
'aǧannit "children", *31*.31
'akallə'at, 'akallə'ət "clay pots", *31*.33
'akarrit(ām) "(a few) hyenas", *31*.37
'akətbat "books", *31*.33
'akətmat "seals", *31*.33
'aklāb "dogs", *31*.31
'a'lāf, 'ālāf "tens of thousands", *35*.22
'alf "thousand", *35*.21
'alwāḥ "boards", *31*.33
'alwaḥat, 'alwəḥat "boards", *31*.33
'am'āt "hundreds", *35*.20
'amdār(āt) "lands", *31*.33
'anaggəl "kids", *31*.31
'anḥās, 'anḥesām "houses", "a few houses", *31*.37
'anqaṭqaṭa "he was shaken", *41*.17
'arwe "serpent", *49*.9; *63*.4
'asbara "he caused to break", *41*.11
'asəgdat "necks", *31*.33
'asək "up to", "until", *48*.17
'asqamqama "he groaned", *41*.14
'atḥādaga "he made leave", *41*.14
'attabala "he caused to be said", *41*.14
'attaqtala "he caused to be killed", *41*.14
'awāləd "daughters", *31*.31
'awḥərat "bulls", *31*.33
'azmata "he caused to raid", *41*.14
'ādad "number", *10*.8

'ala "he was", *38*.26; *42*.25; *49*.24
'allaba, 'allabo(t) "he counted", "counting", "to count", *42*.11
'āmat "year", *31*.20
'arqab "scorpion", *27*.13
'aṣā "he fenced in", *43*.20
'əčay, 'əčyāy "wood", "a piece of wood", *31*.40
'əlatit "little well", *29*.42
ba'at "cave", *30*.6
ba'āy "large cave", *29*.43
bakā "he cried", *43*.20
bet "house", *30*.5
betatit "little house", *29*.43
betāy "ruined house", *29*.43
bet məhro "school", *66*.5
bə'ray "ox", *31*.33
bərə' "pen", *31*.33
bəsəḥənna(t) "maturity", *29*.52
bəšəl "cooked", *42*.14
bun(at) "coffee", "a coffee grain", *31*.41
dabər "mountain", *31*.31
dabanā, damanā "cloud", *11*.6
daqal "mast", *31*.31
dəgəm "tale", *31*.33
dəggə, dəggətāy "town", "small town", *29*.42
'əb "in", *48*.5
'əgāl "calf", *29*.42
'əgar, 'əgər "feet", "foot", *31*.31
'əgəl "for", "to", *38*.26; *39*.12
'əgelat, 'əgelāy "little calf" (fem., masc.), *29*.42
'əl "to", "for", *48*.6
'əlf "ten thousand", *35*.22
'əlli "this", *36*.33-34,41
'ənesat, 'ənesāy "worthless man", "little man", *29*.43
'əntum, 'ənten "you", *36*.9
fagarkum, fagarken "you went out" (plur.), *40*.11

fagraw, fagraya "they went out", *40.*10

gab'a "he will be", *49.*24

gabil "people", *31.*38

gəndāy "log of wood", *30.*6

gərrum "beautiful", *42.*16

ǧabab, ǧəbbat "jackets", "jacket", *31.*31

ǧəna "child", *31.*31

haba "he gave", *43.*7

habbeyām/y "a few monkeys", "a small monkey", *31.*37

halla "he is", *36.*33; *38.*26; *42.*25; *49.*24-25

hatamtam "babbling", *29.*14

hətu, həta "he", "she", *36.*11,33

ḥābara, ḥābaro(t) "he joined", "joining", "to join", *42.*11

ḥada "he was little", *43.*7

ḥadga "to leave", *41.*14

ḥaṣāyər "enclosures", *31.*32

ḥaṣur "enclosure", *31.*32

ḥatte "one" (fem.), *33.*18; *35.*3

ḥaṭa "he devoured", *43.*7

ḥela "he was strong", *31.*32

ḥəd "about", "some", *35.*3

ḥərrād "what is slaughtered", *29.*11

ḥəyal "powers", *31.*32

ḥilat "strength", "power", *31.*32

'i- "not", *47.*11,13

'ifālu "no!", *47.*13

ka- "thus", "so", *49.*9

ka'ā "he spilled", *43.*20

kadādama "he worked on and off", *41.*36

kalə' "clay pot", *31.*33

kaləb "dog", *31.*26,31

karšat, kəraš "belly", "bellys", *31.*31

kawākəb "stars", *31.*32

kəm "when", *58.*2; *59.*6; *60.*1

kətāb "book", *31.*33

kətəm "seal", *31.*33

kokab "star", *31.*32

la "who", "which", "what", *36.*55

ladi "give birth!", *43.*6

lahaṣa "he saved", *27.*12

ləfagra/o "they go out", *40.*29-30

ləssabar "it is broken", *41.*32

luḥ "board", *31.*33

-ma "or", *49.*1,4

ma'amrāy "scientist", *42.*15

madoša "hammer", *30.*6

maktabi "writing implement", *29.*22

malāṣyāy "barber", *42.*15

manāṣəf, manṣaf "carpets", "carpet", *31.*31

manma "nobody", *36.*61

marawi, mawarri "sticks", *27.*12

masallas "third part", *35.*30

masānit, masni "friends", "friend", *31.*31

maṣaddaqi "altar", *29.*22

matqallā' "appearing", *42.*11

məbyāt "dwelling place", *29.*21

mədər "land", *31.*33

məhro "teaching", *29.*50

məkwāl "hiding place", *29.*21

mən "from", *48.*12

məndāq, nadiq "building", *42.*5

nadqa "to build", *42.*5

naggal "kid", *31.*31

naqe "he shouted", *43.*20

nāy- "of", "belonging to", *36.*31

nədqat, nədqo "building", *42.*5

qābəl "former", *42.*13

qadar, qadrāy "gnats", "a gnat", *31.*40

qarš "piaster", *65.*4

qatāl, qatāli, qātlāy "killer", "murderer", *42.*13

qaṭaf "leaves", *31.*38

qawašši "hamlets", *67.*15

qədəsənna "sanctity", *29.*52

qədussām kətubām "Holy Scriptures", *31.*12

qišot "hamlet", *67.*15

ra'ā "he saw", *43.*20

rəšāš(at) "lead", "a piece of lead", *31.*41

sabābara "he broke thoroughly", *41.*36

sadāyat "help", *31.*20

sar "half", *35.*30

səgad "neck", *31.*33

sərəq "theft", *31.*20

səṭṭār "splinter", *29.11*
ṣanḥa "he was", *42.25*
šafattit "rebels", *31.31*
šanaggəl "adults", *31.31*
šəfta "rebel", *31.31*
šəḥ "thousand", *35.21*
šəngul "adult", *31.31*
t- "is", *49.19; 50.9*
taḥat "under", "below", *48.16*
təfagra/o "you go out", *40.29*
təgādabaw "they fought each other", *41.20*
təkān, təkenāy "bugs", "a bug", *31.40*
təmazzana "he was weighed", *41.25*
təqallə'a "he appeared", *42.11*
təšārama "he was cut into strips", *41.27*
tu "he is", *38.26; 39.12; 49.19*

wa "or" *49.4*
wa'at, wa'āt "cow", "a few cows", *31.37*
wad "son", *30.1*
wad ḥal "cousin", *66.5*
wahada "he was little", *43.7*
wahaṭa "he devoured", *43.7*
walat "daughter", *30.1; 31.31*
walatit, waletāt "some girls", "little girl", *31.37*
wəhər "bull", *31.33*
wələdənnat "parentage", *29.52*
woro(t) "one", *33.18; 35.3*
yə- "oh!", *50.3*
zalāyəm "rains", *31.32*
zamta "to raid", *41.14*
zəlām "rain", *31.32*

TIGRINYA

'ab "in", *48.5*
'abatərti "staffs", *31.31*
'abaġəlti "mules", *31.31*
'abay "wild", *23.1*
'abbay "Blue Nile", *23.1*
'adde "mother", *62.2*
'afras "horses", *31.31*
'allä, 'allo "he is", *36.33; 38.26; 49.24-25*
'antum, 'antən "O you!", *36.9*
'arawit "serpent", *63.4*
'asbärä "he caused to break", *41.11*
'ataḥəltat "plants", "trees", *31.33*
'atəḥəltat/ti "plants", "trees", *31.33*
'a'zan "ears", *31.31*
'ay-...-ən "not", *47.8,11*
'azmad "relatives", *31.31*
'ətro "jar", *29.50*
bägli "mule", *27.16; 31.31*
bän^ye "he built", *43.20*
bärtə'e "he become strong", *41.39*
bätri "staff", *31.31*
bə...gəze "at the time", "when", *48.25*
-do interrogative marker, *47.16; 54.5*

'əmbi "no!", *47.13*
'əndə'i "I don't know", *47.13*
'ənglizawi "Englishman", *29.44*
-əs "*up to", *48.10*
'əyyu "he (is)", *38.26*
'əzni "ear", *24.8; 31.31*
'əzom "these", *36.41*
'əzu "this", *36.41*
fälämay "first", *35.24*
färäs "horse", *31.31*
gäza(tat) "house(s)", *31.15,18,20; 63.10*
gäzawətti "houses", *31.18*
g^wädni "rib", *30.11*
habä "he gave", *43.7*
ḥadä "one", *33.18; 35.3*
ḥammuštä "five", *14.9*
ḥantit "one" (fem.), *33.18; 35.3*
ḥaräsä "he ploughed", *45.17*
kälbi "dog", *24.8; 27.16*
käm, kämäzə "that", *60.1*
känfär, känafər "lip", "lips", *31.31*
kə "so that", *59.6*
kəfu' "wicked", *27.9*
konä "he will be", *49.24*
kufu' "wicked", *27.9*

ləbbi, ləbbətat "heart", "hearts", 27.16; *31*.15

mä'alti "day", *31*.30

mädoša "hammer", *27*.9

mändäq, mänadəq "wall", "walls", *31*.31

məs "with", *48*.10

modoša "hammer", *27*.9

näbärä "he was", *38*.26; *49*.24

näfs(a/u) "person", *36*.9,12,36

nay "of", "belonging to", *17*.4; *51*.23

näyru "he was", *38*.26; *49*.24

nə "for", *17*.4; *48*.6; *51*.23

nə "accusative marker", *52*.11

nəgus "king", *27*.9

nəhbi "bee", *30*.10

nəssa, nəssu "she", "he", *36*.12

nəssəkum, nəssəkən "you" (plur.), *36*.9

nugus "king", *27*.9

qätatälä "he slaughtered", *41*.36

qäṭänä "he was small", *23*.1

qäṭṭänä "he liquefied", *23*.1

qədussan "saints", *31*.12

qərsi "piaster", *65*.4

qʷər'a "frog", *29*.27; *30*.10

qʷər'ob "frog", *30*.10

säb(at) "person(s)", *31*.15

säbärä "he broke", *45*.17

səm "name", *14*.9

səwunwun "movement", *29*.14

ṣälot, ṣolot "prayer", *27*.9

šəm "name", *14*.9

šiḥ "thousand", *35*.21

šab'attä "seven", *14*.9

täḫli(tat) "plant(s)", "tree(s)", *31*.33

taḥti "under", "below", *48*.16

täläwä, tälo "he found", *43*.20

täsäb(ä)rä "it was broken", *41*.20

u "or", *49*.4

wäy "or", *49*.4

yəkəffät "it is opened", *41*.32

zämäd "relative", *31*.31

zə "who", "which", "that", *36*.55; *60*.3

zə-səm-u "whose name is", *65*.4

UGARITIC

'aḥd "one", *35*.3

'aḥrtp "brother of Reshef", *13*.6

'aḥd, 'dḫa "he seized", *13*.6; *38*.10

'aḫr "afterwards", *58*.13

'aḫt(t) "sister(s)", *31*.20

'al "not", *47*.9

'alp "ox", "clan", "thousand", *35*.21

'amht "handmaids", *31*.19

'anhb "shellfish" (?), *29*.16

'anḫr "narwhal", *29*.16

'ank, a-na-ku "I", *36*.6

'ap "also", *49*.2

'aqrb "I shall bring near", *40*.34

'arṣh "earthward", *32*.20

'ašhlk "I shall cause to flow", *40*.34; *41*.9

'atwt "she came", *38*.10

'aṭr b'l "settlement of Baal", *32*.12

'd "until", "up to", *48*.17; *58*.11

'l "over", "above", *48*.15

'lt "she is up", *43*.13

'm, 'mn "with", *48*.9,13

'n-qpt "the source is buyoant", *45*.8

'qšr "a kind of snake", *29*.17

'št *"one", *35*.3

'ttr "'Attar", *29*.17

Ba'al-ma-lak "Baal is king", *40*.3; *45*.8

b'l "he made", *10*.8; *11*.4

bhtm "houses", *31*.27

bl "without", "not", *47*.14

bn "between", *48*.21

bn "son", *63*.8

bn(m) 'il "son of El", *33*.16

d "this", "who", "that", *36*.50; *57*.6

dbḥ "sacrifice", *13*.6

dgr "to heap", *29*.29

dt "this", "who", "that" (fem.), *36*.50

du-ú "this", "who", "that", *36*.48

ḏr' "arm", *13*.6

Ga-mi-rad-du "perfect is Haddu", *45.8*

grn(m/t) "threshing floor(s)", *31.14*

ġm' "to be thirsty", *10.9*

ġr "mountain", *10.9*

hl "didn't?", *49.8*

hm "if", *61.2*

hm l "if not", *61.3*

hn "behold", *27.25; 49.6; 60.2*

hkl "palace", *27.16*

hnd "this", *36.33-34*

hyn "Ea", *27.16*

ḥdm "arrows", *13.6*

ḥṣt "half", *35.30*

ḥṭm/t "wheat", *31.14*

ḥṭm "arrows", *13.6*

ḥabbu qualification of ground-plots, *57.5*

Ia-an-ḥa-mu "he comforted...", *40.21*

Ia-pa-milku "splendid is the king", *45.8*

Ig-ma-ra-IM "Haddu has completed", *40.21*

'il'ak "I shall dispatch", *40.21*

'ilht "goddesses", *31.19*

'imtḫṣ "I have seized", *38.4*

'in "there isn't", *47.12*

'iš'al "I shall ask", *40.21*

Iš-la-ma-na "he kept peace...", *40.21*

'ištbm "I have muzzled", *38.4*

'itlk "I have gone", *38.4*

'it "there is", *49.23,25*

'iy "which?", *36.59*

k- "that", "when", "as", *58.2*

kkr "talent" (weight), *27.3*

kl'at "both", *35.4*

kpl "double", *35.4*

ks'at "chairs", *31.15*

ks'u "chair", *31.15*

ky "that", *56.3; 58.2*

l "not", *47.9*

l "to", "for", *48.9*

l'im "people", "clan", *35.21*

l-b "into", *48.24*

ld "give birth!", *43.6*

lm "why?", *58.3*

ln "to", *48.9*

lṭpn, lṭpn "kind", *13.6*

m'aḥd "city", *29.21*

m'at, m'it "hundreds", "hundred", *35.20*

m' "at once", *48.14*

m'lt "height", "step", *29.21*

mġt "I came", *43.13*

mġy "to arrive", *10.9*

mhk "any", *36.61*

mḥrtḥ, mḥrtt "plough-land", *27.28*

mkr "trader", *64.4*

mn "what?", "any", *36.58,61*

mnk "any", *36.61*

mnm "any", *36.61*

mrb't "a fourth", *35.30*

msk "to mix", *65.7*

mṣrm, mṣrym "Egypt", "Egyptians", *29.54*

mṯb(t) "dwelling(s)", *31.15*

mṯltt "a third", *35.30*

Na-qa-ma-du "avenging is Haddu", *45.8*

nbl'at "flames", *29.26*

nġr "to guard", *10.9*

nlqḫt "drawings" (?), *41.16*

npk "well", *10.8*

nš'a, nš'u "he / they lifted up", *40.3; 45.8*

Nūrānu "luminous", *29.36*

p- "and", *49.2*

qrht "towns", *31.19*

qr'itm "you called" (plur.), *45.8*

qrnm/t "two horns", "horns", *31.6*

r'ašm/t "heads", *31.14*

r'iš(t) "head(s)", *31.14*

rbt "ten thousand", *35.22*

ṣhrrt "she was heating", *41.40*

Šapšiyānu "sunny", "small sun", *29.36*

š'tqt "she-who-removes(-evil)", *29.33*

šb''id, šb'd "seven times", *35.31*

šmmh "heavenward", *32.20*

šnm "Shunami", *27.13*

šnpt "two-thirds", *35.30*

šph "posterity", *62.4*

špš "sun", *11.9*

targumyānu "interpreter", *29.30,36*

t'arš "she desires", *38.6*

t'asrn "you will bind", *38.6*
tdgr "store-keeper", *29.29*
tht "under", "below", *48.16*
t'iḥd "she took", *38.6*
tmtḫṣ "she fought", *38.4*
tmtḫṣh "her habit of fighting", *41.35*
tntkn "they pour down", *41.16*
trbṣ "courtyard", *29.31*
trmm "they set up", *41.40*
trmmt "offering", *29.30*
tštḥwy "she prostrated herself", *41.29*
t'uḥd "she held fast", *38.6*
ṯhrm "gems", *13.6*
ṯd "breast", *30.11*
ṯdn "teat", "udder", *30.11*
ṯlḥn "table", *29.37*
ṯlṯ "three", *35.8*
ṯmt "there", *47.7*
ṯnm "two", *35.4*
ṯr "ox", "bull", *65.5*
ṯhrm "gems", *13.6*
'udm't "tears", *27.17*
'Ugārat, 'Ugārit "Ugarit", "fields, plain", *67.11*
'ugr "field", *63.5*

'umht "mothers", *31.19*
'uṣbʿ "finger", *27.17*
'uṯkl "grapes", *31.26*
ʿd "until", "up to", *48.17; 58.11*
wn "and behold", *27.25; 49.1*
wyʿn(y) "and he answered", *43.13*
y'aḥd "he takes", *38.6*
y'arš "he desires", *38.6*
ybmt "daughter-in-law", *11.6*
ydm/t "two hands", "handles", *31.6*
ygrš "expeller", *29.18*
yḥd "to be united", "gathering", *35.3*
y'iḥd "he took", *38.6*
ykllnh "let him complete it", *41.40*
ykrkr "he snapped", *41.38*
yml'u "they filled", *27.24; 38.13*
ymmt "daughter-in-law", *11.6*
yn "wine", *65.5*
yqġ "to be alert", *10.9*
yqḥ "may he take", *38.6*
yrtḥṣ "he washed himself", *41.22*
yṣ'a "he went out", *45.8*
yt ly "I have", *49.25*
y'uḥd "he held fast", *38.6*
zbln "sickness", *29.37*

TABLES, MAPS, AND TEXT FIGURES

Page of David Qimḥi's *Sefer Mikhlol* 2
Hieroglyphic uniconsonantal signs 28
Diagram of Cushitic languages 30
Geographical distribution of Libyco-Berber 35
Libyco-Berber writing 38
Diagram of Chadic languages 40
Diagram of Proto-Afro-Asiatic 41
The spread of the earliest pastoralists in Africa 45
Ebla tablet TM.75.G.1377 Recto 51
Tell Beydar tablet 2629-T-2 52
Fragment of the Gilgamesh Epic 55
Page of the Aleppo Codex 59
Punic inscription from Carthage 60
Alphabetic scripts of the 9th and 8th centuries B.C. 62
Palmyrene inscription 64
Syriac scripts 67
Page from the Canonical Prayerbook of the Mandaeans 68
Ṣafaitic inscriptions 73-74
Arabic script 76
South Arabian alphabet 78
South Arabian languages 79
Semitic and Cushitic languages of the Horn of Africa 82
Evolution of the Semitic alphabet 89
Amharic syllabary 91
Notation systems of consonants 96-98
Notation systems of vowels 98-99
Points of articulation 101
Articulation of vowels 101
Proto-Semitic consonantal system 107
Location of vowels 107
Development of interdentals 118
Development of interdentals and sibilants 119
Development of laterals 132
Development of gutturals 149
Synopsis of the consonantal system 150
Fol. 62/3 of the *Tabulae in grammaticam Hebraeam* by N. Clenardus . 151
Main types of consonantal assimilation 187
Patterns of "broken" plurals in Classical Arabic 248
Paradigm of East Semitic nouns 274
Paradigm of Ugaritic nouns 275
Paradigm of Classical Arabic nouns 275-276
Paradigm of Old Aramaic nouns 276

Paradigm of Hebrew nouns 277
Paradigm of colloquial Cairene nouns. 278
Paradigm of cardinal numerals 282-283
Paradigm of personal pronouns 298-299
Paradigms of the oblique cases of personal pronouns 300-301
Paradigm of pronominal suffixes 306-307
Paradigm of early independent possessive pronouns 312-313
Paradigm of later independent possessive pronouns 314
Paradigm of demonstrative pronouns 316-317
Paradigm of "far" demonstrative pronouns 318-319
Paradigm of affixed "near" demonstrative pronouns 320-321
Paradigm of affixed "far" demonstrative pronouns. 323
Paradigm of determinative-relative pronouns. 325
Paradigm of interrogative pronouns 329
Aramaic ostracon from Elephantine 330
Synoptic table of stem designations 334
Diagram of tenses and aspects 358
The square of fountains at Ghadames 359
Actor affixes of the suffix-conjugation 360-361
Actor affixes of the imperative 366-367
Page from the Samaritan Pentateuch 369
Actor affixes of the prefix-conjugation, Set I 370-371
Actor affixes of the prefix-conjugation, Set II 377
Paradigm of the suffix-conjugation, basic stem 378-379
Paradigms of the prefix-conjugation, basic stem 380-383
Paradigm of the intensive verb-stem 384
Paradigm of the verb-stem with lengthened vowel 385
Paradigm of the N-stem 395
Recapitulative tables of verb-stems. 410-412
Recapitulative table of causative stems 412-413
Recapitulative table of stems with *t*-affix 413-414
Table of Proto-Semitic verb-stems 415
Selected paradigms of Neo-Aramaic conjugation 423
Paradigm of $C\bar{u}C$ verbs, basic-stem 440
Paradigm of $C\bar{\imath}C$ verbs, basic-stem. 440
Paradigm of $C\bar{a}C$ verbs, basic-stem 440-441
Paradigm of CvC_2C_2 verbs, basic-stem 441-442
Page of a Qur'ān manuscript. 444
Paradigm of the South-Ethiopic copula *na-* 477
Old Assyrian envelop with tablet 482
Diagram of conditional particles. 537
Page from a codex with Babylonian vocalization 542
Commemorative medal of Abu Naṣr al-Fārābi 546

ORIENTALIA LOVANIENSIA
ANALECTA

1. E. Lipiński, Studies in Aramaic Inscriptions and Onomastics I.
2. J. Quaegebeur, Le dieu égyptien Shaï dans la religion et l'onomastique.
3. P.H.L. Eggermont, Alexander's Campaigns in Sind and Baluchistan and the Siege of the Brahmin Town of Harmatelia.
4. W.M. Callewaert, The Sarvāṅgī of the Dādūpanthī Rajab.
5. E. Lipiński (ed.), State and Temple Economy in the Ancient Near East I.
6. E. Lipiński (ed.), State and Temple Economy in the Ancient Near East II.
7. M.-C. De Graeve, The Ships of the Ancient Near East (c. 2000-500 B.C.).
8. W.M. Callewaert (ed.), Early Hindī Devotional Literature in Current Research.
9. F.L. Damen, Crisis and Religious Renewal in the Brahmo Samaj Movement (1860-1884).
10. R.Y. Ebied-A. Van Roey-L.R. Wickham, Peter of Callinicum, Anti-Tritheist Dossier.
11. A. Rammant-Peeters, Les pyramidions égyptiens du Nouvel Empire.
12. S. Scheers (ed.), Studia Paulo Naster Oblata I. Numismatica Antiqua.
13. J. Quaegebeur (ed.), Studia Paulo Naster Oblata II. Orientalia Antiqua.
14. E. Platti, Yaḥyā ibn ʿAdī, théologien chrétien et philosophe arabe.
15. E. Gubel-E. Lipiński-B. Servais-Soyez (ed.), Studia Phoenicia I-II.
16. W. Skalmowski-A. Van Tongerloo (ed.), Middle Iranian Studies.
17. M. van Mol, Handboek Modern Arabisch.
18. C. Laga-J.A. Munitiz-L. Van Rompay (ed.), After Chalcedon. Studies in Theology and Church History.
19. E. Lipiński (ed.), The Land of Israel: Cross-Roads of Civilizations.
20. S. Wachsmann, Aegeans in the Theban Tombs.
21. K. Van Lerberghe, Old Babylonian Legal and Administrative Texts from Philadelphia.
22. E. Lipiński (ed.), Phoenicia and the East Mediterranean in the First Millennium B.C.
23. M. Heltzer-E. Lipiński (ed.), Society and Economy in the Eastern Mediterranean (1500-1000 B.C.).
24. M. Van De Mieroop, Crafts in the Early Isin Period.
25. G. Pollet (ed.), India and the Ancient World.
26. E. Lipiński (ed.), Carthago.
27. E. Verreet, Modi Ugaritici.
28. R. Zadok, The Pre-Hellenistic Israelite Anthroponomy and Prosopography.
29. W. Callewaert-M. Lath, The Hindī Songs of Nāmdev.
30. S. Halevy, Coptic Grammatical Chrestomathy.
31. N. Baum, Arbres et arbustes de l'Égypte ancienne.
32. J.-M. Kruchten, Les Annales des prêtres de Karnak.
33. H. Devijver-E. Lipiński (ed.), Punic Wars.
34. E. Vassilika, Ptolemaic Philae.
35. A. Ghaith, La Pensée Religieuse chez Ǧubrân Ḫalil Ǧubrân et Miḫâʾîl Nuʿayma.
36. N. Beaux, Le Cabinet de curiosités de Thoutmosis III.
37. G. Pollet-P. Eggermont-G. Van Damme, Archaeological Sites of Ancient India.
38. S.-A. Naguib, Le Clergé féminin d'Amon thébain à la 21e dynastie.
39. U. Verhoeven-E. Graefe (ed.), Religion und Philosophie im Alten Ägypten.
40. A.R. George, Babylonian Topographical Texts.
41. A. Schoors, The Preacher Sought to Find Pleasing Words.
42. G. Reinink-H.E.J. Van Stiphout (ed.), Dispute Poems and Dialogues in the Ancient and Mediaeval Near East.
43. C. Traunecker, Coptos. Hommes et dieux sur le parvis de Geb.

44. E. LIPIŃSKI (ed.), Phoenicia and the Bible.
45. L. ISEBAERT (ed.), Studia Etymologica Indoeuropaea Memoriae A.J. Van Windekens dicata.
46. F. BRIQUEL-CHATONNET, Les relations entre les cités de la côte phénicienne et les royaumes d'Israël et de Juda.
47. W.J. VAN BEKKUM, A Hebrew Alexander Romance according to MS London, Jews' College no. 145.
48. W. SKALMOWSKI-A. VAN TONGERLOO (ed.), Medioiranica.
49. L. LAUWERS, Igor'-Severjanin, His Life and Work — The Formal Aspects of His Poetry.
50. R.L. VOS, The Apis Embalming Ritual. P. Vindob. 3873.
51. Fr. LABRIQUE, Stylistique et Théologie à Edfou. Le rituel de l'offrande de la campagne: étude de la composition.
52. F. DE JONG (ed.), Miscellanea Arabica et Islamica.
53. G. BREYER, Etruskisches Sprachgut im Lateinischen unter Ausschluß des spezifisch onomastischen Bereiches.
54. P.H.L. EGGERMONT, Alexander's Campaign in Southern Punjab.
55. J. QUAEGEBEUR (ed.), Ritual and Sacrifice in the Ancient Near East.
56. A. VAN ROEY-P. ALLEN, Monophysite Texts of the Sixth Century.
57. E. LIPIŃSKI, Studies in Aramaic Inscriptions and Onomastics II.
58. F.R. HERBIN, Le livre de parcourir l'éternité.
59. K. GEUS, Prosopographie der literarisch bezeugten Karthager.
60. A. SCHOORS-P. VAN DEUN (ed.), Philohistor. Miscellanea in honorem Caroli Laga septuagenarii.
61. M. KRAUSE-S. GIVERSEN-P. NAGEL (ed.), Coptology. Past, Present and Future. Studies in Honour of R. Kasser.
62. C. LEITZ, Altägyptische Sternuhren.
63. J.J. CLÈRE, Les Chauves d'Hathor.
64. E. LIPIŃSKI, Dieux et déesses de l'univers phénicien et punique.
65. K. VAN LERBERGHE-A. SCHOORS (eds.), Immigration and Emigration within the Ancient Near East. Festschrift E. Lipiński.
66. G. POLLET (ed.), Indian Epic Values. *Rāmāyaṇa* and its impact.
67. D. DE SMET, La quiétude de l'Intellect. Néoplatonisme et gnose ismaélienne dans l'œuvre de Ḥamîd ad-Dîn al-Kirmânî (Xᵉ-XIᵉ s.).
68. M.L. FOLMER, The Aramaic Language in the Achaemenid Period. A Study in Linguistic Variation.
69. S. IKRAM, Choice Cuts: Meat Production in Ancient Egypt.
70. H. WILLEMS, The Coffin of Heqata (Cairo JdE 36418). A Case Study of Egyptian Funerary Culture of the Early Middle Kingdom.
71. C. EDER, Die Ägyptischen Motive in der Glyptik des Östlichen Mittelmeerraumes zu Anfang des 2. Jts. v. Chr.
72. J. THIRY, Le Sahara libyen dans l'Afrique du Nord médiévale.
73. U. VERMEULEN, D. DE SMET (eds.), Egypt and Syria in the Fatimid, Ayyubid and Mamluk Eras. Proceedings of the 1st, 2nd and 3rd International Colloquium organized at the Katholieke Universiteit Leuven in May 1992, 1993 and 1994.
74. P. ARÈNES, La déesse Sgrol-Ma (Tara). Recherches sur la nature et le statut d'une divinité du bouddhisme tibétain.
75. K. CIGGAAR, A. DAVIDS, H. TEULE, East and West in the Crusader States. Context - Contacts - Confrontations. Acta of the congress held at Hernen Castle in May 1993.
76. M. BROZE, Mythe et Roman en Egypte ancienne. Les Aventures d'Horus et Seth dans le papyrus Chester Beatty I.
77. L. DEPUYDT, *Civil Calender and Lunar Calendar in Ancient Egypt.*
78. P. WILSON, A Ptolemaic Lexikon. A Lexicographical Study of the Texts in the Temple of Edfu.
79. A. HASNAUI, ELAMRANI Jamal, A., AOUAD, M. (eds.), Perspectives arabes et médievales sur le tradition scientifique et philosophique grecque.
80. E. LIPIŃSKI, Semitic Languages. Outline of a Comparative Grammar.

PRINTED ON PERMANENT PAPER • IMPRIME SUR PAPIER PERMANENT • GEDRUKT OP DUURZAAM PAPIER - ISO 9706

ORIENTALISTE, KLEIN DALENSTRAAT 42, B-3020 HERENT